"If You Love That Lady Don't Marry Her"

"If You Love That Lady Don't Marry Her"

The Courtship Letters of Sally McDowell and John Miller 1854–1856

Edited by Thomas E. Buckley, S.J.

University of Missouri Press
Columbia and London

Library of Congress Cataloging-in-Publication Data

McDowell, Sally Campbell Preston, 1821–1895.
   "If you love that lady don't marry her" : the courtship letters of Sally McDowell
and John Miller, 1854–1856 / edited with an introduction by Thomas E.
Buckley.
      p.   cm.
Icludes index.
   ISBN 0-8262-1278-6 (alk. paper)
   1. McDowell, Sally Campbell Preston, 1821–1895—Correspondence.
2. Miller, John, 1819–1895—Correspondence.   3. Presbyterian Church—
Pennsylvania—Philadelphia—Clergy—Correspondence.   I. Miller, John,
1819–1895. II. Buckley, Thomas E., 1939– . III. Title.
BX9225.M39 A4   2000
975.5'03'0922—dc21
[B]   00-023994

Text Design: Elizabeth K. Young
Jacket Design: Kristie Lee
Typesetter: Bookcomp, Inc.
Printer and Binder: The Maple-Vail Book Manufacturing Group
Typefaces: Bellevue, Bembo

Contents

Preface

Like so many projects that eventually take on lives of their own, this one began almost by chance. I was spending a week in the archives at the Alderman Library of the University of Virginia, searching for sources for a study of legislative divorce in Virginia between the Revolution and the Civil War. Although the file card for the McDowell Family Papers indicated divorce as a subject heading, it also bore the conspicuous red label "Restricted." Initially, I passed it. But after I finished reviewing those manuscript collections that were readily available, half of a Friday remained in my week. So I questioned Michael Plunkett, the gracious director of the archives, who suggested we examine the deposit folder. We discovered that the family had recently lifted the limitation on access. That afternoon's reading introduced me to the courtship letters of Sally McDowell and John Miller.

At the time I did not know the background of either party. Although McDowell's name appeared in my database of Virginia divorces, someone had removed her petition from the collection at the Library of Virginia. In that first brief perusal, I found that her extraordinarily personal letters revealed what had thus far eluded me in my research, a detailed private account of the experience of divorce in the antebellum South and the turmoil and shame it represented in a person's life. Significant as this was in itself, the correspondence offered much more besides. Moreover, the collection was almost completely intact.

The history of the courtship letters can be only surmised. Both principals obviously saved them. Before their marriage, Miller also provided that McDowell's letters would be returned to her in case of his death. At some point she carefully, though not always accurately, dated his letters when he had failed to do so and bound them in paper wrappers stating the month and number. After her father's death, Margaret Miller gave some of his papers to Princeton's Firestone Library, but she and her two unmarried sisters kept the more personal materials. When the three women died in the 1930s, descendants of Sally McDowell's sister, Margaret Cantey McDowell Venable, apparently inherited these manuscripts. In 1948 C. Venable Minor of Charlottesville deposited the McDowell Family Papers at the Alderman Library. This collection included materials related directly to McDowell's divorce in the 1840s. He added the McDowell-Miller-Warner Collection that contained the courtship letters in 1975. His son, C. Venable Minor Jr., opened both collections to researchers and granted permission to publish this volume.

Acknowledgments

My good friend Brent Tarter of the publications staff at the Library of Virginia first suggested this project. For more than two decades Brent has generously instructed me on all things Virginian. No one knows the Old Dominion's history better or where to go or what to read or who to talk to if you have a question about the Mother State. Originally, we planned to edit the letters together. Although a joint enterprise ultimately proved unworkable, Brent has been the best cheerleader one could want. He also read the first transcription in its entirety and proposed chapter divisions and titles that I have generally followed. More than anyone else, this book is for him.

Michael Plunkett and his staff at the archives of the Alderman Library kindly photocopied the entire correspondence collection and sent it to me at Loyola Marymount University in Los Angeles. Over the next four years, with the help of Matthew Cino, Kristin DiBernardo, and Richard Gibson, three excellent student assistants, I deciphered the handwriting and transcribed the letters. On return trips to the Alderman, I located further bits and pieces that had escaped the copy machine and checked my entire text against the originals.

In researching Miller's and McDowell's lives and the people who shared their world, I have received fine support from the staffs of numerous archives and libraries. The Virginia Historical Society, the Perkins Library at Duke University, and the Southern Historical Collection at the University of North Carolina all have collections of McDowell Papers. The Library of Congress holds related collections, and the Maryland Historical Society has some Francis Thomas manuscripts. At Princeton, New Jersey, the Archives and Rare Books at Firestone Library possesses the John Miller Papers, and the Mudd Manuscript Library has extensive information on Princeton alumni. In Philadelphia I drew upon the resources at the Pennsylvania Historical Society and the Presbyterian Historical Society, which possesses an invaluable card catalog for ministers' lives and works. The Library of Virginia offered rich and varied resources for the introduction and the notes. The library at Union Theological Seminary in Richmond contains abundant materials on Virginia presbyteries. The Preston Library at the Virginia Military Institute; the James Graham Leyburn Library at Washington and Lee University; the Huntington Library in San Marino, California; and the Sutro Library in San Francisco were also helpful. And in Berkeley I had the excellent resources of Doe Library at the University of California and the Flora Lamson Hewlett Library at the Graduate Theological Union. I am also grateful to Thomas

H. Smolich, S.J., and the California Province of the Society of Jesus for their generous financial support for this project.

Over lunches, dinners, and gallons of frozen yogurt I have discussed these letters and their subjects with many friends who have offered helpful advice, useful warnings, and strong support. Thanks especially to Sara Bearss, Julie Campbell, Janet Coryell, Jean Friedman, Martha Hodes, Cindy Kierner, John Kneebone, Nelson Lankford, Frances Pollard, and Sandy Treadway. I am also indebted to Jane Censer and Susan Miller for generously reading sections of the correspondence and encouraging the endeavor. Finally, I owe a huge debt of gratitude to Beverly Jarrett, editor-in-chief at the University of Missouri Press, who read the entire text with growing enthusiasm and accepted the responsibility of publishing the entire corpus.

I had not yet completed the transcription when I made my first visit to Colalto. Sally McDowell's old home was unoccupied at the time, but the door was open and the staff at the Lexington visitors center suggested I go inside. I found it just as she described it in her letters, big and empty. Reading her mail made it easy to experience her presence. Colalto has now been tastefully restored as the centerpiece for a Hampton Inn. Four hundred miles away in Princeton, Greg Raschdorf, general manager of the Nassau Club, graciously allowed me to prowl through the home that Samuel Miller built in 1814. In one of its upstairs bedrooms, John Miller scribbled many of his letters to Sally.

My own home changed three times while I was working on this project. It began when I was teaching in the history department at Loyola Marymount, continued during a Bannon Fellowship year at Santa Clara University, and ends at the Jesuit School of Theology at Berkeley. My Jesuit companions and lay colleagues in all three academic communities have listened, as have my family and friends, to the saga of Sally and John for almost eight years. I am immensely grateful for their patience, their charity, and their presence in my life.

Editorial Practices

As far as the requirements of typography permit, I have tried to present the letters as Sally McDowell and John Miller originally exchanged them. Thus, the spelling, capitalization, and punctuation are reproduced as in the originals, although I have substituted periods and commas for small dashes when they were obviously intended for those purposes and supplied missing periods at the ends of sentences. Paragraph indentations and salutations have been regularized. Additions that follow a letter are left in the same position. Marginal and interlined notes designed to fit into the text are placed in the proper location. Notes added as afterthoughts in the margins are placed at the ends of the letters and are noted as marginal notes.

McDowell's handwriting tends to be clear and precise with extensive punctuation. Miller's letters often appear hurried and composed in a stream of consciousness that sometimes defies syntax and grammar. As their correspondence grew, they both frequently used contractions such as wd (would), shd (should), wh (which), yr (your), and fr or fm (from), and so on. I have left these contractions as they wrote them, because they help to explain the mood in which they wrote. Occasionally, they repeated a word, in which case I have eliminated the duplicate and so indicated in a note. When either writer has inadvertently omitted an obvious word in part or whole, I have supplied what is missing and placed it in brackets. I have done the same for quotation marks and parentheses. When they have just as obviously written the wrong word by mistake (as in "thing" instead of "think"), I have made the correction and noted the original. Miller especially tended to write over words. McDowell sometimes found his writing illegible. So have I. At times I have made informed guesses; at other times I have simply given up.

Both McDowell and Miller regularly exchanged letters they had received from others. When these letters were available and pertained significantly to subjects under discussion, I have included them. Otherwise I have simply noted their presence and occasionally provided a summary of the contents.

The notes briefly identify the people referred to in the letters when they are first mentioned. Also, following the Introduction, a reference guide lists the principal family members, friends, and townspeople whose names occur frequently. No sources have been cited for the kind of information to be found in standard dictionaries, directories, family histories, and the like.

Introduction

On the front porch of her Virginia home one warm August evening in 1854, John Miller asked Sally McDowell to marry him. The thirty-five-year-old Presbyterian minister from Philadelphia was a widower with two small children. Two years his junior, she owned and managed a farm in the Shenandoah Valley, and had remained unmarried since her divorce eight years before. The day after John's proposal, Sally refused to see him when he came for a visit. Then she wrote to explain, gently but firmly, her reasons for rejecting his offer of marriage. That letter inaugurated an extraordinary communication. Over the next twenty-seven months, they met only five times, usually for just a very few days and always in carefully orchestrated encounters exposed to public view. Instead of face-to-face conversations, they wrote letters to each other, hundreds of them. From friendship to love to marriage, their relationship ripened through the mail. Through their correspondence, they explained their personal histories and ambitions, exposed their fears and anxieties, and explored their growing passion for each other and the obstacles placed in their path.

It began quite by happenstance. Miller had been vacationing with his older unmarried sister, Mary, at the Alum Springs in the Virginia foothills of the Appalachian Mountains. The summer holiday provided a much needed respite for John, immersed in a strenuous building campaign for a new church for his rapidly expanding congregation. Mary cared for their widowed mother, Sarah Sergeant Miller, at the family home in Princeton. Their father, Samuel Miller, had been a Presbyterian minister as well as a professor of ecclesiastical history and church government at Princeton Theological Seminary. Together with the Reverend Archibald Alexander, the senior Miller had founded the seminary in 1812, and it quickly developed into the most important center for educating Presbyterian ministers in the United States.[1] John Miller had studied there himself.

Miller had not always envisioned himself in the pulpit. As an undergraduate at the College of New Jersey (later Princeton University) and then for a post-graduate year, Miller enjoyed working in the research laboratory of Joseph Henry, a brilliant professor of natural philosophy who would later head the Smithsonian Institution. Henry's enthusiastic support for his protégé and Miller's obvious abilities and interests pointed toward a successful career in teaching and scientific

1. Mark A. Noll, "The Founding of Princeton Seminary," *Westminster Theological Journal* 42 (1979): 72–110.

research. But when a religious awakening swept across Princeton in 1838, he experienced a conversion that redirected his life. Much to the delight of his parents, the young man entered the seminary and, after ordination, accepted an assignment to a small congregation in Frederick, Maryland, in 1843. For the next five years, Miller threw himself into his new ministry with a zeal and enthusiasm that marked his entire life. In addition to the usual rounds of preaching and home visits, he opened two schools, established a board of trustees, and built a parsonage. Years after he had moved to Philadelphia, his Frederick trustees wrote to commend him for the "prosperity" he had brought their church.[2]

Soon after his arrival in Frederick, the young pastor married Margaret Hunter Benedict. Before her death from consumption in 1852, she bore four children.[3] Of these, a daughter, Margaret (Maggie), and a son, Alamby (Allie), survived their mother. By this time Miller had moved to the Philadelphia church, a more prestigious pulpit and a more desirable location in terms of family proximity. The Millers were a large brood—John, born in 1819, was the ninth of ten children. The brother closest in age and affection, E. Spencer Miller, was a practicing attorney in the city, and nearby Princeton held not only his mother and Mary but also his younger married sister, Sarah Miller Hageman, plus assorted other relatives and friends. The extensive Benedict clan also lived nearby and offered emotional support to the lonely young widower. In particular, his deceased wife's oldest sister, Sarah Benedict Potter, and her husband, Alonzo Potter, the Episcopal bishop of Pennsylvania, opened their home and hearts to Miller and his children.

Other friends reached out as well. William Henry Ruffner, a minister in the Shenandoah Valley, wrote Miller in the spring of 1854 urging a summer visit to Virginia and promised to introduce him to a woman designed "to share your busy solitude." "Busy" was an understatement. What Ruffner jokingly called "the Arch St. Cathedral" was a massive project that required extensive fund-raising as well as overseeing the construction of what would be, when completed, the largest church in Philadelphia. The appreciative members of the congregation also thought their pastor deserved a vacation.[4] And so brother and sister Miller traveled to Virginia's Alum Springs. On a whim, the minister passed up an afternoon game of ninepins to visit the nearby town of Lexington.

2. Francis Bazley Lee, ed., *Genealogical and Personal Memorial of Mercer County, New Jersey* (New York and Chicago, 1907), 1:268–69; Nathan Reingold, ed., *The Papers of Joseph Henry*, 8 vols. to date (Washington, D.C., 1972–), 2:478 n, 3:58, 83, 6:609–10; T. J. C. Williams, *History of Frederick County, Maryland* (Baltimore: L. R. Titsworth, 1910), 450; Seth H. Nichols to John Miller, May 26, 1852, Box 1, Correspondence, John Miller Papers, Princeton University Library, Princeton, N.J.

3. John J. Thomson to John Miller, Feb. 10, 1852, Miller Papers; gravestones, Princeton Cemetery, Princeton, N.J.

4. W. H. Ruffner to John Miller, Mar. 28, Sept. 14, 1854, McDowell-Miller-Warner Papers, #2969a, Alderman Library, University of Virginia, Charlottesville (hereafter MMW); C. B. Dungan to H. A. Boardman, Apr. 6, 1854, Miller Papers.

There Miller renewed his acquaintance with Sally Campbell Preston McDowell, and before the week ended he was totally smitten. Her height at five feet, six inches made her tall for women of that time. Possessing a fair complexion, brown eyes, and long brown hair that had been blond in childhood, she was regarded as a handsome, even beautiful woman. But beyond any physical attributes, her warm, engaging personality, acute mind, and deep spirituality drew Miller's affection. Sally's family names—Campbell, Preston, and McDowell—identified her with the South's social and political elite. Her father, James McDowell III, had inherited Colalto, a graceful Georgian plantation home built by his father on the outskirts of Lexington. Preferring politics to farming, McDowell had eventually become governor of Virginia and then a U.S. congressman before his death in 1851. His wife had been a first cousin, Susanna Smith Preston; and, as their letters testify, they had shared a companionate marriage of deep affection and mutual trust and respect. From both her parents, an extensive Preston connection linked Sally McDowell to Breckinridges and Harts, Floyds and Carringtons—politicians, planters, and Presbyterian clergy from Virginia, Maryland, Kentucky, and South Carolina. On her father's side, an uncle by marriage was Thomas Hart Benton, the U.S. senator from Missouri; another was William Taylor, a Virginia congressman.

As a young woman, completing her formal education and just emerging in society, Sally McDowell had lived with her Aunt and Uncle Benton in Washington, D.C., in the mid-1830s. At their home she met and fell in love with Francis Thomas, a bachelor congressman from Maryland, twenty years her senior. Sally's infatuation alarmed her parents. Fearing Thomas's overly serious, suspicious personality would produce an unhappy marriage, the McDowells had not approved of the match, but ultimately they yielded to their oldest daughter's wishes, and soon after her twentieth birthday she and Thomas were wed at Colalto on June 8, 1841. Shortly after the couple returned to his home near Frederick, Maryland, Thomas began to accuse his vivacious young wife of improper conduct and then sexual infidelity with her cousin Robert Taylor. While still courting Sally, Thomas had invited the younger man to move to Maryland and join his law practice. Now, the jealous, paranoid husband badgered his wife until she confronted her cousin with charges of impropriety that all three parties knew to be false. Bewildered and angry, Taylor withdrew to Virginia.[5]

5. For Thomas's career, see Williams, *History of Frederick County, Maryland*, 256–63, and "Miller, John," in *DAB*. Susan S. McDowell to James McDowell, Sept. 2, Dec. 8, 1840, McDowell Family Papers, 1802–1895, #2969, Alderman Library, University of Virginia, Charlottesville (hereafter MFP); "Narrative," in Papers Relating to Divorce, MFP (hereafter Divorce Papers); Sally C. P. McDowell to James McDowell Jr., May 12, 1846, Correspondence Concerning the Divorce, MFP (hereafter Div. Corres.). For an account of the wedding festivities by Sally's cousin, see Jesse Benton Frémont, *Souvenir of My Time* (Boston, 1881), 45–47.

But past was prologue. The marriage deteriorated swiftly as her husband's wild accusations and angry outbursts left Sally increasingly desperate and frightened. Repeatedly, Thomas threatened to send her home to Lexington. Then, inexplicably, the dark mood would lift and he would become tenderness itself, apologizing profusely for his behavior, begging forgiveness, and promising amendment. But his tirades escalated with each such episode. In September, while Thomas was off campaigning for governor, Sally suffered a miscarriage. Upon his return, he accused her of deliberately aborting a child conceived with her cousin, but he pledged absolute forgiveness if she would only admit her sinful conduct. Desperate for some measure of domestic peace, she finally yielded to his bullying only to experience utter rejection. Then, when she immediately retracted her confession, Thomas flew into a violent rage. Isolated in Maryland and reluctant to inform her parents or family of her traumatic situation, Sally McDowell Thomas had become, within six months of her marriage, an emotionally battered wife.[6]

Following Thomas's inauguration on January 3, 1842, the couple moved into the governor's mansion in Annapolis. But Sally's days there were numbered. A week or so later, a frenzied Frank Thomas summoned Elizabeth McDowell Benton to Annapolis to hear his charges against her niece. Returning quickly to Washington she explained the situation to her husband and Sen. William Preston of South Carolina, another of Sally's uncles. Springing to their niece's defense, the family patriarchs at once informed her parents of Thomas's "derangement." This time his predictable change of heart occurred too late. The McDowells sped to Baltimore, scooped up their daughter over their son-in-law's frantic objections, and brought her home to Colalto. Deeply humiliated by the collapse of her marriage, Sally Thomas withdrew into her protective family circle and tried to restore familiar ties. In a profuse apology to her cousin Robert Taylor, she sought "to repair the wrong, which circumstances too painful to detail, but too powerful for an untried woman's heart or nerve to bear up under, led me to do to you."[7]

Governor Thomas did not endure the separation quietly. Over the subsequent years he attacked his estranged wife in the press and public conversations, accusing her of adultery with assorted men. Periodically, he wrote Sally or her father, who had been elected governor of Virginia in 1842, insisting on a personal interview and demanding redress for his grievances, or alternatively, begging that she return to him and let the past be buried in oblivion. On one extraordinary occasion Thomas traveled up the Shenandoah Valley, ostensibly to visit Sally

6. "Narrative," Divorce Papers. There is extensive literature on battery. See, for example, Wini Breines and Linda Gordon, "The New Scholarship on Family Violence," *Signs: Journal of Women in Culture* 8 (1983): 490–531; Leonore E. Walker, *The Battered Woman* (New York: Harper and Row, 1979) and *The Battered Woman Syndrome* (New York: Springer, 1984); and the essays in Richard J. Gelles and Donileen R. Loseke, eds., *Current Controversies on Family Violence* (Newbury Park, London, and New Delhi: Sage Publications, 1997).

7. "Narrative," Divorce Papers. William C. Preston to [James McDowell], [Jan. ?, 1842]; Sally C. P. Thomas to R. J. Taylor, Feb. 20, 1842, Div. Corres.

at Colalto. At a coach stop, he encountered his father-in-law returning home from Richmond. For an awful moment it looked like mortal enemies would be sharing a stage. After they traded harsh words and McDowell attacked Thomas with his umbrella, bystanders intervened. But the violent exchange between the chief magistrates of neighboring states created a public sensation.[8]

An outraged Thomas swore vengeance and increased his public attacks on the McDowells, culminating in a fifty-two-page pamphlet that vividly recounted the crimes his wife and certain of her relatives and friends had committed against him. Up to this point Sally had been unwilling to consider divorce. In Virginia, though the courts had jurisdiction in certain narrowly defined instances, the normal venue lay through the General Assembly. A court hearing would find the facts in the case; then the applicant petitioned the legislature for a private bill of divorce. Relatively few people applied, and even fewer received divorces. The display of a couple's marital trauma furnished grist for press and gossips alike. Sally dreaded the exposure, despite the cogent arguments of her father and others that only such a public action would both vindicate her character and free her legally from any claim Thomas might make against her. But *The Statement of Francis Thomas*, published in 1845, goaded her into action, and she began composing a narrative of her marital troubles to be presented as part of a divorce petition to the state legislature.[9] After a Richmond court verified her version of events, the assembly speedily approved a divorce bill in the early days of 1846 and, in an extraordinary move, restored her maiden name.[10] The next month, in response to a petition from their former governor, the legislators in Annapolis followed suit, though not fixing blame on either party.[11]

Henceforth, she would be styled as "Mrs. McDowell." The "Mrs." branded her a divorcée. Though her situation as the injured party brought widespread sympathy from the "enlightened and virtuous," it made no essential difference in her social status. Prejudice against divorce fixed her reputation. As one Virginia

---

8. Francis Thomas to [S. C. P. Thomas], Feb. 3, 9, 1842, copies in James McDowell to Archibald Graham, May 25, 1843, Graham Family Papers, Box 2, Correspondence and Papers, Perkins Library, Duke University, Durham, N.C.; S. S. McDowell to Mary [McDowell], Apr. 20, [1843], undated file, Carrington-McDowell Family Papers, 1780–1897, Library of Congress. For typical press accounts of the stage incident, see *Daily National Intelligencer* [Washington, D.C.], May 9, 1843; and *Richmond Whig and Public Advertiser*, May 12, 1843.

9. *The Statement of Francis Thomas* (n.p., 1845). James McDowell to Susan S. McDowell, May 27, 30, June 4, 11, 1842, May 20, June 4, 1843; James McDowell to Sally C. P. Thomas, Mar. 5, 1845; Sally C. P. Thomas to James McDowell, Mar. 7, 1845, Div. Corres. "Narrative," Mar. 8, 1845, Divorce Papers.

10. *Richmond Whig and Public Advertiser*, Dec. 25, 1845; Thomas H. Benton to James McDowell, Dec. 30, 1845, Box 2, James McDowell II Papers, Duke University, Durham, N.C. (hereafter McDowell Papers, DU). *Richmond Enquirer*, Jan. 2, 16, 1846; James Lyons to James McDowell, Jan. 10, 1846, Div. Corres.

11. *Journal of the Proceedings of the House of Delegates of the State of Maryland* (Annapolis, 1846), Feb. 12, 13, 17, Mar. 6, 1846, pp. 249, 257, 274, 468.

legislator remarked, after noting all she had suffered at Thomas's hands, "How deplorable her condition. So young and with such prospects to have such a destiny." The stigma she bore as a divorced woman became intrinsic to her identity in southern society. No wonder then that from the beginning of her marital separation, Sally retired from social life. Apart from a single visit to her Aunt Eliza Preston Carrington's family in nearby Fincastle, she remained at Colalto, with her mother her only confidante. She rejected her father's inducements to come to the governor's house in Richmond, and refused her Uncle William Preston's invitations to visit her kin in South Carolina.[12] Years passed before she was willing to travel again.

Meanwhile, her former husband continued to attack on several fronts, with increasingly reckless behavior. His bizarre charges against ever changing targets destroyed his credibility along with what had once been a promising political career. Over the years a growing number of Marylanders came to regard Thomas as an embarrassment. Polite society increasingly ostracized him.[13] Seemingly undaunted by public disapproval, Thomas launched perhaps his most extraordinary assault on one of his own relatives, Dr. William Tyler of Frederick, a physician in his fifties with a wife and grown children. Tyler had initially aroused Thomas's suspicion when he came to treat Sally for a tooth and gum infection in 1841. The friendly banter between doctor and patient convinced the congenitally suspicious husband that they were sexually intimate. Later Thomas accused his kinsman of attempting first to injure him physically and then poison him, and he cited his former wife to appear as a witness in grand jury proceedings in Frederick. Greatly alarmed by what might happen at the trial, Sally realized that this was yet another occasion on which her ex-husband would attempt to embarrass her publicly. But her parents accompanied Sally, and the judge who conducted the hearing in November 1846 kept Thomas in check, much to the latter's disgust. Thomas lost when the jury failed to indict, and the only residual effect for Sally McDowell was that during her brief stay in Frederick, she met the town's Presbyterian pastor, John Miller.[14]

12. Eliza H. Carrington to Susan McDowell, Mar. 6, 1841 [1842], Div. Corres.; Robert S. Brooke to Margaret L. Brooke, Feb. 16, 1842, Brooke Family Papers, Alderman Library, University of Virginia, Charlottesville; James McDowell to Sally C. P. McDowell, Feb. 16, 1843, Div. Corres.; S. C. P. Thomas to Archibald Graham, Apr. 11, 1843, Box 2, Graham Family Papers; James McDowell to Susan S. McDowell, Jan. 5, 1843, Div. Corres.

13. James McDowell [Jr.] to Susanna S. McDowell, Feb. 28, 1842, MMW; George H. Young to James McDowell, Apr. 6, 1842, Box 1, McDowell Papers, DU; for Thomas's concern, see Francis Thomas to John Thompson Mason, Mar. 2, 1842, Box 5, John Thompson Mason Jr. Papers, Maryland Historical Society, Baltimore; S[ophonisba] Breckinridge to Susan S. McDowell, June 25, 1842, Div. Corres.

14. William Tyler to Sally C. P. McDowell, Oct. 13, 1846; Philip R. Fendall to William C. Preston, Mar. 30, 1846; William Tyler to James McDowell, Sept. 29, 1846; William Tyler to S. C. P. McDowell, Sept. 21, Oct. 13, 1846; James McDowell Jr. to S. C. P. McDowell, Nov. 26, 1846, Div. Corres. Francis Thomas to John Thompson Mason, Nov. 12, 1846, Mason Papers.

As the Tyler trial concluded, another major case appeared on the docket in Washington, D.C., at the instance of Thomas Hart Benton. In a circular published in 1844, Thomas had accused Sally's uncle of "a cruel matrimonial fraud." According to his story, his future wife had been seduced while living in the Missouri senator's home, but instead of avenging their niece, the Bentons has foisted Sally off on Thomas. Desiring to vindicate Sally's reputation, Benton sued for libel.[15] Thomas now postponed this suit by suddenly trumping up wild charges against a former protégé, Judge John Legrand. At a sensational impeachment trial in Annapolis, James McDowell spoke eloquently in defense of his daughter. After exonerating Legrand, Maryland legislators opined that their former governor, on the subject of his marriage, was insane. By formal resolution, they affirmed Sally McDowell's irreproachable "conduct and character, both as a maid and wife." Deeply embarrassed by Thomas's reckless attacks, the assembly ordered the written proceedings and evidence destroyed. At this point Thomas's own lawyers withdrew from the Benton libel trial. Their client, they explained, was the victim of his massive delusions. His purpose achieved, Benton dropped the suit.[16]

More than six years after she separated from her husband, Sally McDowell had won a decisive victory. But those traumatic years had extracted an enormous emotional price. Her letters a decade later demonstrate its imprint. The publicity surrounding Thomas's charges and the divorce had made her name a household word and given her a notoriety she despised. Then her mother died in the fall of 1847, leaving Sally the guardian of her youngest sister, Lilly, and the manager of Colalto for her father.[17] James McDowell was now a U.S. congressman. Shortly after his gubernatorial term ended, the Virginia assembly had elected him to replace his recently deceased brother-in-law, William Taylor. Following her mother's death Sally experienced an intense religious conversion that renewed her Presbyterian faith, gave fresh meaning to her life, and left her with a deep awareness of her new responsibilities.[18] With her father immersed in politics and her older brother James a physician in St. Louis, she oversaw the plantation and cared for her younger sisters and brother. Then, when James McDowell died unexpectedly in 1851, Sally became the functional head of her family, even to the extent of buying Colalto from her siblings.[19]

15. The printed circular, dated May 15, 1844, is in the Charles Macgill Papers, 1793–1906, Box 1, Duke University Library, Durham, N.C.

16. *Journal of House of Delegates of Maryland*, Mar. 2, 3, 4, 1847, pp. 413–14, 420, 421, 431; *Baltimore Republican and Argus*, Feb. 19, 20, Mar. 4, 5, 1847; John C. LeGrand to Richard S. Blackburn, Mar. 17, 1847, printed copy, in LeGrand to Charles Macgill, Jan. 18, 1861, Macgill Papers; "United States vs. Francis Thomas," Divorce Papers; *Richmond Watchman and Observer*, Mar. 18, 1847.

17. "Brief Memoranda of requests made by my beloved wife on this, the 3d of Octr. 1847," MFP; James McDowell to S. C. P. McDowell, Feb. 20, 1849, Div. Corres.

18. S. C. P. McDowell to Susan Smith Preston McDowell, Nov. 23, 1848, McDowell Family Papers, 1825–1927, Virginia Historical Society, Richmond (hereafter VHS).

19. S. C. P. McDowell to James McDowell, Apr. 21, 1853, Box 2, McDowell Papers, DU.

This purchase was, after all, the sensible, practical thing to do. Colalto was her home, and she could manage the farm through an overseer. Certainly, she had no future elsewhere. Though Frank Thomas periodically annoyed her with letters proposing reconciliation, Sally usually returned them unopened. This was the advice her uncle, Virginia's governor, John Floyd, urged. When her ex-husband continued his efforts, she wrote that the prospect filled her with "loathing."[20] For emotional support and encouragement, she depended upon her sisters and brothers, an extensive network of aunts, uncles, and other relations, and a wide circle of trusted friends, male and female. Some, like her "Cousin John" Preston and his wife, "Cousin Sally," lived close by in Lexington. There she was a familiar, welcome presence in the town's stores, parlors, and Presbyterian church. She managed Colalto carefully and capably. Her siblings looked to her for advice and direction. In sum, as she approached her mid-thirties, Sally McDowell had achieved a respected position in antebellum society. Throughout the tragedy of her early adulthood, she had maintained her dignity. Now, as the innocent victim of a deranged husband who had robbed her maidenhood and destroyed her prospects for marital happiness, she had emerged as an icon for her extended family and the upper strata of southern womanhood.

Into this carefully managed, emotionally controlled world strolled John Miller to profess his love to the mistress of Colalto. Two inches taller than Sally, with brown hair, blue eyes, and a dark complexion, he was not physically imposing and notably handsome in the way that characterized the Preston men.[21] But he was animated, intelligent, witty, emotionally committed, and a Presbyterian clergyman to boot. Though she initially rebuffed his courtship, the letters soon began, at first cautious, hesitant, and extremely proper. Then, gradually over the months and years, they expanded into intimate explorations of their evolving relationship and the problems their love entailed for both of them. Four hundred miles apart, they spoke to each other through their pens, sometimes as often as five and six times a week. They exchanged all the thoughts and emotions one would expect of a couple in love, but their age, intelligence, and experience gave the correspondence a depth and maturity far above the ordinary letters lovers might write.

They also faced an unusual concern in mid-nineteenth-century America: divorce in all its ethical, religious, social, and legal dimensions. The "moral question," as they styled it, surfaces repeatedly in their writing. McDowell's divorce bill left her legally free to marry again, but the Presbyterian Confession of Faith only admitted remarriage in cases of adultery. She had not charged Thomas with infidelity in her petition for divorce, and the legislative committee's

---

20. Francis Thomas to S. C. P. McDowell, Sept. 3, 1851; John B. Floyd to S. C. P. McDowell, Oct. 6, 1851; S. C. P. McDowell to Francis Thomas, July 19, 1851, Div. Corres.

21. For Miller's physical description, see John Miller Va., filed June 16, 1865, pardoned June 26, 1865, Case Files of Applications from Former Confederates for Presidential Pardons ("Amnesty Papers"), 1865–1867, National Archives, Washington, D.C.

deliberations had not been made public. This fact presented a series of problems. First, as a devout evangelical Presbyterian, was she morally free to marry again during Thomas's lifetime? Equally important in her mind, could she marry a man whose ministry might be jeopardized by his relationship with her? Miller dismissed her concern, but she proved much more prescient when leaders in his congregation questioned openly whether they could be well served by a minister married to a divorcée. Some Miller relations expressed serious reservations, not only because of his career but also for Sally's welfare. Ultimately, he resigned his pastorate at West Arch Street Church in Philadelphia and retired to Princeton to study and write. Meanwhile, members of Sally's family as well as certain close friends also found the prospect of her remarriage socially problematic and warned against it. One sister, writing privately to her husband, compared Sally's situation to someone "under trial for the second time for some penal offence." Another wedding could bring only unhappiness to her sister and injure the entire family's reputation.[22]

Although their personal relationship and the questions raised by the divorce dominate the correspondence, the letters expose the multiple dimensions of their lives. Both are evangelical Christians for whom God's will takes precedence over every other consideration in their lives, though McDowell's letters reflect most demonstrably the struggle to discern it. On the theoretical level Miller wrestles with the conflict between his desires for a retired life of theological scholarship and the duties of pastoral ministry, while practically he interacts with his lay elders, members of his congregation, and other clergymen. Though transplanted into urban Philadelphia, one foot remains in Princeton's village life where he is vitally concerned for his mother's well-being and his children's lives. McDowell's letters are even more expansive in roaming the gamut of southern life. She explores the challenges of farm and household management, encounters with slaves and slavery as an institution, southern and national politics and politicians, contemporary poetry and literature, and the benefits and limitations of southern lifestyles. Their rich exchange provides multiple insights into the social and cultural history of the nation on the eve of the Civil War.

Perhaps the most intriguing dimension of this correspondence, however, lies in its presentation of gender relations among elite women and men in the mid-nineteenth century. McDowell offers the unusual feminist perspective of a divorced woman whose single status left her legally free to manage her own affairs and responsible for the care of family and slaves. Yet, she lived in a society whose political, economic, and religious institutions regarded women as essentially dependent, and divorced women as tainted goods. Though in many respects Miller's attitudes and values are thoroughly traditional, yet he honors McDowell's independence, respects her judgment, and seeks in marriage not dominance but a

22. Sophonisba McDowell Massie to James W. Massie, Sept. 5, 1855, James W. Massie Papers, Archives, Virginia Military Institute, Lexington, Va.

companion and soul mate. Together they examine the full range of their concerns and the potential impact a marriage poses to their families and their religious and social responsibilities. Miller's letters bristle with emotion, while McDowell is more guarded in her response. Constantly reaffirming his undying passion and begging her response, Miller slowly wears down McDowell's defenses. As she probes her own inner world of love and rejection, letter writing becomes a cathartic experience through which she gradually surmounts the limitations imposed by a patriarchal society, recurrent depression, and, most important, the anxieties resulting from her first marriage and the stigma she bore as a divorced woman. Eventually, she matches in intensity his own emotional expression, and then surmounts his fears for her social position. Her self-revelations ultimately lead to their marriage at Colalto on November 3, 1856.

Following a leisurely journey through the mid-Atlantic states to visit Miller's friends and relations, the newlyweds settled at Colalto. There his wife's family and friends graciously welcomed Miller into their company. He transferred easily into the Presbytery of Lexington and ministered on alternating Sundays to congregations in nearby Fairfield, Oxford, and Collierstown. He had originally hoped to make farming his "recreation" and devote the bulk of his time to private study and writing, but that proved impossible when he assumed responsibility for overseeing five hundred acres and six slaves. Yet, letters to his brother demonstrate a newfound happiness. Maggie and Allie Miller now had a mother again, and within a few years they welcomed two new sisters and a brother, Susanna (Susie) McDowell, Elizabeth (Bess), and Preston Miller in 1861.[23]

Though Abraham Lincoln's 1860 election sent rumbles through the Shenandoah, the Millers, like many of their neighbors, at first opposed secession. John had supported the moderate John Bell's Constitutional Union Party, and Sally decried such talk. After Fort Sumter and Lincoln's call for troops to suppress the rebellion, however, the Millers followed, in Sally's words, "our natural and proper allegance" and went with Virginia. Miller recruited a company of soldiers from among his Fairfield congregation that eventually became the Second Rockbridge Artillery. The men promptly elected him their captain. Miller took to military life. In a letter to the front, Sally expressed her pleasure with John's "skill" as an officer, but added, "I beg you wont forget you are chaplain too." At the battle of

23. J. W. Massie to John Miller, Jan. 28, 1857, Box 1, Miller Papers; Susan S. P. Carrington to [Sally C. P. Miller], Jan. 6, 1857, Carrington-McDowell Papers; Lexington Presbytery Records, Apr. 14, Sept. 15, 1857, microfilm, Union Theological Seminary Library, Richmond, Va., pp. 123–24, 152; Howard McKnight Wilson, *The Lexington Presbytery Heritage: The Presbytery of Lexington and Its Churches in the Synod of Virginia, Presbyterian Church in the United States* (Verona, Va.: McClure Press, 1971), 344, 352, 357; John Miller to Samuel Miller, July 3, 1857, Box 1, Miller Papers. The daughters have been identified by their graves at Princeton Cemetery, as well as census records. Preston Miller is identified by a letter he wrote to his mother. See also John Miller to S. C. P. Miller, Oct. 19, 1861, Box 2, Miller Papers. Both sons would die young.

Camp Allegany in December 1861, Miller won high praise for his bravery and leadership, but the following spring his men did not reelect him, and his efforts to raise a partisan cavalry unit were ultimately unsuccessful. One soldier thought he was too uncaring for his men, but another, his brother-in-law Thomas McDowell, praised Miller's competence and attributed his defeat to his insistence on army discipline.[24]

During the war Sally and the children found a new home in Lexington, and in 1864 the Millers finally sold Colalto to James and Nib Massie. Meanwhile, John resigned from the army and resumed the ministry. En route to the Southern Presbyterians' General Assembly in 1863, he passed through Petersburg and preached a Sunday sermon at the Second Presbyterian Church. The impressed congregation immediately invited him to accept their vacant pulpit. Miller consented, but on condition that his mornings would be free for private studies. Over the next eight years his vigorous sermons, delivered up and down the aisles as well as from the pulpit, won the hearts of his congregation. When Union forces besieged Petersburg, Confederate officers and troops, including Cantey's husband, Charles Scott Venable, who was Robert E. Lee's military aide, also beat a path to his church.[25]

After the war, Miller purchased a farm near Petersburg with a "genteel" house and brought his family down from Lexington. Like other southerners, the Millers found themselves low on cash, though the sale of McDowell properties owned by Sally and her siblings in Kentucky and Kansas helped somewhat.[26] Sally found Christmas 1865 a bleak affair. "Who can be merry after all the sorrows and changes of the last year," she wrote Cantey. "I see no merriment with any but children and certainly feel none myself." A few months later she found herself playing hostess to "three Yankees!" Though she praised their good behavior, Sally, like so many southern women, felt the bitterness of defeat as deeply as any beaten soldier. After attending a Fenian meeting one evening, she wrote her sister:

> It made me sad to hear the poor fellows talk of "liberty and a Republic." The ghastly corpse of our Confederacy was staring me in the face all the time: Freedom indeed!

24. John Miller to Samuel Miller, Oct. 26, 1860, Box 1, Miller Papers; Sally C. P. Miller to Edward ?, Apr. 19, 1861, James McDowell Papers, Southern Historical Collection, University of North Carolina, Chapel Hill (hereafter McDowell Papers, UNC); S. C. P. Miller to John Miller, Sept. 21, 1861; Thomas Preston Miller to Constance Warwick McDowell, Apr. 15, 1862, MFP. Robert J. Driver Jr. *The First and Second Rockbridge Artillery* (Lynchburg, Va.: H. E. Howard, 1987), 96–97, 100–102, 104.

25. Deed between John and Sally C. P. Miller and James W. Massie, Oct. 14, 1864, Rockbridge County Deedbook JJ, 1864–1868, p. 34. "Autobiographical notes of John Miller," Box 4; W. Gordon McCabe to Rev. J. Miller, Sept. 28, 1864, Box 1, Miller Papers. C[harles] S. Venable to [Margaret Cantey McDowell Venable], Mar. 19, 1865, in [Francis Preston Venable], "Memoir of Margaret Cantey McDowell Venable, typescript in MMW. [William B. McIlwaine Jr.], *History of the Second Presbyterian Church* (Petersburg: Owen Publishing, [1951?]), 14–15.

26. John Miller to S. C. P. Miller, July 7, 8, 1865, MMW; "Memoir of Margaret Cantey McDowell Venable," 60, 61.

There isn't a free country on the face of this earth, but Liberty stalks abroad a gaunt spectre, whose garments are dripping with the blood of martyred men, and with fair promises and stirring words deludes each nation in its turn, with the belief that her home is in it. Ireland is the deluded one now. She seems determined not only to bear the liberty cap on her head, but to pull it over her eyes.[27]

In the aftermath of the war, John's attention focused on the Church. The war had split the denomination, and in 1866 and 1867 he wrote old friends in New Jersey and Pennsylvania urging reconciliation between northern and southern Presbyterians. His correspondents, though happy to hear from him, thought the time inopportune. The division would persist into the twentieth century. Within his own Virginia presbytery of East Hanover, Miller chaired its committee on domestic missions, raising funds wherever he could to support itinerant clergy and alleviate the poverty of the people.[28] On his own home front, his chief concern was Allie. Though the young man had done brilliantly at the University of Virginia, he had not yet experienced religious conversion. In frequent letters to Allie, Miller anguished over the state of his son's soul. After completing his master's degree, the young man traveled to Germany for advanced studies, but he returned ill in a year, and on November 15, 1869, Allie died of tuberculosis.[29] The Miller family was devastated.

John buried his oldest son in the family plot in Princeton cemetery, and soon after began planning to retire to Princeton himself. The years in the South had never provided the time he sought for writing, and as he approached fifty he had achieved the financial security to follow the mistress that had always eluded him. The ties that held Sally Miller to Virginia were also loosening. After Nib's death in 1870, she returned to Colalto "from which the glory of the McDowell has passed for ever." The next spring Miller resigned his Petersburg charge and moved his family into a Princeton home he called Allamby.[30]

At last Miller could devote himself to his writing. Over the next decade his books and articles rolled off the presses. With publication, however, came the controversy he had predicted years before. His *Commentary on Proverbs*, published in 1873, was received well enough. But the following year he came out with *Fetich in Theology*, an assault on Charles Hodge's recently published *Systematic Theology*.

27. Sally C. P. Miller to Margaret C. M. Venable, [Dec. ?], 1865, Mar. 27, 1866, McDowell Papers, UNC.
28. John Maclean to John Miller, May 18, 1866; George Sharswood to John Miller, Oct. 29, 1867, Box 1, Miller Papers. G[eorge] W. Finley to W[illiam] Brown, Jan. 14, 1868, the *Central Presbyterian*, II. Correspondence, 1868–1873+, Box 181, Brock Collection, Henry E. Huntington Library, San Marino, Calif.
29. See, for example, John Miller to Alamby Millington Miller, Dec. 21, 1866, Feb. 22, 1867, June 22, 1869, Box 2; "Mr Collin's article Sketch of Rev. John Miller," Box 4, Miller Papers.
30. [S. C. P. Miller to John Miller], [Mar. ?, 1870]; John Miller to S. C. P. Miller, June 3, 1871, MMW.

The dominant theologian at Princeton Theological Seminary, Hodge had trained more than two thousand ministers, and befriended Miller from his days in the seminary. Liberal voices in and out of the Church applauded Miller for taking on the "Protestant Pope."[31] Within Miller's own presbytery and at Princeton's seminary the reception was less enthusiastic.

Three years later, Miller published his most controversial work, *Questions Awakened by the Bible*. Until now Hodge's disciples had held their peace. But this challenge not only to Hodge but also to specific tenets of the Westminster Confession roused them to action. The Presbytery of New Brunswick called Miller to answer charges of heresy and in early May 1877 voted unanimously to suspend him from the ministry. That fall, Miller's case came before the Synod of New Jersey on appeal. Afterward Hodge, in a gracious letter to Sally Miller, reported that his son, Alexander Hodge, also a professor at Princeton Theological Seminary, considered Miller's defense before the Synod as "the greatest speech he has ever heard or expects to hear." But John Miller stood condemned. At the trial one speaker had compared him to the revolutionary zealot Tom Paine. But another minister exposed the real concern. Miller had dissented from the Princeton theology and attacked its reigning theologian. The Synod condemned him. Spencer Miller was outraged: "Is Hodge infallible? And for *that* you 'should be tried for heresy.'! monstrous! While they were enlarging Princeton Seminary they should have constructed Inquisition vaults under it, for heretic pupils."[32]

From the Synod's verdict, Miller appealed to the General Assembly. At its May 1878 meeting, the earnest theologian spoke for two hours in his own defense. Though more divided than in the two previous trials, the vote still went against him. Afterward he wrote home to Sally that he was at peace and "thankful to God." Throughout the crisis, she supported him, even sending his books to her relatives in the South for their endorsement. The next year, because he refused to retract his views, his presbytery formally notified Miller that he had been dropped from their membership and could no longer function

31. *Fetich in Theology; or, Doctrinalism Twin to Ritualism* (New York: Dodd and Mead, 1874). W. E. Ijams to John Miller, Sept. 24, 1874 (quote); R. M. Laudie to John Miller, Oct. 7, 1874; R. L. Dabney to John Miller, Feb. 4, 1875; and especially Robert L. Dabney to Messrs. Dodd and Mead, Publishers, Feb. 25, 1875, Box 1, Miller Papers. For a list of his publications, see John Frelinghuysen Hageman, *History of Princeton and Its Institutions*, 2 vols. (Philadelphia, 1879), 396. For Hodge's early interest in Miller, see Charles Hodge to John Miller, July 15, 1845, Box 1, Miller Papers.

32. John Miller, *Questions Awakened by the Bible: I. Are Souls Immortal? II. Was Christ in Adam? III. Is God a Trinity?* (Philadelphia: Lippincott, 1877); *Charge, Specifications, and Proofs in Case of Rev. John Miller* (n.p., n.d.), at Presbyterian Historical Society, Philadelphia; *Attested Copy of the Records of the Presbytery of New Brunswick in the Case of the Rev. John Miller* (Flemington, Apr. 10, 1877), at Presbyterian Historical Society, Philadelphia; Charles Hodge to [Sally McDowell] Miller, Oct. 26, 1877, copied, Box 2, Miller Papers; [E. Spencer Miller to John Miller], Nov. 5, 1877, Box 2, Miller Papers.

as a Presbyterian minister. By then, he had already formally withdrawn from the Church.[33]

But Miller did not abandon the ministry. He continued writing books on Scripture and theology and articles on all sorts of topics. Royalties and fees from this work helped to support his family. After the Methodists refused to allow him to borrow their churches for his preaching, he founded five of his own, building or buying church buildings in Princeton and nearby towns. He also hired, much to the dismay of the seminary faculty, their future ministers to preach to his congregations. Meandering about the village, he loved to corral a group of students from college and seminary, and debate theology and philosophy with them. Though many people regarded him as eccentric, the students called him "Socrates."[34]

Throughout the Princeton area, Miller was noted for his concern for the poor and disadvantaged, many of whom were black. In his early years as a minister, he had traveled to Britain and Europe, fund-raising for the American Colonization Society; later he served on its board of directors. As early as 1854, he had proposed a college for African Americans in the United States.[35] In the 1880s, his interest in Africa revived, now with the possibility of going as a missionary to the continent. He exchanged letters and consulted extensively with various missionaries at work there.[36] Meanwhile, he also opened conversations with the Cumberland Presbyterian Church that led eventually to his acceptance into their Allegany Presbytery and then to his project of forming a New Jersey Presbytery.[37]

But amid his multiple interests, his family contextualized John Miller's life. After his death, an old friend and fellow minister wrote, "in few families are the relation of husband, father, wife & child so intimate, so tender and loving." Sally McDowell Miller also found fulfillment as wife and mother. While supporting her husband's work, she raised her daughters to adulthood, involved herself in church activities and charities, and continued to write articles and poetry for newspapers

33. John Miller to Sally Miller, [May 25, 1878], Box 2, Miller Papers; John Preston to S. C. P. Miller, May 12, 1877, MMW; A. L. Armstrong to John Miller, Apr. 10, 1879, Box 2, Miller Papers; John Miller, *Letter of Withdrawal from the Presbyterian Church* (Princeton, 1878).

34. Lyman Abbott to John Miller, May 10, 1880, Box 1; S. Vansant to John Miller, Apr. 9, 1879, Box 1; the *Cumberland Presbyterian*, May 2, 1895, Box 4; John Miller, "To the Alliance of the Reformed Churches throughout the World Holding the Presbyterian System," Sept. 28, 1880, in "Public Letters," Box 3; [E. Spencer Miller] to "My dear Socrates" [John Miller], Nov. 5, 1877, Box 2; *Newark News*, Apr. 16, 1895, Box 4, Miller Papers.

35. *Princeton Signal*, Apr. 20, 1895, Box 2; Samuel Miller to John Miller, Aug. 22, Nov. 27, 1848, Aug. 20, 1849, Box 1; E. H. Bayly to John Miller, Nov. 24, 1849, Box 1; Alexander T. McGill to John Miller, Jan. 9, 1854, Box 1, Miller Papers.

36. See, for example, Samuel W. Seaton to John Miller, Feb. 1, 1889; Edward W. Blyden to John Miller, Apr. 10, 1889; and J. Augustus Cole to John Miller, July 17, 1889, Aug. 11, 1891, Box 2, Miller Papers.

37. J. I. D. Hinds to John Miller, Dec. 16, 1891; A. B. Miller to John Miller, May 18, 1892; T. C. Blake to John Miller, Apr. 13, 1895, Box 2, Miller Papers.

and journals. Her last major effort, which she had begun to research forty years earlier, was an extended history of her father's political career. Her faith—Jehovah Jireh—that God would provide, grew only stronger with the passage of time. As she wrote in 1886 to a nephew, Lilly's son, extraordinary "vicissitude & agitation" had marked her life, yet she had personally experienced and could proclaim "God's wisdom & goodness." Over the decades of her marriage, her values had not changed, only deepened.[38]

John and Sally Miller shared almost forty years of married life. John died first, on Easter Sunday, April 14, 1895, at the age of seventy-six. Despite a cold, he had been out in typical fashion caring for one of his congregations, developed pneumonia, and passed away quietly. He was buried beneath a gravestone of his own design, a huge white cross on which was inscribed the central tenets he had defended before various Presbyterian tribunals. The tributes at his death emphasized his kindliness, his generosity, and his love for the poor. Sally herself wrote of the loss of her "dear husband."[39] One week later she died, Sunday, April 21, 1895. She was buried with John after a service in which the president, the dean, and a professor of Princeton College eulogized her as an exemplar of Christian life. Her death was completely unexpected. Yet, an old friend, William Henry Ruffner, found in this final linkage of husband and wife "a beautiful fitness."[40]

38. Moses D. Hoge to Sally C. P. Miller, Apr. 19, 1895, MFP; S. C. P. Miller, "James McDowell," *Washington and Lee University, Lexington, Virginia, Historical Papers* 5 (1895); S. C. P. McDowell to Bernard [Woolf], Aug. 22, 1886, McDowell Family Papers, 1777–1963, VHS.

39. Sally C. P. Miller to Moses D. Hoge, Apr. 14 [15], 1895, MMW; the *Princeton Signal*, Apr. 20, 1895; the *Philadelphia Presbyterian*, Apr. 24, 1895, Box 4, Miller Papers.

40. W. H. R., "Death of Mrs. John Miller of Princeton," Apr. 24, 1895; Prayer of Dr. [Francis Landley] Patton; Remarks of Dr. James Armsbec Murray; Eulogy of Dr. John Grier Hibben, section 15, McDowell Family Papers, 1777–1963, VHS.

The Worlds of Sally McDowell and John Miller

Sally McDowell's World

BROTHERS AND SISTERS (IN ORDER OF BIRTH)

James McDowell, a physician in St. Louis, married to Elizabeth (Lizzie) Brant
Mary McDowell, will marry John Ross, a Presbyterian clergyman
Nib (Sophonisba) McDowell, married to James Massie, a lawyer in Lexington. Their son is "Mac"
Susan McDowell, married to Charles Carrington, a lawyer in Halifax, Va.
Tom (Thomas) McDowell
Cantey (Margaret) McDowell, will marry Charles S. Venable
Lilly (Eliza) McDowell

AUNTS, UNCLES, AND COUSINS

"Uncle Robert" Breckinridge, a Presbyterian minister in Kentucky. His first wife, Sophonisba Preston, was deceased. Their children include McDowell's "young cousins":
    Marie Breckinridge
    Willie (William) Breckinridge
"Aunt Eliza" Carrington, married to Edward Carrington; they lived in Fincastle. Their children include:
    Campbell (William Campbell) Carrington
    Jimmy (James) Carrington, lived at Colalto
    Nannie (Ann) Carrington, a frequent houseguest
"Aunt Sally" Floyd, married to former governor John Floyd
"Cousin John" Preston, "the Major," a professor at Virginia Military Institute, married to "Cousin Sally"
Elizabeth Preston Cocke, Cousin John's sister
"Uncle John" Preston, a wealthy planter in South Carolina
"Uncle Tom" Preston, a lawyer and banker, in charge of the Preston family saltworks in Abingdon, Va.
"Uncle William" Preston of South Carolina
Bent (Thomas Benton) Taylor, a law student in Lexington
James Taylor, M.D., of Lexington
Robert Taylor, a Presbyterian minister in Portsmouth, Va.

Section of "A New Map of the United States, 1851."
Courtesy of the Library of Virginia.

LEXINGTON NEIGHBORS AND FRIENDS

Judge John White Brockenbrough

James Dorman Davidson, McDowell's attorney

Junius Fishburn, a professor at Washington College

Archibald Graham, M.D., McDowell's chief adviser, and his wife, Martha Lyle
     Graham

William Booker Morton, of Botetourt, rented a home in Lexington

Samuel McDowell Reid, a lawyer and county clerk

William White, McDowell's Presbyterian pastor

OTHER FRIENDS

John Atkinson, a Presbyterian pastor in Washington, D.C.

John Holmes Bocock, a Presbyterian pastor in Harrisonburg, Va.

William Brown, a Presbyterian pastor in Augusta, Va.

Philip Fendall, an attorney in Washington, D.C.

Miss Jannetta Gordon, a frequent houseguest

Joseph C. G. Kennedy, McDowell's business agent in Washington, D.C.

Miss Polly Moore, a frequent houseguest

SLAVES

Alfred, a house servant, responsible for the mail

Edward, a house servant

Jenny, a house servant, a great favorite of McDowell

John Miller's World

FAMILY

Maggie (Margaret) Breckinridge, his niece

Sarah Miller Hageman, married to John F. Hageman, an attorney in
     Princeton

Allie (Alamby) Miller, his son. The children live with their grandmother.

Dick (J. Dickinson) Miller, his brother, a surgeon in the United States Navy, and
     his wife, Julia

Maggie (Margaret) Miller, his daughter

Mary Miller, his unmarried sister living with their mother

Sam (Samuel) Miller, his brother, a Presbyterian minister and schoolteacher in
     New Holly, N.J.

Sarah Sergeant Miller, his mother in Princeton

Spence (E. Spencer) Miller, his brother, an attorney in Philadelphia, and his
     wife, Annie

IN-LAWS (BY HIS FIRST MARRIAGE TO MARGARET BENEDICT)

"Aunt Hunter" (Margaret Benedict) Hunter, his wife's aunt

Sarah Benedict Potter, his sister-in-law, married to Alonzo Potter, the Episcopal bishop of Pennsylvania

MINISTERIAL COLLEAGUES

Addie (Joseph Addison) Alexander, a professor at Princeton Theological Seminary

Henry Boardman, a pastor in Philadelphia

Charles Hodge, a professor at Princeton Theological Seminary

Thomas Janeway, a pastor in Princeton

John Leyburn, editor of the *Presbyterian* in Philadelphia

John Maclean, president of the College of New Jersey

William McLain, secretary of the American Colonization Society

William Henry Ruffner, a minister at Harrisonburg, Va.

William Schenck, corresponding secretary of the Presbyterian Board of Education in Philadelphia

Courtland Van Rensselaer, a pastor in Burlington, N.J.

MEMBERS OF HIS CONGREGATION

Robert Cornelius, a trustee and businessman

Charles B. Dungan, a trustee and businessman

E. S. Field

Joseph W. Martin, a businessman

Joseph Reinboth, a businessman

FRIENDS

Joseph Henry, a former professor at the College of New Jersey, now director of the Smithsonian Institution, and his wife, Harriet L. Alexander Henry

Arthur Howell, a businessman in Philadelphia, and his wife, Anne Ruffner Howell

Edward Shriver, a former church trustee in Frederick

Samuel Tyler, a former church trustee, lawyer, and writer in Frederick

William Bradley Tyler, M.D., in Frederick

John H. Williams, a lawyer and editor of the *Frederick Examiner*

John Miller about 1851. Special Collections, University of Virginia Library.

Sally McDowell in 1855. Courtesy of Raleigh Colston Minor.

Colalto as viewed up the entry road, the "Straits of Gibralter," where Miller first proposed to McDowell. Colalto is placed on the top of a small knoll.

Colalto. Built of brick in Georgian style, the house has a four-on-four plan. The dining room extends out from the back of the house and opens on the left through two french doors onto a large porch with rounded brick columns.

The Miller home in Princeton, built for Samuel Miller in 1813, is similar in design to Colalto. It is now occupied by the Nassau Club.

The West Arch Street Church in Philadelphia as it looked in 1869. Completed and dedicated in 1855 while John Miller was pastor, it could accommodate more than twelve hundred people. Courtesy of the Presbyterian Historical Society, Presbyterian Church (U.S.A.), Philadelphia.

John Thomas Lewis Preston,
McDowell's "Cousin John."
Courtesy of the Virginia Military
Institute Archives.

Miller's drawing in his letter of July 19, 1855, to Sally McDowell.
McDowell-Miller-Warner Papers (MSS 2969-a), Special Collections,
University of Virginia Library.

Miller's drawing in his letter of August 24, 1856, to Sally McDowell. McDowell-Miller-Warner Papers (MSS 2969-a), Special Collections, University of Virginia Library.

Monday April 30th 1855

Dear John,

At last I come to tell you that I am yours. And I pray God to bless us not only in each other but to each other, and to grant us His favor and protection in the important step we are about to take.

If even to this hour I have fears and misgivings, and am disturbed by doubts and anxieties you must forgive me. They grow out of a condition of things as painful as it is unalterable and out of an anxious temper which is I think, like dear little Allie's ticklishness "constitutional". They are entirely without justification in anything I know or believe of you for I have the very fullest trust in your affection, and every confidence

McDowell's handwriting was more legible than Miller's. She wrote on April 30, 1855, her birthday, accepting his marriage proposal. McDowell-Miller-Warner Papers (MSS 2969-a), Special Collections, University of Virginia Library.

The wax sealer that Sally McDowell used on her letters. Courtesy of Raleigh Colston Minor.

John Miller and Sally
McDowell Miller in 1870.
Courtesy of C. Venable
Minor, Jr.

The graves of John and Sally McDowell Miller lie beneath this large white cross in the Miller family plot at Princeton Cemetery. John Miller inscribed his creed on his tombstone to ensure that his beliefs would not be misinterpreted after his death.

*"If You Love That Lady
Don't Marry Her"*

PART ONE

"*Fearing I say too much, unwilling to say too little.*"

August 1854–January 1855

[John Miller to S. C. P. McDowell]
Friday [August 4, 1854].

Mr Miller's compliments to Mrs McDowell & begs to know, if she or either of her sisters or either of her brothers will ride with him in a little uncomfortable no-top buggy to-day or to-morrow—& at what hour. If neither herself or either member of her family is able to go, he will be obliged to ask the favour of his friend Mr Turveytop.[1]

Aug: 7, 1854

My *dear Sir*,

I found it impossible to grant you a private interview this morning, but thinking it due to you and just to myself that I should explain my views and announce my decision upon the subject of our short conversation last night I avail myself of this, as the only practicable mode, suggested by [my] mind of doing it.

I need not remind you of the peculiarity of my condition in life; nor need I say how exceedingly painful to me, is the *equivocal* nature of it;—nor can I express to you the sensitiveness I feel in regard to every thing that, in the conduct of others refers to, or flows from it:—and thus, I cannot, perhaps, make you understand how my sense of womanly dignity and delicacy is assaulted by such revelations of feeling as those made to me last night. Not that I do not fully acquit you of all intention to offend; not that, on the contrary, I do not believe that true and pure

1. Turveydrop, a character in the novel *Bleak House* by Charles Dickens, was a model of decorum. Miller evidently saw a resemblance in one of his Lexington friends.

1

motives influenced you in the matter, yet I feel that I am greatly misapprehended both by you, and those who may have spoken of me to you, if you and they could suppose that I should feel, for one moment, that proposals like yours to me, in my peculiar circumstances could be otherwise than promptly declined. I could not and would not receive them from any one. The instinct of my nature revolts at any new marriage—and, furthermore, my views of religious truth and duty solemnly forbid it.

I speak, thus frankly, not to wound you in any point whatever—but to prove to you how utterly futile would be any attempt to draw me from the position I have taken.

You will, I am sure, do me the justice to believe that I was entirely unconscious of being in any degree connected with your present visit to our Town.

Our acquaintance has been too brief to have drawn much upon the strong emotions of your heart, and so, whilst your disappointment may be painful, I hope it will, likewise, be short. Your high and solemn office, demands for you such a Wife as I never could have made; and your Motherless children such gentleness and steadiness of temper in the one chosen to fill the now vacant place to them, as I have never possessed. This should entirely reconcile you to a decision, which a better knowledge of me would have prepared you for in the beginning.

I am really sorry to think that our acquaintance, begun in the darkest period of my life, and pleasantly renewed from time to time since should have been subjected to this sad trial,—but I hope, when this episode in it has been forgotten, you will return to the old feeling of friendliness with which it commenced.[2]

> I am, etc. etc.
> S.C.P. McDowell

Tuesday. A.M. [August 8, 1854]

My *dear Madam*,

I beg the privilege when more self possessed of replying to your letter, & expressing my sense of its kindness.

I believe I am acting however as you would desire in conveying to you these assurances.

No friend in Lexington has ever spoken of you in any way, but that of incidental remarks in conversing about the place, always it is true with very peculiar testimonies of respect, but never with the smallest hint of they having the slightest interest in the subject; I have no conception that any one dreams in my going away that I have shown you the least special attention.

---

2. Miller had been pastor of the Presbyterian Church in Frederick, Md., in the 1840s when Sally McDowell was involved in multiple lawsuits brought by her estranged husband, Gov. Francis Thomas of Maryland. Frederick was the site of one of the trials.

I came to Lexington with no idea of what has happened, & without the smallest connection with yourself other than as one of a pleasant company of friends that gave it a different appearance to me from the place I left. This I know makes my haste & *apparent* abruptness of conduct greater but shields me from the weightier charges of repeated dissimulations.

I never thought of such a purpose as that you mention. So little have I talked of you to others that I never heard it suggested. I never dreamed of it till last night. So opposite is it to my own understanding of Scripture, & so little had I given in to any such idea of taste that I had supposed the opposite course would be a clearer expression of principle, & a greater shelter to the mind before the feelings. Do not despise me, dear Madam, for what is so strongly abhorrent to yourself. Perhaps I am rash in uttering it. But it is far better to be under the imputation of an immature or ill considered opinion, than under that of intruding upon you a wrong or even doubtful desire.[3]

I beg your pardon for all that has happened, & while I thank you for the excuses that you make for me, I look back upon the whole occurrence with the most keen regret.

I cannot help loving you. I acted from a sense of honor in telling you at once. And tho' you will not allow me to say this again, yet you will listen to it now as being my great apology. All my memory of what I tho't noble in you before, united with the impressions of the present in suggesting & then fixing in my mind this most unfortunate affection.

Yours very respectfully,
Jno Miller.

Friday morning [August 18, 1854][4]

My *dear* Mrs McDowell,

I have so deep a sense of the violence I have done to your feelings, that I dare not do, as I long to do,—write a free full letter to make what reparation I can for my error, without your express permission. I have no right to infer certainly why it is that I was not able to see you privately on the morning I went over to your house for that purpose; but if it was, as I thought, that it would attract observation & you did not wish that any one should know of what had passed, I might be exposing you to the like notice by such a letter as I would desire to write. If however the reason was different, & referred rather to your feelings, & to your whole aversion to the meeting itself, then a letter ought to be doubly a matter of your own permission, & it was the possibility that this might be the cause, that led me to determine, on finding my sister planning the trip thro' Lexington, to

---

3. At this point in the letter McDowell later placed a number sign and wrote "I cant understand." McDowell returned this letter to Miller on Oct. 13, 1854, and Miller explained it in his letter of Oct. 24, 1854.

4. Miller probably enclosed this letter with the note he wrote the next day.

spend the Sunday elsewhere, & rigorously to observe the rule not to take the matter of a private interview into my own hand, or by a single question, even as to your having received my note, make you feel that I was not to be relied upon to observe your wishes.[5]

I have no confidant on earth, & never had, & have an irrepressible aversion to making any one, even my nearest relatives the repositories of my private feelings. No one suspects me of passing thro' anything on my journey but the sheerest routine of attendance upon my sister's plans & wishes in the whole expedition. And on that account I feel all the more desirous to hear some echo of permission from you before I venture upon writing what I wish should change the somewhat absurd aspect which this whole history must wear now in your mind & what I should write with the utmost pain if, without the chance of consulting others & knowing that we have already so widely differed, I should fear that you might be revolting from it all the time with the most uncontrollable aversion.

Your conduct throughout has been so unsuspecting & delicate, & your recent restoration of me to an outward friendship has been so kind & may, I am quite aware, cover up so great a repugnance of feeling that I feel afraid to write in the dark, tho' my real object is not as I at first desired to present myself a little less preposterously before your mind, but to make reparation for a sin which nevertheless I cannot still repent of except by adopting your principles as mine.

There are wild wishes that come crowding upon me which nevertheless I am resolved to banish. I would like to bend the other judgment to my own by the force of the requisite reasonings. I would like to nurse my usual obstinacy by setting this down as one of the instances in life where obstacles are to be opposed by perseverance. I would like to return to the condition of some time ago when I had no plans but those of a solitary life, & patiently lay siege to the opposition which circumstances & principles have placed before my way. But all this is so instantly checked by my judgment, & so remorselessly silenced, I mean as a thing to be obtruded upon you for a response, that I have now no other idea than that of governing my principles by yours, & of shutting in upon itself my own suffering & disappointed feeling.

Asking to be forgiven in anything in which I give you pain, I am,

Yours very truly & gratefully,
Jno Miller.

Philadelphia
Aug: 19th 1854

My *dear Madam,*

I accepted so almost entirely, (as I said I would,) your kind invitation that would have taken me away from the Hotel in Lexington & from my friend Mr.

---

5. His sister was Mary Miller (1808–1895). Never married, she lived with her mother in Princeton.

Poindexter, that I feel the normal inclination to write to say how pleasant my visit was, & how grateful I am for our share in your Virginia hospitalities.[6]

My sister & I reached Philadelphia on Thursday in the morning line, & my sister went on with a Princeton friend on Thursday evening.[7]

The family at home are well, though Margeret is almost wild with grief at her dreadful bereavement.[8] She has never had such a blow.

Begging to be remembered to the different members of your family, & hoping to meet some of you before long on one of your Northern tours, I am

Yours very truly
Jno Miller.

Colalto
Tuesday August 22, 1854

My *dear Sir,*

Your letter of the 19th was received this morning, and I avoid all delay and spare you all the pain of suspense by an immediate reply.

I am, indeed, troubled to know what to say, and that not, on my own account but on yours. I am not sure that it is kind to you to prolong the consideration of the subject that has opened up a correspondence between us, as will be done by my granting you permission to write the explanatory letter you mention. I known it can have but one result, and I believe that the sooner you learn to look upon that as imperatively fixed, the sooner you will obtain the mastery over the feeling which now causes you so much pain. I cannot recede from the sentiments and determination expressed in my former letter. They are founded upon principle and can not be abandoned, except, as is not probable, my conviction in the power and truth of my own reasoning be first shaken, and yet, I would treat with real kindness and due deference your feelings and opinions, however widely they may differ from, or however strongly they may come athwart my own. That we do differ—honestly differ as to the moral aspect of the subject is certain. I could not have treated you with anything but unmitigated scorn and contempt had I found you advocating *my* views of the matter, at the very time that you were cherishing such feelings and purposes as you have revealed. This has not, however, been your case, and hence I am, even anxious to mitigate the pain I am compelled to inflict.

If then, the letter you desire to write will be any relief to your own feelings I do not deny you permission to write fully and freely; and I grant this with less

6. George B. Poindexter (1797–1860), a lawyer in Lexington.
7. The "morning line" means the morning train.
8. Margaret (Maggie) Elizabeth Breckinridge (1832–1864) was the daughter of Miller's oldest sister, Margaret (1803–1838), and John Breckinridge (1797–1841), Old School Presbyterian minister and controversialist. Orphaned as a child, Margaret lived with her grandmother in Princeton. Her only sister, Mary (Polly) Cabell Breckinridge Porter (1826–1854), had died on Aug. 4. She had been married to Peter Augustus Porter (1827–1864) of Niagara Falls, N.Y.

reluctance because I know you will not misconceive or misconstrue my motive in doing it;—and because I am perfectly persuaded that your sense of honor, and gentlemanly principle will not permit you to utter one word unbecoming a gentleman to speak or a Lady to hear.

But if, after maturer deliberation you conclude to abandon the explanation you now propose to give, I beg you will not consider that I deem it all necessary—or in any sense demand it.

Allow me to thank you for the delicate manner in which you have conducted the whole matter. I do, indeed shrink from public observation and am grateful to you for your generosity in shielding me from it.

And now, tho' I can never be anything more, I am sure I shall never discover in you any quality that will make me anything less than

Your Friend
S.C.P. McDowell

Philadelphia. Sept 5th 1854

My dear Mrs McDowell,

In treading in the sanctuary of your private history even with the lightest & most hasty step, I am cruelly afraid of acting in some way indelicately. And tho' I *see* nothing in the path, yet I have been so mistaken once, & am so ignorant of your interior feelings, that I cannot tell how far the estrangement you have had & the stand you have taken in your previous life, will be my shield in what I have to communicate in respect to my principles.

I am under such painful motives to be honorable, & you have been so good to me in imagining that I intend to be correct, that I am perhaps beyond your suspicion of intentional indelicacy. And I do beg that this may be the case, & that you will attribute to want of sense what you might otherwise attribute to a careless indiscretion.

I came to Virginia without the least thought of you in any way connected with myself, & I went over to Lexington with no other thought than that you made a part of its pleasant society. I had, however, a more thorough acquaintance than our occasional meeting had been able to originate, & had borrowed that singular feeling of respect which the former people of my charge had constantly inspired me with.[9] I had all the principles I have broached settled, & every possibility of doubt forgotten long ago, & by a natural kind of fancy supposed that the same principles reigned, & were obvious everywhere, as prevailed in the circle where I originally formed them.

Now is not that a great deal to say in my own defence?

I came to Lexington & as an entirely undreamed of event was led into the feelings I so soon confessed to you. How I was led to them would be a simple

9. His "charge" refers to his congregation in Frederick.

story, & why they ripened so fast, I think I have sufficiently explained in what I have just communicated. I have tastes which I think you have, & I have aims in the future in which I know you would sympathize.—However, this is not a train that will be agreable to you.

My impulse was the common one, to come again, & mature our acquaintance by other occasions of meeting: but my idle life in Lexington left me whole mornings to think, & I soon made out a point of honor; in which I still agree. I felt this much of the peculiarities of your position; that having your hospitalities turned into occasions of attention, & the public eye attracted upon you as it must be by a second visit, must be singularly unpleasant: & I chose the hard alternative of the hazards of so brief an opportunity. I think I did right. The accident that could drift us together again I could hardly imagine. And leaving your hospitalities to react upon you as occasions of regret, I could not tolerate. Nor could I bear to give up the slender chance of the more early & private avowal. The decision, therefore, to ask the privelege to go on with my attentions before they had attracted the notice of others, is one that I could not have dreamed of a week before, but one which now in my soberest judgment I entirely sanction.

A more serious questions is, why I did not *suspect* the principles which you have since disclosed to me. You will know how helpless I was when I tell you, I do not suspect them now. I cannot imagine what you believe. I spoke to you on Sunday night—without a dream of such an opinion. Your mode of reply startled me when you said.—"I will not waver:"—& a remark casually made next day by Dr. White confirmed the impression that some such feeling might exist. Now how could I suspect it? That you have no thought that there are grounds of a valid divorce, & that that divorce restores one party to an independant & unmarried condition, I cannot have an idea. It would be against the faith of all Protestant churches, & against the Confession in the most set language, of your own.[10] Now, knowing as I do that *no* grounds of the most fastidious casuist are wanting in the case of which we are speaking, & that I am under no possibility of thoughtlessness as to the time or bearing of events; & seeing by your last letter that you derive all your sentiments in the case from principle, & base all your feelings in the case upon the moral and conscientious question, I can hardly express to you how profound my ignorance is, & how little I should be able to conceive any suspicion of such an existing difficulty.

Have I no hope at all that you may be deceived? Or—checking myself in what I have no liberty to ask, Will you not excuse *me*, seeing I am so helplessly seated in the entire certainty of my original opinion?

I have been now three weeks at my post, & my visit to Lexington, instead of appearing like a singular dream, appears more than I would have expected, the

10. William S. White (1800–1878), pastor of the Presbyterian church in Lexington from 1849 to 1867. The Westminster Confession of Faith was the authoritative confessional statement for Presbyterians.

solidest reality. I cannot alter feelings that take possession of my mind. You may tell me of an easy mastery, & of your temper & unsuitableness in many ways, but I have other impressions of a higher & nobler kind. I do not *need* a wife. To all those parts of your letters I can only answer, I love you wildly, & for aught I see more deeply & steadily day by day.

But while I make this honest avowal, I pledge my honor, that I will be governed by the most reserved restraint, & that in any answer you may send me, or in any future or accidental communication or intercourse, you shall never regret your generous & considerate friendliness.

Yours truly
Jno Miller.

Lexington Va.
September 12, 1854

My *dear Sir,*

We are both in fault as to the style of our letters. I have found yours somewhat ambiguous and obscure; and mine, I know now, must have been, as indeed you clearly intimate they were, in some parts, utterly unintelligible to you. The mistake has arisen from the fact that we, with limited personal acquaintance have each, presupposed, such a knowledge upon the past of the other, of our character, principles, and opinions, as have led us to think the generalities and mere allusions we have used amply sufficient upon a subject, which, in truth, demanded the most explicit and unequivocal language. To remedy this error, to some extent, I pray you bear with a very plain recital of my views upon the case at issue between us.

Of course you must know that I enter upon a subject of all others, the most embarrassing to me: there is no other that I handle with such awkwardness,—none that I shrink from with such pain, none upon which I maintain such entire reserve even with my most trusted and familiar friends: and that, I discuss it now is evidence of my respect and confidence in yourself;—a poor return you may deem it, for the stronger feeling you avow, yet all that I can give,—all that you can ever hope to receive.

If, in what I have to say, I should shock you by my plain speech, I shall not mislead you; and I feel that you already know me well enough to be fully satisfied that no *real* propriety and delicacy is wanting, tho' a show of it is not made by a fastidious or over-scrupulous attention to mere forms of expression.

That I may make my letter as satisfactory as possible, I take up, for reply, the points in yours, in the order in which you have presented them.

I find you anxious in your last, as in both your former letters, to convince me that my suspicion, expressed in my first note to you, that your visit here was planned with special reference to myself, and was, in some sort, instigated by the representations made of me to you by others, is without foundation. I believe you implicitly. I am satisfied I was wrong; and beg you will, by way of excuse for me recollect that I could not then know how much, or how favorable had been your previous knowledge of me; and also, that it was impossible for me to attribute to any attractions, I might have dreamed myself possessed of, power to awaken, to develope, to confirm such feelings as you have disclosed, in so short a time.

Then, as to the propriety on *your part* of the indulgence and acknowledgment of such an affection as you avow.

Here I have done you full justice. I could not believe, despite an ambiguous sentence or two in your first note that admitted a different construction,—that you would cherish a feeling to me, that you did not believe to be fully warranted by the most high-toned Scripture morality. I have no doubt you believed it abundantly sanctioned by the severest and most scrupulous religious principle—a belief, in which, I am well aware you are supported by the general consent of society. I do not blame you for your opinions—and think it natural in you, being "entirely certain of their correctness" to act in accordance with them. But they differ, perhaps irreconcilably from my own:—and this brings me to another, and to you, at present, the most important part of your letter.

I believe that the Divine Law, as revealed to us in the Bible, and as apprehended by my plain, common-sense, admits of but *one* plea for annulling any marriage; and this plea my *mind* does not admit in my own case.[11] My judgment may be erroneous; but until I can believe it to be so, it must direct my conduct. That I should, years ago, have taken the stand I did, with this distressing conviction pressing upon me may seem to you a strangely unworthy weakness. But, when the time for action came, I felt that my mind, from intense anxiety & the repeated & violent shocks it had been subjected to, was unequal to the task of directing in my difficulties, and in the terrible exigency to which I was driven, I surrendered my judgment to that of others.

Even then, however, I had no question as to the expediency of the measures adopted. I knew that altho' happiness was wrecked, and peace gone, yet safety and honor alike emphatically demanded a legal separation—a divorce (can you concieve how excessively painful that word is to me?)—yet I have ever had an abiding doubt upon my mind, as to the power of any human Tribunal to annul a marriage, the plea above-referred to being absent, so as to restore the innocent party "to an independant and unmarried condition."

But, did I consider myself, in the eye of God and man absolutely disen-thralled—perfectly free and untramelled in this matter, still, I think the instinct of my nature, I know not what else to call it, would forbid any new connection during the life of the other party. In the formation of a new tie, of this nature, my mind must bear upon it no lingering doubt of its unquestioned, unquestionable propriety;—my heart, enlisted in all its energy & power must feel that its outgoings are sanctioned by every pure and right principle; and that respecting,

11. That is, adultery.

confiding, loving thoroughly I must be assured there is nothing in my present history or circumstances that could by possibility arouse the faintest emotion of shame, or excite the feeblest ruffle in the calm confidence of the One whose honor & happiness was, thenceforth to be inwoven with my own, or the tie would prove to me only a source of anxiety, suspicion, mortification & sorrow. Can I ever have this assurance whilst the thought could force itself into my mind & into his, that another still lived to whom I had once sustained the same near and tender relation? The thought would be agony to me. God grant I never may be so forgetful of what is due to myself & due to others as to place myself in such a mortifying position. But;—yet no—I cannot go on. Have I not already said enough? It may be I have strained the point too far, and have said too much.

One word more: if you suppose I think lightly of the sincerity or strength of your attachment, when I speak of the mastery to be obtained over it, you mistake me. I have no reason to question either its purity or power, but I would render the work of self-conquest easier, by undeceiving you in your impressions of me. Believe me, you idealize far too much about me. Your imagination enriches me with many captivating, but unpossessed qualities. A more extended acquaintance would, perhaps, have shown you this, and have lessened the pain & disappointment you now feel by proving to you that your heart and your home would hardly have been brightened by my presence; nor, yourself aided in the discharge of the lofty duties of the highest & noblest calling upon Earth.

I shall have, no cause, I am sure to regret the confidence, my letters evince, but destroy them all that the memory of everything may perish that could give you pain; and only remember that I will not have you reject my offered friendship, nor disdain my very cordial esteem.

Truly Yours,
S.C.P. McDowell

Philadelphia,
Sept 21st 1854.

My dear Madam,

I can hardly describe to you how I am agitated & interested by your last letter. It reduces the whole question of which we have been writing to one point, in which I have the strongest confidence of being right, & in which I am beginning to have the strongest suspicion that you have been kept in at least partial ignorance.

You say, "Did I consider myself in the eye of God & man absolutely disenthralled still the instinct of my nature would forbid etc." "My mind must bear upon it no lingering doubt."—Now I think I may trust sufficiently to the firmness of your character, to believe that you would devolve this, like all the other judgments of your life, upon the decision of your "mind"; & that when that has clearly established itself, you will not be easily shaken as concerns yourself with doubts or lingering scruples as respects the propriety of your action. Then as concerns another; "the faintest emotion of shame, or the feeblest ruffling of his confidence" can only arise in a person of proper manliness, if he have misjudged the original question. And if, as I am firmly convinced, that question can be conspicuously settled, & *is* so settled with them who have the power to form the public opinion in the case, what sort of a character must he be who from a poor-spirited fastidiousness about the possible understandings of the matter, can be fancied to be disturbed by distant and mistaken analogies?

For myself, if *my* opinion were satisfied I would feel a sort of secret pleasure in having charge of your honour even if other people were in doubt; but as I know that this assurance will be very far from meeting the delicate requirements of your feeling and may result in my case from misanthropy or a wrong contempt, I wish to come in the directest way to the point at issue. I am willing to meet it on the most stringent principle. I am indeed stricter than you in not even having a "doubt upon my mind" that no human tribunal can annul a marriage, except on a single plea. I am excited only by the opening you give me for proving your freedom even on the most rigid grounds. And all I beg is, that no after sentiment or instinct may perplex a decision, if it is possible to derive it from the highest and most simple reason.

You say, "I believe that the Divine law as revealed to us in the Bible admits of but one plea for annulling any marriage, and this plea *my mind* does not admit in my own case". You can come to this last conclusion only in three ways. The plea, of course is that of criminal profligacy in one of the parties to the marriage. You can believe it not admitted in your case only either, first, because you are not aware of any criminality in the case in question; or, second because it does not exist in the form of public & notorious fact, so that it can be acted upon, and be a protection to character; or, thirdly, because it is not admissible in your particularly circumstances. I would have entered upon this less ambiguously before, were it not for the painful apprehension, that while I knew you would abhor a wanton vilifying of the person of whom I am to speak, you might even feel yourself trespassed upon by any severity of charge; especially if your friends, out of a kindred apprehension, had observed the policy of keeping from you any facts in the case.

With no other scrupulosity than this, I mean to throw myself upon your friendship to forgive me, if I fall into any such error; & state in the plainest way why on neither of the grounds I have mentioned can there be a vestige of doubt in respect to your independent position.

In the first place, therefore, your marriage has been entirely annulled, & needed only the action of the state to render it so legally & in fact, by subsequent and long continued profligacy.

In the second place, this profligacy was open & notorious to an extent entirely to justify your acts, in the community best acquainted with the matter; and

Thirdly, the mere fact that this was not the plea before the court (if that *was* the fact, & if that is the doubt in your own mind as to this whole charge being admissible in your particular case,) cannot for one moment be considered, because the church never takes action in this thing, & the state never in any one commonwealth except once; & that would make a marriage that had been dealt with on wrong grounds, inseverable ever afterwards, & give a man repudiated on other charges of wickedness, an immense advantage over one who had never been exposed to previous legislation.

Forgive me if you were not prepared to listen to such charges upon character. And forgive me, on the other hand, if you were not prepared to hear of this particular apprehension. You know I am writing a great deal in the dark; & have only the impressions of Frederick, where I am beginning strongly to believe, the whole case in its mingled monomania & wickedness, is only adequately understood.

I shall look eagerly for your letter, to know, (if nothing else,) that you go on in unruffled kindness to bear with me, & that you impute anything unnecessary that I have said, to some involuntary error, which must soon I think, of course, now, be discovered.

I have one or two things more to say which would make me very sad if you closed this correspondence; but of course I am bound in honour to consider it entirely in your hands.

Yours truly,
Jno Miller.

Colalto,
September 29.1854

My dear Sir,

Your letter has not a little surprised, whilst it has much embarrassed me. I had expected from you acquiescence, not argument; submission, not special pleading.

Until it came I was not aware I was likely to fall, and indeed had fallen into the error of leading you to suppose that the question of ethics was the only one involved in the subject upon which we had been writing; and that if that were triumphantly established in your favor all your difficulties would have been overcome. I had no design or desire to make any such impression for it must be plain to you that there is another point to be considered just as important to us both—, that of a response upon my part to the affection you avow.

My full & free exposition of my views upon this whole matter was, in part, to prove that, with me, this peculiar sentiment did not and could not exist. And you must pardon me, if I say again that if I adopted your opinions, upon your statement of the *facts* in the case, as my own, yet the *instinct of my* nature, however much you may despise it as a contemptible weakness, is not subdued; and it were neither kind nor proper in me to lead you to hope it ever would be.

Our acquaintance has inspired me with no other or stronger feeling than that of my cordial and respectful regard, which I have, without hesitation or disguise, and with as much sincerity as frankness both exhibited and expressed. My letters have given the most unmistakable proof of confidence & esteem— but of nothing more.

Very Truly Yours,
S.C.P. McDowell

Phil. Oct. 6th 1854

My *dear* Madam,

I deeply regret any part of my letter that could be apprehended in the way you indicate. So far from fancying that you have encouraged me in any stage of our correspondence, I have detected nothing in all your letters but a desire to spare my feelings. If I spoke eagerly in my last letter, it was out of the poor comfort of getting *one* difficulty out of the way, and the keen interest I felt even in so small a progress. Your letter brings me to my senses even in that feeling.

The enclosure that I make is one that costs me some pain, and I make not out of any ruffled feeling, but from two well considered motives: one, that I am reading these letters over & over again & I find it not prudent; & the other that I know it will not annoy you if I send them back, but it might annoy you hereafter, with some uncertainty as to their contents, to think of them as being in my possession. The last is perhaps the less well founded consideration of the two.

That your decision makes me *suffer*, I do not deny. That it will cause me suffering for a long time to come, I do not attempt to conceal. It is a new experience; no such desire or proposal having been ever disappointed before. But nevertheless, in respect to my welfare, it restores me only to that loneliness, for years & probably forever, which, till within a few weeks, I invited as the chosen condition of my life.

I have one comfort—that plans of retired study which I have long been cherishing, & which Providence seems to be giving me the means, & may give me the conscientious motive, when I grow older, to realize, will carry into their calm retreats no regrets in respect to this particular transaction of my history, as intentionally blameworthy or dishonorable. I am

Yours very truly
Jno Miller.

Colalto
Oct: 13. 1854.

My *dear* Sir,

After some delay in the mail I have received your letter, with its enclosure. I will make a similar return to you by the next mail.[12]

---

12. Miller had returned her letters to him, and she will reciprocate.

Before our correspondence closes will you patiently bear with another long letter from me?

I do not utter mere words of course when I say how much I feel for you in the pain I have inflicted. I have learned, from the sad events of my life, to be ever covetous of affection, and to return, if nothing more, the warmest gratitude to the bestower of it. Thus I have felt to you & have sought to be truly considerate of your feelings throughout. If in any one instance, I have failed to *appear* thus careful, believe me, it has been thro' sheer awkwardness. I have, in writing, stumbled upon some wrong word, or blundered out some equivocal or obscure sentence or phrase that has clouded or else sadly distorted my meaning. I have fancied, from your last note, that you have felt yourself & your motives, in some way, misapprehended. To this I can only say, that our somewhat peculiar, & certainly very free correspondence has developed traits of character that have won greatly upon my confidence and respect. I have more & more admired the high-toned delicacy, & dignified propriety, and considerate generosity which has characterized your conduct from the beginning. That I could not meet your wishes, by & bye when you look back coolly upon this whole affair, you will not think a fault in me. You know, I did not knowingly draw them out. They had clustered thick about me whilst as yet I was wholly unconscious of their existence. That I should have awakened them was a wonder to me then, is a mystery to me still. But, when they were revealed, I endeavored to treat them with every kindness. For the first time, in many years I have listened to proposals such as yours. Heretofore, for reasons my previous letters have given, I turned from them with a kind of horror. But in your case, (I speak too frankly to be misconceived) I paused, not that my resolution wavered, but because my regard for you indicated a different & a kinder course. I thought you too precipitate. I did not know how you could learn to love me in so short a time. You seemed overtaken & overcome by a feeling, that might exhaust itself in the first outbreak. Yet you were painfully in earnest & I shrank from any semblance of severity in dealing the blow I was forced to give.

Thus, as matters cleared up a little, and difficulties, at first obscurely hinted at, were, at length, plainly stated, I spoke freely my views upon these difficulties, & calmly considered yours. I did more:—for the first time in my life, I invited conversation with a near & dear kinsman upon the moral question involved.[13] Of course we agreed, & you agree with us upon the main point; & strangely enough by a series of coincidences, just then occurring, we had the *facts* of your letter confirmed. So that the *doubt* upon my mind has been dispelled. Yet my decision remains the same. No woman in my circumstances, however free she may be acknowledged to be, may use her liberty without, to a greater or less extent,

13. Her cousin John Thomas Lewis Preston (1811–1890), professor of languages and English literature at Virginia Military Institute and an elder of the Presbyterian church in Lexington. She refers to him as "Cousin John" throughout the correspondence.

losing *caste* in society:—and my pride & delicacy, no less than my generosity recoils from any step that could implicate my own standing, or that of another. This view & others mentioned in it, constrained me to write my last letter. You had desired to "say one or two things more" you said. This made that letter only the more necessary. It left you entirely free to say or not to say them; & rescued me from the false appearance, of encouraging you to go on, whilst yet in the dark as to my sentiments. Did I not do right?

This review of the whole matter I make in the hope of disabusing your mind of any suspicion it may entertain of any unkindness upon my part; & to convince you that I hold no sentiment unfavorable in the slightest degree to your honor, in motive or conduct.

And now, why should not I express my sympathy for you? Is it not natural that I who have known so much of sorrow & disappointment should comprehend what you feel now, & feel for you? Suffering keenly as you think you do now, you have but a shadowy perception of that suffering that has taught me to feel tenderly for the sorrow of others. You do not know, as I have known the agony of having the outpourings of a heart in all its luxuriant fullness & freshness, & purity scornfully trampled upon as utterly valueless: and worse, far worse than this, you know not what it is, despite all your efforts to have the conviction fasten upon you that you have poured out the treasure of your affection upon an unworthy object; & then to have your own right principles, as an iconoclast, come into your heart's inner temple, despoil it & leave it vacant and desolate. You know not what it is to bear thro' weary years a shattered heart with its vacant chambers, its extinguished fires,—its dethroned image,—its broken shrine: with its silent hopelessness,—its terrible struggles,—its anguished longings: with its sad memories,—its humiliating present, and without a future. You know not what it is to live, with the spring of life broken; to live on and on amid the scattered debris of all that you valued in life; to have existence, but to spend it "among the tombs" of every thing that made it a blessing. You know not what it is to have your pure name spoken by polluted lips; to have your high and cherished honor assailed by mouths whose very breath was infamy;—and to have your grief, that sacred thing,—so deep as to be powerless even to throb out an appeal for mercy, denied the last poor privilege of decent privacy. This,—all of this, has been the bitter experience I have garnered up in the very Spring-time of my life.

But these are not the only lessons of the past. This seed time of tears, has brought forth some precious fruits.

When borne down by a sorrow too deep for the reach of human aid however truly & affectionately rendered, my poor heart turned to listen to the tones of One who commended himself to me as being "acquainted with grief," and by his gentle ministrations I was gradually soothed into calmness & peace. A new light burst in upon my darkened heart; a new motive-power was applied to it. I learned that tho' many ties were broken, yet there were enough left to re-connect one with the *duties* of life. I was roused up to a sense of my responsibility, & woke again into energy as the great future with its stupendous realities was spread out, and offered—even to me. I learned, to cast the burden that was heavier than I could bear, upon Him who offered to bear it for me; and, at last gathered courage and strength to take up, I hope unmurmuringly, my cross and bear it. And tho' I often sat down and wept, as I do now, when I looked back upon all the mortification, & trial & struggle of the tedious way, yet the hardest perhaps & best lesson I learned in that stormy period is in practice still, and I bless God, that in tender mercy he did not spare, but has thus "wrung out to me the bitter waters of a full cup."

This is a sad chapter in my history. It seemed pressed upon me by the subject-matter of my letter; and I have so completely exchanged with you the formalities of mere acquaintance for the confidence & abandon of matured friendship, that I allowed my feelings to gush out without restraint.

I shall always feel the greatest interest in your welfare; will always claim a share in your friendly feelings; and will ever be ready to show myself to be, with all sincerity a friend upon whom you may confidently rely.

Very Truly Yours
S.C.P. McDowell

Phil. Oct. 24th 1854.

My *dear Madam*,

Your letter & package have both been received, & your letter has interested & affected me more than I can express. If you have read Bleak House, you remember the character of poor little Jo, the street sweeper. Tho' all that you write has the same melancholy effect that he suffered under of making one "move on"; yet I can't help having his sentence also sometimes in my ear, "She was very kind to me, she was."

I see on one of the letters, which I enclose, the mark, "*I dont understand*". I don't see exactly where the difficulty is, or whether you intend both places where your # is found. I will, therefore, re-write the whole paragraph.

I have never thought of such a purpose, on your part, as that not to marry. I had never heard it suggested that such was your intention. I never so much as thought of such a thing till the night before last, when you used the expression, "I will not waver"—which instantly suggested to me something of the kind. (I wrote the letter at one o'clock at night, & when I came to date it, marked it Tuesday morning, but in the body of the letter meant Sunday night by "last night.") So opposite is such a purpose, on your part, to my understanding of the Bible, & so little had I recognized it as the proper dictate of feeling, that I had supposed the opposite course i.e. practically increasing the distance, would be etc. ["]It is better to be under the imputation of a mistake in opinion, than under that of something that I know or suspect to be wrong."

You may smile perhaps at my diligence in sending on & correcting this old tavern letter, written in that bad time for being very clear, when, if I had not to go early in the morning, (I think at six) I should have been seeking rest from my troubles in what you would think a more innocent way; but my love has one element of goodness which I see very clearly now, when I have no other motive to act for; which is, that I long to stand well in your opinion, even if I never see you again.

I have one little request to make. It is a rule of the seas, when two vessels come into collision, that they shall stay within *speaking distance* till the extent of the damage is determined. As it is very easy to see which is the most suffering party in our case, & the difference is so great that while one is quite uninjured, the other is almost in a sinking condition, I pray that till the great old Wreck-master, Time does something for me in my recent distress, you will stay within sight of my signals, & give me what help you are able. I know that you claim exemption from blame & that as far as you are concerned we came into collision in the fog; but the rule of the seas admits of no apology on such a ground.

You have no conception of the pleasure with which I read over your letter on the evening of the day I received it. I have a lovely little study where, after the labours of the day, I find it a quiet relief to sit dreaming by a good hickory fire, which is really the best comfort I have, & which I sit watching for hours while engaged in my different ruminations. These tho'ts are not all idle but sometimes they ought to be, as a rest from continued study; & tho' the comfort I propose is too much like extracting a poisoned arrow by the barbs of others, yet I cannot bear the thought of never hearing from you again. You see it does not do to praise a poor tried person like me; it gives me a sort of Roman Catholic feeling of goodworks that I can draw upon now as a claim of supererogation. I pray God may comfort & support *you*, my dear Madam, in your long continued distress, & that while your pleasant house seems to you like a place of sepulchers & my great church seems to me like a grand mausoleum of my happiness, I hope that it will all be preparing us at least to meet in another & better condition of being.

Yours truly,
JM.

Colalto
Nov: 2.1854

My dear Sir,

Is your "little request" really small? Is it truly wise? Do we understand each other so perfectly that neither will run any risk if I should grant it? Perhaps you wish to test the truth of my assurance that a better knowledge would give you other less favorable impressions of me, and *complimenting* me by attributing this disenchanting power to my notes you are willing they shall, from time to time, invade your little Sanctum & dispel your evening reveries?

But since you ask only "for such aid as I may be able to give", and as you know exactly the extent of my ability in this case, of course there *must* be no misunderstanding either now or hereafter on this score & so, I promise to "keep within sight of your signals" until I find I am no longer needed.

I thank you for your "diligence" in explaining your first letter. Had you written a sentence in Hebrew & asked me to extract an idea from it, I could not have found it more difficult than I did to get some insight into the meaning of that strange paragraph: I worried over it many times, & ever finished as I commenced with the question—what can Mr Miller mean? It is clear enough now, however, & altogether different from any & every thing I had supposed it to mean.

The returned letters, for whose life you plead, have had their sentence commuted to solitary confinement in a nice niche in my Secretary. They wear, in their imprisonment an air of entire quietude, as if the object of their existence had been successfully achieved.

Let me refer to the past once more & ask a question now that I could not have asked before, & which I beg you will not think impertinent.

In a matter so important as that which has been the subject of our correspondence did you take into careful,—I will not shrink from using the stronger word that forces itself upon me,—*prayerful* consideration the influence which would have been exerted, had your wishes been carried out, upon your character & usefulness as a Christian Minister? Or, did you give the rein to your feelings and allow them to override every suggestion, (remonstrance there may have been too) of prudence upon a point of such vital interest as this?

> *I am,*
> *Very Truly Yours*
> *S.C.P. McDowell*

Phil. Nov: 13th 1854

My *dear Madam*,

I have too much at stake not to be able to answer the question you propose, in my own favour. My dear little children, to say nothing of my ministry, would decide me against anything rash or passionate in what you rightly describe as "a point of such vital interest."[14] I love them with *a sort* of affection that shall be controlling over every other. That is, I shall not answer to my former experience of myself, if I do not take the path of suffering, & endure the utmost loneliness, as I do in sending them from me, rather than sacrifice in any important way my poor orphan son & daughter.

Your question, instead of being an im[pro]per one, might have been asked at any stage of this proceeding; & tho' it may provoke a smile, I will tell you in *detail* how far I was from anything like the over-riding of mere passionate determination.

14. Margaret (Maggie) Miller (1847–1932) and Alamby (Allie) Millington Miller (1849–1869) were the two surviving children of Miller's first marriage to Margaret Benedict (1820–1852).

You know I have always said that that week in the McDowell House was a very *long* one in a great many senses of the word.[15] I had nothing to do but spend it in a way befitting its object as part of my Summer vacation; & what began in listlessness & ennui, ended in some of the deepest & truest & most "prayerful" & most agitated reflections of my life. So unromantic & methodical was I in what you think the "over-riding of every remonstrance", that I absolutely tore from a letter a white margin, & wrote down upon it, I remember, a long catalogue of *points*, in respect to which there might be some question of my wisdom. And in view of my responsibility, not merely as a minister, but as a Christian, which suggests to me something far higher, I did pray that I might be guarded in each of the separate questions that I was called thus plainly to consider; & that God who had loved me hitherto, & had caused his goodness & mercy to follow me in the most trying periods of my life, would keep me from any step that might injure *any* of those who might be implicated in it.

The question to which you particularly refer was not then, in my mind, a very serious one. The feeling of Virginia differs (& I wonder that I have not thought of mentioning this before) from almost any other state. The Legislature more seldom treats such matters; indeed, scarcely ever. There is a feeling about those who are driven to this species of legislation, which is not dreamed of in Northern commonwealths; & apart from any question of a second marriage, a totally different way of regarding the subject from that which prevails, for example, in my native state. Now, if the moral question is one to be decided in the way in which we entirely agree, it may be a doubt whether the feeling prevailing in Virginia, however wholesome it may seem in the majority of cases, may not be oppressive & wrong, & really less desirable in itself, than the one which may have been considered too lax in us at the North.

In respect to the whole subject, now that I have had its most serious aspects brought by our correspondence & by my own reading & reflection very directly before my mind, I say deliberately, that if I thought that I could by any honourable means yet win your hand, I would not hesitate to employ them; & that I would consider my "character & usefulness as a Christian minister", & in my present exposed position, not unfavorably influenced, but rather the contrary.

I do not think the moral difficulty the only one that could injure me, & am ready to consider the mischief of losing caste: & yet not merely for the sake of my family, but for the sake of my ministry, I would not for a moment hesitate. Could I answer your question more fully?

I have plans for the future which may give me feelings of greater independency than most men, & indeed color my thinking with that freedom & retirement in which I hope one day to live, but yet I do not think they affect the integrity of my present judgment. By the way, If I tho't that you would keep my secret & forgive my egotism, I would like to write a great long letter, some day full

15. The McDowell House was a Lexington hotel.

of these dreams which promise to cover with a hue peculiarly their own all the evening of my history.

Yours very truly,
JM

Lexington
Nov: 23. 1854

My *dear Sir,*

No truly, you could not have answered my questions more fully, nor in a way that could more surely have obtained for you my highest regard. For the first time, you have been able to show yourself in your real character in all points, and in the best light. Heretofore there has been an incompleteness in your mental portraiture, as far misled by your own hand, that has made you to look to me *morally* as singularly as would a picture of you physically, that omitted your spectacles,—or rather, that gave you the glasses with but a single eye beneath them.

I have never, until now, in all our correspondence known you to speak of your children. They were present to my mind in the beginning, and in my first letter I ventured to say so,—how was it they seemed absent from yours? But my question has brought you out fully upon that point, as well as upon others, and has exhibited you or made you exhibit yourself more justly & truly than you have ever before done. I claim your thanks for having asked it.

You are perfectly right in all you say and feel about those little children. They have paramount claims upon you, & should exert, as you say a "controlling influence" upon your selection of one to fill the most important & most difficult of all relations to them. If I dare open up the subject again I would tell you how many, in the multitude of my thoughts upon it, had been given to them—especially to the little girl, whose happiness & well-being would be most affected in the matter.

I was hardly prepared to hear of so much "*method*" in your proceedings, yet it was not only necessary, but highly becoming; and certainly does you no discredit. Where so much and so many are involved it was due to all that such deliberation should be used. But, I fear to say more.

I am rather resentful at your skepticism upon my ability to "keep a secret".

I remember with some amusement even yet how I startled you by saying, "I thought silence the refuge of Cowards:"—well, when you confide to me your "dreams", as you half promise to do, you will find me silent enough to prove myself the greatest coward in all Virginia; and as ready with my sympathy as my comprehension of your schemes will allow. You will forgive me, I know, if I should prove very dull, for you will recollect that I am a mere matter-of-fact person—just as much so indeed—as one who inherits my Father's emotional nature can be.[16]

---

16. "Father's" refers to James McDowell III (1795–1851).

Will you give me leave to laugh a little at your "dreams," should they be very fantastic, reassure me you will not feel hurt at it?

My house has been a sort of social kaliedoscope—always changing its figures—for the last five or six months. I had no exemption from company in all that time. Just a week ago, I parted with a party of six & have three yet remaining with me. Though the most insouciante of Hostesses, yet I am obliged to take some thought for my Guests, & so, (pray don't think me inhospitable), I am thinking a period of absolute quiet will be very pleasant. For six months I have done all my thinking by spasms & reading by snatches, until I have well nigh lost the capacity to do either. But during the imprisonment imposed upon me by our Winter climate, I hope to re-learn the art of thinking and reading, and will not despair of getting some new furniture for my "chambers of imagery," which are at present in a sadly impoverished condition.

I am looking with much pleasure to a visit from my friend John Atkinson, (Dr John now, what a parade of D.D's good, bad & mediocre we make!) who comes seeking aid for the National Church at Washington.[17] I have little enthusiasm for the scheme. I know Washington too well to think it will succeed there: but it may. How is your own grand church progressing? Do you like these fine edifices? I do not. But I spare you an *eloquent* defence of my opinion. A day of glorious beauty has subsided into a night of oppressive stillness.—How sad these bright winter days are! Have I not set you an example of egotism?

> *Yours truly,*
> S.C.P. McDowell.

Princeton, Nov: 28th 1854

My *dear Madam*,

Here I am in the house in which I was born. My sister & niece have gone to church. Little Margaret & Allie have just been in to kiss me & bid me good-night. Mother is sitting in her favorite place by a table in the back parlour. And I am up in my chamber, (a great old country room that makes me ashamed of my "little sanctum" in Phila) writing to you. I have just closed the inner shutters upon one of those sad sights you speak of, when by moonlight I can almost fancy I see as far as the distance of your *day* view from Colalto: for you must know that from the ridge on which my mother's house stands, we can see the Navesink hills, which are 30 miles away, & have a broad view besides of much of the intervening country.[18]

17. John Mayo Pleasants Atkinson (1817–1883), Presbyterian minister in Washington, D.C.

18. His sister and niece were Mary Miller and Margaret (Maggie) Breckinridge. His mother, Sarah Sergeant Miller (1778–1861), was the daughter of Jonathan Dickinson Sergeant, lawyer and U.S. congressman from Philadelphia. The Navesink Highlands are located in Monmouth County, N.J.

Your threat about laughing at me has scared away all the little courage I had, & driven back all my dreams about my future hermitage into their ancient hiding place. Suppose that one of the things with which I expect one day to move the world, you should undertake to pronounce "fantastic", what pleasure do you think I would take in my new confidante? And if I should see fit to paint a philosopher with a long robe & venerable beard, you might make an ill-natured copy burying up the philosopher in his hat & spectacles. I c[an']t[19] admit you into my grove of Academus.

But, my dear Madam, why do you approach a part of your letter in which I take the keenest interest, & then turn off from it with the expression, "If I dared open up the subject again I would tell you how many etc"; & why do you say, "But I fear to say more?" There are many things that I dare not say to you,—at least that I dare not ask you; but in your very different position, I see not why you may not approach the subjects of which these sentences were speaking with the greatest freedom.

Your information about the emptying of your house interests me very much. I have been making a sort of sum in Single Rule of Three of it.—If a lady with a house full of company, writes a certain number & length of letters to a friend, how many will she write when all her guests have gone home. And I have fancied that thro' the Winter I might hear every week. Did you not promise to answer all signals?

I cannot say that the particular office for which you said that you destined your letters is going on very rapidly, indeed your letters make me more & more unhappy, but by a strange perverseness of feeling I cannot think of your ceasing to write them without feeling sure that I should be more unhappy still.

I have alluded to there being certain questions that I dare not ask you. Ever since we have corresponded, I have been longing to frame them in some way in which I could dare approve them. But tho' fair enough in the first aspect, they always appeared to me unhandsome & not in the highest tone of gentlemanly feeling when I bro't them to the last analysis. They might lighten my heart, or in another event might serve the part of a merciful sheriff, who adjusts the rope so as to quicken the death of the criminal, but I might no sooner ask them than this correspondence might stop, which would be in itself a great affliction.

Can I never, *never*, *never*, have anything but your highest regard? & if I were faithful thro' long years of manhood & even age, could I *never* exchange this cold esteem for the smallest spark of a warmer & fonder feeling? And if I could, or even if there is no strong assurance that I could not, is there no more cloistered employment of life than that of an exposed public ministry, if it be honorable & equally influential & useful, that could abate your objections on the score of what you think an implication of others in the loss of caste, & indeed present a mode of employment & usefulness answering all the demands of what you think a peculiar condition? What I tho't of telling you of are not dreams, but are in fact

19. The letter is torn here.

the solidest realities of life, & things that I mean in the way that Edwards did & in the way that Butler & Foster did, (tho' with far less power of success) one day to put in practise.[20] Now may not one in the shadow of great libraries, & in the communion of men wiser & more refined than any of our congregations afford, shelter oneself from the ruder traits of a condition which, moreover, I believe you have invariably overwrought & exaggerated? I tremble when I think that I am touching the old chord again: but I am confident that you are sufficiently willing that I should be unreserved & (as you expressed it; it is true, in a very different instance) à la abandon in these communications, to forgive me, if I give you pain, or cause you embarrassment in the feelings I express.

These are not the questions that I have alluded to above, of course, or I would not ask them: but you may think them as hard to bear. Yet I dont know: I am passionately in earnest. What ought you not to excuse in one who makes such an avowal? Will you not write me a letter equally free & equally early in reply?

Yours very truly,
Jno Miller.

Wednesday [November 29, 1854]

My *dear* Mrs. McDowell,

On waking this morning I find the accompanying letter in my drawer as the work of last evening. On reading it, it has so imperfectly the approval of my conscience, & seems to answer so little to the understanding with which we continued our correspondence that I have been afraid to send it. I, therefore, write *this* as my official communication, & send the other just as an instance of what a young man may come to, who trusts himself right, is far better & holier than certain forms either of social or spiritual indifference. Mourning is always a sin because the command is, Rejoice evermore, & there can be no mourning the moment we reach a state of spiritual perfectness tho' occasions of it will still remain. And yet the promise is, "Blessed are they that mourn &c."[21] So I believe building five churches would never be preferred in a state of the most single-minded devotion to the cause. But as a happy intermediate state between spiritual barbarism & refinement, like the temple at Jerusalem, I have no doubt of it.*[22]

Yours very truly
Jno Miller.

[marginal note] My stay in Princeton is but for a day or two.

20. Three clergymen and theologians, the American Jonathan Edwards (1703–1758) and the Englishmen Joseph Butler (1692–1752) and James Foster (1697–1753).

21. Matt. 5:4.

22. Miller placed an asterisk in the letter and in the margin of the last page placed another and wrote "I would not differ from you, but you say, [']silence is the refuge of cowards.'"

Colalto
Dec'r 6. 1854

I am at a loss;—fairly puzzled;—and, my friend, the case stands thus. Two letters came to me from Princeton; one written at night, the other, at that best of all hours for the action of the "sober second thought"—the early morning. The first written under the exhilarating influence of your emancipation from your little Sanctum & its hard work in Phil'a, and under the enkindling power of a reunion at home with home-friends, had imparted to it a warmth and glow, which I do not wonder shocked, at a more sober moment, the nerves of one so (you are so afraid of my "ill-natured copies," I will try your own *fancy sketch*) "methodical & unromantic" as you are. And shocked indeed they must have been to have called forth that stately morning note of most emphatic revocation. The original of the evening's picture, with "flowing robe and venerable beard,"—with solemn step & slow—with measured words and stern, came gravely stepping out to show himself recovered from the overthrow his *impulse* caused the night before. But, seriously, for I would not have you think I could trifle with any feeling that presses you so nearly, you must acknowledge, that I know not what to do. I cannot answer the first letter, because, your second says, "it is only sent as an evidence of the danger of yielding to the feeling of the moment" and, more than that, that it "imperfectly meets the approval of your own conscience." In this state of the matter I shall answer neither, but when you decide what, in either, you would like answered you can write again. By the way, in respect to any questions you may wish to ask, as I am of course, even without conjecture as to what they may be, I can only say that whatever you decide can, in the "highest tone of gentlemanly feeling" be asked; that you will always find me ready to answer. I am quite sure you will ask none that will be improper, tho' they may be painful for me to answer. I feel that you are entitled, from me, to most kind & candid dealing, and I have not a moment's fear of your saying anything that would be, in the slightest degree inconsiderate of my feelings.

And now I shall ask a question out of the sheerest womanly curiosity.—Had you not absolutely forgotten me before your visit this summer, so that you never could have recognized me again? I thought so, & was not a little amused at your blunders in endeavoring, to recall the occasions of our former acquaintance. Yet my vanity was not in the least mortified by having thus sunk into complete oblivion. I am aware that I could not look now as I did when you saw me before. I must then have had an exhausted look, that seemed to appeal to the kindly sympathies of others, for I was always receiving that sort of tender attention that is usually bestowed upon invalids. Moving about constantly for years, with a name that ever told its own sad story, I was necessarily much exposed to remark, yet altho' keenly sensitive, have never had aught to look back upon but kindness, full & free & prompt. But I was weary—heart weary then, and had not nature given me a little sunshine in my temper, that seemed absolutely indestructible; & had not the light of another world somewhat illumined this, life would have been a burden to me.

But I have run unconsciously into this strain. Perhaps I am led into it by my present solitariness. My last Guests left to-day, and my shrunken household (only four now) seem lost in this big house, only the wing of which is to-night occupied. The main building seems converted into an assembly room for the storms, for the wind, this cold night comes whistling, and moaning and sighing thro' it like a despairing Spirit—or rather, like a company of wailing spirits. I know no name so appropriate and descriptive for this place as Bleak House.[23]

And as I sit writing in intense silence, as to human sounds, is it any wonder that the Past should cast its weird spell over me? Is it strange that Memory in this somber hour should come with crow-bar & pick and dig deep, deep into my heart, laying open stratum after stratum, disclosing in each some precious fossils that not only mark the epoch of its convulsive upheavings, but likewise tell its story of decay and death. But, I don't mean to borrow a lament from the sorrowful winds, so pray pardon me.

You give me little chance to sympathize in your dreams; (you are quite behind the times—you should say visions.) Yet from the little peep you vouchsafed me I hope they are only dreams, and not as you sometimes call them "solid realities." The "shadow of a great Library" may afford a pleasant retreat—may wear a wooing aspect to a perplexed, and dispirited and discouraged Minister—may promise a shelter from rude assaults upon his feelings,—yet, after all, it seems more like an asylum for the fleeing, (shall I not say truant?) than a home for the weary: and every Minister who gives all up else for it, except he be disqualified for all else but it, seems to me to be recreant to his high & holy duty. If you can unite ministerial duty, with an author's pleasures, that could not be objected to,—but to give up the pulpit for the pen—would never do. I know that your condition as one of trial but having borne it this long, you do not now grow weary of the burden? There is none other more honorable and honored—none other so important or influential. I do not exaggerate it. I think I am competent to judge in the matter, and I say again as I said to you once before, I think your calling (that's a good Presbyterian word if it be not a very elegant one) the highest and noblest upon earth.

I have lived all my life in the clatter and jingle of titles: my associations have been with those who were among "the powers that be", and I am in no slight degree possessed of the ambitious spirit that characterizes my race, yet I say I esteem no condition in life higher than your own. It involves more self-denial than any other, it is true, yet the rewards of it are often great, and have no bitterness added to them. But you must be wearied out with my—lecture.

23. *Bleak House*, by Charles Dickens (1812–1870), was first published in 1853. It critiqued the brutal features of the British mid-nineteenth-century industrial society.

Does Wadsworth fill your imagination as a great Preacher?[24] I have heard him twice & incline to the opinion that his power is rather in expression than thought. I do not remember to have been struck either time by the originality or boldness, or variety or power of his conceptions, but there was a gushing, rushing, dashing, impetuous flow of language wailed out in his peculiar voice that was very impressive. Would his Thanksgiving sermon be much, stripped of its costume & judged for its mental strength alone? I think not. His satire is keen enough. His declamation only mediocre, & his positions too plain to require great talent either to take or maintain. But I am no judge.

I wish you a pleasant jaunt thro' my long letter, and refreshing rest for your exhausted energies at the end of it. Your calculations, no matter by what Arithmetical process made out, are all wrong. I have no notion of "bestowing my tediousness" in letter form, upon you once a week—Dont you know I am busy all the time? & don't I know that you have no time to waste on such *amplified notes* as mine?

Very truly Yours
S.C.P. McDowell

Sanctum Sanctificorum
Tuesday Evening [December 12, 1854].

My dear Madam,

I have been reading your letter again & again & again, & the only comfortable conviction that it brings me to is that I must send you some good English ink. I am busy in these December weeks in collecting my budget of presents for all even my remoter friends & relatives. As I believe you are related to me thro' the Breckinridges, I have rolled you up the enclosed packet out of my drawer, acting on my principle of giving every one what they seem most to need; for you would seem to me to be as near perfect as I can easily imagine, if you only had better ink. While I am in the same generous mood too, I wish to mail a volume of my brother's poetry. I happened to be reading a part of it the day your letter was handed in (for Spence & I have a bargain to read what each other publishes) & was arrested by a stanza or two as illustrating in some way your letter, & I forget which the stanzas were. You will find a good deal of the sentiment true, & the poetry much better than could be expected. By the way an old English book that I once read *"On Fashions,"* said that no present ought to be given that was of any value, & that presents of *game* or id omne genus were the most

---

24. Charles Wadsworth (1814–1882), Presbyterian minister. He later replaced Miller at West Arch Street Church. Wadsworth published several Thanksgiving Day sermons between 1852 and 1861, the last being *Thanksgiving: A Sermon Preached in the Arch Street Presbyterian Church, on Thursday, November 28, 1861* (Philadelphia, 1861).

recherchés.[25] The first of these prerequisites the book particularly will entirely answer to; for Spencer if I understood him correctly, told me that the last of the edition, especially this copy which he gave me last night, & a few others had not sold: & as to the other prerequisite, you see I can *make* game of ink, & I have no doubt that you will make game of the poetry.

The note I wrote at my brother Spencer's house last night (whom by the way I begin to talk about without having introduced (you) to (him)—he is almost my twin brother, with whom I played and quarrelled for nearly eighteen years) I wrote under the spur of the conviction that it would make your answer date sooner, I hardly know why.[26] By the bye I forget what I write in my letters. I didnt remember having written that "my conscience imperfectly approved" what I sent from Princeton. I have no such feeling of disapproval now. And if you will only let me adopt that letter, & then *try* to answer it, it is all that a poor bewildered *straitened* creature like me can write in the circumstances.

I have been thinking lately of the aid you have given me since the disaster. The first relief you gave me after your promise was to send on board & ask the puzzled penitent captain how he came to run his ship where he did, & to prompt his memory by suggesting that he was "overriding, at the time, all considerations of prudence", & really did not know at the moment where he was driving to. When he had made his statements, & you professed yourself satisfied, (allowing an interval of a week or more, however, before you replied to his signals) he rallied courage to try something again, & this time chose what he thought a *blue* light to set off at night, when all that he received in reply was that the light was not *blue* enough, but of a much brighter tint, & as there was much exhilaration on board at the time the signal could not be answered. But then, that you would be glad if this question could be answered by him, that is, if he ever remembered the times you had met before, & whether just at the dangerous time when you were heaving in sight & were about to engulph him in his troubles he was perfectly ready with the recollection of the times you had sailed by each other previously. Now is not this a perfectly fair representation of all my sufferings.

The misery is that I have no one to condole with me. Here I am in this miserable little cabin, & my ship, which never did sail very well at the best

25. Miller's oldest sister, Margaret Miller, married John Breckinridge. His brother, Robert Jefferson Breckinridge (1800–1871), a Presbyterian minister and professor of theology at Danville Theological Seminary in Kentucky, married McDowell's aunt, Ann Sophonisba Preston (1803–1844). He is "Uncle Robert" in McDowell's letters. Miller's brother, Elihu Spencer Miller (1817–1879), a Philadelphia attorney, published one volume of verse, *Caprices* (New York, 1849). There were at least seven volumes published in England during the eighteenth century and at least three early in the nineteenth century with the title *Fashion* or *Fashions*, some with and some without subtitles. Several of them were satiric verse, and some were quite short, others quite long.

26. There is a small ink numeral 2 above the parenthetical "you" and a small ink numeral 1 above the parenthetical "him" as if to make clearer the antecedents for the numerous pronouns in this sentence.

times, lies almost like a log in the trough of the sea. Can you tell me what your next three questions are to be all together? I would like to know the worst at once.

I will promise you, my dear Mrs McDowell never to desert the pulpit while I live; it is my joy & crown; & never to give up the weekly preparation of sermons except for a higher kind of preaching which is, what Col Preston alluded to, for example, when he said that Dr. Thornwell caught glimpses of a true ethics, & then lost them when he came to follow the light.[27] You said once in your carriage that persons could be *conscious* of their true gifts of mind. I am sure of one thing, that persons can be conscious of their own possession of previously undiscovered truth. And tho' my mind is a very poor machine, of whose faults I am perfectly convinced, yet if it could convince me that it had the clue to some of the more important labyrinths of theological difficulties, & had stood by that conviction for years, & had acted prudently in keeping back its passion for these studies & preventing a metaphysical crust from growing over its popular discourse, I should begin to suspect it, & consider it very wicked if I did not some day give it its turn; Now I do not say that this is the case with me: for whenever I feel tempted to have a vision of any such thing, I remember one of your Virginia Watkins's that told me many years ago that he was sure he should die great. I made some enquiries about him last summer, & could not learn that he had done so, tho' perhaps he may yet.

But from a certain sort of dreaming, I dont know what, I have a sort of irrepressible desire to tell you something about my visions some day when I can rally courage, & when I have got a little ahead with your questions. Will you not admit that if I do feel listed for the rest of life & feel as Spencer says in me of his inimitable lyrics, "Rest? there is no such thing" that an occasion might arise when a man might step aside awhile at least from the pulpit to see if something that has been clamoring in him like Cerberus for twenty years is to be chained any longer or not.[28]

My church is getting on nobly. We worship in the lecture Room & last Sunday morning it was crowded aisles & all & some went away. But this I think will not last. Besides, it is very small. The most hopeful thing of an outward sort to my Methodick unromantic character is, that it is to be paid for before we enter the main building. I wish you could see it.

I think you have heard Mr Wadsworth unfavorably. His T. Sermon is not his best but rather struck off hurriedly & in a popular way.[29] He can preach much better than he usually does. Many people have made the remark you

27. "Col Preston," William Campbell Preston (1794–1860), the oldest brother of McDowell's mother, had been a U.S. senator from South Carolina and president of South Carolina College. James Henley Thornwell (1812–1862) was a southern Presbyterian theologian.

28. Cerberus was the three-headed dog guarding the entrance to Hades in Greek and Roman mythology.

29. That is, his Thanksgiving sermon.

do & perhaps it is fair to estimate a man by the majority of his work: but I have heard Mr Wadsworth when I thought his *mind* was the best part of the performance.

You are hardly right about our first meeting. I had no interest in you whatever such as keeps alive recollections of places & meetings, so as to be thought of in a moment, & you had always appeared to me haggard & worn, but most of the foundation of respect & admiration on which I have built since to carry a structure (which by the way you are always pounding at with your battering rams of disappointment & discouragement) was laid long ago, or else I am very confident that your changed & improved beauty could not have struck me as it did. I am no fool; but

> *yours sincerely,*
> *Jno Miller.*

[marginal note] Please write immediately acknowledging the ink.

Wednesday Morning [December 13, 1854][30]

My *dear Madam,*

I have looked at the young man's letter this morning, as I understand you like me to do & have determined to encourage him in sending it.[31] It has a certain sort of sans souci sauciness about it certainly, & I dissent a little since reading it from his closing remark about his being no fool, but from a long & somewhat unpleasant acquaintance with him, I am convinced he means no mischief. If you send anything in return for his present, let it be a good pen with short directions in six easy lessons for using it, with copious directions at the close for avoiding blots upon the paper. But dont send anything severe, as he *broods* over it. My ward has not been as attentive to his studies since this correspondence began, & unless you send him something for his relief it will diminish his usefulness, which I feel sure was sufficiently small before this correspondence began.

I was elected last night director of the Am[erican] Col[onization] Society, which meets in Washington the third week in January. Is that the time of your annual visit to Georgetown. If it is, I should be glad to meet you & have a talk about the young man, for I cannot conceal that I have a lively interest in him. He has got his head full of the idea that he will be some day a great philosopher & tho' I have checked this for ten years & kept him at the more popular work, yet he can hardly see the back of a copy of Plato or Leibnitz without starting off again.[32] Pity him. He is a great fool. But the letter that night

---

30. This undated letter and the one preceding it, dated Tuesday Evening, are the ones that Sally McDowell received on Friday and answered on Monday, Dec. 18, 1854.

31. That is, the letter Miller wrote the night before.

32. Gottfried Wilhelm Leibniz (1646–1716), German philosopher and mathematician.

in Princeton I was harsh with him in. I wish you could overlook his follies so far as to answer it.

Yours
JM

Colalto
Monday Dec 18. 1854

My *dear Sir,*

A sort of fatality attends my attempts to answer your letter. Friday, the day it arrived, I intended to reply to it, but finding Cantey troubled with an elaborate trimming for her party dress that night I offered my services to her, and thus allowed my spirit of *fun* to ooze out, whence they tell me a man's courage often does, at the ends of my fingers.[33] Notwithstanding this however, I attempted a letter that night, wrote a page or so, & put it aside. Snatching an hour before a dinner-party this afternoon, I picked up the unfinished sheet, found it very flat, yet determined to finish it. I did not however, and since my return from the bridal party I brought it out again, when by a sad mishap, my little Lilly, so ruined it that I was obliged to throw it aside altogether.[34] Perhaps it is quite as well though—it was a miserable affair.

I think it a pretty story for you, at this day to undertake to quarrel with me, first for asking questions—the most natural thing in the world;—and the most moderate I was in the matter too, for by your own showing, I only asked three, & then departed from my usual reserve & complimented you upon your skill in answering one of them:—and next, for not answering *all* questions, whether direct or indirect, whether plain, or somewhat obscure, easy or hard that you choose to ask me.

And then you are ungrateful too. You burlesque my services, & declare I have rendered you no aid at all; and because, forsooth, I wouldn't heed your Princeton "blue" light (how did I know that it was not some Will o' the Wisp glimmering about there) you must get up a regular quarrel with me! Nor is this all.—Without so much as saying "by your leave Ma'am" you presume to cause me a great fright by making me a present! How I looked at that wee package, so carefully wrapped & sealed, and wondered what could be in it, and worried that there should be any thing in it,—and examined again & again, the writing upon it, before I could summon resolution to open it. And yet, when it was opened, how unspeakable the relief to have the little *ink* packet show its face. But what was the matter with my ink? Or what was there in my letters that suggested such a present? I write too rapidly & often too carelessly to be very neat or exact in any way, yet

---

33. McDowell's sister, Margaret Cantey McDowell (1836–1874), lived at Colalto.
34. McDowell's youngest sister and ward, Elizabeth (Lilly) Preston Benton McDowell (1840–1923), lived at Colalto.

I dislike to think of an untidy looking letter reaching you. But I forget. I am not to ask questions. Your philosophic nerves cannot bear them. So dont answer my inquiries, but allow me to find a reason in that spirit of fault-finding, which seems to possess you just now.

"Spence's" little volume came quite safely and looks as demure as possible in its Quaker garb up here in the Mountains. I appreciate the sentiment, that prompted the selection of that book, and value it accordingly.

I don't quite like your old Philosopher. I think he must be spiteful & know how to be very changeable in his notions, so that I can never be sure that what he says to-day, he will remember & stick to to-morrow. And then too, he says, would you believe it! That his ward is—"a great fool". I am much insulted that he should speak thus of my friend, and would do, as you do, quarrel with him for it; if I were not so dreadfully alarmed at the idea of a near approach to so august a personage as a *Philosopher*. Why, they scare me quite as much as Preachers once did. But as you are not afraid, cant you tell the old man that he had better get another view of his ward before he speaks of him to strangers.

Please don't read my letters but once and then kindle your fire with them. I rather shrink from being told that you "read them again & again."

I have been thinking for several months of going down to Washington, and Saturday last received a letter, that I fear will compel me to go in two days or a fortnight. I don't know though—if my Agent can arrange matters without me I shall not go. I had hoped the whole business had been differently arranged, than I find it to be—but these lawyers & speculators, can annoy one greatly.

And now for my Christmas gift. You shall have one, given upon your own principle, of giving what I have long thought you much needed. I slip the pen with which I write from its handle & beg you will throw away those things that, in your hand turn our English words into hieroglyphs, and see how much your penmanship will improve with this new pen. I would send you the *machine* complete but that my name stands conspicuously full upon it. Pray excuse my dullness. I confess to a sort of mental collapse since our evening party.

Very truly Yours
S.C.P. McDowell

[c. December 18, 1854]

It seems to me if I were finding fault with a Lady's writing materials, I should be very careful not to render myself liable to her censure for any want of taste in the selection of my own. Therefore I would not use *blue paper* if I were you—My Banker sends me letters twice a year, & oftener *if I ply him with questions*, written upon blue paper. My Commission Merchants likewise fancy that color—So do all other Merchants—and even your name-sake & fellow-citizen, Mrs Miller, makes an astounding array of silk, & fringe & lace & tassels etc. etc., all upon the same blue paper.[35] So upon the whole it is scarcely a favorite color with me. What do you think upon this important subject? It seems that, Philosopher as you aspire to be, you are yet not unmindful of these lesser matters of fashion.

Yours Truly
S.C.P. McDowell

Phila Dec: 21st 1854

My dear Child,

My ward has been so affected with a letter which he speaks of having received from you, that he is afraid to answer it. He begs me to write & gives me a pen which he wishes me to use, but wishes me not to write on blue paper. As this last is a vanity, I deign to mortify it, & therefore take a sheet left from a sermon that I was stitching together which tho' not as blue, as I would like (I mean the paper) yet will do to speak to him of after the letter is gone by way of lesson. He seems to be specially wounded by the thought of his having "found fault with a lady's writing materials" & says that his only temptation to do it was that your letters stuck together by the dampness perhaps of the mail bag leaving the writing on both sides of the sheet; now tho' he likes to read your letters over, he likes to do it page by page & not two pages at a time & I can easily see that he may be right in this particular. He says that you are right in saying that a man's courage often fails under your fingers. He has repeated to me your whole sentence. "I offered my services to her (Cantey) & thus allowed my spirit of fun to ooze out whence they tell me a man's courage often does, at the ends of my fingers." And he seems to have something too upon his mind about this pen that he has lent me of which he means to write when his courage comes back to him again.

What he meant me to write particularly I cannot tell. He wished me to speak very gratefully of your letter & so I subscribe myself.

Yours very sincerely,
O.P.[36]

Philadelphia
Dec: 25th 1854.

My dear Madam,

I discovered one thing soon after I wrote from Princeton, which was, that tho' I could frame no question, of all I wished to ask, which seemed to me entirely delicate & honorable, yet if I could tell you my whole state of mind & let you in to the whole condition of my feeling, that would be honorable, & would carry along with it all I wished to secure.

35. Mary F. Miller was a dressmaker in Philadelphia.
36. That is, Old Philosopher.

I regretted that the Princeton letter had not been of such a character, & I determined that the next should be, & when I found that there *did* seem to be a way in which even a question that I wished to ask could be framed so as to be free from objection if I only had time to ponder & consider it, I let the last interval pass, or rather filled it with the foolish letter you received, & looked forward to this morning of leisure to write one more serious and unreserved.

I confess this morning has found me quite fixed in my own mind in respect to all the points that came before me in the *stolen* reveries of the previous fortnight. I could shake nothing. I have passed the morning religiously & prayerfully *sanctioning* the deliberations that have intruded upon my hours of study & I am going to write now page after page of my private thinking, taking that prudent course when I am tired after my Sunday preaching of saying over in successive sentences, what I have not wit enough to make clear in a single one.

I shall not fail to be intelligible if I can only tell you in a simple way the convictions that are settled in my mind.

In the first place, (for this is the very serious beginning of all my thinkings) you can have no conception how passionately I love you. When you speak of "controlling my passions" I begin to think how I can get hold of it to control it; when you speak of my "selecting" a wife, I feel that I never had that privilege. I am as helpless under the force of my passions as one can be who has been accustomed to look to religion to guard him when he is going astray, & finds religion siding with him in what he desires. I feel no hope of destroying my affection unless I resist it, & I feel no inclination to do so, & cannot create such an inclination, and like a moth burning himself in the candle I feel a sort of obstinate pleasure at the thought even of a lifetime of defeated affection.

I know of but one thing that could give me any power over my love (& that simply by turning my inclination against it) & that is, if you were to tell me not only that you did not respond to it, but that irrespective of all peculiarities in your condition, you felt sure you never should: that you were entirely indifferent to me: & (as I believe any one may easily decide) that you felt sure from unerring instinct that nothing more than a "cordial esteem" or a "high regard" or a sentiment of "friendliness" could ever possibly be originated.

Now, I am not saying that this would disenchant me immediately: I am only saying that then I should *desire* to be disenchanted, &, *in theory,* for I have no other means of judging, that would appear to be an important difference.

One of the questions, therefore, that I have wished to ask, was, whether you *were*, on my own account, indifferent to my suit, & certain of remaining so. I thought it an improper question. I think so still. Were it not that I had found another question that I can legitimately ask I would not so much as mention it; & for this simple reason:—I would not have a sister whom I loved avow her affection to any man or even the *possibility* of it, so long as there continued in her mind a scruple that decided her that they never could marry; & the man who had drawn from her such an avowal who should afterward desert her, I mean by not remaining unmarried, I should consider as acting a dishonorable part. This may be foolish dogmatism; but I have only to ask *the effect* on my sister's mind to be fixed in the opinion that I am right in such a judgment.

Moreover her *disavowal*, wrong as it might be by the force of the necessary alternative, might border on the very utmost limit of what might be made consistent with conscience & honesty.

Phil. Dec: 26th

Here I am, back at home. I dont like these letters I write in my study. They are more like the waters of the Dead Sea *deep & heavy*. After seeing the simple faces of my children, there are some of these sentences that I can hardly understand myself. Still the *whole paragraphs* are intelligible, & that is what we chiefly need.

I have often been struggling with the question, & half ready to send it in one of my letters, whether you would not allow me to love you, & occasionally to write to you, even tho' the scruples that you mention should prevent us from ever being engaged. There is something dismal in such an idea, & forlorn in the folly, perhaps, of taking a brush & deliberately darkening all a man's prospect of life; but that work is done already, & there is something pleasant, I dont know why, in having some sort of an orbit around what warms us & brightens upon us, even tho' it be like that of a comet, returning at distant intervals.

Then I have thought of asking for an engagement that should be realized only in care of the removal of an *existing obstacle* that I have spoken of in Chester.[37] If the world should find it out, it would be an unhappy connection of events, & indeed an apparent confessing of what you have now convinced yourself, is false, viz that you have no right to marry until that event has occurred.

It was from all these things, & others, the clear enunciation of which I have destroyed my capacity for, by the confusing of these two letters, that I can ask with the most perfect self-approval;—*Will you not entertain the proposal of an engagement which shall leave the whole subject of the time of marriage to your own future decision?*

I must stop this letter, however. Like poor Joe in Bleak House, some pastoral duty is always laying its hand upon me & ordering me to "move on." I dont know that this letter adds anything to the other, but it will show you that other peoples spirits flag sometimes as well as your own. An "elaborate trimming" that I gave my people on Sunday night for some abuses that have grown upon us in church-music is perhaps particularly to blame.

The meeting at Washington is on Tuesday the 16th Jan. If I may call upon you there, & you should chance to be in the city that week, please tell me where you will stay.

Hoping to hear from you very soon, I am.

Yours very truly
Jno Miller.

37. That is, by the death of Francis Thomas (1799–1876), McDowell's ex-husband.

Colalto
Thursday Dec 28. 1854

My *dear Sir,*

I received *both* your letters this afternoon—they should have reached me yesterday, but our mails are somewhat irregular at this season, and my letters have a trick of visiting other Offices before they come to my own.

They have done their work in agitating me much. But I cannot answer them tonight, nor, indeed can I do so for several days, as, owing to a defective mail arrangement & other causes, that I need not trouble you with just now, I shall not be able to send off a letter until next Tuesday. Knowing your anxiety, however, I hurry off this note, in advance of a letter which I intend shall be as "unreserved" as you can possibly desire.

I do not know that your letters attract any special notice, yet I have sometimes wished that certain tell-tale stamps and seals upon them could be omitted. Nobody questions me much in such matters but Lilly, & I make it enough for her to say that I do not choose to tell her who my correspondents are. But it were well, that much privacy should be used, for reasons, the force of which I think you would feel if I had time to state them.

I am even yet doubtful about going to Washington. My visit there was upon *business* (does it seem unladylike for *me* to attend to *matters of business?*) and not for pleasure. But my friend, Mr. Kennedy, can perhaps get on without me; & besides having been upon the sick-list since Sunday I may not deem it quite prudent to go. My old Bachelor Doctor & Kinsman however, was quite willing to give me a discharge to-day, but I *enjoy* being a little sick, as it keeps up the sympathy of friends & prevents one from falling into absolute oblivion, at the same time that it allows me to order the carriage & ride where I please, provided I don't stop to make a visit any where;—a proviso I am not in the slightest danger of forgetting, as I esteem visiting the greatest of the lesser burdens of life. By the bye, Mr. (Rev'd) Tucker Lacy came over yesterday morning at 10 o'clock & remained until nearly five in the afternoon![38] I exhausted all topics of conversation, & all the sewing materials in my work-basket, and even ventured upon, that most consoling of all employments,—knitting. I am no Architect in sock-making, & am sure Trott & Gliddon would be puzzled to find a type of mankind that could be fitted by my specimens, yet my knitting supported my patience astonishingly—But the bell sounded 1 o'clock long ago.

Very truly Yours
S.C.P. McD.

38. Joseph Camp Griffith Kennedy (1813–1887), superintendent of the Federal Census, managed McDowell's property in Washington. "My old Bachelor Doctor & Kinsman" was McDowell's cousin James McDowell Taylor, M.D. (c. 1813–1888). Beverley Tucker Lacy (1819–1900), a Presbyterian minister in Rockbridge County.

Chester. Dec: 29th 1854.

My *dear* Madam

By a singular mishap I have been separated from a letter that I began to you to day. I was interrupted in writing it by a visit & left it to spend a part of Christmas with my children who are here at Bishop Potter's country house staying some weeks. A failure in a train leaves me unable to return & separates me from what I was writing. Maggie & Allie are very well & bright & it makes me happy to have the home feeling which even their Aunts house gives me. The little Potter boys have just come in from Phila to spend the Christmas week with them.[39] I have never been so struck with Maggie's beauty as I have been today. She is now eight years old, & has been more than commonly active & busy lately.

The letter I have left in Philadelphia I will finish & send on, tho' I hope your post-master in Lexington will think these are proof-sheets that are coming in such numbers upon him. I cannot bear the disappointment of not mailing a letter to-night as I have been calculating upon Saturday morning as the time of receiving a reply.

Will you pardon the annoyance I may give you in renewing *once* more the subject that caused you originally so much uneasiness. What those questions are that I feel forbidden to ask I have detailed at length in the letter above referred to & feel relieved in some measure of my hesitation in speaking of them by thinking of a form in which one of them can be presented.

You have passed thro' one change since I first wrote, that is the discovery of the fact that you have *rights* Morally that you did not at first conceive. I do not presume on this in the least. I know you have distinctly said that it does not alter your judgment. But if I convince you that I have nothing at stake that can appeal to your generosity in what you fancy a matter of caste, will you not review your judgment? Have I nothing to hope in the future? Do not accuse me of indirectness, or obscurity; I wish to renew in the most earnest way all my original proposal.

If this is hopeless, then bear with me while I make another proposal. May I not aspire to your hand, if I give up all right to determine as to the *time* when I shall possess it. This makes you the arbiter of the whole question, even after all the inviolableness of a positive engagement. I would *like* to have a time. I would like to say, after I am able conscientiously to retire from my present exposed position. But to this I would object myself, first that I would be fancied to have been decided in such a change of life by this strong temptation, or second, that I *might* be so decided. So solemn a question as what I should do in the fulfillment of my vows as a minister ought not be mingled with such a question.

---

39. Alonzo Potter (1800–1865), the Episcopal bishop of Pennsylvania, was married to Sarah Benedict (1808–1864), the oldest sister of Miller's first wife. Their sons, James Neilson (Nelly) Potter (1841–1906) and William (Willie) Appleton Potter (1842–1909), attended the Episcopal School in Philadelphia.

But, my dear Madam, you will be struck with the presumption of this whole method of speaking.

I have laboured to show in the letter I left at home, how I *must* say something definite in order to shield myself from a worse feeling of indiscretion. I know you will forgive me, seeing as you do the exact difficulties, under which I am acting. I cannot agitate the question, which might seem to be a much more natural one, of your caring anything for me at all; for I know you will not *permit* yourself to care for me unless there is some way in which the scruples in your mind can be set at rest.

I have not asked, what might seem the very most natural question of all, Will you allow me to speak of an engagement that shall be contingent on the removal of obstacles that now exist? for my whole soul revolts from such a life as must follow such an arrangement. It would shake my religious sense & I am sure be intolerable to you. To be waiting, for an event so unwrought in all my sensibilities, for the slow arrival & miseries of such a death as must be all the time contemplated would tinge with the colors of evil all the intervening time & really would make it one of my forbidden questions so much as to hint at an arrangement based on that naked contingency.

What have I then but to ask you, Whether you will not favour my suit if I give it what privacy you direct & leave the time of its being concluded entirely to yourself. There is very little difference between this & a vow for your sake to live unmarried except that you promise similarly & may in the end yield on some change of opinion.

I love my mother better than any being I know besides yourself & my children. I have a feeling that if my mother should die I should be left <u>alone</u> in a weary world with the shadow of a great rock taken away that was my unfailing protection. My mother loves me—more than any of her other children, so my brothers & sisters complain. She loves my children & they could hardly be taken from her in her old age to make parts of another household. If you would only promise me that when that only home I have on earth is broken up & I am cast out into the world entirely desolate you would love me & care for me then I would be perfectly, & then an event that cannot probably happen for many years would be partly provided for in the changes of the future. Resting our marriage, therefore, upon this event far more painful, but not half so horrible as the contingency I spoke of before, would leave me something always to love & prevent the fearful coming together of all species of pain & desolation.

Let me not however become indirect or wild in what I say.

Will you not reconsider your original refusal & allow me to address you again?

Will you not agree to think at least of an engagement conditioned on your own selection of the time?

Will you not encourage the idea of our being married if I survive my mother?

If the last proposal seems a wild one I might add to it the more prosaic justification that it connects itself with family circumstances that would give me more independence in choosing a residence, if there still lingered a feeling that my *public* usefulness or my caste might be interfered with. But with this I will not trouble you yet.

I write this to-night disjointed & naked as it is, for the purpose I mention above as I have lost the use of the other letter. Do answer it immediately & *mercifully*, whichever way the balance turns. I am ashamed that I can so little wait. Whatever manliness I have in other things, I have a girl's feverish inquisitiveness as to my fate & a boy's hot impatience. I will finish the other letter tomorrow (tell me if so many letters attract attention) tho' really I have dashed into most of the things it was to entertain in my hurried writing this evening.

God bless you, my dear Madam. I am liable in any of these letters to be silenced for some hasty or misunderstood speech & never to hear from you again. If this should happen, Remember, I have nothing to reproach you for in all this correspondence & the *extremeness* of my questions to night is in no way connected with any wrong encouragement that you have given me in your letters.

The Colonization Board opens at Washington on Tuesday, Jan: 16th. I will go on on Monday if I know you to be there, but I may be ruining a hope which I so much entertain, (I mean by being allowed to see you there) by this letter. I thank you for the pen, tho' I am writing now with a little steel pen of one of the Potters & see nothing in which to enclose my letter but a brown envelope.

Yours very truly
Jno Miller.

Jan: 1st 1855.(late)

My *dear Sir*,

I wish I could talk to you just now about your last letters. Difficult as I know I should find that to be, I conceive from my present trouble, that it would be far easier than writing. Yet as it cannot be, I will try as much as possible to talk with my pen, giving you, after your own fashion "page after page of my private thinking" in the hope of making out, in the end, something that will be intelligible. The moral difficulty which you encountered at the outset I have since told you, and repeat now is no longer a difficulty. That point is settled so decidedly that no shadow of doubt *rests* upon my mind in regard to it. I need not therefore do more than merely mention it now.

The next obstacle is what you call "a *fancied* loss of caste" by a new marriage. This point is one not of principle but of sentiment, and yet it weighs with me almost as much if it did really involve a grave question of morals—That it does involve one of *duty* has been the trouble with me. I feel,—and I would tell you plainly & simply all that is in my mind about it,—that I have no *right* to do that which would injure my usefulness as a Christian woman; neither have I a right to consent to do that which might, in like manner diminish the influence for good, of another. The step urged by you, would I fear be greatly prejudicial to your influence & perhaps entirely destructive to my own. Would it then be right for me to take it?

Again, my pride could not brook the idea of being, from my painfully peculiar circumstances, an unwelcome addition to any family with which I might choose to connect myself. Neither could I bear, that for the same reason, my family should look coldly upon one whom I might bring into it. My anxiety would be that I might be, at least acceptable to a new household that would be dear to me thro' one of its members. And to that One standing in the tenderest of all relations to me, I would delight to bring undiminished all the respect and confidence & affection, which has surrounded & cheered me thro' all the lights and shadows of my life. Could this be done if I married under present circumstances?

Then, as to your children,—I feel I might sadly mar their future by connecting them with one whose history has been such as mine. I would not be content with anything short of their love, based upon their respect for me. I would assiduously seek it not only for your sake & my own, but also for theirs. Yet as the little girl grew older, her love for me (which it is not impossible that I might attain), would give way, & her respect yield under the sneer that would reach her ear, at her Father's Wife as a Divorcée! And this painful relationship might tinge with an embittering feeling of suspicion all her future intercourse with society.

Now tell me, how much of all this is founded in reason; and how much is to be attributed to a morbid sensitiveness upon a matter that is, of all others the most painful to me. I know you say that you are willing to run the risk of loss of caste;—either you estimate the risk too lightly, or I too greatly. One of us must be in error: which is that one?

It is true that disinterested and warm friends, among the ablest and best Ministers in our State, have strongly advocated the step you propose—one even going so far as to say to my dear old friend Dr. White, that he should make it his business to urge it upon me as a *duty*. But the old gentleman replied, "he would not dare broach the subject to me," tho' he fully agreed in his view of the matter. These, opinions never sought by me, but made known to me thro' a friend, go far to modify my own; but my mind cannot at once, let go what it has grasped so tightly for so long a time.

As to the special subject of your letter,—(I say letter, for I avail myself of the one from Chester as being the plainest & most direct,) I can hardly say anything that would be satisfactory, after what I have already said. And yet, one thing more I may venture to speak of. You speak of an *engagement*. You forget how little personal knowledge I have of you. My impressions are, I am perfectly frank in saying all favorable, but have I not had a very meager opportunity of having those impressions deepened into that sort of feeling which should form the basis of an engagement, whether it be conditional or not? To be sure you write to me, & I have found out a good deal that was acceptable to me in that way, but still I have never seen you in circumstances to reveal those traits of character that enter most into the happiness or misery of domestic life. How do I know that you are not captious, or moody or imperious in temper—and exacting & jealous & morose in disposition? Certainly, I have never seen anything of the kind; on the contrary all I know of you; & that which first won my regard for you, was your unselfishness & generous consideration for the feelings of others. But if I were calling you for my Pastor, you would think it but right in me to inquire into your "gifts & graces," and much more necessary is it that I should do so now, when you would add to that of Pastor another stronger tie.

I am not satisfied with my letter. It imperfectly tells you, what I would like you clearly to understand. But I am cramped in every way, fearing I say too much, unwilling to say too little. But I send it as it is. What you may not understand write to me about, and I shall make another effort to be clear.

My going to Washington is still uncertain, yet I think I shall leave here Thursday, arrive there the next afternoon. You will not, in that case have time to write to me here. Write then to Washington enclosing your letter, to Mr. J.C.G. Kennedy who will keep it, or send it on, as I may direct.[40] I shall be at his house during my short stay, but will probably have left Washington before your meeting comes on.

I hardly know how to date my letter having written it at different times. I finish it however at twilight of as beautiful a day as ever ushered in a New Year—but as usual my spirits flag at the close of a lovely winter day. Can it be that the mind cannot bear excess of loneliness? Or is it the passing away of beauty, with but faint hope of its return that is thus depressing? Anyhow I am sad, & cannot hail the moonlight with joy tonight.

Yet I can with great heartiness wish you many a happy year made up of days as bright as this has been.

Very truly Yours
S.C.P. McDowell

Philadelphia
Jan: 4th 1855.

My *dear Madam*,

Your letter which has just this moment been handed in by the postman is the finest exhibition of your character, *in all respects,* that I have ever seen, & therefore, you will not misunderstand me,—when I say, that it has given me great pain. I do not mean to say, that it is not all & more than all a sane man could expect & ought to satisfy every reasonable feeling, but unfortunately, I aint reasonable. These horses of the Sun that I have been driving for some time past are "imperious" fellows & are in strange contrast with the cool wisdom of your letter.

---

40. Kennedy was McDowell's business agent and good friend in Washington, D.C.

I have yet a chance at the evening mail, & write to say one hasty word about my visit to Washington. I would go on next week. But my duties here are so well known by all my people & my family to be very heavy just now, that for reasons I cannot so briefly explain, every visit that I make any where must give a distinct reason for itself. Still I am not sure but that I can *make* such a reason. Will you only tell me how long you will probably stay *as soon* as you yourself know. If I am unable to go next week & you return before the meeting I shall probably if I can have a Report that I am to prepare looked after by another Director not go to it, for the balance for & against such a visit in the midst of my church year had been turned by the hope of seeing you.

Pardon me for the abruptness of all this for I am writing *post-haste* to get my letter in in time. I would *so much* like to see you. It would be worth in the mere opportunities of explanation some 3000 letters.

If I am unable to go next week & go the week after I shall reach W[ashington] early on Monday & stay all the week.

I am amused & struck with your wisdom about *character*. The modes of intercourse we have had reveal very little & yet perhaps not so very little. I am somewhat of opinion that an entirely uncandid letter cannot be written. If I had not known you in other ways I would not rely upon them. As you know me in no other ways, especially in my private life, you have reason to consider yourself uninformed & I who *do* know myself in much closer ways frankly confess that it would puzzle me to keep up any very good character *all the time*. Do arrange it to stay & please write if possible by return of mail.

> Yours truly
> Jno Miller.

Washington
Jany 6. 1855

My *dear Sir*,

Mr Kennedy gave me your letter late yesterday afternoon as we came over from Alexandria. I hoped to have answered it by this morning's mail, but was not released from the parlor last night till midnight nearly, & after that was too tired to prepare for it. I was sorry to have disappointed you:—but perhaps I exaggerate the disappointment the failure of a letter causes.

There is no imperate[41] necessity for me to return home during the next week; but for several reasons, it would be well for me not to prolong my visit much beyond the time originally fixed upon. My business is a little more intricate than I had anticipated, and may consume more time than I had calculated upon. And besides, for I may as well tell you the whole truth, it scarcely seems to me delicate for *me* to fix the time for your visit. It almost looks as if I had *invited* you to make

---

41. That is, imperative.

it. But as much rests upon it, perhaps a departure from the common course may be granted to a very busy & very "unreasonable" person, and I promise to remain until the Wednesday after your meeting here.

I am sure from the whole tone of your letter that mine fretted and worried you. You even are disposed to find fault with what you call my "*cool wisdom*," a thing I could not believe to be generated in so hot a brain as mine. But perhaps after all, it was only your *hot haste* that gave a little pricking heat to the words you wrote. You had no time to do as I sometimes do when I'm conscious of having written in a little too much warmth of feeling—put your letter by to cool for a day or two.

I do not "misunderstand" you, for I do not understand at all how, for the reasons you give, my letter caused you so much pain.—But I have twice before had you shame me for a quick judgment upon such phrases, by telling me what you really did mean, so now I suspend all judgment, & wait for further developements.

When you come on, you will find Mr Kennedy's house No 470, *H Street,* between 9h & 10th.

You can't tell how I recoil from the entire privacy I use in this matter, and tho' for good reasons I consider it best. Yet I chafe under it quite so much as your "imperious fellows" do under my "cool wisdom." I find my friends rather troubled—Mr. Kennedy by want of business, under the money pressure—and his wife suffering sadly from religious depression, the greatest & most terrible of all kinds of suffering.[42]

Don't feel yourself called upon to bring me another package of ink—my pencil happens to be more convenient just now.

> Very truly Yours
> S.C.P McDowell

Why give up your connection with the Colonization Board? in any contingency of this matter.

Philadelphia,
Jan: 8th 1855.

My *dearest Madam,*

I will have to be to you like the moon, which is so ragged & cusped & *crusty* in its outline, that you have to look through the old beggar's telescope down at the Custom-House, three or four times, before you get any *good* idea of it. We Millers are like Cromwell ("especially John," they would all join in chorus, if they knew what I was writing) a little 'thick in utterance'; which when disconnected with Cromwell's sense, (by the way, dont think of the *moon* again, in connection with what I write) creates a condition of things among us, that Dick, my nautical brother, would describe as being, that "we mean well, but have bad luck."[43]

---

42. Catherine Morrison Kennedy (1815–1897).

43. Oliver Cromwell (1599–1658), English soldier and statesman. Jonathan Dickinson Miller (1810–1891), a surgeon in the United States Navy.

Now, my dear Mrs. McDowell, please read my letters *literally*. I didn't *say* anything that you have put into my last one. On the contrary, I said, it was the highest impression of your character, that I had received from it, that anything I had known in you, had ever given me. It is the least "disenchanting" letter that you have yet written; so much so, that some nights ago, coming home too late to have my usual quiet hour in reading over your letters, I lit a candle & read my self to sleep over this very one, an influence now, which you must not take umbrage at in another way; because this is the honour I put upon the very choicest literature that ever comes into my hand.

It seems to me strange, when I think of it, that the first letter in which you had ever given any evidence of caring anything about me, & which had changed my whole relations so much as to lead me to hope that you had some little regard for me, that *might* "deepen" into something more, should be welcomed by me with the complaint that it gave me great pain. But love is blind. I think you can have no great consciousness of it, or you would understand me better. It is like the lust of fame, it grows by all the aliment it gets. I seize upon all the comfort you give me, *at once*; & that is used up almost as soon as it is experienced; & then come those great frowning batteries that you erect, all about our mutual conscience & our families & worst of all my children, & you really almost make me *hear* the sneers & slights of our acquaintance against my poor innocent Maggie. I confess my heart trembles for a moment under some of your strong sentences; & yet when I get out from the smoke of your battery a little, & reflect, I shake off the misgivings you have created, with this "great pain" however, that the triple wall that you build up so "solidly" again, after I have tried so long to batter it down, seems to make this Sebastopol I have to encounter, appear well nigh impregnable; & seems to promise the slenderest ground of encouragement to the hopes of the alliance.[44]

And then comes the long trial of my gifts & graces. Are you long about that in Virginia before you "make out a call"? I am so afraid you'll find me out, when all my good sermons are preached, & you discover what a poor miserable old creature I am.—But seriously, my dear Madam, I love you & feel warmly grateful for this very letter; & instead of being "chafed & fretted" by it, as you suppose, I am so in no other sense than by *myself*, for I cannot conceive of a letter more kindly & really more gratefully expressed, that is, grateful as far as anything can be that makes me *shudder* at every line.

Jan: 9th Tuesday. I do not feel quite so clear about another part of my letter. Indeed, when I read your reply & reflected how embarrassing in your mind may have been some of the peculiarities of the Washington visit, I felt determined to go on at once, & put an end to all feeling of the kind. A step, however, that

---

44. During the Crimean War (1853–1856) the Anglo-French armies laid seige to Sebastopol, a seaport city on the Crimean Peninsula, for eleven months, from Oct. 17, 1854, to Sept. 11, 1855.

would have satisfied so many impatient feelings, I soon found could only be taken if I could avow its object, & I do feel warmly thankful to you for appreciating the difficulty, & consenting not to hasten your business.

I go on Monday by the very earliest line. The Board will sit three or four days, & tho' I dare not trespass upon a good feeling that I do so genuinely appreciate, yet I wish our friend Kennedy could tie an extra knot in your affairs, for I mean to provide business in the Colonization Office to keep me till Saturday or Monday. And I now promise that my Jersey ingenuity shall go in advance on any like occasion in the future, & provide more *indefinite* excuses for being away so that *your* moon can do as other moons do, move round as an attendant satellite, & not be creating these planetary perturbations.

Now am I forgiven?—I am getting so *brilliant* under the effect of these sorties from Sebastopol, that notwithstanding all the *mud* in the trenches, I shall get to thinking that these poor straggling lines of mine are quite magnificent. Now dont you dispel the illusion by any "ill-natured copies" when you write again.

I can easily imagine that you may be troubled by the question, whether I can be relied upon when we meet, not to embarrass you with a manner, (or mode of speaking) to which, if any one is present, it may be awk[ward] to reply. I wish to say, in respect to that, that nothing would be stranger, after, the repeated meetings of your father & myself, & after our many modes of acquaintance through parishioners & in other ways for so many years; & above all after your kindness to my sister in the Summer, if I did not call upon you, & that more than once while staying in Washington. It is in this aspect of the case I mean to make any visits that you will permit; & tho' I would give anything to have an *undisturbed* interview of hours (poor Lacey!) yet I do not mean to allow the necessity or expectation of such a thing to oppress you in the slightest degree. Cant we go off to some of these meetings? The Anniversary which it is not important that a Director should punctually attend, as it is not a business meeting, occurs on Wednesday night (I think).

Cant we go to it very early, & lose our way round some of those very crooked squares, & reach it very late? But I must not forestall your own womanly judgments & permissions, nor indeed take for granted that I can have even as great an opportunity of speaking with you as I have in these letters.

As to the "privacy", I think your recoil of feeling ought to be entirely modified by its being a privacy *under your own control*. I would be only too happy if it were withdrawn. I agree, that if it exist at all, it ought to be *profoundly kept up* just on the principle that everything that is done ought to be well done; but in a state of things in which you have my entire & joyful acquiescence in your *announcing* an engagement any moment, your chafing at your own "cool wisdom" ought to be very moderate. By the way, why do you scorn my neatly turned expression of respect? If I could get my mother to say that John had a great deal of cool wisdom, it would be an epoch in the house; it would be a sort of knighting from royal hands. I did indeed mean & feel that your letter was eminently wise, &

it added such an element of *value* for you to my already high-wrought sense of admiration, as more than balanced the uneasiness & misgiving that the growl of your cannon gave me, (for the moment,) as they rumbled from those old Lexington hills.

If I dare ask a favour, it would be, that just now when you look so well, you should go to some superior Daguerreotypist, in Washington, & spend some leisure morning of this week in securing a portrait. You would let me see it then. And possibly, as a sort of reward for being so good a reins man of those horses, that are said to dislike so, one of your finest traits of character, you will lend it to me, if I promise to return it in one or two months or whenever you desire. Wont you do it? & I promise that if you ask for Maggie's or Allie's, thinking that you must say something to return the compliment, I will refuse, so as to save you from all embarrassment.

I wish we could find some way of having even more than one quiet interview. There are so many things I would like to talk over. You could get out your knitting, you know:—& if we could only be *sure*, we wouldnt be interrupted, & even if we cant build anything solidly but Spanish Castles, still do that elaborately & well, I should be so glad. Cant you, as you wont let me enter upon the field of planning at all, find out some ingenious way by which with no other opportunities of interview than as old acquaintances, we can nevertheless talk with the leisure & unbroken opportunity of emptying the sewing basket, that belongs to more experienced friends.

I think I will stay at Willards. Is not that near Mr Kennedy's. The President, Mr Latrobe & the five or six Pennsylvania Directors stay at the National.[45] But if I go there they will involve me in afternoon & evening Committees, which I will be less well able to decline.

You will write to me again? a good long letter. If you could see how I watch the window for the postman, & listen for the ringing of the bell, about half past nine some two or three days before your letters usually get to me, you would not doubt whether I was disappointed when your letters failed to reach me. Indeed as you are not a preacher (tho' I am not quite sure about that) & have not to write for your living, as I have, & as letters come to me without the slightest observation from any one, you ought to write me one nearly every night, just throwing into the mail a line or two to give me a pleasant exhilaration. Do you think it would be wrong for me to say yours affectionately or yours somewhat affectionately, or yours almost hopelessly. But perhaps after this garrulous letter I had better just say *yours*

John Miller.

45. John Hazlehurst Boneval Latrobe (1803–1891) was president of the American Colonization Society, which held its thirty-eighth annual meeting in Washington on Jan. 16–18, 1855. Miller was one of six delegates in attendance from Pennsylvania. Willard and the National were Washington hotels.

Wednesday [January 10, 1855]

My *dear Madam*,

Will you not help me in a case of conscience?

The morning line to Baltimore does not go thro' to Washington. The one at 12.45 P.M. is the first that goes thro' except the one that starts at 11 on Sunday night. This would bring me to Washington by daylight on Monday so that I could sleep two or three hours & call to see you at 11 or earlier if it would answer. The other will not bring me to the Hotel till 8 or to Mr Kennedy's till near nine.

Question of Conscience.

If I give a porter my trunk on Saturday to place on storage at the Balt. Depot, & quietly walk down there after preaching on Sunday evening & take the cars, will the hour that I thus take from the midnight of Sunday in view of the whole day I gain by it, make me a great sinner?

Dont laugh at me, now, & say that I was that a long while ago, or that you cant see that the time makes any difference, or that you would quite as willingly see me by the last train, but stick to the question. Do you think travelling just one hour, when you would be otherwise asleep, if it is a work of necessity or mercy to the traveller himself, would be unclerical or wicked?

I really have that sort of instinct that people have when they do too much of a thing in putting *another letter* into the mail, but my conscience will not let me go, unless yours does.

Yours very truly
Jno Miller.

PART TWO

"I have been able to say to you many things with my pen, that I could never have uttered with my tongue."

January 1855–April 1855

[John Miller to S. C. P. McDowell][1]
[January 16, 1855]

Dear Madam,

Greatly to my consternation the Bd meets to-morrow at 9 & has noticed the absence of one or two of us [two illegible words]. I will call at 1 or 2 & if you have gone to George-Town at 5. Can you by your womanly skill secure a quiet talk for us also to-morrow after tea when we shall have no meeting. You must give yourself no further trouble about the portrait nor go there again unless you please. Those you left satisfy me & I will secure them & submit them afterward to your disposal. I feel so *terribly* about this remorseless need of your being carried away.

Yours devotedly
Jno Miller

Cant you put the Major off? What right have these men to be choosing your time?

---

1. Miller penciled this note on his calling card.

Staunton
Thursday Jany 18. 1855

My *dear* Sir,

I fancy you will not quarrel with me for writing so soon. I have an hour of day light yet, & find I can rest & write together.

I groped my way down stairs whilst it was yet dark this morning in prompt response to Cousin John's impatient summons, & by a forlorn gas light in the basement managed to stumble into the Carriage. The stars lighted our way to the Boat, where a hot fire cheerfully welcomed me. By & bye a lovely morning broke upon us; and the sunlight, "by no shadow made tender" has warmed us all the way. An aching head allowed me small chance for enjoyment, & I was obliged to be quite mute & still throughout the forenoon. At Charlottesville the Major left me; but his vacant place at my side was pleasantly, but most unexpectedly filled immediately by my ugly friend Revd Mr. Bocock.[2] I forgot my heavy head in the pleasure of an hour's talk with him,—He is as ugly as the men's faces that adorn earthen ware mugs or terra cotta vases—, & is indeed of that type of mankind. But he is sensible, spicy, rather too censorious, but yet very companionable. I parted with him reluctantly at this depot. A good appetite, sharpened by the long interval of 10 or 11 hours, made a plain dinner most acceptable, & the dinner has somewhat relieved my head, tho' its paroxysms of pain will, I know yeild only to the influence of a good night's rest—a luxury denied me to a great extent during the last week, but which I hope to secure tonight.

A day's journey thro' a Country familiar to you, and performed without accident or annoyance of any kind, furnishes nothing for a letter—the temporary track shook my nerves some what, but makes me feel that I should be truly thankful to have encountered no danger in passing over it.

If I measure time not by hours, but by the number of *sensations* by which it is marked, I should feel that the last week has been a year—& the day, just closed in, a month.—But hours pass on & are lost, whilst the *feelings* that these passing hours brought form indeed the history of one's life.—But I find I am getting into the mist, (I will not say *fog*), & shall descend lest you should lose sight of me altogether.

I shall send this letter to Phil:—& will not write again until next week. You must learn to curb your impatience about my letters; & above all learn to shut me out of your thoughts, when your business requires your whole mind. Bid me be gone *peremptorily;* nor give me liberty of entrance until all important duties have been fulfilled; then sit down quietly & write me a letter in a sort of journal form—a little every day—or whenever you have leisure, until a letter of respectable size has been achieved. I hope you will be very diligent at the Colonization meetings— yet this very diligence might now awaken suspicion. You must remember, I shall feel anxious to hear the result of your talk with your brother on the absorbing subject of our recent walks & rides. I have no fear that you will not be perfectly

2. John Holmes Bocock (1813–1872), Presbyterian pastor in Harrisonburg, Va.

frank in reporting it: I never feel that there is anything held back with you—I know you mean to be, & try to be entirely fair in all you say, & very generous in all you propose.—But my eyes are growing weary & I must say good-night.

Very truly Yours,
S.C.P. McDowell

Some how, my paper has become soiled—but no matter if you can read the words upon it.

Washington
Jan: 18th [1855]
Thursday

"My good Angel"
Here I am in my room in the "National" at half after eleven at night after a day when every body seems to remark how much better a Colonizationist I am than either of the previous days. I called on Mr & Mrs Kennedy at 4 & you can hardly know how sad I felt when I found you gone. You are right in saying that I would bear with no patience whatever a long separation from you after you were once my betrothed wife.

I love you so much that I am going to trouble you with one of my wild rough thoughts the very day it has flashed upon my mind with no leisure to study it & with the wish that you also will send me your first immediate notions about it, as I shall be impatient to hear from you. I am vexed that I did not think of it before you left, it would have been so much better to talk it over fully as we might have done.

Ever since you said, that you were not satisfied that something ought not to be done in respect to some more formal plan for clearing your position in the eye of society I have been thinking of it with the most eager interest. I am your knight errant. And if I could break my way into the Enchanted Castle, & bring out the lady happy and safe, I should feel so proud & in my elation might be intoxicated with the thought that I had done something to deserve her hand.

Now I have carved out this rough plan. An hour's meditation might dispel it all, but while it is coming on with all its illusion & promise, I want to confide it to you.

The State has performed her act, & that, as I have often said, cannot be repeated. Moreover it *need* not be, for your *legal* disenthrallment could not be more complete. The church never performs an act like that of the State. It would be meaningless & vain as that has to do with legal obligations. What we want is that the knowledge we possess of facts deciding the moral question of your position should be *formally* possessed by the community & above all that something like form should be observed *in authorizing you to act upon the fact so that you may not be left to the weak position of having the judgment & authorization & decision of your step all in your own hands*.

Now the body that has your conduct specially in charge is the Church Session.[3] They are the natural authority for you to look to. You would have to be *certain* of their deciding in your favour before you entrusted the matter to them a point which Dr. White could easily ascertain, otherwise by deciding unfavorably or with a minority against us we would suffer more than if nothing had been done. So that my golden thought for delivering one whom I so tenderly love out of what she regards her cruel duress is this. It may be utterly absurd when I come to think of it more cautiously; but I want to send it just as it occurs to me. It is your going to Dr. White & making a confidant of him & asking him whether if Major Preston or some other male friend appeared for you before the Session some such Minute as this could *certainly* be passed & recorded. "Major P. having appeared before the Session in behalf of Mrs. A.B. to ask the judgment of the body &c &c &c & having stated facts & presented certain evidence bearing upon the question, thereupon it was resolved, That in the judgment of this Session Mrs. A.B. is entirely released from all obligation under her former marriage on principles laid done in the Confession of Faith Chap ___ Section ___ & in Scripture Matt: ___ &c &c & that she violates no principle of propriety or right sentiment in contracting a second marriage."[4]

If Dr. White could go so far as to count upon the Presbytery too he might even go the length of introducing there this minute at an interlocutory meeting. "The attention of the Presbytery in examining the Minutes of the Session of the Lexington Church being specially drawn by the session itself to a certain minute expressing the judgment of the session in respect to one of the communicants under their care touching the propriety of her entering upon a second marriage, in peculiar circumstances that were mentioned along with facts on which the judgment had been based, expressed their entire approval of the Session's action both as to the grounds & manner of the decision as it was stated to have been made."

Pardon me for sketching these so hastily. They can be made much more neat & accurate. I send them to you in the very roughest condition that you may think over the whole question of such a reference. Would it not be the really honorable way of rolling off your responsibility upon the body that has your conduct under its care & especially if the Presbytery could be appealed to in addition, giving the furthest sanction that you could have of a public kind.

This may appear to me perfectly unwise to-morrow but to-night it appears to me of sufficient plausibility to refer it to your judgment.

3. In Presbyterian church polity, the session is the local decision-making body. It is made up of the minister and lay elders of a congregation.

4. "Major P." refers to John Thomas Lewis Preston, McDowell's "Cousin John." Chapter 24 of the Westminster Confession of Faith specifies that adultery is grounds for a divorce and that the innocent party may remarry. The Bible verses Miller alluded to are probably Matt. 5:31–32 and 19:8–9.

I wish I could see you again as I did last night. I have both the dagurreotypes on the table by me & am grateful to you for sitting for them. He has coloured their cheeks; & tho' very different they both please me very much.

Dont speak of this proposal, to Dr. White, even if you are struck with it till I hear from you & have written a reply, for I will write a much more careful letter if you feel inclined to show it to him. How delighted I would be if I could call in the voice of the church to clear you from all prejudice in the step I so much desire you to take.

How nice it would be if the Old Keep in which you shut yourself up from me so closely could be broken down, & I could win your hand this very season. It seems to me too charming even to be tho't of in my dreams.

I shall probably go home to-morrow night. I shall not go to Princeton or speak to my brother Spence till this last suggestion is disposed of. It may be better absolutely to let the Session make the decision of which I speak first; & then I really think Mother could be approached with the *absolute certainty* of her acceding to my wishes.

I know she will love you very much when she knows you. And I shall have the wife by far of most character in the family. I write very carelessly, but I begin strongly to suspect that you love me & know you will forgive me. Pray write at once.

Yours affectionately.
JM

1 o'clock.

Philadelphia,
Jan: 20th 1855.

My *dear Darling,*

I dont know what to call you. I am tired of Madam; & "my dear Friend" would sound very sweetly in some cases, but very unmeaningly toward you. Do tell me what I shall say; or else encourage a poor suffering lover, who has brought away from all his visits to you new arrows of uneasiness & distress, to call you what he pleases, as it is only one more way of candidly telling you the truth.

What do you think? I have been to see Spence. I determined to do so last night in the cars. We reached here about 1, & this morning after breakfast I called on him, & told him the main facts of all that it would concern him to know. I began by asking a promise of secrecy which he very pointedly gave. I told him then that he had confided to me the fact of his engagement very soon after it had taken place & that I would act with equal openness to him in confiding to him what was of a far more delicate character but that as he knew that he had often complained of my getting angry &[5] abruptly breaking off a conversation

---

5. Between the lines Miller drew a hand with a pointing finger above the word *angry* and added "N.B. (nota bene)."

on account of his interrupting me with strong expressions before he knew all the facts I must beg of him to hear me patiently till I had quite finished all I had to say. I was half sorry for this last charge for tho' it made us safe against an explosion it made me feel after all was over a wish that I had left him from the very first to the most unguarded manifestation of his feeling.

Spence, unless I am judging sanguinely in my zeal to make everything look favorably to myself, came out *far* more on my side than your letter would have led me to fear. His great attack upon me was, that "in *Philadelphia* it would cost me my church to an unquestionable certainty" & then detailed some of the cares to which I have alluded. But then, on the other hand, he said, (What I did not know before) that he believed "a state divorce satisfied all moral & social claims," a thing which springs out of his legal way of looking at things & which even I do not believe: & secondly, that the town had behaved in the most absurd manner in respect to Mrs. Peace & that he had always & very often stoutly defended her; though he had never allowed himself or his wife to visit her.[6] He also told me of another case where a family of great strength in the city had held up a member entirely & the difficulty was dying out. I thought his first reception of my discovery to him favorable, & tho' his emphatic opinion about my losing my church shows of course a very strong feeling, yet he put it, as you see, solely on the base of a popular error in judging which would hardly affect I should suppose his own personal heartiness of feeling.

He undertook to speak of personal violence as a thing to be apprehended, but this I shamed him out of, & I think I will utter the little piece of egotism of saying, that this is the last thing we Millers would be influenced by. I have a strong faith in the old Presbyterian dogma of self-defence, & I think the blood of an absolute assailant on my hands, or a mortal injury sustained in defending life, would weigh far less heavily upon my conscience, than many a sin that would be considered comparatively light. I have a strong belief of the doctrine that the dying of a bad man is not at all more solemn than his continuing to live.

I told Spence how you had repulsed me, & told him that you had committed yourself in no way to an engagement not even by an avowal of your love to me; & that tho' in my sanguine interest I felt sure you did respond to my affection yet the daguerreotypes which I showed him & which he seemed to devour very approvingly were the greatest instance of your committing yourself that I had known & that these had been stolen from you not as your own gift but by a sort of stratagem.

6. A few years earlier Dr. Edward Peace sued for divorce in the Court of Common Pleas of Philadelphia from his wife, Caroline Willing Peace, on charges of malicious desertion. She had left him for two years, which was legally sufficient for divorce, but she regarded her separation as required by "religious and moral obligation" (Answer of Caroline W. Peace to the Libel of Edward Peace," in the Court of Common Pleas, "Peace v. Peace," John Calwalader Legal Papers, 1552, Pennsylvania Historical Society, Philadelphia).

I say so much to excuse the liberty I have taken in venturing upon this step without consulting with you. The portraits, I think, mollified Spencer's judgments wonderfully; indeed the long, deep look that he took of the first one before he discovered that there were two seemed to be almost as strong in its impression as that first look at the original on that morning that ushered in all our troubles.

I looked upon Spencer (as concerns himself) as gained; for notwithstanding that strong expression about the Church he did not go to work with all his might to dissuade or denounce me as I should have done if I thought my brother was taking a *ruinous* step. Still he may speak differently after reflection.

The more I think of the use of the council of the Session, the better I like it. If they are *quiet* men who will pass the act quickly & without opposition I think it would be of value in many ways. It would meet the argument that people are not to be left to their own discretion in settling whether their case is a legitimate one of separation; & it would be a convenient thing to put promptly before my Session here if any inquiry should arise among the people calculated to compromise us as Spence predicts. Moreover such a convenient shape in which to possess the material for replying to any cavil, would prevent all possible danger of retaliation by renewing slanders on the other side.

Suppose you see Dr White & have a full & most confidential interview. You have a full permission so far as I am concerned: ask him what he thinks of the wisdom of Major Preston or your brother securing the counsel of the Session, whether it would be *certain* to be given in your favor & whether the Presbytery is composed so entirely in your rural region of persons who know each other & their circumstances as that they would just as quietly review the action of the Session & without mentioning names reiterate it. I should suppose this might be done so quietly as not to rouse hostility in Maryland & above all so as not to provoke an appeal to higher ecclesiastical bodies.

If Dr White approves of the step warmly I should like the privilege of preparing both the minutes. If he has the smallest doubt it ought not to be done.

If it is done or whenever it is made certain that it can be done successfully in the Session or not, I will go on at once to Princeton, & lay the whole subject before mother & if Spencer does not disappoint me by harsher judgments than appeared this morning I think my family will no longer stand in the way of my suit.

I beg that Dr White may know that these steps to clear your position are not of my seeking—that I am quite ready to ask your hand at once; & that if the texture of your Session is such as to make such a seeking of its authority unusual & strange I have not a regret & am only scheming such plans to comply with your own sense of difficulty in which I do not share.

And now my dearest Tyrant, show me some mercy. These long waitings of days & weeks for any communication with you, are very heavy upon a poor impatient spoiled worshipper like me. To ride with you & walk with you & visit with you & see you every day & then suddenly to be thrown back into the midst of these, black letter volumes with a letter only once in three weeks is more than I can bear.

Will you not have a steady day for writing? & shall it not be at least once a week. And will you not write as soon as you get this if you have not written already.

In great haste, yours very devotedly
John Miller

[marginal notes] What did Major Preston say on your way home?

Please tell me whether the Wash. letter reached you duly & was paid. The office clerk of the National took it at 2 at night & the money loosely with it.

Colalto
Tuesday Jan'y 23.1855

My *dear Sir,*

Did you get my poor letter from Staunton. The morning (it was pitch dark) after it was written I found myself ensconced in a corner of the Stage jolting over the roughest of plank roads, suffering much from cold and as the day wore on, much more from head-ache. About mid day I reached home; & was glad to assign myself to the mesmeric passes of my little maiden for the next day & a half. I have seldom suffered more violently. But my little maid, (whom I will not agree that you shall colonize) did wonders for me. Cantey laughs when, I say that the touch of her fingers thro' my hair is like dreamy music to me. But no matter whether the touch were musical or mesmeric, it answered the purpose, and I am quite well again.

I was disappointed in getting no letter from you Saturday, for I felt sure you had written from Wash'n. Yesterday however your Phil'a letter came; & this afternoon the expected one from Wash: reached me, *paid,* yet out of time. Now I answer both at once.

I am glad you have had a talk with Spence. I rely upon his cautious & circumspect judgment in a case, in which your feelings are too deeply enlisted to allow you to judge wisely for yourself. In this first interview, he opens the subject just where I left it long ago,—just where it presses me with most power. You cannot have forgotten how earnest I have ever been upon the score of your public usefulness, and will not, therefore, be surprised when I say *I will do nothing!* that will compromise your character & influence as a Minister. The two strongest points in the whole matter, the moral question being settled, are your Ministry & your children. The opposition of friends, should it occur, would be very painful, yet other & more important points having been satisfactorily disposed of, I would not allow my decision to be controlled by it. But hazard your ministerial character by yielding to your wishes, I will not do. I would be unworthy of your love if I did. "Spence" I *feel* must be right in his opinion of the public sentiment of Phil, & you must learn to feel that if you cannot hold your Church & me *together,* you must give me up, or rather, for the trial to your sense of honor & affection united might be too great for you;—I will give you up, that you may cling to your Office. But even in this, be assured, I will not act precipitately—nor without tender consideration of your feelings. As matters at present appear, I will not recede from the recent arrangement between us. But I must impress upon you that if in my judgment, your public usefulness, will be sacrificed by success in your private wishes, then you must submit to that judgment, no matter how painful the effort. You cannot know how precious a thing real affection is to me. It has been the coveted blessing of my life. It has been an unspeakable agony often, that this blessing in its strongest form has, because of my terrible dismemberment from society, been denied me. The most alluring earthly prospect has been that, of stepping down from the exposed stand I now occupy that I may nestle safe & warm and trustingly under the loving shelter of a loving heart. And if, being convinced there was no sin in the feeling, I have yielded to the illusion & dared to dream that there was something in the future besides the ever-deepening isolation of my present lot, I have not only involved myself but you too in difficulty, I have only to draw back before it is too late, no matter at what cost to myself.

If Spencer had said *public* instead of "*personal* violence" was to be apprehended, he would have been I think right. All the machinery that the most intense malice could use to injure & annoy would be brought into action. But I cannot bear to speak to you on this head—Yet one word upon it: I have never, since the first public explosion, been entirely free from a sort of espionage from that quarter, as vigilant as it has been incomprehensible.[7] For years my Father was annoyed & disturbed by letters—and after his death,—not a fortnight after—one came to me which after much thought I answered. Some months after another letter came—then another. This last I answered, & in such manner as to free me from further trouble. Of course I retained copies of my letters—shall I send them to you?

I think favorably of your plan of appealing for Counsel to the Session—& will, at some early day lay the scheme before our friend Dr. White, and write you what he says about it. But this thing of appealing to Church sessions & Courts, looks very terrible to me. I shrink from the slightest observation in a matter so delicate. I have not yet fully taken in the idea that I *can* be married.

You must be patient about my letters. I cannot always write when I would. Unless you could see me as I really am at home I could hardly make you understand my difficulties. But you can write at any time—wont you do it very often?

I am really mortified about those Daguerres. I thought them miserable, & hate to have your brother receive his first impression of me from them. You can bear them, not because they resemble, but because they are *suggestive* of me. By the bye, when you talk to them, by what *name* do you address them? This seems a difficulty with you—but you must not ask me to help you out of it.

7. That is, from Francis Thomas.

I find old Dr Baird's visit has created quite a commotion in this quiet town.[8] The cry of Abolitionist was raised against him, & really things were quite threatening. Another wonder I have to announce, is the fact of a thunder storm Sunday night.

Very truly Yours
S.C.P. McDowell.

Colalto
Friday, Jan'y 25.1855

My *dear Sir,*

When I came home, a week ago I found my house quite full of young Cousins. Tuesday, another visitor appeared in the shape of an "*olden* maid"—a sort of living Encyclopedia—a very pleasant person to me, tho' rather painfully addicted to all printed things from a hand-bill up. She, usually, escapes from the Library, (our winter parlor,) & the boisterous circle of young folk there, & book in hand, takes refuge in my room, sometimes very decidedly to my inconvenience, as her presence imposes upon me no inconsiderable self-denial in the way of writing. Tonight my young Guests are out at a party, and the Library is left to the quiet occupation of Mary, Miss Moore & Cantey, whilst Lilly keeps herself still at my side, with a volume of Poems upon which she seems very intent.[9] And I am glad thus early in the evening to have a chance of drawing my writing table close to the fire, & feel that I can write a letter without fear of being interrupted, or of going to sleep over it, as I happened to do over the last one I wrote to you.

I had a long talk today with Dr. White; full and free and confidential. He disapproves very decidedly of any appeal to the Session, first because he thinks it would look as if *I* were not satisfied of the *propriety* of the step I was about to take; & next, because it would be giving unavoidable & very disagreeable publicity to a proceeding that we desire to keep quiet. So far from presenting an appeal to higher ecclesiastical bodies as you suppose it would, this resort to the Session would, he thinks, just start a ball that would "roll on & on" till it would reach at last, the General Assembly. Thus, as a *preliminary* measure, he thinks it would be very inexpedient; & might be, not from any want of reason & justice in the case submitted, but from want of tone & gentlemanly feeling in some of the individuals who must act upon it, unsuccessful. If the Session or Presbytery are ever called in, in this matter, it should be, in his opinion, *after* *the* step is taken; & then it can be done, he believes most successfully, if it be found to be necessary.

8. Robert Baird (1798–1863), a Presbyterian minister and vigorous advocate of voluntary societies but not an abolitionist.
9. Polly Moore was the "old maid" friend of McDowell.

He does not, however, deem any action necessary now, & quite gratified me by the indignant storm with which he rejected the idea of *my* conduct being submitted to the control or direction of A, B, & C; the common men, who are to be found in our Church Courts. He has as great an estimate of my "cool wisdom" as you can have, & with, perhaps, as little reason for it. Yet he begs that I will be careful not to *step down* in taking a new step. *He* must be a "very clever fellow indeed to whom I would be willing to give you" the dear old gentleman said. I was prudent & said nothing; tho' the fact is that he & Cousin John idealize so much about me that they would be exceedingly hard to please. I greatly doubt whether you, yourself can be much wilder in your fancies than they are. And all three of you are I think a little crazy on the subject, when I consider what a common place person I am.

The Dr wonders at your Brother's fear of your losing your Church. He thinks such a loss would not follow, upon such grounds in my own State—and felt sure that public sentiment could not be more delicate & exacting in any other State in the union.

I have made no revelation of name, and he is quite puzzled & curious about the person whom he is thus, in some sort, counselling.

Cousin John had little to say on the subject as we travelled a half day together after I left Wash: & that little went to show that he believed the suspicions there aroused, were scarcely true.

Such dreary weather we have had. Rain, snow, intense cold, & high winds mark the past week. Tonight I hear the wind blowing most boisterously, tho' it is not so cold as heretofore.

You must be very grateful. I have written you *three* letters in the last 8 or 9 days! Does not that satisfy your craving for them. After all tho', a letter seems a very meager affair after a good talk. And yet I am sure I have been able to say to you many things with my pen, that I could never have uttered with my tongue. But my letter has seen me far into the night. The whole world seems to be asleep, & my eyes are making strong appeals to my compassion on that score themselves. So good night, & all other good things to you.

Very truly Yours
S.C.P. McDowell.

Do use envelopes that are large enough for your letters to go in & out of easily.

You must send back the enclosed scrap as I believe it is Tom's. He carefully preserved it, with a sort of pride not discreditable to him & very pleasant to me. My elder brother had the pleasure of hearing it read & complimented in Brussels I think.[10] My estimate of it was such that I felt ashamed to show it to my Father & ask his sanction in sending it—but he was satisfied—& other friends pleased—&

10. McDowell had sent one of her published poems to her younger brother, Thomas Preston McDowell (1834–1862). Her older brother was James McDowell IV (1820–1879), a physician in St. Louis.

upon the whole I was in much danger from the "puffed up ed ness" from which the man prayed my Father should be delivered.

S.C.P.McD.

Phil, Jan: 27th 1855

My *dearest Madam*

I take your own plan of a pencil for the sheer purpose of moving rapidly over the paper. I am so bankrupt in respect to my Sunday sermons, having employed much of the week in dissipating duties of different sorts that I tho't at first of postponing a reply till Saturday. But if you had tasked your ingenuity to write a letter that would have *moved* me to the utmost possible & deepened as much as one letter could my ardent love for you, you could not have produced one that would have had the effect of this simple artless generous expression of your conscientious feeling. I do love you, my dear darling Madam with all my heart. I go to Princeton with my children (who are well) next Monday week. If you can see Dr White & get his calm dispassionate views about the whole question & then about the session's actions I will be prepared to talk to my mother surely in the whole matter.

If I were not checked by thinking what a fool I would be to commit myself even to you in a thing so unlikely to be realized—indeed if I did not see what a fool I must be to lay myself open by a syllable to any one in a dream of such future expectation—& yet if I was not tempted in all the little I have said in that subject by this very difficulty that you suggest of my *public ministry*—I would *say* just in the Don Quixote spirit in which I sometimes feel—"public ministry! I dont depend upon a public ministry—my ministry is to all climes & to future ages! & anything that would drive me into the seclusion of a cottage life shall be the voice of Providence giving me at last the yearnings of a higher passion." Now this I *know* to be foolish. If I dreamed of such employment hereafter it would be mad to invite after me the taunts of men as to those premature outgivings of important accomplishments & mad to saddle myself with the *impossibility* of accomplishments which like the squaring of the circle, or the discovery of perpetual motion most wise men think to be impossible. Take it then as an evidence of my love to you that I am willing to appear a fool in your eyes that I may urge that my sense of future usefulness does not depend upon my sense of caste in society but upon having four quiet walls around me some 20 or 30 years for the working out (or rather the *proving*—for they are already worked out) of facts that do not depend for their acceptance upon the caste of the preacher but upon their intrinsic truth & which neither your standing nor my standing can ever affect in their independent importance & value. I mean some day to strip all this of the Sybilline look of these rough pencillings & tell you plainly all I mean & all I ask is that you will never upbraid me in the decline of an unsuccessful life for the frank utterance of my dreams to one so dear to me as you are. This is the most costly letter as to time I ever wrote to you, for I *fear* about my pulpit tomorrow, but chiefly in the commotion it causes in my feelings, for I am dashing it thro' in half an hour. I write it because I know that after such an interval in waiting for yours wh has just been sent up by the postman (Sat. morn.) & after such a letter as you have written you may dislike me to let Sunday intervene before my reply. Do send me all letters that you will—all attacks that have been made on you—& by the bye that published letter you promised me.

Do you know that if you were to ask me what caused me most uneasiness in view of my obtaining your hand I would really be at a loss to determine whether it was this that frowns upon you as so appalling or that thing the care of which you most deride—*your health*. I have such a timid terrified shrinking at the thought of anything like sickness in my daughter or anyone I love—such an exaggerated dread of it—that when I hear of you *as cold* in your Staunton ride I feel almost angry at you & tho' I know I am treading on perilous ground considering President McLean's fortune in this matter I must beg that you will take better care of your health & tell me how you are as one of the stereotyped informations of your letter.[11] May I beg that some little dispatch may be given to this seeking of the opinion of Dr White, for waiting for that obstructs the step to which I have alluded & which I want to take. I mean consulting my mother. He can probably tell you just what the result of a reference to the Session or the Presbytery will be.

If it were not for my mother, such is my sense of *conscientious duty* that I would cut my life in two (as I some day *intend & have for years intended* to do) & let the first half go as it has done toward building up the Church & go to you with the humble petition *at once* to share with me what remains in some suitable retreat for study. I am conscious of my power to do good that way more than any other & I desire it as a passion by itself higher than & independent of my passion for you. Meanwhile I do not at all give up the idea that our mutual influence & character (especially *yours*) can sustain us against these attacks even in the most exposed pulpit.

With warmest love *begging you to write often*.

Yours
JM

Colalto,
Monday, Jan'y 29. 1855.

My *dear Sir*,

I begin my letter as, no doubt, you have often had your little Maggie begin hers, with the important announcement that I *am quite well*. I am quite astonished

11. John Maclean Jr. (1800–1886), a Presbyterian minister, had been a professor at the College of New Jersey before becoming its president in 1854. Miller misspelled his name.

at your thought, much more, your care as to my health—a thing that nobody considers or has any fear about now. For years I was, certainly not in firm health; yet I endured so much fatigue, & was capable of such great & constant exertion, & by a sort of indomitable energy effected so much in various ways, that I was ashamed when strangers would remark upon my *"frail* looks." Physicians were consulted from time to time, but they would turn off with the story—"nervous— my dear Madam—nervous." They knew & so did I, that until they could teach me not to think or feel they could do nothing. They might well talk of "nervousness" & deem it hopeless of cure, to one who for 18 months had not half a dozen nights of unbroken sleep; and who for years lived in a state of perpetual & unnatural excitement and unrest.

My Mother was for several years before her death an invalid, and my peculiar troubles, were aggravated by the anxiety I felt for her.[12] I suffered when with her, & could scarcely command my fears & distress when away from her. It seemed to me I died a thousand deaths in the apprehension of hers. And yet when death did come, it was so calm & peaceful as to be stripped of its horrors, and I even saw her buried away from me, without any agony or sorrow; but with an almost joyous realization of the full import of the question "Why seek Ye the living among the dead"?[13] turned away from her grave.

But afflictions deepened upon us. My Father's ill health commenced almost immediately after my Mother's death, and for 3 or 4 years never left me an hour free from anxiety. Then Frank's long illness and death occurred. And my Father's effort to bring her body home, (for she died in Wash'n) for burial, fastened a hitherto unsuspected disease upon him, and in 6 weeks after we reached home he too was dead.[14] And for the first time in all my sorrows I felt that I had been cast out upon life unsheltered and unprotected. Is it any wonder then, that with this accumulation of sorrows, a deep gloom should have settled upon us all.

But, since my Father's death, I have been free from pressing anxiety, and this, together with the necessity for active & steady occupation has given me new health and returned to me the old cheerfulness that belonged to me. I never was in better health than at present. And if I was very cold as I came up from Staunton you should not be angry at me for it, but, like a good philosopher, take a fit of spite at the weather. I was very warmly habited & even availed myself, at the breakfast house of the good Dr's (McLean) previously despised advice and drew a pair of country yarn socks, that would have delighted the old gentleman, over my boots. But I could not make the weather warm,—neither could I make the hotel from which we started warm, so I just did for myself, all that you, had you been there

12. McDowell's mother was Susanna Smith Preston McDowell (1800–1847).

13. Luke 24:5.

14. McDowell's sister Frances Elizabeth Henry McDowell was born about 1825 or 1826 and died on June 15, 1851. James McDowell was serving in the United States House of Representatives when he died on Aug. 24, 1851.

could have done for me,—and was cold notwithstanding. But I am not now any the worse for having been so; so pray dont worry yourself upon this score.

When your letter came this afternoon I thought I would send to Dr White to throw into a letter the opinions he had expressed to me upon the subject of which you write, but the evening was so cold, I did not like to send a servant out with a note. I may get the Dr to do it yet, so that you can have it by Saturday, but in the meantime take my report, in my last letter, of our conversation.

Have you ever marked out a course for yourself in case you should find unrelenting opposition from your Mother? You should do so, that you be not taken unawares. I think it due to your Mother, & due to your affection for her that you should seek her counsel in a matter like this. Her opinion will however come to you *authoritatively*, & you should be ready to meet it by gentle reasonings, or to submit to it with dutiful promptness.

What does Spence say upon more mature consideration?

Do you know you seem to me in a very great hurry?—I am alarmed at it. Another thing—I don't like to hear you speak in so defiant a manner of public sentiment. *It is* of great importance for you, not only for yourself, but for your children, that you should be regardful of the good opinion of the world. I enclose the letters of which I wrote before. The ones to which they are answers are somewhere out of my possession but you will gather the context of them from my answers. Do write from Princeton fully & freely. I shall be restless to hear.

Yours truly
S.C.P. McDowell

Tuesday, Jan'y 30. 1855

My *dear* Sir,

I would not send my last night's letter this morning, thinking I might be able to send you a letter, with it, from Dr White that would be worth having. The Dr gave me his letter tonight as I came out of the Lecture-room, and I enclose it to you. I am disappointed in it,—it is so scant & poor & timid in this last particular singularly unlike the Doctor, whose independence & courage in expressing his opinions I have often admired. But you will do the best you can with it. I have often thought how very unreliable the solemn giver of advice frequently is, and how at last we are, in all matters of consequence left to stand or fall upon the conclusions of our own minds. If these conclusions be to us satisfactory, it seems to me to be both safer & better to follow them. The respect I have for my own opinion is to me the guarantee I have for the respect of others for it. I can only respect the decisions of my mind to influence others, when I perceive they are strongly telling upon my own conduct.

Do you perceive why these truisms are thrust in here? I cannot say that I do.

The first snow of any consequence this winter lies upon the ground now. I had a nice walk thro' it tonight to our regular weekly meeting. I half made up my mind when dark came that it was too cold for me to go out, but my young Cousin, James Carrington, who lives with us at present, persuaded it was not very cold, & the walking quite respectable.[15] So I tried it, in the clear, bright, cloudless moonlight & found it delightful. I thought it likely as I mounted the icy steps, thro' the fields that you would have been "angry" again, had you been witness of my proceeding, but with hundreds of miles between us, I confess I did not fear it very much. Indeed there was no cause for anger. Dr McLean would have been transported at the sight of my preparations.

When you go to Princeton don't take those horrid Daguerres with you. You will be tempted to show them if you do, & they *really* are, to say the least, very *unflattering*.

Do I seem *to talk* to you in my letters, so that the written words, have all the effect of spoken words upon you? Sometimes letters are to me such vivid pictures of their writers, that all their peculiarities of tone and gesture and countenance rise up before me, & I seem to look at them & listen to them.

I thought I had a great deal that was worth saying to you when I began, but it has all oozed out in the various little naps that have happened to me during my writing.

I'm afraid I do not sympathize in your philosophie furors. I cannot precisely understand it. You soar so high above me that I must be excused for thinking that you are in that region in which Commodore Dallas was, to the dismay of his wife whose eager anxiety made search upon *her map* for the place, and never could discover where he was, when the Newspapers said—"he is in nubibus."[16] There is where *you* seem to me to be when you spread your wings.

Very truly Yours
S.C.P. McDowell

Philadelphia Jan: 30th 1855.

My darling Friend,

Your question about the pictures was no help to me; because in my artless way, I call them, "my dear Wife", & you know that would sound very awkwardly in actual writing. I would have called you, "my dear Sally" long ago, but I love you in such a way; that is, my love has so much admiration mingled with it, that I never can free it altogether from certain trying associations. My Uncle Tom's queer wife,[17] a grand-daughter of Dr. Franklin, who loves her soup-societies & her "Christian friends" as she calls them, better than she does her children & my

15. James McDowell Carrington (1838–after 1910).

16. Latin, meaning in the clouds. Alexander James Dallas (1791–1844) of the United States Navy died in Peru.

17. Sarah (Sally) Bache, daughter of Richard Bache and Sarah Franklin Bache, was born in 1788. She married Thomas Sergeant (1782–1860), brother of Miller's mother, Sarah Sargeant Miller.

mother's half-witted chamber-maid long ago when I was a child, & sundry other odd characters were all named Sally & tho' Mother's brothers all called her Sally in olden time when more of them were living than now, yet it always struck us boys as a sort of temerity as tho' some Greek had taken Jupiter Olympus by the nose, or as tho' Father & Dr. Alexander & Dr. Green & the rest of the old Synod had played leap-frog together over the front parlour carpet.[18]

What do you think? This morning out of a sort of pretence as tho' I wanted a little recreation I disobeyed your injunctions so much as to go into a room opening out of my study into the street & throw open the window with a sort of forlorn tho't that possibly tho' you had never done so before you had determined to surprise me with an entire letter. There just at the very moment was the postman at a neighbour's house. The glance seemed to be suggestive for at the moment an idea flashed upon me which I rushed into my study to put in practice. I wrote in a fair hand James Canby, Esq, on a piece of paper & hurried out to him with the request that letters to Mr. Canby, a friend of mine, as the postman was led to infer (that wasnt wrong, was it?) were to be left with me; that they would be addressed to this city for some weeks. The post-man took it up as an every day sort of requirement made of him, & so the matter stands arranged. My words to him were about these;—"letters to that address will be intended for a person who is a fiend of mine who wishes them left with me". Was that a fib? If it was, it was a very gratuitous one; for in any other than such a hurried movement I might easily have thought of saying;—"Please leave Mr. Canby's letters with me. They will be directed to Phila for some weeks to come". Do write me now a whole parcel of *daily* letters. You know they may be ever so short. As my name will disappear from the Post Office Mr. Canby will awaken no attention for weeks. And as to your time, you know they may be so short. Just this for example:—"My dear John, I love you so much that I cant bear to let another of these long days pass without sitting down a moment to write you if it be but a single line. You need have no fears about my health; the cases where you have tho't me careless are rare instances I do assure you. I do not often sit up till "long after one" writing, & the case that has troubled you of my riding in the stage with so few wrappings as to allow myself to feel cold I see the folly of & I will not allow it to occur again. I know I ought to write oftener than you, because you have your sermons; but will you be satisfied with a fair division I writing as much & as often as you. The cat has broke her leg & Roller, the littlest dog of all, went off yesterday in fits. Otherwise we are all well. Yours very affectionately,—.

18. Miller's father was Samuel Miller (1769–1850), Presbyterian minister and professor of ecclesiastical history and church government at Princeton Theological Seminary. His distinguished colleagues were Archibald Alexander (1772–1851), professor of theology and president of Princeton Theological Seminary, and Ashbel Green (1762–1848), professor of theology and then president of the College of New Jersey from 1812 to 1822. He edited the *Christian Advocate*.

And now my dear Mrs. McDowell, what *shall* I say about your letter. I have often been on the eve of writing, *What I firmly believe,* that I have been a far greater sufferer in my life than you have, & have really grown *accustomed* to endurance, so that as I was telling Mrs Potter about another matter not longer ago than yesterday, I scarcely feel comfortable unless some light trouble at least is pressing on my shoulders. I have had a sad life, & have a sad *grey* temperament in place of your bright & happy one. My life is a positive burden & were it not for religious hopes & certain worldly curiosities & ambitions, I would be willing to give it up this very afternoon. The idea of nothingness—the idea of an entire sinking out of being was never dreadful to me as it seems to some persons. But then I have learned to have a sort of *Shame* of talking so, as tho' happiness were a thing that full-grown men ought not to be talking about. *And* I think the more grey I get & the more I go on toward age, the more happy I become under a sort of feeling of contentment under the absence of any positive pleasure. The idea of your refusing me troubles me more than you conceive. I have a sort of hungry passion for everything I love which when denied its proper object turns inward & corrodes itself. When I am going to Princeton to see my children for example & a funeral or some other parish engagement prevents it for another week I can hardly describe to you the *recoil* of my impatience. And now if you can understand such a thing, the sorrows of the past are the things on which I chiefly rely to give me a sort of desperate readiness for the sorrows of the future.

But you will not give me up—will you?

Two things are settled & none of these questions shake them; first, that I love you tenderly; & second, that till you treat me with indifference or I should rather say, till I know you are quite indifferent & averse to me I shall not even *begin* to cease to love you. Then the question of the time of marriage, tho' not secondary *in my feelings* is secondary in *all my thinking* for much is settled before I come to that. But now one thing troubles me. Instead of feeling that "you have involved me in difficulty" I shall feel if you refuse me on the ground of what occurs with my mother & others when I come to consult them, a degree of culpability & fault in having misrepresented the feeling of the North that will amount really to *remorse.* My confidence is strong that such will not be the case but if it is my love to you will make me feel as tho' I had intruded upon what was beginning to be a condition of comparative peace & stirred it up & exposed you again to haggard troubles & anxieties out of sheer folly & ignorance. But God grant that my original estimate may prove the true one. I am so convinced of it up to this point of time that I could get every permission of my will to marry you this very night. But if your judgment on the facts that I shall unfold candidly as they present themselves turns against me, why will you not still accept the offer of my affection & be my plighted Bride even if long years separate us from our day of marriage. My children are in town & *would* send their love. I go to Princeton on Monday & there I will write you a long & I trust hopeful letter. I confess you make me happy & relieve a great many of your harder sentences when you make me feel you love me. I am so *modest an expectant* of happiness that this sort of mail stage love seems to me far better than I deserve.

Yours affectionately,
Jno Miller.

[marginal note] Allow me to say that unless you write often the postman will probably not remember the arrangement about the names.

Colalto
Thursday Feb'y 1. 1855

My *dear Sir,*

I have been writing all day. Letters had accumulated in such numbers upon me that for two days I have been making a desperate effort to deliver myself from the burden of them. I feel almost as tired as if I had been paying a round of visits; but as a gloomy day is drearily closing upon me, I draw my table a little nearer the fire that I may talk a little to you, in the half twilight over your letter received this afternoon.

Somehow, I never dreamt that you were ever *sad*, or pressed by any cares or troubles beyond those that are incident to even the happiest life; and I feel that there is a bond [of] sympathy between us now not the less strong because but just discovered. Yet I will not tell you how heavy my heart feels under all you say. It would scarcely lighten yours to hear it, and might, in a contingency, only add to its weight.

I have little idea—experimentally, I mean of a desponding temper. I see it, painfully exhibited in one of my Sisters; and it belonged somewhat to my Mother—and to them it has been, according of course to the degree in which possessed, a be-clouding sort of thing, dashing darkly allmost their happiest moments. But religious principle & feeling has, in both cases, been applied, not without success as a corrective. In my own case, a stray sunbeam was imprisoned in my nature, which has supplied me with some little warmth & light ever since. Indeed as I grow older, it seems to grow brighter, so that I shall have enough to spare to you, if your wishes and necessities are reasonable & moderate. I remember, as if the thing had happened only yesterday, of coming rather suddenly upon Powers (our famous Sculptor) who was at the moment engaged in modelling a Bust of my Uncle, Col Preston.[19] He turned quickly towards me, fastened his great eyes, the brightest I ever saw, upon me with a gaze under which I shrank, then dropped the clay from his hand & walked up rather smilingly & began his phrenological (phrenology seemed a passion with him then) pressure upon my head. I think he was perhaps disappointed in the matter of intellect, but seemed surprised at "*such* a development of *Hope*!" There may be nothing in Phrenology

---

19. Hiram Powers (1805–1873), an American sculptor, fashioned a bust of McDowell's uncle William Campbell Preston.

generally, but it spoke truly then. In all that I have known of life since, I have found that the solitary blessing of Pandora's box has been mine. Sometimes well-nigh extinguished—but never absolutely;—when it couldn't burn steadily, it would at least flicker up a little.

And now I would fair impart a little of this quality to you—how shall I do it? But I can't think you often feel as you did that afternoon in which you wrote. You spoke as if you had a full knowledge of that sort of suffering that has often made me feel a longing to lay my head in my Mother's lap & take a hearty cry, whilst she stroked my hair in her gentle way & soothed me with such tones as I shall never hear again; and I have it in my heart to speak words of soothing to you in your sad mood that might make it less sad & sombre, but I am checked—Did you ever hear that I had "cool wisdom"? You must be content to know that you do not speak of your sorrows to one who does not feel for you.

Friday night.

You dont seem to fancy my letters as you take the trouble to furnish me a model—Since you can write such ones to yourself, why ask me to send you any? I'm sure if I were to write *just* such a letter as you propose, you would think some mistake had occurred, & would hand it back to the postman with the assurance of its not being yours—it might belong to the *real* "James Canby Esq" for ought you know,—certainly it was not for you. Besides the style being a little too affectionate, the items of information are not altogether true. I do frequently sit up very late at night writing. Are you willing to do without letters that I may give up this bad habit? If not, you must not get angry, and scold at the Lady "on your table" & declare that her name sake in Va is shamefully & even wickedly neglectful of her health. Perhaps it would be well, for me, *here* to assure you *that I am quite well*, notwithstanding the severe cold; & that I seldom venture out without wrappings *almost* sufficient, in number & weight, to defy a Russian climate. But good night.

Saturday

I am writing you, sure enough, a "whole parcel of daily letters" tho' not exactly in the way in which you wish them, as they are not every day, sent off by mail.

I made a great effort to dispose of certain household matters early enough to catch an hour of sunshine for my letter, but I failed, and only begin to write as the sun sets, beyond our hills in unclouded glory. I needed such a cheerful & bright afternoon as this has been to write to you, for I cannot shake off the sad effect of your letter. It was so unexpected to me [in] every way. I had grown fixed in the idea that I had monopolized life's sorrows, but when in such a mournfully earnest tone you tell me that "life is a burden to you,"—& display a sort of longing to "sink into nothingness," I feel that I have overated my own troubles, & not a little blameworthy in not having, somehow or other, come earlier at the knowledge of yours. But even now that you claim a fellowship in suffering with me what can I say or do? Feel for you? that I do, fully & heartily, tho' ignorant of all that has made life sad to you. But—I must not allow myself to say more. But you, my dear Sir, whose business it is to point out the way of *true* comfort to others; why not avail yourself of your own teachings? I have at times, in a tumult of feelings that could not be spoken to any human ear gone like the sorrowing disciples of the beheaded John,[20] and, in such an agony of contenting emotions as I cannot describe and without ability to frame a single petition, have, in sobs & tears looked up with the simple feeling—"Lord! Thou knowest"—and have felt gradually stealing over me such—not calmness—but *peace;*—such peace as the Savior means when he says "My *peace* I give unto you"—such peace as throws a sort of light over past sorrows & animates us with fresh courage to meet & bear the sorrows that are to come.[21] Now, is not this same ear open to you—and is not that same voice ready to speak peace to your troubled heart? As I happen just now to think of it I quote for your benefit two or three very poor stanzas, from a half dozen that I wrote several years ago to a poor woman suffering under a heavy bereavement.

Our Lord & Redeemer
When dwelling below
Was clothed in our nature
And bore all its woe,
Now exalted in Heav'n
That nature still wears,
Still weeps in our sorrows
Still shares in our cares:

Still offers his bosom
Our refuge from harm,
Still places around us
His sheltering arm;
Still whispers of safety
When danger appals,
And lights with hope's promise
Each tear as it falls.

Still speaks in such accents
Of tenderest love
From the throne of his glory
In Heaven above,
And stoops to assure us
Who mourn 'neath his rod
He feels as our Brother
Who reigns as our God.

20. John the Baptist.
21. John 21:17; John 14:27.

My daylight gave out long ago, but I add another line now, & then lay my letter aside till Monday. I will answer the main questions of your letter some time again. To say the least, it might embarrass the whole matter, were I to take them up now. Let me urge that you will keep every thing as silent as possible. You dont know how insecure & apprehensive & fearful I should feel if this matter were buzzed about as such matters usually are.

I am a little mortified at your horror of my name. It is not very musical it is true, but is it not as much so as that downright monosyllable John? And I'm sure "Uncle Tom's queer wife" and "Mother's half-witted chamber maid" can have no more repulsive associations to you than "John Skinner D.D" our ejected Scotch pastor,[22] & John the Bootblack in every hotel in America can have to me. There is some thing so desperately curt in *John*,—it sounds as if one was mad when they said it.

And does the Lady in the picture hear with composure such pet-names as you address to her? Does she never look as tho' she would speak a reproof if she could? I am afraid she is as stupid as she looks to be. I wish I had thought earlier of asking you, when the children were with you, to take them in to see that Talbotype, that Richards has of me. As there are numbers of others there it would have excited no more remark with them for you to have said, "Maggie this is a lady whom your Aunt Mary & I saw in Va last summer—do you think she is pleasant-looking?['] Then it would have done to say "This is Catherine Hayes—wouldn't you like to hear her sing?"[23] And then the child might have gratified you by agreeing that the Lady tho' not pretty *was* rather pleasant-looking.—The one line I set out with has run into—how many?

Monday morning

My old friend, the lady of whom I spoke several days since leaves us today & I add a hurried line before I go out with her to town. I am not sure that you were not guilty of a fib to the postman about—Canby Esq. And, any how, I get so provoked with myself for being drawn into similar errors that I can hardly submit to any thing that entails them upon me. And these deceptions often fail, most mortifyingly. Only think of my dismay, at having Alfred (the servant whose business it is to take the mail & bring it every day) say in answer to my question—"You always drop my letters early in the morning in the letter box?"— "no ma'am—sometimes I think you want to be certain they will go, and I give them to Mr Plunkett (the Postmaster) *in his own hand*."[24] —And this was the end of all my attempt at concealment.

I wish I could enfold in my letter the bright sunshine that gladdens me— and the delightful, almost balmy air, that we have to-day in exchange for the

---

22. John Skinner (1804–1864) was tried by the Lexington Presbytery on the charge of slander in 1847 when he was pastor in Lexington.

23. Catherine Hayes (1820–1861), an Irish soprano, made her debut in New York in 1851.

24. Thomas B. Plunkett (c. 1817–1882), postmaster in Lexington.

piercing cold of the last week. I beg you will pardon all defects that my rapid writing displays in these hurried letters.

Very truly Yours
S.C.P. McDowell

Princeton, Feb: 5th 1855

My *dearest Madam*,

Mother has just left her seat at my chamber fire. I am on the whole in high spirits for tho' she does not withold an unfavorable opinion & that of a some what strong kind, yet she winds up by saying this. I had told her, that I believed I loved her more than any of her children, that I was not yet engaged, that if I thought a marriage of mine would add one grey hair to her temples I would not contract it & that she might prevent this marriage if she chose. These were my *words* as nearly as I can remember. You see they were very strong & ought to save me from a great deal of after anxiety. She replied that she would not assume any such responsibility & desired to be left out of any thought in the case. I think she went so far as to say that it *might* turn out well. Her two grand unfavorable reasons were somewhat curious 1st that your position *must* be somewhat impaired by your passed history & 2nd that from some chance acquaintanceship with you of a slight kind by reputation thro' mutual friends she tho't you had a quick & imperious temper & *as mine was somewhat of the same character*! she tho't the match "might promise little as to character or comfort." Now am I not a fool to tell you all this? I think not; because I would have no right to tell you what was favorable if I did not Daguerreotype the whole scene. Besides I dont think that you will make me pay the penalty of my own candor.

Now the grand fact is this, that my last reserve is removed. And I do earnestly renew the entreaty for your hand & assign to you the choice of the time tho' I beg that it may not be very far distant.

I will write more leisurely to-morrow. Tho' do *pray* & *think* over an immediate reply for I would like you to mail an answer to Phil: the evening after this— certainly after the one to-morrow.

You cant tell how relieved I am. Mother is my great idol. I would not have seriously violated her injunctions for the world & as she distinctly disdains any wish to intervene & really alludes to my "majority" & free agency in the matter & I know will value you & cherish you when she comes to know I feel greatly rejoiced. Mary I do not approach. Spencer did not change his first view seriously. My family I think are very honest spoken & will give their *fullest* disapprovals at the first. All *my* hesitations therefore are all at an end.

I write in the extremist haste fearing I am already too late for the mail. Mother has just left my side & therefore these are fresh impressions.

Yours affecly
John Miller.

Princeton, Feb: 6th 1855.

My *darling Icicle*,

The thermometer is at 4 & as I look out at the snow under my window I cant help thinking how much it is like your letters you do so watchfully keep out of them anything like a *warm* expression. If you have ever seen a poor group of slaves at the South clustered about a few chips trying to get a little comfort out of then in the cold Winter you have a very good notion of the way I go searching among your letters for any little warm spot that I can read over & over again & try to fancy that it means more than it really does. When you say, "The first thing that won my regard" &c or, "good-night & all good things to you," or "I shall be restless to hear," or "that I may nestle safe & warm & trustingly &c &c" I can hardly believe my eyes, & poor as this acorn of sustentation is for my love I devour it & ruminate upon it till its meaning is so *worn* out under my eye that I can hardly see any in it at all. I wish you could draw a pair of "yarn stockings" over *your heart*, & then I might hope for more peace of mind.

Meanwhile tho', I am obliged, however surlily, to say, how much I admire this very thing in you & how properly & with how much delicacy you have written & with how much *necessary* coolness in the peculiar relation to each other in which we have been corresponding & yet dont you think in a chance way you could scatter thro' your letters a few crumbs of affection. And as the poor Lazarus[25] at your gate feasts upon such crusts when you are asleep or when in independance of any such supplies you are faring sumptuously every day I do beg that as tho' by accident you will let a little bread go out to him—or will you not now inaugurate a new dispensation & break up the necessity of keeping up any reserve?

I was so honest in my letter yesterday, that tho' I told everything that was unfavorable I feel sure from the nobility of your character that you will honor me for it & indeed would not have been satisfied with any other plan. My mother naturally would say the worst she could think of under the circumstances to set me on my guard at a point at which I told her I was not yet engaged. I count upon her from the whole tenor of our talk to invite you cordially to her house & *very soon* most admiringly to love you. As to Mary I shall not tell her in any unnecessary haste & after our affair is *settled* (if I may dare to think of such a thing) I shall trust to her, out of regard to Mother's age & infirmity, not to impress her unfavorably & not to add at a stage in which matters cannot be altered to any disagreable feelings. As to Spence what I trust to him for, & what I mean distinctly to settle with him as a business matter is that, (unless he chooses to turn against me, which I do not contemplate tho' in respect to which I shall not importune him) he will be my main dependance in representing us in the right light in Philadelphia & keeping us as far as we choose to extend & observe it in our proper line of social connection. If Spencer turned against me, (which I cant dream of) it would raise the question in my mind of staying in Phila.

25. Luke 16:19–31.

But now as to that—my pastorship—we have reached a point when *before* you commit yourself to me I may speak in a more practical way. When I graduated in '36 I was not a Christian. I was enamored of physical science. So much so that I determined to be a Professor & I entered Prof. Henry's laboratory & spent a year there as his assistant. At the expiration of that time I went to the Moravian settlement at Bethlehem & to get hold of the German literature & science, (under Prof. H's counsel) studied German under an accomplished German teacher. There under the intelligence of Margaret's (Mrs Breckinridge's) sickness & approaching death & under an awakening sermon of Addison Alexander's about that time I became deeply serious & finally joined the church & after a great struggle with my speculative enthusiasms studied for the ministry.[26] I have been loyal to that great office ever since so far as (even against Prof. H's remonstrances often repeated) to banish all study of Natural Philosophy & unspeakably to prefer to *that* my sacred profession. But I was not long a pastor before I found out that theology was a science & a very unexplored & fruitful one. Prof. H. would turn his great honest countenance & say to me sometimes, "Mr Miller, *your* profession has the great philosophy. We have the philosophy of the work. You have the philosophy of the great worker." Nevertheless for ten long years I have mortified even this form of the passion (that is, to an extent you will hardly credit I have put its great studies when they would break in upon me upon the shelf & turned my exclusive study upon the more popular employments of my time) but lately, within 3 years as the result of certain openings of ethical discovery which have occurred in my sermonizing[,] *conscience* is beginning to side with my *passions* & the old promise to be fulfilled "He that giveth up, shall receive *in this world* what he has given up for Christ & in the world to come life everlasting.["][27] I mean distinctly by this that I have grown delighted with the thought not only that I *may* but that I *ought* to do before long as an employment of life what I most thirst to do as a great master passion & nothing on this broad earth not even your own mistress ship of my affections would turn me seriously from a step which wears now the aspect so of a manifest destiny. I am not telling you now *what* it is that I wish to do & that I think so conscientiously important for in that I must be in poor Mrs Dallas' terra incognita till more gradually in immediate intercourse I can explain myself more fully. But if I am ever more distinguished than I am now (which is not much) when my most important work of securing a leading addition to our church-hold upon this great city seems to be put past the danger of defeat & when for years to come I could do no more than build up & retain, it must be as

26. Joseph Henry (1797–1878), formerly of Princeton, N.J., but after 1848 the first secretary and director of the Smithsonian Institution in Washington, D.C. Joseph Addison Alexander (1809–1860), Presbyterian minister, biblical scholar at Princeton, and son of Archibald Alexander.

27. Matt. 19:29.

an originator in the path that Dr Henry marked out for me. This is all very egotistic, but its *dampening* & *uneasy* effect upon you may tell you why I honestly state it.

Now for about two years back I have kept in Phila by the enthusiasm of this prosperous erection of a great church. When I saw you last Summer I had a plan which my sight of you has modified & delayed. I had *determined* past all alteration as I thought to leave Phila & go to Princeton where my mother needed my presence & where a small income of my own independant accumulation of about $250 a year along with my mother's business would have *amply* justified my stay. Indeed we have been obliged to treat Mother rather hardly in leaving her alone in her great house. And then as I had no intention of marrying & as I intended at once to give my whole strength to the steps in ethical discovery which I will one day explain to you, I considered myself as anchored for life, as on my mother's death if I should survive an income of about $1000 or less a year would I know in that country neighborhood along with other sources of reserve furnish my little household with a sort of *philosopher's* support. Now with some shame from my not being able to let you in to the main justification of all this i.e. what & how important these discoveries & these coming years of labour actually are I have forced my way thro' all this & am glad I have done it because you ought to know, that tho' there is one advantage in all this that if ever accomplished it would render us in *some* of the respects we have been speaking of as independant as woodsawyers in public opinion, yet you will in fact be writing your destiny with a man who has already earned whatever *credit* for *popular* enterprise & usefulness he can chiefly claim & who at least in the later part of your life with him will have drawn into the narrower circle of savans & scholars. I am a poor old fellow anyhow & it makes very little difference for the world perhaps where I spend my labour, but I think I ought to be honest with a lady who may have *her* preferences as to where her influences may be extended.

Now of course this passion of mine for you breaks up the immediateness of my Princeton plans. A residence at my mothers is no longer in my eye. It will have the effect of anchoring me more in my present post. I must quit building castles for a time. But tho' one passion must for the present smother & postpone the other. Yet I know which will conquer in the end & I ought in all manliness, hazardous as it may be as to my hold upon your confidence to say that the old fire will break out & that conscience more & more smiles upon it as my ultimate destiny. Dont cast me off for this rival affection. I tell you I love divinity better than I do you; but then I know from the dwellings of your own mind, my darling Madam, that you will one day unite with me in this sympathy & that we will worship this divinity together.

I will go still more practically into all the outlooks of my life in some other letter if you desire it, but I feel that I have told you what is mainly important.

And this is quite tedious enough for you at present: I am again chasing the mail which is here twice a day. Do write at once when you receive this.

I am my dear icicle

Yours affectionly
Jno Miller

Mrs McDowell.

By the way I think these scholarlike plans of mine which for the purpose of having more weight for them before the Presbytery if I should ever act upon them I entrusted confidentially to two leading friends Dr Leyburn & Prof Green some *2 years ago* afford some serious advantages in rendering us more *independent* in the step we take.[28]

Phil. Feb:8th 1855.

My dearest Madam,

I wrote both letters from Princeton so hurriedly that I hardly remember what I said. I think, however, they included all I wish to say. And I will wait to write another till after the *suspense* of your next reply is over. I do hope that you have written me a favorable answer to all my importunities & tho' I am not worthy of such a reply, yet I comfort myself by thinking that I dont know anyone that is. *Any* amiable and lovely woman I have always thought was too great a gift to be bestowed in so intimate a method of possession upon any mortal of our sex.

I began a letter before dinner & wrote half a page on what has struck me as some remarkable Providences in this affair. But an irrepressible repugnance that I feel to certain ways in which religion is introduced into such matters has led me to destroy the letter & I am the more struck by the act, because I believe it is the first letter or fragment of a letter that I have destroyed since we have been writing. I do not remember to have destroyed another sheet.

When I was in Princeton I found my poor mother looking so feeble & wasted with age & care that I made up my mind that her answer forbidding or even refusing to assent to our marriage should be well-nigh decisive during her lifetime. And then under this warm & strong impression I went further & *prayed* that my mother might be in the place of God to me in this matter; that is, that if she used her authority in the way I have said would be decisive to prevent a marriage I would consider it specially as the voice of God. This prayer seemed pressed upon me in a very peculiar way & after pacing the floor for some time *afraid* now to put the matter to the test I at last gathered courage & received the reply I stated to you: the sum of which was that Mother saw painful objections

---

28. John Leyburn (1814–1893), Presbyterian minister in Philadelphia and editor of the *Presbyterian* from 1852 to 1861. William Henry Green (1825–1900), professor of Old Testament and Semitic studies at Princeton Theological Seminary.

but would not interfere—would not accept the offer of my leaving it to her & would even admit that it might turn out better than her fears. *This goes further than I would have required* to relieve my conscience. I am overjoyed at the result & have now no other reserve.

I hope a letter is on the way to increase this pleasure still further. If this is so we shall not need Mr. Canby or the envelopes & may write as often as we please. May we not? The newspaper extract I return. The copies of letters may I ask to keep for some days longer? What you write *does* bring you very vividly before me & I wish you no more retribution for the suspense in which you keep me than that you should be the receiver of such letters & see the *prize* like an ignis fatuus[29] always floating in the distance before you.

Yours affey
JM.

Spencer's Office
Thursday 6 o'clock [February 8, 1855]
Evening

My *dearest Madam*,

In going to mail my letter I stopped at the other window & asked for letters to Mr C. Yours had just arrived & I supposed the interval since I gave the name to the man accounts for the carriers having passed it to the window delivery. I shall drop a note to the postman however & then matters will go right particularly if you will write often.

I do so thank you for your long letter.

The sadness that you sympathize with, with such unexpected kindness is constitutional & does not depend upon a foundation in sorrow, tho' I have had enough of that. Half of my father's family are in the grave & half of my own—that is a life-time of sorrow in a single sentence. I do so thank you for this letter. It is the kindest you have ever written to me. I do believe you are a very good woman as every body tells me. At any rate if you are not you know what goodness is & therefore are very inexcusable.

in haste,
Yours affectionately
Jno Miller

I wish I had the fears you seem to have about the peculiarities of your position. It might make me more prudent if that were possible. Tho' *here* your secret is in as *dead silence* as you could possibly desire. I may be arrogant, but I think I can pilot you safe in this society thro' all the rocks you need care to be delivered from.

---

29. Latin, meaning a deceptive light created by gases in swamps or marshes. Translated as "will-o'-the-wisp."

Colalto
Monday Feb'y 12. 1855

My *dear Sir,*

Your Princeton letters both came together Friday afternoon. I could not answer them earlier tho' I was troubled to occasion you the week of suspense that you have suffered. I had myself just undergone a trial of that kind about these same Princeton letters and could tell very well what you would have to endure in waiting for my reply.

And now what must I say? When I think of how much hangs upon what I say, no wonder I shrink back, with a sort of terror. Even under the most favorable circumstances it would cause me much anxiety, but now, under all I fear—all that I know must be encountered—and right under that scathing foreboding of your Mother's that "the match promises little either of *character or comfort,*" is it strange even to you that I should hesitate and for the present, at least, stand still. How can I take another step when I fear, that step may be one of the greatest danger, not to say ruin to us both. Everything that is dear to me is involved in the matter and I feel if I lose at all, I lose all, and that beyond all hope of recovery. Your unflinching steadiness throughout is greatly gratifying to me, and would be, I think poorly rewarded by obtaining a wife who would, because of her misfortunes, be the means of estranging your family, and impairing your usefulness, and darkening all your prospects. Your calm assured confidence is a great treasure to me and almost the only thing that seems promising in the whole affair. And now wont you let me stand still for a time—let things be, for the next two or three weeks just as they have been for the last two or three. Let me understand my own feelings better too. With me, in yielding to your wishes, everything will be new and strange. I shall have much to learn, much to unlearn. First I have much yet to learn about you—your peculiarities and ways and notions. I must regret that we have actually seen so little of each other, as to be in such ignorance upon these points, which are by no means minor points. If we could dove-tail our peculiarities nicely and make our ways fit smoothly more than half the comfort of everyday life would be secured. These are the things that *try* my temper, and really to a great degree control my affections. I have great *respect* for high virtues—but the highest virtue could not command my love if it were united to anything coarse or low or little in manner & habit. Where my *taste* was offended perpetually it would be impossible for any affection to exist. To be sure, I have not any great fear *here* in the present case, yet it would have been better if we could have known each other a little more closely.

What made your Mother come sweeping over me in such a terrific manner? I declare, my blood boiled for the instant, and indeed is not so very cool yet when I think of what she said. But after all, the supposition was entirely natural. I am so habituated however to expressions of the utmost respect, and to a manner almost deferential wherever I'm thrown that it is hard, and oh! so mortifying to me to think that *anybody* can judge of me otherwise than respectfully. I think you might have told the old Lady that she with all her years & Virtues and the halo of your Father's memory about her did not hold a higher position where she lived, nor have a stronger grasp upon the affectionate respect of the community, than did the Lady whom her Son sought as his Wife hold in her home & among her people. This may all seem very arrogant in me. It is not however, for a sense of gratitude taught me the fact. Then as to temper, I believe she is well-nigh right. I was startled at the words she used in describing me. I rather doubted their correctness but an hour after reading your letter as Mary & Lilly & I were lingering over our dinner, I said—"Mary suppose someone would ask you what kind of temper is Sally's, what would you say?"[30] She paused for a moment & I asked again— "Would you use the word *imperious*"? She laughed & said "Perhaps I might. I have heard it sometimes applied to you by others". So you see what you have to expect. But I imagine your Father had much the same to bear, and your Mother should not have come down so hard upon me, nor have thought the prospect so gloomy for you. Never mind, if you find no greater fault in me than that I shall be perfectly content. We, Prestons (My Parents were first-cousins you know) are all irritable & fiery—but are free from sulkiness & moroseness & malice. We are people of a *grave* & uniform cheerfulness, but of little persistance of disposition, hence, you will not be surprised that where so much talent is possessed, so little has been accomplished. Another characteristic has been remarked, but I dont vouch for its Truth tho' I used to annoy my handsome brother by quoting it— that the men are all handsome—and the women all clever. But, you must pardon this Virginianism.

As you have talked as you say in a "practical way" about this matter to me, I shall just follow up your example. I shall not, in the least, interpose any objection to your "scholarlike plans." As they are not to be immediately carried out, I shall before the time comes for the execution of them have learned to find all my pleasures in yours, and whether my enthusiasm has been kindled by yours or not, I shall at least not make your—what am I to call it? Philosopher's retreat? uncomfortable by any adverse fancies of my own. If I am ever to share your home, whether it be a Parsonage or a (I'm puzzled again for a word, you have taken me into such a strange region—) Student's home I shall undertake only to make it a happy & an honored one. Certainly I prefer the former, yet that would be very *strange* to me, but by & bye I might fairly get into the notion of the other. The only thin[g] I stipulate for, is that the home be absolutely yours. Nothing would ever induce me to live at your Mother's. Don't you know that no matter how much *law* kin love one another they cannot live amicably in the same house unless there is perfect submission on one part, & absolute sway on the other? And do you think that I, who have been so long a sort of Aristocrat could submit unquestioningly to any authority but that that I had myself chosen.

30. McDowell's sister Mary Breckinridge McDowell (1824–1890).

Another thing, in all arrangements for the future you must remember I can accept none that will [not] include my little Lilly. *She belongs to me.* My Mother when she was dying gave her to me and the poor child in her sad condition of entire orphanage clings to me as if I were all that she had left to her on earth. She is spoiled & is at the age when girls are most difficult to manage & most disagreable, but she is kind & affectionate, and my home must be hers.—Is this settled? And will you try & keep a corner in your heart warm for her? I had another matter of business to write about, but I will postpone it.

Such cold weather as we have had. The Thermometer was at zero a day or two ago, and the snow still upon the ground. We are almost completely housed, as walking & riding over the ice are equally unsafe. But I am seldom troubled with loneliness. Indeed I have a kind of scorn at people who are dependent upon others for their amusements, so I take pains to entertain myself & find the task not difficult. Well! and so I am an Icicle? All you have to do then is to melt me.

Let me caution you a little. You must not think that because *you love me* everybody else will. I can't help being pleased to remark this in you, & yet I know you are just preparing yourself for disappointment. Your Mother would love me if you could infuse the feeling into her—not otherwise. Your Sister Mary never will. Spence (do you observe how very familiarly the name comes out?) may—I hope he will. Some how I feel as if I had come into a warmer climate, when he is about. As to the others—I have no idea what they will do. Maggie and Allie—will they ever love such an imperious person as I am? I shall not care so much for the others if I can be sure of winning their hearts. Children dont generally fancy me, but little Susan Taylor last fall while she stayed with me, had a way of clasping me round and round the neck & saying "*You* is my favorite." By the bye Dr. Leyburn has invited my kinsman Rev. R.J. Taylor to preach in Phila.[31] I wish you would do the same. I am concerned he should get a Church in some City, north of us, as his health has failed in Eastern Va & is not strong enough for a County congregation anywhere west of the Mountains.

Have I not written you, what our old folk call "a dish of chat?" Again it is "long after one"; but tonight it is not so cold. Do you think I have made any progress in "drawing the 'yarn stockings' over my heart"? I had almost forgotten—Never mind returning the copies of letters I sent you. Throw them in the fire after you have done with them.

Do you believe in *pre-sentiment*? I have had a painful feeling in my mind all day about Tom, my youngest Brother. I am often anxious about him, poor fellow, but to-day the thought of him is peculiarly pressed upon me. Good night.

Yours truly,
S.C.P. McDowell

31. Robert J. Taylor (1816–1873), McDowell's first cousin, had been a lawyer at the time of her marriage to Francis Thomas, but he later became a Presbyterian minister. Susan Taylor was his daughter.

Colalto
Thursday Feb'y 15, 1855.

My *dear Sir,*

My last letter has probably reached you to-day, and if I waited for you to reply to it before I wrote again another week or more would intervene before you could receive another letter from me. In that interval I *fancy* you would grow *hungry* for one, and so I send off this note as a sort of snack between my regular letters.

I am half-ashamed of writing you such long letters, and therefore, take this small sheet not meaning to go beyond its limits. Sometimes I am rebuked by your very *wee* notes—but then again those great, broad, Princeton sheets, (each one of which looks like a continent) appear & re-assure me.

It seems to me I wrote in my last of every conceivable thing except *one;* and most heartily do I wish you would guess what that one is and in your next letter just plunge right into the subject. You can do it much less awkwardly than I can. Wont you try to guess—& having guessed spare me all feeling and just write plainly & fairly to me.

Pray how many "idols" have I to encounter, in your affections? "I love divinity better than I do you"—whatever else may be unclear in your letters *this* is plain enough. Well—I submit just because that *"divinity"* is an impalpable sort of thing to me—and I cannot consider myself agrieved at its taking first rank with you. So I quite meekly stood No 2.—But then, here comes another. "My Mother is my great idol." I would not detrone the old Lady if I could. I am only the happier that she stands where she does & my heart listens with perfect pleasure to hear you speak of her as you do. (But you must try to keep her from saying or thinking *hard* things of me in the future.) And again with very graceful submission, hardly to be credited in one of such an "imperious temper,["] I come down to no 3. Am I to descend still lower? If so, let me look around and determine whether I *will* do so.

I am still disturbed about my brother. I cannot throw off entirely a somewhat superstitious feeling about him. The impression is so strong upon my mind, that night before last as I sat alone at a very late hour, I turned round half-expecting to see him step from behind a screen that shuts out the air of the porch door, and speak to me. If he is safe & well he will be greatly surprised when he gets my letter to see "how foolish Sister can make herself". I'm afraid you are too. But boys & young men do give one a world of anxiety. They are so exposed to every thing that is bad, and have so many notions & really, tho' they wont believe it, have very little sense. In the last two years I have had *five* boys to be troubled about. All going to college, and getting into scrapes & worrying me to death. No—there was one, who never did any thing wrong. And yet strange to say, the very one who gave me most anxiety is the one that I have the tenderest feeling to. But what interest can you have in all this? Are you not going to give me another chapter in your Autobiography? Lilly said, seeing me read one of those mammoth Princeton papers—"Sister I think B. must be writing his life"—Wasn't she quite right?

Dr. White gave me a letter some time since from Rev. William Brown, giving, in a hurried way, his views upon the moral question involved in this matter—I rather wanted you to have it—but did not send it.[32] I defer much to his good sound sense, and judgment, and was glad to see him state his opinions with firmness & decision.

Would it please you very much if you could cut three inches or more from my height.

My Canby envelopes are out.

Truly Yours
S.C.P. McDowell

Phil. Feb.: 16th 1855.[33]

My dear Sally,

Your letter has just been put into my hands (Friday morning). I read it & lay it down & answer it at once, for at the close of the week I am never so much my own master as at the beginning & as I can only write a short letter now I will postpone a more full reply till Monday.

But, my dear Darling, how could you leave me so long without a letter? I told you how sad I was. Now this doesn't mean "despondent" for I am really hopeful to the extent of obstinacy in all matters that interest me enough to be matters of despondency. But I am melancholy. That is the habit of my temper. And the kind soothings that you would be willing to bestow come to me in no shape more pleasantly than even the briefest letter. Wont you after this reaches you, write me so often that it will relax all my impatience for you can have no idea how I have really *suffered* since the first day that I felt sure that a letter would arrive.

My dear good mother in Princeton, who is the mother of my children, & has been so now for years, even before they became orphans, with devoted & tender affection, has won such an influence over me, that when the sentence *began* in your letter, I tho't you were going to say something severe in respect to her character & you have no conception how it agitated me for a moment. You ended the sentence, however, very differently & I am very anxious not only that you should respect my mother as I know you do, but that you should also love her, for you can have no idea till you see the depth of her character & the trueness of her feelings how much Father owed her for the very halo of honor of which you speak.

32. William Brown (1811–1894), Presbyterian minister in Augusta, Va.

33. A small slip of paper is filed with Miller's letters of Feb. 16 and 19, 1855. On one side it reads: "I have just got your letter & was about to pour wax upon this great number when it came in time to slide this in. If you make me write longer letters than you (as I do) I shall think it *wicked* with [illegible]." The other side reads: "I cant conceive what you would want me to talk about unless it be a certain question of time. I am willing to do all the talking on that question. May I?"

Mary & Mother are neither of them such hopeless dependencies in respect to the warmth hereafter of family affection as those speeches of my mother about things so exaggerated in her mind by over-anxiousness & perhaps so foolishly repeated by me might lead you to imagine. Dick is at sea, & is very much under my influence. His wife, who is also our cousin, is entirely under his. Sam lives in the country from which he rarely comes to town, & is the most manageable of all.[34]

But really, my dear Madam, I am falling too much into your vein. These are persons that will all love you & such is my influence & such *will* be yours that I am strongly confident that six months will end *with them* all discoverable recognition of any peculiarity in our circumstances.

I ought frankly to repeat, however, one fact. I feel about *you* much more strongly than I do about myself. Were I impressed as you fear Mary will be in respect to the marriage I would say to a brother of mine, "John, aint you ashamed to destroy that lady's position, & when the respect & affection in which she is held by her friends is so perfectly complete to mar it by persuading her to marry you." I confess this is the most serious aspect in which the matter presents itself to my conscience & tho' I am singularly *unshaken* in my conscientious decisions about the matter yet nothing would shake me more than such considerations. Because (& now this is what I wish to confess) I am not like other men. I dont care what other men think of me, if I think well of myself. I am not a safe guide for another, perhaps, for I tell you frankly that if I could get my own conscience settled I would marry you to-morrow if every friend turned against me. And this is largely because my highest pleasures are of a solitary kind & I shant really be out of the reach of the highest gratifications of my passions if I live secluded from men.

And yet while this is the fact yet I have not been able to *act* from these feelings at all but have felt constrained as a public man & a pastor to act for others & therefore, I am not *conscious* that this high stand which my feelings take in respect to the opinions of men has any other effect than to make me cool & intrepid in the forming of my judgments.

Mr. Cornelius, the member of my church who is giving over $30,000 toward its completion took me all thro' it on Wednesday & shewed me its completeness & told me of arrangements that they had made for my comfort a dressing-room, hydrant, study & private stairway to each & to the pulpit & how pleased they had been at the report of the pew agent the night before which was larger than they expected & how cheered even some who had tho't the enterprise too heavy were, & I was really humbled as I often am when I thought how loose I was feeling to all this public work & how unimpressed (as ten years ago I would not have been) by a noble entrance to service in the City.[35]

34. Julia Barton Miller (1817–1884) was the daughter of Dr. William P. C. Barton and Esther Rittenhouse Sergeant, a stepsister of Miller's mother. Miller's brother Samuel Miller Jr. (1816–1883), a Presbyterian minister, was principal of a school at Mount Holly, N.J.

35. Robert T. Cornelius (1809–1893) manufactured lamps and chandeliers in Philadelphia. He and Charles B. Dungan had donated the land on which the church was being built.

When you say therefore that you wish to wait two or three weeks before you settle the question in the irrevocable way of which you spoke in Washington I cannot find it in my heart to remonstrate & rebel painful as it is. I feel that I *may* be misleading you as I am not organized like other men. I am a born hermit. I covet the intercourse of the wise & great & that we will have at any rate no matter which way the popular voice might turn against us. But barring a few men like Prof. Henry who will accompany me in any fortunes I dont care how the world turns & therefore am not a safe adviser of one less morbidly or perhaps I should rather say in justice to myself less peculiarly disposed. Give me a little place to stand upon & the usual shelter of the heavens & "my mind a Kingdom is" & I would rather live in tilling its poor acres than in all the public work & popular successes that the world can furnish.

Now dare you trust yourself with such a man? I will love you quite as much as any woman could venture to require for I love you that much now but I will love another thing a vast deal better, I would rather give you up than be divorced from it & I love it so well that I feel almost entirely independant of the favour or the coldness of the world.

But do you know, my dear Sally, when I reflect in the soberest way upon what is wise & best for us, I think sometimes we ought *to be married* in "two or three weeks" or a little more. My church is nearly completed. Mr. Cornelius thinks we shall enter it by April. I feel sure that we shall not enter it till September, but in either case my arguing equally convinces me. We cant marry in the Summer, for then I shall be getting ready for this task of managing in the very best way at so important point as the time of passing out of a small lecture-room or chapel into so large a church. It will require every nerve in visitting & preaching, & getting ready. Then in the Fall you know the work will be at its height. I cant leave a day. Then in the Winter—Why that is too far off. Besides now I am free & comparatively at leisure. Is it not better to go into the City now when I am specially disengaged (I mean comparatively) & when I can spare time to defend you, as I have promised to do from all these phantom obloquies that your imagination is conjuring up & when my congregation is in narrower limits & smaller than it will afterwards be, rather than at a time when you will not have leisure to be known by the leading persons of our community before we will be exposed to the stare of a much larger circle & those comparative strangers even to me.

Now see my plan. Suppose we were married in—I am afraid you'll think me crazy, but if so then just let me imagine it for the sake of argument. Suppose we were married in April. Suppose, with our dear little Lilly, as to whom I almost feel hurt that you should have asked the question, we should return & spend this important two months of which I have been speaking in overcoming all these social difficulties of which we have talked so much. Suppose you leave a part of your family to keep your house. Suppose you return to it & spend the warm weeks in every arrangement that may be necessary for a future residence in Philadelphia. Suppose that in this way all these agitating matters are arranged before the New church is opened. Suppose we are thus in a measure settled & able to turn undivided attention upon that—will this really be so wild a plan as might at first be imagined.

But I am writing too long both for you & me. Just let me say hurriedly.

1st Never again speak of Lilly in the way you did—only beg her to love me & be my own daughter like Maggie.

2d I should in no possible case that I can think of live with mother.

3d Are you going to turn off Cantey & your sister Mary & your brother Tom?

4th I dont believe in presentiments; what has Tom been doing.

5th Ought I to have told you what Mother said? You dont remember how freely a mother would speak to her son & how she would utter in the freest way at her age her admonitory & cautionary councils.

6th Wont you write in your next letter in such a way that I may see the least patch of blue sky in the firmament of your affection.

Lastly, After having put you on your guard as I have done, wont your write me very soon your irrecoverable answer, &

Finally, wont you forgive me for these slaturnly sheets as I am becoming quite ashamed of my share of the correspondence.

Goodbye. *Yours very affectionately*
John Miller

Phil. Feb: 19th [1855]

Having promised that I would pilot you safe, my darling Sally, if you would trust yourself to my hand over the social rocks of which we have spoken so much, I want to go further & tell you *how*. Ladies, I know, hate to travel *at night*; & whatever assurances are given them of care, they like to see where they are going.

Now I know no better use to put this letter to than to give you a little of my policy.

In the first place *silence* is a large element in it. "Das Schweigen ist der Gott der glücklichen". (If you find any difficulty with this send the letter over to the College.)[36] In announcing our engagement to my people I would not in the most distant way either by feature or tone allow them to dream that there is anything peculiar in the circumstances but on the contrary tell them everything favorable in the matter in a pleased & confident way without one lisp to the contrary. I would do this for two eminent reasons. If I tell anything unfavorable I must reply to it & that I dont intend to invite occasions for doing with any but six or eight relatives & family friends for many reasons one of which is that I do not intend to *invite* occasions for provoking by charges of profligacy replies from the

36. German proverb, meaning "The God of the lucky is silence." The "College" refers to Washington College in Lexington.

other quarter. I am going to tell my elders &c that I am engaged to a daughter of Gov. McDowell with every look & expect of being entirely certain of its pleasing them, without another word in the matter. And the other reason is that my own personal judgment & influence is one power I have in the case. If I seem to waver, I give a chance for other peoples' opinions to sweep over me like wild horses. But if I am entirely at ease, I think I have a capital of reputation as respects delicacy & honorableness of behavior that has been gathering as it does about most preachers for a number of years that will carry us very far in the confidence of our congregation.

But then the *recoil*. Well; the recoil of a cannon is never so great as the projection. I gain more by this mode of procedure than I lose by the surprise or disappointment of some in finding that there is some room for question.

Now as to the recoil.

There are certain persons that shape public opinion as to any question & they are those who *know about it*. These in our case will be Dr Leyburn & Mr Dickson & Dr Englis &c.[37] These I will see well posted in a *brief compact* reply to all cavils. This number will increase; for Spencer, for example, if he dont quarrel with me & I have no idea he will, will in self-defence as well as from interest in us deal with skill in the matter. Then if one of my elders should venture to mention the matter to me I will be ready with a distinct answer to any difficulty.

And, by the way, the most manageable answer is this. You *were* set free by the Va legislature on the distinct ground that is Scriptural & right. The matter was entrusted to a Committee & that Committee (for the House acted almost in silence) had before them, & were satisfied by the evidence that our Confession requires. (I wish I knew who furnished those papers & what has become of them.) Now therefore my clear & assured reply would be, that the Legislature of your state tho' scarce ever prevailed on to grant a Divorce granted it in this case without debate, unanimously & on the distinct evidence that our symbols require.

All the time, however, I consider it your wisdom & mine to give as little account of ourselves as possible, to let others defend us, to deal ourselves only with very intimate & important parties & not to say anything that will needlessly exasperate (in a case in which our defence is an attack upon another) the opposite party.

It was for this that I thot it well, if your Session was of a certain texture i.e. a sort of family of country friends, to refer the judgment to them & have their quiet advice. In either of the Sessions I have presided over (with the exception of perhaps one man a very perverse fellow in the one at Frederick) such a quiet giving of consent would go thro' without any difficulty, but I am satisfied by Dr White's letter that it would not be well at Lexington. Indeed the action of the

37. Andrew Flinn Dickson (1825–1879) of Philadelphia. William M. Engles (1797–1867), minister and editor-in-chief for the Presbyterian Board of Publication.

Legislature which actually set you free now strikes me as better. But I entirely differ with Dr White as to any consent *afterward*. That I will never consent to. When you are once married to me (if I should ever be so happy) I want no advice & I will take care not to be seen looking up any justification. A clear conscience, the gift of an assured manner in all my own treatment of the case & the assistance of leading friends & most of all the favor & protection of Heaven are all that we require.

I am serious in thinking we ought to be married at once. If this step *were* to agitate the church in the way Spence fancies, why let us inflict the blow while the church is in her present less exposed position & will be less injured by it. Not at a time when the first cream of success is being gathered which attends an opening building. But having no such notion about a blow & being moreover a better judge than Spence I still think it wiser to marry while my old "body guard" are about me who have built for me this church & not when the larger hall has in it additional groups who might scatter on a sudden flurry like a flock of partridges.

Besides, my darling, I cant be bothered with you next Fall. I shall have too much to do. And I want then to have settled down into a commonplace domestic & hard-working husband.

This is all very saucy I know; but then thro' my strange obstinacy of character I can hardly fancy you are not engaged to me. I would have preferred postponing the above couleur de rose[38] vaticinations about my own success in throwing a shelter about you till after you had accepted me, lest I should be tempting you by prophecies not hereafter fulfilled in making up your mind, but do you know I feel as tho' you were mine already. I could as little think of your being otherwise then of my hand or my foot or my shoulder not being a part of my body. I fall in love so shyly & have been thought to have so little of that proclivity in all my history that when it does occur it seems to me like the voice of God & it would sound strangely if I found myself reproved.

(I guess tho' it dont sound very different to any body.)

I have been thinking too, what I would do if you were attacked in the public papers. *Nothing*, if the attack were insignificant. But if it were serious I think there is a step that can be taken that would check-mate that.—However let us [not] anticipate difficulties.

Do think of the question Whether you & Lillie & whoever else you please cannot spend the months of May & June on a long *visit* to Phila: & whether July & August will not then be sufficient to wind up your residence in Lexington. I know how hurriedly I am handling very sacred subjects & I wonder that so poor a return as I can make to you for such sacrifices should allow me to talk so earnestly but, my dear Sally, I will love you with all my heart & that surely is a good deal to say in this wicked world.

I am half sorry I told you what Mother said, for an honesty not *absolutely*

---

38. French, meaning rose colored.

required has alienated you perhaps from one so dear to me, for a long time to come. Remember that my Mother, knowing I was not engaged, like a lawyer of whose blood she comes, would make the most of her case.

You see how pretty I have come round to your name "Sally". It is on the principle of something I saw last week. My dear little Annie (a child I often play with) wouldnt eat her dinner. It was a very good dinner, but she cried & wanted everything that wasn't on the table. Whereupon her mother (who usually is a very bland mild woman) seeming offended that so good a dinner should be so cavalierly treated scolded her right well; & I was amused with the result. Little Annie plunged into the dishes till her face was almost covered over with everything that had been upon the table, & then ended with a sort of universal crow of profound & general satisfaction.

I will take great pleasure in getting Mr Taylors consent to preach for me. He is thought of in the North Church.

I dont know whether you will need my friend Canby any more after finding that he went the wrong way, but the last time he came directly to hand.

Use him only if you think it necessary.

Wont you sit right down when you get this & tell me in such a letter as you haven't written yet, whether you do care anything about me & when you will be altogether mine? & I will be your most devoted & affectionate—"help", I think they say at the North.

Jno Miller.

Do send Mr. B[rown]'s letter.

I dont know whether I would like you any shorter. You were quite *short* enough in the Sts of Gibralter I remember; tho in posting your letters quite too long.

See how your ink blots.

Colalto,
Monday, Feb'y 19. 1855

Your letter came this afternoon. In my impatience & anxiety it had seemed to me it never would come. But, I was compensated by it for all the disappointments of the last three or four days. I dont think you ever wrote me one that pleased me quite so well—indeed it strongly tempts me to show you a pretty big "patch of blue sky." But that it is not in my nature. I am not very demonstrative, yet for that very reason prize it much in others.

I think if you had known me better you would not have feared a harsh expression against your Mother. I could not, it is true, help the first feeling of indignation, but had you been present, I would have *said* nothing that could have pained you, and certainly *now* I *feel* nothing that would cause you a moments anxiety if you could look right down into my heart & read its feelings for yourself.

I think you did *perfectly right* to tell me what your Mother said. You judged correctly when you thought I would not have been satisfied with any other course.

And I do not blame her for speaking so freely & fully & plainly to you; I think it was clearly her duty to do so. Neither would it be an *unpardonable sin* in her if she *never* should love me. I would mourn over it, because it would be a disappointment & sorrow to you; as well as because it would be the loss of an earnestly coveted thing to me, but still I hope it would never embitter my feelings to her, or render them less respectful & affectionate than they ought to be.

I wont undertake to tell you how much you have gained by the way in which you speak of Lilly. I do hope she will love you with all her heart.

What makes you ask "if I mean to cast off Cantey & Mary & Tom?" Cantey stands to Mary much as Lilly does to me. Tom loves me, I think better than he does any other member of the family. He looks to me for counsel & affection at all times, and is much swayed by my opinion, but he is thrown out upon the world now, poor fellow, almost beyond my reach. His brother & our uncle, his legal Guardian, have always had views in regard to him, very different from mine, and these led to a system, or rather the want of it in his education, that has been to say the least, unsuccessful.[39] Last summer I urged a certain sort of occupation upon him, to which he consented; but my brother just then coming in from St Louis & his Uncle—together persuaded him to abandon it for another. Thus he was taken away from under my eye & thrown into the midst of such temptations as St. Louis could present to him, in his circumstances. I am, sometimes, half-distracted about him—& that not because James writes me of any bad habits, but because I know that no young man is safe who fancies himself in circumstances above the necessity of industry. Laziness seems to me almost the worst thing in the world. I fancy Eve must have had a fit of idleness upon her when she fell into temptation. If she had had a pair of stockings to darn she would not have had the chance to be looking after the forbidden fruit. I feel the greatest spite at her; dont you?

I shall think of all you say about this *plan* of yours for the month of April. You reason it out very plausibly—but dont convince yourself yet, that it is a matter settled. When I think of giving up my own home forever—I almost feel that I *cannot*. But I will write about this again. How do you think you Northern folk can put up with my Southern ways & notions? I'm sure your Sister (do you know I'm more afraid of her than all the rest of you?) will think me—something escaped from Barnums collection.[40]

Such a hospital as my house at times becomes. Two or three sick servants, just able to be out again—& one still sick. Jimmy Carrington too gone to bed sick—& Lilly worrying with a bad cold—and even I am not entirely well—but a good, sound sleep will free me from my ills: so dont write me a letter full of fears about my health. I love to complain & take advantage of the slightest occasion to do so.

---

39. Thomas Lewis Preston (1812–1903), McDowell's "Uncle Tom," a lawyer and banker, managed the family saltworks and lived in Abingdon, Va.

40. Phineas Taylor Barnum (1810–1891), showman and circus operator.

I wish you would reproduce your destroyed letter for my benefit, if it is not to your comfort—It is well I am at the end of my sheet—for I am ever so tired.

I am Very—what? Yours
S.C.P. McDowell

Wednesday (Feb'y 21. 1855)[41]

Darling,

Tell me one thing. I want it answered so much that I can hardly bear to think of a whole week passing before you can reply?

Could you love me so much that if the whole world turned against us, & we were obliged to live alone, given up by society you could live entirely in me? Could I ever become all the world to you?

I dont know what sets me upon this romantic little letter, not a presentiment certainly, for my sense of the difficulty of our position has latterly diminished, but I want to find out how much you are like me. You & my books & my mother & my little children would make me as *satisfied* as a king (happy I dont expect to be) & if all the four were stripped away from me—except you I could live in you in a way of absorbed devotion & affection that I can hardly describe.

Tell me now, my dear dear darling, will you ever love me that way? Do you love me in the least so now? If you had no relations or friends within reach could you love just me—me, all the day?

I dont intend to profane this letter by writing anything else in it. I count it an extra & beg that you will reply to it in the same way without allowing it to diminish the usual series. I stop in the midst of my sermon to write & beg that you will give me out of your heart just as instinctive & impulsive a rejoinder.

Yrs
JM.

[marginal notes] I dont think I ever said I loved mother better than you—for I dont.

(Aint it a funny little letter!)

Colalto,
Feb'y 22. 1855.

I am so wearied with saying "my dear Sir" to you & so impressed with its inappropriateness, that I turn from it and yet know not what else to say. Cant you help me in this very *serious* difficulty?

I wanted to catch an hour of daylight yesterday to write to you, but Dr White came in and made such a long visit that I could not. Then to-day first one thing,

41. McDowell dated this letter.

then another broke up my writing plan. But to-night I felt sure I should be quiet. Mary was spending the evening in town and I had sent Lilly & the boys over to College, and was left alone with my little maid to keep off the hobgoblins in this great house. I was very happy in my solitude & applied myself with infinite satisfaction to my letter, when to my dismay, before a single sentence had been achieved, the Overseer asked admittance. And such an account as he had to give of farming disasters & farming operations. It required all my nerve to hear composedly of lame horses, poor sheep,—my South Downs, that were "poorer than any he had ever saw here before"; of fine "stock" gone "off in fits," of an unusually good tempered & civil servant, who had of late grown sulky and of repairing a servants house. Of a scarcity of grain too he complained, tho' in that we are no *worse* off than our Neighbours—but he brightened up somewhat at our better provision in some other things than our Neighbours. I was glad enough, as I always am, to have him go, & would not have cared if he had carried off with him all the forlorn animals of which he made mention. Before he did go, however, Mary returned & now I just scratch a line or two & then turn round to talk to her about all sort of odd matters. I am so worried in this alternation of writing & talking that I would hardly have courage to go on but that I am going away tomorrow & must need write tonight. Miss Dix once said to me, "I hope my friends will care too much for my reputation to keep my notes"—so, I say to you—or rather I should say I hope you value me for something else than my *ability* in writing.[42] I scarcely think it *respectful* to write so hastily & carelessly as I do, but then how can I accomplish a letter at all if not in this way.

Perhaps a fortnight ago, I destroyed a part of a letter to you having in it a sentence something like this—"if you could only by a sort of violence take possession of me, sparing me the responsibility of giving away myself, I should not etc etc,"—now tho' I fancied this sheet was burnt, yet I think I must have been mistaken. It must by some accident have found its way to your hand, for in this last letter of yours you seem acting upon my suggestion and quite confidently claim me as being as truly one of your belongings as "my hand or foot &c." To tell the truth I hardly know whether to dispute the point or not. I am much in the condition of a client of my Uncle Taylor who, a long time ago, concluded a letter on business to him thus—"I am, my dear Sir, so much yours I am *scarcely* my own."[43] But of this I will tell you again.

As to your question—"Tell me do you care anything about me"? I answer, What do you think would induce me for one moment to think seriously of giving up a home so dear to me as mine is—of hazarding a certain position, & that not a mean one—of risking the loss of friends to whom I am bound by every sentiment of affection & gratitude,—of exchanging all this, for a home with you

---

42. Dorothea Lynde Dix (1802–1887), leader in prison, poorhouse, and insane asylum reform.

43. William Taylor (1788–1846), Virginia congressman. He married Susan Preston Mc-Dowell (1793–1849), James McDowell's sister.

among strangers—or, worse still, among alienated friends & what feeling think you *could* impel me to this?

Is this not answer enough for you? If not, keep quiet and perhaps I may after a while find a way of answering more to your liking.

You are not quite right in saying "you were set free by the Legislature upon the distinct ground that is *scriptural* & right." This Scriptural charge was never made, & that it was not has since been a source of trouble to me. I think I can get the papers upon which the Legislature acted. They were prepared by James Lyons of Rich'd with my Father's aid.[44] The Suit was first brought before the Court & its decision was carried up before the Legislature for its more formal & emphatic action. I am inclined to think I have those papers myself. I will have a search for them if you still wish to see them.

I agree with you that we are to take the dignified & proper stand of being entirely convinced of the correctness of our own views in this matter, and not go about apologizing to the world for what we have done, or, as you say "seeking up any justification" for the step after it is taken! Special friends are, of course, entitled to any and every explanation that we can give, but others are not. And after all, the law of God and not the caprice of man is the safest & truest rule—the only binding rule in this as in all other things. This law we think we have on our side—and William Brown speaks truly when he says, "I always think if we can reach the standard of morals & tone of purity in society which our Saviour set up, we need not trouble ourselves about a *higher*." By the bye I will just enclose his letter. But with all this courageous way of talking, I am I fear the greatest of cowards. I do so dread the gaze & sneer & remark of society. If any thing less delicate & dear to me than my character was assailed I should not care—but just there is the suffering with me. I cannot bear to think that at the very outset you should have to defend my reputation. And then the fear of casting some shadow upon the future of your children—your Church too. I cant help going over the old ground. I am selfish in clinging so madly to your affection in the face of such obstacles. All you say about becoming thro' other pursuits independent of public approval in this matter, does not weigh much with me. If you succeed in the course marked out, you will, to a great extent obliterate the odium of the past & secure to your family their proper places in society, but if not—what will be the fate of your children? When I think of your little Maggie, who is day by day kindling her fire in my heart, suffering from her connection with me, do you wonder that I hesitate & hesitate, and am uncertain what to do. But you must have your patience worn out with this same old story over & over & over again.

The difficulty of an attack thro' the press is one I have always apprehended. If it should be, how would you meet it? Judging of what may be, from what has been, there will be nothing left undone that can be done to annoy, or injure me.

---

44. James Lyons (1801–1882), prominent Virginia attorney.

Private letters, public scandal, secret and open attack of all sorts will be resorted to. Are you willing to bear all this? Ought I to be willing to subject you to it?

I cant tell you, unless I were to say a great deal more than would be proper for me to say, how full my heart gets at seeing you so unshaken in your purpose by all these difficulties. Some times a sort of notion comes up that perhaps the step that may deprive me of the respect of others, may also loosen my hold upon your own. This would be dreadful. Much as I value your affection; it would be absolutely worthless—even scorned, the moment I suspected it could exist without respect.

The one thing of which I have as yet said nothing—is *property*. I wish you to talk with entire unreserve now, & tell me very frankly whether you *would be in the least hurt* if I desired a part or the whole secured (I use the technical phrase) to me by a marriage-contract. I strongly advocated this measure in the cases of my Sisters, not because of any want of confidence in their husbands, but to protect them against some of the accidents of life to which all are liable. I do not like the fact of a trustee coming in between a man & his wife as is necessary in such contracts—but perhaps I exaggerate that disagreeable feature in the case too much. In my own case, I would like a "settlement" simply for the reason given to my Sisters. There would be no separate interests here with us. All the income derived from my property would be thrown into the common fund for common use. I am shocked to hear a wife talking of *her* means as if her husband & herself kept separate purses. As my property, the bulk of it, is in real estate, it as long as it continues so is inalienable, but if it should be sold, then there being no marriage-contract it passes into your absolute possession & in case of your death two thirds of it pass away from me to your heirs-at-law.

Now write me exactly what you would like & what you would not like about this matter. And if there is any thing indelicate in mentioning, pray forgive it, & remember you set me the example of looking at the whole affair in a practical way. I am going up tomorrow to Uncle Carrington's near Fincastle to spend a few days with my Aunt who has been sick for several weeks.[45] Let your letters, however be sent here.

To your list of friends, Dr. Leyburn & Engles & Mr. Dickson why not add Dr. Van Rensselaer?[46] I know him much better & like him greatly more than Dr. Engles who looks as quaint as an old fashioned bit of earthen-ware, & Mr. Dickson who is in a half-evaporated state sighing after a Virginia Wife.

I was amused when I saw my name come out at last. I wondered how many contortions had ushered it in. But it isn't quite so bad now is it? I shall expect in this as in Annie's case to hear by & bye "a crow of profound satisfaction." Is not your Mother's name *Margaret*? How then came her brothers to call her Sally? But if the part of my name you dislike so much had been the changeable part—you

45. Eliza Henry Preston (1796–1877), McDowell's "Aunt Eliza," was married to Edward Codrington Carrington (1790–1855).

46. Courtland Van Rensselaer (1808–1860), of Burlington, N.J., was secretary of the Presbyterian Board of Education.

would have been puzzled, now that you know it belongs to me, to substitute one that would suit better.

I am going to quit writing to you at night, & will limit myself to short notes. I find my eyes pain me from so much use of them at night. You can shade yours by your glasses.

Very truly Yours,
S.C.P. McDowell

Friday morning. I think of your arguments as to *time*, & think them good. I have said not a word to my friends on the subject, & will not until my Brother comes in next month.[47] I cannot write to him because of his uncertain movements. In all his troubles and plans he applies to me for sympathy and advice, and as heretofore, on account [of] his hot temper, I have not been able to allow him to come into my Council when in special difficulty, and as he has felt hurt & complained of it, I mean now to seek his approval or *compel* it thro' his affection & confidence in me first of all my family. Of an immense money project, involving a million of dollars, he writes me in detail during the winter and concludes by asking my *advise* in these terms. "What think you of my plan? I turn to you, my Sister, for counsel: your clear judgment I rely on & there is no one on whom I cast myself for counsel more confidingly than yourself. Your decision will be etc. etc." Now as this matter of mine is greater than *any* money scheme, I mean to return his compliment. My family are not estranged from me by my "*imperious temper*"—so it is not so alarming after all.

I got out of your German puzzle as my friend Fishburn's note will show.[48] Does he do his work of translator well?

I once read a long letter of Jefferson's, a pretty dull one it was too, to a Lady in which he suggested that in order to save time & her patience she should read it by scraps as she was dressing her hair every morning till she got thro': this plan of a little at a time you had better adopt with this letter, & then it will serve you a whole month. In your new study hint to Mr. Cornelius to have a particularly large niche fixed up for such an enormous volume as my letters will make.

Yours
S.C.P. McD.

Philadelphia. Feb: 26th [1855]

My darling Sally,

Let me hasten to say that I really did not know whether you had any serious property or not. A fast young lady that speculates in South downs & Washington lots might well awaken anxieties in her parson-lover on the other side of the

---

47. The brother she refers to is James McDowell.
48. Junius Fishburn (1830–1858), professor of Latin at Washington College.

question & tho' I tho't this *might* be the thing that you were alluding to in your previous letter I durst not write about it lest I might be talking of some chateaux en Espagne.[49] I knew indeed that you had bought your father's estate but *I* am thinking seriously of buying a house but I should pay for it more than half by a mortgage; & I knew that you were living very comfortably at Colalto but so may a group of sisters do by putting their purses together & I fancied that the Lexingtonians tho't you rich but so I knew the Princetonians tho't me I mean the plainer of them tho' I have hardly enough even for a flock of south downs.

But now that your letter comes to me I have a sort of shudder passing all over me at the thought how the grace of loving *you* as I do with a sort of inexplicable passion is dimmed by your property & how I *do* feel a shrinking from the thought of entering upon a defence of you (which by the way is too strong a way of stating it on your part.) with anything like a finger pointed at me about your property. However it is after all only a bull-rush in Niagara. I dont care what people say or what they think.

And now, my dear Sally, I would have a sort of shame of that monosyllable, Yes, by this time if you were not so reasonable in all you ask. "Shall Lilly stay with us?" Why yes, where on earth could our dear little Lilly stay but with you? "Will you agree to what I say about your Mother's?" Why yes I never tho't of anything different. "Will you let me stand still for two or three weeks?" Why yes you are not sacrificing enough for me not to allow you that? "And now will you make this settlement"? Why Sally, I see the need of it in a moment. If I were to die my children or their guardians must take two thirds of your patrimony from you & leave you no means of respectable living. I desire it on my own account: for if I were to try to accomplish the same thing by will the public not knowing which was your property & which mine might think I neglected little Maggie & Allie.

I know little about a Virginia trustee. Does he require an annual percentage all the time? Be on your guard about all these things & I am willing to leave the whole thing to you.

And now I am by no means one of those dishonest talkers that profess to despise money. I am glad you have property. I wish it were twice as great as it can possibly be. If you were a parson's daughter I would put Shady Side in your hands & rely on you to bear with the narrowness of a pastor's maintenance. But as you are a Virginia Preston and a good deal of a queen at that, I should have had some uneasiness about my scholar's treasury. I should have felt a little like Doug my father's man who when he asked him two days after marrying him whether he thought he could support his wife naively confessed that he could not or that he had very sorrowful doubts in respect to the whole adventure.

Still, Sally, these things balance each other for if you had not the property I could ask you with more propriety (*as I have a half wish to do at any rate*) to descend to the frugalities of a Pastor's living.

49. French, meaning castles in Spain.

So now after my homily I say, Yes. Give me by return of mail all right, title, &c to have & to hold for me in fee simple forever all that very desirable piece of property known and remembered as Mrs Sally McDowell, & I so far thoroughly approve of the other step that I would decidedly myself propose it if I could have been certain of the facts.

And now just to show that I am not in a state of universal compliance like a Chinese opium eater or like poor Mr Dickson, I would say that I *do* rebel a little against you reverting to the old charges against the above-mentioned Mrs McDowell. That thing is "done talked over" as your colored people would say; & I *am* getting my dear *dear* Sally a little—just ever so little "tired of it." With the gospel & morality on our side I would do the thing if I were Archbishop of Paris (tho' I believe they dont have any wives) & with my particular purposes and tastes I would marry you if you would only accept me if there were as many miscreants to attack us in the public press as there are leaves in the Navesinks.

Therefore now *do* send me back some good warm assurances & pledges of your love. Who would ever think I was the Northerner & you the Virginian? Because I hardly know now what you mean when you say that telling me just ever so little about this would be so much "more than is proper."

Wont you begin to *get ready*, so that I may come on "to take possession of you" in the way that we agree I had better do without finding your trunk unpacked. My plan will be to make a diversion of the servants by firing one of the barns, & then to drive up with Dr White & be married in the carriage as we are hurrying away. I have *just* received your letter & will answer it in more detail in my next. But will you not write immediately?

My people are threatening to have the church done by the first of May. If that be the case, every week *before* that in which we can be quiet & begin to be settled will be a great gain. Will there be anything in your case my dear Sally, to require time in any preparation.

Thus I have written as fast as my pen would travel over the paper a very hurried & scattered letter. Pardon all its defects & believe me very grateful for all you send me & very true in the devotion with which I am

Yours affectionately
Jno Miller.

If I were sure you were as wise an executive officer as Mrs Jonathan Edwards of happy memory, I would make a sort of vow never to have a care about any property my own or yours after our wedding day.[50] Will you agree to that? so that I shall have even less diversion from my work than I have now! But if I pursued a different course & were meddling incessantly in all the concerns of every body I think the first thing I would attack would be your real estate especially that which requires continual supervision & I would also entreat you to be cautious on the

---

50. Mrs. Jonathan Edwards was Sarah Pierpont Edwards (1710–1758).

marriage of your sisters. I would say, Sally, do you know *well* the person or persons you are intending for either of them. I would say, your own mismanagement in accepting (?) such a forlorn body as me convinces me you need to be greatly cautioned in this particular.

[marginal notes] (Mother's name is Sarah).

Wont you write me now every other day. Tho' in *other* things take care of your eyes.

Phil. Feb: 27th 1855.

My dear Sally,

You must know, I am never sick. With the exception of an ague some five years ago caught in Holland, I dont remember an attack of serious sickness confining me to the house for twenty years. (And yet I am never in the very highest degree of health & have always bad spirits.) Judge then of my surprise when so innocent a thing as writing my yesterdays letter should have made me quite unwell. I had been preaching & writing too hard for two days before & dashing thro' those four sheets of note paper at railroad & very foolishly letting my fire go out & becoming very chilled did me so much mischief that tho' I have been going about the city on my different visits I did not sleep at all, all last night.

But it is an ill wind that blows no one any good & what I want to tell you as the result of all this exordium is that feeling no hope of accomplishing my usual writing this week I determined to dedicate to-day to a careful & prayerful closeting of myself morning & afternoon in close reflection upon this great step in our lives. This I have long intended to do & tho' of course I have continually prayed to be directed yet I have never set apart a whole day before & plunged deep into the close & consecutive reasonings in respect to my duty. I think I came fairly to the feeling of *willingness to do what was exactly right,* & to sacrifice all my plan if I could not go out upon the highway towards it with the firm footing of confirmed assurance.

The day is over & whom have I to communicate the result to but you?

My bones ache too much & my head is too much out of order to tell you all the processes, but of all the questions that came there is not one that I did not settle firmly in our favour. And tho' my mind was all clear before yet my *heart* hereafter will have a new firmness of principle & purpose. The letter that I destroyed has nothing but an allusion to the singular Providences that have led me to you. I destroyed it because I have a wicked aversion to talking on the subject of religion in any close or personal way.

My dear Sally, I feel so strong in my own will & principle in all the steps involved in this matter that I think I must take you in my arms as far as I can at the distance of some hundreds of miles & comfort you in all your discouragements. Let me do your thinking for you & your acting. Do you know I think our case will become a precedent for poor enthralled sufferers such as you have been to help them by such good Presbyterian authority to break their chains. Wont you just confide yourself to me & let my purpose which cant be easily shaken now, for these "*days*" which I consecrate & when after *imploring* that I may be rescued from a step if it is wrong I think it over like a proposition in Euclid for hours together & that my judgment at the close may be the voice of the Almighty. These days are usually final with me & as I shall not have time for another my stand is taken. And I really *dare* not think ill of it.

Let me formally propose a marriage on the 6th day of April. That is my birth-day. If yours comes in the same neighborhood we will choose that. The earlier this thing occurs the better for me as to my church. You know I can leave home on Monday (night) the 2d—reach Lexington on Wednesday the 4th—rest & sign that deed of settlement (by the way another reason I had no idea you had any big serious amount of property was, you said so, dont you remember in the carriage with Mary & spoke of some not very expensive thing I dont remember what that you would get when better off) on Thursday & be married on Friday, which tho' a dies infausta[51] shant scare us on that account. Then shant we stay a day or two in Lexington & secure the affections of that particular stronghold lest we have an enemy in our rear. See how handsomely I plan.

By the way you spoke of espionage &c. There are some degrees of chance that while we are writing sickness & death may actually be removing what has been one great difficulty. Ought we not to have recent information about that. Tho' Cumberland has some of my friends in it yet I would not *ask* on any account.[52] Can the information come to us in any unobserved way. Such a death occurring some weeks after our marriage would lead to obvious regrets.

I speak this way because I have not heard from that quarter for many months.

I still think that you are mistaken about the Legisl: & that evidence of infidelity of a palpable kind *did* come before the Committee who reported the bill & made a profound impression. Indeed I think it about certain. But I feel too unwell to go further.

As to my name call me, Rev and dear Sir, or Rev & dear Brother. Aint you ashamed Sally?

I cant say I have any particular spite at poor Eve just now for I am desperately in love with one of her daughters. She must have been a very pretty woman. "The fairest of her daughters Eve."[53]

On returning fr. Va. we can stay some days here & then go on to Princeton & get possession of all the people there. Dont chide me for settling it all for you wont do it & I am only acting upon your proposal about violence &c.

Your poor sick lover
Mohammed's Coffin Miller.

---

51. Latin, meaning an unfortunate day. It fell on April 13.
52. Francis Thomas lived near Cumberland, Md.
53. This phrase is written between the lines. The reference is to *Paradise Lost* 1.323.

Phil. Feb: 28th 1855.

My dear Sally,

Now that I am so clearly established in my own mind in respect to all the questions of which we have been writing my mind turns more warmly to your own comfort & interest.

A thing came to me last night which set me off upon a new train of thought. And as I have given up this week to unwellness (tho' I am better) & comparative leisure I write just what occurs to me & you must count all these letters in any future delinquency. I must really so manage the direction however on the envelope as to avoid the appearance in the P.O. of such a torrent of letters from the same quarter.

A pastor's life is made up of lights & shadows & while a few days ago I was hearing of the very gratifying condition of everything about our church & really rejoicing in the tho't that considering the boldness of our schemes we were about the most prosperous establishment in the town—receiving from one of our leading laymen the information that the report of a business committee just made showed unexampled soundness in our state. I was last night treated with the knowledge derived incidentally that one of our elders a somewhat illiterate man & one who has always given me anxiety by his New School leanings was disaffected by what he was choosing to call the fatalism of my sermons.[54] An elder *always* has power to do mischief & how far such a thing spreads you can never tell & the incident small as it may seem led me on & on & on into a train of reflection which I will give you.

Now you speak of your always reverting to the *one* great subject with you, that is, what you fancy a stain upon your prospects of respect & standing if you marry in your present circumstances. I have told you how completely I have disposed of that in my own mind. But the moment I have done so I revert again to what is the *one* subject in agitating me & one in respect to which, (when you are obliged to make your response so much in the dark) I am as much gratified by your yielding kindness as you are by what you call my "unflinching purpose".

Now the train of reflection started by what I unexpectedly discovered last night was carried on solely by this "one subject" & that in connection with just one bearing of it which I had never thought of before.

Most preachers, whatever is started in their parish, or whatever cloud no bigger than a man's hand may rise on the horizon, may throw themselves back from the very first thought of anything that dissatisfied them upon the thought that the whole church is open to them, & that in dealing with any question of private or public concernment they can deal with it with the feeling that whatever betides they can go elsewhere if they are not satisfied.

---

54. The Presbyterians had split Old School–New School in the late 1830s. Miller's allegiance was with the Old School strict Calvinist faction embedded at Princeton Theological Seminary. It was also the dominant group in Virginia.

Now I cannot.

This is my last pastoral settlement. My conviction of duty of another sort, as I have often represented it, is so strong that I would consider it trifling with a flock to be settled over them for so brief a time & so much in the way of a convenience. Indeed were it not for some of the results in connection with my own congregation I would sometimes feel wickedly in the way in which I serve myself of *them* in the paintings & chalkings of my future plans.

There is, therefore, that one consideration that I would place before your eyes. If either you or I should be offended or dissatisfied with anything in this particular settlement or should feel ourselves ill to ease on any ground, this is our last charge.

A man's life is written in a sort of hieroglyhic[55] way in his settlements. I have never held but two official posts in my life of any kind & both those so far have been gratifyingly useful. So far as useful reputation is concerned I could pass into the closing phase of my history from this church in Arch Street very reputably; but if I attempted to patch out an intervening time by another pastorate, of a temporary sort, it would wound both my conscience & my good name.

You see what a serious matter in the life you are going to connect yourself with is this "one subject" of mine which, to be sure, *I* think is going to make us both nobles one day, but which in the mean while is carrying me toward itself like a needle to the pole.

I have the sunniest dreams sometimes (clouded only by its connection with the loss of my mother) of a time when all these questions will have solved themselves & when in a way singularly untrammeled & free I shall be able at last to step into a position & do a work that I long after with all my heart. But till that time, the intervening space has to be bridged & I have sometimes thought, tho' the idea is now horrible to me that I ought to bridge that space alone & invite you to join me on the other side.

———————

My! I have just been down to my sick-man's cup of chocolate. I think I can say all this a great deal more plainly. It is this.

Every preacher ought to be in so independant a position as to feel bold to resign. The incident[56] last night led me to feel that there might be such things as I wouldnt tolerate in a church & perhaps it is fair & modest to say, some things that would not be tolerated in me. Were I to resign I would consider it trifling to be solemnly installed over another congregation with the intention whenever I came into possession of what estate is left me by my father, which along with other sources of revenue for incidental labour in authorship &c would support us, to resign again. The intervening time presents a hazard which in searching as *you* have done all possible evils that could result from your "*one* subject," I have

55. That is, hieroglyphic.
56. Miller scratched out the adjective "little."

felt bound to mention in connection with mine. It might require a frugality or care which however distant the danger ought at least to be foreknown.

You cannot enter into the pain with which I say that the word "trifling" which may to you seem a very strong word is suggested to my mind by the very painful evidence we are all receiving every time we visit Princeton of the shortness of the time with which all I am now saying is connected.

I feel not only strongly but solemnly the importance of a work to be done in the field of theology, the means of which have been suggested to me in my last ten years study & which I think in Providence is specially laid at my door. If I can accomplish it in the last thirty years of my life it will be worth a hundred times the first thirty & give a juster reputation for usefulness than any pastoral or even foreign missionary labour. The carrying out of my purpose is therefore a religion with me.

But, my dear Sally, you will be tired of my long letters. The last one, however, has shown how little this is suggested by anything connected with the matter that has weighed upon *your* mind & how entirely by a wish to warn you of any hazard to your own comfort. If it should shake what you call your "mad clinging to my affection" (& you cant tell how grateful I felt to you for writing such a sentence) I should be overwhelmed; Indeed I shall have a panic whenever I think of this letter till it is safely answered. But if you will marry me "for better for worse" & love me as I love you I think we can be happy in spite of the hazard I have conjured up; & I shall then feel glad that I was candid about this theology passion of mine & did not steal you away on false pretences.

Instead of resenting what this elder says (& by the way he doesn't know that I know anything about it) I am going to accomodate myself somewhat to his notions & preach more for a time on those subjects that will conciliate his taste.

Very affectionately yours,
Jno Miller.

Colalto,
Thursday, March 1, 1855

My *dear* Sir,

I was happy to find your two letters waiting for me when I got home last evening. The "extra" one I shall not answer "right at once" as you desire, but will keep you waiting until I shall be able to make you full compensation for it, for it is not a "funny little letter" as you call it, but a very precious little note which I shall put away carefully to *warm* myself by years hence when daily companionship shall have dispelled the illusion, of the present period, and when instead of your finding fault with me for being such an icicle, I shall have to mourn that I once knew you when you were some what warmer & more admiring. Such a time, however, is I hope so far in the future that I may never live to see it. At present

I expect to be "bothered" by a "*parson-lover*" all my life, and have no doubt that I shall be able to bear the infliction with becoming composure & propriety.

I hardly think your sermon could have been profited by your writing your note in the midst of it. If you dont take care you will behave like a minister of whom my Father used to laugh, who being entirely engrossed by his lady-love, one morning, in the course of his sermon, announced to his people something that had been said or done by the "beloved disciple—Susan."

I am greatly obliged to you for your hearty acquiescence in my views about a settlement. It was an awkward thing for me to talk to you of, and I am glad it is so pleasantly over. But I think the mention of the South-Downs must have "set your wits a-wool gathering" or you would scarcely have forgotten an important item in my letter. You do not say whether you desired the whole or a part of the property to be embraced in the settlement. I take it for granted, however, from the tenor of your letter, that you prefer the *whole* shall be secured to me; the power to dispose of it by will I shall insist upon whether the Contract cuts off a portion or covers the whole, as I have no idea of having *my* property, in case of my death, pass into the hands of my brothers—& sisters-in-law, whilst you were living to whom it should properly belong.

I shall apply to my friend Mr. Mosby of Lynchburg to prepare the papers & will then look into all the detail of the matter.[57] I do not think a trustee ever received a per-centage, but of this I am not certain. The selection of a trustee will be a very considerable difficulty with me. I must try to find some one who will be acceptable to the joint-heirs with me to my Father's estate, as well as agreable to you. But after all it need not be a trouble, for he can be changed if he should not please me.

Did I say anything about South Downs in my letter? It was a great piece of presumption in me if I did for my *whole flock* scarcely numbers more than just enough to require me to speak in the plural number. We are too near to town to keep any, and I laughed at your supposing that my meadows were made more beautiful by the show of flocks in them. If you had named any thing besides *sheep*, you would not have found me so poor—By the bye, *how much* do you think this "elect Lady" of yours is possessed of?

I was much amused at your very sage remarks about "descending to the frugalities of a Pastor's means." They were very fine & good, but should have come a little earlier. You will hardly stop to inquire now whether I am extravagant or otherwise,—thrifty or the reverse,—industrious or idle. However that you may not be entirely unwarned I will tell you, that the old Commissioner who has insights into my affairs *hints* to Cousin John in a whisper "that Mrs McDowell is rather extravagant"; & you may believe him for in some things, I am so. Is there any chance of *your* teaching me economy in all things. At any rate I think my extravagance is not of such a nature as will excite the notice or displeasure of

57. Charles Louis Mosby (1810–1879), a Lynchburg attorney.

your flock in Phil'a; and if *you* can put up with certain defects of temper that you have heard of, I think you need have no uneasiness about my confining myself very contentedly, within certain "narrow limits of a pastor's income."

One source of real pain to me in this thing of property is that I have slaves. They are few in number (only nine) and yet I dont know how I can part with them. I am bound to some of them by a strong tie of gratitude and affection, and they preferred a home with me to following the fortunes of any other member of the family. I am not able to set them free, even if that would be a kindness to them, & *sell* them I cannot. I would like to have a certain sett of them always about me—No white servants could be more reliable—nor could any be half as much attached as these. Some of them have been here ever since I was a child & now they are old I have a sort of care over them not to be transferred to another. I said to one the other day "Jenny how would you like to live in a City?['] "I dont know ma'am," she said, "but wherever you choose to live, there I can live with you." And there she would live with me with earnest and real devotion.[58] In the division of servants, when she asked me to select her, I suggested that she had better belong to Lilly whose long minority would secure her a home in the family for many years;—but she objected. Neither would she choose Cantey, who is her great pet, and who tho' a grown young lady she never parts from or meets without kissing—"Let me wash my mouth," she says, "Miss Cantey's going away & I must have a kiss"—and Cantey submits in a way that quite excites my admiration. She was my Mother's special nurse during her last illness & shared with us in her dying injunctions—how can I give her up? One of my Sisters (Mary) would gladly take her but I will not relinquish her to any body except she herself ask me to do so. Then there are others whom I feel much about—You have no idea how startled and grieved they will be to hear that I am going to desert them.

Would you have me sell this home of mine? My plan has been this. A farm is a troublesome and expensive thing to a Lady, but I have thought that just now when agricultural interests were in the ascendant, I would let things remain as they are for a year or two. At the end of that time certain internal improvements running to our town would be completed and land in this vicinity would, of course, have increased in value. Then I will sell, dividing the farm into small portions that may be within the reach of respectable mechanics (who always *pay well*) and only reserve the house & its surroundings some 40 or 50 acres for myself. By that time & in this way I hope to sell at an advance of several thousand dollars and still have the house.

A marriage-contract will require the proceeds of the sale of property of all kinds to be invested in Va State Stock—how would you like that? I think it will do very well. I could not feel more secure in any investment than the guaranteed

58. McDowell misread the relationship. When the Millers took Jenny with them on a visit to Philadelphia in early 1860, she escaped and claimed her freedom. See James White to Samuel McDowell Reid, Mar. 3, 1860, in Charles W. Turner, ed., *Old Zeus: Life and Letters (1860–1862) of James J. White* (Verona, Va.: McClure Press, 1983), 11.

bonds of our State. She will never repudiate, & tho' a great explosion like Selden & Withers' will shake her a little it can never overthrow her entirely.[59] She is a noble, old State after all, & I love her with a sort of enthusiastic admiration. But do you know with all my state-pride & devotion, I am really only a step-child? I was born in Kentucky.

If your Church is to be ready for use by the first of May how will you find time to slip away before that? Your whole argument against waiting until Fall was that *then* you would be so engaged in moving from a chapel to a church that you could "not spare even one day." and yet when the moving is to come off in the Spring you are quite sure you will have a week, or ten days, or a fortnight to devote to your own private affairs. But I will not be unreasonable in the matter, but will see whether I may not be able to agree to your wishes.

The two or three days I was in Fincastle a whole budget of letter came to me here. A long letter from Tom upon two enormous sheets, (that I think must have been procured from some branch-establishment of your Princeton Stationer) quite full of all sorts of things—his private opinions and purposes figure largely in the letter; but, poor fellow, when he gets thro with them in his usual way he says—"now Sister if you will only approve my plans I will feel ten-fold stronger in carrying them out." For years my heart has been hovering over the poor boy with only the more fearful anxiety because he has been the victim of the wrong notions of our very dear, good Uncle, Tom Preston, who would rather cut off his right hand than do the slightest injury to the child, & yet who has done it unconsciously, but irremediably. Tom is the most affectionate and warm-hearted of all my family, with certain gifts of mind, which if they had been vigorously cultivated would have made him a conspicuous man. He was, long ago, set aside for our Preacher, and as his boyish efforts at speaking were unusually successful I hoped "the old man eloquent" was to live thro' him in the pulpit. But thus far I have been disappointed.

James writes that he will leave St. Louis about this time, so I shall begin to look for him in a fortnight.

I enclose a letter of Peyton Harrison, whom you may know as the Father-in-law of our friend Mr John Atkinson.[60] I beg you will understand that I did not seek his opinion. I told Dr White I would not commission him to obtain it, but would not object to his asking it, if he left my name out of the question.

Uncle Carrington was much better when I left yesterday.[61]

I hope in your new Church, the trustees will allow you a pleasantly located pew. Lilly was greatly concerned at the prospect of having her Sister Mary "walk way down to the front pew" if she should be a preacher wife. She thinks front pews are generally given up to beggars, charity scholars & preachers wives.

59. Selden, Withers & Co. was an exchange bank in Washington, D.C., involved in the sale of Virginia state bonds in England.

60. Peyton Harrison (1800–1887), a Presbyterian minister.

61. Edward Carrington, the husband of McDowell's "Aunt Eliza" Carrington.

I shant forgive you for making such a fuss over my name—since your Mother's is much the same;—not half so pleasant many people think. If you had told me you thought mine was Penelope you could not have surprised me more than you did by telling me hers was Sarah.

I am sorry my ink blots so much. I must compel myself to use a different kind, but this is so clear & flowing that it is much pleasanter to me than any other.

Is your little sanctum, (does the phrase bring up any associations to you?) any less dreary now that you have my frequent visits to it, or do you still seek in it that "good hickory fire—which after all is really the best comfort you have"?

But I am determined not to say another word.

Yours,
S.C.P. McDowell.

Phil. Mar. 1st 55.

My *dear Sally,*

While the clouds are rolling about & lying heavy over every part of my horizon in these sleepless nights & *aching* days which are now the order of my experience I think I will write every day (no not to-morrow this week) that you may be able to see me in all moods.

I find more distinctly what it is that I am so earnest to get thoroughly before you. The difficulty that we have talked most about is so far *exploded* in my mind that I find myself never thinking of it, & my love to you is so passionate that I tremble even at being honest & shudder at the tho't. What if in stating my honorable doubts as you have so often stated yours I should find you impressed by them & it should lead even to a delay of our time of marriage.

Now part of what I wish to deal honorably about can be expressed by aid of a sentence in your last letter. "All you say about becoming through other pursuits independant of public approval in this matter does not weigh much with me. If you succeed in the course marked out you will to a great extent obliterate the odium of the past & secure to your family their proper places in society, but if not—what will be the fate of your children?"

Now what is more natural than for an honorable person to say, Then, my dear Sally, I will succeed first & marry you afterward.

I have this great change to make from the Pulpit to the Author's study. It is written on the horoscope of my destiny as plainly as the return of to-morrows Sun. I have prayed over it & waited for it for many years. I am as sure that there has germinated in my mind an important system of ethical truth, which if not containing *all* the reality, ought to be brought out & presented as an important step in the world's thinking. And tho' I know how I would expose myself to ridicule, if I uttered such arrogant things to others, yet I will mention them to you as a step in honorable fairness.

Now there are two paths that open; one is for you to come on in the Fall with Lilly as you proposed, & find all about me, what sort of a person I am in the opinion of others, what sort of relatives I have, what sort of standing I have in the church preserving yourself unengaged & both guarding our secret; allowing me to go alone over the hazardous path of winning public approval to my change from a pastoral life to authorship & at the point where I can safely leave this great & most important church go into student's quarters at my mother's where I am always needed. As long as I remain a Pastor I am investing a thousand a year & when I reach my mother I am improving her estate: Plunge at once into these great subjects that I am yearning after & let you actually see my first success & then marry upon my patrimony. This is one plan. It has the recommendations of perfect safety to you & perfect honor & perfect tranquility to us both in all those respects in which our good name is concerned. For that I can protect you, under God, in circumstances like those from all hurtful aspersions upon your good-name I have not the shadow of a shade of doubt (tho' it is very much the same in respect to any position.)

The other path is for two young persons who wish to be near each other & stand by each other in storms as well as in sunshine to enter upon the battle of life at once & take it as it is, & in spite of this purpose of mine which I must in candour confess is fixed & certain as my destiny, to go over all the intervening steps together: to let health & strength & proper independence with the people regulate the longness or shortness of what remains of pastoral history; if that should be just the time which, in Providence, is suited to our future circumstances well; if not, bridge over the intervening space in such a way as will best subserve the interests of the church & my great end in life & so by a more courageous path reach the preat end which you may think me fanatic when I say, I am *sure* Providence all my life has been preparing me for. If I have manifested an "unflinching purpose" as to the desire of our marriage, you will find I have one that is perfectly "gigantic" (as you very slanderously said about your egotism) in respect to the other.

Now which of these two paths I would prefer it is easy for you to divine. Indeed I tremble when I think of its *being* at this late day a free full offer to you to choose. Nevertheless it is. Every principle of generous honor in my heart dictates this clear exposition. If I felt you were mine by anything like a *blunder* on your part or that while you loved me passionately you were discovering *un*favorable rather than gratifying things in our union thro' all its early period it would make your very image which could not cease to be an object of my passion nevertheless haunt me in my dreams.

If you were a poor girl I would feel very differently but to tell you the whole truth this discovery of your father having divided such an immense estate as he must have done tho' gratifying in one aspect as respects your comfort yet torments me in another. The idea in *any* exigency even of ill health, of being sustained by your means is *withering* to me to an extent that I could not even have foreknown & tho' I had a home at my mother's which you would not occupy, & tho' from your not being poor I could not overcome difficulties for you under any disadvantages of health which I could for one that was, yet my heart *loathes* such circumstances as a poor wounded man on a battle field would shrink from the tramp of the cavalry.

If I had a plain pastors support (even tho' he might be a country pastor) or a plain scholar's support (even tho' it might be like Carlyle's or Wordsworth's far from liberal) & you chose to superadd to it wealth or even splendour I would not care.[62] Or if I were a discoverer, of world-wide fame, & you chose to add your lot to mine & nourish the lamp of a divine philosophy in the way that Salome followed Christ ministering to him of her substance I might not care so much. But to let my wife run all hazards of future usefulness or success & find "ourselves" for any interval of time reversing the order of nature is just a thing I believe that would sink me below the power of producing anything that would be manly or well.

You may ask me then. Would you *prefer* that I should choose the first path that I mark out. I say, *No*, I tremble at the very thought of such a thing. I do still entreat & beg that you will marry me on the sixth of April; but I shall feel partly relieved in the "blue" spirits that ill-appetite & low-health bring with them in having *warned* you, while it is yet time to retract, & before you have spoken to your brother. And it may preface you for a petition that I may one day send in (even on the occurrence of such a casualty as the long continuance of such ill-health, (tho' it is in this case so trifling) as I am now suffering under) to *act* as tho' you were my *poor* wife & to allow me in any embarrassing interval that may occur to be still the maintainer of my family even tho' it may be in some sequestered spot that may for a time turn you from your usual circle of enjoyments.

I smile at the earnestness of this letter when I think that our ship may sail gaily & trimly from the very first. But "forewarned, forearmed." I deliberately think that my student's passion & my emulation of Bacon & Leibnitz & these great thinkers of the old regime is a little like an artist's passion—that it has the air of garrets & very sublimated food: & the very marked peculiarity in a Minister in which he declares that (if it is the will of God) he would never consent to another pastoral settlement is certainly one which just as you iterate & reiterate your fears about a point that *you* make prominent he should be equally express about in stating in all the lights in which it can be threatening.[63]

My church enterprise here is considered somewhat of a wonder & therefore always a risk. It has passed its critical stages but others may at any time arise. It was a New School church in very bad odour & with but a handful of people. My people now are shut into a room or chapel, the former Lecture Room of the Ch. that holds but three hundred. It is crowded in the morning; but in a few months

---

62. Thomas Carlyle (1795–1881), a Scottish philosopher, historian, and essayist. William Wordsworth (1770–1850), English poet.

63. Francis Bacon (1561–1626), English philosopher.

this Spartan band are to move into the larger audience room perhaps the largest in the city. The wide chasm between the three hundred & some four times that many has gradually to be filled up. This, of course, is a *grand* undertaking but it is always a very *great* one & any appearance of a New School feeling remaining especially in an elder & in others round him as I mentioned the other night could not fail to arrest my attention. My philosophic biases & intentions are so well known by one or two of my leading clerical friends that I could withdraw from my church with perfect honor at any time when I chose to take a stand that issued in a way that I would not bear, but then follows all this refusal of my judgment to consent to another settlement.

Thus I have secured for myself the pleasure of placing you in circumstances still for a free election.

And now letting my affection return & take possession of my pen, let me beg you to choose only in one way. What can we not accomplish when our counsels are united together in the way of carrying out a path to the proper retirement that we desire? And as to your hearty sympathy in these ulterior pursuits I can have no doubt of it in the end when I see how I am drawn to you by taste & feeling. I think this is the last of these Jeremiah letters. Write & tell me freely all you think as you have begged me to do as to your whole difficulties of mind.

Yours affectionately
JM

[marginal note] & I am better & have been most triflingly sick.

Colalto
Friday March 2.1855

Poor fellow! how sorry I am for you! I wish I had you snugly fixed under my care: you would not then find it such a bad thing to be sick, but, like Lilly, would *enjoy* the sickness on account of the petting. How could you be so foolish as to sit writing in a cold room without fire on the very coldest day we have had this winter? I thought you had more prudence than that especially after all your lectures to me about my health. But as the cold is taken, pray be careful. Dont let it run into Pneumonia, & remember *my affection* pleads for all the care you can bestow upon yourself, and begs a letter from you every day until you are quite well. And I shall not be content to have you say par parenthèse, "I am better," but you must give a regular account of yourself. Give up chocolate, and if you *can* practice such self-denial all other liquids for 48 hours, and you will be well. Mary is the only person of sufficient power of will to follow out my prescription; & she has been rewarded with success.

As to your trouble about your grumbling elder, and the influence of his disaffection upon others, & the probable influence of that again upon your plans and the effect of all upon me,—why just, so far as I am concerned, dismiss the whole matter from your mind. Dont do anything yourself to hasten the time, but when you find it has come for you to leave your present post, give it up. Conscience & honor & christian integrity will all require it. And having taken one step, from good motives, never fear for a moment that you will not have light enough to see *where* to place your foot next.

As to me—you dont know how well I could struggle with a narrow income if I once had a strong motive for it. I think I am quite fitted to be a *poor* man's wife, and would have half my good qualities undeveloped in any other condition in life. So if you want to love something really worth loving in me, you should not object to see me tried in this way of "frugality."—By the bye that word suggests to me the idea of gruel without salt—it seems so very, very poor.

But after all we need not fear such black poverty as your letter might make one think you were about dropping into, for I am not such a pauper as you suppose. And now I will tell you all about that—that is, I will tell you as much as I can in a letter like this. First then—this farm of mine with its stock etc. is worth at present, even under the money-pressure we are all experiencing, $24 or 25.000. Only about 120 acres of it is under cultivation, & yet the *wheat* alone upon it the last season if it had all been sold would have brought (I believe that is the phrase) $1.200. I could not forbear bragging a little about my flour as it sold at $10 a barrel, whilst my neighbours had to content themselves with something like a dollar less. Well, in addition to this I have 4 small lots in Louisville, at present to be counted at something over $1.000 each. These with the lot you saw in Washington may be estimated now at $10.000. Then, my Grandmother Preston out of special consideration to her namesakes gave to us four Sallys (making us curiously enough heirs of each other in case of death within a specified time, which has well-nigh expired now) a claim upon our Uncles for what is to me now, $4 or 5.000—I cannot tell exactly how much. Still further—there is yet, my Mother's interest in the Salt-works, about $16.500 undivided:—also a tract of land in Missourri, which we have a faint hope may have coal upon it:—also 5 or 6.000 acres of mountain land in our vicinity, which with all its timber does not furnish me with shingles to cover my poor Shanghais & keep them from freezing.[64] Now add these various sums together, leaving out the undivided portions. Let me set them in order.

Colalto	$24.000
Louisville lots	5.000
Washington "	5.000
Remnant of a Legacy	3.000
	$37.000

64. "Grandmother Preston" was Sarah Buchanan Campbell Preston (1778–1846). "My poor Shanghais" refers to McDowell's cats.

I am almost sure a year or two hence that this farm alone will sell for at least $20.000. And I have high hopes of the appreciation of my lots. I am in debt, however, some thousands & I always cut off my lots to meet my liabilities—yet with what I have already in land—and with what I shall probably get from the unsold portions of our estate, for in addition to the Missourri & Salt-works property there is an unsold part of a Kentucky estate—worth some $30 or 40.000—I may safely calculate my *belongings* at $30.000. This invested in State stock (Va) would yield an income of $1.800. Add yours to this & I think we *might* scuffle along & not excite the compassion of the public either. But I dont want to sell for several years—so that, of course I cannot calculate upon any regular income. You will have to make up your mind to be *burdened* with me, as well as "bothered" by me for several years—but I will be as economical as possible & will promise never again to pay your towns-woman, Mrs Miller, $25—for making a dress. I grumbled when I did it, but without the faintest idea that my complaints should ever reach your ear.

I paid my *stipends* this morning, and asked myself as I did it, "shall I ever do such a thing again?" but I hope if I dont it wont be because I am to get preaching that wont be worth paying for. What sort of preaching am I to have? I am somewhat curious to know. Not very, very good tho' I imagine, as I am sometimes myself called in to help it on. However my friend William Brown, who is a very sensible man—none more so in the synod of Va—says I am—can you guess what?—*an Orator*. Wasn't that a pleasant hallucination? I dont know how he came by it tho', for I never make speeches, do I?

Sometimes I fancy you will think me as vain as our friend Lacy, from the frequency with which I repeat such expressions—but you must recollect that I feel quite sure that you will *be pleased* to hear other people say something good of me, and not leave me to descend in solitary stateliness to praise myself.

You ask *me* all sorts of questions: now *I* shall ask you one. What is it that you see in me to love? I want to know how deep & sound is the foundation you have laid.

I am always glad when your envelopes disclose a number of sheets—never dream that your letters are ever tedious or too long or too frequent. I sometimes think mine must be wearying to you. I am occasionally ashamed as Mr. Fendall once wrote to me, to have them transgress into more sheets than one yet I talk away, until you are tired & I—am sleepy.[65]

Do write me you are quite well next time, or I shall have something worse than presentiments about you.

And now "Rev'd & dear Brother,"

I am Yours truly
S.C.P. McDowell.

---

65. Philip Richard Fendall (1794–1868), lawyer and district attorney in Washington, D.C. He had assisted McDowell at the time of her divorce.

Phil. Mar. 5th 55.

My *darling Sally,*

Your letter delights me so that if the Old Philosopher had not been medelling in my affairs & sending out of his sick chair those letters that I must still wait to hear from before I can be perfectly at peace, I would be in the highest spirits.

I am glad the letters went, that is, I shall be if the old fellow dont do mischief with them but if anything, letters or cautions or labour or anything else keeps me much longer from you I think it will break my heart. I do love you so that I think I would submit to anything short of upsetting the whole full beaker of my lifes hopes & purposes (& I think even that assumes a more prosy & *conscientious* aspect in the comparison, than that of a passionate enthusiasm as it has always seemed) to make you mine. There is *one* thing in which I am perfectly *sure* of what is wise & that is that if you will consent to marry me this year at all it ought to be quite as early as the earliest day I have named. It would be better even earlier. The church has actually taken a new start under the increased corps of workmen & tho skeptical still yet I am inclined to think I shall preach the dedication sermon on the 1st Sunday in May. If that be so I can spare *one* or *two* of the intervening weeks but those *nearer* the time & just after it will be like beaten gold. Then in the Summer the weeks we can secure can be so pleasantly employed in looking back over our few weeks residence in the city & arrangements for the future & as my people look a great deal to me in the *religious* orderings of the whole enterprise & will not wish to *close* so new a church thro' the hot months it seems to me so wise to have all our marriage accomplished & settled this long before hand. Then will come on the Winter Campaign which will be long & arduous, when if we are married now we will have lapsed into a quiet & settled condition of things. May I leave here on the 2d of April? I speak I feel sure, my dear Sally, out of the "coolest wisdom" when I say that if it could be even two weeks earlier than that it would be still better.

Now let me take up in detail anything that requires an answer in your full & most pleasant.

I meant of course the *whole* when I spoke of a settlement. I wouldnt dream of anything else.

As to *slaves* Bp. Potter & I have such battles on the slavery question in a laughing way, he inching to abolitionism that I am past all danger of being accused of changing my opinions out of love to a Southern wife; & as to *servants* ours here are so poor in many cases that you can hardly run any risk in retaining as far as strikes you well any that please you. If they live here free as they must do by our free laws a given time you cant return them to Va is not that your law?

I think your plan for your Lexington farm a grand one. I have but one doubt about the Virginia State stock & that tho' strong is a mere theoretic one & you must not let it weigh for more than it is worth. I think *all our states* go thro the same process. They have an interval improvement epoch; then their credit is high. Next follows a reaction from improving too much. Then the state credit falls & the stock can be bought for a fraction of its original value. Then it weathers the storm & probably never repudiates & possibly always pays its interest, but the stock for the whole generation does not climb up again to par & the estate is permanently diminished. So it has been in nearly all the states with as far as I know scarce any exception. Now as Virginia has improved with great *suddenness* & *breadth* of expansion & with a sort of pride of state faith which is not the thing that capitalists look at in after trials (but *assets* & revenue) I have hardly a lingering doubt when I *theorize* that Va securities will decline. I thot so last Summer as I heard of the great Tunnel & other bold acts of the Legislature.[66] She cannot hope for the commerce of Pa & yet you know the result with her. I expect to see the time when Va stock will sell for 80, for she has true so far to the law of other states in her different monetary changes.

But I wouldnt talk so freely my dear Sally, if I didnt wish to inaugurate you as the Mrs Edwards not only in your affairs but in mine. I am only the Old Philosopher meddling & making trouble with my sage remarks.

My brother has lately been investing for my mother in 6 per ct bonds of a perfectly safe character that have *gone through* these trying processes & which have been recently selling at 77 paying their interest (by the 10 years together) with perfect regularity.

Is your contract in Virginia such a thing as you can annul or abandon in case you preferred to substitute another one that would allow you freer action if you became a permanent resident in another state? It is a sort of law I observe with trustees & guardians & executors, in these cities to *scatter* their investments & to keep them lying by smaller parcels in several different things.

There now! Aint that a show of business learning? Did you ever hear a preacher discourse more satisfactorily upon these great questions of finance?

I am on the eve of a concert meeting since I received your letter & am hurrying more than will take up all the lesser points of your letter. You cant tell what pleasure it has given me. My sanctum (which is one of the points I mean) wears a fresh glow from it; & so does my hickory fire.

I shall be *so* happy if the letter comes that has been written *after* those I wrote last & I find you still not afraid to trust yourself in the hands of Le Vieil Sage. I think he's a right meaning old gentleman & I know that in this instance he wrote with that peculiar devotion with which I also Am yours

> *Most affectionately*
> *Jno Miller.*

66. Between 1849 and 1858, the Blue Ridge Railway Company, with state assistance, constructed four tunnels through the mountains. See John Pyntz Nelson, *Four Tunnels in the Blue Ridge Region of Virginia on the Chesapeake and Ohio Railway* (Richmond, Va.: Mitchell and Hotchkiss, 1917).

Lexington,
Monday, March 5. '55

Yes, I am a little *bit* ashamed, nevertheless I mean to say "Rev: & dear Brother." It looks quite nicely, how does it sound to you?

I was much inclined to answer your last letter immediately; but I thought however gratifying the impulsive response might be to you, it would be scarcely so firm and reliable as one written at a cooler moment and after some reflection.

The fact is, you allowed your *mind* to grow feverish under that bad cold you had taken and of course saw every thing in a somewhat exaggerated and unnatural, or *excited* (I had better say) style. Your disaffected elder had so worked upon your feelings as almost to make you ready, the very next day, to give up your Church and go to Princeton. And then, the astounding discovery of my having some property, has increased your sorrows so very greatly that I am really half-inclined to think you would rather give me up, than bear such an odious burden. Now, my dear Sir, make up your mind to put up with some disagreable things in this matter, & try to trim them up to look as well as they can. I appreciate your feeling in this thing of property; & respect them. In our peculiar circumstances it may excite unpleasant remark from some people, but it would be from those who would find something to censure in our proceeding, even if this feature in the case was absent. But it cannot be helped now, and you must not mourn over it. You might as well grieve that my eyes are brown instead of blue,—or over any other unalterable thing connected with the whole affair. I am glad I have it. I wish for all the good it will do us all it were twice as much. And instead of being so *proud* in the matter you should look upon it as one of the Providences, smoothing the way to the gratification of your master-passion. And, after all, for several years it will avail little or nothing, for I want the products of this farm to pay off the debt I have incurred, and thus for several years I shall be a pecuniary burden to you.

As to the other more important subject of your letter. It is scarcely clear to my mind. Do you think of leaving your Church, in this very critical stage of her existence, because of the growling of that one man, and going at once "into student's quarters" as you say. If so, do you mean that your first proposition as to the delay of the marriage shall rest entirely upon your success in the new enterprise? If you do, how long think you it will take to win the success, one year or ten? And then if you do not succeed? Now all this first suggestion of yours is only valuable to me in that it evinces very strongly your anxiety to shield me from all mistakes, & to secure to me every possible degree of pleasure and comfort. But I say however *safe* the course might be I will not accept it. I would not be worthy to reap the benefits of your triumph, if I had not courage enough to meet with you all the dangers of the struggle. If you are to succeed,—I would help you win your success. If you are to fail, I would be with you, to sympathize in your disappointments & thus lighten them. But here is another thing, how much time will you give to the experiment? And if the experiment after—say, ten years fails, what will you do then?

As to the other proposal about the 6th of April, I will write you *fully* next week—can't you wait patiently that long? I am not *inconsiderate* in this delay. I am very fearful as it comes to the final step.

I am not mistaken in what I said of the papers presented for Legislative action. If any facts upon the point you mention came before the Committee I did not hear of them.

It would be well to know something from Md, but I could not, would not make an inquiry for any thing.

Do write me you are quite well again: And dont let your "blue spirits" run away with you.

I am not in condition myself to write tonight being tired—so good night "and all other good things to you"—

Yours truly
S.C.P. McDowell.

You will let me revert to the past once more? I have sometimes thought of saying to you tho' I believe never at the moment of writing that if in regard to that catastrophe of my life there should be anything you would like to be specially informed of, write and ask me without hesitation. Such publicity was given to all things that it seems scarcely possible you can be in ignorance upon any point in the case, & yet you may be. The whole transaction sometimes seems to me like a terrible dream, the horrors of which have followed me in my waking moments. Looking over some old papers yesterday brought the whole matter up again with a sort of night-mare oppression—and the fear again came strong upon me about connecting *you* with such a past—But my "*one subject*" is a *forbidden subject*.

How would you have me "act as your *poor wife*"? In what particulars? I think, (& you may tell me whether I am vain or not,) that just in *myself* I am a koh-a-noor to you & have lost something in beauty & value by having a poor setting of gold.[67]

Yours
S.C.P. McD.

Mar. 6th [1855]

Darling Sally,

I have just about 20 minutes & I am going to write you one or two sentences out of gratitude.

1st I have your letter of the 2nd.

2nd I love you.

3rd You love me. I am now sure of it. I believe you would have me [if] I was old & poor. At least I try to get up such a hallucination.

---

67. The Koh-i-noor ("mountain of light") was one of the oldest and most famous precious stones, an Indian diamond that in 1849 was added to Queen Victoria's crown jewels.

4th You're an angel. I never was so sure of it as since the kindness of your few last letters.

5. You ask me why I love you. I will answer that "again" as you say, because it requires a little philosophic length & system to tell you all. But I love you chiefly because you are an angel. I am sure that is enough. The first buddings in my consciousness of anything like love was in some such soliloquy as this. What a lovely wife this would make for my student's home. How in (a) intellect & (b) beauty & (c) graceful goodness she would adorn it. I don't think now I will write about it again. For this really & seriously, my dear Sallie, is all of the matter. I don't often meet with ladies who understand me in all I say. I am sure you will, & this you supplement so wonderfully with your fine qualities my longings & tastes that I can't help loving you. I think God *made* you for me. I wish he had manufactured me a little better & then I could reverse the statement. I think it will be so lovely for example to sit and hear you talk after a long day of study.

6th I don't understand all your figures, but I see enough to see that along with all your personal loveliness, your property superadded makes you altogether too great a boon for such a poor old match as I am: & yet after all the superaddition of property is a very slight thing. The balance against me was quite bad enough before.

7th I love you.

8th I wish you loved me a great deal better than you do.

9th I see you are a quack like my sister Mary. As she had never entitled herself to a change of name in any other way we call her Mrs Quackenbush.

10th I am a great deal better. I had "miliary fever"; now look in your books.[68]

11th I have no doubt your remedy continued long enough would cure all disease whatever.

12th Oh, what poor preaching you will hear! I get so tired of it!

13th I am so strong in my conviction as to the wisdom of the very earliest day now possible for our marriage. Is it possible for it to be a week earlier? As soon as you have the possibilities of the case settled, my dear Sally, write me & then I will go & have a confidential talk with each of three or four persons, Bp Potter, Spencer, Mary, Julia (Dick's wife) & *one* or *two* of my people. After I have seen them I will be able to report some plans for our reception here eligibly so as to make it wise & unembarrassing.

Darling, when do you mean to answer all the letters that are to be answered "again".

You havnt so much as much as said you would marry me.

> *Yours, always fearing it will be never, "again."*
> Jno Miller

---

68. A fever accompanied by tiny skin eruptions.

Colalto,
Wednesday, March 7.1855.

My *dear* Sir,

It seems we take it by turns to be out of spirits. I am having my turn now; I hope yours is happily over.

I had a short talk with Cousin John this afternoon as we stood in the light of a gorgeous sunset at the end of the shrubbery. It turned upon our matters, and especially upon the one point so frequently talked of between ourselves. He ushered it in by adding, "Have you ever considered that if you marry a Preacher, the marriage, very probably *will* subject him to ecclesiastical notice, & perhaps censure?"

I told him I had—the idea was not a new one to me. Then, said he, do you think a Minister ought to marry where there is a *doubt* as to the propriety of the step? This too you know is no new view of the case to me. But I can't help being depressed by finding *his* opinion agreeing with mine. and I have to fall back upon this old subject tho' you are tired of it.

As he continued to speak of it in its different bearings, he said this—"You will find gentlemen siding with you, whilst ladies will go against you. But let me know in time, that I may be ready to defend you on all sides; for I mean to love you as much as ever." I felt grateful to him for this assurance, but in spite of it I turned off from him with a load upon my spirits scarcely felt before, and now after some three or four hours have passed, it weighs upon me still. And tho' it is no kindness to write in such a mood yet, I am but doing as you desire,—"writing all my difficulties of mind" to you. I do shudder at very thought of being connected with an ecclesiastical trial—(like that of McQueens, something) & being the subject of talk all over America.[69] Only think of the agony endured in that way already. And then if *censure* should follow, I should feel perfectly blighted. Not that the decree of any sett of men would be binding upon my conscience if *it* were fully & firmly fixed upon what to my mind was the meaning of Scripture, but I should feel that the whole Church would form *its* opinion upon this decree & thus we should be "cast out as evil" by the community in which we lived. Why not wait & see what the future may disclose to us?

But I will write no more now. If I am brighter tomorrow morning I will add a line. I hope you are quite well now.

Very Truly Yours
S.C.P. McDowell

69. Archibald McQueen (?–1852) was suspended from active ministry in 1842 by the Fayetteville, N.C., presbytery because he married his deceased wife's sister. Three years later, the General Assembly of the Presbyterian Church restored him to service, and his presbytery reinstated him in 1847. His multiple trials received extensive coverage in the denominational press.

Thursday Morning

I was about to take up my pen when I received a dispatch from Aunt Eliza announcing poor Uncle Carrington's death yesterday at sunset. I hurry off this morning to be with her in her great distress. I shall not be able to write whilst there. Yet if I can I will. I am hungry for a letter from you. Death after death comes rushing thro' our family—yet we rarely "sorrow as those who have no hope".[70] In this case, the poor sufferer we hope is in Heaven. Yet it is sad to know that he is taken away *just before* he was by public profession a Christian.

Yours
S.C.P. McD.

March 9 [1855]
Friday

Koh-i-noor,

The gleam of your blessed light came to me this morning like the day to the Parsee fire-worshipper.[71]

I will make a bargain with you. If you will never mention your 'one subject' to me again till after our wedding day I will never mention mine. We will bury them below deep-sea line in the 'blue', & after our marriage I'll read all the papers you have. I have heard of published attacks against you but if I have ever seen them I dont remember their form or even outward appearance, but, Sally, I love you by a sort of *intuition*. If they were to tell me you had poisoned the Queen of Sheba I wouldnt believe it. And if they had shown me the proof how you had "been & done & gone" & poisoned her I would say you hadnt "done meant it." I know you are very wicked. You keep me hanging between heaven & earth & when I tell you all sorts of things I feel about you, without a moments reservation you never "say turkey" to me at all & I'm getting so tired.

But, darling Sally, your letter puts me in such good spirits. If my fogginess of temper was not so cronic I think I might really say I was a little happy this morning.

I accept with the wildest welcome your decision against the delay policy & now I do beg for a wedding on the 6th of April (or earlier) *indeed* it will not do later. I have secret thoughts that the church will not be done the first of May (or entered this Spring) but all now think it will & I must be ready, & indeed the 6th of April with the dissipations that must follow is very late for such a contingency. On the contrary, if we fail to get in so soon then it is the very time.

My darling, darling Sally, don't let them persuade you not to marry. You have all thot to thro' that.[72] I am so afraid, as you have been talking to none but me,

---

70. 1 Thess. 4:13.
71. Member of a Zoroastrian religious sect in India who had fled Persia during the Muslim persecutions in the seventh and eighth centuries.
72. That is, thought that through.

that others will shake your purpose. I am hot with this last kind letter of yours & the knowledge that we understand each other now so perfectly so bent upon this time that I could hardly bear a disappointment. I *pray* don't subject me to it. If you ask me what setting I would like for my Koh-i-noor I would say that she should be set in her own ways against all comers.

Do not I beg if friends are a little clamorous, think of the quiet path of safety that I opened the other day, for remember, Darling, I close it. It is not open any more. The fact is I am helplessly & hopelessly & (if it ever works you any mischief) haplessly in love. I'm more so than I was yesterday & shall be still more to-morrow. As little Bob Stockton said when he broke his arm, "I'm wus & wus all the time".[73]

I dont think I *can* give you up, & as to this golden setting you talk of the diamond has behaved so under it all that I am sure the gold rim looks as plain now in the contrast as the silver did before.

I am eaten into by this passion of philosophy. I know it makes my life a dangerous one, (tho' I dont look upon it as an experiment). I *possess* what gladdens my own heart; others may think what they please of it. If you will take me just as I am, after 12 years pastoral service *already performed* as my contribution to the great ministerial work I shall be so happy. Indeed Sally, you have allowed me to think of you so much & I have seen you so little that you *must* be mine. And will you not write me very, very soon decisively because I can do a good many things for our pleasanter return here before I leave.

When you do write write *irrevocably* so I may commit no imprudencies in making any arrangements here.

And now, my dear Sally, I wish I could tell you how I love you. It is like a wild tempestuous passion. You are right in surmising that I am jealous even of so much of the sparkle of my Koh i noor as her wealth covers & yet as I told you in another letter I have no contempt for wealth but a great respect for it.

I shall take no step of any sort either for residence or comfort or future plan till you come on & then you must take charge of me & make me behave myself & stay at my work till the time comes.

But ever-more my mind will be turning to the time when we will be domesticated years hence a mile or two from the gothic Library in Princeton & in the light of some pleasant Autumn day telling over our old adventures in their forming periods of Providence.

My dear "Mountain of Light"

Your very happy finder
John Miller.

---

73. Probably Robert Field Stockton (1847–1891) of Princeton. He was the son of John Potter Stockton (1826–1900) and Sarah Marks (1830–1887) and the grandson of Commo. Robert Field Stockton (1795–1866), wealthy landowner and businessman in New Jersey who was involved with John Charles Frémont in the seizure of California during the Mexican War.

I would have you act as my "poor wife" by loving me as much as tho' I was a millionaire.

**Lexington,
Monday, March 12 1855**

I left Aunt Eliza's at two o'clock this morning and reached home about dark, having, by constant effort, accomplished 36 miles! We picked up Lilly, & Cantey in town, & brought them home; The former so much excited by the feat she had performed, during my absence, of writing a letter to Mr Kennedy about my business, that her eyes were "held waking" so long as to give me only a "*skimpt*" allowance of time for you.

I think you are very kind and forbearing. I know you do get worried at my "one subject", I feel you have a right to complain of my indecision; very naturally you are inclined to rebel at it,—and yet you are so considerate & patient that you make me quite ashamed of my weaknesses. Do bear with me a little longer & let me write once more upon that "*one subject.*" Not now how-ever.

It took me some days to recover from the effects of my talk with Cousin John—even now the recovery is by no means complete. You must bear with my difficulties. My mind does not readily cast them aside. And in this case, I want all *doubts* left behind when the decisive step is taken, & would have you *rest* upon *it* with the greatest confidence. You must know, however, that in all matters of importance I suffer in deciding. My mind is suggestive of difficulties, & I fear & fear to decide *with* my *inclination* lest it should be wrong—& dread to decide *against* it because I can not summon up resolution to bear the pain of such a decision. I am ashamed to confess such a weakness, but you must know me as I am.

I have thought much of that sixth of April—always fearing it was too early a day for me, yet not willing to interpose any objections to it, as you had your heart set upon it, if there was a chance of their being overcome. But now, I find it cannot be. We need not even think of it. In fact I don't know when a marriage could take place. I had thought of saying the 30th of April, which is my birthday, but I cannot name any day with any certainty. I feel this uncertainty to be a cruel harrassment to you—to us both—and that instead of subjecting you to it I ought to gather up strength to stop the matter *now*—to set you free absolutely—but how am I to do that. I cant. I shrink from such a struggle. And as long as I confide as I do now in your affection, I shall find myself, as I said before clinging to it with a sort of madness. This insane gratifying of my own feelings, under all the uncertainty and pain caused to you is, I am sure, not honorable in me but whilst there remains even a faint hope for the future I must let things be as at present.

I am pained to write you such a gloomy letter, especially as I have revelled in the pleasure your last two or three have given me. But I may write more cheerfully. Unlike you, after a long cheerless letter like this, I cannot indulge myself and relieve you by any *expressions* of affection. They all seem dammed back in my own heart by a fear that you cannot feel, & by a natural reserve that you can hardly understand. But this reserve will give way, when once all barriers are thrown down:—until then believe me to be—not such an icicle as you have said I was.

Yours
S.C.P.McDowell.

Thursday. [March 16, 1855][74]

My Dear Sally,
     I can hardly express to you the stunning & bewildering effect of the obscure & yet painfully agitating letter that I have just received.
     I ought to be the *stronger* of the two & will be. I will *never* by word or personal "complaint" increase the feelings which are manifested in the very handwriting of what I have received.
     So far I wrote & went back & read the letter over again. My darling Sally, what *is* the matter? What did your cousin John tell you? And what agitates you so much more than ever before? And are you *preparing* me for the black gulf of an entire separation? *Why* can there be only "a faint hope for the future"? And what *has* occurred to spread over your letter a worse gloom than for so many months before?
     Dear Sally, I love you with all the fondness of the most insane devotion. I love you too much to complain of *anything* so long as I see in you the least traces of a return for my affection. And if our marriage were *forbid* by your whole conscience & thro' life I would still love you even if it were the most hapless of all possible attachments. I cant *argue* any more for I have said all I can & tho' I can hardly write any more yet dear Sally, I am yours patiently & fondly

JM.

Colalto
Friday, March 16.1855

My dear Sir,
     I generally receive your letters early in the week—scarcely ever failing to get one on Wednesday, but this week I have had none, and I feel more disappointed than I am willing to express. I have been the more anxious to hear as I felt sure my last letters would be painful to you. I wish I could have avoided giving the pain but indeed I could not. I am so earnest that we should take no wrong step for many reasons, the very strongest of which I cannot speak of even,—and so anxious that no doubt either as to the propriety or expediency of a marriage should linger upon my mind, and hence I am kept unable to decide. You have

74. McDowell dated this letter, but Mar. 16 was Friday rather than Thursday.

cramped my perfectly free expression of feeling upon this "one subject:"—and I hardly think it was kind in you, for it is *the* great trouble in the case. But I dont mean to accept your "bargain", for I am going to write, when less hurried than at present once more fully, that is as much so as I can, upon this my point. So gather up all your strength & patience.

Do you know it half-worries, half-alarms me when you speak so often of your "chronic fogginess of temper". Pray *what* does it mean, & how is it exhibited? Like your Mother, I have a great fear about this thing of temper. I [am] quick, (I dont believe I am imperious after all) but not moody or sullen, and have the greatest aversion to anything like *pouting* in any body—especially in a man. I hope you have no such temper as that to contend with. The only *moody* person I am much acquainted with is Uncle Robt Breckinridge, & dear me! I had rather be beset by a hundred whirlwinds, & as many volcanoes, as be the martyr to one of his moods. Now please devote a page to an answer to this in your next letter.

Sometimes I am quite provoked at your way of evading my questions—for example—You say very gravely in one letter "I shall yet ask you to *act* as my poor wife"—I ask, "*How* shall I do it?" and then you cast off the whole thing by saying—"why, by loving me as much as tho' I were a Millionaire." Now is that fair? You know you had a very different reason for making the remark at first & I was disappointed &—a little mad. I dont care whether you are a Millionaire or not. To be sure I am not romantic enough to think nothing about the means of living respectably—yet you could no more *buy* my affection than you could *buy out* the Emperor of Russia, or possess yourself by purchase of the real Koh-i-noor.

I felt so sorry at the loss of the College building at Princeton. I thought you would feel as tho' some dear friend had been lost. How fared the Gothic Library? Was it burnt too?

I have written you a whole sheet of complaints. The first present I make you I think shall be a—what do you think?—a *seal*! I fancy a "loving letter with a *mystic seal*", which I dont get from you. I write before breakfast & in danger of keeping it waiting. How long before I shall have another letter?

Yours truly
S.C.P. McDowell

[marginal note] Does my ink blot now?

Friday afternoon.

Dear Sir,

I couldn't send my letter this morning, as the servant in the dining room was sick & my mail-carrier had to take his place.

I felt sure I should have a letter from you to day, and cannot bear my disappointment in not getting one quietly. In fact I am greatly disquieted. I wont tell you how much lest you should presume upon it, or perhaps grow a little vain. I am afraid I praised you somewhat too much a few days ago about this very thing of writing. Can it be that you sent a letter to me at Fincastle supposing I would be there long enough to receive one? If so I shall be pleased enough when it gets into my hands to write you "an extra" in return. But if it has not happened so—what must I think of you? Ordinarily I would have more patience but my last letters to you I know gave you so much anxiety & disappointment, that I long to get an answer to them. I would not have written as I did if I could have helped it—would I?

Cant you, as you proposed to me once, have a regular day for writing. Take Monday, & rest yourself after your Sunday duties by paying me a visit—long or short, as according to circumstances.

Such dreary weather as we have. This, with three "ailing" servants does not help one's spirits. I half wish I could do as my Greyhound beside me is doing—go to sleep standing until the sun came out.

We are all alone. Jimmy Carrington not yet returned. My brother, Tom writes left St Louis the 9th—will be here in 16 or 15 days. Tom writes he is a little thin & probably might do to figures so alarming in Sister's dream. Yet quite well. So much for presentiments. But I am busy so, Revd & Dear Brother, Adieu.

S.C.P. McD.

Phil. Mar. 19, 1855

Rev & dear Bother,

Is *this* all?

I am dealt with in strange ways.

Providence never puts my letters into my hands in an expected way. When I have been waiting for one for days & an in a fever of anxious impatience one is[75] thrust into my way in an entirely unlooked for manner. The postman has gone & I have settled down again in utter distress & amazement & little George, a friend of mine, has taken a letter from him, & after standing some fraction of an hour watching the maid washing windows comes up at last in a very leisurely way bringing me the letter all crumpled in his hands. Or the postman neglects the S[unday] mail & brings the letter at night or the servant takes the letter at the door & puts it in some unaccustomed place. I am in a constant process of discipline and now last & crookedest your most important letter of the 7th never came at all. It seemed to be intended that I should receive the blow of your last without any preparation at all & it really shocked me beyond all your comprehension. For the first time the carrier *passed* a letter, & it went to the window & was advertised in to-day's paper & I got it just now.

Now, my dear Sally, Major Preston's idea is this time perfectly absurd. It is the veriest moonshine that ever glimmered on the surface of a lake. I am sorry I did not get your letter sooner. In ecclesiastical matters I am a better judge & it is the veriest phantom that ever entered into the Major's brain.

---

75. Miller repeated "is."

It confirms an impression that I have for some days been beginning to have that for the better protection of peoples reputation it is ordered in Providence that everything shall be exaggeration before any important step, that the lions shall be twice as big as you look up the Hill as after you have past them, and thro' some sort of Providential intimidations lions shall be *painted* where none actually exist. The Major is most certainly wrong. The texture of our Presbyteries is such, at least at the North, & thro' Dr. Leyburn & others the means of knowing better so abundant that if this thing were mentioned in Presbytery I should treat it as a personal affront on the part of the members. It convinces me that *all* these things are exaggerated. By the way, the true moral considerations in the case *were* before the Committee of the house. I have found it out in great fulness.

If Major Preston with such views will love you *as much* as before & will defend you, your conversation was *favorable* & not the reverse.

Meanwhile, My dear Mrs McDowell, tho' I know you love me & tho' I know, to a partial extent, you suffer as I do in these reverses yet I am impelled by every honorable consideration to say that you need never *prepare* me for an entire rejection. I would rather always rely on knowing the utmost of your feeling. If your conscience ever forbids you to go one step further in the matter I shall never upbraid you. Both chivalry & a knowledge of the past convince me that you will act in this matter under great strength of principle & under great distress. And, therefore, I resign all possible claim to you the moment a sense of that claim adds to the sufferings of a checkered life. *I love you too much to act differently.* And tho' I consider myself engaged to you & you *not* engaged to me, and feel that it must remain in sentiment so at least indefinitely in the future, yet I will never even *think* severely of you if you accept even this letter as an entire release. I have grown so accustomed to suffering that it is one of my most familiar companions & I have my expectations so disciplined that I look for nothing else in life.

You will consider me as passing all bounds of submission & forbearance when I say, what nevertheless is consistent with the utmost manliness, which is that our correspondence the longest I believe that I ever continued in my life with anyone not my relative has really improved my character. I am a better man for having lived in expectation of your hand. And if the recoil were fearful I would carry away this form of compensation. This certainly is high praise of one who in case of any disappointment will have caused me so much suffering & may strike you as almost bizarre in its gospel spirit, but I do assure you, my dear Sally, without ever dreaming of its coming out in a letter to you I have again & again remarked the check you were to me on many an occasion of temptation.

But Major Preston is so foolishly & absurdly wrong this time & has given you so much unreasonable agitation that I hardly have patience to think of my being so late in writing this letter.

Let me vaticinate a little.

I. If I am disappointed in this attachment it cannot be long, say, next August a year, (or sooner if matters are sufficiently established) before, under this new burden, I go to Princeton. There in a sense of pleasure that in a certain way I have never before had my marriage will be celebrated "for better for worse," with the Mistress that I love better than you. Unless I can introduce her smoothly into the friendship of those Reverend Doctors which I hardly hope I may (which nevertheless I mean patiently to try to do) rumors will spread about me as a heretic which will give me years of varied controversy. I may be before Presbytery *on that account*. And if there then before the Gen. Assembly, for tho' loyal to my church I would try her last appeals. Controversy would spread the ethical opinion & give it a chance to establish its truth. And after ten years of *endurance* for which you, my dear Sally, are helping to prepare me the opinions will word themselves up to a confessed agreement with the Conf. of Faith & to the point of an important addition to the tho't of the age. All this of course in entire reliance upon the kindness of God in continuing my life & in *causing* me to fulfill my expectations.

II. Or I marry you. Then you marry me with a rival already in my arms. I stay in Phila probably longer. I postpone my other wedding day possibly for years. If it is an ill-omened wedding & the marriage really a heresy you postpone it. You assault your rival & set your fingers upon her defects & scratch out her beauties & show where the whole is a fantasy & instead of getting me before Presbytery, you keep me from it. Or, as I am sure the mistress I worship is *perfect* you find it out, you conceive a high idea of bringing out her fair proportions, you are as impatient as I to get off in her pursuit. You are bridesmaid at her wedding & you share with me the "bother" & the joy of her affection.

It is true I ask you to exercise a most stupendous *faith*, as I have seen the lady but you have not, & I must confess that if we are ever on less terms of confidence than we are now I shall feel very much ashamed of my prophesies, but I do feel sure that I could introduce her to your acquaintance so that you would not be ashamed of my choice.

I cannot yet tell whether the church will be finished by the first of May, but if it is, your birth-day would hardly be a time when I could marry. Cant you still be earlier. Would it be a saucy question if I should ask which of your birth-days it is.

Yours very affectionately
Jno Miller

I enclose you your letter to let you see how I must have felt. Please return it.

[marginal note] Dr Sprague married his wife's sister & the Pres. never noticed it & it is now almost forgotten.[76]

76. William Buell Sprague (1795–1876), pastor of the Second Presbyterian Church in Albany, N.Y., from 1829 to 1876.

Monday [March 20, 1855]

You wicked, wicked Woman,

Quarrelling with you ever since the postman dropped your letter some hours ago, nevertheless I cant help admiring the *grace* with which you evade replying to an unrighteously indistinct inquiry.

Nevertheless, could you be in any doubt as to which letter my conscience would sanction if you would only consent to answer it.

The fact it is your conscience that I am urging, not my own in all this matter.

I write this just to *date* your reply earlier. I mean to write again. Your menise about my first greeting is about half true.

Yours very truly
Jno Miller.

Monday, March 20. 1855[77]

May God bless you abundantly my dear—John for all your steady and considerable & gentle kindness & affection. I find I cannot estimate it too highly, or rely upon it too confidently. It always meets fully the exactions of my exacting nature, & supplies richly the cravings of a heart that is always crying "give, give." I cannot thank you too much for it, tho' I am, at times constrained to think it a misfortune that you should have lavished it on me.

I was sadly troubled when I first wrote you a fortnight ago, and have been since; but if at the moment, out of strong feeling, I used inconsiderately a single strong word that gave you pain, I pray you forgive it, and never remember it again. I do not wilfully give you any uneasiness—on the contrary I think I often err thro' fear of giving it, & in the hope of avoiding it. If I weary you with my difficulties upon a subject, upon which you have none, it is because, under the circumstances, I think it indispensable to the comfort and happiness of both that these difficulties should be removed; and because too, if I am ever to confide in you *as* your wife, I should learn to do so before I become such. Then dont get *very tired* of me & my one subject, but make it easy for me to talk to you upon it first, by inviting me to do it again & then by leading the way: wont you do this?

I scratch off this tonight, but will write tomorrow, if I can. I am under Lilly's care somewhat, as on the sick list. I suffer acute pain & am circumscribed in my moving about. I think I might have been quite well to-day if I had not gone out to Church yesterday morning. But I hope in a few days to be well again. This thing of being a little sick is rather pleasant than otherwise. To be sure I have not the pleasure of going out, but then I look thro' the windows at the yard, just now beginning to look green, & then when the sun comes out throw up the window and welcome back the birds that are my pleasantest companions all the summer long. And then Lilly bustles about as my Housekeeper—rather

---

77. Monday was Mar. 19, 1855.

reluctantly sometimes, it must be confessed, & not always very efficiently, but in the main, quite well.

I received a letter from my old friend Dr Plumer in answer to one to him.[78] I wrote to him knowing (or believing) him to be acquainted with all the facts in the case. I send it to you. Finding Dr White unacquainted with any of the most important facts in the legal proceeding, I sent him some of the papers—his note in reply I enclose too.

Now tell me, have I overpowered you with my tediousness? Will you write one very soon, & assure me that I am something of a koh-i-noor still.

Yours
S.C.P. McDowell

I wont send the letters tonight as your envelope is too small for them. Will the Canby envelopes reach you safely?

1.[79]
Phil. Mar. 20th 1855.

My *"little mad" Darling*,

Yours of the 16th came just now, about 10 or 11 a.m. rattling about me like Kleber's musketry on Mt Carmel.[80] You cant tell what an exhilarating effect it had. And tho' you are the most unreasonable correspondent I care anything about (I hav'nt any other) & your anti-jentaculary feeling must be very different from your post-prandial,[81] yet you can hardly tell what an agreeable change from your recent melancholy communications.

As I am however to make myself the subject in this letter & you expect from me, what certainly is not a small thing to ask, that I should devote a page to what you are "half-alarmed", "half-worried" at as one of my worst faults, I want very naturally to get at that first, especially as it will require my very freshest & best considered tho't. Now I am not *forty*. That I entirely disclaim. And I am not *moody*, if I understand what that means. And I am not *peevish* except when I am *ill*, then Mary says I am perfectly frightful, but as she only saw me so once in a Dutch ague about five years ago, & as I never employ a Doctor & never go to bed or stay in the house even when I am *sallow* or ever so pale with any common sickness, I think this humanly speaking cant come up often enough to interfere with our usual happiness. I am not *morose*. On the contrary I am smiling & pleasant. I am not *sullen*. On the contrary anything that requires to be *kept*

78. William Swan Plumer (1802–1880), a Presbyterian minister in Richmond from 1834 to 1846, had strongly supported McDowell at the time of her divorce. In 1855 he was professor of theology at Western Theological Seminary and pastor of Central Church in Allegany, Pa.

79. Miller will explain the numbering of this letter in his letter of Mar. 27, 1855.

80. Jean-Baptiste Kleber (1753–1800), Napoléon Bonaparte's military commander in the Egyptian campaign. His army defeated the Turks at Mount Tabor, not Mount Carmel.

81. That is, before breakfast and after dinner.

up that I dont possess. I am not *spiteful* or *cross*. On the contrary I am *cool* and *satirical*. Therefore because of this last I am not *stormy*, I dont go off into those fine heats of high passion. Those grander & handsomer exhibitions of excited anger I fear I do not possess. I do not thunder away in a perfect fever passion like a lightning tempest after a clear sky.

But I am something that it will be hard to describe. I hav'nt left much room for myself have I?—I am ill-tempered in the sense of being hotly roused against any-thing I think wrongful or an insult. It is not the sharp flash of electricity but the slow-red heat of galvanism. It is not a thing that storms, but a thing that burns. And, therefore, it is not over in a moment, but keeps burning till the insult is out of sight. It cannot keep itself up, & therefore cools if it be allowed an interval, but it burns steadier than most men's high passions & therefore less spasmodically & with less high demonstrations of temper. It grows pale rather than red with provocation. And when I was a boy it sent me up into my room, or out into the garden paths in a perfect *fume* of indignation at something from father or mother that I tho't unreasonable. It is not troublesome therefore, because it takes itself away out of peoples sight. However it *recurs* again if the same thing recurs, & borrows there a quality which I have often told you [of] something very near bordering on obstinacy. It will not make you unhappy, & I am a little amused at being called to give account for it except in scolding—by the way I *scold* a little sometimes. I will give you an example.

"My darling, darling Sally, how could you treat me so? How could you say, "evade" when I have been so carefully frank in all our correspondence about this matter—*you didnt mean it?*—Yes, but you have explained what you mean, for you say, "You know you had a very different reason for making the remark at first." Now, what reason had I? Dear, dear Sally, aint you ashamed "to quarrel with me at this late day" &c (Curtain falls.)

Now let me go on with this explanation. What I meant by your "acting as my poor wife" was this. Ministers are precarious householders at best, for so dependent are they upon that one possession, health, for example, that they are liable at any moment to be placed in difficult straits. I, tho' not in such precarious circumstances as the generality of ministers, for I have heretofore commanded a better support, am however *more* precariously situated in some respects, for a great Providence of God, that I cannot yet entirely fathom, is this "presentiment" or this inclining of my judgment after years of patient toil in the pulpit to leave it & follow out the path of a great theologic problem the clue of which is already in my hand. This plan will seem Quixottic to many (not to all) till it is accomplished, & therefore I never speak of it, & if I tho't it fair, I would delight to keep it from you. So strong is my conscience for this plan, that if I were dying to night as I might be, I would be plunged into the deepest regrets & almost remorse, for having continued a pastor so long, & would spend my last hours in dictating tho'ts that I have now a great aversion to write without a more thorough leisure to assure myself of their certainty. I wish I could spend an hour or two in *talking* them over with you.

Now this intention of my life makes me curious in respect to you. If you had lived less handsomely, I would have no anxiety whatever. Or if I had not this passion, I would have none, for with the blessing of God I might hope to have one of the ablest churches in the city, & I have rejected posts within the year that would support us handsomely independent of health, that is even if health in the pulpit should fail. So almost in any exigency I am, were I willing to popularize myself, & give up my studious ideas of usefulness, well provided for. But what my perhaps ever cautious spirit was painting for me, was taking charge of you when I was conscious that I had a stronger passion & (within limits) a stronger sense of usefulness, when I was conscious that my pastoral cast & enthusiasm was slowly eaten away by a superior passion, when I was conscious that I had actually to hide my papers & theologizings to keep from being dangerously led away from the ardours of parochial energy, & if from health or any disaffected elder or any casualty now unforseen, but which a prudent man in so great a step as marriage would be thinking of, I should leave this one single charge, I should have at once the ardours of a sort of life-passion clamoring against any other.

Now if, in such an exigency, I felt perfectly able, by means of some congenial office, as for example the "supply" of some country parish (perfectly understood by the Presbytery to be only for a time) or some weekly lectureship in a college that would not like a full professorship take me off too much from my favorite pursuits, to secure for myself not a city maintenance but that of a country pastor, to fill the interval before I receive my patrimony, & still go on with my investigations, my hope was that you would "act as my *poor* wife", that is not be longing for Colalto with its superior luxuries & your ancient habits of Virginia plenty, but live in the plain way of a pastors wife at least for a time, which by the way is not so *very* plain after all, & which I would be the very first to abandon if (what I am sure however would not be the case) the de[te]ction of any flow in my theological reasonings led me to think them not the path of usefulness. You ask if after ten years &—I failed, then what would I do? Why go back of course to the Pastorate.

Now, my darling, you have drawn from me an explanation of this "sick-man's letter" which presents it in altogether an exaggerated light because it seems to say that it deserves this long letter. These exigencies will probably never occur. They are only the scrupulous cautions of a person's who does not *wish* to "evade" anything. I only mean to say that if they should, I *look with jealousy at Colalto*, & want you "to act as my poor wife" in sharing with me my hermitage as a poor scholar with the dignity of self-maintenance rather than in my sharing with you your palace with some few more temporary comforts. Now two words more. First, I think this was all *said* in that first letter. Do read them over & see if, long as this is, it has added one idea. And second, I wrote what you tho't an evasion on a bare spot in my letter just as I was shutting it up (at least I think I did, or was that something else?) & I wrote it just because I had read over your letter & found this unanswered & in the *starved* condition you keep my love in the two ideas (if they are so altogether two) got mingled together in my mind.

I feel so tired after all this. I wouldn't write it over again for anything. My dear darling you must take my letters *just* as you read them. I dash them off generally when yours come in & I mean *just* what I say & *no more*.

I'll tell you what I'll do about writing. I wont write on Monday, but better (?) than that I will write always by the very first mail after receiving any of yours & that will always be the same evening. I will write *on an average* longer letters than yours. Or, if you choose & will solemnly promise to answer *mine* the same day I will agree to that tho' then I will write every day. I *live* upon your letters. They are the only *worldly* pleasure I have. You must have felt amazed at my little short note after so long a silence. But the one since will have explained it. I usually write right after one from you.

And now, my darling Sally, I banish all unwillingness about your one subject. Poor child you do exaggerate it so. Write about it as much as you please however. Major Preston did as misjudged a thing when he expressed to you such an opinion as he ever did in his life. *I assure you this subject will never be breathed in Presbytery.* That I know *confidently* from my whole measure & knowledge of the body & circumstances. If you act upon this fear *you act* upon a perfect vagary. My sense of our whole danger in the circumstances has wonderfully diminished & never was great. I think the most show of danger is from Thomas' *pen*. But here we have several safe-guards. First, his having solicited your hand again. Second, the length of time & the hopelessness of any result. Third, the refusal of decent newspapers to publish & if you say, what certainty is there against a crazy person? then I say, Fourthly, *Pray*. God will shut the lion's mouth. The blessing of our fathers will come upon us. And if you will make the *silencing* of this madman a special subject of daily prayer God will protect us.

If he should attack us, which on common grounds I think he will not we are not without resource. Trust yourself to me. I have *now* not the slenderest fear & it will be a fine form of affection for you to give yourself up into my care.

Suppose I were to say to you that my own & my fathers fidelity in the church was a ground of confidence what would you think of that? Neither my character nor my fathers good-nature & family are things that Philadelphia Presbyterians would like to stain & as I think I have the reputation of high correctness in all these relations there is more than enough capital to draw on even in this particular direction. The whole church in America will wish to protect my father's son & so will they your father's daughter.

You say, why not wait for the disclosures of the future? I have always said you should decide all questions of time. Anything that involves merely *pain* I will agree to. For I am accustomed to that. But darling, unless you mean the far future we ought to be married now. I would rather meet your hobgoblins, if any are left after our marriage, this Spring than any other time. By the way I wholly forgot one thing. The foggy temper I spoke of is a totally different thing from all I have been describing above. It is low spirits. It is in no body's way that I ever heard of. I look so cheerful thro' it all that people laugh at me when I complain of it. It makes me sometimes silent & *indifferent* to things, but my sister Mary's grand complaint of me is (& she is right in it) that I laugh and play the fool so much. Aint you tired? Please send on my seal.

Yours affectionately,
JM.

Give my love to the Shanghais & greyhound. I will put on the mystic seal. I wish yours to be a jay bird picking up a moth miller—the meaning being Jay Miller, or just the "*Blue*" Jay & the letter M. underneath. Or as our family came out of the Ark, I would like you to quarter the arms of Jay Pheth-Pheth being the ancient word for grinder or conductor of a mill as he ground meal for Mrs. OVoak & the young Bacons.[82] Fix it as you please however. You might put me as tho' in the attitude of evading a direct question or guilty of some other blunder & yourself "a little cruel" with the motto, This seals the thing.

Phil. Mar. 21st [1855]

My dearest Sally,

You seem to me more & more like a very wicked woman, but yet for the love I bear you, you bewitch me all the more you do me injury. I turn round in my chair to write to you with a sort of proclivity that I can hardly explain of which you do not deserve to be the object. You are a *very* wicked woman.

But I will forgive you entirely if you will write me a letter confined to the single subject of telling me exactly how you feel about me. If it is at all favorable I promise to return it by the next mail so that it will be as tho' it had never been. I am starving for a little *notice*.

Now I dont mean what you think of me as to character. I'd rather you wouldn't tell me that for I would have to get out 4 of those big white sheets to correct & explain where you flattered me too much or else you would say I had evaded an honest confession. But I mean how much do you love me? *Do* tell me. I dont think since Adam there was ever so unfair a courtship as ours. (By the way you're a pretty woman to ask, Is anything fair? I'd like to know what fair thing you have done since I have been out on this long "trial.") And in his case it was all one-sided, for the very work of getting a wife at that early day, to have him or any one else was all *in his side*. If you will write me an extra telling me just how much you love me, I will forget it as soon afterwards as I can. *Do* write me one. By the way I wish that dam you speak of would break. Cant you get up some sort of a freshet to throw it down just for once. By the way I dont believe there is any. Alas! Alas! What trouble I have got into. You will want to know in your very next letter what it was I cut out here[83] & if I dont tell then you'll say I wished to "evade" the truth & yet I have to go to an engagement presently. What *shall*

---

82. That is, Noah's son, Ham.
83. Miller cut off the bottom of a page after he had written it.

I do? Shall I throw the *extra* away? Oh, I want you too much to answer it.—My wicked brother Spence is always telling me stories & sometimes he tells me one that I dont think a preacher or a lady ought either to hear or to repeat especially in con[nection] with a subject about which I feel so much as this. But I *could* not help thinking & suddenly writing what he told me of in his office the other day of a stream in Jersey that was so very little (like your love as I feared) that when they talked of putting a dam across it, it was pronounced not worth—one. I wish you'd get Spence to quit telling me *all* the stories he hears.

The Gothic Library is not burned down.

Let us begin to write every day. Shant we?

Yours
Jno Miller.

Wednesday, March 22–55[84]

I am dispatching a letter on business, & while my pen is in hand use it to write a line to you.

Altho' fancying myself scarcely well enough yesterday to leave my own room for my usual range thro' the house I was yet occupied all the day; and feeling much better as the evening drew on, did the incautious thing of riding over last night to our weekly lecture, and am in consequence, not so very well this morning. I shall not write more than this note to you until tomorrow; and I write this not that I have anything special to say, but simply because I am sure even the most meager note will not be unwelcome to you now that we are both anxious enough both as to the present and the future.

Now you write me and say that you *will not hereafter*, however you may have felt heretofore, be tired, even "ever so little" of me & my great trouble. Then in return, for that assurance, I will promise (& there is no generosity in it either) that you may batter your Philosophy into my brain every day in the year, if you like, and I shall all the time look as smiling as a May morning.

Affectionately
S.C.P. McDowell

Phil. Thursday 22nd

Darling Sally,
    Put your ear close—
—Oh, a great deal nearer—
—*I am so tired.*
    A lady in an old dominion had a harp which she found in her palace one morning, & which she had never seen there before. She took it up & touched

84. Wednesday was Mar. 21, 1855.

its four old strings with such exquisite gentleness that the harp itself became enamoured of the melody, & begged the lady to keep it in her palace & to let no hand ever touch it but hers.

This fancy of the poor old harp seemed to waken half the merriment, half the anger of the lady, & she coldly rejected it; but the harp, as she threw it away, sighed out so sadly upon her ear its forlorn complaint, that she took it up again with a half curious pity, & tho' she hangs it out upon the willows at her door & leaves it there to sigh in the cold winds nights & days, yet, always since, she has played upon it with a sort of disguised affection, till the poor old harp thinks that she will one day set it at her feet, & keep it as the instrument of her favorite melodies.

But alas! for the mutability of the fondest hopes, the night air as it moaned thro' the willows, & even the soft touches of the gentle harper (especially as she *will* always be harping upon *one* string) have been sighing the poor old harp to rest. The melancholy music is breaking the heart of this good old servant of the palace. And when this gentle lady shall send out into the cold night to bring it in & play on it more cheerful melodies, she will find that it is too late for her compassion, & that there is no home for her poor victim but the grave.

Yours,
Jno Miller.

2 o clock.

O *dear,*

I am so tired. Sally, when *will* you say, Amen. As my poor little niece asked one day in church very much to the discomfiture of her poor grandmother. When matters are like Joe in Bleak House "a movin' on" it dont seem so hard, but my dear *dear* darling we dont now seem to be making any progress at all.

I wish I had the reins for about two weeks; We would travel like Apollo.

I tried so hard to be "clever" in your Virginia sense, that I swore a little & talked a great deal too lightly of your affection in my last letter. And I'm now so much afraid you'll scold me when you write again. Dear Sally, you'll kill me altogether. I wont be worth even hanging on the willows. If you starve me so in your affection & scold me so in your fidelity—why—some morning I'll go and hang *myself*.

I have really written up my part of the correspondence so thoroughly that I have nothing to write but nonsense. May'nt I come on the Monday following the day I first proposed! May'nt we be married Thursday the 12th?

If you do keep me agitated so for weeks & weeks & weeks & weeks—why, all our difficulties & questions will have settled down to one, Whether it will be best to bury me before or after our wedding.

Yours rebelliously & abusively
La Harpe.

Your ink doesnt blot as much. The blot now is upon your kindness of heart.

Phil. Mar. 23rd 1855.

My *dear Sally,*

Your little note came yesterday. Oh, how sweet that sounds,—"My dear John," but then, Sally, it will be the sheerest affectation if you ever go back to the old beginnings. So you'll have to keep it up "Heigho! I'm so glad!"

Now you want me to make it easy for you to get back to the old subject. Well, dear Sally, I have been expecting a long letter from you on it for two weeks. I feel quite envious now that you should write to me all your difficulties. Only dont let it delay our wishes if you are satisfied in other ways. What does my prudish young wife mean by the greatest difficulty of all that "you cant even speak of."? Are you still troubling yourself about Maggie & Allie? or perhaps our grand-children? or perhaps the repute of our house some two centuries hence? I think if *we* can hear all that your fertile imagination has conjured up, those who stand more distant from the scene of trial or come later upon it will be able to endure it. But perhaps you are brooding over some great crime that you have committed the revelation of which you are afraid to make till after our marriage. Now, Sally, by all the trouble it has cost me to draw this[85] I conjure you to tell me. Did you ever murder anybody? Did you ever half murder any poor minister? Did you ever weary out the best months of his life by deferred hopes & by promises that you would write *"fully"* the next week & then writing uncommonly the other way? Is there any crime upon your young heart. Remember you must write clearing yourself or I shall think you have "evaded" the question.

Did you ever shake the understanding of some poor victim & weaken his wits so as to lead him to write whole sheets of nonsense? If you have I dont wonder at the difficulties you have upon your conscience.

But, Sally, what do you mean by being sick again. Do you know, it nearly crazes me. It leads me to run over a hundred things & connect them all together. Why were you so tired in Washington? Why did you walk so slowly? Why did you stop to rest at the stairs of the church? Why when I was expecting you to trip up lightly the stair of the Daguerreotype Gallery did I look back & find you yet at the bottom? Why were you going to the Springs for your health last summer? And why have you been sick two, three, four times since? Oh, I do *shudder* so at such things. If I could know that ten or twelve or even twenty years hence after I had treasured in you all my affection & happiness you would begin to droop & wither under my eye I think nothing earthly could induce me to marry you. And the more I loved you the more I should tremble at the very thought.

But how I do run on!

Sally tell me. Are you sick? And when I have wilfully thought of you & dreamed of you & longed after you & had your image pictured in my very soul, am I to have months & years & *years* of the agony of seeing you fade away out of my eyes.

---

85. At this point Miller drew a large skull and crossbones.

Now tell me when you write. *Do* you get so easily tired? And why do you get so easily tired? And have you any cough? And what persecuting sickness is this that haunts me every day? Dont leave one thing unsaid that will reassure me & tell me distinctly that there are casual indispositions & that you are in the very most perfect health in every respect that I can possibly imagine.

Reply at once for you know I may have no other chance to write much before I go on to be married. Will I? Dr. P[lumer]'s letter &c has not yet come. I do write very foolish letters but I think we have got past the point of quarreling with each other. Havnt we?

Yours affectionately,
Jno Miller.

Please write everyday. I have kept my letter open till I could see the carrier. I have yours of Wednesday, but not Dr. P's. I agree & promise but on the express condition you mention. You dont know how much you have promised but I shall remember all our lives.

Colalto,
Friday, March 23.'55

I demand your congratulations upon the opening of a new bottle of ink. I was so horrified at the appearance of the letter you enclosed me a day or two since, that I made an effort to protect you against such in the future. You would laugh at any writing apparatus, so very plain and quaint it is—and yet I have a fondness for certain parts of it that gives a sort of beauty to the whole. I have often written to you upon & from the very same Secratary at which years ago, when I was a child I have often seen my Grandfather stand & write.[86] Afterwards it became my Fathers; and now for several years, the curious looking old bit of mahogony, with its grim lion heads of brass upon it, is mine. I dip my pen in the same cistern of an inkstand, as it seems to my modern eyes, that served two generations before me, and feel for it a very singular veneration & regard. It is often a trouble to me. I dare not leave it on my table lest some accident should occur. One niche in this old relic, has been emptied of the yellow-tinted papers, that were associated in my mind with my stern & stately old Grandfather of whom we all stood in great fear; and of the more familiar packages with some such labels as these—"Notes for a speech upon the right of Instruction"—"jottings upon the Tariff"—"remarks upon Abolition"—["]Boundary Question"—"Bible Society address" etc etc in the well known writing of my own Father, for your accommodation. There your letters repose, and look as if they felt quite entitled to the honor of such an abode. But they are multiplying so rapidly I shall have to employ another "pigeon-hole" for them. Some day or other I shall let you take a peep at them and then you shall tell me whether you think they have been well cared for.

86. James McDowell II (1770–1835).

An odd little scrap dropped from your letter of the 19th as I opened it having these words upon it—"number your letters in the corner." I can not tell what it means. You must enlighten me. Tho' the words seem very simple they are almost meaningless to me. You told me some queer things in that letter. You make it a matter of conscience always to say something that is pleasant & at the same time to keep within bounds of reason and truth. But sometimes I have *great doubts* about some of your assertions. Thus, when you make such special pains *always* to tell me "you love philosophy better than me," I take just as great pains never to believe a word of it. I would scarcely be a true woman if I did. But yet I dont care very much if you do, if you will just deny yourself the pleasure of telling me. I am entirely satisfied with the warmth and earnestness of your wooing. Seriously, you love me a great deal more that I deserve, tho' not a bit more than I desire. I would not have my *deserts* in this particular, and am not too conscientious to accept all because it is more than my due. I never thought you gave me good reasons for loving me, but as they were only the "(a) (b) (c)" of the matter, I shall probably have developed in its progress more satisfactory ones. Oh, but I forgot, what I set out with—that queer thing you so gravely told me, of my being a kind of safeguard to you in temp[ta]tion. I am as much amazed as if you had said that horrid Daguerre you have was an Amulet. How can I have been of the least help to you, since that famous time that you performed the exploit of dovetailing my letter into your sermon. I wish I could have heard it! How very curiously you must have felt speaking it out Sunday morning for a sermon.[87]

Upon the whole I am satisfied with your Daguerreotype of temper. It is not so *bad* as I feared; but I was scared when I heard you were *satirical.* It seemed unfortunate that this point of resemblance between us should exist. My Father bequeathed me a good share of it; and *it* with a keen sense of the ludicrous & a quick, hot temper, often thrusts a weapon in my hand that is neither dull nor harmless. At least so people say, & so I believe when I sorrow over the pain I have inflicted. It is my misfortune to do as Shakespeare makes his Coward do— "wear a dagger in his *tongue.*"[88] But I am not called upon, (I'm glad you were so prudent) to say anything about *my* temper. Tho' I might & yet not have the revelation result to me as a similar one did, long ago to our friend Dr. Plumer. Long ago, when a student here, he fell in love with a lady much older than himself, & by & bye they became engaged. After a while, the story turns, they agreed to confess to each other their faults, the Doctor of course, to lead the way. This he did very honestly: but unfortunately, honesty, in his case, was not the best policy, for the Lady when called upon to fulfil her part of the contract said, "Well, Sir, if you are such a man as you have just said you are I can have nothing more to do with you." Thereupon they parted. The gentleman all the

87. This episode is not mentioned in the correspondence. Miller must have told McDowell of it when they met in Washington in Jan. 1855.
88. *Cymbeline* 4.2.78.

better in after life for his youthful disappointment; whilst the lady has become the most forlorn looking of hopeless old maids with a physiognomy that would have delighted an Assyrian Sculptor ages ago, and have astonished any modern race of mortal men.

As I am upon this subject of temper, I will just say I'm afraid I shall have to side with your Sister & complain that you are not quite staid enough. In one of your letters you say "if my fogginess of temper were not so *cronic*" &c;—looking over it hastily I read the word—not cronic, but *comic*. From your late account of yourself I am disposed to think my reading was admirably descriptive.

It must have been in a fit of this comic fogginess that you told us last summer of the incident that led to your visit to Lexington. I remember the whole thing perfectly,—have laughed over it a hundred times and every little while hear Cantey repeat it with exact mimicry of your manner and tone. You were telling it one morning as I came into the room, & repeated it for my benefit. "Said I to my sister, Mary, I shall go tomorrow to Lexington. Said she to me, John, I think you had better go: you were playing nine-pins last night and there is no knowing what you will do next." I have often laughed to think *what you did do next;* & how the grave lady will be shocked to hear of the misdemeanor in which her advice resulted. I stand in great awe of her Serene Highness, and am afraid she is not at all predisposed to like me. How am I to charm her?

I cant make any promise to answer your letters regularly; but I will write just as often and just as much as I can. You can have some idea of the difficulty of writing, when I tell you it is sometimes no easy matter to get your letters read. Sometimes I read a sheet, & (as the turning and laying aside of sheet after sheet attracts notice) then put all back in the envelope (which is commonly too small,) and thrust that into my pocket until I can find an unobserved moment & place to read it in. This is a great worry, but can hardly be helped. My room happens to be, as it is in the wing, the most acceptable & most cheerful one in the house, and of late Cantey frequently spends the whole day in it. Mary too finds it an asylum often during the afternoon. Lilly bustles about in it after school hours; even my cousin, the Doctor, prefers coming to it for the chance of a long talk upon family and farming matters, and sometimes the boys pay me a visit; and thus you see I am subject to constant interruption, and, if I am writing, annoyance. Tonight, fancying myself de trop[89] with a pair of lovers in the Library, I seized an auspicious moment and escaped to my writing-table, and have written as well as I could with Cantey & Lilly laughing & talking in a most contagious glee around me.

Your show of seals, quite Mystic enough for any occasion, and any taste, has lost you the one I promised. Why add to such a number? I shall think of something else. I wont have any bird on my seal—'neither jay birds nor parrots, Take care, another such attempt at punning will give you miliary fever again.

---

89. French, meaning in the way.

You must not think Cousin John's notion so absurd. Dr White admitted there was ground for apprehension and said emphatically, "I wish the gentleman was not a preacher."

How came you to the knowledge of the matters that came before *the* Committee? Are you entirely sure of what you say? I am too tired to write more. I am ashamed of the pages already written. Have no fears about the conduct of your *poor* wife. I dont think she will be troublesome. If she is, you must reason her to her senses. What do you mean by the "far-future"? You say, "tell me how much you love me." I answer—Oh, *I couldnt tell how much!* Are you satisfied? But good night—I am as crazy as Gazelle (the greyhound) from sleepiness. She is an ungrateful thing not to return a message to you, but I couldn't get a word out of her. I wish Allie had her. You wont ever go farther North to live than Pennsyla, will you?

Affectionately
S.C.P. McDowell

Sat. 2 o'clock [March 24, 1855]

Dear Sally,

This is the "Rain of Letters." I think you like to get a great many, but I dont think you will entirely relish their appearing so often in your P.O. as there is no such objection in my case let me beg you to write every day. Next week I may not be able.

"Will you write me very soon & assure me that I am something of a Koh-i-noor still?["]
I think I could almost write a sermon in this text. I would divide it somehow in this way.

I. *In what respects the beloved disciple was a genuine Koh-i-noor.*
1. In her beauty.
2. in her large size. (which I like by the way seriously)
3. In her brilliancy.
4. In her intrinsic value.
5. In her being so hard to get possession of: and
6. In her not being set or fixed in any one frame.
II. *How the beloved disciple modestly wished to be reassured that she was a Koh-i-noor though she knew it all the time.* and
III. *How modestly this wish was confessed.* Will you write me very soon & assure me that I am *something* of a Koh-i-noor still?

Which leads me to make the following application. Dear Sally, dont we love each other enough to make it certain that this thing *can* end only in one way? And therefore would it not answer to hasten your deliberations just by that feeling. I know this thing *can* end only in one way & therefore it should end now. So far as your own love of honor is concerned (if your conscience were satisfied) would you not submit to a little loss of honor—would you not endure a little obloquy for my sake? Tell me whether you would when you write.

I have said you need not prepare me if you see fit to cast me off. So will you not promise that you will not delay out of any awkward feeling of overcoming your difficulties too suddenly if you *do* overcome them suddenly.

Yours affectionately
JM

[Interlined note] Write me very long letters. I am getting ready for Thursday the 12th.

Monday, March 26. 1855.

My *dear John,*

How you can trouble yourself about nothing! I am quite well now; and tho' sometimes sick, & occasionally for the very nataral reason of over-exertion, tired, yet, upon the whole, I know of no one who is in more robust health than I am. How could I have been otherwise than tired in Washington? Had I not been walking for days before you came on? I, who had not for weeks walked half a mile a day, *must* soon break down under the city walks of several miles at a time.

No, I have no *cough*, & no tendency so far as I know, to that kind of ill health. Any uncommon degree of emotion, will produce, for a time, labored & uncomfortable respiration,—but the breathing apparatus is, I believe perfectly good, not withstanding. I spoke of going to the Springs last summer to prevent a return of the Erisypelas, that I had suffered from the preceding season at Newport & of which I had great dread. I have twice had it in my hands,—once years ago in Richd, when it was epidemic there; & again in Newport, (the result of sea-bathing) & I feared lest it should become *fixed* upon me. I did not go to the Springs, however, & entirely escaped my old enemy. Nevertheless I am careful or ought to be, not to let the Sun shine too hotly upon me in the summer. The greatest inconvenience I have experienced from erisypelas has been that of being handless for a few days, and looking a fright for a week or more, just at a time when I wanted to look my very best. Dr Leyburn can tell you what a beauty I was under its power. Well then, to go on with this most interesting bulleten of health—I do sometimes have Neuralgia; and have once in the last 8 or 10 months actually cried myself to sleep, like a child, from the pain it gave. Then I once in a while have a sort of sick headache—but isn't this quite enough? I really feel ashamed to be thus holding out my hand to you that you may feel my pulse. When, my Merry Cousin, the Doctor, comes to see me, we soon get into such an uproarious fit of mirth that you would never dream there was anything the matter and indeed there seldom is anything of consequence.[90]

90. Erysipelas is an infectious skin disease caused by bacteria. It results in fever and skin lesions. The cousin she refers to is James McDowell Taylor.

You mistake, we *dont* think it "clever" in Virginia *to swear*—we think it very bad manners to say the least of it, & not at all *smart*. Spence is a pretty fellow to tell you such a story—and *you* are a worse one for enjoying it so much and telling it over to me. Pray what do you mean by swearing *at* my affection *now*, when for, oh, ever so long, you have been complaining that there was none in existence—not even enough for you to *swear by*. But if you will repeat Spence's stories, and apply them to me, I shall just defend myself with your own weapon. I quite enjoyed your *Harp* story the other day, until I had thrust back into my memory an anecdote of my friend Hilliard of Alabama, which a good deal marred my pleasure in your plaintive melody.[91]

I'll tell it to you as a set-off to yours. When crossing the ocean after his Charge-ship was over in Belgium, he met with a young Irishman full of wrath against O'Connell, and venting his anger in very amusing ways;—one of these, curiously enough was conundrums, & one of them was this:—"Why is O'Connell like a *broken harp?*" I'm sure you cant guess, and couldn't if I were to give you as many guesses as Madame de Sevigne in that famous letter of hers that is good for nothing that ever I heard of except for this reference, gave her daughter.[92] Now dont be too much shocked—"because he's a——*blasted Lyre!*"

Your harp isn't as bad as this quite—but it tells a wee bit of a fib, that may I suppose, after all be excused upon the ground of its being a poetic license. Take care, however, & dont have too many of these.

My one subject has not passed out of my mind tho' it has passed from my pen of late. I shall revive it by and bye.

No. I have no murder to confess. I never "poisoned the Queen of Sheba," nor half-killed any "poor Minister" nor upset his wits, nor stole from him the best months of his life—nor told him any injury that I have ever heard of. On the contrary, he tells me sometimes that I have done him some positive good, and he is very anxious to lure me away from my own home & friends that I may take charge of him, and submit to his vagaries & whims, and listen to his philosophizings and live, away off in the North where I shall most probably take a *cough*, and cough myself to death; and where nobody wants me but him, and every body will look cold at me, and I shall feel so very scared & so very, very troubled, and will have nobody to comfort me but him, (and *he*, even now, doesn't like me to tell *him* my troubles;) and nobody to open their heart to me that I may creep in and get warm, and find a home and a welcome. Dont you think mine a hard case? I think it right hard at times, but then there is a something that throws a light over the future in spite of every-thing, which tho' it does not make it very bright, *does* give it *some* attractions, and this thing is not *hope* only, but let me whisper it, for I'm frightened at my temerity it is also—no, I cant say it yet.

91. Henry Washington Hilliard (1808–1892), U.S. congressman.
92. Daniel O'Connell (1775–1847), Irish nationalist. Marie de Rabutin-Chantal, marquise de Sevigne (1626–1696). Her letters to her daughter, Françoise Marguerite de Sevigne, comtesse de Grignan (1646–1705), were published in Paris by 1754.

I am obliged to say the 12th will not do. I could not make the necessary arrangements, or as you say, "get ready" by that time. I am fully persuaded we are not banished for so many hours together from the Library for nothing, but that Mary means it shall result in her accepting a Parsonage in Eastern Virginia.[93] If so, I shall be plunged in new difficulties about Lilly especially. I have thought of asking Aunt Eliza to come down and take the house & children (Cantey & Lilly) until midsummer. But I don't know whether that plan could be carried out. It would lessen the anxiety I should feel about everything connected with a long *visit* to you very greatly, and promises more comfort to all concerned than any yet suggested; but I think it impracticable. Dont fix your heart upon *any* day. When I find the way clear I shall write you & then together we can decide upon the time. Now please dont write & scold me. I do the best I can. I cant just jump up & run off, having nothing to do, but to consult a fashion-plate & order a bonnet, but I must provide for a household; and that cannot be done in a minute. So keep in a good humour & be very reasonable.—An injunction never less needed than in your case.

The few bright, warm days we have had, have brought out the early Spring flowers—I gathered a few violets yesterday that had peeped up thro' the hard ground, with the thought of sending them to you. They are very sweet now, but will be withered & dead when you get them. Yet if you will press them gently & warm them in your hand, they may have enough fragrance left to bear to you a pleasant message of pleasant thoughts.

And now, my dear John, (What shall I come to next?) good night.

Yours
S.C.P. McDowell

Upon second thought, it seems useless to send Dr P's letter.

Monday, Mar 26 [1855]

My *dear Sally,*

Let me say one or two true & very important things:

First, when you dont write to me for some days or when I specially expect a letter I *suffer* & am *dissipated* so much that I cannot attend well to my duty. I really lose hours & *days* sometimes for my parish. I love you so tenderly that with my impatient passions it costs me more pain & loss than you would willingly inflict. I walked three miles yesterday (Sunday) considering it a work of mercy to arrest this feeling & make myself more quiet; & when I reached the Exchange & found no letter I was really alarmed. I thought you were sick. To-day I have none, & probably shall have none this evening. Darling Sally, for my comfortable & cool relaxation of mind, *do* write everyday or at least every other day, if that is

93. McDowell's sister Mary Breckinridge McDowell was engaged to John B. Ross (1813–1871), a Presbyterian clergyman.

impossible. I have written every day for the last 8 except Sunday. And I mean hereafter to begin the rule of writing in reply (the same day) to each letter I receive from you.

Second, if (by any good Providence to me) you should write accepting me & agreeing to a day of our marriage, it ought to be *irrevocable* because I shall at once for various reasons connected with your comfort communicate the fact to various persons, & you see at once that any change afterward would make this very unnecessary & imprudent.

Thirdly, I do love you so much. I'm afraid you dont know what an important fact *that* is. I fairly idolize you, tho' that I know is wicked. As the *decision* is with you I do beg you to be diligent in the work of deliberation. If you mean to reject me I would rather not love you any more that I do. And if you mean to accept me, Oh, how we are lavishing that costliest of all earthly expenditures—*pain & agitation.*

Fourth, kiss our dear little Lilly for me.

Suppose in Washington the night we parted I had kissed you for Goodbye, what would you have done? How would you have felt? Would you ever have forgiven me? You see my heads of discourse grow more important as I advance.

Suppose I were to do as you have half invited me, go right on to Lexington & seize upon you in a sort of guerilla sally. Would you send me home again or would my Sally reward me with success?

Do you know I have *high hopes,* partly from the very delay of which I have been complaining, that your letter to-morrow will tell me of the coming of your brother, of your long & favorable talk with him, of your final purpose, of your actual appointment of a day & of that day being very near. I shall really be *disappointed* if your letter does not contain all this. I have a sort of "presentiment" that it will. I beg you will never be so rash as to show any part of these hurried scrawls to anybody.

Yours affely
Jno Miller.

Phil. Mar. 27th 55.

My *dear* Sally,[94]

I received you letter last evening, but not Dr P's or Dr W's.

Yours was a very nice letter but had a *great many* "queer" things in it. I ask you, Could'nt you just tell me how much you love me? You answer, "*No, I couldnt.*" And then want to know whether I am satisfied!

I *have* tho't of living a little farther North. I have borne a *cool* climate so well this Winter that I have tho't I would try Greenland. I don't think it would be much change for the worse.

---

94. At the top of this page in the left corner, Miller wrote a large roman numeral "I."

But, Sally, where's my letter? You're like Orcus; nothing ever comes back from you.[95] Do send me back the letter; & seriously, let me have those I returned before. Wont you send me ever so little a stray ringlet of your hair? I'll send you nearly all of Allie's if you will & thank you very much besides.

As to the little slip that fell out of one of my envelopes I am really very much afraid that you are—I scarcely know how to express it—just a little—just ever so little—what the Germans would call—a little *Tumm*.[96] If people have been losing letters & the proposal is made to number them in the corner what more natural than to mark them 1, 2, 3, afterward in the order in which they are sent so that a lost one might be missed as I have done in this letter & did in the next one after that from which the slip dropped out. Dear Sally, if you were not so bright I should think you were just ever so little stupid. How do you know, by the way, that some of our letters have not gone to the dead office?

As you are "entirely satisfied with my wooing" I have thought what I would be doing next. I have tho't of politics & controversial theology. How would you like it if I wrote a few letters next on the "Charity & the Clergy question."

I am going to be shrewder than you about *temper*. If I were to ask you for a confession & you gave it, then if I ever complained afterward of your violence you would tell me that you had warned me thoroughly before; now you cant do that, & I have a right to expect that you will be as bland & temperate as a summer morning.

Poor Dr Plumer! But he was better off than I in some respects for his troubles were all on him at a blow.

Aint you ashamed to pick out my bad spelling & tell me of it in as much as two letters. Besides, you know that my bad spelling is not *cronic* but only *sporadic*. Who has a right to say how things shall be spelled if men of my profession havnt.

So you think Mary would have preferred the nine pins if she had know the game I would have been at next.

Your Cousin John's notion *is* absurd. And if Dr White has any such it is entirely for his latitude & not for this. It is as possible that the heavens should fall as that this thing should come before *my* Presbytery. If any member in any strange moment of folly should lisp a word about it I would myself use & rebuke him as not having (as the Book enjoins)[97] a private interview with me & if he had a private interview with me he could'nt go farther for I could give him the distinct Scriptural grounds for my behavior.

Besides I know my Presbytery better. And if you will allow me to add without the imputation of arrogance, they know me better.

Now I must tell you a great secret. I have left the *profoundest silence* in all our matter except with S. & Mother & one other person. Months ago Dr Leyburn

95. Orcus was another name for Pluto, god of the underworld.
96. The German word in *dumm*, meaning stupid.
97. A reference to Matt. 18:15–17, concerning fraternal correction.

mentioned soon after his return from Lexington, when we were talking of the scenes over which we had just travelled, that he had met a Mr. Swinney of Wheeling in the Stage who was speaking of your case before the Legislature.[98] He told him that he was a member of the Committee to whom it was entrusted & that evidence was bro't before them criminating the other party in *the very deepest way*, evidence he said that satisfied him past all shadow of a doubt, that convicted the subject of it with details of the most horrible infamy & left them nothing to do, but to lead the Legislature as far as they could without public exposures to a vote of the unanimous sort that was obtained.

Dr Leyburn did'nt fancy that I was much interested & dropped the matter sooner than he otherwise would.

A few weeks ago under your uneasy anxieties I tho't I would know all more certainly, & yet I dared not approach L. lest he should suspect some special interest & speak of it. I, therefore, determined to break a great law of mine & make a confidant of him. I did so & in the most emphatic way he promised me that he would keep my secret even from his wife. My revelations were very scanty, enough to show that it was not *I* that felt anxiety about such a matter, & I obtained from him these facts. 1st that he could not be mistaken as to Swinney's statement—that it was evidence not in the street but before the Committee. 2nd that it was gross and palpable. 3rd that it was what influenced the Com. & thro' them the Legis: Dr Leyburn, by the way, holds to the morality of another marriage. My reason for not telling you all this before was that I was thinking of having Dr L. write to Swinney & in a careless manner as tho' the subject had recurred in conversations get under his own hand a reaffirmation of the whole thing. Then I would tell you. What think you of it? Can it be had thro' Mr Lyons better? It ought not to be sought for *after* our marriage?

Did I do very wrong in trusting Dr L.

Seriously, I think we shall live at Princeton, not farther North. Shant we? Phila first, & then Princeton. I hear nothing nowadays of my elder or disaffection. I must try & keep it out of sight.

I think this is all that is in your letter.

And now, my dear Sally, come here & put your arm round my neck & tell me how much you love me. You know it is too late for either you or me ever to think of abandoning the other & why not tell me how much you love me. You *do* keep me from temptation; for I am trying all the time to be worthy of you. You have no conception how I *respect* & admire you. I love you for traits of kindness & goodness & *thoroughness of character* which you are rash in wishing to know of for I have told you already enough to ruin you. Darling Sally, wont you treat me a little better than you do. I shall write hereafter the days I receive a letter!

Yours
JM

98. Thomas Sweeney of Wheeling, Va.

I never could understand why you would not *engage* yourself to me even if we could not immediately be married. Please tell me.

[marginal note] I meant by the 'far future' years hence—an infinite time. I tho't that unless we meant leisurely to wait for the disclosures of the distant future we ought to be married now. Dont you think so?

Wednesday, March 28. [1855]

My dear John,

I think you had better change places with me for a time that you may learn all my difficulties in the way of writing. You would be more grateful for my letters, and more lenient to all their faults. You would believe then that I *cannot* write whenever I would, but must wait, sometimes for days to find a time & a place in which to do it.

Your letter of the 26. came to day quite as fresh and nice as a new batch of—baker's bread!

Never fear. When I do write my "final purpose" it will be irrevocable. That it may be so is the great reason for all this delay. When you get the announcement you may make your arrangements as quickly and quietly as possible, for in few days after I shall be ready to take my seat by your side, in that little Sanctum which has figured conspicuously in our correspondence, & in which, if the night be such as to night, we shall need your "only comfort," a good hickory fire. But, remember, if I *do go* to Phil: this Spring it will only be on a visit: you will send me home during the summer?

You give a sorry account of your impatience. I dont know what to do with you to make you attend to your duties?

I delivered your message to Lilly and she said "Tell B, Sister, that *I* think him a very impudent fellow to talk so to me, when I dont even know *his name*! Does he know how *big I am*? But, as you say he plays upon a "broken *Harp*," just tell him that some day, I will mend his harp for him" etc.

Well, I'm something of Lilly's notion. What would I have done at more tender leave-taking in Washington? I should have been as mad as possible at the bare suggestion, and would not have forgiven you very soon. But, of course you did not think of such a thing then. Even the *mute* lady in the picture would *look* shocked if she suspected you would treat her so very affectionately.

Did I ever answer your question about the 30th of April? If not, I say guess how old it will make me. Make a good, *honest*, unromantic, jump at the truth, and then I shall tell you.

I expect every day to hear that my Brother is either in Phil'a or Washington. He always journeys slowly.

Tell me in good earnest, will your Church business make it entirely out of the question for you to leave Phil any time during the month of May? *If the thing is to happen,* somewhere about the middle of May would suit me better than any other. The Episcopal Convention meets here about the 23rd of May, I think, & I would gladly escape its *hospitable troubles*. After James comes, however, I shall be better able to write.

Tell me, will you, for I have often felt curious to know, what did you think of me & my conduct to you when you returned here with your Sister last Summer? Did I seem to you crazy, or just very foolish? One other thing—What did you mean when you said to me in Washington very peculiarly—"They say Mr. Lacy goes over to Colalto to see your Sister Mary." I ask, because I thought my manner of replying was such as to convey to you a different meaning from the one I intended.

Just look at my letter! Did you ever see such a looking sheet.[99] One would think my pen had had several epileptic fits, as it was forced along.

Affectionately
S.C.P McDowell

Mar. 30th [1855]

My dear Sally,

Your letter came to me to-day, & for some cause I know not entirely why made me very happy. It dont say much or promise anything but it spoke to me kindly & I have been so long sitting like patience on a monument that the smallest forms are thankfully received.

"My dear John" sounds so sweetly. I spend some minutes looking at that.

Your account of your health instead of being tedious gave me infinite pleasure. Do take care of it.

I have been thinking what I could send back to Lilly for the violets & have thought that she would like my hair to put in a locket. I send it.

Poor Sally, you do indeed paint a sea of trouble. Then all that is better than that I shall set to the account of my being such a good husband.

The church I think is *unlikely* to be done by the 1st Sab. in May.

So you swear too. Poor old Harp; so you abuse him as well as treat him badly. Well you'll find him buried yet in the tall grass. Requiescat in pace.[100] You'll have to put this epitaph over him.

Hic Jacet[101]
A Precious Old Harpy.

I write in great haste; or I would write more. Do write often & more & send for me to be

Your dear Husband,
Jno Miller.

99. McDowell scratched out several words and wrote over others.
100. Latin, meaning "May he rest in peace."
101. Latin, meaning "Here Lies."

Saturday March 31. [1855]

Dear John,

I scratch a line to you in great haste. I couldnt write last night I was so tired, and this morning the mail closes before our breakfast is *well over.*

What did Dr Leyburn say & how did he look when you unbosomed yourself to him. He, of course wouldnt tell *you* he thought *me* crazy but didnt he look very compassionating, as if he thought "poor fellow you're getting into trouble now." And as to *me,* no doubt he was as much surprised to hear such a piece of news of me, as he would have been to have heard there was a marriage in contemplation between Transe House Mountain and one of your Nevisink hills.[102] Do daguerreotype the scene for me. I think it would be well for him to get Swinney to inform him more accurately and carefully on the subject. My friend, Mr Lyons would do anything I would ask; but I cant bear to approach him on such a topic.

I am glad *some times* to say *yes* to what you ask, and so send you a tress of hair—if you insist on having a "*ringlet*" Lilly will gladly supply you, as she thinks the greatest misfortune of her life has been that she has had her head covered with curls. To have done all things in the most approved style I should have had a "bunch of *blue* ribbons to tie up my bonny brown hair," but as the ribbon is for *use* not sentiments the color will make no difference.

I send you back my letter. *I* didnt think it *worth keeping,* but was rather lazy to get up for it when I was writing. As to the others—why do you want them again? Did they ever give you any special pleasure that you want them back?

Oh, now I think of it let me say—I shall never call you *John* in the world. I feel a sort of shock every time I write the word. It seems unladylike somehow and not respectful; but I excuse myself by thinking it the best under the circumstances that I could do.

What lovely weather we have. What think you of this address to Spring?
"Thou hast farmed the sleeping Earth
Till her dreams are all of flowers,
And the waters look in mirth
For their overhanging bowers;
The forests seem to listen
For the rustling of the leaves,
And very skies to glisten
With the hope of summer eves."

Affectionately
S.C.P. McDowell

---

102. Transe House Mountain was a well-known landmark visible from Lexington.

Saturday March 31. 1855[103]

Dear Sally,

A gentleman who has bo't the house where I study & with whom I board is unable from the state of his family to continue the arrangement & wishes me to move. He would keep me I have no doubt a few weeks if I could tell him confidentially of my marriage at the end of that time. Otherwise I must move on the 8th (prox) I dont wish *this* to hurry you, but I should hate to have the power of such a confidence to come to me a day or two after my removal. Do what you can for me. This is Saturday. If I can hear from you next Thursday or Friday (after your brother may possibly have arrived) so that I may have something to entertain my hostess with & keep her quiet you will have begun your "vigils of mercy."

I cant tell about the middle of May. When I tell you that the Ch. is bargained for the 1st of May & yet is not very likely to be done, I have told you about all I understand myself. I *think* the probabilities are we will not enter it till Fall, but the majority of those immediately overseeing it hope differently & there is a *percentage* of chance for them.

Do you mean only to give me ten days notice. Well, that will be a joyful notice even if I have to be shot out of a cannon to get to you in time. But cant you give me a little more lee-way to take measures here among my friends against the hobgoblins you dread so.

I guess 43, now tell me.

I thought you behaved uncommonly well in the affair of my sister. I gave you credit for great *science* in those things in ignoring your difficulties with me for my sister's sake. I thought you looked very handsome tho' that was no sin & I dont think you could have prevented it.

As to friend Lacy I had no other object than the direct one of knowing whether it *was* so. And I dont remember how you answered except that I didnt find out.

Write as often as you *can*. I wont ask more &[104] I will reply the same day.

I do so feast on these letters in which it is true you are even worse than the *ghosts* as you dont even speak when you are spoken to yet you give me such great hope.

God bless you my dear Sally, & reward you for all your kindness in returning the love of such a poor old creature as I am.

I have the greatest quantity of resolutions on hand about repaying it all; but then Alas! I never did keep my resolutions.

Yours in Sat. haste
Jno Miller.

Monday, April 2. 1855

My dear John,

I am so very, very sad. I dont know why, yet for several days I have been miserably out of spirits. Sometimes I think the bright Spring weather has this

---

103. The day and the date are in McDowell's handwriting.
104. Miller added the word *And* here.

effect,—but it is only when a lovely day is wearing away into night that I generally am thus affected, for I enjoy the sunlight like a bird. Then, Mary's approaching marriage,—which I rejoice at for her sake for I know she will be happier married & in her own home,—yet it breaks another tie. Then *our troubles*—oh, how they do burden my heart. You cant tell how I *feel* about this matter of ours. I am so fearful of so many things; most of all of myself. No shadow ever crosses my mind about your affection. I just quickly repose in it, as a something sure and steady; but when I think of my own variable temper, and strong will and ambitious spirit, I fear—have I not reason to do it? You will suffer from these failings, as will your children & perhaps, to a very diminished extent your church. I suffer enough from them myself, to give me an idea of the effect they will have on others. Suppose you were to see me in one of my sad moods, how would you feel? What would you do with me? Would you scold me sharply & bid me behave myself better? Or would you try a gentler course? Or would it make you half-frantic as I used to be when Lilly would come crying to me about sorrows that she either could not, or would not disclose.

After a long silence a note came to me today from James just as he was leaving Louisville a week ago. He cannot be here for several days yet—probably not until next week. I cannot therefore, say more than I have already said. What a pity!

Why don't your people give you a house of your own? If your Church had cost $15.000 less, it would have been quite handsome. enough, and might have had a Parsonage besides.

I had expected a little *show of sentiment* about the violets, but had my expectations sadly dashed by your provision for Lilly's locket. I feel quite ashamed of you; and have a notion to return your enclosure as I am sure you cannot well *spare* it. Besides I had already made my acquaintance with it; & think it looked much better in its original scattered condition. I have little doubt I could furnish just such myself if I were at all ambitious of becoming your rival in such displays.

No indeed, you must not be "shot out of cannon" to be here in time; for then you w'd be a *spent ball* and would make the ugliest, if not the deadliest wound if I should happen to be in your way. You shall have more than "*ten days* notice.["] You shall have time enough to procure a *black* cravat of the latest style.

What an odd idea you have of "*profound silence*". You have told this affair to "3 persons & Mother and one other." Spence, I suppose you forgot to count. Now a secret seems scarcely one, when committed to the keeping of half a dozen people. But as this particular kind of secret presses very heavily upon one, I admit the necessity of a safety valve. But one thing pray abstain from, and that is, all representations of me to any one of your half dozen who does not know me. Let them see me with their own eyes & not thro' yours—except your Mother, and pray make her see with any other eyes than her own. Dont paint me a beauty—*you* may fancy me so if it pleases you—but it is not really the case;—nor a bel-esprit, for tho' Fishburn & *I* both concluded that if any one did have the temerity to call me *stupid* in German, *nobody could* do it in English: nor a model of excellence, for

I'm as volcanic as Chimboraza.[105] Dont you get tired hearing me talk of myself? I am fairly sick of the subject.

Our Presbytery meets here on Wednesday, and it is to give us no little trouble. Why can't you feign some business & come to it? I wont ask you to be my guest. I would not again shock your nerves by such an invitation.

I had a very nice letter from Dr. Van Rensselaer the other day which took me quite by surprize. I had written to him of Uncle Carrington's death—but the letter, of course required no answer. I had a little spite at him for a piece of neglect, but this dispels it all. I beg you will treat me with more deference since I am so much your Senior. Why did you stop at 43? Why did you not take me off the *muster roll* entirely? I am glad you *can "feast"* on my letters; it shows you have a keen appetite, and a hungry man will eat anything. Do you find any difficulty in reading my letters. Father used to complain much of my writing.

Affectionately
S.C.P McDowell

Phil. April 3rd 55.

My darling Sally,

I have such a way of "unbosoming" myself to others about matters about which I wish to be reserved that they never unbosom themselves to me. Dr. Leyburn said very little. "Well really, you never can tell what will happen in this world. I heard last Autumn that if any one *mentioned* marriage to Mrs McDowell it would mortally offend her. I think you have done a very wonderful thing in reducing that Sebastopol."[106] I remember that much. He seemed to think that Lexington would be a good deal startled out of her propriety at first, but would calm down by degrees into something much more acquiescent. And that people would look *hard* upon me here for a time. By the way, Darling, discharge from your counsels altogether all about me. I'll take care of myself (by the help of a Higher Power). I have no fear of the issue whatever, & scarce ever think of it. Turn all your deliberations upon yourself for I do assure you, small as my reputation is, I think scarce more of a shock to it as imminent in this transaction than I think of the danger of robbers on my journey from this to Lexington.

The hair came to me & quite made me shudder with delight. How heavy & cold it is. The next time Lilly is asleep clip one of her ringlets from her head & send that on & then our little circle will be complete. So she thinks I'm an impudent fellow. I'm afraid she will think me more so if she sees me claiming not only one poor little kiss, but about half of all the family at Colalto & that which in her eyes & in some others' that I know seems very much the whole of Colalto & Lexington put together.

105. A volcano in the Andes Mountains, located in Ecuador.
106. In the margin, without a caret to indicate placement, Miller added, "I didn't tell him any such thing. He meant, that you would listen to me at all."

When *will* that brother of yours get on! Do scold him a little when he comes for not having a presentiment that his journey was a more than usually important one.

It's a pretty story this you tell about my name. If you were obliged to call me, my dear Jack, it would be about on a par with some other names that I know. Dont you know that John, the third in order of the Apostles in the polemics of the Church is the one that has most to say in favor of a certain philosophy in which we are interested, & that while Peter was the man of the first centuries & Paul of the Reformation, with his doctrine of justification by faith, John has to "prophecy *yet* before many kingdoms & nations & tongues & people,[107] or as an ingenious Pole in the Seminary at Princeton recently expressed it, "if I will that he tarry till I come" i.e. be the last of the Apostles in developing the gospel what is that to thee? Follow thou me."[108]

Now I do not mean to give in to all that's fanciful in this, but I do think that John is less understood than either of the three & that he is hereafter to be more prominent than Paul in the teaching of the church.

But I think that a lady who could call her husband a "blasted lyre", might at least be willing to put up with the Saxon plainness of my dear John.

Did you write that poetry? If you did, you are a great deal more than I ever bargained for. If you did not, dear Sally, you ought not only to mark it with quotation marks, but to save me from all pleasant delusions; for I have really so set my heart upon it that it shall turn out yours that it will be hard to sink back to a more prosaic view of your abilities. I do think you are a great preacher, for I know that by experience, but I did not know you were so great a poet.

Seriously, my dear Sally, this is a beautiful gem & I should feel proud & rich to know that I had any such gifts *in my possession.* We Princetonians are all a little blue & I am telling you an unvarnished truth when I say that the fancy that these two verses may be yours has led me with all your previous preciousness in my eyes to look upon you now with an almost Oriental wildness of affection. Did you write it[?]

Yours *affectionately*
JM.

Thursday
April 5. 1855.

My *dear John,*

Well, after your very learned (all incomprehensible talks are such to me,) discussion I admit that John *is* a very good name; much handsomer than Peter & infinitely more musical than Paul. It is decidedly Presbyterian too, inasmuch

107. Rev. 10:11.
108. John 21:22.

as it was the one borne by both Calvin & Knox. It savours too somewhat of poetry as well as religion, for it was Milton's name.[109] There is not much that is regal about it, as only one English King,[110] & he, none of the best, and one Pope & he (?)[111] none of the best either ever united it with Sovreign sway; but then, and this caps the climax of its renown, there is a certain personage, coming, it is true in rather "a questionable shape" yet everwhere known who is spoken of as one "John Barleycorn!"[112] After all, however, I dont ever mean to apply it to *you* otherwise than as at present, And I would have you remember that in spite of all your side thrusts at me, *I* think my name quite as melodious as yours.

What very odd people you must meet! Only think of a *Lady* "calling her husband a blasted ___" oh, I couldn't write such a bad word as that. Does she belong to your Church? You ought to session her for using opprobrious language. Did I ever knew any body to talk that way? It must sound very queer, and be in very bad taste. How do *you* feel when you hear such things?

When you were cast into this world do you think that your whole nature was so completely enveloped in original sin, that there was not a crevice left thro' which the very tiniest stream of *sentiment* could ooze? I'm afraid you have none. I gathered you a very sweet bunch of the earliest Spring violets, and what should you do but mock the sentiment & send, in return a bouquet of—grey hair! Only think of that. But there was some practical wisdom in it after all. You thought the bouquet would be valued because it was made up of *very rare exotics.* Then, after begging like a lover for a "stray ringlet," the only word of thanks upon receiving it was—"how cold & heavy it seems." Now, dont ask me for anything more. I am mad & wont give you a thing. But Lilly is better than I am; for she sends you a curl. She dont wear her hair curled now, but plaits it hoping to get the curl out of it as it is very troublesome; but to-day she opened it & let me cut out a little, which she dampened, as of old, wrapped it tightly round her finger for a minute, and behold, the old ringlets seemed to have come back. Isn't it pretty? It grows or did grow, upon a very sweet head—and a very clever one too, tho' the old Adam in it occasions me an immense amount of trouble, anxiety & vexation.

I am so sorry I sent you the verses. They are not mine: I wish they were. I did mark them with quotation marks. After having work yourself up into a fit of enthusiasm upon the supposition of their being mine, this disappointment will run you to the opposite extreme of believing me a very hum-drum sort

---

109. During the Reformation, John Knox (1505–1572) established John Calvin's (1509–1564) Presbyterian system of church polity in Scotland. John Milton (1608–1674), English poet.

110. King John (1167?–1216), forced by his barons to sign the Magna Carta in 1215.

111. McDowell alludes to a thirteenth-century story of a Pope Joan, a woman reputed to be pope several centuries earlier. By 1855 at least twenty-two popes had taken the name of John.

112. The personification of corn liquor.

of being, just fit to be called Sally. I dont know who they belong to. I have always admired them, & they are very frequently in my mind at this season. The *listening* look of the forest often strikes me where our first warm spring days are preparing them for buds & blossoms. But no, I am no Poet—*that I know of*. I remember now however of our Tom saying to me when we were together in Abingdon—"Sister, Uncle Tom says Uncle William has more poetry in him than anybody in the family; and that you come next to him." But this was all fudge in Uncle Tom, & not worth repeating to anybody but you. I am entitled to some however—as the poetic sentiment was possessed by both my Parents. My Father was full of it & gave expression to it at all times & in all places altho' he never manufactured but one sett of *verses* in his life, and that was—what do you think? an address to a May Queen! It was a long, long time ago, and doubtless I thought them very grand, but they never earned for him a crown of bay. How hard he worked at them. I remember so well how he looked and how he labored. He had an odd way when thoroughly absorbed in mental labor of throwing off his slippers and pacing the room. I think it must have originated in his *diffidence*. He could not bear that anyone should notice him when thus employed & hence he took this way to avoid making any noise. Well these verses I think must have cost him, in addition to more valuable things, a pair of socks. I wish I could get at them again. How this little incident takes me back, to the time when life was all a holiday. And my heart throbs as lightly as if the recollection was the reality, and as if it had not borne a world of sorrow upon it since then.

But I have an unfortunate way of running off the track. Some of these days, some dreadful thing will happen in consequence. I must try to behave better. What was I talking about? I remember now. Well what I want to say is that you must not expect me to be gifted with any uncommon parts in any thing *except in sewing*. I am very skilful and accomplished in the use of the needle.

Our Presbytery is now in session. Mr. Ruffner with his wife are here.[113] The former looks better than when, I saw him, several months ago.

No news since I last wrote from James.

Ain't this a foolish letter?

Affectionately Yours
S.C.P. McDowell.

Why are your last letters so short? have you exhausted your subject or has it exhausted you? Does my ink blot now? What *has* become of your grand plan of numbering your letters, that *you* were so very, very bright about? I wouldn't adopt it for anything. The number would run up too high.

113. William Henry Ruffner (1824–1908), Presbyterian minister at Harrisonburg, Va., and Harriet Ann Gray Ruffner (1824–1895).

Friday April 6. 1855.

My *dear* John,

I have been looking for some weeks to this day as one, in honor of which I meant to answer your famous "Extra," and several other letters that I promised to answer "*again*"; and to accompany my reply with a birth-day gift of no small value. But I am disappointed. I must choose some other time. Perhaps it is as well, for the same day should not bear the honor of commemorating *two* important events in your history.

Thirty-six to-day—how do you feel? Well, I hope the Sixth of April that shall double this number to you may find us together somewhere, either in this world or a better. If in this world, what an odd picture we shall make. By that time you will have mounted *two* p[ai]r of spectacles, and will need only a very little more time to fit you in look, at least for becoming a Myth, as your Father seems to me. Whilst I, with a tight cap drawn closely round a face wrinkled & sunken, will, after the fashion of my Grandmother Preston, occupy a quiet seat in the corner & take *snuff* from a massive gold box! What a handsome pair!

But this looking forward to age is no laughing matter to me. I am often strangely sad at the idea of growing old, & passing away and being forgotten: how is it with you?

I was dining to-day with a small party at Cousin John's, which, after dinner was augmented by a visit from Mr. Fishburn. A casual question of his to Mrs Ruffner led her to mention you. I was alarmed as I found myself half-required to join in the conversation, that became general about "Mr. Miller & his fine church.["] I was much relieved that Cousin John was not present. With all my coolness I could not have borne his meaning smile & covert attacks. However, I attempted to confine Mr. Fishburn to the very entertaining topic of church architecture, and succeeded quite well for a time, but coming, in our progress, upon a Mosque we both broke down completely, & he took refuge with the party opposite, who by this time had poor Mr. Miller in that awful state of suspension in mid-air, in which I have sometimes, known him claim to be. I felt very uneasy, as you may imagine; and suffered under the fear of having the suspended coffin fall upon *my head*. I was, notwithstanding, amused at Mrs Ruffner's expression of her "fear" of you. "I like him extremely, she said, and find him very pleasant, but *he does bewilder me so*. I'm *so* afraid of him too." Wasn't it fortunate I was not called upon to "define my position" upon so important a matter.

I was greatly pleased to find Mr John Atkinson in the Church when I went over this morning. He is to bring up his Metropolitan Church scheme tomorrow, when Church extension comes up for discussion. I have no enthusiasm in his scheme & think I shall content myself with the little I have already done towards it. And as to Church extension—with one Sister married to an Elder, & another going to marry a minister & myself much inclined to do the same thing, I think *we* have demonstrated fully our interest in *it*. By the bye, if our matter is ever carried out, will it not be, sure enough, a Union of Church & State?

Do you read "the Critic"?[114] I am behindhand. I have not yet seen a single number of it. But with Uncle Robert Breckinridge & Stuart Robinson, to write for & manage it, I'm sure it must be hot enough. The bitterness of the one &[115] Kentuckeism, of both, will furnish cayenne enough for any taste—a great deal too much for mine.

I heard an old gentleman 84 years old preach this evening, and his sermon was very good, but too long.

My two letters, should obtain a volume from you—Good night.

Affectionately
S.C.P. McDowell

Please give me something to write about. It is scarcely generous in you to make my letters regulate the number of yours. You can write when you please; I must do it when I can.

I heard incidentally yesterday what I had forgotten before that Dr White's annual visit to the Union Seminary comes off between the 12th & 20th of May.[116] So that time would suit nobody. If we let May slip by, then what is to be done? Wait till Fall? But one question must be settled before that. Am I not a *worry* to you after all? But then if I share in the worry I give, you will not find it so hard to bear.

Yours,
S.C.P. McD.

Phil. *April 6th* 1855.

My *dear Sally*,

I am sitting nearly all day in Presbytery this week & last night did not receive your letter in time to reply. I would so much like to see you. If I knew what your troubles were, I could speak kindly at least for their relief. And I very much regret that (however much for the object of assuring you of *my* impression about it) I should have ever expressed any weariness of the subject that gives you so much concern.

Forgive me all this, my dear Mrs McDowell, & anything else in which I have been thoughtless or have given you pain. And though my affection revolts at any such idea, yet my pride dictates that if in any possible way the tide of your affections burns against me, I forfeit, as my penalty, all claim to the continuance of our present relations.

114. The *Presbyterian Critic*. Stuart Robinson (1814–1881), pastor of the Central Church in Baltimore, helped to edit what his biographer called "a strongly controversial monthly of marked ability" (J. N. Saunders, *Memorial upon the Life of Rev. Stuart Robinson* [Louisville, Ky.: Courier-Journal, 1883], 23).

115. Miller added the word *and* here.

116. Union Theological Seminary was located at Hampden Sydney College in Southside Virginia.

You do me injustice about our secret. My tendency in all such matters is to great reserve & I lock my personal matters in with a silence that is characteristic. I have not committed you in any way. I told my Mother, but scarcely more than that I was seeking your hand; but that we were not engaged; & we have not communicated since. I spoke to Spencer twice within a few days some months ago & told him that a half incidental obtaining of your portrait was your greatest mark of interest in me. And we have not alluded to the subject since. I told Dr Leyburn much more fully (tho' not *all*,) for the sake of gaining an end. I have told no one else. My sentence must have been, "Three persons, viz. <u>S.</u> (meaning Spencer) Mother & one other" (i.e. Dr Leyburn.) All these are under strict obligation not to speak of us.

Hearing from Dr. L. the day before yesterday that your brother, the Doctor was in town with Mrs. McDowell & Thomas I called to see them.[117] They will have told you probably of the time when the Doctor will reach you.

He said, He would leave here on Friday, go to Richmond for a day or two & reach Colalto on Wednesday. I fear from his having business in the different places he will be still later. Knowing into what difficulties his first expressions of feeling may plunge you I wish I could steal in upon you in some unobserved way & sooth any awakened anxieties & comfort you. Remember one thing as an unchanging fact that I love you tenderly & nothing that can possibly happen can easily disturb the respect & affection with which I think of you.

I cannot feign a business with the Presbytery, but I was nominated yesterday to the General Assembly that meets in Nashville.[118] That would have given me an opportunity to pass very near you at least either going or returning. But I declined this year, because I was not altogether sure about our church, but still rather because I hoped I might see you on a more direct & gratifying invitation before the sitting of the Assembly. Dr Leyburn will write to Mr Sweeney & I will let you know the result as soon as I receive it.

If I dared hope that your sadness was of such a character as could be relieved by any sympathy of mine how gladly would I offer it. I cannot *conceive* now of such a thing as "scolding" you. I must see you in a very different light if I *ever* do. I wish the people *would* buy a parsonage. Who knows what they may not do when this $100,000 & over which they spend is a little forgotten. But we can *rent* a house at first; can we not?

I can *truly* say that I never get tired of hearing you talk of yourself & I never talk of you to others, so at least in this last point you will not quarrel with me.

I have been speaking today a good-deal in Presbytery & *fear* I have written a stupid letter, but believe me.

Yours affectionally
JM.

117. "Mrs. McDowell" refers to Elizabeth Lovejoy Brant McDowell (1831–1895).
118. The General Assembly of the Presbyterian Church.

Phil. April 9th 1855.

My *darling Sally*,

Oh how your spirits do transcribe themselves upon your letters.

I thought when I received the one about "Lilly's Locket" either that Colalto had yawned underneath your feet & that you had "gone down to the bottom of the mountains" or that you had suddenly grown weary & utterly uninterested in such a poor unfortunate innocent sufferer as I am. This last supposition was entirely too much for the exhausted remnants of "original sin" that I have in my nature & the picture of you as having no means of intercourse with me except by letters, & as finding these quite insufficient to keep the tide from ebbing back toward misgiving & hesitation, wrought upon me so far as to think of another long & laboured letter *in* which I could put before you all possible proofs of the firmness of *my* affection, but reaffirm as I have often done my unwillingness to bind you by any previous relations of confidence to that in respect to which both your taste & your feeling led you to entertain even at this late hour too much misgiving.

I discarded the thing however, first, because I shrank from running such hazards, second, because I did'nt like even to *suggest* such misgivings to one who has so much "original sin" & thirdly, because there is evermore a lingering suspicion that the party professing to fancy such misgivings in others has them himself & I thought that would be the last feather upon the camels back for whatever else I am chargeable with. I think the sin of not loving you is one for which I will never be condemned & I thought it cruel that I should be even under the most distant suspicion of anything so mournfully aside from the truth.

But now that your next letter comes, scolding as much as ever, but with that sort of singing, laughing tone that leads me to know that you do love me after all[,] I am quite glad that I did not enter upon any such lovers' "See-saw" & I have determined that until you tell me distinctly in some letter, "John I dont love you & I think it hard that I should have to marry you" I mean to be as blind as Justice & to fancy that your "ambitious spirit" & your "variable temper" never carry you out of the region of some little affection for one who loves you so fondly.

You know, Darling, I dont want to marry you if you dont love me. But even this is a feeling of pride; for my affection breaks in and says, "Yes I do: I want to marry her at any rate. If she dont love me I'll bend all my life upon the toil of leading her to love me; & I'll coin all my happiness into the price of buying from her her affection & I know that she *will* love me.["]

I am so much obliged to you for this letter in which after all your regard for me seemed to be slipping away from my grasp you actually add one more title of endearment & say as you have never said before "affectionately *yours*." See how sensitive I am to little things.

But Sally you aint fair. (And yet that produces some confusion of ideas for you blame me in that very letter for saying that you *are* fair & charge me not to tell others so.)

You send me a cluster of violets & tell me by the bye that their fragrance will come back to them. Well I open them eagerly & "press them in my hand" & "warm them" & find them just as I will be some day hopelessly blighted, & as I think of all your cruelty, & think that this emblem of the returning fragrance of your favor is ominously at fault, & remember how withered my hopes are under your long procrastinations & neglects, I determine that I will send you back a token of the havoc that all this severity has made, & as I think of myself but yesterday without a flake of the snow of time rest[ing][119] upon my temples I clip (!) the badges of your cruelty & send them to speak in dumb show their murmurs at your sin.

You have sent me at last something I *never* mean to return to you. If we quarrel & I have to send you back all the letters I ever received & your picture & everything else, Lilly's ringlet I shall certainly keep. What affair will it be of yours? She will never know of it. And it will only tell me how near I came to having another merry foot about my house & a daughter who even tho' coming from so cold a place as Colalto, might learn to love me in these warmer regions of the earth.

Now about the tress of hair. It comes to me & as I open the envelope & see the warm brown wreath lying in the paper I am fairly thrilled with delight. I take it in my hand & am about surprised to see what has been so lately a pait of your very being, "cold & heavy." I start at the thought of its not having the warmth & lightness of actual life. Well I tell you all this poor artless lover as I am & you say in reply that I have no sentiment. That is I tell you "I almost shuddered with delight" & you say I have no sentiment. Well Darling, tell me that about anything of mine & I will promise never to find fault with you on the score of any want of sentiment or feeling.

The poetry was mighty pretty & I wish it had been yours; but I am not certain either. It confounded my notions about you somewhat for I had endowed you with gifts with which such little ringlets of fancy are not altogether consistent. There is no couleur-de-rose on the Koh-i-noor.

I observe that there is no sugar in your ink & it does not blot. I think a *little* sugar, however, makes the character warmer & makes it pleasanter to read. It looks very *black*, however, sometimes now.

By the way your news of James has been delayed by a trifling mishap at the Post Office. I passed thro' its outer Hall on Saturday & as I look for your name everywhere I was glancing along the lists of letters not forwarded because not prepaid & saw as plain as ink could make it. "Mrs. Sally McDowell, Lexington, Va." I called for the letter & found that It was not mine, but one with the Girard House stamp.[120] I could not tell how long it had been lying. The Doctor had paid at the Hotel Office no doubt & the Clerk has neglected the stamp. It cannot reach you till to-day or perhaps tomorrow now.

---

119. The page is torn at this point.
120. The Girard House was a Philadelphia hotel.

Do write me the very first mail after you speak with your brother.

The numbering plan was for you not for me. It is your letters that are important. By the way the last one is *not* a foolish letter.

Do write as often & as much as you can.

Yours most affectionally
Jno Miller.

Mrs. McDowell.

How attentive do you wish me to be to your sister-in-law? I told Spencer of her being at the Girard House & of your attentions to Mary, & he said, he would call.

Monday April 9. 1855.

My *dear John*,

I wish you knew me a little better. I wish you were more familiar with my ways of thinking & talking for then I think, you would not so often mistake me.

You write me as gravely and solemnly about your keeping of our secret as if you were defending your honor from some charge against it. Now what I said about it was said playfully. I was not the least offended at supposing you had confided it to half a dozen friends. I took it for granted they would be discreet, trustworthy folk, and I did not wonder you should bestow such confidence upon some such special friends in a case that I have made so perplexing as this. I thought it due to your Mother that she should know of the thing. And was glad that you consulted with your brother about it, as he, being cool & dispassionate, could look more wisely, perhaps, into all the bearings of the subject than you. Then as to Dr Leyburn—the end in view fully justified the revelation of it to him. And if there had been three others, I should not have blamed you. I would have believed you acted from some good motive, & one which, in all probability, originated in consideration for my feelings, or comfort. Now on my part, Cousin John, until within a few days, is the only person who knows much of the matter. Dr White, has not even a suspicion of the *name* of the "other party" of whom we talk. But within ten days, my old friend, Dr Graham, drew the secret from me. He was, until the last few years our Physician; and I have always been a very special favorite with him. He has been a counselor in my past difficulties, and an active, steady, earnest friend at all times. An evening or two before he left home for New York, he called to see me, & was asking something of Mary's arrangements, and concluded by saying, "You will be left entirely alone. You had better get married yourself." I felt somewhat startled, but asked, What would you think of me if I did? "I should think, he said, you did perfectly right. I think you w'd be happier." "Wouldn't I lose position Doctor?['"] "No I think not, if you married the right sort of person." We then had quite a discussion as to what cons[t]ituted "the right sort of person," and he rather drew from me, I dont know how, the confession, that I had the thing under consideration. Then he was extremely anxious I should go still further & give him some idea as to the person. I objected, saying, "you will be the very first to object to my leaving Virginia and marrying a Preacher." "I shall miss you dreadfully, for I love you very much, but I wont object on either ground." It was a strong proof of his attachment that he would *at all put up with a Preacher*; so I told him. I was much amused at the effect of my information. Like a true Virginian he began to look up your antecedents. He knew of your Father, of course, & had a sort of veneration for him, not so much on account of his own merits as because of his connection with his Uncle, Dr Alexander.[121] "But Sally, who was his Mother?" I soon exhausted my stock of information upon similar points. He seemed quite satisfied, only taking care to add with much emphasis, "I shall find out about the *gentleman himself* when I go to Phila; and I will then write to you". But he has not fulfilled his promise yet. He had seen your Church & remembered with great particularity the fact of its having being paid for. He admitted the fact that there would be many to object to the step upon my part, and seemed much concerned when I told him, Spence thought it would cost you your Church.

I told him your Mother's notion of my temper. He laughed, but evidently did not participate in the old Lady's fears on that score.

Now haven't I told you a budget? Dont get tired of it—forget I have *written* it & imagine I am talking to you. If you could recall my voice & let it take the words in thro' the ear, I think we should get on better.

It is so long since I have figured in your letters as "my dear Mrs. McDowell", that I looked up from the words to see if you were offended; and I thought you were a little, but I couldnt tell at what. I will copy the paragraph & hope you will write it out a little more clearly. To tell you the truth, I *do not* understand it at all.

"Forgive me all this, my dear Mrs. McD—& anything else in which I have been thoughtless & have given you pain. And tho' my affection revolts at any such idea, my pride dictates that if, in any possible way the tide of your affections turns against me, I forfeit, as my penalty, all claim to the continuance of our present relations".

I wish you *could* come in & give me a little aid and comfort under the explosion that will ensue upon the announcement of this matter of ours. James will not, I think say *to me* a single harsh word. He will, probably, not approve; yet he has such respect for my motives & opinions, that he will forbear any harsh judgment in my presence, & maybe, out of it. But he will not, *lead* the others to favor my decision as I should like him to do. Mary will, *say* more than any of the others would venture to do to me directly.

Cantey will explode in words & ways too. Susan (Mrs. Carrington) will feel hurt, but she is moderate, sensible, very strongly attached to me—(more so than any of my Sisters)—& she will reason upon the matter as I do, & then determine to stand by me at all hazards. I don't know about Nib (Mrs. Massie.) Tom will be

---

121. Archibald Graham (1794–1880) of Lexington. Archibald Alexander of Princeton Theological Seminary.

mad for a minute; then he will put his arms round me & kiss me as often as ever, & love me as much, & will take upon himself to keep Cantey in order. Aunt Eliza will, after the first surprize is over, stand by me. Aunt Sally who is a woman of the strongest prejudices, & her husband, Uncle Floyd will give me up.[122] That will grieve me so much. Uncle Tom will think me a lunatic, & Uncle William will believe me to be a fool. Now all this is pretty hard—and I am not made of iron. I shall be very mad—& very sad both, and shall need all the sympathy that you can give.

You mustn't wait for me to ask it either, but just have it always ready.

Our Presbytery is over. Some Members of it are here Still. & Mr Atkinson will remain several days longer. I wonder you fancy Mr Ruffner so much. He dined with some others with me to-day, and really his peculiar *ways* embarrass me to such a degree that I cant like him. But John Atkinson, dont we love him? I am so glad he is coming back to his own quarters, over here tomorrow.

Oh Yes, we can *rent* a house *until a parsonage is provided*. I must get used to things by degrees. A parsonage at first would quite overwhelm me. But I am entirely indifferent about having any house at all. I have not thought much about it, but just now it seems to me it would be better to have none until I have some knowledge of manners & habits of your City. Mr Dickson perhaps would *give us* his Country home. That would suit me very nicely. But whatever you fancy will do for me. Indeed if you will put me in a bird-cage, & hang me outside of the window I shall enjoy it extremely, especially if I am hung too high to be spoken to.

Pray get rested after your Presbytery adjourns and write me a good long letter—and dont talk to me about "quarrelling with you," and remember I'd rather you would *scold* me, than move along with such formal kindness.

Affectionately Yours
S.C.P. McDowell

Phil. April 10th 1855.

My *dear Sally*,

Let me whisper.—My *reason* is going. I knew it would be so. Ever since you told me you would write fully one certain week & that very week gave the forlornest *twinge* to my hopes, I have felt that the great principle to which I have respectfully alluded above was getting dethroned.

Everything looks queer to me. You are *so* queer. Your letters seem to me the queerest letters I have almost ever received—*some of 'em*. Women are *so* queer.

---

122. Susan Smith Preston McDowell (1832–1909) married Charles Scott Carrington (1820–1891) in 1852. He was an attorney at Halifax Court House. Sophonisba Breckinridge McDowell (1827–1870) married James Woods Massie (1826–1872), an attorney in Lexington. "Aunt Sally" was Sarah Buchanan Preston (1802–1879), who married a cousin, John Buchanan Floyd (1806–1863), a Virginia governor and later secretary of war in President James Buchanan's cabinet.

For example here is one that keeps her lover in agonizing suspense for *centuries* & then as tho' he were a poor Bruin of the woods who cared no more about it than if she were a butterfly sailing about his ears, asks him if she "worries him at all"; just when she has given the poor monster some of his worst & hardest troubles & tried his patience & tried his fortitude & tried his courage & tried everything but his temper & left him a sort of shadow among the beasts of the forest she wants to know whether she "worries him at all", & whether the fact that it worries her considerably to keep up this gradual demolition is not an entire amends for all the suffering he endures.

I have no doubt its right, for Pope says, "Whatever is, is right," but it puzzles me in my weak state to get the thing together & see *how* in this fresh instance of "Beauty &—the poor parson" it *comes* to be right that a poor sufferer like me should be so sadly visited.[123]

I *would* have thought when my mind was stronger that if that Archbishop of yours goes to Prince Edward on the 12th (prox.) that a good way to avoid the difficulty is to be married before, but I see in my present weak state that that doesnt necessarily follow.[124] You say, You "never will call me John in the world" & I have begun to think lately that it will not be probably till we get to heaven & indeed you hint at that in your letter just received, for you say You hope we will sit together by a hickory fire if not in this world in a better.

Well, Sally, I am getting too weak to manage this thing myself. I am obliged to commit it to you. I think Providence means to marry us & as, as long as I had my mind, I did all I could to win you.

I am going to hope for the best, keeping a bright look out tho' every morning now for the letter in which you accept me.

I find Julia who is expecting Dick home *kills her impatience* by not thinking of him. I am trying to do the same & in my weak state it would be easy. But I never knew such a determined *spirit* as yours. It presses itself upon my memory & in my weak state comes clamoring to be thought about all the day. It is like the frogs of Egypt. I cant shut it out. It comes *rapping*—on the door of my imagination all the time. I never knew such an omnipresent little spirit in all my life. And if I try to *drive* it out of my mind, it shakes Lilly's curl at me or its own brown tress or a bunch of violets & Julias counsel is no counsel at all.

But "I'm wearing awa" Sally.

Then when I do take it in, it mutters to me that it will write fully the very next week & dont I know now it wont? or that "its ashamed of me" or that it will give me a seal or a portrait or now lately that it *did* think of making me the greatest gift that I ever have had & then when it has served up my feeling to the highest pitch, it suddenly asks, Do I worry you? In my weak state this

123. Alexander Pope (1688–1744), English poet.
124. McDowell's pastor, William White, would visit Union Theological Seminary in Prince Edward County.

naturally gives me a worn feeling, as tho' like a harp the cords had been worn on by too great exhaustion of emotion, & then when I complain ever so little & beg to be touched a little more tenderly I am told that its all a fib & that I am a _____. Oh in my weak state I'm afraid to say.

Dear Sally, treat me a *little* better.

If you want something to write about tell me, all how you came to love me & all the process ever since. Or tell me as you seem burning with impatience to do so what this shocking temper is that you talk so much about & how it will behave when we get to housekeeping. By the way, the next letter will be the <u>Great Letter</u>; you will have seen James (perhaps.)—But Alas! how "mad" you will be. I have written up all my time without replying scarcely to a thing; forgive me this once.

Yours in great feebleness.
Jno Miller

[marginal note] I read *all* 1st Critic, half the 2d & scarce any of the 3d. It is not *positive* enough for me. It deals too much in pulling down & too little in building up. I send it. I see others have read & torn it for me.

Colalto,
Thursday April 12. 1855.

My *dear* John,

I was very glad yesterday to receive a letter which I could recognize as yours. The one immediately preceding it, written the Friday before was strained and stiff and formal and cold enough to have been written by Spence, or any other Miller than John. I tried hard to excuse it. I could not remember enough of the letter to which it *professed* to reply to account for its altered tone and was left to imagine some cause outside of that. I felt much hurt, and much as if it were a case in which "woman's rights" would be yeilded if I did not reply rather sharply. But then I concluded, that after all, some trouble in your Presbytery, or some worry in your day's work, or some other thing had annoyed you & made you feel a little inclined to think that every body's hand was against you, and to determine that you would raise yours against them. So I just let that letter go, & wrote to you, (didn't I?) much as if it had not been received. You dont know how formal you were. You threw up a breastwork of pride and from behind it in the most civil & gentlemanlike manner pelted me, that sunny day with snow balls. However as the balls missed and I was not hurt very seriously I picked them up to see—but no matter what.

James' letter reached me on Monday. I had however heard from him thro' Mary whose letter had been written some days after mine, and had come in good time. I do not look for him until Saturday or early next week. I feel nervous terrors at the very idea of the disclosure to be made. I had half a notion to make an experiment in the matter by telling my Cousin Dr Taylor, and making an ally of him; but when he was here last night I was so overcome with sheer *drowsiness* that he laughingly got up and said he couldnt go on with his talk then, but would come again when I had my eyes open. A proposition to which I, most promptly agreed. I was sorry to lose the chance too, but had no energy to avail myself of it. If I catch him again within a few days I shall have more courage I think.

I was out almost all day yesterday with Mr Atkinson. Mr Lacy had been with him the two preceding days, introducing him to the people, & aiding him in presenting his cause but *he* was called off & Dr White had had a fall & was more lame than usual, & Cousin John was busy and so *I* went with him, more for the pleasure of the drive than for any assistance I could give. It was my first acquaintance with any such proceedings, and I had no idea that *money* could be so gracefully asked for, and sometimes so gracefully refused. Alfred was taken ill a day or two ago, & I could not use my carriage, but I begged Dr White's little affair & made one of my horses perform in single harness. Mr Atkinson proved a very "good whip," and Mc acquitted himself quite handsomely. We did not run *over stumps* as I have known some "extra fine reinsmen" do, and did nothing more awkward than common. Mr A dropped his hat, which I had to run after, and I got my dress well-nigh covered with mud. But we had a very pleasant day, and we were all sorry that it ended in a final leave taking.

I think Mr Atkinson has reason to be satisfied with his success here, tho' the sum of $500 may seem very small to you. Our Church is not a wealthy one—but two really rich men in it—yet during the last year it has given to the different benevolent enterprizes of the Church about $3.700. This with Dr White's salary runs up the year's contributions to very nearly $5.000. Isn't that doing well for a people like ours?

I am perfectly quiet to-day. Every human being in the neighbourhood had gone into Town to hear Mr Wise (our Democratic candidate for Gov'r) and I feel as tho' I had set down to write in a wilderness every thing is so still.[125] If you could step in upon me and look from my window just now you wouldn't wonder that my heart sinks at the thought of giving up a country home, as lovely as this is at present, for the noise, and bustle and dust of a city. So I grow older, and I have long remarked the fact, I enjoy natural objects of beauty more and more and find they can, to some extent, promote my happiness. All country sounds are delightful to me. The number of trees & variety of shrubbery about the yard and garden attracts thousands of birds to us, and all day long I am listening to them with infinite pleasure. The cat-bird, which is the mocking bird of this region, is, from the variety & range of its notes a very great favorite with me. Lilly has learned to imitate its call very successfully. When she hears one, she thrusts her head out of a window, or runs to one of the porches and responds in a clear, sweet note, so like its own that the bird answers her immediately and they then keep up an interchange of sounds for many minutes, much to my wonder and amusement.

125. Henry Alexander Wise (1806–1876).

I love Country sights too. How am I ever to learn to love a city home, a "Number 5" in Philadelphia? Or "the house that Jack built" in Princeton? Princeton seems a sort of old maid of a place to me, stiff, starched & squeamish: is it so?

What makes you say I "*scold*"? If I do, I must do it in a very comic way, for it seems to have the strange effect of putting you in a good humor. Pray send me back a specimen of what you consider scolding. And now as you are pleased once more & have relaxed some of the August hauteur with which you addressed me a week ago, perhaps you *can* "*conceive*" that you may one day find it in your heart or head, or on the tip of your tongue to return my compliment & scold me; how will you do it?

Cantey came in a while ago, and said, as she saw me writing, "Sister I wish you would tell 'B' that I am crazy to know who he is. And you may say too that if his Lady-love ever disappoints him, he has only to come to me. I've got a heart to let, that is his for the asking. If he writes books, tell him please to send me one with the compliments & *name* of the Author". What have you to say to the young Lady? Shall I abdicate in her favor? Or will [you] cast us both aside that we may take our turn at hanging our harps upon the willows?

How did you arrange matters with your Landlord? I'm half sorry you are giving up the little study.

You are right about the Koh-i-noor. It would not have been the *finest* of gems if it had been rose-tinted, but it would have been very beautiful—perhaps the more beautiful for the gentle blush upon it that would, in the eyes of the knowing ones, have lessened its real value.

Do I seem so matter-of-fact to you that "ringlets of fancy" would be out of place upon me? Or do you depreciate them just because I do not possess them, going upon the old lover's notion that I'm "made of every creature's *best.*" That did well enough for Romeo, but we have advanced beyond his illusive period and have learned to look at life as it is. And you with those "snow-flakes" upon your temples, and I with my wealth of hair thinned from its original length of a yard and a half down to scarcely more than half that now, have each had such sober and grave lessons taught us that we will find it difficult to give to our relations such a poetic glow as that. And yet I dont know. The mould that gathers upon the walls of the temple, cannot reach or dim the brightness of the light that burns upon its altar. And time, that makes every thing else hoary *cannot* make the heart grow old. Sorrow does that, and disappointment—but not age.

The paper you use now is very nice, but please get back to the softer sheets that you had before. When a letter comes, if any one is near the rattling of this damask paper as sheet after sheet is opened attracts their notice. And then too, after a letter is read, I slip it in my pocket, and if perchance, *not understanding it* I draw it thence for a *second reading,* it is sure to betray me by its noise, when I endeavor to restore it quickly to its hiding-place.

Have you never a word to say about the children? Does Maggie never bestow a letter upon you? If she does why cant you tear off an unimportant part of it and send it to me so that I may have something that may link the ideal with the real in her case. And why couldn't you have thought of this without my asking, for I feel as diffident about it as I did about that famous marriage-settlement, that seems lost in the abyss of the past.

Did you ever say you would send me home in midsummer if I could go & did go to Phil in May?

Have I anything more to say? Not a word. I am more exhausted than your Original Sin by far. How happy you are to have only "exhausted remnants" of that malady.

You defended yourself so well against my charge of want of sentiment, when I threatened not to give you anything more, that I'm afraid you have something great to ask for. But good bye.

Affectionately Yours
S.C.P. McDowell

Do you call this letter long enough? I opened my letter to say that yours of the 10th was received this afternoon. If you had said, ["]my dear Sally I have lost my senses"—I should have had some idea of the loss sustained. But as you have only lost ["]your *reason*" I must cheer you by assuring you that after all your loss is not very great. Indeed I am surprised that *you* should *miss* a quality that your friends never had thought of your possessing.

I didn't say anything like "sitting by a hickory fire in Heaven." I have several times suspected you of misquoting me in the hope of escaping detection from my want of exact recollection.

As to the amount of attention you are to pay to Lizzie I can only say—certainly a question of no greater magnitude than that is within the grasp of even such feebleness as yours.[126]

Dr Graham tells me Tom is to be here tomorrow, James having made a detour to Richd will not be on for several days.

The Critic came too. Dont send me any more Nos. I am obliged to you for these—But am myself a Subscriber to it.

Dr Graham said to me as I passed him this evening—"Well I have a great deal to say to you. I have quite a feast in store—so if you will be at home tomorrow, I will come out & tell you." I felt somewhat flurried then, but now am preparing with the Dr's aid to dissect you very carefully.

Edward stands waiting for my letter, all in patience.[127]

Yours
S.C.P McD.

I guess you are *32—now* tell me.

126. "Lizzie" was Elizabeth Brant McDowell, James McDowell's wife.
127. Edward was one of McDowell's slaves.

Phil.
April 12th 1855

My *dear Sally,*

I am full of expectation of receiving a letter this afternoon, so I will begin one also, lest I be too late to get one in the mail. Your very bright pleasant letter of the 6th deserves a better answer than I gave it the other day.

I do feel so sorry you let everything rest upon your interview with James. He did not get off from here till Monday. I fear he will not reach you till Saturday or Monday. Who knows that he will for 2 weeks! He tarries so on the road that it would seem almost worth while for you to write to Richmond hurrying him. The reply to that famous "extra" & that inestimable "gift" I do so much want to receive. Dont hesitate to fix the day *suddenly* even if ten full days be all that intervene. I can be ready, if it be any time *before* Dr White's visit to Union Seminary. I have now *no* idea that the Church will be done in May.

I feel no emotion specially at the idea of age. I do not value life as much as most men. And ambition except in its very most exaggerated forms has no power over me. Pulpit celebrity I think I have grown past as an object of worldly ambition. And an ambition which is indeed very powerful at times to be one of the *two* or *three* in each generation who leave an indelible impression upon their age is all the ambition that powerfully excites me. Judge then how little prospect mine is to have my ambition gratified. As I am not happy & care little for inferior successes except as from a better motive than ambition a long or short life is an interest that does not agitate me much & if I can get to heaven I set no very high value upon my continuance in the world. Retired & original speculation is wherein I think I have most to do in the rest of my history & how I can get most speedily to that is the problem that I am most often trying to settle & that in which my value of life chiefly appears. Except in you & our dear little children & this private thirst for a philosophic retirement I have scarce any pleasure except in religion in the world.

Your picture of our fire-side when we get to be old is very alluring because you breathe over it the warmest speech I think you ever made to me, that is, that you hope that thirty six years hence will "find us together somewhere either in this world or a better." God grant that they may my dear, shy, cautious, hesitating Mrs McDowell.

So Mrs Ruffner is afraid of me. I cant conceive how that can spring up. I wish they *had* made you "define your position". *I* never have been able to do so.

There are strange enough in this great city any number of unmarried O.S. Pres. preachers & in the more central churches there are three. Mr Shields of the 2d Church (a Widower), Mr Clarke of the Central Church (a Bachelor) & myself.[128] We adopt different modes of living. Mr Clarke lives in a public

128. O.S. Pres. means "Old School Presbyterian." Charles Woodruff Shields (1825–1904). Henry Steele Clarke (1818–1864).

boarding house, Mr Shields has a housekeeper & keeps house & I live with a private family. My private family, unfortunately, however, are well off & my money cannot tempt them & lately since there has been sickness in the house they grow impatient of the care & restraint of lodging a minister. They are Presbyterians however & I think like me somewhat & I shall certainly stay with them till next Monday week. My "Sanctum" is in a house that they bought about a year ago; hence my introduction to them. If our affair is so far decided that I can communicate it or the fact of my wedding to them next week I shall be able to explain more satisfactorily to them my wish to postpone a removal.

What a nice letter! Oh Sally! *Oh, Oh, Oh!* what a nice letter. I wish you would write me always such gay pleasant, *talking* letters. So Dr Graham wants to know about my blood. I wish everything was as good about me as my stock. The Doctor will probably send you back a better character than I deserve. My *two* great passions are eating upon me so that you must hurry & marry me in order to *help* me to keep up what character I have.

I wish you would apply the match & touch off that explosion of which you speak. I hope it will be more like Etna than Vesuvius & pour out its hot lava fast & clear up the sooner.[129]

I admit, darling Sally, that your position is a trying one & I promise you all the sympathy that such an absent minded, star gazing genius as I has recollection enough to give.

By the way; thats a dreadful fault of mine. I am sometimes absorbed & *possessed* that I seem perfectly indifferent & a stranger would say that I had not a spark of affection even for my dear little children.

I have written a letter *since* that will explain the sentence that you copy. You did write so forlorn a letter about *"your* affection" & your "ambitions" & "variable temper" that I really feared your love had flagged & you were loath to tell me so. That was all. Your letters since have quite reassured me, dear, *dear* Sally.

I wish you *were* hanging out at my window. Tho' I would like to bring you in just for a little while every now & then. By the way I am glad there is a study down at the church, for I never could accomplish much while you were about. Recollect, you are never to come there.

I am glad Dr Graham takes the view he does. There are others who will do the same. I really covet great distinction as a man if for no other purpose to serve as a dignified precedent of the step of delivering a lady out of Coventry unlawfully confined there. I used to be *hotly* ambitious; but I have grown past that & my ambitions are now of the most hyperbolic kind.

God bless you, my dear Sally, & me too, & soon.

JM

I guess you are 32—*Now* tell me.

129. Two volcanic mountains, Etna in Sicily and Vesuvius in southern Italy.

Saturday, April 14. 1855.

Oh, John aint you anxious to know what the Dr & I did with you yesterday?[130] Well if you aint, I am very impatient to tell you. So I begin. The Doctor as soon I came in began "Ah! Sally, I know you are scared now. You dont know what I've got to say." And so he went on for a few minutes till his effervescence passed off, and then he said very soberly—"I hear nothing that isn't favorable. I thought of you all the time, and whenever I could, both in Phila & Princeton inquired about the gentleman, and I hear nothing unfavorable. But one thing I dont like; he is—(think you can bear it?) *too small for you*. Yet if you love him then that is no insuperable objection." I admitted this was a point upon which I was sensitive, but then it was a thing that could not be altered, and so if people only wouldn't call me "John Miller's *bigger-half*", I could stand even it. I think you are less impressed by this thing a great deal than I am. Indeed you have even carried your civility so far as to say you admired me the more because I am a sort of Grenadier.

The Dr told me his Wife[131] who had been several weeks at Mr Howell's (whose wife is her Niece)[132] had gone to hear you preach, and came off quite pleased. He would have gone himself but heard your lecture-room was always crowded. He scolded me (isn't it odd I never can spell that word?) for not having given him a letter of introduction to you, so that he might have seen you himself.

He bids me tell you "*He* thinks you will do *first-rate* if you can persuade me to give up my own home for yours. And if your happiness is never disturbed until *my temper* assails it you will be a most fortunate man." "It isn't true", he went on to say, "that you are bad-tempered. I've known you since I used to nurse you on my knee and have yet to see an outbreak from you;—and I've seen you sorely tried too. You are entirely amenable to reason & have great self-control. And you tell Miller if he doesnt love you & always treat you with the greatest tenderness I think he will deserve to be hung!" And to tell you the Truth, John I think so too,—and I am sure you agree with us, Dont you? Oh, another thing the Doctor said—"I predict Sally, Mr Miller's Mother will love you better than any of the others." I could have said with more than oriental enthusiasm, "Ah Prophet, may you live forever!", but somehow I cant be very hopeful there.

I was glad to hear that *Mrs Graham* expressed no other feeling than surprise when she hears it: it gives me some hope that other ladies may feel as she does, and that I may not realize all my fears. To find the half of them true will be more than I can bear, unless you should be all that I hope to find you.

After we had dispatched you we talked of the probable effect this step would have upon my family, and the Dr sympathized with me in my apprehension of

130. Dr. Archibald Graham.
131. Martha Alexander (Patsy) Lyle Graham (1800–1880).
132. Arthur H. Howell (1818–1877), a Philadelphia merchant and manufacturer, was married to Anne Brumbach Ruffner Howell (1825–1877), a daughter of Henry Ruffner (1790–1861) and his first wife, Sarah Montgomery Lyle Ruffner (1787–1849). Miller's close friend William Henry Ruffner was her brother.

trouble and sorrow, and promised me all the aid he could render. He does not wonder that I am anxious and sad in view of all the difficulties to be met, and all the old ties to be broken and all the new ones to be formed. But I dare not venture to touch upon these things.

Your letter of the 12th came this afternoon. I dont wonder you grow impatient with me. But if you are impatient, I am sometimes almost frantic from anxiety. I cannot express to you the overpowering effect of this thing upon me. At such times if you were only near to meet the thoughts that go out after you and to sustain with a greater strength than mine the energies that then give way, perhaps I might feel the weight less oppressive. But just now, and indeed always there are certain strong feelings that must be met in single combat. No one can give any help. And tho' my heart has learned, I don't know how, to turn to you in its troubles, yet I *know* you can do nothing more than say, "I am so sorry for you. I would relieve you by sharing these troubles, but I cannot even understand them."

Do you know, John, whenever you say, as you did in this last letter, "I am not happy & do not value life as others do" I am sadly discouraged. You never utter such a sentiment, & you do it frequently, that I do not feel it to be a sort of death-knell to my hopes.

Monday afternoon.

Lilly interrupted me, and I had afterwards my Sunday school lesson to look over and laid aside my scribblings until today. I am ashamed to send you such a miserable scrawl, but you may be willing to take the trouble to read it.

About three o'clock Sunday morning a loud knock at my door was quickly followed by Tom's voice asking admittance. I was greatly surprised having given all hope of his coming up until tomorrow. But it seems he came on from Washington & James from Rich'd Saturday morning & reached Staunton at 4 that afternoon. The Town was all agog with Mr Wise, & they determined not to wait for the Stage, but to get a carriage & come directly on; which they did arriving here in the rain at that dismal hour of the night.

James was quite sick yesterday & in his room until nearly dark. To-day he is busy in Court, so I have had no opportunity for our talk. But tomorrow I *must* have it. I find my courage rather strengthens as the time approaches. How I shall feel, however, when the hour has actually come I hardly know. I am so accustomed to having *my* will respected that I hardly can conjecture my sensations at having a universal opposition to it. I ought not to say opposition, for no one will dream of that, but disapproval, & with James perhaps, remonstrance will be expressed. But I will write to you fully and freely after it is all over.

James tells me of Robert Taylor's visit to your city. I cant account for his failure. I never thought him a good Preacher, but then others were much pleased with him and I felt sure he would succeed in pleasing the majority of his hearers. He ought not to preach in such a cold, hum-drum style for he is a man of very warm piety. Some day, if you have any curiosity about it, I'll tell you what I think is the reason he cant preach well—a reason which I dont mean *you* shall ever have.

And you wont let me go near the Church Study? Well, well, we'll see. Before I abandon all claim to having my own way, & give up saying "I will & I wont" we'll have that matter settled. Your Study is the very place for me. I am a new volume to put on your shelf. If I were a "diamond edition", as unfortunately I am not, you could let me lie on your table, and woul[d] sometimes heed my silent appeal for a little notice, and not think I disturbed you in the least, or occasioned you any loss of time. But even tho' I am an enormous great folio, yet if you will take me down to your Study and read me a little day by day I'm sure you will find *more in me* "than you ever dreamed of in *your philosophy*." And wont my rival be dethroned then!

Our mail arrangements have been changed since I last wrote, and I hope my letters will reach you sooner, tho yours will come to me, as they have been doing, on the third day after they are written.

Tuesday afternoon

Company came in just as I had finished my last sentence and kept me engaged until nearly dark, when it was too late for me to send on my letter by that mail. Our new Post office arrangements require our letters to be mailed every evening before dark.

Today I have been fussing over every body's business, but my own. My Brother with his enormous money schemes seeks my advice, and bears with much patience the course, different and more moderate than his own, which my "*cool wisdom*" suggests. This private business, & his business in bringing his connection with our estate to a close, occupies him so much, that thus far I have said not a word as to my own affairs. Then Tom, when James is gone pours *his* troubles, poor fellow, into my ear. Cantey too, who is in special anxiety at present, claims a hearing: and Mary asks for such aid as only my fingers can give. Now haven't I enough to do? And all this is not to show that I am so very *important* a *personage*, but just to prove that I am, as any body else standing to the family as I do would be just as busy as possible.

Now as to our affair; if I can seize James tonight when we get quiet possession of the Library I shall tell him what I may think proper and see how it affects him, and be governed in all my communications by his temper and feeling. I cannot therefore, tell *now* how full or how scant they may be. I think however I shall only ask his opinion as to such a step upon my part; & then tell him I am considering the matter very gravely and carefully, and would be glad to have his approval and support should this consideration issue in immediate action. I think after the first surprize is over he will make up his mind to stand by me, tho' with his extreme sensitiveness to public opinion, he will feel it very deeply.

Now as to yourself—why can't you come & get your answer in person? Suppose you do. Let your people know what you are about, & *who* you are seeking, and thus *test* their feeling in regard to the whole matter. Give your friends in this way an opportunity for thought and decision, and let the thing wear to the world an air of boldness & confidence which it would not otherwise have.

What think you of this? I would be glad on many accounts, if you would just come in upon me next week. James goes to Abingdon on Thursday or Friday, but will return in a short time I suppose. Mary is to be married the 8th of May, and the only quiet days left between this time & the middle of next month will be those of next week. So, I think you had best throw off all concealment and come up then.

Cousin John calling to see James, but finding him out yesterday gave me quite a talk again upon this subject. He finds, some how neither he nor I could tell how, that this *fancy* of yours is not quite so secret as you suppose. Some Lady had mentioned it to his wife, & *she* had had her surmises about it also.[133] I told Cousin John of Spence's opinion of the step—"that it would cost you your Church." "You are worth a great deal,["] he said, "but not worth so much as that. No minister should sacrifice the usefulness of his life for, *even you*". These remarks always tell upon me. But you are not willing I should have any thought even, upon the effect upon you. "You can take care of yourself," you tell me.

I was much disappointed in having no letter to-day. The last one was rather dolorous, and I hoped for another of a more cheerful cast. When you talk of being so absorbed & seemingly indifferent to everybody, a sort of a chill creeps over me, & I wonder how I shall stand that, with my craving after demonstrative affection. But dont you always tell me the *very worst about* yourself?

I pray you dont take a disgust at my letter. I have written it just as I could find time & it bears very much the look of jot work.

Affectionately,
S.C.P. McDowell

Phil. April 17th 1855.

Dear Me,

Tell Cantey, I accept. Tell her, I have been crossed in love; that each week fresh promises have been put before me till I am in a weakly condition of suspense that it is exhausting even to think of. Tell her, that if she will have a heart that is well nigh broken & a hand quite cramped in its beautiful penmanship by cringing replies to crooked & crabbed letters, that both are to be handed over to her together with all my voluminous correspondence which is already in Lexington & which you will please to give her. Tell her that she may reply to it in the order of its dates & that when she has done I will start anew.

Stay, tho' I will write to her myself.

Tell me one thing. Why did John Atkinson let you pick up his hat?

O fie Sally! To think of an old Doctor & a handsome young woman dissecting a poor parson. I hope you had a pleasant time. I know you went to the brain

133. "His wife" refers to Sarah (Sally) Lyle Carothers Preston (1811–1856).

first—for two reasons:—in all post mortems they go to the weak part first, & secondly, young women care very little for any other ailment if the brain is all right. Then you proceeded to the heart & I can fancy your sage diagnosis as that somewhat important organ was actually reached & was at length out in your hand. Poor parson Miller's heart! Dear Sally! Hadnt it just at least a *little* crack in it. Didn't it look broke. As it lay at rest at last after your cruelty didnt your own heart sink a little at the thought of what it had endured? You will of course write me word as *to the detail of your whole examination*. By the way what do you mean to do with the remains?

I didnt throw any snowballs at you. I had no "outside cause." I simply wrote kindly & forgivingly to one of the forlornest & most melancholy letters that ever one of the meekest of men had to help him make increase of his humility.

No one of your letters hardly ever gave me more pleasure than this does by the taste you express for country life. Only *one thing* banishes altogether the thought that would otherwise be coming to me. Can I not in some way arrange to go at once with Dame Miller when we are married & live on the spot where I build all my castles. And where I sincerely hope to spend the major part of the rest of my life. It is one of the loveliest tracts of the earth that the Sun ever shone upon. It is within 3 miles of Princeton (P. is *not* stiff & squeamish). It is a lawn of 60 acres so high that Princeton & a region of 70 miles diameter is *all* spread out in its view. It is surrounded & interspersed with forest & rock & deep ravine & is wild & enchanting beyond conception. Here I wish some day to build. And here the Allamby papers I expect will see the light. Here the new Ethics I expect will be written & under an oak that overhands a chasm of rocks & looks out upon the villages of that part of Jersey I expect that Lady S____ (my dear darling, the name is so *very* plain) will sit at her knitting while *in the afternoon* we will stroll down thro' the forest or drive over to P. Now my *one reason* is this. My church & my means would stagger & delay me & make me wait probably at any rate. But the one thing that is decisive with me is this. I mean to take you to no place *at first* that is not prominently in the view of the public. I do not mean to "hang the cage high where no one can speak to you"; but on the contrary take a house at first (when we settle one) in Chestnut St or near it *& let no one say that your position or standing was such that I sought retirement.*" This is the policy which if you agree in it I mean to observe to live for the first months or years in the very centre of things & then when we have asserted & seized the requisite position go with the friendships we have won into what retired quarters we please. If it were not for this principle the wisdom of wh: grows upon me I would be endlessly wrestling with the question how we could manage at once or soon to build at Allamby. I am going to show you Allamby when we go to P. in the Summer.

Sally, Sally, how can you spoil my letters? I said "winglets of fancy" not ringlets.

I am sorry your hair is not so long. But we will ride on horseback & bring all that back when we get to Allamby. I am *so* glad you like the country.

I have been watching for one of M[aggie]'s letters to send you. But she does not write as carefully as she did & I have been ashamed. I will however.

Darling, I will send you to the *Crimea* in the Summer if you will marry me in May.

I did violence to my own feelings so in violating yours in the matter of the violets, that I have sought out the "rare exotics" that your taste seemed to demand. I thought Japan was about the most foreign & send you a sprig from a bush brought by the Japan exhibition.

What do you mean by my having no "*reason*". I really dont understand.

I will write Cantey in my next.

Yours aff'ly
JM.

Lexington.
Thursday, April 19. 1855

Dear John,

It is so far in the night that I can only write you a note, which I am anxious to do now as I have found out that I can have a letter mailed in the morning.

I began to fear I was never to have a talk with James. An hour after my last letter to you was written I was called off to see my little nephew, Mac Massie, and found him so ill that his Mother & myself were up with him all night.[134] The next morning as he seemed better I came home, but James was at Court until our dinner hour, & after that I had another alarm about Mac that took me over to see him, & again I remained until nearly midnight. To-day in consequence of the unusual fatigue, I was good-for-nothing all morning, and only tonight after nine o'clock when James had discharged his last visitor did I get possession of him. I screwed up my courage & besieged him in his own room, from which I have but just come. I had over-estimated the pain of the interview very extravagantly, and had under-estimated just as greatly James' personal respect and kindness.

I began by abruptly stating the subject of our interview. I then said under the peculiarities of the case I wanted his counsel, and if he could conscientiously grant it his support. But if his views differed from mine & he could not support me in such a step, then he must regard my application to him now, simply as testimony of a confidence that I had extended to no other member of the family. He said, he would think over the subject carefully. That his affections I had already & would always have And that his support & that of his wife should be given. He did not now regard the step as wrong—Does not[135] see why a woman should be cut off from domestic ties because of a *sentiment* against a step of this

134. James MacDowell Massie, born on Nov. 3, 1854, was the son of James and Sophonisba McDowell Massie.
135. McDowell repeated "not."

kind, when the moral question has been satisfactorily met. Yet, he agreed with me that all ladies almost would revolt at it. And mentioned the horror expressed by a kinswoman in Louisville, at hearing a short time ago, that I was actually married—not to you but somebody else. I could but be struck with the outgoings of *sentiment* in different people when the name was mentioned. I have know the Lady ever since I knew anybody, & always thought her lamentably deficient in real delicacy, utterly without elevated principle & without any genuine or high sentiment tho' she is overwhelming with her *sentimentalism*. And yet *she* undertakes to be horrified at *my* doing such a thing as this. Well, this is just what all the "high vulgar" as William Brown calls them, will do.

Well, I could only do as James asked, let him think over the matter, & *then* listen to his advise. So you will have to wait patiently—it may be a *long time*. Tell me seriously would you be willing to wait a long time? or would you weary & wear out under long continued absence. A long engagement is a perilous thing—but, could you, do you think put up with *that* if nothing better should offer?

Never mind about Maggie's letter being a chef d'oeuvre.[136] I know all about such efforts as hers.

Don't write too plainly to Cantey. Lilly is offended that you take no notice of her.

But I dont want day light to dawn upon me so good night.

Affectionately
S.C.P. McDowell.

[marginal note] Oh! I picked up Mr Atkinson's hat, because in a little struggle with his horse it was thrown off & he could not do it for himself. Is that satisfactorily explained?

Phil. April 19th 1855.

My dear Sally,

I am expecting confidently a letter this evening & therefore I begin one in reply. I would write oftener but writing with me is a great tax as I write so much & therefore, I must take those times when I am somewhat fresh for it, & of these I am obliged to be economical in order to accomplish my public duty. Still I hope all need of concealment in writing is already or soon will be at an end & I still promise to write as often as you.

I suppose *just now* you are quite in the midst of the "explosion" of which you spoke. I sincerely hope, my dear Sally, it may be greatly more easily borne than you feared & that your friends will soon turn & half approve the step about which you have been so prudent. I wish I could come & help you in making your defence.

It is I think *certain* now that the Church cannot be opened in May. When it will be it seems hard to decide. They have been working in it through all weathers

---

136. French, meaning a masterpiece.

now for more than two years & at the hour when the workmen dispersed a watchman has taken their place & recently two have watched in it all night. It will be a beautiful building.

I am still in my ancient "sanctum" hallowed by rhyme & prose but Monday is the limit of my present understanding with my landlord. I know not how much grace further he will be able to allow me.

I wish you could go with me on a visit I plan in a few days to Princeton. I mean to go out to Allamby. How I would like to show it to you at this season when the air is like Summer, & the trees which anywhere would interrupt the view are so free of leaves that the whole magnificent panorama lies around you. I have been in the Alps & on the Rhine & near the White Mts & on your Otter Peaks & at Roslyn Castle but as a *residence* it is the most romantic I have ever beheld. A village named Pennington four miles off is singularly beautiful as it lies more fully in view than any other & its spire is situated so as to give it a fine effect. Some 300 acres *walled* in as they can be by the huge stones of the Hills would give a command of all the prospect & would be as fair a hermitage as Leibnitz could have required for the repose of his most perfect investigations. All but the park of 60 acres on the top of the hill which would be level or sloping round from the top is in forest & you know our design would be to let it remain so. I have a Spanish Castle nearly finished on the property & a porters lodge on the corner next to Princeton. Moreover I am saving up my money & in spite of the smile of one of my friends the house that Jack built may one day be a living reality.

They say that N.Y. harbour in one direction & the Atlantic in the other can be seen with a good glass.

Friday, April 20th

I am so disappointed at not receiving a letter. There is no more chance for receiving one to-day & I have received none since that which you wrote yesterday week. Happily I am so convinced of your love for me that this disappointment does not agitate me in that respect & I know that you have either had some good reason for delay or a letter has been lost by some mischance of the mail.

No doubt before this all your immediate family have been made aware of our plan. I trust the shock has been less than you imagined & that after the first "explosion" the disordered elements have settled back into a very agreeable calm. One evidence of my love to you, my dear Sally, is the nervous sympathy I feel for you even at this distance in what you consider so formidable a disclosure. I shall no doubt hear from you tomorrow & then I will write again. The letters that disappoint me in the coming seem always to be those that I am looking to with great anxiety.

Who knows that one wont break into my solitude in the morning untying all the Gordian knot of my difficulties & fixing the day of our marriage? But alas! nothing so good corresponds with the previous inter-weavings of our history: does it?

I am understanding one of your letters in a sort of serio-playful way as ordering off my white cravats. I am going to take my journey to Virginia in those of a different color all out of love & loyalty. If this is not according to your intent you must correct it in a future letter for I am intending to make white black in this instance most religiously. Good-bye. These disappointments about letters are very hard to bear but my affection now burns without much kindling.

Yours affectionately
Jno Miller.

Friday April 20, 1855

My dear John,

I had only written the above scraps of lines when my courage failed, and night drew on and I put by my writing materials for another time. In fact I waited hoping to hear from you last night, but waited only to be disappointed. This morning (Saturday) I write a hurried note as I shall not be able to write again till Tuesday.

I do not mean you to understand that our whole affair rests upon what my Brother may think of it. His opinions and feelings may have the effect of creating a *delay* of the marriage, but cannot, that I can see now, bring about an *abandonment* of it. So you need not make yourself uneasy on that score.

I am *so* glad that famous interview is over—and over so pleasantly too. James is so excessively passionate, and I am so hot myself that I always dread an explosion with him, and fear being drawn into hard & strong & stinging expressions myself when his temper acts like a match upon mine. But in this case, there was not the slightest approach to any irritation. He seemed to feel most concerned to impress me with the strength and ardor of his affection for me, & to assure me of his earnestness in protecting and upholding me. But I am so proud. I can't bear— that is, I can *hardly* bear to think that anybody should feel it to be *necessary* to *uphold me*. Like my Father, I have such intense pride of character that I suffer more than I can Tell from anything that affects it, and shudder at the feeling of scorn that sometimes overpowers me when others stand out and offer to uphold *my character*. I have to school myself to accept such offers gratefully for I do know, that very dark Providences have made them necessary. And I submit. I would do it cheerfully too. I know it is all wisely ordered & well. And if it should happen to cast a shadow over your prospects, why, I shall just have to make a sunny spot for you of your home.

I'm much obliged to you. I have no idea of *going* to the Crimea, much less notion of being *sent* there. So if you cant do better than that with me this summer you must put up with the "bother" of keeping me with you. But I keep breakfast waiting.

Affectionately Yours
S.C.P. McDowell

Jarndyce v. Jarndyce[137]
Court of Chancery
Vernal Sessions
April 21st 1855.

My *dear Sally*,

Yours, the last date of which seemed to be Tuesday is post-marked, the 19th, & reached me just now. It's a nice letter, but Sally, why didn't you *begin* (in talking with him) with your own matters & top off with James' great scheme? I wish I could show James the wrecks of these great agonies as they lie around Philadelphia. The risk is as great as the prize; & I am glad that your "cool wisdom" is in play again to keep you from encouraging him too warmly & from sharing even by so light an endorsement as your counsel, in the dangers of his enterprise. Alas! tho', James mustnt know how sagely I talk about him or he will talk with equal gravity about the other matters.

I am poor St Anthony & you are the Evil One that came to tempt him.[138] St Anthony at his books was trying to do the best he could for the West Arch Street Presbyterian Church when an angel came in & told him of a beautiful spot in Virginia & about birds & Spring weather & how all the dearest treasures of his heart should be within his sight if he would go with him & leave his duties. St Anthony was very tired. Moreover preaching to the West Arch St. people was a thing he had done a great deal of during the Winter, moreover, St Anthony needed relaxation so the world would say & the Evil One greatly tempted St Anthony.

But our friend reasoned this way. The sweet angel is wrong in thinking I had better *try* my people to see how they like anything. I want them to hear as their first knowledge of any step of mine that *I have done it*, not that there is some idea I may do it. In one case I get the full power of my own influence over them before they commit themselves. In the other case they make all sorts of speeches about my *not* doing this or that & the affair becomes so embroiled that there is no straightening it afterward.

My dear Sally, I *mean* to marry you if you will accept me. So that the idea of *trying* the sentiment of my people never for a moment enters my head. I can forecast the state of things sufficiently to come to a conscientious conclusion, & you are right in understanding me as not wishing you to be anxious about *me*. Under God I will take care of myself. If I am in my pulpit one Sunday before we are married & after the thing is announced it will accomplish (what I think is desirable) all the publicity that a minister's marriage need have in order to be distinctly & boldly announced to his people.

Alas! I am forgetting poor St Anthony. Suffice it to say that St Anthony wanted to go but was borne safely thro' the trial & tho't very hard of the bright angel for tempting him to what he could hardly keep from undertaking to do.

---

137. *Jarndyce v. Jarndyce* was the interminable chancery cause that Charles Dickens lampooned in *Bleak House*.

138. Saint Anthony of Egypt (c. 251–356), exemplar for the development of monasticism.

But, Sally, I cant go twice; & if I were to tell my people publicly then you would marry me before Summer wouldnt you. And if we marry before Summer then I must take two holidays & St Anthony would be much spoken against in his management of his domestic engagements.

Alas for poor St Anthony!

Moreover St Anthony has to hang on Monday. There was once a monarch who told a lover that if he would marry his ladye love before a certain time or even have her promise it should save him from the gallows. The lover therefore writ to the ladye & told her how that she could save him from hanging. But the ladye wouldn't. And, therefore, on Monday just at the time when he might have been basking in the ladye's smiles he has to be overlooking his effects & preparing for his departure.

Seriously, I had thought of this thing repeatedly & would have begged you to allow me to do it, & indeed my impatience makes it hard for me to work in my present uncertainty, but if there is anything to apprehend in public opinion (tho' I do not think there is much) I feel sure that my people will *most* decorously submit if they hear directly from *me* (that is from one of my immediate friends) what I *intend to do*.

I think Dr. Graham is right about Mother.

I am not so sure. I think my size *can* "be altered". And if I live to get to Allamby you & I will ride on horseback, & your hair will become so long that it will sweep around the horses feet, & I so stout that I shall have to get a great Flemish horse to carry me. Nous verrons.[139]

Meanwhile take care that I dont exhale in sorrow under these repeated disappointments.

I have family authority for such a match. John Sergeant was I think shorter than I & his wife as large as you.[140] It is from my mother that I get my small size tho' she herself is of the usual size.

No matter, dear Sally, till we get to Allamby we wont walk much in Chestnut St.

My lecture-room is crowded because it is'nt large. If the Dr had come on Wednesday evening wouldnt I have given him room?

Tell him I'm *going* "to be hung" on Monday, all because you wont marry me.

You mus'nt speak so of your letters. They are very nice. I can read them with great ease & I would rather you would scribble away thro' a long letter, than write a shorter one with ever so much care.

How I wish I could be with you under the strong emotions of which you speak. Sally, marry me & then your heart will turn & thrust all its troubles upon me. I am used to bearing trouble. You ought to be glad of that instead of discouraged.

---

139. French, meaning we will see.

140. Miller's maternal grandparents were Jonathan Dickinson Sergeant (1746–1793), a Philadelphia attorney and member of the Continental Congress during the Revolution, and Margaret Spenser Sergeant (1759–1797).

I think when we get to Allamby we shall be happy & then the past will serve as a background to the picture. Don't fear about my indifference. It is only a forgetfulness about the *forms* of affection. In my heart I will be all the world to you.

Mr Taylor's visit here could not have turned out differently. He came quite sick from travelling & would not stay till he was better. I begged him to do so.

Beg Farish to change the mail back.

Yours affectionately
JM.

I have *not* told you the very worst of myself. All men are worse when we know them better. Still Adams children are all a bad brood, & if I had to choose who I would pass my life with, I would choose first you & then myself. You surely wont stop writing in expectation of my coming.

Phil. April 23d 55.

Darling,

You're so queer.

When everything was dark and stormy & uncertain you were intending to write me fully months & months & Months ago. Now that your brother has come & you find you had "extravagant" fears about the interview & he greatly & favorably disappoints you, you are disposed to think we may have to wait a *long time*.

Don't you think I'm a sort of granitic primary formation?

Now "seriously" I would wait for you from one to thirty years. If you *could'nt* marry me I would wait for you forever. If you *would'nt* marry me I would try to forget you as soon as I could. But "seriously" I cant see what gives us this last "crook in our lot" & why we need wait at all.

I shall expect to hear that Cantey & Mary & Lilly have all said they would sustain you & you have had a brand new invoice of first rate testimonials from Philadelphia & some other of your friends without knowing anything of our matter have actually told you you *ought* to marry & that *therefore* you fear it will be a long time before you can have me.

You are *so* queer.

I wish I *could* give you up. I would like to just out of a little spite. But I might as well think of giving up this wicked right hand of mine because it torments me with many a perverseness & deficiency.

Now, Sally, you may put this day off just as long as you please. You may say next Christmas or next Easter or a year from next Whitsuntide or three years from this coming 30th of April or never. *If you will love me* I will be faithful to you on any of these conditions. But if you love me dont keep me in this racking suspense. I think you are just a little cruel to bring me to the eve of the highest expectation six or eight times & then turn off with so little apparent realizing of my share in the common laws of suffering.

But now, my poor darling dear Sally, you suffer so much yourself, I have no doubt, that I ought not to scold you & I have kept back many an impatient utterance on this very account & partly too, because, in my pride, I did not wish to urge either a marriage or an engagement in such a way as to make me feel after our marriage that I had wrung a decision from you unwillingly or one day sooner than you can & give me one day of unnecessary postponement or suspense.

I enclose you a letter from Maggie & one from Mary. I will introduce you by letter to all the members of the family as they write to me. You must know that a friendship has sprung up between Maggie & Willie Potter so ardent that I dont like it. You will smile I know, but nevertheless I dont care about her writing & Mary knows it. Who knows what Willie will be? And as to this affection amounting to nothing you ought to see it.

Write as often as you possibly can. May'nt I as a reward for this great omnibus of a letter get ready for my wedding day & wont you tell me which it is.

I enclose a letter to Cantey. If you think it amiss, keep it, & I will send her another. As to Lilly, take her in your lap & put back her hair from her face, & kiss her on both cheeks for *me*, & say, "To B. or not to B.: that is the question."

I am sorry little Mac has been sick. But I never heard of a lady abusing her health so. To think of you sitting up even to write me a letter after so many vigils.

Never mind at Allamby we will set that all right. I shall remember your promise of "making a sunny spot at home". I am going to have all your letters bound except one or two wh: I mean to hang up in gilt frames about the parlour.

Blessings on you, my dear Sally. I am very angry at you.

> *Yours with great discontent.*
> *Jno Miller.*

[Enclosure: Margaret Miller to John Miller]

April 23. [1855]

Dear Papa,

I have been going to write to you for a long time. Grandmother has most got rid of her cold. Allie uses such big words. The other night Cousin Maggie asked him why he was so ticklish and he said "oh! it is constitutional!"

I want to write to Willie, and Grandmother said I must ask you if I could. David has cleaned the study, and Cousin Maggie is very busy makeing an alphabetical catalogue, and she wants to get it finished before she goes away, and she has composed this verse,

Cousin Maggie like a beaver
In the study works all day
Trying hard to make a catalogue
Before she goes away.
Come and see us soon.

Your affectionate daughter
Maggie Miller.

[Enclosure: Mary Miller to John Miller]

Princeton, April. 23d 55.

Dear John.

Do not you think that Dr Hodge comes out pretty straight in these last articles. I cannot detect any heresy. I heard about your speech in Presbytery first from Mrs Hodge. I am afraid you are carrying the matter too far, especially as I know that you have some bitter feelings in that direction. I think you ought be careful. The children have been unwell a little, for 2, or 3 days, with something like chicken pox. Sam Hageman also has it. Maggie's is very light, but Allie is sore all over & does not bear it very well. Maggie is very lazy about writing to you, but I believe she will accomplish a little at it to'day. She has been wanting to write to Willie Potter lately, but we all told her she had better ask your leave first. I believe she says she promised him to do so, but he has not written to her. I think you had better come up for a little while some time this month. Dr Mc'Gill called once about the Memoir, but said that he did not care to have any of the manuscripts till the vacation.[141] I have heard that he talks of leaving Princeton for the vacation & spending it on a farm that he has. His health has been bad this Spring. It will be 6 weeks on Thursday since Dick sailed. I should think he might arrive any time after that. Hoping to see you soon.

Believe me,

Your affectionate sister,
Mary Miller.

[marginal note with this enclosure]
Don't show this, Sally.

JM.

Dr Hodge has'nt pleased me about an epitaph on my fathers grave but it isn't true that I feel bitterly—& Don't speak of it.

[Enclosure: John Miller to Margaret Cantey McDowell]

Phil. Apr. 24th 1855.

My *dear Miss Cantey,*

I hear from your sister who is a sort of adviser of mine when I am in any difficulty that you own a small tenement in Lexington which you inherited from your mother[142] which you are willing to let & that you have expressed a

141. Charles Hodge (1797–1878), professor of theology at Princeton Theological Seminary and editor of the *Princeton Review*. His wife was Mary Hunter Hodge (1808–1880). Samuel Miller Hageman (1848–1905), the oldest son of Miller's sister, Sarah Sergeant Miller Hageman (c. 1820–1867), and her husband, John Frelinghusen Hageman (1816–1892), a Princeton attorney. Alexander Taggart McGill (1807–1889) of Princeton Theological Seminary.

142. At this point Miller wrote a pound sign (#) and at the bottom of the page another pound sign and wrote, "Eve."

willingness to let it to me. She tells me that it has all the modern conveniences, hot and cold baths which I have *been obliged* to take alternatively lately every two or three days, that it has gas in all its stories & that it is to have a dumb waiter as soon as it is rented.

You are right in supposing that I was badly treated in my former negociation. The house was very cold in Winter & very hot in Summer it had only one story, the way to get up to it was very difficult & I found the landlady so intractable in the engagement. I was to make with her that I have been obliged to give it up.

I agree to take yours.

I learn from your sister that you are willing to take a tenement of mine in exchange. It is old & badly used of late & a good deal injured especially in the upper story, for tho' I am ashamed to tell it, I let the party of whom I was last speaking take possession at once, tho' they refused *me* possession to the very last.

If you wish references as to character or a description of the tenement send on some one from Lexington who can make inquiries here & at Princeton & by all means write soon for my home is sadly injured in the way I tell you & I wish the person that enters it to make repairs.

> *Yours most affectionately,*
> B.

Miss Cantey McDowell.

[Enclosure: William Henry Ruffner to John Miller]

> *Harrisonburg, Rockingham Co, Va.*
> *Ap. 17. 1855*

Dear Sir

The Presbytery of Lex. is to meet next month with a view to ordain & install Mr Cleghorn over a very important charge.[143] There are, I am grieved to say, some unpleasant, tho' not very well defined, suspicions about him in the minds of some members of the Presbytery.

The matter with the Am. Col. Soc. will probably be detailed to us by one that knows. You no doubt comprehend the importance of the case well enough to give your impressions of the *morale* of that transaction; & to furnish any facts or views bearing on the character of Mr C. that will guide us to the right conclusion when we come together. I will make no use of your name that you do not desire.

I have lately been to Lexington!!!! Please give me a call as you pass.—Isn't the 'Critic' the best literature of the day!

> *Briefly your's*
> *Wm. H. Ruffner*

143. Elisha Burnham Cleghorne (1812–1881) was an agent of the American Colonization Society from 1853 to 1855.

April 23d 55.

Oh, Sally, you dont know what you escaped. I have just been writing one of the sharpest letters—so sharp that tho' it lies by me here nearly finished I mean to burn it, not because I do not think you deserve it, but for two reasons, first, that I think you are suffering, & tho' you send shock after shock thro' me first from the positive & then from the negative pole of your battery with the most perfect apparent nonchalance still that I belong to the enduring sex & it is not chivalrous to complain of anything a lady chooses to inflict upon you: then, secondly, that I do not wish, if you marry me, to feel that I wrung from you a decision or destroyed your freedom in judgment.

But indeed, Sally, such an idea as this of "*long delay*" after the repeated hopes of the Writer & after your brother has more than transcended all that those hopes were built upon, makes me feel that you think I am a sort of granitic formation accustomed to pressure & never quite at ease except under a sort of nightmare of superincumbent barriers. I think you are right down unreasonable now, & I wish you would put on your bonnet & go over to Dr. White's & give my compliments to him & ask him if you[144] will scold you a little. Tell him if he has a sermon on,

The Wife

of

The Patriarch Job, or

<u>*The Children & the Bears.*</u>

I wish he would read 'em both to you beginning at the beginning.

Come now, Sally, behave.

You see by what I enclose that Lexington knows all about us & tho' I hear no whisper here, yet it cant be long before the town will be alive with the whole matter. Now my favorite way to kill rumours is to realize them. It keeps your friends from committing themselves against you unwittingly & saves the trouble of all questions. It is my deliberate opinion that the sooner we are married the better, if I may have the courage, my dear darling, to assume that you are willing to marry me at all.

I have relented & will send you a part of the letter but it grew much more violent afterward & was to have ended still more severely. I know you would give anything to see the rest, but I have burnt it & never will tell you.

The fact is, I love you so much that I *cant* scold & when I do, you *know* I love you so much that I believe you laugh at me, & that this moment you are laughing at all these complaints of mine.

Now as to your questions, "Would you be willing to wait a long time?" No; I would'nt. "Would you weary & wear out under long continued absence"? No; I could'nt. I'm as weary as I can be now. "Could you put up with a long engagement if nothing better than that offered?" Yes; I'd have to. But I'd grumble & "go on" so, I'd make you perfectly miserable.

144. Miller meant "he" here instead of "you."

I would'nt write for a month sometimes, & when *you* did'nt write I'd grumble. And I would worry your life out of you.

I'd laugh at you for being so big. I'd write letters beginning "Grannie-dear"

& I'd every now & then profess to wish to bring the engagement to an end & I'd give you no peace.

So now, Sally, be a good girl, & write me word that Mr Lacey & I shall be married on the same night or about a week or ten days after.

If you dont perhaps I shall write to Dr White & ask him to fix an evening & I shall come on & steal you as you invited me to do.

Tuesday Afternoon

I have received your last letter & am delighted to find that you seem to have a little remorse for the one that preceded it.

I did not receive that by the bye till too late to *mail* a reply. I was out in the country at my cousin's.

Tell me, dear Sallie, why is'nt this the time to tell me that you will have me, & when? Hasnt everything turned out better than you feared.

Remember when you feel too proud to accept other peoples offers of support that *I'll* support you. You cant be too proud to accept the protection of your husband.

If you wont go to the Crimea, will you go to Vienna? I think you could help there in befogging the Emperor.

Now what if this galloping foolish letter should come in upon you at some moment of great distress? when you had just been speaking to your sisters? or were distressed by some unexpected embarrassment? How it would jar upon you with all its folly!

Come here Sally. My darling, *I love you more than words can express*. You shall determine time, delay, everything. You shall be entirely supreme. I plight my faith to you whether you delay or not. I leave my peace entirely in your keeping. Now, your *generosity* will do for me all.

Tuesday April 24. 1855

My dear John,

I would not write yesterday hoping I might hear from you by the mail, that now arrived at mid-night. Sure enough this morning your letter came. By our present arrangements my letters should reach you in thirty six hours, and I am annoyed to find them so long delayed. I fancy the delay must occur at this office, yet our Post Master seems careful and efficient, and in my own case, very obliging and accommodating, often mailing letters after the mail has been closed.

I am so sorry you cant come on now, but I acquiesce in your reasonings. I am sure you would fall in love with our country if you could see it now. I have never seen it more beautiful; And my own yard, in grande toilette at present, is as beautiful a spot as I care to see. The weather has been like summer, the Thermometer, a few days since, standing at 92, and the air almost oppressively laden with the perfume of flowers—I am afraid Allamby will never be so sweet a spot to me as this, but I don't know. I have an *odd* way of being pleased with whatever belongs to me. If a thing had no merit before, the instant it becomes mine, I discover some surprising beauty in it, and am satisfied. And apart from any intrinsic value & beauty this is a reason why I shall love Allamby—*because it is mine!* What shall I claim next?

When you go to Princeton tell Allie to send me a name for his—*colt*. I pay him the compliment to give him the first. The little servants make a great "miration" over it, and Lilly is half disposed to claim it; but it is Allie's. When I told Lilly I had given it away, she was quite indignant, suspecting, as she said, that I had given it to my young student—(the young man I am educating.)[145] She will be better pleased when she hears, hereafter, how it has been disposed of. I hope Allie will be pleased with it, and some day find it at least better than a hobby-horse.

Do you remember my writing to you some time ago of a servant whom I was very anxious to keep in case I should go to a free State to live?[146] Well, the other day I stepped out where she was at work to talk to her about going with Mary who, I know, is anxious to have her. To give the poor creature a fair chance for the future I *made her a sort of confidante*. To my surprize she expressed great pleasure at the communication and most emphatically refused to leave me. She would go to Phil, she said or any where that I chose to go, and hoped if she outlived *me* that she might belong to Lilly. I was amused, & no doubt you will be shocked to hear of my confiding so delicate a matter to a *servant;* but she has been a very kind and faithful friend, and under the circumstances was entitled to such a mark of respect and attention. She asked very respectfully after you, and was delighted to hear you were a Preacher. I asked how she thought she could get along with the children? "You know madam, she said, I always did love children; and I will love these. Dont you 'member how Master used to say Miss Lilly would give her very skin for me?" I am glad the matter was so pleasantly settled. I don't know how I could have made up my mind to give her to Mary.

You don't want to give up your *white cravats*, do you? Well—do as you choose in so grave and important a matter. So you give up the *blue hat* you wore last summer, it matters little to me whether the cravat be white or black. I have seen you wear both, and thought each, in its turn looked well. Indeed I used to be struck with your skill in adjusting the white ones. What say you to my wearing a *black* dress?

You say you "cant have two holidays," therefore you cant be married until the summer holiday comes on. Is this what you mean? Or what do you mean? If the marriage does not come off in May—then it *cannot* in *June*. Then I would not

145. Probably James Carrington, her cousin.
146. The slave she refers to is Jenny.

like to go to Phil in mid-summer, or the early fall; so you would have to wait till October. How would you like that? My idea is this—as soon as the thing is absolutely determined upon, then let it be consummated. I would have no talk about it. You shall have *three weeks* to make *your* arrangements & I will take the same time to announce the step to distant friends to whom such attention is due.

Dr Graham talking of the thing to-day takes the same view of it that you do. "Consult nobody—he said,—give no one a chance to express an opinion for or against it. When it is over they will submit. A few persons will regulate public opinion; and in a few days the fuss will all subside, and the peculiarities of the case be forgotten. If any body in his Congregation is disposed to murmur, let Miller send you off to see them when he gets you to Phil'a, & you'll soon bring them safely round." But the Dr. is a partial judge, & you must take all the nice things he says of me with great allowance.

Now when James comes back on Saturday we will have another full talk over the matter and have it brought to an end. But I do, I say it frankly, wish very much I could *see you* before the thing goes further. Cant you *infuse* a little strength into me? For one who stands out with such a show of independence & self-reliance as I do to the world, I have the very most hesitating and undecided being imaginable.

I don't know what you will do with me when you take possession. If the whole truth were told I should know how often this very thing had already tried your temper and perhaps excited a little emotion of contempt. But I cant help it, any more than I can help being five feet, six inches high.

I was amused to have your last letter handed to me side by side with one from Uncle Robert Breckinridge. They looked very amicable, & it happened you both wrote to me upon the same day. I know you dont like one another. My sharp ear caught at your feeling from a single expression in regard to him, the words of which were not very enlightening in this regard, but the tone in which they were uttered told all. But as you both happen to love me I shall have to keep the peace between you. I dont think Uncle Robert loves me *very* much, but he always uses to me the most affectionate expressions and has laid me under heavy obligations for Kindness and real service. These I am always, *not repaying,* but acknowledging by attention to his children; and thus I am more strongly bound to the Breckinridges, than to any other young relations I have, except perhaps the Carringtons.

Tell me, was the Lady whom Mr Wise (our present Candidate for Gov.) married any relation of yours? She was a Philadelphian I remember, and her name was Sergeant.[147]

Dr Graham goes on to your City in ten days and says he means to go to see you, so send me your address that I may give him the letter of introduction he asks for. He says you look "*very queer*" in that book of University Lectures; & sure

147. Henry Alexander Wise's second wife was Sarah Sergeant Wise (1817–1850).

enough you do. I think it is a horrid attempt at a likeness and I wish you could get it expunged which with my old Democratic notions I think might be done.

The Doctor threatens to tell you a great many things when he sees you, the half of which, I tell you before hand you are not to believe.

I find myself writing at a table which Tom had left, and pick up this buff-colored sheet from among his leavings.[148]

I am sorry about your *hanging,* but I couldnt help it. Cantey says what has become of her letter?

Affectionately Yours,
S.C.P. McDowell

Colalto,
Thursday April 26. 1855

Dear John,

Maggie's letter carried the day. Even yours was, this time, only second-best. That odd looking, cramped, straight up & down writing has made a *real* being of the little Lady to me. And wasn't I interested in all its items of news? And didn't I think Allie was *after all,* right smart? And didn't I fancy that Maggie, when she found fault with Allie's "big words" was guilty of a covert charge of the same sort against Allie's Father? And didn't I, with my bias to politics, think it rather ominous that Allie should have stumbled on just the "big word"! that he did? And then the request about the letter to Willie, so very innocently made;—didn't you half relent as you read it? And Cousin Maggie's verse, quite untrammeled by rule, was, I know, an unspeakable comfort to the little writer in her difficult task of getting up a letter. On the whole, I am not a little in love with Maggie & her letter: Do you think she will ever return the compliment? But you must not think I meant to ask for letters from all your family. Of course I would not dream of such an intrusion upon you. I only asked for Maggie's *letter* as any body else would have asked for her *picture.* I wanted to know something more & better of her than that she is very lovely. It is a dangerous thing for a woman to be beautiful, almost unfortunate that she should be extraordinarily clever. "I have *nine* daughters,['] Jefferson Randolph used to say, "and I thank God there is neither a *beauty* nor a *genius* amongst them."[149] I thought the speech very wise, & supposed all men would agree in its sentiment until Mr Fendall said, when I once quoted it to him. "He would have thanked God more heartily if there *had* been a beauty or a Genius among them."

I don't believe Mr Ruffner knows half as much as his very "knowing" remark would lead you to suppose. I don't know how he could.

What makes you say "Don't show this to anybody?—don't speak of this"— who have I to show it to. I'm 'fraid you have no high opinion of my prudence. I

---

148. This letter fills seven pages on two sheets of distinctly different paper.
149. Thomas Jefferson Randolph (1792–1875) was Thomas Jefferson's grandson.

feel almost offended at such cautions. What's the Matter with Mr. Cleghorne? I never heard any suspicion against him except that of his having no brains, and that I believe is not a thing that Presbytery has charge of. He seemed an uncouth creature with a super abundance of hand and arm, that once reached across two pews to demand a peep into my hymn book. I remember too his prying around my carriage as it stood waiting in the street, & excusing himself by asking "whose horses are these"? The horses were not in the best order, and I have little doubt he compassionated them very much.

I didn't give your note to Cantey. I think you can write her a much better one in which you will omit the names of places entirely. However, before you can write again she will know all about the matter. Poor child, she is sadly out of spirits, and I feel concerned at it the more because there is no remedy for her. She is to Mary as Lilly is to me, with the great difference that she does not choose to follow her fortunes. She prefers having her home with me here, or going to Phil with me, as I spoke of going six months ago to any other arrangement at present proposed. But when she knows more of my plans I cant tell what she will do. She wont, I know, wish to go to Phil then, nor would I ask her to go then, but by and bye after her wrath cools off, and after *you* win her over to liking you, I think she will come. I don't want her to go to eastern Virginia and be mixed up with the Carringtons, & Venables & Bruces & Watkins', who tho' good enough and rich enough are yet not exactly of the type I like. I never did like that part of our State. The men in it seem without manly energy and think if they live luxuriously, spend freely, talk learnedly of wines, drive fine horses, dress well & bow handsomely they have accomplished all that is desirable in life. And the women are much of the same stamp, with the very striking difference, that they, with all their thought about it, do *not* dress well.

Mac is quite well again and in anticipation of the forth-coming 30th brought me, the other day, a silver goblet almost as big as himself.[150]

Why didn't you write your Father's epitaph yourself?—and thus escape all chance of collision of feeling with Dr Hodge? What were you talking about in Presbytery that required an admonition from your Sister, of whom I stand in the greatest terror. One admonition from her to me would so mar my fair propositions that you would look in vain for your grenadier after it. I won't inflict another page upon you. How many letters have I written you. I am ashamed any longer to think of counting them. I do laugh at your suspicions of Willie & Maggie, but I think you are right. If you had been half as prudent for yourself it would have saved you a world of trouble. Pray don't scold me about my delays etc. Yet I need not say so for you are *very* good under all the worry I cause you in that way.

> *Yours,*
> S.C.P. McD.

150. The thirtieth was McDowell's birthday.

Thursday [April] 26 [1855]

Darling Sally,

I am not, that I know of so easily moved, but one part of your letter touches me, almost to tears. I know you suffer keenly; that memory & fears for the future & anxiety for the present all distress you, &, therefore, when you think of *me* & calling up this fancy of a "shadow" which you think may obscure my future prospects, turn towards me with pity & tell me that you will "make a sunny spot for me at home," you cant tell how it moves me. Dear, dear Sally; I do believe I am in chase of a Koh-i-noor & if you would only let yourself be caught I do believe *I* at least would possess a very happy home.

What will you do for me if the shadow does'nt descend. If by weight of character & strength of judgment & previous hold upon my friends I do my part toward scattering the shadows altogether. What will you do for me? Will you love me any less? Do you only mean to make a sunny spot at home in case I so fearfully need it as your fears lead you to imagine? Darling, if either your fears or my hopes gain the ascendant, dont you thin[k][151] we will be all the world to each other, either in the one case because we shall be so in fact, or in the other because we shall be so happy?—or chiefest of all because you are so lovely? Sally, that was such a nice speech. I do love you so for it.

I expect your Tuesday's letter to-night & therefore I scratch off these few sentences before going out.

> *Yours most tenderly,*
> *Jno Miller.*

Friday Evening [April 27, 1855].

Dear Sally,

Your letter has just come in.

I feel so grateful for it.

I wish I had more time to answer it.

I cypher it out this way. On Saturday our engagement is to be decided upon & then in three weeks consumated i.e. about May 19th. Is'nt that so?

Poor Allie! I'll have to *break* to him the news about the colt as men do sudden joyful surprises. He's such a young colt himself, that you couldn't have met his vein better. Darling Sally, I'm so much obliged to you for loving my little unknown *invisible* children. No part of my establishment am I more proud of than them. I know that you will be pleased with them & so will our good old friend Jenny to whom I wish to be kindly remembered.

By two holidays I meant two *before* Summer. Oh, I can easily manage the two if Midsummer is included. I meant two this Spring.

I shall be delighted to see Dr Graham.

151. Miller wrote "thing."

Dear Sally, if you marry me in three weeks the intervening time will soon be over & I will comfort & make very clear to you the groundlessness of your anxieties *then*. I am glad Dr G. agrees with me about the boldness one ought to manifest & am only sorry I have to dash thro' this letter to get it into the mail. My watch makes me fear I shall fail. Mrs Wise was my first cousin—uncle John's daughter.[152]

Yrs
JM.

Sunday. 29th. [1855]

Darling Sally,

I must write on Sunday. Tomorrow at 7 I start for Princeton & I wish to mail a letter to you before I leave. I stay a round week. So on writing to Phila All your letters will be forwarded to me the same day they reach here. My landlady when the day came seemed unwilling to part with me and actually herself made overtures to me to stay. If she keeps me in the face of what she conceives an unnecessary trouble I must be a nice sort of person, must'nt I?

Tell Dr Graham, therefore, that I am at 589 Vine St—my old quarters. Tell him it is in the neighborhood of Logan Square & below 17th St. But I sha'nt be home till to-morrow week in the noon train.

Get over all your anxieties for I really now begin to feel that you have monstrously magnified everything, tho' I have made no fresh confidants. I shall tell no one till the day is fixed.

Darling, did you ever wonder that in such a pile of letters that you have received from a Minister of the gospel there is no little mention of religion in any one of them. It is characteristic of me. I *tremble* at it sometimes. I sometimes fear I am not a Christian, & think that if I were no general excuse of a feeling of reserve would keep me out of the abundance of the heart from speaking more & at least *thinking* more of religion. Pray for me.

Yours very fondly,
Jno. Miller

Don't you envy my trip. I shall tell Allie about the colt when you tell me about <u>my present</u>.

Monday *April 30th* 1855.

Dear John,

At last I come to tell you that *I am yours*. And I pray God to bless us not only *in* each other but *to* each other, and to grant us His favor and protection in the important step we are about to take.

152. "Uncle John" refers to John Sergeant (1779–1852).

If even to this hour I have fears and misgivings, and am disturbed by doubts and anxieties you must forgive me. They grow out of a condition of things as painful as it is unalterable, and out of an anxious temper which is, I think, like dear little Allie's ticklishness "constitutional." They are entirely without justification in anything I know or believe of you for I have the very fullest trust in your affection, and every confidence in your high and honorable character. But the cloud that rests upon the past with me *does* obscure the present to us both and looks portentous for the future. Yet you must take me with it all. Perhaps I may by and by prove to be something else than a burden to you; and at any rate, my affection *is* of some value to you, isn't it?

As for me, oh John, as you are the dearest and will hereafter be the nearest of all human beings to me, just let me nestle in your heart "safe & warm & trustingly" and feel that I have, at length found a home and a shelter even on this earth. Life has been so sad to me: so full of trial and change & bereavement that you cannot wonder that a little clearing of its prospects by the light and warmth of your love should be so precious to me.

In commemoration of so important a day as this in our history I send you a ring which you can wear;—or if you prefer it fasten to your watch-chain. It is so plain that even a Preacher need not fear it would be conspicuous, yet even if you had not been a Minister my taste could not have chosen any other.

And now as night closes upon me I can but assure you again that I am

> *Your Own*
> S.C.P. McDowell

James not yet returned. I look for him at noon tomorrow.

PART THREE

"I wonder if I shall love you as much face to face as I do in this 'letter-garb'."

May 1855–July 1855

Tuesday May 1. 1855

Dear John,

I don't know when I have been so worried at not getting a letter. I was really mad & if scolding could have done any good I should have tried it upon Alfred. I was so anxious to have one this morning, and waited & watched for the mail until I was in a perfect fume. I picked up my book, but it might as well have been your Hebrew Testament for all the good it did me. And then when the mail was handed in, and I found no letter among them all from you, I was, as I said before really, & unreasonably mad. Now tell me, why didn't you write? Dont you know you ought to have done it, & not keep me *ever* waiting for a letter. I half determined in my wrath not to write to you at all today but you see I have relented. But as I have only a few minutes to write I scratch off this as quickly as possible.

Dont you think it is a dreadful thing for people to get married? Now here is Mary, just picked up by this Mr Ross, whom I never even heard of until this winter, tho' it seems he has been living in this world for two score years & more, and carried off beyond the Mountains without any regard to how sad it makes me feel, or how much it breaks into our little family circle. But then as she is pleased, I am content, tho' I cannot imagine how any one can fancy a man who doesn't speak his words out clear & plain, but mouthes dreadfully and makes a great mouthful of all the *a*'s he comes across. I know the gentleman very little. He seemed a sensible man, but given far too much to ornament in his sermons—and has a way that tries my fortitude & good manners very greatly of telling stories

189

that *have no point in them:* Now as I'm used to hearing good stories well told, I feel as if my *understanding* was contemptuously treated when a succession of bad ones, poorly delivered are thrust upon me. What think you of my brother-in-law elect?

I wish you could run away from the city and enjoy our delicious Spring. My home never seemed to me as beautiful before. As I am an early riser I have full enjoyment of the birds, & as if conscious they were warbling to a delighted ear they gave me a charming concert this morning. Have you any birds at Allamby? I fear I shall fail to get my letter in. Is Maggie's letter mine or yours now?

Affectionately
S.C.P. McDowell

Princeton
May 2nd [1855]

Darling Sally,

I find my *"express"* from Phila such a slow coach that it brings me no letters at all. And fearing that you'll forget there is such a person & that if I dont write soon I shall see your marriage in the paper to somebody else I write you to beg you not to forget me. I have nothing in the world to tell you. Princeton is all flowers & bright sky & old memories & it keeps me after a more than common interval of absence so excited that I am like a Chinese opium eater all in the clouds. The air seems to me all like old Newark cider which is more exhilarating (*they tell me*) than the best Champagne.

I take refuge from Mary (who tells me off across the hall in Fathers study that "I aint clerical enough") at her own writing desk in the parlor & feel quite *sheltered* in thinking that I am writing to you. You wont scold me much "when you take possession" will you?

The children dont look as well as usual but they are very sweet. I took Allie out of bed last night at 10 to see the eclipse. He looked at it & made his comments & this morning hasn't a trace of any such thing upon his memory. I might have told him of his colt & he could not have betrayed us.

I told Maggie Breckinridge *all,* as she is going West for a time in a few days & I did not wish to expose her to the embarrassment of being ignorant of it when it was mentioned afterward. She *seemed* really *pleased.* But she is young & has a Most Kentucky passion for excitement tho' you know I dont agree with you as to the seriousness of this revelation with any one. I go with Mother on a short trip by rail into the country & will return to night when I am sure of finding a letter, & when I will write again.

Yrs
JM

Wednesday May 2. 1855

Dear John,

Your Sunday's note was received this morning. I hope for a longer one tomorrow. Indeed whilst you are in Princeton why cant you write to me every day. You will, I imagine, have time enough to do it and if you thus devote an hour to me every day you will almost feel that I make one of the family circle.

Jno, I dont envy you the trip; I'm so afraid of every body at Princeton. I fancy every body there will look suspiciously upon me, and from Allie, up that they will regard & treat me as an interloper. But I am glad that you have a chance of seeing the county and breathing the fresh air at this lovely season, and hope you will have a pleasant visit. But I wish you had turned your face in this direction when you were taking a holiday.

Mrs Graham, who was recently in Princeton tells me she heard from the Alexanders that Maggie Breckinridge was to be married some time soon; is it true?—But no, dont answer my question if there is the least privacy about the matter.

What has become of Sweeny's letter? That thing ought to be looked into; and in addition to what he says there should be obtained corroborative testimony from other sources. How this is to be done I dont know; can you suggest a way? We should be ready for defence, for I feel almost sure of attack. You have never convinced me altogether that my fears of ecclesiastical censure were unfounded; and I still feel that this marriage will give you much trouble in your church, even if it should not hold us up as a target for all the sharp-shooters in Presbytery. If your people would only suspend their judgment for a time. If they would only consent to know me a little, they would, I think, upon finding me a plain unobtrusive, quick person, anxious to do what is right, feel more favorably to *me*, & less unkindly to *you*. But this they will not do. We cannot hope for it. I should hope every thing if it could be granted, and hope for nothing as it cannot be.

Cousin John tells me I must expect to hear strong disapprovals, and painful & hard speeches from all my lady friends; and, knowing my temper he warns me, "that I am not to return scorn for scorn, or at all engage in a battle with the world because of its opposition". "But you would be weak, he went on, to allow the opinions of friends to influence you in a step in which you think your happiness involved, after you are satisfied as to its propriety. There will be a great brint, but remember it will be but a *nine day wonder*. I think Miller is a lucky fellow, and knowing you I wonder any people *could* object to their Pastor marrying you". I tell you this last remark, that you may remember when hereafter, so many people are pitying "*poor* Mr Miller" because of his Wife there is *one* at least who congratulates you upon your success.

You know I'm a farmer. For weeks we have been without rain, & yet with summer heat at this season. Every thing has suffered and every body was beginning to feel fearful of such a season as we had last year, but yesterday afternoon we had a delightful shower—another last night, and a hard rain this morning, with steady cloud & occasional showers ever since. It will do us so much good. It has already beautified every thing greatly. If the yard looked less lovely I should feel less at the thought of giving it up. But I dont know, if it were without any beauty I should still feel strongly bound to it. Do you wonder that I sometimes wish you had never assumed the form of the Tempter to me? You must not grow restless for the consummation of *our* engagement. More than "three weeks" must intervene—how many more I cannot say.

I have not been entirely well for a week. I took a cold, I dont know how, which has singularly for me taken the form of a cough, that annoys me a little. Dont make yourself uneasy about me. If it really becomes anything serious I shall write to you everyday—if not, then my not writing everyday will be satisfactory proof so far that I am well.

I do think you are wrong in maintaining such rigid reserve on religious subjects, yet perhaps it is better to be too reserved than the contrary. I know much of the anxiety to which you allude. I believe our nature is incapable of feeling a deeper pang than that caused by a *doubt* on that point, and yet these painful & painfully harrassing fears may be, & are I think of benefit to us, inasmuch as they lead to more self-inspection, & that teaches us humility, and gives us such views of our own helplessness & guilt as impels us to seek constant renewal & constant help from the only renewing power, & the only supplying hand. Does the responsibility of the ministry weigh very heavily upon you? I think the anxieties of a conscientious Minister must be very great, & his cares very oppressive. I would love to be of even the smallest help to you—I pray God I may.

Thursday morning—James not yet returned. He had been disappointed in meeting Uncle Tom. Dr. Graham will not be in Phil before the last of next week. I will give him your address. Do not be surprised to find him very rough, but he is a sensible man & has always loved me very much—*two* good qualities at least.

I dont wonder your Landlady couldn't part with you, for I have no doubt you're a very good *domestic animal*. I am not coughing so much this morning.

> *Affectionately*
> S.C.P. McDowell

[marginal note] Send me a few envelopes.

(Princeton, Thursday May 3.)[1] [1855]

My *dear* Sally,

I have a sort of fancy that the famous 30th will be a great epoch in our eventful history & that a letter is already lying in Phila testifying[2] (a big word) showing *how*. At any rate I am getting up a method to send to the Phil (P.O.) to day &

1. McDowell dated this letter.
2. Miller scratched out this word.

have the results to-night. The 30th seems to have fitted nobly into the train of events i.e. if your brother came back on Saturday; & knowing that you are to speak *irrevocably* when you speak at all I am in high spirits.

So Cantey cant have my letter. My letters are good enough for you, but not for her. Well, tell Miss Cantey in your own language, first, that she is for once just *wasting* her spirits if she is allowing herself to be depressed, second, that one of the nicest homes (in *one* respect) will sue to her that she can well conceive of & that if she deigns to accept it she will never regret preferring the high Jarsies to Lower Virginia. Tell her as Father O'Leary said of purgatory, she "might go farther & fare worse" & then try to *prepossess* her as much as possible in my favor & I will *try* not to let her affection afterward sink lower than I can possibly help.

Dr Hodge wrote my fathers epitaph on a monument built by the Directors with which mother would'nt allow me to meddle. I wanted this.—

Samuel Miller D.D., L.L.D.

Born   ———   ———
Died   ———   ———

but I was over-ruled. And now the family regret it. Dr. Hodge's Epitaph is like Seekonk Plain *long* & *level* & manifests estimates and opinions in Church Polity which (without any of the bitterness Mary imagines) I was trying to arrest in a certain way on the occasion of the examination of one of his pupils in the last Presbytery.

As you wont tell me which birth day it is I am at a loss to tell whether to congratulate you or not.

Alas the mail!

Yours,
Jno Miller

Princeton, May 4th, 1855.

My *dear Sally*,

I have good news for you. Mary turned to me yesterday & said, "John, have you heard anything from Mrs McDowell since we saw her?" "Yes," said I, "I have seen her in Washington." "What did she come to Washington for?" "To see me," said I. Whereupon, Mary, knowing this couldnt be true & seeing that I was so perfectly at my ease seemed to dismiss the whole matter. When I went out, however, she said to Margaret, "I have a suspicion that John has a fancy for Mrs McDowell." "Well, Aunt Mary," said Maggie, "what would you think of it, if he had"? "Why" said, Mary, "I should'nt like it." She very soon, however, appealed to Margaret to know how *she* would like such a match with a tone that Margaret interpreted to mean that she was by no means so bitterly decided against the step as you feared. She gave Maggie two reasons for not liking it, first, the usual one &, second, the same old rumor that another had heard about "imperiousness &c" which I have a shrewd suspicion comes from some one quarter that I will take occasion one of these days to discover. I *like* the presence of this second difficulty in their minds, because I know you will correct *that* & it will serve to make a diversion from the other. Margaret said, Well, Aunt Mary how would you treat her. Would you receive her pleasantly as your sister? "Yes," said Aunt Mary; ["]but I should'nt like the step."

This now, I think, is very well for Mary, & it shows me that in our visit to Princeton which ought to be soon after coming to Phila, the very first day's sojourn will obliterate all unpleasant relations or even impressions as far as they will practically appear. Is'nt this nice? Especially in view of your dark & lowering forebodings?

Now for your questions. "Dont you think it's a dreadful thing for people to get married?" No. I think its a *dreadful* thing for them not to get married in certain circumstances. Dont you see how people are blowing out their brains about the county from not being allowed to marry? Again, What do you think of my brother in law elect?" I think very badly of him. I know him only by your description & if I were he I would get myself described by somebody else. There are, however, two good things about him: one that he loves your sister & the other, that she loves him; both of which go very far to balance all you have said against him.

But Sally, why were you so mad about the letter? I didn't owe you one. Indeed I have written one or two supernumerary ones because you were so slow in writing. I dont know whether to be most flattered or most resentful at you quarrelling with me.

I have been to Allamby. It is magnificent. I want to drive you over to it in a few weeks.

Your letter disappointed me so. I thought the 30th was to be our great family epoch, but I have learned so completely the lesson of submission that I think I would relapse into a condition of silent patience on that subject if that itself might not look as a want of Christian resignation. Therefore I think of getting all that part of my usual letters lithographed so that I can insert it without rewriting on each separate occasion. The children have been with me all the morning & are very well.

Yours affectionately,
Jno Miller

[marginal notes] Keep Maggie's letter.

I wonder at the Tinkling Spring people in electing Mr C[leghorne].[3] He is as you say chiefly to *blame* for being such a blockhead.

---

3. Tinkling Spring was a Presbyterian church near Lexington.

Sunday (May 6)[4] [1855]

God bless you, my darling Sally, for your kindness in making me so happy. I received your letter last night & handed it over to Mary at once. *You will never see in Mary a trace of feeling in respect to our matter.* I have slandered her awfully: all my *first* impressions were true. She still *dont like* some aspects, but it will be a matter buried in herself. You will never know it. And it will soon be all grown over by a sense of sisterly affection. How we can make ourselves unnecessarily unhappy.

I scratch this line *to-day* as a work of mercy thinking it will relieve your mind.

The little children who are well are just to drive with me to Cranbury a village 9 miles off where I am to preach. I mean to tell *them* on the way & Sarah & mother to-morrow & Mrs Potter & Julia & Spencer when I get to the city.

The ring looks so nice to me & fits beautifully. That I may not consign you to one of uncomfortable size, please enclose a card with a circle cut out in it corresponding to the *interior* of the ring that you can comfortably wear & I will wait to see Bailey till I get your letter.[5]

> Yours in warm gratitude.
> JM.

Monday May 7. 1855

Dear John,

Everything is in a fuss & every body hurried and flurried. So much business to arrange, so many "last words" to say, for tomorrow at 9 Mary is to be married, & at 11 James leaves us for Phila. I can hardly snatch a minute to write, but I will dash thro' all I have to say as quickly as possible.

James only reached home on Thursday. Saturday evening we had another talk upon our *business,* (isn't that romantic?) which except upon one or two points was much the same as the previous one. I had withheld from James before the *name* of the other party, wishing him to make up his mind as to the propriety of the contemplated step, without the intervention of personal prejudices. I did not know *how he might feel to you.* Only a passing remark in regard to you had escaped him, which it is true was favorable, yet not strong enough for me to build upon. An accident, however revealed, what my caution had concealed. The morning he left he stepped into the P.O. when the mail was being made up & a letter of mine to you was lying on the table before him. There was no mistaking the writing & so the murder was out. He after thinking over the matter sees no moral difficulty & says his feelings and conduct to me would be unchanged in the event of my marrying you. Yet he shrinks from the noise it will make, and cannot bear to have me subjected to remark & censure. He does not know you, he says, sufficiently to judge how far you would have the moral courage to bear

---

4. McDowell added the date.
5. "Bailey & Co." was a Philadelphia jeweler.

unflinchingly & with unmoved affection the public *sneer*, perhaps, levelled at your Wife. He also suggests that you might by & bye when the flow of the present feeling had subsided into something more sober, begin to enter-tain to me the feeling that the world expressed in the beginning, and think that there was some indecorum connected with my marrying to you. This thing, often present to my mind in the earlier stages of this matter, had grad-ually worn away, & I was startled when James revived it again. I am trust-ing everything to your affection. I am risking everything for it, and the idea of having it swept away from me, & of having your *respect* diminished, is exceedingly painful. I wouldn't have your love without your respect, for *I* couldn't respect you if it were possible for your affection to be without this element in it.

James too says he thinks it would be far better for you to make a visit here, before the marriage. Let people discuss the propriety of the thing for themselves. Cousin John takes the same view—& I am so troubled and anx-ious about the whole thing that I *need to talk* to you about it. I did not tell James we were already engaged.—Somehow I shrank from it—am I not a great coward? I forewarned you that James' views might delay the consummation of the engagement, and sure enough it will. I' do so draw off from public animadversion for the sake of both, and at the same time, (I pray you dont quite despise me for my plain speaking) am so strongly drawn to you, that between my fears & attachment I have lost *my* reason entirely. Cousin John laughs & says to me, "I never knew a more headlong love-affair than this". He evidently thinks we are both determined to[o] madly in the whole thing. But we are not—are we? I am greatly discouraged. I had thought up to the present moment I would tell Mary of the whole affair, but I will wait till *I see you.*

My old maiden friend Miss Moore, sympathizes in my troubles, & gives me some encouragement. Her advice, strange to say, is against the *delay* policy.

Write me a good long letter, & teach me how I am ever to [be] strong enough to go thro the thing courageously—or strong enough, if needs be, to set you free.

I write in a hurry.

> *Very affectionately,*
> S.C.P. McDowell

I add a line this morning. Your letter is just received. I am glad your Sister is not so violently antagonistic, but wait till she knows all, which by the bye, had better not be until the *day* is fixed. The 30th May an important day after. Oh as to the question of age—it only divides me from you by two years. How do you like such an old lady-love?

> *Your*
> S.C.P. McDowell

Phil. May 7th 1855
1 1/2 P.M.

My *dear Sally*,

On a little scrap which perhaps you will receive no sooner than this I told you yesterday how grateful I felt for your "*present*" to me. Here I have the *picture* of it open on the table & it seems to me no truer than a dream that anything so good & lovely *can* really be mine.

I take pleasure in thinking that *some* of the penalties you have tho't to pay for these acts of grace to me are all imaginary & I take pleasure in resolving that if you will "nestle narrow and safe" in an affection which I can hardly describe, I will make up in my own tenderness & love for every friend whom your marriage can possibly repel.

I told Sarah (Mrs Hageman) my married sister; & I am entirely back at the point from which I started. I *told* you Jersey was different from Virginia, & so it is. There is not a person in Princeton who will not receive you with no different air or manner than if all you lament over had never happened. And you will be treated in my mother's house *precisely* as if you were like others in history: at least so I predict. Spencer, & Mrs Potter & Julia I shall talk with to day & write to-morrow. Dont fancy that this is only to encourage you or that I am still striving to win you. You know you are *mine, irrevocably.* But I do mourn over your unnecessary anxiety. You are out of the Enchanted Castle & your knight-errant is only desirous that what you are dreading as tho' it were meeting old Giant Despair himself could take place to-morrow, so sure am I of piloting you safe thro' all your apprehended difficulties. My sister Mary (& Sarah if *well* enough) will write to you as soon as you have communicated more fully with your own family & little Maggie will be sending you one of her notes for I told them both yesterday. And little Allie declared that he would much rather see you than the colt which *also* greatly excited his imagination.

I was able to stay so long in P. by help of an exchange. You know it was very long since I had been there.

Maggie B. is *not* to be married, nor is she engaged. I cant tell how the story could have originated.

Dr Leyburn wrote to Sweeney & has not had any reply. I think he must have soon. I cant tell how we can get other testimony. Is it necessary, if S. writes.

Ecclesiastical censure is no more possible than the falling of the sky. *Do* banish that & never think of it again.

You *will* have the time you desire to make the acquaintance of enough people. I will bring you on & you will see them before most of them know of any peculiarity.

Do write me particularly about your health each time. I hope your next letter will fix our marriage. By the way dont be anxious about my having shown one of your letters to Mary. I looked carefully over it, & there was not one expression that need have been made private.

Yours affectionately
JM

Phil. May 8th 1855

My *darling Sally*,

I have not received any letter to-day or yesterday. I hope to get one this evening.

Philadelphia is not quite so tractable as Princeton. Julia to whom I communicated our affair yesterday, looked on it more sombrely than any one yet & Spencer did not seem much relieved of any of the ideas he had expressed to me. However, neither Julia nor Spencer expressed anything else than a purpose to stand by us & Mary whom you thought so much to be dreaded is really my friend. She came on with me to do some shopping & I find her quite ready to relieve the fears of the others & to take my part. So now what a wrong idea I gave you of her.

I *gave* you so favorable a picture of Princeton, that I can afford to *shade* this a little in order to keep up my entire honesty.

This is Mary's wedding-day. I have faith enough in her own womanly instincts to send her on my warm congratulations in spite of the picture you sent me of Mr Ross. By the way, how *greatly* you surprised me. I tho't all along up to your very last letters that Mr Lacey was the fortunate suitor. How came I to make such a mistake?

I suppose to day you are in the midst of the utmost bustle. I wish I could look in upon you. I infer from my not hearing from you to-day that your health is better tho' of that you must write me.

Julia never for a moment expressed any feeling against me or seemed at all to set herself aloof from me, but on the contrary agreed with Mary at night in saying that both Spence & Dick should espouse & defend the connection. She only quoted to me certain serious cases as she tho't them which however as I soon convinced her were not at all in point.

When I had written so far I was called to dinner, & found a letter waiting for me which has provoked me more than I can easily tell you. How Dr Leyburn could have reiterated, & when I saw him again & questioned him closely could have assured me that his memory was complete—that S. was one of the Com[mittee] of the legislature & that a detail of fact & evidence had come before them so strong that I could not even mention it to you I cannot divine. However, my dear darling Sally, I am sorry that uprightness of dealing obliges me to send you the letter. It makes no difference whatever with me. And indeed as just the sort of evidence that S. found to be rife in Richmond & that he *must* have presented in some detail to Dr Leyburn is already in our possession & is enough to satisfy our friends, it is perhaps *better* that no detailed charge such as this would have been, should have been brought as it would be far more apt to awaken opposition. You see I am something of a philosopher. Dear, dear Sally leave yourself to me. I will carry you safely, by God's help, thro' all difficulties. I feel (I dont know how *you* feel, for you are very shy yet in telling me of your love) as if the idea of finishing my life without you was utterly impossible. And as my conscience tells me that the step is right & that my particular intentions as to the bestowment of my life make me more independant than others of popular favour I would marry you even if the difficulties of that sort in the way were very formidable. But as I dont conceive them to be so, no slight occurrence of difficulty can easily ruffle me.

I hope I shall receive a letter this evening fixing our time of marriage.

I called on Mrs Potter yesterday & she was out. I mean to see her this evening.

I am *serious* in what I say about my not much regretting the failure of this testimony of Sweeney. Our being in the habit of saying that such & such distinct facts occurred in Richmond would be heard of in Maryland & might create a desire to reply. Our saying or leaving our friends to say that the character that those facts involve was notoriously licentious could create no such definite occasion to reply & for conscience & for public suspicion would be almost as effective. Write me freely whether this letter at all disturbs you. I hold you bound by no promise that you have made under any false information.

But yet, Sally, dont let these things *delay* you.

Spencer's Office

I kept my letter open till I could see if I had one in the Office. I hope I shall get one to-morrow. I am more & more convinced of the wisdom of an early marriage if we are married at all this year both on account of the duties of my church & on account of a bold prompt meeting of any of the difficulties that you fear. But, darling you have been so good to me already that I must not be restless. If you will resign all your difficulties to me I will resign all other things to you.

Affectly,
Jno Miller

[Enclosure: T. Sweeney to John Leyburn]

Wheeling April 30/55

Rev John Leyburn
Dear Sir

I received (on my return home), your letter of the 9th Inst. making some inquiry in relation to Mr Thomas who married Miss McDowel.

In reply have to say, that, I was not a member of the Legislature at the time of the proceedings, but was in Richmond attending to other business—I heard a good deal said on the Subject, the general opinion seemed to be that he had behaved badly—my knowledge or rememberance of the affair is not *such* as to enable me to give you any positive information on the subject.

[Respectfully Yours]
T. Sweeney

Phil. May 9th 1855

My darling Sally,

I have something to communicate that I think will give you real pleasure, & if you are not very unreasonable ought to go far to abate your anxiety about coming to Phila. I have seen Mrs Potter. You know Mrs Potter is just in a position as respects me to judge very rigidly our whole undertaking. She *told* me, "You know, John, *my* interest is about the children. That is a thing I would naturally think about before anything else". Well, I told her all with the utmost candour & fulness, leaving out as of course we must now do that about the committee of the Legislature, (tho' I still believe from its being so rife in Richmond that that information was before them.) and when I had gotten through & had told her of Major Preston's remark that he tho't it would be only a "nine day's wonder" she said to my great gratification, "John, I dont believe it will be even that". "Well, but," said I "What will the Bishop think?" Now I had some fear of the Bishop because he encouraged a nephew to break an engagement with a very estimable young lady here because she had been divorced. "Why," said Mrs Potter, "he thinks just as I do. He was discussing the whole subject the other day. Some friends of Mrs Peace were complaining to him of the treatment she met with in society in being entirely neglected &c when he replied, that the treatment was right, that Dr P. & his former wife had been separated from mere *"incompatibility"* & therefore they were not truly divorced & so in his nephew's case, the lady had never made known *any* cause for a divorce & there was none known in the society of the City. But," said Mrs P. "the Bishop distinctly declared that a divorce under circumstances such as those described in Scripture would both in morals & sentiment justify another marriage & that he would perform the ceremony in such a case". Now I never tho't before what an important spoke the Bishop might be in my wheel. His way of feeling would have great influence with the Episcopalians here who very much control society & that along with my relations & the Virginia gentlemen who are here will I think make our course a comparatively smooth one.

Now am I not *"infusing strength into you"* as you wished me to do.

I think it not improbable as the time approaches that Mrs P. will invite us to stay some time at her house. At least I mean to play my cards that way. She has represented herself as under obligation to me in certain ways & I shall not feel disinclined to accept such an invitation.

Dick came home last night. There is great rejoicing. The *St. Louis* is beating up the bay. He got off at Jersies & came on in the Rail Road. I mean to secure from him the warmest cordiality. So long as I am moving about in this way among my friends I will write every day. But, Sally, be kind to me & dont let our wedding day be later than the 17th or at least the 24th.

Yours affectionately,
Jno. Miller.

Spencer's Office.

As I have appointed myself helmsman in this voyage of ours I must in deference to the crew tell everything as I go along. I saw Mrs P. just now on my way down & she tells me that she has told all our affair to the Bishop & he takes the precise view that she had told me. He says moreover that he remembers the whole history in Maryland & that it accords entirely with my step, & he characterizes Gov. Thomas in terms even more severe than I would like to repeat to you. Mrs P. expresses real pleasure at the promise of her little nephew & niece having so good a mother & she lays before me a plan which I am to communicate methodically to you.

She wants you to stay with her some time when you come to the North. She proposes it at once as an idea she had been conceiving since I saw her. She wishes it exceedingly, so much so that when I tell her how late you may be in fixing a day for marriage, she says that she was going out to her country place for the Summer on the week after next, but that she will stay in till the first of June or after to secure you as her guest. Now, my darling Sally, you *must* choose the 23d or the week before if possible: for just think every day that you postpone our wedding now, you keep a worthy family in town. Mrs P. is bent on welcoming you & I believe she will stay waiting for you some distance in June unless you decide earlier. The only redeeming fact I know is that her Aunt dont *wish* her to go out so soon on account of the chilly weather.

When I spoke of Mrs P. representing herself as under obligation to *me*, I forget that you are not aware of the fact that I am under vastly greater obligation to her. I have been a boarder in the Bishop's house with my whole family for months & months together when sickness made it extremely desirable that we should be with Mrs P. & when nothing would compensate for the trouble. I shall be sorry however to injure your health by any over exertion & remember you must not yield to request if any such *danger* threatens.

Yours
JM.

[marginal note] Spence has just come in & says that you must come *first* to *his* house, that the Bishop has no right to you. Dick will no doubt follow suit & I see not that we shall get any chance to *flaunt* ourselves any where before our return to Virginia.

Thursday May 10.1855

My dear John,

I was so good-for-nothing on Tuesday after Mary was married that I could not write a line even to you. We were all lonely and depressed and huddled together over the fire to keep warm and keep up the little spirit that was left. In our forlorn condition little Mac was an invaluable visitor and I was glad enough to devote myself to him. We should have felt much under any circumstances, but I think the sudden re-appearance of Winter added greatly to the sombreness of the occasion.

Yesterday was cold enough for a February day, and I drew down my wrappings for a morning walk. Today is still cool and *frosty*. The dreaded frost came this morning and we, farmers & gardeners, do not feel our cares at all lessened by its appearance.

Let me bestow upon you a recital of one of my household troubles. Last Spring I drove a beautiful pair of young horses, but as they had once certainly run off & were once suspected of having done so, I grew too much afraid of them to keep them. They were sold. All summer I was put to inconvenience for want of another pair. Uncle Tom undertook to buy them, & I waited patiently until about the last of August they made their appearance here. One of them however was lame, but it was thought would soon recover. I was greatly rejoiced that they were here, & hoped, as usual that every thing would soon be right again. But the lame horse for months performed no other service than that of drawing a poor, sick stranger at the Hotel a mile or two once a week, and about Winter he was even unfit for that. I called in for him during the winter the most *skilful doctors* of the county but with no success. Finally Alfred had recourse to quackery, and the horse about six weeks ago was put in the Carriage looking quite bright and *hopeful*. I began to think he was entirely well & so gave the Carriage to Mary to go to Staunton with only a caution to have the horses driven gently. I stood at the door & admired my young bays, as only a Virginia woman can admire horses, and felt a sort of satisfaction in them not to be described. But 24 hours cured me of all that. The first words I heard next morning were to announce the *breakdown* of the lame horse about 18 miles from town. And here they are lame and useless and I am disappointed & worried & vexed.

I dont think I shall ever have another pair. It most makes me mad to hear of a horse. Isn't it very annoying? And just now when the warm weather is coming on, & the Episcopal Convention next week is to throw into our little Town some 500 strangers I feel the annoyance to be much *"aggravated."*

My friend, Miss Moore, left us this morning. You cant tell how very quick and forlorn we look.

Your Princeton letters (the last of them) came yesterday, & Tuesday's letter from Phil'a this morning. As to the ring, I mention it now lest I should forget it, the one I sent you will do well enough as a measure. It is rather large, but I would rather not have one smaller. In case it should prove too large, I shall make Lilly get me a smaller one as a guard for it. The one I sent you should have the day of the month engraved on it—I shall have that done some day.

I am so grateful to your little Sister for her conduct in this matter. I had dreaded her antagonism more than that of any of the others, and feared its effect upon your Mother, and your children very greatly. I did not dream for [a] moment that she would allow herself by any direct influence to render the children adverse to me, but strong disapprobation cannot ever be felt without in some unguarded moment betraying itself. And children are so quick to perceive and adopt such feelings. And you know, there is no relationship so peculiarly requiring prudence and wisdom (*cool wisdom?*) in all the parties as that which I shall sustain to these children. Much of the heartburning and discomfort generally arising out of it, is, I am sure, attributable to outside influences. A very great deal depends upon the new relative herself—so much that I tremble to think of it—but she can be materially aided in her work, and just as much thwarted and disheartened in it by the conduct of the near friends of her new charge. Here if your Sister espouses our cause *heartily* she can do—oh, ever so much for the peace & comfort of us all. Just here I should like to have her aid, and feel that I could depend upon receiving it. Of course I shall look to you always and unreservedly for your support and counsel, but then often you *could not* judge where she might.

But of all, this I will write "*again.*" You dont mind hearing the word now, do you?

How does your Mother hear the news? And Maggie? Let the child's feelings whatever they may be, have full vent. If she is disposed to be worried—why let her be so. It is perfectly natural she should be; and any restrictions laid upon the expression of such a feeling would only make matters worse. Let it come out, & it will the sooner be over. I rather think I shall woo her successfully without any aid. Send her to little Julia Howell if she would like to know something of my charms. As to Allie I have no doubt he feels as if I were a sort of Van Amberg, with a collection of colts & monkeys which will be made to *perform* together for his amusement.[6] To make myself the more acceptable to him I would like to send him Gazelle. A colt and a greyhound could not fail to overcome *all of his* scruples. By the way I hear the colt is a beauty—has he no name for it yet?

I was really provoked about Sweeny's drawing back. But I have known so much of that thing in my life, I wonder now that I placed any reliance upon him, in the beginning. It is the rarest thing in the world to get a man to stand up, as a *witness* to facts which he will state with the utmost fullness & emphasis in conversation. My old friend, Miss English of Geo:Town, is the only *perfectly reliable* person in that way that I have ever seen. But I hope we will be independent of Sweeny. Thro' a friend, I have applied to Mr Lyons, who was not only, one of the Lawyers in the case, but also a member of the Legislature at the time the matter was acted upon, and no doubt, he can and will furnish all the information necessary. If he does not, it must be obtained from other quarters. Mere *rumor* will not answer. My friend, William Brown's father-in-law, Mr Smith, who immediately preceded you in Frederick, I think could be made available, if other means should fail.[7] Mr Fendall of Washington, will put himself to any trouble to serve me, and I think,

6. Julia Ruffner Howell was a daughter of Arthur and Anne Ruffner Howell. She died young. Isaac A. Van Amburgh (1811–1865), wild-animal trainer and proprietor of Van Amburgh's Menagerie.

7. Lydia S. English was the principal of Georgetown Female Seminary where McDowell had studied in 1837–1838. Joseph Smith (1796–1868) was pastor of the Presbyterian church

in a very quiet, unobserved way, could secure what we wish. I dont like to write to him about it however. I hate to open the subject to any body. I consider it a terrible calamity that I have to speak of it to you. But we *must* have facts—*well substantiated facts*, else we wait till the end of time as we are.

Cousin John suggests another difficulty, which may have occurred to the friends with whom you talk, but which did not arise in my mind at all. It is this—that persons who were unfavorably disposed to me years ago, might have, by a marriage now their impressions confirmed, and do me much injury by a free expression of them. Now such difficulties as these are scarcely conceivable to me. I can hardly imagine downright, cold-blooded assaults upon my character. I reckon I am stupid about that, dont you think I am? I have no thought but that many persons believed there was much that was wrong about me then—but that that *wrong* was in *principle* I cannot believe that any human being who ever knew me could, for a moment think. Half the world considered me high-tempered and rather given to levity—neither of which charges, were true at the time.—But why go over the old thing again. You know what the world thought of me, better than I do.

I dont know how you came to make the mistake about Mr Lacy. He never had any views that Mr Ross at all interfered with or disappointed, tho' the town thought and spoke differently. What did I say about Brother Ross that makes you "not like him". He is a very good person—rather lumbering and lounging &, *for the sake of the alliteration only*, lazy for my taste. He is somewhat slow in his stories, the *point* of which like the wits of the man of whom Hamilton writes, "will come up by the next arrival". When I talk to him too, he looks at me with a puzzled air, as if he did not know what I was driving at; or if he did, was entirely in despair of keeping up with me. And this makes me flounder, and flounder & fall down;— and then I get mad & cant get up any more. And I dont think that's agreable. But Mr Ross does very well. He wears overshoes religiously, (I wish Dr McLean could rejoice his heart with a sight of them) and has an uncommonly good appetite; which two things will I am sure, secure his light to this lower world for a long, long time.[8] He gives us the gospel too, very gorgeously apparalled and very showily bedecked with gold & jewels (pinch back & paste I think) and uttered most sonorously. And the people admire him & his sermons exceedingly I hear.

Now the half of all this is mere fun. I like the gentleman quite as well as could be expected upon so short an acquaintance, and have not one disrespectful feeling to him. I have no doubt he will prove a very kind, & affectionate & unromantic husband and if Mary will be content with this, she will be happy. But I want you to know that I shall need a little spice of romance in your affection, and shall *hope* to have a "parson-lover" all the time—even after I get to be as old as the

---

in Frederick from 1838 to 1843. McDowell lived in or near Frederick for six months after her marriage to Francis Thomas on June 8, 1841.

8. John Maclean Jr., president of the College of New Jersey.

hills & as ugly as Meg Merrilies.[9]

I am waiting to have your answer to my last letters.

I was sure I had something quite important to say this morning (Friday) but the appearance of a Bank account has entirely deprived me of my ordinary composure. I had forgotten to send on a deposit to the Bank, and was checking upon it as if I had, until the Cashier having paid $240 over a former deposit undertook to give me warning. So now I have remedied my forgetfulness, & I hope not lost my credit. You need have no fears on the score of property. I shall be your "poor wife" after all.

I am almost well of my curious cough; but it scared me a little more than I acknowledged.

I did shrink from your Sister seeing my letter. Why couldn't you have told her without showing it to her?

Affectionately Yours
S.C.P. McDowell

Phil. May 10th 1855.

Ma chere Fiancée

I think never a lady accepted her suitor & then dropped him as you have done me. I have had no letter since Saturday. I have been living all that time on *mere faith* & you cant tell how desolate I feel. I know this is a momentous week & that your sister Mary must have engrossed much of your care: but, Darling, just a chip of a letter thrown to me would keep me in good spirits for many a long hour.

I have something to tell you that never occurred to me before. Our communion is on the 2d Sabbath in June. This in the city is never postponed & the minister is not expected to be absent: And the Sunday & week before are also important times. If we are not married on the 23d or near that day we can hardly be the week following & there seems no practicable time till the third week in June when Mrs Potter will be out of town & the time when you wish to go South not far off.

Darling, if you have written appointing the time later than the week after next wont you reconsider it? That is the week in which the 23d occurs. It would really scarcely be proper for me to leave at a time nearer to our communion. This letter will reach you on Saturday. Wont you break your rule in such an emergency & write by next Sunday's mail? I will receive the letter then on Wednesday. And that Wednesday or even Thursday is all the notice I ask of you if you will be married the Wednesday or Thursday or even Saturday following (i.e. about the 23d)

Yours very affectionately
JM

9. Character in Sir Walter Scott's novel *Guy Mannering*, published in 1815.

Phil. May 11th 1855.

Darling,

I do begin to blame you. It shows the ardour of my attachment that I devour even such letters as this & love you more & more whatever I hear from you.

I am going to put all your love & confidence to the proof in what I consider a vital proposal. It is <u>that you will marry me on the 23rd</u>. Trusting that you will do it I am going to make every preparation & tho' the 24th or 25th or 26th or even the 28th might almost do yet hear me now, however much it may startle you at first, while I give the reasons for so bold a measure.

The fact is we are on the brink of a great *gaucherie*. I *cannot* be married between the 28th (inst) & the 13th of June on account of the communion.[10] The 13th of June will find all the *influential* part of Phil. disappearing into the country. If there be any truth in your fears my great hope to dispel them is to bring you to the city while Spencer & Mrs Potter are here & *I have leisure* to turn some attention that way. We *ought* not to be married in the Summer. Because we shall be for weeks away & people without any help from any body will have full leisure to talk & that for weeks before any measures can be taken to prepossess them. We *cannot* be married in the Fall for my people would *stare* at my choosing for my wedding a time for opening a great city church. I would have no time to pay a visit scarcely & would be driven too much in mind & body to attend to the double anxieties even of making the ordinary arrangements of marriage. Then toward January or Spring might do but Sally trusting to your will that the marriage should be consummated in "three weeks" or as you said in Washington "as soon as possible after our engagement" I have told more persons than I would be willing to trust for such a long array of months. I have told Bp & Mrs P. my two brothers, my sisters & sister-in-law & a lady a matronly friend of mine one of the old friends & members of the church. Besides it is known in Lexington & will be know in that way here.

Now I am abundantly at leisure; hereafter I shall be overwhelmed with extra work.

Moreover what have we to gain. Your Brother & Major Preston may be wise as respects their doubt of me & therefore the prudence of seeing me again but, Darling, you dont share in this doubt. I think a lover who can bear the sweep & desolation of this letter & yet love you heart & soul without a ruffle of displeasure is a good reliable husband. And as to respect I tell you Sally, *I respect our match itself*. If there is one quality I possess more than another it is an obstinacy of opinion. And fixed as I am in respect for the step I am proposing I have contempt enough for the sneers of the world to be all the more settled in affection for you.

I write this on Friday. It will reach you on Monday. I can hear from you by Thursday. I will set out for Lex: on the Monday following or later one day or two as you determine. But I begin to prepare at once & if you write unfavorably darling Sally I shall be so much disappointed.

---

10. "Gaucherie" means awkward or tactless behavior. Miller interlined this last phrase.

You may say it is not a proper interval to write to friends. Then tell them the circumstances that my communion occurred to hasten us.

You may say, you cannot be ready. You know you will be back in the Summer. Tell *me* what you want. I will bring it on to you.

You may say, you are so distracted & in doubt. *You dare not.* Darling, trust to me. If I am to be your husband, this may be one of the greatest marks of confidence I may ever ask you to bestow. Instead of being headlong, *I think it headlong to let this leisure season pass.* As to the distraction of "fear" of which you speak I dont possess it. I scarcely ever *think* of what you regard so great a bugbear. Whether it be moral courage or no I am as perfectly cool & even indifferent about this whole fear as I ever was about anything in my life. And as to "love" it is not love that is driving me I am conscious. If it were merely that I loved you so much I would have many things to balance my impatience in the engrossment of present pursuits & in the constant prospect of times equally eligible. It is the profound conviction that if we let that week pass it will be a *calamity* as you yourself will feel, great in proportion to all the reasons of anxiety you have felt on this subject.

If you say, your brother will now expect you to wait, I will convince your brother if you direct me to do so while he is here.

If your letters that I will receive before you can reply to this, are such as mention another time, I will pay no attention to them. *I will steadily get ready to be married on the 23d* (or thereabouts) & will feel greatly disappointed & distressed if you write refusing it.

Darling, dont quarrel with me for taking your rights out of your hand. You know in my case there was a great deal for a sanguine lover to build upon even as early as the 6th of April & if I didn't scorn such selfish considerations I would complain of the "hope deferred" & the real distractions in my work of so many painful disappointments. I dont *entreat* this thing, for I wont let you feel that I selfishly precipitated your judgment but I do *counsel* it & that with the most solemn assurance. Letting May pass without our marriage will be a grievous practical blunder. And if there is anything in what you fear about the public (which by the way is all that you plead for a delay) we may regret it all our lives.

If you *finally reject this* then the 13th of June is a far inferior time but it appears to me the next in order. Pardon me, Darling for being so urgent after all your kindness. I would marry you in the clock of St. Peters if it were to strike in the midst of the ceremony if I could not win you in a better time & place. "How are you ever to be strong enough?" Only by remembering that next Wednesday week if you assent you will have no further occasion for strength: all the difficulties will be in my hand. *Remember: You need have no fear of a misunderstanding. I will certainly be on before the 23-4-5-6 or 8th if you say in a letter mailed on next Tuesday morning that that shall be our wedding day.*

Yours affly
JM.

[marginal note] The settlement I will sign *after* if that is legal if you are prevented as you hardly can be in 10 days from preparing it before.

Colalto
Saturday May 12/55

My *dear* John,

I write in extreme haste, I took up your letter last this morning as the three others I have dispatched were upon business requiring great promptness. I would not write at all now but that Sunday coming in, I could not write again for several days.

I am really glad Dick is safe at home again. I am amazed to find how *naturally* I participate in the pleasures of your family, and how I have rising up a sort of anxiety in all its concerns from Maggie and Willie Potter's *up*—or *down* as the case may be. When Dick knows me a little favorably, I shall send to him & his wife my very warm congratulations. Tell me what he looks like, & do add the comforting intelligence that he is no taller than you, & his wife is more of a grenadier than I.

You cant think how your account of the Potters relieved me. I begin to think *perhaps* things may not be so very, very bad after all. I am most anxious to have Spence propitiated, as I think much of the pleasure of *your* continuance in Phila will depend upon the keeping up of perfect good feeling between you. I would be so pained at any coolness growing out of your marriage which would occur if he neither approved the marriage nor liked your wife. I want him to like me very much. Until I see him, he must take my good qualities upon trust.

And now about Maggie. Did you *require* her to write to me? If so don't you think you had better withdraw the *command,* and *ask* her to do it as a sort of special gratification to you? It will be very hard for her to do it any how, & if it be done just as an act of obedience, I rather think any bitterness of feeling that she may have to me, will only be strengthened. I wish she would do it, as I should be glad of the chance to write to her, but I would run no risk of exciting any unkind feeling.

As to fixing a day for the marriage, I dont know what to say. My business arrangements are somewhat worrying. And now, that Mary is married, I dont know what to do with Lilly & Cantey. I have no idea of taking either to Phil: till fall. In the mean time I dont know what to do with them. Aunt Eliza can't leave her house & take mine. Nib (Mrs Massie, whose real name is Sophonisba—the only evidence of bad taste I ever knew my Mother guilty of) might be willing to come over & occupy it & keep the children for a month or two, but I dont know when she could come, as she is to pay a visit of some length soon to her husbands family. How long do you mean me to stay in Phila?

Give my very special thanks to your Sister for every lecture she gives you on "clerical gravity."

Very affectionately
S.C.P. McDowell

Phil. May 12th 55.

My *dear Sally*,

I have just come from a long talk with Mrs Potter. She is so wrought up to the conviction that much depends upon your answer in respect to the 23d that she is urging me to start off on Monday & carry the point by a personal interview. I would do it if I had felt the necessity as I now do a little earlier & could have disposed of some things that fix me here through next week.

But you know, if I came I could only bring you orally what I do assure you of now, that if we let the week of the 23d pass there is no good wedding time till December or January. I know I should begin to clamour again for the next possible occasion, but *my judgment* would dictate that a serious contretemps had occurred to us.

Besides December & January are hardly in the question, for it is so known in Lexington & elsewhere that we cant trust people to be talking of us all that time.

I believe the greatest number of inducements for a malicious person insidiously or publicly to attack you exist before marriage.

Now may I not beg of you *as a great act of confidence in me* even if you are all distracted & in doubt yourself to submit to what inconveniences it may occasion & boldly trust to me in fixing that day.

Mrs P. goes to Niagara & White Mts on the 12th of June or thereabouts & as I told you to her country place sooner. She reiterates the opinions of the Bishop & speaks in the most cordial way of the whole engagement. The whole look of things is brighter, I am sure than you have anticipated.

Even if you shall have written an unfavorable reply when this reaches you reconsider it *& dont let any household or wardrobe difficulties* stand in the way of what if I had all the fears that you have I would consider a most critical juncture.

You need have no fears of a fixed understanding. One of those days is in my own arrangements already fixed: and a letter from you received even as late as Saturday (the 19th) will see me on my way the following Thursday. By the way it need not be the 23rd. The 28th would answer tho' badly. So would the 26th.

What I ask of you is to resign your judgment this once, & give yourself up into my hand. I cannot approach a period which strikes me as so very important without the utmost anxiety & Mrs Potter & I were speculating upon the probabilities of your answer with all the feeling of the most critical determination.

However I have gone quite far enough. If you write back, No, I will still love you with all my heart & be

your affectionate suitor,
JM

[Added-on leaf] These postage stamps were put on by mistake. You can pay me when I see you!

Mon (May 14)[11] [1855]

"Why go over this old thing again?" So say I. It is indeed an "old *thing*". I wish "Cousin John" was in the Pacific & I wish you were in my charge. Oh, how I will steep & saturate you with my philosophy some day till you are perfectly sick & tired of it.

I like very well the idea of getting any facts that you can & placing them within the reach of our family hereafter. But you are to remember that notorious public rumour is one of the soundest species of evidence & one that weighs most with enlightened people. Be very careful too in your inquiries lest it should come to hostile ears.

My darling dear Sally you have talked on this thing till it makes me giddy. All that about impressions against you is *practically* the veriest nonsense. I am *really* as proud as I can be. Mrs Potter will tell you when you see her how "ridiculously proud John is." I wouldnt marry you if it would touch a feather of my *self*-respect if I loved you five hundred times as much as I do. Nothing in my family blood or present standing as a minister & future wild hopes of usefulness on a still higher scale would have allowed me one moment to tolerate falling in love with you if I had any grave fear of a *real* compromise. That men & women should talk about me in that ephemeral way in which the mass may impress themselves or others I dont care a farthing. I have often told you that I have the *coolest* contempt for it; but that grave influences in society such as I swear by & appeal to can be permanently compromised <u>I know is not the case</u>. Now, Sally, you are going to make this I see the means of a negative in your letter to day. Well, *to me*, this sign of a retrograde when we are known to have advanced so far is a greater evil than all your cousin speaks about, still everything is fated & if you write me, No, it is the voice of God.

Poor little Maggie! Why she was highly gratified & so was Allie. Mother I almost laughed at. She told Mary with such an air of Oriental indolence that John must really manage those things himself. Dick even, just from sea & hearing of all entirely fresh told me that he tho't any excitement would soon blow over.

However, I wont weary you.

The horses really seem to have had some fetish charm upon them. And as to the Banks. Why, Sally, you must be a mighty careless lady. How much do you owe? You spoke of "several thousands." How do you manage to keep the sheriff away from you? Dear Sally, I am sorry about the horse. You ought to be riding all the time. What *kind* of a cough was it? Tell me all about it. Do tell me when you write just what it was & why you were frightened.

Yrs affly.
JM

[marginal notes] I am still trusting on our wedding next week.

What views *had* brother Lacey?

11. McDowell added the date later.

Poor Alley! Gazelle would meet the cold shoulder from every body at P. You might as well send a white elephant.

I will get a letter of thanks & a name from Allie. How would [illegible word] do?

**Tuesday,
May 14.1855.**[12]

My *dear John*,

I received two letters Saturday late at night; and one written on Saturday last night. You ought not to plead quite so hard for I can hardly resist the temptation to yeild. But we must wait. I am strongly inclined on some accounts, to bring the matter to a close next week as you propose, but cannot. And as your earnestness seems principally to spring from a desire to remove *my fears*, I am less troubled at creating the delay than I would have been had it proceeded from other motives.

We must have, I think, the facts which Sweeny has failed to re-iterate. It would never do to look them up after we are married.

Then we must do nothing that looks as if we were ashamed of the step we were taking. A sudden descent upon me here & the *bold* carrying me off would look somewhat so—so they tell me. I dont know myself how things look, or how they are, for I have at last, got to that condition that I know nothing at all with any sort of certainty.

Then we must do nothing unusual. Let things proceed as in most cases of the kind, and if people talk—just let them do it. *I* shall not hear, & *you* will not listen, and we will not be greatly disturbed by what they say.

If I married you next week, I could only stay in Phil a few weeks, & then must come back to wind up my affairs here—Now let me get rid of all business matters first, & then as soon as you think it practicable after August let the marriage take place. Your people may "stare" at the opening of a Church & a marriage at the same moment, but it will make no difference if they do. And having the opening of the Church to talk about they will be too engrossed to think "& wonder" about the peculiarities of the other. Then I shall be with you, and not half as much of a bother to you as you think now. It seems a long time, (I am half ashamed to say *how long* it looks to me) to wait, but let me name the 5th of September. In the meantime pay me a visit and write as often as you can. Now if this suits you, dont be clamorous for an earlier time, unless something should turn up making an earlier one, on all accounts, more proper & desirable. My own feelings rebel at my decision, and I shall not wonder at your disappointment, but we must look at it as favorably as possible. If I *could* tell you as unreservedly as you do me of the strong affection that underlies all this coolness perhaps you might have more patience with me.

Say to Mrs Potter all that is proper & kind to be said for me. Some time I may

12. Tuesday was May 15, 1855.

have a chance of showing her how much I appreciate all her considerable and most unexpected kindness at so trying and anxious a time as this is to me.

I am beginning to think the prospect brightens a little. Even Cousin John said to me last night—"I' am beginning to be quite courageous about you." And he has come round with a degree of heartiness that surprises me. His Psychology which has been his hobby for some time, fails to furnish him with the whole process "but of one thing he is certain—you've had a famous victory!"

I am writing as hard as I can for Nib has unexpectedly come over to breakfast with me and is yet waiting to see me. I will write this evening again. Dont send me any more envelopes, until I ask for them, & dont imagine that I am going to write very soon a letter that will demand two stamps. Caution your friends to be quiet & write to Margaret Breckinridge to be silent.

> *Affectionately*
> *S.C.P. McDowell*

Colalto
Tuesday May 15. 1855

Dear John,

You know I promised to write to you this afternoon, hoping I should have leisure to do so. But I have been busied with company, servants & household arrangements ever since. I had made up my mind that I would not invite anybody to my house during the Episcopal Convention if I could possibly help it, & hence had been very sluggish in making any Spring changes. To my dismay, however, Col Smith sent me word last night that the Rev Mr Dana of Alexandria considered himself my guest.[13] I had no knowledge whatever of the gentleman except that he had said to Mary last fall "that he would accept her invitation to be my Guest at Con'n." Mary was amazed, not having given him one. How the mistake occurred we cant tell; but I am determined to make the best of it. This afternoon the Rev gentleman presented himself, and I was very pleasantly impressed by our short talk. Fearing he would find me rather tedious, I petitioned for another guest to keep him alive over here, & tonight am to have one sent. So I am fairly in for the fuss. I begin to think I am public property and that my hospitality is as much calculated upon as if, like my far-off ancestress old John Preston's very clever wife I had given up my life to the keeping of a way-side tavern.[14] Uncle William tells me I keep a "family hotel", but I think my house is more emphatically a "house of refuge" or Orphan Asylum than anything else.

But I do get so tired of playing hostess; & just now with other anxieties pressing upon me I wish my friend had found other quarters. But he will never be disturbed

13. Francis H. Smith (1812–1917), superintendant of the Virginia Military Institute in Lexington. Charles Backus Dana (1807–1873).

14. McDowell's great-great-grandfather John Preston (c. 1700–1747) married Elizabeth Patton (1700–1776).

by this bit of selfishness, but will, if I can so manage it, go off very well pleased with Mrs McDowell & her establishment.

Cant I complain well? Dont I weary you with all this stuff? It ought to bear Judge Harper's great name for Foreign Missions—"fiddle-faddle", and would be much better applied.

Wednesday

If it wasn't easier to go on just here I should tear off the above. I am but just returned (7 1/2 o'clock) with Mr Dana from his morning service & keep him waiting for prayers & breakfast whilst I finish this to you. Isn't it odd to hear a Minister talk gravely from the Pulpit of the "advantage of *prayers.*" But I like their doings extremely.

When your letters come, I am ready to say Yes, I'll marry you tomorrow—as Dr White is absent we'll send for old Dr McFarland.[15] Or perhaps you'll fancy Mr Lacy? But then, I repress every thing in my own heart that would second your own pleadings, and feel a little, *just ever so little*, regret, but say, I cant agree to next week.

I know you get worried with Cousin John, but if you knew how steadily & freely he has loved me, & how anxious his love for me makes him just now, you would think very differently of him. "My respect for Mr Miller is greatly increased" he laughingly said the other day, "since I hear your decision. I am conscious of a nascent affection for him already." I pray you get up the same feeling to him.

I cant make out the name you suggest for Allie's colt—but I wont have it if it is of your choosing. Allie must name it himself.

Aren't you ashamed to call me "careless." I enclose Mr Marx's letter just received.[16] He knows better than you. "How much are you in debt?" A good deal. I dont quite know myself. I have paid in the last 10 or 12 days about $5000 and feel as poor as—I am in such a hurry, I dont know what.

I was afraid of Pneumonia—but I am pretty well now. I am easily scared, and love greatly to complain. I shant give Gazelle to Allie. She is too troublesome for any mortal, I think. She would fight him for a kiss twenty times a day—lean her head on him at table, lie down beside him at night, follow him at all times & annoy him to death as she does me. I wish she would die, as I dont like to play executioner.

Brother Dana is quite bright and smiling as a May morning.

"My *love to all inquiring friends*" & believe Me—what you please.

S.C.P. McDowell

---

15. Francis McFarland (1788–1871), Presbyterian pastor in Bethel, Va.
16. Samuel Marx (1797–1860), McDowell's Richmond banker.

[Enclosure: Samuel Marx Jr. to S. C. P. McDowell]

Bank of Virginia

Richmond 14 May 1855.
Dear Madam

I am favored with your letters of 11th & 12th Inst, and return herein your check for $1913.54, as your Brother had already placed the same amount to your credit.

In handing you a statement of your a/c, I was well aware that you could satisfactorily explain the Cause of the apparent over draft, and I only wish that all the Customers of the Bank were equally prompt and correct as yourself.

I am
very respectfully
Your obd Ser
Saml Marx Jr

(May 15)[17] [1855]

Dear Sally,

How intensely concerned I feel!

I never was so strongly confirmed, that I remember in any judgment of my life.

If we are not married next week or on Monday of the week after we make a grand blunder. Afterwards I cannot *move* till the middle of June & then Spence & Dick & Mrs P. & all the more influential of my people are either out of town or just starting & we leave broad sheets of the summer for people to be misinformed & grumbling about us without knowing who you are or what are the distinct bearings of any reports they hear. Then we come home to see *all* under these difficult circumstances for the first time; to pay visits; to be distracted with *forms*, just at a time when I am crazy with the amount of work in the first weeks of opening this new church. Really in spite of the publicity already given to our attachment I shall be staggered to find *any early time* after next week when it will *do* for us to take the step. And I think it wd be so sad to wait till January.

And yet I am so helpless! Here I am hundreds of miles away from you & the whole decision is with you. Darling, I shall be so rebellious if you choose wrong. If we were in a Turkish country I think I should begin to dream about sacks and bow-strings.

And yet on Thursday I have the greatest pain lest I shall hear from you saying, No!

Now even if I do, reconsider it, my darling Sally. Choose the 26th or the 28th & write me word the morning you get this & I will get it on Sat. or Mon. & it shall be in time. Dont take the responsibility of a mistake that I am sure we both of us shall continually regret.

As to the Convention. It is a thing in which we have no concern.

17. McDowell supplied the date later.

As to the difficulties the Major starts, if your plan is to get information *quietly* you can do that as well after as before. I have enough information to justify me in marrying, tho' as a reasonable man I would be glad of any amount of more. For our children's sake we can seize upon any facts that meet us for years to come.

As to your business 4 weeks cant ruin it & rather than fail you may return in a month.

As to Cantey & Lilly we will bring them if no perfectly comfortable plan occurs for leaving them at C[olalto.] I would *like* to bring them if I did not mean[18] to accept *every wise invitation* that occurs till the time of your return & the presence of your sisters might swell our numbers too much in certain cases *where* we might feel specialy interested to go. Still it is a perfect bagatelle *comparatively* whether they come or stay, so dont let that keep you.

As to any business arrangements you have to make cant I help you make them. Write me frankly anything I can do. You know in the event of our being married *ever* I am the nearest person to you in being & you ought to be willing to tell me anything in which I can assist you to arrange your affairs.

Need you arrange anything for a four or eight weeks absence?

Spence I have no fears about such as you mention & Maggie has no shade upon her mind of consciousness that there can be anything undesirable in what she hears. I will ask the letter fr: her in the way you mention.

And now, my dear Sally, I dont know how these letters sound. They seem to me after finishing one of them like most warlike love letters as tho' your parson lover was wooing you in iron gloves. But seriously, if I could carry you off as you most prophetically said in a sort of hurried assault that is, quite bodily away as they did the Sabine women, I would trust to securing your acquiescence after the 23d of May.

I can conceive of no earthly cause that <u>ought</u> *to prevent our Marriage next week.*

And recollect, a woman tho partly the superior of her husband in chief respects yet is a good deal like an ivy never quite herself till she has some old dumb wall to lean upon & beautify. We are scarcely married before half your troubles are transferred to me & I can tell you boldly that I have the coolest contempt for about half of them. Not that I do not love you more for feeling sensitive about them, but they are the ivy's troubles which she loses the moment she throws her arms around the poor old wall & buries up in her beauty & her cheerfulness the *gloomy* old keep that she thought at one time she would only cover with deformity.

I have the most murderous ideas about your free will. I would like to kill it for about two weeks & with the most Moslem fatalism resign yourself to the will of

18. At this point Miller interlined some phrases for an alternative reading: "I did not mean to beg you if you are willing to accept."

another who undertakes to affirm in a case in which he is willing to risk all your confidence that he sees *coolly* thro' the mazes of yr: difficulty.

Now dont distractedly & timidly shrink & even if you have to be married in a torn gown & in a man's straw hat write promptly to your friends & throw all the hazards upon me.

Yours confidently
Jno Miller.

This is the last & imperfect sheet of a half ream of this good for nothing paper. I think it is prophetic that I shant have to use any more such but that when I write again if my note cracks like black tin it wont alarm any one.

Dick is tall & handsome & Julia just a proper size to be his wife. Wont we look odd walking together. You know it will be so *dreadfully* out of proportion; & Spencer tho a half inch shorter than I, yet has taken care to have a nice little apple faced wife just dropping the right length beneath him (both in mind & person.)[19] Dont you think we are precipitating things too much & that we ought to take time to consider this. I think as we have not known each other for more than 12 years & have not thot of marrying for more than 10 months we are going in a very headlong way & ought to pause if for nothing else than this <u>disproportion in our heights. How will it look</u> in Chestnut St.! Thats the point. And then some who "once thought you" tall, wont they "have their impressions revived" & secretly sneer at us. There goes the giraffe. I cant tell you how often I think of these things.

Phil. May 17th 1855.

My darling Sally,

I have fibbed a little I find about the paper. I find it "in spots" about the study & may for aught I know discover more.

I enclose a ring which is marked so beautifully especially in the closing letter of the "Miller" that I instantly placed my own in the hands of the jeweller who by a strange perverseness marked the "April 30th" on it all straight & regular & in exact correspondence with what was already there. If you like mine better when we meet I will make our friend retouch yours & take out of the letter its romantic twist.

I sent to him this marking. J.M. S.C.P. McD. April 30th 1855. telling him to let the marking run all round the inside of the ring. But the idea struck me that it was a great piece of rebellion against the taste of one I love to mark it differently from my own & moreover that yours was the true idea, & so (realizing what you said that I should find more in you than in the books of my philosophy,) I walked a square or two & made the alteration. The jeweller seems to have tho't it was an ugly name & that it would be out of character to make it prettier. But Sally I am in

19. Anna (Annie) Emlen Hare Miller (1833–1914).

such a terrible anxiety about a letter. I got none this morning & when one comes I fear it will be all marked crooked like the ring. Well I hope it will be for the best.

Yrs
JM.

Spence's Office.

You vile,

Base black-hearted miserable—angel; I've a great mind to—love you more than ever. I dont know what is meant by all this clamour about woman's rights & mean to get up a society to take steps in the opposite direction. Here am I perfectly helpless & you absolute mistress of all times & histories of me so wholly that I absolutely love the hand that strikes me. I dont agree to any of your reasonings or any of your arrangements. If I am not married next Wednesday night I am going to be like Lucy Stone *un*married "under protest" & I dont see how a woman who says she "knows nothing" & is out of her reasons should undertake to tell me when I shall get married or not.[20] I am in a terrible frame of mind. Watch the (sui)side columns of the paper for some days to come, & you may "see something to your advantage".

Yours in utter disappointment
JM.

Thursday May 17. 1855

You write to me, my dear John, like you were crazy. And yet I cant help loving you the more for all your "clamor" tho' it does trouble me. But indeed, indeed it cannot be. What,—next week! Oh, John give me a little more time. It would never do for me to *seem* to falter in this thing—and just now indeed I have not the calm courage to meet so suddenly the great family explosion this will make. Besides it scarcely looks proper to be *torn* away as you propose. I *could* leave everything & go off for a month or two without any injury, but rather the contrary, but then to return and meet all the feeling of the community here, is a little more than I can bear *alone*. I cannot appreciate the difficulties you suggest about being married in the fall. I know nothing of the labor attendant upon the opening of a new Church, but I think *ordinaryly* when a man is bent upon having his Wife, he can find time to secure her, no matter what his work may be. I told you in Washington that you would not bear an engagement of any length. I was right. You are tormenting yourself now with your restlessness to have it consummated. And *I* have been wrong in saying heretofore anything as to the immediate termination of it as I have thereby encouraged you to urge all this haste upon me. But whilst I talk of your anxiety as restlessness, I beg

20. Lucy Stone (1818–1893), feminist and abolitionist.

you will not misunderstand me. I do think along with that you are seeking most earnestly to have all things arranged so as best to promote *my* ease and comfort at the outset. All this motive I can appreciate and feel grateful for, and if we had been engaged a month earlier I should have yielded to your wishes, and have been now quietly seated by your side.

I cannot see, as you do, that so much *would* be gained by a marriage next week. If everything could be smoothly arranged—Cantey & Lilly disposed of for 8 weeks, & the servants &c provided for and the marriage over by the 28th we couldn't reach Phil earlier than the 1st of June. The next week, (the week preceding your Communion) you would be busy—The week after, your friends would all be going or gone, and we left just where we would be if we married some half dozen weeks later.

Now we will take matters in a more orderly way—giving the summer to all necessary business arrangements, and then in the fall, after your friends re-assemble, be married and settled like rational people. I named the 5th of Sep't—I made a mistake—it should have been the 7th, partly because it is a family epoch with us, being the wedding-day of my Parents, and partly because it seems about the close of your summer vacation. But if it does not suit, we can choose another. After that time any day that would be best for you will suit me.

My letter will be a sad disappointment to you I know. I feel that it is selfish not to yield, and at times I murmur at my own decision, but it must be.

It is from no want of confidence in you that I dont yield: and I have already given you a stronger proof of my confidence than the acquiescence now could do. Never fear *about that—I do confide* in most fully. If you could help me I would ask you without a moment's delay recognizing the new relation existing between us. I have written this under very great difficulty.

Friday morning

I add a line in a hurry this morning. It troubles me much to think of the pain of your disappointment, but as I cannot change, I do not know what to say to relieve it.

You have spoiled me by writing so often; Now I am not content unless I hear from you every day. The failure of your letter this morning disappointed me as much as tho' I had thought it reasonable to expect one every day.

I am so harassed with company. All day long I am in it, until when night comes I am weary, and depressed and good for nothing. I find Mr Dana an acquaintance of Bishop Potter. I was curious to know about them, but could not venture to inquire with any particularity. Mr Peterkin too—wasn't he in Frederick when you were there? Recently he has been living in Princeton, & speaks with a glowing sort of admiration(!) and affection of old Dr McLean.[21] At the dinner table

---

21. Joshua Peterkin (1814–1892), rector of the Episcopal church in Frederick from 1841 to 1847 and then rector in Princeton from 1852 to 1855. John Maclean, Miller's friend, was president of the College of New Jersey from 1795 to 1812.

yesterday he began a remark about one John Miller, that I was afraid would lead on to another, and I was quite scared out of my composure. Fortunately, I was skilful enough to turn off the gentleman by a well-timed question upon a kindred topic, and my fears blew over.

What do they have a Convention for? This one does no business. And when they appoint business hours, they seem dreadfully at a loss to know what to fill them up with. Bishop Meade looks as if he did the work of the whole Church, and in reply to my question yesterday, "Can't an Old Man & a Bishop find leisure to do what he pleases?" assured me "he could not if he were a *Bishop*."[22]

"What views *had* brother Lacy?" Ask him yourself. "Am *I* my brother's keeper?" We always have a sharp encounter of wits when we meet, and he tells me "I am the cleverest woman he ever saw—except one—Yes, there is *one* other, just one in all his knowledge of the world who is *smarter*"—but he does not confide to me his secrets. So, if you are curious, ask him about his "views", and tell him at the same time that Mrs McDowell doesnt think it the highest compliment to be called the *cleverest* woman he knows.

I shall be so anxious to hear from you after all these worrying letters. Dont keep me waiting for an answer.

Yes, I think we had better give some months to the great question of our unequal size. If I could have foreseen all this before I was Lilly's age, I might have taken measures to prevent it. What a wee woman Spence's wife must be. And *so pretty!* (from your description). Now when I get to Phil I suppose Spence should say—"Well, John's Wife, after all the worry he had about her, is a Yahoo!" wouldnt you be particularly grateful to him? But, my dear John, good bye.

Affec'ly
S.C.P. McDowell

Phil. May 21st 55.

Dear Sally,

I am so tired every Monday that I dont feel enterprising enough to tell you all I feel about the "23d of May", but there never was a finer plan more ruthlessly exploded. *Suppose* we had been here June 1st. We would have gone to Spence's a few days, then to Mrs P's, then to Princeton & you would have felt entirely *at home* before returning to Lexington. My communion week requires me *to be here* & to be the preacher, but it has no other services than usual in the week & one less on the Sunday. As it is Mrs Potter will not be back by Sept 7th from Chester, nor will Mrs Hunter our Aunt who comes from her country seat late, nor perhaps will Spencer.[23] Besides the distractions & cares of such a time in my

22. William Meade (1789–1862), bishop of the Episcopal Diocese of Virginia.
23. Margaret Benedict Hunter (1791–1865), an aunt of Miller's first wife.

own case are greater than you imagine. And moreover my communion which is quarterly is on the 9th of the very month that you have selected. Still, my darling, I "guess" we'll manage it in some way. We *cant* be married the week of Sept 7th; that's certain. But perhaps I'll beg you to let it be Aug: 22d or perhaps Sept 12th. Will you agree to Aug: 22d? Then we can go to Princeton for a few days & return when others are coming in. If I am *within reach of my pulpit* in warm months, that is often sufficient.

I defer so to a lady's privileges, My darling Sally, that I have not a word of complaint; so excuse me for the incivility of having fallen into the old train.

Now that man, Peterkin that you have had at your table is one of the noblest of men. I am glad that you have seen him. He was in F. nearly all my pastorate there & I greatly valued his friendship. As to Lacy his "views" seem to be mysterious & deep but on *one* point they strike me as both orthodox & intelligle; but Sally, I'm afraid they'll spoil you.

Spence, I fear would think you a sort of Topsey if he knew how much trouble I had with you. I wish I could hear you saying, "I'm so wicked." By the way, Mrs Potter, on whom I called after seeing your first letter begged to send her compliments & to say you were a "naughty woman". So you see I shall have them all on my side.

I mean now to work back into my old plan of doing as I was taught to do when I was *little*—I mean to "speak when I am spoken to". Your sister Mary is away & the younger ladies will think you are writing to B. & you have no sermons to write. Wont you employ the time between this & August in overtaking the number of my letters.

Yours Most affectionately
Jno Miller.

Monday May 21. 1855.

My *dear John,*

I am so tired of Preachers. If you were to present yourself just now I dont think I could make up my mind to see you,—especially if I suspected you had on a white cravat. I am rather glad, in my wearied condition, that there was a ministerial stampede this morning. And yet with all the trouble and bustle I *find now* that I really enjoyed the Convention. Some of the brethren were old acquaintances—others have become very pleasant new ones. We all got to liking Mr Dana very much. He gave us much occasion for speculation & amusement. "I dont know" said Cantey "whether he is a Bachelor or not; but of one thing I'm certain—he is a *something without a wife,* for he looks (copying his grimace) very sweet at me". "Yes,["] added Lilly emphatically "He is very civil to *me*(!); sits by me at table, and is very attentive." Lilly's suspicions were very overcoming to us all, but proved nothing. By & bye however in a quiet tete à tête with me, he brought me to Canteys conclusion—and now that he is gone I hear he is an old

Bachelor. Well, his visit here will not do him any harm. I dont think his *young* affections have been at all tricked. He has too good an appetite for a lover in any stage of the passion. He is very *funny* to me—looks in his straight coat, like a Jesuit and adopts in conversation a *low* tone as being the *heighth* of elegance, which is in fact the greatest inconvenience, as it often leaves me in ignorance of the names of people to whom I was obliged to say something.

Mr Woodbridge, of the Monumental Church Richd, dined with us yesterday.[24] Your name, in connection with that fine church of yours being mentioned, he asked very particularly, & with much friendly interest after your Sisters—your Sister Mary especially. Upon which occasion I allowed myself a very innocent laugh at the dear Lady and our *Motherly* old friend, Dr McLean. That is a stereotyped love affair, the fame of which is quite gigantic, but you must never allow any remark of mine about it to go beyond your own ear. And it isn't wrong to laugh a little bit about it, is it?

Old Dr Sparrow, of the Alexandria Theological Seminary also, bestowed upon us very condescendingly his company.[25] I didn't like him much. He had too much the air—of "*I do you the honor, Madam*, to address my remark to you". If I had not been his hostess I should have felt like responding, "& I, Sir, do *you* the honor to listen to them", for they were not of the most striking ability in any respect. Did you ever see him? Well, he looks just like an old-fashioned pedagogue elevated suddenly into an August Professor of Theology—6 feet, 2 or 3 inches high & 16 or 18 inches broad; with a face that looks as tho' the skin grew to the bones of it and a voice that utters slowly and with great nicety his sublime conceptions. I liked him less than any of the celebrities.

Old Bishop Meade has always been a striking and very noble character to me. And now that he is thin, and his hair grey & combed entirely back from the face, he has in his canonicals, a very picturesque appearance, and as apostolic as it is picturesque. His Assistant, is not so much to my mind, tho' he is I think, a very good man despite his mannerism, which is peculiarly unpleasant to me.[26]

There were some clever men—I mean men of high talent—in their body, but very few. Bishop Meade himself, I think it likely, is the ablest amongst them. I have no idea, as a body it can, at all compare in this respect, with the *Synod* of Virginia.

You remember Miss Tyler of Frederick who married a Mr Baker, an Episcopal Minister?[27] They are living about 25 miles from us, and have made me their first visit this morning. It was a real pleasure to me to see them. But am I not boring you insufferably? I sometimes wonder you dont send my letters back to me with a request that I will send you no more. But in writing I try to get up the feeling of talking to you, so as to render this "mail-coach love" of ours, as

24. George Woodbridge (1804–1878).
25. William Sparrow (1801–1874).
26. John Johns (1796–1876), later the fourth bishop of Virginia.
27. Francis Mason Baker (1822–?) married Lucy H. Tyler (1829–?).

you call it, as little formal as possible. And I am going to *write* to you about things that happen around me, just as I would talk to you of them, if you were here. And if this tires you, you must tell me so. I will not pay you the poor compliment of bringing all the rules & instructions of "the perfect letter writer" to bear upon my letters to you, as "very admirable productions", in the form of epistles, would be more acceptable to some other reader, & look better in print, than they would be pleasant to you, or suited to my skratchy style of penmanship.

By no means the least noticeable fact during the past week was a good, hard rain, that we needed extremely. Farmers were suffering for it. Many were re-planting their Corn; and our gardens were entirely without promise. But the night's rain did a great deal of good last week, and the hope of another tonight is an additional pleasure.

But the sun and rain that make such *good crops* upon this farm, does not secure them *to*[28] *me*; I am afraid the chief benefit of successful farming is to be found in the increased comfort of my Overseer's family, who in consequence, is rather too Lordly to be retained in my employment.[29] I have been dissatisfied with him for some time, and from time to time have suspected him of unfair dealing, and of drinking and of harshness to the few servants he has had to manage. These suspicions have increased of late and I am resolved to rent out the farm & get rid of its harassments and of him at the same time. He was much trusted by my Father who had him for 8 or 10 years, and we retained him on that account. But no Overseer can be kept with safety over five years. They all become rich, in suspicious contrast with the diminishing property of their employers; and a little "brief authority" ruins them. If this happens with *men* for *their* Masters, how can it fail to occur under a woman's *gentle sway*; and ignorant supervision?

I asked Cousin John a few weeks ago, if he would act as Trustee under the marriage settlement of which we spoke some time since. He was inclined to do it at first, but has since told me that he could not. My property is so diverse in kind & so scattered that, he, with his engrossments here, fears he would be unable to attend to it efficiently. I dont know who to look to now, and am somewhat worried about it. If James was residing in Virginia, and not full of his own business he might accept; but I would rather have a Stranger who would be acceptable to other members of the family, and with whom money difficulties, if any should arise, could produce no painful estrangement.

You once asked me about the pay of the Trustee. I was mistaken in telling you they received none: they receive, according to circumstances, from 1 1/2 to 5 per cent, and this, upon arrangement between the parties, not by any

28. McDowell repeated "to."
29. The overseer was Henry E. Morgan.

special requirement of the law as in the case of Guardians etc. This apparent division of interests on a matter so prolific of trouble as property, is not altogether agreable to me, and yet we both agree as to the prudence of this precautionary measure. In case of disaster or death to you I'm sure it will be best for us all round: and if life wears smoothly to us, we will never think of it.

The ring came safely and suits beautifully. You have succeeded in getting it to suit my taste exactly. Sometimes they are unhandsomely broad, but this is just right in that particular. I wish it had been better marked, but that is a little matter. I agree with you that the name was *not handsome enough* to inspire the engraver with any enthusiasm in preserving it on metal, and therefore am rather lenient to him. I dont wear it without very strange sensations & a very peculiar emotion.

Tuesday morning.

I hoped for a letter this morning, but none came. *Of course,* I cant quarrel as I know you write just as often as you can, but I *may* say I am disappointed.

James writes me a long letter on our affair. It much disquiets him, and he urges very strongly a year's delay. He is, as all the men of my family are, excessively sensitive to public opinion, and is more easily made to suffer by public disapproval & what he might esteem, slight than any one I know. Hence he dreads the world's talk in this matter. He fears the revival of the old scandal, & a renewal of old troubles—Personal violence & fatal rencoutres fill his mind. These are the spectres that, you know have often haunted me, so that when he mentions them in his strong way, I am again terrified by them.

Then he foresees the loss of your Church; etc etc;—going over the same old beaten path of ecclesiastical troubles with which you are, already so familiar. I confess my heart quakes under it all, and I feel very like a poor man, I once saw, struggling up to the waist in muddy water, under a burning summer Sun, to get a boat dislodged. He worked mind & body to accomplish his end; but his ingenuity failed & his strength too, so letting go, he threw up his hands exclaiming in the most despairing tone—"*this day do I wish I was in Heaven.*"

I shall fail entirely, if I am much longer to depend upon the *mail* to bring me all the strength you can give. Dont you feel very like giving me up yourself, and getting back to a state of mental quietude once more.

Have you read Hypatia?[30] If you have, tell me what you think of it. I am rather groping through it. I mean to write James a volume of a letter to-day, but with no idea that it will dissipate his fears.

Affectionately Yours,
S.C.P. McDowell

30. Charles Kingsley (1819–1875) published *Hypatia; or, New Foes in an Old Face,* in 1853.

Phil. May. 24th. 1855.

My dear Sally,

I have come from the country just as the mail closes. I have received your letter & write with great haste knowing you would be disappointed without a letter on Saturday.

The ecclesiastical difficulties to which your brother alludes I do assure you are entirely chimeras. There *can* be no such thing. It distresses me to think there should be trouble on that score.

All you write about the Convention is very amusing to me. You have the idiosyncrisy, my dear Sally of always wishing to give up & leave out *some* of the most interesting parts of your letter. If you saw how I *devoured* your letters & how often I read them you would quit slandering them & make them longer.

yours affly,
Jno Miller.

Colalto
May 24, 1855

Dear John,

It isn't often I indulge myself in writing in the morning after breakfast, but to-day the boys are all gone, Cantey is occupied in her own room & Lilly at the Piano, and I have a quiet hour vouchsafed me.

I have suffered under a sort of collapse all week. The bustle of Mary's marriage, my own anxiety about these last days of May, and the noise & fuss of the Convention, kept up for five or six weeks the greatest state of excitement. And since it is all over I am as stupid and heavy and dull as possible. If you hadn't mentioned the 22d of August in your last letter I am sure I should not have had energy to look at a pen, much less to use it. Now, please settle down to the conviction that nothing more is to be done until fall. I would be afraid to go to Philadelphia in the heat of the summer, and as September is a busy month to you, and not the very best for the contemplated event, we will pass it over, and afterwards be ruled by circumstances. I could give you an additional most satisfactory reason against August & September too, but I am sure you would laugh at me for it.

How forgetful I am! I never thanked you, I believe, for your very kind and timely offers in the *shopping line*. They were very thoughtful, and I was very grateful and exceedingly amused. If I were much given to the vanities of dress, what a job you would have had! I'm afraid you would have been completely lost in the mazes of tissues & silks, & bêrèges and laces & embroidery and all manner of gim-cracks. But fortunately I am not irrational in such things, & will only be careful to manage so as to attract no special observation or remark. By the way, I half suspect that one reason why you judged me to be a sort of a pauper, was because you have always seen me dressed so plainly. I adopted, long ago, a plain style because I found that any trimmings such as other ladies wore, made me, from some cause or other, probably because I am so tall, look rather showy & conspicuous. The world has paid me the compliment to say that I was handsome and attractive, and I shuddered at the thought of seeming for one moment to presume upon it, and so made dress rather a matter of principle than of taste. Hence tho' I dressed becoming my position, yet always very plainly. Now isn't this a most interesting topic for a letter, and a very plain-spoken piece of— what? vanity? No, it isn't vanity; I never believed what the world said in that matter of beauty; and as to the other, tho' I dont know what it consists in, yet I honestly confess, I am fully aware of possessing it. It is a *Talent* put in my hand for usefulness, and therefore I have no right to have any feeling about it, but that of responsibility for its proper use. I have observed its effect upon all classes & ages of people, and see it every Sunday as I pass an old, grim, iron-faced man in the aisle, whose rigid muscles relax into an almost caressing smile as we exchange salutations. And why is it? I don't know. But one thing I do know, that it has been a great friend to me in my peculiar circumstances. After this, will you wonder to hear me speak of my *egotism* as being of colossal proportions?

"I'm afraid they'll spoil you"! Does my letter give any real ground for such a fear? At any rate *you* wont have your conscience to upbraid you with aiding in the ruin. Listen, to a few of your honied phrases, and flattering comparisons.—"I never saw such a Spirit as yours: It is like the *frogs* of Egypt I cant *drive* it out". "You are a base, black-hearted, miserable angel." "*I* am St Anthony (indeed!) and *you* are the *Evil One* come to tempt him". "What right has a woman who has *no reason* to tell me whether I should or should not be married on the 23rd?" "Mrs Potter says you're a naughty woman; and Spence would think you a sort of Topsey if he knew how much trouble I had with you." "And Mother says you are high-tempered, and so does Mary", and, you should have added to complete the picture, Julia is not pleased & Dick is indifferent. And Sarah thinks your name is enough to condemn *any* lady,—*she* dont want any more such in the family; and Sam *would* think hard thoughts if he had the chance; and Maggie and Allie have *alone* favored you, one by a heriditary, the other by a "constitutional" bias. Now isn't this a glittering display of jewels!

Mr Peterkin is an old acquaintance, and I like him & respect him very much. I was ready fully to coincide with friend Dana in his remark about him—"Peterkin" said he "always brings to my mind the apostle John." But perhaps, the pleasantest member of Convention that I saw was a little man, about five feet high, who went slipping about most unpretendingly, tho' he is regarded, I hear, as the most learned man of their Church in Virginia—A Mr Chisholm of Portsmouth.[31] I took a great fancy to the little man, and we grew to be very cordial, upon Robert

31. James Chisholm (1815–1855).

Taylor's letter of introduction. I liked every body better than Dr Sparrow, who I hope *is a rare bird,* in his Church.

Mr Kennedy writes me very sad accounts of his Wife. He is greatly discouraged about her, and troubled to know what to do with her or for her. I have urged him to bring her here for a few weeks, & then take her to the Alum Spring, for I am convinced that physical ill-health & feebleness is at the bottom of her present suffering. Hers is an awful malady. We have had two cases of it amongst us, that were fearful. But, both, were at last successfully treated. In Nib's present cheerfulness, not a shade of the past is discernible, and Robert Taylor you have seen—a grave, but not melancholy man.

I am so much afraid of thunder-storms, that the summer is never all together pleasant to me. For two successive nights I have been roused and alarmed by the thunder & lightning. I never make any commotion or disturb any one with my fears, yet I sometimes suffer very much. With my Sister Frank, it was almost like derangement; but I always thought if my Father hadn't indulged her but had *made* her control herself, she would by and by have gained some ascendancy over her terrors.

The election of State officers comes off today. I'm surprised to find how indifferent I am to all such things. I was indignant at my party for choosing Wise, and except that I have a sort of dislike to Know Nothingism, would not care to see him beaten. He is an extremist, and therefore unfit for a Governor, especially in exciting times. He was the most violent of Whigs when I knew him, and seemed to think of Democracy as of the Leprosy, & of Democrats as social as well as political lepers. But now that he has the plague-spot upon him, he is determined to make it advantageous, if it isn't very ornamental.

I know all he is struggling for. I have tried it all, and I can tell him what a shadow he is chasing. I am glad it is all over with me, tho' now & then I confess to the bubbling up, for a moment, of the old ambition.

Tell me, what is a Philosopher's ambition like?

You ought not to keep count with me in your letters, for when I do write, it seems to me I send you a whole volume. How long does it take for you to read such a one as this? Cousin John laughed & said the other day—"Well, Mr Miller is preaching his *old sermons* now": is it true? Does this private affair at all interfere with your public duties? If it does, I'm doing you great disservice. But I can't help it, and certainly you brought the evil on yourself.

Princeton will never be troubled by Gazelle. The house rose in rebellion against her, and this morning, she was presented by one of the servants to a Wagoner as he drove by, and we shall never see her again.

I shall put my letter aside until the mail comes in tomorrow morning. But if I do get a letter from you then, you must consider that you owe me *two* for this double one, & I will not write again until Monday. By the way, I wish you would write me a *book,* as at present I have nothing to read having waded, or *groped* rather, thro' Kingsley's Hypatia.

Wont you tell me what Mrs Potter is like. Dont treat me as you did about "Dick"—"What is Dick like?" said I. "Dick is tall & handsome," was your very comprehensive and satisfactory reply. If any of them should ask what I am like,— you can say, "Oh nothing that you ever saw or imagined":—and they will be as satisfied as I am. Isn't Dick a Doctor? Well, I am going to call him Dr here after as I dont like to say Dick, & Spence & Julia, etc. etc.

Friday morning.

No letter came by last night's mail, and I am very much disappointed. Perhaps tonight I may fare better.

The boys came home quite excited after the election returns came in last night. I grew uneasy about them as 11 o'clock approached and they were still absent, but towards midnight they came with their wrath somewhat cooled down. "How goes the election boys"? I asked as they came into my room—"Oh, pshaw! we're beat. The Know Nothings are 47 ahead." "Well, I hope you kept cool under your defeat"? "I liked to have had a fight," said Bent whose brother is one of the defeated candidates for the Legislature, "But I didn't. I was mad enough to have fought any how". This County has always been Whig, & therefore we were to expect it would slide into Know Nothingism. Yet I am sorry too. Old Dr Junkin has been I hear a very loud-spoken & electioneering Know Nothing; and he, & Dr White both voted that ticket yesterday, which I think, was scarcely right or seemly in either of them.[32] Presidents of Colleges should keep out of politics, & so should Pastors of churches, except in times of the very greatest emergency.

Tom goes to Abingdon in a few days, and we will feel lonely enough. I think we had better rent out the front of the house. I might, if I hadn't such an aversion to having people near me.

Affectionately Yours
S.C.P. McDowell

Phil. May 25th 1855.

My *dear Sally,*

I went out after dinner yesterday to the county seat of one of my people. On returning I found the time for the dispatch post already past & on enquiring & finding that the carrier had not been punctual I seized a sheet of paper & a envelope & went over to the office & wrote till the carrier came. What sort of a letter I wrote I hardly know for I had to wrap it up & send it.

The Winter has been so wearing a one that tho' I think it hardly chivalrous to complain of what a lady chooses to inflict upon you especially when she in any measure shares it herself, yet I begin to feel the effects of its various excitements & disappointments & tho' I think it necessary to stay closely at my work for

---

32. "Bent" was McDowell's cousin Thomas Benton Taylor (1832–?). George Junkin (1790–1868), Presbyterian minister and president of Washington College in Lexington.

about a month, yet I am already beginning to agitate various plans for including in the weeks of the Summer different things that I wish to accomplish.

I have mentioned our marriage (*privately*) to one of the leading ladies of my church & find in her no such revulsion of feeling as you have been led to apprehend.

How differently you & I feel on this whole matter. I think I am not indifferent to family standing especially in all aspects of it in which it would react upon self-respect & yet so little does this whole matter weigh with me that I never think of it. And the slightest anxiety for health either for yourself or me, & the slightest fear for our engagement in which so much of my happiness is now embarked has more weight in disturbing my comfort than all the peculiarities of which I have talked so much in our different letters.

I want to accomplish two things before I die. One is to write a certain treatise on ethical science the other is to marry you. & anything in health or life or sorrow or circumstances of whatever sort that alters either of these results affects me even in the conception of it with a degree of feeling that I can hardly express.

I wish in your next letter, Sally, you would either cast me off or else go thro' some form of bethrothal to me that should be as inviolable as the seal of death. I wish you would either say, "My courage flags & really I am not sure I altogether love you. I wish you would let me off." Or, "God do so to me & more also if aught but death part me & thee." I know you have talked of the engagement being "irrevocable" but somehow I dont think it so. Indeed no engagement would be irrevocable that you wished to break. But I wish you would plight yourself so that I should feel we were married & that it would be just as unnatural to *wish* to separate as after marriage. So my heart yearns to have it. I am vesting an amount of feeling in this thing which is truly *awful* & if you are ever to scatter it to the winds I do beg & entreat you to do it now.

I dont know what has got into me this morning. I came home from the country yesterday a little unwell & my mind under such circumstances works always upon a sort of minor key or as you roguishly might say a flat but there is nothing in all this that I will not stand by & that I do not *wish* to say, as it may give me in your reply either an utter shipwreck, which I wish might come now, or else such an anchorage as would make me feel exactly as if I were married to you. I think that ought to be in the peculiarities of our case.

I dont *like* you to say, "I have not strength enough &c to release you"; or as you write in this last letter, "Dont you feel very like giving me up?" You might as well ask, Dont you feel very like having your head chopped off? The fact is, my dear darling Sally, I always feel that it is *you* that have these wicked notions, & then I feel Oh, so recklessly & desperately, "I wish she would do it *now*."

Therefore, Sally, do write marrying yourself to me for ever & age, for it is the wildest folly in me, with my mad hot temperament, to go on storing away whole oceans of affection & passion in you with any chance that these ruminating difficulties which have led you once or twice to change your mind about minor points should lead you some day to change your mind in the whole matter.

Dont I write "like I was crazy?" Well, Sally, isn't it wise & right, & didn't you first suggest that *our* engagement of all other hot-blooded acquaintances & lovers on the planet ought to be "written in vermillion?" & be as inexorable as death.

I have not read Hypatia & indeed little except the Bible & your letters & I read them very much in the same way trying to get as much comfort from both of them as the letter of the oracle will allow.

As to your business troubles I wish I could help you. The watch I wear was given me for skill in farming. I am really a very good practical farmer. My father had 17 acres in the midst of Princeton & while I was in the College I took his place & directed the work. Instead of buying hay as we had before done I gave mother a stack to give to an Orphan Asylum & she was so much pleased that she gave me $100 for a watch. When we get to Allamby which God grant may not be long I'll show you some things.

The trustee I cant help you in. I wish you would make me *your* trustee (i.e. the trustee of you,) but the other I can only say this about. 1st there is a recent *law* of Pa. that settles *every* wife's property. I will enquire about it. 2d. Dont let difficulties on this score delay our marriage. If no person whom you dare to trust or would like to associate with us in this relation occurs postpone the matter, *if it is legal*, I will settle the property any time after the marriage. You would trust me that far wouldnt you? 3d. If you should utterly fail to secure anybody it needn't dishearten you. You may after a time. And meanwhile I will make a will leaving all your property to you. This will guard against everything but *bankruptcy* & that a parson has very little chance to suffer under. Still dont flag in your effort to secure the *right* trustee if one can be had. Can you have such a deed of settlement as you can cancel or transfer to another trustee or State at any time?

What do you think of this paper. It is made of the same material with bank-notes. It is so tough you can hardly tear it. Try it. I bought it for a retiring young woman I know who dont like her letters to rustle.

By the way that lady's letters are quite right as they are. She needn't alter them except to make them a little more loving. By the way, Sally, I thought when we were engaged you were going to reward me for all my patience & fondness in previous months. Virginia women must have queer notions of volcanoes if you think that any thing in your affection so far is so dangerously "volcanic." I was quite startled the other day when you said, "Do not utterly despise me", & I thought something singularly confessed & passionate was now at the end of so much reserve at last to escape you, when lo & behold, all you had to say was that you loved me too much to give me up!

Dear Sally, Virginia people must be so funny. Mr Ruffner once remarked that he would like to hear a northern person making love. I am beginning to think that matters are quite reversed & that all the icicles are down by the Equator.

I sympathize with you in your wish about heaven but when you go I would like to go with you: *Dear* Sally pray that I may ever get there.

> *I am most affectionately yours*
> *Jno Miller.*

Dont receive the impression from this letter that I am sick. I meant literally & only just a little unwell.

Phil, May 26th 55.

My *darling Sally,*

I feel so contrite for the poor letter you have received to day that I think I will mail one to night. I hope to get one this evening & then I can add a reply to anything it may bring.

There are two sorts of judgments in my church—one that the church will be finished & opened on the first of Aug: & one that it will neither be finished nor opened till Oct: In either case I think our wedding day need not be seriously altered from the time you mentioned. If it is opened Aug: 1st I can get matters so settled as to come on the last of Sept, & if it is opened in October then I can come the first of Sept.

I want so much to see you. Dear Sally, it would be a treat such as you with your *less tropical temperament* could hardly understand. If it were not for the very short time between that & my holiday I think I would try to persuade you to encourage me to come somewhere about next Monday fortnight, that is, the day after our communion. But then a fortnight after that I hope to be entirely free.

What do you think I am planning. As your cruelties to me thro' the Winter have reduced me below my usual mark of activity & spirits I am contemplating the purchase of a horse. I think if I set out in a chariot & _____ one some month hence & drive over the country to Lexington I shall be so tanned & rustic a lover when I meet you at Lexington that you will marry me out of sheer compassion. I will send over from the hotel to have myself announced so that my first visit may not overcome you with surprise & I will take a few lessons from Cantey in Mr Dana's method of arranging his looks so that I am not altogether hopeless of my enterprise.

6 1/2 P.M.

I am so disappointed.

You aint fair.

And yet I am always puzzled when I say that for somehow I have always tho't you *were* fair.

But, Sally, why cant we quit tormenting each other in failing of letters when I at least am feasting on them all day in advance. Why cant you write every other day. I have twice tried to introduce the practice of daily writing. And tho' it impoverishes my sermons which at the best are not sermons that would bear much depletion I am still ready to write every day yet you never would follow my example. Wont you *please* to improve a little in these respects?

What do you think of my Summer plan? How would you like to receive missives from me as I was working my way nearer to you day by day. I would spend the first Sunday in Frederick & then reach you somewhere about Thursday.

But I forgot. You dont want to see any preachers for some time to come. O very well; I will postpone my visit then till I go on to be married & spend the Summer in driving about New Jersey.

I mean to have a good long talk with you about philosophy. I would give worlds if you & I could steal away with our four children to some cool retreat not far from Princeton library & begin at once the incubation of these magnificent ideas. Let us bend all our life that way.

Still this is idle talk & will be till this church is more thoroughly under way. You will have to be a parsons wife for some time yet.

Yours affectionately,
Jno Miller.

I do love you so much. I wish I could see you, Dear Sally, you & I are just tormenting ourselves for nothing. We might as well have been married the day before yesterday as not. But perhaps you dont love me enough.

Sunday May 27. 1855

My *dear John,*

In all the exigencies of our correspondence I have never before written to you on Sunday; but I could not bear to make you wait a single day for an answer to your last letter.

What makes you so gloomy? and what makes you bear with so little confidence upon what I say to you? Dont you think I feel wounded by this want of trust? I have told you very distinctly that I meant to marry you. I am making all my arrangements to meet such an event. I am breaking down the barriers of my own feelings which my painful circumstances have thrown up, and I am giving up early friends & running the risk of position & to a certain degree of usefulness that I pray by & bye from this marriage—& yet you tell me that you are fearful I may yet fail thro' want of courage, or want of affection. Well if you could even conceive of all the pain, and intense and agonizing mortification of the past to me, you would have some sympathy for me, in the dread I feel of incurring open remark again. And I feel it on your account as well as my own. And I am weak not from having too little, but rather too much feeling in the matter.

And now, John, let me tell you. I love you as I love no other human being. My last, and first conscious thought as the day closes and opens again is of you; and if you were to see how my energy in things around me had decayed, & how little interest I have in matters that formerly engrossed me, you would believe me when I say how much—almost how exclusively my mind & heart are with you in your little sanction. And when a fear comes over me, that something I know not what may interpose & prevent our marriage, I shudder at the rebellion of my heart against any such dispensation of Providence. Yet I do not love you now as much as I shall hereafter. I would not marry you, if I didn't feel that I should find out in the future much in you to increase my affection. I wouldn't bring to you on our wedding day all the love I was capable of feeling for you, or all that you now yearn to possess. I want you, as we live together to love me more & more & more—and thus I would treat you. I write in a hurry but I hope my letter will dispel much of your sadness & many of your fears. May God bless you, my dear John, always.

Very affectionately
S.C.P. McDowell

Do write to me how you are. I feel anxious about you as the warm weather comes on, and would very gladly throw a noose over you & drag you into the Country. I'm sure if you were really sick I should forget I was not yet your wife and would pretty soon find myself beside you.

Monday, 9 o clock
May 28,[33] [1855]

My dear Sally,

I have just reached home from the country where I have been all day. I have your last letter & have read it once, but that is only about the twentieth part of the pleasure I get out of your letters. How you do abuse me. You have collected all the impudence that a whole Winter's correspondence furnishes & strung it together in one letter. Dear Sally you're so wicked. You will be startled to find so portentous a law paper.[34] I hired a scrivener to copy it & send it, tho' my sense of its importance is very slight first, because we will not always live in Pennsylvania & second from something Spencer remarked to me when I had a word with him this morning that "the great practical value of a settlement was usually considered to be the preventing of the husband from *persuading* his wife to make over her property to him after their marriage" which of course this Pennsylvania law does not prevent. That is, Sally, the danger practically is that I will pinch you or scold you or threaten you after we are married & make you give your property up. This Spencer says is the great *practical danger.* Now of course I dont fear that; yet who can tell what an old miser I might become? Still as it is best to do these things regularly Spencers thought is worth listening to. And yet on the other hand if a settlement is made such that you cannot undo it which is what Spencer's law

33. McDowell dated this letter.
34. Miller wrote this letter at the end of a law titled "Of the Rights of Married Women" that he sent to McDowell.

custom contemplates there seems to be an evil on that side, for how do you know how enamoured you might be of the North & how desirous you might be to transfer to Northern investments the mass of your money. There is an evil either. The effect of this Pennsylvania law is that *as long as we live in Pa.* it applies to all your personal property & so much of real property as might be in Pa. But Va real estate would remain under Va law. It would protect you as long as you staid in Pa & after that you could have a settlement. Still I am in favour of a settlement now if you can find an eligible trustee. In great haste.

Yours affectionately
Jno Miller

Monday
May 28. 1855

Good evening, my dear John. You are better this bright afternoon? Quite recovered from that fit of the blues which your unfortunate country visit last Thursday entailed upon you? And the Evil Spirit which possessed you last Friday morning, has St Anthony, or your patron Saint of some other name, been kind enough to exorcise it? And this afternoon, does not your returning strength & tone both of mind & body somewhat brighten your views of the world in general, and of a certain Lady in particular, who seems unwittingly to have given you a terrible idea of the utter faithlessness of human nature? And under this truer and pleasanter perception of things don't you feel a little like recalling a certain painfully doubting & gloomy letter written under the influence of an Evil Spirit some days ago to this same poor troubled lady away off in Virginia whose difficulties were great enough & varied enough, without your adding *doubt and distrust* to the number & the pain of them. And dont you see now how wounded that Lady must be by your suspicions and fears?

Indeed, John, I am hurt—and if I didn't, in my "cool wisdom" and forbearance make some excuses for you I should be angry as well as hurt. As to any stronger *form* of betrothal—what stronger could be made? *I have promised to marry you.* If you could not confide in that, then you would not confide in any thing else; and you should scorn to require any woman to bind herself to you by an oath, who has already plighted herself to you by her word and promise. If you have no confidence in her *word*, how *could* you have any in her *oath*. I am sure you could not have been quite yourself or you would not have so written.

Now I know there have [been] many harassments in this affair of ours. It could not have been otherwise from the very nature of the case. It is one of peculiar difficulty. Every step in it had been one of importance, and the engagement, after much anxious thought and feeling at length formed, means a thousand times more with us than with any other persons known to either one of us. It implies a giving up on both sides, each for the sake of the other, of more that enters into individual comfort, than half the world can even conceive of. And it attests, by this very relinquishment, a sincerity and strength and reality of affection, which *ought* to place it beyond all the cavil & question of the most captious & the most skeptical. It never occurs to me to doubt your affection any more than it occurs to me to question your identity. I couldn't imagine *why* you should wish to marry me if you didn't love me. And, in my turn, who should I wish to consent to marry you or anybody else if it were not from this same impelling power of affection? And pray John, what makes you think that I don't love you? Haven't I given you the strongest evidence of it. And if I have as you say changed my mind several times upon "minor points", may I not be allowed to do that without exciting your fear as to my steadiness upon the main point. You are scarcely a proper judge of the feeling that occasions these changes with me as you so frankly acknowledge you have no participation in it.

We must have no lovers quarrel on this point. Too much of happiness is embarked in the matter by both of us for any thing like that, but I say, if your fears as to the fulfilment of our engagement arise from any want of confidence in my affection or my promise to you, then tell me so distinctly and in the same hour you shall be free. As to myself—*when I want to be unbound, I shall tell you so;* so be good enough to wait for that & don't make yourself miserable & me too by, every little while, offering me my "free papers".

You Northern folk are very queer, that is if you fitly represent them. Here you were, for months more clamorous for an engagement than any lover ever saw, and yet no sooner is your wish granted, than you turn round and quarrel with me for not making the engagement (what it is already) a sort of marrying of myself to you, & declare you had rather not be engaged at all, than to be so, in such way as you are now. And then you complain that I am an icicle and a coward and I dont know how many things besides.

Poor fellow! You have had a right hard time I really do think, but then you make things worse than they would have been, by being so hotly impatient.

Tell me, do I really seem so cold to you, or do you just complain of that that you may, occasionally bring me to confession. I am not as hot as you, I admit: and it is well I am not. You should be glad of this difference. But I can assure you I am warm enough. Somehow I have always felt a reluctance to drag into the daylight the secrets buried down, down in my heart. I cannot well form into words the feelings that lie there not idle, but in restless activity keeping the whole machine of the "inner man" in full employment. Yet I dont mean to love you as much as ever I can *now*, for I would have that pleasure increase as we live longer together.

So with you—I hope you are not expending *all* upon me just now. I shall be greatly disappointed, & shall feel that I have not redeemed my promises to you, if you dont tell me after we have been married five years that I am infinitely dearer to you then, than I was when you first folded me in your arms and claimed me as your wife.

Tuesday morning

Well, I am glad to find you have some conscience left, and that you are "so contrite" about your Friday's letter. Tom waked me up last night to "read Brother James' letter and tell him what he said"; but upon looking at the letter I found it was from you. Tom's mistake was no compliment to your penmanship, I assure you, and if I had had time to think about it I should have thought it less of a comfort to me than the quiet it disturbed.

But the letter taught me one thing;—that the next time you get worried or sick, or sit down to write with the wrong spectacles on, not to disturb myself very greatly about any thing you may choose to say. You are not then a responsible being. But if the fit should last long enough to produce two letters, why then I shall write to Spence to have you put in some insane asylum, or else apply to the Court to appoint a guardian for you. Do you know I am a little fearful for your mind any how. I am [fearful] it is a crazy machine that will give us a great deal of trouble yet. I'm afraid it's got cob-webs in it that catch flies. And from the noise I hear now I'm afraid when I look a little closer I shall find a "bee in your bonnet" as our Scotch friends say.

I think your plan for your summer's jaunts a very nice one, provided your *equipage* be well & tastefully appointed. You wouldn't have a light-colored horse would you, even if he trotted forty miles an hour over the worst corduroy road in all Virginia? I wouldn't, I know. And I wouldn't have an open affair, (I don't know what you call them,) and get sun-burnt on that Winchester turnpike, either. I would get a—but indeed I dont know what I should get in such very delicate circumstances. At present horses are much trouble to me. My lame horse is getting well enough for short drives, but the other, the handsomest of the two, is threatened with blindness. I have not yet seen Allie's colt but they tell me it is very pretty. It is an "f.f.v."[35] and entitled to good qualities & good looks, but if it stays here some thing will certainly befall it.

You dont know how I am annoyed by my Overseer. I am some times so "aggravated" that I feel like calling in an Auctioneer & selling every thing I possess. He lets all the horses get poor and works them too hard; and sells off the calves, when I dont want them sold; and keeps 10 or 15 cows yet cant let me swim in butter and milk, but gives me an uncertain feeling about its sufficiency, & makes me take counsel with Edward, when the breakfast hour comes round, and he has, unexpectedly, to lengthen his table & add to his plates. And then he cuts down all the best wood for his own use, & I *suspect* for the payment of his own bills—and does a variety of disagreable things, about which I would be quite eloquent, if I had you for a listener. However I must not complain of the Dairy so greatly, for friend Dana used to turn his bright, little brown eyes up to me, with such a *sweetly* pleased look every morning, as he took his glass of cream, and shake

35. That is, first families of Virginia. The horse evidently possessed a distinguished pedigree.

his head half-reproachfully & murmur very musically, ["]Ah! Mrs McDowell, you will spoil me!" And I, would smile behind the urn very politely, and assure him in the most earnest tones possible, that the thing was impossible. Again the brown eyes were raised very gently & an expressive gesture closed the episode. You ought to see Dana. He is very funny and very Episcopal. He couldn't help telling me though, with all his gravity, and *straight coat to boot,* that he had met with one lady up in the Mountains who could use her tongue well & his brown eyes in their, "liquid sweetness," made the application unmistakably. That wasn't right in him, was it? He didn't know but that *I might* be vain & that he was doing me harm by talking so. To tell you the truth, John, I was in danger of being spoiled at Convention—*Any other woman, I think would have been.* I could tell you some very nice things that were said, if my modesty would allow. I confess my *courage* rather increased under them, & I began to think, perhaps some of those Phil'a folk, whose names figure in our correspondence, might have the same taste, and that I should not be voted a Yahoo after all. I wouldn't like Spence & Dick & the rest of them to think they had the best wives in the family—and the handsomest too, But I suppose they will. Each of my brothers-in-law thinks he has borne away the prize of the family. Mr Massie says to be sure, & only the other day too to Cantey—"I dont think Nib has the talent or genius of your sister Sally, but she has better judgment & better *reasoning powers* than any of you". I laughed at his discrimination—& didnt think it much for a woman to be a genius any how. If you should ever be so mistaken as to imagine me one, please get my neck broken, for that very minute you will feel that your domestic happiness is gone. Men dont ever like very gifted (I mean intellectually) wives. Fathers always enjoy, and are even proud of clever daughters—and sometimes a son will value intellect in his Mother—but brothers & husbands, in the main, have a sort of aversion to such sisters & wives. Now isn't this true?

Tell me, John, is there any woman in Philadelphia as tall as I am? Has your new Church got a spire to it? If it has, have it knocked down immediately, for people will be sure to say, "the tallest things in our City are John Miller's wife & his church steeple."

I hear that John Atkinson is going over to the Episcopal church. I can hardly credit it; but there is no knowing what his Episcopal wife may do with him. He seemed to me, however, as staunch as old John Knox himself.

I cant write to you everyday: it takes too much time. But that need make no difference with you, if you can find a spare minute every day to write to me. Count my letters to you some day & send me the number of them. If you are bent on keeping them, pray put them away carefully & dont let any other eyes than your own ever see them. I havent quite forgiven you for letting your Sister get a peep at one of them. Would you ever imagine that anybody would apply to me for literary aid? And yet, some three years ago I was very much urged by the Editor of what was meant to be a very striking book, to furnish him with *an Article* for it. And afterwards, the Editor of a leading Newspaper begged I would try my hand in a series of—what do you think—*satirical* articles upon a specified subject. The first application after some time I determined to accept. I didn't believe I had any *gift* in that way, but as I was restless to do something, I thought I might as well make the experiment and if any power in that way developed by it, why, I should have *something* to do for the rest of my life; and if it failed, then, I was just where I was before. Perhaps too I was somewhat taken with the Editor's remark that "the best talent in Virginia had been secured" in the getting up of the book. They were very complimentary to my part of the thing & myself, and I was very anxious that my contribution to this State Monument should be fit to stand side by side with those of Professor Washington, & Mr Holmes.[36] But by & bye the Originator of the whole affair grew tired, & sold out to Mr Holmes, who offended me, and I have given up the whole thing. I shall tell you some thing about it more fully. I always thought it rather absurd in me to undertake it, & but for the private point involved, which I intended should be reached without any public failure or injury, I never would have mixed myself up with it.

As to the other—I declined it quick enough.

Tell me, where do you get your hot blood? I thought you all in New Jersey were the coolest & calmest people extant.

Wednesday morning.

What is the reason I got no letter from you this morning? I am, without any affectation, ashamed of the length of my letters, but as this one has been written day after day in three days, it ought to pass for three letters of proper length.

I did a most economical thing the other day. I walked into a store & bought a sett (I think they say—a *pair* is it?) of letter scales. I fear have been a little too generous to the gov't in that matter, & so determined to draw in. I find them very convenient, especially as the mail does many a job for me, besides carrying my letters. In fact, it is less expensive & much quicker and safer than Adam's Express: & as such I use it.

I wish you a pleasant jaunt thro my long letter with its corduroy road.

Affectionately
S.C.P. McDowell

May 29th 1855.

My *Darling Sally*,

I do love you so for that long letter. Oh, if you knew what a pleasure you give me & what a comfort I take in such a good long talk which seems to be so full

---

36. Henry Augustine Washington (1820–1858), professor of history and political economy at the College of William and Mary. George Frederick Holmes (1820–1897), professor at William and Mary in 1848, then president at the University of Mississippi briefly before returning to Virginia to write. In 1857 he became professor of history and general literature at the University of Virginia.

of your own kind feeling & character you would write every day, more specially as it seems to carry to you to put down what you wish upon paper & to express everything that is kind & good except affection.

You say, tell me, ["]What is a Philosopher's ambition like?" I would so like to describe it so as to attract you.

New-England I suppose is a part of the country for which you have very little comparative favor & therein you are not altogether unlike me. And yet you cannot deny that this Eastern corner of America has a very peculiar character & has made that character felt over great interests of man. Now a Philosopher's ambition is to *make* that character, to let his own thought & will live in whole nations of men, to let his own system of belief & pervade society & to let it mould & alter whole masses of the people.

Now I mention New England because Jonathan Edwards has done this very thing. Dwight & Emmons & Hopkins & Edwards & Bellamy have *begotten* New England & these all are the one mans pupils & actual disciples.[37] And tho' the faults of New England spring from the same philosophy yet there is something glorious in having named in the quiet of a study by one individual intelligence the thoughts & the character of whole generations of the people.

Accordingly a Philosopher's ambition is to be known when Wise & Houston & Pinckney & Randolph & Everett & Douglas & Marcy & Buchanan & all that class of secondary men are forgotten & when Jackson & Webster & Henry Clay are known only in the dim distance & are heard of only in an imperfect history.[38]

The ambition of a Philosopher is to be what Edwards now is a man absolutely growing brighter & better known as the times advance: whose M.S.S. were absolutely considered too precious on a recent occasion for the chances of a voyage & were copied out to avoid the danger: more books are now publishing in Edinburgh like Shakespeares with "various readings; & of whom people speak in this way—Paul, Augustine, Edwards," skipping clean over Calvin when they come to enumerate the giant theologians.

Such an ambition scorns such a man as Wise & the place he aspires to & scorns all secondary honors, & would as lief die unknown as die with all of them. It *was* very greedy of them etc etc, but unless it can set its name among the

37. Timothy Dwight (1752–1817), Nathaniel Emmons (1745–1840), Samuel Hopkins (1721–1803), Jonathan Edwards Jr. (1745–1801), and Joseph Bellamy (1719–1790) were all Congregational clergymen and theologians.

38. Henry Alexander Wise; Samuel Houston (1793–1863), Texas senator and governor; Charles Coatsworth Pinckney (1746–1825), American diplomat; John Randolph (1773–1833), Virginia congressman; Edward Everett (1794–1865), Massachusetts senator, orator, and scholar; Stephen Arnold Douglas (1813–1861), Illinois senator; William Learned Marcy (1786–1857), New York senator and governor, cabinet member; and James Buchanan (1791–1868), Pennsylvania politician and fifteenth president of the United States. Andrew Jackson (1767–1845), seventh president of the United States; Daniel Webster (1782–1852), Massachusetts senator; and Henry Clay (1777–1852), Kentucky senator and congressman.

one or *two* who are remembered in all time as having controlled the thinking of the world it is *un*ambitious. It plays for great stakes & unless it wins those it will die broken & indeed has a towering contempt for any of those who will set themselves to court mere popularity.

Now this is the worldly aspect of the thing; but a philosopher in a Christian sense is one who to be sure is troubled with these hungry cravings, but who the more he is a Christian delights in the philosophy itself. Who cares less whether he is *ever* great & cares more & more for the *pleasures* of his thinking. "A fool hath no delight in *understanding*, but that his heart (or intellect) may discover (or show) *itself*". But, "*through desire*, a man having separated himself, seeketh & intermeddleth with all wisdom." There is the very thing uttered clearly enough by Solomon.

Lewis Littleluck was a man much affected with these ambitions with two peculiarities however, one that he had wasted too much of his life upon the distractions of a laborious profession & the other that he lacked too much the talent requisite for these high philosophies. This last defect he never seemed to be aware of himself but having an inordinate passion for philosophy he was ever indulging the dream that he might one day have an humble share in it. And tho' obliged to nurse these children of his fancy in great secrecy for fear of his friends yet he never even in the grey of age could be got out of the idea that he was born for a great philosopher, & tho' the size of what he was to accomplish naturally dwindled with the dwindling of his years yet Lewis Littleluck never gave up the dream & when he ceased to be ambitious as to others he continued to be greedy for himself to enjoy the pleasures & taste the sweets of a Philosophic retirement.

Lewis Littleluck had only one misgiving, as to *absolute solitude*. There had crossed his path an angel who had confused his ideas as to the pleasures of absolute retirement. She was an angel who smiled upon him with engaging beauty & seemed to promise bright hours with him in the seclusions of his philosophic paradise. Happily she was an angel not deaf to his entreaties for her affection. And tho' she always seemed to him like one who smiled on him rather out of compassion, yet she allowed him to paint her image in his heart & to prepare her chamber in the castle he was building.

Our friend Lewis however was born under an unwholesome star, for tho' this angel became more & more rooted in his affection & displayed more & more her singular loveliness yet Lewis seemed less & less able actually to imprison her. She would fly past him in the most bewildering beauty & when he would reach out his hand to touch this image of his fancy it would vanish, & poor Littleluck was left to mourn over the sally of his hopes when at a brighter age they went out after this chosen object.

His idea was that God who had sadly tried him by all kinds of uncongenial scenes & employments was about to bless his philosophic retreat not only with liberty to enter it, but also with this lovely image to be enshrined in its recess, &

that in musings that might issue in something great he might have the presence of an angel to sooth & to cheer him.

Poor Littleluck!

Sally, aint I a fool? What will you think when you read all this rigmarol. But, Sally, I *do* mean that being a philosopher usefully & well is *the very most prolific of human services*. And that in the weight of it & the solitude of it I can conceive of nothing more perfectly enchanting than the love & intelligent sympathy of an angel such as I have been sketching.

Mrs Potter is the granddaughter of an old Doctor of Divinity of the last century in Connecticut—the daughter of that man's youngest son who settled on a tract of his father's in the backwoods of New York.[39] She is a Lady of great strength of character, of great fixedness of will, of fine powers of family government & provision, of no beauty, of a rugged sort of countenance & of about 45 years of age. She likes me, & yet we laugh at each other all the time. She is the decided leader in her own family & of great & excellent influence among the ladies of the church. She is a lady of plain matters, of excellent sense & distinguished judgment & loves Maggie & Allie as if they were her children & did love you till you disappointed her so & will love you I think again if you are a good girl & dont break your husband's heart before she sees you. Dick ("the Doctor") is neither very tall nor at all handsome. I fear I fibbed if I said he was either. He is a little tall & a very little handsome sometime. I am considered the ugliest of the family. I will send you on the first chapters of the book you asked for in my next. *Do* tell me your "satisfactory reason against August or September for our marriage." *Do.* I want so to hear. I'm a Whig & have voted the Whig ticket all my life (tho' I hate these K.N.s how will you like that?[)]

> Yours affectionately
> JM.

Phil. May 30th 1855.

My *dear darling Sally*.

My heart yearns to you so much that I cant help writing you another letter. I do beg pardon for sending you so many of my scrawls but I do love you so much that I cant help telling you so all the time. I ought'nt to do it, for tho' Major Preston is wrong in fancying I am preaching all my old sermons yet I *am* interrupted by my courtship. I sit in my chair listlessly dreaming of you & this very moment I ought to be out visiting some orphan children & instead of that am writing this "extra" to you.

39. The "Doctor of Divinity" was Joel Benedict (1745–1816), Congregational pastor in Plainfield, Conn. The "youngest son" was Robert Benedict (1776–1855), a farmer in New York until he retired to Chester, Pa.

Still, I must be honest. The image of you has improved me & made me a better man I hope than I have been before. I have written more sermons since Aug: than ever in an equal time & tho' this results in part from my *exigency* being greater yet I do thin[k] it results in part from my trying to be worthy of you.

Dear, dear Sally; my fate has been always to love people more than they loved me. I wish you would love me more. I wish you would some day forget yourself so far as to tell me all the little affection you have for me & I wish, (for I might as well wish much as little) that you would write to me every day at least for one week.

You have Cantey & Lilly & a host of townspeople & a nice warm place in a pleasant household circle all to yourself. I have no body. My children are at P. You are off hundreds of miles. My brothers are in other houses & immersed in business. I am alone. And when I write to you to try to make you feel how much I love you you write back in perhaps four days laughing at me & telling me you will answer anything affectionate "again." Sally do treat me better. Nobody ever loved you as I do, & yet I have to write whole pages of letters to win back from you the least expression of attachment.

Yours affectionately
JM.

Tell me honestly, had you not a little feeling of *fatigue* when this thousand and first letter was handed out by Alfred.[40]

Phil. May 31st 55.

Sally, dear, dear, *dear* Sally, if you knew how easy it was to make a poor forlorn man like me happy, how few things affect me & how little of those I do long after serves to alter the whole tone of my feelings you would write such letters as this often. My whole being is wrapped up in you far more perhaps than if my children or any Lady I cared to love were immediately with me & Oh, the thot of anything occurring that could part us for ever has grown to be insupportable.

God reward you therefore for plighting your faith to me again so warm & truly. Now you are *mine* passed all danger of a separation & I do offer you, my darling, the warmth & the strength & the fervor of the very most earnest affection.

Do you know you never wrote me such a letter before. I shall begin really to think that you *are* penning up in your heart far more emotion & love than you have ever told me of. I have just gotten out of a carriage that has brought me back from the Alms House which is over in Blockley. The Mail is just closing. Wont you write at least for a week or two every day.

Yours affly.
JM.

[marginal note] I am quite well.

40. This addition was written on a separate piece of paper.

Colalto
Friday June 1, 1855

Dear John,

I had made up my mind not to write to you this morning, but you beg so hard for a letter every day, that I have changed my plans, and scratch off a note in haste for to-day's mail.

I wrote to you on Sunday last a hurried letter which you have not acknowledged; and as your last, received an hour ago, was written on Wednesday and makes no mention of it, I am afraid it has not reached you. It wasn't worth much—yet as it was worth writing, it was worth getting.

I shall be pretty busy all day to-day, for I have invited a cluster of old Ladies, whose ages range along from 45 to 70 to spend this evening with me. Their evening to begin at 5 o'clock and close at half past eight I suppose, after which hour I may go out myself. And as Cantey goes to this large evening party she fancied a new dress, about the trimming of which she rather needs my assistance. So between the old ladies & the flounces I shall have my hands full.

Have you any old maids among your people? Please pay them an extra visit round, as quick as you can, for I am afraid of them, and shall not be able to go see them for a very great while. There are so many of that class here, that they quite hold the balance of power in society.

You behaved very well about Mrs Potter. But you might have saved yourself such an elaborate description of her, by comprehending everything in this one phrase: "Mrs P. is a very superior woman",—for that, I discover is exactly what you want to say about her. Now, I'm very sorry to make any such discovery, for *superior women*, in any opinion, are in some sort, Monsters. They are so disagreeable— indeed, it is their prerogative to be so;—they are so dictatorial; they are so ill-mannered & rough under the plea of being sincere and candid. And they have always such very *meek* looking husbands, and such forlorn, poorly clad children, with their shoes flapping open without strings, their aprons tied on the wrong way, and their faces, poor things, with a shiny look as if a little water had been hastily *smeared* over them for the occasion. Now, you dont want Mrs Potter to hear such an image to me as that to me, do you? Well, dont make out to me then that she is a superior woman. I hate them all,—those *"superior women"*,—with their hooked noses, and thin visages, and sharp voices & self-satisfied looks, and prying ways, and unending homilies.

But John, you are terribly given to "fibbing". And the worst of it is, there is no hope of curing you, for you think if the sin is *acknowledged* nothing more is needed. And you are a dreadful punster, and seem greatly obliged with your efforts in that way. And I dont like at all, at all, that you should be a Whig, for now, you will turn K. N.[41] And then you complain so much: I think you're a fearful Grumbler. And you say, "Maybe I may become a *Miser* by & by"; and

41. That is, Know-Nothing.

that is worse than all. And then,—are you anything more that is bad? Oh yes! You're bad enough to wish me to love you just as hard as ever I can, with all these faults, and worry me to death if I don't do it, as if, forsooth, *bad people* were to be loved as much as *good ones*.

The rain is coming down delightfully. No thunder & lightening, but just heavy clouds and steady, gentle rain. I met an old farmer the other day, and wishing to have something to say to him, & yet not quite knowing what to say, I ventured to ask about his farming, and was rewarded for my efforts at civility, by his telling me that my wheat was "the brag" of the place. I hope it may be so indeed. Much, pecuniarily, depends upon it.

I dont much like your bank-bill paper. It "rustles", or rattles as I would say, worse than any other.

1 o'clock P.M.

I failed to get my letter off in time, and because of the rain, my old ladies write me they will not be here this afternoon, so I shall write along very leisurely and send my letter off tomorrow morning. Some day, I mean to note every interruption that occurs to me during the writing of a single letter, for I suspect you think I fib a little on that subject.

Oh, John, dont you wish you were a farmer just that you might enjoy such a rain as this. I sit by an open window & look at it as it falls & listen to it with such a sense of quiet pleasure as I cannot describe. But do you like to hear me talk about farming? Don't you think it a little manish? I think it is rather so, but then I am bound to be interested in all that belongs to me. To tell you the truth I know very little about farming. It was only this Spring I think, I was riding a little distance in the Country & was much struck with the beauty of a large field, and exclaimed, "Alfred isn't that very fine grass! What kind is it?" "La! Madam", said he, "that aint grass, it's a grain field!"

As to the famous settlement. Any settlement that I have had any interest at all in preparing has secured to the Wife her property in such manner, as that she, herself *can never* part with it either upon the persuasions or threats (!) of her husband. She may, or may not be, according to circumstances, consulted as to its investment, but whatever change of investments occur, and they are allowed, she is still protected in her rights. Marriage settlements, I assure you, are all based upon the one idea of the *depravity of Man's nature*, and the conviction that all husbands are grasping & unworthy of trust. The romance of affection never sheds its radiance upon a law paper. The existence of la belle passion is ignored in all deeds of settlement, or if recognized, is supposed [to] be a sort of craziness that seizes upon *women* and sometime induces them to give everything in the world they possess to their Husbands. Therefore the law interposes & prevents that, by thrusting a cool, sensible, disinterested Trustee between the parties, and makes him the guardian of *her money*, whilst it allows her, poor thing, to do what she pleases with those trifling things herself & her affections. She may give *them* to her husband. The law makes him welcome to *that much*. Well, after all it is right, tho' not the most pleasant thing in the world. The less power too, a woman has under such an arrangement the better. Eighteen months ago, I rejected quite vehemently a paper of this sort, prepared for one of my Sisters, by my old friend Fendall, at my request, because it was too *liberal* upon that very point. I had Spencer's idea of the thing entirely, and I still think it the true one. But then, and this is my case, a woman doesn't want to be protected *against her husband, but against the accidents of life*. This, of course you understand; If you don't know you are—Oh! that german word, I remember now, that you flung at me once upon a time, and that meant something—not bright—and looked under your skilful use of the pen just so—"TUM"—How do [you] like its "physiag"? I have no doubt it would look better if you had spelled it right, which *Fishburn* says you don't do. Generally *English* words look well when the spelling is good—so I suppose it will be with this German fellow. But as my pen often comes down, with its spelling blunders upon the fair countenance of an innocent old Saxon word, and mars its beauty like a stroke of paralysis by drawing its mouth all array, I have no right to quarrel with you about your Misdemeanor's in that way whether they be frequent or infrequent, "*cronic*" or sporadic.

But haven't I run away from my text! If you run off from yours in the same way when you get in the pulpit, I'm afraid your people wont long run *after* you. Or rather they will, if they are bent upon hearing what you have to say; and wont they have a hot chase!

But one word more about the settlement. The *Trustee* can be changed at will, but his powers are always the same. By consultation with him, under *your* advice, I could at any time sell out in Virginia and invest in Pennsylvania or N.J.: but the money thus invested would still be mine, & you would have no more control over it than you would have had if no change had been made. And I believe that these deeds secure property to the wife no matter what may be the law of the State in which the property lies. But I will find out fully about these points & let you know. But don't Spence know? What right have I to think that our man, Mr. Davidson is any better lawyer than he.[42] Go, ask him someday all about it, & then write me what he says.

My young student is to be licensed in a few days. At the same time Mr Cleghorne is to be installed. I dont now believe him to be a blockhead *only*. Perhaps that is the chief of his merits. He goes thro' our neighbourhood, they say, counting all the *rich* girls he can force himself upon. What do you think ought to be done with such a creature? I am always so mad when I hear of these coarse, vulgar Preachers, presuming upon the fact of their being Preachers, to force an entrance into a gentleman's family, and think themselves entitled to alliance with it. I have known several of that kind,—one of whom tho' we grew up together in the same town, never will *condescend* now to speak to me even. I wish Cleghorne

---

42. James Dorman Davidson (1812–1889), Lexington attorney.

was out of the country. He's so big too—looks some horrid old Masterdon. And when I hear of his asking about Cantey—how much property she has etc. etc. I feel like he ought to have his throat cut. I think it such an indignity for such a creature as he even to dream of a high-bred, high-born woman.

I did not think I should again fall into the folly & indiscretion of a letter of three sheets. But you perceive I am a great talker. What will you do with me when you go out to Allamby. Do you think you could have me tongue-tied?

For a week or ten days Mrs Leyburn, Sister-in-law of Dr John Leyburn, has been extremely ill.[43] So hopelessly ill that her husband was telegraphed at Nashville a week ago to return with all possible haste. He reached here Monday night. She revived somewhat after he came—indeed rallied so greatly that her friends caught again a hope of recovery, but she sunk again, and last night died. In a little place like this the death of an acquaintance seems almost like it had occurred in your own household. In this particular case, death has come as an Angel of Mercy. The poor Lady has been a sufferer for many years, and was ready and willing to go when she was called. But, she leaves a family of little children, with very few near relatives to care for them. Their Father, to be sure; but no female friend who could take them. I am often made to feel the nothingness of life with the engrossment of "things seen",[44] but when life temporal is thus made to issue in life eternal, I know that the gift of existence is the noblest boon upon earth. And if when death comes to me, I shall be found like this poor lady able to say truly, "Notwithstanding all my ties to earth, and they are many and strong, I believe I would rather go than stay", I shall have accomplished the highest object of life and shall have nothing to fear, but every thing to gain in the future.

I wish I was an earnest, industrious Christian, always impressed by the truth that all christians should be, *God's witnesses* in this world. But to grope along and mope along, and feel duty to be a burden, and obedience to the will of God a sore grievance, and to sigh for the forbidden things of time & sense, and to murmur all the way—oh!; these things make this life gloomy indeed, and forbid us to hope for less of gloom in another.

Friday night

Tom & Cantey have, at last, gone off to the party, neither of them very much inclined to the task. Tom has been delayed some days & will not now leave us until Tuesday. I am sorry to see him so out of spirits. I have never seen him so much depressed. He is naturally grave & despondent and reserved to a fault, but kind, and affectionate. Somehow I have a feeling of sadness for the child—but that may arise from my anxiety about him. He has not been wisely dealt with of late, and has had a pretty trying time for years. I am apprehensive as to the result

---

43. Ann Pope Price (c. 1808–1855) was the second wife of Dr. Alfred Leyburn (1803–1878), a Lexington physician, farmer, and Whig legislator.

44. 2 Cor. 4:18.

of it all. The perpetual changing of plans for him, dispirits him and destroys his energy. However, I must hope for all that is favorable.

Where is Maggie Breckinridge? With Cousin William in Louisville, or Uncle Robert?[45]

I must say a Philosopher's ambition is of the most sublimated sort. A little more towering he is, than the most aspiring person I ever knew. I think it rather odd, that your friend Littlebeck should so frankly confess that the only tie to the world he had, was that which his very ethical Lady-love had woven for him—making her a clog upon him. But dont I tire you to death?

Saturday 6 A.M.

Didn't I have a time last night! When 2 o'clock came and Cantey & Tom, did not make their appearance I became very uneasy, and waked up Lilly to share my anxiety with me. I was utterly unable to do anything. She & I were the sole occupants of the house. The hard rain had prevented Jimmy's return and we were then entirely alone without hope of making the servants in their houses hear a bell or anything else.[46] I thought of all sorts of things for & against the probability of an accident, and at last made up my mind to be quiet. Twice I fancied I heard the carriage returning, & at length I really did hear them. And, in a moment they stood before me in great wrath, both of them. They soon told their worry & Lilly & I shared in it. A young Lawyer here, whom none of us like, & whom I have for a year just quietly dropped from my acquaintance, has within a few weeks re-commenced his attentions to Cantey.[47] I dont know that they were ever anything special, but I didn't choose they should be continued to her, or ever bestowed upon anybody in my house. Well last night, he even went so far as to insist, in spite of downright rudeness upon her part & Toms too, to take a seat in the Carriage. But, for consideration for his Host Tom would not have permitted it at all. I am really provoked about it. I gave up my fur cloak, because he was impudent enough, out of my presence, to throw it round his shoulders; and now I have a disgust at the Carriage because he rode in it.

No, I'm never *"fatigued"* at the sight of your letters. You need never fear they come too often. The next time you write send me a model of just such a letter as you would have *me* write to you. And the next letter *I* write shall be the tiniest little wee thing you ever saw. Not a great volume like this. Some day I shall tell you how much I love you & it will not be such a "very little" amount of affection you will then discover either.

Dear John I am affectionately Yours
S.C.P. McDowell

45. "Cousin William" refers to William Campbell Preston Breckinridge (1837–1904).
46. Jimmy Carrington.
47. The young lawyer referred to is Dabney Cosby Jr. (1836–1886), a law student in Lexington.

Sat. (June 2) [1855][48]

My *dear darling Sally*,

How you do misconceive me! I didn't want your "oath" & never dreamt of such a thing & would have looked strangely at the letter if it had attempted to confirm in any way *your word* which is quite enough for me on any occasion on which you give it. But darling, of what value is your word to me if you didn't love me & tho' I know your word to me in such a promise is the highest proof of your love yet dear dear Sally I cant live by *my reason* when I aint well. I want you to *tell* me you love me & now that you have told me so, so fondly & even passionately, I can tell you it's far nicer than when I had to walk by faith & not by sight. I do feel very penitent for having hurt your feelings but somehow I cant get to feeling *sorry* about it. Because I cant help thinking how nice my letter drawer is with those last two letters in it & how if I had to choose between losing those two or all the rest I would be puzzled to know whether I wouldn't keep those two. I respect Mr. Dana for finding out the conversational gifts of a certain lady in the Mountains but I have found out something far better, that she has a *good warm heart*. I *knew* it before, but I didn't *feel* it, & what I meant by a new betrothal was not an oath, but some certainty to a poor sad man that when I had endowed this lady with all the gold of my affections she would not find she loved me so little as really by her looks to appeal to my pity to release her from so ill-starred a bethrothal. But Darling, you do love me now & I love you more than I can possibly tell you. Dont let us have any more "lovers' quarrels;" & remember if you ever wish to shed a little sun-light of cheerfulness into what is at best rather a dark chamber you will tell me just in the most unvarnished phrase how much you love me & how sorry you are to be away.

There now we are reconciled: aint we?

I never doubted your word: but what is the word worth when affections change? What would I care if you came with all the punctuality of light & gave yourself up into my arms on our appointed wedding day if I found you were sacrificing to your word what I had asked you from your pure affection.

But, Sally, it was all foolish and you have forgiven me. You ought'nt to have talked of "releasing me" & whether "I wouldn't like to be released" it is like breaking the third commandment. I cant bear to *think* of you in another relation than my own darling wife.

I intended not to write till Monday as I am very busy, but I couldn't refrain from this much. I am indeed a poor "crazy machine" & you ought to have been on your guard but, Sally, I have intellect enough for one thing, & that will answer one of your questions, *to long after you for nothing more than I long after you as a companion in my studies*. So far from being able to realize what you say of undervaluing talent in a wife, if I didn't thin[k][49] everyone was conspiring to spoil you I would say

48. McDowell dated this letter.
49. Miller wrote "thing."

that you *first* presented your self in my path as so beautiful an ornament to my *Cloisters* which I was diligently building all thro' the idleness of the Summer. When I have wrestled away with things for which I have a passion all thro' the hours of the morning it will be so sweet to have one in the afternoon who will not weary me with the platitudes of life, but will keep me still in the companionship of the *"wise"* & good. *And this I really thought of.*

It will never do for you to dampen me in philosophical studies, for you first kindled my affection as part of the same picture with Allamby & these ethical & metaphysical objects of my life.

Now dont be scared Sally. I dont mean to take it for granted that you will ever touch a philosophical book. What I mean is that whether from arrogance at the thought of having any sense myself or the passion (& no envy) for "those" who have I loved you *first* as I would a statue for the grounds of Allamby & because *I had a taste for you* & I loved you next & I have loved you ever since on all accounts & because I couldn't help it. But recollect you have forgiven me, Sally,

> *yours affectly*
> *Jno Miller.*

Tell me "some of the nice things that were said of you at Convention". Only tell me without thinking. "Open your mouth & shut your eyes". I'm afraid they'll spoil you.

Some of the absurdest things you say in your letters you say oftener than anything else. I think of getting an answer printed that I may just slide it into each letter in reply. For example this, "I am ashamed of the length of my letters".

Where do I "get my hot blood"? Why, from you.

[marginal note] Your notions about the settlement are just my own, & they are also Spence's & Spence is not a K. N.

> *Phil. June 5, 1855.*

My dear Sally,

Your most abusive letter came this morning & gave me great delight. There is a wood that grows in Africa that is called "sassy wood". It is given to females to chew & produces in them the greatest tirade of abuse & excitement but then as it is too much for the nerves the effect does not last & it ends in syncope & death. Does any grow at Colalto? These highly wrought fictions about "misers" & "grumblers" & "bad people" that "wish to be loved as well as good people["] & about "superior women" & their "meek looking husbands" that go potter-ing about with "shiny faces" & about "punsters" & "ministers" & about "cutting preachers throats" & "breaking my own darling Sally's handsome neck" & then "anything more that is bad" may be very pleasant but my dear darling Sally what if you shouldn't live long? Such efforts may not exhaust you now but may not the sword cut the scabbard & life ebb away in the end. Remember those that take the "sassy wood" dont think "it's hurten of 'em" at the time but it carries them off before they know it.

Dear, dear, Sally I dont like even to laugh at you. You have me so under your witchery that I dont like to write any other way than this fashion as I am writing now. I hardly laugh at you for two sentences before I want to catch you in my arms & see whether you aint offended. Never mind, Sally, I'll be a good husband in spite of all your ridicule. I love *you*; & that's a great deal of capital to begin with. It is true I play the fool & that will vex you to death sometimes. And then when I aint playing the fool I am absent & have to be shaken almost to get an answer from me. And then tho' I am steady as the sun about all the larger passions & purposes of life I am whimsical as the wind about all the lesser things & ringlets & tendrils of behaviour. Oh, I'm a terrible fellow. But I dont drink or chew or smoke or snuff or swear or cheat & I'm going to be particularly careful about breaking your heart in any other way than with bad puns.

As for Cantey, dear Sally, dont you think you had better hurry her to the North. I have thought since I read your letter that the sooner you come with her the better. There are ways we have here for keeping people out of our cloaks & carriages that we dont want to ride in them.

As to "superior women" those that live in glass houses oughtnt to throw stones, but I am glad that you have these notions about shoestrings & meek husbands as I see these things will be avoided when we get to Allamby.

Your abuse about the paper I shall follow by taking it from you & as I pass Lawrence & Rimby's I will buy enough of the flimsy kind to last us till we are married.[50] Talking of paper I might as well say here that I despise the K. N.s & "wish I was a farmer" & that your Sundays letter didn't come to me any sooner than if it had been written on Monday. But I think its a heap nicer than any of your Monday's letters.

Darling didn't I say "tumm"? or didnt I at least say "Tum"? Just look again. "Cronic" is so neat a word to remember that I wouldn't like you to be burdened with more than that one.

No you *dont* "tire me". Sally, how foolish you are. Maggie B. is in Niagara. Why cant you "tell me how much you love me" *now*? I'm going to "strike" for higher pay wages in this love contract. You keep me on the slenderest allowance. This is *not* my "model letter" but one in great haste from your dearest

John.

Monday June 4, 1855

No, John I cant send off a letter every day. I think of you enough to send you double that number daily, but I must do something beside scribble, scribble all the time. Tho' I have no sermons to write, nor pastoral visits to pay, nor a new Church to look after, yet I have occupations just as varied as yours & just as imperatively calling upon me for attention. As it is, I write oftener than I should,

50. Lawrence & Rimby's was a paper supplier in Philadelphia.

and such long letters, that I should not be at all surprised if, some day you would ask me to shorten them one half.

What is all this about Cleghorn? Do you know our Presbytery has refused to ordain him until he answers some charges relating to the Colonization Society, satisfactorily. I dont want him to turn out a ___ (what is he?) but I wish they would *never* ordain him here.

I have a party on hand for tonight. I undertook it without the least enthusiasm, & have not yet obtained any. They are very wearisome to me some times, and in the country, are always somewhat troublesome. Then to-day Cantey is sick, and I am assailed by a sharp pain thro' one eye that makes me wish our dear friends were in Japan. But the girls are both in for it, & strawberries will not last a week and I am going thro' with it just as well as I can.

It is *so* cold. I have fire in my room & have hung up my linen dresses & brought out worsted ones again. A little frost was reported this morning, & certainly I have been chilly enough to think it might have been snow.

What think you of the enclosed? I found it in an old Indian basket in my Mother's wardrobe, only a few weeks ago. Doesn't it speak Time's changes very fully? Can you possibly imagine that there ever was a time when my head was covered with golden curls like these. Such a very demure, grave, unattractive child as they represent me to have been, whom nobody especially loved but my Father. I was so ugly too, & therefore stood in such strong contrast with my beautiful brother. My Mother loved me, of course, but not with the decided preference that my Father then exhibited, and everybody thought me stupid. About the time these curls were cut, I was a sort of plaything for the Aunt, who afterwards became Mrs Breckinridge, and thus first fell under Uncle Robert's notice.[51] He relieves the barrenness of that early period of my existence by his kindly sentiment for me & describes me thus "I remember you, Sally, when you used to sit in your Aunt's lap, and when I would come in, would in the most ladylike tone & manner salute me with—"damn your soul Robert"—Wasn't that a specimen of the old Adam? I suspect it was the overflowing of his own badness that I was giving back to him & not any that was inherent in me. But in a late letter from him he alludes very affectionately to this early acquaintance, begun when I was first learning to connect words into short sentences at 18 months old.

I can hardly tell why it was, yet childhood was not a happy period of life to me. I look back to it without the pleasant feeling that beautifies it to most people; I am conscious of much pain, and disappointment, & nervous sensibility during the whole time, that marred my pleasure & gave me wrong & distorted views of everything. I was eager then as now for affection, yet too proud ever to seek it. I was ambitious, yet absolutely self-distrustful. I was possessed with the idea that no body loved me and it often made me irritable and miserable. And I had the most

---

51. McDowell's maternal aunt Ann Sophonisba Preston married Robert Jefferson Breckinridge.

painful sense of a conspicuous deficiency in beauty and attractiveness. I have no recollection now either of ever having thought myself clever. I have often, often felt as I would catch an eye earnestly fastened upon me,—"how that person pities me for being so ugly"; and my heart would sink & checks glow with the most painful emotion. Yet I never remember a time when I was not treated with more than common consideration, and was not thought by some body or other to have possessed the very qualities, the absence of which I so much lamented. But I have never had the conviction in all my life that I possessed in any considerable degree either beauty or talent. I believe some people over-rate me greatly; but whilst I am grateful for their opinion, it doesn't at all affect my own, and hence I am not in danger of "being spoiled" by anything I hear on these points. Now, as you seem to value both these things very much, I should like to have both, and am as pleased as possible to repeat the pretty nothings that people say of me & to me, and am treasuring them up as if they were of some value. But if I do this wont I spoil *you*? I'm afraid *I shall make you vain*.

June 5th

I thought our guests were never going away last night; but they did at last. Cantey was sick all night & at 4 o'clock this morning I sent for a Physician. Her attack is something like Quinsy.[52] This afternoon she is much better and I hope will soon be entirely well. It is still very cool, and another frost this morning was very trying to every thing that grows on the earth.

Oh John, if you were near, I think I would come to you for a little advice,—in fact I'm half tempted to write to you how puzzled I am, but I think you would laugh and say "why, Sally it is [a] pretty story that you can't manage such things yourself"; and then I would feel "*so bad*".

Mr. Lacy was among our guests last night. He has uncommon conversational ability—is the best raconteur I know. But then conversation is a profession with him. He studies for it, reads for it, arranges for it, and is indeed very successful in it. I dont think he ever touches a pen, and does not seem industrious any way. Yet he has improved in his preaching & his addresses that are somewhat conversational, are uncommonly good. But for all that he needn't think he is going to succeed over here.

Wednesday morning

I was so stupid yesterday I couldn't even write. My head was a lumbering affair that could make no progress whatever.

Why didn't you write on Monday? In fact why dont you write every day? Do you know I am growing impatient for your holiday to commence? When does it begin? And how long will it take you to get here? Im afraid you will come just in the bustle of the early part of July. The first week in July the town is full of strangers, full of bustle and excitement. The College Commencement &

---

52. An inflammation of the tonsils.

that of the Institute take place then & the Trustees of the one & Visitors of the other, with parents & friends flood the place.[53] It is usually a time when every thing & every body, servants & all are as busy as bees. Will this make the least difference with you? Oh Yes! of course, write to me as you come along, but dont "have yourself announced" after you reach here. There is no danger of my not knowing you if you are "sun burnt & rustic". By the way, we dont think it makes people *rustic* to come up to our Mountains. We think it helps you city-folk to come amongst us amazingly.

This next Sunday is the day for our Communion too. It happens so accidentally this year, but fortunately I think as it occurs in a quiet season & not amid the bustle of the Commencements. My thoughts are always straying out after you— following you in all that I know of your duties, and into your pulpit, and I am worried that they are not better governed & reined in, yet when this time comes I will let them, to a certain extent, go to meet you unrebuked.

I am glad to report the weather a little warmer, tho' I am now, in the early morning, writing by the fire.

I wish you would, sometimes, write me about the children; Perhaps you think, my heart is only large to take you in? I tell you, it wouldn't be worth you having if it wasn't large enough for all. When I opened the door of it to you, it just opened of itself to them and they *would* come in. Oh John, do you think they will ever love me. What sort of children are they? Am I not the very greatest beggar for love that you ever saw? But the hour has come, so goodbye.

Affectionately Yours
S.C.P. McDowell

Thursday P.M.
June 7, 1855[54]

Dear Sally,

I am always checking myself in my terms of endearment. I think if I allowed my pen to run it would make so many of them that my letters would look like old banknotes in which—one dollar—one dollar—one dollar & __ used to run all over the page. Why is it, Sally, cant you tell me? It isnt so in other letters that I write. And it is'nt so in yours. It must annoy you a great deal. I will really try to break myself of it. But it is a species of weed that grows in the soil of my affection that it is very hard to root out. Can you tell me how I can get rid of it.

Who do you think came in upon me yesterday but Mr Cleghorne. He really seemed to be summoned from the bounty deep by reading your letter. Sally, why do you dislike big people? Do you like little people because you are in love with me? Or are you in love with me because [you] like little people?

53. Washington College and Virginia Military Institute.
54. McDowell dated this letter.

Well, Cleghorne came to get me to white-wash his character, & I told him I wouldn't. I told him I had replied to three letters from Va ministers in a way that greatly exculpated him that he had better let it rest there for that I might not be as favorable in another letter. What a great big savage he is! And yet do you know I'd like to be as big.

I send you a chip from one of Spence's notes partly to give you some little notion of him from his good hand writing & partly like a model husband to do nothing without my wife. I have not seen Spence & I dont know how he came by the information or how it arose that I was nominated. I have never dreamed of the office. It is the Univ. of which Dr Ewing was Provost & of which Prof. Reed who perished in the Arctic was Professor.[55] The salary on the strength of old endowments is $2000. There are two classes a day & no such leisure for private study as I long after. If you will allow me, my darling Sally,[56] I will write a respectful note begging that my name may be withdrawn before the election which occurs a month hence. This too will save the shame of a defeat, for tho' there are no very formidable candidates in the field yet their might be before a month. I cross my hands upon my heart & wait for my wife's decision.

What will you do with me if I come to Lexington? Will you confess before the whole town your interest in me, & battle out (as you fear) the months afterward before our marriage? or are you secretly willing that I shouldn't come till nearer the day of our wedding. Tell me frankly in your next letter. You know my appearance in the town & my frequent visits to you will divulge the whole matter at once. Will the pleasure of seeing me overbalance the pain of so long a gossip on the subject?

I will try to see Spence before I send this letter & tell you about what you ask. If the deed does as you think admit of a change of trustees & a transfer of property to Pa or N.J. I dont see what more you could ask. My *only* difficulty is removed. For I think it would have been a hardship to tie you hopelessly to a trustee with whom, for example, you have had a difference & through a long life at the North to bind you to investments in Va. Tho' very probably both trustee & investment may of choice remain the same.

Maggie B. is in Niagara & visits the West afterwards. Poor thing, she has never been the same since Polly's death.

I will keep the rest of this sheet & finish it in Spence's office. Rimby & Lawrence have sold all your favorite paper & told me they could have sold cuts more of it. So there must be other lovers in the world who cant bear their letters to rattle.

55. Enclosed is a brief note, dated June 6, 1855, that John Miller had been nominated as professor of moral philosophy at the University of Pennsylvania. John Miller added, "The rest of the note was just impudence & I cut it off." John Ewing (1732–1802), provost of the University of Pennsylvania from 1779 to 1802. Henry Hope Reed (1808–1854), professor of English literature and rhetoric, died in the steamer *Arctic* on Sept. 27, 1854.

56. These three words are circled in the letter.

By the way, your letters number 55 leaving out the purloined ones. How many have I written? Dont forget to tell me the "reason why you would not like our wedding-day to be in August or September".

Spence's Office 8 o'clock

No letter. Bad girl. Stop too. Spence in. Little man. Lighter hair. More curled. Man of the world. Better dressed—at least was, before married. About equal now.

Settlement good against any law; unless by its terms it contravenes the law of the state which is not likely.

Judge Thompson nominated me.[57] Spence says, "Show me your letter of declinature if you write one! I want to see that you are not too rough about it". Aint that cool?

Bad girl. No letter. Mad. I wonder some people aint ashamed. Good night

Dearest Sally[58]
your poor John.

Colalto
Thursday June 7. '55

"Dear, dear Sally I can't bear even to laugh at you". Dear, dear John, what an outrageous fib. You *do* love to laugh at me. You love it dearly. You are glad of a chance to do it. And Sometimes I don't altogether feel So cool under it, but at other Times I rather enjoy it and laugh too. I shall pay off old scores when I *see* you. So you better take care. I dont mean to have you all the time laughing at me, and slandering me & saying I eat Sassy wood & grow first, furious then, foolish.

I have been all day with Nib who is sick, and, in consequence am not very bright tonight. And I started Tom, poor fellow, out to Abingdon this morning & that doesn't make me at all merry. And then, I am really sorry for friend Lacy, but I couldn't help him, could I? It does seem hard to demolish at a blow the work he has spent years upon, but then I did not even suspect what he was at for a very long time, and after I did, I could do nothing. But I really am sorry: dont you feel a little bit so too? By & by tho' he will look round and find somebody else who will strike his fancy as being the embodiment of all that is lovely & loveable. *They say* Presbyterian Ministers, of all people, are the most susceptible of consolation in such matters. I dont know. I know little that class, but am inclined to believe them somewhat slandered in this particular.

June 8th

Tell me how it is you "play the fool", that I may be prepared for the infliction, or find some way to escape from it. I foresee I shall have a terrible time, between

---

57. John Oswald Thompson (1809–1866), judge of the Court of Common Pleas of Pennsylvania.
58. These two words are circled.

that awful absent-mindedness, and mountebankism and punning and grumbling. But then after all you have some negative virtues! You dont "chew, nor smoke nor snuff nor swear nor cheat"—aint you very free from all disagreablenesses? Now if you dont snuff, I hope you will have no objection to my doing that after while when I get to be as old as my Grandmother Preston, who always looked very grand to me in her use of snuff. I shall never be so troublesome or picturesque, however, as she was about it. She had a collection of beautiful & costly & curious snuff boxes, from the Scotch Mall with its silver thistle, up to the most elegant things that could be made of gold, or rare kinds of wood inlaid with gold, yet she was notionate about the quality of her snuff, & never thought it good if it was in a very close box. Bottles of it were, therefore, all about the house & a very odd, dwarfish, & deformed servant boy, who could do nothing scarcely & was rather tenderly cared for by the old Lady, found his labor & his delight in following his Mistress thro' the garden & grounds, with her common paper-snuff box, from which she frequently regaled herself during her morning walks.

She was a very superb woman, both in appearance and in character, and I greatly admired her, tho' there was a want of something in her to draw out my affection very warmly. She was, perhaps, a little stern, but yet very strongly and tenderly attached to her family. She was very Majestic in her movement and manner—a sort of Juno—but not winning.[59] Very unlike my own Mother, who was eminently lovely in person, and very gentle in her manner and tones, and gave in everything the very best justification for my Father's extravagant love for her, from childhood to the grave. James Taylor, only the other [day] was laughing about it. "Sally" said he, "did you ever see such lovers as your Parents were! Theirs was a perpetual courtship".

Dont I run on dreadfully. I forget you are not interested in such matters. But then, you will have to be, so make up your mind to it now. I shall never forgive you if you show any indifference in such things.

You never saw such weather as we have. Cold & hot all the time—not steadily one or the other.

When you go to Frederick, are you & Mr Sam Tyler on such terms of intimacy as would permit you to ask his aid in our matter?[60] I dont know what else to do. or think of. The difficulties in the case seem rather to diminish to me too as I get more accustomed to looking at them. So I perceive, they do to Cousin John also, who speaks encouragingly and will not allow me to say that my *courage* ever flags in the thing now.

Why dont you, as you seem fastidious about your paper get some like this. It is much pleasanter to write upon than white, not being so glaring. The Post Master of the House of Representatives furnishes me with such things generally, which

59. In Roman mythology, Juno was the principal goddess, the wife and sister of Jupiter.

60. Samuel Tyler (1809–1877), attorney and writer, had been a church trustee when Miller was in Frederick.

he is at perfect liberty to do, and it has been more convenient to me to send to him than to trouble a friend about it. I believe, however, the last package that came from Washington was not *Congressional*.

I haven't a single word more to say. I am as dull as Col Reid, who is a mighty good man, notwithstanding, and as heavy as Judge Brockenbrough, who is, nevertheless, very gallant.[61] I wish you would write to me every day. I get hungry for a letter when you miss a day, and I confess to a right strong desire to see you.

What becomes of your brothers when they leave Phil for the summer?

Affectionately Yours
S.C.P. McDowell

Friday 7 P.M. [June 8, 1855]

Dear Sally,
Tell me all your troubles. I shant say any such thing.

Affectionately
Jno Miller

What a dear little golden relic.[62]

You must *see* my children. I shrink from *beginning* to tell you anything about them.

Saturday, June 9. 1855

I do believe, John, you *do* spoil me. I am greatly astonished now when *two* days pass by without hearing from you; and indeed as the second wears heavily on I, in spite of my reasons, get restless and anxious. I know you are busy, and feel that I am unreasonable but—*I do want a letter every day.*

Some time ago—perhaps a year, Cousin John & I stood, late at night talking in the front porch upon the subject that has been the burden of my letters to you. As we talked on & on, I unbosoming myself to him as I did to no other friend, I remember saying,—"I stand in awe of the power of my own feelings. If they should ever be aroused, nothing could stop them. They would come, sweeping over all obstacles, breaking down all barriers, defying all control: I should have no hope but in the restraining grace of God". I spoke, I suppose with great emphasis, for he seemed startled & turned and spoke impressively of the might of that only restraint to which I had attended.

I might in the excitement of the moment have exaggerated the strength of feeling, but I dont know. When I see how my heart goes out to you—how absolutely possessed I am by this whole thing—how you have in fact become

61. Col. Samuel McDowell Reid (1790–1869), attorney and major landowner in Rockbridge County. John White Brockenbrough (1806–1877), judge in Lexington.
62. She had sent him a curl of her hair, cut when she was a child.

"The ocean to the river of my thoughts which terminates them all", I dont think I did over-rate the feeling & I dont wonder that,[63] I am agitated at every occurrence, no matter how slight, that could by any torturing of my imagination be made prognostic of ill to us. Sometimes, I am half inclined to regret that I was so positive about that 23d of May; but it cant be remedied now. When I am bright and cheerful, altho' it would be a great addition to my pleasure to be with you, yet I *can* do without you; but when I am dispirited and a little heart-weary I do wish for you so earnestly. I feel very much as tho' I should be ready at any moment to go back with you. And wouldn't I "shake" you well if I found you slow about answering. I wouldn't give you a chance to have an absent fit, except when I took one myself, and that would not happen very often.

I have had so many ups & downs in my life that I never have my feelings strongly set upon any thing, that it does not cause me some uneasiness. I am so afraid of disappointment and disaster. And the more I find myself drawn to you, the more anxious I get. But we will wait patiently until Fall; and we shall both be the better able to wait after your July visit.

I am anxious you should know and esteem my dear Cousin, the Major, and not cast him into the Pacific as you threatened some time since. We had a very merry talk about you last night, and he in the course of it said, "Well I think if Mr Miller could see you now, he w'd be content!. I always had a high respect for him, and all you tell me about him makes me like him more. And then, I like the marriage better as I look at [it] the oftener." I was much pleased for he is cautious in what he says, and has not heretofore been as well satisfied as I was eager he should be. But I told you before he was rather foolish in his notions about me & would think King David himself entirely below the notice of so August a personage as my Ladyship. In fact, he has tried to magnify me into something very—I dont know what.—Let him speak for himself. "Here I have been", said he "for years studying you, and admiring you and loving you and thinking of you as one of those bright stars yonder that could stand and shine alone. I thought of you as self-supported—living *in duty* & *for duty* alone;—elevated above common affections and giving yourself absolutely to the discharge of high christian obligations. But I find you are, after all, nothing but a *woman*, who must have another to love & protect you, whilst you love and lean upon him. And", he added dropping from the height to which he had ascended "if his heart doesn't beat true to you as you lean upon it, he will be sure to have one enemy in me".

Dear me! I almost laugh, when any body suggests the possibility of that heart of yours not beating full and true. I repose upon it with such unquestioning confidence, and feel as safe in it as I can feel in any thing below the skies. And wrap myself up in its affections and feel quite warm even in this cold world of ours. Oh John, dear John, how came you even to think of throwing such a priceless mantle as that over my head.

63. McDowell repeated "that."

But how I do go on. Pray, where I am I? down at the equator? I used to feel so pleased when you wd say "My darling Icicle", for I was afraid of seeming too warm, but now, I dont care if you do know how much I love you, tho' I am rather awkward at expressing it. I have been writing an hour, when I ought to have been with Nib, who is still quite unwell. I couldn't stay with her this morning, but promised to go over this afternoon, and must go now; so "Rev & dear Brother" for the present adieu.

Oh John, I shall behave so nicely when you come up in July. I shall say "Mr Miller" to you just as formally and primly as if you were Spence who had stepped in upon me; and I shant "abuse" you in the least, and altogether I shall be so "pretty-behaved" that you will hardly recognize your old correspondent.

Monday June 10. 1855[64]

I very seldom send to the Post Office on Sunday, but as my arrangement for getting the mail Saturday night was an utter failure, and as I was more anxious than usual to hear from you, I sent yesterday, and received your letter with one also from Maggie & her Aunt Mary. I had rather given up Maggie's letter. I thought Your Mother & Sister had concluded it would be most *prudent* for her not to write, and tho' I felt sorry to think of not hearing from her, yet the prudential motives that I thought were going to deny me the pleasure, were too natural to be blame worthy. But now that both letters have come I am very much pleased and have nothing more to ask. But, John, I am *really* vexed with you about yours. What *does* make you so careless? Do you know what you did? Why you put your letter in a thin envelope, and instead of turning the blank side of it out, you turned the written side next [to] the envelope, & there were the last words of it standing out to the P.M's eye almost as plainly as if nothing covered it. I was aghast when I saw it, and very much provoked at you for your thoughtlessness. You know in a little place like this all such things are Talked about. Curious eyes like nothing better than to have private letters to pry into, and vulgar tongues rejoice to get hold of such secrets and spread them abroad. But even if nothing worse was done, I didn't want Plunkett's eyes to profane my letter by looking upon it. I am in good earnest in my scolding,—pray, how do you like it? Think you can stand such for a life time?

Now as to the *inside* of this letter, the *outside* of which annoyed me so much; I have only to say as to the "terms of endearment" you use, that you need not trouble yourself to restrain them from any notion of their being annoying to me. *I would not impose any such self-denial upon you.* There is no great variety in them, but such as they are, they are very acceptable.

I dont dislike *big* people. I wish I did. But Cleghorne is a great Masterdon of a Man. Did you ever hear him preach? Well, if you have the chance go & hear him preach his favorite sermon upon the World's progress. It is the most astonishing

---

64. Monday was June 11, 1855.

production of original genius that I have ever known. But do what you can for his character even if we shall have to cut his throat if he looks over here.

Fifty five letters! I dont wonder that "the winter has been a wearing" one to you. But, tell me honestly, have those 55 letters told you anything about me that you did not know before? Have they taught you as much as you think 55 visits would have done? Have they given you any thing of a picture of me? If they have, they are worth something, if not burn them up, right away.

You're a pretty fellow to talk to me about "purloined letters". Purloined indeed! when they were hurled back at me as hard as you could throw, because they didn't please you & "you wouldn't read them again" for any thing. And what became of my "purloined ones" pray! I never asked for them. I thought it would make you too vain; But I thought someday, when you would give me permission to rummage about in your sanctum, & "tidy up" a little, I might come across them in the rubbish and secure them without asking your leave. And so I will yet.

I cant tell you why I dont want to be married in Augt or Sept. I'm afraid you would laugh at me. But you may guess, if you can.

I'm sure Spence is too prim. His writing looks so precise. I'm not sure that I like it as well as your scraggy style, which has the merit of being, I am glad to say, entirely your own. It is perfectly individualized. Do you think I will like Spence? What will I like him for? I always thought you all behaved badly to Spence about his marriage, with your Know Nothing proscription of Episcopalians, and I wish he would make *you* feel ashamed of it and heap coals upon your head by loving me right warmly.[65]

As to the Professorship, isn't it worth considering? Would you like it? Would it suit Your task and at all, fall in with your other plans? When must the new Professor enter upon his duties? If some time must intervene between the election of the Pro: & his taking his Chair; and if you are, (if your people dont give you up before that) determined to give up your Church a year hence, why not now make an effort to get this place. If, however, you have not fully made up your mind to leave your present post, & if your charge seems satisfied with you, you should do nothing that would loosen the tie between you. A show of willingness on your part to leave your people wd very soon bring about an anxiety upon theirs to let you go.

Now if you are *useful* where you are, and if we can get along quietly and usefully with the people after we are married, I prefer the Church to the Professorship. But then, would not the professorship chime in better with your peculiar *notions*, and ultimate designs? But, I talk as gravely, as if I really had such knowledge of all circumstances of the case, as to make my opinion of any value whatever. I cant tell what you ought to do. I am chiefly concerned that you should do what

---

65. Spencer Miller's wife, Anna Emlen Hare, was the daughter of an Episcopalian clergyman, George Emlen Hare. Her mother, Elizabeth Catherine Hobart, was a daughter of Episcopal bishop John Henry Hobart of New York.

is *right*. If you decline,—just give Spence a chance to use his polishing brush upon your note;—not that it will *need* it, oh no! I wouldn't hint such a thing as that, but because he asks the favor, and anybody who reads his "Caprices" will soon discover that he is addicted to the use of sand paper. One other thing upon this subject. If you are ever to be a Professor, let it be *now*, whilst Maggie is little. I think no girl should be brought up in a College Campus if it can possibly be avoided. A very accomplished gentleman of our State refused a Chair at the University for no other reason than that he had a family of Daughters: And I think he was right.

What upon earth made you send me "Sister Rose"?[66] I wonder you haven't long ago sent me a copy of Bleak House, wh seems so special a favorite of yours. But for an allusion to it in one of your letters, I never should have read it.

Dr Addison Alexander is here & preaches for us tomorrow night.

I enclose a letter to Maggie, which you will please send on to her. I do not like to have it mailed here. I leave it open. You may make it more acceptable to her by adding a line yourself. By & by I shall write to Allie, as it seems hard that because he can't write he shouldn't be written to, and in a few days to your Sister. Did you ever see such writing: I'm afraid I am falling into dreadful carelessness.

Tuesday morn'g.

Your tiny letter came last night. I had disposed of my difficulties before it came. "What shall I do with you when you come to Lexington?" Why, be very glad to see you, and treat you accordingly.

Affectionately Yours
S.C.P. McDowell.

[Mary Miller to S. C. P. McDowell]

Princeton, June 6th 1855.

My *dear Mrs Mc'Dowell.*

I feel as if I would like to write a few lines, to accompany Maggie's letter, not only to apologise for the defects of her epistle, but to renew the intercourse that was so pleasant to me last summer. Maggie is very much of a beginner in letter writing & has had but little regular instruction. Her Grandmother has always been averse to any thing like a public school for such little ones as they are, & she has suffered so much from bad health within a few years, that she has not been able to be quite as regular, as she could have wished, in their home education. Their cousin, Margaret Breckinridge has assisted a good deal in this matter, & I think, that while they have not been as regularly at their school books as some other children of their age, perhaps their mental & moral habits & especially their scriptural knowledge will be found not so much deficient.

66. *Sister Rose; or, The Ominous Marriage*, by Wilkie Collins, was first serialized in *Household Words*, Apr. 7–28, 1855. T. B. Peterson and Brothers in Philadelphia published it in book form in 1855, but mistakenly attributed it to Charles Dickens.

I look back with a great deal of pleasure, on my journey to Virginia last Summer, & I think it was of great benefit to my health. It ended however very sadly, & when I saw you, I was so anxious about them all at home, & especially Margaret, who I knew would be in such deep affliction, that it was very hard to turn my mind to any thing else but the distressing scenes connected with that bereavement. Margaret has again left us, to be absent probably a year. She is now at Niagara & she expects to go farther West, in a few months. She is with her little nephew there, who is a very interesting child & I hope the care of him will do her some good.[67] Her spirits are still very much depressed & we have all been anxious about her.

I hope I shall see you again in less troubled times, & that an acquaintance begun so unexpectedly may grow into a long & intimate friendship. Believe me

Your's sincerely.
Mary Miller.

Phil. June 12th 1855.

My *dearest Sally*,

It aint possible that Mr Lacy dared to court you. I cant make out yet about him. Do let me know. Last week I thought it was Cantey, for you said, "Nevertheless he aint going to succeed over here", as if under such inducements as his great skill in conversation such a thing were imaginable. So I said, it cant be Sally for she, poor thing, has committed herself too far for the charms of any conversational powers. But to-day your whole letter looks as tho' it were you. And yet it cant be you, for how then would you have invited him so recently to a party & nursed his hopes with strawberries & cream. I am in a perfect "fog." Have you got any body else there at Colalto that I dont know of.

And then, Sally, I'm in so much trouble. May not Lacy use personal violence? Who can tell what he may do in the height of his disappointment? Had we not better postpone our marriage till we see what the future may disclose? My mind had become somewhat calm & serene & accustomed to look as this event as certain. But I am now plunged back into all my uncertainties & fears.

Do write & let me know whether it was you. And, Sally, as you & I are very much the same person tell me all how it was. Did Mr Lacy tell his anxieties, in the "Straits of Gibralter"? Did he do it any more skillfully than I & had you the same queenly gait when you made him feel as if the whole vault of heaven was one dome of solid indigo?

Poor Lacy! I know exactly how he feels. And yet so proud have you made me that I almost think it was insolent in him to dream of you.

But perhaps it was Cantey. Why cant you save trouble by telling all about things at once?

67. The "little nephew" was Peter Augustus Porter Jr. (1853–1925).

What queer letters mine must be as *you* read them: the few sentences you quote from them being so many of them misread. I said "Sassy wood" not "Gassy wood" & all I told you about it was literally true. And Sally, I *dont* love to laugh at you.

I am sorry Mrs Massey is sick. Please tell me how all are when you write.

I "play the fool" by getting into humors of perfect abandon; when too tired perhaps to be witty (even if I could be so ever) & too off my dignity to be reserved I just behave like a drunken man & allow nature to recover from some fit of over exertion by an entire handing myself over to a sort of maudlin appetite for fun. Now must not that be nice for a preacher. But, Sally, I mean to behave better when you're by.

Tell me more about your Grandmother. Who was she? What was her maiden name? Where was she from? And give me more of these still pictures of yours. I dont mean to say anything about you ever that I think will spoil you, but I am quite willing you should devote whole pages of letters to such portraits.

I will *sound* Sam Tyler & see how I can use him. Col. Shriver was here yesterday, but I did not see him.[68] I shall without doubt go to Frederick during the Summer.

You mustn't press the question about the yellow paper. Why I don't write on it is a great secret. I'll tell you why, some day when we are sitting together at Allamby. This, tho' a half ream of it has been lying in my drawer for more than a year I think I have never written to you on before. But Sally, I dont intend to write letters much longer.

My brothers both go into the country with their families—Dick with his wife & two children, Julia and Ned go to Cape May & Spence with his wife (Annie) & little Sam to a place a few miles out.[69] Spence has just bought a country place of a modest sort, but whether he can get released from some boarding that he has engaged he told me last night was doubtful. And now, my darling, I have gone thro' all your letter. A friend yesterday was warning me against my 'over-land' project & advising the cars.[70] I dont want to give up the drive however. I am sure it would do me good.

My children are parts of my establishment that I am so sure you will like that I never give myself a moments uneasiness about them. Maggie is certainly a great beauty & you know that is a bold speech to make for it leads usually to such a certain disappointment. Allie is smart & handsome too. They are well trained at Princeton. But I have one grave objection. I dont think the style of their training promotes their health. I think they are too much with old people there. I think it dries them up & gives them sheepish, nursery ways. Allie looks too much like an old man. And Maggie who has not as good a natural character looks afraid of a *free expression of herself* if you know what that means, & take it all in all I think they are nobly circumstanced, but just with these somewhat grave drawbacks.

68. Edward Shriver (1812–1896) had been a church trustee when Miller was in Frederick.

69. The three children were Julia Miller, Edward (Ned) Rittenhouse Miller, and Samuel Millington Miller (1854–1891).

70. That is, the railroad.

And yet I know so little myself that I may be quite mistaken. These are faults that are soon cured & balanced by over powering excellencies. I have thought however that if God spared their lives & they grew up robust & blooming my children would be singularly beautiful.

My children *are* the finest in the family & my wife will quite distance all comparison. The fact is, the thing of slenderest promise about your future ménage is, I am sorry to say

Yours very truly & affectionately
Jno Miller.

Phil. June 14th 1855

My *dear Sally*,

The other day I passed down by the Office to mail a letter to you & as I recollected seeing in an advertisement that there was a new story by Dickens I bot it & after walking back a step or two it struck me that you & I were very much the same & that you ought to read it too. I therefore went back to the store & told the man to roll me up another copy ready for mailing & I marked it & sent it you. On coming again up the street I called on some ladies one of whom spoke of Sister Rose & expressed her intention to get it, whereupon I left her the copy & on going on home I bought again another copy & to-day & yesterday have been reading it. I am a little startled at my having chanced to send you such a book & that I should thus to you & to the other ladies seem to take it under my special patronage. I like it exceedingly on reading it, but tho' it contains nothing but some harmless & unmeaning coincidences as respects ourselves, I am not sure it is just the book I should have sent you or that I should like to lie under the idea of having known what was in it when I threw it in the mail. Still I am glad I sent it. Isn't it beautiful? Each of the characters is so finely drawn & it is so free from Dickens' tediousness.

Mother & Maggie are in town to-day both on a visit to the Dentist. They are just now at Spencers & return to-night. Maggie is so beautiful! I want very much to hear your estimate of her character as compared with Allie.

Sally, when you said, there was "another reason" against your marrying me which you "could not ever mention" I wonder what you meant. I wonder if I surmised it in a subsequent letter. It struck me the other day that perhaps I didn't. If so I wonder if our intimacy hasn't ripened so that you could entrust it to me even if it embarrasses you a little. I write this with about *half* a feeling of indelicacy in alluding to a thing again which a lady says she can't tell me.

I have no letter to-day, but surely I shall get one to-night. I begin to think this church will never be done. It has never been without its full complement of men for more than two years & yet some of these last columns & capitals seem to me as if they absorbed labour like a sponge. Still, Sally, Wont it be nice, if they dont finish it till November to have the early part of October or the last part of September to be married in. But I dont know how it will be. The builders themselves seem a good deal at sea.

I am so forlorn. I want you so to come & live with me. The hours then which are now most dismal would be then most happy & surely that ought to make a difference in my spirits. I love to *think,* but I hate the hours when I am too tired to think & Oh, in the evening & after dinner & on Sunday afternoon & on long Sundays when some one else is to preach for me & on Mondays & on Saturdays & indeed on most any day & in most any hour of the day what a comfort you would be to me! I wonder if you are really as nice as I think you. I have before me the ideal of a peerless woman. If I am deceived in the painting "my" what a disappointment. Sally, are you *the* Sally I dream of; just tell me that. If you are you are a sort of angel. If you are not you will be jealous of me, for I shall be always shutting my eyes & trying to conjure up the old ideal. "You better take care."

Yours *affectionately*
Jno Miller.

Spence's Office 4 o'clock

Oh, Sally, I do enjoy your scolding so. I can hardly describe the pleasure it gives, to you. It is like the ringing of clear steel lively & exhilarating beyond anything you can conceive. I wish I could get this letter wrong in some way.

And Oh, what a nice letter. My dear Sally, how foolish you are not to write such letters always. With such hot earnest feelings to keep them pent up & suppressed all this long long Winter when the very object of writing letters I always thought was to give the person all the pleasure you conscientiously were able. I'm going to take this letter home & study it as I would a play of Shakespeare & one of the conclusions I have already come to is to be very mad at you for saying that you loved me to call you, My darling Icicle. So it seems you are proud of not loving me. And so must be a much worse person than I, for I'm proud of loving you all I do & find only one difficulty in my letters & that is that from my very meager vocabulary, an embarrassment on my part which I observe you notice. I cant tell you all the love I have.

Dear darling Sally, it is so sweet to know you love me & that you love me warmly & that you do feel more of that passionate desire to see me & to be with me with which I look upon this visit in July.

But, Sally, how shall we behave if we ever do actually meet. I suppose we must go all the way back to our modes of behaviour in Washington. Let me see I think you frowned only every other sentence; was not that the distance our reconciliation had gotten. Our intimacies are so altogether postal that I suppose that tete a tete we are almost as far back as ever. By the way I dont intend to go up the *steep lane* in front of your house.

Yrs *affly*
JM.

Colalto,
June 14. 1855

My *dear John*,

It is nearly a week since your last note of a few lines only was written; is anything the matter? Do your "absent fits" extend to your writing as well as talking? Or are you just very busy?

I wearied thro' a long evening at Col Reid's yesterday, having consented to go to a large party of very young people, in hope of meeting the Sisters of the Col, a pair of old ladies who are now making him a visit.[71] I was disappointed in meeting the younger of the two, and wished myself at home, tho' I found things pleasanter than I could have expected. I met Dr Addison Alexander there, who bore the presence of some 4 or 5 biddies with most heroic resignation. He is not so odd as I expected to find him. And when, to relieve a somewhat awkward silence, I ventured to address him he did not shuffle me off with a surly monosyllable, but answered so promptly & at so much length that I was much surprised, & ventured still further, & met with the most, distinguished success. If I had had the energy & ability to push my advantage I think I might have found him as conversible as most folk. I fancied, from finding his eye frequently wandering to me that he was a little curious about me, and that on *your* account. Do you know that this matter of ours is quite the Talk of my friends & acquaintances? These Sisters of Col Reid's during a recent visit to Harrisonburg heard it from William Henry Ruffner, not as a thing of conjecture with him, but of certainty. He also being in Staunton, a few weeks since, mentioned it there to the McClungs, who are Alexander's also.[72] How he obtained his information I dont know. But you might as well proclaim things thro' a trumpet as confide them to an Alexander. I can't say I care much about it. I am glad to find, that the rumor, makes not the slightest perceptible difference in the manner of my friends to me. The Reids are the only people I feared here, but they seem suddenly warmed to me within a few days. I shall gratify and *overcome* them by divulging the whole thing to them myself, sometime soon.

Friday morning.

I have less than an hour to write on now, so you must be content with what I can give in that time. I intended writing both to your Sister & yourself yesterday, but found Nib so unwell when I went over early in the morning, that I remained with her almost all day. She was better when I left—so much so, that I did not think it worth while to go back again at night, tho' Mr Massie is absent. She is

---

71. The sisters were Magdalena Reid (c. 1795–1867) and Nancy Reid (c. 1798–?).
72. Elizabeth Alexander McClung (1783–1869), widow of Henry McClung (1773–1846), was a sister of Andrew and John Alexander of Rockbridge County, and the Reverend Archibald Alexander of Princeton. Her son, James A. McClung, owned the major hotel, the Virginia House, in Staunton.

by no means alarmingly ill; yet is nervous & anxious about her health, which has not been very good for several months.

It is *you* that are wrong now. I did say Sassy wood, not "Gassy." I had had an acquaintance with "the article" previous to your letter.

It is true that Mr Lacy has dared to do, just what you charge against him. And he did not do it at the "Straits of Gibralter", and did do it much better than a certain person we know of. He did the thing very handsomely indeed; he showed more emotion than I believed he possessed, and managed his appeal very skillfully and eloquently, but unfortunately for him, unsuccessfully. I felt strongly moved myself. This feeling has been growing & strengthening for years, and tho, long ago, suspected by his friends was yet entirely unsuspected by me until within the last 5 or 6 months, when it was too late to remedy the matter. He begs I will always command his friendly aid, and assures me "he will love me 'till I am married; will then love me *differently,* but will love me always." I thought—yes till some other face dethrones mine. With all Lacy's vanity he has some high & striking qualities and I like him very much, and have, of late, thought more respectfully & approvingly of him as a Christian man and Minister. All he needs to sober him is a good, steady, sensible wife, such as one I fear he will not have the judgment to select. Poor fellow! "I shall need", said he "all the power of religion to keep me from envying the man who has obtained all that I wanted. I know *I* am not worthy—I feel it to be presumptuous in me to dream of you, but then I know no man who is not *unworthy* such distinction and such happiness." How do *you* feel about that piece of hyperbole? But isn't this a great rigmarol for me to tell you? If it were not, as you say, that "we are very much the same person", I wouldn't tell you all this stuff. I dont think any lady should causelessly make such revelations.

And so you dont like my buff paper! I shant like it either if you call it "yellow", but I must say your want of liking for it just now, when it has the stamp of fashion upon it, is rather incomprehensible. I have a good deal of it and I mean to bestow it upon you until you will declare it be the most beautiful paper to be found in the U.S.

I can tell you my Grandmother Preston was a very striking woman. She came nearer to my idea of an old Roman Matron than any one I ever saw:—grave & solid & stern in character, of majestic presence and superb manner. Her Father was the Col William Campbell who commanded our troops at King's Mountain, during the Revolution; and her Mother was a Sister of Patrick Henry, and possessed in conversation, the eloquence which he displayed at the Bar & elsewhere.[73] Col. Campbell, afterwards Genl Campbell died a few years after the King's Mountain affair, leaving two children, my Grandmother (who was Sally Campbell) then 5 years of age & a brother, several years younger, heirs to his immense estate. Their Mother, 9 months after his death married another

---

73. William Campbell (1745–1781) married Elizabeth Henry.

Revolutionary Officer—one General Russell, whom the world respected, but the family heartily abhorred. This was pretty bad, in the old Lady, but those were "troublous times", and in a remote corner of South West Va the protection of a husband was very necessary for a young, & rich, & charming woman. Genl Russell made her home insupportable to my Grandmother, by his unkindness to her Mother & brother, and as, in addition to his badness, she had to encounter the violence (whether resulting from motives of affection to her or her wealth I cannot now remember) of her Uncle, Arthur Campbell, who, once stole her from her Mother.[74] She, after the death of her brother, left her Mother & came to Botetourt County, to live with her Uncle-in-law and Guardian, Bishop Madison, the first Bp of Va.[75] Here when scarcely 15 she married my grandfather, who took her back to reside upon her paternal estate—the Salt Works. Her Father's family was a plain one, tho' they number among their kin across the water Campbell the Poet & Robertson the Historian & old Buchanan the Scotch Divine.[76]

My Grandmother, from early difficulties & struggles, acquired the greatest amount of self-dependence & resolution & decision of character. I imagine she inherited too, these qualities from her Father. Her mental endowments were of the same order. She had not the peculiar eloquence of her Mother, but talked in a stately style and with great point & emphasis. To these mental & moral characteristics she united a very imposing physique. She was two inches taller than I am, very large, and the old people say, extremely beautiful. Certainly a miniature of her taken when she went with her husband, then a Member of Congress, to Phil, is very lovely. She was brought up in the formalities of that period, had her manners & motions formed in the days of the Minuet, and thro' life there was the air of a Court ceremonial about her, and a majestic swell in her movements that was quite awful to me. I used to think no parlour was spacious enough for the superb sweep of the old Lady's curtsy. As she advanced in life, the family afflictions she had to endure, together with the influence of religion softened her character and made her much more loveable, than I think she could have been in early & middle life. She possessed the greatest power over her whole family, & has impressed her own strong points of character—truth & honor, and honesty, upon every member of it. She has left no child, of the 10 who were grown & married, in all points equal to her. My Mother excelled her in personal beauty & in all the gentle & attractive qualities of a woman, and perhaps was not

74. William Russell (1735–1793). By his will, which the court upheld, William Campbell had given his brother Arthur (1743–1811) the guardianship of his children (Hartwell L. Quinn, *Arthur Campbell: Pioneer and Patriot of the "Old Southwest"* [Jefferson, N.C., and London: McFarland, 1990], 77–78).

75. Second cousin of the future president, this James Madison (1749–1812) was president of the College of William and Mary and first bishop of the Protestant Episcopal Church in Virginia.

76. "My grandfather" refers to Francis Preston (1765–1835). Thomas Campbell (1777–1844), Scottish poet; William Robertson (1721–1793), Scottish historian; and George Buchanan (1506–1582), Scottish humanist and educator.

inferior to her intellectually. Aunt Eliza, (Mrs. Carrington) was greatly superior to her in mind, but not equal in force of character. As to the others, they all equalled her in moral, but were inferior to her in all other qualities.

Grandmama's Mother, was by far, the most remarkable woman of our family, but we do not consider that the Henry blood she transmitted did anything towards the present repute of her descendants for Oratory. Patrick Henry, & Thomas Jefferson are remarkable for having left to no one, in either of their families the Talent they, themselves possessed. Eloquence, with us is from the Prestons. My Grandfather Preston spoke well; his youngest Brother, (Cousin John's Father) who died very early, was quite gifted in that way. In the generation below him, were his own Son, Uncle William; my Father, the son of one sister, & Uncle Floyd, the son of another: the late Secratery of the Navy, Ballard Preston, & Tom Preston of Ky,—the sons of younger brothers. Then, there are the Breckinridges, & Tom Marshall of Ky. The Browns, one of whom James Brown, the Uncle of Mrs. Charles Ingarsell, resided in your City & others all of the same Preston stock to which we belong.[77] But, I am so tired—ain't you too?

What odd phrases you do use! I am one of the ladies who find you somewhat incomprehensible. What sort of pictures are "still pictures". You tell me "give me more of those still pictures of yours". I dont know what you mean. I never heard of *painted* pictures that were otherwise than still, except those that are in Catholic churches. And *word picturing,* if commended at all, is said to have a sort of *moving* power, but mine, must be "still". What is that, & how is it to be?

Never fear that you are in danger of spoiling me. You compliment me with such conscientious reserve, that I sometimes doubt whether I oughtn't to be mad at it.

I have been so interrupted that I could not finish my letter for the mail. If ever I am so pushed for time as to put off writing till after breakfast, I must give my letter up for that day's mail. When I was in the midst of the other sheets, Mr. Morton called, & I heard the hour for closing the mail rung out, some time before he left.[78]

For the first time I begin vividly to realize that I am to give up my home for yours. Mr. Morton wants my house. He heard, he said in town that I was going to Phila, & he came to see if I would rent out to him for a year! What must I

77. "Cousin John's Father" was Thomas Lewis Preston (1781–1812). McDowell's paternal grandparents were James McDowell II and Sarah Preston (1767–1841), a sister of Francis Preston, her maternal grandfather. John Buchanan Floyd (1806–1863) was the son of John Floyd (1783–1837), an earlier Virginia governor, and Letitia Preston (1779–1852), another of Francis Preston's sisters. William Ballard Preston (1805–1862), Virginia congressman, secretary of the navy under President Zachary Taylor. Thomas Francis Marshall (1801–1864), attorney and former U.S. congressman from Kentucky. James Brown (1776–1835), U.S. senator from Louisiana who later lived in Philadelphia. Mary Wilcocks Ingersoll (1805–1882), the wife of Charles Jared Ingersoll (1782–1862), lawyer, author, and U.S. congressman from Pennsylvania.

78. William Booker Morton (1811–1885), a prosperous farmer and Presbyterian elder in neighboring Botetourt County.

do? Wont you want me to come home next June? And wont you let the children come with me? And in that case I would need all the house myself. And yet for the pleasure of having it three months, would it be well to shut it up for nine? Tell me, what you think I had better do, just as quickly as you can. When it comes to all such arrangements, a sort of dismay creeps over me. I reckon you will have to take me away blindfold. My heart sinks at giving up my old home forever. But I have husbanded, (I am the farthest in the world from attempting a pun—I wouldn't invade your territory,) so much of happiness and hope in you, that when the time comes for the sacrifice, doubtless I shall be ready to make it composedly.

I know exactly what you mean by your expression about Maggie, and I should judge from it that she was sensitive & shrinking, and that living with, "old people", as you say would unavoidably occasion it. Or perhaps, it is only to you, that this constrained look is apparent, and if so, may be naturally explained by the fact of your being so little with her. Is she affectionate? And do you let her be so to you, by being yourself demonstrative to her? I dont know how I shall feel when I see them, but in advance of any personal acquaintance, my anxiety and interest is much deeper and warmer for Maggie than for her brother. I cant tell you, how tenderly I feel for her; I never think of her, but with the impulse to take her in my arms and shelter her with my affection. Your Sister writes me she is delicate & speaks in a tone of regret of their having been so little at school. I dont know what your Northern notions are, but *I* dont think there is anything to be regretted in such a fact in regard to a child of her age. If she hadn't learned to read, much less to write at 8 years of age, I shouldn't have cared, especially where there is any delicacy of constitution. Slip her into your packet and smuggle her up to me, and when I am tired of her I'll send her back under envelope to her Grandmother. In the mean time, however, dont get up the idea of any want of affection on my part for Allie.

Mr Ruffner was here a day or two since. I met him accidentally in town. He looks so very big and awkward, and is rabid about "The Critic". Do you know that Bocock has had a blow up with Robinson because of Uncle Robert's article—"the American Party?" I never thought much good could come of any paper under the control of such firebrands as Robinson, Bocock, Vaughan,[79] Uncle Robert & others. I dont like such violent tempered people. I cannot believe them to be altogether reliable.

What are your Summer plans? How long a holiday have you? When you come here how long will you stay? Suppose you come up to the College Commencement, which is on the 3d of July and stay a few days; then go off to some of the Springs and return again before you go back against to Phil:

Have you told your landlady, of your new domestic arrangements, as you desired to do some months ago? If you have, tell me what she says.

---

79. Probably Clement Read Vaughan (1827–1911), of Lynchburg, Va.

How do you like this paper? Dont you think *it* nice? I fancy it very much, yet it has a troublesome way of getting filled up too quick. After a whole sheet of family history, I think you will never again be so imprudent as to ask a question about any of my kin, whether it be from politeness or curiosity only.

Saturday 8 A.M.

Your letter of the 14th came to me so late last night that it nearly put my eyes out to read it and conveyed to me scarcely anything more than a feeling of satisfaction at having received it. But I read it again this morning, and find the longest sort of apology about "Sister Rose". I dont agree with you about it. I like the Brother very much, yet cannot see anything in the namby-pambyism of Sister Rose to justify his devotion to her. In fact, the Brother in his high discharge of his obligations as *Son* & *Brother*, is the only *real* character in the book. The Land-Steward & his Master may be well drawn, but I am happy to say I have never had the misfortune to number such folk among my acquaintants, & therefore cannot tell whether the sketches are life-like or not.

No, I am sure I am not all you fancy me to be. I am rather sorry to see you making such a beautiful image, & calling it by my name. You will find many defects, when you come to know me, to which you will have to be "a little blind", and will mark the absence of many qualities you now invest me with. But if you will manage well, I think we shall get along very comfortably. It will take me some time to learn that the sovereign power has passed into your hand, & that I am to be *at last* only a subject. This will be a great struggle for a time, but if you will rule a little gently, but at the same time very firmly, at first, I shall soon grow into habits of cheerful submission. And I should never love you if you didn't *make* me feel that it was your *right* to *govern me* along with the rest of the establishment, tho' if you dont exercise your power wisely I shall only submit from principle—not from pleasure.

I impose this additional half sheet upon you just to say—what do you think I meant by that strange sentence you quote from one of my old letters to you? Tell me, and then I shall write back to you whether you have hit upon the right reason or not.

I laugh at your notions about your children & wife. "Mine *are* the finest children in the family & my wife will distance all comparison"! Ask Spence to give his opinion upon the subject; and the Doctor his, & each man will pick out his own wife & his own child as being handsomest and best. Never mind, if your Mother, can be won over to your opinion, we wont care who else may think Dick's wife or Spence's handsomer than yours; will we? Of one thing you may boast—that your Virginia importation is none of the smallest. But I am late.

Affectionately Yours
S.C.P. McDowell

Phil. June 15th 1855.

Dear Sally,

I go to Princeton on Monday & was so foolish as to forget it yesterday when I wrote. I stay till Monday (the 25th) but shall leave too early to get anything from the Office on that day. Write to me there up to next Thursday. That is if you can get a letter in the mail from Lexington of Thursday morning early do so; for letters reach there nearly as soon as they do here & I shall send to the office on Sunday.

I mean now to tell you all I think about the Professorship.

When I had the good fortune to fall in love with you my plan of life was this, to stay as Pastor till I had thoroughly started the new church & well established it (which I supposed would be about next August a year) & then either try extempore preaching for which I have a fondness & which would give me leisure for my studies or resign & go to Princeton, knowing that by that time my investments here & the constant demand upon unsettled ministers for occasional labour (when they are within reach of both cities as I would be at Princeton) would fully support & pay my way as an inmate of my mothers family. Now I hate to repeat even to you the reasons why I would do this & when I came to do it I would not have unfolded them to the world, because I would not go into retirement *with anything expected of me*. There is no *reason* why I should have people smiling at me & saying, "They wonder what John Miller is going to hatch out". I can give some other *real* reason & retain all the luxury of retirement without anything publicly expected from it, of the kind that *I* should expect. For my own real object would be to test the truth of certain ideas in intellectual philosophy which have been forcing themselves upon me for ten years past, & if I found them reliable (as I am sure I shall) to spend some years in establishing them & giving them currency among men. You have no idea tho' how Quixotic this would appear to *all* others than myself & hence how wise it is to take such a step silently, & without holding out any expectations.

There are certain plans too of Biblical exposition that have greatly arrested me.

Now the catastrophe I speak of at Lexington has broken in upon this plan a little & set me at sea a little again. I must keep up an independent home as long as the life time of my mother which I hope may be very long. And, therefore, I *have* no very settled plan. If you wish to know what my *aim* is, as far as I have light it is this:—*After* I have seen this church into a comfortable condition which will be in a year or so I trust, then to attain the point of a private residence in Princeton (or near there) as soon as I *can*, letting that word *can* take in the idea of honor & comfort to you & duty to my children & all other kindred obligations. I have no idea that this plan will ever disappear from me for I have nursed it for years & yet I am more & more impressed with its difficulty in some respects & some times when I think of the good I might do if I could accomplish it & the passion I have to hurry it on I feel amazed at the loyalty with which I cling to my new passion & exult at what it has won for me & at the resignation with which I waive its rival for the present. Yet, Sally, it is only a question of life. If I were sure I would live I would be satisfied. If I were suddenly confronted with my *end* I should feel a remorse that I had not done this work of my history sooner. Now you have it all. Dont laugh at me for what I confess I should consider visionary in others & remember I always warned you of the fact that I had this particular *vision* which I must some day obey.

I always think of you as a wife that I must *make comfortable* & that heightens my difficulty. If I had a wife that had spent her whole life in "tidying up" her father's study, I could take some liberties with her & for the sake of la belle science we could endure hardness together. But you I must continue somewhere within hailing distance of your old Va comforts, & tho' you have property yet there again come in some other hardships & I never could take much satisfaction in that till I had something like a maintenance without it.

Now as to the Professorship it is a distinguished post & in very close propinquity to the Provostship which in fact ought to embrace it & the University is in the City & the Professors' daughters need never see the Campus & the branch is just the one I like & I feel sanguine from something I heard last night that I could get the post, but then one thing destroys it all. I must leave my church just at a time when I cant honorably leave it & moreover I must meet two classes a day & teach three branches & spend an amount of time utterly inconsistent with profounder studies. I can really study more in my present post.

So I see nothing but holding on where I am. I hold metaphysics at bay & dont allow it to attack my sermons; I preach diligently (tho' always with a longing another way wh: is bad) & I havn't heard a breath of my disaffected elder since I wrote you. If there is not the most unbroken harmony in my church no lisp to the contrary has come to me since my miliary fever.

So, Sally, let us do this. Let us manage each our money matters & household plans with a view to a residence in P. if the future opens the way for it. Meanwhile I will work away as plain Parson (*silently* as of course prudence obliges me to do even as to a *wish* of any change) & then if Providence opens my way so that I can retire with honor & proper independance I can yet in spite of all your jealousy bring your rival into her appropriate position.[80] By the way I would not *commit* myself publicly to anything. Even if I went into the country my present *prospectings* in ethics should turn out all illusory (as I know they wont) I could return to the pulpit & that with a fine culture of intermediate investigation. Do you think I talk sanely?

Poor Capt Ingraham, Dicks celebrated friend of the St Louis comes home to a house desolated by entire bankruptcy.[81] I hope you never endorse. He endorsed

---

80. At this point, Miller wrote in the margin, "Tell me what you think of all this."

81. Duncan Nathaniel Ingraham (1802–1891), naval officer, commanded the *St. Louis* in the Mediterranean in 1853 where he secured the release of Martin Koszta, a Hungarian patriot. He became a hero in Europe and America, and Congress voted him a gold medal in 1854. His wife was Harriott Horry Laurens of South Carolina.

for a brother-in-law & his whole property, his own & his wife's chiefly in real estate, is all swept & he perhaps brought in for a permanent indebtedness. And what is worse too his creditor is his own South Carolina, his native state.

Here I have read over my letter & there is one thing I dont like in it & that is that it seems to convey the impression that *you* are an embarrassment to my plans. The fact is, Sally, I never can get thro' a letter without a *dangerous* amount of flattery. But still I must tell you how my heart has leaped lately with the idea that God was going to be better to me than my own poor solitary plans & whereas I had dedicated myself to him in the loneliness of what I thought are important & arduous investigation he meant to send me company & therefore I bow to the *infliction* as from the hand of God. Perhaps he will spare us to grow old together & still further improve my mother's estate & then we shall have time for being Pastor first & then have leisure & means for study afterward.

Yrs affly
JM.

Monday [June] 18th [1855]

Darling Sally,
    You're such a naughty child that I hardly want to speak to you. Here am I after all the disappointment of Saturday 'glowering' over the idea of all I am to have to day & when the postman passes he dont so much as look at me. Oh, you bad, bad girl, & just think that I have to live with you thro' all the years of my terrestrial probation!
    But, dear Sally, I want to tell you of one of the feelings I have about you. I dont think I ever told you before. I feel so <u>thankful</u> about you. The feeling that I have is one of such strong admiration & love that I shudder almost at the profaneness of thinking that you ever can be entirely mine; & when I think of you as going with me thro' all the future changes of my history you can hardly think of the *gratitude* with which I bless God for so kind an allotment.
    But Sally, aint you afraid that you will get very tired of me? You ask me whether I can know as much of you by 55 letters as by 55 visits. I think not. I would hardly grudge *all* my letters for the few hours I have been in your company. Besides Sally, how do you know that *my* letters are not the very best presenting of myself. How do you know that half I say in my letters is sincere? And how do you know it is not all in a style of taste & caution much above what I usually command. Dear Sally, how do you know you'll love me always? And have *you* such an idea as you suggest to me, that you have me entirely as I am in my letters, & that you know me altogether as you know yourself, now that I have written to you so long a period? *I* know *you* because I've seen you, because I've heard of you & admired you long before (with that haggard woe-begone face of yours) I ever dreamed I could love you & because every body speaks well of you & because you are a dear

good sweet, tho' very naughty girl & because its utterly impossible to *conceive* of your not being all you seem to be even in these very letters.

But Sally, it was very foolish about the 23d of May. How people can torment each other & heap on their own shoulders long months of dreariness just out of a sort of R[oman] C[atholic] penance. I wish you had let me carry my point & then you would have been snugly here at my side & then perhaps I would have gone *with* you to Va, tho' that perhaps you wouldn't have liked.

By the way, how long may I stay in Lexington? Suppose I hover about there three or four weeks or to bring it before you in a more actual light suppose I should *stay* there three or four weeks till I became quite a habitue at the old Hotel—till Old McDowell really began to consider me as a sort of son how would you like it?[82] Then, however, you would be bothered with me every day. You might pack me off to the Nat[ural] Bridge or the Rock Alum when you became thoroughly rebellious at the idea of such a trespasser upon your quiet, but like remorseless fate I might be back again till perhaps by the middle of August or the anniversary of the delightful walk we had, you remember, in the Straits you might begin decidedly to "waver" & beg in utter revolting for a sight of those "free papers".

Then too *when* must I get to Lexington. I fear I cant start till the 8th or 17th of July. I will stay some days perhaps a week in Frederick, but when I come to Lexington I want you *all myself*. Dear Sally, wont you promise me? that you'll have no guests, not even an unnecessary dog or cat, that I may have you all undisdracted for *good* long talks & unembarrassed meetings. Think of going to see you & finding your porch & hall filled with visitors! & think of dining at your house with your table all full of company. Oh awful! Sally, I wont come unless you can promise me that your place will be as still as an old garret & that seeing me in the "Straits" will be pleasant if for no other reason than some little relief from absolute loneliness. You & Cantey & Lilly & an occasional visit from Mrs Massey & the Major are surely enough in 1855 for a Lady who in 1854 did hostess duty enough for the whole county. Now write & tell me. And if you are going to invite company or they are going to come without invitation tell me which those weeks are, for, dear Sally, you know you were really mine on the 23d of May & the least you can do for me is to let me have a sense of peace & quietness the few days I can visit you.

How the Major has improved. I thought I would have to take his care into my own hand when I came to L. But as he shows signs of returning sanity I hope his reason will be entirely restored to him. You seem to have treated his case mildly. I told you we would have to resort to the Pacific with him.

I am just on the wing for P[rinceton]. Good-bye. In any second by looking at my watch.

Yrs
Jno Miller.

82. Robert M. McDowell owned the McDowell Hotel in Lexington.

Colalto
Monday, June 18. 1855.

My dear Mr Miller—Don't that look nice and pretty-behaved! I think it looks uncommonly well. I am already enamored of the new and prim style. It seems so Northern & precise that I think it will suit your taste much better than any other. And at any sake it ushers in nicely the new régime to which you say, our July meeting, is to be subject.

Upon second thought, I have determined not to write to you upon the buff paper, but to keep it and give it to you when you come up in July. You will want something, when you go away as a don d'amour, and I think a box of that paper will, of all things, please you best. So I shall put it aside carefully for that purpose.

I am going to write to-day to Susan & Mary telling them of our engagement. I would have them hear it first from me, & if I wait a day longer the news of it will be carried to them by the same old Ladies, I mentioned to you, as having set it afloat here. I suppose every body talks of it here. Yesterday, at Sunday School Mr. Lyle, came sidling up to me with a mysterious air and whispered gravely, "I have heard very bad news". I was thrown off my guard by his manner, & asked earnestly, what is the matter? "I hear you're going to Phila". "Indeed! Who told you that?" "Fishburn told me; Nelson told him, who heard it from Mrs. Estell, the Dr. (her husband) having caught it up some where".[83] "Well, I have been talking of that for a year. But if you want to know anything of my movements, you had better come to head-quarters for information". That was a blunder, for he laughed & said "*That's* exactly what I am doing:—have you made up your mind to go,—tell me". Something stopped us, fortunately, right here. I am surprised to find how little affected I am by the mention of this thing now. What is the reason? I used to shrink away with horror at the bare idea of any one *thinking* I could ever be willing to marry.

One thing I want you to tell me, seriously & soberly: how is it you expect me "to be such a comfort to you?" Sketch me in your next a home picture in which you paint me just what you *expect* me to be—then give me another showing just what you want me to be. To be a very great comfort to you is exactly what I desire to be, but *how* to be that I dont yet know. After I know you & all your idiosyncrasies better, I shall judge for myself, but in advance of that tell me in what way I am most likely to please you. Think of me as a real woman, not an ideal one, and tell me how you will feel when, some day I shall "shake" you out of a reverie and bid you in no very gentle tone to "get up, and go to your work and not sit dreaming in your chair like a lover or a lunatic". Then you'll scold roundly and I—shall retreat very meekly.

83. John Blair Lyle (1807–1858), a Presbyterian elder, owned a bookstore in Lexington. Alexander L. Nelson (c. 1827–1910), professor of mathematics at Washington College. Mary J. Patrick Estill (1812–1882) was the wife of Henry M. Estill (1811–1867), a Lexington physician.

Dr Alexander is here still. He preached yesterday and preaches, probably, tonight, again. Last Summer I was much disappointed in him. Dont you remember hearing him here? I remember very distinctly all about that famous Tuesday evening, when old Dr Junkin escorted you to our pew, & I got into such a spell of laughter that I could hardly behave decently. But not of that, it is of the Dr I was speaking. He pleases me now extremely. His manner is peculiar, and the rising inflection of his voice very singular to my ear which is, unfortunately sensitive, but the sermon itself is a real treat. I think too, I like him better since I have found out that he is neither a boor or a bear, one or both of which I expected to find him. I was amused at him yesterday. I had scarcely thought of his doing anything more than recollecting me after our single meeting, but there he stood in the door so very ready that he seemed almost *waiting* to shake hands with me as I passed. Cantey & I both laughed at his manner after we got out.

Did I tell you that Uncle William had come on from Carolina & was now at Aunt Eliza's? He has been there 8 or 10 days and says he expects "shortly" to see us here. I hope he wont come until the middle of next month when all the hubbub of Commencement and of harvest is over. And especially I hope you & he wont come together: I cant attend to both at the same time. Oh John, let me tell you one thing, & you mustn't think it very bad, for indeed I couldn't help it. When Uncle comes here, he will have prayers, & he will read the same morning & evening prayer out of the Prayer Book every day—& a little scrap of Scripture out of the Prayer Book too. And he wont wear any Spectacles, and he reads, oh! so very fine & disagreably, but owing to his want of glasses he sometimes has to stop in the midst of the prayer, & stops so long that I think he will never begin again, & then I get nervous and want to say, "Amen", myself. Well, the whole thing was so unpleasant to me last Summer that I would 'most take a fit when the prayer bell was rung; and I think it likely I manoevoured to get out of the way at such times; but no, there was no escape for me, Uncle would wait, wait until I came; as he deemed it disrespectful to proceed in my absence.

I think the *feeling* was wrong, but my *behavior* was quite good, and I never expressed the least worry on the subject to any one, until this Winter I talked it over very feelingly with Mary, & found her *exercises* were much the same as mine had been. Do you think was *powerful bad* in me to feel so? Uncle, before he was anything of a Christian, was sublimely High Church, but of late since he has learned the need of *real religion*, I think he is more disposed to seek it in the gospel & not in the Church, and to like the exhibition of it that he meets among the despised Dissenters. I dont know how my Uncles came to be Episcopalians, unless it was because they thought it *elegant* to be so. Uncle Tom is a very sincere and energetic Christian and would have been so much helped by being a Presbyterian. It is *such* a pity, he is not. Episcopal piety is very good, no doubt, as far as it goes, but unfortunately it dont go very far. It has an air of elegant repose about it, much at variance, with the up-

&-be doing bustle of an earnest Presbyterian. It wears its gloves, nicely fitted, but never sees Itself called upon for such work as will require the use of an ungloved hand, & may too endanger the purity of the white cuff above it. I like to see people at work—and dont think it either becoming or beautiful to be idle.

How long before you'll be up—two weeks? I am growing impatient as the time approaches I want so much to see you. But I think, may be, when you do come I shall feel, at first, as if you were a *stranger* yet. If I should you mustn't be annoyed at it, for it will wear off as I get used to your looks & voice. And whilst this feeling is wearing off with me you will have the same to get rid of yourself, unless indeed the possession of those lovely Daguerre's has made it impossible for you to regard my face as strange. By the way, have those pictures improved in beauty since the famous 30th of April. Tell me, John, what do you say to them, & what does the lady say to you? And how often do you draw them from their hiding-place? Once a week? Every miserable Monday? Or, once a month, when you write me a doleful letter, and tell me you have never been accepted yet, and you're just so worn out by the uncertainty of my doings & feelings, that you cant stand it, & wont stand it any longer. Poor fellow, you do make yourself very wretched then, and I feel like patting you on the head and quieting you, tho' I do think all the time you're behaving very bad. Next time you do so, I shall get mad and not answer, and then you'll be fixed.

When we get settled in the Winter, wont we take the Children home? Or what will you do? What would your Mother like? Wouldn't she think it natural & proper that they should be with you, even tho' it might be painful to her to part with them? I was mistaken in writing to you that your Sister said Maggie's health was delicate. I found on reading her letter again, that it was your Mother of whom she spoke.

Nib is recovering slowly. Mr. Massie means to take her to his Father's in a few days & thence to the Springs—the Alum, I believe. I think they would all be better if they had a house of their own, & Nib was forced to more active occupation. What has become of Mr. Dickson? Do you know I dont like him much. I dont think him honorable in his love-affairs. Where does his *love* come from? I doubted whether he had any more of *heart* than that given to his children; & as to his *head* would it be heterodox and uncharitable to question whether he had—*much* of that. He has been however, extremely attentive to me; quite overpowering me with flowers & fruits & visits, & so I entertain a sort of gratitude to him, on that account, but I dont think him clever, which is no sin in Philadelphia, I hope.

This is to be, my last long letter to you. I find as mine grow longer, yours grow[84] (!) shorter and less frequent. Tomorrow morning I hope to have one from you & then I shall finish my sheet.

84. McDowell interlined the word *become*.

Tuesday 8 A.M.

I have had your letter for an hour. It came opportunely for I was about to send this to Phil. It would be useless for me to say a word about your "Quixotic" plans. I know too little. I must take them all upon trust. One thing however I must say, the whole of that plan has, from the beginning, given me more uneasiness than I have ever heretofore acknowledged. But as you are very sensitive to any thing like want of liking for it, and would give me up in a minute, if I really interfered with it, I shall let it alone.

But indeed, John, I never altogether like to hear you say such things as these— "I always think of you as a Wife that *I must make comfortable*"—and "*You,* I must continue somewhere within hailing distance of your old Va comforts etc". It does seem, as if you rather thought I would add to your cares & exertions, and would be, therefore, something of a burden to you. Now, give up all your exaggerated notions about such things, and just believe that the greatest discomfort in the world to me, would be to find myself giving you any additional labor or anxiety. You let me alone. It is all nonsense about Va women being so inefficient & self-indulgent. I dont believe yr Northern ladies *do* do or *can* do more than we do. And I believe I can do without, what it seems necessary to give up, in the way of personal ease & attention quite as well & cheerfully as anybody. If I dont, you must teach me to do it, & not *spoil me* sure enough, by foolish indulgences.

What will you say to Maggie & Allie for me? Will you have anything to do at Princeton that will prevent your writing every day?

Affectionately Yours
S.C.P. McDowell

Colalto,
Wednesday June 20. 1855

Dear John,

I went over to Nib's this morning to aid in getting her ready for her journey tomorrow, and have just returned. I found her quite cheerful and much better than heretofore. I hope the visit will be of decided benefit, tho' do you know I think the first visit to one's law kin rather too trying to the nerves to be altogether pleasant.

As I have only an hour till night I wont fill it up with a little business. I want to have a little of *your wisdom* in the regulation of my affairs. I enclose you Mr Kennedy's letter about my Washington lot.[85] Tell me what you think of it. I shall give him no instructions until I hear from you, which must be pretty soon, as I dont like to keep him waiting. I incline to keep the lot, & lease it upon the conditions he speaks of, unless I can sell it for 65 A. pr ft and invest advantageously in Pennsyl'a State Stock. Didn't you write to me, that Spence had invested some money of your Mother's in some such stock & that you thought it a good & safe

---

85. This letter has not been located.

investment? Wouldn't it suit me too? However, I think, it perhaps it maybe best not to sell. The rent, Mr K, speaks of will be about $400—; somewhere very near 10 per ct upon the $4.200 the lot actually cost me. Deducting City Taxes and Commission, I could certainly calculate upon $300 a year from it, which is, however, not so good, as 6 percent upon[86] $6.300 in Bank or State Stock wd be. But then, the ground may increase in value; & some how City lots in an improving City seem very well worth keeping. Do you at all understand me?

Until Mr K.'s letter came, I did not know that the Ellicotts were yet unpaid. I left him Chesapeake & Ohio Canal Bonds, with which, at a very reduced price, to pay them, & afterwards sent him $7. or 800: but it seems I am still in their debt $4 or 500.

I am going to have a long talk with you on money matters when you come here. I want you to give up your notions—or rather your way of talking of my property as if it was Julia's or Annie's, to which you had no right or concern, I cant bear you to feel that we are to have separate interests in anything. If you are so very foolish about this thing why not go a little further, & refuse to marry me because I happen to have a few thousand? Would you love me any more if I had nothing? Do you love me any the less because I have some little?

Wednesday night 9 1/2 o'clock

I never like to do any thing after night at this season. We sometimes sit in the porch all the evening. Tonight we found it very delightful—cool & clear. I wished you were with us, more than once. I was really disappointed in this morning's letter to find you delaying your visit until the middle of July. I thought you could have come & *gone* by that time, and I had fixed upon that for the time of Uncle's visit. The Kennedy's are not coming up: Uncle, I suppose will only stay a few days: the Howells will be here, I dont know when, nor indeed do I know certainly that they will stay any time with me; but besides these I know of no one likely to visit me, so that I may safely promise that you will not be greeted either on the porch or in the hall by a fearful array of visitors. My old friend, Miss Moore, I forgot to mention but she will not in the least incommode you, if I can find a book or Newspaper for her.

I dont know whether I shall "love you always", I think tho' it is likely I shall *if* you will always make yourself loveable. I have many misgivings too about your "being sincere in all you say". Indeed, I have known you to say & unsay things very curiously. And I have some very well defined fears of, by & by getting, oh, so very, very "tired of you" & your *philosophy* which, if I was ready for my "free papers" I should say I was a little, wee bit tired of already.

Your Mastodon, Cleghorne is to have his trial tomorrow. Tell me, John, do you like Mr McLain, the Sec'y of the Coln: Socy as a Man?[87] I believe he is a

86. McDowell repeated "upon."

87. William McLain (1806–1873), Presbyterian minister and secretary of the American Colonization Society, lived in Washington, D.C. His wife was Louisa Mosby.

good Officer, but I dont like him at all. I have known him since I was a little girl, He married an Assistant Teacher in the School at which I was, & from that time to this, I have had much of the same opinion of him.

How do you behave when you get deeply into the *blues*? Are you fretful & ill-tempered? I shall find out a good deal about you, I think when you come up. I am a little afraid I have over-rated you and shall be disappointed, but pray *never* let me suspect that you dont love me a very great deal. And if I *never* should love you more than I do at present, you ought to be content with that, but I expect to *improve* even in this particular, which is little more than you promise me.

Thursday

I am hurrying 6 A.M. to see Nib off. When I parted with her she didn't expect to leave so early.

I am affectionately Yours
S.C.P. McDowell

Princeton, June 20th 55.

O my darling Sallie,

How you do torment your poor old husband. Here am I without a scrap of a letter since next Wednesday fortnight & I dont see that I am any more likely to get one tonight than this morning. I wish I was old Cerberus our dog except that he died some two years ago & even that I think is hardly worse than some of the trials you subject me to. Our Parson here, good Dr McDonald saw a Jack in a lantern in the Jug Town swamp last Autumn & if there was not so heavy a rain at the time he would have chased it.[88] I'm glad he didn't; for I know it's very bad for the clergy. In spite of the hard reign which is almost like an old fashioned tyranny, a kind of aristocracy in which a man hasn't command even of his own thoughts & his heart & his life are completely stolen away from him, here have I been chasing this ignis fatuus for near a year & sometimes it doesn't even take the pains to shine. It is the most nonchalant Will o' the Wisp I ever chased & really for whole days expects me to follow on over bog & moor without even taking the pains to dance & glimmer to let me know where it is. or whether I shall ever see it again. And then I'm so helpless. If I were to say I wont stand it any more & were to stop chasing it, then I'd die, & if I go on chasing it then I'll die that way & I think its hard for a Will O' the Wisp to take pleasure in killing a poor preacher.

I rode out this morning on horse back & I mean to ride out again this afternoon & my children, who send their love, are very sweet & my Mother is as good to me as she has always been since I've been born, but what is all this so long as this horrid old Mordecai of disappointment & delay sits at the gate.[89] You ought to have said, March! & then I should have been happy some three months ago. Or

88. James Madison McDonald (1812–1876).
89. In the Hebrew Scriptures, Mordecai is the uncle of Esther.

if you had only said May, when the thing was so neatly reasoned out for you once or twice, or if you would only write to me instead of keeping up this perpetual silence I could get along, but as it is I'm just "going off" as our old Phillis used to say, "like snuff" & you dont pity me a bit.

Now I'm going to run get little Maggie & set her to work to finish this letter. Good-bye. I can show her my writing you know as a sort of copy.

> *Yours very affly*
> *Jno Miller.*

Maggie I find takes more than one sitting for her performances, so good bye, Darling,

> *affectionately*
> *JM.*

Princeton, June 21st [1855]

My *dear Sally,*

I turn right back from the P.O. where I have just mailed the last, to begin another letter. Maggie will have hers ready to enclose by this afternoon's mail. All the comments I have to make upon your modest speeches about the "sketches" you sent me is that you are very naughty for not having made better use of your time for the last dozen years & *published* some similar productions. I want to know now where your own name came from & who the stately gentleman was who looms up before my mind as your paternal grandfather. Tell me tho' one thing, just here. Does my writing so badly annoy you? I can write much better; but not near so easily as when I just race over the paper scratching off the letters carelessly. My hand is a nervous one & when I confine it to smooth penmanship it rebels.

My darling, *I did not know* I was so long without writing. Are you sure I was? The buff paper I dare not trust myself to speak of. Two weeks ago I ordered some more of that sort that I wrote on some months ago (very much like these square sheets of yours) & when I get home I shall have it.

Still pictures, Sally, is just what your word will explain—"word-picturing". I have no say of authority for it, but like many expressions of mine to *you* whom I begin to consider a person who ought to understand me almost without any words at all, I send it on its errand without stopping to ask whether any body ever used it before. "Still life", of course, in the fine arts is altogether a different expression. "Still pictures" meant just as it came rolling & tumbling out of my mind such quiet scenes as you had once or twice put graphically before me, of you & me for example under the frosts of four-score winters sitting quietly by our chimney-fire or your grand old grandmother in her garden walks with the poor humpback & the snuff boxes. Sally, if you dont understand any of my letters lock 'em up & when I go on to be married I'll take you in my arms & we'll get them out from the old lion-head secretary & I'll explain 'em at great length.

In return for all I ask you of your family history I am going to begin before long the book I promised you. It is going to consist of such chapters as these. "John Adams", or "the Maid of the May Flower". "The Divine Doctor & the Doctor the Divine". "Abigail Dickinson or Where all the bad blood came from". "The Wine But or Two Marriages in One". "Beilby Grange or the Serpent in the Garden". "The Sad Millionaire". & "The Spencers or Aunt Biddle & the Duke of Marlborough".

Whenever my letters get stupid as, I am quite sure they would have done long ago were it not for the feeling of warm affection that breathes through the whole of them, just choose any one of these chapters that I have thus, (hastily & out of their true chronological order) jotted down & I will begin at once to put it into my excellent English. You are such a naughty woman however that I have no doubt you'll want to begin at once with "Abigail Dickinson" & remember, *that* I wont do.

The chapters when they are finished will contain a complete resumé of family matters & I will begin them as soon as your complaints that my letters "convey to you scarcely anything" become more outspoken & emphatic.

My darling, what I thought you meant when you said, There was a reason for our not marrying that "you could not even mention" was the effect of such a step upon the standing of your children? Have you any other reason?

As to Lacy, I have not recovered sufficiently from the shock about the comparison you make. So you plainly say that I did not address you handsomely. Did I not "manifest emotion"? Please tell me when you write, how, considering the unevenness of the path I could have done better. I feel a little like Lacy that no body is worthy of you, but also a little like the old lady in the "Pines" who complained to Dr Alexander that she was so wicked. "Yes", said the Dr "I have heard people say, Madam, that you were not what you ought to be". Whereupon she flew into a towering passion & swore soundly that she was as good as he any day & drove him out of the house with a broom-stick. We all like to confess *our own* unworthiness & not to have these disappointed lovers do it for us.

I told my landlady & she will keep me till my marriage. I think I have grown in her eyes & get better tea & larger strawberries ever since I showed her your portrait. It may be fancy.

Tell me more stories about your family.

What I say to you is *true* & you will please hereafter not to question it. You are worth a whole stack of Julias & Annies & as to my children I feel cheapened in even *comparing* them with my nephews & nieces.

Sally, dont I write very trifling letters? But I have no time or spirit to write more learned ones & it is too late for you to laugh at your poor young lover. So you must tell me when you get tired.

Yours very affectionately
JM.

[Enclosure: Margaret Miller to S. C. P. McDowell]

Princeton, June 21, 1855

My Dear Mrs McDowell

Your letter came here on Friday, and perhaps it is too soon for me to write again, but Father is here, and thought that I had better have my letter off before he went.

You told me in your letter that you wanted Allie to send you a name for the little colt that you were keeping for him, and he says he will call it Lilly.

There was a great fire here last night which burnt up the printing office, and the machine factory, and the owners Dwelling House.

I long to see you, and hope Father will take me to see you soon.

Allie and I both send our love to you.

Yours affectionately,
Margaret Miller.

Princeton June 21st [1855]

My dear Sally,

Were I you I would rent my house. Houses are more exposed to injury in all ways—from fire from mould & from thieves when they are uninhabited or occupied only by a house-keeper. I do not *"want you"* to go to Va next Summer for any other reason than there springing up in your mind a strong desire to do so; on the contrary by the time the long confinements of the Winter have passed again there will be seeing to us three or four ways of passing the Summer. There will be Princeton; there will be the Sea-shore where especially in some of the quieter corners of it it would be pleasant sometimes to go; there will be Bethlehem, of which I will tell you & a greater variety of other places. Rent your house without hesitation. If you prefer going to Va we can do without the house; & Maggie however much she would like to go with her mother to her old home will by that time be made very happy by going with you anywhere.

The mauvaise honte[90] of which I speak in Maggie does not arise from any shyness of me. If you saw how Allie & she climb about me & with what perfect ecstasy they run out to the gate when I come & really upset me on the pavement as they did the other day in their eager attempts to kiss me you would not think they were under any special embarrassment in that direction. But, Darling, I am under so much obligation to these ladies here that it violates all my sense even of decency to criticise any part of their management. It is in all solid respects admirable. You will find the children very *good* children. But since you have been mine & my tho'ts have worked for themselves a new channel I give up a sentence that I once wrote to you. I said, "I do not *need* a wife". *I think I do.* Mary says, Margaret is delicate. She was a magnificent child. She is still. But if I might be allowed after expressing *the thorough & chief obligation* I am under to my Mother

90. French, meaning false shame.

& niece & sister in all this passage of my life to make just one criticism would be this, that my children in *the one matter* of *health* have been for the last three or four years too much *undercover* & *under restraint* too much like the sea-kale (is that the way to spell it?) that Father used to whiten under dark boxes in the garden too much *wilted* & checked in their motions by over training. I believe this is all the delicateness of health that Margaret labours under. And Sallie, if I did not love you so much & respect & trust you so entirely I would not say this. I am telling you a thing which I never lisped to any mortal before, & which would violate my taste as a gentleman & my obligation & gratitude as a son & brother did I not feel my dear dear Sally that your mind & heart were just the *higher story* of my own & that you are so warmly & truly near to me that I may pour things into your mind with the same freeness that I may revolve them in my own. I know that you will have sense enough to love mother the more for her over care over my poor little orphans & yet sense enough when they become entirely yours to unwrap some of their swaddling clothes & with the same care over their morals & the same horror of spoiled children & the same foretaste of the disgraces of the future if we let them spoil in our hands still to allow them *more play* for their feelings & more liberty to work out their own particular impulses & character.

God bless you. *Yours affectionately*
JM.

[On a separate sheet] It will be awkward for you to have me very much in Lexington this summer. Will it not? Tell me honestly. You will be too busy to see after me & too embarrassed by so long a series of visits as would result from my coming over from McDowell's every day. And yet, Sally, where ought I go to be but with you when I am not absolutely prevented?

Princeton, June 22d [1855]

O *Sally,*

Where do you think we've been. Old Dr McGill, of blessed memory, has been up the highest tree in Allamby. Allie & I & Maggie carried him out there. He didn't "go off" as much as I would have liked, but still for so heavy a body of divinity became quite exalted as you may judge from the tree. Oh, Allamby is *so* nice!

There, Sally, I told you so. *Your* trouble is hardly disposed of before you come upon mine. I told you *I* had a "Crook in my Lot" more serious in some respects than yours that is that I was sold to a rival who was more lovely & enchanting than any one in the wide creation but herself & that I *was* passionately fond of her & *must* one day find my way to her feet.

You made light of it. And comforted me & said you would never pull her hair or interfere with our amours & yet scarcely are you out of your troubles & your Exodus is almost accomplished before you turn & point to me & say, "As for this

Moses I dont know what's going to become of him". Now "you let me alone". Didn't I tell you that I was an enthusiast on one point? & that having denied myself to it so long I meant one day to make up for all my ancient sacrifices. "You better take care". Think what a soothsayer I am. Havn't I by successful auguries prophesied you in 8 months out of all the hobgoblins of years & after having for my skill as a fortune teller crossed my palm with a gold ring after a world of incredulousness & doubt you are going now to alienate me from my other mistress & question all the auguries of good that I have made from our connection with her.

Dear Sally, I dont wonder that you are a little doubtful. I wouldnt trust my nearest friend to bring anything out of so vague a field as private study in metaphysical philosophy. But cant you love me so hard as to repose upon me in this one matter of trust especially as I told you almost in the first week of our courtship that I had just this one demand to make upon your confidence?

We are all amused with the news of Dr A.[91] By the way, your fame is quite spreading in our family as a letter writer. Your note to Maggie is thought on all sides to be a sort of "chef d'oeuvre" & this to Mary scarcely behind it. Now that you are writing to Mrs Ross & Mrs Carrington I mean to set some other pens in motion & in reply I think you will take the whole citadel with care. I think Mary feels a spite already at any one who could have said you had the slightest imperiousness of temper.

By the way, you ask me "how you are to be a great comfort to me". Now that's a question I dont mean even to try to answer. I dont know how you do it, Sally. But if you'll only sit by me & talk to me quietly as you did that day you had the great yellow sheet in your hand & seemed to be freer than usual from family troubles that's the way you can be a comfort to me. You looked hard at the sewing but you talked so quietly & cosily to me. I cant tell how you manage to be so nice, but, Sally, I guess you cant help it. The *chief* thing I ever want you to do for me you have done already & that is to promise to marry me & being kind to me & letting me sit down by you when you are sewing & lie down on the sofa when you are reading to me on Sunday night & ramble with you over the rocks when we come out to Allamby is my beau ideal of all human comfort.

Now dont break in upon me & say I'm evading the question. "You let me alone". I have answered all you asked with the best light I have on the subject. For everything culinary & disciplinary & fiduciary & necessary in other ways I'll trust you with the utmost confidence.

I cant tell when I'll be up yet. When will Col. Preston go?

Oh, Sally, the children will go home with us almost at once. The children expect it & so does Mother. Mother says she thinks she will go to the *poor-house* & get two more. What do you think of that?

91. Joseph Addison Alexander.

Your dare, not to write any more long letters.

What did Dickson do?

O Sally! & you did really try to stay away from prayers! How will you do if you get thoroughly tired of *me*?

Sally, dont ask so many questions when you write. You dont allow me enough room for original matter. And I know thats a great deprivation to you. I do so wish you were here. Oh how I longed after you this morning as we were chasing thro' the woods. If you hadn't been so—cautious[92] about the 23d of May what a nice time we might have had. Now we cant *see* Allamby in its best dress for a year.

I tell the ladies in the portrait case Oh, the nicest things about you. I put my lips very near to them & whisper to them Oh, the daintiest little notions in their ears. They are the nicest women. One always looks pleased & the other Oh, so solemn & tho' I shut 'em up in the dark together they are people of the evenest temper I know; they always looked pleased. One has just the least bit of a saucy look & the other looks Oh, so stately I'm almost afraid to look at her. They've both promised to have me & I'm so embarrassed to know how I shall get rid of one of them. I have thot of smothering her, but when I've tried it once or twice she doesn't change a feature & the fact is if they weren't such nice people I should think they were not so easily abashed as they might be.

Good bye! This is my last foolish letter. But think! I've been on Rocky Hill all day.

Yours most fondly
Jno Miller.

I send you an old envelope [for] your museum.

Colalto,
Saturday, June 23. 1855

My *dear John,*

I dont know why you don't get my letters. I write often enough to keep you always supplied with *light reading*. Yet I often forget what I write & cannot by your references to my letters either make out which letter you received, or what that particular one you speak of, was about. After they are sent off a glimmering idea of their content only, remains. But, last Monday, a week ago, I sent you a letter enclosing one to Maggie: Then the Friday after, (but it did not go until the next day) I wrote you again, asking a little help in deciding what to do with my house; did you ever get either of those? Then I've written to you twice at Princeton this present week, so if you receive all I write you get plenty of letters, and only amuse yourself, as usual, by fibbing, when you talk of "perpetual silence". By the way, how are you ever to be broken of that bad habit? And punning too? When I find a pun coming my strength fails entirely and a sense of hopeless helplessness

---

92. In lines above Miller scratched out the following: "obst — wick — fool — naught—."

steals over me. But, just this morning a light broke upon me, about that failing of yours, which will, hereafter, reconcile me somewhat to it. I perceive it is a sort of safety-valve for all your impatience, & restlessness and worry & ill-humor, and as it is an innocent thing I can well put up with it, if you does you such service.

I have rarely ever in summer felt a more delightful morning—such a long one as it has even now (6 1/2 A.M.) been to me. The birds were in full chorus at 4 o'clock, and the air almost chilly, but I am tired, and out of spirits, & with a very little encouragement would quarrel with every body.

I have heard nothing yet of Cleghorne, but from the buzzing about before Presbytery met, suppose they changed their mode of proceeding and instead of refusing to ordain him because of this Colonization business, will throw him back upon your Presbytery as unfit by his total want of education for the Ministry. I dont like that way of acting. I dont believe in that sort of *charity* which for the sake of the feelings of an erring man, covers up his offence & sets him loose upon society. If I were C_ I would *demand* a trial upon the original charge. Or if I were a man & one of his people I would insist upon it.

We are ever so quiet, & the weather so warm as to keep off all visitors except a few Students & Cadets who are an annoyance to me. I am glad of it, for I get sometimes so wearied with company that I wish I could live in a Cave, provided I had light & air in it.

As you perceive, I am utterly without ideas to-day. I think I must, pack up & go off to the Springs for a few days, for the reason Victor Hugo assigns for his sail down the Rhine—"renovation of ideas and sensations".

I hope you are back in Phil. I find you are always a little bit dull at Princeton, & never get a letter from you from there that altogether pleases me. Dear John, I'm in a such a forlorn sort of humor. I shall go & hurry breakfast & see what good my French repast of Raspberries & cream will do.

Affectionately
S.C.P. McD.

Phil. June 25th 1855.

My *dearest*,

I love the very table I usually write to you on.

Here I am back in my study & shut up in the heat of the city. The cause of my going to P. was that Dr Janeway proposed to exchange with me.[93] I had a good long pleasant visit to our dear little Maggie & Allie riding & driving & visiting some old friends & then yesterday I managed to supply Dr J's place without preaching myself & as I declined all other preachings I had a good Sundays rest the first for a very long time. (I see by consulting my record the first since last May a year!) Such continued preaching is very foolish & I mean to avoid it hereafter. You cant tell what a strange effect it has upon me to sit in a church as

93. Thomas Leiper Janeway (1805–1895), Presbyterian pastor in Princeton.

I did yesterday three times a day & do nothing. So I mean to manage as much as possible through the Summer.

We went almost every day to Allamby & have become still more enamored of it. We wished you were with us again & again.

Mr K[ennedy]'s letter came on Sat. This is my first chance to answer yours that came with it. You delight me my dear Sally, with your *thorough judgments* in these matters & I really have nothing to suggest so entirely do I agree with you in your reasoning. Instead of thinking it unladylike to be wise in such things (as you have so repeatedly suggested) I consider them my dear Sally as really heightening your beauty & your grace. Indeed I can hardly conceive of the higher attributes of feminine loveliness without connecting them with a fitness to the place they occupy just as I cannot conceive of grace in an arch or column without fitness to the superincumbent building.

It is not the only fresh admiration of you that the letter gave. You have been kind to Mrs K. & very warmly & intelligently kind & attentive & the only tinge of pain your letter gave me, my Darling, was in thinking how doubtful it was whether I was entirely worthy of you.

As to the lot, the renting of it at 75 cts strikes me as the wisest. You gave your lessee it is true a great speculative advantage in enabling him to seize any appreciated value that five years may develope but still in return you draw rent at once & fix a somewhat high price for the final purchase. Still, these suggestions occur to me,

1. I would prefer leasing the lot at 65 or even 60 *without* the right to purchase in the end if such a lease is possible.

2. I would bargain (if possible) should the 75 cts lease be agreed upon that any laying of water pipe or similar *heavy* tax that the city may order thro' the five years may be borne in whole or in part by the lessee in case he finally purchases; otherwise round that triangular lot the laying of pipe may be so heavy a charge as to make your gain little or nothing. If he would let you lay on before the ultimate price the additional heavy expenses that the City might bring you under during the five years you will be safe enough. "Do you understand me?"

3. Dont *sacrifice* any of your property for the lack of any small sum needed for your immediate payments without letting me know; that is, my Darling, if you are willing to show me such a mark of confidence as to let me into your counsels at such a time. I am a great speculator myself, tho' in a very small way. I am just now reflecting over a little miniature purchase in the Toltec Lake Superior Copper Co. But it might very well arise that an investment of mine was very much less promising than one of yours; In which case you might *honor* me so far as to let me sell out one of mine & help you "carry" one of yours where there was a prospect of its rapid appreciation.

I want when I see you to tell you all what I am worth both at present & prospectively. As nearly as I can calculate it will be about $1000 per an. But if certain estates of my mother remain long unsold or divided it will probably be more. But I want to tell you all about it when I can do it at more length than by writing. My mother must be worth very nearly if not quite $100.000 tho' her income is about that which might be derived from half that sum.

The history of her property & indeed of my Father's also, is somewhat romantic. A little farm of 12 acres of which she owns three tenths is right in the heart of West Philadelphia. Her share is already worth $30.000 is *quite* unproductive & is rising with great rapidity. It was taken as a bad debt by her father in 1814 & has not been touched or visited by the majority of the family since. It lies in its old farm state & is in the hands of some sheep grazer who pays the taxes & keeps up the fences.

But dont rest on my judgment in the slightest, Sally, till I am living with you. Your property is so far off that I cant judge of it discreetly & your letter quite convinces me that you & I are both very wise for we quite agree in our modes of judging.

Let me say, however this in our direction is not so very good a time for "reinvesting". Money is very cheap & stocks are quite high. I send you the quotations. The Pa loans that Spence buys are 5ˢ & are not so very eligible at present prices. Money in New York commands only 5 pr ct loaned 'on call'.

I am glad that your sister is better. If you have established my right with her by this time of doing any such thing I would be happy to send the expression of my affectionate sympathy in her sickness & my sincere hope that her journey & visit to her friends may be the means of her recovery.

Tell me as often as you write, of the prospects of the Summer as respects your time for being at leisure & I on my part will tell you when I can set out for Lexington as soon as my holiday is determined.

Why, Sally, as to the "blues" you are actually beginning to ask your questions all over again.

I haven't any "fits" of the blues strictly so called. I am always a little dull in my spirits, but I never have *fits* of melancholy. I never am more depressed at one time than another except thro: sorrow or fatigue or decided ill-health. I dont think I'm cross. I dont think I *could* be cross to some people I know & moreover, Sally, I love you with all my strength & beg that you will pay me back with all the love & all the confidence & all the *valuing pleasure in me* that you can possibly feel.

Yours affly.
JM.

[marginal note] I cant promise to love you any more than I do now for I dont see how its to be done. You needn't return Maggie B's letter.

Monday, June 25. 1855.

My *dear John,*

I demand your congratulations upon my recovered spirits and temper. And yet I was not out of temper, only a little—I don't know what—when I last wrote.

But every body is out of humor sometimes; and no wonder, for as long as we have such wicked hearts, a pestilent miasma will rise from them & show itself in bad Tempers and bad spirits. I am very quick in discovering the freaks of *your* spirits, and can tell generally by the first line of your letter, almost as accurately as if I looked right into your face, whether you are gay or gloomy. This I put down to the power of sympathy,—whose subtle power no man questions, & no man can explain. I am amazed to see its operations in our case. You may not have observed, but I have noticed repeatedly, how often our thoughts are directed at the same time to the very same subject, & that before either could have guided the other by an expression of their own. If I am much anxious upon any of the points involved in our matter, & sit down to write to you about it, *before* my letter can reach you, I receive one from you upon the very thing that troubled me.

No, your writing doesn't annoy me in the least. I would have you write just as you do; and beg you will never be guilty of the bad taste of writing a fine letter to me. I would have you write, just as you would talk to me if I were near you, and I should very soon weary of labored & learned & long discourses: yet not a bit sooner than I wd of long & fine, letters.

Mr. Morton wants my house in September; but I have no idea I can let him have it before the middle of November. I think it wise and proper to rent it. And if it is rented & we cant have it next Summer, I shall not want to come to Va at all. I couldn't bear to be here and not in it, & it is well now to make it impossible to have it. I shall then be ready to go wherever you may think best.

What do you think John, somebody, (I never mean to tell you who, so you need never ask,) came whispering in my ear the other day, just this—"Mr. Miller is reputed to be a gentleman & a scholar &c &c, but he is also very generally regarded as being somewhat *eccentric,* and both *pedantic* & *affected.* If you love him these things are nothing even if true, but if you dont love him *enough* then you ought to know them etc etc". Now what *do* you think of such very grave charges? Come, clear Yourself, or we *may* have some trouble yet. Is it true you're eccentric? What sort of eccentricity is it? That of wearing a green scarf with little palms over it, instead of the clerical black or Presbyterian blue? If that's all, it will soon be remedied: put the scarf away & give it to me, I shall find it very comfortable & becoming some cool evening in the Fall, & then I will give you one in its place that will set all such notions at defiance. And are you pedantic? I hope not. It's in very bad taste. And are you affected? "Honor bright", *are* you affected! If you are, hand over all your affectation to me, as it belongs *naturally* to a woman, and I'll wear it as long as you'll admire it. Genl Waddy Thompson used to say my Father was affected, and it was as great a piece of nonsense as

"That little old busy-body
Our Ex-Minister General Waddy"

was ever guilty of.[94] But you must clear yourself of all these heinous sins, for it may be, I dont "love you enough" to put up with them.

Did I ever find fault with your letters as "conveying scarcely anything". I used to think, to tell the truth & set you an example, as you are somewhat deficient in this great cardinal virtue, that the Princeton letters were always a little mystifying—& sometimes as during the May visit, they *were* rather scant of meaning. Now I'm sure if you were equally frank you would say this of a great many of mine, & I dont think I would feel—only a *little* "bad" about it. But if we never have any more serious thing to quarrel over than this, life will flow along only too smoothly—I shall long for some ripple upon its surface. Deliver me, from that state of being which is of unbroken serenity and unruffled quiet.

"Shining on, shining on by no shadow made tender, 'Till love falls asleep in its sameness of splendour".[95]

"Who was your Grandfather McDowell?" Just the very one, of all my Grandparents whom I loved the most; and yet feared a good deal. I remember him only after he was much broken down in mind and body by paralysis, yet I remember him as being even then of very uncommon personal beauty. He was much in character such a man as Genl Jackson. He had the same inflexible, iron will; the same unbending purpose; the same daring spirit; the same cool & determined courage; the same hot, impetuous, explosive temper. But to these, he united a very high order of talent; very good conversational ability, great generosity, a high sense of honor & justice—and a power of sarcasm, that is enough to taint his whole race for ten generations. (So you had better take care: you don't know how keen my tongue is.) He was an only son, and brought up by his Mother alone, who became a Widow, when he was two years of age. His Father was a gay young man, addicted to all sorts of fooleries and the one vice of gambling.[96] He seemed not to have inherited in the slightest degree the grave character of *his* Father,[97] who shared, as far as a boy of 15 could share, in the struggle, & sorrows of the famous siege of Derry, but dying at 32 bequeathed to his family a considerable property in land, with a number of silver shoe & knee buckles, and the reputation of being, a fop, a gambler and a beauty.[98]

I believe, I once told you the Preston men were all handsome & the women all clever. Beauty runs in the male line, among the McDowell's too. My Grandfather was, exceedingly handsome. He towered up 6 ft 3, as erect as an Indian, with the stately step and martial air of one of Bonaparte's veterans. And when he spoke, his word, not only to his family, but to his neighborhood, was as the decree of Fate. He was without public office, but possessed very great influence in this

94. Gen. Waddy Thompson (1798–1868), a political friend of McDowell's father.

95. From "Lalla Rookh," by Thomas Moore (1779–1852), Irish poet.

96. Elizabeth McClung married James McDowell I (1740–1771).

97. John McDowell (?–1740).

98. Following the Glorious Revolution, the Protestant supporters of William of Orange were besiged in Derry in 1689 by the Catholic forces of James II.

region of country. During the last war, he responded to the call of the Gov, &
went, with his regiment, first to Ellicott's Mills—then to Norfolk: but for some
reason, I dont know what, was never called into active service. When he came of
age, he waived his rights under the old law of primogeniture & divided, tho' not
equally, his property with his two Sisters.[99] One of these Sisters, long, long after
her marriage, tho' in delicate health made the journey from Tennessee where
she lived, to this place to see him. He was when she arrived with his regiment
at Norfolk, but returned unexpectedly two or three days after her Arrival. The
fatigues of the journey & the joyful surprise of his coming were too much for
the feeble lady,—and she died a few hours after seeing him. I think she had
been the favorite Sister of my Grandfather—or perhaps the circumstances of
her death made him cling tenderly to her memory, for he showed to me as a
child special partiality, which, my Grandmother attributed to my likeness to this
Sister. Any how, the stern old man loved me, and he lives in my recollection,
with a pleasant freshness, that none of the other do. I was going to school here
& ambitiously contending with my friend, Julia Ruffner, for the gold medal for
composition, the summer before Grandpapa's death, and when the stroke of
paralysis came & struck him down almost in an instant, there was taken from
his pocket a composition of mine which, I think the very week before he had
been looking into, with, I reckon, a *little satisfaction,* as well as a good deal of
curiosity.[100]

My father was very unlike him. He was possessed of the Preston traits of his
Mother, whilst his Sister, my Aunt Benton, was more than either of the others like
her Father, tho' by no means so much of a despot.[101] In politics my Grandfather
was a Federalist of the bitterest kind; but Grandmama (who was Sarah Preston,
the Sister of my Mother's Father) whose strong mind led her to take the greatest
interest in such things imbibed different opinions and imbued her only son, the
youngest of three children, with her own Republican principles. He did her no
little credit in after life, and from his babyhood *he* was her darling as she was, next
to his wife & children the dearest being on earth to him. When a little fellow,
he was her housekeeper and companion and pet; and as he grew older the pet
became her pride, and by & by all her hopes & pleasures centered in him. She
was very energetic & industrious, and after Father became conspicuous in the
Legislature we used to laugh at her struggles between her work & the Newspapers,
and tell her she was like some other old lady similarly circumstanced who would
say "Wherever you see Jimmy's name stick a pin" that she might find time to
read that much any how. Her familiarity with the English classics was wonderful
to me. I dont think I have ever seen any woman so much at home with our old
Poets as she.

99. Sarah McDowell and Elizabeth McDowell.

100. Julia Elizabeth Stuart Ruffner (1822–1864), sister of William Henry Ruffner.

101. Elizabeth McDowell Benton (1794–1854), wife of Thomas Hart Benton (1782–
1858), U.S. senator from Missouri.

You needn't be shocked by the comparison between yourself & Lacy on certain occasions. You dont suffer in any way I assure you, tho' I do admit he managed the dénouement more handsomely & skillfully than you. But what was the use of his skill if he didn't succeed. I felt sorry enough for him at first; but he has within a few days bestowed upon me a letter, which has not pleased me at all, at all. I think I shall answer it, in the "queenly style" he attributes to me. Oh, John, I wonder if I could have felt the very least particle of love for you when I wrote you that sermon of a letter?

Tuesday 7 A.M.

"Please don't ask so many questions". I wont. I'm mad. I wouldn't ask another— no—not even "how do you do, Sir?" not for any thing in the world. I'm sure you needn't make a fuss about that for you dont trouble yourself much to answer them. I 'spect You are like a Student we had here once at an Examination, who *couldn't* answer any questions put to him. But he had some Spirit, if he had no learning and felt himself insulted to such a degree by this interminable questioning that, at last he rose in his wrath and said sternly to the Questioner, "I think, Sir, for a gentleman, you are entirely too inquisitive".

I wouldn't send you this *long* letter, if I had time to write a short one.

Affectionately Yours
S.C.P. McDowell

Phil. June 26th [1855]

Dear, dear Sally,

I'll behave. Only go back to those good old letters that were so long & loving & I wont laugh at you any more. The fact is I love you so much that I dont even like you to laugh at me. I know you're in fun, but, O Sally, I love you too much to like any parts of your letters that are spent in scolding me or slandering me even in fun. Such a cross little letter as this is you've just written to me. And, Sally, I love you now & then to say just by way of episode, "O John I do love you so much". Come now, as you write these letters for me do make them a little more after my mind. I go back over those you have already written & wherever there is anything like such a sentence I read it over. & over. And Sally, Ill stop punning & I'll stop (I never do fib) being saucy & I'll stop being "dull". *if I can,* tho' that is the hardest of all, if you'll just quit scolding me & be a little more loving than you are.

I saw two little kittens a while ago playing on the floor. I found their heartiest caresses were blows on the head with each other's paws & biting each others ears; & I began to make up my mind that a little mock fighting was the highest development of instinctive affection. But then, I observed, every now & then the kittens got mad at each other. One bit the other too hard or scratched him with her claws. And the dearest little pussy you ever saw, as white as the driven snow & as graceful as a tame gazelle was almost always the offender & nearly broke the heart of the other poor little cat who seemed sometimes in a perfect panic & yet in spite of a very disfigured face & very uneasy ears seemed to find it quite impossible to give up the pleasure even of being quarrelled with.

But, Darling, you were not well the morning you wrote that letter? Why did you get up at 4? & why were you low spirited? & why dont you do as I do? I sleep 8 hours whenever I can & find that not a bit too much to recover my wasted spirits. I sleep always very profoundly. Indeed I never dream unless I have worked too hard or am indisposed. So that, as I am sorry to confess, I am yet to have my very first dream of you. Dont despise me for my want of romance. I suppose, I think so much of you in the day time, that Nature who is jealous of all our pleasures expels you from her domain at night.

Dont go to the Springs in any way that will make me less rich in letters. I am doing now with just as few as I can get along with. Why cant you, when you write shorter ones write every day? I love you more than I can describe. I picture you as I saw you at different times, in the carriage when I was walking with my sister & we met you near the carriage makers—on your porch as I was taking leave of you when my sister was in the carriage—in the door of McDowell's when we were alone for the first time as I walked away with you from your visit to my sister & when you looked at me with such a wild worried look in your anxiety probably lest I should embarrass you by some fresh allusion to my discomfiture in the "Straits" or to the letter with which you disciplined me—then your quiet demure look as you were sewing that big yellow clothes-bag or table cover, I dont know what it was—then your feeling of profound relief when I took myself off that Monday morning when I waited in vain for an interview (by the way, Sally, why wouldn't you see me?) then all our Washington meetings—your anxious & almost tearful distress at the question I was pressing upon you & your sudden resolution in the carriage to give up your visits & have it settled, then instead of settling it your hurling it on quite out of your reach into the future—your looking so handsome at Miss English's your looking so handsome at Mrs L's, your looking *so* handsome the evening we parted & your looking so handsome almost everywhere—then my picturing of how you *will* look when I see you in L. These are my dreams dear Sally & hundreds of times when you have quite forgotten that there is such a person as I in the world I am feasting upon all my memories of you. God bless you, Sally. Tell me always when you will probably be most at leisure.

JM.

I wonder if Mr Turveytop isn't going East this Summer.

Wednesday, June 27. 1855.

My *dear* John,

Do you remember my bringing yourself & your Sister from the parlor to an "upper chamber" to see the Mountain view from its window? Just by that window I sit and write as long as the warm weather lasts. It is always cool and pleasant in the morning, and tho' the Sun shines hotly in it all the afternoon, yet I am so wedded to the spot & have been for years, that I put up with all its inconveniences. My own room is a perfect thoroughfare. Cantey says I am the "trouble depositary" of the family, & my room the gathering-place for all the troubled ones. Even Mr Massie finds his way to it, and only, last night we all sat there for an hour or two after we came home from Church. I sometimes am much cramped by this state of things, but after all it suits very well, as it drives me away from all family concerns & faces to this distant room where I can read or write quietly at least one hour in the day.

You never saw me sew "a great yellow sheet" in your life. I remember how I laughed at my parlor-work when you were here, but it was not a sheet I was so earnest upon. I was very busy then; Tom & Benton had bought a farm & were going to housekeeping & having, in vain, tried to get seamstresses in the Town to make up their *Napary*, I believe the Scotch call it, I came to their relief with my own hands. My own Seamstress was dividing her time, just then, between the laundry & the kitchen, and I was obliged to lend my own fingers to the boys. And often if you had stepped in between 9 & 11 in the morning you would have found Susan and Nannie Carrington and I sitting in the Hall sewing *sheets* & towels etc etc, whilst Uncle sat reading.[102] And I shouldn't have cared very much if you had, in as much as the work was one of necessity. This thing of sewing is a great blessing to us, poor women. It is very consolatory. I know nothing more soothing than *darning*, to excited nerves. My only trouble in regard to it as I was complaining only yesterday, is that I am *too accomplished* in the art. I would be a little vain about it, but that I am like a Chinaman, confined to my patterns always—having no ingenuity whatever, and therefore an Artisan only—not an Artist.

You tell your Sister that I can sew a great deal better than I can write; a fact which will I think make you value me rather more highly too.

And so, after you've *preached* to me, Sunday night I am to *read* to you! I shall read you a lecture with pleasure. It's quite in my line; & I've, no doubt, I shall find frequent occasion for the exercise of my talent. But if you ever want to get any good from being read to I advise you before hand not to employ me, as my reading has the effect of putting, both myself & my auditors to sleep.

Thursday morning.

I am so obliged to you for your two last letters, which came together last night. I had been overcome almost all day with a kind of low spirits that made every thing in the future black enough, and I was glad to have a little comfort from any source. But, John, I don't really scold—and was not really cross, when I wrote you that "little letter", I just felt *so* badly. If I ever am spiteful to you, it will be after the fashion of a lunatic, who always turns first & with all his fury upon

102. McDowell's cousin Ann Lightfoot (Nannie) Carrington (1831–1863). Her father was Edward Codington Carrington.

the very one he loves best. But I shall try and keep down any such proofs of affection; yet if they should come you will know how to account for them. One great value to me in your love is that it gives me a right to pour into your heart all my troubles, and every time I use you in this way I love you the better. This is very selfish isn't it? but I have not the least objection to your doing likewise if it produces the same result.

I'm in a hurry this morning, & will write again this afternoon or tomorrow.

Affectionately Yours,
S.C.P. McDowell

Colalto
June 28. 1855

My *dear* John,

I was so sorry about my letter this morning. It wasn't worth any thing & yet I knew you wd be so disappointed at getting nothing Saturday. But I couldn't help it. Edward was called off from the breakfast table to the harvest field, & I did not like to give it to Jimmy Carrington. But I am writing now (5. P.M.) that I may be sure to get my letter off by putting it in the Office to-night. Now that I think of it in time, tell me, are my letters to you ever underpaid? I had rather be in your debt $1.000 than one letter stamp. At present I dont want to be in your debt for anything but love, and that debt I am daily diminishing until in a little while we will stand quite equal. As it may be, I shall, after we are married, bring you round to the place I now occupy. Will it ever burden you, do you think to discharge such obligations? I find it my greatest pleasure to pay you all I owe of this commodity.

But indeed, John, you are right odd. A week or two ago you wrote to me "O Sally, how I do enjoy your scolding". Today you speak so gravely & say "tho' I know you're in fun yet I dont like you to scold or slander me even in fun", and seem so hurt about it, that I feel sorry too & wish the fun had never done so imprudent & unkind a thing as to "ooze out at the ends of my fingers". Well, I wont worry you anymore, for I do, most seriously think you are very kind and very good, and I love you more than I do any body in the world. & I love you more now than I did a month ago; and have no doubt I will love you more & more the longer & the better I know you. Now, aint you ashamed to make me tell you all this so plainly? I feel that you ought to find it out without words; and yet when I come to judge of you by myself I see that words, if not very necessary, *are* extremely pleasant, and so I come to confession. And as to "*confidence*", my dear John, how *much* would you have me show? Can I show one particle more than I have shown? Haven't I just grown into speaking to you almost as freely as I wd to myself? And dont my mind gather up its thoughts, and my heart its affections & all its emotions that they may be, some day, poured into your ear? And as to anything more, dont I often tell you of my worry & trouble just that I may have the highest enjoyment I now have, of being a little bit petted by you. But, I wont tell you any more. I'm ashamed now that I am so outspoken.

The reason I didn't see you that famous Monday, (that must have been one of the miserable Mondays you talk of) was that *I couldn't*.[103] I was not in when you came, & some one had to take my place in receiving you. When I did come you were, therefore, in a room with two or three people in it, who couldn't be invited out. Feeling for your suspense & anxiety I stepped across the Hall into the Library, thinking I could lure you there without exciting anybody's suspicions. But then, I found Susan lying on the sofa reading, and the door communicating with the dining-room, (which had been hastily fitted up for Uncle's chamber as it was on the first floor), wide open & Uncle sitting very near it. I couldn't ask Susan out of the Library; neither could I shut its door & consign Uncle to imprisonment, and I just had to give up the idea of helping you. I was troubled too, but I tried to get on as smoothly as possible, and no one that I know of suspected we had any secret between us. And now, in return for this, tell me what induced you to choose Sunday night for your purpose? You deserved to fail just for that. And one other thing I was always worried at you for—that you let your Sister stay all day long in that noisy, hot house of McDowell's without letting me know that she was there.[104] It was by the merest accident that, at last, I learned she was in town. O John ask her some day, whether she still thinks it was wise in her to send you off from Nine Pins at the Warm Springs, to "evils that she knew not of" in Lexington? I wonder if she will ever be reconciled thoroughly to all that has happened there since.

I declare I feel right badly that you all should think Sally such a horrid name. Here's Margaret too with her aversion to it, only more emphatically pronounced than yours. I cant change *it*, but I shall have my revenge in changing your opinion of it. And I shall make "little Julia & Ned & little Sam" grow up to believe that "Aunt Sally" is just the very sweetest of all names. But, mean time, if you all dont behave I shall follow your Mother to her room some day, & sit down on a low chair beside her, and tell her how badly I'm treated and beg her to make her children & grandchildren quit talking so, and hurtin' a body's feelings about things that cant be helped.

Poor Margaret! I do feel sorry for her. I dont wonder she feels so desolate and sad. Has she ever spent any time with Sam? I hope if she does visit him, she will find Virginia pleasant & affectionate. I dont know her, but Cousin Frances spoke favorably of her, & I hope for Margaret's sake, she is a fine woman. Her Father, old Mr Castleman, was one of my Father's best friends in Ky.[105] He was in bad health, when I was there three years ago, & cd not come to see me, but I went

103. McDowell recaps here the events that began their courtship.

104. The McDowell hotel in Lexington.

105. Margaret Breckinridge. Her brother was Samuel Miller Breckinridge (1828–1891), an attorney in St. Louis and serving in the Missouri legislature in 1854–1855. He was married to Virginia Harrison Castleman (1827–?). "Cousin Frances" possibly refers to Frances

several times to see him, & was extremely gratified by his manner to me. I liked him the more because I found nothing attractive in any of the family except, I believe in Robert, who was afterwards killed in a railroad Car. He was a very fine young man I have heard.

John's unfortunate duel will be a heavy distress to his family.[106] I have no patience with such things & wish the Law could be enforced in some conspicuous cases, & stop the practice. I feel very much for Cousin Tom's family in this case, especially for his Wife, who will suffer under it greatly. That Breckinridge blood is very inflammable & given to all sorts of fighting: I am called off. I don't know when I can finish. My "call" deprived me of all that was left to me of day light & I am now writing, as fast as I can by lamp light. I stepped to the end of the back porch a moment ago, & found the harvesters waiting for their supper. I inquired as to their progress, & was glad to hear them say "Ourn is the best wheat in the Country". I am pretty sure Negroes are contented when they are so prompt to claim the preference for things that are "Ourn". "How long before you will get thro'?" I asked. "About ten days" John replied, to my sorrow. I am tired of it already. But then if the Wheat alone upon this little place will nett $2.000, that will be nice, wont it?

I am so much obliged to you for *all* you say about my Washington lot. I shall write to Mr. K___ as soon as I can. But oh no, I could never think of your "sacrificing" any piece of property to "carry" on my speculations; and then to have it tied up from you by a settlement! And yet it was so kind of you to propose it!

You must take all Mr. K. says of me with much caution. He uses very strong terms I know when he speaks of me, which convey more than he means. I wish I was only half as good as you think me.

You mustn't let Maggie be urged to write to me too often. She'll get to thinking it a burden and be disgusted with writing and tired of me if you do. I know exactly how much trouble it is to her, & really think it a great triumph of principle in her to have made two efforts already.

I have not written to Mr Lacy. Upon second thoughts I concluded it would be best not. He says he expected to be refused, but did not suppose any body could succeed, & is therefore the more pained to find "his loss is your (or any other body's) gain".

I am hurried half out of my life.

Good bye. "Don't I write you very trifling letters"?

Affec'ly Yours
S.C.P McD.

Prevost Breckinridge (1836–1900). David Castleman (1786–1852), merchant, planter, and Presbyterian church elder, lived at "Castleton" near Lexington, Ky.

106. John Bartlow Breckinridge (1826–?), while a newspaper editor in New Orleans, was wounded in a duel and remained an invalid for the rest of his life.

Thursday (June 29)[107] [1855]

Well? Sally, did you? That's the very thing I want to know. *Did* you love me when you wrote that letter? And when did you *begin* to love me? I want to know all about it.

You're a pretty woman! I shant do any such thing. Give you my scarf! You'll have to bring a whole heap more of charges against me before you into so forlorn a condition as to sacrifice my scarf.

Why, Sally, *I never in my whole life before heard that I was either affected or pedantic*. I think that the strongest *probable* evidence that I could possibly adduce I have been in the midst of the Sergeants whole rafts of whom would have laughed at me if I had those faults & I do assure you on my word as a "gentleman" that I never heard the charge before. I bet anything it was my friend Ruffner, tho' I wont be so uncivil as to ask you. But if it was, just put it into your pipe & smoke it for friend Ruffner is not altogether reliable in this particular case.

But, Sally, I have far worse faults than either of these could possibly be. I am not conscious of being "affected" in either of the senses which your informant imputes to me, but it may be that I am in both. I have a great contempt for either. And yet I have been surprised at my self at the little zeal I manifest to correct your impression. For Sally, I have far worse faults. I have nearly *all* faults. And what is the use of my laying out strength to deny these particular ones when I am really impatient to be married to see how you will get on with some of my failings.

But then, Sally, I think you'll like me, I think you'll *love* me. Instead of being affected Spence tells me I am *slouching* & too outspoken & careless in all my ways. And as I know I shall most artlessly & simply *love you* I think we shall have the nicest time of it. Only I tell you that I believe all men "have a devil" & that I have two or three.

Then as to the other I plead guilty to that. People say to me (sometimes, not often) John, you know you're eccentric. So I'm quite convinced there must be something in this. And yet I strive against it. I greatly despise it. I have the utmost *contempt* for a man who willfully encourages it. And all I have to say is that the circle of those who bring the charge is not large, for that in my public acts I am singularly straight forward & simple. Sally, I guess it's I joke so much. And I joke often with a sad & careworn face & people think I'm in earnest. I dont *act* eccentrically. I wish I could abate the "general impression". Hurry & marry me, dear Sally, & we'll break all these miserable failings.

I'm getting very much as you were. I have a sort of feeling that nothing will estrange you from me. I know its very presumptuous but I have grown almost indifferent to what you hear about me I'm so sure you love me & will marry me.

As to Mr Morton I would most respectfully suggest that its cruel to keep the poor man out of all house & home till November. Suppose you let him have the house just whenever he wants it, & I at "great personal sacrifice" as they say in

107. McDowell added the date, but Thursday was actually June 28, 1855.

politics will take up my cross & come on for you in September. Think how cruel it will be to make him move in November!

That must have been a nice old lady that grandmother of yours. With a few strokes of your pen you quite eclipsed all the other portraits in your picture. Sally, go on & tell me more about—Tell me something about the Henrys. Only tell me now & then how much you love [me]. For if I am like the poor demoniac who had all that great number of badnesses that went by the name of Legion,[108] you *must* love me & there's no help for it.

I send you a missive that has just come in by Blood. It will give you another glimpse of Spence & show you too how miniature-like are my investments.[109]

As to my holiday it is yet undecided. One elder wants it to be five weeks the rest less & one says that if Mr. Miller will stay & preach for them he would be glad to keep the church open thro' the whole Summer for, "the poor have the gospel preached to them".[110] comforting; aint it? I agree with Tallys and "Never do to-day what you can put off till tomorrow". The longer I leave it undetermined the more will they be oppressed with the heat & the longer will they let me be absent. I can go when I please but then till the church is shut I have to see that the pulpit is supplied which is troublesome. Tell me always what your prospects are for being alone. It is most probable now that I may get to you toward the last of July, but I cant tell. Do I incommode you by this uncertainty? Write & tell me also what Mr Morton seems to insist upon.

Yours very affectionately,
Jno Miller.

Friday, June 29. 1855

My dear John,

I am always complaining I have no time to write to any body, Yet some how I manage to find time almost every day to write to you. It comes to me very naturally. It was my practice during the last years of my Father's life to write to him daily when absent from him, unless some one was with me, who could alternate with me. You have no conception of his anxiety about us. It was always great, yet after his health failed it became fearfully excessive. In fact, sometimes it seemed almost like insanity. I have known him, grow uneasy if the girls were later than usual returning from Church Sunday afternoon, when he lived in Washington, & in a few minutes allow himself to be so overcome by his undefined fears, as to get up & go after them, tho' scarcely able to undergo any extra fatigue. Oh, such a time as we had there! Frank was sick for a year, some times so ill that

---

108. Mark 5:1–20; Luke 8:26–39.

109. An enclosed note from his brother Spencer informed Miller that his rental property had paid $25.00. Blood was a local postal service.

110. Luke 7:22.

we would be for weeks apprehensive of immediate death—then she recovered enough to walk several squares—then became worse & died. We sat up night after night for weeks together. At that very time, Father was confined to bed with an attack of Sciatica, and I spent my nights, first with one, then the other, & would rest as I could by lying on the floor with a chair turned down for a pillow. If we had had more time to give to Father I think his life might have been prolonged. The disease, of which he died, must have commenced long before we suspected it. It must have been one night early in March, I stepped into his room as I generally did, the last thing at night, and found him propped up in bed struggling for breath. I was instantly alarmed, but as composedly as possible did what I could & sent for the Doctor, whose immediate attendance probably saved his life. But I think that was the beginning of the end with him. He afterwards went to Phil to speak & took cold; then came to Rich'd where I had gone with Frank & became more unwell, & so with little recovery of strength he lingered until after Frank's burial, & then suddenly gave way. So sad we all were for years. Our house seemed always shrouded in mourning. A perpetual gloom rested upon it. Even the children, Lilly especially were not cheerful like others. I believe I was about the merriest of the concern. Mary is naturally grave; Nib subject to fits of depression; Susan gravely cheerful—never gay; Cantey gay, & Lilly grave & gay by turns. James too, tho' a great talker is not very cheerful, And Tom is very grave. As for me, you know pretty well what *I* am—a little spiteful, a little given to scolding, a little merry very seldom, yet generally calm & cheerful. And now haven't I tired you out?

I had a letter from Uncle William last night, but he says nothing as to the *time* of his promised visit. I cant, at all tell when he'll be here. Do you know Uncle is a good deal of a sentimentalist? He used to say, "he thought it very strange that none of his Sisters had any sentiment". "Uncle mistakes his Sisters", said I to Genl Thompson "about that: They are all women of very high *sentiment,* but without the least *sentimentality*". He agreed. But Uncle's Wives were like himself—they would languish all day over a rose leaf, and go into ecstacies about a dew drop. All of which he thought was so sweet. Tell me John wd you like your wife to be of that stamp? If you would you mustn't marry me. My sentiment is not of that syllabut order, it is rather more practical, & *substantial.* Uncle's style of thought & feeling is to me like the old fashioned love novels—such as the "Children of the Abbey".[111]

I enclose a letter to—Allie! Send it to him if it's fit to go. Now that I have *something* to *lose* as a letter-writer I should be more cautious. "We wished you were with us at Allamby". Who wished it but you? Don't you say "*We*" Ministerially? I should be glad enough to believe the children even so much as thought of

111. William Campbell Preston was married twice. His first wife was Maria Eliza Coalter (?–1829); his second was Louisa Penelope Davis (1807–1853). *The Children of the Abbey: A Tale in Four Volumes* was written by Regina Maria Roche (1764?–1845) and published originally in London toward the end of the eighteenth century.

me. Do they express any curiosity or special interest about me? You see I can't help asking questions. Some day when "I let you sit beside me as I sew" I will allow you the further privilege asking me questions, out of gratitude for all your *forbearance* with mine.

Your number of letters will soon run up to 100. Let the hundredth one be an "extra". I haven't had a real good "extra" since—I wont tell you when, because it isn't as far back as I thought when I began. But good-night. O John when *are* you coming! I want to see you *so* much.

I wrote the above nearly 2 1/2 hours ago and came off not dreaming, of course that I should add another line tonight. I had only 5 hours sleep in the last 24, but hoped for more now. But I can't sleep, & in a fit of desperation I am going to write myself sleepy, if I send you a whole quire of a letter. If I spend 3 hours upon it I will have the birds to cheer its close. Do I seem crazy?

Since I gave up all attempts to woo sleep by gentle means, I opened the Presbyterian that came tonight. What does make Dr Leyburn inflict so much of his trash in shape of letters upon the public. I never do more than glance at his articles, yet even a glance takes in a great deal of the flatest sort of thing. Suppose we offer to write some letters for him. We are in high practice, and I know our letters would effectually rouse up all his readers. No such ever were seen there before. Do you know his brother George?[112] He is just the very best man in the world. But he went out a Missionary to Greece a long time ago, & he said, forgot for a time after his return, the use of his own language. Then when he went away he was cross-eyed, but after he came back he had his eyes straightened & I think the operation did not improve his beauty, whilst it may have diminished his very small amount of brains. But he's very good & I think will go right to Heaven when he dies, where he will increase in intelligence.

I enclose Susan's letter.[113] It is just what I predicted of her. Her older Sisters have always accused me of loving her better than them. It was natural I should, as she has always been the most affectionate & considerate & attached to me. I think you will love her a good deal when you know her. She is less clever than Cantey, but of far higher moral qualities. When my Mother died, Susan & Tom & Lilly seemed to fall entirely to me, whilst Mary had Cantey, and I couldn't desire a stronger return of affection than they make. Lilly is wayward, & just at the very hardest age to manage—neither a child to be completely governed, by another, nor a women to know how to govern herself. She gives me a great deal of trouble with her notions, and fancies but I hope she will grow out of them. She is very devoted to me, and that, of course gives me a good deal of influence & power over her. My great

---

112. George William Leyburn (1809–1875), a former missionary to Greece, was an agent of the Virginia Colonization Society from 1852 to 1855.

113. This letter has not been located.

trouble is to keep her at her books, which she detests as much as old Govn Berkley did.[114]

To tell you the truth, I have some fears about our mixed household. It is a pretty bold undertaking. Ain't you afraid of the trial? I'm afraid your "philosophy" will be greatly exercised. I have heard much of your Mother's management, suppose we ask her to manage us all.

James writes me, if I lease my farm, I must let him come in with his bid. I would like right well for him to have it.

I haven't had any letter from you for two days, & unless by accident the mail is brought over tomorrow night I shall not hear until Monday. I hate these gaps in your letters, tho' I know you write just as often as any reasonable person could wish, & yet I *need* one every day. If our affair had only the ordinary anxieties about it, this would be unreasonable, but when I am burdened by all of my cares and fears, I wonder I am not more depressed often than I am, & do not wonder at all, that I should need a little help from you every day. When is your holiday ever to come. Just tell your people next Sunday, you think it is high time you should be allowed a few weeks to attend to your own private affairs; and if they wont let you off, why just come off & let them get somebody else, and assure them they might ["]go farther & fare worse" if they attempted that. I want very much to talk our whole matter over with you. I wonder if I can do it just as I would like. Do you know I'm a little bit afraid of you. You'll talk to me about it all & save me the pain of making all the points, wont you? O John I hope we are not sinfully bent on this thing. Sometimes I am so fearful. I am wholly engrossed by it, and that isn't right. I am bound by it, oh, so strongly to earth, that I almost feel as if I didn't care for any thing beside; and that is wrong. And I'm so rebellious at the *thought* of a separation—& that's wrong too. How *can* any good ever come out of all these wrong things?

All nature is asleep—in such profound slumber that not even the rustle of a leaf is to be heard, yet my eyes are as wide awake as ever. My watch ticks away with a sorry effort at companionship, & occasionally a dog barks to remind me of other existences than you & I—and a cow-bell heard in the distance is a pleasant disturbance of the deep quiet I am in. I welcome the faint breeze that has just sprung up with a forlorn hope of its fanning me to sleep.

Saturday morning.

The clock struck 2 just as I finished. Of course, I am not so well this morning, yet 3 hours of absolute unconsciousness has done wonders for me. I am quite bright enough to write you as much more, but have too much consideration to think of such a thing.

Very affectionately,
S.C.P. McDowell

114. Sir William Berkeley (1605–1677).

Phil. Sat. June 30.'55[115]

My *dear* Wife,

As I am just mailing some letters my fingers clutch the pen & *insist* upon my adding one to you.

I dont know why I do it as I cant *make a practise* of writing every day except under heavy inducements but my fingers clamor to be allowed & why should I forbid them. They are dainty-fellows these little digits of mine & one of them, the smallest I have on either hand, glitters in a fillet of gold, which he takes punctually from a drawer every time I come in from my parish. Poor little fellows! I give them a great deal of work to do, & what do you think they are asking of me? Why that I(!) will hasten the time when they may tangle themselves all up in some fingers that they once saw in a dainty brown glove & which five of them are always bragging that they one day touched & that they mean some day to claim as their own.

So, Sally, I have determined to humour them; so please be ready to give up these pretty white fingers of yours to the little savages who claim them at your hand at the very earliest possible day.

Aint it warm?

I try to comfort myself under my recent misfortune by thinking that if we were married you would be now going to Virginia & yet if you had only allowed I would be going too; for do you know I am glad you are willing to stay next Summer for when we are married I dont want ever to be separated again.

What do you think I did yesterday? Why I drank near a tumbler of port wine. I was so exhausted by heat which has come upon us uncommonly soon that I drank more wine in an afternoon than I think I have drunk in whole years. Dont you think I had better take care?

The first tide of the *rumour* reached me yesterday. Mr Newkirk had heard it somehow at Princeton or in the cars coming away. Addison has written on I fancy or some of the ladies.[116] Who told Ruffner I cant divine. He heard it in Lexington he said.

But, Sally, who cares? Shall I tell every body right & left & make myself as I predict I will be, an object of envy by all our acquaintance.

I believe the oftener I write the less you care for me, that is, for the time. You become tired of me. If I quit writing you love me a great deal better.

Besides my letters dispel every time they come a beau ideal you have been forming of me.

Dear Sally, whenever you love me the least—I mean whenever you love me at all—let me know would you.

Yours tenderly
Jno Miller.

115. McDowell added the date.

116. Matthew Newkirk (1794–1868), Philadelphia businessman and Presbyterian elder. Joseph Addison Alexander.

[marginal notes] Did you steal my gloves in Washington & take the measure of this ring of mine? 'Honor bright!'

Don't be afraid of the buff paper. Write on that every other day.

July 2, 1855

My *dear John,*

And so you think it would be a "sacrifice" to give me your scarf! That's very civil. But pray do not be alarmed, perhaps I *wouldn't* have it. (I dont know though; If you don't want me to have it, you had better not make me the offer of it.) I'm disappointed however, I thought you were going to be so highly delighted that I would *condescend* so much as even to think of it.

I am troubled about your coming. I proposed to you to come up to the College Commencement that comes off tomorrow, not that *it* was anything of an inducement, but because the fuss at that time secured to us two quiet, uninterrupted days, which I am now entirely hopeless of obtaining. If you were here now, you could come over tomorrow at 10 and stay until 2 or 3 without finding any body in the house but myself—not even "a dog or cat." Then if you didn't choose to dine with us, after the girls came home, you could go back to McDowell's[117] & return at 6 or 7 & stay until midnight if you fancied.—& so of the day following. But now I am liable to interruptions every day until September. Susan will be here the last of July or the first of August. I shall have to renew my invitation to the Howells about that same time, which it is not unlikely they will accept. Then Uncle may make a descent upon me at any time, and I am always called upon for a certain sort of attention to acquaintances passing thro' our Town. You will just have to take your chance now, & be content with things as you find them, & come just when you get ready. But I want you to appoint your visit as we do our Synods by the moon, for when the moon shines then I can walk with you & get beyond the eye and ear of others.

Have you given up your plan of a "chariot & one"? It would be slow and somewhat annoying to you to travel in that way, but the constant exercise might be so beneficial as to overbalance other inconveniences. I thought when you came if you found me unpleasantly full of company, you could run over to Lynchburg, or across to the Alum for a few days. How would you like that?

You are much mistaken in supposing that I feel "that nothing could ever estrange you from me". I dont feel so certain as all that. I am afraid, when you find me stripped of the many beauties you bedeck me with, you will love me less than you do, and may find the keeping up of your affection rather a thing of principle than of impulse. You'll have to love me with all my faults; and must love me a very, very great deal, not because I deserve it, but because I long for it above everything else. As to my loving you—I don't know when

117. The hotel in Lexington.

it began. Cousin John says "I think, Sally, your feelings were interested from the very first". I didn't know it then. I cant tell you how much I love you. You musn't ask me. I feel that it isn't a thing to be dragged into the day-light, tho' it need not shrink from its glare. You must not *pump* it up from my heart, but just let alone and it will flow out of itself. But I think you must have a poor idea of my taste when you think it possible for me to love such a person as you represent yourself to be. By the way, John, what does Spence mean by saying you are "slouching"? You all use such odd terms. I think you are rather too formal and precise wh I take it is just the opposite of Spence's charge. I am sure Spence is as formal as an old maid, and will, in one half hour, be shocked beyond recovery by my informality & incorrigible insouciance.

I don't know anything about the Henrys that is worth telling. My Grandmother Preston's mother was a woman of very extraordinary talent, but with very great peculiarities.[118] She was raised an Episcopalian, but became a Methodist of the very hottest kind. Her husband, old Genl Russell was also a Methodist, but did nothing to advance his denominational faith in the eyes of his wife's family. She was a good & sincere Christian, but no doubt mixed up much of will-worship, & other absurdities with her piety. But we are in the habit of tracing much of the signal success of her family to the prayers of this good woman on one side, & to the piety of one old John Preston on the other. Somehow I'm not [in] the humor for talking of them tonight. Dont you percieve how poorly I get along? Of Patrick Henry, this old Lady's brother, you know as much as I do. He married unfortunately, into a family tarnished by insanity, and has left no child or grand-child, or great grandchild, that can be pointed out as any thing uncommon. His sons, one or more of whom live yet, are very great fools—& add to their silliness great eccentricity. They are aptly described by a compound word we apply to an odd kinswoman of ours—idle-lunatic. Wm H. Roane, a grandson of Henry's & a Senator from this State was a man of very moderate ability & left no mark any where. Young Aylett, a grandson, now a lawyer in Rich'd is the most promising of the blood that I have ever heard of.[119] I have had some very clever kin and some very stupid, & many of a happy(?) mediocrity, yet they none of them came from the Henrys. I had an old Aunt, who in the olden times was tried for a *witch*—and another, who came to her end rather unfortunately for her reputation in a Still house. My Father's demonstration for temperance however will prove to you that, that blood was exhausted before it came to my turn to have it so you needn't be scared. But—I'm tired, I cant tell you any more now. I am afraid to ask for your chapters on family history lest you should think your letters had become dull. You remember, it was only

---

118. Elizabeth Henry Campbell Russell.
119. William Henry Roane (1787–1845). William Roane Aylett (1833–1900).

when I complained that they were so, that you were to relieve them by the family papers.

If I had some disguise for my letters to you I would write every day. But I dont like the P.M.[120] & every body else who chooses to be present when the mail is fixed up, remarking upon the frequency of my letters to you.

Tuesday morning

My dear John, get out of Phil as quick as ever you can. You are not made of wood or iron, so as to be able to preach, and talk, and visit, and bustle about in this warm weather, without feeling it. Just quit, & come off, & let your elders, who do nothing all the rest of the year, supply your Pulpit and manage things themselves until Sept: Come up here & try the Alum Spring, and if you must do a little preaching do it to me.

And you never found your gloves? That is a pity. I noticed how nice they were, & how much prettier than those that took their place. By the way, dont make a point of wearing a *black* cravat. If you do, I shall feel called upon to supply white ones after you come up. The ring was all guess work. Why not fasten it to your watch chain, if you dont like to wear it. By & by I shall fall upon something that you can use all the time.

Mr Morton does not *insist* upon anything as to the house, but seemed content to wait till the middle of Nov. I cant be married in Sept: it's *too expensive*. So keep quiet about it. I write in such a hurry.

Very affectionately
S.C.P. McDowell

[John Miller to S. C. P. McDowell]
[July 2, 1855]

Good lazy soul that I am, not for any other reason, Oh no, I have taken Spencer's word for word with one only regret that I didnt spend the time of writing mine in writing some letter to you.

I'll return Mrs C's letter in my next.[121] I want to read it again.

[Enclosure: John Miller to E. Spencer Miller]
Project of a letter, intended to be very fine, sent for the purpose of having Spencer Miller spoil it,

by his affectionate Bro:
JM.[122]

120. That is, postmaster.
121. "Mrs. C." refers to Susan McDowell Carrington.
122. Miller wrote this note to his brother at the top of his draft.

Philadelphia
July 1st 1855.

To the Board of Trustees of the
University of Penna.
Gentlemen,

The very unexpected information that my name has been presented to you in connection with the Chair of Moral Philosophy, obliges me to say, that the cares of an important parish, & the peculiar juncture in its history in which I am called to be its Pastor, would forbid me to think of any change in my present relation.

I feel very sensible of the honor, & the more so because I have never thought of it. & have never spoken of the post except in behalf of another gentleman in whose fitness for its duties I have felt an uncommon degree of confidence. But the department is one in which I am so deeply interested, & the Institution one which I have been taught always so greatly to venerate, that I feel peculiarly the kindness that has suggested the nomination & desire to express to the Trustee who may have offered it & to yourselves, the Members of the Board generally, the grateful appreciation with which I am, Gentlemen,

Yours, very sincerely
Jno Miller.

Beat that if you can.

[Enclosure: E. Spencer Miller to John Miller]
Gentlemen:

Will you allow me to take the liberty of asking that my name may be withdrawn from nomination for the chair of Moral Philosophy in the University of Pa.

I feel sincerely the honor that has been done to me, but my duties of another Character are such that I could not with propriety accept the chair if I was elected.

JMiller

Monday (July 3) [1855][123]

Sally, My Darling,

You're such a funny queer girl. "I am so obliged to [you] for your two letters" you say, "I had been overcome with low spirits & was glad to have a *little* comfort from *any* source". So it takes two of my letters to give you even a *little* comfort—& that at a time when you are glad to have a little even from any source. Well, I *am* getting on finely. I suppose when my letters fail to be sufficient, "darning" comes in in the more serious cares.

---

123. McDowell dated this letter, but Monday was July 2, 1855.

(I ought'nt to write this letter. I have been at Presbytery all day & have a speech to-night in Dr Boardman's Church.[124] Still I will scribble on a little for I know how accustomed you are to a Wednesday letter.)

Then, Sally, the "confession" you talk about. Why I never heard of such a thing. Dont engaged people love each other all they can & tell each other all they know & yet you say, "I'm ashamed now that I am so outspoken". And yet if you knew how happy it made me; how I read this letter this morn: how I hurried home from Pres: to read it again. How I shall come to night & read it again and how to-morrow morning I shall get into a nice cosy position in my study—take it out & read it all over again you'd write me such letters every day.

But my! what a homily this is!

But now about the Sunday. Doesn't the Bible say that "If a sheep has fallen into a pit you are to help it out on the Sabbath day?"[125] I really think it was right especially if you had shown the mercy you might have done. I was in great trouble. I did not know when I would see you again as privately even if I waited several days & besides if you knew how much I really loved you you would have graver views of the matter as consistent with the day that you possibly can have.

Now as to Mary. I was not soaring off on any high shadow-[outage] when I failed to write you a note telling you of her being there. On the contrary I proposed that very thing to Mary & she objected. The fact is her conscience was a little troubled at taking a route even one day longer in returning to Maggie B. & as she stated to you she did not feel inclined to see anybody. Still I knew it would look awkwardly not to go near you on my return when I had seen you so often previously & tho' I rather caught at Mary's reason because I tho't you would not like to see *me* again yet I demurred to it greatly on the other account & so *I proposed the walk* & in that direction, hoping that you would be in town in the evening & see us. If you had not I should have over-persuaded Mary, perhaps, and written you the note after all. My *great* motive in hesitating was not wishing to embarrass you after you had so entirely dismissed me. For this I caught at Mary's objection. Still the publicity of *not* seeing you was quite as awkward & I resorted to the walk to get rid [of] the difficulty. Was I right?

Lacy's a "dog in the manger" aint he? Oughtn't he to be glad that somebody can be happy if he isn't.

In haste, yours affectionately
JM.

If I didnt know how uncivil it was I would ask you to send me Lacy's letter. Was he saucy to you? I dont know yet about the holiday. I'll tell you when I do.

124. Henry Augustus Boardman (1808–1880), pastor of Tenth Presbyterian Church, Philadelphia.
125. Matt. 12:11.

Phil. July 3rd, 1855

Now, Darling, I'm going to scold. Get ready! I'll give you just five minutes grace.

You foolish wicked woman: to sit up till 2! When you are in the midst of a most trying summer & have so much tho't & care upon your hands. You're not fit to take care of yourself. The fact is I never felt more disposed to throw up all here for a week & come right on, & send Alfred over for Dr White & go through the ceremony of packing & handing over the keys to Mr Morton & the little word or two of contract with you & Dr White & come right on where I can make you behave yourself. The fact is there are only two things I ever did like & that is sound sense & entire nonsense & this comes so near the category of the last that I wonder that I dont feel for it my usual affection. Now, Sally, just remember that you are to behave yourself hereafter. Go to bed at ten. Begin to undress punctually when the clock growls for that hour, & by the time it strikes be entirely put away, & be paying attention to your first sleep.

The fact is I am not sure *even now* that you'll do it more than a night or two. Poor, Sally! I dont think you're right entirely. If I had been there I would have mildly corked your inkstand, blandly shut up your desk, gently tweaked one of your pretty ears & given you just five minutes to be in bed. And when I came back if you were not I would have fanned you, if you were nervous and restless. I would have sat by your bed & played with your hair, if you were feverish I would have brought your basin & let you get to sleep while I squeezed water on your hand and if you were just wicked I would have pulled the mosquito net over your posts & just left you to Satan & yourself.

I hate sentimentalistic people (except when its funny) & a woman who turns up a chair on the floor in the low heavy currents of the chamber & sacrifices herself in one slightest step in which she can avoid it is worse than one that exhales over rose leaves for this last can be done in the day time with a good healthy appetite & warm clothes on while the lady who sits up to two is like a man that borrowed my watch & then took it to pieces, she's abusing what dont belong to her, for you knew perfectly well while you sat by that window that you were *mine,* & you had no more right to excite yourself & make yourself more wakeful by writing a letter than I would have to preach three times on Sunday after I had plighted myself to you. You're a wicked deceitful disappointing hussy & I've no patience with you. Here endeth the first lesson.

And now while I am about it I may as well say that there are parts of your letters that I dont wish continued: where you say, "And now haven't I tired you out?" or, "aint you tired; I am". or, "aint this egotistic!" & a heap of other matter that I cant remember. Just leave all that out.

And now, my darling, when I whip Ally which I never did in my life that I remember ('cause grandmother does it) I mean to take him in my lap & look kind at him & wipe his cheeks with my handkerchief & talk gravely & mildly to him & I know he'll understand what I have been doing better. So all dissolved in tears as you now are, my sweet erring Sally, I would wipe your swollen imploring eyes & tell you how much I love you & kiss your wet cheeks & tell you how I *know* you can do better & comfort your sobbing & tell you how sorry I am & then turn your weary wicked heart off into some different channel.

There now, dont cry; but never do so again.

11 o clock A.M.

I am so glad you love me. It's a great nicer to love a person you're engaged to, isnt it Sally?

Your sister, Mrs Carrington's, letter is very kind, & I love her very much for it, but then I cant help thinking that she makes entirely too much of the matter. (Of course *I* do) But then I think that *she* will after a little intervening acquaintance with it. The fact is Sally, I hate to flatter. My Mother frowned that all out of me when I was little. And when I go to Princeton now she always takes care to put out every spark of good opinion of myself that Satan or some soft-headed parishioner has given me but I have been *trembling* to tell you for some time past that you are a different being from any of the rest of the family (except it be Lilly; I haven't made her out yet). You have more sense than all of them put together. You ought to have been the man (No, no—no, no, I forgot. There are reasons why this wouldn't have answered. Then what would have become of Allamby with the little arbour & the knitting basket under the hill. No, I was absolutely rubbing out the *light* of my own philosophy. Wouldn't you rather be my wife than a man, Sally?) No, but the man ought to have been like you. (Dont tell James this.) These children have all the notions that *you* gave them. And the same hand that turned them crooked must set them straight again. Now, Sally, dont run wild with this. You have faults enough in all conscience. But if as much were said to *me* Mother would mark off ten of my Princeton visits as necessary to get one humble again.

Tell me, darling Sally, if it wont give you pain, all about your sister Frances. Which was *she* like? Were you near the same age & were you much together? Your Father had the glazed eye of pulmonary disease when he spoke. I *told* a friend who was standing with me near him in the Chinese Museum that it was a shame to exact a speech from one who seemed to me to be really dying.

Only think if from my coldness & uncommunicativeness & real *lack* in the matter of piety, along with all you say of the *engrossment* of your love you should be the *loser* for marrying me. It would have been better then for you if I had never known your father. Pray for me, Sally. That is your only resource. *Do* you pray for me Sally? How often? & when?

Allie, who is a polite youth, will be very grateful for his letter & were he a letter writer would very civilly thank you. His will start this afternoon or in the morning. Poor Leyburn! his letters have a worse fault than flatness. I pity the ladies the wings of whose *taste* have to be so fingered by him. Still, Sally, dont let's slander him for Providence has put L. in a position here where he will do *us* an important service & his mind is *right* on our subject.

Yours affectionately,
Jno Miller.

"A cow bell heard in the distance" has to me the *wildest melody*. If that is sentimentalistic I fear I'm a little so too. I could not think of it for an hour.

Wednesday, July 4, 1855

My Dear John,

I feel entirely out of employment if I dont steal off an hour almost every day to write to you. You make me waste a great deal of time, with these trashy letters, yet if they give you the least pleasure the time *is not* absolutely wasted.

Last evening Mr. Lacy and I sitting quietly in the midst of a crowd talking of you he said, somewhat laughingly to be sure, and in no connection that could make it serious to any body uninterested—"Well, I noticed last Summer, Mr Miller looked delicate"—yet I felt it at the moment & it has recurred to me frequently since with a feeling of uneasiness not before experienced. It may be, your account of the exhaustion you felt under the heat, made it the more impressive to me—or it may have been some premonition. I dont know what it is, but I am anxious about you with a new anxiety. I remember now too you have incidentally said little things, that give reason to my fears. Now John, please come off from Phil and get yourself entirely well and strong in the Mountains. Uncle, I hear, is going to the Springs but did not hear exactly when. I suppose, however, some time this month. Whenever I ascertain the time I will write to you, for as he will probably pay me a visit either going or returning, I should like you to come, just when he does not. When you come I dont want any body in the house, who will be the least restraint to me, or make any demands upon my time. I want to feel entirely free to put on my bonnet & walk with you, without being obliged to return to the minute lest my Guests should find their Tea cold. And I want to ride with you, without feeling myself called upon to offer a seat to any body. And I want to do just as I please & have nobody observe me. And above all, I want you to get rested and well. Dont bring any sermons with you, that you may have an excuse for not preaching, and just make up your mind to do nothing, but talk to me, for the next 6 weeks. You wont find that very hard work for I shall listen very encouragingly all the time.

I heard Cousin John make an admirable offhand address to the Cadet Gradu-ates this morning.[126] He always speaks well, with much animation & enthusiasm. And I never hear a speech that rouses me at all without wishing I was a man and had the right & ability to speak. I think I ought to have been one of the Sons in the family. My brothers dont care for such things & are not easily roused by

---

126. At the Virginia Military Academy.

them, whilst I am always kindling & think I should like to try my power (?) in a stump-speech. Cousin John once very gallantly told me, "the world would have lost a great deal if you had not been a woman", yet I fancy I should have gained something if I had been a man. But I don't know. I might have been only a man mediocre, whilst as I am you say (& I dont thank you for it) that I am a "superior woman". Tell me honestly, Dont you wish I could get rid of such intense egotism?

O' John I wish I could transfer to my paper the lovely Sunset I am enjoying. I wish you could come here and learn all the spots that I am familiar with, and get fully acquainted with all the peculiarities of our bit of Earth & sky & climate so that you could have some sympathy with me hereafter, when I get sad and wearied & dispirited in your City and have a longing, home-sick feeling for all that I love in Virginia. It will take a long time to cover up these old places to me so that they can be thought of without real sorrow. When I go with you, you must be wise enough not to let me come back for a long, long time. You must keep me tied to your side until I shall think it the greatest pain in the world ever to be let loose.

What do you think Lacy says? He says "he is sure *you dont love me as much as he does*, for he loves hopelessly & you never have been subjected to that test". He is an imprudent fellow, isn't he? He behaves very well & I am sure will do a good deal to help us on smoothly, which is more than can be said of many disappointed lovers. He insists that I asked him, what sort of a body you were, last summer; but I tell him I did no such thing. And I know he is mistaken. But I dont care. He knows there is no chance for him, & therefore if he loves me *so mighty much*, he must love you too.

Friday morning

I didn't send my letter yesterday, partly because I couldn't. I felt a good deal too for your disappointment in not getting it tomorrow, but was obliged to let it go. An hour ago, your *three* letters came all together. I wondered I had received none for two or three days, but I now find the fault was in the mail not in you.

I am not so much affected as you would suppose by the scolding. It scarcely seems done in *good earnest*. When you do scold in all solemnity, I shall feel very like Lilly did, when she was a very little thing.—Mother found it necessary to bring her under more decided control than usual, & by stern means, and the punishment was inflicted in one of a suite of rooms at the Gov't House; Lilly was not so hurt as she was astonished at the thing, & spying me at the farthest end of the most remote room from her, she came running to me & jumped in my lap & looked most earnestly in my face—"O Sister, what *is* the matter with my Ma". She evidently thought her deranged. Just so, I shall think of you & your scolding.

What made you take Spence's note? Yours was too long, & rather too full of detail; but his was too short & too general. The fact is, Spence is too outrageously nice. Does he ever let his hair get frizzled in the least. And his office, isn't it all as nicely arranged & as methodically put together as a bit of Mosaic. I expect to find him just one of those people who can use a handkerchief of the finest lawn for a whole week, without in the least rumpling or soiling it. Does he wear spectacles too, John?

The bustle is all over, and our town has subsided into its usual quiet. I am glad of it. I soon weary of the noise & trouble of these "occasions". And you must know *I* am one of the curiosities of this town, and asked for & pointed out to Strangers as such. It used to be excessively painful, but I have become so accustomed to it as not to mind it now. The world is very easily humbuged, & if by accident, you once get up a name for anything special, it just sticks to you without any effort upon your part.

I dont know, that I am any cleverer than my Sisters or brothers, yet is natural enough that you should wish to think me so. Mr Carrington thinks Susan the smartest and handsomest—Mr Massie is sure his wife is the prettiest, tho' he hasn't quite made up his mind that she "has as much genius as her Sister". Mr Ross, I imagine, feels the same, if he feels at all. And you—you are just like the rest. Wait till you get Phil: to decide upon my "gifts & graces", before you pronounce judgment upon so important a subject. And wait till Spence says in the neatest of phrases, "I think John your Wife will do, tho' she is from the backwoods of Virginia.["]

I shall be, I think now entirely quiet & free from company the remainder of this Month. Mr Morton becomes houseless the first of September, but he cant have my house till Nov. Make Spence direct some envelopes & send them to me.

I went to see Mrs Dr James Alexander the other night. She is Cousin, or something of the Reids. I wasn't particularly pleased, but she was anxious about her little boy, who was sick. The grown son looks feeble in health and not strong in mind.[127]

I am hurried to breakfast. I wish you could come in & join us. I'd give you—I don't know what, as Lilly is housekeeper—but I suppose a hot roll & *black tea* by way of compliment to you. Do you like that bill of fare.

> *Affectionately*
> S.C.P. McDowell

Phil July 4th 1855.

My *Darling*,

Do you know you now are almost as cruel with your love as you were before with your coldness? You nearly set me wild with pleasure. Dear, *dear* Sally how lovely

---

127. Elizabeth Clarentine Cabell Alexander (1809–1885). Her husband was James Waddel Alexander (1804–1859), Presbyterian pastor of Fifth Avenue and Nineteenth Street Church, New York. The Reid family in Lexington intermarried with the Cabells of Virginia. James Waddel Alexander Jr. (1839–1915) later wrote *Princeton—Old and New: Recollections of Undergraduate Life* (New York, 1898). His older brother, Henry Carrington Alexander (1835–1894), graduated from Princeton College in 1854 and from Princeton Seminary in 1858. He later became a professor at Union Theological Seminary in Virginia.

you are! Before you seemed to lack a certain womanly softness & tenderness. But now that you have thrown all that away & are my own undisguised & lovely treasure I am almost crazed that I cannot see you & very unhappy that I do not hear from you all the time. My Darling, I have determined to do as you ask about writing. I mean to write, thenceforth, every day. I think you might do the same & I mean to trust to your generosity that you will after receiving this letter. If you have scarce any leisure write *a line* & O Sally, never again be afraid to tell me all you feel. I live upon it. I love you for it so much more, & it does help to keep me from being so entirely miserable.

Your sentences of warm simple affection in which you tell me that our loves are your great bond to earth & that the idea of our union engrosses you more than anything beside sweep over me with a feeling that is almost cruelly wild & are in such strange contrast with my forlorn life & the cold chill atmosphere in which my heart always lies buried that I can hardly endure it.

Dear Sally, how could you be so cold to me so long? Why when I notice your fondnesses & rashly talk a little of your gleams of affection do you grow cold again as you did some weeks ago & begin to scold or talk harshly to me.

You're my great tie to life. You're the greatest prop I have to keep me from being sternly & coldly wretched. And tho' half my heart is frozen with sadness now, it is only because I am too helplessly forlorn to be lifted up even by these almost painful excitements of affection.

Dear Sally! Aint you almost *afraid* to marry me? I'm such a poor suffering old man.

And yet Sally! I laugh now with the wildest derision at the thought of anything else than our marriage. I know you love me. I know you love me wildly. I have no doubt of your fervent & reigning affection. I know you will marry me. I know you would marry me if I could get before you all my most serious defects & blemishes & tho' I tremble sometimes at the idea of the responsibility of your happiness yet even the honesties of doubt seem to have flown entirely away. You seem helplessly mine & our union seems one of those things already existing the opposite of which seems as impossible as the changeableness of God.

Isnt it so, Sally?

Dont you love me wide & independent of my defects? & wouldn't you have me even if you discovered great weaknesses of character?

I have nothing to communicate yet about the church. But tell me when you write when you *think* you will be most alone? Dont be afraid about our matters. We'll talk 'em over like we were old people that had been married forty years. I'll not promise to *start* on all the points of *myself*. I will need prompting a little. I dont know what they all are. It would seem to me like riding backward, for we have talk 'em over so often, it would seem awkward to consider ourselves as starting. But how foolish! Sally, I *will* do all you say. And I will take care in all our interviews that you shall not feel awkward in anything of wh. you may wish to speak.

Your sister, Mrs Carrington, is a dear good woman & whenever the time comes when I am to write to any of your sisters, I will tell her so.

I know very little about practical housekeeping or the management of young people, but I augur much more favorably than you of Lilly & Maggie & our mixed household. By the way the children *did* want you at Allam[by] & *are* very often anxious to have you with them.

Do you mean by Mothers "managing us all" to give up your decided views of living alone? Poor Mother! I wish she were younger & stronger.

You will love her, tho' she is a stern old lady & very strict & serious.

Good-bye, Sally. Giving me very little to feed upon in the way of love dont do me any good. I am one of those poor shivering creatures that require a great deal of affection.

Yrs fondly
JM.

July 5th [1855]

Dear Sally,

Did you get my yesterday's letter. Blood was not running.[128] And so I gave it to a 'bus who if he drank the fee & read the letter would have had no authority to bring him into trouble.

5 1/4 P.M.

So far in the day I have no letter & begin sadly to gather up my energies to bear the pain of not having any. Dear Sally, if you have just to send me Sally McDowell, her X mark do write now every day.

Terrible news this from the Crimea! I cant resist the impulse to clip it out & enclose it to one whose sympathy I long for in all high excitement. Dont laugh at me for you are no where near a telegraph & this may be your first-intelligence. That Pelissier must be a madcap.[129] I mourn over the repulse as if it were a family bereavement. Sally, I aint a bit of a Russian & this loss has made me more of a—Tarter.

I'm afraid you're sick. How could you send off your last letter by telling me you were not & then not write for several days—this when I was just coming to such generous resolutions? The fact is the Sally that I suffer under is almost as bad as the Sally from the Malakoff & will end some day in leaving me dead upon the field.[130]

Dear Sally, I am so dull this afternoon. I am never so unvaryingly capable of writing a letter as some people I know but this afternoon I am really stupid. How

128. Blood operated a postal service in Philadelphia.
129. Aimable-Jean-Jacques Pelissier (1794–1864), French commander in the Crimean War.
130. Malakhov was a Russian fort, besieged by French forces under Pelissier. It eventually fell in Aug. 1855.

would you like to be a man, Sally? & Sally, if you were a man can you think of me as transmogrified into a woman with any such tolerable character as that you would have me for.

Friday, July 6th

Then you shall have no excuses for not doing it, for here, Darling, are the complete disguises. So now I shall have a letter every day!

I can say more now about the visit. We have had no formal meeting yet & I have thought it wise to let the weather get quite unbearable knowing that it would produce a better result. My elders would *give* me anything I asked, but dont you see how much wiser it is to let it be no gift for me but an arrangement for themselves by waiting a little. The plan now seems to be to close the church after the 4th Sunday in July which is the 22nd & *all* of August. The Friday service is already omitted, or made one with that of Wednesday.

I *never* looked into the Almanac before for the changes of the moon. Dont that seem queer for a man of near 50. And tho' I now dont exactly know how to look yet I think there will be full moon some where about that last week of July.

Now Sally my plan would be to *hover about you.* Whenever I saw you getting tired of me I would go: and then when I decently could I would come in on you again from wherever I might be chancing to rusticate. I dont think you can tell me that I shant be in that part of Va in all that month if I please. May not that very week—the last week of July be one of entire freedom to you.

Sally, you're teasing me about the gloves. I dont think now you took them. I should feel so flattered if I thought you had.

"Slouching"!—why Sally McDowell, you're so—(what is that word that Fishburn applied to you?) Dont you know what "slouching" is? Why its the opposite of particular. So if I am your particular friend, Spence slanders me when he says I'm slouching.

The still picture you drew of me of your aunts surprises me for I had not observed any thing of that sort in the family but the trial of one of them as a witch dont surprise me at all. I wish another of the family could be indicted for the same offence.

My sister Sarah (Mrs. Hageman of Princeton) is in such circumstances of health that she has not been able to write to you. Mary alludes to it in a letter this morning. Mother, whose infirmity led me scarcely to expect such a thing writes me that (tho' I never even suggested such a thing to her) she means soon to write you & as I know two things of Mother, first, that she *wouldn't write* unless she could give us something like a cordial blessing &, second, that every word she sends you will be like tried silver the expression of the very *honestest reality of feeling.* I greatly rejoice at it. Please send me her letter when it comes. For I love Mother next best to you. O those moonlight walks you talk of are too nice to think of. I wish you hadn't mention'd em.

Yours affectionately

Jon Miller.

[marginal note] Well really old as I am I never knew that about September. Is it so in Jersey too, do you know? What makes it? Is November reasonable?

Colalto
July 7. 1855

My *dear* John,

Saturday evening is not the best time ever to write, yet I seize the few minutes between sunset and dark to dash off a few lines.

About ten o'clock yesterday morning I was[131] walking on the street, when Lacy reigned in his horse & buggy & asked, "Do you know Mr. Chevalier is at your house?" "Indeed! then pick me up and take me home, if you are not going to Salem". (I had lent my horses to Bent & a favorite young student to go to the Bridge, & it was almost too muddy to walk.)[132] He picked me up in a hurry & I found Mr. C. ready to receive me in the hall. I had not seen him for many months, and as I am very fond of him, we spent a very quiet & pleasant day. Every body thinks him dull & dry but me, and some how I find him sensible and enjoy a visit from him more than from many others who are reputed to be of brighter parts. He was in great concern to hear you had any right to take me away, as he thinks I belong to Virginia, and at last said you must come to a meeting of our Synod here in October & let it decide whether I shall go. He had not heard pleasant things about you, and that really was the reason he was so disquieted. "I am so glad I came over to-day", he said. "I am so much relieved by what I hear you say. My mind was perfectly burdened by the thing before". And so, he went off, better content with the whole affair, & left a very cordial invitation to you to go & see him, when we could go together. I asked him about the difficulty of ecclesiastical censure. He thought there was nothing to be apprehended there. He is very kind & good & has always been singularly attached to me.

I received your letters yesterday morning, and am sorry to say, that I so far profited by them as to sit up till midnight last night. But I do mean to behave better in that respect.

O John tell me how came you ever to think I was "deficient in a certain womanly softness & tenderness?" You dont know how such a sentence as that wounds me. And Lacy too, seeing me, unexpectedly & to him, almost unaccountably agitated & overcome, said "You have always been so self-controlled I did not know till then, that you could be so strongly moved". I don't know how it happens, with this strong power within I *look* so collected & cool. But I

131. McDowell repeated "was."

132. Nicholas Washington Chevalier (1809–1868), Presbyterian pastor in Christiansburg, Va. Natural Bridge, an extraordinary rock formation fifteen miles south of Lexington from which Rockbridge County derived its name.

long ago learned or tried to learn to keep out of view all feeling that I did not wish others to observe & remark upon. But I thought you knew me better. I cant bear to think I should seem to you "deficient" in any thing a woman ought to possess, even down to her numberless weaknesses. Indeed I thought I had made full display of enough of these already. But you will find me out some of these days. If you will only love me as much after the discoveries you will make as you do now, I shall be satisfied.

One thing *always* falls heavily on my heart that is, the feeling you express by such terms as these—"you keep me from being coldly & sternly wretched"—"my heart is half frozen in sadness now & so helplessly forlorn as to be scarce able to endure even the excitement of affection". Now what does all this mean? It always pains me so to hear you talk in this way. I cannot understand how this can be a *habit* of mine—a constitutional peculiarity, that will not be overcome. Can't I melt you in the least? What am I to do for you? You, some how have learned the art of comforting me in my troubles, so that now I feel like going right to you when I get sad and disturbed, and would always do it but for the fear of selfishly thrusting upon you any thing that I can bear myself. And I am so used to standing alone, that it looks almost like affectation to lean upon another. And yet, at this very moment, I wish I could put my head in your lap & take a good, hearty cry. I wouldn't do it for the world, & yet it would be *such* a relief.—I have been depressed all day. Mr Morton has been here again about the house. & Mr Myers wants to *buy*, plantation & all for $18.000. And James wants to rent: so does Morgan; and altogether I have a homeless sort of feeling.[133] And the future is such a risk for me. It is much the same to you too, tho' not quite so bad.

I didn't know I *ever* talked harshly to you. You have misunderstood me. You give me no cause for any such thing, and I love you too much to seek out any cause for myself.

Cantey & Lilly go to Aunt Eliza's Wednesday or Thursday for a week or so, and leave me absolutely alone, unless Bent will stay at night. Nib & Mr Massie will be absent too. Cousin John also, having been called to see his Sister, Mrs Cocke, of Cumberland, who has just lost her husband.[134] So for a fortnight, so far as I can now see, I shall not only be alone, but cut off from visitors. I wish you could be here then.

What do you think? Mr Chevalier urges me to write a biography of my Father! He has been very earnest about it for some time, but I always say to him, & say truly that I have not the ability. But now he is more urgent & insists that such a thing will be well received. "I'll give you" said he, "$1.000 for the Manuscript, & run all the risk myself". What think you? Will you give me a year to make

133. John H. Myers (1806-1869), a Lexington merchant. Henry E. Morgan, McDowell's overseer.

134. Elizabeth Randolph Preston (1808–1889) married William Armistead Cocke (1798–1855). He died July 1, 1855.

the experiment and _____ the thousand dollars? No; I am sure you wouldn't. You would be horrified to see your wife's name in print. But don't be alarmed. I shall never disturb your quiet in that way. Books and book-making belong to your domain, not mine.

Virginia is very squeamish about such things. A Lady seems to become manish to Va eyes, the moment she writes a book—& to receive *pay* for her writings would immediately place her without the pale of decent society! How is it with you? At least, this is what my Uncles would think. They are so transcendental in their views of womanly delicacy, that I fear they are in the danger in which Shakespeare places "vaulting ambition"—Your own memory will furnish the quotation without my writing it.[135]

Monday afternoon.

Whilst in Church yesterday morning I was seized with violent headache which continued all morning & was accompanied with chilliness & impeded circulation which lasting for several hours, induced me to send for my Doctor. He threw himself upon the sofa, discoursed me a long time, left a prescription & expected to see me well this morning. But he was mistaken. My brain felt as sore as possible & my eyes too heavy & painful to keep open. Some how, I had got up a fear of congestion of the brain,—but he had no belief in it at all. He bade me quit thinking & be quiet; neither of which things I have done. But I am better this afternoon, can lie on the Dr's sofa to write to you quite comfortably & hope to write you tomorrow that I am entirely well. A little sickness scares me more than most people, because I am so unused to any *real* illness.

My friends, the Grahams, are in great trouble. One of their sons, for the last week or ten days has been drinking incessantly, and is now, poor fellow, just alive. His Father was sent for at the Alum Spring last night, his brother (also a physician) having given up his case as hopeless. The Dr, however, entertains some slight hope for him, which goes a great way with me, as he is usually the very first to despair of his patients. This one, is the cleverest of all the sons, (& I am drawn to him specially because he is named for my Father) and they have tried hard to educate him, but his propensity for drinking, has thus far been unconquerable.[136] Isn't it dreadful? Poor Mrs Graham suffers beyond all expression. Her boys have well-nigh killed her, many a time before this.

My Father did not die of consumption but of dropsy of the chest.[137] He suffered very intensely, as all persons do from that disease, and died, at last suddenly.

Frank came between Mary & Nib; and in early childhood & youth she & Nib were inseparable. After she was grown however, Mary became her constant

135. *Macbeth* 1.7.27.
136. Dr. Archibald Graham and his wife, Martha (Patsy) Alexander Lyle Graham. Two of their sons became doctors: Edward Lacy Graham (c. 1830–1876) and John Alexander Graham (c. 1833–c. 1895). The one in trouble refers to James McDowell Graham (1835–1861).
137. Dropsy refers to an accumulation of fluids. James McDowell may have died from congestive heart failure.

companion. She was not much like any of us whom you know, but Cantey. Lilly is something like her too, tho' much larger. Frank & Cantey are the smallest & merriest amongst us, tho' Cantey is prettier & sprightier than ever her Sister was. Among the older members of the family, she seemed an odd one, we were all so much graver & steadier, & hence she was the only one of the number who had intimacies out of the house. After Mother's death she seemed to feel very painfully the dissimilarity between herself & Sisters & devoted herself very strongly to my Father. She was extremely fond of company, & like our Aunt Taylor, much dependent upon others for her pleasures.[138] She was pretty & pleasing and kind, much more impulsive & less under the guidance of *reason* than any of us. She was sick a long, long time—18 months I think, during which time she developed traits of character which none of us had dreamed of, and a strength & clearness of mind that surprised us. She passed thro' the most excruciating suffering with great fortitude & met death with perfect calmness & peace—And I had no doubt upon my mind that she had exchanged earth for Heaven.

O John I am so provoked at you! How came you to tell me your Mother was going to write to me? I should have enjoyed the surprise so much. And now I cant be surprised. But I am extremely pleased that she even thinks of it, & hope she will be able to do it. I think it so very kind of her. Are you sure you didn't hint to her what a gratification it would be?

Tuesday 7 1/2 A.M.

If I could get the mist to rise from my mind as it is just now doing from the Mountains I should report myself perfectly well. But I am a little foggy yet.

The letter you gave the *irregular* Carrier has never reached. I suppose he thought the 4th entitled him to the largest liberty & so he read the letter & lost it. Please dont give any more to the " 'bus" men.

I have been worried about an inscription for our Grandfather's monument. Uncle Benton's was so miserably out of taste that we rejected it instantly.[139] James wouldn't do anything & so it fell to me. How do you like the enclosed. Just run your pen thro' the parts you dont like; and as you *have nothing to do*, recast it & compress it into half its present dimensions, & let me have it forthwith.

Affectionately Yours
S.C.P. McDowell

"Do you ever pray for me?" Why not ask, "do you ever pray for yourself? . . .".

Phil. July 7th 55.

Now see, Sally; you do nothing but get me into trouble. Here this silken noose you have got me to put my head in is bringing down my people upon me

138. Aunt Taylor was Susan Preston McDowell Taylor, oldest sister of McDowell's father.
139. Thomas Hart Benton.

& the pleasant days I had when I wore white cravats & had all the good people minding their own business are all at an end.[140]

I must most respectfully beg that without making any difficulty you will send me on my free papers. I can then wear what clothes I please & moreover I hadn't had a day of entire quiet of mind since last August.

The letter I will reply to presently. I will say first that the umbrella is found; second, (I *might* say) that all about the umbrella was a pretext to write the other; thirdly that I usually have no more involved in my cravat then my throat & collar & 4thly that if some of my friends were more sensitive about their own throats than other peoples they might keep them some day out of a tie that they would find much worse than a black cravat.

What sort of an old gentleman would you judge this to be from his hand writing? Can you judge anything by autographs?

I am beginning to think I wont *drive* to L. It would take ten days & ten to return & it would keep me too long from you & drag me away too soon. Dont be afraid, my darling, I wont embarrass you. I will go off some where for days, whenever my visits become awkwardly long.

I am not "made of iron or wood" & I am somewhat thin & worn out & I have one fear about you, Sally, that the excitements of my visit to L. & those long & happy interviews especially if I borrow your fondness for the small hours of the night & the excitements of meeting others are just the worst thing for a poor fellow who goes to rally from that same sort of excitement which he endures all the rest of the year. This was only I thought a long *quiet lonely* drive would be the very thing for me. But, Sally, I cant endure it. I want to see you. Only I want you to begin to take care of me. I want you to keep me in the shade & quiet & not ask me too many questions & let me sit by you while you sew & sit a whole hour without saying a word only looking at you & then send me home by about the time the chickens go to roost & not let any of your friends invite me out anywhere.

Tell 'em I'm modest like Addy Alexander.[141] Tell 'em I'm very much afraid of women especially since one Sunday evening last August. And then between-whiles I'll ride on horseback & drive out from the tavern where I chance to be.

How would it do for us to meet at one of the watering places? Have you even tho't of that? Or even go there together? Or how would it do for me at least to drive you over to the Nat. Bridge & dine there some day? I'm going to make free use of McDowell's horse while I'm there if he has the same, & will hire it.

Oh, wont it be nice to see each other again! I think I'll love you so; I'll have so much clearer *ideality* of my fair correspondent after this next visit.—I forgot

---

140. Miller enclosed a letter he had received from a parishioner, E. S. Field (c. 1818–?).
141. Joseph Addison Alexander.

about the free papers tho'. Please send them right on. I dont get any letter to day but I'll wait.—Perhaps one will come this evening.

6 1/2 P.M.

No letter! Just when I'm acting in the most generous way. She's mean. I never told her so. But she is.

Jno Miller, His + Mark.

[Enclosure: E. S. Field to John Miller] [July 7, 1855]
My *dear* Mr. *Miller*

You told me that if your umbrella *was here* to "drop you a line", but it is not here. I have concluded to do likewise, that you may prosecute your inquiries as to its whereabouts.

I intended last evening, in *defiance* of the laws of etiquette, and of your being my pastor, to have rallied you about that *black* cravat; but the discussion with regard to the umbrella dissipated the thought, for I begin to suspect from the pertinacity with which you cling to it, that more is involved in the wearing of it than I have any idea of. Am I right? With kind regards believe me

Very truly yr friend
E.S. Field.

Phil. July 9th 55.

My *dear Sally,*

No; I like black tea with sugar & no cream, & dry toast. I will have that, Mrs. Miller, if you please, the year round.

I wrote my note to the Trustees so much in detail because I wanted to edge in a word for my friend Connell. I had written him a long letter of commendation & I wished to do more for him & connect it with my own declining. And, moreover, as Father was a Graduate & for a long time the oldest living graduate & had been honored in a good many ways I wanted delicately to say how well I tho't of the University. But as Spencer's note was neater & moreover was obligingly written & offered to me & as I always like to yield to people when I can for the very reason that I so often obstinately (as they think) cant do it, I took Spence's note. I copied it word for word; & now the election has come off & the Provost old Mr. Vethake is returned & has that department.[142]

I cant tell *certainly* yet, but I think I shall be free on Monday the 23d. Shall I go to Frederick first or shall I come right on to you. That would bring me to you on the morning of Wednesday (or if detained here a day Thursday) the 25th.

---

142. John Martin Connell (1819–1855), Presbyterian minister. Henry Vethake (1792–1866), provost of the University of Pennsylvania and former professor of natural philosophy at Princeton and then president of Washington College.

I like your plan for me. Oh, so much. Do Sally clear the way altogether for our having a long & leisurely visitation. Why cant you throw yourself upon an engaged persons rights & have your time at liberty *for the very purpose* of receiving me. And therefore why need you invite the Howells or above all why be attentive to passing visitors. Sally, do you know, that my confidence in you is such that I am sure you can arrange it all & that we shall have the most charmingly quiet time, so that you will get tired of me from the very number & freeness of our interviews.

Spencer's hair by the way *is* frizzled. Tis just that, one general frizzle all over his head. He dresses neatly & keeps his office trim & is I often tell him most obstructingly & awkwardly fastidious. He does *not* wear spectacles & has a hardier look than I have is a handsomer man & is withall a pretty clever fellow. At least for the sake of his wife & child will tolerate him for some time yet. He is 37 years old (you're 34 I think you told me?) & has had for some years part (even before his marriage) one of the large old homes in 4th St. south of Walnut within a door or two of Uncle John's.[143] And there with his apple faced young wife (who is about 23) & his little good natured big-eyed little Sammy he manages to bring life along with some tolerable degree of equanimity. He is off now in the country & Dick goes tomorrow to Cape May. I am so glad I shall have daily letters after this.

Yours affly
Jno Miller

Phil. July 10th 55.

Dear Sally,

Did you ever read the fable of the man & the boy & the donkey? Well, its very evident that I cant please every body. Here is one man that wants me to be a Catholic.[144]

He has done every thing else but go down on his knees to me for the last five years. And I cant tell you the charms he has sent & the little gilded Madonnas & the weighty books & blessed crosses on cards. He has tried faithfully to make me a Christian in his own way & told me confidently I think more than once that he would one day succeed. I take all he sends simply because I once distributed tracts & didnt like it if the Papists wouldn't take them & so out of fair play I feel bound to admit the light as they understand it. But alas! for me I am as great a heretic as ever tho' I see traces of some of the dogmas as for example auricular confession & the worship of angels slowly creeping over me for about a year past.

Then my other friend! Sally, what sort of an old man would you think he was. Tell me when you write. Would you think him a bright old gentleman with silver hair? or would you think him sour & cynical & prone to find fault with his young pastor. Tell me all what you would think.

143. John Sergeant.
144. Miller enclosed a letter from Damon Brown dated July 7, 1855, in which he urged Miller to read some controversial Catholic literature.

I tho't a word in the vestibule the other day in which I told about the umbrella & how the rest of the letter was mysterious & needed explanation would be enough. But it seems it is not. And instead of "straws showing the wind to be blowing from the South["] my good member is possessed with the fear that I doff the white from not magnifying my office. Well, if the *martyrs* are to be clothed in white I think I had better put on mine now.[145]

Then, Sally, you're so mean. I dont love you as much as usual to day. I feel quite injured. Just in the midst of my handsome impulses in response to what you said about "needing" letters, you are disappointing me now almost at every mail. And I really *suffer* from it. I cant tell you how much. The fact is if I had a telegraph I would complain quite bitterly. But as I cant tell over these hundred miles what you are doing & I might be scolding my darling Sally when she was sick or in great trouble or when just after my letter might come one all warm fondness & affection, I cant find it in my heart. See here, Sally. Do you think you treat me right generously. Bishop Potters son is a student at Alexandria & his lady love *writes nearly all the letters* because forsooth he's busy & cant do it.[146] And *I* to whom a pen is a sort of night mare, write such a pile of letters, that you tell me carelessly that there are a hundred, & some days after, that you "really need one every day", & when I in the kindest compliance begin & write daily *you* drop off to one or two a week & those with scarce one good kind word of old fashioned love in all of them. Oh my! Well it'll do no good now for by the time you get this your writing days will be ended pretty much. I suppose when I get to Lexington Edward (or Alfred is it?) will come to the door to say, Please Master, missus is very much engaged, could you call day after to-morrow. Oh Sally, here is all my paper gone & I nothing but this cross letter. Dear, dear Sally. If you'll put these wicked letters by themselves I'll kiss you & make a profound apology for every one of them.

JM.

[marginal note] I use this envelope for one letter. Stamp over Blood's.

Phil July 10th 55
6 1/2 p.m.

My *darling Sally,*

I came home just now with more compunction for my scolding letter & with an intention to write another to make amends. But when I found that even by

---

145. Miller refers to a second letter from E. S. Field that he included. While complimenting his sermon, it complains of the choir's lengthy hymns and the general failure of clergy to value sufficiently their call to the ministry.

146. Henry Codman Potter (1835–1908), son of Bishop Alonzo Potter and his first wife, Sarah Maria Nott, graduated from Alexandria Seminary in Virginia in 1857. He later became the Episcopal Bishop of New York.

the evening's mail there was no letter my heart died within me. No letter till Thursday! Really it dont seem possible to bear.

When you remember that letters from you are almost my only pleasure, & that I read each over & over till the new one comes, really you ought to show me more mercy.

I still hope to leave here next Monday week tho' it aint certain yet. I will tell you as the matter goes on.

Dear Sally, wont it be nice to throw away these quills & ink bottles & substitute a right pleasant face to face talk. I wonder you aint hearty tired of me in this voluminous letter garb. I half suspect you are.

Do Lilly & Cantey know who B. is. If I tho't they did I would send my love.

Yours most affectionaly,
Jno Miller.

Coltalto
Tuesday, July 10. 1855.

Give you your "free-papers"! Oh no; I couldn't do you such disservice as that. You've got too much liberty now; a little more would make you a burden to yourself and a *pest* to society. Indeed, Philadelphia, & that Arch St Church in particular, owes me, at least a note of thanks, for having reduced you to slavery, and kept you in bonds even this long. And give you your free papers now & turn you adrift upon society! Never dream of such a thing; I am too philanthropic ever to be drawn into so hurtful a scheme.

But as, for some reason or other, I dont know what, you are a sort of a favorite with me, I'll treat you as I do other favorite slaves whom I hardly think worthy of their freedom. I'll indulge you in all *reasonable* fancies. And as your desire for freedom seems to turn upon the color of your cravat, I'll grant perfect liberty to wear it white or black as you choose. Or we'll compromise upon gray—as a mixture of white & black, which will suit every body's taste and excite nobody's remark. Will you consent to this? If not, then wear black to the end of the chapter, and tell that lady (something or other "Field"—either a pleasant Matron with half-grown daughters, or an Old Maid arrived at that age when "she accepts resignation instead of hope") that it is neither *your* business nor *hers* that you wear a *black* cravat.

Look here, John, how does it happen you didn't fall in love with some body in Phil, instead of coming way off here to an impregnable (?) fortress in Va? I really do think a Northern woman would suit you better, tho' I know you are wise in going outside of your own Church for one. I am *so* afraid you are extravagantly particular about little things & little notions like—*your Father.* I would be frantic in a week if you worried over all the bits of thread that dropped from my sewing on the carpet, and made a fuss whenever a newspaper was torn up, or not put on the right shelf, & fretted every time a chair was left standing out in the floor, and scolded if your slippers were found in the evening just where they had been left in the morning, and fumed if Allie's hair wasn't always as nice as his Uncle Spence's, and blazed out if Maggie's apron was the least awry,—and towered up into the most terrible wrath at every particle of dust to be detected any where—these things would make *me* crazy in a week. Now tell me honestly are you going to be fussy about such things, for if you are, please send me my free papers without the least delay. I haven't the least intention of risking the little sense I've got. And I want to know I may sit with "Ledgers" & "Pennsylvanians" & "Intelligencers" & "Richmond Enquirers" & "Presbyterians" & "Critics" & "Reviews" of all sorts & sizes & creeds up to my very eyes if I choose and you wont even whimper at it. And as for Allie if he gets his hair all tangled up like a frizzled Chicken (did you ever see one?) why you aint to say a word, for such a "superior woman" as I am holds these mirror like heads for little boys in great abhorrence. I'll promise however, to keep Maggie's aprons in order and make her look very sweet always.

No, I cant go to any of the Springs. I have a great dislike to all watering-places. But I'll manage to secure you a day's journey without much trouble. I dont think I can go to the Bridge with you. It would look so very *juvenile*.

Please dont get any thinner. I once heard of a poor husband who suffered *so* under his wife's sovreignty, that at last he was obliged to put a dime in each pocket to keep from being blown away. Wasn't that bad?

Mrs James Alexander returned my visit yesterday afternoon, & I liked her much better than before. But all the Reids came with her. I like them all very much, but they are great talkers, & all talk to me at once, and my politeness is sadly tortured with the effort to render to each one their one. I look at the oldest, & answer the younger, &, if a 3d one is present, make a graceful gesture there; but these three things, with the mental operations of hearing & replying are too much for my strength. How do you manage in such circumstances?

You never told me whether I guessed right about Spence:—but I know I did.

Poor Jimmy Graham is living still, tho' suffering greatly, and with the very feeblest hope of life. Poor fellow! But boys are a terrible trouble. I wish they were all in Heaven now. If I am not grey long before that, I am sure the first year Allie spends at College will make my head white as snow. Wont I be a pretty old Lady with my white hair & prim cap & gold snuff box? And how stern I'll be by that time. I shall speak as short & hard as Mary Breckinridge.[147]

You see how economical I am with my buff paper.[148] I want you to have a large supply & will not diminish it by taking unnecessarily a single sheet. I wish you would do me the favor to write up this.

I am not the least bit particular about anything, but I have some *notions* that I like not to be intruded upon. One is about my pen. I take care that every guest in my house shall be furnished with pens, ink, tapers etc etc, & make Lilly keep her

---

147. Mary Hopkins Cabell Breckinridge (1769–1858).
148. McDowell cut off half of the double-folded stationary.

own writing table supplied with such things, just that nobody may touch mine. I use the ugliest sort of a pen, but it differs from every other in the house, & I am as much put out if any accident befalls it as if it were always of the utmost importance to me. Several days ago, I laid it carelessly on my Secretary, & it fell behind it. I looked & looked for it, & only this afternoon found it. In my rejoicing I set it to work, & how do you like its performance?

Affectionately Yours
S.C.P. McDowell

Phil. July 11th 1855.

My dear Sally,

I write to announce the birth of your young nephew a son of my sister Sarah, who, as you will see by the accompanying Bulletin is doing well & likely to do honour to his line & kindred.[149] Poor little fellow! he has *all* his path yet to travel. I can find no one how ever many I question who are willing to go back & live over their lives if they must endure the same evils again.

Something has reminded me of what you lately said in regard to your misgivings about our prosperity, because you saw so much sin in your own heart in regard to our love for each other & our whole engagement—that you felt so engrossed in it & indeed so weaned from better things by it. It did not occur to me to say in reply, what I always feel when such things come into my own mind:—What a pity that I cant *bring* God into all my pleasures. It is right & natural that some things should engross us more than others, & that our life should be woven of variant colors of which some must stand out most prominently in different parts of the fabric. What a pity it is that we cant bring God into all our intenser feelings. We dont see him. We dont *know* him except by his works. We cant adore him except by what we see of him in his different Providences. Now as this affection of ours is certainly one of his Providences, why not be able to indulge it to the very extent & save it from estranging us from God by bringing him into it: By thanking him for it & trusting him in it?

Why, Sally, if I love you I ought to be able to love God a great deal more for *God made you.* If I think, you're so unspeakably agreeable to me as I unquestionably do, I ought only to use that for a higher affection of God, for all that is lovely in you He gave you. And I think that you might love me a great deal more than you do & be even more engrossed in our engagement & yet love God only the more on that account, for, Sally, if you & I get to heaven we shall love each other more there & I'm sure it wont prevent our loving our Maker.

I do feel so sad to day about having no letter. *Please* write every day as long as I stay here. I am quite well with the exception of a sort of *scraped* feeling in my

---

149. Miller enclosed a short note from his sister Mary happily reporting the birth of Edward Hageman, "a fine large boy." The child died in Mar. 1856.

healthing machinery, & for that I think of riding on horseback all the Summer. Will you ride sometimes with me? If you will prepare a skirt or a riding dress. I hope about a weeks ride will make me quite stout but wherever I am I want to ride daily all Summer & not preach much.

Yrs affly-
JM

Wednesday July 11.1855

My *dear John:*

And so *"old Mr Vethake*["] is your Provost! When I was a little girl going to school with the longest sort of a bonnet on my head, & I thought, the heaviest sort of a book under my arm *he* was the President of our College, then in no very favorable condition.[150] The very mention of his name takes me down, down in the abyss of the Past until I seem to have gone down further than any human being ever did before. I remember so well how he used to stumble along in his nearsightedness and awkwardness, which together made his ungainly figure more ungainly, and his *abstracted* countenance more *distracted* still. He soon got tired here—not sooner however I believe than the people tired of him. Our boys were decidedly unmanagable, & your friend Turveydrop's brother-in-law I think even ventured to propose to this stiff, starched Northern President a regular fist-fight. His dignity (not his person) was so wounded by the proceeding that he soon after resigned. And from that time to this, except when he sent a copy of his work on Political Economy to my Father, I dont think I have heard of him. And then your Friend *Connell* or *Cannell* is it? If he is the husband of one Sarah Skipwith, I have the sort of interest in him which a slight acquaintance with her long ago, can give. But I must say, en passant, that I hope your friend is a little cleverer than his Wife, other wise your letter would have done little good with me had I been one of your Trustees, or Visitors or whatever you call them.

Didn't I guess well about Spence? If I have guessed as well about your correspondent "Field", your question as to my skill in reading Autographs is answered. I am so sorry Spence is prim and fastidious. I wish we could get him into Virginia & make him pitch quoits outside of Richmond for a month.[151] He would be much improved, I know, by the scuffle & dust of the game. I shall shock him terribly, & in return, he will chill me completely. You know I think you dont like Annie particularly well? I dont want you to tell me any thing about it, but I know you dont; & I know you think she isn't quite bright enough for Spence, and that's the worry.

I had a very sweet little letter from Maggie Breckinridge this morning, which she says I am not to thank *you* for, as she intended writing before you proposed

150. Washington College.
151. Pitch quoits is a game in which participants throw a ring of either rope or flat metal at a peg in the ground, with the objective of encircling it or coming as close as possible to it.

to her to do it. All this smoothing of my entrance into your family is so very thoughtful and kind on your part,—& almost as much so on theirs, considering their want of hearty concurrence in your choice.

I have a very little box I want to send to you for the children, but I hesitate to do it, first because the little present it contains for Maggie will be too large for her, & I cant well have it remedied without getting you to attend to it; and then next, because I think, perhaps, they might be better pleased to have you take it to them when you return from Va. Yet if they are to be pleased at all, in so small a way, *I* am impatient they should have the pleasure now. So, if you will write me that you are not too *diffident* to take so important a matter in hand, I will *honor* you with a commission, & send the things on in time for you to take them to Princeton when you go again.

If I have the prospect of being free from company all this month, still fair, why, come here first.

To-day is Lilly's birthday. I wish she were five instead of fifteen, but then if we lived she would have to be fifteen—there is no skipping that disagreable age, & I much submit to it.

Why dont you get my letter from the "'bus" man?

Affectionately Yours
S.C.P. McDowell

Thursday,
July 12./55

Indeed, John your lady—"Field" is painfully pertinacious. What difference does it make to her, I should like to know whether you wear a white cravat or a black one. I am afraid, in spite of all she says about your preaching, that she's more occupied with your cravat than with your sermon. Please tell her you wear it just because you choose to do it. *Why* you choose to do it is another affair.

I dont like the lady so much. I think she is what Susie Taylor calls "too *sufficious.*" I know she buzzes about all the week among sewing societies, and wonders every where she goes over "poor dear Mr Miller's" cravats; & reckons or *guesses* rather, that the white ones are all gone & he's got nobody, poor fellow, to hem any new ones; & proposes to have a new set made up, forthwith, by all the idle young ladies of the Congregation. And then, that subject disposed of, she fusses about the long services, that dont *tire her,* but may keep the young people from coming to the Church, or else bring them there from the improper motive of hearing three hymns of 8 verses each sung by a good choir. And more than all, John isn't there a little too much *cant* about the dear, active, bustling, earnest, "sufficious" Dame Field?

If *I* were a Man, as I sometimes wish I was, I wouldn't have *my* lady-love do all the writing. I dont think the Student you speak of shows good taste or much zeal in his love affair. No matter how busy he is, he ought to have time to do his part, & that the larger, of the writing. And as for you, you are right much of a grumbler. You have a great ambition to be a Martyr in this affair of ours, and are always exaggerating your woes. I'm afraid you'll never be content till you get somebody to say—"Well, poor John Miller; that Mrs. McD, has been the death of him after all." But I dont mean to kill you quite. I am going to write up the Canby envelopes, & then play "quits" for awhile. Dear John, I shall be so glad to see you. I begin to count the intervening days between this & your arrival with some agitation already, and as the time grows shorter & shorter, I shall get more & more excited. And yet I am sure, you will feel disappointed when you see me, & fancy I am rather cooler than you expected, unless indeed a sudden gust of feeling should break down all my collectedness at once. I wonder if I shall love you as much face to face as I do in this "letter garb" that I am so used to seeing you in. I have become so much attached to this ragged writing of yours, that I may not, in a minute, love you as much in any other guise, and yet I may learn, in a very little time to love you better. I dont know how it will be till I see the black cravat. You'll bring some white cravats too, wont you?

Owing to the heavy & frequent rains we have been in danger of losing our wheat. The most of mine I am glad is under shelter, and hope this afternoon's shower was too slight to do much damage to the remainder.

The girls & Benton go up to Fincastle tomorrow. I shall be entirely alone unless Miss Moore comes up. If she does not come I'll go over to Cousin John's & stay at night until Bent returns. I'm a real coward. I am afraid of men, & horses & cows & witches & the dark.

Dont you think Mr Kennedy writes me that I am taxed $300—for the paving of my Washington lot? I felt really provoked and astonished by his whole statement. Never mind, *you* are to look after it next year, and if it is to be a worry to any body it must be to you, for I am heartily tired of it.

No letter from your Mother yet. It was right unkind in you to tell me one was coming. But you mustn't let the old Lady know that you've told me, for then she'll feel obliged to write, which wont be pleasant to her.

Aint I too stupid this evening? Dont forget to bring an Overcoat with you, when you come to the Mountains. I think you are very saucy—do you know it? Do you know *why* I think so? Then take care, you dont know what might happen if you dont behave better.

Affectionately Yours
S.C.P. McD

[July 12, 1855]
Spence's Office

My *darling Sally*,

The mail has broken down or something has happened for I have no letter again. I trust you are not sick. But Darling, if you were sick somebody else would write. It is now since Monday that I have no letter. This is Thursday evening. Oh how unfortunate that just at the time when I had brot myself up to the mark of a letter a day from the strong inducement of hearing every day from you I should be so specially badly off. A little worn out as I am at the close of our long campaign I would drop back to the measure of writing less often, but then it would not be honorable would it?[152] Oh! I shall hear every day here after till I see you: shall I not?

The holiday matter is decided. The Session have voted to shut the church the whole of August. I shall get some one else, if I am spared, to preach the 29th of July & shall set out from here next Monday week at 11 P.M. Need I go to Frederick till my return? I do so much want to see you. Write & tell me. Spence is out in the country or on his way there, but I set his office boy who was at a table near the pens to scribbling my name. You see with what success. Either will find its way to me. These last two Sundays are utterly burdensome to me. I feel quite a repugnance to the writing & the preaching that remain. How we are all alike & how we do tease ourselves.

Yours affectionally
Jno Miller.

Friday, July 13, 1855.

My *dear* John,

What *is* the reason you dont get my letters? No letter on Wednesday from me & none the Monday before? I cant think how it happens. It seems to me I am all the time writing to you.

Your Mother's letter came this morning—I enclose it to you, but you must send it back to me after you read it. I am really grateful to her for making the effort to write to me and tho' the letter is, it seems to me, rather formal, (it may be I mistake it even in that particular,) yet it is meant to be kind, John, out and out? If she had only said "my dear Sally," as so old a Lady & *your* Mother might have said, I should have felt at once like throwing my arms round her neck and claiming her as *my* Mother too. But it is all my fault if I am a little disappointed. It is so foolish in me to have thought she could have any other than just that sort of interest that must naturally be felt for one who is entering her family unwelcomed by her. But I think I shall surprise her into a welcome yet—and at any rate, I love you enough to feel very affectionately to her, whether she likes me or not. I shall write to her this evening.

I am all by myself. I cant remember ever before to have dined alone. I compassionated myself a little I looked so solitary. Edward went thro' all the form of setting the dinner table & ringing the bell & I sat down & very leisurely went thro' the ceremony of dining. And yet I might have taken up Longfellow's Swedenborgian verse, occurring, I forget in which of his short pieces—

---

152. The "long campaign" refers to the fund drive for the new church building.

"Take, O boatman! *Thrice* thy fee,
For, tho' all unseen by thee
Spirits *three* have crossed with me."

Lilly asked with great concern, *who* I should have to talk to when they were gone, but when I assured her I could "talk to myself", she was entirely satisfied.

Have you suffered much from heat this summer? I scarcely remember a cooler season than this has been here. Nor, have I noticed for many years such frequent & violent thunder storms as we have had. The fields instead of being parched as is usual, at this time, are as fresh & green & beautiful as in May.

My friend Fishburn goes to Germany for a little while, to spend a year or 18 months.—meantime Cousin John's son, Tom Preston takes his place at College. He goes to study the language not the philosophy of Germany, yet I fear he will dabble a little in the latter too, in which case he will be ruined, as he has not the sort of mind to engage in anything so subtle as german Metaphysics without danger. I hear that he is engaged to be married to Dr Junkin's youngest daughter.[153] One of our other young Professor's was married the other day—young Mr. Nelson Prof: of Mathematics, & respected to be wonderfully clever in his line; but I think him wonderfully stupid out of it. I dont admire these extraordinary developments of a single faculty. I think it a mental deformity. To have a mind that exhibits but one faculty, even tho' that be to its greatest extent is as bad to me, as a dwindling little body appended to a great rickety head.

Do you know, John, your Mother scares me a good deal about you? She evidently means to apprize me of the necessity I shall have to "*endure*" a good deal of something from you—what is it? Are you arbitrary & exacting? But to tell you the truth I am more afraid of *myself* than of any body else concerned. I'm so used to the sovreignty that I fear we shall have a "fight for the crown" yet.

How many more letters am I to write you? Let me see—Monday, Tuesday, Wednesday, Thursday—4! You can keep up your patience till then. I do wish you were here now. We could have had such a nice cozy day "with none to molest or make us afraid." I may add a line tomorrow morning.

Saturday 7 1/2 A.M.

I am surprised you dont get my letters. The Canby envelopes cannot answer well. But you'll soon be here now, & I need not quarrel about the mails. It may be too, that yesterday you got a whole budget of letters, & are to-day rather sorry that the mail brought so many.

I did not go over to Cousin John's last night, but remained very unfearingly at home.

I am sure you are just as anxious as you can be to see my letter to your Mother, and I have half a notion to let you have the first reading of it that you may be

---

153. Thomas Lewis Preston (1835–1895). Junius Fishburn later married Julia Rush Junkin (1835–1915).

satisfied that I have no want of kind feeling there, but I will not; if you are very curious about it, ask for it.

Such delightful weather we have! I know it will be all over by the time you come on.

I shant write again till Monday evening.

Very affectionately,
S.C.P. McDowell

[Enclosure: Sarah Miller to Sally C. P. McDowell]

Princeton July 10th/55.

My *Dear Madam,*

My son, with whom you have lately become interestingly acquainted, will have told you, by this time, of his mother's increasing infirmities; and given this as a reason why I was not among the number of those whom you had lately added to the list of your correspondents. The truth is, that the writing of any letter about which I am to be cautious, and must have all my facilities—or rather, felicities of mind and body in exercise, is one of the most trying things to do. I have resolved, however, with my son's consent, to send you such an one as shall be the honest expression of my views and feelings.

I have thought, for some time, that nobody wanted a good wife more then he does. He has compassed himself about with so much and various business, abroad, that I think he cannot be, at home, what he ought to be; and if I did not think that you would sometimes make him a firm—and sometimes a yielding wife "bearing all things, enduring all things"—as he needed—for His sake who does this for us, I should advise you not to cast in your Lot with his. But if you can, through all this be to him a helper in advancing the Gospel, and a blessing to the Church, I shall love you, not only for your own sake—and for his sake—but for the *Gospel's* sake.

My desire is that neither you nor he shall retake one step in the progress which is made in your interesting engagement; but that in the face of every untoward circumstance which does not interpose a strong and Christian reason for so doing—you come, and as soon as you can, make one of our family circle.

Remember me to your sisters, and believe me, my dear Madam—yours sincerely,

Sarah Miller.

[July 13, 1855]

Darling

Just in from some visits. Write hard to catch the mail. Your letter just in *Friday evening.*

You misapprehend my speech about deficiency in womanly softness. I mean just another way of saying you didnt love me enough or didnt express it. Would I a *Northerner* dare to take up such a fancy as the other? I love you with a fondness that clothes you with a tenderness in other respects that I cannot exaggerate.

Yours fondly
Jno Miller

Phil. July 13th 1855.

My *dear Sally*,

I came in late from writing & scratched off this & found it too late.[154] I mean to try another 'bus man rather than fail utterly as I am 2 miles or near that from the P.O. I dont like to omit one day of the 7 writing days that remain. I hope to leave here Monday week. Need I go to F[rederick] first? Otherwise I can see you on the morning of Wednesday.

What had Mr. Chevalier heard of me? Tell me in all honesty. I never before heard anything of myself put in so serious a form & of a nature to "disquiet" any one in a relation like ours & it has *pleased* me in one respect that it confirms an impression I have long had of myself, that I dont *care* as much as most men what people think of me. It annoys me just so far as I fear it annoys you but even in this relation I would rather you should hear it before our marriage than after. And indeed, Sally, I have a sort of passion that you should have me before you in all possible lights so as even to hesitate about the marriage, rather than have a tinge of misgiving after it has been consummated. Please tell me what Mr C. said, for tho' I am telling you a literal truth when I say, I care very little what he said, yet I would like to know that I might mend my ways & not have such rumours commencing upon me in my old age.

Reputation, tho' (perhaps from a melancholy temperament) I greatly scorn it, yet is a priceless gift & the nursing of it a conscientious duty.

The epitaph I will keep & write about on Monday. I like this too well to alter it. Tho' when I read your letter again I may make up my mind that you really *want* me to shorten it whether I like it as it is or not.

Now my darling, darling Darling, how came you to make such a mistake about what I said. It makes me grieve to think I should have so awkwardly given you distress. I had hung the charges so upon your not loving me that I was only presenting the old idea in different language. Do read the letter again, Sally. I have no such conviction about you as that you have understood & yet here you have been grieving about me as tho' I had.

The sadness I tell you of I cannot prevent or deny. But, Sally, you wont feel it. I am cheerful & buoyant in *purpose* & I help up others spirits even when I have none of my own. Perhaps when I am older & your husband & get among my congenial philosophies I shall be happier. I *think* I *am* happier than when I was younger. Dont let it grieve you, Sally. It is a part of my physique. You will not have to bear it.

154. A reference to the preceeding note.

Dont be rash about your place. If you are eager to sell anything, sell your wheat crop. The sooner that is sold the better, I *think*.

Cant you postpone C & L's visit a week. However they have gone I suppose. It is quite settled now that I leave here next Monday week at 11 o'clock at night. I push on next day to Staunton & reach L. Tuesday night; dont I? Or might I to go to F.?

By all means write your father's life. It is a sacred & honorable authorship. And take the $1000. A Northern lady would regard it as a patent of nobility. I should feel *proud* of you if you won that much even if you threw it into the James river the day after. I cant answer for Va. But it will make more of a lady (& of a woman) of you where I live I can assure you. But what do you mean by "taking a year for it"? You will never see in me a trace of what you think literary jealousy in husbands. Overtop me if you can; & you easily may & do. Dont I tell you I *despise* reputation unless it be of the most etherial & exalted kind.

I am so sorry about your sickness. I want you to gather up your best looks for my visit. I shall be sallow enough for both of us.

I hope the driver wont lose this. By the way I feel badly about the other. I forget what was in it.

I shall be in town till the *night* of Monday week, so you must write so that I can have a letter that day before you stop. Wont you also write to Staunton care of the McClungs, for Tuesday afternoon?

Your affly
JM

Phil. July 14th [1855]

Dear Sally,

I am going to write you the genteelest little note, because its Saturday. Your letter comes frolicking & romping into my sanctum & is gay enough really to dance on my great ponderous looking table. God bless you for it, Sally. Right about what? Spences being a little old maidish? Oh yes. But you are wrong about Father who was quite slip shod in his study & pile every exposed surface with books. Father would have lived in dust (& as it was just brushed away books enough for writing space) if it had not been for Mary. I am a terrible sloven. Spence & I are antipodes. I allow not only litter but dust & expect my wife to improve me in those things. O Sally, you are not in earnest about Allie. I do like other people to keep other people neat & in order, & I mean to brush up & pretend clean so as to keep you from starting low in these respects. There is a Lady here (in Phil) [who][155] leaves everything just as she is done with it. She leaves the queerest looking sorts of dresses on the floor just as she has stepped all out of them & her shoes & brushes are just where she last used them & of course

---

155. The page is torn here.

just where she is most likely to use them again. But Sally just you do so. We all love our opposites. I am a shocking sloven & I want my wife to be a what? There ought to be a word for that. But haven't I been in yr rooms & dont I know better?

Be sure to tell me what Chevalier said of me when you write.

yrs affy
Jno Miller

Phil. July 16th 1855

Ha! that's all abortive.

Dear Sally, I have been trying to show my faithfulness by seizing upon the Epitaph this morning after my Sunday's work & trying to get off to you my paraphrase of it. But like most things that you do I find it very hard to improve on you & very difficult even to make you *shorter*. I send off to you just my first jottings before getting into that boat to go to Chester. I will get at it again this evening & have something further in my to-morrow's letter. I wish, however, thus far in advance to engage you to write my Epitaph. Will you do it Sally?

Yes Miss Field is a single lady a little over my age. I dont exactly approve of such correspondences & therefore, you perhaps will scold me when you hear that I have answered neither letter. I answer viva voce somehow & save my autograph. Am I prim? like Spence? By the way, I never said he was so. Primness is fastidiousness on a small scale. He is fastidious on a great scale. I dont think we could persuade him into quoits.

Your letters now are one day later in reaching me. The letter marked the 12th I have just gotten. The box, therefore, you can hardly send me bef. I leave. Yet I will be glad to receive it if you think it well to trust it to the last moment. I leave here next Monday(!!!!.) I hope Providence will be kind to me & not prevent or disturb what looks so pleasant to me.

I dont know which 'bus it was. If I did they would own to nothing in the past. You might as well go after peace to the Crimea.

I'm going to see Mrs Potter.

In Haste
Yours affly
Jno Miller.

Monday
July 16. 1855

My *dear John*,

I have been bustling and worrying almost all day over old accounts that I am anxious to have disposed of. As I rolled up bundle after bundle I was struck with their unsightly appearance in my secretary, & determined to bestow them elsewhere. So, I gathered them all up & brought them to a little closet in which

Father kept such papers, & there I put mine. As I was about shutting the door my eye fell upon an odd-looking package which I dragged out & in a few minutes grew interested in reading. It was the rough draft of a speech, delivered at Amherst College, I think; tho' of that I am not sure. At random I draw out two sheets & send them to you. Perhaps they may give you some idea of my Father, in his work of preparation.

I was glad yesterday morning to have the tolling bell announce the death of an old man—my nearest neighbor, who has been suffering the most excruciating pain for months.[156] He was 83—had outlived all his children—had buried the most beloved of the 2 or 3 grandchildren he had—had become very, very deaf, and had been obliged to bear, as best he could for 20 years the terrible affliction of having a deranged wife. Poor old Man! I was rejoiced to hear that he was in heaven. I went over to his funeral at 9 o'clock. Two grandchildren were there & two nieces, & a great grandson. No tears were shed;—why should there have been? No one looked grieved. I should have been mad if they had. A recital of the old man's gentle patience to his poor wife touched us all, yet we thanked God that he had lived a life of faith & had died a death of perfect peace. It was, it seemed to me a time & place for praise & I was annoyed at Dr White's talking of "the house of mourning" to which we had come. And yet, there was one real mourner, in the poor old woman. Just before the body was carried out, the old lady, oh so thin & miserable looking came slowly in, half-supported by the kind arm of a gentleman thrown round her, & with a low, moaning, sobbing cry stood for a moment looking at the face of the dead, & then bent over it with a last, sad embrace. She had sense enough left, poor creature to feel her loss. She has had sense enough all along to love her husband & to be kind to him, tho she has, of course, been an unspeakably great burden to him.

You intermitted one day in your letters;—I didn't get one on Saturday. Were you mad or tired, or a little of both? Have all of my last week's epistles reached you? If they have please answer some of them, and tell me all about the settlement of the Cravat difficulty. I am quite curious to know the end of so important a matter.

You cant think how impatient I grow, as your absence diminishes. I wish you could get some one to preach for you next Sunday, & you come right up now.

Dr Ben Smith preached for us yesterday.[157] He is something like Uncle Robert a little too eloquent upon the subject of his own maladies. I dont know what they would do if they couldn't use that pretty phrase about "spending & being spent in the Master's service". However he looks badly. I get so provoked with him for telling me with professional minuteness all about his illness & the remedies prescribed for it, when I ask how he is, as happened yesterday in the vestibule. He has a child threatened with scarlet fever, into whose case, he also plunged

---

156. John McCleland (c. 1770–1855). His wife was Mary Brownlee McCleland.
157. Benjamin Mosby Smith (1811–1893), professor of Oriental literature at Union Theological Seminary in Virginia.

with great particularity. Aint his wife too ugly & too—not agreeable? But he preaches finely.

I am so delighted with my solitariness as to be rather sorry that Bent & Miss Moore will be up tomorrow. I think you would feel a little sorry for me if you were to see me at my meals. I have no companion at anytime but a little servant, who with a great air, asks "if I want her to take care of me?" While I write, she mounts a large arm chair at the writing table, & amuses herself with the pictures in Froissart, (as well she may) until her eyes give out entirely.[158]

I wish you were here during all this quiet time. I should have felt so entirely untrammeled and free. Next week Cousin John will be back & then you must give some time to him—& Dr White, & Col Reid—But I suppose it cant be helped & therefore mustn't be mourned over.

Tuesday

I shall venture to send the children's box either by this morning's mail or tomorrow. Maggie's thimble is too large & rather too old-womanish for her. So take it back to Bailey, from whom it came a week ago, & exchange it for another, somewhat smaller & more ornamented. I put mine in the box as a guide in size & looks. Do not get one with any more chasing upon it than mine has.[159] I think they look out of taste; & as these things last a lifetime I want one that will always look well. Have the name marked in full, and in distinct letters—not like those in your ring, but like the enclosed card. Am I not very minute? I think there will be room on the scroll on the back of the knife for Allie's name—A.M. Miller,— in small capitals. If not, arrange it as best you can, only let him be pleased by having the whole name & not the initials merely. If you think Maggie would like it better make Bailey put up her thimble in a case of ivory, either egg-shaped like mine, or in the shape of an acorn. I like the morocco case best, as the vegetable ivory, of which the others are made become discolored by handling & exposure to the air & light.

James brought the things from Bailey, & they were to be exchanged if they did not suit: so you will have no difficulty about that—And they ought to have new marked at the beginning, but I didn't choose to let James know their destination.

Bring my thimble up with you, dont return it by mail. As for the pencil the box contains, put it in your pocket & use it till I can get you a better. I wont give it to you—first, because I dont think it good enough—and next because Susan gave it to me: but you may use it as a sort of Amulet.

I am writing in a great hurry, but will write again by tomorrow's mail.

Affectionately Yours,
S.C.P. McD.

158. Jean Froissart (1338?–1410?). His work was translated into English and published repeatedly in England and the United States. See, for example, *Chronicles of England, France, Spain, and Adjoining Countries*, 2 vols. (London: H. G. Bohn, 1852).

159. "Chasing" here means "engraving."

Colalto
July 17. 1855

Dear John,

I've just finished a letter to Maggie Breckenridge, & the enclosed notes to the children; so it follows naturally that you should come next. I have neglected, all along, to say you had better come here first, & take Frederick on your return. You will be free six weeks? The last one, then you can best give to your old parish. I am impatient for you to come, and then you need rest and quiet now more than anything else. But it will be just as I feared. All the cool, pleasant weather will be over when you come, & you will have to alternate between roasting & melting all the time you'll be here. To-day is the first real summer day I have felt for weeks, & I fear it is to usher in just such a season as that of the past year. What a pity! Warm weather is so unpleasant to me. But no matter, our *warm* days are cooler than yours & I hope you will find the change both pleasant & beneficial. And I'll keep you in the shade as you ask, and quiet; & will allow you to "bestow your tediousness" upon me day after day without ever discovering that you are dull, or ever showing that I am drowsy. Sometimes I have been so uncivil as to take a nap whilst a friend was talking to me; but I managed so skilfully that my nods were but a graceful assent to his propositions & opinions. Dr Smith said to me yesterday, "I preached under the influence of a opiate to-day"—In cases like that referred to, I must excuse myself by saying I *listened* under the same influence, with this difference, however, that my opiate was mental, not material.

I wonder you are not utterly worn out with my letters. They are as stupid as my good friend, Col Reid, is heavy & prosy. I doubt whether I ought to tell you what Mr Chevalier said. He has not known you personally, since you were a lad at College, (when he remembered you had *temper enough*!!), and what he told me he had obtained from some *lady,* I think, whose name he would not give, tho' he said, she had said, she would tell me what she told him. However as you ask very urgently—& as any hesitancy on my part might induce you to think it had left some unfavorable impression on my mind,—I gather up the disjointed remarks into a sentence that conveyed the charge. "So Mrs McDowell is going to marry John Miller! Well, I'm sorry for it. He was not—(or, "was not thought to be," I forget the exact language) a *good husband*".

Now John let me tell you. I haven't a fear of you in this regard. I dont believe one word of what was said. I did feel at the moment. You would not have wished me to feel, & to feel a good deal under such an accusation; yet it was but for the moment. In my cool wisdom, & abundant caution, I never even submitted it to you for a denial, as I would have felt called upon to do, if it had at all unsettled my mind. I dont expect to find you *perfect* by any means; & I fancy you will sometimes turn right *sharply* upon me, & make me have a vision of my old home & its quiet, but for all that I know you love me enough to be considerate & kind & affectionate, & forbearing. And I, in turn love you quite enough to have my affection, whether expressed or unexpressed, a sufficient prop under all the exigencies of life. No doubt I shall tax your forbearance & patience very often, by faults that I am aware of, and in ways that I am unaware of, but a little gentleness & entire frankness will go far to remedy much that is amiss. I hardly know what particularly bad qualities I am to be on the lookout for in you. I haven't made up my mind *how* I am to be martyred, but I pray you it may be neither by petulance or indifference—the one is so mean & the other so iniquitous.

I was interrupted an hour or so ago by a young Tinner who brought a bill to be paid. Hoping he would only sit long enough for me to get his money, I hurried to pay him his $5.00. But I was sadly disappointed. He commenced a brisk talk upon the wheat crop of the Valley—thence to that of the United States, and travelled on, on till he quite settled it, that no wheat could be, at present, raised in the Crimea. Here he gave me a few eloquent remarks upon the war in its present aspect, & also a prophetic glance at its future history. This of course brought us on a homeward march, & after he had decided that in the great future struggle *we* have to be *the* people, he suddenly plunged into all the intricacies of union or disunion, amongst us. Like an expert politician I fought equally well & acceptably on both sides of the question, & got paid for my eloquence, not by a profound silence as I hoped, but by a significant return to first principles:,—"Is it right for every man to vote". As the right of suffrage was outside of my sphere, I had not much to say, theoretically, on so controverted a point. Now didn't I have a time?

When you get to Staunton you will find two sets of coaches, that will contest the honor of bringing you, their contest founded upon a principle of dollars & cents. One set runs from McClung's; the other from the American.[160] Those McClungs are very kind & *I* always go there, but I don't like to do it. They are such terrible Talkers, and have such a *gift* at finding out things! If there was any thing stowed away back in your mind, or hid under your cravat even, why, they are worse than Mrs (?) Field in dragging it to light. How about the Princeton Alexanders? But the infusion of Waddle blood has elevated them above the rest of their Kith & Kin.[161]

Oh no! I shant write to you at McClung's. James McClung is just as certain of my handwriting as you could be after my hecatomb of letters to la belle passion. Every little while I carry on an animated correspondence with him about some package or box by Adams' Express. By the way if you see a package in his barroom bearing my name, say nothing to him but take possession & bring it up.

The Engraver sent me a proof of Father's a day or two since. The likeness is as good as we could expect to get—& the work very handsome.

I'm afraid your Mother will not be pleased with my letter to her. I have a sort of impression, she will think it hardly deferential or grave enough.

160. McClung's hotel was the Virginia House; the American was another hotel.
161. Janetta Waddel, wife of Archibald Alexander of Princeton, was the daughter of the Reverend James Waddel (1739–1805), the famous "blind preacher" of William Wirt's *Spy*. Her sister-in-law was Elizabeth Alexander McClung.

I am worried about the lost letter too. Cant you make the 'bus man tell you something about it.

Well now, Goodbye

Yours affectionately
S.C.P. McD.

Wednesday
July 18. 1855

Dear John,

Never fear that you will ever be in want of a "brushing" when once you get me to Philadelphia. Neither need you grieve about Allie; for I have no doubt, that out of an abundance of tender care I shall sometimes (precious seldom tho' I imagine if it's left in my hands) work myself up to the necessity of bestowing upon him, "a *little dressing*": not enough, however to excite any apprehension for his morals. Poor little fellow! This piece of fame places him in a new light to me. I feel as if I had done him an injury already.

Such a warm day we have had; and so busy I have been. I was not fully emancipated till 6 o'clock & then out of a little looking after something new, I spent a little while at the Piano—a thing I do so seldom that it actually brought my pair of little servants in from their weeding to be my astonished auditors. I gave up music a long time ago, & have since much regretted it. But as I thought nobody cared for my music, and as life was at the time a sort of jot work with me, done by the day, I became a Utilitarian & devoted myself to the doing of things that were of immediate use. It was a wrong notion—I am sure. I gave up almost every thing that was simply a thing of taste & pleasure, & tried to live upon the rigid realities of existence. My Mother sometimes remonstrated a little, but no one had the heart to check me. They let me do as I pleased. I was a great burden to everybody, but greatest of all to myself. Your life has been smoother than mine; how much of it would you live over again?

Have you read Uncle Robert's letter to Sumner?[162] I think it a superb specimen of his great mind. What do you think of it? There's a majes[tic] swell in much that he writes that is very impressive to me. How different from Robinson's chop-sea style! I am out of patience with his *smartness*, of which he has undeniably a great deal.

I am so surprised at what you say of your Father. I thought he was what Uncle Benton calls, "the quintessential distillation" of particularity. But I'm glad of it. I dont like these very disagreably neat & fastidious men. They seem to me to fritter away their sense upon nothing, but, at the same time I detest a want of proper neatness. My Carrington Kin think it an evidence of genius to be absent

---

162. Published in the *Presbyterian Critic*. Senator Charles Sumner (1811–1874).

& careless in their dress. Edward, when at the Institute, in a hurry picked up a sock & tied it on for a cravat![163] He shouldn't have sat at my table, tho' his Mother & Sisters thought it a good joke.

I think you will never refresh your eyes with the spectacle of my dresses on the floor or my gaiters left where they were taken off. The nicest & most commodious of shoe-bags, all ornamented with blue braid, is the home of my boots & slippers, when they are of a kind to be cared about. But I am not the least bit crazy with particularity. I wont let you use my pen, & there may be a few other *notions* that are things of partnership usually, that you need never think it possible you could touch. But beyond these, I care little.

Am I not very interesting? In fact I am really stupid. I sent the box off by this morning's mail & hope it will reach you safely & not give you much trouble. By the way, do as you think best about sending it on to the children.

It has just occurred to me that it may be that Aunt Eliza is detaining my Carriage, as it hasn't returned yet, that she may come down in it, in which case Uncle will come too. Wont that be bad just now when I am so anxious to have no one in the house. I have an impression that something is going to mar the pleasure of your visit.

If you dont choose to go to McClung's the American, rather a poor place tho', is just at the depot:—reason enough for your going to it.

My letter about the epitaph was so long getting to you, that I am afraid I am troubling you about it for nothing. I put mine in the stone cutters hands, but hoped he would not progress too far to make yours unavailable when it came. I disliked to keep Jenks waiting, as under the agreement between he & James I can advance no part of his pay.[164] He is not to be paid until the work is completed, & every day's delay he feels. I wish you could see Jenks holding a talk with me. He is an Englishman, & always defers to me with the air of one who is about to address me as "My Lady". I believe he has quite made up his mind that the Queen of Sheeba is a fool in comparison with my Ladyship, & quite grieves that so smart a woman, could not be sent as a man to enlighten & elevate the race. I was amused with him about the epitaph—"No doubt the Dr. could have done it as well as Col Benton;—or yourself, Madam, better than either". He is very fond of flowers, & has several times this summer brought me a bouquet from his little garden. This sort of attention & respect from worthy, plain people has always been very pleasant to me. His sincerity makes it very acceptable. But goodbye—God bless you my dear John. I wonder if I shall ever learn to say Mr Miller again? I reckon I shall when I get right down mad with you.

Yours
S.C.P. McD

163. Edward C. Carrington (1825–1892), McDowell's first cousin.
164. Francis Jenks, a stonecutter in Lexington.

Phil. July 18th 1855.

I can assure you, my darling Sally, with the utmost honesty that Mother *means* by this letter something very cordial, or to express the thing still more practically that the mother who writes this letter indicates by it a state of feeling that will give *you* the pleasantest & most satisfying welcome. She wouldnt say anything than My dear Madam or My dear Miss—if she were writing to whole stacks of daughters-in-law who were not yet married & whom she had never seen. I know Mother so well that I know each word of that letter means about four times as much as such words would ordinarily mean in the mouths of most old ladies.

But then, on the contrary, you know dear Sally, she knows *me* so well. Just think of that. My *own mother* tells you you had better not have me. Think of that! Oh Sally I'm forlorn. You cant *tell* how troublesome I am. I never have had such trouble with any one as with this very lover of yours & as to Mary she had to send me away from her last Summer & told me with great earnestness she did'nt know what I would do next.

Monday morn:

I went to Chester. I found Mrs P[otter] wishing to drive to Aunt Hunter's country seat which was 18 miles. I, therefore, staid & the next day sent for a horse & drove her over & back & did not return to Phil. till yesterday. Hence you had no letter yesterday. I receive yours now daily but four days after date. That is your letter of Friday reached me this evening. They are so pleasant to me getting them every day, they dont become so *feverish* to me in the waiting & in the reading as they used to be. I send you back the epitaph. Let us retouch it when we can talk over it together. I find it very hard to improve it. Sincerely, Sally, I think you greatly excel in such things. As to the Wash. Lot dont be troubled about it this hot weather. The payment you speak of is a reasonable one & will all go into the selling price of the lot. Dont be anxious. I wish they'd send in three or four more bills & make you right poor so that you may have a more *parsonage* feeling before you enter into near relations to the high office so that afterwards if you should grow very rich you may have the pleasure of thinking that you entered a low door in the great ecclesiastical edifice.

Mrs. Hunter, who is a dear old Aunt of Mrs. P's commissioned me very particularly to offer you her sincerest regards.

It is *intensely* hot here. The thermometer in my cool study is 89. A bright tho't has struck me about my five weeks. When you are tired of me & think its time for me to leave a while I meant to go to some hotel in the Mountain *nearest* to Lexington & there establish my head quarters get a saddle horse & ride in by that lane near Colalto every day to see you. It will make *every ride* a pleasure & so satisfy all the doctors notions of healthy exercise. What do you think of my plan? But alas! I neednt ask questions. You cant answer any more.

Yours affectionately
Jno Miller.

[marginal notes] Dont forget to write to Staunton.

How late does the stage reach Lexington. If by 11 1/2 I will run over a moment that night. May I?

Really, Sally, I musnt tease you this hot weather. Mother means nothing more about me than that I am absent & careless & sometimes indifferent (to every body) as I have confessed to you. I think Mother loves me more than any of her children & would give you the best character of me than any one else would in the family.

[Enclosure]

To commemorate
the virtues of
Their Grand-parents
James & Sarah McDowell
& to record
their reverence for the honored
name & high example
that has been
transmitted by their ancestors
this Monument
(in the year 1855)
is erected
by the surviving children
of
S.P. Taylor, E- Benton & Jas McD.
(Col)? James McDowell
was born Aug 1. 1770
& died Sept 1835

Distinguished by native talent of a high order; a gallant spirit; a noble justice; a lofty courage & a determined will he lived honorably discharging with singular ability both civil & military trusts & died universally esteemed & regretted.

———

Sarah McDowell

———

———

———

Her character formed in the stormy period of our National History was desirent for truth & patriotism she was_____

Yet to these traits she added the gentler qualities of her sex & the tenderness & devotion of the Christian.

———

James McDowell, the Third
in the order of descent

———

Also a Daughter
Elizabeth McGavick

———

Phil. July 19th 1855.

My *dear* Mrs. McDowell,

Dont it look solemn our old way of addressing each other? And yet, My dear Madam, it was very respectable & Spence, if all you suspect of him were true might never have emerged into the more artless & loving expressions. So what you say about my grumbling I have only to reply by the Rule of Three. If being "right much of a grumbler" produces 50 letters in a round year how many would not grumbling at all produce. I "reckon" grumbling "like I was crazy["] was all that kept me out of the poor-house in respect to letters; so "you let me alone". I reckon "you better take care" because after Thursday (Today) this week all the letters I write are *thrown in*. They will feel very much like works of supererogation & it will only be in order to get into a good glow of "martyr" feeling that I shall produce them at all.

As to my being saucy I'd like to know in what. I never knew so reserved & *distant* a lover. Here am I, (like a man who is alive & reading the newspapers after his funeral) treated as tho' every word of endearment to me was a sort of forgetfulness, when I have been as good as married ever since the 23d of May; my own darling Wife absolutely asking "if I am not ashamed to have drawn from her" one or two straggling expressions of affection; & now actually charging me with being saucy, when she who within a month or two is to be with me all the time, to sit at my table, to live in my home & to keep out of my study has only received from me one or two words of quiet endearment, such as, for example, how much I loved her, such as, for example, (having scolded her a good deal) how I would like to be with her to wipe the tears away from her cheeks & comfort her poor broken heart & encourage her to do better—forsooth I'm saucy. Well, it's very hard. Why, Sally, suppose you were my wife this minute. You know you might have been. And if you love me about enough to have been my wife two months ago next Monday I can hardly conceive how I *could* be saucy by any way I could twist the English into an expression of the very tenderest affection. I wish you'd be a little saucy. Now, Sally, lets fix it all. Dont you know you've been in the habit of sitting up late at night. If the stage comes in by 12 Tuesday night I'm going over to your house unless your man at McDowell's (havent you a servant there yet?) thrusts a note into my hand forbidding it or I get one at Staunton. So now take care that you be up & ready to receive me & Sally, I'll pay the shortest sort of a visit so you neednt be afraid of your night's sleep. Dont wait up later for I will come right over from the stage & I wont come if the stage hour is later than 12. It will be so forlorn to wait till next day, & besides I dont think I can sleep till I have seen you. And I shall want sleep for in a martyr spirit I mean to travel from 11 the night before. Oh, it is so near! My poor ricketty head & dwindled strength is hardly a match for this gnawing impatience & as to sermons my mind refuses to produce them this week.

Your faithful Martyr
Jno Miller.[165]

Colalto
July 20. 1855

Oh well! My dear John I wish I were able
To come and sit down by your "ponderous table"
Instead of thus being thrust in at the door,
Or hurl'd thro' the window or dropped on the floor,
Or pull'd out of your pocket all crumpled & torn
With my visage all *stamped* by the Care it has borne,
And read—read again, & re-read at your leisure
Until I could no longer give any pleasure
Then bound with red tape & put up on a shelf
Out of sight, like a bit of crack'd china or delft:—
Or, like an old Bill that has run all its readings
And borne all the starts, stops & sudden recedings
Of Bills whose supporters are not strong or able
To force a safe passage—"I'm laid on the table."
The sadest of fates! for Oblivious pall
Then shuts in the picture & covers up all.
    But if, in my own proper person & voice
I'd call for admittance & leave you no choice
But to open the door & most cordially greet
The daring intruder, and offer a seat,
And hope, as in most civil phase you would say
"That you'll take off your bonnet & spend the whole day.
And indeed, since you've done me the honor to come
I beg, my dear Madam, you'll feel quite at home."
Then, I'd take off my bonnet, & smooth down my hair
And fold up my mantle & take the arm-chair
And throw aside gauntlets & veil & all that
And make myself ready to have a good chat.
Oh! Then how we'd ramble along thro the year!
Pause again at its stand-points of hope & of fear,—
Till over our changes and wondrous vagaries—
And the converse we've held with "blue devils" & fairies
Till at last, we look out from your Vine (?) St retreat
And view old Mount Difficult calm at our feet.

165. Here Miller drew a self-portait as a martyr.

With its rugged ascent,—with its brow lost on cloud,
With its muttering thunders portentous & loud,
No wonder we feared as its steep we ascended,—
No wonder our path was with sorrows attended,
No wonder we paused—no wonder we quailed,
The wonder of all is, that we have not failed
But a brave heart I've found in this hard world of ours
Is the greatest & best of man's conquering powers.
 To descend from the top & go back to the road
Won't you tell me your dangers by *Field* & by flood?
I'll list like the fair Desdamona of old
To the hair-breath escapes that your story'll unfold
And grieve in your griefs & be glad in your pleasure
As well as I can in my very long measure.
But I honestly tell you before you commence
If my sympathy's scant you must take no offense
For my words are so tightly corsetted by verse
That the half that I feel I can never rehearse.
Yet I'll manage to shudder & draw my breath short
When I hear you were actually seized by the throat
Sorely collared, & furiously held to the question
That's filling our Country with wrath & contention
And made to proclaim on no field for fair fight
Which cause you espouse—the black, Sir or the white!
 But pshaw! I must stop—for a friend has come in So good-bye—

I am Yours in a state of chagrin.
S.C.P. McDowell

Phil. Spencer's Office
July 20th 1855.

My darling Sally,
 Your packet has just reached me. I can hardly describe to you the pain of what you communicate from Mr. Chevalier. I find I *do* care for whether it be because of the justice of the charge or the keen anguish such a charge *must* occasion whether just or unjust it plunges me into the saddest feelings & strange to say not on your account or the worlds account or even my own account but on account of one who if the charge is true is so terribly avenged by the very silence & defencelessness of the tomb.
 And Sally, I would be afraid to appeal to our Creator & *say that the charge is untrue.* Death is a terrible accuser, & the very helplessness & absence of the dead so quicken conscience & make every memory of an unkind word or look so full of misgiving & remorse.—But Sally, I dont mean to draw you

into the circle of anguish than *this* rumour occasions me.—I never felt so like entirely confessing that *I was guilty*, & yet I would have to tell you of one whom I have never spoken to you of before of her loveliness & kindness & self-sacrifice for these children of ours to make you know the cause of my sensitiveness & how *inferior* I feel in any estimate that my own conscience makes in the question whether I was a good husband or no. But, Sally, I will say one thing. This charge *is entirely new to me*. I never heard the lisp even of such a rumor. My mother & my sisters never so much as *counselled* me in the matter. And Mrs Potter & the Bishop & Louisa & my parents-in-law cling to me with an affection & an interest & with an invitation so late as just before our engagement to come live with them less which would seem to me inconsistent with such an accusation.[166] Yet they may do it for my children's sake. Sally, I was not *always* kind (& yet who is?) & my great experience is that Death so fixes the barbed arrows of such a memory & gives a husband so weak a *will* to defend himself from just such an accusation. I fear you will not understand all this but God bless you Sally, for being so kind to me & for so affectionately defending me against such an idea. But Oh, I cant tell you the pain it gives me to think of this finger above the ground pointing at me unseen all this time for a crime which my conscience groans under at the very tho't of its even possible commission. Sally, I wont trifle you again with the idea of giving you back your liberty, but when I think how unworthy I may be of you even in the opinion of friends I do burn so with the impulse of preserving to you a longer & a farther liberty of choice—not binding you by any engagement. But this subject is forbidden to me.

I love you passionately. I *think* I was kind & self-sacrificing in my things over all the time that this charge covers. And if starting with so large a fund of affection can be any safeguard to you, I *cannot* be afraid that I shall treat you unkindly. But Oh, the tomb, My darling Sally, it makes so much even of so measly a *misgiving* & puts you so helplessly in the wrong & leaves you so little zeal in your own vindication.

I thank you so much for your kindness to me thro' the children. The gifts will be as welcome as any you could select & I love you for your affection in making them in the kind terms you do. I will do all at Bailey's this very evening.

I received your other letter—but pardon me from writing more to-night.

My dear darling Sally, good-bye. I *tried* to be a good husband *that I can say conscientiously*.

Yours most fondly,
Jno Miller

166. Clarissa Louisa Benedict (1830–?), the sister of Miller's deceased wife. She later married Alfred Potter (1817–1881). Miller's parents-in-law were Robert Benedict and his wife, Clarissa Dow Benedict (1789–1868).

Phil, July 21st 1855.

My *dearest* Sally,

This is my last letter!

Yours have come very regularly to hand for some days & have been very good & kind. The letter to the 'bus man I cant recall for there are a whole army of drivers & I dont know which was the one. But I have worse news for you yet. I was so hard driven last week as to trust *two men* to the same conveyance under the assurance of my friend the Druggist that he knew the particular one & that they would go safe. I very much fear that Saturday's letter that you missed went by such conveyance.

Nor can I remember what the 4th of July letter or either of these contained, but no harm I guess. Besides if they were a little too loving for the public gaze the chances are not more than one to fifty that any other than the driver would ever see them. He would pick off the Postage stamp & then destroy them to conceal his crime. They *certainly* would not confess or give up anything to me.

Alas I feel I am too late for the Despatch. I was called out.

Good bye!

I will soon see you. I have your last Cantey letter.

Yrs
JM.

Dear Sally,[167]

I failed. Whether this will reach you or not I know not. I enclose you a letter of Dr. Janeway.[168] I have your thimble &c & will arrange all satisfactorily. Jenks is a discerning man I must see him. I shall go to McClurgs. I wish they would put me in the room you last occupied. Oh! but I forgot. I dont stay happily for that.

Yours devotedly,
Jno Miller.

Only think! Our next word to each other will be absolutely face to face.

Io paean! Io te quaeso![169]

---

167. This is written on the back of the previous letter. A final sheet of writing paper is empty except for the heading "Phil: July 23, 1855" written by McDowell and a single word, "Bravo!" written by Miller. The July 21 letter that missed the mail may have been folded and sent in this sheet.

168. In this friendly letter, Janeway discussed arrangements to fill Miller's pulpit while he was on vacation and asked, "What are you going off for—is it to Virginia! I heard something like this—Is it the natural bridge, or some softer formation, which you go to see? Virginia has remarkable specimens, from the old church in Jamestown, to Rockbridge Co" (Thomas L. Janeway to John Miller, July 14 [1855], MFP).

169. Latin, meaning "Oh how completely! Oh how totally I desire you!"

PART FOUR

"Letters are poor substitutes for long talks, but we must put up with them."

August 1855–November 1855

[John Miller to S. C. P. McDowell, July–August 1855][1]

Darling Sally,

You couldn't have waked me out of the profoundest slumber with pleasanter news

Yours affly

[John Miller to S. C. P. McDowell, July–August 1855]

My dear Sally,

It is so pleasant an afternoon for riding that I have begun to-day.

I will not come over till after tea.

Yours affectionately
Jno Miller.

Tuesday Aug. 7. 1855

Dear John,

I have changed my mind about our trip to-day, and will go at 9 instead of 12, as we intended yesterday. Will you give up your ride on horseback for a drive with me?

Affecly
S.C.P. McDowell

1. These notes were sent during Miller's extended vacation in Lexington.

Colalto
Saturday Augt 18. 1855

My *dear John*

Here we are, back at the old thing of writing, writing,—with this difference however that I go at it with much less zest than formerly. Letters are poor substitutes for long talks, but we must put up with them.

I haven't yet cast off the fit of low spirits that made me guilty of the unbecoming spell of crying the morning you left, and as you are not here to talk me into something better, I must just let time exhaust, then cure. I wish you were here, and yet I am glad you are looking after your disaffected folk & disturbed plans at home. I am sure even Country air and exercise would have availed you nothing so long as your mind was harassed by these difficulties, the exact extent of which you did not know. And then, every day's delay in looking after them allowed them to increase and strengthen; and so I'm glad you are gone, now that the actual pain of the parting is over.

I beg you will be cautious in all you do & say, be specially guarded in giving an opinion at *the moment* of hearing anything unpleasant of your people's feeling or conduct to you. Take such time & care to make up your mind upon all you see & hear as will enable you to stand firmly upon your conclusions. This thing, of talking impulsively, gives one the appearance of a changeling in his opinions & sentiments, which doesn't suit in any case, especially not in yours. But this is all nonsense to you—your own mind & better knowledge of all involved will suggest all necessary prudence.

I felt a sort of momentary panic when I thought of you as crossing the Blue Ridge. I have a terror of that temporary track. But you are, I hope safe in Frederick now buzzing about among your friends there. By Tuesday I shall grow anxious for a letter from you there. Meantime I shall be busy with Col Reid and Mr Lewis, and have no thought for anything but figures, which I stand in great terror of.[2]

We are a good deal uneasy about Robt Taylor & his family. When they reached Staunton on Wednesday the Sister-in-law, who was with them became sick with every symptom, Robt writes, of yellow fever.[3] We have heard nothing further to-day & argue favorably from his silence.

Susan here still—Also Mr Venable, who now has full & fair success.[4]

How is the mark, our friend, the Dog, left? No signs of madness about you?[5]

O John, I would like to see you so much. I would behave so nice & grave & never "frolic" nor be "a fool" nor "nothing" that would worry you. I am quite penitent about all such things, & really think I have much improved since my

2. William C. Lewis (1796–1868), Lexington attorney and Rockbridge County commissioner.

3. Robert J. Taylor's wife, Eliza McNaught Taylor (1822–1855), died in September.

4. Charles Scott Venable (1827–1900) was courting Cantey McDowell.

5. Miller had been bitten by a dog while on vacation in Lexington.

little man went away. By the time you come back I shall be as staid as an olden maid, and as agreable as the screech-owl that serenades me here, after "love's winning notes" are out of my ear.

It is so cold this morning, that I find an open window chilly.

God bless you, my dear, dear John.

Affectionately
S.C.P. McDowell

August 18.[6] [1855]
Frederick
Saturday Morn.

My *darling Sally,*

I have important news to tell you.

I have had a long talk with Mr. Williams, a retired lawyer, Judge Shriver's son-in-law & have judged it wise as the result to make a partial confidant of him & to enlist him in our service.[7] He told me last night that the notorious belief here was[8] that Thomas had been a libertine since his marriage & spoke so strongly of this & in such a way as to convince me that his testimony came fully up to the whole of the Major's requirement.

But then he went a great deal further. He said that *facts* had once been in his possession, but that they had chiefly faded from his memory—but that he recollected this, that (a known courtezan) a woman of bad repute from abroad whose person he described a large fine looking woman, had been in Frederick & out (he tho't for some time) at Thomas' place & that O'Leery the Lottery dealer here told him that she came into his office with a ticket that Thomas had bought & demanded a small prize of $20 or 30 which it had drawn. You see the strength of all this statement taken together. This was after your separation.

Williams proposed that after I had gone & not in undue haste connection with my visit he should ascertain this & other facts more clearly in casual & apparent careless conversations with these men & that observing a perfect & permanent privacy in the whole he should write & let me know. This I have consented to & he promises to be exceedingly carefully not to mention my desire or interest or connection on the matter not even to his wife.

S. Tyler I have sounded & find him certain (in absolute facts) of T's criminality before his marriage & under the usual impression afterward but not possessed of any absolute histories.

6. McDowell dated this letter.

7. John H. Williams (1814–1896), attorney and editor of the *Frederick Examiner;* he married Eleanor Shriver (1814–1892), daughter of Judge Abraham Colbert Shriver (1771–1848).

8. Miller wrote this word twice, at the bottom of one page and the top of the other.

All this removes the least trace of doubt in my own mind as at present & I advised so far as the course I would take if the wedding were now & as it draws nearer I fancy my means of knowing will be still further encreased.

Williams is very reliable & his testimony far more reliable than Tyler's. Is not this a happy development? & was it not well I did not yield to any dread of the present feelings of Frederick but scrupulously & punctiliously came? No one knew of our engagement or attachment when I came. Mr & Mrs W. & Mr T. had not even a change of countenance when the marriage was broached. They seemed to approve it roundly & they are my most intimate & interested friends.

All this I know will gratify you. And I *hope* I may write you confortingly from Phil.

I write in extreme haste
My *darling Sally*

> Yours *Affly*
> Jno Miller

Will write again tomorrow. I stay at Mr. W and go on Monday.

Don't let us use the facts we get too boldly, lest it produce the other evil of hostility from Thomas.

Frederick
Monday. (August 20. 1855)[9]

Dearest Sally,

I go at 2 to-day. There was no mail yesterday. Williams reassures me of what I wrote as he searches more deeply into his memory,—says it is unquestionable as to time & general facts & tells me that with great quiet & *prudence* he will pick up other information & let me know.

I was the bearer of the news here myself. Col & Mrs Shriver who had heard it on Sat. evening gave us yesterday a warm & cordial invitation to their house at any time after our marriage, & the step seems met in the same way whenever your friends here hear it. Old Dr. Tyler introduced the subject this morning—told me facts of T's criminality before his marriage but like Sam knew more afterward as he had not been in the way of hearing any.[10] I have approached no one else.

I have fully realized my hope of learning all I wanted without appearing to go for it. Mr Williams is the only person with whom I have entered into any confidential relation.

Darling Sally, my life in L. seems to me now like a dream. I love you with a warmth that seems to invest you with the colors of romance. You seem to me like a sort of naiad whom I saw in some wild forest home & whose image floats

---

9. McDowell dated this letter.

10. Edward Shriver's wife was Elizabeth Lydia Reigart (?–1860). William Bradley Tyler (1788–1863), Frederick physician.

wildly before me.[11] I am bro't a little back to sober life by my throat that dont behave quite as well since I have been visiting these people. Let us trust love to take care of us however

yours warmly
JM

Tuesday,
Augt 21. 1855

My Dear John,

I have been busy with Lilly's accounts for some time; and as I shut up my Guardian's book, I turn my pen to the pleasanter work of writing to you. I am balked in my business arrangements by Col Reid's absence. He left town before you did & will not return for some days. This is a worry, especially as besides the delay, I fear I shall be hindered much next week by company. However Mr Lewis can do much for me without Col Reid's presence.

I am growing impatient to hear from you. My calculations upon your prompt writing made me feel *sure* of a letter this morning; but none came. I was sorely disappointed. However, a nice, long letter tomorrow morning will go far to make amends for today's disappointment. Not hearing from you, I don't know what to write about any plan for the future. Indeed all the planning is yours now, I have no power, but a sort of *veto power*, which I shall use with much caution & moderation. In all your Church movements, I beg you will remember that *its* interests, are above your own. I cannot bear to think of our allowing our own private wishes and designs to have any undue influence in so important a matter as that of your Church connection. If possible, keep our affair out of sight, in making your decision, especially if your find that the disaffection of your people is mainly attributed to your style of preaching, & not except, by way of giving weight to one objection by adding another, to your marriage. I could not advocate any undignified hesitation in your actions, yet I am fearful of a little miff or the smart of wounded feeling making you too precipitate. Is there no chance of your striking between these two points?

You may think it excessively foolish, yet I *do* have some painfully uneasy feelings about your adventure with the dog. Just today I had a talk with James Taylor about it, that renewed my anxiety, tho' I dissented strongly from the most serious view he takes of it. Can you tell me how to find my way to the house where the accident occurred? Or do you remember the name of the man to whom the dog belonged, & whom you saw in town the next day. Do look after the injured spot, & take care of it. James tells me, he feels now, or rather, felt until recently the effects of a similar accident to him some 20 or 25 years ago.

11. In Greek and Roman mythology, naiads are the nymphs who live in and give life to fountains, springs, rivers, and lakes.

Susan, Mr Carrington & Mr Venable left us last night at 9. & Mr. C_ has been quite unwell for several days, but was well enough to undertake a journey that he fancied would cure him by carrying him out of a limestone region.

Wednesday 8 1/2 A.M.

Your letter from Frederick came two hours ago. My *impressions* had been so very strong on the point of which you write, that I was sure they *must* be based on *fact,* and if the facts did not appear, it was only because we had not skill enough to draw them from their hiding-place. Your mention of the woman with the lottery ticket, recalls to me some troubled scenes with the German Gardener & his Wife, whom Mr Thomas had living on his place when I first went to it. As well as I recollect, Mr Thomas *obliged* the man to marry his Wife, then I think the Mother of a very young child, the morning after we reached the Town, & some weeks before we went out to his place to live: I frequently saw the woman after, I went to the farm, tho' I don't think I ever employed her, except perhaps to do a little sewing that was sent to her; but she was something of an annoyance from the fact of her bad temper. Once, long after dark, her husband who was the chief sufferer from her temper, came running in great agitation & fear into our sitting-room, & besought Mr Thomas to go & quiet his Wife who had exploded upon him so terribly as to make him fear for his life. Mr T_ went with him & hushed up the noise. I had no suspicion that he (Mr T) had any connection with the woman at the time; but my mind now slowly wakes up the old story about her, and presents it in a new & suspicious light. But even if it were true that the poor creature had been lured away from her home in Washington, by him, then to cover her shame forced upon Reynolds, (the gardener) it would avail nothing to us now. I mention this just because it occurs to me & not that I think it of any special value. I may wrong the man by my suspicion which I would not do. He is bad enough as he is.

I think of you with the greatest tenderness & anxious affection, so you needn't say, "Sally so you love me?" quite so doubtingly as heretofore.

Lilly sends her love to you, as she finds out to whom I am writing.

Affectionately,
S.C.P. McDowell

Phil. Aug 21 1855.
Tuesday.

My *dear Sally,*

I have just finished a long talk with Spence. His letters were I find to the very extreme of unfavorableness, as he says from what he knew of my character he was afraid I would be disposed to show fight & not come to prudent terms. He tells me that Mr Dungan defined my unpopularity by telling him that I was not *generally* understood, that he understood me & greatly enjoyed the preaching.[12] Now I know that you have no patience with these unintelligible people, but still as there was something consolatory in these views they ought to have been communicated, especially as Spence told Dungan in one part of the conversation that he (Spence) preferred hearing me to any one else, a sentence that a particular turn in the interview led him naturally to.

I have seen none of my people. I see Cornelius to-morrow. I have won over Spence entirely to your way of thinking. He says that if my plan was (at all) to resign in August he thinks that is probably time enough to think about resigning if Cornelius is still disposed to resist it, so that I have the advantage of pursuing my own policy & carrying Spence along with me. A great deal depends upon Cornelius. I will write you after I see him. I shall not *mention* next August perhaps as any time of decision, nor perhaps will I *intend* any such epoch but I think by that time I shall *long* for scholastic life. *I love you Sally.* Your letter has just come. God bless you.

Yours aftly
Jno Miller

[marginal notes] I agree in your counsels entirely & shall not act in haste.

I am not mad, most noble Sally.

Colalto
Thursday Augt 23. 1855

My *dear* John

Does Mr Dungan tell Spencer that the disaffection among your people is at all formidable? Is your "unpopularity" wide spread in the Congregation? You know, I told you Mrs. Graham heard (I suppose from the Howells) "that you preached over the heads of the people", and therefore I am not surprised at the charge Dungan makes against you—but the thing is, do *many* thus complain of you? If comparatively *many* do, then it seems clear you should leave your post;—if the number is small, then let the majority rule. No Pastor is ever universally acceptable; and if you should be weak enough to allow 40 dissentients out of a charge of 400, if they be of the ordinary mixed kind—good, bad & mediocre,— turn you away from your parish I should think you very weak. Where you can please 360 people, I think you may afford to be without influence over the remaining forty.

However I know too little of such matters to be relied upon at all for an opinion.

12. Charles Bird Dungan (1813–1888), the treasurer of the Northern Liberties Gas Works in Philadelphia. A joint owner with Robert Cornelius of the land on which the West Arch Street Presbyterian Church was built, he and Cornelius each contributed $50,000 to the building fund.

I think John you are a little unfair to Dungan: I thought so when you were here. I dont like *temporizing* with anybody; but there is so much of misconception & mistake as to peoples motives and conduct, that being *very* <u>slow</u> to judge unfavorably is, I think, in the main, a good rule. Spence's letter placed Dungan rather favorably before me, and your report of his interview with Spence as related by him, is still more acceptable to me. If he had, at all concurred in the opinions he says others in your Church hold, then he might be somewhat suspected, but as he not only disclaims them, but expresses others very strongly opposed to them, he is placed in the attitude of one who is rather reluctantly telling of a state of things that he regrets. Now if this be true of him, then he seems to me entitled to no small consideration. With your feelings to him, you ought *never* I think to be specially confidential with him but you can be & ought to be friendly & considerate. He is, as an Elder in such close connection with you, that you ought to be as harmonious as possible.

I am glad you have made an ally of Spence, with his string of curt sentences that come across a body like so many chain shot.[13] By the by John how does "Ward" come on, & a certain "little apple-faced lady" of whom I have heard?

Jimmy Carrington & John Preston came down yesterday to pay me a visit.[14] They go off this afternoon, when I shall be entirely alone Cantey & Lilly having gone down this morning to Bent's to see his Sister. I enjoy the absolute quiet astonishingly, and am almost, if not quite, inhospitable in my wrath at having it invaded.

I am impatiently waiting to hear more from your people. My own arrangements a good deal depend upon what you write me.

This is a sad anniversary to me. Just four years to-day since my Father died; and my mind goes back & brings again the scene of suffering and sorrow as vividly as if it had but just transpired. These 4 years have scattered us as a family; and one more will find none here to bear the name, or own the home that then belonged to us. *Dear* Me! I wish I was in Heaven. And yet, John I love you enough to make earth only too attractive to me just now.

Why dont you make your throat behave? What makes you talk so much as to irritate it? Never mind when I get to Phil, I shall do the week-days talking; & will do it especially well since you compliment me by intimating that the reasons my "trains of thought" run so rapidly is because they are not (like yours?) heavily freighted! But you'll put up steam & carry your load—["]*oh me! it is so heavy!*—a little faster, wont you!"

There is no disputing the fact:—we do suit admirably. Was there ever such a nicely adjusted pair.—*I've* got all the weight of body, whilst you have all the weight of mind! Well—goodbye. Write me a nice letter—love me with all your

13. Two cannonballs or half balls connected by a chain. Used especially in naval warfare to bring down masts and sails.

14. John Preston (1836–1880), the son of McDowell's uncle John Smith Preston (1809–1881) of South Carolina.

heart—behave yourself with great propriety & prudence, and believe me to be "so much yours that I am scarcely my own."

S.C.P. McDowell

Colalto
Saturday, Aug. 25. 1855

My *dear John*,

Of course, you know you don't deserve a letter, but I write you one because if I pass this mail I cant write again until Tuesday.

I was confident of getting a letter from you this morning that would give me some better knowledge of your troubles in Phil, and some information as to your management of them, and some idea of what was ahead of us. But I got no letter of any kind, and am rather troubled at it, tho' not, in the least disposed to find fault with you about it.

Mr Massie came over last night to relieve my loneliness and sat until 11 o'clock. I was pretty tired, but his visit was very kind. He told me Judge Brockenbrough had talked to him about our matter very approvingly, and said, "well if I could approach Mrs M D I would urge her to an immediate marriage". I was glad to have his distinct avowal in favor not only because as a Judge his opinion carries weight, but because his chivalrous Eastern Virginia sentiments, are worth a good deal. By the bye did you ever receive his card? I hear that he called on you—tho' there may have been some mistake.

I asked James Taylor yesterday why he hadn't been to see you, and he gave me this reply and desires I would report it to you. When you first came he was unusually busy with his country practice; after some days, however, when he had leisure, he went several times to see you but always found you out, & would not leave a card as he wished to see & apologize when he met for what seemed want of attention at the beginning.

James writes me he has been very unwell for several weeks: confined all that time to his room & a part of it to his bed. His health has been delicate for five or six years; his system never having recovered tone or strength since an attack of Cholera in 48 or 9; and I am always uneasy when I hear of him being sick. He wants my home, but the more I think of it, the less I am disposed to sell it to any one. If I can keep it so that it will not bring me in debt, I think it will be best. The accidents of life are so many that a home kept in reserve may be found in the future to have been very wise.

I would give a great deal for a nice long talk with you this pleasant, quiet morning. I begin already to hunger for it, and am quite sure that I love you with more animation & warmth now than when we parted. I think of you coming home wearied and worried and dispirited from your walks and talks and visits to your people, and wish I was there to lessen or lighten your cares by my sympathy. If you were too tired to talk to me, why, I could talk to you; if you were too troubled to listen, then I could be sympathizingly silent; if you were vexed with all the world and believed every man's hand turned against you, and would not be reasoned into any better opinion, why,—what could I do then? In such an extreme case would there be any virtue in a "candy wabbit"? Could it sweeten any of life's ills in a gloomy moment?

I foolishly linger over my letters to you, forgetting the *foolishness* in the mere pleasure of the sort of chat they give.

Now I think of it let me say—dont take the tumbler I gave you to Princeton, it will seem such a ridiculous gift, but use it as a shaving-cup, or stand for your tooth-brush.

Affectionately,
S.C.P. McDowell

Princeton Aug. 25th 1855.

My *dear Sally,*

I was disappointed in dispatching a letter to you yesterday by an unlucky visitor who had the gift of continuance far beyond the mail hour.

I have to write to you now in *entire confidence*. My visit to Mr Cornelius which was most gratifying as far as my personal feeling was concerned gave me a full explanation if I had still needed it of all Mr Dungan's restless disquietude. My anxiety was entirely turned into a new channel. I find all my fears about the financial condition of the church have a foundation & that Mr Dungan is untrue to Mr Cornelius to an extent that gives me the new concern lest they quarrel & the whole matter is overturned. For example Mr C. reminds me that Mr D. was to have borne the larger share of the pecuniary burden & that $30.000 which he at last promised to provide was to be fully matched & made sufficient by larger provisions on the fact of Mr D. & that instead of that he has been obliged to pay $37.000 & that Mr D. is casting everything upon him. He also tells me that when he writes & asks for information about the whole thing Mr D. replies in such a way as would satisfy many people (Mr C. says) of its being a reply to the question presented. "But," says Mr C. "I see that it is not, but only a skilful turning aside from the whole matter. And I *dont* think that either gentlemanly or honest; do you"? He tells me also that he finds that Mr D. has encouraged at least one person (a Mr Henry)[15] to subscribe on the subscription to the church merely "so as to give his name" without intending to pay & yet the subscription list was brot to Mr C. as all valid. Mr D. keeps away from him also & leaves all the bills to be brought to him.

You may know how this surprises & enlightens me. I understand now if I did not understand before all Mr D's movements & intrigues & tho' I mean

15. Probably Alexander Henry (1823–1883), a Philadelphia attorney and rising politician who was elected the city's mayor in 1858.

sedulously to keep out of all *appearance* even of antagonism (unless it is forced upon me) yet it changed the entire question before my mind. It makes it to be now, whether I will consent to retain the church, not whether I think the church ought to be expected to retain me;—in other words as everything now depends upon the good nature of Mr Cornelius, whether I will meet the risk of a quarrel & financial explosion.

Mr C. when I unfolded before him my reasonings spoke pointedly of the conduct in making my marriage a consideration in the case & agreed with me that now was not the right time even to *consider* the matter of a resignation; nay he advised me to leave the question entirely open & not even to consider such a step *in my own mind* till I had occupied the church several months.

I told him however that as Mr D. was an active & untiring man his behaviour in the case was particularly formidable & that on finding the condition of things I felt afraid to marry & bring a wife to such a financial scene of disquietude. I asked if he would, as my personal adviser, take time to look into the whole state of the affair & tell me whether with perfect security to yourself & me I could marry & occupy the new church without danger from Mr D's influence for another year leaving the question undecided. He undertook this cheerfully. I am to see him on Tuesday. Nothing could be kinder than his own opinions. And as I now see the Church must be ruined but for his *prodigious* liberality to complete I feel that it is particularly proper to consult him. Reinboth had just come from Dungan's cottage at Cafe May when he saw Spence & Cornelius tells me that the whole disaffection has its centre in D. and now as his financial methods are such as C. mentions you can understand the whole thing.[16] M & A. are well. God bless you.

Yours affly
JM.

[marginal note] I have read your letter to Mother & like it much. She herself pronounced it excellent. I wish I could see you. I have not time to read over this letter before the mail which is very early.

Phil. Aug. 27th 55.
Monday.

My *dearest Sally,*

I came back from Princeton this morning & am now settled in my study ready for my first service which is on Wednesday night. Your charity for Dungan will not I am afraid, cover all his sins for in addition to those you will have heard of by this time fr: Mr Cornelius there are occurring to me now every little while in the memory of the past months, proofs that I am able to put together of his being untrue to me.

16. Joseph D. Reinboth, Philadelphia real estate businessman and member of Miller's congregation.

However I will not revive that matter at any length till my next letter. I see Mr C. tomorrow & what he tells me will then help me in entering upon the whole decision. I will write to-morrow evening.

The point I find most difficulty with is this. Suppose I stay as I incline now very much to do till next August after marrying this Fall; & suppose we secure a perfectly comfortable reception & position in the city as concerns our marriage, & a comfortable year's labour & residence in the pastorship of the church till the expiration of the year, & then resign, how can I be sure of making you safe from embarrassment in the interval that occurs between that & some quiet settlement in my peculiar studies? Dungan I now know so well that I have little hope that he will behave in a way that I can endure longer than this year & indeed I am now pressingly anxious about the whole finances of the church. They depend entirely upon Cornelius. However, dearest Sally, I will not anticipate to-morrow's deliberations. Write me fully your own opinions whenever you write.

The dog lived at the first house to the right after leaving the woods on the road that crosses the Covington turn-pike just before it descends from the mountain on which you got out to take that view. But, Sally, how foolish Dr T. is. Do not dogs bite people every day. It is one of the commonest of accidents & yet how often does any one go mad? I wish my throat was as sound as my limb even after my black friend had paid his respects to it.

By the way I have not answered your question. Mr D. did *not* say to S. that *many* were disaffected. He mentioned some others than Hall & Martin with whom he is in constant intercourse.[17] I have no reason to believe in *any* general disaffection. If it exists the persons do not express it to me in any way.

I hear that Dr Backus in passing thro' here lately spoke of my marriage to Dr Leyburn & said that he had not the remotest doubt of its propriety, & quoted Dr. Hodge in defence of it.[18]

You dont know how my heart went out after you all the time I was in Princeton & with my little children. I so pray & long that we might be clustered altogether. Oh, if I could begin my divings into ethics at once with all of us sheltered in a snug home in P. what a charm life would wear. Give my love to Lilly & to others who may be with you. Take a great deal of it for yourself my darling darling Sally, for I am

yours most fondly & devotedly.
JM

P.S. Take care in the hesitations that are occurring in our plans that I do not defraud you of your regular Fall sowing. You will have to set Morgan to work in time even if it be still as your overseer or else you will lose a year's revenue of your farm. Dont take my tho't of buying the place into any immediate account,

17. Wilfred Hall, agent for the American Bible Society in Philadelphia, and Joseph W. Martin, a banker, were members of Miller's congregation.
18. John Chester Backus (1810–1884), pastor of First Presbyterian Church, Baltimore.

but in consultation with Col Reid. Do the very best with the farm irrespective of any such plan of mine. Either rent, sell, or hold just as strikes you but for the property I have tho't too that you would have to be careful even of your *words* to Morgan for he might begin to sow & then claim that you had promised to rent to him & that even before you had mentioned any conditions. But, Darling I know all this you have thot.

[marginal note] Dr Leyburn begged me to say when I write that Welch the engraver has seen him two or three times & seems very impatient to hear from you.[19]

Colalto
Tuesday, Aug: 28. 1855

My *dear John*,

Perhaps I dont fully understand, yet it does not seem to me that, should the financial affairs of the Church turn out to be just as bad, or even worse than you now fear, this is the time for you to give up. As long as there was no doubt of the Church getting on well:—no doubt of its being a work fully established you might freely consider the question of remaining, or quitting it; but since the whole enterprize is jeopardized by Dungan's faithlessness, and likely to fall thro' just at the moment you were "going up to possess the land," I *wouldn't* abandon it. If Cornelius *could* and *would* assume Dungan's subscription, & by a sale of the pews or other means, be secured against the ultimate loss of it, would it not be best to so arrange it & thus throw D— overboard? Or if, which would be better 30 persons could be found, who would pay $1000 each, & thus liberate Mr Dungan. But even if he was released from the money pressure he suffers under just now, he would still be an elder and have power to annoy and injure you, and this money trouble will always give him the *wish* or any how the *will* to use it. But you could put up with that for a year or so, especially if an explosion between he & Mr Cornelius should enlighten the public as to his (D's) Motives.

One thing I am very anxious about—and that is, that you should not do or say any thing that wd give the slightest ground for suspicion of your having had any hand in fomenting or furthering a quarrel between these two men. Dungan, who seems absolutely unreliable, might suspect you of it—or lead others to do it—& his conversation with Spence be given as the cause of your hostility to him. Let them fight over their money matters if they are bent upon it,—but you keep out of the fight. You are so circumstanced that I doubt whether you could even attempt to be a peacemaker between them, as one standing in your relation to them ought, under other circumstances to do. Such a mistake it was, to have such large contributors. It was a fact of ill omen to me when I first heard of the church.

---

19. Thomas B. Welch, engraver, of Philadelphia.

Do you think Spence will be prudent and say nothing about Mr Dungan's communication to him? Anticipating an explosion it seems to me that policy as well as propriety demands entire—the deadest silence on the part of your family about this man and his movements.

I cant bear that the Church should fall thro' just now. I feel all the shame of those "who began to build and were not able to finish",[20] and if aught can be gained by hanging to it, I would not think of giving it up. If you hold to it you might, at least, purchase in that way a little delay for its recuperation; if you give up, might that not accelerate its downfall. Mr Cornelius by his personal friendship & munificence to the Church demands something of you, but God forbid that considerations of such a nature should shape your course, as a Minister of the Gospel.

My dear John you need to be circumspect and prudent in your difficulties—I hope you seek diligently for the only true wisdom, and seek it from the unfailing Source of all Wisdom.

Wouldn't Cornelius *lend* the money you need to finish the Church, & give Dungan time to mend his finances? But Dungan is a dangerous man to have a large pecuniary interest in the thing & if he were out of it altogether, it would be best in every point of view. But don't you have any hand in getting him out.

I write in a hurry this morning, and not very intelligibly I fear.

How is your throat? Quite well again? Write as often as you can. Col Reid not yet returned. I want very much to see you. Shall I write again to your Mother?

With all my heart Yours
S.C.P. McDowell

Phil. Aug. 29th 1855[21]

My *darling Sally.*

I have had my important interview with Mr C. It was long & full & turned out just as I anticipated. I spread before him all my difficulties & told him my greatest was a fear to injure a church which depended now so entirely upon his particular contributions. He gave me what I verily believe are his honest convictions—that my judgment about postponing the question of resigning was decidedly judicious—that it met both his judgment & his preference—that he had formed an opinion of my preaching which he still had no cause to change— that he did not wish to "force open the rose-bud" as he expressed it prematurely to see how it was growing, but wished to wait the natural course of events for his judgment of our success—that Dungan was acting very improperly—that he was *sure* he was now wrong in other things in his relations with him & hence was quite prepared for these steps about me—& that he was quite unchanged in the

---

20. Luke 14:30.
21. The date was actually Aug. 28, 1855.

advice he had all along given me [to] go on actively in my work & make every arrangement for entering the church.

He told me one thing that provoked me—that one of the ladies of his connection had heard among the ladies of the church, "that Mr M. was going to marry a lady who had been divorced whose husband was still living & *that the session were going to try him for it*". This could only have sprung from one quarter in existing circumstances & tho' I still am not willing to give D. up as an honest man yet I fear he is a desperate intriguer when under financial difficulty. Mr C. tells me what I did not know before that while I was in Va the work on the church actually stopped, D. failing in his part of the payments & failing to tell him of the difficulty & that it was then that he told the painter to draw on him whenever he required. Dungan has avoided him lately, so he tells me. I am only giving you his own statements, & tho' I feel the wisdom of your caution yet I cant help giving D. up as a man to be relied on.

On the other hand Mr C. says that he (Mr C.) has prospered unprecedently in his business & is willing to complete the church (alone if need be) that $20 or $30.000 more or less he feels it to be his duty not to consider & that the early expenses of the church, *which he does not expect to be met by the pews at once* he is ready to manage.[22] He gave me counsel also as to my interview with D. advised me to conciliate him but told me that if he *directly advised* a resignation (which he knew he would not) he would tell him that others differed from him & not be impressed by it. He told me that if I were his son he would assure me that my own state of mind as I unveiled it to him contemplating a marriage in Nov. & a continuance in the parish was judicious & right. He could not have said more. $40.000 he contemplates giving & $20.000 more if needed & that whatever Mr D. may do on his side. He could not tell me how much Mr D. had given. I infer somewhere about $20.000. When I told him of your advice that I should look solely at the church he told me he did so in saying that "he wished the rose-bud to be allowed to bloom as it was"—that he had provided a certain kite string for his kite & ["]he wished to fly it with no other" & then when I pressed the question upon him as to his own motives in the case he said it was not from friendliness that if I were an entire stranger to him he would give me the same advice & think it for the interest of the church. What could I expect more from him?

Now I must see D. & when I have had that interview I will write you my judgment. Write me from time to time what *you* think, and be diligent in your business arrangements for I suppose whatever the time of our marriage you have now pretty much the same things to do. I would have my own judgment fully formed tonight (& it is nearly formed) were it not for these ugly proofs of my *danger* in Dungan's hands. Of him my fear is greater than it was. Yet fear may hold *him* too. Let us pray for divine direction. The "trial" has not in it a particle of

---

22. Written crossways on the page: "Remember the secrecy of these matters."

danger & I hope soon to stop the report. Things have happened as I predicted in the main so far. Trust me as much as you can farther. Love me with all your heart—

yrs affy
JM.

[marginal notes] Make yourself as safe & clear as you can in financial matters & write me a clear report. We must try to get our sails well reefed in all respects if we are to try a difficult passage. God bless you. How I wish you were with me now.

Never doubt my love. I still say that I would continue to love you even if I could never see you again for years.

Phil: 29th Aug: 55

My *Darling,*

I ought not to write to you every day but I cant help doing it. My visit instead of dissipating the ideal I had formed of you brightens it & I love you with a passion that remorselessly follows me every moment. I wish sometimes I could shake you out of my mind.

My confidence is so shaken in the ship in which I am embarked that I feel no pleasure any more in sailing it, & tho' I am rousing myself to what fidelity I can muster for the Winter's work, yet you are all my *pleasure* & I do long after you with the most intemperate impatience to make you my wife.

I cant see Dungan (or Reinboth). He returns to town next Wednesday or Thursday. Tho' I *think* I shall keep my post this coming season (not longer) I cannot be *sure* till I have felt D's pulse & judged of how much mischief he is *able* to do me. I think he fears me & I hope he will be quiet, but that last speech in the lady's mouth which I know D. must have had a hand in takes him quite out of the list of my dependencies except as under some selfish restraint. I am sorry to speak so of a Christian but you cant understand our case unless I do. Be very careful to be profoundly silent on all these things. Having to wait as I do for a final opinion another week cant you still go on just as tho' we were certainly to be married in Nov. (without announcing etc.). Am I right in supposing that the things you have to do are the same whether we marry then or not. You know the alternative of delay is this:—If I go on (which is far the most probable) then we ought to marry. I would not consent to go on without. If I resign (which will now require very *strong* inducements since the speech I heard of from the lady I am as near decided to go on as I can be, well) then I will have to refer the question to you whether we *dare* marry till I have made the representation I intend to the Presbytery & am dismissed, have gone to Princeton & from there have fallen upon some light office that will allow me time to study & yet supplement our support. It is true that We have a hazard to run of this last kind if I stay & marry & resign next *Spring,* but then we will have more leisure to look about us, will be a year nearer to greater command of our own means, & will have a *powerful* motive for running the hazard. What think you of my reasonings? You are so skilled in reading people by their letters that I send you one of Mrs Potter's.[23]

Yours tenderly
JM.

[marginal notes] Mr Cornelius urges me not to offend D. but to keep up terms of friendliness with him & it agrees with my own judgment.

Dismiss fr your mind as the merest chimera any fear of a "trial" (or of the dog). There is a mail now, *from* your place on Monday.

Phil. Aug: 31st 55.

My *darling Sally,*

Your letter of Saturday did not reach me till yesterday thro' some mistake here. You are a kind good girl. The way you fold me to your bosom & offer me the best caresses that a letter written a hundred leagues off can convey is good beyond my deservings, but then it makes me love you with a passion that I can hardly describe. You are my own dear darling darling Sally & the idea of being separated from you after being with you so long & often is distressing beyond what I can express.

I did not get the Judge's card.

What you say about the "deadness" of the secrecy that ought to be observed about Mr D. is just after my notion. You remember from what I entrusted to you that it would be a crime as well as an imprudence if I turned any suspicion upon him.

After my visit on Wednesday next, I have no doubt that this will be the case:—I have no doubt that by passing a petty narrow ordeal of labour & risk I can keep down the discordant elements & remain by the aid of Providence comfortably till Spring. I have no doubt that that will be enough to give you all your position & to give me all the occasion to retire that my most fastidious self-respect would lead me to need. I have little doubt that I will then be led to resign. I think so first because my health will unquestionably suffer with the advance of the season. I cannot altogether eradicate that uneasiness from my throat & with the advance of my work anxiety & disgust will wear upon me by the expiration of the season. Dungan will give me more trouble after awhile & about by next March I shall begin to arrange for a departure & this season will be my closing year. Of this I feel almost sure. Then I am quite sure that philosophizing is the best work for the remainder of my life & that the sooner I set about it in a calm & perfectly arranged way the better for my usefulness & self respect. This therefore I take it is my last *full* charge if such is the pleasure of God. And therefore, by Spring or perhaps as late as August I expect the hazard

---

23. Miller enclosed a friendly note from Sarah Potter dated Aug. 28, 1855, asking for McDowell's address so she could write to her.

of that economy & straitened circumstances for a time that a resignation made in those special circumstances might be in danger to produce. And I expect my darling Sally who has been trained up in the easiest wealth with scarce a thought as to the need of forbearing in expence, may wake up & find her newly married husband out of a position & with plans of so peculiar a fixedness that he can only seek one of a peculiar character. Now what do you think of all this? Tell me again & again. Have I a right to involve a lady in such a risk? Dare I do it for my own self-respect? And if I dare, will you distinctly contemplate it & when the trial comes will you be that quiet hopeful & enduring wife which the interval before the death of my mother may very probably call you to be.

This plan carries I see some very great advantages.

But then on the other hand I have no doubt that I could resign now without any very *fatal* influence upon the good-name of either yourself or me—that I could go to Princeton—that I could begin my studies—that I could form a settled life that would be our future permanent history—that I could secure a position light enough for my arrangements of study—that when all was safe & understood we could marry & then escape all the intervening hazards & difficulties. How I would bear a year or 18 months delay I cannot say but it would cast our honey-moon before more quiet times & lead us to *begin* our life in the calmness of this "divine philosophy."

I will not tell you this time which way my own opinion turns. I wish you to write a letter of unbiased opinion. If you choose wrong I will remonstrate. Whichever way we decide the fact that you were most honestly consulted will have a fine effect upon my mind.

Reinboth I have seen. He reddened a good deal & seemed a good deal disposed to explain, but I said little to him. He intimated the idea that he felt bound to tell me of the disaffection but that he did not think the way was clear for me to act upon it in any serious way at this stage in the history of the church.

As soon as you are *certain* that you do not owe more than $15.000 dollars *in all* will you not let me know. Your debts weigh upon my mind entirely as tho they were my own.

Yrs affly
JM

Thursday, September 1. 1855[24]

My *dear* John,

I am rejoiced that Mr. Cornelius proved kind and true to you personally and to the Church. If I thought it any great praise I would say "he gives like a Prince"— but I have no opinion of the liberality of Kings and no belief in the purity of

24. This is incorrect. The date was actually Aug. 30, 1855.

their motives when they do give. But I hope our friend gives like a Christian—I wish however, it had so happened that such large contributions were not needed from one man:—but that can't be helped now.

At present, the great good to *you* derivable from Mr C's promised additions of \$20.000, is that it will free Dungan from his money pressure and *for a while* make a better elder of him. So far as you tell me, he is the only formidable opponent you have to contend with, and that because he maintains to you & preserves before others that sort of manner which prevents your breaking with him, or their penetrating his disguise. This he will continue to the end of the chapter—he is too wary and politic to do otherwise, at least, as long your knowledge of his pecuniary matters gives you a sort of power over him. If however he ever gets out of his money difficulties he will turn against you openly. For my part I wish he was—in Abraham's bosom, and his wife & children & friends and a bereaved public were already comforted by the thought that their loss was his gain. Anything wrong in that John? I think it's *right* to wish the very best we can for ourselves and others; don't you? But I pray you be wise and true in all your dealings with him. *Policy* seems highly commendable in most cases;—but somehow I cant get over the idea that it savors of duplicity. I used to hear an old song of a "false lover, who washed his '*cateful* face with 'sembling water"—which furnishes a pretty accurate description of one who, in anything acts from motives of policy alone. I think perfect frankness is likely to prove in almost every condition of things the *best policy*. Of course you will write as soon as your talk with Dungan is over.

Do you hear nothing from Williams yet? Cousin John gave me another talk about the necessity of having well-attested facts. He has just returned from Harrisonburg from a meeting of Presbytery. Our matter is as a topic of universal talk. Nobody questioning its propriety so far as he stated but Mrs Howell, if these impressions as to the existence of the facts referred to be true. William Henry Ruffner lauded you beyond all belief to Cousin John; & Dr Ben Smith is reported to say that he liked you better than any man in Phil. "But what can induce Mrs McD"—(they say,—"to give up all she really has—and that so much, and run any risk for the future?" "I don't know": said Cousin John, "but I believe it to be a desperate case of real old-fashioned love." What do think of that, Sir? Is it true?

Col Reid not yet returned. In case he refuses to become my Trustee, I shall ask Mr Lewis. He is cognizant of all my money matters anyhow, and is conversant with these particular kinds of pecuniary transactions. He is an honest & reliable man; an elder in our Church and sings thro' his nose with a power and spirit that would have caused any "Praise-God barebones" in the time of Claverhouse to have retired from the Conventicle in envious disgust and despair.[25]

25. John Graham of Claverhouse, Viscount Dundee (c. 1649–1689), Scottish royalist who repressed the conventicles in favor of episcopacy.

You are so busy I dislike to claim the fulfilment of your promise to ask a little about a suitable school for Lilly—Could I apply to your Sister for some information on this subject with propriety? She would know more than you can, & just now, be better able to attend to me.

Morgan is putting in the next year's crop. James offers to take the whole establishment and pay me $1.200 annually. I am sorry his offer only came this morning. I fancy I am bound now irrevocably for this year to Mrs Cocke for the house.

Do my letters reach you regularly and in good time? Yours come as punctually as the "St. Louis Evening News", which rain or shine, never fails to come, & rarely fails to be dull when it does come.

I *do* love you with all my heart—aint you ashamed to doubt it.

> *Affectionately,*
> S.C.P. McDowell

Saturday
Sept 1. 1855

My *dear* John,

"What think you of my reasonings?" you ask. I can not clearly make them out. I copy a string of sentences that mystify me somewhat. "If I resign, then I will have to refer the question to you whether we *dare* marry till I have made the representation I intend to the Presb'y & am dismissed; have gone to Princeton & from there have fallen upon some light office that will allow me time to study & yet supplement our support. It is time that we have a hazard of this last kind if I stay & marry & resign next Spring, but then we will have more leisure to look about us, will be a year nearer to greater command of our own means & will have a *powerful* motive for running the hazard." Now I cant make out what period this last sentence refers to—whether it will be before or after we are married that we are to have so "powerful a motive" for running such a terrible hazard. And pray tell me what "*powerful* motive" you allude to.

I have full comprehension of all reasons for delay that grow out of consider-ations of a social kind, but not much *patience even*, with those that are simply pecuniary. And yet I feel how essential it will be to you, whether as Pastor or Student, to have your mind free from money anxieties. But you are exaggerated in your ideas of what constitutes a comfortable support for such a person as I am. I *fancy* I can live upon very moderate means, tho', of course, I have had no experience of real struggle of this kind. One thing I never will do, and that I have told you before, that is, I never will live with your Mother; and that not because I have one single feeling of prejudice or unkindness, but from a conviction long entertained that law-kin in that particular relationship cannot live unjarringly under the same roof. And in our case the difficulties would be greater because of the children. I am sure you will not misunderstand me, and suspect me of any latent dislike to the dear old Lady whom you love so much. So far from any such feeling, I cant help having a tender sort of drawing to her.

As to our being in any such terrible strait, even if you should resign next Spring & have no immediate prospect of the half-occupation you want, I have no idea of it. As long as this house stands it is a home for us, which *your means* can support, if you continue to be so foolish about it. But it is very absurd in you to have such notions about my property—However—we will not talk of that.

Take good care of your throat. I dont like you find it so constantly troublesome. I wish I was near enough to take care of you. I am ashamed even to whisper to you how much I long to be with you.

I am rather restless till you write me your momentous interview with Dungan is happily over. What a man for an Elder. Perhaps, after all, he isn't quite so bad.

How long were you in Princeton? Do the children still look upon me as a sort of myth; or are they now satisfied of the reality of my being?

Do you know John I think it very queer that you never told me anything about Sam? Why don't you? Is there an apple-faced lady there too? But—I have a great deal to do. God bless you my very dear little man.

Affecly,
S.C.P. McDowell

September 1[26] [1855]
Sat. Eve.

My dearest Love,

Those fellows at Harrisonburg seem to have been in a wonderful complimentary humour. I know myself far better than to be led away by any such high talk as they seem to have been having of me. I am a little, weary old man with an elder always astride of me like a night-mare & the greatest treasure I have far off from me in the mountains.

I will attend to the school matter with great pleasure, but write to mother or Mary either or both. I should have answered that question before.

If your brother means $1200 without your stock (which I suppose is too perishable to rent) & knows exactly all he is undertaking, I should think Mrs C. if you desired it would not insist upon her bargain. I am a very poor judge tho' at this distance.

Lewis if he has more *comprehensiveness* as well as accuracy of detail may be your very man. Your trustee ought to be a man capable of getting a fair idea of all your rights.

God bless you my dear Sally.

26. McDowell dated this letter.

I preach my first sermon to-morrow for five weeks.
Good night. Yours in haste

affectionately
Jno Miller.

Colalto
Monday, Sept: 3. 1855.

My *dear John*

No man can map out his life with perfect clearness.—No man can mark out his path so as to see its end from its beginning. Reason is a sort of *lamp* only, and of course, gives but just light enough for us to take *one step* at a time. This fact, it seems to me you have entirely forgotten in making your plans. You are bent upon improving upon the old story & instead of putting on boots that step 7 *miles*, you are for donning a pair that will take in years at a stride. For my own part I'd rather walk more slowly & naturally. I'd rather step along from spot to spot as each spot was clearly pointed out. Therefore I am quite decided, that if nothing but pecuniary considerations interpose, if we are to be married at all it had better be now. I am not afraid of a struggle with straitened means. I sincerely think it would do me good. And I quite scorn the idea of estimating by dollars & cents the pain and anxiety that a delay of 12 or 18 months would occasion me. If there was any thing to be gained by the delay but more ample means for mere physical comfort, I would have not a word to say; but when that is all—& that too is sought for with an eye to *me* principally I *do* demur to it. I know I shall feel, perhaps a very great deal, the necessity that would impose a very rigid, self-denying economy upon me, but then I would be more than compensated for it all if you would gather me up in your arms & let me nestle in your heart and feel that you loved me well and warmly all the time.

I dont think I should be at all in your way, if you should resign next Spring and set about your "divine philosophy";—on the contrary, I fancy as this same philosophy is at least in the outset going to make your life rather forlorn you will be somewhat happier for having me by your side loving you very heartily, even tho' I may not love it at all. Are you answered now?

Oh John, I do wish your throat was right well. Can't you do something for it? I wish you had mine, which is larger than common anyhow, and just as strong as—as there's any need for a throat to be. But as we cant make the exchange, do take good care of your own.

Tuesday 9 a.m.

I could not see Col Reid as he was busy in Court all day, and I'm afraid I shall not see him today as it rains too much for me to go over to see him, or for him to come over here. I am inclined to believe Lewis will suit better than the Col and shall not be at all reluctant to fall back upon him.

Your Saturday's letter came last night. Also one from Annie, who by the by, I observe spells her name *Anna* which makes it no prettier than mine, and one, very kind and pleasant, from Mrs Potter.[27] I shall get them all answered in a few days.

Robert Taylor succeeded in gathering his poor wife to the Alum Spring a week ago, but he will never bring her thence alive. She has been gradually sinking since and a few days must close her history here. I am going out to see her tomorrow if the weather permits—would have gone on Sunday, but James dissuaded me from it.

Dont you think our little town very liberal—last night there was a meeting for the relief of the sick at Norfolk & P[ortsmouth] and some $5 or 600 subscribed, and old Dr William Graham offered his services as nurse if they wd send him.[28]

God bless you dear John

Affec'ly
S.C.P. McDowell

[Enclosure: Sarah Benedict Potter to Sally C. P. McDowell]

Springhurst Aug 28 '55

My dear Mrs McDowell

Sometime since Mr Miller entrusted me with a secret which inspired me with great interest in you & prompted me to write to you at once & without reserve. I felt a little doubtful, however how far I might presume upon my knowledge of a fact which had not yet transpired generally among his friends. While in this State of hesitancy I started with my Husband on a distant journey—& have only been established again in my own home within the last two weeks.

Finding that Mr Millers hopes & plans have in the meantime become public I write to say with what sincere pleasure we are looking forward to the prospect of welcoming you here & with what unaffected endearment & affection we shall number you on our list of friends.

I hope Mr Miller has long since conveyed to you an invitation with which I charged him last Spring & I would now say that when you come on we shall rely upon your accepting it. We are at our little home in the country & we hope that it will not be inconvenient for you to pass a few days there on your way North.

With my Husbands most kind & cordial regards. I am dear Ms. McDowell

Most Sincerely & affy yrs
Sarah B Potter

Phil. Sep. 4th 1855
1 1/2 o'clock

My darling Sally,

I am looking forward to the rich treat of a letter at 5. I hope it will be a loving one. You cant tell how I read over the *warm* parts of every letter. It has made my

---

27. The letter from Anna Hare Miller has not been located.
28. William Alexander Graham, M.D. (1796–1856).

afternoon seem right pleasant to me & I mean on the strength of the anticipated pleasure to push thro' a great deal of hard work.

Mr. D. I do not expect till Friday. I have no fresh facts. My congregation seem kind & pleasant & on Sunday we began our regular services. If this congregation are so largely disaffected they are the most *cordial* church to be in that condition that I know.

The other day I could hardly have dared to write to you. It blew so stiff a gale in the matrimonial line that one might have tho't everything was coming about our ears. One of my people a lady told me that every body was expressing astonishment about us & making inquiries & that there seemed a deal of anxious feeling about it. Another lady said that all thro' the summer her door had been rung at by visitors of other churches asking what it all meant; & that some Princeton people had wondered that one of *our* family who usually were so fastidious in such matters should take such a step. Did my mother sanction it? &c &c. This all happened to come at once so shrill did the storm whistle & I forebore to mention it to you lest my poor dear Sally should think the heavens were falling. But, my darling, it was just a little sort of equinoctial that particular day. At least It did not disturb my equilibrium & since then I hear nothing. People are unchanged & these very ladies quite comforted when I talk a little. I believe all I have ever said will be realized & that the very fastidiousness of which they speak will help, for I hear already of the defence set up for me by my people who dont know any of the circumstances, "Mr. Miller *must* know what he's about".

Williams, I have not heard from. I spoke of *three weeks* & I suppose he means to take that.

Nor having seen Dungan I have purposely forborne to form a fixed opinion. But the *tendencies* of my purpose are all toward what it has been before—to face down (by God's help) this movement of D. & this assault upon our marriage & to win you here if I can when we purposed. I state this now freely because *your* opinion which I hope has been unbiassed has by this time been sent off. I trust we shall be found to agree. My church will be opened about Oct. 1st. And the first excitement about it will be soon over. Choose almost any subsequent day.

I mean to be very *unreserved* in my surrender to all God seems to make my duty. I think I am honest in this, & tho' I love you passionately yet I think you will come to my arms under the very *conscious* permission & protection of a Governing Power. So let us pray that it may be.

yrs affy
JM

6 o'clock

"The *powerful* motive" I allude to is the disproving the charges of disaffection & the contradicting of the fears of Reinboth & his friend about our marriage. I meant our marriage promptly when we planned & my *not* resigning have "the powerful motive" of securing an unchallenged position.

I forget what I write from time to time but I think that my letter *last* written will have explained by this time the letter about which you write.

I was in Princeton three days & found the children about as usual. Mrs P. had paid them a long visit & spoke in high terms of their health tho' I thot they looked paler after the Summer.

Sam I will begin upon in some letter soon & go all thro' with him. He is a subject by himself.

The children seem hardly able to grasp the idea of Mrs McDowell as an actual woman but I think they are getting to it gradually.

I dont wish exactly I was in Abraham's bosom for I have a world to do yet & some books to write before I wish to go quite so far but I wish I had some of his flocks & herds, & a certain Sarah that I know of to bake cakes for me on the hearth. I think It was Abraham wasnt it that entertained angels unawares. I think I shall differ from him in doing it without any such modest ignorance.

Yours truly
the Father *of the* Faithful

Phil. Sept 5th 1855.

Dearest Sally,

Dungan came unexpectedly yesterday & I have had a long interview with him. It turned out about as I excepted, less pleasantly in some things & more safely in others. I was very prudent & said as little as I could. What was not so pleasant as I had expected was 1st that he was not *personally* as cordial as usual which is perhaps not to be wondered especially as I fancy I may have been more constrained. 2d that he did not say as R[einboth] did it would be rash to act hastily but on the contrary carefully avoided giving an opinion either way tho' my opinion is unchanged as to his really desiring at least during the present year to produce a change. 3d He wielded the matter of my marriage much more severely & pertinaciously than I expected.

Still on the other hand he professes all that he ever did, declares that he will never lift a finger to produce any other result than the successful continuance & prosperity of my labours, reiterates his intention to help me all he can & declares that he considers the whole matter entirely in my hands & a decision to resign under these discouragements must be at any time a thing entirely of my own.

The most unpleasant thing he said was a hint that three months or a year hence *might* be a more embarrassed time to leave off than now.

I cant give you much point in the talk for really it had very little. We were both on our guard. He assured me I had no personal enemy in the church & admitted the great awkwardness of any decision now.

One consequence of his exceedingly mild & at times kind expression & of his deprecating the idea of certain things of which I still suspect him was a remorse on my part for any possible wrong I may have done. I have spoken only to Mr C.

& my family, but still I will avoid *unnecessary* charges in the future. Tho' I cant very clearly retract anything I have said.

Mrs S. one of his family remarked afterward upon the goodness of our audience on Sabbath & seems I think unaffected with opposition; & this talk with D. is the last *means* I am going to wait for for forming my judgment.

Now as to the judgment itself it is nearly formed. It waits only for one of my periods of *serious* & more *prayerful* reflection to "become a law." *It is that we alter our plan not one particle.* I have no serious fear that the searchings of that particular time of devotion will change it; & I think you may reflect upon it as almost certain to be my plan. Now will you consent to it? Will you marry me as soon after the last of October as you intended & will you write fixing the wedding-day at least making a project of one in view of the fact that the tho't I still wish conscientiously to give within a few days will almost certainly be as I have stated. I cannot give my reasons for my judgment for I write in haste but they are the old ones why next Spring is a *far* better time if I resign than now.

> Yours most *affly*
> in haste
> Jno Miller.

I am closing so hastily because I am preparing a lecture. My judgment seems to form itself with *great decisiveness* tho' it beckons me to a path which is certainly the most narrow & precarious that I ever walked upon. Let us pray that God will help us. One safety I ought to seek is to be very prayerful & faithful to my duties.

Lexington
Thursday Sept: 6. 1855

Dear John,

Having written my answer to Annie I was a little troubled about her address. I did not like to have it lie for days in the Office in Phil, and so I conclude to enclose it to you.

I haven't a single word to say this morning. I am as stupid as a heavy head and a pair of painful eyes can make me. A lowering sort of head-ache since yesterday morning has unfitted me for any real work by affecting my eyes very painfully.

We are as quiet as can be. Nothing has specially excited us except the announcement James makes today of the advent of another James McDowell.[29] This is pleasant news to me.

In the fuss other lady friends choose to make about your marriage what does your friend of the white cravat say?

I wrote yesterday to your Sister about Miss Giles' school for Lilly.[30]

29. James McDowell V (1855–1856).
30. Mary Harvey Gill operated a school for young women in Philadelphia. Mary Miller responded on Sept. 8, 1855, recommending especially the school's "religious influence."

I don't know how to tell you how much I love you. I am almost ashamed to come to a full confession; and besides you must be tired of the old story told in the same old phrases. Anyhow I love you a very, very great deal—if that be news to you then I hope it is pleasant.

Yours
S.C.P. McDowell

Fr. (Sept 7)[31] [1855]

Dear Sally,

I [am] very busy to-day. I must tho' tell you one or two things. Your letter that I have just received is one of the pleasantest I ever broke open. I am rejoiced by it beyond what I can tell you. Go on now & get everything ready for our bans & I hope we will be very happy.

I say this—tho' I ought not to talk quite so unreservedly when at our communion which is on Sun. I mean specially to ask counsel of God in this matter, but every day leads me to think that the decision must eventuate as I have said & I can hardly see how it can otherwise. I will write about it my Monday's mail.

Mr. Gerhard (husband of Anna S., Mrs. Wise's sister) called on Bp Potter lately & asked about our marriage.[32] The Bp explained it with great decision. I saw him yesterday & thanked him & spoke for the first time of the matter. He is very firm & Mrs. P. renews her invit. to her house *in the* city for from what G says she thinks she will be there before we marry, that is bef. Nov:

I am encouraged in my church as I begin to labor. My throat was well till— to-day.—troubles me a little not much.

Dear dear Sally: I wish I could see you "juss a minnit" as Ally says.

Yrs affly.
JM.

Lexington
Friday Sept. 7 1855.

My dear John,

Cant you tell me *what* Dungan said about our marriage? I am glad you are safely thro' with him; but what did he mean by your "possibly finding it more awkward 3 months or a year hence to resign than now"? I wish I could understand all you say, and all other people say just at first, and not have to write back for explanations. I most forget what I wanted by the time the explanations return.

Mr Lewis called while I was at breakfast this morning to settle up a worrying account between Mary, Nib, & myself & to look after my Guardian's account.

31. McDowell added this date later.
32. Benjamin Gerhard (1812–1864), a Philadelphia attorney. His wife was Anna Sergeant, the sister of Sarah Sergeant Wise.

Whilst he sat here, I almost made up my mind to ask him to become my Trustee, yet I thought I would wait & take a fuller talk with Cousin John about his fitness for such an office. He is conversant already with the main part of my business; is conscientious and accurate & efficient as an accountant; is well-judging and observant as a business man & I think I fancy him altogether more than Col Reid. Cousin John prefers him he told me this evening to the Col; who of late years, he says, has become somewhat negligent & very dilatory about business matters. The weather has been so bad that I could not have seen the Col except by a great effort before today & my wavering in Lewis' favor determined me not to seek an interview with him. I think now I will fix upon Lewis & engage him if possible at once. He is our lawyer Davidson's Uncle & they have their offices in the same building, &, in our matters assist each other.

I have been disappointed heretofore in making my visit to poor Eliza Taylor at the Alum; but Mr Massie drives me over tomorrow morning. Hence I scratch off a line tonight. Next week I am going to make a desperate effort to see Uncle William, who has declined making me a visit. I shall be absent 3 or 4 days only. I am too busy to leave home. One of my servants, has been sick too for 10 or 12 days. During her sickness Lilly & I have done the chief part of the cleaning up of our room—in which service to tell the truth, I am no novice.

My courage flags at the prospect of quitting here—"for good"—I can't help having a sort of shudder at it, but I shudder a thousand fold more at the idea of giving you up. Why cant you love me all the time & come & pay me a visit every summer & just let me live here. But no; I really would not like to think of *living here* all my life. I shall follow your fortunes as courageously and cheerfully as possible.

Tell me, how much time can you give for despatching the actual marriage ceremony? A week? Send me a programme of the affair.

Take care not to excite Dungan's suspicions as to your faith in his peculiar matters—& that for the reason, that you are reliable, & ought not *so appear* to be otherwise.

I haven't quite shaken off my headache, but am just sick enough to be irritable and uncomfortable. Good night.

Affectionately Yours
S.C.P. McDowell

Monday,
Sept. 10th 1855

Do you know, John, I am really mad every time I think of our last famous drive. I thought you a heedless, reckless sort of driver then and felt a little unsafe all the time; but I am fully convinced now that you were too careless. Dont you know that little bay horse is given to running off! Just the other day Professor White barely succeeded in extricating himself from the buggy when the horse, (that same one) started off at full speed down the street and ran a mile or more.[33] Now, I have two reasons for being mad with you—first *fright* always makes me mad; and then, I attribute your heedlessness to the influence of that Philosophy of yours, which I plainly see, will be the death of us yet. I expect to wither away under its "divine" influence until for some month preceding the actual passing off, I shall have nothing left but a pair of staring eyes & a scolding tongue.

Mr Massie drove me over Saturday to the Alum. I found Robert improved by the water and fresh air; but Eliza, poor thing, looking shockingly, and apparently, just living. She has lost all interest in everything—even in her children who are separated from her. And yet, ill as she is, and as much as she labors for breath Robert cannot make her comprehend the danger she is in.

I thought of going up tomorrow to see Uncle Wm, but cannot. Perhaps I may go on Wednesday taking Paul Morton & Robert Carrington as a sort of bodyguard.[34] I cannot well spare even the three days the visit will take, for I am very busy getting Lilly ready for school. She objects to going on the first of next month with James, and I'm afraid I'll have to go with her. It will be rather awkward, but I hardly know how to avoid it.

I'm a good deal troubled about Tom. He writes despondingly & as if dissatisfied. I never did like him to be where he is, but James & his Uncle thought their heads wiser than mine. As Tom referred his difficulties to his brother, I wrote some days ago urgently stating my objections to his continuance with Uncle Tom, hoping that he (James) wd adopt them. Not so however. Yesterday he replies to me that Tom had better stay where he is at present. I am mad about it out & out; and am well-nigh determined to write to Tom urging him to come here for awhile; & to Uncle Tom giving fully and fairly all my objections to Tom's remaining with him. Don't you think that will be right? I *cannot* be quiet and see that boy just losing time and character between the pre-occupation of his Uncle & the want of judgment in his brother, neither of whom have had half the anxiety, or feel half the interest in him that I do. I wish you could help me even by a suggestion; but, of course, you cannot. We, Sisters, all feel alike about Tom, and we are right, but the *power* is not in us. I think *men* as a general rule are much less straightforward & independent than women, and are more given to temporizing:—and at this moment, I incline to the belief that they not only have less sense, but in fact have no sense at all.

I met, to my great surprise, at the Alum the other day, Frank Etting—the son of a Jew in your City, who was one of our party from Newport 2 years ago.[35] He & Tom & Cantey quarrelled & fussed during all our journeyings, and poor Frank

33. James Jones White (1828–1893), professor of Greek at Washington College and son of William S. White, McDowell's pastor.

34. Paul Carrington Morton (1837–?) was the oldest of the seven sons of William Booker Morton. He and Robert G. Carrington (1836–?) were students at Washington College.

35. Frank Marx Etting (1833–1890), a Philadelphia lawyer, was the son of Benjamin Etting and Harriet Marx.

has no one to like him specially, tho' Anna & I were always civil.[36] He stepped up just as I was leaving the Alum to regret having but a moment to see me, "but," said he "I hear we are soon to have you in our City." If he had said he expected me to take a balloon ascension I could not have been more stunned. Do you know his family? I never saw his Father; but his Mother belongs to the Marx's of Richd, who are extremely well-bred, well-informed agreable people:—originally wealthy, but now poor, & old & as ugly as only Jews & especially Jewesses *can* be.

I don't much expect one, yet hope I may have a letter from you tonight, & therefore leave this half page for a paragraph after it comes. But before I stop, allow me to say that I think you have shocking taste in the matter of envelopes. Your writing, rather fantastic than artistic at best, is much disfigured by the running of the ink in these tough paper envelopes and sometimes when Mr Massie happens to see one, I dont wonder he exclaims "Well! That's dreadful for a lover!" I say "Yes it's very bad;" but then while near the air of entire satisfaction with is very badness; which is only about four-fifths true.

Tuesday 7 1/2 A.M.

No letter—Well no matter, I shall have one tomorrow. I had one from your Sister, very kind, only a wee bit formal.[37] What think you of the enclosed scrap— The weather is intensely warm for 10 AM till 9 PM: how is it with you?

I have no news, except that I love you very much. I had almost said, extravagantly.

Yours aff'ly
S.C.P.McD.

Sept 10th 1855.

My darling Sally,

I am in the habit where anything grave is to be determined of submitting it to a sort of test. I go into my study & lock myself in & spend the whole day till dinner in prayer & thought. I bring myself first to feel sure *that I am willing to do right* & really *want to know* what is the path that God would approve. I then beg that the result of that morning's thought may be the will of God as directly as the Old Testament Urim & Thummim.[38] And I have *great faith* that an honest desire to do right followed up by such a methodical period of reflection always succeeds in its end & absolutely obtains the direction of God.

Now my judgment *clearly* is *to go on in my church & to marry you as soon as you will permit.* This judgment seems conclusive & final & is reached with an

36. Probably Anna Maria Saunders Preston (1825–1911), the second wife of McDowell's "Uncle Tom."

37. McDowell enclosed a letter from Mary Miller dated Sept. 7, 1855. She mentioned family illnesses, recalled her visit to Lexington the previous summer, and commented sadly on the yellow fever epidemic in Norfolk.

38. A primitive oracular device for discovering God's will.

accumulated certainty which makes me almost sorry that I ever showed you the letters. However I am *not* sorry. I am glad that you have passed with me thro' all the questioning.

I saw Mr. Cornelius just now & he seemed anxious to hear from me & *most manifestly* relieved & satisfied when I told him what I had determined. I am very sure from his manner that he at least is cordially pleased.

Now, Sally, our wedding day! Only think of it! Will we ever be so happy! May I really consider you in love with me, & say *we* instead of *I?* The people seem cordial. Our Lecture Room is full. And those I meet seem uninfluenced by D. When will you marry me? Now that it is settled I am troubled with this other devil of hungry impatience.

Let me congratulate you on another James McDowell. May the mantle of his grand-father rest upon him.

I enclose Wm's old letter of which I spoke.[39] I have no new one. *This* is pretty strong: tho' written carelessly with no dream that I cared to know.

My brother Sam took the first honor in college—studied law—practiced—became a Xtn—studied for the ministry & is settled in Mt Holly. To rival Bp. Doane who was educating the Quaker children of that region he established a Pres[byteria]n school & when he found teachers incompetent he entered it himself—very much to the annoyance of Father who thought his preaching enough for him & very much to the discomfort of all of us who find him harrassed & worn down & failing to accomplish all he should in his parish.[40] We seldom see him because he is so immersed. He is a bachelor older than Spence—larger & better looking than I am. I think Sam is very pious, but he's very stubborn too: tho' he & I are fond of each other. I dont mean to bother you now with any more questions of casuistry unless Providence forces them upon me. Good-bye. Dont injure your health by over exertion of any kind & be ever what I am to you your true lover

JM.

I trust you that you dont speak to any one of disaffection with D. or the others.

Phil. Sept. 11th 1855.

Poor darling cross little Sally,

Come here & let me kiss you.—What makes you in such a bad humour?—There;—poor dear darling, what makes you "feel so bad."

There; *there*—Dont stir, Sally.—Dont it make you feel better, to have my hand all thro' your hair, over your temples, & my arm round & round you? You dont deserve it—you bad wicked girl.

39. This letter from John Williams of Frederick has not been located.
40. "Xtn" is an abbreviation for Christian. George Washington Doane (1799–1859), Episcopal bishop of New Jersey.

What did Dungan say? Why he said, He was *so* afraid things might be said to hurt your feelings if you came. To which I replied that I had no fear of the sort but a strong certainty the other way; & when he still harped upon the idea, I said I *did* feel annoyed this much, that a lady so accustomed to respect should even be spoken of as in danger of anything different & that among my own people; but that I had no fear of the sort.

The fact is, Dungan is in bad health & I cant tell in what degree of other distress. I feel badly about him, always checking myself for whatever I have said & yet unable to think differently. *I think him a good man* & yet for many months he has been to me a sort of Pharaoh expecting as Cornelius expressed it lately impossible results to be achieved thro' a failure of looking at things exactly as they are. I feel greatly strengthened. It becomes me to be modest & distrustful of myself. But I *doubt* whether I have not made too much of all this difficulty. I would think so more confidently if it were not for D's power along with the elders whom he must more or less influence still to do mischief.

D's remark about the awkwardness 3 mos hence was suggested by *mine*. I told him I could not consider his informations in that talk five months ago because it was an awkward time, when he rather tryingly suggested that if disaffection existed & my marriage added to it might it not be *more* awkward at some future time. It was not a threat on his part & yet I confess I don't understand him. May God keep me from wronging him. He is a poor sick looking man & has done noble actions. Pray that I may [be] kept from all unnecessary judgments.

Well—my cross sweetheart—you know I always told you you would do better if you kept me at a distance. What if they open a bombardment upon your husband as a heretic & cut off his supplies & he is looked upon for 15 years as a poor brain-struck visionary as Kant was, What then? Will that be leaving Lexington "for *good?*" So there, my dear little cross darling, I agree—"I will love you all the time & come & pay you a visit every summer & just let you live where you are" *till*, but here is *your* promise, I have made myself worthy of a marriage & then you are to marry me. And yet do you know, my dear Darling, that I think myself worthy of you now. I have the greatest boilings of the highest sort of pride. If I were to tell you all I mean one day to do, even you would be ashamed of me. And if I were to tell you how *easy* & *confident* some of the feelings of mine were in the midst of the strokes of Providence you would think me far more enthusiast than Xtn. Well, Sally, I cant help it. You are a lady who must take your husband if you take him at all, & make the best of him; & therefore it is that I am always standing at the gateway of my humility with your "free papers" & giving you the benefit of your last & uttermost misgiving.

Still, Sally, let me give you a programme of our wedding. If we dont need it it will answer for somebody else. How will it do to be married some Wednesday. I can take a week for it. i.e. I can leave home on Monday & spare till next Monday. Whether we shall be married morning or night depends upon your house. Shall we stay in it or not after the wedding. If we return at once then it should be before stage time in the forenoon. Now, Sally, you fill out the rest. I would rather kiss you than write you a letter. So then if you were here in spite of all your crossness & wry faces I'd bid you goodbye that way my own _dear darling_ Sally.

JM.

Lexington
Wednesday Sept 12. 1855

My _dear John_,

I have had much worry and repeated disappointments about my Botetourt trip; but I think I shall get off tomorrow morning at 8, so I write you a note to-night.[41] That is, I am attempting to write in the midst of the noise & talking & singing that Cantey & Lilly are at.

I have been reluctant all along to engage Mr Lewis, or anyone else as my Trustee until our marriage was absolutely settled, and the time for it approaching. There was, manifestly, no propriety in employing a Trustee, when his duties as such could not commence for 12 or 18 months. But when I received your letter of Monday I determined to send over for him & engage him as Trustee as soon, of course as the marriage is over; and as Agent from this time till then. I accordingly sent for him this afternoon; but unfortunately he was not at home. I suppose he has gone to the Alum Spring for his Wife who has been a pitiable invalid for years. This delay is not so bad however—for he already has Lilly's accounts in his hand. I left a message for him to come over early Monday morning.

And now, John, what do you say to the fourteenth of November for our wedding-day? I observe it comes on Wednesday. You can leave Phil. Monday night, get here Tuesday night, sign that famous settlement Wednesday morning, & be married that night. Or, if you prefer it, rest all of Wednesday & be married Thursday morning. In either case could you spend the remainder of the week here? If not, then could you leave home the Friday before, and be married Monday, the 12th, and leave here the next day. I cannot think of an earlier day—indeed we may have to change to one a week or two later. The coming on of Synod the last of October makes a serious break in my time.

The servants are uneasy & anxious about their fate. I dont know what to do with them. Malinda continues very feeble & I am growing apprehensive of her recovery. These sudden and powerful changes make apparent to us every now & then some of the heavy evils of slavery. I am gratified by their interest and liking for you. I stood some days ago talking to Mary, when she rather suddenly broke in upon her talk by say "I forgot my manners Ma'am, have you heard from Mr Miller, & is he well?" And Jenny too asks after you, & this morning rather called me to account for hiding those Daguerre's of the children. She had looked all about for

---

41. McDowell refers to her trip to see her uncle William Preston, who was staying near Fincastle in Botetourt County.

them, she said, but couldn't find them. "I can't help kissing them, tho' I know that don't do me no good, for they aint nothing but pictures—but I jus' has to do that. That little boy! Aint he so sweet. I just wants to mash his eyes out:"—& so on, & so on. You perceive the children constitute your great attraction to her.

I am always, night & day, fearful that every quick step, or unusual noise is a messenger from the Alum announcing Eliza's death. I hate to leave home under the uncertainty about her, and wouldn't do it, but that Uncle leaves Virginia very soon, & my movements must accord with his.

No, of course, I dont lisp the faintest whisper of disaffection in your Church.

While I think of it let me say, if you carry out your threat of having cards printed for me, remember to have them exactly like yours—no smaller. Somehow, I have an aversion to small cards, small type, & small pencils & small everything that ladies generally have small, except a small watch.

And Sam is a Bachelor! Well, I dont wonder. I cant imagine how anybody can marry a man named "Sam". But still, I thought he was the happy possessor of a fat wife & half a dozen children who were not guilty of casting unpleasant aspersions upon their family by having any great share of personal beauty themselves. But good-night to you & all the world. My eyes are weary & midnight is rapidly advancing upon me.

Thursday morning

I'm just starting—Mr Morton & I in a nice, new covered buggy.—Your Tuesday's letter came an hour or so ago. I ain't cross—you mistake. You are sure enough awfully ambitious—& if that be my failing too—why dear me! What a future we shall have. I am right sorry for Dungan—poor fellow. But John it's desperately hard for anybody to do right.

I shant write till Monday's mail. God bless my dear little man. Dont you think I love you very much John?

Your S.C.P. McD

Sept. 13th 1855

My dear Sally,

I feel *almost* sorry that I troubled you with this episode in my clerical life for tho' I more than ever think that D. has opportunities of mischief yet the care is not so bad as even *I* originally supposed. Dick told me yesterday that he thought I was "*safe*" & that because D. had not sufficient *material* for doing evil, but I will not think so too confidently & desire to be humble & prayerful & to take the lesson as it has been sent to me in Providence. A discovery that I made on Tuesday has helped to show Dungan's spirit. He reached over to me at a meeting of the Trustees of the church, at which I was called to be present in connection with the opening of the church & asked me if I had thought of anyone to preach in the after parts of that first day. (It is the habit for the Pastor to preach in the morning

& dedicate the church & to invite others for the afternoon & evening.) I told him I had tho't of Dr Addison Alexander, but observing some sort of demurrer upon his countenance I asked him whether he had been thinking of anyone, when he replied that he had *written* to Dr Palmer of S. Carolina to propose to him to come on & take a share in the service. Palmer had declined for other engagements.[42] You may not know enough of clerical matters to know the impropriety of such an act, but to me it showed a great deal more than impropriety & gave me a still easier feeling in respect to how all this that had been called disaffection was to be accounted for.

I am disposed now to a course of entire *silence* & of simple & faithful *service* without troubling my mind about these different Manoeuvres.

Thinking over the matter of our marriage the other day I thought how much relief it might be to you if we left Lexington in the morning right after the wedding. If I am right in this suspicion by all means let us have it so. It may make your whole trouble lighter to have no thought of a provision for the wedding except just a parlour for the ceremony to occur in & to have no need of any entertainment for *me* of any sort who in that case would have been only at the Tavern. I would like on some accounts to stay a day or two, but they are very trivial accounts & not to be compared with the troubles of keeping up whole parts of your establishment or perhaps keeping it out of Mrs C's or your brother's hands or retaining unnecessary servants, just for that which nothing even in its effect upon the conciliation of the town (of wh. we spoke) furnishes a sufficient ground.

If I leave here some Monday night, I reach L. Tuesday night, can be married on Wednesday morning, can return by that morning's stage & can reach Spencer's or Mrs Potters on Thursday night at 11. It would of course be somewhat tiresome, but more to me than to you & that will make no difference. I shall be in good enough spirits to bear a little fatigue.

So go to work with this feeling if you choose that you need *keep up* nothing for the wedding but liberty for a hasty concourse in the parlours in the morning. It may save you too invitations & hospitalities which with the cares to which you have to attend may be a decided relief.

Pardon me for a simple word. In winding up at L. you will have need for all the money within your reach. I know you are too well provided to need any of my somewhat Quixotic offers in that respect, but I wish to settle your mind as to the need of the *retention* of any money for use after our wedding. I beg that you will spend *all* that is in your purse in the needful settlement of your affairs & not be embarrassing yourself by keeping any under the impression that it will not do to be *entirely without* on leaving Lexington. Let me ask it as a favour that you will spend the last sou, knowing as I do that you will have a great deal to disburse in straightening your accounts & that you will allow me the satisfaction as long

---

42. Benjamin Morgan Palmer (1818–1902) taught church history at Columbia Theological Seminary and edited the *Southern Presbyterian Review*. This sentence is interlined.

as my salary shall last which you know may not be always to find you entirely giving up to me the care of the expense.

I know young people like you are very foolish &, therefore, I repeat again spend right & left toward all your most immediate liabilities & let me have the pleasure of knowing that there is not a cent in your purse when we start together from Lexington.

Aint I a matter of fact old gentleman?

And now, Sally, I'll keep what space is left till I see whether I get a letter. I love you more than I can express. I believe our marriage will turn out nobly even as respects its impression on this very city. I think I am more worthy of you than you imagine & sometimes in my pride I fancy that you could hardly have done better than to marry his divine philosophership, poor old

Jno Miller.

6 o clock alas! poor me, I have no letter & have had none since [word blotted out]

[marginal note] I doubt whether you had better bring Jenny either now or very soon, at all, but *you* must choose.

Phil. Sept. 14th 1855
589 Vine St.

My *darling Sally*,

Am I to understand you to mean that you think of coming on *here* with Lilly?[43] This is by all odds the greatest news of your letter! How happy I shall be! Why do you utter such an important fact & then not explain it more & tell when it is to be? Then our marriage Sally; you seem about to have dropped the subject. When will you marry me? I am getting into that state of settled feeling myself which makes the settling of that question seem very much to be desired.

And do you really think of coming on? O Sally, how can you utter an announcement like that & leave me so excited by suspense.

I wish all this separation was at an end.

As to the bay horse I would like to know whose philosophy is best, Professor White's, who let him run off or mine that caught him or to come nearer to the truth yours to be "really mad" or mine to be very thankful. If Professor White had driven you he would have turned still Whiter,[44] & you probably would both have been killed.

As to poor Tom my ignorance is such that as you say I cant in the nature of things advise. I see this however that if you interfere & anything goes wrong the responsibility will be thrown upon you. This is not a conclusive argument in all cases, but still it is universally true that if you interrupt a plan that is in progress

43. That is, to bring Lilly to school in Philadelphia.
44. Miller wrote here "than I did" and put a line through it.

& substitute one of your own the mischiefs of the first plan as well as all that follow are laid at your door. Still it may be your duty to do this very thing.

Young Etting I dont know. I never heard of him.

See what dandy envelopes I will have hereafter. I know some other people that are a little formal as well as some other people. (I get this buff paper all twisted wrong side out.)[45]

I have enquired about schools & Misses Gill's, Mrs Bagards's, Mrs Gardelle's & a Mr Collot's have the best name.[46] I can't hear of any tho', as yet, more highly spoken of than the first. Give my love to Lilly, indeed to all your sisters. I will be glad to help in the matter in any way I can.

I think the poetry beautiful but, Darling, how crazy you are about little boys.[47]

It has been very hot here for some days & gives me the same wilted feeling that we had earlier in the season. I hope the heat is over.

The "news" you send me is very pleasant, &, Sally, though I cant give it the fresh look of news yet I can say in return that I love you most tenderly & truly. I thank God, for one blessing, Sally, that we do love each other at last with the most thorough & absorbed affection. Do we not?

Yours impatiently
Jno Miller.

Write me very often & if you [go] to Fincastle write from there. Tell me all about our marriage when you write next. Do you find you have much to do?

By the way: Have you an autograph letter of Washington's within your reach?

Saturday Sept. 15, 1855

Dear John,

I shall not have time to write by Monday's mail, for I saw Mr Lewis Thursday morning & I drove out of town & made an engagement with him for that morning.

Mr Morton & I had a tiresome drive from Aunt Eliza's to-day thro' mud and rain. However, here I am safe & satisfied. To my surprise, I found myself arriving at Aunt Eliza's on the eve of a sale. Upon looking into her affairs, Uncle had advised this disagreeable proceeding, & it came off the only day I had to spend with them. It was a trying thing, in some of its details even to me.—Negroes had to be sold—and for the first time in my life I was present at such a time. I stood

45. Miller had written first on the back of a folded sheet of stationery.
46. In addition to the school operated by "the Misses" Gill, the 1855 Philadelphia directory included B. Gardel as a teacher on Chestnut St. and Professor A. G. Collot at West Penn Square. Miller did not mention a women's school operated by Mr. C. D. Cleveland, probably because, as Mary Miller had noted in her letter to McDowell on Sept. 10, Cleveland vociferously opposed slavery.
47. In her letter of Sept. 10, 1855, McDowell had enclosed a newspaper clipping of a poem "By the Alma River," which dealt with an English boy's concern for his father away at the Crimean War.

within the room, outside of which the thing went on. Some of the negroes I had known all their lives—some had known me all of mine, and, of course, it was painful to see them subjected to this trial. They were all bought by the family. It is very shocking this traffic in human beings—but I think slavery will exist as long as the world. My heart bleeds for the poor creatures very often, but I don't think their condition will ever be remedied.

I found everybody in such a fuss that I said nothing of my plans. Uncle William leaves there on Monday for the King's Mountain celebration the 4th of Oct: Mr. Bancroft, who is collecting materials for a continuation of his History, joins him 12 or 13 miles beyond Fincastle & they journey slowly to the Mountain, on the confines of the two Carolinas. $9.000 has been given to get up the celebration; & Uncle John is to make the speech.[48] I wish them joy upon the occasion: but I think it great nonsense. They had much better give the money to Norfolk. By the way—my little friend, Rev: Mr Chisholm of the Episcopal Church in Portsmouth is dead. We are all grieved of it. He has been all the season attending to his ministerial duties, & having escaped thus far, I had hardly a thought that the Fever *could* attack him. But, poor fellow, he has not been spared. A more excellent Christian could not have been called to his reward however, and there is no cause for regret except on account of his motherless children.

As I write lying down my right hand gets tired and I'm trying my left.[49] I think you so funny about the money. I don't mean to mind you. I mean to have $1 in my purse "to keep the devil out." Indeed, John, you are very thoughtful, but I cant take your advice & offer except under great pressure of circumstances. But I'm so tired—I cant write another line—good night—

Monday Morning

Poor Eliza Taylor died yesterday at 2 A.M. and is to be buried at 2 p.m. today. Eddie & the children came up yesterday from Benton's place, and are playing about enjoying the sight of strangers and a new place.[50] I am sorry for them, poor things, yet in my inmost soul I think that both for them & their Father this event is full of Mercy. But Robert, of course, thinks differently at present. He has had a sorrowful life—but is a most excellent Christian.

My old friend, Mr. Armstrong, in Norfolk, is down with the fever by last accounts—I hope he may be spared.[51] The world has need of so good a man &

48. The King's Mountain celebration refers to the seventy-fifth anniversary of the victory that occurred on Oct. 7, 1780. Col. William Campbell, the American commander, was McDowell's great-grandfather. George Bancroft (1800–1891) wrote the ten-volume *History of the United States*. "Uncle John" is John Smith Preston.

49. Instead of her typically neat and precise handwriting, this paragraph is a scrawl.

50. McDowell's cousin Edmonia (Eddie) Taylor (1835–?) was the youngest sister of Thomas Benton Taylor and Robert J. Taylor, the husband of Eliza McNaught Taylor.

51. George Dod Armstrong (1813–1899), Presbyterian minister, professor of chemistry and mechanics at Washington College, and then pastor of the First Presbyterian Church in Norfolk from 1851 to 1891.

I can't cheerfully give up so cherished a friend.

I write in great haste being busy with the children's mourning.

You're an impudent fellow—it was the wife not the child that took my fancy in the "Alma" verses.

I'll write tomorrow.

Yours,
S.C.P. McDowell.

Phil. Sept. 15th 1855

My dear Sally,

My d (I was going to say that right over again by a sort of proclivity of fondness.)

God bless you, Sally for this most welcome letter. Will you believe me I had that very number 14 crossed backward & forward for my wedding day in my little almanac. It steers clear of all my meetings & lands me upon a time when above all others there seems to be a happy juncture of the constellations. I mean to cross out all the intervening days as they pass as a criminal does where he's to be led to execution—only "vicy versy".

And now, Darling, you're mine past all recovery! What a present! Soul & body of such a lovely creature as I *fancy*! Do you know you're image has all faded from my mind. I cant recall it. I can only catch glimpses of you as I saw you at different points—in the meadow & on the steps of the porch. God bless you, dear Sally, for such a peerless gift to such a poor old man.

You will have received my letter asking if it will not be easier for you not to keep up an establishment for our stay *after* the wedding. Judge as you think fit. I can easily secure the week.

Think what a great day this will be in our family history!

<u>*November 14.*</u>

As to the cards I will be careful to make them alike. Please send me one. I find none of mine are left. What do you say about a ring?

Last night Dungan spoke to me again about the preacher & told me that *the elders did not like Addison Alexander*—that he was not as acceptable to them as his brother—that his preaching was instructive but not sufficiently profitable![52] Every such speech eases my mind wonderfully for it relieves me of a feeling of personal depression. I said nothing from which he could infer anything & so I do always. My own deer Sally good night.

Yours lovingly
JM.

I dont know how much you love me Sally, but if you dont love me passionately its an ill balanced couple we are, my dear big woman.

52. The brother referred to is James Waddel Alexander.

Monday 1 1/2
September 17, 1855.[53]

Darling Sally,

Long before this you are safely back in L. & I hope have dispatched me a letter. You know there is a mail that leaves on Monday.

You can hardly conceive how unhappy I am. The ennui of living without you & the nearness of living with you blend together in a sort of impatient mixture that render me perfectly wretched.

I find matters very much to my mind in the church—all except this—that just at the time when I want to rob all conspirators of every plea for opposition I am preaching remarkably ill. It is hard to stand up with a sense, for the first time, of any such declared hostility on the part of any one of your hearers, but still I dont think that accounts for it. I dont feel *conscious* of any such embarrassment, but somehow either from want of practice or what I dont know I have been writing good sermons & murdering them when they came to be delivered. This is unfortunate for one gets *demoralized* as the French say by doing so & loses gradually the power of doing better. I am in the hands of Providence however & no man can preach beyond "the ability that God giveth".

I hope your uncle William gave you a warm patriarchal blessing.

Williams I have not heard from yet but I have written to his wife to-day & shall hear soon.

Spence was regretting Sat. night that he couldnt go on with me to our wedding. Dont pattern after my short letters. I write in haste. I write many more than you.

My *darling* Sally. Yrs.

John Miller.

Tuesday Sept. 18. 1855

Dear John,

I thought I should secure an hour to write to you last night as every body would feel like going to their rooms early; but I was mistaken & when 10 o'clock came I was too tired to do anything but say my prayers & go to bed. I have not been for weeks so worn out.

Mrs. Swann, Eddie, Robert & his three children are all with me at present.[54] My table once more stretches across the dining room. Of course, at such a time I cannot complain, but these constant interruptions try both my temper and patience. Robert, poor fellow, is quite calm and bears this heavy sorrow as he does all other trials & afflictions without a murmur. I never thought him suitably married, & always wondered what a refined, shrinking person like he should have chosen a _____ one so startling his opposite.

53. McDowell added this date.
54. Elizabeth Gilmor Sherlock Swann (1813–1876) was married to Thomas Swann (1809–1883), the president of the Northwestern Virginia Rail Road Company. He was elected mayor of Baltimore in 1856.

Why do you ask about "an autograph letter of Washington's"? Have you turned Antiquarian? Yes, I have one in possession: do you want it? If you do, you can't have it. I'll *lend* it to you, but you must be sure to return it before the 14th of Nov: otherwise it will be yours. Foreseeing that we are, in consequence of your Philosophy, to live paupers that we may *die famous*, I shall put up this letter to *sell for bread* some dark day in the future. Old Mrs Madison, gave me long ago, 3 or 4 or 5 Autograph letters—this one & one of La Fayette's among them.[55]

Ah! John—you don't like to be called a "dear little man"! You are very foolish. I'm quite ashamed of you. *I do* mind being a "big woman" on some accounts; but then you know folly is bound up in the heart of a woman & you can make allowances for her.

By the first of next month I shall probably be in Phil: with Lilly. I have not fully decided upon it, however. It is awkward, and, as I am such a pauper, rather expensive, but I fancy I shall have to incur it all. I cannot keep Lilly 6 or 8 weeks longer from School. And even if I did, it wd be an annoyance to the child to go on with us.

O John—I do hate so much to give up my home here. I'm in a strait betwixt two—to stay or go. And yet I wish I was with you now, if it were only a little cooler.

Mr. Dungan is very *sensible* about Addison Alexander. He's "*instructive* but not *profitable* in his preaching"! Maybe he meant to say "popular"? Dr. James Alexander preached for *us* Sunday. He is ever so far, inferior to his brother I think. I have been amazed at Palmer's reputation. He preached the winter I spent in Columbia, & tho' I heard him often I never was especially impressed by him. In fact I bore away with me only an idea of the physical man. I know nothing of clerical etiquette, but my recollections of old Dr Laurie's chagrin at Dr Junkin's (then Junior Pastor) inviting without his knowledge a Minister to preach the dedication sermon for him, gives me some conception of the annoyance one wd feel at an Elder doing such a thing.[56] I reckon Dungan will worry me as thin as the heroine of a Poets dream. Not such a poet as Byron, tho' for his beauties were wonderfully substantial. I think he must have had a vision of our Preston women.

I can't tell you how often I've been interrupted since I commenced. I give up now in despair. I enclose the Card—Oh—the ring—I'd rather have it—but do as you please.

I keep a man waiting till I finish.

Do you mean to make out that *I am formal*? But good-bye.

Affectionately Yours
S.C.P. McDowell

55. Dolley Payne Todd Madison (1768–1849), wife of President James Madison. Marquis de Lafayette (1757–1834).

56. James Laurie (1778–1853) and David Xavier Junkin (1808–1880) were Presbyterian ministers.

Wednesday, Sept. 19. 1855

My dear John what a treat it is to get into a quiet corner and have a cozy talk with you! Last night I thought I would steal an hour after every body else was in bed,—but suffering to step into Mrs Swann's room to see that she had everything she needed, I sat down, and was rather invited to remain as the lady "was a sort of an owl" and had no thought of going to sleep immediately. I did so, and, in consequence, heard the clock ring out *one* just after my own head was on the pillow. So I missed the chance of writing. But now, as the evening is fast deepening into twilight, I draw my little, low chair close beside you that I may half whisper a little bit of my mind to your ear. I wish I could tell you a great many thoughts that agitate me—but I cant. I dont know how. I shall never be able to make you know, how my heart, almost stands still, when a return of old fears, brings up the question whether after all, I may not have to give you up. I am allowing you to absorb so exclusively my whole heart; I am just recklessly lavishing upon all my affection.—I am just storing in you all my hopes as tho' change or death could never darken or destroy them. And I know perfectly well, that you cannot be all I fancy you to be, yet I am just loving you with an earnestness & power that sometimes alarms me. What makes me do it John? Is it because there is in you that which will justify all this, or is it just the hungering of my nature for its proper aliments?

Months ago—I was anxious to know how I cd be as your Mother says "a helper" to you in your work: and then the children came in for their share of my thoughts, but now every thing is dismissed but the one feeling of loving, & being loved by you. I think it wrong to a certain extent, for one who has any sense of Christian obligation, yet here it is. I can never say "I can't help" anything that ought to be helped—and I might have helped this, but it would have been by turning my feelings out of their natural channel. Some times it is a very merry, glowing sort of emotion;—then very sober—again very sad. Some times it is very, very hopeful—then full of fear. I am for the most part entirely confident of your affection,—but occasionally a half-formed, but quickly abandoned *doubt* troubles me. If there be sin in it, God forgive it, and teach me to feel again as I did months ago—"If thy presence go not with me carry me not up hence".

Thursday morning.

Robert's family are still here, having been detained by bad weather yesterday, and being detained by the same cause to-day. To these Miss Jannetta Gordon & her little Niece were added yesterday;[57] You see I have a house full of people just now when I am very busy in both mind & body. I take it, however, with as little concern as possible & let every body take care of himself.

---

57. Jannetta McKenzie Gordon (c. 1805–?) had been a close friend of McDowell's mother who, on her deathbed, instructed her family to care for her. Her niece was Lelia T. Gordon (c. 1827–?).

So cold it is! In ten minutes yesterday morning about 8 the clouds gathered, & a cold, raw damp day was bestowed upon us. It feels like winter again. The trees are fast dropping their leaves, and some how my spirits are taking the hue of the falling leaf.

I wish Spence wd come on with you. It had never occurred to me that he would have even a desire to do so. Perhaps the Dr will?

I saw Uncle in such a fuss that I said nothing to him of our matters. He had heard of us, however, I am sure from Cousin John. I have not met him for a long time before when I thought him so little affectionate, but he was busy all the day & much fatigued the last night I was with him. If, however, the absence of his usual manner grew out of my plans, I am very indifferent about it. James wrote some time ago—"You ought to consult your Uncles in this matter of yours: they have been very kind to you always".—I replied— "When my affairs are arranged, I shall announce the result to my Uncles. *That* I consider respectful—but as to *consulting* them & shaping my course to meet their feelings & opinions, when the moral question is settled, would be very absurd, and I have not the slightest intention of doing it". They ought to know me well enough by this time, to *respect my opinions & decisions*, and if they don't—why let them not.

Dont you think I'm right? I haven't half as much confidence in Uncle William's opinions upon the right & wrong of any point of morals as I have in my own, because I know that I turn to "the Law & the Testimony" for mine whilst *he* submits his to natural reason, the world—and it may be, in extreme cases *the Church*. And yet perhaps if he had been near I might have talked over the thing with him. Tho' I dont know—he is not one to whom I feel drawn in such manner as to disburden myself to him. I really love Uncle Tom much more. Uncle John is much of a stranger to me & of very reserved manners.

I wrote to Tom to quit his Uncle forthwith, & not be seduced by any promise of pecuniary advantage to enter into any money arrangements with him. I find my strong terms & representation of things to James, has not been after all ineffective. His last letters have been more & more after my own way of thinking, & the very last says "I will try to get Tom out of his present position". Our men are very queer folk. They invariably object to & reject the *first* showing that we women make to them, upon any matter of importance—& then they come gradually round for they know—put your ear down, & let me whisper it, & dont you tell your Mother what I say, you hear?—they know we have more sense & better sense too than they have. But they just like to make a *show* of having more:—

It was a great shame in you not to give me that famous scarf last summer, for now I want it, it's so cold & damp.

God bless you. Affectionately Yours
S.C.P. McDowell

Phil. Sept 19th 1855.

My *dear Sally,*

I know I shall get a letter this afternoon. Till it comes I will busy myself in writing whatever occurs to me. Enclosed is a scrap from a letter of Spencers. He seems half inclined to pack his trunk & come along, but I suppose his business will prevent him. You have never gotten me thoroughly aroused in any anxieties about our position & therefore I havnt any hearty zeal in feeling the *necessity* of any such steps as these. Spencer would gratify me just as he would by going with me in any circumstances of a wedding, but I have grown past the idea of its necessity, or of the necessity of anything but my own good judgment & management & the blessing of God. The gale has blown pretty stiff in some quarters but it is subsiding already. "Nemo noceteur nisi ex se".[58]

The fact is, Sally, I am a perfect worshipper of *silence.* I believe nearly all *catastrophes* grow out of the want of it & that fighting these intestine foes such as the disaffection that Dungan has in charge & this marriage difficulty by one or two clear wise talks & then remaining always silent perfectly bewilders people. You seem to them perfectly unmanageable. They cant assault you. And just so far as you have them under influence your cool & settled manner gives them the feeling that every difficulty is removed. Believe me, dearest Lady, "speech is silver, but silence is golden."

Yours affty
Jno Miller

Thursday 6 P.M.

Heigho! I forgot my letter & left it in my drawer. Yours never came till to-day & then was so exhausted by heat & travel that it had shrunk into the smallest sort of a note the only thing piquant in which was "You're an impudent fellow".

I do hope another will come tomorrow & that it will be "good & fat" like that pretty shoulder of yours.

I am getting quite out of patience for my wedding day. It seems to me as if it would never come. The days move so slowly that I am really uncomfortable from impatience all the time. However, there's one thing that comforts me that the day *will come* some day or other, if something terrible dont occur.

Maggie B. writes from Kentucky that our affair is all abroad there & that she is quite an object of attention from being the niece of the happy man.

Wont we have a nice place in Princeton some day if we live. I have been thinking of it lately much. You do wrong to undervalue my philosophy. It will greaten us both some day. Perhaps tho' metaphysics is so ungrateful to you that

---

58. Latin, meaning "You can only be hurt by yourself."

being the wife even of a *distinguished* metaphysician would be no pride to you. Everything goes on pleasantly in the Church.

Yours devotedly
JM

[Enclosure: Elihu Spencer Miller to John Miller]

I am sincerely sorry that I cannot go to Lexington. I say this, without an invitation, because I regret that no one of the family will, as I fear, be there. There ought to be a representation, for many reasons.

Yours very affly
E Spencer Miller
Sept. 17/55

September 22d/55
Saturday

My *dear* John,

I am really ashamed of my letters. They are to the last degree trashy, and I cheerfully pardon you for so plainly intimating as you do in your last letter, that they are very dull and poor. But then look up some excuse for me, and be merciful in your judgment.

I began a letter to you before breakfast, but was called from it to breakfast, & from that again to a talk with Mr Lewis first, and James (who came at daylight this morning) afterward. I thought of my unfinished letter & your disappointment as I sat talking, but could not civilly break away to finish it.

Then tonight when I took it up again I was disgusted with it, tore it up and have begun afresh.

Mr Lewis refuses to act as my Agent. He will have nothing to do with Morgan in that capacity, yet strangely enough seems willing to become my Trustee. I proposed to James to relieve me of my difficulties by renting the place, & keeping Cousin Elizabeth as his tenant, & managing Morgan himself but he declined: his head is full of other projects.[59] So I am at sea again. Do tell me, John, what I must do with my servants. Hiring, is a sad thing for their well-being; & selling is unpleasant to me. Such a pity it is you dont live in Virginia and despise Philosophy.

By the by what do you mean to do with me in Phil:? Am I to find a home down in your study, or where? You know I dont want any house. I should, thro' ignorance, break you in a month by my housekeeping—and the *white servants*! I don't know what to think of them. And we don't like large boarding-houses, do we? There is so much gossip among a set of idle women and so many cliques

59. That is, Elizabeth Cocke.

that are neither safe nor pleasant. I prefer—or think I should, despite the greater restraint it imposes on one, living in a private family, provided it is one not belonging to your Church. I don't want you to place me where all the tittle-tattle of the Church will come to my ears and give me prejudices against any of its members.

And the children: what about them? A large boarding-house wouldn't suit them at all, do you think it would? What would suit? Such a fuss as this thing of getting married makes! I wish it was all over. But it will be over some day.

I wish Spence would come on with you. What does he mean by "not being invited to do so".

Please John, write me a letter *all* in good English. I'm rather stupid about it, and decidedly foolish when Latin comes into play.

My old friend Miss Jannette Gordon has been sick for several days, and I begin to feel uneasy about her. Hers is a very sad case.

Monday morning.

Such a fuss as I have to get a letter written! I go thro' one as one goes thro' the Country on an accommodation train, stopping every five minutes to pick up a passenger.

I begin to think our matter is going to succeed after all. James, who himself was very timorous at first, is now so strengthened by the opinion of friends abroad, that he is quite indignant at James Taylor's expression of fear as to its success! Uncle Benton volunteered a very cordial approval of it—also other friends, male & *female!*

James & Lilly & I leave here next Wednesday for Phil: I find Professor Henry interests himself very unexpectedly in this school matter, & half secured Miss Gill's favor in Lilly's behalf. He writes me very kindly offering to look after my matters in Washington during Mr Kennedy's absence. But I shant trouble him.

I am ever so busy—Company, sick servants & other things interrupt & distract me greatly. Lilly's fixing too is very troublesome.

When I go to Phil, I don't want to see anybody except yourself. I have engaged, in the person of Miss Brinton, all the aid & *society* I shall need,— and mean to spend a little time in Trenton with Lizzie.[60] So you can write me a note every day & pay me a visit of half an hour every three days—which will be two visits during my stay.—Wont that be time enough for a busy Pastor to waste?

So cold & damp it has become again.

Very affectionately
S.C.P. McDowell

60. Elizabeth Brinton operated a women's clothing store in Philadelphia. Lizzie refers to Elizabeth Brant McDowell, McDowell's sister-in-law.

Phil. Sept 22d 55

Darling Sally,

Write now & tell me all about your contemplated visit, when you will come & where you will stay & how long you will remain & whether I may fasten myself to you & stay with you all the time & whether after all it is not a vision & I am altogether bewitched by somebody in fancying you will come at all. It will be a sort of half way house in my long pilgrimage from August to November.

But Sally, I shall leave here on the 16th of Oct for Synod. Then the week before that I shall be busy with the opening of the church. Cant you come on the first week of Oct just as you say. If you can stay on thro' the second so much the better—or come next week. Give my love to Lilly & tell her I am glad I can see her. What can I do for you in advance of your coming.

I enclose Wms' letter.[61] It disappoints me but not much. It does not crumble away my foundations & I am still as far as I can search my own conscience much in my sense of the propriety of my step. Dont show this letter for it has a little something ungallant in it about the ladies. Still it reiterates W's *own* convictions which is the sort of evidence the Major calls for. If the Major complains put him up to writing to Lyons—not for proof of recent facts for that of course is impossible but to know what was had at the time & how far he & the committee knew of T's failings *then.*—I mean, to bear on the point whether the divorce was given with any such knowledge.[62] I dont think this *necessary* but still ask the Major to do it if he reiterates his old troubles.

I have written right back to W. to ask if he has seen any reason to abandon the lottery-man's story which he said he would look into & also to caution him to great secrecy.[63] I shall hear on Wednesday. Take great care of these letters. Whatever conscientious scruples you have tell freely of from time to time.

Please bring on the autograph or send it even if you wont give it. I will tell you why "again".

Dungan *did* say instructive but not profitable but that is a common complaint with him. He's New School.[64]

Did you get a former letter from Wms & two from Miss Field?

The cards I will have ready when you come & I will also get from you the lettering of the ring. Good bye

Yours very fondly
John Miller.

Dont forget the autograph. Have you one of Franklin.[65]

61. This letter has not been located.
62. In the margin, Miller added, "Did he see Wm Brown as he said he would."
63. The "lottery-man" is O'Leery.
64. That is, New School Presbyterian. This may account for his conflict with John Miller and dislike for Addison Alexander, both Old School Presbyterians.
65. Benjamin Franklin (1706–1790).

Phil. Sept. 24th 55.

Dear Sally,

How *could* you send me such a letter altogether unannounced? Why it's the sweetest & dearest I ever received. Do you know it is about the first full disclosure of passionate affection for me that you have ever made. I feel as if I had inherited a kingdom. Darling Sally, I love you ever since I broke the seal with an entirely new devotion. I will live for you. A woman that endows me with so much passion shall be my warmly cherished & highest pleasure in life & I differ from you in such things for I think we love God *thro'* the good things he gives us. I cant think it my duty to love you less & I *know* it isnt yours for I think you have been concealing from me & keeping back a sort of devotion which God approves & which he intended should be planted in all married relations.

But, Sally, I'm so happy. Do you love me so all the time, or was it just the gushing up of a sudden fondness. Oh, I love that letter so! I have read it over & over this morning. I keep it by itself. And Oh, I love you so. It does seem so inexpressibly sweet to have you coming up to my side upon the same level of absorbed affection.

Dear Sally, why havent you written such letters before. They would have made me love you so much more, & if you knew how inexpressibly dear you seem to me this morning, dear for the first time in ways which I could not realize before, you would have told me all that was in your heart long ago.

But now I know it & I feel as proud of your passion as any miser. It really makes me feel like a king &, Sally, I'm sure it's safe & fixed. I feel for the first time as if you were mine forever & ever as concerns your love for me & that I can trust you in it. And Oh, I long so now to have you at my side & entirely to appropriate you as my own & to keep you near me, & to beg off from all separations & long journeys away from each other or absences for many years to come.

How did this inarticulate passion of yours get a tongue at last. Tell me all about the birth of this warm disclosure, & Oh, tell me whether you think you will love me so always for I am most crazy to day for the mere pleasure of your love.

You must give people to understand how busy & engaged you are & not *let* them come to see you.—However I dont feel in the humour of writing anything but about the pleasure you have given me. Dear, dear, dear, *dear*, Sally. I could hardly have conceived that being the object of such a fervour of affection even from one I love so much could surprise & intoxicate me so. But, Sally, I am admitted now into the very sanctuary of your heart & I am never to move out of it again. Am I?

Yours devotedly
John Miller.

This seems a high day with me. I preached well yesterday & everything looks promising. *May God* take care of us.

I have read over my letter. It seems more like the spasms of the Delphic Priestess than a grave clergyman but still it's *true* & that's the main thing—either in raint or sibyl.

Colalto
Tuesday Sept: 25. 1855.

Dear John,

Lest I should forget it in the bustle of daylight, I went up to-night and drew from its hiding place—the Autograph letter you ask for. Several others were in the same package; and fancying you might have some curiosity about LaFayette's I brought it along. Also a note of old Mrs Madison's which happened to be there too, & which tho' not worthy of a place in such august society is yet worth preserving as a specimen of a lady of the older time, and as much illustrates the peculiarities of society fifty years ago as the hoop or minuet. I pay you no small compliment by trusting my Washington letter to you:—but I hope to see it "after many days". I have no letter of Franklin.

Your letter, enclosing a recent one from Mr Williams came this morning. You had before sent me an old one of his, and *one* had *two* as you suppose, from Miss Field.

Williams' letter is entirely valueless to us except so far as his own *conviction* on the point of worry, is clearly & decidedly expressed. I have said nothing to Cousin John about it, nor he to me since I wrote you of our talk on the subject a month ago. He had seen Wm Brown, at the then recent Presbytery at Harrisonburg, & asked as to the extent of his Father-in-law's information; but heard nothing more satisfactory than you hear constantly from others. All that he knew, was anterior to the period that we are anxious about.

I am not disposed to ask aid from Mr Lyons, but wd rather go to my old friend Fendall of Washington City. He is nearer the true sources of information, & would manage the thing more sagaciously. If you think it would be well I'll stop a day in Washington as I go on next week, & see Mr Fendall about it. He has been warm & true in his friendship & I'd like to get his help now if necessary. He is quiet in his ways & could go poking about with his inquiries so as to arouse nobody's suspicions or curiosity. He is an odd man—a sort of book-worm with an eccentric invalid of a wife & a houseful of noisy lawless children. Somehow or other he has grown cold in his domestic atmosphere, and the only warmth *I* ever witnessed in him was that that oozed out to me.

We *must* have, I think, this point that Cousin John makes, & that we all make, *established* before we are married, if it does occasion some delay and annoyance. We can't tell what may occur to make absolute testimony indispensable. I am proud about *asking* aid from near friends—nor indeed do I think it would look well to do it, but such help as friends like Mr Fendall can render I have no feeling in requesting.

My dear John, I think you fib a little. My affection must have spoken to you before. I cannot believe it was "inarticulate" all this time.—How could I when it is everlastingly talking to me. I can't silence it, and of late I have submitted to its clatter so much that I am really beginning to find it quite pleasant. But I don't know that it will continue all my life: that depends entirely upon you. If you supply the fuel, there will be no danger of the fire going out—but if you don't—what then?

Miss Jannetta begrudges you the possession of me, and wants to disenchant you & get me back by abusing me to you. For instance, she says "Well, Sally, Mr Miller, will get *old Harry* when he gets you".—Yet for all that she believes you wd do uncommon well to get "old Harry". As she sits near with a book I asked if she had a message to you, and she replies—"give my best respects to him, & tell him I say he mustn't spoil you".

After we are married I shall rid your study of my elegant letters by making a bonfire of them. I am ashamed of them now & will be more so then.

Affectionately Yours,
S.C.P. McDowell

Wednesday Sep't 26.[66] [1855]

My own sweet Darling,

I love you so for that letter. I cant get over thanking & kissing you for it. It is so ineffably pleasant to have one all my own in this cold sad world who loves me passionately; (I may use that word now, mayn't I, my Darling?) & to pour back upon such a one, as I do from the overflowings of a most exclusive affection all the tender fondness that this impatient heart of mine is capable of. But, Sally, was it just a bubbling up of a sudden gush of a half factitious fountain of endearment, or is it a deep well-tide of true & perpetual devotion? Is it a clinging fondness, Sally, that will seal your arms about my neck in sunshine & in storm & that will make you passionately fond even when the world contends with me & when I have no earthly pleasure but what is to be found in your own warm embrace. Oh, Sally, I'm afraid that was a rash proffer of yours & that when you see me clutch at it with such a heated earnestness, you will gently take it out of my sight & I shall "see it no more."

Wed. Aft. 2. oclock.

I expect that this letter from F. will be very welcome to you.[67] Before you open it see what a "free & easy" look it has as you read it thro' the envelope. Isnt it rather public for a private letter; but what is visible could not I think be understood & the P.M. would not dream of stopping to inspect. This is certainly much of what the Major could demand. Can you not show it to him? Dont show

---

66. McDowell dated this letter.
67. This letter has not been located.

him my letter tho' for that one sentence in which I express surprise that "nothing should have—"for fourteen years" &c is too strongly expressed. It does not give a fair account of Wms' letters & would be too discouraging. I was led into it in order to draw Williams fully out.

My own mind is very much impressed with this one, now well attested, fact. You can find my letter in which the fact is accurately stated, I believe, & lay them away together for our grand-children; & now I hope, my Darling, that this piece of evidence will help to still that unquiet heart of yours & sooth that poor fluttering scared conscience weeks hence when you find yourself quietly lying in my arms.

I mean to quit now (& I advise you to be cautious & to tell the Major not to allow statements to trace themselves to us). I mean to quit charging Thomas right & left in respect to his character. I have done it enough. Others will do it now. If a well attested case of my denouncing him were to come to Thomas' ears he might like no better revenge than a slander suit. When the same statement traced to any one else than you or me might not rouse him; for we are the parties that could be chiefly mortified by being brot into court. I do not anticipate such a thing for my friends would not allow him to trace any speeches to me, nor do I think at his age that he will move at all, still it is best to be guarded.

And now, Darling, I say further that I have tho't over all our moral questions very studiously of late & have most accurately pondered every legitimate doubt & no thorough difficulty could I find but that sort of contradicted evidence that I feared Wms' letters might bring. They bring no such thing you see. I have been openly & frankly to F. I have resisted the half temptation we spoke of in L. to shirk that danger of adverse discoveries & stay away. I have been there faithfully & honestly. I have written to Wms. as you see clearly & searchingly & the result is that Providence has not brought us any adverse discoveries & we have dug out one well remembered & to my mind considering that it was heard from first hands most exclusive & satisfying fact. Therefore, come here & let me kiss you.—There. Dear, *dear,* Darling. Providence & your own passion & my tender love & all the circumstances of the case seem to conspire together to bring you to my arms. Dont they, Sally? God grant that our lives may be preserved & that he may not find it necessary to thwart us. Let us humble ourselves before him & ask Him to spare us till we meet. Alas! alas! I hardly feel willing to die, till I have been some years, *dearest* Sally,

> *Your own darling*
> *Husband.*

P.S. Dont laugh at my letters. If you do I will think you are not so near the shrine of the fair goddess as I am & cant appreciate them; whereas I am just waking up to a sort of capture of discovery that you are quite as near (are you Sally?) & that we are worshipping hand-in-hand close by the coals of her altar so as about to be singed by them. Whenever you love me as you did the other day <u>do tell me</u>. Do it from selfishness for it makes me love *you* more. JM.

6 P.M.

I have no letter from you wh makes me sad. I went out onto Chestnut St to Moore's to get your plate & cards.[68] I ordered but a pack to allow for alterations & its well I did. Moore had the audacity to tell me that ladies' cards ought to be bigger than gentlemen's & as he had none smaller cut he made yours as within. When you come on next week I will have others printed on the right size. I have another criticism see if you find it out. I think the engraving admirable but the tout ensemble displeases me in one thing. Moore can alter it.

Friday Sept 28. 1855

Dear John,

I am so in the habit of writing every other day that I naturally go to the work even tho' I have nothing to say. You are a sort of Pharaoh in the letter-business, with unrelenting cruelty expecting me to make bricks without straw. But as you fancy my brick for your air-castles, the work after all, isn't so very, very hard.

I am ever so busy. It wd take two heads & a dozen hands to accomplish all I have to do; of course then my one head will leave much undone. I shall be in Phil: Thursday or Friday next; I will be at the Girard. If I delay a day in Washington I'll write from there.

If Myers will [pay] me $12.000 in State Stock, & his house in town I think I'll sell my premises at once. What do you think? I shall then have an interest-bearing fund just ready to-begin with. And as to this old home of mine—why, I give it up with all things else & henceforth *your* home shall be mine, and I'll get up for it all the attachment that I now bestow upon the other. But it's a struggle after all my reasoning—and even tho' I'm in a hurry now, I cant help stopping to take a little cry.

The remnant of the Military (our Kentucky place) James thinks can now be sold for $40.000, & I mean to sell that too:—are you willing?[69]

You'll write so that I may have a letter Wednesday morning before I go?

I was distressed yesterday to hear of the death of my old Sunday School scholar, Dr Armstrong's Sister-in-law. She was a very lovely girl. From some mistaken feeling she wd stay with her Sister in Norfolk, & has thus fallen a victim to the fever. Mrs A. is now ill with it—& two of her children.[70] The eldest child died of it ten days ago. Isn't it terrible.

I grow impatient to see you.

Affectionately Yours
S.C.P. McDowell

I have directed several letters to be enclosed to you for me—so don't be surprised when they come, but keep them for me.

68. A. D. R. Moore operated a fancy stationery store on Chestnut St. in Philadelphia.
69. The "Military" was a Kentucky plantation jointly owned by McDowell and her siblings.
70. Mehitabel H. Porter Armstrong (?–1855).

Friday Eve.
Sept 28th 55.

Dearest Sally,

A pretty wild-goose chase!—Bright & early this morn: I Sallied out & went to the La Pierre & Girard & then to Miss Gill's & then to Mrs Howell's but my visits were all disappointed & I waited till this afternoon & then repeated the search at the Girard & La Pierre.[71] For when in your Monday's letter you say, "James & Lilly & I go to Phil. *next Wednesday*" of course how could I know you meant *Wednesday week*. Your letter of Tuesday which have just recd says "when I come on next week" so I have determined to let the tavern registers be for just one week from this morning.

Well I am accustomed to it. This same "pretty wild—duck" has been hovering before me now more than a twelve-month & it is full half that time since I thought I had her very palpably under my hand. However, "faint heart &c &c" & I mean to persevere for three or four years yet.

Darling, you frighten me about Miss Field's letters. I have sent you two within three or four weeks. The one written on Sat. long & severe & the one written on Monday after my visit taking all back & saying "no one whose opinion I valued could blame me;"[72] which did you get?

As to Wms what do you think of what I last sent. *I* consider it very strong. I dislike to discourage you in any step necessary to your repose of conscience but suppose you wait till on your return to see Fendall. Do as your conscience moves you, however. My conscience allows me to marry you & this *one* testified fact is to me very palpable indeed more in distinctness than I thought I should obtain. I hesitate about Fendall, because nothing could exasperate Thomas more than such a step if he could possibly hear of it.

By the way if we have lost a letter we ought to quit writing anything private in our correspondence (& I would propose that we do so) that hereafter we write nothing that could *damage* us if by any possibility it got into the most hostile hands. I shall try to observe that rule. Which Field letter did you get?

Tell me all about your visit, where you stay & when exactly you come. By the way Spence whom I just left was trying to persuade himself that it was proper for you to stay at his house & was quite on the eve of writing to you & sending the invitation but Northern manners won the ascendant & we *all* voted in solemn conclave that it wouldnt do. You must expect to see the young gentleman tho' & his apple-faced wife whose letter (from you) by the way I have read & feel very proud of.

71. La Pierre and the Girard were two Philadelphia hotels.

72. Field wrote Miller a stern letter on Sept. 8 that apparently criticized his engagement to McDowell. That letter has been lost. Miller immediately confronted her. Afterward, on Sept. 10, she wrote, "I have thought over all you said, and feel certain that no blame will be attached to you by any one whose opinion you may value." In his brief reply, Miller thanked her and noted, "my mind has long ago been made up & my conscience at rest."

The autographs I have received.

I never said or hinted or thought that your letters were empty. What a little suspicious jealous hizzy you are. Behave; & go on writing.

I think I must write to Miss Gordon to beg her to warn me & save me if I am making a misstep.

Give my respects to her & remember me affectionately to Lilly & your sisters and to the Doctor.

Yours affly
Jno Miller.

Lexington,
Monday, Oct. 1. 1855

My *dear John*,

Somehow your letters do not come as punctually as heretofore:—they are a day behind hand. This may account for my not getting one as I expected yesterday.

My Brother Tom came on Saturday and we look for Uncle Tom this evening. If he comes, we will not leave before Wednesday as we have all along decided; but if he does not & nothing is heard from him we will probably go tomorrow. James tells me, we reach Phil: about 10 P.M—but you need not *trouble* yourself about me till next morning, when you can come round for half an hour about breakfast time. I have been writing a half hour and in that time I have been interrupted half a dozen times. First James—"I think I shall wait for news from Staunton about the Bank business; & shall I go to Rich's about my boxes etc then!"—I answer, take my pen, write a word, & Tom comes—"Sister, what can I do for you in town?"—"Nothing"—I begin again—Miss Jannetta—"Sally I'll take this collar & sleeves for a pattern"—"Well Ma'am"—again the pen goes. Alfred appears at the window—"Here's some Sage Ma'am"—"Hang it in the pantry"—By this time I'm desperate—Lilly comes regardless of my occupation—"Sister my trunk needs a new cover"—& Cantey then appears & Mary Leabrook, and so my time is consumed & my temper ignited.[73]

But I've nothing to say after all, John. I have written myself out. It's no news to you that I love you with all my heart, tho' you do *pretend* to doubt the fact sometimes.

I don't quite like to stay at the Girard just with Lilly after James leaves us:—can you suggest any thing else? I so dislike the surveillance of a boarding-house even for a week, that I am reluctant to try it. In a hotel *you* can come in & out without remark—which you cd not do any where else, & that is something of a consideration at the Girard. If I am delayed beyond Wednesday I will write.

In haste & confusion
I am Yours most wholly & truly
S.C.P. McDowell

73. Mary Leabrook, probably the wife of John Leabrook of Halifax County.

Colalto
Tuesday Oct. 2d/55

Dear John,

I write a hurried line that there may be no more mistakes about my movements. We leave tomorrow. If James doesn't go, I'll go on with a gentleman from here, as I cannot well delay longer.

I am amused at Spence's delusion about the invitation. Nothing wd have induced me to accept it, but I appreciate the kindness notwithstanding.

But I wish they wouldn't come to see me. I shall be terribly busy & like Talleyrand's friends having but one fault—"that they are unbearable".[74]

Look about for Miss Field's letter. The one saying "no one whose opinion was of value, would blame you"—is the one I received. Do find the other. I'd like to see the production. It's very odd in her, anyhow, to be expressing *any opinion* on such a subject to you. If she don't take care I'll make a face at her some of these days.

I'm not well, having a throat as troublesome as yours.

Affectionately,
S.C.P. McDowell

Lexington,
Monday Oct 15. 1855

Dear John,

I am safe at home again, having made the whole journey in just 24 hours. I suffered greatly from the cold from Phil to Baltimore, and would have done so from Staunton home, but that an acquaintance who adopted me at Alexandria pressed his plaid upon me and made me very comfortable all the day long. A snake head, on that miserable Louisa road alarmed me and made me nervous & timid, but on the whole I had a very successful trip.

I found Nib returned, and Mac sick. I hope he is better today. He is a lovely little fellow, and I love him astonishingly.

Everything looks very lovely here after Philadelphia. I am sure six months in Phil: will sweep away every objection to Allamby or any other Country residence.

Look after my poor child at Miss Gill's sometimes. I felt very, very sad at leaving her.

How did the dedication pass off?[75] I found my mind wandering after you all the day yesterday with no little anxiety. I think you would never ask—"Sally do you love me"? if you could get right into my heart and see how snugly my little Man was ensconced there; and how he orders about in it, just as tho' he were sole Master.

---

74. Charles de Talleyrand (1754–1838), French diplomat and Bishop of Autun.
75. Miller's church was dedicated on Oct. 14, 1855.

I write you a line today in a hurry; but will write again tomorrow. I begin to tremble for the 14 N;[76] and think we have to push it off just one week more.

God bless you my dear John

Affect'y
S.C.P. McDowell

Please go to Wilson, have the Communion service marked, Presbyterian Church, Lex: Va:, either in full or abbreviated as you may fancy, & tell him to send it by Express to "James McClung. Virginia House, Staunton Va.["][77]

Urge him to send it off by the 19th or 20th.—

Tuesday.
October 16. '55[78]

Dearest Sally,

I will not tell you how much we miss you or it would make you vain, & I will not tell you how well we get on without you or it might make you mad.

So we will proceed to business.

What am I to do with two queer looking pieces of lace which I find in my pocket-book.

I paid Scullshaver & Hairmister $9.50 & told Wilson to mark the *goblets* (not the others) "Presbyterian Church Lexington, Va.["] & to send the service to "Mrs. S.C.P. McDowell, care of James McClung Staunton.["] Moreover I called at Borhek's & was told *by him* that the spectacles would make a spectacle of me i.e. he said the sense of that.[79] And he soon brought me down to narrower shape & less metal. He told me If you had told him that I was a poor wilted dome shrunken up & gathered in specimen of mortality it would have cost you far less money at the first. As it was he returned me $3. I lay awake last night thinking of this money. It seems hard that I should return it to you & yet I'm afraid you'll extinguish me if I spend it myself. And so I am in great trouble. He tells me a lady came into his store & told him she wanted the most expensive spectacle he had & he said that this pair which he kept for me such occasions & which was the only one he had he handed over to you thinking it was for the N.H. Giant whom Barnum has here exhibited as a woman & that he charged you $15 for it, but that as the pair he brot me down to were but $12 tho' of very fine gold & very handsome he would return me $3. This he said of his own motive. I consulted him as to what I should do with the money & he told me to give it to the poor, so in obedience to, that I keep it myself.

---

76. The date assigned for their wedding.
77. William Wilson was a Philadelphia silversmith.
78. McDowell added the date.
79. The Philadelphia directories do not list such a firm as Scullshaver & Hairmister. Miller may have invented this name as a joke. Edward Borheck was a Philadelphia optician.

But, dear darling Sally, how it does *chill* me to laugh in my letters. I want to be telling you all the time how much I love you & how dear you are to me in all my memories. These spectacles will be my favorite pair. After a week or two I will wear them all the time & I thank you very much for them.

Our church was opened yesterday & was ended in a way that gratified me much.

Tell me when you write whether the 14th seems still the fixed day for our marriage for I am counting those that intervene most impatiently.

God bless you, my dear Sally.

Yours most devotedly
Jno Miller.

I will send you two ledgers for the sake of yr friend Dr Van R.[80]

Colalto,
Wednesday Oct: 17./55

Dear John,

Wont you tell me why you don't write. I am so troubled at not hearing from you. Your letters should come as soon as James' from Trenton, & yet I have one from him & none from you. I feel it the more as I was anxious about the dedication experiment.

I am busy making arrangements with Cousin Elizabeth. I am glad to find she wants to buy my place, and begs that, when I sell, I will make her the first offer. I prefer her to any other purchaser. She is rich, and abundantly able to pay; and then is attached to this spot, because it was the home of my Parents.

Do you think your people will ever be so foolish as to make a difficulty with you because of *my slaves* if by any chance they should hear I owned any? If they do, tell them they are great numskulls and do not deserve to be answered even "according to their folly".

Every body is in a fuss about Synod—& I find the Committee of arrangements has a notion of cramming my house. I refused, out & out to entertain a single lady—ladies were too troublesome & my servants were sick—and so they send a squad of men over to me. I am going to remonstrate & limit them to 6— who with my own invited guests & family will swell my number to, at least, 15 persons.

I am not to give up the house till the first of Dec:—

Since the loss of the Field letter I have been anxious about our mail communications.

Affectionately Yours
S.C.P. McDowell

80. Courtland Van Rensselaer.

Colalto,
Friday Oct: 19. 1855

My *dear John*,

Keep the "two queer-looking pieces of lace" you found in yr pocket-book very securely till I call for them,—and use the $3.00 Borhek returned to you in purchasing *letter-stamps*. It may be I shall then hear from you a little oftener.

I send you a paper with a notice of the 'King's Mountain' celebration in it. Uncle John is thought to speak as well as Uncle William. I don't know how that it is, but certainly the reported speech in the Examiner is no great thing—not at all comparable to Bancroft.

Mr Lewis refuses to become my Trustee, and I'm at a loss to know who to turn to. He advises, that a settlement shall be made, signed by us both in the presence of Magistrates, *but not recorded*. This gives *me* the full management of all my property, and at the same time protects it against any *designs you* may have upon it. I think, Mr Lewis can scarcely be correct or as Spence says, "*accurate*" in this notion, so I am going to ask Judge Brockenbrough about it. Poor Mr Davidson is too unwell to attend to any business.

I am busy night and day. I give up my house the first of December, and we will be married the 20th Nov:, just a week later than the day first named. If I cant get all the ragged ends of my business gathered up by that time, I'll come back again and attend to it.

Poor Lilly writes very sorrowfully. She begs I will write to you to go & see her. I hope you will.

I am glad you mean to wear the spectacles right at once for do you know your own are much more unusual than the gold ones, & have more a look of affectation about them. I've had but one letter from you—that with the bracelets.

Affectionately Yours,
S.C.P. McDowell

Phil. Oct. 19th 55.

My *dear Sally*,

I have just been walking two hours with Lilly. She is a good deal home-sick, but seems to like the school *as* a school & highly to approve of it. She was very glad to see me & had thought of sending word to Mrs Hunter's that she would be glad if I would call.

My people would have no feeling about the slaves & if they had I wouldnt care. By the bye the Ded. passed off well. I would say *nobly* if you had not discreetly checked me once or twice for encouraging you too much about my own managements. Still every-body talks most encouragingly to me. Many went away from all the services, unable to get seats.

I wrote on Tuesday sending a box of bracelets. I hope all has gone safe. Dear Sally, Why do you write such short letters? I expected one yesterday.

To-day Mr Sneeder intimated to me that house-cleaning would make it necessary for me to leave here on Monday.[81] I regret it for I must move twice & it makes me in a desperate hurry.

I have taken the liberty to introduce to you, Mr Schenck, Sec. of the Bd. of Pub.[82] He is a Princetonian & an old play-mate & a former Pastor at Princeton, & has it in his power to make himself very agreable to us in various ways. If you *mean* to have any one of the Syn. (tho' I think it wild) & it is a matter of indifference I dont know but that it would be wise to invite him to your house. You will find him a gentleman.

Dear Sally. I am I am in such a desperate hurry.

I preach twice in the New Church next Sunday & think I shall find it not unpracticable as a place to fill with my voice.

Yours desperately
Jno Miller.

I move on Monday I dont know where.

Schenck is the son of a Princeton farmer, married to a niece of Dr. Torry the Botanist.[83]

Phil. Oct. 20th 1855.

Darling Sally,

I suppose either now or on Monday you will have the Com. set. It was sent off to Mr McClung's care on the 18th. Lilly went with me to Wilson's. She is eagerly looking for the Dr, who, she says, is about to take a house here.[84]

I am in the bustle of moving & where I shall board these few weeks I am still uncertain. I mean to try to select some place that will possibly suit *us*, so that with no pledge of any sort, by my temporary residence in it, I may try how it will answer permanently.

Spencer & Dick have not delivered themselves on the subject of what sort of person their new sister seems to be. Mrs Hunter, however, whose habits are less reserved in all such matters & Cousin Benedict express their satisfaction with wonderful *empressement*. But, Sally, you know you're very nice & people cant help being a good deal pleased, at least *I* cant. Nor can these brothers of mine I am very sure.

Lilly, moreover, unburdened her heart to me yesterday & told me that you were the most attractive woman she had ever known. She said, if she ever was

81. E. J. Sneeder owned the home at 389 Vine St. in Philadelphia where Miller lived.

82. William Edward Schenck (1819–1903), corresponding secretary of the board of education of the Presbyterian Church.

83. Jane Torrey Schenck (c. 1821–1856). Her uncle was John Torrey (1796–1873), eminent botanist and professor of chemistry and natural history at the College of New Jersey from 1830 to 1854.

84. "Com. set" means communion set. The doctor is James McDowell, M.D., her brother.

near you again she would be too wise to consent to leave you & that when you came she meant instantly to leave Miss Gill's & board where you did. By the way, I have no house to offer, but I hope you will remember me most kindly to Miss Cantey & assure her of the pleasure I would have if she would live with us this Winter. Dont speak of my having heard so, but Lilly spoke of her feeling unsettled & forlorn in view of your breaking up.

I am sorry for the delay of a week you spoke of & hope it need not occur, but Dearest Sally dont fatigue yourself & injure your health, by fixing the day imprudently early & perhaps in the end failing to keep your appointment & injuring yourself beside.

My spectacles suit grandly. I am going to make my first appearance in them on the road between this & Baltimore.

Schenck is a social man & makes a good many friends here. He lives in the City. I was led to disoblige him necessarily some months ago; & tho' he is drawing towards me again, he is just the sort of man I would like heartily with us after we are married. He has a great big family, big enough for six men.

Poor Lilly is so home sick that I mean to see her often. As it rains & looks gloomy I may go over to night.

I love you Sally.

Do you care to know it? & I am yours even in my dreams,

Most affly
Jno Miller.

Colalto
Monday Oct 22d. 1855

My dear John,

I am entirely too busy to write to you. You mustn't expect more than one letter in the next ten days.

Such a worry to me this Synod business is. My house is to be filled just as if I had nothing to do but entertain company. Miss Jannetta relieves me, however of much housekeeping trouble, by taking the keys and looking after matters herself. I have no idea of how many gentlemen are today here, or of who they are. Mr Van Zandt wrote accepting an invitation but I know none of the rest.[85]

Your letter with its enclosure,—a letter from Dr. Leibermann came Saturday night.[86] Yesterday I stopped Professor White, one of the Committee of arrangements, to ask if your friend, Mr Schenck could be given to me, and found he had, already been put down on my list. So that is settled.

---

85. Abraham Brooks Van Zandt (1816–1881), pastor of Tabb Street Presbyterian Church in Petersburg, Va.

86. Charles H. Liebermann, M.D., of Washington, D.C., had written McDowell in care of Miller, congratulating her on her forthcoming marriage and asking her to solicit the intervention of her uncle John Floyd in a pending lawsuit.

I made a mistake about the day of our marriage—I meant the *22d*—not 21st as I said. Dont we wish it was over?

Write a little oftener. Can't you?

I think Leyburn noticed yr Dedication very stingily.[87]

I am glad you've been to see Lilly. Do let her learn to turn to you, while I am absent for affection and attention. Poor child! She has nobody to lean upon but me, and I am anxious she should love you very much. She complains that you are "formal"—but I think even that will wear off after awhile.

Mary & Susan will both be here tomorrow or the next day.

I am annoyed that you should have to move just now. Cant you send all your books & papers right off to the Church Study & have that job over. Or if the Study is not ready couldn't they be tumbled into the committee room below it, until it is ready.

But I'm in a hurry—So good-bye.

> *With all my heart Your*
> *Own little woman*
> *S.C.P. McDowell*

Colalto
Wednesday Oct 24. 1855

My *dear John,*

Mere habit, if I had no affection for you would lead me to write every day or two to you, but when both come together I find I cant jostle my letter out of its usual time, I have nothing special to say, and am getting my house filled with Synodical visitors. Aunt Eliza sits by me, & the Library is full of girls.

I am disappointed in not hearing from you this morning. Your letters are fewer of late, and shorter; but I make all due allowance for your moving bustle just now. But, John, I am always hungering after a letter from you & find *reason* not the surest correction.

Aunt Sally Floyd writes me a tremendous letter about our marriage. Thinks it a shocking proceeding & begs me, by every thing sacred to me, to give it up. My whole family, she says disapproves and is outraged by it. She speaks very strongly, but with much affection, and I bear her no unkind feeling for anything she has written. I shall so write to her, and at the same time, I shall enclose her husbands letter to me in which he says "he heartily approves my step" & that "there will be amongst us many earnest partisans to applaud & sanction" it.

I begin to think I am *pretty* steady against such attacks, tho' at the same time they wound and annoy me. I am thoroughly engrossed by my own love to you, and content perfectly to be wrapped in your warm affection for me, and so; tho'

---

87. In the *Presbyterian,* which he edited in Philadelphia.

the attachment of old friends is to be somewhat coveted, yet it is not now a necessity of my existence.

I dont know how I should feel if you ever get cooler—but you never will get cooler, will you? I tremble to think the thing even possible. I am a perfect Salamander in this matter of affection—it cannot be too hot for me. And I don't return you a *little* for all you give. You may think it poor & faint, but if it is, you, at least have the pleasure of knowing that I have poured out to you all I have.

Judge Brockenbrough was here yesterday about the marriage settlement. It is to give me the control of my property as far *as is wise*, and the right to dispose of it by will. And, in case of sudden death without a will, and without children secures the whole to you during your lifetime. I would rather you should have it absolutely & that it should pass, like your own to Maggie & Allie, but Lilly comes in & tho' I may not fancy her husband, yet I might not fancy Maggie's either—so, in the far future it is wiser to let the Law take its usual course. In property concerns I have an irrepressible reluctance to allowing anything of mine to pass to my brothers-in-law or their children. Your children seen nearer to me than all other human beings except yourself & Lilly; and indeed I am surprised to find, how they are threatening to push my own poor child out of her natural place in my heart.

Susan is here & Mary will come tonight. You know Susan is my favorite Sister among the grown ones. She is so affectionate and considerate.

Dont you call this a long letter? I dont know what's in it—I write with perpetual interruption.

God bless you my own darling "little man."

Yours
S.C.P. McDowell

Sanctum Sanctissimum
Oct: 24th 1855.

Darling Sally,

The long agony is over. I expected to move my study in about half a day; instead of that I occupied two & the labour was concluded late last night by a gradual swelling of my force to four men & two carts & horses. Must not that have been a portentous little study. Late yesterday afternoon I went to my new boarding house which is as starched & stiff & yet as comfortable as one could desire. It is, I think, the most pleasant in the City. It is a large double house, a square from the La Pierre House & was the house of the Misses Henop of whom you have probably heard, ladies in reduced circumstances from the South. They have lately transferred the house to a friend, Mrs. Griffith. I find uninteresting but well-bred people at the table among others a son & grand-daughter of Bp White.[88] The Misses H. were accused of a little too much ceremony at their meals

---

88. Mrs. P. Henop operated a boarding house at 194 South Broad St. William White (1748–1836), first Episcopal bishop of Pennsylvania.

& in other respects but I see none of it now. It is within a Square of Lilly whom I saw last night after my troubles were over & who seems in better spirits. I told her of our wedding day & assured her that it was now fixed & she was not a little comforted. Darling Sally, my heart leaps so at the idea of actually having you in my possession & when you talk of leaving again to look after what remains of your business I am quite jealous of such a movement already. Still it is better to do that than to get sick by struggling thro' too much business. The paper came & I think you hardly do your Uncle justice in his speech. There is a sort of rank richness in the growth of that Preston eloquence which to me is always very striking. I have promised Lilly the paper. I will keep the lace. So 589 Vine St is among the things of the part. Well, I regret it. Tho' those were sad years as all mine are. Lilly was telling me what a frolicksome lass you had been the last six months; such as you had never been before in *her* knowledge. Do you know it quite made me vain? Tell me, if it ought to have done so. She tells me you have played with Cantey & her like one of themselves. God bless you, Dear Sally, I hope nothing will occur to damp those spirits again till white hair is on your temples.

Sunday was a rainy day which I considered a misfortune on freshly opening our church. At night we *had* a good audience. I preached both times. I will write oftener now.

Yours *affly*,
JM.

Church Study Thursday
Oct 25[89] [1855]

My *dear Little Woman*,

You can hardly think how nice it seems up here. You remember the large Franklin?[90] Well it *draws* to a charm. And when I think that perhaps on rare occasions you will be up here & that I probably will work in this room until my promotion to Princeton it gives me a most tranquil & happy feeling.

I saw Lilly this morning. She seems happier. But she says she fears you have entered her for the year as a boarder & wishes much that if you have done so you would write on to Miss Gill arranging for her leaving when you come that Miss Gill may have time to fill her space.

I enclose you our Governor's Thanksgiving appointment. You see he has chosen our wedding day. Dr Potts has also agreed (as you know) to exchange with me on the 25th the Sunday following & that of course implies my being in New York.[91]

89. McDowell added the date.
90. His stove.
91. George Potts (1802–1864), pastor of University Place Church, New York.

Now my sweet little woman if you were *sure*[92] you would marry me on the 22d I would adjust both these matters. I would write to Dr. Potts postponing our exchange & I would get some one to preach my Thanksgiving sermon. But if you are obliged to postpone the day hereafter, you know you may postpone it right into the day that Dr P. selected a second time.

What do you think of these ideas?—If you were to say the <u>21</u>st (Wednesday) we could reach Phil. by Thursday night go to Princeton on Friday & I or both of us could go on to N.Y. on Saturday & so keep the exchange as it is. Or if you are *sure* of the 22d I might propose an exchange with Dr Gurley of Washn or Dr Backus of Balto for the 25th & stay in one of those two cities on our way North— go to Princeton from there on Monday the 26th & to New York from there the following Saturday if the week's postponement suits Dr Potts. Or I can go on to Phil: you know in either case.[93] You know, My Darling, you must make me certain now one way or the other or that particular week crowded with appointments that have to be arranged beforehand wont answer. Still dont postpone if you can help, for both Lilly & I will be tired of waiting by the 22d.

I am glad Schenck is with you. I *wish* I was.

Yours affy
JM.

Colalto
Friday Oct 26.1856

My *dear John*,

It is nearly one o'clock, and the whole house is asleep, but as I shall have no time to-morrow morning to write, & as I was too busy to do it this morning, I write to-night.

My house is pretty full, with a constant change of company at meals. We all like Mr Schenck very much. *I* think him rather too formal & Northern, but am pleased with him, *notwithstanding*. He seems rather pleased with things & people here, tho' he is not very demonstrative.

Dr Musgrave is getting himself into trouble with our East Hanover Presbytery. This afternoon & till 11 tonight they had a warm debate upon the matter. The old man looks as *hard* as a piece of cast iron, but is very jovial & pleasant as a Visitor. In reply to my inquiry this evening after Tea—"Shan't I see you again Dr?" he said—"if not *here*, I shall see you soon in Phila!" I was surprised at his cool & confident allusion to our private affairs.—He couldn't have been cooler if he had been talking to me about a scheme of Church extension. Dr Van Rensselaer too—but then it was to be expected from him. Brother Schenck, however makes no allusions, and beyond an expression of thanks to you "for the pleasure of my acquaintance" has ignored all knowledge of any peculiarity in our relation to

---

92. This word is underlined five times.
93. Phineas Densmore Gurley (1816–1868), pastor of New York Avenue Presbyterian Church, Washington, D.C. Miller added this sentence in the margin.

each other. I observe, however, that he watches me curiously, & has made up his mind that I am a very independent & defiant sort of a Yahoo.

Oct 27th 1855.

I am so much obliged to you for the trouble you take about Lilly. She writes to Cantey—"Mr Miller is very kind to me, & I love him very much".

My heart sinks at the idea of pulling my house to pieces next week & packing up & giving up. I am fearfully engrossed by the whole thing.

"Old Jigger", after all, is admirably descriptive of the individual to whom it was applied—I have a sensation almost approaching disgust when I look at him.

Mr Carrington came today. He is a nice person—as is Susan too.[94]

Mary[95] is as quiet as ever—I wonder she isn't quieter. I think with that mass of mortality at my side, I should shrink away into absolute silence, & become as dull as he. He dont like me—and evidently thinks I think myself too clever & ought to be brought down a little.

Well, John, I don't mean to offend anybody in Princeton that way, but I want to enjoy the thing a little before I take leave of it. I am *tolerable humble*, when I am in bad spirits,—& that ought to content you.

But good night—I'm sorry now I didn't see the Vine St Study.

Affectionately Yours
S.C.P. McDowell

Phil. Oct: 29th 1855.
Study

My Dearest,

I feel to you tenderly in a way that I cannot at all express in a letter. Your letter almost made me cry. The true woman's devotion with which you throw yourself in my arms when one of your relatives so strongly upbraids you moves me beyond what I can tell. Dear Sally; *you are mine forever.* I did not once love you strongly enough to bear everything that was not sinful in your behalf; but now I do: & I accept the absorbed & self-contented affection with which you cast yourself entirely upon me. Dear Sally, I will be all the world to you.

You ask me if I will ever love you less. I think only in one contingency. And that is, if you ever grow cooler yourself. Nothing warms me so much as affection. I am a sort of *girl* in that respect. I once told you I would marry you if you did not love me. So I would. I would marry you because you have grown fast to me. I cannot do without you. But then I would marry you to be very forlorn & in time indifferent myself. The way in which you manifestly turn to me whenever the world chills toward you in any direction & warms yourself in our mutual

---

94. Charles S. Carrington, the husband of Susan Preston McDowell.
95. Mary Breckinridge McDowell Ross and her husband, John Ross.

love touches me beyond measure, & makes the whole warm garment of affection spread itself around me in thicker & warmer folds. God bless you for that true heart of yours, Dearest. It feeds my own love more than I can tell you, for I do think that of all feeling in the world indifference is the one that most entirely repels me.

You will have received my letter about Thanksgiving &c. If it has become certain that you must return some time in the Winter to see about your affairs (which I hope it has not) why not go back to the 14th as that week is remarkably free & will bring you to me seven days the earlier.

I saw Lilly on Thursday evening. I shall not call again till Monday for she goes out the last days of this week to spend a part of the day. My study is noble. I think I must relax a little & let you come sometimes to it with your knitting. Oh if I could only see you one minute each day, how happy I should be. You seem my only *happy* bond to life. And indeed you will soon be in my arms, dear, dear Sally, unless *Providence* thwarts, will you not?

Yours affectionately
Jno Miller.

[marginal note] Is it *true* that all yr family "feel outraged"?

Colalto
Thursday, Oct. 30: 1855

Dear John,

I was too tired last night to write. My house is still full of people. I write now in great haste.

Yesterday morning a letter in Mr Thomas' handwriting was handed to me. By the merest accidents, Miss Janetta Gordon was prevented from tearing it open as hers. I instantly threw it aside determining to return it unopened by today's mail. For the greater security I counseled with Cousin John & enclose you the result of our talk. Please keep what I send as I have kept no other copy myself. Whether the letter be hostile or amicable it is alike impertinent & obtrusive in him to write it. It gives warning of trouble from that quarter, and serves to put us on our guard against it. It is a worry and mortification to me to feel that, with me, you are to take this sort of annoyance & public notoriety. I long ago thought, & said I ought not to subject you to it—as a man it is bad enough—as a Minister greatly worse. And even yet, if you have any feeling that would suggest a retreat from such difficulties as seem in the future for you if you marry me, I will give you back your liberty in a moment. I could not say, it would cost me nothing;—very far from it, but you know I have had long experience in the matter of keeping my feelings controlled, and tho' the lesson of such self-denial has been out of practise for a year, yet if it be necessary I can learn it again. I feel your duty as a Minister to be superior to my claims upon you, and if that duty is in conflict with your affection to me & all that grows out of it, why, my dear John I submit without one word.

No, it is not true that my family "feel outraged" by our marriage. I never heard any such opinion from any but Aunt Sally, & never received any evidence of the existence of any thing strongly adverse to it from any one but Cousin Elizabeth Cocke, who is an excitable, prejudiced, eccentric woman. Aunt Eliza said Aunt Sally had no right to say such was the sentiments of the family, for she knew nothing about her opinions on the subject. I mean to enclose Uncle Floyd's letter to Aunt Sally, that she may see that she & her husband think very differently.

Susan leaves to-day. Lilly writes me very gratefully & affectionately of your kindness & attention to her. I thank you for it too. I rejoice you are so pleasantly fixed in the new Study. Somehow this morning, the little Sanctum, with its "great Franklin" and its air of comfort & peace, and all the delightful imagining with which I have invested it, seems almost out of sight—certainly beyond my grasp, and almost the sorrow of leave-taking comes over me.

I am barely in time for the mail.

God bless you, my dear John

Affectionately
S.C.P. McDowell

[Enclosure: Sally C. P. McDowell to Francis Thomas]

Lexington, Va.
Oct. 29th. 1855.

The enclosed letter was received this morning. The handwriting of the address discloses you as its Author, and hence I return it to you unopened. Everything in the past demands this course; and everything in the present sanctions and approves it.

Sally C.P. McDowell

[Enclosure: Sally C. P. McDowell to John T. L. Preston]
Dear Cousin,

On the page within you will find my answer to the letter we were speaking of yesterday. Please suggest any alterations,—

Affectionately
S.C.P. McDowell[96]

Study.
(Oct: 30)[97] [1855]

My darling Woman,

I wish you were here in this red plush arm chair that I might kiss & caress you as a relief from a long morning's work instead of the poorer reality of scribbling a letter. I am sorry you and Lord Rosse dont get on: perhaps he has visions that are above you like his namesake over the water & you are too microsropic to interest

---

96. Sideways on the page, Preston penciled a reply: "D. Sally, In every possible contingency, this reply will be exactly appropriate. J.T.L.P."

97. McDowell added the date.

him. Perhaps you are altogether in a different walk & fall naturally to me who am on an humbler scale & from not living on such spiritual food as he, have notions of a practical sort that make me love you. You know you said you were matter of fact & of course you know I am. Poor Rosse! He is a god in his own world, but a perfect Yahoo in ours aint he? Communicate to Mary this offering of poetry

lines to Mrs Rosse
"Mary, Mary;
"Quite contrary,
"How does your garden grow?
"Full of weeds
"And cockle seeds
"And up to your knees in <u>snow</u>.[98]

No matter we're warm enough, aint we? We're the people. And as to a great mass of humanity about you that you certainly wont have if you have me, for you know you're quite slender & I scarcely larger. Give my love to Mr Rosse & tell him that you & I are both heavenly bodies, you because you're so sweet & I because I require one of his best mounted glasses to bring me into vision at all.

I am glad Lilly loves me. It's a new desiare with her. I saw her yesterday. What d'ye think? She wants to go on to the wedding with me, & is willing to travel all night & to turn & come right back with us. That's a metamorphosis from a lady who wanted to be away at the time of the explosion, isn't it? Shall I roll her up in my plaid & bring her.

Sally, be very sure that this week or a least as soon as you get this letter you *fix* the wedding day. *I cant afford* in the midst of my engagements to have it slide again especially that week. What would you think of an exchange at Balto on our way?

Yours affly
Jno Miller.

Colalto
Nov: 1. 1855

My *dear John,*

I am always bustling and am compelled to snatch a half hour before breakfast to write to you.

Mary, Mr Ross & Miss Polly Moore leave this morning; Aunt Eliza & her two girls tomorrow. I can hardly get to business with so many about.

I am worried about the house. Cousin Elizabeth is disinclined to give the rent I ask, altho' all who speak to me of it consider it moderate enough. I would compromise in the matter, however, if her demeanor to me had not been so offensive. I know she will be troubled not to have the house, but then I have

---

98. "Lord Rosse" refers to John Ross, McDowell's brother-in-law. "His namesake over the water" refers to Sir John Ross (1777–1856), British explorer of the Artic. Mary refers to Mary Breckinridge McDowell Ross.

refused two offers for it for her, & now if she chooses to throw it back upon me, I am quite willing. Indeed I prefer now to have no relations of any kind with her. I am to hear finally from her agent here to-day. Mr Lewis insists I shall not lower my rent "as it would depreciate the property in the eyes of the community.["]

Col Reid declines the Trusteeship. He is too old he says for such business. Yesterday in a sort of desperation I applied to a Young Merchant here to take it. He is a man of good sense, uncompromising integrity, great resolution, & with very considerable business talent. He is terribly bad-tempered, but I warned him if we quarreled I could discharge him. He is to think of the subject, learn the duties of a Trustee & let me have his answer pretty soon.

I see no reason very strong for changing the day—the 21st will suit me as well as any other, tho' after a week's travel night & day you could do yourself no credit on Sunday in N. York. I will write about that however when I get an answer to my last letter.

I believe I go about offending the whole community. Brother Ross looked dyspeptic at me the other day; & Miss Polly asked me last night what I was mad at her for, & Aunt Eliza made me mad last night about you & my old rocking chair, which was my Grand Father McDowell's & which as a great favor I said I would lend to her. She said she wd keep it & give it to James—that you shouldn't have it. I told her *She* shouldn't have it; & tho' it all was carried on as a joke, I was mad and she shant have it. And I'm mad yet—and of course you'll laugh at me.

I must hurry Brother Ross & his prayers—So I go—I am pretty worried & angry—but mad or pleased I am yet all

your own
S.C.P. McDowell

Phil. Nov 1.st [1855]

Dear Sally,

I am spinning a web that is shutting me down & giving me no time even for a letter to you. I saw Lilly this morn: I called to invite her to go over with me this afternoon & when I found her engaged, then, this evening to my study that she might see it & sit down by my great wood fire & & write a letter to you. She seemed quite full of it, but Miss Gill, when she went to enquire for a permission asked her who were to be at the church & what was going on & when she told her nothing, her whole maidenly nature seemed to be revolted & she told Lilly to tell him *politely* that it couldn't be. She is possibly right, but when I found my pastoral trust-worthiness so entirely set at naught & my parental relation so entirely ignored & Lilly at 15 elevated into a lady as to whom *I*, the pastor of a Church, was not to be deferred to in my opinions of propriety I felt quite reduced in stature & left the house feeling that the New School authority in this case at least was too much for the Old.[99] Send me some notes & comments on my proposal & the Misses Gill's fidelity to the trust committed to them.

99. Miss Gill was a New School Presbyterian.

To confess the real truth I was never so taken by the gills in my life.

I saw Mr Schenck last night he is a reserved man, but I learned enough to see that he had been pleased. He was greatly shocked at his awkwardness in having left you without thanking you for your Va hospitality.

I have spoken confidentially with the Pastor of the Cumberland Ch. T[homas] it seems dont live in town but 50 m[ile]s off & *he knows nothing* except a *previous impression* of character.

Yours fondly
Jno Miller

Nov 1.[100] **[1855]**
Thursday, Night.
10 o'clock.

Darling Sally,

I have just opened your letter & on laying it down I feel more anxious about next Sunday's sermon than all the Thomases in the wide creation. I rejoice that in a few weeks a lady & one so tenderly & devotedly loved will no longer have charge of such unmutable things, but that they will pass into other & much less solicitous hands. I wish the whole matter left to myself not only by you but by the Major. I have my opinions formed on all the exigencies that may arise & have nothing in my religion that would prevent me from going to any extreme in defence either of myself or you. I think you have done just right in your reply. I dont *care* what the letter contains & am only touched that you should speak so sadly of taking leave of the "old Franklin" or of the old Franklin's *most impatient* proprietor. I have had half a notion to write to the Major but if you will say to him that clerical life in Jersey is not considered as making a man dependant upon his friends in unpleasant emergencies & that I wish all the responsibilities of what Thomas may do left to myself—I mean if you will convey this to him not as a message from me but as what you understand of my *feeling*, it may save us from having both the trouble of thinking of these things & it may save him from the wonder whether I am distinctly realizing this part of my position.

But, Sally, you dont say anything of our wedding day. You know, I must settle it with Dr Potts. Cant we be married on the 21st & return so as to get to New York.[101] You know you must settle the day now fixedly.

Whatever anxieties you may feel about leaving Colalto I have but one counsel to give you & that is *prayer*. I believe that prayer has more to do to bless people & give them prosperity than we ever possibly imagine. I think it is a shield over them in all the trials of life.

I write in great haste, but I love you so much & feel unwilling that you should spend the Sabbath under the sadness of that melancholy letter that I mean to

---

100. McDowell added the date.
101. Miller added a marginal note: "I can leave home on Sunday night, if necessary.

walk out in the rain & get this in at the Depot. God bless you my darling. I love you with the fondest tenderness. I feel as tho' you were my hand or my arm & have no more idea of ever parting with you than I have of life nor near so much. You are my sweet, lovely, darling, bride & I am,

Your own
JM.

Phil. Nov. 3d 1855.[102]

My *dear Child*,

"Scorn no man's love tho' of a mean degree; much less make any man thine enemy; love is a present for a mighty king; As guns destroy, so may a little sting."[103]

Dont offend anybody if you can possibly help it. You made a good impression here among all you met. Dont lose any friend in Virginia. If you have certain *cool* terms for your house &c. Mrs C[ocke] cant object to your insisting upon them; & I wouldnt quarrel with her for that or anything else. Beware of sharp words at the last. You know all these people you will see at intervals again. As to the trustee I should trust a good deal to the opinion of others. If Col Reid approves the young man, then you are tolerably safe.

I have seen Lilly. She has not heard fr. the Dr. She seems cheerful. I wrote to you yesterday twice & took the last to the Depot. I hope you got it. It was to say that the whole difficulty of which it speaks falls naturally to *me* when we are married & that I beg you will drive it all out of your mind. You had enough of these things to think of before you had one to whom you must confide them as you must to me. Your little irritations at Lexington give me more immediate anxiety than all this about the letter.

Good-bye, dear Sally, I am tired to-night. Be a good child & pray for me to-night when you go to bed. And dont let Aunt Eliza or any body else diminish your cool self-possession or your firm self-respect.

I am your own dear darling John whom you love very much. Dont you Sally? Good bye!

Be sure & *fix* the day.

Lexington,
Saturday, Nov: 3. 1855

My *dear John*,

Why, certainly, Miss Gill did right. I am glad she is so powerful proper. I wish she would take you for a pupil for a few weeks. You need a great deal of teaching in such things.

Sure enough Mr Schenck *is* a "reserved man", and if you will just let me *whisper* it to you, I didn't altogether like him. Every body in the house fancied

---

102. This was actually written on Nov. 2, 1855.
103. Lines are from "The Church Porch," by George Herbert (1593–1633).

him and I didn't utter a hint of the kind, but some how, there was a sediment of something unfavorable left in my mind. He was extremely gentleman like and polite, and tho' divested of everything like impulse in his manner, was, I thought, rather pleased than otherwise. He does not impress me as a man of ability, but as possessing a mind the very counterpart of his physique—cool, cautious, & constrained.

I answered Aunt Sally's hot epistle last night in a very calm, dispassionate way. I am sorry she is so hot against me for I love her very much, & I think she loves me almost more than any one else.

I am much annoyed by the fact of Mr Thomas' writing to me. I hear, he has threatened vengeance against us, & I know his malice is an undying passion. The malice of a brave man is not so much to be dreaded—but the assassin spirit of a coward you cannot protect yourself against.

Miss Jannetta wishes you would look in some of your book-stores for a book the title of which you will find in the waste of words on the enclosed scrap.[104] When you get it you will find a chance for disposing of the great return that Borhek made you.

Dont go too often to see Lilly; the Gills may complain that you interrupt her in her studies.

Such delightful weather we have! So warm that I sit with open windows and a poor slumbering fire.

Do you know I am opposed to your going to N. York or any where else the first Sunday after we are married. I think it would be best for you to be in your own pulpit and among your own people as soon after as possible. Besides I dont think everything can be accomplished here as soon as you think. You reach here at Midnight Tuesday night—the stage leaves next morning between 10 & 11—How can we get the marriage settlement, read & signed, and the marriage ceremony concluded, & the leave taking accomplished by 11 o'clock? But I am ready to make the effort to do it all.

What are you so busy about? Does Maggie never write to you now?

Affectionately Yours
S.C.P. McDowell

If you can, conveniently, please give the enclosed note to Lilly & offer to go with her to Brinton's on an errand of business. I feel much like apologizing for my frequent calls upon—tell me how I shall do it.

Colalto
Monday Nov: 5. 1855

My *dear John,*

To relieve you of all further anxiety about Dr. Potts & other engagements I say to you now that the *21st is the day fixed.* I will try to get thro' with all my business

---

104. This enclosed note has not been found.

by that time, and if I dont succeed you will send me back in the Spring to look after what remains. This arrangement requires you to do nothing but travel all the week if you carry out your plan of going to New York by the 25th, and on that account is a bad one. I would not like you to leave home on Sunday, tho' the one hour that you would take from it would give you a day's rest here.

I am beginning to realize that I am going away and the prospect assails my resolution very strongly. You asked if my family were "outraged" by my marriage. Mary said to me the morning she left, that tho' she had a sort of *feeling* about it still, "Yet she was entirely reconciled to it". And Mr Ross most cordially approves it. I remark no change but one of increased respect & affection with both Susan & Mr Carrington and old Mrs C___ (Susan's Mother-in-law) bestirs herself kindly in making plans to shield me from all unpleasant remark. Catherine too is far more affectionate than ever before.[105] I have *seen* no demonstration against it but from Cousin Elizabeth Cocke, & if I had treated her according to the dictates of the Old Adam I sh have ordered her out of my house in very few words. I am rather sorry Cousin John has taken my house for her, but I put up with her, & her bad manners & all rather than have any outbreak. She is eccentric, any how; but until now was a very kind & attached friend to *me*, & all her life warmly devoted to my Parents, who loved her greatly.

Hadn't you better reconsider the plan of going to New York. I think we wd gain by being immediately in Phil. If you go to N. Y. you will be absent nearly two weeks (for you wd stop two or three days at Princeton on your return) and thus give you proper time to huddle together & talk over the marriage & concert plans of action.

How would it do for me not to sell any of my furniture now? It will be sold at a sacrifice, & perhaps in a few months you may make such arrangements as will make it useful to us. I half wish I had not rented the house, so that in case of difficulty in Philadelphia we could come back to it next Spring.

I am hurried & must get to my work.

Affectionately Yours
S.C.P. McDowell

(Nov 6. 1855)[106]
Tuesday.

My darling Daughter,

I am getting quite accustomed to my altered study; & so impatient for the time when I shall fold you in my warm possession that I have made you contraband in my thinking. I have a rule against ever bringing you into my mind. And as you know you are no homoepathic dose & always insist upon coming into my

---

105. "Mrs. C___" is Sarah E. Scott Carrington (1800–1870). Catherine Scott Carrington (1825–1893) was Charles Carrington's sister.
106. McDowell added the date.

notice in anything else than an infinitessimal way I keep you out all together. In my studies in my visits & in my chamber I never think of you if *I can help it*; & as the result of my effort I only think of you about three quarters of the time.

Seriously; you have no idea how *uncomfortable* you are. You are not contented with a decent share of attention that ought to content any Xtn woman. But wherever I let in to my mind you pull & haul at me as if you were distracted. You shut up my books & thrust me down into an arm chair near my Franklin & there make me idle my time in mere reveries. You love my umbrellas & scatter my gloves to the four winds & sit on my spectacles & it is only by shutting you out close that I can keep brains in my head, sermons on my desk or money in my pocket. You are all idle, worthless, uneasy *spirit* & unless you lie quieter when you actually get into my embrace my usefulness is at an end.

I meet no trouble in my parish & my people so far are pleased with our success. Our church was well filled on Sunday tho' it rained. How long it will last, dont know.

I have not yet written to Dr. Potts, but hope to after your letter this evening. You are not a useful wife so far. I dont know how you'll be after your inauguration but tho' I particularly asked you to write *fixing* the day, so it wouldnt slide again you haven't done it & haven't *mentioned* any such matter for several letters & youre a wicked nasty thing.

Good bye: I'm going to whip you every day about dinner time after you come to Phil.

> *Yours affectionately*
> +John.[107]

Colalto
Nov 7. 1855

Dear John,

I write in the extremest haste & without having an idea in my head, & in just such condition of being as makes me hopeless of ever having one again.

Would it be worth while for me to take my silver with me to Phil:? There is no great quantity of it, but such as there is, is unusually handsome & I wd not like to run any risk of losing it. As we wont need it immediately, wouldn't it be better for me to lend it to Mary who really wants it, if she is willing to take it?

I progress very slowly with all my affairs. My Trustee-elect has not yet answered. If he accepts, I shall think "God put it into my heart" to ask him, for I now feel sure he is the best selection I could have made at all.

I am behaving very nicely to people & will try to keep them in good humor with me. Nib & I are rather cool to each other, but I will endeavor to warm her up a little & keep myself a bit cooler & see if that wont remedy things.

---

107. The greeting and the cross before the signature concluding the letter affected the episcopal style.

Two weeks from today, John, settles things with us for life. Only think of it! Well, the prospect is full of hope to me, dear little man, tho' I have many a fear about it too. And I dont mean that the venture shall be such a bad one for you, & at the end of the first decade you will tell me so of your own free will.

With all my heart Yours
S.C.P. McDowell

Thursday,
Nov. 8. 1855.

My dear Sally,

I am just going to Chester. I was shocked yesterday to receive a note from Bp P. that our father-in-law who was quite aged had died suddenly of heart disease. Poor Nelly, the Bishop's son, was so overcome by it that when sent over to me at my boarding house before I received my note he could not tell me what had happened, but simply conveyed a message from Mrs H. to come & see her.[108]

There is trouble all around me. Poor Annie is suffering under a sad mishap to her prospects of health & Dick has been quite sick & Spence in a good deal of anxiety so that just now I am the only one who am in good spirits.

Miss Brinton sent your box on the 20 ult. I hope you have it.

The book I will get.

Before your letter came I had sent to Dr Potts altering our arrangements for an exchange, so that I am free to arrange that Sunday as I please.

I think I will not set out till Monday night the 19th for I dont see that I can help you in any cares of *yours* by my presence, & *my* work consists of nothing but signing my name which I can do in a minute & taking leave of your friends in which I suppose we shall be hurried let it be what morning you please. Still I am under your command in the matter.

I agree in your idea of being at once in Phil. & also in its not being desirable to be all the week travelling.

As to the furniture I cant intelligently advise. The great thing is storage. If you cant store it safely & well & out of the reach of damp & children you had better sell it. It is a very perishable species of property.

I saw Lilly this morning. She is well. I will be guarded about going too often.

I have half a notion to say that I will *not* go over to see you the night of my arrival. It will disturb that night's rest at a time when you are full of fatigue & excitement. But I will see how my resolution holds out. God bless you. Tell me now & then whether you love me at all,

for I am yours fondly,
Jno Miller.

108. Robert Benedict died on Nov. 5, 1855. "Mrs. H." is Margaret Benedict Hunter, Robert Benedict's sister.

Colalto
Friday Nov: 9. 1855

Indeed, John, you are a cross fellow, sure enough. If it were not that matters had gone so far I should feel like turning back and turning against you. But I am without help now: I shall have to put up with you and all the faults I know and all I suspect, and all I am yet to discover! What an undertaking! I'm as scared *as I can be.*

I did write you that the 21st was the day fixed. I wish you could make your exchange with Dr Potts later in the Winter. I think it would be better and pleasanter. I don't want to go to New York and yet could not well do otherwise. I couldn't stay in Philadelphia without you, and would feel very awkward at Princeton if you were away. By the by, do tell me a programme from the 21st, on.

I have written to Lilly that *she* must give all orders to Brinton about the things she has, but that those orders must all depend upon *your consent* to have a box sent to you at Mrs Griffith's. So you will please tell Lilly whether you will or will not have Brinton's box sent to you. If you will allow it, then, when it reaches you, open it & take out of it a cashmere dress that you find on the top, wrap it up nicely in a large towel, (which you must get somewhere or other), put it in your trunk & bring it to me. You will distinguish this, from another Cashmere in the box if it sh not be on top, by its lining of a pinkish kind of silk. There is another thing that I want too, which may be in the box, but I will write to Lilly about it, & have it rolled in a long package so that there can be no mistake about it.

Robert White refuses my trusteeship, for no other reason that I can see, but that Judge Brockenbrough has been so slow in giving him an insight into the duties that would devolve upon him.[109] I am sorry for it, as I'm sure he has been, by far the best choice I have made.

I have applied to his Kinsman Wm White & aim to receive his answer this morning.[110] I think he will refuse too. I am fortunate in not having succeeded with Col Reid.

If you think it best to conclude your arrangements with Dr Potts for the 25th, of course you must not be influenced by my notions, for *at present* you know more & better about such things than I can do. But John wouldnt it be very nice to be entirely quiet for a week, & not hear a car whistle, nor think of a even an hour's journey.

My days of letter writing are nearly over—two more or three will conclude them. I shall not be greatly grieved, yet I shall have some regrets about them.

Goodbye my dear John. When I next see you I hope you will be in a better humor.

Affectionately
S.C.P. McDowell

---

109. Robert I. White (1818–1890), a Lexington merchant.
110. William C. White (1812–1897), also a merchant in Lexington.

Sat.
Nov 10. 1855

Dear Giraffe,[111]

How is your Highness this morning? Your dear little man sends you his love & hopes you are enjoying life up there better than he is, for darling Sally, the truth is these last days are very hard to endure. And it requires all my philosophy which you say "is not much" to carry me over this dead point in my life.

The silver I would by all means send to Mrs Ross. *I* have some also which would help us to begin if we woke up suddenly some morning and found ourselves housekeeping. Just think of my having so few days now to be separated from you, not more than (I am afraid) you will run away from me for, after we are married. Tho', Sally, let us be like Dick & Julia, always most romantically together except—when I am in my study.

I enclose Dr P.s letter. He dont write as tho' he were "outraged" does he? Dr Van Rensellaer gave me the highest account of you & wound up by saying, you were "a great gift from the Almighty". I think you are a great gift myself; 160 lbs avoir dupous did'nt you say?

Near 7 P.M.

I have only to send you a Sat. even: salut: Good bye

affly
JM.

[Enclosure: George Potts to John Miller]

9 Nov. 1855.
To the Rev John Miller.

My dear Sir

"Cedunt arma toga"[112]—by a loose translation—All things give way to a wedding. No excuses were needed as to the postponement of the arrange for an exchange. I agree with you in hoping it may be effected at some future day— but not able so far ahead, to say at present, what day of next month will be convenient.

Will you permit me to offer my best wishes in advance of your marriage with a lady for whom I have a great respect. May blessing attend you.

Yours very truly
Geo Potts.

Lexington
Monday Nov: 12. 1855

My dear John,

Mr William White has at length accepted the Trusteeship, and to-day he will be duly inaugurated.

---

111. A reference to McDowell's height.
112. Latin, meaning "weapons yield to a toga," that is, we give up warfare for politics.

This is a heavy burden off my mind, and I hope my Man will be a comfort to me. He is not so efficient as Robert White, whom I first chose, but he is quite as conscientious, and sensible & prudent, and much better tempered, and is therefore, a more pleasant person to come in contact with. The Carriage waits at the door & I am excessively hurried.

Lilly is to have a long package put in Brinton's box, just by the Cashmere dress, about which I wrote, for you to bring to me. If a cord & tassel is lying near the dress bring it too—the dress wd be useless without it. And as I am on the subject of dress I may say, I have a fancy for your wearing the frock coat I saw you wear in Phil, when we are married; and a *black* cravat.

I shall write again when I'm less hurried.

You need not require me to tell you "now & then" that I love you, but believe that I do it very warmly all the time. I find it hot enough & strong enough to bear down every other attachment.

I hope soon to see you & yet I grow nervous & alarmed sometimes, as the time approaches.

Very affectionately Yours
S.C.P McDowell

Church Study
Nov: 12th 1855.

My *darling Sally*,

The time of my *rapture* comes so near as to make me tremble. I am so constituted that high joys are more painful than deep sorrows. I have been so bereaved & saddened all thro' life that a marriage wears to me half the semblance of another offering on the shrine of trouble. You are so dear to me that I dread to possess you lest you be torn away. And you are so precious in my eyes in your actual *value* to me apart from my affection, that if I love you (& Darling I have lost everything in this world that I loved except my Mother & my two little children) I should not be able to reason myself into any intelligent acquiescence in such a sorrow.

Darling, put a new petition in your prayers for my sake, that God will spare you long as my darling wife & that in the riches of his goodness he will never give *me* the distress of ever parting with you.

But Alas! for a poor old man like me this is sad talk on the eve of a marriage. Well, Sally, I talk just as I feel, & I think that's the way letters should be written. I love you with the most ardent passion & the tho't that this marriage not only brings you to my arms but *keeps* you there & that you are to be my own sweet bride as long as we live seems to me entirely too good for such a poor sinner as I, & not in keeping with the rest of my melancholy history.

I saw Lilly yesterday & she spoke of the parcels & also of a box that *she* has to send. I will be very careful to have all right.

As to the Trustee take care that at the last moment you dont make a rash selection. Your power to *discharge* is not a full protection for a trustee can easily so entangle himself in your estate that you cant discharge him.

Annie is so sick that I cant give you a programme yet. If she is sufficiently recovered we will go to Spencer's on Thursday night from the cars & stay some days. Mrs Potter is not in town. She hopes to be some week or more from this. I will probably know more when I write again.

Mrs Benedict (their grand-mother) has been making a most formal & affecting appeal to me to let the children be with *her* this Winter. She still means to live in Chester, &, of course, alone. Mother, also, advises that the children be left at Princeton while we are boarding. I, of course, would like them in Phil. How it will be we can tell better when time has drifted us a little further on. God bless you. We have not much longer to be away from each other. Have we, Sally? God bless you. I didn't know this *old* heart of mine could love any one now so dearly.

Yours with deep Affection
JM.

Phil. Nov : 14th [1855]

My *dearest Sally,*

Spencer saw me yesterday & told me that he *hoped* he would not be defeated in his wish to have us there at once from the cars but that Annie was still so unwell as to make him anxious. She is not up yet. And every one is charging him to be careful of her—and so I mean to let a few days more pass before I form a programme that I can send on to you. Mrs P. is not in yet. If Spence (who insists that if defeated in his wish to have us at first, we will go to his house when Annie is enough recovered) is out of the question, I think I will propose to you to go at once to Princeton, a step which I think has many things in it desirable in its own account, but which I would agree with you in preferring to postpone if A. were well.

Does it not seem strange that I should be writing the *last* letter that it will be in your power to reply to.

I find the French book with a long name not in our city. I went to all the leading bookstores of that class last afternoon & they assured me I would not find it. But I will get it yet. Tho' not in time to take with me.

Blessings on you, my Darling; you seem fearfully near my grasp. The sea I sail on now is tossed by the wildest impatience & yet at the bottom of this heart of mind is a sort of leaden unbelief that God in his Providence *can* intend for me so rich a treasure. I never shall *exult* over my happiness till you are actually in my arms.

Yours Sincerely
Jno Miller

Wed. Eve, 6' o clock, I have received your letter & will attend to all its commissions with more than [illegible] more pleasure.

Colalto,
Nov: 14. 1855

My *dear John*,

I am in no state of exuberant spirits myself, and your letter really makes me sad. But it hardly seems right for me to add any thing to your depression by any expression of my own. And besides it is not true, that just now I am always below par. Notwithstanding all my fears, life is happier to me now than for many, many years before. I find myself getting back the joyousness of Lilly's age, without the pain that a morbid sensitivity imposed upon me then. Somehow I have rolled off the burden I have borne for such a long time, and am happier—really happier now, than I ever was. I am not so merry as of yore but the *grave* & steady cheerfulness that belongs to my race, is fully in possession. And for the most of all this, I must thank you.

I wish we could go *first* to some Hotel or Boarding house. I hate to go to any private houses at midnight under any circumstances; but especially now as Annie is not well, & Spence anxious about her, & worse than all, since I have such an amount of baggage. However arrange it to suit yourself and friends.

Pray don't commit yourself to Mrs Benedict about the children. Make them a New Year's gift to me. I want them; and I know that the sooner they are with me the better for us all.

Don't let Lilly put too large a box upon you. I dont know what she has in it, but if it is too large for your trunk, tell her so, for like all girls, she may be inconsiderate of such things.

When you come, you must come over the night of your arrival for if we are married at 10 next day I wont have time for some arrangements unless you do. I am getting so impatient to see you.

God bless you, my dear John

Affecly
S.C.P. McDowell

Phil. Nov: 15th [1855]

My *darling Sally*,

I have my pulpit supplied for Sunday & I have determined not to wait till Monday but to leave here tomorrow night. At least I think of it very seriously.

If I reach Lexington on Sat night I will come over to Colalto unless it is very late.

Lilly tells me your things will be ready tomorrow.

Yours most affectionately
Jno Miller.

PART FIVE

"If you love that lady dont marry her."

November 1855–March 1856

When John Miller arrived in Lexington for the wedding, he found major obstacles to his marriage to Sally McDowell. Members of her family, especially her older brother James, expressed strong objections. Miller also received disturbing news from Philadelphia. The elders of West Arch Street Church had passed a resolution stating that his marriage to a divorced woman would "injure and interfere with our Success as a Church and our Pastors influence among us."[1]

Yielding to these multiple pressures, the couple determined to postpone their marriage. Miller left Virginia and returned to confront his congregation in Philadelphia.

Colalto
Friday, Nov: 23. 1855.

John, darling, I am so grieved at our disappointment. I find, as I often suspected before, that I have loved you too engrossingly. I have been pouring out upon you all the affection that was in my own heart. It may not be passionate—I always stop, & hesitate whether I can describe it by such a word as that, but it is just that sort of feeling which is ready to undertake any thing for your sake, to endure any thing, and sacrifice every thing, not absolutely sinful, to your wish and will. I mourn with bitterness that I am so yeilding to you. And yet I would not feel for you, even if I could, any less confidence & trust than I do. I am *painfully* anxious for your whole love, and so jealous of every thing that can abate its warmth and respectful tenderness.

---

1. "At a meeting of the Board of Trustees . . ." (Nov. 13, 1855, McDowell Family Papers, #2969, folder 1848–1859, Alderman Library, University of Virginia).

Now, that you are gone, and my mind is more free to act, I begin to look back over this last year, and to feel how I have allowed all the fervor & strength of religious principle & feeling to diminish under this new affection. Tho' I often and often thanked God with all my heart that he had sent you here and allowed me the happiness of loving you & being loved by you, yet this favor I did not let draw me more humbly & decidedly to Him & his service; but, on the contrary, permitted to wean me from Him. And now, I mourn over all this, and pray that I may truly repent of it. And if I have been the occasion of any such sin in you, I hope it may be forgiven, & the evils consequent upon it averted from you. And for the future, let us be more decided and steady in endeavoring to know and to do the will of God. I would have my love to you sanctified by a feeling & purpose like this. I love you John with more power than you dream of, or than I dreamt of until now, and I long after your love with a keenness of desire, you do not begin to comprehend.

I enclose all of Williams letters that you have sent me—& James', & one of Wm Brown's to Dr White which has a paragraph in it devoted to us.[2] By the bye I have written to Mr Brown to repeat in a letter to me the expressions he had expressed on the subject of our marriage to Dr White, that you may have this letter to use privately in the Phil: Presbytery, in case you have mislaid those I sent you in the Spring.

Please send me Spence's address that in case of emergence, I may enclose a letter for you to him.

Go & comfort Lilly as well as you can. And be careful in all things. And may God protect you & bless you Darling and give us a happy issue out of all our troubles.

Affec'y
S.C.P. McDowell

Colalto
Saturday Nov 24. 1855

My *dear* John,

The morning is a bad time for me to write to you. I get up in uncontrollable agony after a night of restlessness and anxiety, and am scarcely fit for any effort of any kind. Yet I find it a momentary relief to come and pour out my heart to you. I am beset with a thousand fears, yet the greatest of all, and the most terrible of all is that of your affection. And I want you to tell me John with the utmost solemnity & truth *just* how much you love me, & what sort of love it is. Do re-assure me on this point, for every thing future hinges upon it. However much I love you, under our threatened embarrassment & difficulties, I could not, I think, with any hope

---

2. William Brown, the Presbyterian minister in Augusta, had earlier written of his support. These letters have not been found.

of happiness to myself or you, venture to marry you if I doubted the fervency and respect & tenderness of your love. So tell me about it: and tell me truly. I wont bind you by any refined notion of honor to any engagement between us, if your affection wanes. It is *that* that I want & want it as I have described it to you a hundred times. When the world grows cold & the storm beats, if I cannot wrap myself up warmly in it, then nothing human can avail me.

I have always wanted to stand by you as a helper in your work. I dont sympathize in your Studies because I dont understand them, but feeling to you as to my husband I should I hope soon [to] learn to concentrate all my pleasures in you and yours.

I find my present trouble brings me back stronger & stronger, to the true source of comfort—and I am more willing to submit all to the disposal of the great Disposer of all: and I pray for Guidance, and have the words Jehovah-jireh strongly sounding in my ears.[3]

Do write to me every day & as fully as you can. And May God bless & protect you

> My *darling* John
> S.C.P. McDowell

Sat [November 24, 1855]

Dear Sally,

Desperately hurry—sudden call to Burlington. Expected to write tonight. I <u>pledge</u> myself never to marry another unless you desire it in some most unexpected circumstances or forbid it in circumstances of malice which with you are impossible. God bless you! Will write from Burlington.

> JM

[marginal note] No news. Keep up your courage. mine does not flag.

Nov 24. [1855]
Steamer Edwin Forrest
Delaware River
Sat. Evening.

Darling Sally,

I reached S[taunton] with more than usual speed. At the table at McClung's I was treated to the following conversation.
Gentleman. Well why didnt it come off?
Lady. (Something sotto voce)
Gent. They couldnt have loved each other much.

3. "Jehovah-Yir'eh" means "The Lord will provide."

Lady. (unheard)

Gent. It only increases the notoriety.

Lady. ——————

Gent. The truth is both are afraid of Thomas. They had better have him bound over to keep the peace.

I thought it time just at this point to interpose. So I touch my neighbor (the gentleman) quietly & said—"I'll explain that matter to you, Sir, after tea." (silence)

A Col Ruff with whom I rode all day, & who I found was from your town went in with me over the Blue Ridge & I thought I would tell him of this affair at the table. I found Mr Locher (the gentleman I sat with) had already told him & seemed much mortified. What sort of a man is Rough. I tho't I would explain to him the cause of the delay & I did so. He rode with me all the way to Balto. I had a talk also with Mrs McClung & explained the matter to her distinctly.[4]

I reached Phil last night. This morning I saw Cornelius. He told me the paper of the Trustees would not be recorded. I saw also Dr Musgrave who took a very sombre view of our affair. What do you think he advised me? To be dismissed to the Lex: Presbytery & take a Va charge. He is however a warm friend & yielded to my considerations for not doing so & has entered into my counsels. I then saw Mr Happersett, who told me that in N.Y. Drs Potts & McElroy had both asked him about me & expressed their indignation at my church & belief that the Pastors should rally round us & sustain us under the attack. He said also that here there was a good deal said of the same sort. The modes of talking are however diverse in different cases. Mrs Boardman, for example I find dont mean to visit you, to which I had the wickedness to reply that I did not care if she did not.[5]

I have, however, determined to *sound* the different prominent members of the Presbytery as to whether a minute *some what* in our favour may not be passed. Dr Musgrave tho't *not* at first, but afterward yielded a little. I have just been to Burlington to see Dr Van Rensellaer. He & I drafted the form of a minute which *he tho't would pass.* He is to see Dr Boardman about it on Monday. I will then write to you. If I find Dr B. & one or two others opposing I will recede from any further steps lest my effort should become known as having been defeated. I hear that Dr Cheeseman says he means to make a snite in Presbytery about the action of my church & have it rebuked, but that will not answer.[6]

4. Jacob M. Ruff (1809–c. 1880), Lexington hat manufacturer and former treasurer of the Virginia Military Institute. Charles H. Locher (c. 1822–1889), cement manufacturer in Lexington. Elizabeth Alexander McClung, mother of the hotel proprietor in Staunton.

5. George Washington Musgrave (1804–1882), Presbyterian minister in Baltimore. Reese Happersett (1810–1866), assistant secretary for the Presbyterian Board of Domestic Missions, Philadelphia. Joseph McElroy (1792–1876), pastor of the Scotch Presbyterian Church in New York City. Eliza Beach Jones Boardman (1810–1874).

6. A minute was a motion passed in a meeting of presbytery. Lewis Cheeseman (1803–1861) of Fourth Presbyterian Church, Philadelphia.

This table shakes so that I can hardly jot down my words. My head aches & I feel tired. But Darling you are the object of all my love & my most passionate desires. I wrote before I left the city *my* side of the marriage covenant we were speaking of. *Your* side you need not care for. I will not bind you.

I have not seen Spence yet nor the Dr (James) nor Dick.[7] I shall see James this evening & beg him not to *talk* about this thing himself.

I did not know till this visit that I loved you so much. These preachers tell me that I must act with the most *painful sense* this week & I shall do so: Pray for me. I will do the best for both of us I can. I would like to go on living in Phil. These ministers are fond of me.

Yours very affly
Jno Miller.

Church Study[8]
Nov: 26th 1855

My darling Sally,

I have debated how I could keep from disturbing you by the see-saw thro' which I pass in meeting with different persons in respect to our difficulties— whether I should tell you what was pleasant alone—that would be dishonest whether I should delay telling you anything till after all is settled—that would hold you in suspense, or whether I should tell you *all* just as it happens that I know you would prefer. And, Darling, it ought to be like my own arm under your head to hold you up when I assure you thro' all rebuffs of the passion & ardour with which I love you.

After writing on Sat. I staid in my room on Sunday thinking over our matter prayerfully till late at night when I went over to Mrs Hunter's. She was *more* kind even than usual but told me that the moment the church acted the whole town seemed to break out in a common blaze about our affair & that the fire all seemed to burn one way. This does not surprise me after what the ch. did except in its intensity. I am mortified however that I seem such a false prophet to you & take fully to myself the shame of misjudging the strength of the popular mind, but then, Sally, I *in part* predicted it when I urged you to marry me in the Spring so as to bring your personal influence to bear even before the trouble rose up. Mrs Hunter concluded by advising me, *if I loved you not to marry you & so destroy your position.* Lou also, tho' kind as usual had settled into a strong feeling against our marriage.[9] I next even went to Dick's who had also his unfavorable stories of excitement & who said that preachers were *not* the leading men in the community & hence their advice was not as good as influential laymen. This is

---

7. McDowell's brother was visiting Philadelphia.
8. In the top margin, Miller added, "Just direct to 'Phila.'"
9. Clarissa Louisa Benedict, younger sister of Miller's first wife.

fudge. He did not, however, undertake to say one word in the way of counter advice.

I then went to see Dr Van R. who had been disappointed in getting in & will come to-morrow. I met Mr Schenck. He espouses our cause warmly. He has not a *doubt* of my step. He says it is his deliberate judgment that my step will *not* affect your social standing. *He* says, many of the ladies speak in your favor. He thinks a minute such as I described to him will pass & he offers all possible help & denounced the idea of postponement. I then met Dr Cheeseman who thundered away at my church, said his daughter (who is in it) would leave it & that there was a good deal of excitement in it against the elders & that he had no doubt of my step. I calmed him as much as I could & he promised to behave himself.

Sally, Darling, I have two great fears about this thing now, both ending in you. first, lest I fill myself with remorse for bringing down your social position & second, lest I beggar you by turning the public against us. I would not care for the last so much as in its connection with the first. Still I have high hopes of doing neither one thing nor the other, but of shielding you in both respects. I mean to act with great care & will tell you more to-morrow night. If the Pres. treats us with a favoring minute which I hope & I shall risk no other, then I shall also *want* to stay in Phil sometime after our marriage & face this bug-bear of Phil society. I would like it if it be but six months. I want also to see how Mrs Potter stands, kindly I have no doubt. I am wholly yours whatever difficulties ensue & I have much hope.

Yours Affy
Jno Miller.

Church Study
Nov: 27th 55.

My *Darling,*

You cant conceive what pleasure these new expressions of love give me. You never *wrote*—"Darling" before. If you could feel the gush of tenderness that such an endearment awakens you would not bind me so solemnly to tell you of my love.

Now, Sally, listen! If I *knew* that I must wait twenty years to marry you & that all that time you would love me & that occasionally I might see you, I would rather be in that relation to *you* than have all the past steeped in the waters of oblivion & have the warmest love of any other woman I have ever seen. As to the tinges of bitterness that my wild love for you has occasioned I say with the most honest certainty, Darling, that I *never* loved you with so much respectful tenderness as the morning I looked back at you as you stood in the front door bidding me good bye as I left you. Indeed, Sally, I love you still so much better than you love me that the anxiety ought to be all the other way. I was describing my feelings towards you this morning to Mrs Potter & I was quite ashamed of the warmth & glow of my expressions.

But, Sally, my heart *bleeds* when I hear of such a thing as your "uncontrollable agony". *Think* of it: you *possess* me entirely. I am yours beyond the hope or wish of recall. I shall live for you alone (if you will allow me) the rest of my life. I am *sure* of this. And in *my* feelings of love this is the *great* thing. If you were not *mine* I should be plunged in the deepest depression. As you *are* mine I look upon this *arrest* of our marriage only as a painful self-denial.

You ask me *how* I love you. I will tell you. If I could live in the same house with you. If you would sit by my fire while I studied. If you would ramble with me thro' the woods in the Summer afternoons. If you would talk with me about my peculiar passions & ambitions. If you would lean as you did at Colalto upon my side & let me kiss you, & our relations, therefore, were like the relations of sisters nine tenths of the yearnings of my heart would be fully satisfied— so much of my love consists of that very tenderness & respect, & let me say, congenialtly, about which you raise the question. My whole passion for you is built upon a substratum of respect & could not exist without it. So behave, Child, & keep quiet.

Now about my mornings work I feel sad. I write most shrinkingly, but I will tell you all. Dr Van R. is still sick. I saw Bp. Potter. As I feared when Mrs H. spoke as she did he has changed very much. He speaks with the utmost kindness, but began by advising our settling in Va a thing which for this reason I cant abide. He says he has been near Frederick & there is a difference of opinion there about the *expediency* of the marriage (well, that is not a very serious thing). But then he implies that he has scruples about the step itself because the divorce was not on the right ground. He says public opinion here is strongly against us. He hears it on every side. He says he is grieved that he gave me a wrong impression. He could not have conceived that he could have changed so, & yet he said he was not *sure* that excitement might not blow over in time. I saw Mrs P. She was under the same influence said that it would not influence *her* conduct in the heart but on the contrary she would insist on all we had promised as to her house but still she seemed to say as Mrs H. did, if you *love* the lady dont marry. One of Bp Potters emphatic speeches was, If I were Mrs M D with such a position as she has I wouldnt marry you. And they told me what seemed to have surprised them both, that the public seemed to make no distinction between the different cases of divorce.

Now, to-morrow, I shall probably hear something just as strong on the other side. I am determined no *light* thing shall shake me in my own convictions. I am determined to marry no one *else* than you. And I beg you, Darling, not to desert me as you threatened to do if sheer *certainty* that you will lose your position should raise an outcry against the marriage & force you to decide that you will postpone it further.

It seems cruel that with all the pain I feel I should have this additional that I give you so much. But, Sally, if I love you so tenderly that in the sight of God I still prize your affection to me in spite of all its pains as my greatest treasure, is that no support to you? I will write daily without exception. Keep up your spirits & I shall still hope to send you good news. I wish we had taken the Potters in their first mood & yet perhaps they would have turned then more unpleasantly. I may get a *minute* in our favour. I have some hopes.

Tell me if my love seems of any value to you if we have to postpone our marriage.

Yours fondly
Jno Miller

[marginal note] I am convinced we ought to marry *soon* if we venture upon it under existing circumstances. And but *the certain loss of your position socially* will deter me for a moment. Dare we incur that with our eyes open?

Colalto,
Thursday, Nov 27. 1855.

Dear John,

I cannot express to you all the pain and anguish of the last three or four days. Some day, if God ever throws us together again, I shall tell you about it. Mean time I write off in a hurry the things that fill my mind in regard to our present circumstances.

First of all, I want to impress upon my own mind and yours, the Truth, that we are not blindly to seek our own happiness either in this, or in any other act in life. The question with us *now* sh be, not "May I seek my happiness in this marriage if it be in accordance with God's will"?, but, happiness aside, "How shall I act so as most to glorify God?" This is, the highest standard of Christian action, & the most difficult; yet it is the one I want to reach myself, and the one I want you to attain too. Weak as I am in this sort of piety and strong as I am in the degree of my love to you, I find it excessively difficult,—as yet impossible, to decide by which feeling, in looking to further action, I am biassed. But I pray for guidance for us both, and am hoping that it may be given clearly and decidedly.

If your plans of study stretched over a lifetime—there might be little or no hesitation; but as they have to be tested, and may be exploded, and then you wd like to return to the pulpit, the case becomes very different. This marriage, will *probably*, Cousin John thinks *certainly*, cast you off always from the Ministry. He says, you could not find a Church in Virginia even, tho' he thinks, the more closely he considers it, that the marriage is in full accordance with Scripture & with both points made in the Confession of Faith. Now, the question is Have you a right to give up the Ministry for the selfish promotion of your own happiness? Years hence, should your Studies, prove delusive dreams, wouldn't your conscience upbraid you with wicked disloyalty to your high Office?

This is for you to settle. My motives of action, & range of inquiry must be somewhat different, tho' at some points meeting these questions of yours. I need not press them upon you now. I haven't time, nor ability at present to do it.

If these questions, on your part, are settled clearly & conscientiously in favor of a marriage, then, if the strongest love on my part, and the most earnest desire to promote your personal, & public (as much of it as you have) usefulness, can be, in any sort a guarantee of happiness, you shall have it just whenever you choose to claim it. But I hope never to love you in a way to be the occasion of injury to you. I mourn now, that heretofore, I have loved you so much as a Man, & so little as Minister. I hope it will be different hereafter; I pray you help me to make it so.

And now, my darling John, we need to be watchful and prayerful—do let us become so.

I hear no news, & see nobody, but men on business & Cousin John & Benton. I have been totally unfit for any business arrangements, and don't know what kind to make even if I were able.

God bless & guide you.

> *Affectionately*
> *S.C.P. McDowell*

Wednesday.
Nov. 28. [1855]

My darling Sally,

Last night in going to my room at the boarding house I lay awake a long time reading & thinking of your letters. Tell me, Sally, why do you feel such uneasiness about my love. When I know how much I long after you & how again & again within a few hours I have longed to be with you to take you in my lap & tell you whatever was sorrowful *myself* so that I could sooth & comfort you it feels to me so *useless* for you to be suffering one moment about my love. I love you better than I *remember* loving any mortal. And I love & respect you more since my last visit & since these last letters than ever before. If *my love* is to you *the great thing*, as yours is to me; Do I beg you rely upon it for it is as much in your own control as anything which only your own indifference can remove from me.

I have better news today. Dr Rogers has expressed himself entirely with me & prepared a minute in a talk with Dr Leyburn which suits them both.[10] Dr Van R. has seen Dr Boardman who says greatly to my pleasure, that my step is right (tho' imprudent) & the "monkish sensibility" of the public to use his own

---

10. Ebenezer Platt Rogers (1817–1881), pastor of Seventh Presbyterian Church in Philadelphia.

phrase should be resisted. He is in favour of a minute but suggests that it should distinguish this case from others which indeed would be better for us. I dont know whether my hope or my fear now most preponderates about the minute. I shall not push it to a decision if in weighing it further I find any to oppose it.

Dearest, I agree with you about our return to God & our duty. Pray for me that I may be helped in these matters. I will always be yours whatever the issue of these things is. Tell me is that any comfort. God bless you. I hate to stop writing to you.

Yours warmly
Jno Miller.

Lexington,
Wednesday Nov 28. 1855

My *dear John*,

I think our troubles over & over until I have no longer power to do anything but suffer about them. If we were alone in this thing I should view it very differently: but with my poor Lilly on my side, and your Maggie upon yours, I shrink from anything likely to injure them. And then yourself, John, I *wont* compromise your usefulness for me. I can't undo the action of your Church, nor retract your resignation, but I wont consummate our engagement in any way to injure you or at all if there is danger of injury. Therefore if, to loose you fully and decidedly from all bonds to me will avail you, then you are free, & free to say so. Having done so much & being willing to do still more for me, I would be ashamed not to do my part in helping you out of these difficulties, even tho' it be that of giving you up forever—an act which would cost me more, than you can possibly conceive of. Yet I distinctly make you the tender of your liberty now, & shall have no uprising even of emotion against you, if you accept it. And may God guide you in your decision.

You know I love you: you can never know how much, yet I would sacrifice it, and all it has promised me rather than have you suffer under the evils it may entail upon you, if under, the present state of things a marriage should prove disastrous.

Write as often as you can; and act as wisely as you can. *I* have needed all the pain of the last 10 or 12 days, and pray that the lesson may be profitable to me. And for you John darling! I pray with the utmost earnestness that you may act becoming your profession, and according to the will and in order to the glory of God.

God bless you, & guide you.

Affec'ly
S.C.P. McDowell

I enclose a note from Lacy received yesterday: shall I answer it?[11] He can do us service and we have no friends to spare.

11. The note has not been located.

Nov: 29th 1855.

Darling, Darling,

How can you write so? I feel all the yearning tenderness that would lead me to throw everything away & come right off to you. I could pillow your poor head upon my side & tell you all that was painful as well as hopeful in our lot with some hope of soothing you into comfortable feelings. I never so admired you for true nobility of character.

I conjure you to believe me in one thing. I consecrate the rest of my life to you whatever that life may be. I *beg* you not to cast me off in the midst of such feelings as you now suffer. I see no law that can force us from each other as betrothed even if you would reject me for fear of a marriage.

When I wrote last I was in the midst of an effort which I still continue. I have scarcely any news today. My wish trembles in the poise of an even balance as to its being realized. I think it will decide itself this evening. I mean this minute. My great fear now is a development of feelings that would utterly shake your *position* if you married. I confess my purposes are so *fixed* upon private study that the idea of that *ever* ceasing never enters my mind.

Darling, why cant you take comfort even if *all* your fears were realized in *this* picture. I *give* myself to you. I am yours perpetually. I am your slave. You shall *say* whether we shall be married unless my conscience yet finds something to forbid.

Now, toiling in my work of study on which I am about to enter & struggling for your sake to win respect & power by what I become & announcing myself always as engaged to you & seeing you from time to time & folding you to my bosom & being yours always & writing to you & proving to you more & more month after month how I love you, why not in the worst event that you can fear is there not some comfort. I declare myself forever yours unless you cast me of. Did you really mean that if we could not marry in four years you would rather suspend all relations with me.

Dear Sally, I may be strangely constituted, but I feel as if you were more than half mine & as if I had more than half of all the comfort & delight in you & in merely knowing that you love me. Not *possessing* you, would be an agony to me; not *marrying* you is only a self-denial.

But I am giving in too much to your vein. When you write tell me if you have any such satisfaction & dont let your *health* be corroded by pain & above all by sad tearful watchings; & utter abandonment of rest & health.

Yours affly
Jno Miller

I give in entirely to your notions about God & returning to him of duty, but Alas! I never could tell even what *little* I *feel* on those subjects in writing. I have strong hopes yet.

Colalto,
Thursday Nov 29. '55

John, Darling, your letter is a great comfort to me as it regards your affection. In our present difficulties that is all I have to cheer me, and when, for a moment, I fancy that it is not of the sort I want—warm & steady—and respectful, you cant imagine the anguish I feel.

I have written to you, in view of the embarrassment & trouble I cause you, setting you free. And again, I say if you conscientiously accept the offer I shall never reproach you for it, but will consider it the will of God in regard to this matter.

I depend upon you, as you are in the midst of all the trouble and see things as they are transpiring, to do all the deciding upon them that is necessary. I am too far off even to be counselled with. But we must be careful & willing to be taught our duty in a case involving so much & so many as this does. If it seems best to give up the marriage:—I submit. If a short postponement will be wise—I yield to that—If a long one—and you wish it, I consent to that too.

As to the Potters John—I am disappointed. The Bp had no right to speak so strongly to you months ago, upon what he admits now, was insufficient evidence. This shakes my reliance upon his fairness & strength too. Then, as to his Wife—of course, I thank her for all that she would do that is kind, but I could not & would not accept any hospitality from her except it could be given with conscientious approval of our step—not as to its wisdom (people may think as they choose about that,) but as to its Scripture legality.

Cousin John says the more he thinks on it, the more clearly it meets the requirements of our Confession. And Dr White has not shaken in his opinion since he saw you, & told me yesterday that he thinks, if he could have seen us Tuesday, he would have advised the marriage to take place, as proposed, the next day. He expresses very great indignation at the "scoundrels" in your Session & "hoots at the idea of a parcel of vulgar men, second or third rate city people, setting up their notions of propriety against those of the highest, & most honorable & pious gentlemen of Virginia." He says moreover he is quite sure, from reliable information received before you came on the other day, that the *sale of pews* had more to do with the Sessional action than the purity & spiritual welfare of the Church—or as much anyhow. So you see, he knows a good deal. As I told you, I have been annoyed, at the Dr's frequent assent to my opinions—as destroying my reliance upon his fair judgment—but he is esteemed in our Synod for *"his wisdom"*—you frequently hear the remark of him—"Oh! Dr White, he has a great deal of worldly wisdom." He shows his sagacity here at any rate.

Write to me every day, and write just as you wd talk to me. What does your Mother say? All these things trouble me so. Yet I am better every way than I was. I had no idea, for some days of the effect of this thing upon me. Wakefulness, anxiety, loss of strength and intense suffering reduced me in three days to a degree that astonished me. I am thinner, than I have been for two years. But I am so much better now, that I can tell you this, without your having cause for any anxiety about me. I am gradually getting to business again with some energy.

God bless you my Darling

Affec'ly
S.C.P. McDowell

Colalto,
Thursday, Nov 29. '55

My *dear John,*

I write tonight, when I have a quiet hour, & my room to myself.

Dr. White did not come over today as he promised, and I have nothing more to say to you from him. Having misjudged public sentiment about this thing he means to be more careful, he intimated the other evening, in what he says, either by way of suggestion or advice hereafter. How he learned—or rather *from whom* he learned enough of your Church matters to lead him to the conclusion I have mentioned about the action of yr Session, he did not tell me; but I conjectured John Leyburn was his informant. Whoever it was, *I think* he spoke truly, and I am indignant that this session, with the outside show of caring so much for the *spiritualities* of the Church, in fact with a keen eye to its *temporalities* should have done you such an injury. Had *it* kept quiet, all this stir would not have been made in your Society. However, all these things are ordered by a Higher Power, and we do wisely to seek after their meaning. It may be, *we are* wrong in our conclusions; and if so, we ought to be willing to be set right both in thought and act. The voice of the multitudes does not always, I know utter the *Truth;* nor does it always maintain tomorrow what it asserts today, yet there are times, I believe, when the voice of the people *is* the voice of God, and I stand now and wonder, with anxious thought, if this be one of those times. I have thought the *word* of God sanctioned our step fully; I have thought the *ways* of God as I have read them in my relation to it now to my family & society was an exponent of His will & an interpreter of His word, yet it may all be wrong. Despite my care I may be mistaken; and if I am, why, I must take up again my old burden of sorrow & disappointment and wear along thro' the remainder of life as best I can. Then your love will be of value to me—the very greatest value even if we never are married. I shall always want it to warm me, and encourage me to effort and to give something like a *future* to my troubled life. It will be to me the only good in *my* box of earthy ills. Hasn't life been a sad story to me? My unfortunate marriage was a sort of drop-curtain upon it, shutting out everything that was prospective in it.—Doesn't it seem very strange that I should ever have been born? That existence was given me for some wise end I cant doubt,—but what that end is, I cannot, thus far, discover. I am of no *use* to anybody: I never become a *pleasure* to anyone that,

that moment I become a terrible evil to them, and I can't make out why I was born, or wherefore I live. Yet I dare not complain. In fact, I have no reason to complain: my "good things" even in this life are wonderfully beyond my merits—and so I wont say another murmuring word. It would be both a sin & a shame to do it.

As Bp Potter changed about so unexpectedly, (and I confess I am more irritated by his change than by any other I have heard of;) wd it not be well, when you counsel with other gentlemen to give them the prominant & distinct particulars of my difficulties, so that they may make up an opinion from which they will not recede when their time comes for that opinion to be of any service to us. And keep to men of your own Church.[12] As a body, I believe them to be the best-informed, the most sincere in their desire for the purity of the Church & society, the most liberal-minded and best men in the Country, and if *I* am wrong, for *my* part I choose that *they* shall tell me so. In our present emergence too, they have a bond of relationship to us, which will make them interested as well as discreet advisers.

But,—haven't I run away from my subject? No matter,—I believe I said all that was necessary. (and more too?)

In our last talk, Cousin John, said he believed it wd be impossible for you to get *any* office in our Church:—that this marriage wd cut you off, not only from a Pastorate but every other office that a Minister can ordinarily, hold:—is it true?

You are right about rejecting even the mention, *at present*, of coming to Virginia to live. Id rather see you go to Kamskaca, where I suppose you would, at least, be free, during its night of six months from the sight of a Church Session and the worry of its surveillance.[13] But, I dont mean to find fault with your session for its act, if it *really* acted from proper motives; on the contrary, I could but respect it even tho I suffered from it.

I have had new discoveries of my man, Morgan, and, I think, now he begins to think, after my long nap, I have waked up in a sort of fury. Mr White declines being my Agent, but will give me all the aid he can.[14] He is too full of business to carry on mine. This is a worry to me. I must try someone else.

Lilly writes me you have been to see her. I thought it so kind in you when you were tired & troubled even to think of going. By the bye, tell me, where are you living now? Are you comfortably fixed? O John isn't it hard that I cant even have the care of these lesser comforts for you.—Like poor old Dr Musgrave "you deserve a better lot" than this, of having loved a woman, whose love to you seems to carry a blight instead of a blessing with it. Poor fellow! 'twas a sad accident that changed, a year ago your game of nine pins at the Hot

12. Presbyterian ministers.
13. By "Kamskaca" is meant Kamchatka, a peninsula in northeast Siberia.
14. William White had originally agreed to be her trustee. See McDowell's letter of Nov. 12, 1855.

Springs into this game of hearts over here, in which your *heaviest loss was in the winning.*

But God bless you, my Darling John, & make all these troubles issue in your greatest good.

Affectionately
S.C.P. McDowell

Friday morning.

There were two or three things I wanted to tell you this morning, but now, that I sit down to write I cant recall them. The least important, however, I believe was this—that a man named *Christian,* who is now I think the Pastor of the North Church on North St is it?, is an old acquaintance of mine, and as he is a Member of Presbytery might, perhaps, be made available to you by that circumstance.[15] He was Dr Laurie's Assistant part of the time that we lived in Washington; and I thought him a good man, tho' none of the brightest. He lived, I think previous to his settlement in Washington somewhere in Maryland,—and has good reason to know me, & know about me.

"Why am I so anxious about your love"? Why, because it is natural & right that I should watch over my treasure with all vigilance and solicitude. I thank you, Darling, for all you say about it. It is my greatest earthly comfort, and I hope God may never let it be lost to me.

Thinking Lilly wd suffer from the incautious remarks of her school-fellows about us, I wrote last week to Miss Gill, asking her special care over the child's feelings & this morning have received, in reply an extremely kind letter, which contains this sentence:—"As for the rest the floating rumors that reach us are calculated only to excite feeling for you & indignation against your persecutors." *This* from ladies in your City, and from that most straitest of all classes of women— old maids—is particularly acceptable to me.

But, in all these changes of sentiment & feeling about us, and in all the pain and anxiety these swelling floods give us, I calm myself down for us both in the imperishable, unchangeable truth "that our times are the hand of the Judge of all the earth, who can do no wrong. And just here, under this shelter, I would stay till these "troubles be over past". And, I hope I dont want more to be delivered from the trouble, than I do to be improved by it. I tremble at the idea of an *unsanctified sorrow.* I dont want my heart to come, like a bit of Asbestos, out of the fire, only the harder because of the flame—but like a pure metal—with its dross consumed, and ready to receive a new stamp & to bear a new image. If this can be the case now, I shall not murmur no matter what be the trial.—Is it so with you? God bless you,

Affec'ly
S.C.P. McDowell

15. Levi Hunt Christian (1817–1864) of North Church in Philadelphia.

Dec. 1. 1855
Saturday morning 8 o'clock

My *dear John,*

I was sure I should get a letter from you last night and waited for the mail till a late hour;—but it brought me nothing.

I had a long talk with Dr White yesterday afternoon. He stands firmly to what he has said before, and gave me a synopsis of a conversation held, some days since, between himself William Brown & Rev Mr Wilson of Staunton, who was Professor lately at Union T.S., which was entirely & strongly in our favor.[16] My ugly friend, Mr Bocock, who by the bye is, to my thinking, the cleverest man in the Virginia Synod, also espouses our cause with his customary vigorous heat. Dr White, scorns the idea of your Session having been actuated by motives of high regard for the purity of the Church, or *real offence* that this marriage was to be to their "righteous souls". The sale of pews, and a *poor negro* looming up in the far distance, *he thinks,* were the things that warmed their zeal, and quickened their Graces. However that may be, the Act is done. I hate to impugn their motives, and am self-upbraided when I do it. I have no anger against them; & not a particle of resentment roused in me. I look beyond their Acts, to see why God permits it, & what *He* means to teach us by it.

I enclose you a letter received last night. I have no suspicion as to its Author; and very little interest.

Dear John, I cant express to you how much and how lovingly I think of you:— yet I am often checked in these outgoings of my heart after you by the desire *not* to be too far influenced by them. And I would not be *selfish* either in seeking their gratification, but wish to consult *your* good, as well as my own pleasure. And, indeed, would have both these held in submission to the highest dictates of Christian obligation. But this is very hard: shall we ever reach such a height of pure purpose as that? You must help me to do it. And you must bear with me if I repeat this again and again.

I write to you with the utmost freeness here, where my thoughts all tend, and my religious sense is most busily at work. I speak to you, of these internal anxieties, much as I do to myself, acknowledging the fact, that there is no other human being so near or so dear to me.

You'll write *every day*? You see I *inflict* a daily letter upon you, & yet never dream that it will be unacceptable.

God bless you my dear John.

Affe'ly
S.C.P. McDowell

---

16. Joseph Ruggles Wilson (1825–1903), pastor in Staunton, Va., and father of President Woodrow Wilson. "Union T.S." is Union Theological Seminary in Virginia.

Phil. Dec. 1st [1855][17]
Saturday

My darling Sally,

I have this moment received your letter & on the very moment without a thought of reflection I reply. My liberty in the midst of all my passion for you & hope to be your cherished & happy husband would be a blow unspeakably worse than the disappointment of our marriage. It would be a worse *instalment* of pain if you know what that means, that is it would be a far heavier blow *in addition* than my original suffering. I not only tremble at the thought of your discarding me but I value my existing relations to you beyond what I can express. Next to marrying me the thing I most desire is that you should *have the same love* to be my betrothed bride & let me have some one on this green earth to love & think of, whom I may write to & visit & who *possibly* one day might be my bride.

Let me say to you, not for the *sake* of *comfort* or as a thing I *think* or *feel* or as a mere warm lover's expression but as a *fact* which I long that you would realize, that in the bottom of my heart there is a seal upon you as my wife, I am sure I shall never lose the feeling. I judge so from my past history. I am not capricious in passions of this sort. I have never addressed or *desired* besides yourself any other than the mother of my children. And while I am quite sure that your indifference would break the seal, I am quite sure that while you continue to love me you have complete power over me & will prevent the germ of any other affection.

I labour so with this idea that you will think the impediments to our marriage are in my mind settled. They are so by no means; I have yet strong hopes. But what alarms me is the shifting of men's opinions. Between ourselves & binding on you *secresy* even from the Major in the matter, *Leyburn* is now one of my greatest obstacles in the way of public opinion. I hate to tell you this because you will be angry with L. & there you would be wronging him. He says I never did get a favouring opinion from him but then he confesses that he did not dream that public opinion would be what he finds it to be & he is grieved that he had not the means of advising me better some months ago. The thing I most blame him for is that while I was managing carefully in respect to Dr Boardman & waiting till Van R. could influence & after he had done so & I had invited Dr B. & his support was pledged Leyburn actually *called* & undid what we had done & left B. quite indisposed to his own original minute.[18] It would take me too long to tell you all the motives he professes for this step. They are such as to lead me to forgive him, but it does from a man so related to us unmixed mischief. I beg you dont mention all this to a *second person*. Should he ever hear of it it would do us great harm.

You naturally are in suspense as to the exact state of the thing in my mind & as to why I have ceased from the *confidence* & *resolute certainty* that I have always

17. On the top margin, Miller wrote, "Spence's address is 99 South 4 Street. I forgot it before."

18. "Van R." refers to Courtland Van Rensselaer. Miller originally hoped that the ministers would condemn the actions of the Arch Street Church's session.

hitherto expressed. I cannot tell you plainly because my mind is all at sea from the fact that the materials of judgment & those very discordant are coming in to me every hour, but I assure you that my *greatest* anxiety is one in which I have no other duty than to lay the facts before *you*, if *you* are satisfied the thing that now gives me the greatest agony is no impediment at all. It is the much heightened danger of your social position. I feel less to blame for my own false judgment in this respect (which nevertheless gives me remorse) because what has shaken *me* is the marvellously changed judgment of other people & the expression of "grief" that when they first spoke of it they had no dream of existing prejudices.

Sally, darling; *if the pain of social rebuffs that you might meet were greater than the pleasure of being married to me as compared with the pleasure of being betrothed to me* our marriage would be not as good as a betrothal. This is the great bugbear now in my path. Expressed as it was by Mrs Hunter it is this:—"Mr Miller; if you love that lady dont marry her"; & Mrs Hunter like all the rest was taken by surprise by her own judgment.

It may surprise you that I, a minister, should talk so little about the sacrifice of my high vocation. The real fact is that I am kept from talking on that subject & have no fears upon it from a state of purpose as to my labour for Christ which common modesty forbids me to go to the bottom of. If I spoke in a way of conceit that would be unproper even with you I would say that these are plans of future success in theological discovery that would make all this matter like a fly on the horn of an ox. I secretly expect to be great. I am telling you out of passion & love for you what it is silly to tell any one, & that for which some day you may bring me into decision. But I thereby show you my love for you. I value my life each year of it that remains by a price that is perfectly conceited. And yet with the earnest aim & intention *with the help of Christ* to be a totally different man on both sides of the Atlantic from any of these that are now judging me & with a supreme indifference therefore to popular clamour I wish to live entirely for you & even in my proudest moments of—conceit you are always seated at my side as the queen & witness of all my labours. I *cant* feel therefore a *conscientious* trouble about losing my pastorate because 1st the thing that disturbs it is a wicked unscriptural prejudice that is making tyrants & libertines much more than the more liberal view & 2d the prudence that expediency might enjoin as to what absolute *does* sacrifice the pastorate I do not feel because my ambitious conceits lift me above it.

Now tho' in all this I am only showing you that in all judgments of common sense you have linked your destiny with a *vain* fellow who is mostly certain to run himself to nothing or at least to *appear* nothing but a country gentleman who has lost the pastoral office & is busy about private studies which never come to anything yet what can I do but with a sort of soft-minded amorousness tell you of the dreams of mine & so show you what sort of a heart my actions are springing out of.

I want to revolutionize philosophy. I want to be an Augustine or an Edwards.

I have never told you so so plainly before. I shrink from telling you so so plainly now. But why shouldnt two lovers entirely mingle their minds together. Dont laugh at me to others. And as to yourself I would be willing that you should explore all the recesses of my mind. If I succeed this prejudice of divorce you & our children will easily carry. If I fail I really have no heart for being or doing anything else in the history that remains to me.

Still, Sally, I dare not madly spoil your position. And if you only loved as I did to be a lover (if not a wife) & to wait till God removes our obstacle, if you would take back the expression of the other day (which however, if you *feel* it I dont wish you to take back,) & continue my affianced bride I shall be half-happy & shall consecrate all my poor lunatic greatness to you & give you an opportunity really to *experiment* upon my dreams & see if I really bring anything to pass before you marry me. And I am not sure that I should not be even happier than in that drivelled & remorseful state in which I should see you either turned from or *patronized*.

There are other things I would like to say but I am afraid for once at least I have tired you out. I wish I could see you. The minute I fear will not be encouraged. The few I speak to, tell me that entire silence on all my domestic matter is certain as I always supposed, but if I introduce it willfully they are afraid. So I pause. I am still deriving light from all sides.

The tendency of private opinion is to *your reprieve* & an act from them but dont speak of it, for it ought to come to them freshly & without agitation beforehand. Be assured I will act wisely. I love you with an undying passion. If you love me in return cant you fall *into a cheerful condition of waiting* whether it be weeks or years if I only satisfy you that I will remain your lover. My life is always a burden. Yours is not. Cant you face the delay far more easily than I. This I say with some hopes yet that we shall be married within the month. The simple fact is this. *I will collect the facts; & you* shall make the decision.

Now as to Lacey's letter I shall not say one word. A Northerner cant judge of a Southerner. I have no jealousy of him, not because I know him, but I know you.

I offer you your entire liberty. If you accept it the release from my church places me just where on the receipt of such a blow I would place myself. So that in any possible view you have done me no harm. You are as free to leave me as to the air you breathe. I shall not *feel* a reproach to you. But if you accept your liberty it will be the worst stroke of my life (certainly except one) & it will be long before I stagger up under the blow. Still I forbid your continuing our engagement out of compassion. I refuse to break it. I long to keep it. I prize it even more than what is additional in our marriage. Still I would prefer your liberty than that you should continue it out of any other motive than sheer love to me.

Sally, tell me, if you knew that I would love you always & was just perfectly safe & certain of my being *happiest* betrothed to you even up till my own death, would you be sorry that you had ever seen me? Are you now sorry you ever saw me? I will bring this matter to such a searching issue: I will find out so safely &

certainly now the issue both to yourself & children that if you could *marry anyone safely, we* should marry. Then if we still could not would you be sorry we had met?

Oh, Sally, let me implore you not to brood over this thing so as to overwhelm me with its consequences to your health. Think of one thing. My love you are <u>certain</u> of as long as you choose to tolerate it. Then, marriage, if you feel obliged to defer it, carries with it all chagrins & mortifications that might fasten upon it at this time & who knows but God intends it for us at a far more auspicious season. As betrothed no body can whisper against us. As married we would certainly have somethings to fear.

Let us not, however, antedate our troubles.

I will gather up anything unpleasant that may come to me in the intervening days & keep it out of my letters for I want till I see you or write more fully to have my letters for pleasanter things.

I have not heard from Mother.

Come here, Darling. Poor, poor Sally I wish I could smooth your hair & tell you all I feel that is peaceful & confident. If you would only love me so as to make a treasure of my *love,* even if we should have to submit to the self-denial of postponing the marriage how happy I should be!

You know we would have great license as lovers. The world would think well of us for seeing each other as often as we could. The taste that would forbid our nuptials would admire our attachment as betrothed people. My respectful acknowledgment of you as my affianced wife would be my testimony as far as I could bear it against every ancient slander. We should have no fear of Thomas & none of public censure & none of church remarks. I should dream of tolerating none. You might even live at the North & I would adore you as next to the Almighty my great tie to bind me in the world. This however only if we cant marry which you must decide.

Yours affy
Jno Miller

[marginal note] Be careful to write at once.

Sat. Evening 5 o'clock

Dear Sally,

I hate to send you the enclosed, because it is a dealing with circumstances that I would fain hope we could avoid but tho' I have had half a notion to burn it yet I send it to show the firm state of my affection in the very last extreme.[19]

I have new reason to mistrust Dungan. He has lost largely within a few weeks & begins to press upon his friends at bank. I have no doubt if I had less chicane from him I could have continued longer as indeed we could have done in the present case but what has alarmed me is, that Dr Rogers who favors a minute of sanction & is warmly friendly says that about the discretion

19. He enclosed the letter he had composed earlier that day.

of the step he must speak frankly that he believes it would cost any man his pulpit in the City. Still luckily we have not to decide upon the balance of causes, the step is taken & I have no doubt of its propriety & do not regret it.

I find the feeling such that I cannot succeed in the minute I wanted & if I secure any it will have to be modified. But, Darling, dont care for that. It seems to be the opinion of all that no hostile move will be ventured upon & that itself will be something in our favour.

I mourn over your accounts of your health. Dear, dear, Sally, you make me tremble. How <u>could</u> you doubt my love after it had been so steady. Suppose you should allow yourself to brood over this, so as to injure your strength. What remorse you would fill me with.

Tell me this. The Presbytery sits on Thursday. Shall I go on at once after it rises to Lexington & take your head into my lap as I used to do & tell you all the result whatever it proves to be or shall I write it to you & postpone visiting you again till some other time. I would not ask you, but you may not wish me to be seen on the road so soon again, & you may not be able conveniently to entertain me in my visits. Which had I better do. This letter will reach you on Monday night. If you write by Tuesday morning's mail it will reach me by Thursday evenings mail & I could see you that week. Do you wish me to do it?

Dec: 2d 1855

Dearest Sally,

I am sitting in my room at Mrs. Griffith's. I have been thoughtfully pondering our matter all day.

I can not answer your letters which speak of your resort to a blessed Saviour in our troubles. I never could write on those subjects. I can only say that those letters fill me with love & regard for you. I warmly turn to the same comforts when you write so & in the midst of much to agonize me reach after the same blessings.

I beg you say nothing of Leyburn. I have seen him again. He has had a long & very candid talk with me. I left him no longer feeling anything against him, but really much the other way.

I long to see you. I love you with a passion that I cannot describe. I rejoice to find my love standing all these fires & really becoming a source of pleasure & joy even in the midst of its disconfitures. I look now with great suspense to your reply to my inquiries as to whether you would live an engaged life to me if we had to put off our wedding; & whether you love me with such a love as would make that better than nothing. Indeed, if you could trust *me* whether there would be any charm to you in that sort of relation above your entirely isolated life. I must wait for the Presbytery to convey you any news.

Yours perpetually
Jno Miller.

Phil. Dec: 3d 1855.

My *dearest Sally,*

I have been led to give up the idea of a minute & to expect an entire silence on all private matters. It seems to be as *certain* as anything earthly can be that *nothing* will be said or written either at the Church's meeting tonight or the Pres' on Thursday that will at all allude to our matter or indeed to *any* reasons in the case. You may, therefore, I think consider yourself as knowing all before-hand.

I do suffer so from thinking of what you said of your health.

Come here, child. Lean your head there in its old place. Now listen. A great deal of your pain springs from what you call the "trouble you give me" & the "shade you cast &c." Now, listen. I do declare in the presence of our Maker that I have not one regret, & not one sense of mischief to me in all that has happened. That I am grieved by the delay of our marriage I cannot deny: & that I am pained to think of you as suffering; but saving these two things I do assure you nothing that has occurred either disconcerts or ruffles me. I look life in the face with exactly the same equanimity as ever. Now brush away that difficulty. Then as to my love it is as certain to you as the beating of your heart. I shall be your lover just as long as you will tolerate me in that relation. And as to trammelling you in that way if you postpone our marriage I have no compunction about doing that because *I mean to marry you, if any one else be he lawyer or planter here in Va or Ky could with your present light upon the dangers of your social position.*

I would have some compunctions about occupying your affections as a mere lover when some one else less publicly situated might peacefully & pleasantly marry you, were it not that I am determined to postpone (willingly) for no causes that would not operate just as powerfully upon any other. Indeed *more powerfully* because from my hermit tentencies we could bear social persecution better than other persons.

So cheer up, Darling. I have done you no harm, *I hope;* & you have done me no harm *I know.* And all your talk about being of no use is sheer fudge ridiculous & wicked. You are of use *to me* this minute & of use to Lilly, & you shall continue to say, mark my words, that you are happier as my betrothed wife than you used to be.

Dont speak to White or commit yourself in talking about the Session till I either see or write to you. This angry speaking in L. will be heard of here & will do harm. There are facts that bear on the case that I want to tell you that show a feeling that my church could not have produced.

But, Sally, cheer up & put on your old looks again else you will be a real burden to me. My Sergeant friends speak with great interest of you. I board at Miss Henop's or (Griffiths) on Broad St & my great relief will be to hear that you are happy again. I hope you have written directing me to come to you on Thursday.

I wish the Major instead of philosophizing about what places I can get would manage your business for you. Why dont he do it? I say this half in fun, but why dont he?

Yours fondly
Jno Miller.

Monday Dec 3. 1855.

Dear John,

Altho' yesterday was Sunday I intended to write you a *little* letter, but James Taylor came over in the afternoon to see a sick servant & disturbed me; & at night I went to church. I had nothing special to say however. I only wanted to give you such pleasure as a constant remembrance of you could give. I have only that to prompt my letter now, for I hear nothing & see nobody and have no workings of mind that would be worth mentioning.

Until a day or two ago, I thought *to-day* was the day for the meeting of your Presbytery—but I find it will not come on till Thursday. I am surprised to find how calm I am as to its action. Perhaps as the day approaches still nearer I shall be more agitated; but I think not. My anxiety is that *you* shall act wisely in all respects, and be influenced by the highest & best motives in all that you do. As to the rest—I have not so great solicitude. Indeed, I have just rolled off the whole burden upon a Stronger than any human arm, and only ask for willingness to submit to His decision, & strength to do *His* will.

Your Friday's letter came yesterday morning. I am sure I must have lost a letter of the day before, as the "effort" you allude to, in this letter last received, was not mentioned by you in any previous one that has reached me. By the by, John, do be careful about your letters to me, & give up you old *bad* habit of entrusting them to Omnibus drivers & such like good-for-nothing people. Miss Fields' lost note always comes up as a sort of scare crow on this subject.

Another thing—don't get worried with Spence & his ways; and, even if he is a little too short & fiery, don't exclude him from your counsels. A little forbearance & self-control on your part will make all things smooth, especially as a deference to *his* opinion, will please him & pre-dispose him to be kind & considerate. *I am* the very person to advise here, for *I* know how much one loses by an eruption now & then of a pretty hot temper. You have *seen me* right mad,—and have heard how I could blaze out, haven't you? But John, I don't often flame out, as I did that morning.

Write to me every day. God bless you my dear John.

Affectionately
S.C.P. McDowell

Lexington,
Tuesday Dec: 4. 1855.

My own darling John; I don't want to be free. I have no wish whatever, as connected with my own feelings or purposes to change our present relations to each other; and when I have spoken of setting *you* free it was out of a strong desire to *do* what was—or seemed, best for *you* and not for any *pleasure* that the rupture was likely to bring to *me*. Oh No! Your affection is almost every thing to me now. The exclusion of it from my life would envelope me in such a "horror of darkness" as I cannot describe, and dread to look at even for a moment. I gave myself to you in more hopeful times than the present, but with fears even then that the gift would prove a great trouble to you, yet, if you want it still with all the sorrows it has brought upon you, why just keep it. After all, it is only a heart that will love you, and go hovering over you with a sort of painful anxiety thro' the years to come, with little ability to give any pleasure as do you any real service. One great pleasure in my attachment was the hope of being *useful* to you,—this is all dispelled now:— another, was that of *your* being a support to me. I wanted to lean upon you, and rest in you and be guided by you, and give up this thing of being self-sustained, and independent which my nature struggles against. To a great extent, situated as we are, you can yet be this to me. And, at any rate, I think we *may* avail ourselves of the comfort of remaining as we are, until further developments in Providence will teach us what to do. Is that settled then? And you won't think it worth while to offer my "free papers" again? I don't know *how much* I am *capable* of loving any one. I can only judge from actual experience of my ability in that way; and certainly I have known no feeling in the past, any stronger than that I am moved by at present. In some respects, I am sure, my affection for you is more valuable, and has more power and just as much warmth as that of an earlier day. And tho' I gave the *best* I had then, yet the offering I bring to you, *I* think a worthier one than that.

I dont think it has ever crossed my mind "to wish I had never seen you". This past year, with all its cares & solicitudes has been, take it all and all, perhaps the happiest of my life. The mere pleasure of loving you has been very great. It has given a rich glow to all my feelings. And then the happiness of being warmly and engrossingly loved by you—has been just such as I could not make you comprehend unless I could open to you my heart of hearts & show you what was there.

I hardly know what to say about your coming. If the marriage is postponed, as seems to me inevitable, from all you write to me, then you had best come as quickly after the meeting of Presbytery as you conveniently can. It would suit me best for you to come before the 1st of January, for I must make new arrangements for myself by that time, and you could perhaps help me about them. But you must judge for yourself about coming. I want to see you, and think we had better determine our plans in an interview than by writing.

I know so much of the changeableness of men's opinions, that what you tell me, does not surprise me. We must learn to put up with these things.

I hope you will allow *no* feeling to interfere with your clear sense of duty, when Presbytery meets. It becomes you to be calm, self-poised, yet ready for any emergency, which the ill will, or wrong judgment, or vulgar doggedness of any member of it, may occasion.

If you do come up, ask Lilly to get Brinton to send you a green cashmere & a raw silk morning dress to bring with you—my cloak also.—About the rest I will write to Brinton & Lilly when I am not so hurried. I may pay Susan a visit later in the Winter & shall need these things.

Also—do another job, for me. Step to Wilson the Silversmith and give him the enclosed check. I dont know his name, so I leave it blank & you can insert it. Ask him to make out a regular bill for the spoons & forks I bought, with a receipt to it.

God bless you, my dear John.

Affectionately,
S.C.P. McDowell.

Why don't your Mother write to you? Wouldn't it be most respectful in you to go & see her before you come on again?

Tuesday,
Dec. 4 [1855]

Dearest Darling,

You should have gotten a letter every day except the one on which Friday's mail would fall. That day I didnt write for I did not get home in time. I shall have a great deal to tell you on all these matters when we meet again. Meanwhile there are relations of it to others, as for example to Dr L & through him to Dr White that seem to make it wise to let it sleep as a matter of counsel till I see you.

You need fear nothing worse in all that I am encountering here but a postponement of our marriage. My own fervent love to you & our good name & your social position & my ecclesiastical standing are as yet quite unassailed.

The congregational Meeting occurred last night & our private affair or *anything* private was in no way mentioned, the meeting was a short & simple one.[20] So I determine will be the Presbytery. I *think* I can almost picture it before I enter it.

If you have written favorably to my coming on I shall see you on Friday or Saturday night. I want to take your head in my lap & talk the whole thing over with you & we will get ready to set out on that path that God dictates to us. My love burns brighter under trouble. You are my *own* darling Sally.

JM

20. At this meeting on Dec. 3, 1855, Miller and the congregation mutually agreed to dissolve their relationship. The Philadelphia presbytery concurred on Dec. 6, 1855 (Presbytery of Philadelphia, Minutes, vol. 5 [1850–1855], pp. 390, 391, Presbyterian Historical Society, Philadelphia, Pa.).

Phil. Dec: 5th 1855.

Dearest,

I trust you have told me to come on to you. If so I shall not write again.

I have just received your Mondays letter. God bless you, dear Sally, for your love to me. It is my greatest earthly treasure.

Since the congregational meeting I have been visiting the people. I am pleased with the general expressions of regret. Just now at table this was handed in & is a specimen of what I meet with at the houses of the people. This people will always love me & I shall have the credit of having built them up & served them faithfully. A man in my disappointed situation may be excused for feeling satisfaction at such assurances. Already they begin to speak to me of the harm the paper has done & the struggle they shall have to fill up the church.

I hope God may bless them. I love them after all very dearly: & find that the pastoral tie has its nerves of very keen devotion.

God bless *you*, Darling. Good bye

Affly
Jno Miller.

Up to this time I have not *one* regret about resigning the church or my game of hearts. How is it with you.

I am sorry about my letter. I fear we must give up *dangerous* writings. I feel anxious about the lost letters.

[Enclosure: C. R. Garrett to John Miller]
Dear Mr Miller,

I cannot refrain from writing a line to you, to express my deep regret at losing you as a Pastor, and to thank you for your friendly Pastoral care over us during the short time we were privileged to attend upon your ministry.

Your resignation was as unexpected as painful to us. I had hoped we should long enjoy your faithful instructions. May God bless and reward you for your labor of love. Pray for us.

With our best wishes for your future happiness and the kindest regards of myself and family I remain your

sincerely attached friend
Mrs C. R. Garrett

Tuesday eve Dec 4th. 19th st

[December 7, 1855]

My dear John,

The Stage comes in late I know, but I will be up and wait for you until 12 o'clock. If you are even a little later than that come over; for I feel anxious about your serious determination to come just now, and fancy it arose out of something unpleasant.

Dont wait at McDowell's for a cup of tea. I'll supply you when you come over.

affec'y
S.C.P. McDowell

Saturday night[21]

December [8,] 1855.

Dear John,
   I send my letter to Mr Bocock. If you approve it, put it in the mail—if not then keep it.
   Come over about 12 o'clock.[22] The enclosed newspaper scraps James sent this morning to Cantey.

Affec'ly
S.C.P. McDowell.

Saturday morning.
Presbyterian has nothing in it.[23]

McClung's, Lex.
December 19. 1855[24]

Dearest Sally
   Here I am as forlorn as possible in what seems to have been fitted up as our bridal chamber. It is the best room I ever had here. I have past the ordeal of Mrs McClung's parlour & by breaking away in pretence of hurrying my supper have got thro' it without giving any account of myself at all. I am better off than others for I heard her ask an old lady if her son married to please her. A Mrs & Miss Preston of Missouri came with us.
   I scribble these line to assure you of my love & to cheer you in the horror of great darkness of which you speak. Jehovah-jireh. That is your own saying. I will hold you to it, Sally.
   God bless you

Yours fondly
Jno Miller.

21. This should be Friday, Dec. 7.
22. Miller had arrived in Lexington and was in a hotel.
23. "Saturday morning" was Dec. 8, 1855. Not until Feb. 2, 1856, did the *Central Presbyterian* carry the following announcement: "The pastoral relation has been dissolved between Rev. John Miller and the West Arch Street Church, Philadelphia, at his request, Dec. 6th, 1855."
24. McClung's hotel was in Staunton. McDowell dated this note.

[McDowell wrote the following verse on this letter]

Jehovah-jireh

The Lord will provide.
Judge not the Lord by feeble sense
But trust him for his grace
Behind a frowning Providence
He hides a smiling face.
Good when he gives—supremely good
Nor less when he denies
And crosses from his "sovreign hand
Are blessings in disguise."

Princeton, Thursday
Dec: 21. 1855[25]

Dearest Sally,

I reached Princeton Depot about a mile & a half from the village about 3 this morning. I left my trunk in charge of an old watchman & walked up to a certain window in mother's piazza which I had begged might be left unbarred. On a table in the dining room was a little twinkling night lamp & a candle standing by it which I lit & some cold refreshments. And upstairs was an open door & a nicely prepared bed & my famous Navesink windows & some right good sleep which I fell heir to about 4. I found the town just where I left it & no one mentions to me my troubles. Mother & Mary tell me (as I supposed) that no one speaks to them of our matter. So I do not learn a thing about the excitement that was talked of here. Mother I find very much disposed to take up cudgels for me against what she calls the unscriptural opposition of the people & yet I think not unsatisfied with the tho't that the marriage is delayed.

I find I am elected again to the Col. Bd at Washington.[26] Alas! I shant have as pleasant a visit this year.

I cannot at all reconcile myself to the Major's fears about the engagement. I see no ground in them. I feel that a settled firm betrothal will be a great comfort to us both (to me certainly) & entirely proper. I do trust you will not rupture it. I write, my Darling, in the most hurried way on this old scrap of paper & will write more fully when I hear from you.

God bless you

Yours Affly
JM.

25. McDowell dated this letter.
26. The board of the American Colonization Society.

Colalto,
Saturday, Dec 22. 1855.

My *dear John,*

I have not been able to make the effort to write before. When the night comes I am weary; and when the early morning rolls round, the wakefulness of the last hours of the night leaves me too much depressed to attempt a letter.

I am, however, endeavoring to make arrangements for the future, blank as it is. Thus far, my plans have failed; but to-day I am going to appeal to Mr Morton to take my house, & give me two rooms in it, for the next year. If he declines, I am at the end of my rope. Dr Graham, who came the day you left, has been over to offer his services in any way that I may choose to accept. And he has done it so promptly and affectionately and earnestly as to make it all very gratifying. I mean to accept his offer, & put the farm & Morgan into his hands. I am pressed for time in all these things, as everything must be completed before the 1st of January. And I have no heart for it all.

Miss Jannetta will stay with me until Cantey is married, which will probably be the 15th of next month. After that, I think a little of going to see Susan & Mary, and to wear along thro' the Winter. And yet I am ashamed to speak so—for I hope to gather up my strength again, and look about me for something to do, and not waste my time & energies in lamenting over my misfortunes.

Dr Graham tells me & so also Cousin Sally says that they believe most of the opposition to our marriage grew out of your being a Preacher—you say differently.[27] I dont know—but I am mystified at my kinsfolk for their doings. Uncle Tom said again & again to Nib this summer that he wondered I didn't marry—and saw no impropriety in it—& yet when the time comes, instead of helping—goes against me. However, the deed is done now—it is no use to look up its causes.

I cant tell you, John, how absolutely dark the future looks to me. And our present relations to each other are so unsteady that I am pained by them. When I would come to you & pour out my heart to you & lean upon you for comfort, a shade of reserve creeps over me & I fall back to such support as my own feelings, writhing in agony as they do can give. And yet, when I think of giving up wholly our engagement, I shrink from it, tho' my judgment dictates that it would be wisest to do it. Do you remember Spence telling us of the rainbows in the Cave of the Winds? This engagement to me is something like one of those. It is the only light to me in the storm & dreariness of life, and yet is so faint & small that like one [of] those, it can in an instant, be shut out with the hand.

I am ashamed, in our troubles, to have so little faith in God's Mercy to us.—and yet the little I have is of great comfort.

Write some of your plans. And may God guide & bless you my dear John—for you are dearer than you dream of.

27. Sarah (Sally) Preston, wife of "Cousin John" Preston.

I feel anxious about your philosophizing after all—I think it dangerous. Men are so ambitious of the discovery of *truth* whether, in Science Moral or Thyeical, that their minds are in danger of being blinded.[28] And I could not bear you to get into such error as might shake your religious belief.

Affecly
S.C.P. McDowell

Princeton, Dec: 24th [1855]

My dear Sally,

I cant surmise why you dont write to me.

I have felt a little fear about writing myself, lest as I have not heard from you since I left L. it is a sign that you dread the publicity of a continued correspondence.

Perhaps you have written to Phil. If so I shall hear to-morrow.

Meanwhile, my Darling, (for I cant give up my fond way of thinking of you) I have talked with Mother about our engagement, & tho' I did not tell her all the doubt you had yet I brought to her mind the *question* as to the delicacy of an engagement. *She had not a doubt of it.* Indeed Mother is more disposed than others to rebel against the popular feeling & (tho' she is glad we are not married) still to sympathize with the feeling that would claim a *right* to marry in any given moment in the future when we might choose to do so.

Besides her I hear no one speak. I have not talked with Mary & no one has mentioned the subject except a Mr Blodgett who told me that public opinion here was *divided* about the step, tho' he smiled at the idea of an *excitement*.[29]

Spencer seems to have heard very directly that your brother the Doctor "was opposed" to the match.

I have planted myself already to my work. I feel more than I can tell you now *the sadness* of my disappointment. It is harder to bear than it was at first. I fear I will grow more & more *weary* of the separation; but, Darling, I *live* upon the engagement & I do entreat you not to sunder it. Perhaps my pride would revolt at my talking so if I knew that my want of a letter was due to your not having written but till all conjectures of the cause as having been different are ended. I must assure you of this:—I have not one doubt about our right to remain engaged. *No person has spoke to me against it.* And I do beg you not to bring our relations to an end.

My studies I have already entered upon & am charmed with them so far. I feel lonely & depressed, but I am used to that. My great pleasure would be to write to you often so that I might as often hear from you; And make this my great entertainment.

28. "Thyeical" should be "ethical."

29. Herman Miller Blodgett (1796–1877), Presbyterian minister and secretary of the New Jersey Colonization Society from 1853 to 1860. He lived in Princeton.

I go to Washington on the 15th of Jan to the Col. Bd. I wish it were with the same hopes as last year. My P.O. will be this now permanently. I am boarding in my mother's house.

Yours affly
Jno Miller.

I have not read Lilly's letter. You put it back into the black letter case. The other letter will explain itself.[30]

Princeton, Dec: 24th [1855]

My darling Sally,

I have received your letter & am just writhing in the pains it gives me. It distresses me that I am away from you. You say, "When I would come to you & lean upon you for comfort, a shade of reserve creeps over me & I fall back to such support as my own feelings &c can give". Dear Darling, it is very different with me. I long after you with the greatest confidence of love. I would like to fold you in my arms & win from you a complete unburdening of all your sorrows. And even now, if you will only dispel all these notions about our betrothal which I utterly reject & deny & tell me all you think & feel & treat me as tho' I were what I really am your nearest natural protector I would so much delight in the relation.

How strange it is that your letter warning me about my philosophy should have come in just at an hour when I was sitting by the fire thinking of that very thing. I think I *am* in danger. And while I am charmed with the opening that these few days have given me into truths that I love I have a very distinct idea that I shall not be able to publish what I think without the usual opposition to discovery.

Pray for me.

I mean myself to spend a day of prayer before long that I may be kept from heretical belief.

As to my plans they are all formed & entered on. I am boarding at home with my children & am about to furnish a study with the debris of that in Phil & plunge at once into these long cherished investigations. I have already begun them.

Tuesday Eve.

So far I wrote yesterday. And now my dear Child, I feel this evening in a much more scolding mood. I would like so much to sit down by your side & chide you for your faithlessness. I love you more than you dream. I live upon my love. It is one of the blessings of my life. You are as really useful to me & in many of the same ways as tho you were my wife. And while I am indulging this feeling & doting

---

30. Miller enclosed a friendly letter dated Dec. 20, 1855, from John H. Williams in Frederick, congratulating him on remaining engaged to McDowell despite the "clamor." Though Williams had learned nothing further about Thomas's infidelities while married to McDowell, he reported that the ex-governor was immersed in financial problems and selling property in Allegany County.

upon it, giving it root & room in my mind as tho' it were for long occupancy, you speak of it as a thing to be "shut out with your hand" & actually pronouncing it in your judgment unwise. You naughty wicked Sally. I dont wonder you dont sleep well & that time hangs heavy upon you.

Seriously, I reiterate the assurance that the Major is quite deceived about our engagement & that it is both proper & delicate. I believe it not only delicate but *graceful* & that people of right heart will admire it. And now after I am settled down long enough in part to try my feelings I assure you that I can offer you the continuance of my whole affection with no doubt as to the permanency of my feeling.

But good-bye. I have assured you of this till I think my own darling Sally ought to believe me & therefore beg you to dismiss all question & to settle down upon our undisturbed relations.

Yours ever affy
Jno Miller.

Write often

Colalto,
Dec 25. 1855.

Dear John,

Your letter from Princeton did not reach me till Sunday, and I was disappointed in finding it hurried and short. However it sufficed to tell me of your safe arrival; and helped to stir up my spirits a little. I had a feeling of sorrowful compassion come over me at the picture you drew of your midnight entrance—but the stumbling along thro' silence & darkness was not half so forlorn a thing as I feel the wearing away of these dreary disappointed days to be to me. Is it any sin to mourn over my troubles? I try not to murmur under them—but at present, that is all that I can do.

Do you remember about a year ago, writing me a great sheet of a letter from Princeton, begging to know "if you were faithful thro' manhood & even age would I not then give you a fonder" feeling than I had ever expressed?[31] How well I recollect that letter. How it came thrilling thro' me, as again & again, when alone, either during the day, or at a late hour at night I wd take it out of my pocket and read it! I refused to answer it—tho' not then fully aware of the nature of the feeling it had so roused in me, and on Christmas day—just a year ago, you wrote again more fully & explicitly; and in a few days I answered that, yielding to its wishes tho' with heavy forebodings, which alas! I have lived to realize. I was much troubled with that thing then, John, as you know, but for all, it was a pleasant dreamy period to me, which, with all its ups & downs grew more & more a joy and a happiness. It may have been an error—the whole thing—yet it

31. See Miller to McDowell, Nov. 28, 1854.

illuminated many a month of the past year, with such a glow & warmth, that even now saddened & despondent as I am, I am brightened by the recollection of it.

But that unfortunate letter of mine last New Year's day has wrought sad changes for the present. If it had never been written you wd have been working away in Arch Street, with, in all probability, more practicable and promising domestic schemes buzzing in your brain; and I should have been—I can't conjecture where. It cant be undone now however; and what it may yet do in the future is far beyond any imagining of mine.

As yet I have accomplished nothing in my arrangements. I incline to Dr Graham's advice to advertise for a tenant and sell off everything on the farm, & hire my Negroes.[32] The proceeds of the sale wd nearly if not quite extinguish my debt to Mary & Nib. Then if Mr Morton will rent my house & allow me rooms in it, for the rent that will be an economical & convenient arrangement, & will allow me all the rents, hires etc. from other properties, except that of the Louisville lots ($300) which I mean shall defray all personal expenses, & pay off a part of my subscriptions to the Metropolitan Church, & Union Seminary as I find necessary. These rents etc will be some thing like $1.500 or 2.000. If, I conclude to sell two negroes to aid in repaying Lilly, then that sum will be lessened about $250, which wd be the hire of them—but even then, with Mary's debt cancelled, it will enable me to pay Lilly's interest and have something beside. I think too, I shall turn over to Lilly the $12 or 1.300 that Uncle Tom owes me. If the exact amount of my legacy was ascertained, I would do likewise with that. These sums would, probably be entirely safe, inasmuch as I should be compelled to insist upon their payment, not for myself, but as her Guardian. I prefer too giving her these

32. McDowell used the blank sections of Miller's letter on Dec. 19, 1855, to list her debts and sources of income.

14,000 @6 p ct _____ $ 840 [debt & payments on Colalto]
To Mary _____ 120
To Nib _____ 30
                       990

Rents-
Louisville _____ $300
House _____ 300
Farm _____   500
Hire of servants _____   570
                       $1670
                         990
                         680

Washington lot—doubtful—
Legacy & $1180 in Uncle Tom's hands—worthless
Military—unsold.
Saline— "
In addition to the "Military" in Kentucky, McDowell and her siblings jointly owned the Saline property in Kansas.

bonds which meet the requirements of the law in the way of 6 p. ct interest, to sacrificing my City lots by thrusting them at a wrong time into market; or by making them over to her as they now stand and debarring my self from their appreciation. The sale of the Military in the Spring, if it is sold will more than meet my last payment on Colalto. If, however, I find it wisest not to sell the Military, & if as June (the time for my last payment) draws on, I see no other way of meeting it, I will make the effort to sell the place itself, either in lots or as a whole. I must get from under the pressure of this load of debt.

Cousin Elizabeth Cocke is here—a little warmer than in the fall, but still cool. I take no notice of her manner & dont mean to give her any opportunity for specially bad treatment, by being very polite, & yet omitting everything in which she could be marked in her show of antagonism.

She is entitled to forbearance for me, for she has hitherto been a most kind friend. But she is violent & prejudiced—& I fancy implacable. At any rate, my affection for her received a very severe shock several years ago, from hearing her outburst of feeling against a friend of 40 years standing. I couldnt excuse her then & really sorrowed over the affair as if I had a personal interest in it,—but I never have recovered from the feeling against Cousin E then excited, tho' to be sure it never aroused any anger to her, but a sort of fear.

Aunt Sally Floyd sends me word by her, "that if I will write & ask her, she will come & see me". She couldn't have given a stronger proof of her affection for me, & I felt much moved by her kindness. I shall write as soon as I know my arrangements.

I have not written to James yet; but I shall do it. I am rejoiced to hear he is going to leave Phil, & go out to Abingdon. I am so glad you refused his letter. I don't know what was in it, but Cousin Sally, speaking of it, said she had told Cousin John that Massie (for it seems he consulted the Major about it) should not present such a letter—but should have returned it to James & told him, if he wanted to communicate with you he should do it thro' the mail". I made no inquiry as to its contents. The remark was made in connection with another to this effect—"that James had changed about several times, & had long ago transcended all proper bounds in his deportment to me"—that is—that *his right* to interfere had been pushed far beyond what was proper. I don't know that she meant that the letter of which M___ was "the Conduit" was insulting—it may have been only obtrusive.

Are you settled yet? And the children—tell me about them. I may be an awful croaker, but do be cautious about that new Scheme of yours, & if a Church, suitable for you offers,—don't thoughtlessly reject it.

God bless you darling.

Affec'ly
S.C.P. McDowell.

Princeton, Dec: 29th [1855]

Dearest Sally,

You cant tell how your letter had comforted me.

It wears the tone of energy & spirits & seems to say that you are treating our troubles & bearing them in such a way as to escape being injured by them.

I hoped to have a long evening to answer both your letter & Mr Ruffner's, but as it is I have been kept out till so near the mail time that I will have to postpone till next week a fuller letter. Why dont you write to me oftener. I would like a line from you every day.

I have fallen already into a regular system of spending my time & I should not be surprised if it should last the rest of my life. I study from breakfast till dinner & *read* at other times in the day. At three I walk out with the children who by the way are much more rosy & stout than they were in the Summer. I wish you could see them. In spite of all your croaking I am greatly enamored of my studies & were it not for my Va troubles I think I should be happier than I have been for a long time.

Dear Sally, I love you in a way that I think would satisfy a peri. I cant have the pabulum that most love demands that is the hope of a speedy possession & yet my love seems to grow like some bad weed or like one of those air plants that seem to flourish like Mohammeds coffin.[33] I love you with the fondest passion. And, Sally, when you talk of bringing our relations to an end what do you exactly mean by it. You cant expect that my love will weaken by mere affliction & disappointment. And if not, what then? Suppose you *did* rupture the engagement. I cant quit loving you. And what then? Where is the use of talking about ceasing all relations when we love each other with all our hearts.

But, Sally, perhaps it isn't so. Tell me how much you love me after all this trouble & disappointment.

Tell me particularly how you are when you write again. I have been thinking of writing to Miss Gordon to know how you really are.

I am not sure that it is right to be turning an eye at all toward the removal of the obstacle in our way. But I cant resist the temptation to copy & send you this paper. Let us try & keep our hearts unspotted from anything murderous or wicked. I love you enough even to make our present relations a source of pleasure. The Com are,

Willis P. Bocock	Buckingham
Rob. E. Scott.	Fauquier
Isaac I. Leftwich	Wythe
David Funston	Warren
James L. Gordon	Louisa
Whitner P. Turnstall	Pittsylvania
R. D. Turnbull	Brunswick
John L. Wooton	Henry

33. A "peri" is a fairy or elf; a "pabulum" is food or nourishment.

Alexander R. Holladay	Spottsylvania
John R. Edwards	Halifax
Muscoe Garnett	Essex
Richmond L. Lacy	Charles City
John B. Baldwin[34]	Augusta

I *did* send Bococks letter. Good bye. Write oftener.

Yours affly
Jno Miller.

When Miller returned to Lexington in early December, the couple had set out with renewed determination to discover the facts underlying McDowell's case for a divorce in 1845–1846. Writing from Lexington, Miller contacted John Williams in Frederick but learned nothing further, as Williams's response of December 20, 1855, explained. McDowell had written her friend John Holmes Bocock on December 8, 1855, but she had sent the letter to Miller for his approval first and asked him to forward it. McDowell had requested Bocock's help in determining whether the issue of Frank Thomas's adultery had come before the Virginia legislature. She regarded the Presbyterian pastor at Harrisonburg as the "cleverest" minister in the state. But more important, his brother, Willis Perry Bocock, Virginia's attorney general, had chaired the legislative committee that sifted the evidence and prepared McDowell's divorce bill. Yet weeks passed and she heard nothing back from the minister.

In a letter to Miller that has been lost, she evidently asked whether he had sent the Bocock letter. Miller now asserts that he did mail her letter to Bocock. But he also sends her the full committee roster should McDowell desire information from any of them. McDowell did not need to write further, however, because as December ended her clergyman friend finally replied that he was gathering data. Another month would elapse, and she would write the minister again before he finally responded in February. At that time he enclosed a portion of a letter from his brother in Richmond. McDowell would post this information to Miller on February 26, 1856. By that time, this avenue of inquiry had proven to be a dead end.

Lexington,
Dec: 31. 1855.

Dear John,

It is almost a week since I wrote, and I know you begin to feel a little hungry for a letter. I have no time for anything but a note, having occupied the greater part of the hour in writing to Aunt Sally declining her offered visit, on account of my unsettled condition.

---

34. Some of these politicians may be further identified: Willis Perry Bocock (1806–1887), Robert Eden Scott (1803–1862), Isaac Jefferson Leftwich (1799–1893), David Funsten (1819–1866), James Lindsay Gordon (1813–?), Robert D. Turnbull (1820–1880), Alexander Richmond Holladay (1811–?), Muscoe Russell Hunter Garnett (1821–1864), and John Brown Baldwin (1820–1873).

Since I last wrote I paid another visit to Mrs Cocke on business, and have never been so disrespectfully & insultingly treated in all my life. I kept my temper & civility thro' it all, but it has brought all relations between us to an end. Cousin Sally was present during the whole conference, & as she followed me to the passage when I left, I remarked to her my notice of Cousin Elizabeth's manner, & told her, that tho' I didn't mean to quarrel with her, yet I wouldn't subject myself to insult & wd never to go to her house when she was there. She seemed much hurt, & wept as she talked to me. Among other things she said was this—"To do you justice you have behaved beautifully whilst she does not behave well at all." I was gratified at the emphasis with which she defended me & blamed her. She has behaved as I did not dream one lady cd to another. However it will make no difference between Cousin John & myself. He has been to see me since & to help me with my affairs and is as kind as ever.

I am inclined to offer my home for sale by the 1st of June. I don't know what else to do—& I have got into such a shake of despondency about every thing, that it matters not what befalls me. Life is ever so gloomy to me: and except that it is sinful to fall into entire inaction & listlessness I wd just yield to my troubles until I had lost both sense & sensation.

Dear John pray for me. I don't excuse this spirit of complaint—& do not always feel it; yet as long as I am a human being I must feel with a human feeling the sorrows that have befallen me.

God bless you Darling.

Affectionately
S.C.P. McD.

Colalto.
January 2. 1856.

My *dear John,*

I wrote you a long letter yesterday, but somehow it didn't suit me, and this morning I refused to send it. It is possible, however, that I would have reconsidered my refusal, if a sort of headache hadnt unfitted me for any active work and left me time to write again this afternoon.

A year has made sad changes with us, Darling. As I sat here, twelve months ago, and wrote to you a letter favouring your suit, I ushered in no little trouble to us both. Yet the past year, stands out to me from the many dark ones that preceded it with a sort of unnatural brightness as I look back upon it from my present stand-point.—How it will seem, when half a dozen years more divide me from it, I can't even dream. It may be only an episode in my history—and it may be too the introduction to a very important era in it. It has been very peculiar in all its incidents; and marked, I think by singularly emphatic Providences, which I wish I could read aright.

With less knowledge of the world than you, I made a truer estimate of its judgment upon our affairs. It was a sad day to us, when I submitted my opinion to yours. Yet even I did not fully realize the extent of opposition we have received, for, on some points, my worst fears have been Transcended by the reality. I am inclined to believe that our case does to American Morality the service which Macauley says Byron's did to British virtue—(Turn to his review of Moore's life &c of Byron, & see what he says.)[35] However, we cannot alter the past. But my good judgment heretofore, makes me a little confident in it now as to our engagement.—That is, if I can be said to have confidence in any thing which involves so much feeling.

I am much troubled about it, & am distressed by many fears & anxieties in regard to it. Some of the objections to it, I mentioned to you, chafe my spirit terribly. At times I am so harrassed by these fears as to have my affection severely taxed. Under their power, I feel as tho' my love was utterly extinguished, and believe that it would be even easy to give you up. But then comes the reflux tide, and I am overwhelmed. I cling to you as before and shudder at the thought of giving you up.

Two or three reasons against it weigh upon me heavily. First—the fact that the marriage is *based* upon the death of another.[36] I scarcely admit this in my own thinking, yet it is true. I rebel against it, and shudder at it, and shrink from it. I do not believe it any sin to marry during the life of that other—I feel I could do it, under certain circumstances, & claim God's blessing upon the act:—but to refuse to marry because of the continuance of that man's life, and yet *contract* to marry as soon as his death shall occur has a coloring of wickedness to me in it now, which at first sight did not appear. To avoid the appearance *to the World* of breaking one Commandment, we are absolutely encouraging ourselves in the real transgression of another, by deliberately doing that which, *I fear* directly tends to it. Is this the real tendency of our engagement, John, or is it the aspect my anxieties make it wear? It is true, I am often surprised to see how little I think of that death as a means of relief from my troubles—but it, sometimes, does start up before me, and make me tremble; and I am sure that the presence of such a feeling in my heart, would sap away both solid principle & true comfort. And yet, I am not willing to yield to this objection until, by actual experience, I find there is validity in it. I would not have that experience, however, to attain any great extent—far from it.

Again: you labor to impress upon me the fact, that God has wonderfully interposed to stop our marriage. I believe it fully—& did from the day beginning, and under all the sorrow it has caused have tried, to submit uncomplainingly—or rather have acknowledged it to be my duty to do so. Admitting this fact, is it right in us to attempt to regulate the future in regard to it? I don't know how you feel, but I think it want of faith in me, & perhaps a want of real submission, not

35. Thomas Moore, the Irish poet, edited *The Works of Lord Byron; with Notices of his Life* in 1830. The next year Thomas Babington, Baron Macaulay (1800–1859), English historian, essayist, and statesman, published an essay, "Moore's Life of Lord Byron," in the *Edinburgh Review.*

36. Francis Thomas.

to leave this whole matter implicitly in God's hand. To do this fully, I should give up all promises & engagements, and let the events of the time to come be left free from any attempted control on my part. I believe that, if it is best, He will, in his own way & time bring us together and marry us to one another: if not—we will, ourselves, live to see the wisdom and good of our present disappointment; and if we have submitted promptly to it, will reap all the benefit & pleasure which an unquestioning obedience, in advance of all providential developments, will undoubtedly secure to us. This view of the matter has more power over me, than any other:—and yet I would not be rash in acting under it. It may, after all, not be the true one. It may have—(I use the word reverently) a dash of Quixotism about it, which appeals to my imagination, under the sober guise of simple faith. And yet, John, I still believe I am right. Tell me what you think?

With two reasons, such as these, against an engagement, don't you wonder I should hesitate to dissolve it? If my mind was fully made up upon them it would be blameable, not to say criminal weakness in me not to do it;—but until then, is it so? And O John, it is so terribly hard to gather up strength to collect the dèbris of hope & affection left me, & make a sacrifice of them. And yet I am ashamed to speak as if a sacrifice of feeling were a more difficult thing, than a sacrifice of principle. I am not sure that it isn't true tho', and I ought to be humbled by the fact, & struggle the harder against it.

Other considerations press upon me too. I think it wrong to shut you out from the pleasure of a more promising and successful attachment, & from the comforts of your own home, which wd grow up under it. It seems selfish and ungenerous to tie you to me for years, and then, it might be if I married you, I should not be able to make you happy;—for the struggle of life, and the wear of its cares, and the battle with its storms, and the suffering under its sorrows may destroy in me all that you see to love now, and leave me a stern-tempered, cold-hearted, imbittered woman. Here, I fear, my love has a taint of meanness in it. If I was capable of loving you with the purest & best affection, I would be capable too of doing what I thought wd advance your happiness, no matter at what cost to myself. But I can't do it. Other considerations must be added to that before I *can* give up the selfish gratification of having you to love me—& of having you to love. It is true, you may tell me, as you do that you promote your own pleasure by loving me, & remaining bound to me as at present. But my dear John, you are only a human being; and this feeling may wear out under the effect of time, & absence, and other things—And if it should, how painful, and terrible your bonds would become!

No: the sundering of our relations would not *impose* upon either you or I the *necessity* of giving up our attachment:—but it would leave both *free* to do so, if in the future it seemed best to them to stifle it. If I thought you loved me, (& of that I should love to guess) I could love you just as warmly and truly, I *think* without an engagement, as with one under our circumstances:—indeed I am not sure that I could not do it more warmly. But the pain of never hearing from you would be excessive;—and the agony of feeling that I had no longer any claim upon you, or any right to you very great—and the denial of any utterance of affection to both, a very severely trying one.

But, John, Darling, I have allowed my love to you to engross me too exclusively. It has unnerved me for the stern realities of every day existence. I have just luxuriated in it with a kind of intoxication of delight. I have let it overspread my whole heart & mind, and usurp a place it ought never to have attacked. And now isn't it time to curb it, and let higher duties come in for thought, & effort, & attention.

Tell me what you think of all I say Darling, & don't let it worry you with suspicions as to whether I have loved you or not, as you sometimes do.

My effort with Mr Morton failed. Today, he seemed to think there might be chance some weeks hence of disposing of his house but it was rather remote. I don't know what to do. To live here alone is rather fearful. To visit about unpleasant, and a waste of time. To board in town impracticable I think. But to keep house, retain my servants,—& keep Morgan as an Overseer on the other hand, seems criminally extravagant. What am I to do? Can you do a little thinking for me? I encourage the idea of selling Colalto; but there are serious objections to that, which I will mention when I write again.

You are right about my letter. Mr Bocock received it, & sends me a message to the effect that he is collecting information upon the subject of it, before he replies. I hope he will be cautious, & not compromise us either in delicacy or dignity. The Committee was an able one, & I perceive made up of the best gentlemen in the Legislature. Turnstall, poor fellow, is dead. I think Holliday too: but the others are accessible, no doubt.

Why don't you tell me about the children. I wish so much I *could* have Maggie. She would be a great comfort to me, a sunbeam to my dreary home all thro' the winter.

How is the Church getting on? & Dungan & Co? And, (I may as well mention all bad things together) Your philosophy.

I have written a letter of unreasonable length, but shan't regret it, if it brings me an answer just as long.

God bless you Dear John.

Affec'ly
S.C.P. McDowell

[marginal note] Please send the enclosed to Maggie B. I'm afraid to trust it in the Western line from here.

**Philadelphia
Church Study**
Jan: 3d 185[6].

My Darling Sally,

Here I am in my old quarters. I came yesterday with Mother. Why *do* you write so seldom. One of the pleasures of my love for you is to hear from you nearly every day. I have seen no one of the old parish since I came last evening & my visit to the church has to do with the removal of all my trass from the study. It is a disagreeable business. I hope to dispatch it & get back to P. today or to-morrow. I have a sort of feeling that it will be a long long time before I drop the studies I am now enamoured of & go back again to the preparations of sermons. Still I shall do it at a day's notice if I think it my duty.

I mean to call to see Lilly while I am here. Poor thing! Her hopes have been sadly involved with ours. Still under her present promptings I suppose she feels vastly relieved by the turn things have taken & willing to endure her present position away from you on that account. I love you with a degree of steadiness that makes your infrequent writing a great trial to me. Do write every other day.

Yours very affectionately
Jno Miller.

Colalto
Saturday Jany 5. 1856

John, dear John, I wish I could lay my head in your lap to-night and be quiet. Today has been a sad, sad day to me. Before I was dressed this morning, I was shocked by the announcement of Cousin Sally Preston's death.[37] With a faint hope that it was not true, I hurried over, when almost the first object that presented itself as I opened the door was the body prepared for burial. I had not heard of her illness tho' she had been sick since Tuesday night. Indeed no fears of a very serious kind were entertained by her Physician until after 9 o'clock Friday night. She then sunk rapidly and in two hours was dead. The impossible birth of an infant cost her her life.

Hasty preparations were made for the burial, and at five this afternoon in the midst of a fall of snow that has been increasing all day, we have buried her out of our sight.

Poor Cousin John is in terrible distress—as well he may be—Few men ever had such a wife.

And I too have lost heavily. I have never had a more steady, reliable, considerate, & affectionate friend.

But, good night.

Monday.

I jot a line this morning 9 o'clock. The weather is intensely cold—& the roads in such condition that we cannot receive our mails from Staunton. Do write often John. In spite of our unsteady relations I turn to you only the more & more as other friends fall off or die.

God bless you my darling John & keep you from all evil, & especially from the mischiefs & perils of a "vain philosophy."

Affec'ly
S.C.P. McDowell

37. Sarah (Sally) Lyle Carothers Preston died Jan. 4, 1856.

Princeton, Jan: 7th 56.

My *darling Sally,*

You are an incorrigible carper at all existing relations. Things venerable for age like our engagement & like me seem to meet no more mercy at your hands than things of yesterday. I have been thinking so long & earnestly about our matter, (thinking, as I paced the floor that this long letter *must* have some reason in it,) that my mind which you know naturally is none of the best is so strained that I can hardly write. I *see* no reasons for ending our engagement.

Your first is, that it tempts you to wish a man dead. So would your being heiress to a crabbed wicked old uncle, but should that make you throw up the estate. *Pray* for this person night & morning & it will keep you from any such wickedness. Recollect we are not "*contracting*" to marry as your letter would allege but simply considering how to treat a contract already formed. *We are only postponing a marriage from day to day as long as we please for the reason that our usefulness & comfort unmarried is the greater that is all*. And all the question is, would our usefulness & comfort be greater *unengaged*. That is all our present question.

Your second point is that an unengaged state would be one of more entire submission to Providence. I dont see that. If God by most marked Providences were to arrest you in collecting a debt would you say that you ought out of submission to Providence to throw away the claim. Recollect we are not engaging ourselves to marry trusting to God to remove a certain obstacle out of the way, but we *find* ourselves engaged and the question is have we any reason to separate. You yourself say that if we rupture the engagement we must quit hearing from each other & exist in blank silence. *That is awful*. I could not stand it. I would not know where I was resting. I might be *nursing* my affection to one who had grown entirely indifferent.

Then if we love each other we must hear from each other; & if we hear from each other we must be engaged & if we are engaged we must lie quiet & behave ourselves & a certain restless child I know must settle down more composedly in her lot.

Darling Sally, I am very unhappy; but my unhappiness is a much more sullen sort of unhappiness than yours. I look at my fate & see no help for it & just quietly settle down upon it the first week.

Now I am not willing to hold you to your engagement if your conscience rejects it. Indeed, in spite of all your brother says, I do offer to resign the bond with one hand & to uphold it with the other. *If it costs you a rightful standing with your Preston friends* I bind you not at all. Only, Sally, as it would crush me to give you up dont keep me under the impending fear of the thing for weeks & weeks & dont I do entreat you my Darling, torment yourself with the fear that there is anything in *my* conscience or in *my* feelings that would encourage you in thinking the rupture necessary.

I love you this moment *more* (as well as I am able to judge) than I ever loved you before. And I would be willing to wait for you for ten years if I knew you could be mine at the end of that time.

I go [to] Washington on Monday. If I had not seen you so lately I would go on from there & see you. By the way write to me there twice. I shall stay till Friday. Mary goes with me.

I did not see Lilly when I called. I left with her a Nube which Miss White worked for *Maggie*, tho' I half suspect she knew she was working it for you.[38] Maggie sends it to you. It is in the old box Miss W. gave it to me in & which she apologized for.

I cant advise you very prudently about your estate. Only this I say. I would tell the Major *candidly* all my indebtedness & embarrassments. I would banish all pride in the matter. Your estate can easily be made a good one but it must be done wisely & by someone who has your good at heart. The plan of Morton's living with you strikes me as singularly good. You ought to act with vigor & *promptness* & with the wisest counsel. & Darling may not this be the very thing for your health & spirits. Take care of yourself. The bitterest tho't of this engagement is that it may chafe & wear upon you. Rouse yourself my Darling Sally to your tasks & rest confidently in the love with which I am yours fondly

JM.

[marginal note] Wont you write oftener. I will.

Colalto,
Thursday Jan'ry 10. 1856

My *dear John*,

I have just received your note of the 3d inst from Phil. It will be a fortnight on Sunday since I received one before, & this is the *fourth* letter I have written since then. You see I am not so remiss after all. But our mails are terribly deranged by the weather. We have not had regular arrivals for ten days: and have had no mail North of Rich'd I suspect for several days until this morning.

Cousin Sally's death has given another shock to my plans. I feel more reluctant than ever to plant myself here, when my interest is gradually lessening & yet I have no special interest anywhere—& recent events have proved that I have few reliable friends. Do you think it a wonder John, that I am weary of the storms of life, & wonder why God lengthens out existence to one who has so little in it to make it happy. If I could only feel strength to give up you absolutely, & forever renounce all feeling for domestic ties, and look around & see *what* I could do outside of myself & get at it I sh be happier. Perhaps after all, this is what God intends me to do. And yet I can't do it. It were far easier to give up life. At least

---

38. A "Nube" is a nubia, a woman's head scarf.

so it seems now. I may change however. Cantey is to be married on Tuesday, & go off immediately. Miss Jannetta will remain awhile after: & then—?

The weather is intensely cold—12 degrees below zero yesterday, & I think colder to-day. Everything freezes in my room except my heart, which I wish wd freeze too.

It looks like old times to see yr Phil stamps.

I am going to write you again when I'm not so hurried. Why don't you write oftener? Tell me if you received my little package to Maggie Breckenridge.

God bless you my darling & send you back to the pulpit.

Affec'ly
S.C.P. McDowell

Princeton, Jan: 12th [1856]

My darling Sally,

I am truly grieved to hear of the death of Mrs Preston & so are Mother & Mary who remember her in her visits to P. with great interest. Your letter has just reached me tho' mailed on the 7th. I hope therefore I will have another tonight. Darling Sally, *wont you write to me every other day?* I do beg it as a favour. I love you with a degree of *tenderness* which I did not use to feel & these long silences are very trying to me. I would have written yesterday but as I was sure I would have a letter at night I waited & when the postman came it was too late to write.

You asked me two or three things in your long letter which I did not reply to. You asked me about Dungan &c. I *know* very little, as I do not inquire. Mr C. however is increasingly anxious about Mr D's solvency & is quietly taking precautions against the effects of it. I have to be extremely careful tho' that nothing of the sort should be heard of from me. They have no Pastor in view & seem to have some difficulties in their path.[39]

My "philosophy," Darling Sally, is my joy & my wealth. *You* neglect me so that your rival has full sway. I am so enamoured that I make love all day long sitting at her feet & blandished by her smiles. If there is anything improper in *this* marriage alliance I fear I am irrecoverably undone, for the poor nymph & I are hopelessly espoused & there is no depth of her loveliness that she does not seem willing to unmask as I come to her for her benefactions in all possible ways.

I *do* believe this philosophizing is a very solemn business, but then, Sally, I have some hopes about it. 1st I am so old. There's an advantage. 2d I am so thorough a Calvinist. I become so more as I study. 3d I have you to pray for me. 4th I trust in Christ & hope he will deliver me from ruin. 5th I pray to be made very humble.

Still, I mean to be very *thorough*. And I think one ought to be very *bold* where they *ponder* as I do, & give their whole time to a certain pursuit. And I see I differ in some respects from what is usually taught. And all that I brought with

---

39. "They" refers to the elders of Arch Street Presbyterian Church.

me to Princeton a month or more ago I have become more settled in. I am now thoroughly convinced of the conscientious propriety of studying & remaining unsettled as I do.

Still I ought to be self distrustful & I pray God that I may be kept from anything foolish & as the chances, others being judge, would be endlessly against my finding out anything, I ought to be quiet about my plans & silent in my steps that I may not be mortified by a failure.

You ask me about your farm. I hesitate about even "thinking" in the case because I am so far off; but what thinking I do leads me to this.

1st You ought not to farm yourself. That is certain.

2d You ought not to live *alone* in the house at Colalto, nor keep up the establishment.

3d You ought not to sell it at a sacrifice.

4th You ought not to go farther into debt.

Therefore these steps strike me.

1st to rent your house, (if possible to some one who will furnish you rooms.)

2d to rent your farm as the Misses Banter do theirs.

3d to sell whatever is perishable such as furniture, stock, farming implements &c acting under the advice of others & selling in the most eligible way.

4th To sell your place *whenever a full price is offered by anybody*—to sell the whole or any part—& to sell farm servants whenever a relative or friend or man with whom you can trust them offers their value.

5th to be exceedingly careful about Lilly's interests & watchful of her accounts, &

6th what you do to do promptly & with vigor.

My hesitations, Darling, about this advice are

1st that it is so easy to give it.

2d that I would hate so to *appear* to be advising you at all about such matters.

3d that you might suffer in some of these steps & then I should feel mortified, &

4th that I think your business requires wisdom & you should resort to that of some one wiser & nearer to Lexington than I.

But dont sit idly & let matters take their course. That is *the* worst of all.

Dont follow my advice. Consider it merely as a suggestion.

And now as to what is more properly *my* burden in these recent letters that I write, let me beg you to think how wrapped up I am in this passion I have for you—how it haunts me—how I long for more of the pleasures of it—how you deny these to me by sending such few letters—how I would like a more *settled* & loving correspondence—how entirely I am unchanged in my love by our disappointment in marriage—& how sure I am of my affection if you will only nurse it & enjoy it & return it & reassure it by considering it a thing fated & by reciprocating it with all your heart. I do long for your love, Darling; & I do rebel against the thot of your being so infrequent in your letters now when I have so little else to cheer me. The children are well & in[quire] often about you. I am puzzled sometimes to know how to answer. I walk with them every day. Did Dr White hear from Dr Hodge. No one speaks to me about our matter here.

Yours affly
Jno Miller.

Colalto
Jan'ry 12. 1856

My dear John,

I take your fidelity as to your share of our correspondence for the last fortnight upon *faith* as I have not had anything but a note from Phil, in all that time. However, my *faith* is in stronger exercise from my absolute knowledge of the state of the roads & weather, both of which are terrible. To-day the temperature is more moderate than for 6 or 8 days previous. But, even in my chamber where a fire never goes out, everything freezes. I am afraid to indulge in the luxury of a fit of crying lest my eyes should be adorned with ice-jewels.

It was Cantey's own will and proposal to send the enclosed cards to you & the children, so tho' they bear my writing I had naught beside to do with them.

I wish I cd tell you some of my annoyances in the shape of letters. They rouse my wrath notwithstanding they come pleading "a sense of duty" as the motive. I am ready to paraphrase poor Madam Roland's famous exclamation "A liberty! eh' A Duty! how many insults are offered in thy name!"[40] However I hear them silently thus far:—but if ever they urge me to the point of speaking, they will not be spared, & they know themselves to be very vulnerable.

Poor old Dr Wm. Graham is, at last dead & buried. Except for a fear as his future, I imagine nobody cares particularly. Such a pity it is; that a man richly endowed mentally sh'd come to lead a vagabond life, & die an unlamented death.

Can't you write me letters that are longer, & fuller.

God bless you.

Affc'ly
S.C.P. McDowell

Phil. Jan: 14th 56.

Poor darling Sally,

How my heart aches at this sad wailing letter. Why *dear* Sally is my *love* nothing; & is looking forward to being my wife & writing to me & trying with me to serve God & do your duty—is that nothing to live for? I have the most yearning desire for that calm settled love from you & secure of rest as to all doubts

---

40. Madam (Manon Jeanne Phlipon) Roland de la Platière (1754–1793). When her husband supported the Revolution, her salon became the headquarters for republicans and Girondists. Arrested in May 1793, she was guillotined in November. She composed her memoirs in prison.

of our engagement that would bring about your old cheerfulness of temper & quiet feeling.

I have written so many letters that I can hardly realize your not having enough of them. I think I have written two after the receipt of each of yours. I have also written one to Miss G. which I would be glad if either she or you would answer very honestly.[41] For dear Sally I would like to know how the lady looks that writes me such sad letters, whether you are haggard & pale. I should scold you so if I thought you were. Do keep your health. And if you need employment go out & walk & learn more athletic habits. As to your business a lady of your fine sense is just the very person to have such an estate to manage—to get it out of its emergencies & to make an employment of managing your own & Lilly's.

I was the first to tell the Alexanders of Mrs Preston's death. They are much shocked.

I am here en route for Washn with Mary.

The N.J. line was late & missed the junction & we go on tonight. I wish you were to be there.

I am glad you cant give me up. God dont ask it of you. Cherish me & love me as I do you & it will make us both happy.

I sent Maggies package to St Louis.

I shall hope to get letters from you in Washn.

I have read your letter over again. It is so fearfully gloomy that it saddens me beyond expression. Dear Sally, let us not despair of the goodness of God. If we are happily married in a year or two you would be ashamed of your ingratitude to God.

My philosophy which you attack so is one of my great comforts. It realizes all in solid truth that I expected. It looks very much to me as tho' it would give me work & usefulness for a long time. I will send you my book when it is printed.

In haste yours my blessed Sally

Jno Miller.

Colalto,
Jan'ry 16. 1856.

My darling John,

How does it happen that you don't get my letters? I am really ashamed to write you any more, in the absence of any from you. Yet I know this blocking up of snow, delays all our mails.

I have written you, let me see how many letters. One on the 31st, one on the 3d, one again the 6 or 7th one the 10 or 11th, one with Cantey's invitation, & now another—*six* in all. And to these I have had a short note of the 29th from Princeton, & one of the 3d from Phil. This morning your note to Miss Jannetta came, and I was rejoiced to see it.

Cantey was to have been married yesterday, but Mr V. after five days journey

---

41. "Miss G." is Jannetta Gordon.

only reached here at 10 last night—so the marriage will come off tonight. Mr Ross came over with Mr V. to officiate.[42]

Mr Venable asked if *you* were not here, as he always meets you when he comes. He says he prefers you "infinitely" to Brother Ross.

I shall be wretched when Cantey goes. I am very troubled,—so much so as to be ashamed of myself. If I were a good Christian as I ought to be these things wd not worry me so.

Dear John I do love you, and think so of you far too much.

Can't you write to me a little oftener, and a little more in detail as to your pursuits & pleasures.

Take the children on your lap and kiss them for me.

God bless you.

Affec'ly
S.C.P. McDowell

I write in a great hurry by the breakfast table,—having left Mr. Ross in the parlor alone.

Jan: 18th 1855
Washington[43]
Friday.

My darling Sally,

I am so disappointed in not hearing from you while here. You must have lost one of my letters. I begged for two while in W.[44] Everything reminds me of you here.—Mrs Kennedy's house where I went on Wednesday—the little parlour—the high steps—the place where the carriage stood that carried us off—the lounge where I saw you last—how pretty you looked—the landmarks round the house—the old church—Dr McLean who is here again—Prof: Henry—all seem to be in a sort of cloud of love & glory. Darling Sally these things instead of giving me pain as I thot they would give me pleasure & I think of you now as my great earthly prize. Oh that God would give you to me in some way or other. I fear to pray for it. & yet I cant help having a sort of confidence that he will. I love you, with all my strength. Do write very often. Let us enjoy what we can of our present relations. Mrs K. received me very cordially; so did Mrs Linsley.[45] Prof. Henry spoke very cordially of you & said that your father first took him by the hand in Washington. Mr K. is not expected home soon.

Yours affectionately
JM.

42. Margaret Cantey McDowell married Charles Scott Venable on Jan. 16, 1856. McDowell's brother-in-law, John Ross, was a Presbyterian minister.

43. Miller was attending a meeting of the board of the American Colonization Society.

44. Washington, D.C.

45. Emeline Coney Webster Lindsly (1808–1892), wife of Dr. Harvey Lindsly, M.D. (1804–1889).

Colalto,
Monday Jan'ry 21. 1856.

My *dear John*,

Three letters—of the 7th, 12th & 14th—reached me Friday morning. I would have answered them then, but that Miss Jannetta promised to write by the next morning's mail, & I had just written the day before; However Miss 'Netta failed, & I scratch off a line in a hurry this morning. I feel very sorry that I did not write on Saturday, for yesterday's heavy fall of snow, will render the Mountain impassible again, & I don't know when this will reach you. However, it will be in Staunton until the Cars run, & thus be a day nearer to you.

I wanted to write to you at Washington; but we had such accounts of the snow & ice beyond, that I thought it likely you wd not be able to go on. Your note from there received yesterday, makes me regret that I did not venture upon a letter.

The snow & ice so blocked up all routes to us, that Mr Venable & suite were *five days* making the journey from Prince Edward—a thing that is usually accomplished in two. They were detained two days on top of the Mountain; and when the Cars did run, the snow was so deep that they ran upon it for several miles without touching the rails. It was a perilous trip altogether: but brother Ross had a very plethoric and comfortable look when he reached us. He has an air of great *creature-comfort* about him, which naturally suggests to me the *fact* that *Man* is, after all, very much of an animal. He was very kind in his invitations, & apparent interest in my affairs; and I *liked* him better, (tho' I had no increase of respect,) than formerly.

The marriage instead of coming off in the morning, took place at night. I never heard so awkward an affair as Mr Ross made of it. Everybody laughed, but Nib & I—even the parties themselves, which, I confess, I was much displeased at. Next morning they all left, and I felt as tho' I had buried Cantey, I was so desolate & grieved. I was sick too, for I had been up till nearly 2 the night before finishing her packing. The day wd have been insupportable, but that an hour or so after she left, my kind friend, William Brown walked in & sat several hours. I don't think, John, you know Mr Brown? I am very fond of him, & we have been good friends for half a dozen years or more. His visit was a real treat to me. He talked of our affairs freely and candidly; but thinks we committed a faux pas in allowing the 21st of Nov to pass without the marriage. I am not sure that he isn't right. We had no business to defer to the world's opinion, at that stage of affairs, especially, as with due notice previously, it had kept quiet. We might have known that, as soon as it was appealed to as Judge, it would become rampant & unreasonable. Mr Brown, sd nothing of this kind, but simply expressed the opinion I have mentioned.

I see little of Cousin John's family. The weather is too cold & the roads too dangerous for me to venture out a great deal. And then, Cousin Elizabeth, tho' she has come down to entire civility in her deportment to me, makes it unpleasant for me to go there. I send very frequently, some little thing, to Cousin John, but have only seen him once since Cousin Sally's death. Then he sent for me to his room; but in half an hour seemed too much excited to stand the presence of anybody, and asked me to leave him. I felt uneasy about him—for loss of sleep, & his overwhelming distress had brought on a sort of nervous affection that was very disturbing. Every few minutes, as he talked to me, a spasm would convulse his whole frame. I think now, he is better, & goes part of the day to the Institute. He sends all his children except Tom & Frank home with his Sister, as soon as she can safely travel.[46]

Miss Jannetta & Mary are here yet; and will not leave me for some weeks I think.

What do the children ask about me? If you will give me Maggie, I think I shall give *you* up very cheerfully, and fancy I have profited by the bargain.

I mean to write more fully (about what?) by tomorrow's mail.

Dear John, I love you a great deal—what is the use of my doing it? I don't percieve that it makes me any happier, yet if I didn't do it, I fancy I might be more unhappy? Don't you think it wd be well for me & you too to pray that God wd fit me to die, & then, as quick, as possible take me out of this world. Indeed John, I can't see that I am of the least use in the World. I think life a precious boon, but really *I enjoy* nothing in it, but the sunshine, & sky, & the song of birds as they occasionally even in this season trill out a merry note as if for my benefit,—and the warm assurance you give now & then, of your affection. But I find this scarcely enough to relieve the weariness & burden of existence. I am conscious all this is wrong. *Duty* not pleasure or even happiness is the end of life here—and I err in reversing the natural order—of duty first & then happiness. But year after year I have been struggling with all sorts of sorrow, & tho' I dont complain that it is sent upon me, yet I can't help mourning under it. And I *do* feel very like sitting down in the most abject despondency. Sometimes I make a great effort to shake off such feelings, & to get the "loins of my mind girt" up to bear the burden quietly and steadily, but it is a fitful—& spasmodic sort of strength I get rather indicative of disease than health of mind. Pray for me, Darling. And may God bless you my dear John.

Yours
S.C.P. McDowell.

Princeton,
Jan: 21st 1856.

Sweetest love,

When my letters give you pleasure & you say, "Write longer ones" & more frequently, why will you not come into my arrangement of writing steadily every other day. It would be such a relief to me. I hope by this time you have received

---

46. His oldest sons were Thomas Lewis Preston and Franklin Preston (1841–1869).

all my back letters. I have written, I think, as many again as you have. And now, darling Sally, will you not agree to dismiss all thought of retracting our engagement & leave yourself in my possession so far as that I may feel that you are mine & may hear from you at least every other day.

I have received Cantey's invitation. When you write remember me to her & present to Mr V my very warm congratulations. If I knew exactly how I stood with the different members of your family I would write to Cantey myself. If you think well of my doing so, give me her address in Georgia.

In all respects but my disappointed affection I am more comfortable in my present mode of living than I have been for many years—perhaps ever. The pleasantness of these pursuits exceeds my expectation & if you were with me I would begin to think that even *I* could at length be happy. One source of my discomfort is my impatience to see you again. It was a trial to turn back in Washington without seeing you. Another Bd meeting occurs in March. I can hardly resist a desire to promise myself a visit then. I know it will not answer: but it is astonishing how long it seems since I last saw you on the porch of your house.

The children are well & often talk about you. Maggie is teasing me to take her with me when I next go to L. & I am longing for the day to come when you shall first see her. If I were rich I would take you at your word & encourage you to adopt her.

My philosophical pursuits fully answer my expectations & employ me every day. If you are hoping that I will give them up I am afraid you will grow grey before you are gratified. I do so wish you were with me that I could tease you a little with my studies in the evening after the labours of the day.

How do you look Sally? Tell me whether all these worries have made you thin & destroyed your good looks. Tell me how you are. I love you with all my heart. Why should not you & I be happy (even if we are disappointed in marriage) by at least realizing the thoroughness with which we possess each others love. Do you love me, Sally? Tell me whether you do all the time. Nothing makes me more happy than a sense of your affection.

Yours fondly
John Miller

I read this over & find it rather a prosy affair but agree to write every other day & I will write you the nicest letters alive.

Colalto,
Tuesday, Jan'y 22d. 1856.

My *dear John,*

I don't write every other day it is true, yet it seems to me, I write very often. I generally put off writing until the mail comes in in the morning so that I may answer any letter that comes from you immediately. I find this a bad plan, as it hurries my writing until it must often be not only illegible, but unintelligible. So I take a new purpose, and write *tonight*, when I have both leisure and quiet.

You don't fully satisfy my anxieties as to our engagement. You answer my objections plausibly enough, yet my mind is not entirely relieved of its difficulties, and I fear, John, you somewhat deceive yourself in the matter. However [I] will let it rest now. But as I am on the subject, I will mention another thing that often gives me much concern. As long as this engagement lasts don't you feel it as much cuts you off from pastoral usefulness, as if the marriage had taken place? And, in case, your philosophy fails and your conscience requires you to return to the pulpit, this wd prove, I am pretty sure an insufferable barrier to any settlement:—dont you think so? What then?

I think you foolish to offer to me my liberty, if it wd secure a firm footing with my Preston friends. Do you think I'm going to *sue* to them for their favor & support? They know me better than to expect any such thing from me; and I should rather scorn myself if I assumed the attitude of an apologist to them, or anyone else for purposing what I thought I had every right to perform. They have not been so very *kind* to me either, in these recent troubles; for instead of helping me whilst in the midst of them, they only offer to support me when I get out of them. A piece of affectionate consideration, for which I hope I am duly grateful; & of which I am sensible appreciative. Not one of them, except Aunt Sally & Aunt Eliza have uttered one word of sympathy in the whole matter, which, considering all things, is as neglectful as they could well be. However I won't quarrel with them if, by chance, we should come together. And I hope to be able to get along without their aid.

Do you think all this feeling wrong John?

I am still at sea about my movements. When Miss Jannetta leaves, I don't know how I shall be able to stay here alone, and yet I see nothing else to be done. I can't rent my house in any way. If I sell, I am still thrown out of a home, and out of the means of support; for the payment of the place must be paid over to my creditors & not re-invested for me. Henning writes me, that the City Taxes, & repairs on my Louisville lots & their buildings, have diminished my rents for the last 6 months *one third*. This is very unexpected and annoying. I am hemmed in on all sides, & see no door of escape. And when I ask counsel from my friends, they invariably say—"You can't live in that big house alone—that is certain". "What then?" I ask. "I don't know". A reply wh does little to dispel my difficulties or suppress my anxieties.

But I am getting to be a dreadful croaker I am ashamed of it—but John, Darling, haven't I *some* excuse for my lamentations? Our disappointment was, one wd think enough for one person to bear at a time. Add to that, pecuniary embarrassment—and to that again the fact, that I sit night after night in my old home, the solitary one of my blood under its roof. Indeed I am indebted, in this emergence, to a stranger for a deliverance from absolute solitude, and for every kindness that cheers me. My dear old friend, Miss Jannetta, has allowed her Sister & Niece to break up their house, & go off to other friends, without leaving me a day that she might go to them. And she stays with me, and cares for me, with an incessant watchfulness and affection, that is more like my Mother's solicitude than anything I have known since her death. Sometimes, I am worried & an impatient, sharp word assails the old lady and wounds her—and then I am troubled too. But tho' I apologize, yet I can't get the words back. I fancy my tongue is longer than any other woman's tongue in the world. And it has such a way of slipping its bridle, & doing mischief. I wish you had it in charge. But how *wd* you feel, if, in a moment of sudden impatience, I should turn with a sharp tone & sharper word upon you? Dear John, I cant imagine I *could* do it—very *often*.

I enclose you Julia's letter—send it back to me.[47] Don't you think she wd have suited you better than I? By the bye,—tell me *how much* you love me now-a-days; And if there is any romance in it, or if it is a plain humdrum passion suggestive of missing buttons, and undarned socks. For my own part, I want no pleasanter suggestions, & wd delight in such employment as they point to; but then with you, it may be different.

The snow lies a foot deep as far as my eye can reach, & the wind blows over it cold enough. It has been a terrible winter.

I am disappointed in hearing from you this morning, Wedn'day. God bless you my own darling little man.

Affecly
S.C.P. McDowell

No. I.
Princeton, Jan: 24th 56.

My *darling Sally,*

I have been waiting again for a letter. I really fear that some one takes out my letters from the post. At all events I have determined to put my "bright ideas" into practice & to number my letters from this time on. This, therefore, is No. I. I should be glad if you would do so too, tho' the list you sent me I see by looking at the pack have all come.

You cant tell how I long for the day to come when my note shall have brought an answer in which I propose a letter every other day. I do so wish the time to be settled so that I can settle into what is now the greatest luxury that I hope to possess. Mother, in a word of counsel the other day startled me by saying that I thot more of this correspondence than I did about the duties of religion. I had declined going to church on two occasions & about the same time had been inquiring very eagerly about the arrival of black Sam with the post. She put the rest together.

---

47. This letter has not been located.

My philosophy that you hate so I am humming away at with all my might. Your prayers are not answered. I am becoming entirely absorbed & still have the inspiration of believing that something may be done in this way as a means of usefulness. At any rate, Sally, it makes me happier; & who would grudge me a little glimmer of relief after so sad a life & so cruel a disappointment. I feel much better able to bear the brunt of sorrow, now that I have the comforts of study than when I was tasked with the more uncongenial work of preaching to the people.

I love you so that I cant bear to think of the long months before I see you again. God give me strength to bear whatever he intends for me & give you, Darling, help in trouble, tho' I hope not "a happy issue, out of *all* your afflictions."

> Yours most tenderly
> John Miller.

Princeton, Jan: 26th 56

Darling Sally,

In spite of all that Mr Brown says & in spite of all your sadness (tho' it distressed me beyond measure) I do believe that everything that has happened is for the best, & this not because that is the promise but because I *see* good in what has occurred. It would not have done for us to marry. Your family & my family & Lexington & Princeton & the church & finally we ourselves would have felt the effects of a strong public opposition, which each of these separate sources of influence would have imputed to the other but which would have been too strong for our married comfort. This is all against the convictions into which I tried to lead you in the beginning, but nevertheless mortifying as it is to my own correctness of judgment it is most certainly true.

Then, Sally, I cant regret I ever saw you. I love you with a passion that renders such an idea impossible, just as impossible as regretting I ever saw my mother or my dearest sister or my very hand or arm. I start at the idea of having bro't *you* into trouble, but O Darling if you would only live in my love distant as it is at all with the faith with which I live in mine to you—if you would dote on me & dream of me & live in me & for me & in hope of seeing me as I live for you—if you would only consider our failure to be married as a grievous disappointment & a hard self denial & trouble but as leaving you *me* & as leaving unimpaired our love & our mutual devotion & value that as I value it as something worth living for & as indeed a treasure fitted to make one happy I should be so much more in love with our present relations. If you could just *settle down* if you know what that means & share with me the means broken as they are that we have of happiness I should feel so much more as if I had you in possession.

For, Sally, as a third thing I am far happier engaged to you than I could be in any other way than married & I *couldnt* be engaged to you unless we had gone thro' the very course of mistake & disappointment by which our wedding was brought to an end.

But it does so sadden me to think of you as unhappy. I torture myself with the idea that you are pale & thin & haggard again & then I think of my *remorse* if I were to hear that you were dead. Darling, *for my sake* rouse yourself from all this despondency. You say you are of no use. Do you know I think that a dreadful sin. You have Lilly & you have both her fortunes & your own & you have a church & you have a circle of friends & you have me & my children at least to pray for, & you have your father's family & name & more—*far more* than most ladies have in their keeping to be engaged for & to manage. O Sally, do make me happy by being more entirely mine—that is, by taking our circumstances just as they are & while we weave our histories still more actually together let us abide by whatever delays or embarrassments Providence may order as our destiny. I love you with all my heart. I shall always love you unless you *repel* me. I *submit* to my misfortunes & therein I show that I am more accustomed to suffer than you are & as I have often said have really endured a more saddened & a more melancholy history.

Maggie "asks" one thing very often & that is to "go to Lexington" & I am going to take her some day. I hope Miss J. will write & that you will write every other day. Let us be as happy as we can be. Our engagement is perfectly proper. Whenever you get tired of me tell me, but till then let us try and cheer each other in our present relations.

Yrs af.
Jno Miller

Colalto
Saturday, Jany 26. 1856

My *dear John*,

I put off my letter to you from the morning yesterday until night, and thereby lost the chance of writing. *Your* letters don't reach me with any regularity—some, of them, I fear, not at all. I have had none since, the one from Washington until the one of the 21st from Princeton came half an hour ago. If I compare all I have written with the number of those I have received, I rather think you are in my debt.

I find life a wee bit more cheerful in the last few days; as the bright, calm weather has wooed me to a walk every day over the snow, which, the first day allowed me to sink in it to depth of 18 inches or more. Since then, I have made Alfred scrape me a path from the front door to the gate on the Lynchburg road; there I find the snow firmly pressed by wagons, and can walk with comparative ease to town. Somehow, I took cold in my first excursion, and am a good deal worried with it yet, tho' I never let it stop me in my going out.

Dr White was here yesterday, the first time he has been able to pay me a visit since you were here. He spoke, as usual, about our matter, and brought me a very affectionate message from Mr Peyton Harrison in regard to it. Mr Schen—(Oh John! how *does* your townsman of the Bd of Publication *spell* his horrid name?) also has written a strong paragraph against Phil: The more important thing, however, was what he *volunteered* about Dr. Hodge. It was this almost verbatim:—"Upon the question of Divorce *en thesi,* nothing can have been suggested to my mind which had not occurred to you. But as your question, is meant, doubtless, to apply to a particular case, I must say that owing to my peculiar relations to Mr Miller's family, and to the fact that my opinion has not been asked by any member of it, I could not now give it now without seeming to them to be officious." Cautious, cool, & as you, percieve entirely non-committal. An exhibition of himself, I think, in no very attractive guise. Dr. White remarked, that he did not know when, he recieved the letter, but Mr Brown told him afterwards "that there had been some jarring between the Millers & Dr Hodge"! wh accounted for this discreet epistle.

I was greatly surprised and gratified about dark yesterday to have a little sleigh drive to the door & Nannie Carrington walk in. She had been anxious for some time to pay me a visit, & yesterday took a seat with Mr Morton & came 40 miles on the snow to see me. She & Campbell you know came on in Nov: They are my staunch friends.[48] Campbell says, like a hot tempered, generous fellow as he is, "I don't care what you say, but right or wrong *I'm* going to support Cousin Sally, and the first man that utters one word to me against her, I'll knock him down".

Aunt Sally, has recently been at Aunt Eliza & I gather from what Nannie drops unconsciously that her antagonism has been more rampant than I had supposed. She, even, I suspect, used her influence with *Tom* to prevent his coming on to our wedding. What think you of the kindness of an Aunt who *could be willing* to encourage a young Brother bound to me by strong ties of obligation, as she knows, to treat me in a painful emergence in such a manner. But no matter. It may be, I have not heard accurately, certainly I do not know *fully* what she did. However I shall take Longfellow's advice—

> "As one by one thy hopes depart
> Be resolute and calm.

> "Oh, fear not in a world like this
> And thou shalt know ere long,
> Know how sublime a thing it is
> To suffer & be strong."[49]

But I am at the end of my sheet. No, darling, I cant write every other day—

48. McDowell's cousins, Ann Lightfoot (Nannie) Carrington (1831–1863) and her brother, William Campbell Carrington (1835–1863).

49. Henry Wadsworth Longfellow (1807–1882), "The Light of Stars" ("A Second Psalm of Life"), published in 1839.

twice a week will do, won't it? Kiss the children for me. I love you—as my servants say—*"powerful."*

Such intense cold! Two days ago the mercury was 14° below zero, & a glass of water actually had a portion of ice upon it in its quick passage from my room thro' the dining room to me in the Library. God bless you *and* your philosophy,

Your
S.C.P. McD.

Princeton, Jan: 28th
1856.

My dearest Sally,

I think so too. Do write on the evening before & then when your morning postscript is added I have a good long letter.

I am so much obliged to Miss Gordon.[50] Tell her so & with my most cordial respects beg to know whether I may not write some day again. But. Sally, *are* you right down handsome. Honour bright. Do you look as well as that day with the brown dress on in the piazza?

As to our engagement I am glad you are willing at last to "let it rest". If you *want* to be free you may be free at once with a stroke of the pen. But if you are willing to be mine do say so, my Darling, & let us be easy about all that matter.

The danger of self-deception & effect upon preaching &c I will risk. My philosophy is not likely to "fail". Certainly if you mean by "failing" my running it out & finding it empty, there is no danger, for I am more enamoured than ever of it.

You ask me *how much* I love you. I will tell you. So much as to think of you morning, noon & night & to have a little sense of what Mrs Hunter spoke of the *weariness* of a long engagement. If you lived within forty miles of me I could endure it better; but now I am crazy already to see you. As to buttons &c my conviction is that we dont gain in these respects by marriage. My idea is that a bachelor is apt to have a straighter wardrobe than a husband. At least I have generally found that a few shillings & a seamstress within a block or two made up all these exigencies of marriage.

But *Sally* I should be *happier* if you were my wife. I feel it. I feel it a great sacrifice to give it up too for a social integrity that is one of the things I make very little practical use of. And tho' for our children's sake & above all for you I know I am doing right to preserve our social strength unimpaired yet I make the sacrifice grudgingly & with a great deal of gloomy discontentedness of feeling.

I think you are "just a tinsy winsy bit" wrong about the Prestons. They tho't your step a bad one. So now do we. Not bad in character but bad in policy. Their

---

50. Jannetta MacKenzie Gordon wrote to John Miller on Jan. 22, 1856, reassuring him of McDowell's health and appearance.

being silent & not *helping* you was perhaps to them the height of delicacy & deference. Dont blame them. I would keep friendly with all. Nay more I would attribute to the very kindliest motives all such things as silence & absence which *may* flow from the kindliest sense.

Sally, as to your home I am at a loss always to speak. Because I have the awkwardness of only a partial knowledge. But certain things are plain to me. first—you could not have a worthier & more proper *business* to occupy you & to answer the question which seems to trouble you, what good you can do & of what use you can be to any body, than to rouse yourself & bring you matured energies to the work of extricating yourself from impending difficulties. You owe it to your proper guardianship of Lilly as well as to yourself.

Second, you cannot live alone at Colalto & every day you are living there may be increasing your difficulties.

Third, the Major, or some similar friend in L. ought to advise & help you, & Darling, you ought frankly to tell them the length & breadth of your difficulty.

Your difficulty that if you sell Colalto you must pay away its price to others *may* not be a sufficient argument against it. For the expenses incident to so large a house may if you continue them bring you into much greater embarrassments.

If you feel unequal to the task of managing your own business yourself, then you ought to search out perseveringly some competent agent & pay him his fees. The only thing against this seems to be that if you could rouse yourself to accomplish all yourself with the advice of your relatives, you would be securing yourself the very occupation you want & saving the fees for your own immediate support.

You know, servants' hire & the saving of large household expenses & the saving of inevitable hospitalities & the rent of your house are all things you are kept back from by going on to live at Colalto & the want of these as means of liquidation may be plunging you deeper in debt.

The Major might still rent your house to his sister, taking the thing quite off your hand & attending to the duty himself—or Morton may take it & give you rooms in it or some one else. Then your servants you might hire or some one or two of them perhaps give over to some members of your family in part payment of debt. As to yourself, Darling, if you could not board where Mrs Carrington your sister is boarding or any where in Lexington or anywhere else, which you ought very carefully to consider still you could set up housekeeping elsewhere in Lexington much more inexpensively than in that great big & hospitable Col-alto.

Now, Darling, I am almost out of breath & if I were near I might have one of those cross retorts with which you accuse yourself toward poor Miss G., but if you really saw into my heart you would see how great a sacrifice this is to my affection. I hate to advise any body about their private affairs, first, because I do it in the dark &, second, because I do it at the hazard of misleading you &, third, because it is not the most graceful business for a lover. But, Darling, you *must* for some months to come *make a business* of these embarrassments of yours. It is[51] a *sin* with so much to do to be asking of "what use you are" to any body & what you have to live for. And now as your sisters have all left you & you have no one to guard but Lilly & yourself even *your own immediate residence* important as it is as to its comfort both to you & to me is of less consequence than the integrity of your credit & your own smooth command of your circumstances for years to come.

The idea that if you take certain steps you will have no immediate means is dreadful illusory. Better borrow immediate means or learn the most rigid habits of frugality than secure just the mere provisions of your purse thro' the means of great & most threatening expenditures.

Whoa! dont I scold. But, Sally, one of the pains of my own disappointment is that embarrassments wh. look to me so simple & so easily resolved & wh. would leave you with so good an estate are for the lack of some efficient friend or perhaps a more awakened decision in yourself giving you so much uneasiness. Perhaps you had better not let me *appear* as one of your advisers but do think of my advice.

Yrs trly
JM.

I will make a bargain with you. If you as your share of our partnership will cheer up & get out of your despondencies & bring your affairs by prompt & well devised means into complete command I on my part will promise to make this poor despised philosophy of mine a real pleasure & a pride to you. And even if we are never married to make it a matter of real romantic interest that we lived & died wedded to each other under the shadow of this divine philosophy.

Write me back word just how you felt on reading this cross letter & tell me what you did the first day toward turning the tide of your income so that it shall flow in the direction of liquidation.

The Major I suppose is not in a condition to help any one. Do offer him my sincere sympathies when you see him & let me remain, Darling, you own scolding but faithful lover

JM

I will send Julias letter again. She writes a mighty nice letter but there is a vast difference between that & a wife.

Princeton, Jan: 30th [1856]

Dear Heart,

Unless you are wholly I & I am so wholly you as to be no longer *any different* I ought not to have told you about R. & as it is I have a great deal of compunction. To show it I send you his letter; for like the man that "jumped into the quick set hedge" I have a proclivity when I feel a remorse about anything just to do

51. "almost" is scratched out.

the same thing over again. Indeed I will send you two or three letters & keep Julias till another time.[52] Perhaps the "tout ensemble" will appear better than just the naked statement I made to you. But, Sally, never lisp anything about, & put these letters right into the fire.

Dearest Darling, "God bless my philosophy" is the first kind word you ever spoke of it. You will feel ashamed of the way you have treated it when it has made us both, great & useful.

Schenck, my Dear, *Schenck*. As to Dr Hodge, there is no "jar" except with me. I wrote a little article about him in the paper & challenged one of his students in his examination & it offended them particularly Mrs Hodge. I am so glad you walk. Keep at it, & tell me all about it when you write.

These letters I have just fished out of a pile some of which I have burned. I thot I had burned these.

Bravo, for your cousin Campbell. I like those two cousins just from the glimpse I had of them in the buggy. Remember me to them when you write.

Yours in haste
Jno Miller.

Colalto,
January 30. 1856.

My dear John, you know I always did have sad fears of your Philosophy. I thought it crept in like a wedge between you and the pulpit and, to an alarming degree, destroyed your usefulness. I am sure it was that thing that made my Kentucky friend assure us, "that John Miller was a fool". I fear now it is seducing you away from your duty, and alluring you into forbidden parts of speculative inquiry. I anticipate disappointment to you from it, and look forward to the time when you, yourself will look back sorrowfully upon the time & energy you have lost in your chase after this Will o'Wisp. But there is something worse than all this. *I* can bear composedly your constant wooing of this rival-love; I can bear, since it is a sort of relief to one habitually depressed in spirits, that you should for a while indulge this gorgeously-tinted day-dream; but, my dear John, I shudder, when I perceive that *your mind*, is to be the sacrifice of your passion, and I can no longer forbear to warn you of your danger, and earnestly entreat you to stop now, while there is yet some hope of recovery.

You cannot see, as I do, how alarmingly some of the powers of your mind are suffering:—how your judgment is warped—your discrimination, degenerated from strength to the saddest exhibition of feebleness—your *moral* discernment still more decayed & all such traits as taste & true & high sentiments entirely

---

52. William Henry Ruffner had written to Miller. Evidently McDowell destroyed these letters, because they have not been located. She comments on them in her letter of February 2, 1856.

obliterated! Dear John, how grieved I am! I want *so* much to be with you. I *so* mourn that I can't be near to throw away those horrid books, that have been the great Tempter & Destroyer to you, & persuade you to entire abandonment of every thing like study for some time to come. My poor little man! I wonder I was so much shocked at the bursting of these terrible facts upon me yesterday when I read your last letter, for now, that I look back I can trace quite clearly the steady & rapid progress of your malady. But it was not till I read your last letter in the first long paragraph in which you gravely and solemnly assure me with all the emphasis of sober trust & real conviction, that "it is your *number one* letter" that the fact of your mental decay was forced upon me! So great was the blow, that my own mind was well-nigh overthrown by it. I am not sure yet that I have my wits about me. But it's no wonder. I was repeating all night in my agonizing wakefulness—"number one—number one".—Poor John! to tell me with such a grave tone—"Sally this is my bright idea—and this my number one letter"! "All this is of a piece with his philosophy, I thought. Or rather this is the lunacy to which it has led. But he must be humoured, the poor lunatic": and my heart bled for him—and for myself to whose woes was added this yet more terrible one. John, tell me when you take a flight and get pretty high, how do you get down again? Let off steam, as they do, in a balloon among the clouds? I wd do that, but for the misfortune of having the steam turn & let me off, before I was ready to part with it. But suppose I am to drop—where must it be? in the water? I am weak enough now without further dilution. On *dry ground* then? O no! I too often stand there. Well then I must have a *terra-firma*, so I'll fall on old Dr Hodge as he thinks he is that to us & the world both: what do you think of him?

Thursday 31. 8 1/2 a.m.

I am more than commonly hurried this morning. I was worried at being stopped in my letter last night; I find having Miss Jannetta for so near a neighbour is sometimes a trouble to me, as my room (which by the by is the Library) is no longer a Sanctum to me.

Your letter of the 28th came an hour ago. It is very wise as to my difficulties, if I could only act upon its suggestions. Cousin John can't help me, & there is no chance of renting my house at present. Three servants I am obliged to keep, or support if I left them with others. That is Malinda is a confirmed invalid: Mary so frequently sick as to preclude the possibility of hiring her & her youngest child too young to be subjected to such usage as generally falls upon hired little negroes. Edward, I send to Susan as soon as I can.

I am right glad to hear you speak of being "discontented" at our disappointment. I thought you were entirely too well pleased at it, and have been rather mad when I *did* admit the thoughts.

No: I am not handsome, and am nervous about your laying so much stress upon my being so. You must love me for something more decided and more durable than that, or you'll wake up some morning and find all your affection gone. I have had, a very bad cold too, which hangs about me yet, & does not improve my looks in the least. Miss Jannetta is sick too, & I feel uneasy about her.

Write a short note [to] Cantey: I am sure she'll be pleased at it. She was so unfortunate as to break John Miller's[53] head before she left, and almost the last thing she did was to go to a Jeweller and ask him to mend it, & ornament it with a bit of her watch chain with the tiniest heart suspended to it. She couldn't take it however. Isn't it extraordinary her passion for dolls. As I was locking her trunk, she inquired about a little Negro doll—"Jim Massie" & wanted it thrown in.

I have a nice letter from Maggie B. today.

Tell me, John, what Professor Henry said of me—you see the old passion.

I am Darling, very affectionately
S.C.P. McDowell

II
Princeton
Feb: 2d

My *dearest Sally*,

I am hoping for a letter to-night, but as it will be too late to allow a reply before Monday I write one in the interval.

I am getting matters gradually reduced to order here. My household god a big Franklin which I have just bought discarding one of smaller dimension I have this day inaugurated in one of these big square rooms. My books are yet in great boxes in the middle of the floor. The carpenter has been fixing shelves & I am gradually sinking into a confirmed recluse.

The children come into my room & climb about my chair at certain privileged times but besides these it is astonishing how few I see.

Gentlemen call to see me, professors in college &c & I mark down their names intending to go when I need a little socializing but that time seems never to come. My walks & my despised philosophy make up the sum of my Princ: existence. But then there is all my Lex: existence. I live there much of the time. I take the *train* & travel there every evening & a certain packet in red tape helps my expedition wonderfully.

I preach sometimes—tomorrow for Dr Janeway. I want you so much to see my children. I am going to manage in some of these months some day or other.

Would you like Maggie to write you a letter?

What does Bocock say? My judg[ment] says we did right but I have sometimes great rebelliousness at our not having gone forward.

It was a sacrifice of happiness to social peace.

God bless you Darling.

Yours affy
Jno Miller

53. The name given to one of her dolls.

Princeton
Feb: 2d 1856.

My dear Sally,

I have already written a letter to-day. But yours just brot late at night is such an enigma that I hurry a reply that I may hear from you again as soon as possible.

What *do* you mean?

Some weeks ago I spoke of *numbering* my letters because some were lost so that this miscarriage of any one might be noticed. You called it laughingly at the time my "bright idea" & there, you remember the matter dropped.

The other day feeling uneasy again about our letters I determined again to number mine & in the letter of which you speak told you so, alluded to the plan playfully as my "bright idea" & said this letter is number one & marked it so (I.) just over the date as you will see, intending to go on numbering them that you might see when one was lost. I forgot to do so in one or two that followed but this afternoon marked the one I sent number two (II.) What *do* you mean, my Darling? And what do you mean by "my judgment being warped" & "my moral discernment decayed"? What has gotten over you Sally? I write in great haste, but do reply at once & send your letter by the very speediest mail.

I cant tell you what a riddle your letter seems to me.

God bless you

Yours warmly
Jno Miller.

Colalto
Thursday, Feb 2. 1856.

I declare, John, I was really worried when I opened your letter this morning, and found, instead of the nice, long letter from you that the two stamps predicted, only those great, rough, blue sheets of your friend with an overseer look about them, & the merest dwarf of a note from yourself.[54] I am even mad now as I think of my disappointment & beg that you wont subject me to any such in future.

They are very coarse letters, those in their handling of the subject you mentioned. If there had been any long, & very special & very affectionate intimacy between you, I can comprehend the feeling that would have induced him to make to you the suggestion he did; but then it would have been done more delicately and cautiously. I don't know that the matter has been at all improved by your allowing him the privilege of speaking for himself. But are you quite sure you are right in your suspicion of the person alluded to by him? I cant think he wd speak, of *my* friend, as possessing "a physique of

---

54. McDowell refers to the enclosures in Miller's letter of Jan. 30, 1856. His friend was William Henry Ruffner.

the most refined beauty". The other parts of his description *may* be entirely true; I think them much more nearly so than such high-sounding phrases generally are—indeed, I wd not abate the warmth of any of the terms he has used in speaking of "her mind & heart," but I cannot think any affection cd be blind enough to subscribe to his talk about her beauty; and his extravagance on this point makes me think you may be mistaken in the person he means. But John, tho' I am annoyed, & feel that he has *belittled* my friend, by thrusting her as he has done into yr presence, yet as he expresses himself, not only in his letters to you, but at all times and to all persons most kindly and admiringly of you, I can forgive a great many things in him. Yet, do you know in spite of these kind expressions, I wouldn't like you to open to him the secrets of that "heart-chamber" he speaks of; and that just because he wd unintentionally, pain you by his manner of handling its contents. I was much surprised and pleased this morning to hear of the arrival of our friend Dr D. X. Junkin; yet sorry to learn that his coming South was on account of his health. I saw him this afternoon, and was impressed by his look of ill health. At present, however, he is more unwell than usual, having had the other day in Rich'd an attack of Pneumonia, which has left him with weak voice & an anxious & dispirited countenance. He was extremely kind to us in Washington when Frank was ill and died there. And when they were all gone, & Susan & I left to pack up & have things moved from our temporary dwelling there, he came every night and staid with us; which was a real kindness & comfort.

Put your ear down here, little man, and let me whisper something to you, which you must be sure not to tell anybody; will you? It isn't any *great* secret, after all, but then you mustn't tell "Mary" nor "Mother", nor any one else, unless you get crazy to speak it out, like I do, and then you may tell Allie when he's asleep. I am hungry for a sight of you. I am ashamed to use words strong enough to tell you how much, this day, I have wanted to see you. Dear John, don't our fate *seem* right hard. It *feels* so to me often & often I wish I had a love of a philosophy to fill my heart & reconcile me to my destiny. But, philosophy is no more meant for a woman, than hat & boots. Indeed I don't know what *is* meant for her but suffering and sorrow and submission to every thing and every body. Don't you believe that it is much better to be a man? I do; tho' if I were a good woman, I wouldn't care to be a *great* man.

Do you know, John, I think I behave *mighty* bad to you about your philosophy. I feel self-reproachful about it; for inasmuch as it is *your* passion, it ought to be my pleasure; and instead of speaking slightingly of it, I ought to possess every desire to sympathize with you in it: and I mean to try to do it, tho' in all honesty I must say, I think some other pursuit wd be more useful. But, Darling, good-night—and remember not to ring me back for some toe-toe.

Monday 8 A.M.

It is almost too cold to write this morning. Altho' I am sitting almost in the fire, yet I cannot hope to be comfortable even, for the half hour I shall have to write to you. This terribly cold weather suggested to me the notion of so unsentimental & homely a present to you, as a pair of socks of my own knitting. They are nothing like so nice, as to the mere fine quality of the yarn, as I wanted, but still they felt soft and pleasant, as I slipped one on this morning to satisfy myself of its architectural beauty & judge of its probable fit and so if I can get them put up in time I will send them by today's mail. I will send one pair, & if you write me they fit nicely and answer well, I'll make others follow them. And, to avoid all remark at our gossiping little P.O. I shall take the liberty of putting your Mother's name on your package. Be careful not to let any *body* know what the package contains. I haven't quite recovered from the revelation of the silver tumbler.

Cantey's address, which I believe I neglected to give you is "Athens, Georgia."

Dr D. X. dines with me today, & I anticipate as much pleasure from the visit as the intense cold will allow. The Dr is rather snappish but always to me very kind.

Do you know, it is a great pain to me to find that Preachers are not all gentlemen: and more than this, that they don't care to be so.

Dear John, I love you with the most painful emotion—with a restless, suspicious, anxious affection that, whilst it gives me much pleasure, gives much pain too.

Affectionately Yours
S.C.P. McDowell

III
Wed. Feb: 6 [1856]

So Sally,

You think I am "well pleased" with our disappointment. That is the refinement of cruelty: For fortune first to defraud me of what I was looking forward to as my happiness & then to have it cast upon me as a reproach that it is no unhappiness at all.

Alas! Alas! I have fallen upon evil times. You mock me & jeer me & trick me. By the way, I hope you have answered by this time my very serious letter of Sat. night. I hope you considered it as thoroughly in earnest & that you had no rest until you went into a long explanation & vindication of your last letter.

How cold it is. I fear this letter will lie long on the way before it reaches you. I expected one from you last night; but I suppose it was delayed by the snow upon the Ridge.

Darling, how much of that letter was really earnest. I know you have no mercy for my other passion. If it ever amounts to anything, you will have no credit for our success. My fame as a philosopher will be altogether my own.

But, Sally, dont write me any more *such* letters. They really make me feel crazy. Had you not a little "tinsy winsee bit" of seriousness in what you wrote. God bless you. Write oftener.

Yours affly
Jno Miller

Colalto
Wednesday Feb'y 6. 1856.

I have been worried & troubled, & withal not well all day, and tonight, John, I beg for a little petting. I was vexed with you too—*really vexed,* I believe for the very first time. I may have been unreasonable, but I could not repress a pretty strong uprising of my temper, & if you had been present, in all probability, we would have quarrelled in good earnest. I only received your letter of the 26th this morning. It was evidently, in answer to some comment of mine upon a remark of William Brown's, and did not please me. It touched upon a point that I am excessively sensitive about—much more so than you have ever dreamed—and I felt both wounded and worried. If I have dealt with you, with ·any want of perfect candor, in any part of our whole matter, it has been just here—& that for two reasons:- first, because my own opinion was constantly fluctuating as to your *real*—not your expressed—feelings—not that I thought you uttered what you didn't feel—but I feared you held in reserve a stronger feeling, & a different one, which some regard to *my* feelings forbade you to express. And, then next because it was always too painful for me to speak even to you the fears that I could not always reason away, and could scarcely reveal without the hazard of having my motives misconceived in a way most unpleasant to me.

One thing however, I can say very distinctly—that I don't want you, out of mere compassion, to feel bound to me;—nor, do I want, a mere sense of honor, as you all call it, to form the tie between us. But either of these reasons alone, or both together would prevent your acknowledging either one of them or the powerful motive on your part for continuing our engagement, so long as *I*, on my part, seemed actuated by affection; and hence I feel the great difficulty of discovering exactly how & what you *do* feel; and, of conforming my course to your wishes. Sometimes I think I have banished entirely all this painful questioning of your feelings; but then it returns again, and I go thro' the same anxious tossings as before. And these are helped on, occasionally, by your saying such things as these:—"You know you can be free with the dust of the pen whenever you wish it". "Whenever you are tired of me, tell me". &c. I always feel when such things are said, that, after all, it is not my liberty that you want to return—but *your own* that you wish me to restore to you. Now, John, this engagement of ours would be far worse than nothing to me, without your affection. It is *that* that is precious to me; and without it this bond of ours would be to me unspeakably burdensome & revolting. And, whenever I find out that this is wanting, of course, it will be no struggle for me to set you free.

Miss Jannetta s'd to me early this morning, "Why Sally, I don't think you are in an amiable mood to-day". I'm afraid you'll think so too. Well, if I'm unreasonable, scold me soundly & set me right: if I am not—what?

I can't help getting troubled. I am pressed and annoyed by really heavy cares and anxieties, and feel that I have no human being to turn to for help, and so when my suspicious anxiety is roused upon a point so tender as your love, I sometimes, I know unreasonably, give way. But Darling,—good-night.

Thursday morning.

Dear John, draw me right close to your heart and forgive me if I said one word last night that pained you. I am wayward it may be, and know I am exacting, but John darling, I am always hoping that your love will be to me, what your philosophy seems to you—an exhaustless mine all my own. You must be a woman to be able to understand all these quirks & requirements of temper; & as you can never be that—wont you bear with me patiently & make the best of me? I love you with all the tenderness & strength and steadiness of my nature; and if you do think the amount small, you have, at least, the comfort of knowing that what I have given has been dealt with no niggardly hand, but it is *all* that I possess.

And so my *number one* letter mystified you! I meant nothing more than to laugh at you for having accidentally bestowed the number that, in the common phrase of the day, indicates the perfection of excellence in every thing from a game-cock up to an Orator—& from a primer up to—to—(help me out, please)—to a treatise on Moral Science, to a very nice note, which tho' it was very pleasant & acceptable to me wd by no means have illustrated to you as a writer. If *you* were mystified, now *I* am mortified that my mock gravity should have failed so completely. However, be relieved now—your "judgment" is as good as ever; & your "moral discernment" not all less clear than formerly. Do write to me some times when you are not in a hurry, & pray discard the wee sheets you have written on lately. And if Maggie would like, let her write me a letter. It wd be a pleasure to me that I wd not dare to ask for. By the by Maggie's Nube, as you spell it has never reached me. I think it may be in a box I am daily expecting from Phil: The weather & roads are so bad & the mails so irregular that you ought to write without waiting to receive my letters—Campbell came down yesterday. God bless you dear John.

Affec'ly
S.C.P. McDowell

Princeton, Feb: 8th
1856.

My lovely, darling Sally,

I do so love you for that earnest letter. Then you do care for me? O Sally, if you only knew how I longed for all affection that pours itself out to me without one suspicion or reserve, & gives itself up to me as tho' it trusted itself in my keeping & my love without one thought of concealing itself or keeping the whole strength of its existence from me you would write such letters more often than you do. I bring them out from their hiding place day & night & read them & think about them & feast on them sentence by sentence & the moment I lay them down I am wondering when such another letter (which I have no doubt it is very easy for you to write) will come again in the list of those in which you half conceal from me these secret feelings.

Sally, do you *really* love me. You say, you love me "with painful emotion". That may be because you love me so little. You say, you want to see me. That may be because you want to see whether you love me at all. So I *poison* even your nicest letters.

I laugh at myself sometimes for the perfect *witchcraft* of my love. When you told me in sending the socks that you had slipped *one* of them on your foot I felt right sorry there were two of them & that when they came I should not know which was the happy foot that was wrapped round in anything that had been so highly honored. I must be very far gone. And, Sally, that you should care to see me, & that I shall ever see you again & that I shall fold you in my arms & that I *may* some day possess you as all my own & that you *are* all my own, these are thots, the pleasure of which I can hardly express to you & that give a tinge of romance & a certain sort of disappointed bitter rapture to all my life.

Wont you *write every other day*. I really desire it enough to warrant your doing so.

My philosophy goes always on. I do wish you would love it. I send you the skeleton of my book. How is it possible that you love me when you do not love that which *characterizes* me & that has taken possession of all my life.

When I write again I will tell you more of my everyday life.

The socks I very much want. I shall certainly "ask for more". So by the time I can receive these & write to you again, get your needles ready for another trial. I am an ungraceful person at receiving presents, but *such* presents I greatly enjoy.

Now, Darling, let that love of yours of which you speak be a little more outspoken & confiding & a little less restless & suspicious. You may let your whole heart lavish upon me its fullest treasures. You need never fear that after you have loaded me with your love, the peculiarities of our lot can in any possibility defraud you of mine.

Darling, what *is* your suspicion? Are you *afraid* to love me? And is the mortification of having committed yourself to my affection & being one day *deserted* one of the bugbears that troubles your path.

Tell me all you think & feel. Love me a great deal more than you have loved me before. And dont be afraid to pour out upon me all your thought, for Darling, *the first indifference you may rely upon it must* begin with you.

By the way, dont send anything to Mother which you do not wish her to open for her mail goes at once to her often. This tho' will make no difference as to the socks.

Take care of your health.

Yours affectionately
Jno Miller.

I am too late for the skeleton.

Colalto,
Saturday Feb'y 8.[55] **1856.**

My own darling John, I am really sorry about that foolish letter. I had no "seriousness" in anything I said about your philosophy, but was laughing harmlessly tho' it at yr No 1 letter, & never dreamed that my assumed gravity had vraisemblance enough to deceive you. But I won't do it any more. I shan't write "*any such* letters" in future. I have, as I have often said, very serious anxiety about your "other passion", but whenever I express it has been, & will be done in a manner very different from the silly letter that has annoyed you. So now have no more troubles on that score: burn up the letter & forget it ever was written.

My troubles press more heavily upon me within a few days. I have had another offer for my farm; & hear of still another gentleman that wishes to have it. I am making up my mind gradually to give it up. I have so many heart-aches about other things it seems extraordinary folly in me, to allow the parting with a bit of ground to be a grief to me. But the giving up Colalto involves much more than the mere selling of a piece of land. It leaves me afloat in this world. If I can so arrange it, & by a *very* advantageous sale can acquire, without injustice to others, the means, what do you say to my accepting Mr Kennedy's invitation to go with his family in a few months to Europe? I have no strong ties any where. Life is almost a blank to me. Except yourself & Lilly I have no strong affection to any body. And Lilly must be at school—or it may be, I cd take her with me:—and you are away any how: As distant almost as if the Ocean was between us. O John, can you imagine *why* God gave me this mad-hot heart of mine, without any ability to diffuse its heat, & without the privilege of the very meanest of the race to concentrate it with any result but pain.

Miss Jannetta has been offered a school in Fincastle, & I think she ought to accept it. Nannie returns home in a fortnight and when they all go, I shall comfort myself as best I can, with such things as are within reach.

I never see Cousin John—He is always absent when I go to his house, & tho' I want to see him, yet I have an undefinable shrinking from it. I love him more than all my kin put together, and mourn that this blow has been dealt to him.

Dr D. X. Junkin still here, I think, tho' he was uncertain two days ago about remaining. He says very flattering things, for which I am obliged to him, and is very warm & kind in his expressions of interest. My brother Tom writes me he has been successful in his wooing & demands my congratulations.[56] I shall

---

55. Saturday was Feb. 9, 1855.
56. Thomas Preston McDowell later married Louisa Constance Warwick (c. 1835–?).

write to him, I am glad to hear it for his sake—but Heaven help the poor girl. I don't like the projected alliance; but, of course, will have nothing to say. Tom has behaved so badly to me, that my interest in him has greatly waned, tho' I will not intermit any civil kindness. Poor fellow! I can't help having my heart ache for him, & I can forget his bad treatment, I believe after all, tho' I shall never love him as before.

Dear John have I written you a miserably complaining, & bitter-flavored letter. Well pardon it & pray for me—& write me a letter on a big sheet of paper.

God bless you my Darling.

Aff'y
S.C.P. McDowell

Colalto.
Saturday Feb'y 9. 1856.

My *dear John,*

I wrote to you this morning and did not intend to write again until Monday or Tuesday, but I have borne all day upon my mind a painful sense of having really wounded you by my foolish letter of last week; and tonight in reading over your note of Wednesday which came this morn'g, I have this impression deepened. I think, John, you speak of the thing too seriously, when even before you receive my letter telling you that it was but an awkward jest, you, yourself perceive it was not meant in earnest, for you ask *"how much* of it was serious." I had really *no seriousness* in anything I then said about your philosophy—but simply drew upon my imagination for all the evils I ascribed to its influence, that I might laugh, in a way that I did not think wd worry you in the least; about your calling your little note—"my number one letter". It was a foolish thing; but utterly meaningly beyond what I tell you. But as I am awkward about it, I'll never again write you such a letter. I wish you were here that I might talk to you of it.

No, Darling, I dont *always* think you are "well pleased" with our disappointment". Sometimes I do, and it is great torture to me. I can't exactly tell *why* the feeling comes over me, unless it is, that from my peculiar trials in life, I have become a little suspicious. And then my affection is exacting,—and sorrow & disappointment, & a certain kind of hopelessness, and cares of various sorts all combine to make me unreasonable. No doubt, I trouble & pain you very often. It seems strange that I should, for I believe all the tenderness of my nature is centered in you; & certainly I love no one else with anything like the absorbing emotion that I do you. I am ashamed even to *think* of you so unceasingly; and agree with your Mother in believing, so far as I am concerned, that this correspondence of ours, is drawing sinfully upon my time & thought.—But no more tonight, as the bell rung out 12 some minutes ago.

Monday morning 8 o'clock.

I mean to try to be more reasonable and better-tempered in future: Are you glad to hear it? or are you skeptical as to my power to reform in these particulars? You oughtn't to allow me to complain so much. A good scolding now & then, I fancy would do me real good; yet I think, I would look upon anyone as very cruel, or else wonderfully disinterested & virtuous in their friendship who *could* give *me* a real, hard scolding.

You remember we heard that old Dr Junkin was opposed to our marriage & had said *he* wd not perform the ceremony?

I think even Dr White believed the report—and indeed it met with general acceptance. Well, Dr D. X. told me the other day that he had heard the same in Penn'a, and had, since he came here, asked his brother about it, & the old man had replied—"He saw nothing wrong in it, & would have married us any time we had asked him to do it". D. X. himself is very indignant at your treatment, but thinks you acted too hastily in resigning. He intimates too, that you may have disobliged some of the City Pastors, who wd rather augment the marriage difficulty to get you out of their way. This seems to me a shocking suspicion against any men who profess to [be] actuated & controlled by Christian principles. Young George Junkin (the lawyer in Phil), I fancy from what his Uncle says, turned to us very warmly.[57]

I write in a great hurry; & Edward has just appeared with breakfast, for which Miss Jannetta has, already, proclaimed her readiness.

I shall look eagerly for Maggie's letter—Did you get the socks? How did they fit? I have another beautiful pair on hand. God bless you, my darling.

Affectionately
S.C.P. McDowell

Princeton, Feb: 11th 1856.

So you have been "vexed" with me, Darling. Well I dont know what that old letter had in it, but if it was half as awkward as it seems to have been it ought to be burnt in effigy.

But, Sally; you are a little like that Slough of Despond it tells of in Pilgrim's Progress.[58] "The Lord of the country" by which I now understand *me*, had poured into that deceitful marsh all sorts of good material, whole wagon loads of promises, oaths, covenants & yet they had all been swallowed up & the ground was as hungry & as unsteady as before. Darling Sally, what can I do for you? If there is any possible form of speech by which I can convince you that I do fondly love

---

57. George Junkin (1827–1902).
58. The classic Christian story by John Bunyan (1628–1688). The "Slough of Despond" was one of the places visited by the Christian on his way from the "City of Destruction" to the "Heavenly City."

you & prize this engagement beyond what I can express I am sure I would like to employ it.

Now let me tell you.

I will open to you all that is in my heart. I. I *do* feel in honour bound to you & if a son of mine should win a woman as I have won you & then desert her I would think badly of him. I *do* have a remorse about our disappointment & if I didnt dare to remain engaged & you were to find it out & dismiss me & I were to hear of you in any way as a sufferer either in your own affection or in your pride I would feel painfully self condemned. I won you in spite of your remonstrances. I repelled arguments which have turned out to be sound. I seduced you into an engagement & got possession of your affections in the face of strong resistances of your judgment. And I do confess that all that you have fancied, exists, that is, a strong sense of honor & a most thoroughly implanted feeling both binding me not to bring our relations to an end. If I tho't you didnt love me that would release me. Or if I felt that I didnt love you that would terribly perplex me; for I could not long keep it in concealment without unworthy maneuvres or without perjuring myself with declarations of affection which the fact did not legitimately warrant. Now, Sally, all this I confess. I confess, that after winning my way to your love through assurances all of which have found themselves deceived, & after beating down your resistances & winning you into my arms in the face of your constantly expressed misgivings when you were honest with me & indeed very wearisome in your different difficulties, then to desert you, *would* violate every honorable sense & if Allie should treat a lady so I should be ashamed of him to the last hour of my life.

But Sally, what on earth has this to do with the business? II. I have told you in a way in which I could not deceive you without the grossest falsehood that I am held to our engagement by another & an infinitely stronger bond—that I love you past expression—that I long after you with the most yearning & anxious desire—that I am as incapable of any other affection so long as you love me as if you were the only human creature that I *could* love in the world—that I value our engagement on its own account—that I am willing to wait for you for ten years if that be necessary—that I am willing to give up even the tho't of "waiting" & settle down upon the mere pleasure of our present relations if Christianity demands it & that all this does not weigh at all upon the bond of honor but would exist & would bind me to your affection even if there were no principle or feeling in the case.

Now, Sally, what *can* I have "in reserve". A *great* lie, as Dr Breckinridge would say, most certainly, & nothing else. I cannot be holding in reserve anything that could possibly move your uneasiness or make you suspicious unless I am one of the most treacherous or inconsistent of men.

You say there is danger in a long engagement by which I can only understand that one's affection is exposed to change. Well Sally, what's the use of putting the devil into one's mind. There never was a woman who had a fairer chance to settle down in the whole possession of a man's affections. I love you with all my nature. And what I am longing for is what my affection has never had & that is the entire surrender to me of your firm & unsuspecting devotion.

Before this subject is put away tell me in the next letter you write all that was "too fanciful to speak of even to me & that you could not reveal without hazard of having your motives misconceived". Tell me all that is in your heart, Sally. Tell me what those "silly things are in which you have not been candid with me". And then after that love me with an unwavering passion & never till the day of my death tell me anything that can ruffle the waters of our affection.

I go to Phil. to-morrow & hope to see Lilly. I received the socks & they fit nicely. Cant you make the leg an inch longer? Tell Miss J. the children were in a great 'miration over the toe-toe. If she were 400 miles nearer I would add that they expressed a decided wish for more.

You talk about suspicion Sally, but do you know I *still* have a suspicion you dont love me very much. I know you are a woman of strong feeling. And yet when you talk of your love to me you always say it is "as strong as you are capable of" & such talk as that. But I hope you may be forgiven.

Yours affly
Jno Miller

Colalto,
Thursday, Feb'y 14. 1856

O, John, I would give so much to have you here now. I have been suffering all day with my face—either from cold or neuralgia I cannot yet tell which, and as I sat drearily looking into the fire as the day wore away into night I longed for you with much more than common earnestness. I think of you with the most absorbed and engrossing thought at all times, almost—yet there are hours when the feeling is intensified beyond my power to express. I feel sure I give up a great deal too much time to you: I know I am giving you too strong and influential a power over my affections—but how am I to help it? I had rather not love you at all than love you a little.

I hoped we were to have no more cold weather a few days since, but yesterday it snowed a little & this afternoon has been snowing again. I wish it were in the condition I once heard a servant announce it to be in. "Charles,["] said Aunt Sally, at the breakfast table to a large solemn looking servant behind her chair—"Charles is it snowing still?" Charles was always slow & dignified, but this morning was more so than usual as he collected himself for a reply—"No madam," said he; ["]the snow is *deceased*". There seems little prospect of its ever arriving at so remarkable a conclusion as that with us. A continuance of such weather much longer will put us to very serious trouble. We are so blocked in by ice that our usual supplies are cut off. There is scarcity now of groceries in town, and I begin to fear we may even suffer for flour.

There is to be a change in our mail arrangements—in fact, I think it has already taken place, as no mail came to me today. We are to have the mails arrive at mid-day instead of midnight—a change I am extremely glad of. I have found the arrival of Alfred & the mail at 7 1/2 every morning made terribly inroads upon my long established practice of reading etc an hour every morning. And then when I had several letters to answer by 10 o'clock, why it kept breakfast late, & the servants late & everything out of order. I am glad it is over, & hope now for better things.

I send you another pair of socks, much finer than the others. An accident put me in possession of some extremely fine yarn from a factory in Richd, of which I knit them. I don't think I shall knit any more of it however, it is so very fine & takes me so very long, & besides I fear they will do you little service. But they are soft & pleasant, and if they could speak wd tell you many a thing that was— or ought to be, most welcome to you. They are not perfectly white, which is a defect but that will make no material difference as a gaiter or boot will entirely conceal them. As there was some slight difference in the size, this time I tried on *both*—there will therefore be no jealousy as to which shall have the honor of following me—the right foot or the left.

My dear John, what does make you torment yourself, by twisting my letters in all sorts of ways? You are just as suspicious as I am, notwithstanding you do lecture me at such a rate. By the way, I begin to think we are a little alike in some things. But I don't care to have the resemblance either decided or extensive: I had rather you'd be something a great deal better. John, what *do* you love me for any how?

You cant imagine how much anxiety I feel about your book. I have a sort of terror every time I think of it. That it should be successful in the mere matter of acquiring for you a certain kind of distinction—is, I am afraid, doubtful. If this success *did* await you, it is not, it seems to me, either the highest order of reward, or the highest aim of ambition. That it should be successful in establishing new & important truths and thereby adding to your usefulness, I am even yet more discouraged about. You ought not to publish any thing without a certain measure of success:—failure, absolute failure, I fancy wd be ruinous. But I'm a terrible croaker. If I didn't feel like a *silent* ? partner in the concern, perhaps I wouldn't give myself so much uneasiness. But do as you please—Whenever you say philosophy to me, I feel like responding with my usual fondness for *alliteration*—"O fiddlesticks John"!

> God bless you. Yours affec'y
> S.C.P. McDowell.

Princeton Feb: 15 1856.

Sally My Daughter,
    You are right. Come here, my child; kneel down & put your hands in my lap I want to give you your first scolding. Now listen!

Did you ever know any one who *said* he loved you more than I do? Did you ever know anyone, especially any preacher whose *word* you cast into doubt more than you do mine? Is there any *possible* way within all the stores of the English tongue in which I can convey to you the fact that I can not willingly release you from our engagement, & that from the selfish value I set upon it? And if I say, "You can be free with the dash of the pen"; would you not think it natural that sometimes I should say that when I have betrayed you into a betrothal that I cannot fulfil, & when I am obliged to say to Mr Brown's idea that we might have been married that I am persuaded we were right in *not* being.

I am troubled sometimes with a craving sort of passion for more of your love. You have never poured your whole soul out to me with ardent affection. You have never "settled down" in your love if you know what that means. You have never ceased to be begetting scruples & misgivings & yet, Darling, tho' I know that this has many extenuations yet I do so long to bring it to an end. I say, "when you get tired of me, tell me," for when the temperature of your love seems to fall a little or when the idea occurs to me that some one else would not have paused at the social scruples which you and I at last came to entertain so seriously, I feel almost as tho' I were a burden to you, & then I feel ready to say anything that will lead you to feel how entirely free you are to extricate yourself from this barren engagement.

But Darling, if you poured upon me a fuller tide of affection I would not feel so. You speak at one time of this "hot heart" of yours & at another of your love if it be not as passionate as I desire being all you have to bestow. Dearest, I want you to forget all possible reserves & love me without any "shame" or "misgiving" or "suspicion" or "restlessness" or anything of the kind. And as we are giving these disquietudes of ours their *last discussion* (ain't we Sally?) let us love each other hereafter with a pure heart fervently & come weal or come woe let us forget everything else in each others affection & never stopping to ask whether one is a burden to the other (for "there is no fear in love") let us lavish upon ourselves in this cold winter of a life, all the love that we mutually possess. There, Sally, is it a bargain?

Let all scruples expressed or implied, be considered contraband of war, or else let us break the whole thing up, because you know Sally, we have been long enough living upon each others affection to have had a thorough opportunity of trying what sort of a *home* we can count upon in each others devotion.

Now, my wicked little Daughter, tell me, are you willing to come to terms? Tell me in your next letter. "Let dogs delight to bark & bite &c." If you say, Yes; remember, you are never again to say one word about misgiving or vexation. You are *mine* for better for worse. And that chilled little heart of yours is to go on with the trickling stream of its love, encouraging your lovers hopes that some day it may be a *little* more free in flowing.

The No 1 letter business was funny. It shows the difficulty of joking over 400 miles. When I first received your letter it was so long & serious that I was thunderstruck & took it all for granted. I thot my No 1. letter must from your not understanding the arrangement have worn some wonderful air of conceit & lunacy. I therefore, seized my pen & as I was hurried in going to the office I scribbled off the note in which I express my wonder.

Afterward I made up my mind that the letter was a hoax—indeed not 20 mins after my note had gone. But then the wicked tho't occurred to me, Why is'nt my note as fit a jest as Sally's. I to be sure was completely "quizzed" when I wrote it but still that only gave it an air of sincerity which I am sure Sally's has to perfection. Then I began in my soft-hearted tenderness for you to feel "bad" as you said about worrying you & so when I wrote again I only *half* kept up my seriousness. So you see Sally, a righteous Providence has visited you for hoaxing a poor heart-broken old man. *He* has suffered but half an hour; while you have been reduced to all manner of remorse & sorrow.

As to Europe, Sally, if you can exert your executive ability so as to sell your farm for so much secure money as to make yourself *safe* in maintenance & credit in time to come I dont know what you might not do. But I still think that your indebtednesses make your estate so precarious that your utmost wisdom should be given to *ascertain* & make safe for all coming time your own & Lilly's provision for maintenance. I think a trip to Europe would do *you* good, but would *hurt* Lilly. But then, Sally, you would go off like a comet & I dont know how many months or years it would be before I should get hold of you again.

But, Sally, I think your sale ought to be "*very* advantageous["] to justify you in seeming to your creditors to be spending money so freely just now. Foreign travel is a little like building a house. It costs more than we ever anticipated. And it costs ladies more than gentlemen. Still I think the question put as you state it might be answered in the affirmative. If you "can sell your farm so *very* advantageously" as to pay all your debts to Lilly & to others & give you a safe *income* to travel upon besides without spending what is properly your future principal I know no one who might more suitably go on an expedition like this. And yet, Sally, I tho't I heard Mrs K. say that she would stay a year or two. I would be pained at such a long separation & at the diminution of our correspondence.

Whom does Tom marry?

By the bye, you're not up from your knees yet. I want to scold you a little more. You do wrong in saying you have "no strong affection for any one but Lilly & me". You do wrong in saying you cant love Tom as much as you used to. He is very young. You ought to forgive him. He needs a sisters counsel. It makes me feel guilty when I find I have separated you from your friends. My experience of life is that people separate *themselves* from their families not their families from them. All men have infirmities. You must cultivate your old friendships. And be as you have always been a centre & an ornament among your numerous kindred. Without the slightest wavering of my purpose to keep James at a distance from insulting or annoying *me* I still never for a moment doubt that it is *your* duty if possible to lead him into proper acknowledgements to you & to be his friend.

I never heard that about the *Phil.* preachers before. The catalogue of *explana-*

tions is getting to be pretty long, isnt it?

How do you *feel* when you get vexed with me? I saw Lilly in Phil. She was well. I go to Washington on the 4th of March to an adjourned meeting of the Col Board. I shall stay there some days. Write often.

Yrs aff
JM.

Princeton, Feb: 17th 1856.

My dearest Sally

Some odds & ends that I forgot in my last letters I want to put down while I think of them. The socks fitted nicely. I said so in one of my letters, but lest it should miscarry I would send word again. They fit beautifully. And one of them that had a sort of opened look when I put it on went tingling through my flesh as tho' I had been taking opium, my whole sole seemed to be warmed by it & I stood upon a better footing tho' I confess I felt *worsted* the moment I put the stocking on. Please make the legs a little longer. I begged for this before & I must needs repeat the request. I dont expect it will make me any taller; but it will make me less of a calf & help to keep me at my knees. I have always liked your yarns to be longer & now you will have a chance to gratify me. Please make me an extra rib. And as I have waited long I hope the match will prove a good one. And that when the pair are bro't together all that is back will be found to be healed & all—. ha, ha. Aint I a fool? Sally, it comes over me so sometimes that I scarce have any peace.

But, what did you mean by saying "I agree with your mother in believing so far as I am concerned that this correspondence of ours is drawing sinfully from my time & tho't". When did Mother say that? I never heard it before.

And about the *nube*. Why havent I a right to spell that as I please. I never saw it written & I dont know how other people spell it or exactly how they pronounce it. But I know that the Latin *nubes* means a cloud & that you with one of these on looks as tho' you were in a cloud & therefore I spell the word this way.

I send you my book. I think it more important than the big church. I shall think it a greater accomplishment than the church. I wish you would think so too. Kiss me for good night.

Yours &c
JM

**Colalto,
Monday Feb'y 18. 1856.**

Dear John

I completely burdened you with letters last week, and so, did well to resist the temptation to add another to the number this morning. I oughtn't to write tonight, for I dont feel much in a writing humor, but tomorrow I shall be busy, and indeed don't know when I shall be able to write again.

Miss Jannetta has accepted a place as Teacher in a gentleman's family in Fincastle, and will go to her new home the first of March. I am busy helping her in her preparations. I am sad to part, with her, and she is pained to leave me alone, but she ought to go and I do all I can to reconcile her to the plan.

Nannie leaves me, about the same time. If I cd have foreseen this arrangement of Mr Miller's,[59] I wd have begged Nannie to have postponed her visit until Miss Jannetta was gone so that I might not have been entirely alone. But I see no remedy for the thing—I *must* stay here—and by myself—at least for the present. I may go to Aunt Eliza's with Nannie but not unless the weather is more moderate than it has been. At any rate, I had best get accustomed to being alone before I go any where, for I sh never have courage to come back, if I did not. I am still in difficulty as to a decided plan for the future. I can't think of anything for myself that seems feasible and am not willing to ask aid from others for I don't think they care what becomes of me. I rather think I am the poor bird with which the world chooses just now, to play a game of shuttlecock.

I often feel it to be very wrong to sit thus moping & pouting under the dispensations of Providence, and I try to rouse myself & shake it off and get something to do. Then comes the question: "What can I do"? And the same unvarying reply—"I don't know."

The great mistakes—for I dont know that I can exactly call them errors—of my life have, strangely enough originated in my affections. *Why* I loved that man who was afterwards my husband with such impetuous & yet abiding and strong attachment I never could tell. By what spell he acquired his perfect mastery over me I do not, even now, know. How it was that for years & years this affection triumphed over his worthlessness and wickedness (repelling earnestly all belief in both,) and seemed as tho' it cd not die, is a mystery to me yet. But it did die at last; and has not been buried away in my heart in its secrecy and sacredness as the object of its early love, tho' it does treasure as a holy thing the memory of the affection bestowed upon it—but has been cast out utterly as unworthy. My heart has not in any of its secret chambers a mouldering form that may ever again have breathed into it the breath of life, and become instinct with energy and warmth and power.

After this, tho' always conscious of the existence and strength of the feeling that slept like a Giant in my heart, I felt that early prejudice, & a sort of womanly instinct, and social sentiment had bound it down with chains that cd never be broken. But I was mistaken. I don't know where you got the torch that lighted up these fires again, and melted down these heavy chains, and once more, in spite of all the sufferings of the past and all the misgivings of the present made me yield to an influence I cd not resist.

59. Miss Jannetta Gordon's employer in Fincastle.

And, John, Darling, I have brought to you a love just as warm and as pure as that of my early girlhood. If it is less impetuous (and I doubt whether it is) in its bounding emotion, it is far more valuable because of its deep & steady swell. If it is less sportive—it is not less ardent—and tho' it may be more sedate is not the less tinged with a certain sort of romance that brightens it as much as ever. It is more reposeful, in its confidence, and more calm in its happy surrender to you. But It is for all this, subject too, as before to storms, and at times, rushes and roars with an impetuous sort of fury. And yet, why is it? Why does God give me such a heart and yet not allow me to use it?

The world thinks me ambitious—& so I am—yet the strongest yearning of my nature as far back as I can remember was for *love*,—love. And a happy home of my own has been always the most coveted of earthly blessings. And yet, I have long thought, it will never be my destiny to possess it. I have been permitted to look into it, but will never be allowed to obtain it. As my heart comes welling out to you, as if all its flood gates were opened, and in an agony of pleasure I wd throw my arms round you and claim you as my husband—the words almost trembling on my lips—I fall back to the belief that it is all a dream, & to the conviction that it will never be anything more. I shall never be your wife. The thought is unspeakable agony to me often, but I may, by and by, learn to submit. This disappointment, is a part of God's plan for me; & I wd like to submit to it, not in the spirit of one, who yields because he is obliged to, but with willing obedience, as to an appointment of wisdom and love. Dear John, it had been far better for us, if you had kept at your game of Ninepins. And yet, I do not regret what is past. It has given me many a pleasure I sh not otherwise have had, and I have suffered no loss of self-respect in loving you.

Tuesday morning

I had written away slowly until my fire had well-nigh burned down last night. And this morning I am too late, I fear, for the mail.

Make your socks an "inch longer in the leg"! Truly John, they are aspiring fellows those socks of yours. I'm afraid they're ambitious of an Order of Knighthood, and wd fain wear "stars & garters". However I'll do as you desire about them. I hoped all day for a letter yesterday but was disappointed—I fear a similar fate today. God bless you, my own precious little man.

Affectionately
S.C.P. McDowell

Princeton, Feb: (21) [1856]
Thursday.

Dearest Sally,

I go to Wash: next Monday week to attend the Col. Board. I shall stay several days. Please mark the time in your Almanac so that at least two letters neatly calculated shall strike me at the beginning & end of my visit. Suppose you roll a certain Lady up in some appropriate way & send her on some errands to the City choosing that time.

How you do run on. You told me last week you meant to like my studies & speak differently of them & now by way of practice in the improved mode you say, "O fiddlesticks, John." And by a strange running together of ideas, "O fiddlesticks, John. God bless you".

Well, so you are discouraged & think a failure would be ruinous. Why, Sally, I dont feel as if I depended upon success in anything, especially in this, for any such result as being kept from ruin. I take real pleasure in this philosophy irrespective of other men. If the whole world should turn against it, that would not ruin me. If the whole world should slight it or the book should be still-born I would not call myself ruined. I dont venture to predict how it will be treated. I dont feel dependent upon how men choose to receive what I think or teach. If *I* enjoy it, & my duty seems to me to be to think it & teach it that is all I ask in the matter. I yield in the matter of my marriage because other peoples' opinion uttered in a very clamorous way would affect me *thro' my wife* & incommode me in the interest of your children.

But my! how solemnly I am talking. Aint I a worrying fellow. Kiss me dearest.

JM.

Let me worry you "just a tinsy wincy bit" more. Honor bright, now, Sally. Answer me. Dont you observe that in saying you love me you always use some expression that is troubled with a little ambiguity? You never say, "John, I do love you intensely & fervently". Sally, do you *strongly* love me? Just give me one answer that I canst possibly pervert.

Colalto,
Feb'y 23. 1856.

My *dear John*,

As Jimmy Carrington and I sit alone, waiting for breakfast I let him entertain himself with a book, whilst I scribble a nice note to you. I want a good long hour to write you my *last letter upon* "the subject of our disquietudes," and will get it some day next week:—meantime you may have a "spell", as you Yankees say, of peace.

Another pair of socks I'm pretty sure will overturn your mind even more certainly than your thousand-leaved philosophy. Pray, John, where did you get such a horrible propensity for puns. I have heard that the disease was peculiar to Phil: but now that you have left the big church & big city, why not leave puns behind, with Dungan & Co. Tell me, in plain terms, how the last pair of socks suited. I'm afraid they were too small; and certainly thought I could never summon energy enough to make another pair;—but I've already commenced another on a larger & longer scale.

I feel much relieved by the breaking up of the winter. The snow is fast melting off and I hope before many days to see the earth once more.

I enclose you James' letter; you see he is inclined to more proper behavior in future.[60] Poor fellow! I'm sorry for him, with his extravagance, and temper & unsteadiness. And he has always had a way of coming to me, in his difficulties for sympathy, and I know must feel that *he* loses *something* in cutting himself off from that. I have written to him repeatedly since you were here; but confined myself exclusively to the business subjects upon which he wd write—Not replying to any other matter, except in a single instance, when I undertook to express my satisfaction at the rupture of a recent business arrangement between he & Uncle Tom, & to say how little his Uncle *should* be depended upon by him. I have no idea of any breaking of our natural ties—but I have no idea, either of adding any intimacy to that wh nature has furnished.

As to Tom—I don't know the lady he is engaged to. Her family are Rich'd people of wealth, & fashion,—illiterate and stupid. Her branch of it, has lived in N. York & N. Orleans—& her Mother is an Englishwoman. Her father has failed lately, & the other day fell on the sleet & broke his leg. I remember the lady as a poor, affected, miserable-looking little girl, whose great accomplishment, & ambition was dancing fancy dances, which she did to the astonishment of our children, in the great drawing room at the Gov't House. Of course, time may have remedied much that was unpleasant in her then—. may have taught her to wear loose shoes—& not dance like an Artiste, & not bend about like her head was light and empty as I suspect it is, if she be like the kin I know—those Warwicks of Rich[mond].[61]

But here comes breakfast. With a great deal of love

Your Own
S.C.P. McDowell

Send back James' letter.

Princeton Feb: 23d
1855.[62]

Darling Sally,

Your letter has banished all my lingering doubts of your love into the farthest exile. I take you to my heart without one lingering suspicion now that you are not all my own.

You have no idea how my mind treads over the same never ending path of tho't ever scheming whether you cannot in some way be my wife. I am getting

---

60. This letter has not been located.

61. Louisa Constance Warwick's father was William B. Warwick. The Richmond Warwicks were wealthy tobacco manufacturers and merchants, and Abraham Warwick owned Gallego Flour Mills, the largest plant in the city.

62. The year is misdated. It was 1856.

up all sorts of impracticable schemes. Now I think I will collect facts & go boldly before my own Presbytery & refer the whole question to them. Now I think I will write thro' some one or another to all the Com. men who had a hand in the matter before the Legislature. Now I think I will beg Mrs Hunter to adopt you so that I may have you near. Then I think of bringing all the debris of a family together yourself & my children & planting you down in a house of your own as soon as I shall have my patrimony & going off myself to Edinburgh & not returning till I can return & be married in my own house. Wouldnt that be romantic? So I wear the incessant round of thought, & endlessly yearn after you with a warmer & fonder affection. How you mock me when you say that I seem glad of our disappointment. Still Sally, your last letter is such a frank surrender of yourself to me in all your being that I cant help feeling as if you were married to me. Now you are mine soul & body. I claim all of you, Darling, in every sense in which you are not given up to your Creator. I love you with the most fervent passion; & all I beg is that you will never again express any suspicion or reserve but pour out in your letters the full tide of all your feelings & desires. I meant to scold you a little about the sacrifice you are making of *your friends*, but I cannot bear to say anything but that I am yours

ardent Jno Miller.

Colalto,
Monday Feb'y 25. 1856.

My *dear John,*

Observation & experience have both taught me, long ago, the truth of the remark, "that the horse that is sure to run away with a man is his *hobby-horse*". I am not surprised therefore to see the race your philosophy is giving you. It bids fair to run off with *your* wits, & run *me* distracted. How you do talk about it! But have I not been respectful to it of late? I have great anxiety about it I can tell you, on more accounts than that of its success when done up into book form.

I will manage to have a letter reach you in Wash: tho' to tell you the truth I shall have nothing to write about. In future, however, I mean to make my letters correspond in size to yours, and will find them easier to accomplish. Yet I don't want them to wear, at any time, the *manufactured* look that yours sometimes do.

Nannie left me this morning. I miss her, & wd miss her more but that I am so busy with Miss Jannetta's preparations.

"You never say, 'John I *do* love you intensely & fervently' ". I have said as much fully a hundred times, in every variety of phrase, & in such strong terms as have often, come back upon me with almost a shock. And yet you never will believe me: what is the reason you wont? I am beginning to think you have made up your mind that you are not worth loving, & can't credit such deplorable ignorance of you as wd lead any body to love you. However, I answer your question:—"Sally do you *strongly* love me"? I say, *Yes; I do*. Can you pervert that? I do love you with all my heart. And, when I wipe away the mists that my painful suspicions sometimes dim my eyes with, I am sure I love you now much more than I did some months ago.

Do you know I am a little offended at yr continued skepticism on this subject. I think you ungrateful & unkind too in it. And now tell me, in turn *why* do you want me to love you so very very much? Of what special value can *my* affection be to you?

The world is as quiet here, as tho' we lived in the "happy Valley of Rasselas.["][63] I am cheered by the melting away of the snow, and hope now for Spring and out-door pleasures.

I enclose Mr Bocock's letter; also one from his brother.

Good-night—I am altogether yours

S.C.P. McDowell

[Enclosures: John H. Bocock to Sally C. P. McDowell]

Harrisonburg, Va.
Feb 4, 1856

My *Dear Madam,*

Yours of Jany 29 is received, and yours of the previous date had *not been forgotten*. But I had written a letter of inquiry to an older brother, who was a Member of the House of Delegates, during the Session of '45-'46, and of the Committee which reported the bill.[64] And owing to his absence from Richmond on business, the letter, of which I enclose you a copy of the most relevant part, was not received till lately.

You will find that the divorce was granted on fact, brought before a jury by *your own Counsel*. And that of course the action of the Legislature was based on your own allegation of fact, which might have been greater or less, as you might have been able to prove. I am positively persuaded that I heard the cause so often alluded to mentioned in conversation at the time but have no other proof of it than my own memory. It could not have been before the legislature, unless you had alleged it. Could a *lady ever* allege such a cause, if there were other grounds of allegation sufficient without it?

Truly we have had a most severe winter. So severe that I hardly care a great deal whether they elect a Speaker at Washington or not—being full persuaded

---

63. *Rasselas* is a philosophical romance by Dr. Samuel Johnson (1709–1784), published in 1759. Rasselas and his siblings live in a secluded place called Happy Valley.

64. The older brother was Willis P. Bocock.

that such a body is, in all probability, more innocuously employed in ballotting for a Speaker than they are likely to be after the election of that officer.[65]

Dr. White will be glad to hear from Henry.—He has been threatened with pneumonia—but is better, his cold, I think, passing away.

I called on him to *pray in public* yesterday for the first time at a little missionary meeting of our Sunday school. Tell his papa that his prayer was one of much decency & dignity in manner;—and that it would have done his *heart good* to hear Henry plead with God earnestly & frequently, for *the Souls of the Children* of the Sunday School.

My best, true, & deepest love for my poor friend Preston.[66] May God be with him & up hold him. My wife sends you her kind regards.[67] Yours most truly & fraternally

Jn H. Bocock

"A copy"

Richmond Va
Jan. 19. 1856

"I was a member (of the Legislature) at the time of her (Mrs McD's) divorce, and the bill was reported by me on examination of the fact as presented. There was then a provision of law that petitions of divorce should be accompanied either by the record of a chancery-suit in which a divorce from bed and board had been granted, or by a statement of fact in the case formed by a jury on evidence adduced before a circuit court. The latter course was taken in this case. A jury in judge Nicholas's court found certain fact, and these were with the petition. I looked today in the Clerk's office of the House of Delegates, but find that the facts found by the jury have been withdrawn by Miss McDowell's Counsel, and nothing remains but the petition which makes no mention of adultery as one of the grounds."

"Since writing the above I have looked in the Clerk's office of the court & found the facts alleged by the then Mrs Thomas & the verdict. The latter finds her facts true, & bears testimony to her innocence. The facts she stated do not charge adultery on him, but cruelty and defamation, in unkind treatment to her and in charging her with adultery with diverse persons, Showing a case, in its kind, I think, unparalleled. The legislative act had no foundation but these facts so far as appears, nor do I remember that any other cause was suggested in committee, or in either house".

"W. P. Bocock"

65. After the passage of the Kansas-Nebraska Act, the Democrats lost control of the House of Representatives, but the opposition could not coalesce. A two-month struggle over the Speakership finally ended with the election by plurality of Nathaniel P. Banks of Massachusetts.

66. McDowell's "Cousin John," whose wife had died in January.

67. Sarah Margaret Kemper Bocock.

Princeton Feb: 25th 1856
Monday Morning.

Sally Dear,

I have had a great secret. I have been nursing the project of taking you by surprise with a visit. This child of my hopes has had diverse & cruel fortunes & has four great enemies. 1st the Major's scruples & the fear that my frequent visits will be de trop. 2d a bad division of the time. If I run on now from Washn it will be so long before I dare go again. 3d the dissipation caused in the fiddlesticks & 4th the extravagance.[68] These monsters have gone far to throttle the infant plan in the very cradle. I do so *long* to see you.

Your tho't of going to Fincastle leads me at least to resign the spell of secresy & admit you into my counsels. Suppose I cant go on again till Christmas; would you rather see me now or in June. Do you mean to go to Fincastle & if so when & when will you return. Write to this place *as soon as you get this* & then write at the close of the week to Washington. I shall start for there next Monday.

I scribble this off in haste in time for Sam (the boy). Dont call me little man. It is a disagreeable word to me. Dont say "I burden you with letters." But write more & oftener. Dont speak despairingly of your friends. They love you more than most men do their relatives.

Dont consider my visit fixed even if you approve of it; for I may not be able to get off.

God bless you

Yours fondly
Jno Miller.

Suppose, as this is leap year, you come off to see me (at Washn). I know a little man, a sort of relative of yours, who, if your purse is not plethoric & you will agree to pay back to some favorite charity of his when money is more plenty, will hand over the amount for the journey. But then you must start next Sat or Monday if you do that.

Lexington,
Thursday Feb'y 28. 1856.

My dear John,

Your letter of the 25th, & yours & Maggie's of the Saturday before came together yesterday.

I am very glad you decided to ask me about the visit just now,—otherwise you would have come & found the house shut up. I often long to see you, but it won't do for you to come now on any account. We must wait till May or June. It

---

68. "De trop" means in the way. "Fiddlesticks" refers to his philosophical writings.

wouldn't do for you to come when I am entirely alone here as I may be for awhile after Miss Jannetta goes, unless indeed Nannie returns with me as she promised. And then the distance is too great between March & December. And then we ought not to raise a hubbub about our affairs again so soon. So, Darling, you wont come now. And yet I think it right hard that I have to deny myself such a pleasure.

John, what made you think I didn't love you? Do you doubt that I can love anybody with all my heart? Or, perhaps you think I haven't any heart to bestow upon any body? Some times I think so, & but for the pain I feel would come near settling down upon the conviction that I have none.

Do I speak "disparagingly" of my friends? It may be I do; but I know them well enough to know their faults, & just now they stand out to me, as the faces in that old puzzle of the Napoleon Violets, so that I can see nothing else.[69] And at any rate I am not bound to love people, any more than I find something in them to love. I can't & wont love disingenuousness, cringing, selfishness & stupidity whether it be of a sportive or stolid kind, no matter in whose body it be put up. But, as we are all both by "original sin" & "actual transgression" far from being perfect, I can bear these evils when they form only a sort of background to other & fine traits of character—but when they stand out, the main figure in the picture, do you 'spect me to love them?

I think, my folk, all in all, are as good as the rest of fallen men—and not any better, as they think themselves.

I'm afraid my letter wont reach you before you leave Princeton, so I'll write to Wash: by Saturday's mail.

Take Maggie in your lap & kiss her for her letter. Did she write it without any urging from you.

Affectionately
S.C.P. McDowell

Miss 'Netta says—"Mr Miller ask Sally if she's got no faults of her own? And please explain to her what this text means: [']Be ye perfect ever as I am perfect[']".[70] Now if you cd hear the good lady talk of me & to me you wd think I was a whole bundle of faults, with the solitary merit of being my Mother's child. She uses me terribly. But I'm too amiable to fight her back.

Colalto,
Friday, Feb'y 29. 1856.

My dear John I am so tired. I have been worrying over business letters all day, and just begin to write to you as the Sun is about to set. I don't write without some pain either, as my hand and wrist trouble me, and I think have a little

---

69. *Napoléon Violets* was a painting of violets that contained a large number of portraits or drawings of Napoléon. The objective of the puzzle was to locate all of them in the painting.

70. Matt. 5:48.

touch of rheumatism in them. I am very stupid too, and if you were to come in, I should just take a low seat & sit down beside you & never speak a word—first because I should be too glad to be in a talking humor, & then, unless the sight of you brightened me up a little, I should be too dull. Isn't it very strange that real happiness should make one so quiet? The fullness of content (which I suppose means happiness) never with me, in its rare visits, admits of words. I am silent, not because I have nothing to say, but because my heart is too full to speak. But it will be a long, long time before I shall have the luxury of such a quiet hour with you. Yet, as I have the memory of some such I have no right to grumble. And as for the future, we know not what it may bring; tho' as I speak the words I have these lines come to my mind.

" 'Tis ever thus with happiness: It is the gay tomorrow of the mind that never, never comes".[71]

Did I ever tell you that I received your "Skeleton"?[72] It seemed to me to have as many bones in it as a human body. Do you ever dream that you will be able to breathe life into those dry bones? But we'll talk of that again.

Take a walk up to my lot corner of K & 7th & tell me if it seems good for anything—that is, if you can do it, without asking questions.

What a notion that I should go to Wash: & let you play purser to me! "You can pay back the sum to some *favorite charity* of mine", which means, "Keep it altogether Sally, for *you* are my favorite charity". O John, you're so "funny." I think "little man", sounds very sweet, and you are very foolish for not liking it. What do you like better[,] pray?

We go on Monday to Aunt Eliza's & stay a week. Send your letters here.

The Spring is paying us capricious but very refreshing visits—The dark has caught me.

With all my heart Yours,
S.C.P. McDowell

Princeton, Feb: 29th 1856

Darling Sally,

Sam Breckenridge is here. He is (last) from the K.N. Convention that nominated Fillmore.[73] With his overgrown beard & moustache he looks quite old, & makes me *feel* quite old by calling me all the time Uncle John. What a cross letter you wrote me. I cry, Quarter! on the subject of the philosophy & on condition of your not attacking me again. I promise to make a fool of myself as little as I can possibly help. What all I send that distracts you so I have almost forgotten but if you think I am in such great danger I feel most discreetly & becomingly sorry.

71. Barry Cornwall (1787–1874), *Mirandola: A Tragedy,* 3.1, published in 1821.
72. The outline of his book.
73. Samuel Miller Breckinridge was Miller's nephew. "K.N." stands for the Know-Nothing or American Party that nominated former president Millard Fillmore (1800–1874).

So my letters look "manufactured." Well Sally, I plead guilty to that. I do hate writing. It is only to you that I can *endure* to write. And it is only for your letters & to make them come large & often that I write at all.

I *do* believe you love me & I will never trespass in doubting it again.

I have great misgivings as to the Lexn trip. I long to go & yet feel sure I shant. I know it would be hard to make the next visit any more distant because of this & therefore perhaps I had better wait till a longer interval occurs.

Dear Sally, I wish you lived nearer to me.

Why do I wish you to love me? Because I live upon it. I feel bound to you by a most natural chain i.e. the bond of an affection so strong that you seem constantly my wife. I can no more banish you from my memory than I can Maggie or Allie or my own mother. You seem part of the being that the Almighty has given me.

Yours Affectionately
Jno Miller.

Colalto,
Tuesday, March 4. 1856

My *dear* John,

I am so hurried. A visit on business from Dr Taylor kept breakfast at a distance for ever so long, & has left me only a half hour to write.

I was grievously disappointed at getting no letter from you yesterday. I hoped you had written often enough since the "25th of Feb" the date of your last letter, for me to have had two letters by the last mail. However, I am expecting one to-day. We could not get off yesterday; & owing to some work-woman of Miss Jannetta's cannot go today; for which I am [not] sorry, as it gives me the chance of to-day's mail bringing me something from you.

I have given up my promised letter to you—because I have given up fully all my painful suspicions. I am sure I did you wrong John; but then nobody suffered in the wrong but myself. I wont have any more, if I can possibly help it. But, I believe I love you only the more because of my injustice—so, after all, some good (if that be good) has come out of the evil.

I would give a great deal to see you. I am denying myself more than I thought at first, by discouraging your visit. And when I think of the same reasons applying again when another visit is proposed, I feel hopelessly sad at the dreary prospect ahead.

Dear John, I feel I am wrong in Vesting as I do so recklessly, all my happiness in you. I think of it, and pray over it, and weep over it, & yet the thing goes on & on, with an accelerating flow & increasing strength.

We go to-morrow. God bless you my dear John.

Affectionately Yours
S.C.P. McDowell

National Hotel
Mar: 5th 1856

My Sweetest Darling,

I never loved you more than I do this moment; & what is very hard to bear I am losing so my power to *wait* in all this restless affection of mine that it seems to me utterly *impossible* that we should be separated for years longer.

O Sally I cant describe to you how sad I have felt since I came to Washington. I never felt so *sorrowfully* the extent of our misfortunes. I do so passionately long to see you. I never felt so poignantly the misery of our separation as when I was obliged to give up all thoughts of going on to you as utterly hopeless. You have completely wound yourself around my heart. And I am really beginning to look with *agony* at the tho't of *long long long* years of separation.

I think this prohibition of my coming has woke me up to new tho'ts of my unhappiness for I have never felt so the utter anguish of my absence as in these days in Washn. I feel almost tempted to break thru' all laws social & prudential & beg you to put an end to my misery.

Sally, can you give me one spark of gentle comfort. I feel like one who has gotten into some wider drearier arid part of the great Sahara of life & I never felt so disposed to write as tho' you were the lover & I a poor weak woman longing to lean upon your knees & to look up into your face & beg you for some strength & consolation. And there seems to be no time when we can look for anything better. Dear Sally, write me a good long patient strengthening letter. I love you with a passion that in this long suspense I can hardly tolerate. As you love letter writing & I do not, do write me some long kind letters & tell me how much you love me, for tho' this passion just now is making me very unhappy yet I cherish it as I do my life itself & it feeds upon *your* affection as its choicest aliment.

I feel a little wild this evening a little crazed by my helpless love. Write a good womanly letter telling me all the things that look to you bright & comforting in our case & at least giving me the painful delight of being sure of your own passionate attachment.

I shall go home tomorrow. I *wish* I could go the other way. "What shall you call me?" Call me "*Dearest*".

Good night! God bless you.

Your poor unhappy husband.
Jno Miller.

Philadelphia
Mar: 7th 1856.

My Darling Sally,

I do love you so tenderly & I am so endlessly thinking of where you are & when I shall hear from you next that I make an excuse of being in a new place,

(Phila) to break one of your commands & write to you twice at your Aunt Eliza's. Where would have been the use of my writing every day at Washn if I could only write once to Fincastle & then my letters should accumulate as tho' your own tried lover did not so much as know where you were.

What do you think? I meant to leave Washn yesterday at 6 a.m. But lying awake thinking of you so wore upon me that I put off starting till (8 1/2) half past eight. The train I was thus kept from was *smashed* between Wilmington & this city & two of the cars driven over the locomotive & dashed apart. See there what your love does for me. It is true no body was killed but the fireman but think how your poor little friend might have been frightened & what fear he might always have afterward of going on the Southern route. Our own train was detained till night & hence my being still in Phila.

Sally, dear, write me longer letters.

I am almost sorry you did not write the letter you spoke of, & then repent of doing me so much wrong afterward. Do tell me, Darling, what all your thoughts were, what you suspected me of. Tell me literally all. Tell me what you feared & exactly why you feared it for I can assure you Sally, that a sort of manifest destiny ties me to you & that I am *absorbed* in the attachment & held fast to it, as to my continued being. I do love you so much that you may pour out all you thought into my mind. Tell me all, Sally. And never say again, "If I have been uncandid with you in anything it has been &c" for Darling your being & mine are one. We must learn to love each other more than other mortals to be tied to each other by threads of adamant, to live in each others life & for each others happiness & to pour out all that we think into each others minds as tho' we had no separate existence whatever. Do you do so, Sally?

I go to Prinn to-day. I have written to Washn to have forwarded here any letter that may have been sent later.

I received two. God bless you, dearest.

Yours
zJno Miller.

Friday, March 7, 1856

Dear John,

I do not find it so easy to write away from home; and you must patiently wait for my letters, not feeling worried if the interval between them should be longer than you are accustomed to. We are two miles, or more of very bad road from Fincastle, and, tho' I have Alfred to do my bidding yet it will often occur that I cannot send him in to the P.O. just when I wish.

To my surprise, we found the road almost perfectly good till within 6 miles of the house, when it became so heavy & bad, & the horses grew so tired, & the night overtook us, & we lost our way—or rather took the wrong road, & I became uneasy & frightened and got out of the carriage, and walked with Mary thro' the plantation to the house. The carriage lamp was of some assistance to us, & we walked by the side of it, or just behind it until, at length, we reached the house. I was anxious about the horses, as they had never made such a journey before, but they were sufficiently well the next day to take Aunt Eliza & Miss Jannetta into town. And today we took a ride of fourteen miles to bury an old acquaintance, without any bad effect, that I have heard of to them.

I had a short letter from you the day before I came up—It was a long time before I cd recall what I had said to you about yr philosophy. That is one of the evils of a correspondence—it is so long before I can get a response to anything I say, that I really forget what I did say in the beginning. By the bye, John, I don't mean to find fault with yr letters, when I talk of their being "manufactured". I think you write very much better than most gentlemen, if you do despise it. But I don't want you to find it such a task to write to me. Why can't writing be as much of a pleasure to you, as talking to me would be?

I hope to hear from you tomorrow morning when the Lex: mail will be up. It is a great disappointment when yr letters fail. And John, darling, don't send me any letters that will worry me, for getting along with even moderate quietness is often a great struggle with me. And if I am, sometimes, "cross", just excuse it for it don't last long any how, and I'm very much oftener sad than cross.

I saw Cousin John for a little while the evening before I left home. I have not done more than speak to him once before since the morning or two after his wife was buried. He looks thin, & sad enough, with his hair greatly whitened. I am glad to have seen him, that we were both *moved* too much to find the meeting otherwise than somewhat painful. Somehow I always have that sort of painful shrinking from seeing friends under such circumstances of great sorrow. But, hereafter, I shant have it, but will find Cousin John, just all that he has ever been in the way of help, and counsel & comfort. Poor fellow! this has been a terrible stroke to him; & yet he bears himself nobly under it—as I expected he would.

I think I shall leave here next Thursday—I find my old acquaintances as cordial as ever—What do you think? Aunt Sally says Uncle Floyd has entirely changed his sentiments since he wrote to me in the summer. He's used to that—he has tried it *successfully* in politics, & no doubt thinks he can do it now in such an inferior thing as moral principles. But I don't perceive that my sky is any the darker on account of his change. We don't care; do we?

Dear John, I would give ever so much for an hours talk with you.

Yours
S.C.P. McDowell.

**Princeton,
March 10th 1856.**

My *dear Sally*,

Little Edward, Mrs Hageman's (Sarah) youngest child died last night of scarlet fever. He was a sickly little fellow & yet little as we any of us expected he would live death always seems a great robber. Sammy & Johnny are both sick & I am beginning to tremble for your little children, my own darling Allie & Maggie.[74]

What an interesting sight it would be to see you first get a glimpse of these little people. How do you think you would behave? Would you gaze at them much? Or would you take the little creatures *for granted* & just give them a passing notice. Maggie is not losing a particle of her beauty but is I think more thoroughly lovely than ever.

I am beginning to chafe a good deal under our wearying restraints & tho' I feel more than ever *sealed* in my attachment, yet I [am] beginning only on that account the more restlessly to pace round the cage bars of our difficulties. I feel sad & restive under our various restraints. And do you know that under my eager longing for our marriage I have actually resorted to the expedient of praying night & morning for *one who might little expect such a habit from me* in order to keep down the murderous & hardening thoughts that would take possession of me in my desire for your hand. Sally, do you not pity me?

My philosophy ought to be your delight, for it comforts me in this horrible separation.

I am becoming not a misanthrope, but a hermit. I find I can bear any amount of solitude. Visits that I am not obliged to pay I postpone endlessly. And if Allamby were tenable & I felt no bond to keep the children with Mother I would move out there & begin to beautify & settle what I would expect to occupy the rest of my life.

By the way when you talked of my book not succeeding & you pronounced it ruinous & I said the utmost failure would not disconcert or ruin what I expected from my studies & you then tho't I was going crazy, I did not think I should so soon fall on what would show that I am not alone in the feeling. I am sorry the slip I send you is from so bad a source as Beecher,[75] but still there is a world of truth in it whoever is the author. I do not confess to ill-success in my history hitherto. If I have it in my history hereafter, behold what I may comfort myself with.

The mail has just come in. From Dick I learn that poor Schenck has lost his

---

74. "Sammy and Johnny" are Samuel Miller Hageman and John Frelinghuysen Hageman Jr. (1849–1893).

75. Lyman Beecher (1775–1863) or his son, Henry Ward Beecher (1813–1887).

wife & I also receive these cards which I enclose you.[76] I am sad that I get no letter. God bless you.

Yours affly
Jno Miller.

Mrs Carrington's[77]
March 10. 1856.

John, Dearest, ours *is* a sad lot; and yet I would think it robbed of half its sorrows if, sometimes, in your hours of sadness, I could sit down beside you & minister to you with all the tenderness with which my heart overflows. You know, in our circumstances, I can speak no word of promise or of hope; but I would love to draw that troubled head of yours into my arms and bend my own beside it, that, at least, we might mourn together over our disappointments and sorrows. And if it wd be any comfort to you, I wd tell you how dearly and engrossingly I love you, and how heavy a grief our separation is to me. If you suffer, as I see you do, from our ruptured marriage, when you have all the gratification that mental occupation of a favorite kind can afford, how must it be with me John, with nothing to interest or occupy! I can't express to you the agony of the last few months; and instead of things improving under the effect of time, I have scarcely ever felt our circumstances press more heavily & painfully upon me than in the last fortnight. But John we do wrong. We are both too rebellious & unsubmissive. We are both too much bent upon carrying out, what we think the best plan for securing our happiness, and too little willing to do or submit to God's will, when it is adverse to our own. Instead of mourning so deeply & bitterly and incessantly, as I do over this thing—wasting my time & spending my energy in mere hopeless grief, I feel that I ought cheerfully to rouse up to useful & steady occupation of some sort, & calmly leave the disposal of things to One who, I know, does right always. I have tried Him a thousand times—& many of those times, when I seemed to be trampling upon my heart, all quivering with anguish—and found myself wise & well, & happy in doing it. But John, when it comes to you I fail.

When I see you suffer, and feel the helplessness of our condition, I am always revived the conviction that it is ungenerous in me, to bind you to so hopeless a thing as my affection. I would help you dearest, if I could, that you know. Few women could have been willing to have encountered so many difficulties, to prove this. But all my love to you, cannot bring me to you, and make me your Wife. But, somebody else might make you happy in their

76. Schenck's wife was Jane Torrey Schenck.
77. McDowell was visiting the home of her aunt, Eliza Henry Preston Carrington, near Fincastle, Va.

love; and I am, as so often, made to feel, that for that reason I ought to relinquish you. I am sad to think of your forlorn, half-home in Princeton; and know how much happier you would be in your own house, with your own little family around you. I don't know, of course, what is to be in the future, but I have given up my old dreams of ever being one at your fireside. To be your Wife, John, was a pleasure too much coveted, ever to be granted. It may have been sinfully longed for; & therefore withheld:—at any rate, I think, that is, I fear greatly it will never be. I must learn other lessons, & try to have these heavy, heavy disappointments, serve the good end, for which I hope Providence designed them. I have been loving you, as if this world contained nothing else to be loved. I am thinking of you as tho' my waking thoughts were never meant for any other purpose than to go musing & hovering round you. I am concentrating my *all* in you, just as if you could neither change nor die; and as if all the ends of my life would be answered in being yours. This is all sinful; & much of it, is irrational; and I ought, as a christian duty seek after a reformation. And for you too, I wd seek after & pray for something better. I can't, *now* wish you to love me less, but I want very earnestly that our affection should be no snare, but, in the far-away future, a blessing to us.

Do you know, John Dearest, I have a strangely strong longing for your little Maggie? I wish you could give her to me, if it could be done without the least injury to her.

I am writing away in the cold, and find my fingers are getting very uncomfortably frosty. Don't make longer intervals than formerly between your letters; and I'll write, whenever I can.

John, put your ear down here I want to whisper to you. Do you behave any better about your duties of private devotion than you used to? You said you were going to change for the better about that—therefore I venture to ask.

And now, darling, may God bless you always as all good things.

With all my heart Your own
S.C.P. McDowell

I may not write again till I get home.

[John Miller to Sally C. P. McDowell]

I.

Release thee! How? The doom of Heaven
      May frown upon our dream;
But passion's self must move the spell,
      That passion made supreme.

II.

Release thee! When? When pain has set
    Her seal upon thy brow?
When love, that patient mystery
    Is wavering less than now?

III.

Release thee! Why? For vulgar calls
    of home & happier ties,
That all our better thought rejects
    And ancient vows despise.

IV.

Release thee! Good! That wedded wrong
    May rule with iron rod,
And Cant, the ancient harlequin,
    Put on the face of God.

V.

Release thee! Where? From all the scenes,
    Where love hath made thee reign,
From all my hours of happiness,
    And all my years of pain.

VI.

Release thee! Yes! When courage faints,
    And grace denies her aid,
And Love prefers the wilderness,
    That blighted truth has made.

VII.

Release thee! _No._ Thy doom is fixed
    Unalterably with mine;
And fate may weave our destiny;
    It shall be ruled by thine.
Princeton, Mar. 14th 1856.

March 17th [1856]
Maggie's Birth Day.

My darling Sally,

I feel so unwilling to make the intervals of my writing so long as to make you uncomfortable that I sit down among these pictures on a hasty visit to New York just to kiss you & tell you how much I love you.[78] It's an old story isn't it Sally. We have worn it into each other's faith by constant attrition. I dont doubt (as in respect to me I am sure you dont doubt) that you love me passionately. You have

78. Miller wrote this letter on stationery inscribed "the Dusseldorf Gallery, No. 497 Broadway, New York."

always declined the word & perhaps on that very account made me suspicious, but you have said all that I care to hear in other & sweeter ways. I feel sad about this engagement because I love it with all my heart & soul; & it seems such a sad child of our affection. Isn't it Sally. It never brings us together. It never gives us the unalloyed bliss of our attachment. It never ceases to be disappointed & forlorn. I mourn over you Sally as one always away from my reach & always a subject of sorrow. I mourn over the fate of having been so nearly married to you & then painfully driven back. I repine at my banishment. And tho you are dearer to me than all the world beside & I value my love as one of my choicest gifts, yet it is beginning to wear upon me with the ceaseless recurrence of the thoughts by which I am dreaming of you as in some way my bride & go over the same hopeless modes of obtaining you again & again & again & I get perfectly wearied out with my hopes which are building their castles almost every hour of the day.

Yet I *love* to love you Sally & my life wears a wilder tinge by it. It fills up the dead parts of the picture. I love to dream & put you in the foreground of the picture & see my children with you & I never cease to pray, not that we may be married I shudder at that prayer: but that God would bless us in his own chosen way & give us rich blessings in this engagement & in each other.

Yrs
Jno Miller.

Colalto,
Monday March 17. 1856.

My *dear John*,

I did not leave Fincastle as soon as I expected, but delayed one day on Miss Jannetta's account, so that I only got home Saturday evening.

I found your letter of the 10th waiting for me, and was troubled to hear of the appearance of Scarlet Fever amongst you. I do wish you could bring the children out of the danger, up to me. If you could, I should, if no sorrow had or should yet result to your Sister from it, be almost glad it had come. But no; I can't feel that. I want those children with a most unreasonable sort of longing, but I don't wish them mine by any misfortune, or sorrow to any body.

I have a great terror of Scarlet fever—not only because life is always endangered by it, but because, if the life is spared, the constitution is more frequently than not, greatly injured. Do write to me until the danger is over, I feel agitated even now at the idea of what news the mail today may bring me of you all. It seems hard that mere conventualisms should prevent my having them here in safety.

Poor Schenck—I am sorry for him. Dear Me! I wish we could all die and go to Heaven right now, and leave the world and philosophy & everything else behind that worries & distresses us.

Nannie came home with me, very kindly.

I picked up a "Memmorand" of our family some days before I left home & intended sending it to you, but forgot it. I send it now. It is faulty in many of its details, but perhaps as correct as genealogies usually are. Take care of it, & after your curiosity is satisfied return it to me.

God bless you. Affec'ly
S.C.P. McDowell

[Sally C. P. McDowell to John Miller]

"Release me!" My affection came
    Responsive to thy call,
Upspringing from the wreck that lay
    'Neath Sorrow's heavy pall.
When *thy* voice stirred its lowest depths
    And *thou* the call had given,
It gushed as stream from out the rock
    The prophet's rod had riven.
And as it poured its gurgling song
    Along Life's dreary plain,
Love sparkled in its rippling light
    And Hope beam'd bright again.

The world once more bloom'd fresh & gay;
    Old fires were lit again;
My days seem'd each a holy day,
    And sorrow all a dream.
Ev'n Youth came back with frolic step
    And, as in days of old
With tuneful voice & glowing phrase
    Our future joys foretold:—
Its promises once more were fair;
    Its prospects bathed in light;
Its flatteries were sweet, & teem'd
    With Visions of delight.

O Then, around this heart of mine
    The tenderest tie was spun
So sure and strong it cannot be
    By mortal hands undone.
For like that rock-bound desert spring
    The prophet's rod revealed,
God's will evoked the stream & ne'er
    Again its flow upsealed;

But on it flowed, nor spent the pow'r
    With years that o'er it pass'd—
The life-gift of its earliest hour
    Still present at its last;—
So, shall the gushing, swelling flood
    My riven heart out-pours
Come sweeping down each barrier-word
    The world would interpose;
And dashing on thro' months & years
    With a resistless force Shall feel no falter of decay
    To stem its outward course.

"Release me!" No. You could not tear
    Your image from my heart;—
You could not ope its temple gate
    And bid *that* guest depart:
You could not hush its whisperings
    Those murmuring tones that bear
Like Ocean-shell, in ceaseless sign
    One loved name to my ear:
You could not calm its longings wild,
    Those earnest wailing notes—
Nor speak into forgetfulness
    The memory of its hopes:—
You could not still its throbbing pulse
    Of anxious love and fear
Nor lift its burden of destress
    Nor take away its care:
Oh No! You can't release me now
    From all the heart-bound ties
That Faith has told in utter'd vow
    And Love in mysteries

Release *thee*! Yes; at duty's call
    From every bond and vow—
And give thee back the promises
    So precious to me now;—
Return each dear memorial
    Of all that makes my joy
And sacrifice the cherish'd hopes
    My waking thoughts employ:
Shut out with stern decision
    The visions that will rise
Of home and fireside pleasures

To my enraptured eyes:—
Put down the earnest longing
　　To nestle at thy side
To share with thee life's pleasures—
　　With thee its cares divide:—
Yes, these and every feeling
　　That would link yr fate to mine
I'd tear away, and free you
　　At a mandate that's divine.

Release *thee*! Yes; at duty's call
　　Nor taint the sacrifice,
By Sin's rebellious murmurings;—
　　Grief's unsubmissive sighs.
[No].[79] The stern decree once given,—
　　In anguish I would bow;
Yet with eye upturned to Heaven
　　Beg for strength to strike the blow:—
Beg for such a loyal clinging
　　To a higher love than this
As would shed o'er earth's lost treasure
　　Some beams of Heaven's bliss.
March 18. 1856.

---

79. The sheet is torn here, but the word is supplied in pencil.

PART SIX

"Shall I tell you all that goes in at the golden gate of Fancy or only of what goes out at the iron door of Fate?"

March 1856–June 1856

Colalto,
Thursday, March 20. 1856.

Dear John,

Do you mean to limit me to one letter a week? As you sit in your study every day for hours together, without interruption of any kind, what can be easier than to take up yr pen, and by way of recreation, write me a note two or three times a week. However, I wont quarrel unless I find, when the mail comes to-day that I have no letter from you.

James has written, offering to rent my house & all its belongings for six months. I am inclined to agree to his proposition, provided I can spend the time he mentions, agreeably, elsewhere than here. I can't—that is, would rather not live in my own house, as a boarder with my Brother, and if I can get Lilly to agree to it, and find the expense of such a plan not great, I prefer spending the Summer out of Virginia. I have always had a hankering after New Haven; and thought, at one time, of sending Lilly there to school. I am a good deal, in that notion like Cousin John, who means to send his daughter this summer to Vermont, that she may wear off all prejudices against the North. That is one end to be gained in such a plan for Lilly. I am worn out with the nonsense I am continually hearing on that subject. I never had any sympathy with it, and do utterly despise it. I see just as much want of high tone, and right feeling, & strong principle,

531

and good manners here, in Virginia, as I can conceive could exist in any one of our Northern States. I was glad to hear Aunt Eliza say the other day, if it came to her for decision "she would rather her daughters would marry Yankees than Virginians." Aunt Sally wd have ordered her out to execution immediately if she had been present, as she wanted to do me, some years ago when I warmly advocated a Northern school for Thomas.

I am as quiet as a hermit, and strange to say, entirely content with my solitude. I think Nannie enjoys it too; and I feel so grateful to her for coming down with me that I am glad she is not suffering under the dreariness of my home.

Why don't you sometimes write to me about the children? When is Maggie's birthday?

Affectionately Yours
S.C.P. McDowell

Princeton, Mar. 22d 56.

Oh, Sally,

I'm so tired. I've been chopping wood. What do you think of your brave gallant being engaged in a thing like that. Did your big brother ever touch an axe or a hickory log?

But, Sally, I'm *so* tired. Come take me in your arms & let me get my youth & strength back again by the inspiration of your sweet lips. I've been reading St Ronan's Well.[1] Get it Sally & read it all thro' & see what sorrow like ours ends in in this poor sick world. By the way, wood-chopping is a fine thing to get one over the romance of novels. It was quite timely. I never tho't of it. It brings one down to the sober realities of life.

I feel reproached sometimes for not bringing you more, in my letters, into the common acts of my life. I have no talent that way. I mean to begin to reform, however, by telling you of the castle I have been building for some days part. Part of Allamby is for sale. Half the most important part. The price is $20 pr acre & there are forty three acres. I am greatly in the mood to buy. It has no house on it, but it is an exquisite spot & I am greatly tempted: so much so that I have been building castles up there all the week.

Darling; I argue this way. If I am ever obliged to provide myself a house & I dont know how soon that may be. Allamby is the spot of all others where I would choose to locate it. It is a perfect paradise. And do you know? Put your ear down here very close. I have a foolish notion that some day when I get all fixed & my children are out there under the care of a certain matronly housekeeper whom I have in view—Ann Heinekin—who nursed me when a boy. I mean to step aside off the stage & go on a trip to Georgia or St Louis or the moon & persuade you to come & pay my little establishment a long visit. What think you of it. Perhaps

---

1. *St. Ronan's Well*, a novel by Sir Walter Scott, was published in 1828.

I'll get Maggie Breckinridge to matronize you & welcome you to the lawns of Allamby. Bravo! You see I have a little twang of the novel about me yet. Then I couldnt help as a sort of outgrowth of my novel-reading the plan of clandestine returns & secret meetings in the rocks beyond the hill & a separation—a là old times at Lexington somewhere about ten you to go up to the Ha'[2] & I to go off again into a cold world. Tell me how you like the whole plan from top to bottom. My immediate dream is to buy the 43 acres & use it as a sort of recreation trying to improve it & part pay for it by setting somebody to farm it, & without any building hold on to it & if it seems to become more & more like home buy the rest of the hill & some day live there. I am becoming so wedded to this mistress of mine, your favorite Metaphysics, that I have little tho't of ever being in a mood to leave Princeton at least for many years. Sally, do you love to hear me tell all my wild dreams or would you prefer hearing only of those that are put in practice. Shall I tell you all that goes in at the golden gate of Fancy or only of what goes out at the iron door of Fate?

Dear Sally, your question about my prayers I can answer favorably I think. I am a little better than I was. I have returned to more regular hours & I hope more fully to return to what I think the great *decisive* remedy for trouble & sin.

And now, Darling, why were you so long writing. Since the long letter partly in pencil which I think I have read 20 times, I have none but a little scrap written on Saturday. Do let us write oftener. As poor Clara says in St Ronan's, there are only two of us on earth Darling & we ought to relieve as much as possible the agony of these long separations. Why not write every other day. I would have written yesterday but came in late from a ride.

Yours devoutly
Jno Miller.

[marginal note] I received the Preston Memoir & am glad to lay hold. I shall return it much obliged.

Colalto,
March 26. 1856.

Do you know, John, I valued yr letter from New York more than common, just because it made me feel as tho' you were taking me with you in your wanderings, and, in some sort, making me to share in yr pleasures. You are so in the habit of giving me a place with yr books in yr Study, that I felt when you left it, you would throw me off with the books that you might have all pleasure of perfect disenthralment. And yet that Dusseldorf letter made me *sad* too as, in fact, many of yr letters have done of late. I almost wish I could wear out the capacity for feeling troubled.

2. That is, ha-ha, a garden or park where the surrounding fence or wall is set down in a ditch, in order to provide a view of the countryside from within.

I thought of writing yesterday, but grew interested in & by & bye exhausted by some calculations and gave out the notion.

I have[3] written to Aunt Sally asking her to make the visit now that she offered in Jan'y, as I am more in condition to receive it, and am daily expecting to hear from her. I don't care much whether she makes it or not. I asked her to do it, because I wdn't be a laggard in civility, & because I wd be no aggressor in the difficulties between us.—I am more than ever outraged by her recent conduct, but put a great deal of it to the account of want of judgment, prejudice, & want of true information. She used to love me much; even says now that next to her husband she loves me, but she has behaved unhandsomely in some things, improperly in others, & avows a motive for her conduct that is far from being elevated.

However, we all act amiss, & feel amiss, and therefore I ought to be and try to be *forgiving,* tho' it wd be folly to endeavor to controvert the decisions of my mind, about these people and their acts, by vamping up *excuses* for them & calling them by so sweet & acceptable a name as—*charity.*

John, tell me how harsh and bad tempered you think me in all this.

I feel some reluctance to answer Maggie's letter, and yet a strong wish to write to her. A week ago, I walked about in search of some Violets, and was impatient they sh bloom, just that I might send the first I gathered to her. But now that they are here, I pause, and feel that even in so small a thing as this I must deny myself. They wd all have been withered and without fragrance when they reached her, yet it was a sort of perfumed pleasure to me to gather them with my thoughts full of the little lady, and I wanted to send them. But No; here they are in the tiniest, & prettiest white porcelain goblet, no bigger than an egg, looking Spring like and sweet, but seeming to mock me, & deride me for an attempt to grasp pleasure of any kind.

I read the papers, and conclude that our Legislature is all a humbug, Congress a bear-garden, and all men and women distractedly walking in a vain show. If I read a book that is a true picture of life, I turn from it as you wd from all inanimate representations of that original, whose throbs & agonies you are everyday feeling: and if I get a fancy sketch I sicken at a painting of happiness which, *I* at least never can attain; and so reading is not always a pleasure—nor is anything else. How long will it be, do you think before I become a regular built misanthrope of colossal proportions. After all, however, I am not so discontented and gloomy & spiteful as all this wd indicate—but, John, I do grow weary oh, so weary of this life-long burden. Yet I know, & it is my only comfort, that God knows best, & does the best for me.

God bless you. Affecty
S.C.P. McDowell

3. McDowell originally wrote "am going" but left in the word "am" when she scratched out the word "going."

Princeton, Mar: 26th 56.

My dearest Darling,

I would give a great deal to see your first meeting with my little children. How would you behave. Would you look carelessly at them as tho' they were much what you had supposed. Or would you give them a long earnest look as tho' you had thought often of your first encounter with the poor little things. If all conventualisms, as you say, were out of the way, I would give them to you without a moments anxiety. Indeed if I were rich & Mother would part with her, I would give you Maggie as it is, & be only too glad that so much of my flesh & blood was so continually with you. I would miss her often but I would only make it a more frequently apology for going to see how she was coming on.

I am sad to find no letter to night. I have been riding from 2 till 6 looking after my unpurchased rights in the direction of Allamby. Did you ever know a man talk so much about a farm that did not belong to him? Indeed it is very much like you, Sally, a thing to tempt me with its fair face but voilà tout.[4] It is the most enchanting spot I ever saw & I *must* show it to you some day.

I was so flattered by your response to my poetizings. You have the credit of having moved me to the first poetry I have perpetrated for twenty years. I suppose it will be twenty years before I am so wrought upon again. I write poetry very much as a machine that has been shaking our barn all day shells corn, by a sort of grinding process. If your numbers had reached me first, mine would never have dared to set in motion.

Poor Sarah's own John is slowly climbing up from the Scarlet Fever & is very weak. Allie & Mag have entirely escaped. I am very thankful. Maggie has the winningest habit of creeping into my room all day long & establishing herself hour after hour at my great big Franklin. She is getting to be a stout hearty child & as pretty as she can be. She has a great curiosity to see you & flatters me sometimes by saying that she would rather see you than any living person. I know you would grow very fond of her.

Sally, why dont you write oftener. I really *suffer* for want of a letter to-night. Do you ever feel when it is raining as tho' you didnt know how it could possibly clear. So I have felt to-night as tho' I could hardly realize how letters would ever begin to come again.

As to New Haven I should be delighted. Take care in your arrangements with your brother not to endorse or to involve yourself in mutual securities. Such things are never wise. If you come to New Haven, (the very thought of which exhilarates me) I shall see you on your way & then I will be an occasional pilgrim there myself. Maynt I be? I wish we were country youths & our fathers lived "across lots". I think it hard we should be not only un-married but separated.

---

4. French, meaning that's all.

But, Sally, there must be some good end in it all. Let us pray that it may be safely reached.

Yours fondly
J. Miller.

Princeton, Mar. 28th 56

Darling Sally,

I have actually made an offer for 43 acres of land embracing the position of the Coast surveyors & being the actual spot of highest land in all this 60 miles square of Jersey. It is not quite a quarter of what you have heard me run wild about under the name of Allamby. I buy it not because I have any money to throw away but because I think it as good an investment as any other & because I *have lived there so much* with you & the children that I have grown attached to the place by mere castle building. Who knows but that in these throes & tossings of this naughty world, you & I, a gray old pair of lovers will be actually quartered up there & be spending the evening of our lives in looking out upon those far scenes which might almost remind one by their glory of something better for us beyond the grave.

But, Sally, I ought to defer to you somewhat. If you are to be a captive living up in that beautiful cage between heaven & earth you ought to be consulted about it. Most persons might say that three miles & a half or four miles from P. was too far from ones friends; but I always answer this by thinking that you are a Virginian accustomed to a ride of some miles to pay your visits & moreover when one or two years more are over our heads we will both be like Charles V, pretty well prepared for enjoying at least the possibilities of being quiet.[5] What think you?

Tho' still my talk is a little on the [illegible] order for my offer of a purchase has not been accepted yet tho' I hear the owner wants badly to sell.

Sally, Darling, I write this letter chiefly to persuade you to write oftener. I have not had a letter from you since last Saturday (near a week). Do write to me Sally. I am not happy. And when you fail to write it makes me miserable. The children have just left me & gone to bed. I am by my eternal Franklin & the never ending stream of smoke is sending its way up its black forehead. No one is ever with me. No chere amie[6] ever was so faithfully treated as you. You are ever with me. I have your sweet image in the embers. And this old stove if it would speak would tell how sometimes I tell out audibly my sorrows when one I love so much treats me unfairly & neglects me.

I live for you, Sally, more than you think—more perhaps than you desire, & if we are ever married which I leave entirely to the Almighty, the actual possession

---

5. Holy Roman Emperor Charles V (1500–1558) resigned in 1556 and retired to a monastery in Spain.

6. French, meaning dear love.

will be like one of those ideal ecstasies the real experience of which will seem to me too sweet to be believed. God bless you.

Yours fondly
JM.

Oh, Sally, why didnt you make it longer. I have just received your letter & it only tantalizes me. Do write a little every day & send me long letters. You do abuse your relatives right roundly. I know they love you & I mean some of these days to take their part. Come here & let me kiss you for good night as I do my children. Write to Maggie & send the violets. You are my betrothed wife & they all know, & every body shall know it till the end of the chapter. You are all the mother that I shall ever furnish these children with.

Colalto,
Saturday March 29. 1856.

Dear John,

What shall I write to you? I hate to weary you with the platitudes of my every day existence, or disgust you with the constant relation of its pains & troubles. I don't want to make my letter a burden to you, and yet, if they are at all to you, what I am to myself, surely they must be a burden of the heaviest kind. However, let that pass.

I think I would buy Allamby, especially if you are to divide the purchase money into 3 payments, as is common with us. If the place has timber upon it, I think you wd find it easy to sell it off in such quantities as wd improve its beauty, and liquidate in part, the original cost of it. However, I dont know much about it:—all I know is, that I want you to have it, if you desire it. When you speak of "*farming*" 43 acres, I don't know what you mean. I can't imagine how that many acres cd, unless it be of the very best kind, be so cultivated as to pay the expense of hands & farming implements etc, and still yield any thing worth talking of besides. But, if it wd only pay you back 6 pr cent upon yr investment, it would do double as much for you as the majority of the farms in Western Va do for their owners.

At any rate, it will afford you some amusement, and give you a solid foundation for some of yr air-castles; if you can spare the money, buy it. But *I* shall never see it, except as I see other pleasures—in my dreams:—yet I shall have a certain degree of participation in your enjoyment of it.

No; I have not read St. Ronan's Well. I am obliged to confess the bad taste of not liking Scott's novels, tho' I have so far conformed to the opinions of others as to read a good number of them. I have a suspicion of St Ronan, being a disastrous story, something after the order of the Bride of Lammermoor, and as I am, only too well acquainted with real troubles, I can't make up my mind to bear the recital of fictitious sorrows.[7]

7. Sir Walter Scott (1771–1832), Scottist poet and novelist, published *The Bride of Lammermoor* in 1819.

Have you read Hiawatha? Such melodious nonsense as it seems to me! Let me whisper to you, John, that, besides a short piece now & then of great beauty, I think Longfellow writes such trash as would render any Poet *without* a reputation, perfectly ridiculous. But the absurdest of all his absurd things that I know, is this Hiawatha—this "Indian-Edda", as he calls it. But I dont like any of the poems of the last few years—Smith's "Life drama," shocked me by its want of moral tone: Tennyson's "Maud" seemed a long-drawn out bit of namby-pambyism, and this Hiawatha comes *condescendingly* bestowed upon the gaping public—a mass of affectation & nonsense.[8]

Do you still belong to the Philadelphia Presbytery?

John, dearest, does no body ever mention me to you—And do you never mention me to any one? I ask from the sheerest curiosity—No, not quite that either—for I want to see if there is the least resemblance between us in our habits of speaking & thinking & doing.

God bless you my dear John, & send you happier days than the present. Don't you think, after the first shock was over, it would be a *comfort* yes, a real comfort to you to know that I was dead, & to *hope* (I don't pretend to say with any great reason) that I was in Heaven.

Affectionately
S.C.P. McDowell

Colalto.
April 1. 1856.

My *dear John*,

Sometimes I am hurried in the morning, and hate to send you off a mere note, and decide it is better not to write at all.

I had only succeeded in writing the single sentence above; when a man called upon business, and remained too long for me [to] write by the morning mail. I felt sorry for it as I knew you would be disappointed and troubled at the length of the interval between my letters.

Since I last wrote, James has written to me declining to take my house. He is rather changeable, but I am disposed to think I shall be happier to be here alone. There were it seemed to me insurmountable barriers of temper, &c, to my remaining here *after* I had rented to James; and, on the other hand, there were very strong objections to my going North,—not the least strong, of which was the fact of my being almost in yr neighbourhood, in any spot I could fix upon. So, after all, it is best as it seems to have turned out—I say "seems" for I am not sure that James will not turn round yet, and ask to come here.

---

8. Henry Wadsworth Longfellow composed *The Song of Hiawatha* in 1855. A long narrative poem, the first edition comprised 316 pages. Scottish poet and essayist Alexander Smith (c. 1830–1867) published *A Life Drama and Other Poems* in 1853. Alfred, first Baron Tennyson (1809–1892), the English poet, published *Maud* in 1855.

No: I wouldn't let you pay me a visit at New Haven if there was any reason why that same visit could not have been made to me here. Indeed, I should feel more anxiety about receiving one there, than here. However we wont discuss that point until it becomes necessary.

I am glad you are actually going to buy Allamby. You can set to work upon at once, & before *we* shall need it you may have it as highly improved & beautified as Shenstone's Sea Towers.[9] But you are right in part as to the distance being too great from town. If you were about to build a house with the prospect of soon occupying it, I would urge some pretty strong objections to it; but since we only dwell there in fancy, what is the use of speaking a word against your scheme?—:

But I must say good night, I can scarcely keep my eyes open; But tomorrow morning I will add a little.

Wednesday. 8 A.M.

Somehow, my brain is wonderfully poor—I am a sort of mental pauper; and feel my destitution, this morning very much indeed. Can you help me any?

I wish you were here during this delightful weather. It is still too cool to abandon fires even during the warm hours of the day, but a light wrapping keeps me warm enough, & the roads are as dusty as they are in midsummer. The yard begins to look green again, & the trees are full of birds; So, upon the whole out-door life is much increased in its pleasantness. I have a sick servant, however, who is often upon my mind & has been "upon my hands" for nearly a year. Of late she has become more feeble & is very desponding. Poor creature—Men may say what they please on the stump & in the Newspapers, & in Congress, but I tell you slavery *is* a terrible calamity and dreadful evil. I am no Abolitionist—but I heartily wish all our slaves were in Africa. Yet negroes are worse off by far, as free people, in our land than as slaves; and as a matter of philanthropic principle I would have them all in bondage here;—I go further & say I would not live among them & be obliged to have their services, without owning them as slaves. But I feel it a heavy burden notwithstanding.

I shall write to Maggie in a day or two.

Do you never weary of your Philosophy? Don't be in too great a hurry about your book. Let it have two or three calm revisions, before it is out. I feel, of course, anxious that it should not fail—anxious that it should not make you a subject of ridicule as a "setter forth of strange doctrines," or of ecclesiastical censure for heterodoxy—but far more than that, I feel concerned for the *truth's* sake. I have a heavy sense of responsibility in the utterance of any sentiment, & I tremble at the thought of your holding yourself, & teaching to others errors which may be fatal. But I am hurried. Write to me whenever you can. I am often, & often hungry for a letter, and am daily struggling with a feeling of despondency & sadness that I cannot make you at all acquainted with.

I want to send you a likeness of my Father:—how shall I get it to you.

9. William Shenstone (1714–1763), English poet, essayist, and landscape gardener.

I enclose you a letter from Aunt Sally.[10] I think she is getting pleased again. I am cooling off myself somewhat—whether it be because I can't keep mad a great while anyhow, or whether I have been successful in my faint efforts to keep my feeling subject to my principle I don't know—but I hope a little of both. Kiss the children for me.

Affectionately Yours
S.C.P. McDowell

Table of the Presbytery
Philadelphia, April 3d [1856]

Darling Sally,

You will see that I am yet in the old Presbytery. I mean before very long to go to the Presbytery of New Brunswick, but not yet as I feel a hesitation about taking a step which some of my co-presbyters are kind enough to deprecate.[11]

You ask whether I ever speak of you to others.—I never do. And as people take their cue from my manner they never introduce the subject. I move along in entire silence as to our whole affair. How do you do?

Do I wish you dead? Not till I die. Then I am not sure but that I should be willing that you should.—But, Sally, seriously you are interwoven into all my future. I am an obstinate being & my mind holds its claim upon you with a tenacity that I cannot describe. I paint a great many castles but in every one of them sooner or later you step in as a part of the great masquerade. In the Kitchen you are installed with a bunch of keys & a cross objurgatory look & a general aspect of matronly management. In the parlour a perfect queen—in the dining room old McDowell's beau ideal of the first lady in Virginia—in the nursery the sum & centre of all Allie's regard as a first rate *story-teller*—in your chamber—a perfect—Mrs Candle;—apparently one of the most suffering & hard used women that were ever cursed with a hard husband. So you see for weal or for woe you are mine in all possible circumstances. I tell every one who obtrudes the subject upon me that we are engaged & treat the relation as a settle[d] & established one.

Darling, I entreat you to treat it so. Treat it so in your letters. Treat it so in all your statements to others. Treat it so in all your dreams. Treat it so in your feelings; for I do assure you now it will never be otherwise. You never will alter your feeling to me & we never will quarrel. And some day tho' it may be very late we shall be married; unless an early death which is what you sometime desperately wish should separate us in a stern way. God bless you.

Promise to talk more hereafter of our marriage for I think we innocently may. If we live (& if we dont live why it makes less matter)—if we live we shall almost certainly one day be brot into each others arms & I love you fondly enough to

10. This letter has not been located.
11. New Brunswick, N.J.

covet the privilege of waiting for you if it be many years. But, Sally, how is it with you? I stay at Dick's. I think I will see Lilly to-night.

Yours affectionately
Jno Miller.

April 4 1856.

Dear John,

I am hurried as the mail hour is drawing rapidly upon me. I enclose Maggie's letter to you. Life wears along much as usual.

I am concerned about a sad accident in Mr Morton's family. An orphan nephew living with them and going to College here, was accidently shot by his room-mate four days ago.[12] He has lingered so long that we hoped he would survive altho' the wound was in the lungs. Within an hour, however, a messenger has come to say he is thought to be dying. Poor fellow—as I looked at his marble face the other day, it seemed there was yet enough of life in it, despite its paleness & languor to give some hope. But his Drs think not even then.

God bless you, my dear John.

Affecly,
S.C.P. McD.

Friday night.

My letter was too late for the mail this morning, so I kept it to add a line before I send it off tomorrow.

Poor young Booker died about noon, without the comfort of seeing his Father, who was expected last night. He was shot by the accidental discharge of a pistol, the ball entering the right lung it is supposed. He has suffered little from the pain of his wound, but much from fever & thirst.

I scarcely knew the boy, tho' his Sisters were frequently here with Cantey & Lilly; yet he seemed to have a fancy for me, & wd think of me as one to do him a kindness. Last night, as Col Smith went to his bedside & soothingly stroked his head, he asked "Is it Mrs McDowell."[13] And afterward several times attributed the little comforts that were specially acceptable to him to me, tho' in fact I had not furnished them. An occurrence of this kind that wd excite no remark in a City makes a great sensation here.

John, how much do you love me? You haven't told me for some time. And John tell me do you love me—but no, I wont ask. But I wish you would guess and then tell me what I want to know so much.

12. William Green Booker (1837–1856) was the oldest son of John Booker (1810–after 1860) and the late Lucilla Elliott Booker (1813–185?). She was the sister of Margaret Irene Elliott Morton (1811–?), the wife of William Booker Morton.

13. Francis H. Smith.

Tell me about Allamby: is it yours in reality? Are you sure it won't lose half its value by belonging to you: You know there are some people that undervalue everything that they possess, while another set over estimate their possessions. They tell me I belong to this last class, & find the fact of ownership gives charms where none previously existed. How is it with you?

But good night. I love you very much, if you care to have so old an assurance repeated, and am

Yours
S.C.P. McD

Saturday 7 a.m. I am so disappointed in getting no letter from you. I was sure one wd come to-day. O John, what makes you so far between in your letters. Now I can't hear till Monday, for I dont send to the Post Office on Sunday. This is so bad in you.

Colalto,
Sunday, April 6. 1856.

My *dear* John,

You know I never write on Sunday; but I write a few lines to-day just because it is to-day.[14] I need no other justification for it.

We are rather too old, Dearest, and know too much of the sad reality of life, and have felt too deeply its vicissitudes, to think of ushering in a new year of life with mere ceremonious gratulation. It is an occasion of thankfulness to be sure, but it is a time too, and I generally try to make it so, of very anxious, and solemn reflection. The survey of the past and future from such a stand-point, cannot be otherwise than solemn. And, strange to say, I have become so identified with you in feeling and interest that I have, for days looked for the coming of your birthday, with very much the same sort of feeling with which I would recognize my own. And now that it has come, & is almost over, for I see the long shadows from my window, I write just to say how much & how prayerfully, I have thought of you this day. It may never do *you* any good—but it is *my* pleasure, & I think does *me* good thus to bear you on my mind and heart in its strivings after better things and loftier hopes than this world can give. Dear John, when my heart wells up in a moment like this, how I would rejoice that there was no barrier to my saying to you all that I would so much like to say, and that you would freely speak to me of such things as I wd like to hear.

I am interrupted.

Monday 8. A.M.

O, John, what *is* the reason you dont write. I am fairly wearied with the constant suspense & repeated disappointment. I had almost rather make up my

14. Miller's birthday.

mind never to have any more letters than be thus worried and troubled when they don't come, when I think they ought. I am so annoyed. After waiting, hopefully all day yesterday, thinking surely a letter wd be here this morning here comes a whole budget from other people & not one from you. I was so worried, I just wouldn't for a while read my letters, but took up a newspaper to see what comfort I could find in it. Pshaw! So long I am so worried. What do you think you deserve for all this.

Tell me, do you think life a great boon? I would not undervalue it, but often and often it seems a heavy burden under wh I hopelessly struggle. And yet even I have some pleasures—more than a great many people, & many more than I deserve. And after all

"The battle of our life is brief—

"The alarm—the struggle—the relief—

Then sleep we side by side."[15]

I am far from feeling that the mere pursuit & the mere attainment of happiness, is the noblest of occupations or achievements. I aspire to something less selfish & more elevating—but at the same time I suffer under the loss or denial of it. However I am at the end of my paper. God bless you & make you as happy as He sees best for you.

Affec'ly
S.C.P. McDowell

Princeton, Ap. 7th 1856.

My sweet Sally,

I have been looking at this as my long letter to tell you all about our marriage, but Everett lectures here to-night & I have just been dining with him & am driven to overtake the mail with such a letter as I can scribble.[16]

But Sally, *give* your objections against the distance of Allamby. I want to see them. I dont want Allamby unless we are to live there. I have tho't of many objections & have fancied I met them; but Sally, tell me those that strike you for seriously if I buy Allamby it is as a home & only so; & I meant to do that very thing beautify & prepare it that we might live there together.

What do *you* think about the future? Does it seem to you all against me. Does it strike you I shall never possess you. Honestly when you seriously reflect do you not think you will one day be in my arms?

I enclose your Aunts letter & feel a pleasure at everything that is kind & friendly to you. I observe around me a great deal of respect for your character & learn to value you every day.

15. The concluding lines of "The Goblet of Life" by Henry Wadsworth Longfellow, composed in 1841 and originally titled "Fennel."
16. Edward Everett.

The children often talk of you & Maggie particularly wants to be taken to see you. She will be delighted with your letter.

As to my book dont trouble yourself. I will be very careful. I never tire of this philosophy & am bent upon pursuing it more than ever.

Yours in haste

Jno

Princeton Mar: 8th 1856

(April)[17]

So Sally,

I have kindled a big fire, got down a famous sheet, taken out my favorite pen & begun my great letter.

You ask me whether I love you. I'll speak to that point first. I have been thinking what a vast deal of feeling we have wasted in anxious misgivings & how grand it would be if we could set all doubt about each other at rest. Shant we do it, Darling? I know you secretly repine at that sort of distance & uncertainty that leaves you a prey to what you think a grand probability that this whole engagement will one day vanish into nothing. Cant I convince you in some way of the contrary. How much happier you would be if you would give up all further doubts of our stability, & if you would lavish upon me the full tide of your affection without one lingering thought that we can ever possibly be separated. I tell you Darling, I love you with a passionate fervor & if it is possible that any assurance of mine can convince you of my feeling I can tell you with the most earnest sincerity that I love you more each month than I have ever loved you before. Can you say the same of me? And tell me also, Was this what you wanted to ask me?

I never felt more thoroughly a bond than I do my bond to you. It is one of honor & of truth & of strong affection all combined; & it has grown into a sort of tie which is in some sense more delicate & constant than the tie of marriage. It may be obstinacy. I dont know what all is concerned in its composition; but dear Sally, let me entreat you to rely upon it, & to bend on me the force of your affection with as much assurance as if I was already your husband.

I do not mean by all this to take the extraordinary ground that I am so important to your happiness, but only to beg that you will not be always in doubt whether I am worthy of you at all & whether it is safe in you to waste the warmth of your affection upon one who by the very drifting of his purpose may manifest the poorness of his nature & how unworthy he is to be the object of your passion.

Now as to our marriage I want *you* to write & tell me all you think about it. I think it wrong to be longing for another's calamity; but I am not sure that we may not practically talk sometimes of certain future probabilities. We are twenty years

---

17. McDowell corrected the month.

younger than that poor unfortunate man who is the ground of our difficulty. Well, Sally, we may die before him & *then* you know it makes very little difference. But according to all human chance we have to arrange for 20 years longer life after this particular difficulty has gone out of our way. Now I am willing to wait thro' all this contingency. And, Sally, what I like is to arrange all the rest of my life with this particular anticipation. You quarrel with my philosophy, but you have no idea now fixed I am in it. *I have been regretting that I did not begin it sooner.* I have scarce a doubt that it will occupy the rest of my life. Then I am best fixed in Princeton. And Allamby that we have laughed over often becomes a real object. I want you to think all about it. I intend it as a home for both of us. I want you to advise against it if it wont suit you as well as me. I want you to talk always in the most practical way about all our affairs. I do not want to buy Allamby if it wont suit you in the end; for as I said before, if we die, it makes no difference; but if we live it seems certain that we shall marry & certain that we shall need some place where we may live.

Then, Sally, I want you to take care of your health. And I want you to manage your estate. I cant tell, now, how you are living, & my fear that you will wear upon your spirits by embarrassments makes me so anxious sometimes I dont know what to do. I do wish that you would clear up your business & make me easy on all that subject. When you write speak to me freely about your own forecastings of our future lot & let us get more close to each other in all the habits of more entire dependance upon our affection. What did you mean when you wanted me to guess what you desired to ask? Maggie was quite absorbed in your letter & reads it over & over. I wish she could see you. You will spoil your father's portrait if you send it by mail & I know nothing else. Wont you let me come & see you & then get it?

Dearest Sally I predict that God will *make us glad* in all this disappointing delay & that we shall see the advantage some day when we are living peacefully together. I cant help having the arrogant feeling that God has made you for me & just as he means me to bring out some important truths so he means as part of my hire to give me one of the loveliest of wives. Dont you think that?

Yours fondly
Jno

April 10th 1856

My *dearest Darling*,

I am going to write you a love of an extra just for the love I bear you. Did you keep my birth-day?

Come here, Sally. Put your head—there—in its old place. Now kiss me. Do you care the least bit about me?

I do get so forlorn just out of the weariness of longing to be with you. And tho' when I come to reason about it I remember that I never *was* happy, yet under the sadness of this hope deferred I am ever cheating myself with the fancy that it makes up the whole of my unhappiness. I have a sort of feeling that if I actually married you I would settle down still upon some method of unhappiness: & yet I am persuaded that if I were actually yours you would chase away more than half my melancholy broodings & smile upon me in such a way as to make my life unspeakably more happy. Did the madness never come over you of planning a flight from all these embarrassments & of our burying ourselves together away from all these clamorings of public talk in some land where we could be known only to each other. How often have I thought of the Maggiores & Comos & Lemans of that old sky of Italy & Switzerland or cozy corners of Scotland or even Holland & thought how happy we might be away from all foreign interference & away from all accountability to any one.[18] But, Darling, all these things are a chafing against our fate & I, for one, have such a deep venturing often of all my hopes upon a faith in the Almighty & such a warm love for you as the mere object of hope & expectation that I am willing to wait. I pray God that I may be always as willing to trust him as I have felt thus far whenever I composed myself to think over all our disappointments.

So far I had written when your birth-day letter came in. God bless you, Sally. You are a dear kind girl. But I am so mad about my letter. I wrote one in Phila on Thursday & mailed it with my own hand at the P.O. on Thursday night. You should have gotten it on Sat. No matter you will have had two others before this reaches you. Poor child!, but I will write every other day if you will.

Tell me, Sally, Are you happier than before I courted you? Or is our present disappointed life worse than that in which you were two years ago. Is our engagement a happiness to you? & do you look forward to a marriage day however distant with any pleasure.

Yours affly
JM.

What barriers are those you speak of that keep you from telling me just what you feel.

Colalto,
Friday April 11. 1856.

My *dear John*,

In all our correspondence I have never before been so long without a letter from you. I was dreadfully annoyed by it at first, and then as day after day passed on, tho' I felt it none the less, yet I grew accustomed to being without, just as I have grown accustomed to all other denials. I wondered at you, & tried to imagine an excuse for what I didn't like to think was mere carelessness, and

---

18. Lake Maggiore in northern Italy and southern Switzerland; Lake Como in northern Italy; and Lac Leman, the French name for Lake Geneva in Switzerland.

wouldn't think was designed neglect, and at last settled down quietly on the belief that I should be satisfied sometime or other when I did learn what had become of your pen during the last fortnight.

Yesterday yr note came—and I *am* satisfied in all reasonable calculations. I am selfish in my demands upon you, & yet I shrink from the idea of your finding, even with all yr aversion to writing, a letter to me every few days a burden to you. I don't wonder you should sometimes feel reluctant to undertake it, for, I know if you were here, you wd often think it a worry to talk to me when you had rather be silent; (and I too—you know how hard it is for me to talk when a sleepy fit overtakes me,) and yet—and yet—what John? Why, just this,—I want the letter anyhow & will thank you for it abundantly.

Do tell me about Everett—What kind of a man is he, out of the newspapers, and when he is not sitting for his portrait, as all great men are, when they are paraded about, and fêted to death? I am glad he came to Va; and hope he will come again, as he promises to do in May to Lynchburg. But if he gives the same lecture everywhere I should stand a little in fear of hearing it, lest I shd be disappointed with its artificial excitement & a[t] that sort of phosphorescent enthusiasm which exudes from the decay of real feeling & genuine eloquence. I am much of a skeptic about these great men. I have known so many of them, that turned out, under the analysing power of close acquaintance, to be French paste or at best chrystal, instead of Diamond—pinchback instead of fine gold. However, this may not be Everett's case.

Oh! As to Allamby—why, I can't say that I have any such serious objections that a carriage & horses may not dissipate them, or, at least, greatly diminish them. I am anxious you should have the place if you want it, & think you can get it without pecuniary entanglements or inconvenience. It will be a long time before you will live there, & perhaps, still longer before you will have to make Allie mount a p[ai]r of "Seven League boots" to enable him to be present at "rollcall" in the morning. So never worry about it—but get the place & let the future take care of itself;—as, indeed, it certainly will do without, so much as saying "By yr leave, Sir?" to you.

I am much annoyed here, & have been for weeks by _____ but never mind.

How will you manage, now when yr "big Franklin" will have to be set aside? Everyone feels at a loss, what to do with themselves when the weather first becomes warm enough to put out the fire. I am troubled, I know, & sad at the close of these long, balmy evenings, when everything is quiet, and I have nothing to do, but look at the clear sky & bright stars above me. I am a great debtor to the birds at this season—indeed at all seasons. They often furnish *society* enough for me. A few days since, I opened a very unpretending little book on Physical Science, & was soon engrossed for hours, with all the mysteries of *nest-building*. It was genuine castle-building this, of a substantial kind too, for their "castles in the air" were real homes.

I am afraid Nannie will leave me in a few days. I can't urge her stay, for I feel she has been too kind for me to impose upon her further. Tom writes to say he will be here next week, so that I shall not be entirely alone; tho', I can't say, that his visit *in prospect* is much of a pleasure to me.

With all my heart, Dear John, I am

Yours
S.C.P. McDowell.

Colalto, Saturday April 12./56.

Say, John, will you let me write you
A long letter in trochaics,
Full of words of gentle music
Gently rippling—flowing gently
Like some brook in grassy meadow—
Or, like some clear Mountain streamlet
Laughing, murmuring, sparkling, gurgling
Underneath the clustering branches
Of huge trees and tangled bushes
Such as we have seen & heard of;
Such as I have lately read of
In the Song of Hiawatha?

Will you thank me for a letter—
A long letter in trochaics.
Full of sound & song & legend,
Full of tales & story telling,—
Sounds and songs and legends hoary
That have naught but Music in them,
Like those dainty, measured verses;—
Measured, but unrhyming verses;
Measured, but unmeaning verses
In the Song of Hiawatha?

Yes! Well then I'll write a letter—
Write a letter in trochaics:
And, if you will take and read it
As you sit in the grey twilight,
And have thoughts, like fairy music,
Floating thro' your dreamy brain;—
And have none but Spirits near you,
None but Spirits for yr hearers,—
Read aloud and read it slowly
Till you get its flow & cadence

And its sounds come mellowed to you
Like the twilight lamentation
Of the pleading "Wawonaissa";—
Or like far-off note of herd-boy
Urging home his lagging cattle;—
Or, like the sad, plaintive striking
Of the bell, as home-returning
Herds are sauntering thro' the fields
When the eve is lost in night:—
You will find as much of meaning;
(Perchance not such artistic music)
Have yr mind as much enlightened
As mine was, I think, by reading
the strange Song of Hiawatha.

    And now for my Songs & Legends
    And my show of story telling!

John, I fear I was mistaken
When I thought that I possessed them,
And could draw them forth & tell them
With the cunning, Power & Vim
"Of Iagoo, the great Boaster—
He, the Monstrous Storyteller."
But I find I bear no likeness
To that famous Indian Talker
Save in the unlikely seeming
Of a stupid, barren Boaster.

But, what is the use of Fancy,
With its gaudy tints portraying
Life's unreal histories,
When our hearts and lives are teeming
with mysterious enfoldings
That no art has yet revealed.
When our chapter in our story,
One act in our own life-drama
Has as much of strangeness in it,
Much of planning & adventure,
Much of mishap & misfortune,
Much of change, & chance & sorrow
As would spread such air of fiction
Oe'r the plain recital of it
That it would try any Author's

Fame, to Father it.

"Of the Here & the Hereafter?"
No, I cannot tell you of it;
For it all is clothed in darkness;—
Safely hidden from our view
All I know, and all I learn is
That we must submit in patience.
Time will do its own unfoldings,
And perhaps—dear John, we know not
But that soon or late we'll open
To a page of light and pleasure
Having our hopes written on it,—
Brighter in their full fruition
Than erst in their presages.
Then we'll see a Jersey Castle
On the rocks of Allamby;
Neat, & snug, and very home-like,
For the evening of our lives.
And the children gathered round us
With their books and noisy sports;
With their school day toils and wrangles
And their heedless, headstrong ways;—
Talking fast—and oh so wisely
Of what is—and what will be!

And ourselves, now all-quiescent
As the storms of Life subside.
With our white locks smoothly lying
Over calm but wrinkled brows:
Two old figures by the fireside
Looking thro' their different glasses
At the Past—so long and painful;
At the Future—just at hand
We will, then have no emotions
Save the two in exercise;—
That which warms the tie that binds us
Stronger then, and still more dearly
To each others as the Sun sinks
And the Shadows, deeply lengthened
Tell us of our day's decline,
And that which is interwoven
With the gambols on the floor!

But, there may not be this picture,

But one that I dare not paint.—
Then—we must look on, look further.
Upward—onward then our race
Till the clouds that overshadow
All our life here, shall be lost
In a blaze of noontide glory
In the home beyond the skies.
There, there will be no repining
For the pleasures lost below;
There, relations the most tender
The most precious to us now
All are centered in our Union
That can know nor change—nor end.

Thus we must learn patience, Darling—
Learn to "suffer and be strong"—
Strong in Faith, and in devotion;
Strong in Hope—in purpose strong:
Loyal to our Lord & Master,
Doing *His* will, not our own.
Till our happiness is given
In the hour *He* seeth best.

John, I tell you when I'm waxing
Hot with strong impulsive feeling
I don't like these measured verses;
For they come astride emotion
With no more concern or feeling
Than a nightmare;—throttling it
Or sadly pressing it in bounds
Too scant for its expansion,
For fear one word too short might make,
The reader hobble in his course—
Or one too long would spoil the flow
Of all its melody. So turn
The leaf and we'll hear prose again
That is, when next I write for now,
I am too tired for more than
This—Dear John I'm all your own.

Monday, April 14. 1856.

My *dear John*,
     Don't you think your letter of the 3d from Phil:, reached me Saturday morning?
I felt ashamed of my quarreling after it did come—and indeed before; for to tell

you the truth, you very, very seldom give me any real reason for worry on that score—not much on any other.

I thank you very much for that letter from Presbytery. I always value yr letter *from* home much more than those written *at* home. This morning I had one written the 10th.

You often ask me, and I have often answered you, "whether I am happier since I knew you?" Now, let me ask you—Are you any the happier since you knew me?

I have been very much happier on account of our strange coming together; but I don't know how it will be hereafter. It is true, I was not subject to the anxiety, and sadness that I have borne in the last six months, before you deserted yr nine pins; but then I was without all the pleasures that have come bubbling up in our peculiar relations, and these probably turn the balance in yr favor.

Yes, I have sometimes, thought of a foreign home; but then have rejected the idea of it as an unworthy one. I wd be too proud ever to seek another Country as a refuge from the public Sentiment of my own. I write to you more fully about our Marriage question, *again*. Do you remember how that word used to worry you?

To my surprise & dismay, Saturday evening, Virginia Carrington, & Miss Jannetta Gordon came upon us.[19] Miss Jannetta to see me, & Virginia to take Nannie home. This Morning they have all gone and I am entirely alone. I have looked at this state of things whilst it was yet, future with great sinking of heart; but now that it has actually come, and seems inevitable, my mind & fears will gradually accommodate themselves to it.

Mr Bocock is here preaching. You don't know him at all, I believe. I think him the cleverest man—that is the one of most genius in our Synod. He has, some ways that are annoying, but I like him & admire him, as a Preacher very greatly.

Do bear my long letter, to which, this is appended with composure; for it is to be the last of the kind.[20] I don't think, I'll worry you again in any *measured* letters, but will content myself by writing them *without measure*. A boundless pun certainly, tho' skimpt enough as to its amount of wit.

Dear John, I pray God may have something pleasant for us in the future—but we must learn to be patient & uncomplaining. Meantime draw me close to you[r] heart and keep me warm in its affection.

Affectionately
S.C.P. McDowell

April 14th 1856. Princeton

Poor Darling Dear Sally

What wretches we are! The poorest ditchers have more liberty of life & pleasure than we have. Your letter came to me in my usual dismal spirits & I

---

19. Virginia Preston Carrington (1833–1893) was McDowell's cousin.

20. McDowell wrote this letter on the same piece of stationery on which she had written the poem-letter dated two days earlier.

was saddened not only that you should have had no letter & that my lonely Sally should have been worn out with annoyance, but that, even now, or at least when your letter was written you should not know but that I had utterly neglected you. Let me beg you *never again in any circumstances to dream that I have absolutely written no letter for a fortnight or even for a week*. Such a thing shall never happen. And if I am sick or crazy or even dead I will take care that somebody writes to you, so that my letters in such a case as this last may always be known to have miscarried. You have learned by this time that I wrote you three in a certain interval covered by the silence of which you complain. And now, Darling, what shall we do about all these lost letters. It torments me to know that I have forgotten what was in them; &—what hands they may be in! Is your P.M a Democrat? Is it possible that Gov T. could bribe him or that any one could abstract our letters.[21] I dont think it safe hereafter to write anything confidential in this exposed way;—& yet I would like you to write more confidentially than you ever do. I shall always seal my letters hereafter & stamp them with this seal (JM). If they haven't it on please tell me.

And, Sally, I send you a little paper of Muriate of Cobalt. Dont swallow it. I dont want to get rid of you in that way. But put it in a little phial—very small— holding one or two thimbles full & put water over it. It will make a pale pink solution. Take care you dont make it too pale. Then write away all that is loving & secret in your affection for me. If *this* letter reaches you unopened no mortal will ever suspect you. Write with common ink & a pen not used before all that you would not be *too* unwilling to have broken open & read and everything that is more private write in some remaining paper in this ink. All I have to do is to toast it at the fire or pass a hot iron over it &—Voila! The ink when heated will be blue & when cold will disappear again. And if in old age & when I am dead you want to read these letters again all you will have to do will be to heat them at the fire. I thought of a cypher, but that is troublesome so I hope this will answer. And now Sally, write to me the kindest & sweetest most generous devotions of your heart & as I think you are not yet quite unreserved enough in this correspondence please tell your poor lover all your love for him.

Let me beg another thing. You say, I am much annoyed here, & have been for weeks by _____ but never mind. Now, Darling, this distresses me. I want to know what this is. I want to know this afternoon. And it worries me that I must wait a whole week. Please tell me always what you hint at in this way. You know we are so far off & I am so troubled & so anxious about you in many ways. Always tell me everything. You have my whole heart. And you need never fear that it will be different. By the way when you add anything in invisible ink in your letters put my name as I here put yours at the bottom of what you write put

Mrs. McDowell.[22]

> *Yours Affectionately*
> *Jno Miller*

21. "P.M." stands for "Postmaster." "Gov. T." refers to Francis Thomas.
22. Here McDowell wrote "(over)" to indicate the addition to his letter.

I will always do the same. If I put your name at the left corner of my letter you may know that there is something on the blank sheet. So please heat this.

[marginal note] Write where the light may glisten on the paper & then you may where the stroke is perfect.

**Colalto,
Thursday April 17. 1856.**

My *dear* John,

Your letter of the 15th post marked "Phila" came within an hour. To relieve all anxiety about the missing letters, I shall tell you that I think, they have, after some delay, all come to hand.

I am often anxious myself about the safety of our letters, especially, now, since from what I'll tell you by & by, I find there is some one here who is inclined to pursue me with most malicious annoyance. And yet I don't know where, in regard to our letters, shd any evil befall them, to let my suspicions rest. Our Post Master is not, I believe a Democrat; and could not I think be bribed to interfere with the private interests of his Office. He is an excellent Officer, & manages this Office with more prudence and privacy than any of his predecessors within my recollection, or that of my Father, whose post office reminiscences, were very astonishing. He is too, so far as I know or hear a worthy and reliable man. Now, as to his clerk, I know nothing beyond the facts of his youth and his very prompt obligingness when I, in person, ask him to do me a favor in his line of business. I think it may happen, that some cunning or malicious creature might obtain when he fancied my mail from this young Clerk, or out of my box—but these are all notions. So far as I really know, nothing adverse has as yet overtaken our correspondence. The letters lost in Phil, except those that were taken to yr Study after you left last Nov. & were never again heard of, were lost thro' your own imprudence in giving them to Omnibus drivers; who were, no doubt, edified by their contents, if indeed they had enough of the Skill of Champollion to decypher them.[23]

As to this muriate of cobalt—I have a sort of shrinking from anything that looks like improper & unusual secrecy. It is true, we might say many things, that wd be proper enough between ourselves, which wd be exceedingly injurious in the hands of an enemy. In such cases, under our circumstances, we might, very, very rarely though, resort to this invisible ink; but in the common run of things it ought to be to us contraband. We ought not to think thoughts that are wrong, much less ought we to speak them—or get in the habit of speaking them. And I think you do me injustice. I cannot conceive how I could be more unreserved or confidential than I am. I write all that it seems to me possible to write. I speak

---

23. Jean François Champollion (1790–1832), French Egyptologist who deciphered the Rosetta stone.

with perfect openness of my affection. I have nothing to make me ashamed of its existence—on the contrary, I should be much more ashamed if it didn't exist and I tell you about as well as I can. Indeed I am sometimes afraid you will turn with a sort of disgust from the unreserve I exhibit on this very point. If I were your Wife, I doubt whether I wd be any more communicative in words. You would sometimes be surprised at my coming in quietly to yr study, & throwing my arms round you as if I meant to *smother* you and yr philosophy, in that one embrace:—but I would never speak a word. Or, if you were weary and lying down I would kneel beside you & very gently put back the hair from yr brow & press my lips upon it—but it wd be done in perfect silence; And you would never know, unless you had learned to know me, that there was anything more than common affection under so calm an exterior. You wd never dream that those bubbles on the surface *could* only be there, when the depths beneath were stirred to their very foundations. An affection that is always coming out in words is very different from that absorbing sort of emotion that is wordless. Did you never notice or have you been enough in the South to know, the portentous silence which is often the characteristic of our most violent storms? Everything is still, not a leaf moves, not a breath of air stirs;—everything is silent—oppressively silent—but we all know that the storm in its might is in that very stillness & silence.

But John, when the *heat* makes reactations even upon blank pages, I have fears of another & deeper kind. I feel that I am assuming the form of the Tempter to you more than I ought; and the question always comes up, can a condition of things which leads to so much—or such wrong feelings be, in itself right? I never can bear the thought of being your "evil genius." The very love I bear you forbids it. I have always loved you for all that was honest & honorable & true in you, & I cd not love you, if there was any decay in these qualities—and more than that, I could not do otherwise than shrink with a kind of horror from yr love to me if I thought it could be undermining your character in what are to me—the highest points in any character.

I am hurried to catch the mail, & have been much interrupted by little Mac, who is my guest this morning and comes slipping up to my side, & rubbing his hands over my paper without any ceremony.

The annoyance to which I alluded in my last letter, comes to me in the shape of anonymous thrusts, sometimes of one kind,—then of another. I have been at a loss who to suspect, but at length my mind has settled down, not fully, but almost so, upon a young student, to whom I gave offence last Fall.[24] He wrote, as I thought an offensive note to Cantey—and I took it out of her hands, told her she shouldn't answer it, & myself returned it to him, without one word of remark—one way or the other. I was very indignant, & expressed myself pretty strongly in the presence of young Morton, who, out of kindness to Cantey, had rather brought on the difficulty. The returned note, occasioned very great wrath,

24. Dabney Cosby Jr. of Halifax.

especially at me; for it seems Paul Morton told the young man of my agency in the matter. He desired a sort of explanation with Cantey thro' Paul, of which, when Cantey told me, I said "You must have nothing more to say or do with that young man—and if he wants to make any explanations he must make them to me." Without my knowing of it, I believe, just at the time, she repeated my words to Paul, & he again to this miserable fellow. From a supposed similarity between the penmanship upon the envelopes to me, altho' it is somewhat disguised, and that of the note to Cantey, I infer they all have the same origin. Some weeks ago however, this fellow was dismissed from College for being found in a drunken frolic. Since then, & since he has gone home, I have had another one of these anonymous missives, bearing no postmark, but thrown into my box as a drop letter, showing that if *he* is the author of them, he must have a coadjutor resident here. I enclose a scrap of one of the wrappings, so that if similar ones ever reach you, you may have all the advantage that previous acquaintance can give.

I am in a perfect race after the mail. Are you going to let Maggie write to me again?

God bless you, my dear John.

Affectionately
S.C.P. McDowell

Have you & Spence quarrelled that you stay with Dick?

Princeton, Ap. 18th 1856.

My *dear Sally*,

Everett is a plain homespun Puritan. He looks demure & steady past anything I had expected. He has neither the polish or vivacity, neither the manner nor the mind that I had exactly expected tho' I think in the solid parts & therefore on the whole as concerns my expectations of him he has gone in advance of what I thought. Father knew him when he was an orthodox clergyman & tho' we did not of course touch upon this yet he alluded to that early acquaintance. You must hear his speech. It was superlatively fine. You must know that Whitefield said that a man could not preach a sermon till he had preached it seven or eight times. Talma & Garrick are evidences of the fact that your phosphorous theory is not the true one.[25]

When we get poor I am going to sell your poetry for bread. Indeed this last is so good a satire upon L[ongfellow] that I have a notion to send it to the Knickerbocker as it is.[26]

Am I happier than before I saw you? I cant say I am. Everything that occurs to me my mind feeds on for its morbid discomforts. I dont know whether I am

25. George Whitefield (1715–1770), evangelist. François Joseph Talma (1763–1826), French actor. David Garrick (1717–1779), English actor.
26. The *Knickerbocker*, a literary journal published in New York.

happier or not. I think if I married you the thrill of felicity in your possession would not be unalloyed with a melancholy that seems to make its banquet of the most rapturous pleasures. Aint I a brute? No matter; you are engaged to me. You are thoroughly "enmeshed" as Mad. de Maintenon says.[27] I sometimes think it was well that I am released from preaching on account of health. Such deep melancholy must have its rest in delicacy of structure of some sort or another & perhaps I shall live longer for being just as I am. Ni importe[28] therefore. We will trust to the Almighty.

Yours most egotistically
JOHN MILLER.

Colalto,
Monday, April 21. 1856.

My *dear John,*

I meant to have written the last days of the past week, but some how my mind had got into a spell of self-torture, and I couldn't do it. There are times, when this engagement of ours, is a source of the very keenest suffering to me. My anxieties rise to a height that is beyond all expression painful; and this not because they originate in any doubt of my affection for you,—a doubt which grown to anything approaching certainty, wd be insupportable,—but just the contrary;—so much the contrary, that I feel, with agony, that perhaps God requires me to make a sacrifice of it to Him. In all this matter of ours, I have earnestly desired that I might unquestioningly and fully commit the whole to Him, not dictating as to its issue in the smallest degree; for I have felt that our relations to each other, whether remaining as at present, or whether matured by a Marriage could be no blessing to me or to you either, if it were unaccompanied by His favor & His blessing. And therefore, when I have fears of God's withholding his blessing, because I fail to commit the whole thing entirely to Him, I am wretched. When I pray for entire consecration—and then turn & look at how large a part of my heart you occupy:—When I pray for Faith and then have even a lingering reluctance to make this sacrifice to it—is it any wonder I am troubled, day and night.

But then, John, all my anxieties are not of this personal kind: I fear for you. I don't know, of course, whether any such feelings as these ever creep into your mind and cause you uneasiness & pain, but I fear, that perhaps, our relations wear upon your spirits, which from yr own account, are bad enough without this additional burden, and prove a torment to you;—and this pains both my affection and my pride. So between my fears for myself and my anxieties for you, I am sometimes half-crazy. And then again the clouds break away, & the Sun

---

27. Françoise d'Aubigné, Marquise de Maintenon (1635–1719), second wife of Louis XIV.
28. Italian, meaning not important.

comes out a little, & its warmth lures me to throw off for a time, my mantle of care, and I sit down quietly in our circumstances as they are, & get from them all the pleasure they can give.

It distresses, me to hear you speak so often of low spirits. Months ago, it was a trouble to me, but I hoped to have a chance to chase them away; Now I feel powerless to do anything but sympathize with you. It may be constitutional, perhaps is, but there may still be some remedy. Don't you think you live too secluded and inactive, I mean physically inactive, a life? Suppose you give up your books, and desert Princeton for awhile this summer, & try surf bathing somewhere, and get strong and stout, and well.

What news from Allamby? How do your negotiations come on?

I am beginning to love my Anchorite existence so much that any visit seems an invasion of my privileges and pleasures. When these horrible spells of despondency come over me, I can't bear to have anybody in the house, but prefer putting on my bonnet & going over to town.

There is a great deal of religious feeling aroused and existing in our Church— principally among the young people, & Students. Our meetings are frequent and very full—yesterday afternoon there was scarcely a seat to be found in the Lecture room, but they are without that sort of noisy excitement that somehow, always terrifies me. They are solemn & breathlessly silent. I wish so much you could be here.

We have no Preacher but Dr White—Mr Ramsey is too unwell to come.[29] Dr Junkin preaches occasionally but has other duties, of course. I am glad, in this state of things to find the Dr. calling upon his elders for aid. Several of them speak well, and I like to see them do it. Cousin John gave us a capital address yesterday afternoon. I have often wished I was a man & a preacher, with the heart and ability to come in, in just such a time as this and preach from a text like this—"If any man sin he hath an Advocate with the Father &c".[30]

I am afraid we would be in extremes if my "poetry" had to buy us bread— bad bread, it would be I reckon, recommended by the fact of its being sold for half-price.

My yard is a source of constant enjoyment to me. It is indeed a thing of beauty. And at night, when the moon shines out so peacefully & beautifully, and I step out on the back porch the air is laden with the perfume of the trees now in full bloom. I often wish for you, John. An enjoyment of any sort, makes me turn to you, with a sense of incompleteness without you: And these bright nights, and blooming tress, & singing birds, and springing grass are all great pleasures to me. But if you are not here, I fancy how much greater this quiet enjoyment of mine

29. James Bevelin Ramsey (1814–1871), Presbyterian minister in New Monmouth near Lexington.
30. 1 John 2:1.

wd be if you were, & thus you get to be mixed up with all that is agreable to me. God forbid, it should ever be otherwise.

God bless you, my dear John.

Affecly
S.C.P. McDowell.

Princeton, April 21st 56.

Darling Minerva,

Since you came from the brain of Jupiter I doubt whether you have preached a more wholesome homily on badness & invisible ink than you have done on the present occasion. If I am never spoiled more than I promise to be by my poor Sally's prudery & shy affection I think I shall be a sort of perfect Mother & you are having the finest influence on me. And if it is heat that is bringing out the *deep blue* upon me it must be a queer kind of heat. For, Sally, I think your love is a little like the Northern lights which are monstrous pretty, but never killed anybody that I ever hear by 'eating him as an Englishman would say. Dont be afraid, Sally. I dont think you spoil me a bit.

The cowardly scamp that sent you those letters roused me at first very much. But when I tho't how in all cases discretion is the better part of valour I became more anxious to tell you not for the world to refrain from taking them all from the office & not for the world to say anything about it to *anybody*. They ought not to be allowed to go to the dead office. And they ought not to be lisped of by anybody. If they fall dead from the student's hand he will get tired of sending them to you. Indeed I half fancy he sent you the last to prevent your identifying him by their stopping short now that he has gone away.

But, Sally, you & I have no secrets (except of other people) send them all to me. You know I cannot intrude upon your privacy, for you have none when I am in the case. Enclose them all to me, & dont be afraid to let me discover how vilely anybody can abuse you.

Dearest, you oughtnt to talk as you do about coming in to my study. It makes me perfectly black with wretchedness. When I think of your white arms round me & your beautiful hair flowing all over my shoulders & your smothering me with kisses all as a volunteer visit to me after we are happily married it makes me perfectly desperate. To think of your coming in when I am sleepy & kneeling over your poor ____ but Sally, I must stop. I can neither bear the thought of you or your absence. And I think for a poor lover sad as I am to be lectured about being dangerously spoiled is like reproving some poor dead person. I am just as forlorn Sally as I can very easily be.

I was yesterday at Trenton. I staid with Dr Hall & saw a good deal of the lady your brother warned you about.[31] She is as tall as you are & I think growing ugly.

---

31. John Hall (1806–1894), Presbyterian pastor in Trenton.

I sent my love by her to a mutual relative whose wedding she is about to attend. And her sisters all laughed & she half-laughed stammered out some reasons why she couldnt do it. I have a grudge against you Sally. You make every other person look uninteresting to me.

Have I quarrelled with Spence? No. Dick is my older brother. Spence & I have dropped all this subject of our marriage. He didnt please me last Jan: when I was in my troubles, but began to tell me one morning how Ben Gerhard had said "Spence we must close around John & help him out of this difficulty & was going on." Whereupon I told him I suppose with a little too much feeling that I would hear no more of the sort. He has not lisped the subject since.

But good-bye. *Write every other* day.
My Darling Sally.

Yours fondly
Jno Miller.

Wednesday April 23./56

Dear John,

I have only 15 minutes for my letter, & I take a pencil to expedite matters.

I don't know *why* I write at all this morning, for I have no special reason for it. I covet the pleasure of writing to you every day, and would luxuriate in more frequent letters from you; but I don't think it quite right to send you a daily letter; and as you make yours to correspond in number to mine, of course this self-denial is two fold—cutting off my own letter, and yrs too.

I am much more dispirited than usual, and account for it upon the ground, of not being well. I doubt somewhat whether I am right to stay so much alone—my mind wears itself out in ceaseless action upon its own troubles.—Yet I see no remedy for this, beyond the one I have already prescribed to myself—that of occupation; as little with my hands & as much with my head as possible.

Oh! I want to ask you something—You know I didn't send you any birth-day present, not from forgetfulness but design. I preferred sending it on my birthday which, you know is the anniversary of this engagement of ours, about which we write & feel so much. Now, what I want to ask is this, *what shall I send you?* I want it to be something you will wear, & tho't of proposing to you to take one of my sleeve buttons, wh you have seen me wear, so often and use it to fasten your collar, under the cravat, where no eye, not even Miss Field's would spy it—And then, you cd have one made exactly like it, & send it to me, to restore my pair of buttons and be *my present.*—Or if you don't like that—then what else?

My time is up—do write a wee bit more cheerfully.

Affectionately
S.C.P. McDowell.

Princeton April 24th 56.

My Sweet One,

What do you think of my greeting your whole long letter as I read it, with nothing else than—"Foolish child!" And yet if you had been with me in my old sanctum as I sat with the first sheet in my hand you would actually have heard me expressing all my feelings about it in that quiet ejaculation. Whoever heard of a woman breaking her heart because her lover was breaking his? And who ever heard of a woman being "pained not only in her affection but her *pride*" because her lover was depressed & sorry that he couldnt marry her.

Sally, Darling, why do you manufacture troubles? Suppose I were to get into a terrible self-torture, because I tho't that Providence might want me to give up this philosophy—or might want me to give up burning wood in winter—or might want me to give up going out into the sunshine—or anything no reason for which I could possibly imagine; would not your case & my case be nearly on a par? You dont tell one reason *why* you should make this sacrifice, & yet it seems always disturbing & disordering your mind.

Darling Sally, let us discard everything but our own love for each other & our patient determination to wait till some mercy is shown us in our distress, & let us save all the drops of comfort & encourage all the means of hope & at least of quiet till all this sorrowful life of ours is either made better or else brot to an end.

I made an offer for Allamby which was rejected. Forty-three acres are now offered for $860 i.e. $20 acre. But then it covers only half of the hill. The other half is in law & I cant buy it yet, & perhaps if I am too eager about the other I cant buy it at all. Still I have a great notion to make this first purchase. What do you think? Your love of the grass & birds, & your taste for an anchorite's life make me think this place would be very pleasant to you. Its capabilities strike me more & more. Would you like it *best* of all other residences, considering it settled that your husband is to be a student? Or would you rather wait & choose for yourself? Sally, tell me all about these things. You know you said you would write about our marriage & you have never done it. I would so like your telling me all your private thots about our hopes & probabilities.

It is a great blessing that revivals should occur so often at the seat of colleges & it is a golden opportunity to do great good & secure important ends for the church. I wish you *could* preach, only, Sally, I dont think I could love you as much if you did.

Now come here, Darling. Put your arms round & round my neck & kiss me with all the tenderness of your passion. When may I come to see you? Why cant we write to each other oftener? I think if I could get a letter every day I would have some chance to get a little tired of you, & that would be a great relief to me. Even Cupid I think ought sometimes to unstring his bow. Aint I getting foolish in my old age?

Yours fondly
Jno Miller.

Princton April 25th 1856

My darling Sally,

Why *dont* you write every day? And why do you think it not right? I think I enjoy your letters more when they come oftener. For when they come seldom they excite me so & the pleasure is so long expected & so greedily devoured that it is like the meal of a poor starved man, a thing that I really sit a moment & consider that I may not so feverishly break the seal & hurry through the letter.

I know I write sorrowfully, & Sally, I have long accustomed myself to keep my sad spirits to myself, but you are like another life to me. I can no more keep anything from you than I can conceal a pain of one part of my body from another.

You have untied a Gordian knot. I have always been *tumm* about presents. And I have been often ruminating some *amulet* for our engagement—anniversary— not so much a keep-sake as a fresh *promise* of some sort. And as I cannot cover your fingers with rings, or call one by one name & another by another, so I like much the thought of the sleeve buttons. They shall be the clasp by which I take possession of your hand. The one I send you I will mark with my name—may'nt I—to show that you are my property. And the one you send me I suppose is already marked with yours. So please commit yours to Uncle J & let it come on. But Sally, you musnt always choose my birth-day present for me. Give me stupid as I am some chance.

So, Sally, write every day. Where did you get that sentence you once put into your letter about "Mother thinking it a waste of time &c" I never you told you that. Dont you wish people could kiss each other in their letters. I always feel inclined to kiss you Good bye before I sign my name. Isnt it queer I should feel so?

Yours fondly
Jno Miller.

Mrs Anti-invisible Ink McDowell.

P.S. How are you unwell? Tell me if you look as handsome as when I saw you last.

Colalto
Monday April 28. 1856.

My dear John,

I write you a hurried line this morning. So far from my last letter being *"foolish"* to me, its subject has cost me the greatest possible anxiety and distress. I feel the effects of my mental torture in such physical nervousness that even now, when my mind is calmer, I can scarcely hold my pen steadily. I have had such long paroxysms before—One, I remember, to such an extent as to alarm my Father terribly, and make him take me in hand with all the power of his authority. I am inclined to think, it results greatly from some physical cause. I am conscious of not being well, and that united to my entire solitariness, & the two combined, their strength in attacking me in a weak, or rather morbidly sensitive point of feeling. But I am better now—and when I recover from this nervous quivering will be quite strong again. Tom too, is here now & I will have somebody in the house with me, to cheer me. Dr Graham came over yesterday morning, & actually compassionated me so much, & made such a fuss over my looking pale & thin, that I began to think I *really* was more sick than I had thought. I *am* thinner than I have been for a long time, but not enough so to occasion any anxiety.

I walk over to town every afternoon, and am not the worse for it—but, no doubt, the better. Our religious meetings are kept up with much spirit and earnestness. And the religious feeling is not confined to the College and our Church, but seems general;—other churches participating in it, and the Institute likewise coming in for its share. Mr Lacy is here, preaching frequently, and sometimes uncommon well. We have no one else. I have never seen such a time any where. There is no tumult or excitement, but intense stillness and solemnity.

If I had any doubt as to the justice of my suspicion as to my anonymous insulter when I wrote last, I have none now. I am sure it is that young student, Cosby. Last week, there came another attack from him. This time not a *drop letter*. He had taken pains however that it should bear no postmark and it was slipped in as a *way* letter. I glanced at a line or two of the note as I drew it out of the envelope, & found it purported to be written by you,—but those few lines were enough—I read no more & nothing wd induce me to read it thro'. I was again, however, struck with the similarity of the handwriting to that of Cantey's note, and am confident I have made no mistake as to the person. He is a base-born and vile creature. I had a dislike to him last Fall; and I think Lilly had too, & was always worried at seeing Cantey with him. My fear is, that he will, by & bye, undertake to *say* things against me. However I take no notice of these attacks, & hereafter think I will not even open the envelopes that contain them, and as to the future why I hope to be taken care of by a Higher Power than Man.

It takes yr letters a long time to reach me. The last (of the 24th,) only came Saturday night, & I did not get it until this morning. John what makes you use such fine paper in writing to *me*? I am getting so poor, & have to write to you so often I think I shall get some Congressional wrapping paper at 75 cts a ream! Please praise my economy. I wont write you any more long letters. I never send you one that you don't note it *foolish*, which *might* hurt my *vanity*, if I had any. But good-bye for the present. O John dearest, do draw me close to yr heart, and give me a wee bit of comfort.

Affectionately
S.C.P. McDowell

Princeton April 30th 1856.

My dear Sally,

I am pushing on slowly with my book, preparing, I am afraid you think, to gain nothing but ridicule, & so great is my constancy that if this book were met with a perfect storm of derision I would push on & never rest till I had gained a foothold for what I think a true Ethical Philosophy. If I am a fool, I am sternly & soundly a fool for I mean to give the rest of my life to it & it is a sad thing for a man at thirty seven, with a beautiful wife, in expectancy at least, linked in with his fate, to spend all his life making himself & declaring himself a fool. Dont you sigh over me? And Sally, I dont see anything that greatly encourages me. I only see deeper & more deep as I look down into myself that unconquerable purpose. It seems perfectly remorseless. It seems saturated with all the life of my being. It seems to grow by my very bodings of reverse. And I am sure that it will never lose its hold short of some wonderful appearance of duty or the yielding of life itself.

I am afraid I scare you dearest. Yet you told me once that you were accustomed to *idle* husbands & if I keep always busy you know it will be at least as respectable a passage thro' life as merely to vegetate & do nothing.

My Poor Darling enters today upon her 35th year. I'd give a rouble to know what you are thinking about just at this very moment. Do you ever fear that you have been unwise in entangling yourself with such a poor old man as I am? And above all do you think these birth-days are drifting you onward past any of your old affection. I send you an old friend of ours busy about something which they say the old Vandal does sometimes even for the best of us. Honor bright! Sally, is he working any such change upon you.

Thus you see I am harping upon the old idea. And yet I firmly believe you love me. And I believe at your next birth-day you will love me more. I believe you love me tenderly & I believe there is something wonderful in your attachment, inasmuch as it does seem to grow & grow beyond all my expectation & deserving.

Yet, Sally, I will tell you how I account for it. Never a woman was wooed so with such a tender & continual attachment. I think I have earned you by my very passion. And I think nothing but my affection could deserve that here at another birth-day a round year from our engagement my own darling Sally should be just as steadily in my possession as she ever was since we first plighted our engagement.

affy
JM.

Princeton Ap. 30th 1856.

Dearest Sally,

I am so grieved to-night. I have no letter. You spoke of "every day" when you wrote last as tho' I might hope for a more frequent letter & these are the first results.

I can tell you, Darling, the Anniversary of our engagement makes me conscious of one result, & that is that I cant do without letters from you. I think that love may be counted to be very solid & reliable which makes the object of it seem like a part of your own being & therefore makes you feel lost & anxious in these long intervals of silence.

Still I feel very mad about having no letter & tho' it is our engagement day I dont feel at all inclined to write much.

Just be assured that I love you more than you dream & that your prosy nature doesnt conceive of the amount of affection I lavish upon you & when you remember how little you love me feel condemned by the thot of how [illegible] I am

> Yours ever
> Jno Miller.

Colalto,
Thursday May 1. 1856.

My *dear John*

I couldn't seize a half hour to write to you yesterday, and indeed I have hardly one at my disposal this morning, for Tom leaves at 11 o'clock, and I just snatch at the time he takes for a walk over to town for my letter.

After I came to look narrowly at my buttons, I feared they were too large for the purpose I mentioned. However I send you two buttons from different sets and of different kinds, that you may choose the one *you can wear*. The blue enamel is not what my *taste* wd select for you, yet I think it will suit for a collar better than the other, and if it does keep it, & don't send me one like it, for there were *three* in the set, and as I have only two wrists, of course I dont use this extra. But if you keep the other, have the date engraved on the under side of one of the pieces. If you choose to send me a match to the odd-fellow that I will then have left in my possession, have it engraved precisely like the one you keep, having yr own name with the date put below, out of sight. These buttons are the playthings often of little children, and I don't care that they should attract attention by any difference in their outside show of letters. However, if you would rather, & I would be just as well pleased if you did, send me something else that would suit your own fancy, why do so & I'll have another button made, which I can have done very easily. I only proposed this exchange, first because I wanted something I could wear, & then, I only wanted a trifle. I believe, on the whole, I would prefer you should select something yourself—only let it be a thing that I can have in my hand every day. And if you don't mean to wear either of these buttons send them both back, for I wont give you anything that you either cant or wont use. But don't I talk gravely of this matter, as tho' it were of the greatest importance to us?

Did I ever say yr Mother considered our correspondence *waste of time?* Your expression about it was this, as nearly as I can recollect, for I cant put my hand on the letter just now—"Mother hinted to me that I was more concerned about this correspondence of ours than I was about the duties of religion".

So, my affection for you exceeds all yr expectations and deserts both in its degree and steadiness! What makes you so ungrateful about it then? And why do you rate me so about it, and suspect it so often? You're a sad fellow, John after all, and I'm not sure that I have not acted unwisely in ever loving you at all. But I wouldn't have done it, if I could have helped myself; would I? And as you don't deserve as much as I give you; & didn't expect to receive it, would you advise me to try the effect of a little clipping of wings too?

I have not been quite honest as to the Philosophy business. I do admire, & respect your adherence to it, but I fear as to its results. However, whenever I approach it with any degree of seriousness, I am sure in yr next letter to get a civil sort of rebuff about it. Very civil yr words will be, but when I translate them into plain English they are very apt to be these—"Come, come Sally, this is *my* business. You know nothing in the world about it—I'll hear nothing against it; & upon the whole, I think it will be best for you to let it alone & attend to yr own affairs". And so I retire as gracefully as I can, under the circumstances. By the bye, I was startled some days ago to find in one of Byron's poems just such an onslaught on philosophy as I had been guilty of myself, & I thought I'd remember it for yr benefit. But I can't just now; I'll look it up however.

I am better than I was a week ago. I don't know what is the matter, except that I am often weary, with a fluttering sort of nervousness, and occasionally an unpleasant sense of oppression upon the lungs, not any great deal, not of long continuance but unpleasant—the fact is, I imagine, that I am just troubled, & being much alone, my troubles wear upon my spirits.

Do write to me always just as you feel—if you are sad, why not let me help you to bear it by my sympathy. God bless you, my dear John. Isn't it strange that all the world should seem to me to be centered in you—at least so far as my affection goes.

Affect'y
S.C.P. McDowell

May 1st 1856.
Princeton

My *dear Sally,*

I wrote you a shabby letter last night which your sad note this morning makes me quite repent of. As letters written like that late at night are not taken till early next morning I hope to get this in time to go with it.

Dearest Sally, come to me in your old way & put your arms round my neck & let me whisper in your ear all I would reply to this letter. It has made me very sad. My romantic character, the name of which I would not like entirely to disown runs in very unromantic channels. Your pain about "our relations" &c I felt very much inclined to make sport of; & hence what you naughtily call my calling all your long letters foolish. But so unetherial a subject as your growing pale & thin really distresses me. Indeed, Sally, I am *always* anxious about you, & I find my anxiety turning to two very homespun realities. One is your health, & the other is your freedom from pecuniary embarrassment. When my *great* anxiety & that is when & how the Almighty is meaning to bring us together—when that is out of view, then these others come in to trouble me. I cant help mourning over the thought of the decay of your physical beauty & I cant help connecting with it as an occasion & aggravation worries which I constantly suspect from the glimpse I had of the recent state of your affairs.

Now how can I "comfort" you in all this? If I were with you I would take you in my arms & kiss & cherish you with my warm & fond embraces & *just pour out upon you the true feelings of my heart* & I would trust to them to be the best comfort I could possibly give. I would tell you that health & freedom from distraction had nothing to do with the growth of my affection: that your wan pale looks the moment they became an object of my pity would warm me more with an undying attachment; &, Sally, that poverty & reproach & even insults heaped upon your head would throw me more upon that unyielding obstinacy of heart which makes the growth of my affections go on better in seasons of calamity.

But, Sally, remember I rebel against all your bad looks & against all your reasons of embarrassment. I think that my own darling girl who has nothing under the sun to engage her attention but her own comfortable health & her own better directed circumstances, & who in the *regularity* that one demands & in the *economy* necessary to the other may really be going thro' a discipline which is essential to fit her for some post of duty that she is yet to fill; who has a constant, however much disappointed lover & one on whom she can perfectly rely however long this disappointment & postponement may be protracted—I say that such a dear, darling wife, ought to be fatter & ought to look more cheerily upon the facts as they exist & ought above all never to distrust her relations to me & never for one moment to forget that she is more important to me (for this world at least) than she can possibly be any moment to her self.

I do love you with the most unchanging treasures of affection. And, Sally, when I think of you as pale & thin & weak I mourn over you as I would over a child. It seems to strip my affection of all the gay colours in which it clothes itself & tho' it diminishes its gayer feeling of delight it lays bare one fact & that is that I love you in your own lovely spirit & in your own gentle & loving heart no matter what blight may fall upon your outward loveliness.

And now, Sally, write & tell me how thin you are & how sick you are & how you are each time you write. Tell me all about your affairs & what troubles you. Tell me why you are still upon your estate & what has become of all your plans, & tell me, Darling, if at the bottom of your heart of hearts you have the least misgiving or the least distress about your own or my affection.

I tried to get some brown wrapping paper to write this letter on; but failing of that I got some pieces of old sermons which I think will keep you countenance in your utmost fits of economy in paper. Darling, I havent bought a particle of paper for more than a year. I have a large supply & I write to few other people than yourself.

When am I to come to see you?

Dont speak of those letters to others—not to one other person, & take them all from the P.O. And, Dearest, send them all to me. You & I are one in all adversities.

God bless you. Suppose while your spirits are so low we write every day.

Yours fondly
Jno Miller.

Colalto,
Friday, May 2. 1856.

Look John! did you ever see such a great Leviathan of a sheet as this! The idea of completely covering it is almost appalling to me. And I fancy I can see the look of weariness with which you greet it, and the air of resignation with which you address yourself to the task of reading it. But I am not at all alarmed by such looks;—a distance of 400 miles makes me quite calm under them, and saves me from any embarrassment or irritation. But I would willingly suffer both, just now, if we could only wipe away these 400 miles, and sit here quietly together under the acknowledged right to do so.

I am sure, John, I don't know what to say about Allamby. I want you to have the pleasure of the possession of it, and of such occupation as you may find it yield. As to its becoming a home, and above all, *our* home, and as to yr regarding it as such & preparing it with any such view, that is just the point where I can say nothing;—not because I have no feeling about it, but because I have so little hope. And besides I know so little of that country that I am no judge as to the convenience of such a spot for a residence. In this country, the distance (3 1/2 miles isn't it from Princeton?) would be to me, on many accounts objectionable, no matter what your business was. Whilst it wd diminish some of the expenses of town living, that is, if it has anything of the capacity of a small farm, it would entail upon you expenses of another kind, which might prove greater than those from which it relieved you, and, in addition, subject you to many inconveniences. Even if you are to be a student all your life, and think Princeton the best residence for so "eccentric" a character, and Allamby the choicest spot about Princeton, I still think you may be mistaken. But, John, do as your own judgment dictates in this thing. If ever I am your Wife, I shall find my happiness in being with you; wherever you may choose that to be, making in regard to the whole thing but a single requirement; & that,—that the house we live in, be your own.

But, John how do you mean to provide for yr family if you are going to be a student always, and write books which you, yourself say are unlikely to prove profitable, or bring in anything but trouble? Do you expect yours to be of the family of air-plants? Or do yr calculations ever take in the necessities of flesh and blood, and such indispensables as shoes & stockings etc?

You so often ask me of my thoughts about our marriage. If you were here, no doubt, I could talk to you of all that is in my mind upon the subject, but when I begin to write it seems as if I would grasp nothing long enough to send it off at the point of my pen. And, at any rate, I'd rather you wd do all the talking that is to be done, for you are more hopeful about it than I am. And really, I have suffered so intensely in the whole affair, that I feel as if I cd not inflict upon myself the pain of collecting and arranging in any intelligible way, my own fears and forebodings. Sometimes the distinct presenting of my painful doubts, even for a moment, so overcomes me that I can scarcely stand. I almost tremble under the agony of the thing, and, for a time, without even physical strength to oppose it. Yet, there are some seasons of hopefulness too—but not many—nor are they long when they do come. But, in spite of it all, I love you still with all my heart—just as if there was nothing else to love in the world. Sometimes, when I get into one of my spells of trouble about you, and feel called upon by so many considerations to set you free—and have the fear creep over me that, after all you may not love me & wd rejoice to be relieved from such a burden as I must be to you—then, in the tumult and torture of these fears & doubts, my affection seems hurled back at me that I may crush out its very existence. But when these subside; and, above all, when your love comes back upon me as with the consciousness of a real presence, then here comes this affection of mine, leaping and bounding, not only with recovered but augmented vigor.

Do you think, John, I *could* love you any more if I was your wife? I sometimes think marriage would disappoint me sadly, tho' I try to be reasonable, and certainly do not, even now, believe you to be faultless. Yet I'm so afraid I might get a little chilled; that I might discover something in you that would jar upon me. And then, in turn, I might disappoint you, and no doubt I shall if ever we are married, in many things. I know I'm better in some things than you now think, & not so good in others.

I think I shall go next week to Halifax to see Susan. I feel somewhat anxious to make a little change on my own account. I get no better really, tho' some days, I feel less uncomfortably than on others.—Yesterday I was more unwell than I had been for a week. I am perfectly able to walk to town every day, but I am weary & palpitating, and come home and feel inert and dejected; and in this condition do not consider my solitary life advisable. I dont think this indisposition a serious one; it seems the natural relaxing of the system after the highly-wrought excitements of the Winter; and after a little rest, it will recover its tone again. But good-night now. I'll keep the rest of my big sheet till tomorrow;—it may be the mail will bring me a letter from you. I had a nice letter from Maggie Breckinridge to-day from Louisville. It had been so long since I had written to her, that I had almost concluded she didn't intend to write again.

Saturday 7 1/2 A.M.

O John, what a disappointment! No letter to-day. I am sorry, but will have to wait till Monday for another chance. I am better this morning—indeed feel more like being well than I've done for a fortnight or more.

Yes; I do utterly despise *idle* husbands, and have seen an abundance of them; but when men do work, I *prefer* they shd do it to some purpose. I have little idea of how agreable a husband buried in books all the time could be. What do you think about such an one?

If I take the Richmond route to Halifax, I shall want to send you a little box for the children from Rich'd, how shall I do it? Put it in the Express to you at Princeton, or how else? Don't be alarmed & refuse to let me do it, for who knows that the box will contain anything but toe-toe after all. When you get this, for the greater safety, write to me at Rich'd, care of Walter D. Blair Esq.[32] If I go that way the letter will be there ready for me; if not, 12 hours will bring it to me at Halifax. I shall, of course, write from here again, & give all instructions about yr letters for the future.

I amused myself in putting away yr letters the other day. There are 200 of them. Some day count mine & tell me the number of them. And do, John, have a care over them, so that in any accident to you they may not fall into other hands. After this experiment of Mammoth paper I expect you will suggest to me very evilly a week hence, that white paper is most *fashionable* at present. Well, I'll pardon you if you do, but will say by way of justification that I only do as I wd be done by.

God bless you my own precious—just let me say, little man, this once John, because I love to say it.

Yours
S.C.P. McDowell

Princeton, May 5th 1856.

Dearest,

How beautiful! The blue ones, however, are such an ethereal blue that I can hardly see it; & the gold like most of the gold I ever came across is so evanescent that you can hardly take it in your hand. I'll tell you what the whole contents of the box have reminded me of, ever since they came—the substance out of which the world is said to have been made & if they ever produce corresponding results why Sally—all I can say is, We shall be very happy in our buttons. They will indeed be all the world to us.

---

32. Walter Dabrey Blair (1797–1878).

I have looked on the undermost side of the gold ones & cant find room enough for either name or date & indeed, Sally, they are altogether too delicate; for what—you know—would be altogether sufficient for your delicate proportions would seem somewhat out of place when employed for mine.

I wonder, if All fool's day comes on the 30th or 1st down where you live for, Darling, nothing that is pledged or promised to me on that day seems ever to turn up straight for once on a time when I was promised not only a sleeve button but the very hand to which it belonged, I got—a box & very little more.

Seriously, Sally, I hope you aint one of these absent minded people. I suffer enough from your absence of body. I dont know how I should endure your absence of mind. And I think if you & I are ever responsible for other beings, (which I hope a good Providence will not altogether deny) we must get over this hereditary taint or they will have no minds at all. Indeed I think I see it already in them. Poor little Allie & Maggie.

Well, Sally, all I mean to say is I love you buttons or no buttons. Burn this letter & believe yours very devotedly

John.

By the way, Sally, I'm afraid this aint the first experience of you. I'm afraid I shall often find the buttons missing after we are married.

Colalto,
Monday, May 5. 1856.

My *dear John,*

Your letter of the 1st, with the note of the preceding night, both came this morning. Somehow yr letters are long getting to me. I think they shd come in 36 hours, but it takes them twice that time usually. However these last, laid in the Office here all day yesterday.

I don't think I ever promised to write every day. I regretted being unable to do it. I don't know exactly *why.* I think that wd be wrong. It may be my conscientiousness about it, only extends to the avoidance of all remark by our Post Master & his clerk—a thing somewhat to be considered in a little place like this. As it is, I write frequently, and you mustn't complain of occasional irregularities & delays.

I still think of leaving home on Wednesday or Thursday, therefore after you get this letter write to me at Richd until I advise you further. Send yr letters to me *under envelope* to Walter D. Blair Esq, having the envelope of my letter *stamped* and only bearing my name; so that if I am not in Rich'd, all Mr Blair will have to do will be to send it to me, at Halifax or Charlotte.

I suffer less from nervousness than when I wrote last, tho' I don't think I am really better. I fancy change of air, & the giving up of my solitude for a time will entirely restore me. I have almost every day to struggle thro' the morning—but after that is over, am ready for a sort of lame service in the afternoon. I get up pretty bright, but as the day becomes warm, my weariness overtakes me. But, in writing the whole assumes a much graver & more serious aspect than it is, at all entitled to. You must not let it decieve you, for one can feel very uncomfortably & still not be much sick.

I do take all these anonymous missives from the Office. Another came today. It was done up like a package in coarse wrapping paper. I ran a pr of scizzors along the side of it, & finding what seemed to be a book, with a note, I just let both rest as they were, not drawing either out from the cover. I wouldn't think of reading them, nor of sending them to you. It seems hard, that in attempting to shield Cantey, I should become the sufferer myself. But I believe that is my fate—I am always getting myself into trouble for others.

O, I forgot to say before, what I have thought of several times—don't use the seal with JM on it;—choose another that will baffle the curiosity of curious folk.

I shall write to you again about my arrangements here—at present I'm something in a hurry.

You're a pretty fellow to talk to me about my *"prosy nature."* I must have exchanged with you. I don't know how else I obtained it. What makes me prosy, John? Is it the old story of my affection so often repeated that has made me so? Never mind! When I get you in possession, (if that time ever comes,) I'll have my revenge for all this—Are you disposed to put off the evil day.

But good-bye now.

With all my heart Yours
S.C.P. McDowell

Colalto,
Tuesday, May 6. 1856.

Dear John,

I generally write to you in the morning; but this is a dreary, dismal afternoon and I am tempted to seize now upon the comfort that writing to you affords. So raw & damp & cold as it has been for two days! But we needed the rain greatly and can easily bear with the inconvenience it causes.

I am still here, because I can decide upon no plan that offers fewer objections to my mind than just this of keeping this farm. I think with the rest of my property I can pay my debts. Still, there are formidable reasons against this arrangement; the greatest of which is, that I cannot live here alone, if I am to judge of the future by the experiment I am now making. It is true this experiment is not a fair one,—for it is made in a condition of mental depression which must secure its failure. But I think it can never be successful. If I were sure of having Lilly with me for even three years longer, I might with more courage & confidence either make up my mind to this arrangement, or enter upon some other; but you see there are many things that make her continuance with me very questionable. You have seen her brothers & Aunt Sally tamper with my guardianship & jeopardize my influence over her, & yet, so far as I know at any rate, propose nothing in the way of home or shelter for her when they cut her loose from me. And, in truth, I fear so much my inability to protect her that I dread, with a fear I never exactly realized before, to have her committed, in this perilous period of her life to my hands alone; and for her own sake, poor child, I heartily wish she had the affectionate watchfulness & care of some Male protector. This recent affair of Cantey's shows that I am not able to shield either myself or my child from the insult of the low & vulgar. Once, before Susan was married, I interposed in some slight difficulty with a young gentleman, putting her aside & taking the thing in hand myself, and found I managed it successfully, & without rousing any unkind feeling,—but, occasionally a low-bred fellow finds his way to yr house, & makes you suffer for the notice you have extended to him.—However, to get back to my subject—if Lilly were to live with me, I think *this* would be the best place for her; and I wd like to keep it as a home for us both, until she gets one for herself, and I have, *at last* a quiet resting place, in that old corner of the burying-ground. But, in my present state of health & spirits I am really unable to decide upon anything of importance. Everything, wears a certain tinge of gloom, and sombre views grow darker, until, I suppose nothing shows its true face to me.

I dont know whether I'm better or not. The sense of weariness is somewhat modified, & my nervousness to some extent abated. I am not actually sick, in the common acceptation of the word, but am dejected, with a weight upon my spirits that rarely intermits its pressure, and produces a physical sensation that is perhaps best described by the words, "worn down." I have never, I think, before possessed so little elasticity of mind;—but I have never before been subjected to so severe a trial as my present solitary life. However I am hoping entire recovery from my proposed visit.

The great evil of my low spirits is that of being incapacitated for occupation. I cant for any length of time, confine my attention to anything. Reading, by & bye tires me—writing also—& as for sewing—it require the utmost strength of will to force me to it, unless, which doesn't often happen, I am driven to it by necessity. And yet, when I think over all these things, I condemn myself, and hope to do differently & do better. I know it is a great sin thus to waste my time & health, under the disappointments God thinks best to send upon me, and so I do, daily make an effort to gather up my strength—but it is a spasmodic & feeble & futile effort, that seems but to collect power for its death-struggle. In this state of things don't you think John if I just keep from complaining, that that is all that is required of me? I can't help suffering—I am sure it is intended I should suffer,—but if I bear it quietly, & hate nobody on account of it, will not that do?

They tell me—"the darkest hour is the hour before dawn"—It may be—but then the "dawn" may be of that morning which succeeds the night of death, and will never be upon this world. Well, certainly that wd be an assurance full of comfort, & unspeakably beyond my deserts; yet John, is it any sin to wish that a day of happiness might break upon us here? Not that I deserve it, but I do so long for it. But I don't want it at all hazards. O No! I want to have it safely as well as truly.

I don't know how Tom is to arrange his affairs. He feels anxious himself as to his pecuniary matters, and is in favor, I think, of some delay as to his other projects.

What did Spence or "Ben Gerhard" mean, "by getting you out of yr difficulty?" I thought of asking you before, but forgot it.

Wednesday 8 A.M.

I am much brighter this morning, and hope before midday my spirits will come up to some few degrees above yrs. I am sorry not to have a letter from you today, but it may be you thought it was useless to write to me here again. Hereafter write to me at Halifax Court House Va, care of Charles S. Carrington.[33] Your letters will reach me a day earlier there than here, which is no small comfort, in prospect.

Do you know, I often think I would be far happier if I could just consider our engagement as fixed and unalterable a thing as a marriage would be, and if I would rely upon it with the same faith & spirit. My feelings would then relax into an assured repose, which they do need exceedingly, and I could bear our separation less repiningly & despondently. It is true you are often urging me to this very sort of confidence, by every assurance of yr present and continued affection, and you would allow no doubt of it to linger in my mind by failing to speak any word that could dispel it; but John, I am so fearful. You are but a human being, and changes come over every body. And I have known so much of change, that the only wonder you should have, ought to be, that I should be so weak as to trust any body. And yet it is my nature, and I do it in spite of every experience it seems. Not that I don't think you *worthy* of all my confidence to a greater degree than any one else I know, but I ought to accustom myself to the idea of change even in you.

But I think I'm getting some what stupid—do you think so too? Perhaps it would be better for me. I don't see any great use of women generally, or me in particular, having any more sense than is necessary to make bread, & patch & darn, & keep a clean house & neat children. And as but one, in all this catalogue of female duties falls to my lot, why a very meager supply will suffice for me. I am no genius however, & need not worry about having too much sense. And I am sure if Mrs McDowell had been less unfortunate, she wd have had less reputation for cleverness; but heroines are always tricked out with beauty & talent, tho' they have themselves, but little consciousness of anything but suffering.

John, how much scolding do you think it will take to make me a reasonable woman? And *what* ought I to be scolded for? This is your prerogative; & I shall love you all the better if you will exercise it. Why wouldn't you love me as much if I cd preach? Is there anything unloveable to you in preachers as a class? But I'm writing a volume. I still think of going tomorrow. The idea is not very exhilarating, but I am settled in my opinion as to the necessity of the move.

---

33. McDowell's brother-in-law.

I beg you will come up to the measure of my letters, as well as thier number. I hope to meet a letter from you in Rich'd, if I determine to stop there, after seeing Nannie tomorrow night.

Isn't it very strange, that when my thoughts are so full of loving epithets to you that I can with difficulty repress the utterance of them, I should yet use them so sparingly in writing? It seems ungracious in me too, since upon yr tongue they have such a charm, & are so full of exquisite pleasure to me. But, in writing, & even in speaking your name simply is very sweet to me & I don't know indeed that you care for anything additional. This old, silent house of mine, is yet very familiar with that plain, monosyllable, "John," which is sometimes for hours together the only sound that breaks its stillness: and I have learned to love it until every letter in it seems a note of music.—But now, Adieu.

Affectionately
S.C.P. McDowell.

Princeton May 7th 1856.

My dear Sally,

I was thunderstruck on hearing again to find from you no mention of the buttons. Do you know the box was empty & no signs as far as I could see of the letter having been opened. However I send you a part of it & you could see if the seals have been tampered with. I observe the mark of a finger upon one of them but I thot it was one of your blessed little digits, Sally. I set it down to your absent-mindedness & thot you had got the box & forgot to put the things into it.

About the things for the children. Darling, why do you spend money when you are using *all* your stray capital in arranging your estate? I dont like you to do so. It is true, Sally, I wait with the greatest curiosity for anything you ever send & would watch for the box with even more eagerness than the children but then my judgment dictates that you ought not to be lavishing your means in your old-fashioned generous habits & that I ought to scold at you for it whenever I see you trespass in that way.

Aint I a cross old fellow?

Our difficulty here in P. is that Adams dont so much as look at us here.[34] We never can use him farther than Phila or at most at Trenton. But, Sally, anything ever addressed to me care of E. Spencer Miller Esq, 99 S. 4th Street, Philadelphia will find its way to me without fail.

Mr Moore or some friend of his will be coming on to the Assembly, but probably you may not wish to communicate in any such way with a messenger to him as would show that the box was from you.[35] You're so queer about these things.

Aint I an ungracious fellow in receiving presents. I would write this letter all over again if I could spare the time. But, Darling, if you send anything send the

34. Adams & Co. Express, a mail service in Philadelphia.
35. Samuel McDowell Moore (1796–1875).

merest trifle & if you can something you have now or long owned. They will like it better. I dont write only for the present, but for all time coming.

I mourn over your accounts of your health & feel sad that I cannot be with you. Darling, Sally, grant me one favor. It is more than all presents you could possibly give me. It is, to believe me when I assure you by all that is sacred that all your fears about my affection & vain night-mares about the future & my regrets &c are *utterly* imaginative. There never was a man who *prized* more than I do as a selfish pleasure the progress he had made in winning a lady's hand. I would not resign the chances I have of marrying you & my right to your present affection, for any most prosperous match that I can possibly imagine. Dont waste your sorrows upon what is unreal.

Yrs in haste
JM

I will write *again* more fully.

Richmond,
Saturday May 8. 1856.

My *dear John*,

After a variety of misadventures Nannie & I reached here last evening about dark. We did not decide to make this detour from our route until we got to Lynchburg; when we found ourselves so perplexed by railroad arrangements that we came straight on to this place that we might preserve our minds and baggage.

Your letter came last night too. I am so grieved about the buttons. They were both put in the box. But as they were heavy for so small a box it is likely the Motion of the letter, jostled off the top, & then the buttons worked their way out of the ends of the package. These ends however were sealed too, & I think the outer wrapping was folded on, so as to protect the Enclosure. I feared, after they were sent, they were not securely put up as I was hurried about it. I know something of the P. Office fixing of letter packages & think if you will ask yr P.M. if there was an Article of the kind I described, loose, in any package when it came to his office, you might yet find it. Indeed I enclose the odd button I have that you may see what kind of thing it was.

And now, John, if you had written me a sensible letter, at first, telling me you had not rec'd the buttons I cd have asked my Post Master to have inquired after them;—but instead of that you wrote me a note that mystified me from beginning to end, & left me no chance to do anything.

I am amused at yr grave scolding about the children's box. The great thing it was to have contained was *maple sugar*! I had some unusually fine & nice, & brought it to Fincastle to bring here for them; but, before we left Aunt Eliza's, we gave out coming by Richmond, & I left the sugar, for which now I am so sorry.

How do you feel now about your scolding? Don't worry yrself about any expensive presents from me. I don't think it wd be in good taste for me to make such, at present, even if I were able, tho' I would like extremely to do it.

Everybody is very kind here, & I meet with great attention as a general thing, wherever I go.

But I'm sick yet. When I was travelling I was almost well, but today I am heavy-headed & just now hearted too. Everyone says I look well, however, so there can be nothing very serious. I hurry, for I am just dressing to go out.

I shall leave here Monday or Tuesday. About 15 hours run between us, but it might as well be as many months except in the matters of letters.

> *God bless you. Yours affec'ly*
> *S.C.P. McDowell*

I incline to think my seals on the letter containing the buttons were stamped—& if you will examine them closely you will find some marks of a stamp, where an extra drop of wax has covered the initials. But I may have done it myself:—I don't remember about that.

Upon second thought I wont send my buttons. If the missing pr is presented it will bear my initials.

I find it difficult to get my letters sent to you, as I don't want to excite remark by them. O John, ours is a sad lot & pains me so.

How much do you love me? Tell me, as tho' you had never told me before.

Princeton, May 9th 1856.

My dear Sally,

I sincerely hope you will keep up the practice of writing every other day. It really makes me happier. I know you love me enough, if you remember how sad I am, to do anything so easy as writing a letter, if you were sure it would make me less melancholy.

Your broodings over being a burden to me are all waste anxiousness. If you were all intermingled with my mind (as I wish you were) you would find that we had grown together so much that it would seem strange to me if we were separated. You seem entirely like my wife. I fear that my affection has outgrown yours & Sally it makes me feel "*bad*". I wish my sweet-heart loved me more than I loved her. I think I would be happier. Sally, cant you produce this state of things in some way.

You ask me how we are to live at Allamby & whether my books will get us shoes & stockings &c. Darling, you have a lower estimate of my practical judgment than the fact. If Allamby itself is not able to support us along with what inheritance I shall have, I trust I am not such a fool if I have a wife & children as not to take a parish again & arrange for our support. You dont know what a good husband you have in more ways than you now are aware of.

Do tell me how you are in all your letters. I feel very sad about your health. If you were to meet[36]

Richmond,
Monday May 12. 1856.

Dear John,

I have been so worried about getting my letters off to you, and, in fact, have not yet been able to send one. The first one I wrote is still in *my* possession instead of yours; and does nothing but migrate from the pocket of one dress to that of another. I think however I shall get both off today, for if other means fail I will enclose this to your Mother. This seems foolish & even ungenerous particularity, but I fancy it is best to keep our matter entirely at rest. No one thrusts it upon me, & therefore I make no revelations in regard to it.

I hope still to send my homely present to the children, for I find Tom left a supply of sugar which he had intended for Mary & Susan here for me to take to them; but as I can't do that I shall just appropriate myself for Maggie & Allie.

I am much better since I came down. I think being among people once more has been of service to me. I find my old friends, of whom there are only a few here now, very cordial & attentive, and I enjoy this beautiful city with all the zest of an earlier day. You wd have been amused at the meeting I had yesterday with an old acquaintance whom I found in Mr Hoge's Church.[37] It was an old negro woman. I hung back until she came out of the gallery & then spoke to her. She was greatly delighted to meet me—"one of her darling friends" she said, & grew so noisy in her welcome as to embarrass me. I tried to stop her—saying "Aunt Alsie I knew you wd make a fuss over me, & therefore waited till the crowd passed out before I'd speak to you." "O honey!" said she, ["]I don't make fuss enough—if I wasn't so weak I'd make a heap more than this." But she gave me her blessing, poor old creature, & discharged me.

I shall leave here tomorrow or the next day. I feel oppressed at the idea of going back to my solitude, but I reckon it's best for me to be shut out from people—otherwise I should be spoiled! By the bye, let me tell you for your comfort that I believe I am thought quite as handsome as ever; so don't worry yourself about my having grown to be a fright.

I shall send the box to Spence.

You are crazy to make a martyr of yourself in this thing of affection:—that you give all, & get, precious little in return, is the burden of all yr complaints, which like, most complaints have many little real truth in them. I love you abundantly,—too much for you to worry about, even under the guise of most anxious, sentiment. My affection is like Sancho Panza's notion of sleep—"it

---

36. The conclusion of this letter is missing.
37. Moses Drury Hoge (1818–1899) was the pastor of Second Presbyterian Church.

covers you all over like a blanket.["]³⁸ And I have no belief whatever in yr having outstripped me in it. I fancy you don't love me, all the time just as hard as you can.

I enclose you the odd button; but don't send me another pair. Mine are gentleman's buttons as you perceive, & more expensive than you imagine. As you lecture me on such things, it is but fair for me to return the compliment. I am so sorry for the loss of the others. Make out my letter as you can.

I write in a hurry. God bless you.

Affectionately
S.C.P. McDowell

Princeton May 12 1856.

My *dearest Darling*

I cannot talk to you with any comfort unless you are sitting in my lap. So tho' you are hundreds of miles away you must put your arms round my neck, & quit making such wry faces, & just patiently endure from me at least one kiss & one gentle fond pressure to this poor helpless old heart of mine & one long steady gaze into those bright I'es, which Sally, are the great arguments I use whenever the least doubt springs up in my mind whether or no you are not perfectly beautiful. And tho', Sally, I can just picture to myself the twisted lips & sour looks that you have at the very mention of such liberties as these yet at this distance I can do just what I please with my arms & my lips. I can kiss you all over your cheeks & eyes & pretty round shoulders without so much as paying, by your leave & I can sit whole hours taking entire possession of your time & ease & I can make you five times as patient with me as you ever were in Lexington & ten times more *wakeful* & twenty times more fond & affectionate in every way. Oh this imagination is a capital device instead of stages & locomotives, & instead of a cross, cold, uninterested & hard hearted mistress, I can have one as bland as a summer zephyr, one who smiles upon me & throws her arms round my shoulder & climbs up on the sofa to my lips & lavishes upon me all her love; & when I think in a half coward way, What would, Sally think if she saw us? I can roll back to that most luxurious idea that, Sally, has no earthly power to interfere & that this lovely Sally of mine & that cross Virginia prototype of hers are utterly independent of each other & that if this one chooses to be a little more amiable & good, why it's none of the other's business. So, my Darling (its this one here) put that white arm round under my shoulder & let me tell you all I think (you other Sally, dont you listen) & if I say anything at all that you approve dont do as that wicked Lexington girl, just hear it & drink it all in & treat me worse than ever, but tell me that you love me with all your heart & that you always will love me, please God to keep you from going mad.

---

38. Sancho Panza, the squire of Cervantes's *Don Quixote*.

Now, Sally, (not you old bad Lexington there), indeed you are so foolish about what you say of your not trusting our engagement. Why what dare you trust? I believe you'll get to doubting the sun in heaven. Why, Sally, how can I make this firmer? Tell me some way in which I can seal the thing more firmly than it is now & I will do it with all my heart. Havent I *solemnly promised* that I will marry no other than you unless for your own reasons you change yourself & desire otherwise, or unless you are wickedly unfaithful & contumacious. I am sure I cannot go farther. Dont you believe my word Sally? I have had a notion to write you a distinct & solemn vow in the name of heaven that I will never marry any one else in your life-time. But what good would it do? The other has all the same advantage. And inasmuch, as I have often told you my love would diminish & die if *you* became indifferent why should I take an oath that would seal me to a certain destiny even tho' your love & attachment were altogether emptied out of my heart. Still if I thought such an oath would conduce to your happiness & health & above all to your safety & your life I would seal it beyond all earthly or even heavenly powers to excuse me from it. I am anxious about your health. I am so tried by it. I think about *you* with sadness. I think about *your health* with fear & a kind of terror. Darling, when am I to come to see you. I cant come as well in the summer as in cooler weather. Why maynt I come now? If you don't answer my questions when I write I'll come without asking you.

"Ben Gerhard" only meant that as they chose to think my marriage dangerous & mischievous he & Spence ought to close in & win me away from it. So I *suppose;* I would not hear Spence any further. I have no letter fr you to-day. Do write oftener. I preach nearly every Sunday. Indeed somewhat oftener than I like. This letter is so foolish that I *beg* you to burn it. *Dont you think it foolish?* Tell me.

Yours fondly
Jno

Sally, do you *really* love me? It seems to me *hard* that one who loves you so passionately & constantly as I should be deceived in the slightest degree about your affection? Solemnly & before God, Sally, do you love me? And if you love me why *dont* you use some of those fond & earnest expressions that you say are wrong to your lips. *Certainly* its "ungracious."

Princeton May 14th 1856.

Well Sally,

I have read your letter & my mind is made up. You put the buttons safely in & they were taken neatly out (probably at the Phila P.O.) & the letter sealed up again. There is a seal under each of these as I now see of the lighter coloured wax. Moreover the letter has been searched in resealing & there can be no doubt the buttons have been stolen. I have given the seals & envelope & a description of the stolen property (not the initials) into the hand of the proper officer & there is a bare possibility they may be recovered. The man who has them goes to Phila to-morrow.

I have received the buttons, & unless your notions of expense are very high I want to match them. You would not like anything else *better* would you? If not I want to match these. Have you any changes to suggest in the new pair?

Darling, I am such a homespun country-man that I dont dare to tell you what I would like to present to you. You would laugh at me at the very least. Or perhaps curl your pretty lip at me (& Sally, if I could see it I wouldnt care.) I am most crazy on the subject of teeth. I think all people are mad about their teeth. (By the way that's where dogs are mad about.) I would like to give my darling love, first, a good scolding & then a carte blanche to some first rate Richmond dentist to over haul all her teeth. Darling, why may I not present you some of my gold set in your ivory as well as in any other form in which you can wear it? Not that I mean for one moment to say that I think you need the dentists care more than any one else—Oh no! but that I am crazy about the whole subject & that Ally & Maggie & their father & every one within their reach had to bear the brunt of my anxiety.

I cannot get the buttons till I go to Phila. When do you mean to go home?

"How much do I love you?" Why, this much that when you tell me you are well I have a *thrill* all thro' my frame. I am a little jealous about your beauty, & if I dare pray on so light a subject I would pray our good Father who made it, "please to keep it for his poor servant" till I can see it every day.

I am glad about the maple sugar. & the children will no doubt think more of their Great Unknown than ever. Children are best approached thro' the same portal out of which civil speeches come, only in the opposite direction. I shall keep a sharp look out on Spence, for he has a bright little fellow, who I think has great taste for those Southern delicacies. Dont say on the box that there is any maple sugar in it. I have grown sensitive to this thing of empty boxes. So my letters are not sensible. Well I have long tho't so myself. But, Sally, I'm not like you. I'm not bound to be very sensible in anything.

Sally, Dearest, why dont you tell every body we love each other. If you *knew* I would never alter in the slightest would you express your love & allow me more priveleges of a lover? Tell me, Sally. Tell me too whether you love me—tell me fresh—just "as if you had never told me before.["]

Yours doubtingly
Jno Miller

May I send your dentist a present for his faithful services past & to come.

Richmond
Monday May 14. 56.
Midnight

Dear John,

Here I am still; but in five hours I shall be en route to Halifax. I have been detained simply by the pleasure of being here, and am sorry to go tomorrow. I have just packed the children's box, & will have it in Mr Blair's hands to be sent by Express to Spence tomorrow morning.

You must unpack it *very carefully* yourself. I am half ashamed of my presents; but in truth I did not know what to get for Allie. I wish I could have sent him a full supply of real agates, but in this great city could only find a few, from which I chose the prettiest:—but if nobody will tell him the contrary, I imagine he is scarcely wise enough yet to know the difference between glass & stone agate. They are all scattered thro' Maggie's box, & you must look out for them in all wee corners.—The largest cake of sugar is his.

The socks on top are yours. I had no way of sending them to you before. They will do for next winter.

These little things are rather for my pleasure, than the children's, and it seems almost silly to send such to city children. However I hope they will give some amusement to both.

My visit has been one of most unmixed pleasure. I only wish it cd be prolonged.

Mr Blair followed me from the parlor to the hall this afternoon, & for the first time broached our matter, laughingly demanding confessions, & telling me my letters were rather suspicious to him. I acknowledged they were just & stated the present condition of affairs. He was sorry the marriage had not taken place, & expressed himself strongly, & decidedly in favor of it. He asked what kind of a man is that any how—so he had heard he was a clever sort of a fellow, with book-learning enough; but he didn't care for the head he had, if he only had heart enough to love me well & strongly & sincerely. *I spoke the truth*, of course, even on so delicate a point saying—"O! as to looks, he's something of a fright—and as to other things—he meddles with philosophy wh is to me a proof of want of wisdom, & gives me much anxiety by having his head too hot & his heart too cold." How do you like that? *Might I not* have said it all? But I didn't say any of it; but was very proper and becomingly reserved.

I hope to hear from you at Susan's. But good night. God bless you.

Affectionately
S.C.P. McDowell

Princeton, May 16th 1856.

Darling Sally,

I dont know why I love you so. You never have been very kind to me. You never have loved me very hard. You never have invited me to come & see you, &, now when I am dying for an invitation, echo answers—you shant do it, Sir.

Sally, can you tell me anything, about this strange phenomenon? I dont see that youre so very loveable—in that highest of all ways a perfectly invincible predestination to love me & load me with your tenderness; & yet all the while I'm loving *you* as tho' you were an angel, & I am settling down in deeper depths of love & in stronger persuasions that you have become to me a kind of necessity.

Only yesterday, I was thinking, why does Sally vex herself about my altering my wish, when all the time her fetters are getting heavier & heavier, & I am now quite incapable of spending one single hour without some thought of that tyrant of mine away off there in the hills.

Sally, I do love you so. I love you to a point in which the thought of marrying you seems almost painful from the excess of exquisite anticipation. I can hardly bear the thought of being with you every day—of being anchored by you so that I shall never post away again thro' all our history—of having you as my own darling friend & child & comforter, my darling wife—my lovely "good angel" (Do you remember how horrified you were when I called you that once before?) my better spirit, to make me hope when I am so dreary as I every day am & to make me still & peaceful when I am engaged with the crooked things in my history. It seems too good that I can ever throw my arms around you & claim you as my own dear wife, & that when in these times when I feel outraged by these social oppressions, I feel careless of all ties social or in the church I shall have one to breath her own loving spirit into mine & to warm me into better affections.

But, Sally, when am I to see you again? Indeed you better take care. Dont you see a little tinge of insanity in what I write? Aint you afraid Ill get crazy from being too long out of the company of what is more than half of all the being & all the intelligence I possess. And do you think it altogether right when I am a sort of semi-annual body at the very most, that when the time of my perihelion should approach, I should be still left flying disconsolately thro the labyrinths of space.[39]

Darling, you'll find me some day like one of the Pleiades & when you look for me in the spot I used to occupy in the heavens you'll feel sad when you see how the poor lost Pleiad has twinkled itself from your vision.[40]

I have no letter to-day. Indeed, I have no nothing. I feel as forlorn as one can possibly do. I feel the same strong yearning for what is ever fading from my grasp, but not one comfort. All I know is that I love you better than you deserve &

am yrs
JM

Princeton, May 17th 1856.

Dearest Sally,

I dont know why I write this afternoon—only because (I believe) I am not fit for anything else. Still I will not inflict the letter by mail till Monday afternoon.

I wonder I dont tell you more of the affairs around me. I find from my hermit life I have grown careless about my dress & if you could look in upon me some afternoon as worn out with writing I am lounging over a book you could tell Blair with a safe conscience I was a "perfect fright". I go unshaved for days together. And as our man-servant is under my direction & I have uses for his time in great

39. A "perihelion" is the point nearest the sun in the orbit of a planet.

40. A cluster of stars in the constellation Taurus. In Greek mythology, Zeus placed the seven daughters of Atlas and Pleinone among the stars. Six are plainly visible; the seventh is the "lost" Pleiad.

works I want to finish about the place I fail to give him my shoes in the morning & altogether look like distraction. It's sometimes a pleasure to me when I am such a scare crow that I know somebody that can keep up appearance for us both.

Well, you must know that sometimes somebody gives a party. Dr McLean gave one the other evening. It was a perfect jam—much grander than that party where you were so saucy to Mrs Pendleton.[41] I overhauled Hasper our man & made him improve my understanding & I removed all the venerableness of an ancient beard & drew myself out of a state of abandonment which even you would be startled at & sallied out to the party. I cant tell you all who were there but Sally one thing I was greatly struck with & that was that there was not *one* really interesting lady in the room. Miss Waddell a young lady from your state was certainly the most so. I was thinking—& yet Sally I'm afraid I shall spoil you—I was thinking how grandly I should have felt if *my wife* could have been pointed out as the most interesting lady in the room. Darling Sally, how I wish you could have been there.

Monday Evening.

Ha! it was well that I scribbled a little on Sat. aft. Here I am as tired as a pelican & so hot I couldnt take my tea. I have been out finding a new place to build Spanish castles. You quarrelled with Allamby because it was too far out & I am trying to get a foundation for air castles two miles nearer. Or perhaps you would like to be in town better. I have found a new spot & my fancies cluster about it right wildly already. The mania seems to rise & rage quite finely & I dont see but my chateaux are as handsome on this new plateau as the other.

Never mind, Sally; some of these plans will one day be realized for you know we must live somewhere.

But I must hurry my little messages to the mail

Yours Affectionately
Jno Miller.

You could not have made a better selection of presents. I shant tell Allie or he'll worry me till they come.

None of your Blair's Rhetoric when you write again.

Halifax
Monday May 18.[42] 1856.

Well, John; what next? You first offer to pay my dressmaker,—then you would bear my travelling expenses to a certain point this Spring—now, shocking to relate, you would sweep away a dentist's bill! Is it any wonder I ask what you will

41. Anzolette Elizabeth Page Pendleton (1807–1884), wife of William Nelson Pendleton (1809–1883), Episcopal rector of Grace Church, Latimer Parish, in Lexington.
42. Monday was May 19.

wish *me* to do with *your* money next! However I had almost anticipated your matter of fact proposal before it came. I was too short a time in Richd tho' to allow Dr Pleasants a chance to do anything.[43] The only reason I prefer him, is that he *makes* you submit to all that is necessary, which is a great recommendation in my case.

I gave Mr Blair directions about the box for you, which I hope has reached you safely. It was packed, with no great skill, & at last left to the tender mercy of a servant, after I was gone to mail the box on, & convey it from a "sky-chamber" to the Express Office. I didn't prepay it, because I didn't know how much it wd be, & disliked giving Mr Blair too small a sum for the purpose lest I shd feel badly about it, or too large, lest he wd be annoyed with the small remainder left in his hand; therefore I thought you cd best do it yourself.

I feel a little regret at having sent the children anything but the sugar, but I could not resist the temptation; & smoothed over the bad taste of it, by sending the merest trifles I could think of. You must write me how they fancy them. By the bye, home-made sugar is something of a rarity even to us now, & the cakes I sent were brought 200 miles from the South West to Lexington.

I begin to feel lighter about my money matters, for Mr Carrington has very kindly offered to take charge of my worries in that line, and deliver me from debt. He is as good a lawyer as I can get, and is so concerned about my difficulties that I am entirely willing to confide the whole to him. I breathe freely once more at the prospect even of having this burden unbound & thrown down. I begin to feel as if the door of escape from the debtor's prison was open, & my free papers almost in my hand. You cant tell how much anxiety these things have given me. I wish I was a man, any how & could attend to my own business & fight my own battles—But I don't know either—I might be a mean man (as mean as others you know) & that wd be bad; so I had better stay contentedly the forlorn woman I am.

Yesterday, after I was quietly seated in church, a young man walked in across the house from me, who upon turning round I found to be my anonymous correspondent.[44] I am sure I have made no mistake in my suspicions. He looks like a young imp, & I have no doubt is. *Here*, he is, I suppose, kept in his place. Look here John! do some day, take a fresh sheet of paper, & tell me honestly, like a preacher, what is meant by "loving our enemies." I have my own views about it, it is true, and they are very hard upon poor human nature, but I want to know yours.

No, I don't *prefer* the buttons to anything you could send me; but a good many pair of sleeves would be useless to me almost, without them. I don't know either that I care to have them new *exactly* like the old pair, since my old fancy that you should wear one & I the other of that pair cannot be carried out. You can therefore do as you please in the selection of another pair, only get them about the size of the one you have. If I had expressed a fancy special for anything, it

43. William B. Pleasants (1814–?), a Richmond dentist.
44. Dabney Cosby Jr.

would have been a gold thimble which would have been, of all others, except a pen, the thing I most use. But I wanted you to share my buttons with me, & I have been so unfortunate in thimbles, having had several that didn't suit, that I gave up the notion of such a choice. Sometime again, perhaps, you can send me one, unless indeed you run out of funds entirely by making me your beneficiary in some other extraordinary way.

I go home early in June, probably before the 5th, tho' of that I cannot yet be absolutely certain. I want to see you, sometimes dreadfully; but it always wakes me to a renewed sense of our unhappy condition, when you ask about making a visit. Of course, I am sensitive to remark as to our affair, & shrink from anybody thinking it indelicate in us to continue our engagement. You remember Cousin John's remark—tho' to be sure he does not represent every body's opinion. But I will write to you more fully about this. I have been interrupted since I began my letter first by Tom, who came over from Powhatan a day or two since, & then by Susan.

Indeed, John, I do love you, and as I have never loved any human being more, I think I have no ability to love any harder or warmer. I don't think you really can doubt me; but you just like to hear this same thing over & over again: isn't it so? How much would you like me to love you, when you are reasonable on the subject? Do you think if we were married *you* would love me more or less than now? I think after one right sound strong quarrel in which you had convinced me that "woman's rights" were not in the ascendant in your house, I should love you a very great deal more. But if you were to quarrel for a "little brief authority" upon wrong grounds or low grounds, I should love you a very great deal less, and find a wife's duty anything but a pleasure. But that's a far off picture, which need give me no trouble now.

You never saw such a miserable country as this is, tho' I am here among the Nabobs of Virginia. I don't know how they make their money, but they spend it curiously. Instead of having fine pictures or other works of the fine Arts, James Bruce for example, has solid silver toilet seats in his chambers—yr soap lies in a silver stand—yr toothbrush in a silver holder,—water from A silver pitcher, is emptied into a superb silver basin, & that again into a massive silver jar: A silver mug stands upon the marble slab, and ones little feet are cooled & cleansed in a silver bath. Silver finger-bowls, wine glasses, etc adorn the dinner table whilst the gentleman himself is plain as a pipe stem and ugly—oh so ugly.[45]

Never mind *enclosing* letters to Mr Carrington—send them simply to his care. He left home this morning & enclosed letters might not reach me. My own dear John goodbye

S.C.P. McDowell

---

45. James Coles Bruce (1806–1865), one of Virginia's wealthiest merchants and planters, lived at "Berry Hill."

Halifax
Thursday May 22. 1856

My *dear John*,

Do you know you gain upon me a stronger and stronger hold every time you write me such a letter as your last. I mean the one written on Friday last, for I have had none since. If my affection, tho' as deep as ever, *is* sometimes sluggish in its flow, such a letter quickens it into a sort of leaping motion, that, since you are far away & cannot receive its demonstrations, becomes a real and great & pure pleasure to me, just all by myself. When you make me believe that I really am something, and that, not a little, to you in this thing of happiness that we are always longing for & pursuing, my heart opens to you immediately, & oh, so fully. And yet you are always *pretending* to doubt my love to you. You're an ungrateful fellow, and some day when I can, I shall turn round upon you, and tell you to be gone for I don't care the least bit in the world for you. How will you like that?

I wish you would be careful to note whether my letters reach you in proper time. I would write at regular periods, but I am so often interrupted, that I must write just when I can. The reason I am careful in this thing is that yesterday going into a Store here in which the Post Office is kept, I perceived my young enemy hanging about with a very 'at home' air, & I immediately suspected he might be not only willing but able both to withdraw my letters from the mail, and to withold yours, distinguishing them by their postmark, which wd be in accordance with the address of mine to you. I think him quite up to any price of villainy which he thinks he may be able to conceal. As the only protection I can think of is a seal, you will always find my letters with one.

You cant tell how much better I am since I came here. Indeed I feel quite well again, and am some what inclined to think myself, in a fanciful white-crepe bonnet, no poor compliment to your good taste. By the bye that famous nube of Miss White's only found its way to me last night. I admired it much & wrapping it round my head & throat turned to Susan & Catherine for an opinion of it—"O! how becoming!" they both said;[46] and *I* had my own notions, which you know, John, I didn't like to express, lest I might excite the vanity of that lady in the glass who, you tell me, belongs to you. However I suppose it's no harm to tell you that the lady looked uncommon well in her shadowy head-gear, and felt a little sad that you were not present to bear your testimony to its effect, & receive her thanks for it by her looks as well as in her words. I don't exactly know who I am to thank for it—you said Maggie sent it, but I didn't believe you altogether. If that was true, why thank the little lady for it.

I begin to-day a regular round of Va Country hospitality. I go 8 miles to dine at Mr Clark's at 3 o'clock. Saturday I am to go 10 miles to Mr Tom Bruce's for the same purpose. After that I am to arrange for another day at Mr Clayborne's so I

46. Catherine Scott Carrington was Susan McDowell Carrington's sister-in-law.

see nothing ahead for some time now but dinners.[47] Night before last we went to spend the evening at our nearest neighbour's, where I distinguished myself by a regular spell of drowsiness. I grew uneasy under its power, & wondered how it would look if [I] should really drop to sleep while "mine host" was talking to me. It seemed utterly probable that I should do it in spite of my efforts to the contrary. Isn't it strange that I should not be able to keep awake in company, when everybody else has sense enough to keep their eyes open. And yet I don't know: I was so uninterested. I shouldn't have made any effort at all under ordinary circumstances, but last night I really felt so impressed & unfeignedly pleased by the prompt civility of these Strangers, that I did my best to please them and myself too. They were plain people too, with much in their domestic story that appealed to my sympathy, and I hadn't the heart to omit any effort to recompense them for their hospitality. But I couldn't help being sleepy—This world is full of trouble, and every one has his peculiar sorrows. I sat by that poor lady (our hostess) the other night and had my compassion so excited for her. She looks withered & old under the loss of health & property and of her children one after another until only a half-idiot son is left who of course, is a living grief to her: and yet she spoke in such a tenderness to me of "our boy." The poor fellow seemed willing to talk, & as he sat beside his Mother I talked to him of birds, of which he said the Parrot was his favorite, tho mocking-birds (which belong to this region) were sweet too;—& of the Washington Monument that he was curious about, but thought tho' it was to be 600 feet high it wouldn't still be as high as the tower of Babel. Isn't it terrible, this thing of idiocy! I don't think I could bear it; & yet we are able to bear whatever God decrees to us. My Father's greatest friend in this section of the State, an elegant old gentleman, has an idiot son, with a half dozen eccentric children besides. My rampant Cousin, Mrs Cocke, has also a brother-in-law of the same sort—& Sister-in-law too, there was I have heard idiotic also. I wonder if it belong to Eastern Va, like Cretanism to Switzerland?[48]

I am just rattling along, expecting every few minutes to be disturbed, & not willing therefore to do anything more serious than chat with you. Wouldn't I give a great deal to have a real chat, face to face, with—hold you[r] ear down here, John, and don't you get mad,—my dear little man.

Don't you think this is nice paper? Your Phil: folk can't do everything. I wrote to Lilly to have my paper stamped simply M D. & she couldn't get it done. They don't know how to mark surnames of that kind, and so Lilly had these letters put on. I believe tho' I ordered them. It don't look like my name as it stands thus & I am not satisfied with them.

47. William Howson Clark (1805–1873) lived at Bannister Lodge in Halifax County. Thomas Bruce (1830–1861), a wealthy planter and oldest son of James Coles Bruce. David Augustine Claiborne (c. 1823–1892), a Halifax planter.

48. That is, cretinism; a form of idiocy and deformity resulting from a congenital deficiency of thyroid secretion.

I am hurried to an end. So take care of yourself, and love me so hard as possible, and believe me I am, with all my heart

Yours
S.C.P. McDowell

Princeton May 23. 1856.

Come here, Darling. You wish yourself a man? Think again one moment. You love me so "that you have never loved any human being more" & yet you wish yourself a man?

Dearest Sally, when you write again take that all back; for if you love me so very much, you ought to be thankful that you are a woman just for the pleasure of nestling in my arms & living one day entirely in my affection. Sally, do you know, I am jealous of that man that you wish yourself so earnestly to be. I beg you recant all this; & tell me you are *so* glad you're a woman, for whatever you thirst for independance it would be a far higher luxury to live under the shelter of a heart that you have learned to love with all the energy of the most absorbing devotion.

That's the way to talk, Sally.

My love when it began, lived on rain drops & myrtle leaves. But now it has become a perfectly omnivorous Comaro. It takes in whole loads of vows & conjurations as tho' they were sun-beams & unless you take all that back about being a man it will give me such a sense of starvation & famine as would excite the pity even of my bitterest enemy (which, by the bye I think that man would be if you ever carried your cruel prayer into actual accomplishment[)].

Now, Sally, moreover. I once remember a beautiful white duck, that it would have feasted your eyes to look upon. I tried to throw water on it. By the most consummate grace & courtesy of motion it seemed to say that it was perfectly at my service & that nothing could be more agreable to it than to have that water thrown upon it just in that particular way. And the fair white creature scarcely moved an inch or seemed at all to object to my throwing all the cup full on it just whenever I might be so disposed & yet strange to say not a drop ever touched its feathers, or if it bid by a gentle undulating motion my dear duck managed gracefully to get from under it & leave me just as disappointed as ever. Now, Darling, as Nathan said unto David, "Thou art the—(—not a man quite yet but)—the duck.[49] Dr Pleasants is a "wonderful good dentist" & "just the dentist for me" & "just the thing I thought of" & all, so, just like the curtseys of the duck but not a bit of success have I in getting you into the dentist's chair. So I beg for a little curl of yellow hair. Its a trifling little thing, like a curl I remember on that ducks crown—growing near your shoulder & therefore not far from your heart, a harmless little curl of no possible value to you, nay one would think you would be glad to give it to me & like the duck you bow & curtsy with all kind of true

49. 2 Sam. 12:7.

& most graceful expressions one would think you were all ready to send the gift & have not a word against it, but without any other sign of disappointment or sorrow the only mercy is that the curls dont come & the beautiful white duck goes on curtseying & bowing as tho' all the world were just one wide symbol of her benevolence & affection. Then the visit—but I leave off. As Col Crockett said, "my sufferings is intolerable".[50] That duck'll kill me. And I have to stand by & see her in all the grace of her snow-white beauty agree to every thing I say, but neither Pleasants chair or my pretty cherished curl, of no use to anybody but me or my Lexington trip or those sweet words of love which you say are just on your lip are ever the better or the wiser, for all the graceful smoothness of my snow white companion &—plague. Now, Sally, take that. You're what the students used to say of Johnny McLean a sort of necessary evil. And if I didn't love you till the very blood chills in my veins with the thrill & the splendor of my romantic passion I wouldn't stand it a day, but would begin to throw stones at the duck as the sequel of all my admiration.

Sally the box has come. So Spence writes. I have not got it yet. Darling, clip off that little curl & send it to me *wont* you? I did not get a letter from Friday till Thursday.

Blessings on you, Sally. I love you with all my heart.

Yours aff.
JM.

Princeton, May: 26th 1856

My *dear Sally*,

I wish I knew what letter that was. I think I would get it lithographed & mail it regularly every other day. What did it say? Suppose you send it to me. If I knew what would make you love me only a "tinsy winsy bit" I would write that sort of a letter all the time.

By the way you have written 166 letters. Indeed Sally, it aint fair. I mean to stop till you catch up to me. I do get so tired writing some times. You like it, & I do not. I like only getting letters. The moment one comes I am in a fever to have another. Strange to say the old ones dont answer. I have a whole pack of the sweetest letters, that once on a time have given me the sweetest pleasure. And, indeed, the second time often more pleasure than the first. But when I resort to them weeks after or months for some comfort in your long silence, they are not like fresh news from you.

Darling, why is it that I love you so much? It is a sort of enigma. Can you tell me why it is?

What do you think of Brooks caning Sumner?[51] Do you know tho I hate

50. David (Davy) Crockett (1786–1836).
51. In a speech titled "The Crime against Kansas," Sen. Charles Sumner of Massachusetts had grossly insulted Sen. Andrew Pickens Butler (1796–1857) of South Carolina. Two days

that sort of thing. I have such a contempt for Sumner & his bombastic & scrappy speech that I thinks he more deserves his caning than Brooks would being turned out of the House for it. These times look squally. You & I will have to break over our scruples of pride get married & go live up among the rocks. I wouldnt shoulder a musket or risk your pretty neck either to preserve slavery or to emancipate the slaves. I feel the profoundest nausea at all that these Yankees are doing in this matter.

I am so sorry I cant see you in that crepe bonnet. What a pretty little woman you must be.

"Isn't it terrible, this thing of ideocy? I dont think I could bear it." Why, Sally, Providence adapts our backs to the burden. Its astonishing how bravely you do bear it sometimes. In some of the paroxysms of this terrible ailment when you have treated me as tho' I was utterly faithless & unworthy & made me hold down my ear that you might whisper invidious & disparaging epithets, I have thought that you lived under the malady with considerable contentment. It is a species of cretinism however which seems to lurk in the mts for since you have descended into the plains I think you are better.

sweet Sally, what a letter!

Yours fondly
JM.

Halifax
Monday May 26. 1856.

My dear John,

I can write only a note this morning as I am hurried to get ready to take it in myself to the Village as soon as the carriage is ready. But I shall write this afternoon and have my letter mailed tomorrow evening. It is such a distance to the Post Office that I never like to send off a special messenger with my letters.

I am rather wearied already of my country hospitalities. Riding 8 or 10 miles to dine is somewhat fatiguing; and, somehow, I cannot get up an interest in people after I meet them. Those whom I see, are pleasant enough but they excite no emotion of interest with me. And I have little doubt, tho' I try to please them, that they find me wonderfully dull.

The families among whom I have been visiting are descendants of Patrick Henry—one of them his granddaughter; and they claim, on that score, relationship with me. This lady, the grand-daughter, a Mrs Clark, is I hear the cleverest descendent, male or female in a direct line, of the old gentleman.[52] I don't fancy

---

later, on May 22, 1856, Preston Smith Brooks (1819–1857), congressman from South Carolina and a relative of Butler, assaulted and seriously injured Sumner on the floor of the Senate. The incident created a national sensation.

52. William Howson Clark married Elvira Ann Henry (1804–1870), only child of Patrick Henry Jr.

particularly this Henry blood they boast of; but consider it the meanest I have. They, however, are proud of it, and as they have a great deal more of it than I, I have no objection to their valuing it as highly as they please. These old Virginia families here, in the East, amuse me with their pride of birth & consequence. They are plain looking people, of plain manners, & with no uncommon gifts of mind, & no special cultivation of such minds as they have:—indeed, I find no reason *in themselves* for pride of any sort, & doubt whether they wd be greatly regarded if it were not for what Willis calls, "their bright originals in Heaven."[53]

Did I ever tell you "your letters were not sensible?" I am sure I never did, tho' it may be, I *might* have done it sometimes. But I am very glad to get them, any how.

I believe I did not thank you for yr great compliment—Speaking of Dr McLean's party, at which you gravely assure me there was no particularly interesting lady, you break out with the sudden exclamation, "I wish you had been there that you might have been noticed as the most interesting lady present." I felt duly flattered, & becomingly grateful for the compliment of being the least dull among dull people! O John! how came you to make such a failure that time. I am not the least spoiled as you feared I'd be, by the remark. But I have a great fancy for compliments, provided they have in some degree, the true expressions of opinion. I treasure them up, with a new pleasure now, inasmuch as I think they wd be some pleasure to you. And I find myself much influenced in all things by the thoughts of what would please you. It is not a little surprising that any one, so defiant of control, should bend so lovingly, as I assure you I do, to the drawings of this noose you have succeeded in throwing over my head. Of course, I don't know how it wd be, if the drawings were greater & the checks more frequent, but as it is, no poor woman ever enjoyed a surrender more than I. So, Dearest, just put me away in yr heart, & I'm content in this world, which has become very forlorn to me.

> *God bless you. Affec'ly*
> *S.C.P. McDowell*

Halifax,
Wednesday May 28. 1856.

My *dear John*,

I break all my promises about writing at particular times; but I can't always help it. It was dark when we came home from Mr Claiborne's yesterday, and I was so tired and sleepy after ten that, if you had been near I would have quarreled with you, if you had even spoken to me. This morning to be sure, I might have written but Catherine was going away, & I didn't like to steal off to my own room until she had gone.

---

53. Nathaniel Parker Willis (1806–1867), writer and editor of the *Home Journal*.

But here I am now, as quiet as the mocking-bird that nestles in the cedar tree below me, and enjoying the gathering of the clouds with their promise of rain. But I am hurried nevertheless, for Susan is inexperienced in some kinds of work that have just now come upon her, & whenever I can I am lending her my wisdom & my hands.

I had hardly written the last word when Susan called announcing an arrival. Mr Carrington, his Mother, & Nannie. So I am hurried to an end. I have nothing special to write about. Beyond my own dear self, there is nothing here to interest you, and I rather enjoy the thought of being the solitary object of *your* thought in this great State of ours. Everything is in shocking dilapidation in this region. I wouldn't live here. The people too seem so lazy and slow and supercilious. Don't you tell any body *I* say so, but I am greatly disenchanted of late years with Va & her people, especially those east of the Blue Ridge.

O John, I am mortified at your asking for such things as you do. I thought you wd understand that I didn't like it from my silence. Please don't do it any more.

I shall leave next week probably but until I write you certainly of going, you continue to write to me here.

I do want to see you; yet the very thought of your coming makes me sad. I love you fearfully and absorbingly. You don't dream how much: I don't always know myself. Are you worth loving so much? And do you value this affection that I am pouring out upon you in what, if you are what I believe you to be, will be an exhaustless stream?

I tell you, John, you will have much to answer for, if you ever turn its tide back upon my own heart again.

I am afraid you don't love me as you ought or you wd not mourn as you do over the loss of my beauty—at least of what beauty you think I possess. I felt such a pang some weeks ago, in having Mr Bowyer Miller[54] say—"Mrs McDowell is changed since I saw her last:—she was just grown then, & I thought her beautiful." I didn't care for myself much; but I so coveted for you all the charm in that way that I had ever had.

Ha! There's the dinner bell!

Tell me how Maggie fancies her tea things. Tell Allie, he must unwrap his Sugar and put it out on the porch, or somewhere in the Sun, that it may dry. I am sure it will be damp from the unusual quantity of sap that was in it. I must get some more for them as soon as the season for making it comes round.

Oh! I had almost forgotten to tell you; I wish I was a man just as much as ever. It wd be a great Matter to get rid of my woman's nature, & a great pride to be possessed of a Man's independance.

I hope to hear from you this afternoon.

Always Yours,
S.C.P. McDowell.

54. Fleming Bowyer Miller (1793–1874).

What makes you use *green wax?* Why, it looks as if it had had yellow fever at least a dozen times.

Princeton, May 31st 1856.

Sally, you're so cross. If it were not for those sentences of your letter that are so exquisitely sweet that I have been reading them over & over again, I think I would quarrel with you. So I am to judge by your silence when you dont like a thing; Why then, Darling, I would have judged long ago that you didn't like myself. Still a lady that will lavish upon me such an undeserved fulness of affection, & a lady whom I so tenderly love shall be consulted even in her crossnesses; &, Darling, I'll be like that mocking-bird under your window, capable of saying a good deal, but quiet, probably because you have treated him badly in some way, thrown cold water on him perhaps, or given him to understand that you are so sad he ever thought of coming to see you.

But Dearest, you are my own darling wife. I can no more quarrel with you than I can with my shadow, & tho' my life is a very hard one (isn't it, Dearest?) yet if you will only love me, I will forget that all I love dearest in the world is wasting away in its years of loveliness, & remember only that it shuts out from me by its very beauty & its tenderness the possibility of any other affection.

Sally, I know nothing about how other people are constituted or how I would be if I were under other circumstances of attachment, but you have me in a great barred dungeon with lock & key. I can no more go out than the charmed lady in Comus.[55] I dont know any other existence than that within the walls of my barred prison. And whenever I begin to commiserate my lot my honour stands by my affection & the two declare I never can be released.

So when you say, "I tell you, John, you will have much to answer for, if you ever turn its tide back upon my own heart" the old Keep rings all its bells with approbation & the jailor a grim old tyrant shakes all his keys in my face & gives me to feel that I am his prisoner forever.

But, Darling, if they would only let you in. How hard a case, to turn a palace into a cold sepulchre! But I have always been a sufferer & tho' I long sometimes with perfect intemperance of passion for one year of simple affection with you, yet probably it's all a blunder. These prison doors are probably as happy as anything to hold *me* can be. And perhaps God in kindness weaves on the changes of my life, knowing that anticipation is a happier thing for *me* than the ardours & perversenesses of a melancholy nature.

At any rate, Sally, I bow to the will of God. I claim you as mine, & beg you to treat me as well as you can seeing I am a poor helpless beggar. And as all my treasure is always from me locked up in an old Chancery—abomination & I am like poor Mrs Flite hovering about these court days & whispering to the Justices all about my sorrows, I do hope *you* wont laugh at me, but that you will

55. A pastoral drama, composed in 1634 by John Milton.

shelter my madness & not be "mortified" about me if I do talk a little strangely & wildly in my sufferings.[56]

Come here Sally. Put your arms round & round my neck. See how grey my hair is. Aint I old & worn &—strange in what God has given me for the horizon & every day prospect of my life. dont talk *cross* to me, Sally. And if I ask anything that aint actually wicked; even if I ask a little blood out of your heart or a pound of flesh out of your cheek or out of your pretty round shoulder, dont speak quick to me, Dearest. But remember I am a poor broken old man. And give me what I want & comfort me in my madness & my misery.

Sally, the box has come. Voici:

I. Two large cakes of sugar, the largest for Allie.

II. Twenty-one *glass* marbles (four of them of stone.) Allie as bad since they came as can be.

III. A complete set of tea china. Maggie promises us all an invitation to a tea party.

IIII. One letter weight. But, Sally, you said my letters were heavy enough before.

V. One pair of socks.

Dearest, everybody is satisfied except me. Mother has gotten hold of the sugar & deals it out at an established hour every day. Allie is shooting his marbles all over the carpet & Maggie is demurely ruminating a great entertainment. The letter weight I kiss now & then tho it has a very unpleasant resemblance to a certain heart that I know & is nearly as heavy as mine. But what dissatisfies me is the stockings. I expected ten or a dozen pair & indeed was anxious about your health in close confinement in making them. & lo & behold you have made me only one. Well, I suppose Virginia dont rain much wool any more.

As to old Bowyer Miller, whoever he is, tell him, its none of his business. As to the green wax I have lost two long sticks of fine red wax & found this green glue fast to a chocolate piece in an old secretary. Ill try the chocolate! So you still wish to be a man, why, Sally, how do you reconcile that with loving me so hard. *Tell me when you write.* Indeed I'm in earnest. How can you be so "*absorbed*" in loving me & yet wish you were a man?

Yours *affly*
JM.

Maggie began a letter some ten days ago.

Write oftener, Dearest, & dont tell me you'll write, when you dont.

Halifax,
Saturday, May 31. 1856.

My *dear* John,

I thought when I came here your letters would come to me so quickly that the ink wd be scarcely dry upon them; but it is far otherwise: they rarely come

---

56. In Charles Dickens's *Bleak House*, Miss Flite is an old woman driven insane by the interminable wait for her chancery lawsuit to be settled.

in less than four days after they are written. However; that they come at all is something to be thankful for.

By the bye, I think you must have made a mistake in counting my letters to you,—or have lost some of them; for I can't believe I am so far behind you. It is impossible you can have written 50 letters more than I have. Why, I am all the time writing to you. A letter is perpetually buzzing on my brain; tho' I believe it is true that *all* of these brain letters are *not* sent off to you.

Did you ever know anything more cowardly than Brook's attack upon Sumner! I admit Sumner was insulting; but that was no excuse for the dastardly conduct of the other. However, I am prejudiced. I despise South Carolina, and have a dislike to Judge Butler on account of his obstreperous coarseness of manner;[57] and think Brooks himself one of those quarrelsome men who are always belittling themselves by getting into fights. If Sumner had knocked them both down (out of the Senate Chamber, of course) & given them a good drubbing, I think I should have been well pleased. In fact, it wd be well if all S. Carolina could have a whipping. She is so troublesome and supercilious; so full of airs and swell and bombast; so exacting and so lazy; so presuming and so good-for-nothing; she seems to me like a petted, spoiled, selfish, irritable silly woman—the very most despicable thing I know, unconnected with absolute vice.

But these things look alarming; and if I didn't believe in the good sound strong sense and feeling of the masses North & South, I wd have no hope of the continuance of any connection between. Our Southern gentlemen can not approve Brooks' course; and yet the Southern press is full of cheering to the cowardly creature, and Southern men are getting up meetings & disgracing themselves by sending him tokens of approval. For myself, I shd rejoice to see him expelled by acclamation—somehow, there comes faintly buzzing thro' my brain a line of Shakespeare's—something about, "putting a lash in every honest hand"—but I can't get it all, or get it straight;—but no matter—it wouldn't suit, for if the whip is only to be used by "*honest* hands,["] I'm sure Brooks wouldn't be punished as he deserves or I desire. But Sumner too, went too far, as do all yr junto of Abolitionists, Black Republicans, Free-soilers & Northern fanatics, by whatever name they may be called. They have no business to meddle with our private affairs, or attempt to teach us our duty. This burden of slavery (& a heavy one it is) is ours, not theirs, & if we choose to bear it, just as it is, why let us do it, & let them keep quiet, & "mind their own business"—a piece of advice not the less valuable that it bears the apostolic Stamp upon it.

It is so cold we are obliged to have fires again. Everything suffers much for rain. The wheat looks miserably; not worth the cutting. The hot, dry weather has done it some harm, & the fly & chinch bug has, it seems to me made the land look, for miles together, loathesome & leprous. Altogether, "the face of the

---

57. Butler had been a judge on the South Carolina Court of Common Pleas before his election to the Senate.

Country" as our geographies used to say, is very unattractive in this part of Va. I think it's contiguity to N. Carolina must be the cause of its bad looks.

Have you really abandoned Allamby. I had a feeling of regret come over me at yr saying you were looking out for some other site for your Air-Castles. But, at the distance, at which I am I do think Allamby ineligible for a residence for a poor person, or what is worse, a poor student. But how does the book come on? Any flesh upon its bones yet? Any symmetry & grace in its proportions? Any breath—any faint vitality percepitable upon a careful and anxious examination? Is it to be a veiled figure John, instinct with genius like the Veiled prophet of Khorassin[58]—or is it to show its grave face, sublime in its thoughtfulness, and self-sustained in its exalted mission of revolutionizing the world's thinking.

Oh John, I tremble for you and for it. I admire yr steadiness about it, but you must sometimes let me tell you I have anxious fears in spite of all you say.

Monday 7 1/2 A.M.

It was too late after I returned from dinner at Col Carrington's on Saturday to finish my letter—except I had done it thro' mists of sleepiness. By the bye as I was riding out there all alone the quotation I could not catch while I was writing, popped into my head, and here it is:

"I'd put a lash in every honest hand,
    And whip the scoundrel naked thro' the land."[59]

I want to write to you about your visit. When I can find a quiet hour to do it in. I long to see you. Don't you think you could bring Maggie with you? I do want so much to have that little thing in my arms. I think of her a great deal, and tho' I have no feelings of "propriety" in her, yet I would like to have a real possession of her for a little while.

Your letters come slowly to me. What makes you hate to write them so?

But I'm hurried—So good-bye.

With all my heart Yours
S.C.P. McDowell

Princeton June 4th 56.

Dearest Darling Sally,

No letter! No letter since, Oh I dont know when. You bad girl. I write under protest & in a sort of pity. If I didnt think you'd feel "bad" if you didnt hear & if I wasnt reminded by my present sufferings how bad one feels when they feel "bad" I wouldnt write at all.

Who do you think have been in our parlour to-night. I've been helping 'em all to ice cream & sending 'em off with umbrellas.

58. "The Veiled Prophet of Khorassan" is part 1 of a long poem titled *Lalla Rookh; an Eastern Romance*, published by Thomas Moore in 1817.
59. *Othello* 4.2.141.

Mrs McClung. Dr. Dabney. Miss McClurity. Dr Jas. Alexander. Mrs. Jas. Alexander. Miss Reid. (daughter of the Col.) (Miss Waddel daughter of the Blind Preacher).[60] [A] Miss Hazard (from Jamaica Long Island).

Old Mrs McClung is as talkative as ever & evidently wants a quiet piece of gossip with me about our concerns. Poor woman! I am beginning to hope she may leave town without it.

By the way, Sally, how slow you are at taking compliments. When I told you that not a lady at Dr McLean's party interested me at-all how could you not feel the force of the intimation. Dont you know, Jersey is celebrated for her beauty; & in that very room there were fine examples of Jersey good looks & attractiveness; & yet because I say, I was not interested, you dont see the delicate point of the compliment—especially when I tell you, how proud I would have been if you could have been there. O Sally, "how could you make such a mistake that time"?

I was glad to be able to return a little to Col. Reid the kind attention for which I am grateful.

Sally, you are the Moses that strikes the rock of my letter writing till the waters flow out. When you fail to strike (as you have done, Sally, dreadfully these "four days in the wilderness") I murmur like the Israelites & moreover, the waters dry up & so I have precious little to say.[61] So, dear Moses (—Ha! Sally, who would ever think of you in connection with *Moses*—except poor darling, Sally, we should climb Mt Nebo to look over into the promised land &—*die there*.[62] I am more like Moses for you know Moses was the meekest man & you know how meekly I bear all your fitful & interrupted writings. Moreover I think it would have been so fine if I had been found in an ark of bulrushes; it could have been said, as a sort of type of the sorrows & disappointments of my life, "When they saw the child, *behold the child wept.*"[63]

Yours sadly
Jno Miller.

Halifax.
Wednesday, June 4. 1856.

Such a pleasant evening this is! We have, for several days been almost exhausted by the scorching heat, and the ground is parched until almost every growing thing seems threatened with death; but a rain this afternoon has

---

60. Elizabeth Alexander McClung from Staunton, Va., was the aunt of James Waddel Alexander. Robert Lewis Dabney (1820–1898), professor of church history and polity at Union Theological Seminary in Virginia. Agnes Reid (1838–1923), the youngest daughter of Col. Samuel McDowell Reid. The "Blind Preacher" refers to the Reverend James Waddel.

61. The reference to Moses striking the rock and the people complaining is found in Num. 20:2–13.

62. Deut. 34:1–4. Moses climbed Mount Nebo and saw the Promised Land before his death.

63. Miller refers to the discovery of Moses in Exod. 2:6.

freshened all green things and refreshed us amazingly. And now as I sit quietly by my window, and hear the birds as the twilight is deepening, I find my heart taking its every day excursion to you, with a longing for you to be here. Such a treat it would be to me to take a low seat beside you now, and feel your hand gently laid upon my head, (which is often heavy enough under its burden of anxiety,) and have a consciousness of yr real presence, and a sense of repose once more, that that presence has, sometimes, before given me. But—and it always ends so—these wishes are mere dreams, which fade away just as the day is doing now—into darkness.

Friday, June 6. 8:A.M.

My *dear John,*

I have yr letter of last Saturday. I can't well make it out. I don't exactly know what you mean; but I have been troubled by it, and old anxieties, for awhile quieted come back again. But, perhaps, another letter may explain this one more clearly.

Now, John, come, be fair for once; did you ever find me "cross" to you? On the contrary, are you not perfectly sure, that often you've been treated with a little more gentleness than you could fairly lay claim to? But then, I claim nothing as due to me for such forbearance, for I loved you too much to quarrel with you, while there was the least possibility of shielding you by any plausible excuse that my own mind could frame.

And have you ever found me [to] "speak quick to you"? And do you think I would begin it now, when we have neither of us, any large stock of happiness, to sport with.

You little know, how much of wealth, (if affection be a treasure to you) is laid away for you in this heart of mine, nor how strong the foundation it lays for the sort of happiness that is decreed to us. But it would not be an affection worth having, if it had not, in its nature, the power of overturning its own authority and conquering itself should the necessity for doing so ever arise. Sometimes, I think, that a mere disinterested consideration for you, ought to call upon me for the exercise of the inherent power; but then, I pause:—it may be that what I think of, as securing your happiness apart from me, might be a mistake, and so I let my anxieties on that point be whipped away from me time after time. O John, I wish I could know you thoroughly. I am often hampered, beyond your most distant imagining in the mere expression of attachment, by the fear of mistaking your feelings, and fastening a cord about you which perhaps some other feeling than affection upon your part, is making to press too heavily & painfully upon you.

It doesn't matter to me, John, that your "hair *is* grey". My love to you, did not originate in anything that changes, as Time lays his hand upon it from year to year, as that does. That dear head of yours is just as dear to me as if its locks were as full & glossy & dark as when I first remember them. Indeed, I rather think I love it all the more, not, of course, *for* the grey hair that lies upon yr temples, but because by its resting there, it appeals to the highest and best & strongest element of my affection.

I find I can't leave here until the latter part of next week, or perhaps first of the week after. I half wish you could meet me in Rich'd then, & go on with Lilly & I home. But that can hardly be.

Did Maggie's things reach her in perfect safety? I laughed about the letter-weight. I did not send it to you, but left it on the table in my room [at] Mr Blair's, & doubtless, it was put in your box by some of the family who thought I had forgotten to do it. It is made of Gypsum from a bank of Tom's, & he brought it on as a specimen of the purity & good quality of his plaster. But keep it, & don't despise it since you hear of the mistake. God bless you, my own dear John!

Yours
S.C.P. McD.

Princeton June 6th 56.

I have no doubt if the truth were known, Darling Sally, that you have many an anxious hour about my book & the chances of its being neglected or disgraced. And tho' you try to think you are anxious about the truth & my usefulness yet the caustic of that speech in Kentucky,—"John Miller's a fool" & the dwindled look I would have if the book fell dead all arise to trouble you.

Now, Darling, I mean to publish that book. I have it half written; that is, I have written to what I suppose is a page past the middle of the volume & all the rest is arranged & ready to be composed. I have no sanguine ideas. I would publish if I knew it would be unnoticed. I mean to publish & follow it up with publishing other things even if I have to screw out of my narrowed means the price to help issue unremunerative & barren publications. The fact is I am irreclaimably resolute in this undertaking. And, it grieves me to think of my poor Sally who has linked her being with me in so important a way having the *crawlings* of distrust & apprehension in respect to her share of the dishonor.

Now, Darling, I'll tell you what I have been thinking. Paul you know made some sort of a vow. (I forget what it was) that time when he had shorn his head in Cenchrea & I am tempted to do that very thing—to say that I will never see Sally McDowell in this world again till my book is done & published & sent for her to read & till the world indulges it enough to make it safe for her to own her relation to its author.[64] How would you like that, Darling! I could get all this accomplished perhaps, by October, & tho' I would find it very hard to take up my burden of expectation & carry it thro' four months yet I am accustomed to that sort of discomfiture. And besides, Sally, it would be so comfortable to take you in my arms after all this book question was decided & you knew what you must expect.

64. Cenchreae, the port city for Corinth, on the Saronic Gulf. Paul had his hair cut there to fulfill a Nazarite vow. See Acts 18:18.

It is true I do not prognosticate any of that success which will declare itself in so short a time. As for you I dont expect you to *read* more than the first twenty pages & probably when I visit you in October you will be just in the torpor of disappointment & regret, but still you will see then what your poor lover means all this time & he will know that you are tolerating him with your eyes open (or more probably with your eyes shut!) when you have again reason to know that John Miller is a fool.

Dearest, suppose I were to come up to your expression, & really conceive the enterprise & cast my life accordingly of being, in "self-sustained efforts to revolutionize the world's thinking" & suppose I were after great precèdent contempt & years of slowness absolutely to accomplish something of the kind, how would the "grave face & sublime thoughtfulness" you speak of fill your fancy in a lover & a husband. I wonder if, with me, you regard a new thinker, if his field be an important one the very highest prince among men, or whether if you could choose you would rather choose some other husband as your idea of what is highest in your species.

Sally dear, you have often asked why I loved you. Now, I'll tell you. I have always pined after a solitary life. That is by no means a life that would exclude society, but a life of unbroken power to *command* solitude in the working hours of the day. I have always painted hermitages when ever I began to erect anything in the air. Now knowing how much I *depend* upon society for some of my few highest pleasures & how fastidious & disinclined long study makes one to society not after ones likings, my passion for you kindled itself in the shelter of one of my own air castles I folded you to my heart in my own future hermitage & I became enamoured of the picture of such a lovely stranger (as you then were) in the field of my scholarly pursuits. You were preeminently ["]la fille de l'hermitage"[65] & So I began to babble to you of my Spanish castles almost as soon as I knew you & that, I still say, as I have often told you before, knowing that there were many things in which you & I in these very matters of intellectual taste would be entirely different.

Darling, suppose you *knew* I would never write a book that was worth reading. Suppose you knew I would never cut a figure in the world that was worth the least remembrance after I was laid in the grave. Suppose my present pursuits shwd grow to be thot imbecile & queer & suppose you never read a line of mine with any satisfaction but my letters to you. How then, Sally? Would you love me? Would you wish to marry me? Are you bolstering up your love to me on the *hope* that I may be something more than those Kentucky gentlemen were aware. Tell me all these things Darling, And answer me whether you would nestle in my arms & lie quietly in my embrace if you knew I was dear to no one but yourself & was dwelling in our little cottage in a prospect of oblivion as entire as the Kentucky verdict would so far secure. Tell me Sally, all these things. And tell me what you

---

65. French, meaning the girl of the hermitage.

think of my vow. I would feel effeminate & idle in going on to take you in my arms after these challenges you give me as to the future.

Yours passionately
Jno Miller.

By the way, you are mistaken about my not liking you to speak of my book. I like you to speak of everything. Do write oftener! I am still writing one third more than you.

Do you love me?

Princeton June 9th [1856]

My Sweetest Sally,

If you could know how I yearn over you with a sort of loving, fondling, protective tenderness, & how I grieve over anything that wounds you, or annoys you, like that letter, you would never have the power of being wounded or annoyed by anything that I could write again.

Now, all this that you have harrassed yourself with is mere *conjuration*. I wrote that letter so idly & carelessly that I cant recall what I said in it & I *do* think Dearest, that your love is a jealous little urchin to call up so many phantoms as he has done thro' our long correspondence.

Dearest, put your pretty shoulder near to me—there—Put your cheek against my lips—now—let me tell you something. You *are* cross—& you dont deserve this letter—but now listen. *I loved you once so that if you had given me up I could have endured the separation & men could not have seen by my looks that I had borne any suffering.* I love you now so that I think wildly of all schemes that could bring you to my side & *I have no possible thought of how I could endure to lose you.* If you had kept me at a distance after I returned your letters I could slowly have weaned myself away. But now I have a totally different feeling. Dearest, I am honest with you _before God,_ when I say that you seem to have grown to me as the fondest part of my existence.

Stay—dont leave me—nestle close to me, Sally—I want to tell you more. I have been so *drearily* yours—so wild in my passion for you for some weeks past more than ever before, & under the influence of some generous letters of yours more frank & unjealous than you had yet written, that I cant tell you how much I have suffered & how much I now daily suffer in the mere denial of being separated from you. And, Darling, it is so cruel when I need so much your fondness when I live so much upon your frank unshrinking professions of affection when I love you so to cast yourself in my arms without one reserve of that sort of half-calculating hesitation to hear you say that "you are conscious that you do not tell me all that you feel & that there is welling up upon your lips more than you ever tell me in your very tenderest letters."

Darling, you say, "I am often hampered beyond your most distant imagining in the mere expression of attachment by the fear of mistaking your feelings."

Now *I complain of this*. You know I have observed it. You know I have said you didn't love me & you have, laughed at me as only *pretending* to feel so, when here you confess that you are keeping back from me the very bread on which I live & the very joys that might help to balance our continual separation. Dearest, come to me, & be my own darling wife hereafter. Throw yourself in my arms without reserve & without need of untrusting prudence, & believe me when I assure you that a love as tender as mine & that is always increasing ought long ago to have passed its probation & to have been treated with the cordiality that I so constantly propose.

But *Poor Sally* I pity you. You have indeed a hard time. Throw your arms round my neck & love me.

I meant to write only two sentences. You do manage so as to get the warmest & the marry-est letters. I think I'll write one of these Slough of Despond letters myself some day just to get pulled out by an angel. And yet Sally, I wont doubt you. I mean to believe that you are pouring out upon me the fullness of the very most passionate affection. Isnt it so? Now kiss me. I'm going to ride.

I am suffering to see you & yet my judgment is interposing some barriers connected with my book that I fear now will embarrass your invitation even should it come, for a month, or, two.

> *Your poor injured lover.*
> *Jno Miller.*

I couldnt get to you now till July. And *then* it wont be long till September or Oct. And yet it will be very long. By the way I read a good deal of your letter before I opened it.

Halifax,
Tuesday, June 10. 1856.

My dear John,

Your letter, about yr forthcoming book, came late yesterday afternoon; and as it is so very serious about its subject-matter I intended to answer it in the same spirit; but find I am too hurried this morning to do it, and must decide either to write you a note by to-day's mail, or wait till tomorrow's for a long letter. I have no hesitation in believing, you wd rather have the note than wait.

How little you know me if you think I would wait for the world to stamp your book with success before "I would own my relations to its Author". If I loved you only in the light of other people's opinions you might reasonably take your irrational vow, and pin your faith, and build your dependence upon an affection as shifting as the clouds. No, no: if you succeed, nobody, not even yourself would luxuriate in that success with richer enjoyment than I would; but if you fail, just as others draw off, my affection will lead me to draw nearer and nearer to you; and I shall love you all the better that I find you then establishing my attachment as a sort of necessity to you. As long as I see in you what I think justifies a strong affection, I am independent of "philosophy" in any form; but when I lose this, I had rather cut off my hand than give it to you, and break my neck rather than you should draw my head into to your bosom.

At the same time however, a capacity for usefulness, in whatever high form it is developed increases my admiration & respect, and that far only heightens my affection. But, John, you might be a very good writer, & yet a very bad husband, and I'm pretty sure then the extolled book, would not make my home happy. But the contrary of that might be very happily true.

"Do you love me"? What makes you ask me? Are you not tired of the same unvarying answer for these 12 or 18 months past. *I* don't get tired, because I'm a woman; but a man must, by & by, have a sort of disgust to such repetitions.

But, as you tell me you are a forlorn sort of a man, I'll tell you, I do love you hard enough to keep you warm for a whole lifetime even in so cold a place as this world of ours.

Are you going to bring Maggie to see me?

I can't exactly say when I shall go home—but am getting uneasy at my prolonged absence.

I do write quite often, all things considered—you don't know the difficulties of a postal kind here.

With all my heart yours
S.C.P. McDowell

Halifax,
Tuesday June 10. 1856.

My *dear* John,

How do you feel when you draw out of an envelope such an enormous sheet as this? Do you ever feel weary at the very sight of it, especially if it seems to be closely written? Well, *I* feel as tho' I had launched out into the ocean when I begin upon it; but I think it will suit my present purpose well; for I mean to take your last letter and answer its questions, one after another as well as I can, and begin by saying, I *do* feel anxious about your book, and "the chances of its being neglected & disgraced". That I am really anxious about it for "the truth's sake, and the sake of your usefulness", often when I have no consciousness of intermingling with that anxiety any thought of myself as sharing either in the failure or triumph of it. That a failure would greatly distress me I cannot deny;—(you wouldn't have me unmoved by it, would you?) but that it would alienate my affection, if there was nothing wrong—morally wrong, as a cause of that failure, and you loved me still, I do not think. If I were convinced you were teaching "damnable heresies", I wouldn't ever marry you; but if you were only unsuccessful, I would have every call of honorable affection to love you more tenderly, if it were possible for my nature to do so, than I do now. And so far from disowning our relations *because* the world took up a Kentucky cry, which by the bye I had no business telling you, I would think meanly of myself if I did not, on fit occasions avow them. My love is not dependent upon the sunshine for its existence: I think it was meant for storms and darkness; and don't you see, John, without my telling you, how well it is accomplishing its destiny. It was a delicate thing in the beginning that required constant and careful watching, but it has grown very hardy and vigorous, by the very storm-life it has led. It has had many a blast that you knew nothing about; but always after these tempests, there come again its "still, small voice" and gentle whisperings. And so now, if we have to bear this book-blast, we'll bear it together: if it brings any triumph you'll let me be, the prouder of the two—or I'll be so without your permission:—if a failure, why then let me sorrow over it with you, and if it be right, help to buckle on your armor for a new trial, and give you a word of cheering as you march out to the conflict. But never do you think of my deserting in the hour of difficulty and darkness. I am not a little "snapped with the" coward, but I try not to allow it to be cowardice of that kind, tho' to tell the truth, John, I don't always come up to my own standard of courage.

Now, as to the vow—pshaw! You don't know what you are talking about John; nor who you are talking to. Not come till October, just on account of a foolish notion, when I am so anxious to see you, that I think I detect a little recklessness about it even now, and am constantly turning in my mind the question of the best time for you to come, & find an early day after I leave here the card that frequently turns up. But I am so hampered, at present, I can't carry out my wishes on that point.

I don't know that I would "read more than 20 pages of your book"; but you would tell me the rest some day when you had nothing to talk about and I was dull; wouldn't you? I would listen with gratifying attention for one hour; and then, John, Dearest, the rest would come to me in dreams, oh, so sweetly!

But John, have patience with me: tho' I do talk so, *it isn't every bit true;* some of it (which part do you reckon that is?) is a sort of a wee fib. But one thing is true, & that is, that, of all things, I would like to go in & out of that sanctum of yours, and rummage amongst your manuscripts, and have *my* word to say about the divine philosophy, as it lies in its crude state—a chaos of wisdom—on your table. How I covet the honor of being tire-woman to this august lady! And, John, when you were tired, think how nice it would be, to throw yourself at ease upon a sofa, and leave me to take the pen and play Amannensis. How pleased I would be! And the printer too, wouldn't he rejoice to see p's & f's & g's & h's & e's behaving themselves, and not looking as if they had all had St Vitus's dance on the paper. Then, too, you would, sometimes, tho' rarely, of course, allow me to use my skill in adjusting the drapery of this new divinity; and altogether those morning jobs, over this little volume you talk of would be very delightful—if they could but be realized.

You ask some right hard questions of a poor piece of flesh & blood, & sin and pride like myself. I don't know how to answer them exactly, as they all require me to be placed in such circumstances as are entirely new to me, and as to which all that I could say wd be conjectural. But I fancy I can judge of the future, somewhat by the present and the past.

I am a little wayward in temper; but not discontented. I am ambitious; yet not greatly dependent for happiness upon the success of my ambitious projects. I would mourn over life-long ill success to you; but at the same time, if we loved one another very warmly, I think I could bear with oblivion, straightened means, a cottage etc.—I would have spasms of rebellion at it, it may be, quite violent; but the "even current" of every day life, if I were your wife, wd be guided by your plans & pursuits, whatever they were, & I would, soon learn to be content with them. But I can hardly judge what I might do. So much wd depend upon *you*, that I have thought less of these outside influences than I, perhaps, should do. But you can never doubt, how I will answer yr last question: I love you with all my heart. And if I am ever dissevered from you, it will be from reasons more stringent and influential than any yet offered as having grown out of your philosophy.

Wednesday 7 1/2 A.M.

Unless you are prepared to court the gossip of, I dont know how many different sections of this country, I advise you never to tell anything to old Mrs McClung, or any other Alexander in Virginia. They mean to do no harm; but they love to talk, & do talk without any restraint being imposed upon them by any acute perceptions or principles of delicacy. They are kind people, & trustworthy barring this one propensity.

You mistake, John; you don't write oftener, but just as often as I do. I think we keep an even balance now. Every day I look for Maggie's letter; & am every day disappointed it doesn't come.

Under Mr Carrington's counsel, I am taking steps for the settlement of my business, wh I hope will be successful. God bless you.

Affec'ly.
S.C.P. McDowell

Halifax,
Friday, June 13. 1856.

My *dear* John,

You have had no scarcity of letters this week—this, being the 3d I have written. But you seem not to tire of them; & I am more at leisure than heretofore—and, any how, it is one of my few pleasures, this of writing, to you.

You ought not to be very impatient with what you think my "*jealous* affection". It may be, just what you call it,—I don't know that it is—but it seems very natural that, with me, it should be so. And then John I am so sad, and have been so terribly tired, that it is not strange that I look at things thro' a cloud suspiciously. The great wonder is that I should have left any capacity for loving; or any for confiding.

But for the strength & ardor of my affection for you, my heart might well have been an extinct volcano. Sometimes I am almost ready to wish it would burn out & leave me an impassive being. But, I believe there is no such thing as making one's heart "fire-proof",—unless, indeed I could be changed into a man. Oh! by the bye I forgot to tell you *why* I would like to be a man. I won't tell you all the reasons, for they say "a woman's reasons always make up in number what they want in weight", but I'll tell you some.—1st—Men are intellectually, of a higher order of beings than women. 2d—They are more useful—have a wider range for the exercise of all their powers. 3d They are independent—as women never are in this country without loss—4th—but I won't tell you any more.

When Lilly was a little thing—indeed until she was 8 or 10 years old, she was crazy to be a boy, and called herself "Willie", and would snatch up Tom's hat & coat whenever she could get a chance. I don't wish she had been as I've had the care of her; but if she had been she would have been the cleverest boy of the name by far.

Do you think if I had been a man & had fallen any where near you in this world, you would have liked me at all—that is supposing I had as a man, the mental & moral characteristics you perceive now? but I wouldn't be content to be that sort of a man. I would be something sterner and more resolute & more persistent & every way superior. Yet as I am a woman, I try to make the best of it, and bear all that is to be borne in such a lot patiently, if not as gracefully as I would do, if I were entirely content with it.

Do you know, John, in one of your letters recently you spoke of your great wish that "we could live one year of simple affection together", as if at the end of that time you would be perfectly willing to send me to Heaven, but hadn't the least notion of leaving this earth so soon yourself! I rebelled right at the moment, and wondered if you were entirely demented.

Isn't it amazing what a quantity of trash I can write you, and often too when I feel as sombre as possible.

I get sad in spite of everything. As soon as the freshness of people & things wears off, which it does in a little time, I sink down, down. By the use of reason & the influence of higher considerations I sometimes wind up my spirits like a watch; but they run down before the 24 hours are gone. I get to work & am as busy as if my life depended upon what I as doing; but the job finished, my spirits are done too. I have no interest in people either—scarcely enough, when I'm talking to them, to keep my thoughts civilly present. They are pleasant enough, no doubt, if I could but be attracted to them. Sometimes I get much interested in the subject I am talking of, and perceive from the countenances of others that my animation is attractive to them; & my enthusiasm contagious—but they don't wake me up often if ever.

All this is wrong.—And then John, I am objectless in life. My nature is somewhat enterprizing & adventurous—and a thing undertaken, is pursued with energy, and I suffer for want of real occupation upon which to set these qualities to work. I often think of *what* I am to do; and arrive at no conclusion. Everything is empracticable that my mind suggest. And I am just running thro' the days and weeks doing nothing. I am of no earthly account to any human being so far as I can see. You wd be far happier if you had never seen me. & Lilly—yes, it may be, I *am* some little use to her just now; but if we both live a year or so longer I'll be of none. No doubt, if I ever get to Heaven, I shall know why I have been so troubled & tortured here—but I want to know about it right now, this minute, that I may have more patience under it. And yet, I don't know—I wouldn't know either, for I might be less patient than I am now. And I want to be submit, as a true christian woman should, to whatever is sent upon me, for, in truth, I have no reason for complaint under all my troubles.

And besides I have not a few blessings even in the midst of my sorrows. But John, I think I would exchange all the things about me that others covet for a quiet happy home. People tell me & I can't help knowing it, for I'm not blind, that the world thinks me vastly cleverer than most women. I think it's mistaken in the extent to which it goes, but if I were the most sublime of geniuses, with this woman's heart, I'd have no hesitation in sacrificing the genius, if that cd purchase the calmer & steadier & obscurer & purer pleasures that such a home as I want wd give. If you loved me the better for being highly gifted, tho' I don't think men like clever wives as a general thing, why I'd be ambitious to be a—Queen of Sheba—no—I wouldn't be that—I never did like that woman—with her dull grand, Miss Martineau style with her old political economy—but a Sappho—or, O! now I've got it! a Hypatia—I'd be Hypathia—that lovely Greek philosopher, and then I'd suit your taste pre-cise-ly.[66]

But John, about your book. Are you not in too great a hurry to publish? Suppose you lay it aside after it is ready for publication for awhile, and then throw the whole subject out of your mind for some months until your thinking powers get entirely free from any pressure & are strong again; then pick up your Mss and revise it carefully. It may be yr own mind will be in a condition to play Critic upon it then, & may be of valuable aid to you.

I fancy, you may have fallen into the error of having first set up to [illegible] a *theory* upon this particular branch of philosophy, and then have made all your search for the means of *fortifying your positions*—instead of making your search to be for *the truth*, in advance, & indeed in defiance of any theory. I have the idea of what I want to tell you in my mind; but I fear I have not made it appear to you.

However a book, upon so grave & abstruce a science as the one you have chosen, ought not to be hurried before the public.—it ought not to be sent hot from the steam of yr own brain into the press,—but laid away to cool first—If you'd keep at it long enough to add a wrinkle to yr brow it wd promise more,

---

66. The Queen of Sheba paid Solomon a visit in 1 Kings 10:1–13. Harriet Martineau (1802–1876), English writer. Sappho (seventh century B.C.), Greek lyric poetess. Hypatia, a neoplatonic philosopher and teacher in Alexandria in the late fourth and early fifth centuries, famous for her beauty and tragic death.

than if it is so hastened as to have the fresh ink upon its pages blurred by the hands of the type-setter.

I've written upon these scraps accidentally.

Yours Affec'ly
S.C.P. McDowell

Princeton June 13th 1856.

My darling Sally,

I have been thinking of you a great deal. If I did not feel so much like your husband I would feel more like your father. I do mourn over you so in everything that is giving you pain & disquiet. You have a right to know that you have won my entire affection. *How* you have done it I can't altogether tell, but the fact seems to be the thing you chiefly desire to know, & I do mourn, my sweet Child, when you needlessly vex yourself about a thing that is so apparent. And yet I know, & this is what I have been thinking about, that if you *were* my daughter I would have anxieties about a relation such as that which you sustain to me, & it is by throwing myself into this sort of fancy that I arrive a little at the anxieties that you have all along expressed:

You feel that a long engagement is perilous—that if a relation, usually of few months, is extended into as many years there is fearful danger that something may occur to interrupt our relation, you feel that I am exposed all this time to some other affection, you feel that I am sacrificing the endearments of a wife & a guardian for my children at a time & for a length when such endearments would seem specially necessary & that I am in fact condemning myself not to marry & that with many ways of reasoning myself out of it by the idea that my remaining faithful can be of no benefit to you, may be a harm to my children & could best be adjusted by the earliest acceptance of your many offers for a release,—that you are obliged to leave me away & exposed to many other temptations of society & that you can never know when my carefully concealed defection begins first to seek for itself a path away from my hastily found obligations. These all pass in review before me about my poor darling daughter, Sally McDowell & show how she vexes *herself* about the chances of this engagement. Now, Darling, I have been thinking of all these things. I have been longing for some path to bring them all to an end. I would marry you in some secret interview & really bring in some trustworthy witness to attend the ceremony if I did not thin[k] such a procedure rash in view of certain chances as for example *my* becoming offensive to you in which case the bond would be intolerable & would be different from usual marriage. I know, Darling, you dont tell me all the workings of your trouble because a certain womanly pride keeps you from some avowals—as for example how you fear to be seen again as engaged to me lest in some subsequent year the public should see I had deserted you & how you shrink from pouring out upon me your ardours lest having told me unguardedly of all your love I should put you to shame some day by throwing it all back upon yourself. Now, Darling, I'll tell you what I will do. When I see you Ill make you put your arms round my neck & give yourself up to me in actual consecration. I'll make you feel that you are relieved from the odium of holding me to a hard bargain because I have asked you [to] do so (that is, if you think it hard—&, Darling, *I* think it hard in some respects). I'll ask you to grant me *the fresh devotion of trusting to my faithfulness* just as some poor women do with feebler bonds even than ours, & we'll enter upon some sort of new relation—it shall be the firmest possible short of actual marriage—it shall place you, Darling as the very bond & mistress of my destiny & it shall admit of but one possible release that is, a condition in which we hated each other & would look upon the last impossibility of a release as a horrible oppression. I mean, Sally, a solemn oath to each other to consider ourselves fixed in each others keeping, but with that one exception. Now what you are waiting to hear out of all this is that *I love you enough to do this*. I love you passionately. I am satisfied now as to your love. I am an obstinate man. I know my endurance. As long as you *live for me* I am yours. *I could not release myself*. You hold me invincibly as long as you choose to love me. I am constituted not to love another as long as *I am sure* of a cherished affection. And as to your being anxious so long as you will pour upon me the treasures of your heart it is idle folly in view of the very statutes of my nature. But, Darling, I want you to do for me all you can for I resign much in living without you. I resign much for you & your children in delaying our marriage & sacrificing to our children's fame the pleasures of our history. And Sally, I want you to be kind to me. I want you to tell me all your love even when you think your pride suffers. I want you never again to say you are "hampered" in speaking of your passion but to feed my delight the exquisiteness of which I cannot unveil to you when you love me with passionate affection. Moreover I want you to submit— to my authority. What do you think of that Sally? You know I am almost your husband dearest—& have been so, both in time & near relation. And now I will give you an instance. <u>I want you to write to me every other day from this time.</u> I can almost say with truth that I have been angry at you for your long delays. I think I have never felt so dissatisfied with you about any act of yours. You have found me writing near sixty more letters & lately I have written in order to relieve sad feelings on your part I have written when you have written me none. You say you like to write. I dislike it & am relieved by any omission. I dont want to burden you with letters. I want it to be a pleasure, else the letters will be marked with the appearance of constraint, but, Darling, "postal arrangements" are not so hard as any failing of a letter & such a little note as I have just received is not any easier to send to the Post Office than a good long letter such as you ought to write. I love you with all my being & so wrought on is my life & so wrought in the mould of your influence that your letters are my *blood*. I feel it when they have been insufficient just as much as tho' I were fainting with hunger. And Darling, do at last cast away all reserves. Why be shrinking & calculating to your very husband when you are lying in his bosom. Tell me all your dreams of me, why you love me, what you hope about me, what you picture about the future & what you quarrel with in the past & be my own fond & confiding wife just as I am your

> *Own Husband*
> *Jno Miller.*

P.S. Dont forget now. Its my desire that you write every other day. Let's see if you will assume the relation of an obedient wife.

Halifax,
Monday, June 16. 1865.

My *dear John,*

I am very uneasy about my Sister Mary, who has within a few days returned from a visit to Dr Smith of Baltimore whom[67] she went on to consult about a neuralgic affiction, as we thought of the neck, from which she has suffered for a year or more. He gives a different opinion from ours, & I think pronounces unfavorably in regard to it. I am going off, as soon as I can to see her. I would have gone this morning but Nib & her little boy came on Saturday, & as Mac was threatened yesterday with convulsion I fear to leave him (or his Mother rather) to-day. It may be however that the Dr will give so cheering an opinion of him when he comes that I shall be able to go this afternoon.

I shall be gone only two or three days. Nib is so easily upset by anxiety and apparent danger that, I shall hurry back.

I am not very bright myself this morning.

Uncle Robert Breckinridge is opening the way for me to have a settlement of my business with Uncle Tom, by calling peremptorily for a settlement of his children's. I am glad of it—it will be a great relief to me. Mr Carrington has been urging me by all means to have it done by my own Agent, but Uncle Robert's notice to me of his proceedings has just come in to stop individual effort on my part. On the whole I am encouraged about my business. Dr Lindsley writes me an unexpectedly favorable opinion of my Washington lot; & I am hoping to hear something cheering from those in Louisville. I shall probably sell them all, with the Military in the Fall, & might hope to realize from those 3 pieces of property $18 or 20.000.

Mr Carrington is very kind & helpful, and anxious to serve me; and I love him very much. However, Mr Massie too, is at work for me just now, very kindly.

I write in a hurry. You must learn not to think that it is improper in you to be interested in my property matters. I shall be greatly agrieved if you don't.

> *With all my heart Yours*
> *S.C.P. McDowell*

---

67. McDowell then wrote "you" but failed to scratch it out. Dr. Nathan Ryno Smith (1797–1877) was Baltimore's most prominent physician and surgeon.

Princeton June 16th 1856.

Here I am, back from a ride with Mother. I got a letter on Friday & I got a letter on Saturday & I got a letter to day, & I'm as happy as a prince. Kiss me, Sally. How *can* you let me sit looking at you so long & not fold me to your lips & kiss me? Sit nearer to me, Dearest. See here: put your hand under your pretty boddice & feel where your heart beats. Now, Darling, I want to ask you about some things that are under there. Tell me all I ask you. Tell me, first of all, how that little heart of yours manages to talk so contradictorily. First, you say you love me *Oh!* so much. And yet in the next sentence you say, You wish you were a man. Now, Sally, you have still not answered me that. How can you wish yourself a man when your highest passion is to love me as your husband. Tell me, Darling. I can see how you could have *once* wished you were a man. But now if your passion is that absorbing thing, how can you avoid thanking God every hour you breathe that he should have loved you & me so much as to make you a woman. That is the first question.

Now the second is, what that little hypocrite of a heart means by beating so lovingly against my bosom when the very next moment it sets you to writing this sentence, "If you were to write 'damnable heresy['] I wouldnt marry you". That's where the starved passion that you have speaks out. Then if I were a poor lost apostate, with no friend, & the church blackening around me & my soul in danger that loving heart would flutter quite away from me & oaths & troths & sweet memories—all—would be just nothing. Ha! Is that the way I love you Darling?—

Again, you say, "You <u>think</u> you *detect* a <u>little</u> restlessness about it <u>even</u> now;" that is my passionate little sweet-heart there beating under your boddice *thinks* it detects "*juss a little*," after six months separation, when I fear it will be continued to near a year. Bravo! What a tender heart that must be! Dear Sally, I often wondered what you meant by saying you were so volcanic but now I see. The fact is I wonder how you restrain such a love as that at all.

Again—however—Poor little heart. Kiss me Sally—& I'll promise not to say anymore. Now tell me also—What do you mean when you say your love has had so many trials that I know nothing about; &, Darling, (Remember, I never feel that I must be *polite* to you. The person I love best on earth I lose all courtesy for in certain things. For example, I wouldnt dare to ask anybody else what they meant by a sentence they had began—[&] scratched out in a letter) but Dearest, what did you mean when you said, "It will be from reasons more stringent than any yet offered or those originated in Mr Massie's"—What do you mean by Mr Massie &c?

Again, for I mean to make a Shorter Catechism out of these last letters. When you turn your miscroscope upon me & keep thinking as you say you do all day. Do you think its quite right to tell me at night when you come to write that your life is quite *objectless*. O Sally, I wish I was a woman & then I wouldnt have such a negligent & unflattering sort of a Dulcinea.[68] But good-bye. I'll forgive you if your own little heart will & when I write again Ill tell you all about the book. Write every other day. And write me just every now & then in your letters a sentence or two like this:—"Oh, John, how I do love you. You cant conceive how necessary you are to my existence. &c &c" & so good-bye, Darling,

Jno Miller.

As I past the book store yesterday, I thought of the green wax & lo! what a pretty substitute!

Princeton, June 17th 1856.

My Sweetest Sally,

I think writing is such a stupid business. If I had you here at my side, to look into your _____ Sally, what's the colour of your eyes. I don't think I ever observed. No matter, tho' if they were only here bending over your poor lover how much nicer it would be than this formal copper-plate sort of writing on this great big paper.

Dearest, I am so tried by this absence. I dont know why it is, but just at this time when I had supposed I should be in L. I find it almost *impossible* to endure our continued separation. I suffer much more than I did a month ago. Indeed I suffer poignantly. The sense of loneliness & desertion has become almost unsupportable & either because I am a little worse with long study or the powers of longer suspense are failing me, I find it impossible to make myself easy in this constant distance fr you.

At such times I do think our lot so hard a one. Sally, why did you marry? Why didn't you just forecast your horoscope better. I'm so mad at you. My star if you had just watched it a little would have saved you from all the troubles of your history.

My life settles itself more & more in a path in which with God's blessing much usefulness as I expect & that of a very high order seems more & more to be had for the labour.

When I wrote to you about that Kentucky cry, you must not give me the credit of being so humble as[69] at all to believe in it. Nor, Sally, do I think all your stories about me that you had collected together were quite in that solid phalanx you made them out to be. I think you were teasing me a little. I dont anticipate a certain sort of success with my book. I dont expect that I will *sell* or be popular. I should think it very strange if it did; but I think it will so far take root as to give me something to watch and cultivate afterward in the way of a public opinion. I think it is a question of industry now rather than of sudden or critical decision. I dont expect a certain sort of succeeding. And I have no expectation at all of any deciding failing.

---

68. The idealized woman with whom Don Quixote falls in love.
69. Miller repeated "as."

I wish you *were* here, Dearest. That implies now all I covet:—to dig into philosophy the rest of life & to have you near me in my lighter & more social hours. It was so good in you to wish to be Hypatia. Now, Darling, honour bright. Is that really your taste? I have thought you liked eloquence & strength rather than profoundness and nobleness of intellect. I wish you could do some writing for me now. I have finished the first two books of the volume & the third will be short. I wish you could copy what I have written so that I could send it for the prudence of the thing, to one or two friends to judge of it.

When I see you I want to throw our engagement into a more certain form. I mean to make your feelings more easy under it. I want to arrange so that you can speak of it more freely, & I want to speak of what I covet very much that you should seek a more Northern house & be nearer to me. What do you think of all this Sally. Instead of being uninterested about your business arrangements I have been thinking of them with trepidation & you vastly relieve me by *any probability* that you will be saved from pressing embarrassments.

Yours affly,
Jno Miller

Roanoke Parsonage
June 18. 1856.

My *dear John,*

Owing to a late start from Halifax, I did not reach here until 10 o'clock yesterday morning. I find Mary better than I had expected, but looking badly and obliged to lie down 20 out of the 24 hours of the day. Dr Smith's prescription is to ward off a spinal affection.

This afternoon or evening if the rain does not fall, & the river is not too full to cross, I go over to Mildendo (the residence of Mr Carringtons Mother) & thence to Susan's tomorrow morning. I regret to stay so short a time, for my visit to Mary has been a great treat to me.

Mr Ross is very kind & as cordial as I could expect him to be.

I received your letter of the 13th, the afternoon I came over, but have no time to attempt to answer it now.

I love you more & more, Dearest, the more I know you; tho' I won't flatter you by saying that I go as far [as] Dickens and make you out "next door, *but one* to a cherubim." But my very affection for you augments the pain I feel at my unfortunate circumstances. I am so grieved there should be anything about me that could be a source of trouble to you. My love for you demands that your wife should have all possible perfection; & that these demands are not met by nature, and that such attractions as may be acknowledged, are darkened by so much of sorrow, are both a distress to me. But I can't give you all I want to have—you must, therefore, be content with what I can give.

It is only to show you that I am coming in to your own measures that I write at all to-day. I wrote on Monday—this is Wednesday; so you see what a promising beginning I make. While Mary went out to look after her dinner, I contented myself to send you this short note.

Mary tells me she heard in Baltimore, that your Mother had said publicly, "that if our Marriage had been consummated (after that public explosion) she would never have allowed either of us to Come into her house again!" She might have *felt* so to me but I doubt whether she ever wd have expressed the feeling,—and disbelieve entirely that she would ever have spoken so of you. O! how my pride has suffered in so many thousand ways! I feel its coils about my heart until I bear the torture, & seem to myself too near the countenounce of the Laocoon.

Maggie wrote to me at Lexington, and the letter only reached me two or three days since. I didn't know the children were in Chester:—you never tell me anything in the shape of news, about them. I noticed a little girl in church the other day, whom I fancied *must* be like Maggie. I gazed at her with the greatest interest. I suppose the resemblance was to the picture of my flower-girl; & then what struck me very much was that the child's eyes—so large, & bright, & dark recalled to me all that I had particularly remembered of Maggie's Mother so strongly, that they seemed to be such as might belong to her child.

The child was beautiful—but not fair as Maggie may be—& with long dark curls hanging about her face which, too I believe, is unlike her.

God bless you. Affec'ly.
S.C.P. McDowell

Halifax
Friday, June 20. 1856.

My *dear John*,

I wrote you a letter this morning—that is, it was the joint-product of a sleepy hour late last night & a hurried one after breakfast today, but as I found it could not be mailed till this evening, I wouldn't send it, but determined to write a fresh one for to-night's mail. So you see I have been honest, but unfortunate in coming up fully to your *requirement* of a letter every other day. I hope my letter from Charlotte will reach you; tho' yesterday after I left Mary's I found the Post Office closed, & had to trust my letter to the care of a gentlemanly looking boy whom I met half an hour after, to drop in the Office as he passed, when I hoped, breakfast being over, the P.M. wd have returned to his duty.

I reached here at noon, or about that, yesterday having my heart full of sorrow & fear about Mary. She looked so mournfully, and was so unwell & so lonely it makes me sad to think of her. The Parsonage is in the woods, & looks very desolate. I laughed & told her she looked to me as tho' she were "roughing it in the bush" sure enough. But she seems content with it; & if she were well wd be very happy. Mr Ross is a kind man—but I know I cd not love him with any sort of animation; but that's no proof, of course, that he isn't loveable: and if he'll make Mary happy, that's all I'll ask of him.

John, my own darling John, you do state my difficulties in our engagement very truly; and you do, most nobly meet & endeavor to reconcile me to them: and you do succeed in making me love you all the more for what you do. It may be poor pay, Dearest, but it seems to be the kind you ask, & it is a sort of pay which makes me feel the happier and richer in giving out. But, John, I think it a hard lot, as you say, that you've chosen, and my sense of generosity reproaches me for permitting you to bear it, especially when I fear that after years it may be, of lonely self-denial on your part, I may not be able to meet your hopes and prove to you just such a comfort as you would need, and as my affection, so exacting from myself for you, as it has grown to be, would demand. And then too, notwithstanding all you do & say—I can't get rid of this strong element of suspicious anxiety in my affection; nor keep my mind from working away upon its long-established distrust of tired human nature. If I loved you less, I imagine my anxiety would be less, alike as to the reality & extent & steadiness of your attachment to me. But I love you so much that yr love seems a necessity to me; & I long for a full & constant flow of it with insatiable longings. And while I am asking this of you, I am claiming from myself for you everything that can gratify yr taste & justify yr affection, & be worthy your care & tenderness, and am worried & distressed to find my claims not fully answered.

But, John, when, as within the range of possibilities that might please me, you even mention such a thing as a private marriage, you can't think how you sting my pride, & how my nature revolts at the supposition. In the present condition of things I want you bound to me by affection; and I want to feel that there *can* be no stronger bond than that: & I want to believe, away down in the very bottom of my heart, that in that bond there *can* be no decay, at least, this side the grave. And further, John, I want you to feel & know that your honor & your high name & your usefulness are all alike dear to me, & that my affection however mad it may seem, *can* ask nothing that would seriously jeopard any of these things, or be inconsistent with them;—indeed it cd not be pleased or promoted by any sacrifice of them on yr part. I couldn't love you—I would scorn myself if I could, & would hate you if *you* were willing I should love you without fully respecting you. Besides, John, you must recollect, that I have become so identified with you, that you ought not to speak as if, in this marriage matter, I hold a separate & independent existence. If our engagement, in the face & with a full sense of the dangers of it, fully & freely & frequently discussed between us, is yet of choice, & from a strong affection which we think, or hope will over-ride these dangers, continued, then we stand on equal terms, & you have no right to propose to me any scheme which may, protect my affection *apparently*, but not maintain my position, (as I think a private marriage could not)—nor have I, any right to risk your honor & usefulness by any exactions from a strong & restless, but most warm & anxious attachment. I don't know that I make you understand me—I wish I were near enough to talk to you.

Of some of our difficulties, I have taken a different view from yours—but as my opinion has never been made up with entire decision, I have submitted to yours,—not always unquestioningly and unmurmuringly, but silently. And as long as I choose to be silent, John, you mustn't ask any questions. I love you with all my heart, & I confide in you with all the faith of my nature, which I have told you has a certain amount of distrust in it—not a large one though, and I respect you fully. Now, Darling, this three-fold cord binds me to you with a strength which only unworthiness in you can relax, and gives you a power over me, greater far than you dream of, & so tremendous as I view it, that I beg John you will pray fervently to be directed & restrained in the use of it; & I too will pray that I may not be so weak as to allow my love to you to be a blind passion. I want it to be a blessing & not an evil to us—& in the dangers and delays & temptations that open upon the future to us, I am so earnest that we may each be an aid & not a clog to the other. As ours is a tried affection, I am anxious it shall be a worthy one; and that it be so, we should be honest & frank in all intercourse—without annoying reserves & secret ill-feeling—and each, with a high sense of responsibility holding as a sacred trust the affection & honor of the other. Don't you agree with me?

And now, my own precious,[70] John, if you require me "to submit to your authority" which I've been doing by the by for some time past, won't you yield a little [to] my reason and judgment? You know I love you. You know if I do that I can't be inconsiderate of your feelings, but, on the contrary, will be eager to gratify you & spare you pain, then why make me feel that you will take no excuse for a delay in a letter which under circumstances that you can't judge of or comprehend, may seem proper to me? You *will* leave me some liberty of judgment in that matter, wont you? And you will take my good purposes on trust, sometimes when they are not apparent to actual vision? And you will love me all the time? And won't be suspicious about my love to you? And you will be careful about that new Primer of Metaphysics you are about to put into the hands of our grey headed philosophers? And, above all, John you will be a good christian man, with aspirations & exertions beyond popular favor & scientific fame? I am so scared about the book—& its heresies. By the way I only said I wouldn't marry you if you taught & imbibed "damnable heresy". I didn't say I wouldn't love you, & would draw away from you. I meant what I said—for I couldn't put myself & perhaps others, outside of God's covenant even for the greatly coveted pleasure of being nestled by your side as your wife.

But ain't you tired with such a long letter?—Goodbye.

Mr Massie's name, I think must have been written in my letter to you when I nodded over it, for I was surprised to see it where it was myself—& certainly has no thought of him in the connection in which I was writing. I never speak to him

70. After "precious" McDowell wrote "little man" but then put a single line through it.

of you or our affairs & have not since you left Lexington except incidentally once or twice in the way of business—once I remember, in connection with Cantey's marriage-contract. Wasn't there a good deal of scratching out, just in the same lines in the letter in which the name was? I recollect, how sleepy I felt when I wrote a sentence or two just there. However—I am done.

> *God bless you. Affec'ly*
> *S.C.P McDowell.*

Halifax
June 21. 1856.

My *dear John,*

I foresee I shall not be able to write to you on Monday morning as I generally do, for a new nephew came upon us at noon today, who with his Mother, will take all our time & care for some days to come.[71] He is a fine fellow & these first 10 or 12 hours of his existence have been entirely comfortable to him & to us.

I am getting somewhat impatient to get home, & shall go, I think Saturday or the Monday after. The weather is becoming intensely warm; & I think I am thinner than when I came here, tho' I am feeling better. My Spirits wear upon me, & I can't keep them in a healthy condition.

I look for Lilly on Wednesday or Thursday, and am much comforted at the thought of taking her home with me, tho' Willie & Marie Breckinridge will pay me a visit, & relieve my solitude somewhat, I suppose early in July.[72]

I want to see you, John, very much; but the thought of your coming is full of sadness to me, nevertheless. But I'm sad any how, and when a little fatigued as at present, find it natural enough to sink down to a low key. It is a poor compliment to you, these low spirits—but I can't help it. If I were a man I should escape half my troubles. But good night—I'll see what a little rest & sleep will do for me.

The fact of my life being objectless is not inconsistent with my loving you—tho' an objectless life if I didn't love you would be a more tranquil & passive one, and I'm beginning to think that perhaps, freedom from pain is happiness.

> *Monday morning.*

I now think I shall leave here the last of this week, and beg you will have a letter waiting to meet me at home on Monday evening. So regulate your writing that I shall have one on Thursday at this place. Altho' I am impatient to get home, I rather shrink from it too. I look back to the last 3 or 4 weeks there as I do to the crossing of the Appomattox bridge, with a shudder, and a desire never to be obliged to do the same thing again.

---

71. Charles Scott Carrington (1856–1898).
72. McDowell's "young cousins," William Campbell Preston Breckinridge and his sister, Marie Lettice Breckinridge (1836–1905).

The heat is intense. The walls of the house are warm to the touch, and a dress thrown upon a chair soon becomes too warm to put on again with any comfort. It will be cooler at home, & my eyes will have something green to rest upon. Tho' the flowers of this region are wonderfully abundant & beautiful, yet there is little or no grass.

Can't you suggest some employment for me. I am a beggar for work.

I had no letter from you Saturday, none the day before; but hope for one today.

Affectionately Yours,
S.C.P. McDowell

Princeton June. 23d [1856]

My Sweetest Darling Sally,

If you knew how easy it was to make your poor lover happy you would write such letters as I have just read all the time. My lovely daughter! I do love you so for your kindness to a poor old man. Sally, Dearest tell me how you came first to love me. You didnt love me in the *Straits*. And you didnt love me till I had quit Lexington. And you didnt love me when that proud letter came in which you gave me to understand you didnt care a baubee for me & when I sent back your letters. And you didnt seem to care *much* for me for a long long time. Come Sally, you say very righteously "we are to be honest & frank &c" "without annoying reserves &"—come now & tell all how your love arose when you *first* began to love me just a little & what you loved me for & what your experience was afterward & all; *do*, Sally, that's a good girl.

This letter has fairly intoxicated me with pleasure. So you do love me. Why didnt you tell me that long ago?

And yet here is the "white duck" again (Did you get that letter, Sally?) See what an exquisite courtesy—Listen—"And now, my own precious[73] John, if you require me to submit to your authority which I've been *doing by the bye*[74] for some time past; wont you yield a little to my reason & judgment?" (Not a particle. I've been trying that long enough.) "You know I love you" (Yes, that I admit) "You know if I do that, I cant be inconsiderate of your feelings (!) but on the contrary will be eager to gratify you & spare you pain (!!)["] "You *will* leave me some liberty"—(Indeed I shant.) "And you will take my good <u>purposes</u> on trust" (Yes, Darling, I've great practice in that) "even when they are not apparent to actual vision". "And you will love me all the time?" (I will if I cant help it.) "And wont be suspicious about my love to you?["] (I wont if I can help it.) "And you will be careful about that new Primer" (Now, Sally, thats none—) "I only said I wouldnt *marry* you if you imbibed & taught "damnable heresy" (by the way that's

---

73. As in her previous letter, he writes "little man" and then draws a line through it.

74. At this point, Miller placed a note and added at the bottom of the page, "I suppose the same that we mean in Jersey when we say, [']*giving a thing the go-bye*['] i.e. not doing it at all."

a pretty compliment to pay to my theory) "I couldnt put myself & perhaps others" (There it is, Sally. You're always preferring others to me. Besides how could your *not* marrying me keep you from "putting others outside of God's covenant?") "But aint you tired with such a long letter". (No Darling) "Writing to you is one of my few pleasures. Mr Massie's name must have been written when I nodded over my letter. I recollect how sleepy I felt." (Well, Darling, that's a peculiarity of yours. Talking to me is one of "your few pleasures," & do you remember how sleepy you used to get?)

But, Oh, Sally, what a shame to laugh at so sweet a letter. Come here; & kiss me. And never write me any other than just such a letter Darling, all the time.

I am going to write you a long answer some other time. This afternoon I have a head-ache. Your letters came both together to day. Your "gentlemanly boy" must have carried your letter a long time in his pocket for it is postmarked June 21st & smells strongly of tobacco. Dearest if you will "submit" in the matter of writing & I miss a letter at any time I will take for granted you have written & not wait till I receive a letter. I tho't I had told you about the children. The Bishop & Sarah (Mrs P.) made a descent upon us three Saturdays ago & carried them off bodily. Their grandmother (Benedict) has been complaining it seems of their staying too long with their grandmother here. I wish I had seen the little girl you speak of.

Oh. I came near forgetting. The story you heard about Mother is singularly untrue. Mother rather piqued me at my submission. And tho' when everything was going smoothly she uttered some dissatisfaction, yet when others were turning against me she said, that, if *she* were in my place she would have the thing referred to the *courts* of the church quietly & prudently. There is *nothing* to answer to Mary's rumour.

Good-bye. Excuse me for this foolish letter.

Yours tenderly.
JM.

Princeton, June 24th 1856.

My dearest Sally,

I must be very much in love for there is a sort of *aroma* about your last letter that makes the memory of it a constant enjoyment. I find myself quite childlike in my merriment & when I come to consider what it is that makes some trifle amuse me so, I find the great artery that is supplying so much good spirits comes strait from the region of your letter.

Darling, I *have* had something to complain of heretofore. You know you have *told* me you were "hampered" in expressing all your affection. That is, I take it, that that little heart of yours was always out like a wary sentinel afraid of the least *abandon* of endearment, lest that terrible catastrophe of our some day ceasing our relation to each other should after all shame all your liberality. Now Darling, I'll tell you what I deliberately think. I think the least you can do for so fond a lover as I am is to abandon every reserve to cast yourself in my arms without one feeling of care

& to deliver yourself over to my embrace without one thought of whether we ever can be separated. You see, Darling, you have always been on your guard against me. You watch your words & measure out your expressions of fondness as tho' I were a sort of wild Arab; or rather as if you & I were diplomatists seated at a board & were weighing each expression as it falls. Now Dearest I invite you to all the freedom of the most entire & wife-like reliance &, Sally, *if I invite you to this* dont you see that I deliberately take the responsibility of it; & throw myself under the mightiest obligations of honour to understand my own passion & be sure of the firmness of its texture. Nay, Darling, I *beg* you to be my own dear daughter, that I may fold you to my bosom without one thought of your feverish anxieties, that I may have you living upon my honour, nay even forgetting that there is such a word in the entireness of your childlike consecration, so that I may have one person at least in this weary world speaking to me without restraint & pouring out on me the treasures of her faith without so much as asking whether we *could* have an independant being.

Darling, I have a picture of a woman that I would so much like to be engaged to. She should write letters just as an ivy climbs upon an oak throwing the tendrils of her affection everywhere wherever they might choose to cling. Not numbed & shrinking & seeming to climb upon the oak with the fewest possible supports but throwing its wild arms round & round the tree & burying it in the weight of its luxuriance.

Darling, I wish you & I could change places for a week. You'd see what an era would arrive in correspondence.

Besides, Sally, do you know I have a sort of tyrant notion that the lady should *articulate* nearly all the fondness. Men are so stupid. And then they hate to write so. I think it would be so fine to live with a sort of stupid ecstacy & have your wife or your affianced bride feed you with affection just as the Esquimaux' wifes do with seals flesh. I dont know how to express it. I wouldnt have the woman love the most. Oh no! I wouldnt have the woman volunteer the soonest. But I have a sort of feeling like this that just as an Indian sits in his cabin & smokes while his wife does the corn so it would be so nice for me to sit in my study & write niver a letter & you, now that we have settled into staid every day lovers,— hoe the corn of our affections. But Alas! I am like all poor starved beggars, the moment I get a little crumb of comfort in the shape of a long delayed & single feast of affection I feel like a prince & have all sorts of tyrannous & exacting tho'ts come into my head.

So, Darling, if you'll love me half as fondly as I love you & write me half as fondly in your letters I'll be *a king* & be more than satisfied.

Yours fondly
Jno Miller.

Do you love me?

Promise me Sally, when you write next that you never will have a reserved feeling again but will give me your *entire* confidence & pour your whole heart without reserve into your letters.

Halifax,
Wednesday June 25. 1856

Dear John,

I wonder if I have been so obscure in speaking of my movements as to have led you to think it was the Monday past instead of next Monday that I was to be at home! I can't think of any other reason for the failure of your letters during the last four or five days.

I have telegraphed Lilly at Wash- to meet me in Rich'd Friday evening where I shall be, if nothing unforeseen happens to delay or prevent my going. Can't you contrive a letter to me there, addressing it to me at the Exchange Hotel, care of R. W. Hughes Esq for it may be, a little business with Mr Hughes, or a detention on Lilly's part may keep me in Rich till Monday morning.[75] And I want a letter very much now, & don't want to think of waiting for it a day longer than possible.

You must be content with short notes now—for I am a good deal wearied with hot weather & nursing. Our little Charlie is a nice fellow, and very sweet to me in all his unconsciousness and redness.

Mac, who is here, is however my great pet & play thing—He talks slowly, but makes out to tell me he loves me "a heartful."

Somehow when yr letters fail, I find [I] have nothing to write to you about—my mind seem to dry up—I half wish my heart would too.

Mr Logan writes me a pretty good account of my Louisville property—but I'm going to sell any how.

What think you of Fremont for President?[76] I, who know him, think it the greatest farce upon earth—or as Morgan once told me of a man who failed some how in his contract with him; "Why Madam, it's ridiklous—it's a burlesque on human nature."

I shall write hereafter as I have time until I get to Richmond.

With all my heart Yours
S.C.P. MD.

Halifax,
Friday June 27. 1856.

My dear John,

I scratch off a note which I hope to mail this evening in Rich'd. I set off in an hour or two but take a half hour to meet my regular writing engagement with you, about which, after all you *are* unreasonable.

75. Robert W. Hughes (1821–1901), a Richmond attorney and editor of the *Examiner* from 1850 to 1857.

76. John Charles Frémont (1813–1890), Republican candidate for president in 1856, was married to McDowell's cousin, Jessie Benton Frémont (1824–1902).

There was an unaccountable delay in yr letter of the 17. or 19th. I couldn't well make out its date, for you said *17th* & the P.M. 19th. It only reached me Wednesday. I was glad it came then. Do, John contrive me the MS you want copied. I shall want something to do, & that will suit me very well. If these mss are not *too precious*, you might send them to me by Express—& I could return them in the same. Taking the precaution of not pre-paying in either case.

Look here;—what do you mean by tearing my letters to pieces as you do! I always did think you couldn't bear the least indulgence, and were the most easily spoiled of all mortals. Take care, or I'll bring you down to low diet again. It is best for you any how, as it keeps you properly humble.

I don't know when I began to love you. Cousin John says from the beginning, which I don't think quite true. I don't know what I love you for either, unless I account for it, as a rhyming Alphabet long ago rung thro' my brain has done it;—

"I love my love with an *E*

Because my love loves me."

No I dont specially admire Hypatia—but would choose to be like her only because I fancied you wd love me the more for the resemblance. But you should love me that I am the opposite to you in all things—philosophy in chief.

I shall add a line if not too tired tonight in Rich'd.

Meantime—adieu.

Richmond

Here I am, defeated in all my plans, Lilly not having come—nor Nannie either. I am worried as you may be sure but have determined to wait here until Monday morning & then run the risk of meeting Lilly at Gordonsville. I shall be here by myself—Mr Hughes leaving with his family tomorrow. Now if I was a man, I could have avoided this scrape.

O John; I do long for you so much sometimes. I find myself turning to you, when I tire of everybody else, with a feeling of resting myself in your love. And then at such times it wd be such an unspeakable comfort to sit by you quietly in this sense of support & shelter, that the fact of belonging to you wd give. And I do need that—that is—it wd be such a luxury to me, for I am so very, very tired of always living a strained & exposed life. But good night—it must be morning tho!—God bless you, Darling,

S.C.P. McDowell.

Princeton June 27th 56.

You will have found by this time, Dearest, that from falling into my old habit, I waited till your letter came & therefore failed to write till your Cub Creek note had taken its five or six days to reach me. I am sorry for your suspence, but have hardly yet learned that my letters are so dear to you.

I have five or six things I want to write to you of. The fact is I am never at a loss for something & tho' I write you many a foolish letter yet, Darling, my love is like these strawberries that have been bearing so prodigiously in our garden. My thought seems hardly to touch a spot upon that paper that it does not branch out into innumerable roots from which, fresh things come up to be talked about.

If my letters are necessary "to keep your mind from drying up," may it not be true, Darling, that my love sustains both yours & mine & that if my love should for a moment falter (an experience that would seem to me very queer) yours would droop & we should bury both in the same grave. Is it so, Dearest. If I should treat you badly would you bear with me. Or if I should waver a little would you try to win me back again or would you send me a cold & last repulse?

I have such a profusion of things to say I dont know what to do. I haven't patience to wait for successive letters & yet I cant say them all in this so I'll jot a little at them just, & you must understand me from very little.

First, as to some of your troubles. Your ill health terrifies me. Linked as I am with you it seems to me as tho' I were your jailor & you were grieving & pining under a heavy dungeon. And when you say, first, that you would be more happy if you didnt love me because you would be more passive &, second, that you are under higher idea of our right to marry & therefore more restless & tried than you otherwise would be at our separation from each other (because, my Love, that is what you mean when you tell me to "ask you no questions") it makes me feel like a poor scrupulous monk torturing myself by unnecessary steps & torturing another by the relation into which I have seduced her. I do quake sometimes at the thought of your losing health & I do beg you Sally to be cheerful for my sake. I mean to cease writing lugubrious letters & *I mean to make it perfectly evident to you first that you __cannot__ marry me or any one now & second that you have given yourself to me in circumstances in which I know we have been disappointed but in which you have grown to be the treasure of my life & in which you have inspired me with a passion which grows with the vigor of a life long & certain principle.* I may not ever marry you. I feel no compunction at standing in the way of another first because with the feeling of a tyrant I take possession of you __for myself__ & cant dream of any one possessing you. If *I* were tied & *you* were free I would have that same feeling:—"Sally must wait *for me.* She is my arm or my leg or my whole self: God made her for me. It is absurd to think of her in the arms of another":—but second, because I know you cant marry one any sooner. I stand in your way as concerns another marriage in no other sense than as a real friend: for by stopping up the channels of affection & interposing in the way of any other passion that you might have conceived—Darling—I have been your angel—holding you up in my arms lest you dashed your foot against a stone.[77] Now I say this with some shame for it was I who told you "you might marry" & that "I despised public

77. A reference to Matt. 4:6.

opinion" & all that & as concerns the breaking up of your peace & quiet, of that I might feel remorse. But as concerns my being the wolf in the manger appropriating a lovely creature & keeping her in a life long suspense, of that I feel no remorse at all. I hold you just in the state in which you ought to be, and your children some day will rise up & call me blessed for these years of denial & suspense which I am mortified to think I so strongly once protested must end.

Now I want to tell you of some of the things you feel. You feel that all this time we could be living peacefully together & you feel cruelly the thought that we should be bearing (if unnecessary) so much distress. You paint often the scene, if we should have married & come to the North & appropriated the friendships that we had & put all this in the past; & the pleasure that starts up half tortures you & you chide me as the cause of the delay. Now, Darling, I want some day to take you in my arms & in a few quiet hours go over all these events, go over the difficulties of your life. *I long to marry you.* The thought that I <u>might</u> has been the rock that obstinately I have been chafing. I long after you with the most torturing regrets. But I have passed the point when I think of such a thing, & all the idea I am conceiving now, is, how sweet you are to me! How sweet you are solely in your love! How sweet you are as my poor banished bride. How dear you are in this long wilderness of suspense. And how raptured & yet tortured I am to think of our connection. <u>*Now, Dearest, I am willing to put our bonds solely on the ground of my mere entreaty.*</u> That is the honorable ground. I am willing to put my arms round your neck & beg you not to forsake me. If you say, "the suspense is too great: the dangers are too terrible, the exposures such as I speak of to your power are too terrible & too often repeated to be tho't of for long years together: it is unwise in me & a dangerous sacrifice of my peace & my safety," I am willing, Darling, to take your hand in mine & beg it as a sacrifice *for me*—to *let* these years of your life be the victims of suspense as a pure tribute of your bounty to one who perfectly adores you. Darling, if *I* were the hindrance, if *I* were the person who was sealed with these painful embarrassments & were unable to marry you & yet had won you & you were recovering from the dismal mistake, would you desert me? Or, Dearest, would you utterly repel me if I then tried to awake your pity & move you to the dreary waste of waiting for me thro' the long years for our expected marriage? I *would* beg you? I would not think it dishonorable to resort to any entreaty to force you to yield? I would have no compunction for engrossing you & absorbing your affection even if it condemned you to long years of dreary engagement. And if you ask me Why? I answer, Because I have reached a pass where I cant think of you as in the arms of another & where it seems to me as even romantically my honor to guard you for myself & to keep you from even the dream of any other alliance. The fact is I think man's love is holier than woman's in one sense. It absorbs & absolutely embodies with it its own object & like the Roman Catholic Religion it seems to consider all means commendable not to imitate indeed but to keep in existence even an ill gotten

& disappointed possession.

Now, Darling, you feel several things. You feel that I may seduce you into farther & farther affection & then when you love me passionately & well & have given all up in a thousand letters of confession & have formed the habit of emptying upon me from its depths just wildly & madly your affection that some day we will be dissevered. Yet how you dont entirely picture; but you think of me in the embrace of another & you think of me as carrying away in absolute recollection vows & wild speeches of your all abandoning attachment. Now, Darling, I want to say of this I will not *take an oath* that this shall never be the case for that you say would humble you & "sting your pride," but I mean to take another oath, *I declare as God make me & as I hope for mercy at his great Account* that it is my solemn purpose, as far as I can divine what my purpose is, to wait for you till we can happily marry & *that I am led to this purpose* by several things either one of which would be enough to be its foundation & among them this—*that I selfishly desire to live absorbed in this inevitable & extraordinary passion & that I am entirely convinced that nothing will unseat it but your own long continued indifference*.

Now, Darling, what could you have more? You are tormented with the thought that we *might* marry. Now trust me, till I can see you, & talk with you of all my wrestlings with this subject & you will find that it is not the case.

Now if I could settle it that we would always be attached; & if I could convince you that a postponement is *necessary*; & if I cease to write dismal letters & give myself up to cheer & comfort you, cant I at least make it true that you shall be happier than before our engagement? & then as to my coming to see you would you not have less fear of that if all these other points were settled & it was the plan of your life to wait patiently as you are?

Well, another thing I want to speak to you about is my book. You know me now better privately than you do publicly & your ambition makes you anxious to know what a public character you have linked yourself with. Dearest, I am sorry I have spoken so slightingly to you of myself & that I ever showed you that letter from Spence. You have got a wrong view of your husbands character. A weeks life in Phila would give you perfectly another. Spence's own statements to me when I saw him were of a different cast. I spoke carelessly of myself, for we were soon to be married & you would hear for yourself,—but as it is, you may spend years under foolish untrue ideas. My book has not the heretic & eccentric dangers that I have tempted you to suppose. I am very careful of my own reputation & am this moment as much on the high road of all I ever aimed at & as much on my guard as ever in my life. I am distinct in my plans, have no foolish notions about being a recluse, but should return in a day to the pulpit if I thot it necessary. I deliberately think it never will be. My frame is not robust & I can preach better to a different audience. My book is nearly finished so nearly so that I had a plan (when you asked for something to do) of sending to you at Lexington & asking you to copy the first forty seven chapters or short sections. (There are but fifteen more.) I wanted you to see it & tho' it is rather dry for your reading I wanted you to catch a glimpse of it as safe & respectable. Indeed I have a half notion *to give you the book* & let you hold your fate in your own hand. How would you like that? This defence of myself is rather [illegible] but Sally, I hate you to feel as I know you sometimes do at the tho't of how little you know me in public or useful life. I wish you could be my own darling wife now so that you might get over some of your fears. So you see, Sally, how my plans of brief! writing turn out. Well write to me as freely & I *will* be still more,

> Yours fondly,
> JM

I had this letter enclosed to Hughes & stamped with a note asking him in case &c to forward. But fearing Hughes might not be in town to give it [to] you, or if he was *might* or *might not* stay at the Exchange Hotel I broke it open again & determined it to be the safer plan just to do as I now do.

(June 27)[78]
Princeton June 7th 1856
Evening

My Sweetest love,

I wrote the longest queerest hardest looking letter a few hours ago that I ever wrote, so bad that I could hardly read it & so long in the effort to be short that it will tire your patience & perhaps alarms you for my reason. But, Sally, it violates neither Syntax nor Prosody & as to Etymology & spelling why, Dearest, you are so good at those that I think it can do you no harm even if it does trip a little. Do you know that when you get thoroughly *down* or what is worse out of temper with your poor hermit lover you begin to spell, (Sally I'm afraid to say it—still you're 400 miles off—I mean to venture) like a—fish-woman. I am actually in earnest. Usually you are very correct. But whether it is that you cant get at *me* & therefore fall foul of the King's English, or whether you have thrown your dictionary at the cook or cant keep your temper & your polysyllables both at the same time, Dearest love, my spelling is nothing to yours when you get agoing. I always try to spell *short*, that is if I dont know the word, to gain by it in getting over the ground, but the way you do pack in the consonants & bring in the dipthongs & the tripthongs & all that sort of vegetable, is perfectly refreshing. Dearest, I'd give—Oh, I dont know what—to see you read this letter. I believe you'll look grave at your poor rash lover. But, Dearest, I cant "*yeild*" you the palm of being a perfect speller "miser*i*able" a speller as I am.

I thought on Wednesday of sending you my book. I heard Col Reid was going to Lexington. I wanted you to copy & read it. I could not get hold of the Col. I fear to trust it by mail, as, if it were lost, I could not rewrite it. I have nearly finished it, & about fifteen chapters that remain are all thought out. It is a very

---

78. McDowell corrected Miller's date.

little book; the chapters are very short. I want to complete it before I see you, and I want to see you as soon as it is cool weather.

I intended to go to Philadelphia & meant then to get & send on those buttons, but Dick does what else I wanted & as to the buttons I should fear a little to send them by mail. Dick may disappoint me & then I shall go; & send on one at a time. If not I shall go in some weeks. Dearest tell me quite all you think about my letter to Richmond & answer its different points in a way that shall cheer & assure me. I want to see you contented & happy & tho' I dont want you to tell me so when you are not, yet I want you to tell me *all* of your feelings & to enter into your thoughts so that I can more entirely understand you.

Above all tell me *distinctly* what you meant by your submitting your judgments to mine & tell me all about it frankly for you might actually change some of my opinions.

And now, Dearest, let me tell you what I never told you before. I believe firmly that there is something very extraordinary about my love. I believe that firmer every day. I love you with the wildness of an entire surrender. I give up everything but God for you. I think of you all day long & love you to the exclusion of all other interest in society. I am constantly planning, planting & building & setting you in the midst of all my creations. I am proud of you in society. I am charmed by you in private. I am nursing you in sickness—reading to you—walking with you—living for you—*praying against you* lest you rob me of my very conscience & lest in that sweet fascination that steals away every sense I forget there is such a thing as any other obligation.

I believe I should be *happier* if I married you & remembering how much I sacrifice of daily & constant enjoyment I feel a sort of *virtue* in my fear of your own & our children's dishonor.

Now with all this witchery of my desires [illegible] as I do some day our happy marriage & loving you all the more for our disappointments & embarrassments when you write & talk about *liberating* me I can hardly express to you my feeling. It is that all your anxiety is so entirely gratuitous, your compassion so entirely wasted & your fear of imposing upon me or of endangering yourself so entirely unpractical, so completely have you stripped me of the power of loving or imagining any other relations. Sally, take me to your heart & love me without one thought of our ever being sundered. Indeed, I cannot let you go. If you were to say, I repent, & beg to be released from your condition, I would think, "C'est trop tard"[79] as they said to the poor Duchess of Orleans, & Sally, I would beg you to continue your engagement. In fact I am losing all mercy for you in respect to loosing you from the coil that is over your head & if I could fancy I had any such "power" as you speak of to charm you into submission I think I would exert it to hold you as the slave of my devotion. So, Dearest, give up all thots of leaving

79. French, meaning it is too late.

me. Let us consider our relation fixed & seek as much happiness & contentment as hard Providence & obscure prospects can possibly give.

Yours finally
Jno Miller

June 28th.

[marginal note] Can you *read* all my letters. I cant always.

Sometimes when I read my letters I think *these* may make you unhappy. There is such an air of restlessness & fever about them. Is it so?

PART SEVEN

"I may just talk to you about all things, as tho' you were only another self."

July 1856–August 1856

Colalto
July 1. 1856.

Dear John,

Here I am as quiet and cool as if this were the 1st of May instead of July. It was 11 o'clock when we reached here, after a day's journey of great discomfort from heat & dust. I met Lilly at Gordonsville much to my relief. She looks very thin, but seems entirely well—and I am so glad to have her again.

Oh John, such a lovely spot this is! I think it never looked cooler & sweeter & more refreshing than at present. After the ruggedness, and want of grass in Eastern Va, this green country is perfectly charming. My own home too, is very attractive. And I was pleased to hear Lilly exclaim as we sat down to table "O, Sister, what a nice breakfast. I go to other peoples houses where every thing is very grand & handsome, but it doesn't please me like our own." And sure enough our breakfast was nice with all country delicacies—a dish of newly gathered raspberries & rich, fresh cream, making its great charm to me.

What odd letters *you* write! And what fits you tell about my spelling. I confess I do get the vowels transposed in such words as "yield", but I don't add syllables nor multiply consonants nor do any of the other things you charge me with. I never spelt "miseriable" in that style in my life. And another thing I dont do—I never leave you in uncertainty as to the date of my letters—But you—just look here. Here is this letter dated "June 7th" at the beginning. I read it in wonder & felt mystified at its tone & allusions, but when I get to the end of it what turns up but this—"June 28th".

631

I never received the Richmond letter, but will write to Mr Blair or Hughes to send it on to me—& will answer it when it comes.

I hear Cousin John has suddenly determined to go to Europe again—or rather he is to decide the question to go or not, today. I shall feel broken up if he goes, tho' of late, I have not seen much of him.

I am so sorry you didn't send me the book. Do [send][1] it to me, if possible. I find my servants sick & harvest going on, so it is well I am here. I write in a hurry to catch the mail. Dont you like this paper? It is pleasant to write upon & of good size.

I love you astonishingly Darling—so if you mean to quarrel with me for anything, it can't be for that. I wrote you a note at 5 A.M. yesterday but slipped it in my pocket & brought it on with me.

Always Yours
S.C.P. McDowell.

Princeton, July 1st 1856.

My *Dearest*,

Isn't it strange that I talk so little to you of the children? The idea has just struck me that my little jealous Sally might some day begin to suspect me, & think that I have not yet admitted her into my heart of hearts or I would share with her these little children. Well, Sally, I dont know why it is, but I never feel led to talk to you about them. I think it is because you have never seen them. How sad that Mother didnt carry them to you that day. I wish you could see them just for an hour. I think they would help me to court you. They are nicer than I am particularly in all respects except philosophy & that divine personage you have no heart for#.[2]

Why, as to bringing Maggie, Sally how could I? I have no nurse for her & I cant take her on so long a journey & then what would I do with her there? I wouldnt like to quarter her at Colalto. Moreover Sally, I want to stay a great while. What do you think of that? I want to take my papers & have that as a sort of studying place for two or three weeks. Darling, I want to have just as much of your company this time as you & others will possibly tolerate. And I would like to give my visit that sort of leisure look as tho' I must be staying somewhere & here is where I choose to stay for some weeks.

I think also of another thing. I not only dont talk to you much of Maggie but I dont talk to you *at all* of what ought to be still dearer. I sometimes think that it is a *shame* for a minister of the gospel to go thro' trying scenes & to need comfort & to give it without one mention of the noblest & best things. Indeed

1. McDowell wrote "plan."
2. Miller originally wrote "have no heart for" at the top of what would be the third page. But he scratched them out, placed this mark (#), and rewrote them here at the top of page two with the same mark.

I shudder sometimes at the thought that if it were of the abundance of my heart my mouth *would* speak of it. And how poor my letters, Indeed, how wonderful, viewed as the long continued utterances of my saddest & most tried moments of life. Dearest you once drew my attention to that name Jehovah Jireh & tho' I did not even respond yet I have never forgot that letter from that day to this. Such is my great comfort. I have committed *you* & yours & Maggie & Allie & myself *all* to the Almighty, I am renewing that confidence from day to day. Indeed, I have committed you, Darling, to God in so express a manner that I seem *waiting* to see what he will do for us. I take comfort in believing that you are a very good woman; you know Dr White told me so; & that the son of such a mother as I have & the lover of such a woman would not be deserted but would have a common blessing from a covenant keeping God. Dear Sally; try to make me better. Dont quit writing serious letters even if I do. You havn't the same excuse as I in a habit of singular reserve. And moreover you have far more real piety than I. I am expecting great things from Providence from the mere fact that He has mixed my destiny with yours.[3]

Colalto,
Wednesday, July 2. 1856.

My *dear John*,

It was only yesterday morning I wrote to you; but I shall not be able to write a line tomorrow, so I bring my writing apparatus into the front porch, just as the Institute drum beats for supper to do what I can towards accomplishing a letter.

I found my servants sick when I got here. Edward & Alfred turned into the harvest field, with only Jenny & the little girl & boy you used to see here available of my whole corps of house servants. I was expecting the Breckinridges & Uncle Tom too, & my house being dreadfully out of order, I turned maid-of-all-work myself yesterday, cleaned up & set to rights 3 chambers, and then broke down. I laid down for an hour or two to rest as the evening came on, but was roused by the report of the illness of one of my harvest hands. I hurried round to see him, & much alarmed at his case sent off in haste for a Physician, & instituted a search for such simple remedies as I knew were necessary. It was a search sure enough, for my house was emptied of every thing of the sort, by my own indifference or carelessness before I went away. In the midst of my anxiety Mr Davidson called. I excused myself upon the plea of this illness, when he kindly offered to turn Dr himself & go & see the poor creature. By this time the cholera symptoms were much heightened, but Mr Davidson, who, there being a good deal of this sort of disease in the town just now, was experienced & calm prescribed & administered medicine himself very successfully. Another Dr was sent for, the first not having come, who after awhile arrived, & added his wisdom, so by 11

---

3. The conclusion to this letter appears to be missing.

o'clock, I was almost free from uneasiness about our patient. And to-day he has been recovering apparently. But the fatigue of the day had been too much for me, and almost all of this day I have been unfit for any thing. This evening I am pretty well again, and hope to be entirely well to-morrow.

But John, I do grow so sad & despondent, and I long after you, as one to whom I would like to go with all my troubles. Cares & anxieties seem to multiply upon me, & my energy & strength gives way under them. And I suffer so much under the torture of a growing distrust of every human being. I am afraid of everybody; and yearn with inexpressible yearning just to lay my head in your lap & be assured I need have no fear there & that you were so far unlike other people that you *couldn't* change. You so often accuse me of reserve, John. And the charge is true, to some extent. Yet I can't help it. It just fastens like a compress on my heart, which throb as it may & as it does cannot get free. I've always had this temper; and yet always had longings for some one who could sound the depths of my heart, without my *telling* of its workings. That person I always thought *could* only be my husband. No other relation seemed near enough or dear enough for such entire confidence & intimacy. No other could lure me to such perfect abandon of affection. No other, could to my mind, even justify it; and this relation without such oneness of being, would be insupportable. I should sink under it, & perhaps, loathe it. And now, more that ever I need the comfort & support that such free interchange of thought & feeling would give—that is, I think it a necessary, but as it is denied, it may after all, be only a *luxury* of life that I am asking. But, I believe, I really do need some real friend now. I am troubled about matters, & need counsel upon things that, it may be, I have no right to speak of to you—not that I wouldn't rather go to you, than any body else, but you wd feel it unwise & unseemly in you to have any word of advice to give—& I think it wrong to ask it from you. But, John, Dearest, you can, at least, pray for me. I need wisdom & prudence & firmness. O, John I would be so relieved if you cd bear my burdens with me—or teach me how to bear them alone.

Your letter of the 24th & the one sent to Rich'd both came to-day. I am, you say to take some things in this last, on "trust till you see me";—then why need I say any thing in reply to them? However, I think I shall some day soon, write you a whole volume of a letter on those very things. I am expecting another letter from you tomorrow morning—Three letters in three days will make me quite rich. By the bye you never did me justice about my share of our correspondence. One reason of the greater number of yr letters was that during our troubles last winter you wrote once & sometime twice a day, when, of course you couldn't expect me to write as often. You were just sending me dispatches from scene of war, & did not require an answer to each one. It was very kind & thoughtful, but just what I expected you would do. You are considerate and generous well-nigh all the time—Sometimes you start off rather obstinately, but when I get broken to yr ways, it's all pleasant enough. But I wish you cd devise some method of getting yr letters differently. I *do* so dislike to send 3 letters a week to you thro' this Office.

Besides, I have a suspicion my buttons were lost here & not in Princeton & Phil'a.

Our Commencements are going on with very universal pomp & display. The Gov. is to speak tomorrow, when the bronze Washington (a copy of Houdon's) is to be erected. Mr Massie follows him, & Kiett, the coadjutor of Brooks in the Sumner affair speaks last.—But good-night.[4] I am nodding over my paper.

Thursday 6 A.M.

I have received no mail yet, & will not before I send this off, as I have no servants to do the double errand.

Lilly tells me she heard in Washington that you were applying for the George-town Church, to which Mr Bocock has been called. I felt quite indignant at the rumour. By the bye Bocock is here—also William Brown & Lacy—but I have, as yet, seen nobody. The Carringtons came down yesterday, but fortunately are not staying with me. I wish they wd a part of their time; but my house is so out of gear I could not make them comfortable all the time, & wd be very uncomfortable myself.

But I am in a hurry so good-bye.

Affectionately Yours
S.C.P. McDowell.

Princeton July 2d 1856.

My Sweetest Darling,

I argue this way:—Saturday Sally wrote, or Friday midnight that letter I had Monday. Sunday she would not *think* of me. Monday she would start. Monday noon be tired at Stanton Monday night be late at home. And Tuesday morning late in bed. So poor John would have no letter till Tuesday night. See how I *follow* you. And that would not leave till Wednesday morning. Then I shouldnt get it till to-night. So tho' I have had no letter since Monday, still, kiss me, & I'll try to wait. But Sally its so hard when you expect a letter.

Tell me now what you think of this:—Last night I went to see Mr Blodgett. Mr B. is a brother-in-law of Mrs Tom Potters & is on a visit to her home. I went at 8 1/2 & was ushered into a parlour & presently a pretty little daughter of Mrs P. came to say that her mother would have me go into tea.[5] I was there introduced to a Miss Hall & after talking a while with Mrs P. turned to this lady & addressed her as Miss Dickinson. They got me straight on that subject & after we had chatted a while went to the parlour & talked a long while on

4. The "Gov" refers to Henry Alexander Wise. Jean Antoine Houdon (1741–1828), French sculptor. His life statute of George Washington, commissioned by the State of Virginia, stands in the rotunda of the capitol in Richmond. Lawrence Massilon Keitt (1824–1864), congressman from South Carolina.

5. Sarah Jane Hall Potter (1818–1877). Her husband, Thomas Fuller Potter, M.D. (1806–1855), had died the previous September. The "pretty little daughter" was either Elizabeth Potter (1844–?) or Alice Potter (1846–1894).

Allamby & a whole pack of other things. When presently at a remark of mine about some musicians Mrs P asked me if I liked music & asked it in such a way as to lead me to fancy that at some time or other I had been telling her of the special distaste I had for music. Whereupon I said, Why, do you ask because of any peculiarity of mine & then had to explain how I hated music & before I had done my explanation woke up to the fact that the whole thing was a polite overture of Mrs P's for the opening of the piano & the performing of this young niece of hers—Miss Hall.

Very shrewdly & with that prudent thought at the time I held myself quite unconscious of any such thought on her part & went on talking about other things when by a mad fatality such strangeness as comes over all at times & with a kind of hope of recovering from my found mistake I turned to Mrs P. & said that tho' I had so little taste & everybody laughed at me at home & refused to play for me yet if she would let me open the piano I should be very glad &c &c. Whereupon in an awkward way she declined intimated it was not herself that she had thot of as playing & inasmuch as "I dont like music" she rather emphatically forbid the piano to be opened. Now what do you think of such things? Do you ever tumble into them? How do you feel after them? And oughtn't an old man of near forty to have wit enough even when so far in the pit by some dexterous speech to drag himself out again? These very serious points I submit to your consideration.

Mrs P. did one thing that I thought strangely sensible. She praised Maggie. Said she was the most beautiful child she had ever seen. And what is more agreed with Dr Hodge that she ought to be told so.

Now Dearest, the old fashion Lexington mails will bring me my letters just like the sun in heaven. God bless you.

Yours affly
Jno Miller.

Can you read all my writing?

Colalto, July 5. 1856.

My *dear* John,

I never was reduced to such straits in housekeeping in all my life before. I can hire nobody, and am just obliged to do all sorts of things myself. Lilly helps some; but still I have had a pretty tough time. You wd fancy me the most bustling of Northern housekeepers if you could see me sweeping, & setting the table & fixing chambers & worrying generally. On going to town Thursday I found Mr Massie sick in bed, & persuaded him to come over here, which he did next day. The place has been so thronged with strangers that I could not hire a servant for him, & had my own all in the harvest field—consequently I wait upon him a good deal in person, & run from his room to the kitchen oftener now in one day than heretofore in a month. To-night, however, his own servant comes to take care of him, & I am much relieved. He is not dangerously ill, but suffering a good deal, & like all men, very impatient & despondent when sick.

I am pretty tired, yet I think the exercise in spite of the fatigue is good for me.

Monday 7 A.M.

I purposely avoided writing Saturday morning for I wanted to change my writing day to others that wd suit better—every other day then will be, Monday, Wednesday & Friday.

Mr Massie continues sick. I fear his disease is assuming a more serious aspect. Last night the Dr remained with him all night—I have not seen him this morning however to inquire how his patient really is. I have thought him, heretofore, more alarmed than ill & the Drs spoke lightly rather of his attack; but I begin to grow uneasy. I hope Nib will be at home in a few days.

My sick servant has recovered;—but the Overseer is ill. Another servant too is sick enough to require special nursing; and altogether every thing is in confusion.

Gov Wise made half a dozen speeches during his visit, & seems to have given general satisfaction. I heard his set oration, tho' not perfectly, and was not particularly pleased—especially as two or three times in the course of it the "gizzard-foot" was protruded offensively to my taste. I was glad to find, however, that his one or two allusions to Massachusetts & "Senator Sumner" fell flat with his audience, tho' from his manner I knew he expected them to be loudly cheered. By the bye Kiett (Brooks friend in the Sumner affair) came on to address the Institute Literary Societies—a great, bluff, moustached fellow with a conspicuous cane in his hand which I thought instantly must be one of Brooks' & found out afterwards was, that I half wished could have been well used upon the backs of them both. I don't think he took well here, particularly as he got drunk at the Cadets ball. It is astonishing the animosity I feel against South Carolina.

My friend Bocock, who is I think, with great satisfaction, just learning to an-swer to his newly-conferred Doctorate, is a rabid Southern man; and is expressing such sentiments in regard to our political agitation & on the subject of personal redress as quite shock me, & disturb his brother Ministers—at least Mr Brown expresses himself so. Just think, with such violent manner & feelings how much mischief he may do in Geo:town. He looks better than I ever saw him—& would, with his new wig, look entirely like a gentleman, if he could be persuaded to keep his sleeves clean—but his cuffs are all crumpled & soiled and look so ugly.

I have been interrupted in my letter and must send this off as quickly as possible that it may go this morning. I am disappointed, at being stopped, for John, Darling, I had my heart full of things to say to you. But I shall write again, perhaps this evening & tomorrow both, so, as to get off to you a long letter by Wednesday's mail. Meantime I thank you, more than you can tell for yr last letter, that, by an accident came to me yesterday, Sunday as it was. I treasure it very much. It answers a little, & promises more to my most earnest longings upon a subject, that yr reserve has somehow seemed to lay an embargo upon. I am glad these barriers are being broken down, & that I may just talk to you about all things, as tho' you were only another self.

God bless you Love.

Affecly
S.C.P. McD.

New York, July 7 1856.

My dearest Sally,

So we go floating about the world, you at Cub Creek & Halifax & I at Rocky Hill & Gotham. I wonder if the weird sisters ever mean to bring us together.[6] I came here to preach in the Grand st Church on Sunday & have been treated as tho' I were a sort of Napoleon 4th. How very little it takes to spoil some people.

I go back to Princeton at 2.

I sally out after breakfast to mail this letter & to look for your sleeve buttons. I marked down the odd one on my [illegible], & Miller like forgot them. & all so that I am here with no pattern. Still as I dont want to match that exactly I am going to see what I can do without it.

Do you know I would give—I think about a half inch off of one of my fingers if I could just see you, especially if the meeting could be so far extended as that I could steal from you even in the most fleeting possible way the slightest sort of a kiss.

God bless you, Darling, & send us better times.

Yours very sincerely
Jno Miller.

Colalto,
Tuesday, July 8. 1856.

O, yes John; I've often thought, & thought with pain how we had banished, as by a tacit compact, almost all mention of religious duties, & motives & feelings from our letters—We have almost ignored, in our complicated troubles & sorrows, all reference to the highest & truest source of comfort & support. And all the time I've felt it was wrong; & yet, shrunk from every free utterance of the kind, as tho' it were sinful. Somehow I feared you would look upon it as mere cant; and, my own consciousness of so much that was sinful in my own heart, made the expression of feeling on the subject seem like hypocracy; and, then, every body has a natural reserve about it. But there have been times when I have longed to talk to you freely, & have you speak to me freely—when my heart has just come gushing with emotion, & I felt so like throwing my arms around

---

6. The "weird sisters" refers to the witches in Shakespeare's *Macbeth*.

you, & begging permission to unburden it to you. And yet I would restrain it, & endeavor to speak it into silence again. And if, as I remember once to have done, I'd half utter a sentence, & you, in reply, ask *what* I meant, I have not answered—I had not the courage. Isn't it a shame that I should speak of *needing courage* to talk to you on such a topic,—you, whom I love more than all the world beside. If I had never thought of it at all I should have been blameworthy; but to have my heart and head so often filled with it, & yet resist it, is, I think, inexcusable. But we won't let this neglect be permitted in the future, John? I long to have our affection elevated and guided by this principle. I am so anxious that we should do good & not evil to each other, and that our attachment should have in it the element of christian fellowship to make it more useful more happy more safe & more steady & unwavering. You cant tell, how glad I am to have our reserve broken up. I feel that I am drawn more closely to you than ever before and I am more ready to yield, an almost unquestioning confidence.

Wednesday morning.

I am hurried with my letter by Nib's unexpected descent upon us within the last half hour. I expected her last night & she wd have been here but for the bad roads. I am greatly disappointed at having no letter to-day. I wish you would be particular in noticing the arrival or detention of mine, for somehow, I am suspicious about them.

I did feel a little hurt about Maggie, & thought I would never ask to see her again. I know there are difficulties in getting her here, & scarcely expected to have them overcome; but I longed to see the child, & pleased myself by dreaming that I should. My great difficulty about her was that her friends would object, & fancy some evil wd grow out of it: and it was awkward & on that score might be abandoned. But if yr objections are only those you mention, why, they are easily set aside. Maggie would need nobody but you with you. You could bring her to Phil: one day—the next, leave there, get to Staunton at 3 P.M, & take the Cars there to a place called Goshen, & thence come 17 miles to Lexington;—reaching here about 8 o' 9 o'clock that same evening. Then bring her straight over to me: where else shd she stay? I would fear, the child would feel like a prisoner, & suffer from loneliness here, but if you could bring Allie with her they might be as happy here as at Princeton—and I, O, John it would be such a happiness to me to have them.

One of the servants called me just before breakfast to see a new colt—A Sister to Allie's, and the two were driven into the yard. Allie's is a fine thing, & but for the color, wd be even to my taste a beauty. The other as exactly like it as if it were a twin; & Lilly asked if I meant to call it "Maggie".

But I'm in such a hurry. God bless you Darling.

Affection'y
S.C.P. McDowell.

Princeton, July 10th 1856.

My *dear Sally,*

For the first time since our correspondence began I have written a long letter & enclosed it, & then torn it open & burnt it, not for any fault in the letter other than its being so perfectly inane. I have half a notion to send it as a curiosity. It occupied three large pages & as near as I can make it out it rejoices that you will at last treat me as tho' I were another self & mourns that you have so long grieved & chilled me with treating me with reserve. Dear Sally, act upon this suggestion & write to me just as tho' I were your own precious self & save the need of long tiresome folios, that's a good girl.

I wish I could take a part of your burdens & I give you carte blanche to tell me all your business. You know, Sally, you never took any of my advice. So it will be of small account. I advised you long ago not to keep up a $500 home & a retinue of servants & not to run in debt, but Sally, you do both. And, moreover, you dont take your own advice for you meant to send Edward away & to make some other solid retrenchments & you have done nothing. And, Dearest, money is of more consequence than you even *yet* dream. For in the first place you will lose your health by it which to me is a most *distressing* anxiety & moreover you will lose your hold upon your different sources of influence.

Still, Darling, I musnt worry you. I am not the tasteful person to help you manage, &, Dearest, you are so wicked that I should feel very helpless if I was.

God bless you. If I *knew* that your health would be young & blooming eight years hence & then you would be entirely my own I would feel less anxious about these intermediate managements.

But let me whisper something to you. Put your head down very low—I love you. Do you feel anything like that to me?

Yours the second time this afternoon.

JM.

Colalto,
Thursday, July 10. 1856.

Dear John,

And so you don't wear my buttons! I suspected you wouldn't. Why didn't you tell me you wouldn't in advance of my sending them? I inferred from what you said, when I wrote to you about them that you would, & so sent them on; but, afterwards I had suspicions of being mistaken. I think it very ungracious of you— & next time I won't send you anything; and won't agree to receive anything—not even such a trifle as this single button was.

I think I ought to have had a letter between the one written on the 2d & that of the 7th from New York which came to-day. Our letters cause me, at times, a good deal of anxiety—I'm afraid I shall become a monomaniac about them yet.

Who are you preaching for in New York? Do you do much preaching now? Is it pleasant to you to do any? I should so much like to be a preacher: but I suppose my ambition wd come in to spoil it; for I would aspire to do a noble work, in the noblest way. And it would never do for me to carry my heart & head into the Ministry—I would do more harm than good. However, as no such charge can ever come, I must content myself by listening to other people's preaching.

Yes; I read all yr letters without any great difficulty—at least none greater than I have in reading my own. Occasionally a word baffles all my skill; but in such a case, I call in my imagination, & that settles the matter.

One thing, I long ago meant to say to you, but always forget it when I was writing, which is, that I want you always to write to me just as you feel. You spoke some time ago of endeavouring, hereafter, always to write cheerfully; and I felt pained at the thought of any restraint upon our letters, even tho' you were using it out of kindness to me. It wouldn't be kindness tho' John. It would make my heart ache to think you were writing a cheerful letter to me, when your own feelings were as sad as they could be. I would infinitely rather you wd write sadly, when you feel so. It makes me love you a great deal more, & feel a great deal nearer to you when you treat me in a perfectly natural & unrestrained way. You are not acting a part to me, Darling, now any more than if I were your wife. And if I am not to share your hours of gloom, I am worth nothing to you; and am denied my very highest & dearest privilege. I am too far away to show my sympathy just at the moment it is needed—but when those sad letters of yours come, how my heart yearns over you, & oh, how warmly all my affection glows. If you ever really doubted my love, I think, if you would see within then, yr doubts would very quickly vanish.

Friday 7 A.M.

I have no letter to-day. Mr Massie continues convalescent, &, in a day or two will, I think be able to leave his room & come down stairs.

I sometimes, as you know, amuse myself, & occupy myself by making my lines jingle, and two months or more ago, *took compassion* (!) upon our Presbyterian and sent them some verses.[7] I cut them out, or rather since I came home, Lilly cut them out of a copy of the Paper I found here, and I intended to send them to you—laying them beside me yesterday when I commenced this letter, but, I suppose I forgot the scrap & this morning it is gone. If I can find it I'll send it not that I think much of it, but still fancied sending it to you.

Our Town is as quiet as old Nineveh; which, however, is no trouble to me. I think the Breckinridges are scared at the epidemic here, & may not come down from Aunt Eliza's to see me. I had a letter from Willie an hour ago, asking as to the safety of their coming.[8]

7. The *Central Presbyterian* was published in Richmond.
8. McDowell's cousin, William Campbell Preston Breckinridge.

It is true there is a good deal of sickness, but I have heard of no fatal case yet. Cousin John was in bed several days; but is out again. My Overseer is still sick. I imagine his is the worst case as yet; but I don't know that Dr Taylor considers him in danger. I was afraid my turn had come last night; but this morning I am quite well. Lilly too is well. Benton was complaining a little all the time he was with us, but took no special care of himself, & grew better, rather than worse.

I am called off on business.

God bless you, dear John.

Affec'ly
S.C.P. McDowell.

Princeton, July 12th 1856.

My darling dear Sally,

When I consider our circumstances & remember how entirely dependent we are upon a Higher Power I agree with you that religion ought to be one of our most constant ideas. There is no comfort for us but in the conviction that God is planing for us a comfortable life & that this bond of ours is necessary to its eventual history. I *am* not sure that you would have entered into it if you could have foreseen all the results[9] but God has surprised us into it as the necessary steps toward what he intends eventually as very delightful. And, Dearest, we may yet be living in all the glow of a surprised & most gratified deliverance to pick out this very letter & see how we *ought* to have trusted that the Almighty had *something* beneficent in store for us.

Now, Dearest, I know this may be in another world & yet I have a feeling that if it is so it will be because of our peculiar sins, that we will see some day when we come to look back upon Providences that God would have been true to us in this world if we had been more true to ourselves. Indeed Sally, I am actually reforming certain faults as a sort of Catholic penance to win from God our Great Indulgence. Not entirely so either—I am using the great Protestant privilege of pleasing God with a better life that he may give me what I so much desire or rather, in the words of the apostle I am "judging myself that I may not be judged".[10] My great earthly Paradise is my marriage and so strong is my desire that the idea of it as never granted is one that I cannot think of. The thought even of Heaven without an intervening history with you would seem almost intolerable & this often frightens me & leads me to ask how this differs from an *idol* & how I can expect that God will be gracious to me in that which seems itself so great an injury. Thus *Sally* the good influence & the bad influence seem to unite together in your single person & yet I have an overshadowing & constant feeling that God *will* some day give you to me & tho' I have no faith in impressions yet I cannot help having this hope in our affair & present with me nearly all the time.

9. Miller interlined here the question: "would you, Sally?"

10. Matt. 7:1. Actually the text reads "Do not judge, so that you may not be judged"; and in Luke 6:37 "Do not judge, and you will not be judged."

Sometimes, too, I have very queer feelings. You must know Sally I am going to tell you everything almost that ever occurs to me. I have been thinking of the Major. I have been thinking how I came to disturb the quiet of that little village where the Major & you would have been thrown together in such near & continual intimacy. I have been thinking how you were there both products of the same soil & knowing each other with the thoroughness of the most complete acquaintance. And then, Sally, the strength with which he seemed to appeal from my sentence when I said that if I didnt marry you no body could; a sentence which he did not rebel against on any personal grounds at the time of course, but which indicated his spirit. And then a thousand other things—his not being a minister—& his not being a pauper—& his not being a Yankee, but there with you right at home & able to be with you & to help you. Darling, I shudder almost to write so. Tell me if your love drags its anchor in the least. I know you oughtn't to marry. I know you can marry no one sooner than you can marry me. I rejoice, all things considered, to have saved you from the chance of marrying any one (as I now think) foolishly, that is the marriage would have been foolish, but yet, Darling, you might have done it, & the queer wonder comes over my mind whether you love me more than any one beside & whether you would rather be my poor suffering betrothed & anxious friend, than the Major's safely carried home & conscientiously married bride. Tell me Sally. Tell me how much of this is fancy or how much of it if I were to treat you a little badly for example might soon be fact, how much you *exclusively* love me, how soon you would love some body else if I were to desert you, how much your love for me is a mere love to be loved, how much of it is love that you would have lavished upon L[illy] for example if I had not been in the way, how much of it was a mere matter of matronly choice as Chevalier said to "take John Miller" all things considered & how firmly it would stand if the most admired friend you have in the world should clear away from you all harrowing scruples & woo you as his bride & I was still only your poor absent & intending to be absent & afraid to marry you, but accepted lover.

Sally, in all honesty, suppose, there was no honor to bind you or no pity for me, how much would sheer love to me individually & for myself make you averse to such a marriage. Dearest this is a hard question but answer it *with absolute candour & in the fear of God.*

It's odd I should have turned my letter into such an inquisition but as I have fallen into it do Sally, answer me sincerely.

Yours affectionately
JM

Saturday 5 P.M.

Dear Sally,

I suspected this letter a little as I wrote it. On looking at it now I think it not delicate or handsome. Neither in respect to your relations to your cousin or Mrs P. or me or—your own self. But, Sally, yet I am wild enough to send it first because I havent a letter on Thursday, second because it wont make me any kinder or more delicate to hide my impulses fm you & thirdly, because I am mad to get an answer. Dear, good, Sally, write to me & tell me whether you think it an unhandsome & cruel letter & then write me a full answer to all its questions.

As to Maggie you are mistaken about going from Phil to Staunton by 3 the same day. You must start the night before. Is the way by Goshen the common way now?

Yours truly & affly,
Jno Miller

Monday morning
July 14. 1856.

My *dear John,*

I wish you had sent me the long letter you burnt; this little one seems very like a bottle of champagne which had been carefully corked *after* the gas had escaped. However it isn't becoming in me to complain; & an old proverb comes to your support, reminding me that "beggars are not to be choosers".

You somewhat mistake about my rejecting yr advice. I don't think, on the very points, on which you bring the charge you ever went all the length that the case required in giving yr advice. You did tell me it is true, that I ought not to keep up this establishment; but you never advised me what to do, or where to go, if I broke it up. And I am very anxiously considering this very question now, & have been all the time. And so, in other things you don't know all the circumstances & difficulties as I do. At any rate, for an independent, unconnected, forlorn sort of being as I am, it wd be very stupid to ask or to take advice. Every body disappoints me; and I never make the experiment, that my nature is continually impelling me to, by a sort of headlong power, of confiding in people, that I do not suffer from it in some way or other. And actually I grow sick & weary of the constant arguing with myself, that I must take the world as I find it, & be contented. I can't help giving way sometimes, for I have no recollection in all the past of suffering as I have done during the last 6 or eight months. I am bringing to bear upon it all of reason & religion that I can, but I am but a human being, after all, & tho' I shame to do it as cowardly & mean, yet I do often sink under a burden which seems to increase in its pressure every year of my life.

I wish I was more anxious than I am, to bear my troubles well, than to get rid of them—more submissive & patient—more intent upon getting some good out of them. I feel as if every nerve was exposed, just that the world might walk rough shod over them. But there is some reason why this is all needful for me, as none of these things happen by chance, and tho' I now & then am overcome by my feelings yet I do struggle against both the spirit & language of complaint.

I think a little of going to Fincastle on Wednesday to see Marie & Willie Breckinridge, if they decide not to come to see me. Uncle William is there; & promises me a visit later in the season. I don't like to go there. When I paid Aunt

Eliza a visit in the Spring, I half lost my senses. I don't know why, but it has a depressing effect upon me.

I am afraid you will hate the sight of my letters, if they are ever so doleful in future, as this one; but please take me as I am and have a little patience with me. You little know how sad I am, & yet I tell you often enough to worry you to death.

Oh yes! I love you—but you ought to pray that I should be released from the power of the spell that the chances of unhappiness to us both might be diminished.

God bless you, my precious, & forgive us our restiveness & murmuring.

Your
S.C.P. McD.

Princeton, July 14th 1856.

My *dearest Darling,*

You women are too intolerably shrewd for any comfort. Who would ever dream you would have laid things together & found out I had not worn the buttons by such a stray sentence in a letter? Especially as I was keeping it as a grand secret.

Now, Dearest, listen. You often tell me I have no idea of ladies' engagements that prevent them from writing a letter. Now I say you have no idea of a gentleman's trials that prevent him from wearing buttons. Why, Sally, I'm a perfect martyr to buttons. I'd give I dont know how much to set you down in this room & pull out a great map of all kinds of linen & make you sew on all the buttons. It would be a sort of Paradise that I never expect. And, Dearest, if you would only be quiet & wouldnt talk so much I would keep you there for two or three weeks just in the continual employment of sewing on buttons. And do you think in such a condition of things I'm going to leave a whole host of buttonless sorrows unmended & go off upon the fancy work of having holes cut for those two.

Besides, Sally, I dont intend ever to wear them that way. I'm going to get *three* new ones all alike—two for you & one for me & then some of these days I'm going to wear them like a sober Christian in my sleeves. If I could have matched them the other day fr. memory I would have done it in N.Y. Now my poor little restless pigeon, can you keep quiet?

My! how you frighten me about the letters! Did you get one addressed inside to Mrs John Miller? Do tell me for I wouldnt like that to be floating about the world. It was a very proper letter a little too reserved & modest as mine always are but then I hate to think of it as read by strangers.

In N.Y. I preached for a Dr Thompson.[11] He is gone to Europe. I am to preach next month in Rutger's St Ch, & also in Market St. There are just random engagements filled by an absence from Sat. night to Mon. morn. & tho' I like them much I would not like anything longer. Yes, Sally, I love preaching, but I love what I am now busy at a great deal more.

11. John Thompson (1819-?), pastor of Thirty-fourth Street Presbyterian Church, New York.

I have searched all the Presbyterians & cant find your piece. Do send it. Why do you try me so, Sally, by exciting me with a wish & not adding a line that would have told me the subject & date of the article?

It's terribly hot here & if I could find anything to quarrel with you for I would but you are so sweet & in most respects so kind that tho' you dont care for me half as much as you ought & dont write me long enough letters I cant bear to get up a feud.

Dearest, you havent invited me to come & see you. And tho' I cant come till after those engagements in N.Y. yet you know one likes to have an invitation. Cant you tell me that you positively cant live a month without seeing me & that if I dont come in that time you wont be responsible for the consequences.

Tell me whether you got the letter I speak of.

The children are back & send their love.

> Yours very affly
> Jno Miller.

Maggie Breckinridge wrote me what nice letters she had had from you. I wrote to her to send them to me & she wont. Maynt she? I enclose you a letter to mail to Spence when I am dead.

[Enclosure: John Miller to E. Spencer Miller]

> Princeton July 14th 1856.

My *dear Spence,*

In a locked drawer of a walnut secretary in my room are all my letters from Mrs McDowell. In the event of my sudden death before our marriage she will send you this letter & on the receipt of it please seal up both packages & send them to her.

The presents she has given me I wish kept for my children till an age when they will not destroy them.

> Yours very affectionately
> Jno Miller.

Tuesday, July 15. 1856.

My dear John, are you perfectly demented? What, upon earth made you write me such a letter? I wish you hadn't done it: it was wrong in you, for any but the very strongest reasons, to say a word likely to jeopard the very most intimate friendship I think I ever had. I have never known Cousin John but as a married man. For years before he was married, he was off at College; and my first distinct recollection of him, is dated a few days before his marriage. As I grew up, he took a kindly sort of interest in me, probably growing out of his affection for my Parents, and often worried me with quiet aside remarks upon serious subjects. I didn't like him, & felt afraid of him, & restrained by him. I admired him, nevertheless, for many fine traits of character that impressed themselves upon me, without my exactly knowing what they were; if you can understand such a paradoxical feeling as that. After I left school, he grew more interested in me—I was the nearest of his blood here, & he acknowledged our relationship quite warmly. I wonder why he liked me. I often thought he didn't then, & my vanity was greatly wounded by it. He disliked my marriage; and once came as near telling me so as he thought he could venture. But after it turned out so disastrously, no friends could have been more steadily and warmly considerate and kind than both he & Cousin Sally. Perhaps, taking them all in all, I have never had two friends as reliable and unremitting in their kindness as they. They were strongly attached to my parents—& since their death seem to give to me, in addition to the affection they felt for me individually, most of that they had given to them. I used to go to them, not for advice so much as sympathy, until by & bye Cousin John became my chief almost only Counsellor in any special & private matter of importance. I loved him very much; more than any of his name or my blood. I loved him a great deal more than my own brothers, or than any other male friend. I suppose I have said as much a hundred times before, whenever the subject came up—no doubt you have heard me yourself say it a dozen times. And it is just because I have this free, full and candid sort of affection for him, that I repudiate all idea of the *possibility* of the existence of any other kind: and O John, I shrink from putting into words such a denial as this. If you could have seen how I shrunk away from yr words as I read them you would never have written them; but would have crushed, at its birth, the thought that they express. I would not have this one tie loosened or broken by any such absurd suspicions.

And yet, painful as it was to me, I have noticed, I couldn't tell why, a sort of reserve growing up between us. Just the other day, feeling hurt, at what impressed me as an evidence of this, I found my mind turning the thing over & over, and this suspicion, as if the Devil had whispered it in my ear, creeping up to show a reason for it; and I found myself, speaking almost aloud, in my indignation against it. I tell you it is impossible with either of us. Now pray in future, just let me love, my dear Cousin, as I have done; & I hope, the world will allow him to love me as he has done; and not deny me every thing in the way of affection; & cut me off from every body who cares for me, or whom I care for.

But John I wish you hadn't asked me all these things,—they are not proper or pleasant subjects to write about.

I can't tell why I love you—or whether I love you with the same sort of love, or to the same degree, that I would have loved any other, or *the other* you mention, for it wd take an experiment to teach me, & furnish me the ground of comparison, which I have not made: one thing however ought to satisfy you, and that is the *fact* that I do love you—and love you as much, if not more than I ever loved any human being. And this fact has been pretty well attested: that, under all the circumstances of our case I am writing to you now as I do, is not the least strong or the least conclusive proof of it. It is true, if I had seen 18 months ago the sorrows and troubles of the last six or eight months, I would never have purchased the year of pleasure, at such an immense cost, yet in spite of it all, I love you a great deal more now than at the beginning. My pride has had terrible conflicts with my affection too. I wonder how it ever yielded. But here we are, after all sorts of difficulties, & drawbacks, together yet. And I think of you & dream of you as much as ever; & as much as if it were not the most insane sort of unreasonableness imaginable. But I had learned to think of you as my husband, and you were so near being so, that I have so inwoven you with all my thoughts, and hopes and anxieties, that when, as in a recent letter you are speaking of our troubles & use a phrase like this—"I cannot bear to think of you in the arms of another"—I hide away from the expression as tho' it were dishonoring.

"How long would yr love last if I treated you a little badly &c, &c?". Not an hour after I became convinced of it. It might take some time, to convince me you treated me ill designedly—but the conviction once fastened on my mind, that moment my affection is throttled. I couldn't love you if I found you *capable* of a cold-blooded purpose of the kind. I could forgive you for being suddenly surprised & overcome, for you are only a human being, but as to the other, it wd be inexcusable. You are right in yr surmises: I don't agree with you that *I can't marry*. The greatest bar against it, in the future so far as any other than yrself is concerned is, that I love *you*, & unless I am, in some way or other, disenchanted—I can never marry another. The breaking of the spell is in yr own hands. Convince me that you don't love me,—& that moment you are free. Or convince me, that you are unworthy of my love, & by a single flash of lightning you would have yr liberty restored to you. But I fancy this latter thing you would find very hard to teach me; whilst the other, from my suspicious and anxious affection you would find an easy lesson.

How odd of you to ask me so often how I love you, as compared with the love I *might* have to some other. And yet I very often ask the question of myself— and find the needle, invariably turning straight back to you—sometimes with an exhilarated sort of feeling—oftener with a quiet, rational sort of very enjoyable contentment. And then again, when I get a little worried with you, & am fretful & suspicious, & my affection seems baffled & agrieved, and I hem it up, I find by & bye, the old feeling comes sweeping down all my barriers, and asserting its own place, with the utmost strength. Then too, I am ashamed of the intermitted pulse, and make amends for it, by too great warmth. But, John, it's all very sad to me; and well-nigh hopeless. I am often hoping that God will make a straight and plain path for me, not only in this, but in other troubles & difficulties.—As yet, however, I see nothing, and every day seems to bring fresh perplexities.

Wednesday morning.

I have given up going to Aunt Eliza's for the present, as I can't hear whether the Breckinridges are still there or not.

The Goshen route is a good deal travelled: I don't know whether or not it is the common route however. Nib & Mr Massie left an hour or so ago for the

Alum Springs, & thence Nib goes by Goshen to Waynesboro.

If you want to send me the buttons there is no difficulty in sending them to this Office. I find the P.M. has discharged his clerk. I don't know why. I had no reason to suspect him, only the disappearance of my buttons, & re-sealing of my envelope were suspicious. God bless you, my dear John

Affectionately
S.C.P. McDowell.

Princeton, July 17th 1856.

My dearest Sally,

How I would like to have you nearer to me. The greatest sadness that all your distress is to me is that I am so helpless & must listen to your account & cannot possibly comfort you. It would be such a luxury to hold you in our old fashion on my lap & *make* you tell me all that is in your heart. And then piece by piece go over all your distress & find where any relief could be applied.

What, if after all you write me a long letter as you tho't you sometime would & tell me where you differed from me in respect to our conclusion? Who knows but your woman's wit might cut the link that chains us in this unnatural position & give us into each others arms. If you will I will raise a monument to you as high as the College—to the Great Disenchantress.

How like we are to the old story of the poor somebody that was changed into a myrtle. All the love we are allowed to make is through the Post Office &, Darling, tho' your letters are powerful yet your bodily presence unlike that of Paul is far from being (weak)[12] or your speech contemptible.

Dearest, what do you mean by saying that you were never so unhappy as the last eight months. Do you mean that you would have been less miserable if you had never seen me. I am always trembling over that sort of idea. If I thought I had invaded your peace by courting you I should begin *for the first time* to feel sad that I ever left the nine pins. Am I no necessity to you Darling? Am I no help to bear these long despondencies? Would you have kept on in an even, better state if we had never seen each other again after visiting in that shop in Geo Town? Tell me all these things. And tell me when you write how you look exactly, whether you have lost your young looks & whether you look pale & haggard & whether you are thin & exactly how thin you are & if you answer unfavorably to all these things, then tell me how much of all this distress springs from me & how much remorse & sorrow I should have for invading your former contentedness.

I am looking forward eagerly to the time when I can come & see you. I have engagements to preach till the last of August. And if you will invite me then after that or by the first of the next month after I would be glad to come. I say the first of Oct. because I have an engagement I think about the third day of that

---

12. Above "weak," Miller interlined "little."

month in Phila & I wish no engagements ahead when I come to see you. By the way I *do* preach a great deal, I forgot to answer that question.

I could hardly have staid from you so long had I not determined I would make an effort to hold out to the end of the Summer. I have such queer memories of those tavern rooms & was so half-sick half the time of those Summer visits that I was half *ashamed* to go & see you, & used to encourage myself that if in that wretched guise, so sallow & forlorn I could make you pity me enough to love me, I might possibly succeed better under more favorable circumstances. And yet, Sally, I regret the cool moon-light walks & that broken stone threshold at the door: even with all the vigils of the Hotel there was something sweet about those Summer months. And when I reach you in October, if you let me come, we shall be shut up in the parlour & delivered over to the tender-mercies of Edward & the fire.

Still, Darling, life anywhere with you is a Paradise, & do you know I am telling you the sober verity when I say that a life *always* with you seems so Eutopian & impossible that I am half reconciled to my banishment by an idea of the absurdity of any actual possession. And yet Darling, I was within three days of marrying you & indeed the idea of my *name* on your trunks which seems to be the nearest embodiment of the idea of our being each others fairly sets me crazy with vexation when I coupled the slenderness of the balance that seemed then to turn against it.

But, God bless you. You are mine still, Sally my Love, are you not?

JM.

[marginal note] As to the M.S.S.[13] I dare not risk them by express.

Colalto,
Thursday, July 17. 1856.

My *dear John,*

I limit myself to half an hour this afternoon, in which time I may write a whole letter, or only a part, according to the spirit with which I am inspired as I progress.

To my surprise, Marie & Willie came an hour ago, and as I have sent them to their rooms to rest after their hot ride from Fincastle I get this minute for my letter to you.

First & foremost, I'm worried about the buttons; and laugh at that logic of yours which whilst it makes it impossible for a gentleman, who is a Martyr to buttons, in the midst of his sorrows to add *one* more for his collar, very plainly to himself proves that it is perfectly easy for him "like a sober Christian" to add *two* more for his sleeves. This reasoning may all be according to the books, but my mind finds it to have its origin in a certain temper, which always does as it fancies in spite of everything. Well, when you do fancy to wear them in yr sleeves won't you let me give you the pair complete?

13. That is, the manuscript of his book.

The letter to "Mrs John Miller" came safely. Indeed John you do worry: don't write me any more such.

I lost the printed copy—but enclose you one in writing, slightly different. It was in *our* (the Central) Presbyterian, which I suppose you never see. Please criticize it. I make no pretensions to any *gift* in that way; but almost every body, I imagine, can sometimes measure their lines & make them jingle.

You can't tell how often my mind wanders back to your letter & its queer topic. John, *honestly*, what put such a notion in yr head, & what made you think of telling it to me? Would you fancy turning the channel of my affection from yourself, that it might flow out to somebody else, and thus set you free without the slightest ruffle of the most sensitive notions of honor? And I shame to ask such a question, but, tell me, if it is just the notion of my own busy & anxious brain? Any how, if such *could* be yr wish, you must choose some other person; with this one, the thing could not be. Love him as a friend, I have done with all my heart, & with much admiration, but to love him in any other way is impossible. I never could feel for him that sort of emotion which made me willing to brave so much to be your wife. There's Lacy too, whom I like very much, but whether you were in the way or not, I could never have given him any other answer than I did. If I ever *cd* have loved him, whether I would have done it in my different way from that in which I love you is another question, which I could not answer even in theory. But do you know when we come down to individuals in speaking on such a subject, that I shrink from it with a sort of disgust. I can't help turning away from it. And then it rouses any anxieties & disquiets me as to yr feelings. John, my own darling John, don't you love me with all your heart, or as you say, "exclusively"? It would be a great deal better to tell me if you didn't. I am always slow to use the word "passionately" myself, yet you say I have said in other words all that that one could convey, but as to this of yours—this exclusivity—I can use no other with more freedom or greater truth. I am so scared tho' as the long future stretches out before us, for our steadiness and warmth. The Lord help us, John, in our difficulties.

No, Maggie, mayn't send you my letters. Why don't I write enough to you, your own precious self to make you willing for other people to keep *theirs* to themselves. Or, are you alarmed about the "*yeilds* & miseriables", etc, etc." O! did I write hypocrity with an *a* to you the other day? If I didn't, then be alarmed, man, for I wrote it so to somebody else, & had the horrors in consequence. I hope Maggie won't call me in question for anything in my letters for I remember scarcely a word of them.

Yes, John; come and see me just when you can. If more occasions for preaching spring up in N.Y. or elsewhere, during the next month, why stay & meet them, and afterwards take yr holiday and make yr visit to me. To be sure I want to see you, yet the idea of yr coming is always mixed with pain. I mean soon to tell you some of the things I think of as connected with it, that make me anxious.

The weather is very hot here; but so much cooler than in Halifax that I can scarcely complain of it, or indeed feel it. In fact last week, I felt so chilly one day that I threw a large shawl round me & found it comfortable. My yard looks very green & fresh & lovely and is coveted by many a poor body who don't know the sadness and troubles of its forlorn, tho' envied Owner.

Nib & Mr Massie & Mac left me yesterday for the Alum. My letter has taken me just within 5 minutes of an hour—so much for resolutions where my little man is concerned.

Your own
S.C.P. McDowell.

[Enclosure]
    "I will not leave you comfortless."
Amid earth's darkest struggles,
    When sorrow's billows roll,
And Sin, in rushing torrents
    Comes sweeping o'er the soul:
When anguish rend our heart strings,
    And cares upon us press
Remember, Lord, thy promise—
    Leave us not comfortless.

When, at thy sovereign mandate
    Death comes with fearful stride
And snatches, with relentless grasp,
    Our dearest from our side;
As o'er their cold forms bending
    In grief's lone bitterness
And full hearts plead thy promise—
    Leave us not comfortless.

When o'er our heart's are stealing
    Life's shadows deep and long;
And hopes are set in darkness
    That once beam'd bright & strong;
When joy is quench'd in sadness,
    And mirth hush'd in distress,
Our refuge is thy promise—
    Leave us not comfortless.

And when alone, heart-weary
    Life's storms we meet and bear;
Deserted by earth's changelings
    Friendless & bow'd with care:
Without one tear of sympathy

To make our burdens less,
Father! We claim thy promise,—
   Leave us not comfortless.

And when our dark'ning senses
   Proclaim our work is done;
And the spent pulse faintly flutt'ring
   Tells us our course is run;
O, then when flesh is failing,
   And fears our spirits press
Fulfil, Lord, thine own promise,—
   Leave us not comfortless.
March, 1856.

Princeton July 19th 1856.

My honest darling Sally,

   I dont know that it *can* be so, but I feel as if I never knew what love was till I got your letter. If you knew the irrepressible tenderness with which I clasp you, *Dearest*—leaning upon this letter which seems to take you from all other possible possessions & give you entirely to me, you would hardly regret that in a moment of wild & somewhat wicked impulse I should have asked you those foolish questions.[14] I really think I never loved you half as much as since yesterday evening. And I feel more than ever the sacredness of a relation that makes you all in all to me. If it fills me in all my waking thoughts & makes me dream of you & yearn over you with such tenderness of love & if your own warm feeling, Sally, honestly expressed is so deep & so constant in its nature, then, Darling, a great many things of which we speak ought never to be mentioned by us again. When you talk to me of my changing how foolish & how like a mere *formality* it sounds. And when you talk of any reserves between us—Why Sally we *must* get these things away. You must break down that rampart that you say separates you from an entire expression of your feelings. You must give up all that you might wish to have reserved if you ever discover my want of affection. That is you must trust me. You must let our fondness flow on into the smooth waters of entire & trustful interdependance. If you lose anything, Sally, by my ultimately deceiving you, that is, if you lavish upon me a perfectly unreserved & as you seem to call it, "too warm" affection & fall into ways of speaking & of feeling that entirely resign you to me as having confessed your passion & then I some day prove false or unworthy—why, Darling, you must brook all that mortification. You *must* give up all precautionary coldness that would provide for such a day as that &, Darling, now be mine entirely. Why, not

---

14. Miller interlined here the question: "Do you?"

in this cold & wicked world when as you say we have few pleasures & when both in heart & speech & in appearance even we must avoid all temptations, why not seize & appropriate that one innocent pleasure which an entire trust in each other both suffers & creates; & why not when all that could prohibit such a feeling must be some defection of ourselves why not cast the fear of it to the winds & risk at least this much as to our permanent happiness.

A distinct invitation to you deliberately to change in all your fears of me, & deliberately to consecrate yourself, come what risk there may, to an ardent & avowed attachment involves on my part, at this late day, an entire forfeiture of honour if you find in me any thing you ever regret.

Be mine, Darling. And be mine in your letters. Soul & spirit—let me feel that your whole nature is flowing out to me without reserve. And Darling, I promise that nothing in which you ever trust me in a letter shall ever flow back upon your memory to shame or to disappoint you.

I know you are a woman. I see this in women. I know it is instinctive to oppose barriers to affection. But, Darling, think of our situation. It is now two years since that I have been dreaming of you. We are actually walking down the main high road of life & making this hampered & disappointed love our chief existence, ought you not to relent a little & make the instincts of your sex yield a little if it be merely in the abandon of a letter. Why cant you say, John, I love you, without caring about it lest it should be too frequent or express. And why if such freedom is kept solely for the privelege of the married, why cant you count me as married solely in this privelege, viz. that I should hear all that you feel without your stopping to think how it will be remembered, if we are ever separated.

Sally, *wouldn't* you "have purchased that year of pleasure" &—Do you wish you had never listened to me?

Do you ever "dream of me". Tell me, What?

When has your love been ever "baffled or agrieved or fretted or made suspicious"[?]

And, Darling, how has your "pride come in conflict with your affection & been obliged to yield". I dont know whether you will understand this letter. I have been in one of my inarticulate fits & couldnt say all I want. *Dear* Sally, I wish I could really feel the breath of a warm good-bye.

Yours affly
JM

[marginal notes] When I come on, if not before, I think I must penetrate more into your confidence in respect to your affairs, but of this again.

Tell me when you will if you remember me.

Colalto,
Monday July 21. 1856.

Dear John,

I thought of getting up a little earlier this morning that I might accomplish my letter to you & our little arrangements for going to the Bridge; but the cool weather made a nap rather too inviting & instead of being earlier, I am later than common.

So cool as it has been for two or three days! I feel like the winter was coming back, & find myself running to the sunny spots on the porch to get comfortably warm. It suits nicely for one trip however, & stirs me up a good deal.

I feel somewhat like murmuring at the delay of yr visit until October; but if you will, you will, you know, & I am shut up to silence. It may be our tavern here is better than before. It has passed into new hands & I hear has been overhauled and improved. I am thinking of plans which may turn me out of house & home by October; & then Lilly must go back to school somewhere about that time. However I'll write about it all when I have more time.

I hear Addison Alexander is coming to Waynesboro very soon. Why not give him the book done up in a secure package to bring to me, for no doubt he will come on this far. I'm so afraid I'll never read it, if I don't do it before it's printed! No, John, I'm going to behave good about it, & read it thro & thro', taking a little every day, just as I wd a dose of Quinine to fight off a chill & keep down a fever. I shall have to do something you know to restore me to the health which this book of yrs threatens to destroy. I have an ague every time I think of it, & hope to cure it, by reading the book—you told me it was a *littler* volume didn't you?

Marie & Willie go tomorrow & my brother Tom comes in a day or two. When my brothers get into difficulties, they are mighty apt to come to me, forgetting that they ignore & abuse me when I get into trouble—but like a good Episcopal brother I heard of—"I'll have my revenge—*I'll forgive them*".

God bless you my dear John.

Yrs S.C.P. McD.

Princeton, July 21st 1856.

Dearest, your two last letters have had a strange effect upon me. I dont know why it is, but I think they have doubled my love. The self-surrender of entire confession by which you give yourself up as *dependant* so to speak upon a power that has taken entire possession of you is responded to as tho' my frame were part of yours & as tho' the entire disclosure were unnecessary in such oneness of relation. My love has such a *solemnness* about it. I cant express it by any better word. The feeling seems to have reached some of its deeper & more heavy chords; &, Dearest, the idea of abandoning you, the idea of ever losing by any fault of mine such a lovely trust, the idea of its ever being possible that one who has ever trusted herself to me in all the guilelessness of womanly affection should ever be other than mine seems to me so incredible even to you, that I would love you more if you would never think of it. I invite you to my arms without a doubt or cloud about my affection & as you say, Sally, that you have a proclivity to confide in people do indulge it in this harmless instance of your life, where if in other cases it has done you harm, in this case it may make some amends by making you happy.

If you say your *pride* revolts at your position, dearest Sally, then love me with the homage of humility, & let me know, if it requires any mortifications to pride, that I am possessed of an affection that brings you all shamefaced to my knees.

Now, on the other hand, I am the safest person to treat with such entire surrender, because I have a feeling of *necessity*. I cant debate any longer my affection. It has gone thro' three stages; first, I tho't I could be separated from you. Tho' that was long ago. I thot if you repelled me, I would suffer, but I could *endure* it. I told you so. This was when we first met,—or rather separated. My love was all new & light & has a sort of instinctive feeling of its own power to subdue itself. And yet I loved you tenderly.

Next, I loved you with a feeling that concluded all my debates. It was a feeling that just threw a large portentous balance in the scale whenever I dared to question the strength of my attachment. It was a feeling that made me willing to die without marrying you rather than marry another. And it was a feeling that made me long for more of your fondness so that I could roll myself up in your affection & keep warm against the chills of life.

And now, Darling, this fondness comes & two letters in which you unburdened yourself to me & tell me more than ever before & place yourself in a condition in which both your affection & mine must be shamefully violated if we are ever left to trifle &, Dearest, it has the strangest effect upon all my feelings. It gives me a feeling of a man's tenderness for you that I can hardly describe. It makes you mine in a way the feeling of which gives me the keenest pleasure. It gives you so *entirely* to me. And, Dearest, it makes me feel as tho' you were glad to be mine, & glad even to disencumber yourself even of anxiety, that you may sink down trustfully & unthinkingly in my arms.

Now the fruit of all this is in me a love that is perfectly *unyielding*. It seems the third great stage in the growth of a singular passion. It will not debate any more. It looks at such questions as you put, as tho' they were asking whether I would be rent asunder or whether I would give up one of these children of mine to be poisoned. I cant describe how impossible it seems. You have become not only a part of myself, but I, my own being, in a remarkable way. I never intend to give you up. If you leave me it must be by the blankest fatality or by an indifference which is impossible also in you. Sally, we are made for each other, & tho' you may not follow me in this rhapsody, (which nevertheless I dare not laugh at, for it is the religious feeling of my heart) yet I feel *strong* from these letters that you are with me, that wisely or unwisely, as worthy or unworthy you love me tenderly & with that warm species of affection that can conceive itself possible to no other object.

Then as to your definite question it is no longer necessary for me to answer it. It shows what a jealous thing love is that in one week two passionate lovers should have asked each other—one whether he might not one day be supplanted by another person & the other, whether this very question was not a profoundly gentle way of getting rid of her altogether. And yet, Dearest, to leave you no lurking suspicion I will say frankly that in your two letters I *have* all the object in asking the question. So far from wishing to get off from you or from ever dreaming of such a thing there has been no time from the first of our attachment when I would have been willing to lose you even if your own feeling were entirely provided for—*no time for two minutes*—Can you say as much! And now—And now after all these mutual jealousies, come here, Love, & put your arms warmly & trustfully round me. I do love you, Sally, enough for any woman with the most exacting jealousy of nature. To meet your own question I love you "with *all* my heart". I think our circumstances will produce a singular passion for we have all the consecrations of marriage without its differences. And however this passion may end Remember Dearest, I am as much yours as tho' I were actually your husband. I invite you to as absolute a thot of me as perpetually your own as if we were fettered by the most absolute bonds of actual marriage.

In your very next letter tell me all "the things you think of as connected with my visit that make you anxious." Tell me all that you fear about it.

The poetry is beautiful. I am a little jealous of the Presbyterian. I think it is even handsomer than what you sent to me. Why dont you write me more? But when you do—let me tell you one thing—dont let it make your letter any shorter. If you will send me as beautiful a piece (unpublished) I will send it to Blackwood. I am sorry this is spoiled by having been printed. It is [unquestionably?] beautiful.

Laughably enough this letter which is so full of honest tenderness—which does so seem to confide in me & surrender you to me—has the first hard word you ever uttered;—"My mind finds it to have its origin in a certain temper which always does as it fancies in spite of everything!" Oh, Sally, what a character! I think you are like Robt Breckenridge who sometimes finishes a sentence *strong* just for the sake of the jingle. I know you didnt *mean* it.

Because, Sally, about the buttons I am entirely innocent. I mean to wear them in my sleeves which I know you would like better. And therefore I forbear to fix the collars which would cost me a great deal of fuss & explanation. Moreover I have been hit once in a store where I could buy them & then by a strange fatality. I had forgot to have them along. I go to N.Y. next Sat. week. I mean to get all three then, mark them, & if I dare venture it, again send them by mail. If you will only love me half as much as I love you I'll never quarrel with you about buttons. I cant let you give me the pair first because you cant get 'em where you [live?] & second because you *did* give 'em.

yours

JM

Colalto,
Tuesday July 22. 1856.

My *dear John*,

I had no idea I should feel as much as I do the parting with my young cousins. After they left us this morning I gave up to a real spell of depression. Willie is wonderfully clever; and I think the most attractive young man of his age I ever saw. He is not handsome, but so easy and graceful in his carriage & manner, and so gifted in voice, (which if it be a charm in a woman is just as great a one in a man) and conversation that I scarcely remark, & certainly am not affected by the absence of mere physical beauty. But Marie is my special favorite among all the children. When she was an outlaw of a child, whom everybody felt privileged to abuse, I remember her singular affection for me, and of her creeping up to my side & as she looked up in my face saying with very gratifying emphasis, "Cousin I'm going to have you for my Sister". She evidently thought that relationship wd justify the full expenditure of all her love to me. She is just the same affectionate, impulsive eager thing now, and professes to love me as much as ever! "O Cousin" she called to me from the carriage as they drove off—"dont you change any before I see you again". I made no promises; for you know "time & tide &c. &c.["]

It was very cool and pleasant yesterday, & we had a nice time at the Bridge; but I thought of our visit there a year ago, & tried to recall all the incidents of it, and catch again a little of its pleasure. I didn't venture to the large rock on which we sat, & where you had the talk with the man about lovers visits to the place; nor did I go farther down to a deeper place in the little stream where, as I looked at you going thro' the unromantic & very commonplace business of washing yr hands I could hardly keep from saying—"Pray, John, don't waste all that soap". That old tavern looks the same as ever—dingy and dirty; but I sat down at the window where I waited for you, as you took yr solitary stroll to the top of the Bridge and thought of you, and my heart, like a Magic Mirror, gave me a sight of you once more. But I have so poor a memory of localities that tho' I tried it, I couldn't identify the stretch of good road where you left me to drive after you. I'm afraid, John, you didn't value my neck very much in those days, for two or three times you left me to the mercy of strange horses, and my own unskilful management of the reins.

By the way this resurrecting of by-gone pleasures is something of an occupation with me now. It is just a year this very night, I believe, since I watched with such anxiety for the passing away of the day light, and, after the night closed in and Cantey & Lilly were asleep, sat down in the porch, and listened & listened with such restless emotion for the coming stages which I knew 11 o'clock wd bring; and for the coming footsteps that something else wd bring, the sound of which my quickened sense cd catch at a long distance. I waited and watched & listened and thought they were *so* long coming. But at last a quick, decided step on the stile by the hedge was unmistakable, and hardly knowing or thinking what I should say or do, I hurried from the door to meet you. Do *you* remember it all John? How vivid it is to me! I must have had it impressed by sunlight upon my memory instead of that beautiful moonlight, it is so clearly and strongly there. I almost hear now yr exclamation of surprise at my sudden apparition, and feel again the eager & warm clasp of my hand as you drew it within yr arm where I turned you back to the steps. I don't remember what you sd, if indeed you said anything, for I was agitated; and that you were really come was almost my only distinct consciousness. How I shivered as we sat on that step in the night air, not so much from cold, tho' it was cool, as from nervous excitement which the shawl that you wrapt round me,—that friendly gray plaid, which on account of these associations I have an attachment for,—could not quiet however warm it kept me.

And, John, as I think of it, you stand before now just as clearly defined by that clear sky as you were then. And you look just the same as when I asked you to take off yr hat and let me see whether I knew you again. I feel that I can put out my hand and smooth down the hair which the night breeze lifted from its place. I didn't dare to do it then. I didn't dare lay claim to that dear head as mine then; I would feel differently now. I hardly had suggested to me then, the idea of your belonging to me, but my mind was engrossed by thought of my belonging to you. No unpleasant thought either, but one full of anxiety both then and now.

How long did we stay on that step John, do you remember? Half an hour was it? I am sure I don't know; but one thing I recollect; as we came back and *I* stood in the light you said, "Why, Sally, I don't think, after all, you are such a *big* woman". The name, spoken as tho' you had made a great effort to get it out, went tingling thro' me; and then I was amused at the relief you evidently experienced at finding me somewhat smaller than the house I lived in. I have no doubt you had magnified my proportions to those of a giantess.

We walked along pretty soberly to the porch, & as I wouldn't let you come in stopt on the step to say good night. And I recollect, dear John, I wonder if you do? of yr leaning against the porch and giving me, in a tone & manner of strong emotion the warmest assurances of yr affection; and then as we parted, of your putting you hand on my head & gently bending it that you might lightly press yr lips on my forehead. O, John, I feel almost ashamed to say that that light kiss lingers there yet.

I don't know how you fared—whether the fatigue of yr journey overcame all other things and thrust sleep upon you; but I know the excitement held my eyes waking many an hour after you were gone. And I know too that my mind has been just as busy with the recollections of that moonlight meeting many a quiet hour since as it was then. Tell me, John, does that hour ever steal back pleasantly upon your sober, philosophizing life now. Or has it been blotted out by our troubles since, or become hateful as having ushered in their troubles? It is so pleasant a memory to me, I wonder if a time ever *can* come when I shall wish it never had been!

Wednesday morning

While I think of it let me ask you. Look in yr music stores, if you have such places in Princeton for a song called "Linger not long" dedicated or inscribed or whatever they call it, "to Mrs McDowell of Va". Marie was asking me about it, telling me that her Cousin Dr (M.D.) Robt Breckinridge[15] had found it in New York, had understood that the dedication was to me and fancying it as a song, had sent it to some of his Ky cousins to learn. I have not seen it, & she promised to send me a copy. I hardly think I am the Mrs M D meant; but any how I am a little curious about it.

John *don't* you wish I could write you more sensible letters. Do you think I would talk this sort of things to you if I was sitting quietly by you employed upon that buttonless linen you speak of? If I didn't then, I think it very likely I should find some other time to do it in. O John, who loves you besides me and Maggie and Allie, any body? And what do they love you for? And how much do they love you? I have come down in my notions: I don't think any body hardly really loves me. But so long as I think you love me, I feel very independent of the affection of other people.

Mary writes me very sadly of herself, & I feel very sad about her. She is naturally despondent, and her struggle against this temper, in the midst of so much to strengthen it, is very touching [to] me. I hope we will all get to Heaven someday and find peace & happiness there. Yet I don't think we are earnestly seeking after that rest: we are so bent upon the happiness that we fancy this world is capable of giving. In your last letter you bid me write you about something, but I cd not possibly make out what. I wish I cd send you a facsimile of the word. You laid great stress upon my doing it too. Next time write better.

Yrs
S.C.P. McD.

Thursday 1856. July (24)[16]

Dear Sally,

This is the first time for a long long time that I write in a hurry. But I have been driving Julia out who is here & have but a moment before the mail. I will write just what comes uppermost. I would be happier than I am a great deal if

15. Robert James Breckinridge (1828–1866), a physician in Louisville, was the son of William Lewis Breckinridge (1803–1876), a brother of "Uncle Robert" Breckinridge.

16. McDowell added the date in parentheses.

you were nearer to me. If we were so happily off as be [poor?] country people in neighbouring hamlets & were embarrassed as we now are how sweet it would be to lie down at night with your cottage so near that I could see the smoke of it curling up in the morning. But still God is the Judge. I suppose all these things are right. I love you with a passion more than I can tell you of & wonder whether I would have loved you so much by this time if we had been married. Do you know I think these romantic histories of ours have a tendency favorable to a very elevated sort of passion. I am anxious about you in many ways. Do you know that I will not endure more than a certain amount of suffering & embarrassment on your part of a pecuniary sort. I must know all down to the very bottom if your pressure becomes much greater. For, Dearest, you are *mine*. By all that is sacred in my mind & thought of you, you are *my wife* in a vast many respects of association & feeling. And before you shall be shamed by exposures of your self-respect or feel the extreme need of aid *I* am the person to be made your confidant. I would rather return to the pulpit on that very express errand & consider it a call in Providence than not have you feel that substantially & in the dernier resort you & I after all are but one & that I am determined to try & win you to the feeling that we are launched in the same boat & that [we] are perfectly safe from the *extremes* of embarrassment so long as I am kept from them.

I know, Dearest, that this may sound strange to you & you may laugh at it & think that I am wiping away all romance from our attachment. But, Dearest, I have a strong belief in romance but a strong belief also in the unity of lovers. So come weal or come woe. If you consider it impossible then consider it as a sort of rod held over you to make you vigilant in your own estate. For think how preposterous it would be for me to profess to love you like abstraction & yet to *dream* of such a thing as letting you suffer from anything from which I am exempt.

I *feel* toward you in all these respects as towards my children & Sally dear, dont quarrel with me when you write. I have grown anxious about you. I wouldnt care if you would hurry my visit. I love you with a calmness of certainty that this passion will have its hold upon me all thro' this life.

In extreme haste

Yrs
JM.

Colalto,
Thursday, July 24. 1856.

My *dear John*,

I think it *is* pleasanter to get my letters with some regularity every other day. It allays a good deal the constant excitement I used to be in from morning to morning. Often, I have suffered inexpressibly when the letters failed, and couldn't recover from the disappointment for hours. Now I pretty well know, how to bear the intervals between them; and can make one real good letter serve for several comfortable meals. How do you treat my letters when they reach you? Read them once, then stuff them in an old wrapper of old papers, or carelessly thrust them in yr pocket & let them stay there till you are tired of having them take up the room of something more valuable. Do you ever find them troublesome to read? Sometimes they seem to me almost illegible in places. However, if ever we are married they will help to kindle many a fire of a more material kind than the one they keep alive now. And if we ain't, why somebody else may make an Auto da fé of them if they please.[17] By the way, I am obliged to you for yr letter to Spence about these same letters. I would not like in any circumstances to have strange or curious eyes looking into our correspondence.

I have gathered all yr letters in one place. They are tied up in seperate packages, each one bearing the date & number, on the outside wrapping. Latterly, I collect them by the month and mark them thus—"May 1856.—11" or "June. 1856–12"—As they come, one after another, I throw them in a little drawer in my work stand, until the month is up, then tie them together, mark them, & put with them with the rest. Then sometimes, when I think I won't be disturbed, for do you know I can't bear a servant even to come in & catch me at such employment, I sit down *on the floor*, & take out these letters, & read them. Not all of them, or perhaps, many of them at a time, but some of them. But it does not always have the same effect; for it happens occasionally I am made much sadder than merrier by the pastime. I had my fancy pleased a long time ago by reading a little story of Sir Phillip Sydney.[18] Being absent from his ladye-love, he was excessively anxious about her remembrance of him, and longed to know how she employed herself while he was away. *Somehow*, perhaps by the kind interposition of fairies, his wish was granted; and he beheld the dear lady quietly sleeping with a volume of his poems in her hand! He was satisfied. Here was proof positive that her waking thoughts were his; & proof presumptive that her sleeping ones were too. But John, Darling, if ever you were to find me asleep over *yr philosophy*, would you be content? What reason wd you impute to me for being caught napping? Oh John, I often laugh at the thought of how dreadful sleepy I am when that philosophy's about.

But, "turn about is fair play", you know: & very early in our correspondence you wrote to me that one night, you had drawn yr table to the side of yr bed, & had taken out my letters to read, & had actually fallen asleep with one in yr hand! I forgave you that offence a great while ago—but you mustn't be too hard on me in future about such delinquencies.

I hardly know how to write to Maggie. Tell me how. Does she ever ask about me of her own accord, or do you suggest her inquiries?

Unless you particularly fancy, don't send me the sleeve-buttons, but any thing

17. An "auto-da-fé" is a public burning, used during the Inquisition to execute heretics.
18. Sir Philip Sidney (1554–1586), English soldier, poet, and statesman.

else *you* would like me to wear. Lilly has two setts of buttons, & I can use one of them, especially as I gave them to her, whenever I want.

I have inaugurated a new Overseer, who begins with some promise. I'm afraid Morgan is a great scamp. He comes & talks & cries over his devotion to Father & fidelity to me until I am, sometimes so full of contempt for him that I can hardly put up with him. Yesterday we had that scene repeated, with an addition, in which if there be no truth, there is much villany—but I will not trouble you with it.

I have turned Edward out of the house on the farm. He is not strong & I thought outdoor work would strengthen him;—besides a man-servant is too expensive a luxury for me, at present. He saves me the hiring of an out hand, & I am willing to bear the inconvenience of his absence. He will not be out all the time. I can recall him when I have company.

People tell me I look very well. And, by way of pleasing you, let me tell you, that I hear quite nice things said about me yet. Mr Flournoy, the K.N. defeated candidate for Governor, speaks quite enthusiastically of what he calls "Mrs M D's fascinations"; & Mrs Clarke declares that that same lady "is the most elegant woman in Va".[19] But she always speaks extravagantly—however her praise is worth something, for she has a reputation for talent &c, &c, herself. We are remote kin thro' the Henrys. She is a charming musician, & perhaps her oratory is at the end of her fingers, more conspicuously, than at the end of her tongue.

I did mean all I said about the buttons—:

"If you will, you will: I may depend on't.

If you wont, you wont, & there's the end on't."

A most descriptive couplet, you must acknowledge—tho' somewhat lacking in melody.

But, good-bye. I long to call you by all sorts of sweet names, but am really ashamed.

Yrs
S.C.P. McD.

Princeton July 26th 1856.

My *darling love*,

I always feel when I begin to write to you as if I had a vast amount to say, &, as in my old visits to Colalto, I always end by letting everything I had thought of lie, in the far more engrossing pleasure of caressing you & telling you my affection. Do you never get tired of hearing that I love you?—But I must break off & try to crowd a great deal in my letter by little short broken sentences.

I am growing unhappy from impatience. I am engaged to preach in N.Y. the 2d Sun. Aug.—After that I want earnestly to come as soon as you will allow. Tell

19. Thomas Stanhope Flournoy (1811–1883) had run for governor on the Know-Nothing or American Party ticket. Elvira Ann Henry Clark.

me when the *best* time will be. Above all dont let it postpone any business plan. Do you still think of breaking up in Oct?

How *long* may I stay? Do you think it would be quite out of the question for me to come with the avowed purpose of staying some time in Lex: & going on with my studies? I do so hate these wrong separations. Indeed I have staid away so long that my visit now is an occasion partly of pain from the fever of suspense & impatience. Have you any of these persevenesses of character that change your pleasures into pain by mere excess.

Mon. week. It is not here.

I dont know what word it was you couldnt decypher. You spoke of two subjects you would some day write me long letters upon. One was the pain in some respects my visit would give you, & the other was the feelings that agitate you about our marriage, in which you said you acquiesced in the judgment of others without entire certainty of conviction. Darling, write me freely on all these subjects. My love is so perfectly inveterate & fixed & my fondness for you in your love to me & all your frankness of character so excessive that I do beg you to treat me in all matters of confidence as if we had been long married.

I was touched by your last letter. How much, after all you have been concealing from me. What I want to ask & I can merely mention it—in this omnibus letter you must consider me as very earnest in *all* I say—I want to beg you to go back over all our love—go back to that morning at Colalto or even if you please to our first meeting at Fred. & Geo. Town & give me your own kind & loving thoughts of all our Virginia interviews. Indeed Sally you could hardly write to me sweeter letters than such as that yesterday extended thro' all our courtship. You do so win upon me when you express your passion in these unexpected ways, & now when I read over your old letters which I am beginning more to do those written at the time you speak of glow with fresh light & I see more in their expressions of affection.

Do you ever read over my letters, Sally? Then I want you also to *send back* to me those letters that wounded you. I think you were a little hard upon me, Sally: & that you dont judge me by any very even standard, but then that letter whose reception you lately kept so quiet & that one in which I tease you for a keepsake to which I had taken a fancy I would like you if you will to send back to me & indeed any others that present me, at any disadvantage in your eyes. I think you judge me a little rigidly & perhaps under some misapprehension of which I know nothing, but no matter, I want to weed out from your bundle of letters any that worry you.

Have I worried you much, Dearest?

Be sure to forecast your movements well & choose for me the most convenient time & in every respect the most pleasant to you for my visit.

My book is nearly done. Shall I publish at once or give the M.S. to you?

Your letters are not alike on one point as to whether you are glad or sorry you ever saw me.

I have been thinking some day of beginning a diary, to bring you into closer relations with my every day life.

Last Sunday night I fell into a long rumination upon you & plans for your comfort. I thot of yr N. Haven plan—of the pleasure I would have in closer relations with you for my poor daughter Maggie—of how probable it was that you were really *suffering* with banks & moneyed embarrassments—but out of it all I would reach but three points—1st that you were mine & that with a feeling of confidence both in your affection & mine which gives me no doubt.[20] Have I cause for any? Sally? 2d that you must not & *shall* not be left to struggle too much alone & unprotected. Your health & your self-respect & your pleasant cheerful temperament to say nothing of your comfort are all pieces of my property which I must look after with something more than the spirit of a silent partner.

I thank you so for regular writing. But, Dearest, beggars like me are always unreasonable. You asked the other day for employment. Let me propose some. The interval caused by Sunday troubles me. I find I cant *bear* more than an interval of two days. Now as a great favour, will you not in some way secure me *one* more letter in the week. And then will you not avoid the short hasty letter of Mon. morn which I get on Wednesday.

Tell me how you are when you write. Are you fat? You know you told me at Halifax you were thinner than you had been for a long time. Be particular to tell me how you look.

I have had half a notion to write to Lilly asking her. How is she? Is her dislike for me very great?

Did you ever hear whether that letter I returned to the Doctor was a proper sort of letter or not & how the Dr liked its being declined?

Act energetically about your business. And dont let my projected visit enervate or distract your attention to that sort of duty.

Sally, what is the pleasantest hour you & I ever spent together? I do hope, Dearest, you will sketch our whole progress thro' these eventful years as you did in this letter I have just received. Whatever, unveils you to me fills me with love to you & makes me if such a thing can be more complete in your allegiance. You ask me Does any body love me? I dont know; but, if some dozens of people don't they're great hypocrites.

Yours affly
JM

[marginal notes] Ha! Sally, you amused me so about the spelling. The demure way in which you *count* your mishaps in that line is quite refreshing. Tho' you *simplify* certainly sometimes. You say "schold" for scold & that certainly looks righter than the other. You say cretanism for cretinism. O, Sally.

20. In March, McDowell had considered spending the summer in New Haven, Conn. (McDowell to Miller, Mar. 20, 1856).

Dont *you* write your letters this way. I dont like scrappy letters.

Colalto,
July 28 1856.

My *dear John,*

I am always hurried when I write in the morning and have every number & variety of interruptions. However before the breakfast bell rings I may be able to write a little.

My new Overseer has set to work very industriously, and with a great idea of retrenchment! He is not a *gentleman* like Morgan, (nor such a scamp either I hope) but works himself, thus saving me the expense of an additional hand. He found Edward, who is not well this summer, too delicate for farm service, and has returned him to me, taking Alfred in exchange. This suits me better. I have been greatly annoyed by Alfred, who tho' honest and faithful, is yet sullen & simper truant, to a degree that I found extremely hard to endure. However as Edward is to go into the garden, it still leaves me only these two little worries of children to wait in the house. They irritate me incessantly like a pair of mosquitoes, but I can put up with I think, especially as they are growing in knowledge & skill.

But my servants are, from feeble health, almost valueless to me. It is wrong, but I grow so impatient under, first, their being sick, & then, the privileges they claim in consequence that I heartily wish the State would provide an Asylum for good-for-nothing negroes. When they grow old & worn out from faithful service you are bound to take care of them by every sentiment of humanity & honor; but when, as in the case of one of mine, they have never been of special value for their industry & fidelity, & have always been imprudent, & have grown more so as age & infirmities increase, they become a great burden.

Your letter of Thursday came an hour ago. How strange you should think I could find it in me "to quarrel" with you about it. It is just like you John; & I love you all the better for it. I should feel it hard & awkward if you didn't sympathize with me, & were not anxious as to the issue of my pecuniary difficulties. And I do thank you with all my heart for all you say and all you offer and all you feel about me in these money troubles. And I can tell you I value far more that sort of attachment that leads you to look into & desire to provide for me in my real embarrassments, than that, that stands off and addresses me in all the "airy nothings" of mere romance. Besides, I really do think this helpful sort of affection is after all, more deeply colored with *genuine romance* than the other. But whether it be the real romantic, or just the practical real, it is all the same to me, inasmuch as it teaches me that you love me in such a ways as, not to *inspire,* for that you have done already in many ways, but *to confirm* my confidence in you. You can't think how I need to have a vent for this impulse of my nature. I have been so shocked by the exhibitions of selfishness & treachery & faithlessness, that my proclivities to confidence have been rudely checked, and I have had a doubt of every body. Oh, John, if you can never spare me any other pain, do spare me the dreadful agony of finding my Trust in you misplaced. I have no reason to question it now; I have entire faith in your trueness, (which word has a highest & broader meaning to me than mere *truth*) of character, and I rely upon you,—don't you see me do it?, with all the faith of my nature.

I can't write to you about my affairs. I will tell you, as much as you want to know, about them when you come on. I am taking such steps towards the adjustment of them that I can. But I find, this thing of transacting business with men several hundred miles distant, is very slow & unsatisfactory. My Louisville Agent has again disappointed me in his remittance. But I have more hope of the real and beneficial results of the sale of our Ky land than heretofore, and am glad that my decided refusal to commit the sale of it to James, has, as I think saved to us, some thousands of dollars. However, I cannot tell yet very accurately about it: I am waiting to hear from Uncle Robt Breckinridge, before I ask for a sale & employ an agent. My opinion, just now, is drawn from Willie Br's statement. Our Missouri land too—I hear has risen from $5 to 12 p acre; which is somewhat inspiriting.

If you can meet with it, please read a little memoir, just published, of my highly esteemed acquaintance, Mr Chisholm of the Episcopal church of Portsmouth. I was reading it yesterday with very great pleasure. It is written by an eminent lawyer of Va, who has fairly and I think, with uncommon truthfulness, drawn the character of a very noble christian Minister:—or rather he has allowed Mr Chisholm in his quiet, unobtrusive way to show himself to us in his letters, memoranda &c, for Mr Conrad's part of the book is entirely a secondary affair— but the cement that fastens Mr C's own materials together.[21]

My enthusiasm is always roused by the earnest attempt of an immortal man, *to be useful:*—not to be distinguished, but to be useful;—and when, in some instances, as in this, I find usefulness *achieved* by firm, unostentatious, patient, labor; by unyielding, unswerving, elevated principle; by the self-sacrificing, heroic devotion to the noblest of all duties, I can hardly tell you how stirred and glowing my admiration becomes. What a blessing that such men live! Ay! & what a blessing too, strange as it may seem, *that they die.*

Next time you drive Julia, go earlier or make your drive shorter, that I may have my regular letter in its proper size. By the by, does Julia like me any better now that I am afar off. O John you are partial critic. But the verses were really not much. God bless you.

Aff'y
S.C.P McD.

---

21. David Holmes Conrad (1800–1877), *Memoir of Rev. James Chisholm, A.J., Late Rector of St. John's Church, Portsmouth, Va.* (New York: Protestant Episcopal Society for the Promotion of Evangelical Knowledge, 1856).

Princeton, July 28th 1856.
Maggie's sick chamber.

My *Charmer*,

I would *so* like to have you here now. Night before last Maggie was taken sick & yesterday morning it was pronounced Scarlet Fever! You must know that my sister Sarah, (Mrs Hageman) lost an infant with this disease this Spring & has another son I fear seriously lamed by it. I was in a great panic & began at once the closest application as a nurse. What do you think of Maggie's liking no body to nurse her like me. Indeed she asks questions now & then to see if I am going to give out or be with her still. I would so like you to help me. I think I could nurse Maggie for a fortnight without the slightest disposition to leave her, if I had you just to mix the medicines & put your smooth white hand upon her cheek & speak a word of comfort to—both of us now & then. Maggie is getting off wonderfully well & I with my dread of the disease am beginning to be quite glad that she has taken it. I hope poor little Allie will either not take it or do as well.

My darling Sally, what do you think of this notion of Maggies about my nursing her. Suppose you were dreadfully sick. Suppose that foolish head of yours was free of all notions about, what shall I call it?—not "the expulsive power of a new affection", as some religious book heads itself—but the expulsive power of my poor Sally's prudish notions to keep her lover at arms length. Or suppose you were so far, far worn away by a long decline that you had very little expulsive force about anything—tell me Dearest would you have the least notion like my poor Maggies—would you think it quite a luxury to have me smooth your pillow & hand you your neat little pieces of broken ice—or would I be like all worldly pomps & vanities a thing that you couldnt abide in your hour of misery.

Poor little Maggie! Little Ned & Julie (who, by the way, had quite a stampede this morning to Phil with their father & mother) have been playing Indian with her lately, & as she looked down a while ago at her bosom & arms all flaming with scarlet, she said, Now she'd make a good Indian. What shall you write to her? Why write her a letter of comfort in her sickness. The poor little thing quite touched me when she asked so anxiously whether I would sit up to-night again as her nurse & turned me into the channel of thinking how significant that is of certain kinds of liking. A practical solid liking—a sort of liking that lasts. I have a great curiosity to know whether you are at all like her in this respect & I beg you dont forget to tell me. You ask me what I do with your letters.— The thing that *agitates* me most is the *first* reading. I have found beyond the possibility of doubt that the second reading gives me most pleasure. The first reading I thought I could mellow into something more pleasant by keeping the letter in my pocket—by looking at it & turning it in my hand as a cat does a mouse. Indeed I thought there was philosophy in the thought of prolonging the pleasure by keeping my treasures sealed as a miser does his money & thinking of the pleasure in the future. But I found this like stemming a torrent of wild horses.

Every eager passion would be threatening to lynch me. Curiosity would reach her long finger over my shoulder & say, John, what is that you've got in your pocket. And I have found that *this* stage of the enjoyment was all parched up to nothing. So usually I read it. But then it is, with the vexing thot that it is all *going going* & presently like a dream it will be all wasted. Then fancy is always wanting me to wait till I get into a nice place to read it. If I am walking in the moonlight as I was one evening fancy wants me to wait to some point in the meadow more beautiful than the rest & I actually placed myself in a new spot in the moonlight four times before I feverishly drew out the letter & rifled it of its contents. *Then* if it is short (& of that perhaps I have already had notice by the thin feeling that it has) I feel so *dispirited*. And if it is about somebody else than you & your love I am so disappointed but if it any says in some artless way, I love you I'm as happy as a prince & I feel as if the whole meadow & the moon that hangs over it & the night air were all mine & I had the world pretty much at my feet. But the second reading is quite different. I calmly enjoy it. And then I read it over & over—& at last like all worldly pleasures get it so worn out & so crumpled under the fingers of memory that I cant get any fresh or tingling emotion from it.

Sally, this is an unvarnished tale. I have not enough worldly providence to look six days ahead & try to coax you out of a warmer letter but if you knew how you could cheer your lover & set him upon his tasks with fresh hope & life, you would whisper in your own sweet maidenly way into his ear all your passion for him. When your letters are read I throw away the envelope & fold them all their length with their date uppermost & out & tie them all together with red tape in the order in which they come.

Sally, when you say you are "ashamed" just in the midst of some little pleasant expression of your love please tell me what you are ashamed of. I think women are so funny.

Yours very impatiently
Jno Miller.

[marginal note] When had I best come & how long may I stay?

Colalto,
July 29. 1856.

Well, John, I've tried my very best; and I can no more make out the word in your letter which is to tell me how I am not to write mine, than if it was written in Sanscrit or Chinese, and intended for Ancients or Celestrals. But I'll give you the context and try to do you justice in my attempt at drawing the hieroglyph. "Don't *you* write yr letters this way. I don't like—scappy-letters."[22] Be kind enough to send me a translation either literal or free. And in future, when you would lay your commands upon me in the form of an expressed wish,

---

22. McDowell's word for "scrappy" is actually illegible.

pray write or *print* the important word or words in the sentence. I think I have seen you show some capacity for printing.

And then as to the spelling—what an array of new words you bring against me! But pshaw! John, it isn't genteel to spell every word exactly according to rule. It is only a literary *parvenue* that finds it necessary to be so intensely and punctiliously accurate. And if I do introduce poor harmless, silent letters now & then into a word, it is only done from the over flowings of my amiably sociable spirit, and from that charitable temper that seeks to make the *most* even of a *scold*! And do you sure enough, notice these sort of "mishaps" as you call them? And what effect do they have upon you? I confess I am somewhat sensitive about them. I don't at all like to make such mistakes, and that because I am so susceptible of an unfavorable impression by such on my own feelings. I am sure, I could not have loved you, if I had been receiving from you all this time letters that looked to me illiterate and unscholarly: not that I like an essay of a letter; but I like, even the careless execution of such letters, as a correspondence like ours countenances, to bear the mark of some cultivation. I am so easily disgusted by the want of this, that, very naturally, I am averse to any such exhibition of it on my own part. But, of course, you are not to understand, that I would have you exhaust all yr mind in writing a *fine* letter to me, any more than you wd understand me to wish you to make elegant set speeches to me, if I were to tell you that I objected to having a gentleman talk like a peasant & preferred he sh speak like a scholar.

You know, John, I have often remarked to you what seemed to be the oneness of thought between us. I am often struck with it myself. Your letter this morning gives, in a little matter, another instance of it. Almost at the same moment that I write to you, somewhat anxiously, as to how you read and treat my letters, you are writing to me exactly in the same spirit & on the same subject:—our letters cross each other. It may be, in other and more important things, we have this same "community of sensation" (isn't that what they call it?) which, however, is unuttered.

I can't write you such letters, as the one you ask me to repeat, except when I'm in the humor for it; and, indeed, not always then. And it's well I cant: you would get dreadfully tired of them. They wouldn't be natural either; for, if I remember the one you allude to, it was not speaking of an every-day occurrence, but with great speciality of one or two pleasant meetings only. If you will just let me turn Quakeress in our love-affairs, and only speak when the spirit moves me, you will like it better:—then these will be true fire in my censer, and not that false fire, which might have light enough, but could have no heat. So, John, my own dear John, you will just leave me to do as I please about that.

Another thing.—I can't write any oftener than I do. I couldn't contrive a letter on Sunday; you, must put up with that *tremendous interval of three days*. I think I practise a good deal of self-denial about yr Sunday letters; for the second letter you write in the week almost always comes by Saturday night's mail. But all day Sunday there it lies quietly in my box. I long for it, & think of it, and reason about it, but unless my conscience seizes upon some justification for the act as connected with somebody else, there it *rests* till Monday morning. I remember, last summer, getting a letter from you on Sunday & punishing myself for taking it out, by only, reading a line or two of it, & then locking it up till Monday. If I had been a Catholic that penance wd have canonized me—elevated me to the honor of being your patron Saint! Then you would have had the pleasure of knowing, & loving and apostrophizing me under some, sweeter name, than that which you say belongs to me in common with "Uncle Tom's queer wife"[23] and some forlorn chamber maid in the remote past.

No: I never tire of hearing, do you ever tire of telling me that you love me? It is a fresh & pleasant thing every time it comes;—and if it wasn't why, surely a good story may be very much oftener than twice told.

I have taken up almost the whole of my "broad page" with mere flimsiness. I wanted to talk to you too about important matters in a serious way. However, I'll first dispose of yr questions, as just at this moment they come to mind. I don't know that Lilly dislikes you at all. She cautiously avoided expressing herself about our affair. Poor child! it was natural, under all the circumstances, she should feel a shrinking from our marriage. Occasionally, she lets things drop, that show me something of the violence, to use a moderate word, that her brother used in speaking of me. By the way, Aunt Sally had a great story to tell Aunt Eliza & Susan of James having one day met Lilly on the Street with a dress of mine in her hand, which she said I had told her to take *to your room to you:* and of his taking it from her & being horrified at my want of care and thought for the child. Aunt Eliza contradicted it plump, upon what she knew of me in the general, & told me of it, asking authority from me to put a stop to it. I asked Lilly if there was any foundation for the story whatever. She sd, of course, I had never sent her on any such errand; if I had she wouldn't have gone; & that she never had any such meeting with her brother; or any meeting at all that she cd remember on the street with him during the winter. So much for the tender care my friends have for me!

As to the letter you returned to James, all I know of its character, I gathered from a conversation with Cousin Sally Preston in December. Massie showed the letter to Cousin John, & he to his wife, who asked, as she told me, if Massie was going to present it to you; adding that, she thought, he ought to return such a letter as it was to James & tell him if he meant to send it to you, he must do it thro' the mail. From this I inferred that the letter was violent not to say denunciatory in its character. In the same conversation, Cousin Sally, said "In her opinion James had long ago transcended any right that his relationship gave him—and had changed about in his views of the matter two or three times". But all this is in the past. I were less or more than a human being not to have felt greatly indignant and greatly outraged at James' conduct; but I have been struggling against all bitterness & revengeful feeling to him on account of it. I

23. Sarah Bache Sergeant, the wife of Miller's uncle, Thomas Sergeant.

remember that we are children of the same Parents—and that, of all men he & Tom are the nearest of my blood:—and more than that, from christian principle I wd restrain the feeling—and christian duty & propriety wd urge me to keep from the *exhibition* of any such domestic hostility. Besides this, from my heart I do so compassionate James in his many difficulties & weaknesses, that I am surprised to find, at times, that I wholly forget that I have any cause of complaint against him on my own account. We write to each other, much less frequently than formerly; but generally in a tone of civil kindliness. I never speak to him of my plans, or difficulties—never ask him of his. If he tells me voluntarily *his* arrangements, I respond with a sufficient degree of interest in them—but only do it, to assure him that he can rely upon my kind services & sympathy when he feels that he needs them. And I have a sort of feeling that a time will come, when he will find himself returning to me as almost his only disinterested & reliable friend. I am often anxious about him. No man stands more in need of a real friend I think, than he does. And I desire to hold myself ready to be that to him at any moment that he calls, or that I find he needs one. But; I tell you, John, this thing of forgiveness, is not so easy. I never wonder, when I read of the Apostle, when he is taught the duty in its length & breadth, praying for *an increase of faith*. You remember those lines in Marmion?

"Vengeance alone to God belongs,
Yet, when I think on all my wrongs
My blood is liquid fire."[24]

They often come to my mind: but whilst they are descriptive of the natural feeling, they ought not be allowed to awaken the slightest desire that God wd assume his prerogative and avenge our injuries. Our hearts are terribly deceitful on this very point. If we look into them very narrowly we find we forgive others, rather hoping that God won't, but will reckon with them *fully* for their misdeeds to us— instead of coming out nobly like Stephen & Paul (if we wd confine ourselves to the standard set up by men of like passions with ourselves) and praying that God "would not lay this to their charge."[25]

One wd think I hadn't written to you for a month from the length of my letter. I believe, if I had time I would tare it up & write another. I am tired now, & can't go into all I thought of saying about yr visit, etc.

You will be in New York next Sunday & the Sunday after too? I am glad you are going, and glad that I know beforehand of yr engagements. Somehow, I like my thoughts to follow you into the pulpit. They learned the habit long ago, and I am sorry they have had to unlearn it since.

How do those New York folk treat you? I mean how do they threaten "to spoil" as you say, my retired preacher? Tell me the *Minister* for whom you preach, for you know, I don't know city churches, except thro' their Pastors. Do the best you can

24. *Marmion*, a narrative poem by Sir Walter Scott, published in 1808.
25. Acts 7:60.

my dear John, not only because a noble work deserves yr best efforts, but because away off, hundreds of miles distant, there is one heart anxiously looking to the performance, and oh, so earnestly concerned as to its results. Think John, how I should feel, if I were in any way to know, that your visit to N.Y. was a Mission of Mercy to even one soul. And why may it not be so? That is, to you *Missionary ground;* and you ought to go to it in the spirit with all necessary preparation to do the work of a Missionary.

We are suffering for rain. The corn is almost ruined. Our mills have all stopped: there is not a barrel of flour in one of them. Water too is not abundant in town, and altogether, a continuance of dry weather may bring very great distress.

God bless you my own precious John.

Yrs
S.C.P. McDowell.

Thursday[26]

Dear John

I didn't intend to write today, but thought Maggie wd be pleased to get a letter from me, & so have hurried myself to catch the mail.

I am so sorry to hear she is sick, and alarmed too: for Scarlet fever is a terror to me.

I don't mean that Maggie's letter shall cheat you out of yr regular one tomorrow. Do *you* read my letter to her, & don't let it go floating about for every body to read, who cares to take the trouble.

Yes; I have much the same fancy as Maggie, & in an exigence of health wd make the same exactions upon you without much more thought than she has about its being proper & all that.

Yours
S.C.P. McDowell

Maggie's Room
July 31st 1856.

I give you joy, Sally upon the recovery of our little Maggie. She is not well yet, but as near it as children in this dis. ever are so soon. As she is as much yours as she is mine at least in contract I know this will give you great pleasure.

I have now been nursing her night & day since she was taken on Sat. night. I have not left her room for any great length once & no one else has had any serious charge of her. I would not have supposed before that this was possible but I have been led along from less to more till I found on wishing to try my liberty a

26. This letter was probably written on Wednesday, July 30, 1856. Her "regular one tomorrow" would be written on Thursday, July 31. McDowell usually wrote Miller on Thursday.

day or two ago that I was *fixed*. I said to her, "Maggie, Aunt Mary will sit up with you to-night". "No, you Poppa" was her immediate & very emphatic reply. It is not sitting up exactly, however. On the contrary the night begins by my going regularly to bed. But the little lady manages to call me every little while & I had little good sleep till last night when she was so much better as to disturb me very little. I wish you would remember, my dear Mrs McDowell, that this makes me so much the more an eligible match; for my daughter having had the scarlet fever will subtract so much from your cares when you favour us with your presidence. Mag. in the pulse of her returning enterprise has seized her crochet needle & sent me out for worsted & our combined labours have produced this mat this morning & afternoon. In acknowledging it & thanking us for it please remember that I went for the worsted & gave the crochet-ter broken ice &—her dinner while she made it. Take care however! It may be Pandora's box! What if all the little niggers should turn flaming scarlet in ten calendar days after you receive it.

I am so glad to see the proofs of thrift & retrenchment that your last letter gives. Often when you have told me like another of my darling children that "you had nothing to do", I have thought, Does my darling Sally really know how clearly a man's vocation is defined in nearly every case, & how manifestly hers is to rid herself by patient management of fiduciary & personal embarrassment & danger. How do I know that God is not intending this to be the last lesson of your unmarried life & that in giving you into my arms as my angel he means first to teach you to live upon that angels food which you will find in the cabin of a hermit & an anchorite like me. I have a sort of persuasion that God means me to do a certain work. I *grow* in the persuasion. I believe if you could peer into his great decrees you would find our history interblended, & I think you would discover that no year of this awkward & pitiable delay but has its own purpose to answer in arranging a history that we are yet to live in the world.

But Sally, speaking of Maggie. She is stealing away all my good looks. I was keeping it for you as a great surprise that I had grown a handsome & robust young man. The summer had already begun to spread a sort of saffron hue over my beauty, and most haplessly this sick room has finished it. When you see me you will know me instantly whereas I wanted to throw you into a panic by coming in upon your prudery in the guise of an entire stranger. What would you have thought if some evening a handsome young man rather under the highest stature with a profusion of brown hair & fine animated features had sent up his name & surprised you when you came into the parlour with all the appearance of an impudent imposture. Suppose that instead of your *acute* visaged lover you were folded in the arms of one in the hey day of youth & health & that with the exception of a little too much eyebrow point & a trifle too broad a face you were claimed as having given up soul & body to one as much like me as your "Watch" (isnt that his name) is like the little black dog that bit me last summer—what would you do? Would you be faithful to me & turn me out of the house or would you see thro' the optical illusion & by a sort of instinct release your poor lover.

This sort of trial I was preparing to surprise you with. But in an evil hour, Maggie, took this fever & restored to me the features that you loved.

One word more. You have a trick when you write to Maggie, of enclosing her letter in mine. Now I dont like that. I have no objection to your doing it if you will put an extra stamp on but what with Monday morning letters with their pinched look & these that are made to carry double I do get the veriest crumbs that ever fell from the rich man's table. I was thinking the other day, "How happy the woman that *I* court! If I could only get the letters that I write to her—My! how happy I should be! I take one of your little thin ones sometimes & put it in my drawer & keep one of mine an hour or two after it is written & fancy you wrote it to me. You cant think how nice it reads. If you cant do better I wish you would copy one of mine & sign your name.

Yours affly
JM.

Colalto,
Friday July 31. 1856.[27]

My *dear John,*

You know Lilly and I are here entirely alone; and when I think of your visit I feel this to be something of a difficulty. However I wrote to Miss Jannetta some days since to come down and stay with me, as soon as her school was out—not to meet this difficulty of ours, but on her own account, & my pleasure in having her with me.—She has not yet replied to me. If *she* comes, then I can better fix a time for yr coming. You know, John, this is mere deference to the world, which is too censorious to be much defied. Indeed all my anxieties spring from the same source. I shrink, in spite of my hope of yr coming, from rousing up another fuss & talk about us. I *fear* it with a deeper concern on Lilly's account than on my own. I don't like to do anything that may compromise her in any way. Do you think it cd be done by your visit? That, in any public sensation adverse to it, her brother James would assault her by violent abuse of me, & represent to her that she would lose caste by a continued connexion with me, & in such ways endeavor to drag her from me, I have no doubt. That Massie would have the audacity & indelicacy to follow the same course, tho' more moderately, I hardly question; especially if by doing or attempting to do it he can have promise of favor with James or Uncle Tom. Now, if they should succeed in tearing that child from me, I should be in the deepest distress, not on my own account so much as hers. That my affection wd be outraged by such an act, is true; that I should suffer greatly at the mere absence of my child, is true too; but these I could bear: I have borne heavier woes than they *cd* be. But to have her given over to her brother in such

---

27. This day was Thursday. The postscript McDowell added on Friday morning is correctly dated Aug. 1, 1856.

sense as that he should have the power of authority over her, wd fill me with more alarm and anguish for her than I can tell you. I would look upon it as *fatal* to her happiness, at least so far as human forethought can see. I speak strongly, John. I would not do it—for every principle of Sisterly honor ought to make me shelter my brother—lest this is involved in our own affairs: and, besides, I recognize your right to my confidence, even in so delicate a matter as this. James' fault that I always look to with such unmitigated distrust, is not such as would lessen his standing as a gentleman; or that people think of as implicating his honor on principle; but it is one that I am not willing to subject Lilly to. He is kind enough, when he happens to be in the humor; but, you know no degree of calm can ever undo the destruction of the hurricane.

Now to go back to where I began, ought I to run the risk of what I consider so much evil to Lilly? Or am I bound to sacrifice my happiness, to a conjectured ill to her. I rebel strongly at *yielding* (observe I am right this time) so much of the little pleasure left me in this world to the unreasonable whims and *selfish*, (for recollect I don't flatter them by supposing they were actuated by any special & disinterested feeling for my welfare) requirements of those who happen to be kin to me. Whatever I conceive to be my duty to Lilly, I will try to perform—and whatever is best for you as a Minister,—I don't feel myself much called upon to regard yr interest as a simple member of Society,—I am ready to submit to, at almost any sacrifice of private feeling; but exactions outside of these, I regard as great impertinence, no matter who makes them. Write to me all you think about these difficulties.

You must not think, that my pecuniary involvements with Lilly, excite, or even form a feature, in my anxiety about her. So far from it, I tell you, painful as it wd be to me to be separated from her, I would not hesitate, if she had any male friend who wd be a good protector to her, to yield her to his charge. I wd consider it my highest duty to her to do it; for I feel that with me, as I am now, she is too unprotected & exposed.

I want to see you John, ever so much: do you see any thing to forbid it, in all I say and all you think? It seems to me that so sad a pleasure as that might be granted me. I long to talk over all our troubles with you. I want some help too in clearing up the future. And I yearn for the gratification of *hearing* you say once more "My dear Sally, I do indeed love you with all my heart." I want to be sure that you can say it as heartily as of old. All my life I have been so eager for affection, that when I get a little it only whets my appetite for more. I think men & women are, happily, very different in their feelings:—a man's happiness is in loving—a woman's in being loved—le besoin d'etre Aimé, is almost the earliest & strongest *necessity* of her nature. At least this is the opinion I draw from my own experience. My greatest *pleasure* is to love you; but, after all, it is *only* my *highest pleasure*: my *happiness is in having you to love me*. But with you, it is just the reverse; isn't it? Don't you think if you loved me extravagantly you would be really happy tho' you knew that I, in return only loved you a little? I hope you will upset my theory by saying, "No"; for I wd not be willing that my love should be counted out, in calculating the sources of yr happiness. But all metaphysics aside—I love you too much; that is, if my constant & engrossing thought of you be the true index of my feeling. I fear a higher affection cools under the ardor of this: which ought not to be: the exact reverse should be the case. How can we make it so, My Darling?

Altho' you spoke so cheerfully of Maggie's case, I feel uneasy about her. That S. Fever is so insidious & deceitful that as long as it lasts it is to be feared; & none of its promises are fully to be relied on. I wish I was with you now. Do you imagine John, that any Step-Mother ever had the same outgoings of affection to a child that I have to her? She seems very dear to me. I love little Mac dearly; but not with the nearness of feeling I have to this child of yrs. But Good night. & may God bless you all.

S.C.P. McDowell.

Friday Morning Aug: 1. 1856.

I received this letter from Robert an hour since.[28] You see it shows only a gloomy prospect of any immediate settlement with Uncle Tom. If, however, I could get a settlement that wd be certain & safe with him, & yet require no payment of money before the first of Jan'y '57: but wd require the interest from July 1. '56 I think I should be satisfied. Then I wd have the whole sum arranged in Lilly's name, thereby paying her several thousand dollars of my debt to her. After that, I should demand, by every power that the Law would give, punctual semi-annual payments of interest. My great anxiety is to get it absolutely out of his hands, & have no further money dealings with him: but, at present that seems impossible; & under the circumstances I must do the best I can, which seems what I have stated above.

I enclose also a letter from Uncle Robert. Upon the strength of it I incline not to sell; but have the land valued and transfer, if it be possible, & there are some legal difficulties in doing that, my portion in it to Lilly that wd then leave my Washington lot & the Louisville lots & the Saline property, & my farm & negroes here to pay other debts & make my own living. Such a burden debt is. Send me back these letters that I may file them away.[29] They may be important hereafter.

If Maggie is well enough you will be in New York on Sunday, & will not get this letter before Tuesday. I have some remorseful thoughts about sending it. I feel badly at saying so much against James; but, John, I am only doing it that I may show you how my mind works about our own difficulties. Write to me about Maggie; & if you go to N.Y. remember I'm a woman & tell me all about yr visit.

Affec'ly
S.C.P. McDowell.

28. Robert W. Hughes.
29. These letters have not been located.

Princeton, Aug 2d 1856.

My *darling Love*,

I am not sure but that if I wrote in the morning instead of the evening my letter would reach you *a day* sooner. I am going to try the experiment. I get your letters late on Wednesday & Friday nights & at 10 1/2 on Monday morning. I reply to them on Monday Thursday & Sat: evenings & it seems, that, on Thursday, does not reach you till Monday morning. I mean now to write on Monday evening & on Thursday & Sat. morning & see what effect it will have. I would like you to get my letters a day sooner for then *every* letter would be an answer to the one before the last. The Sat. letter, tho', I fancy will make no difference for Sunday I suppose makes that late at any rate. I suppose the only advantage gained will be in that written on Thursday.

Thanks for your good long letter. If I had you here I would acknowledge it in a sort of unspoken manner very common in Jersey but which I suppose would shock your weak Virginia nerves. I have been practising this method of compensation all the week upon poor little sick Maggie & I am not sure if her lips could testify they could bear witness that my administrations have been at least quite as pleasant as some of the other things that have passed through them in the course of the week.

Are you ever so sick that the world seems to travel back & wave from you until you seem to consider your hold on it quite nothing. I was, last night. For a man like me who is *never* ill & indeed never confined by any unwellness there are once or twice in my life the very fiercest attacks that I can easily conceive of. And tho' it seems as tho' I could not *endure* it for an hour yet I know all the time that it is one of my least serious unwellnesses & that I shall be more than commonly well in a few hours. The attack when at its height presents your poor lover in a plight like this. In the first place so deadly pale & livid that a somewhat long beard such as I had last night & a sort of *exaggerated* look of the eye makes me look quite horrid. In the second place a shivering coldness which in this intense heat makes me put on a stuffed gown & sit in some sheltered corner. Then a cold dripping perspiration falling in large drops as you have seen in some summer shower. Then a romping headache that seems to be stabing at my skull as tho' it would batter it to pieces. And then last & worst a mortal sickness lifting a man quite off of the earth & making him think as it always does me of the punishments of eternal wrath. All this, which tho' the worst *perhaps* of all bodily afflictions is one which I believe is the simplest, which I know will all be over in a few hours or in a night, which neither racks my frame or leaves me weak or indisposed & which I think I can bring on almost at any time by going without my breakfast as I did yesterday or by a skillful use of the multiplication & then the sudden & entire omission of my cups of coffee. Are not we poor weak creatures to tremble almost at the door of another world, (for I think with a little dramatic gesticulation at such times I could make a stranger feel that I was almost going out at it) & yet be brought to such a pass by some trifle of every day existence. Do you know at such times when the religious element comes in & I tremble at *eternal* suffering & think how readily I am searched by the fingers of that old bony messenger that will one day come for all of us I feel a sort of mortal shame of humbling myself & penitently confessing under the idea of the meanness of doing it under the reminder of bodily suffering. I know this is very wicked but one advantage the devil gets over me to push me over such times which of course are sent for a religious purpose is to represent how mean it is to fall at such times upon repentance & how much better it is to turn to my duty more cheerfully when I am well.

Maggie is a great deal better & we are back in our rooms tho' her sickness has drawn me toward the little lady as you call her & her room which is between mine & Mary's & connects with them each by a door I have determined shall open into mine & that I will watch over the poor little thing hereafter in all those things in which she cannot take care of herself. Mary has done & would do it very cheerfully but these sicknesses give me a sort of panic about the little things & give me a sort of pity for them as poor motherless children.

I wish you could help me. Dont you?

Yours *affly*
Jno Miller.

Colalto,
Aug. 4. 1856.

My *dear John,*

I thought I wouldn't give you a chance to grumble over yr Monday's letter, by writing Saturday night; and so while Lilly was writing at my table, I thought I would take a nap & wake up in time to write after she had finished; but alas! I was too sleepy to do anything, when the hour came, and you are thrown upon the tender mercies of this morning again. And, I think, you deserve less mercy even than usual to-day, for having the audacity to complain of the shortness &c of my *extra* letter to you last week. You should have been glad to get it, instead of turning to quarrel about it. But, John, you are terribly spoiled. When this correspondence began, you could wait *three weeks* for a letter, with quite a show of patience—afterwards, you begged for just *one a week*—then two, then three, then one every day. Soon you will ask me to write two every day, & move into some region of country where there would be two mails a day by wh to send them. The worst of it is that you quarrel with me so, and are so impudent about my letter:—They are not frequent enough, nor long enough, nor warm enough: they are not well-spelled, nor free enough to satisfy very unreasonable requests in that way; and altogether they are so defective that you beg I will copy one of yrs & send it to you! I thank you, sir; I think I can "do better" than that.

I am glad Maggie has escaped so lightly. But, John, you do wrong to let her use her eyes at any sort of work, even the crochet. All eruptive diseases affect the eyes; I am more anxious upon this point than almost any other, & for this reason. When I was a child 8 or 10 years old I had the measles, not very badly, but bad enough to keep me in bed for some days. After I was able to play about, I, (for there were others sick & Mama was too much engaged with them to look after me so well as I seemed to be) got possession of a book—the Chronicles of Canongate, for I remember it to this day,—and screwed myself up in a large, easy-chair, and read to my heart's content.[30] My eyes suffered from it greatly, as the immediate consequence; & tho' they grew better, they never became strong enough for me to use them regularly & moderately at night until long after I was grown. All the time I was at school in Geo:Town, I was excused from any amount of night-study in consequence of this weakness of my eyes. Another thing, be careful of cold with Maggie; and watch closely the glands of the neck that the slightest swelling there may be instantly attended to. It was a long time before Lilly recovered from that effort of the disease. But, dear Me! I talk to you as if there were no Drs to give you all these cautions.

We have been nearly burnt up. The corn seemed irretrievably gone, which, as owing to the fly, &c, our wheat-crop was nearly a failure, would have been a calamitous loss. But Saturday night we had a fine rain; and all yesterday afternoon & night & this morning it has been raining, until our hopes about the forlorn corn & vegitables begin to revive. My farming has, almost entirely failed this year, from bad seasons & Morgan's stealages. Just this morning I hear of his having stolen $100. worth of clover seed. I shall take means to recover that, however.

I tremble to think how near Alfred was being killed two or three days ago. He was engaged at the threshing machine & some how his apron was caught by it, & he drawn so near to it, that nothing but the tearing off of his clothes saved his life. He was cut on one side, and bled some, but the wound was not dangerous. I asked him, yesterday about [it] & he told me, with great solemnity—"A little more, Madam, & I should have been sent to judgment, & have received my reward." He is, what he calls a "sufficient member" of the Methodist Church North, and is very full of the phrases & peculiarities of his sect; tho' he, is nevertheless, I think, a sincere christian.

I wish, John, you would carry into practice your thought of a Diary. But, John, I have long wished to propose to you a plan for a daily meeting, different from that; but I have hesitated & drawn back from doing it from a certain sort of diffidence & a certain kind of pride too. For many years, I was in the habit of taking my Bible & going off to a quiet room in the house, usually the one over the Library, when it was unoccupied, & spending an hour there before breakfast. Last summer, (& it was a sad interruption) yr letters were brought to me then & there. This last

30. *The Chronicles of the Canongate,* by Sir Walter Scott, was published in two series in 1827 and 1828.

winter & this summer, this habit has been a good deal broken. I have been trying to restore it. Now, Darling, can't you meet me that hour, that we may, *every day*, spend it together. I am an early riser, & from half past five to half past six would suit me best; but if a little later wd be most convenient for you—but no, then the hour wd have to be cut off one quarter or more or more to be accommodated to my household arrangements. I prefer the morning, because I am fresh, and free from all kinds of interruptions, that wd assail me at any other time. I think we both need this. And I am sure I should feel better content to *know* that we were, at least, making the effort to get some good out of this engagement of ours; And that we were trying to elevate our affection by mingling it with an higher affection; and cementing it by higher principles & higher duties.

Do you know, it almost makes me tremble when I think of yr publishing. I reckon I'm foolish, but I can't help it. I thank you very much for all that is signified by yr offer to place the Ms in my hand; but I couldn't assume the responsibility of deciding what to do with it.[31] God bless you my dear John.

Always Yours
S.C.P. McDowell.

[marginal note] Do you ever hear anything of a Mr George Morrison of Baltimore—a teacher or superintendent of the free schools there? Sally Breckinridge is to marry him in a few days, & I want to know something of him.[32]

Princeton Aug 4th 1856.

I admire you greatly & value you more, my darling Sally, for the zeal with which you are addressing yourself to what I think just now is the great vocation of your mind. I hope God in his Providence will guide you in such a way that you will see your difficulties as you look back all provided for. Two or three things strike me. First, if I am ever your husband I will be perfectly dissatisfied if any *doubt* even in respect to your accounts with Lilly be not adjusted in her favour. And, therefore, tho' I think you have every right to make her bear her own & even *your* expenses in cases where she is interested yet I feel glad that you are carefully considering her interests & watching the equities of her right as you go along.

Second, so long as you pay Lilly 6 per cent on all you owe her, & do not derive 6 per cent from what you are relying on to meet her claim Dr B's arguing is not altogether good. That is, it is only good this far, that the Bourbon tract may be a very good investment for Lilly & a very bad one for you.[33] If, therefore, you can with *perfect propriety* & the counsel of others transfer that interest to

31. "Ms" means the manuscript of Miller's book.
32. George Morrison (1831–1898), principal of Baltimore City College from 1854 to 1857, married McDowell's cousin Sarah (Sally) Campbell Breckinridge (1832–1865).
33. "Dr. B" is Robert Jefferson Breckinridge. McDowell had sent Miller his letter (McDowell to Miller, Aug. 1, 1856). The Bourbon tract refers to the land in Kentucky.

her I should think very well of it. It has all the safety that she wants, while at the same time it rids you of a process which just now you cannot afford namely of steadily emptying your property into hers. In other words *now* you are both making her sure & giving her the large interest, whereas *you* are becoming less sure & drawing the small interest; a state of things which, by *the advice* of *others*, I would consider it quite proper to end by making her property *secure* itself in the way Dr B. indicates.

Thirdly, I think what Mr H. says is favorable about the other, only, Darling, I give you two pieces of urgent advice, 1st Be sure of your man in Mr H.[34] You know I know nothing about him. If he take him all in all the best & truest & surest lawyer within your reach he may be *invaluable* to you. You may attach yourself to him in *all* your affairs. He may help you as to Lilly & as to this Kentucky tract. You *need* such a man, & need one whom you can keep to without changing. On the other hand if he is not reliable he may ravel out your property as an old knitter ravels out a stocking & when he once begins you may not be able to stop him. Is he a *vigilant, common sense, honest* lawyer & do *other people* trust him. I know I may be calling in question here one of your very household gods; but you know I know nothing.

The 2d advice I urge is that you *never* quarrel with your uncle Tom. Law business especially when once in the hand of a lawyer need never estrange any body. The closest pushing of a right can then be done with the closest continuance of relations. And it is your interest to hold *all* your friends to you by silken bonds. Here is the beauty of a skillful management that it empties the purse without breaking the threads.

First & foremost, tho' & above all other things is you need a skillful *helper*— one to whom you will be perfectly *honest* & tell all your circumstances—one who will enter into your care & treat it as tho' it were his own—one who will not take more than you confide to him & will not be pursuing you with fees for parts of your business which you did not consider in his hand one that will conciliate James & yet keep him at a distance—& one that will keep you from some sad endorsement or some wrong signing of your name which may cut off half your property. If Hughes is such a man I am glad he makes you so direct an offer about your Uncle. Do you know, Sally, you're very proud, & your uncle really may not know that you want your means. He may think you are about the most comfortable of any of them or at least not pressed. You must have some immediately around you with whom you must be candid & above all you must never contrive expence for the value of pride when it is becoming dangerous to your actual safety.

But My! how I do run on.—I have no doubt you are right & that James may one day need your help & others may, Tom or any of them. Now, when you *need*

---

34. Robert N. Hughes, whose letter McDowell also enclosed when she wrote to Miller on Aug. 1, 1856.

have the least expense of all of them is undoubtedly the time so handsomely to manage as to become by Gods help *mistress of your own position*.

The above sheet I sat down to write *at once* after coming in from N.Y. It is rather abrupt counsel to offer in such delicate matters. But, Darling, all I say must be the mere *suggestion* of your "alter ego." You know I am far off & can hardly do more than conjecture what is wisest.

I pray that I may not "estrange you from higher affections" & I pray for things like this oftener than you know.

I'm the funniest fellow about jewelry. I made careful inquiries & went to the best place I could hear of on Broadway near the Astor H.[35] & op. the Park & the buttons he has furnished me are really beautiful, an exact match to yours tho' a little heavier. I was so pleased to see them look so well that I was foolish enough to let him attempt to mark them all before I left instead of waiting a week longer. The result is that he has marked them somewhat hastily & that in marking one the tool slipped & cut the inside of the button so that I refused to take it. The outside of the button was right, but the inside I tho't ought at least to *start* right in such a thing as you wear all your life. The result was that I took an unmarked button in the place of the spoiled one determining not to risk the same hand again & mean to employ next Monday a man in Cortlandt street whom I know to spend his best skill upon that particular button. As it happened to be one of yours I kept its mate to copy from & as like most dilatory people I am very much in a hurry at the last moment, I wont wait till next week, but send you *my* pair in this letter. Yours are *exactly* like them except that they are marked S.M. underneath before the date. We will exchange again when I come. The advantage will be that you will then have worn both these, & I (if I can settle the button hole question) will have worn both yours. Then we will actually exchange them from each others visits.

I must tell you about N.Y. in my next. But, Sally, when I do *well*! I find egotism a hard thing to manage. But when I do ill I have a great disposition to [illegible] myself. Does it not, therefore, encourage you to hear that I now feel a strong indisposition to tell you "*how* the people spoil me"? God bless you, Dearest. I love you with a sort of blended fondness for you, as both my child & wife.

Yours
JM.

[written on a small envelope] I forgot tho' the funniest part of my jewelry adventure. I took your button in your own square box into which I had also put my engagement ring. Coming home in the cars just now I reflected that I had not seen that box since! & am quite without the ring you gave me. I hope the Jeweler has it, but if not, what then! I drew it out on his counter & feel sure I did not bring it away.

35. Astor Hotel.

Will you ever give me another?

[marginal notes] Of course I know some more matronly friend than Lilly would be with you. Dearest, what makes you think James would feel so? About me you need not have a care. But as to you, Sally, I should be so sad if your friends were estranged from you by my visit. Write again about it.

Scrappy letter that was the word. Maggie is well.

Colalto,
Tuesday Augt: 5. 1856.

My dear John,

I have neglected heretofore to correct a mistake you have fallen into about my plans. I have no fixed purpose, as yet, of breaking up here in October. Indeed I don't know what to do. I can't think of living here alone all Winter; and want of means, and other reasons seem to press strongly against my going elsewhere. I am hesitating about sending Lilly again to Miss Gill. Her expenses were enormous there; and the returns in the way of education extremely small. She has acquired a tremendous amount of affectation, which I don't consider worth purchasing, at any rate; and the shrill Northern tone & sharp accentuation, which is not pleasant, but greatly the reverse in her to my ear, and which, with the mixture of our Southern peculiarities produces a most unmusical & mongrel dialect. However, *these* Phil accomplishments I hope to see laid aside in a little while.

I started off at 6 this afternoon to write to you, when just at the door I met Bent. After tea, we went over to prayer-meeting, & Mr Massie returning with me, entirely broke up my plan of writing by sitting til 11 o'clock. Now, after writing thus far, I must give up my letter till tomorrow morning; which, by the by, some 10 or 15 minutes will usher in.

I beg you will not be critical as to Maggie's letter. I find it badly divided in one part; but was too lazy &c, to remedy it by re-writing the whole. But this, the little lady will not discover herself; & if the jingling letter pleases her, don't you mar her pleasure by telling her of its faults. I think I should have made it shorter, if I had given more time to it: as it is, it is rather an unwieldy great thing—But good-night.

Wednesday morning

I half expected a letter this morning; but none came. I have been trying to make out why a letter that can come from Phil: in just 24 hours, should take two or three days to come from Princeton, which is only a short distance beyond. I think our difficulty is in making the connection at Washington, from which place there are two daily mails to Rich'd; but only one, & but one in the early morning to us. However, we can't change or remedy these things.

I am sorry to hear of your being sick,—not that you give me any cause for uneasiness about you on that score, but I am both sorry and surprised to hear of such spells of suffering. *What* is the matter with my little man? Do you ever wish for me, John, when you get sick and troubled, & shiver away crouched in a corner by yr-self? This thing of eating & fasting is very curious. The most alarming & suffering hours I have ever spent have been occasioned by want of food. The first attack I remember was in Rich'd, when we lived there; and I look back to it now with a sort of shuddering. My *brain*, strange to say, is the seat of the suffering, such as it is, tho' I am, at the same time well-nigh frantic for food. It was suffering, similar to this, and every day repeated this Spring, for several weeks, that reduced me to that forlorn condition which Nib told Mary had resulted in "my looking wretchedly".

Pray don't lose your *beauty*, my dear John. You know I told you I didn't consider you any regular "tea-party beauty," to use Uncle Floyd's phrase, but still I don't want you to grow to be the reverse. I don't value this thing of beauty in a man. It is so seldom united with any strong gifts of either mind or morals: and when a man is weak in mind & morals, and is very handsome, at the same time, he might as well be a woman. Oftentimes countenance, if it bears the stamp of refinement & intelligence is more attractive to me, than physical beauty.

Did you give up your New York engagements? I find from the Presbyterian that Dr McGill is to supply the Market & Rutgers St Churches for the 3 first Sundays of this month. I thought those were your preaching places. Was Maggie not well enough for you to leave her? Do be particular, & accept invitations whenever they come, & you can possibly do it: I can't bear the idea of your being over slaughed or set aside.

It is just two years tomorrow since I wrote you my first famous letter, and denied you the promised interview. What a time we have had since then! Suppose, John, you had never repeated yr visit here, that summer, and we had never met, would you have rested quite quiet under that letter? Was it a mistake on yr part of supposing that, when I parted with you & yr Sister here on the porch, I was demonstrative of some special feeling to you, that led you to write to me when you got back to Phil? Or what was it? You had no reason for yr conjecture then, & your mistake was entirely gratuitous. I always liked you; tho' my Mother & I did amuse ourselves, that morning in Frederick with yr great cane, and the fancied resemblance between you & it to the wood-cuts of Martin Luther: yet I have no idea now *when* it was that that "liking" assumed a warmer & brighter coloring. I am certainly indebted to you for many, many hours of exquisite pleasure, Darling; but then there have been many hours too, of intense pain. Perhaps, the balance is an even one between them. What think you of the future?

I don't remember, John, that I was when I first knew you, at all impressed by what every body else feels to be your *formal manner.* I have no recollection of having even remarked it, tho' I think now, there must be some ground for the charge against you. I don't know how it is; but when we show ourselves to outsiders, you wear the look of *formality,* & I of great frankness & unreserve; but when we look deeper than the surface, I think we change entirely, and you are really far the least formal of the two. Don't you think so?

When you come on you had better take the Cars to Goshen, which is two or three miles from the Alum Spring, and come from there here in the Stage. The road is rough, but not more so than the plank road from Staunton; and besides there is only 18 miles of it. The great advantage of that route, however, is that it brings you here several hours sooner: instead of getting in at 11 1/2 or 12 o'clock, you come at 9 1/2 or 10, which will give you the chance of paying me a visit the night you arrive, & of getting back *reasonably early* to the Hotel. Mr Mann, a great friend & supporter of Mr Massie's keeps the hotel now; and they say, has much improved it.[36]

Does Maggie ever ask for me of her own thought,—not from yr suggestion? And Allie, John; tell me something about him. You know I have always thought I should love Allie the most of the two? And yet I don't now think of him half as often or as affect'y as Maggie.

Yours
S.C.P. McDowell.

Princeton Aug: 6th [1856]

My *fair Deceiver,*

No letter to-night. This is the first blank after a long series of prizes & a disappointment hard to bear. Sally, how could you? Still on the coals of fire principle I am going to try the morning's mail as I promised you. Tell me if it reaches you earlier.

Now as to my visit, Dearest, I feel quite at a loss. Left to myself I would say it was all nonsense. But, left to myself, I said that about our wedding & it turned out to be sober truth. So therefore I say as follows:—

I. As concerns *me* & *my* family I choose to come & see you & have no idea it will compromise me in the least.

II. Concerning *you* & *your* family I *am of opinion* that it will not compromise you, but

III. if it did & your comfort in your family was less & Lilly was taken from you I should feel wretchedly & the pleasure of our meeting would be dearly purchased.

IV. Now, as to going *farther* than an *opinion* I cannot, first, because I have been mistaken before. Second, because I dont know James & dont know your family & really dont know their present attitude in the whole case. Third, because I have never thot of asking you what givings out you have made yourself as to our present relations with each other.

I feel clear tho' about these suggestions:

I. That *I* feel more inclined to *press* our right to see each other than I did our right to be married, & to run the risk of consequences, particularly as they cannot involve your *whole* standing as the other might & the standing of your children.

---

36. William A. Mann (c. 1824–?) operated the Lexington House.

II. I think it would do no harm to ask Dr White & also Miss Gordon herself, taking care to ask them in such a way as that their opinion shall not embarrass you if given adversely.

III. My *dropping* you & appearing to the public to have given you up might be susceptible of just as illnatured an interpretation as that acknowledgement of you which I would make by a public visit. Tell me what you think of this. I have not as high an opinion of the astuteness of your Brother James as you have & yet have wondered that in his disposition as he represents it to "shelter" you his sister he has never thought of it. He might wisely not speak of such a thing & you, Darling, ought never to argue for my visit on such a consideration to him, but I wonder he has not seemed more under the influence of it. I confess here has lain (apart from my affection for you which is intense) my strongest consideration in honor not to give you up.

IV. Therefore, I have always said & again & again suggested it to you that our true course was, to be perfectly above board, to *obtrude* nothing, but to answer all questions about each other frankly & in one way viz. that we are of *course* still engaged, but that our marriage is deferred that my visits should not be too long separated that they should be in circumstances of quiet & settled purpose & plan that would make people accustomed to them & should silence all gainsayers. I am sure that we have but two policies either to vow never to see each other or else to throw away all reserve & determine that we *will* see each & that with sufficient frequency & insouciance as to the public eye to fatigue & wear out the press & public sensation of which you speak. How have you talked of me? If you have concealed our relations or rather resented the subject when suggested even by ill mannered people, I think it makes the danger of my visit greater.

Darling, my love grows. Hardly has it accomplished a measure which I think is about all it is capable of when it takes a new start & grows in some quite new direction. I seem to have lost all guard against you as tho' you & I were partners & I must be careful of not offending you but I have grown to love you with a fondness which makes me free with you as a child, which makes me guard you as tho' you were my daughter & which makes me as free to speak to you of our household sorrows & even of your own mortifications & defencelessnesses as tho' you were my own Maggie grown to woman's stature & looking to me for protection.

Now listen:—your husband repelled you. He loaded you with insults which your own youth & yielding disposition gave him the execrable power to force on you almost to the point of submission & confession. Your own fine character & his notorious infamy saved you & rolled back the charges perhaps to a miraculous degree. Men are so slanderous & the adage is so fixed that there are two sides to every story & *some* people are so certain to believe evil of a woman if her husband gives her up that I consider the Frederick impression about you almost a miracle. It is more like the Mask of Comus business than anything of which I have ever heard. Be that as it may you passed unscathed & when I wooed you you were standing as *perfectly* as concerns everything in the past or present as the purest

Christian I have ever known. I pressed my visit & you yielded. I didnt *know* some things I now know of our difficulties & I didnt *think* certain others. No matter; you remonstrated, & even entreated my forbearance & I overbore your scruples & found you in my possession. The very first impulse of an honorable man when he found that marriage was voted down would be to remember the delicacies of your position & to strive to guard two things, first, your feelings &, next, your honour. Both these I tho't involved in the continuance of our engagement. If you were my sister & another man your suitor I think I would have thot so: your feelings, if you ever loved him & your honour, lest some one should say, he found her out & rejected her like her husband. Now, mark me, Sally, I do not mean that this would be a *serious* danger. A lady who could ride out the first could ride out the last trial of her life. I have no idea that if some ill-natured foe should start such a scandal it would live any more than those of your husband except in a few of the basest minds. But I mean to say that *if left to my own opinion* it would seem *more* serious than the *other*. I would rather Maggie, if divorced, & then engaged to be married & then prevented from having that engagement consummated should remain the plighted lover of her affianced husband if he were worthy of her, than be cast back upon herself with no shelter to her spirit from whatever free remarks might be made about her. And I wonder your brother hasn't thot of this. That is, I *would* wonder so if I had the same opinion of his knowledge of the world that you have sometimes had. I would have courted the friendship of my sisters affianced husband & made his relation to my family a comfort to my sister & a shelter to her general reputation.

Now, Sally, I dont say this in the way of a particular plea for in the first place I have no fear of your love. I feel just as sure of it as of the sky over my head. Things in your letters lately have led me to feel that you are far gone in love, my poor dear Daughter, & my heart bleeds that your love is so violated & that I cannot shelter it in my actual possession. I sometimes think that if you were actually my wife you would yearn over me with less fervent tenderness than you do at present (Is it so, Sally,) At any rate I am not afraid of your affection. Nor am I pleading for a visit. You are sufficiently yielding, my dear girl, to make me confident that you would not resist, if I strove to see you even at the peril of your highest position. That is not what I aim at. What I aim at, is to give you my real convictions about what your honour exacts from you: And at the same time to say, you know your relatives better than I do. And you know the town. I would not see you at the sacrifice of Lilly or of your good name, if I were never to see you again. And the same argument that weighed hard against my marrying you would weigh seriously also here: the arg: Mrs H: used, wh. she said John, if you love that lady dont marry her. Now think of all these things & tell me how they strike you. I am beginning to say just what I please to you, for I know my own *self* cant be offended with me; can it Dearest?

Now as to N.Y. I have left no room. I preach sometimes for Dr. Thompson a Scotch man & who has gone to Europe & sometimes for the united churches of

Dr Krebs & Theo: Cuyler who are also away. Dr McGill is with me in the supply. I am to preach just as often yet as I was to have when I began. The work grows. I go to Grand St next Sunday & to Dr Krebs church the *4th* & 5th Sundays of Aug. By the bye remember that in writing to Miss J.G. she must not come yet. I think I will be disengaged in Sept: but am not sure. Wont Miss Polly matronize you ever?[37] I dont know what to say about my preaching. I could tell you some things, but what would they amount to. By the way your letter to Maggie I found on my table this morning unopened. God bless you for it. It had come in my absence & it was supposed I had it. Mag: was delighted & talks with much zeal of her answer.

Your
JM

[accompanying note] Suppose I were to direct "Mrs McDowell Lexington Virginia" would it be safe? Has Mrs Hotel McDowell left the town & are you the only Mrs McDowell there?[38]

[marginal note] I looked up & down Broadway for the music & cannot find it. I will look again.

Thursday night
Aug. 7. 1856.

My *dear John*,
    You are right I *do* need a considerate & wise adviser here on the spot; but as to getting one who will be inclined to treat my affairs as tho' they were his own, I have no expectation. Mr Davidson has been a cautious, capable, honest *lawyer*, and in some respects, I prefer him to any one else as a lawyer, yet it is only in that character that I can call upon him. I have employed him in all the legal business I have had, since my Father's death, until last Fall when from ill health he declined any further service. Afterwards, I felt badly with Massie here to employ a strange lawyer; but had determined if Robt Hughes would not act for me with Uncle Tom, to apply again to Mr Davidson, whose health & spirits seem re-established.
    In this business with my right worshipful Uncle I was prompted to engage Robt because he was friend to us both; and because in this moment of his excessive money pressure, I did not wish to *appear* to act in an *aggressive* spirit—as tho' the securing of oneself was aggression! I know little of Robt's qualifications. He was, I believe, quite successful in Rich: before he became the Editor of "the Examiner"—is a sensible man & I believe honest. I have no idea of employing him in any other case than this. I don't like his Wife, who is a patronizing little

37. John Michael Krebs (1804–1867), pastor of Rutgers Street Church, New York. Theodore L. Cuyler (1822–1909), pastor of Market Street Church in Brooklyn. Miss J.G. is Jannetta Gordon. Miss Polly is Polly Moore.
    38. Margaret McDowell, wife of Robert M. McDowell who had previously operated the McDowell Hotel in Lexington.

body about as big as a humming bird, & don't intend to give her an insight into my affairs. *She* is our Kinswoman; an adopted daughter too of Aunt Sally.[39] Robert, tho' not adopted by Uncle Carrington was taken by him when 2 or 3 years old, an orphan child of an old college acquaintance whose dissipated habits left his children at his death almost penniless, and brought up in his house, and educated by him, more expensively than he was, afterwards, able to educate his own son. I have not been pleased that Eliza Hughes has seemed unwilling to acknowledge her husband's obligation to Aunt Eliza—Indeed I am the more displeased at this, since Eliza's own brother was, for years, with her husband the beneficiary of Aunt Eliza's. And Robt I have feared for a year past, has too much sympathized with his wife, in this feeling. However, I could do no better than employ him. Our personal relations are very kind. I meet with no one more prompt & heartsome than he in his offers of Service and Kindness.

I think he looks on the bright side of Uncle Tom's affairs, tho' it is probable he knows them accurately. Yet, John, a man $300.000 in debt, with no great business capacity, and a heavy annual rent of $23,000 to pay cannot be the very safest depository of yr money. He has, in vain, tried to sell the Salt works for $750.000. It will take a prodigious amount of salt & plaster to pay his rent & debts, and the current expenses of his Works.

I don't quarrel with him: but I talk pretty strong against his money proceedings in my case, & laugh at his *elegance* &c, &c; but we all do that; yet I have, no doubt, if my sharp speeches were to come to his ears he would scarcely forgive them, first, because, he would have a consciousness of, in part, deserving them; and next because I have been a sort of favorite of his; & he wd berate me for want of appreciation of that honor. My Mother was fonder of him than any of her brothers; and Father loved him too, and so did I till these dollars & our marriage difficulties scraped it all away. He is an amiable man of very kind feelings, and I reproach myself that I have lost my love for him, when I think of the affectionate things he has done for us in the past. But, John, I never thought the dear man was a *genius;* & when he undertakes to oppose me in any matter [of] opinion I feel like coming down upon him & demanding a fair fight tho' I am a woman. Or rather I feel that *my* capacity for forming an opinion is as good as his, & entitled to as much respect, tho' I am denied the Knockdown Arguments of hat & boots. Uncle Tom is very nice tho'. He would have made a *love* of an episcopal preacher as he once thought being; lawn would have been so cruelly becoming to him; and in the flowing sleeves & bands he would have looked so sweet! But laughing aside, and indeed now I am only good humouredly caricaturing him, he is an honorable gentleman, for[gett]ing his weaknesses, & affectionate & considered clever by a great many sensible people, and with no small talent for public speaking.

39. Eliza Mary Johnston Hughes (1825–?). Her parents were Charles C. Johnston and Eliza Mary Preston.

The buttons came safely. I am so sorry about the ring. Do try to get it—the loss of it seems ominous. How careless of you to put it in the same box with the button any how. No, of course, I wouldn't give you another; what wd be the use? By the way John, do you ever use anything I ever gave you? If you don't please bundle them all up & send them back to me.

Friday morning

Things have gone hard with me this past year, in every way. My farming has been almost a complete failure: I suppose there has never been so small a crop of wheat raised on the farm; and probably there never before had been as much sowed. the amount of corn planted would have been insufficient, even if it had turned out well; but to have an indifferent supply only yield about half looks very disastrous. The meadows have produced well—but I suspect Morgan stole my clover seed (which here sells for $8 or 9 a bushel) as there is so little to show for it, where there ought to have been, at least, some thing respectable. Cows & horses are poor, and I have had to buy within a day or two other kinds of stock. This is all very disheartening, but I think I am fast approaching a condition which will at least have this satisfaction in it—that it *cant be any worse*. However, I ought not to talk so; for in these farming disasters, I have only shared as my neighbors have done.

Do you know, John, I've felt hurt that Cousin John seems to have almost entirely abandoned his interest in my affairs. To be sure he has been gone some weeks, & before that I was away two months; but prior to that I felt worried that he should have intermitted any of his old habits in this particular. A week ago he came over one evening, a day or two after his return, but there were several gentlemen present, he said nothing, of course, about my matters until all left but Mr Massie, when he turned to me, "Well, Sally have you got anything to tell me about yourself and what interests you?", or something to that effect, I don't quote the very precise words perhaps. But I haven't seen him since except as I came out of church Tuesday evening. And my mind must change from its present mood, if I do soon go to him for counsel. I have no idea of thrusting my cares upon him, or asking him to share the responsibility of my decisions. I love him very much too—and therefore I am the more hurt.

Tom writes yesterday he will be here as soon as he can. His brother James writes to me much dissatisfied with his project of going West, & very coolly tells me "I had better rent him my farm for a year *as an experiment*". In which time as it requires very peculiar & watchful tillage, it might be so ruined as to lessen the sale, if I wanted that, several thousand dollars, or render it unproductive for a year or two. But, of course, it didn't matter as *I* only would suffer from that.

Sometimes, when I think of what I consider the unkind treatment of my Brothers & their total disregard of my welfare, I do feel bitter to them;—but it's like a spasm of pain that is over in a little while, & I am soon ready for their service again. That poor miserable boy, Randolph Benton when a child, irritated by my Father's teasing, went to his Mother, & gravely told her, "He did wish that as God had given her only one brother, he had made him a better one than his Uncle James."[40] I feel inclined to wish with him, that God had made mine of a different stamp. I may do them injustice however, & would not allow others to speak of them as I do. That very thing is one of my annoyances with Uncle Tom. Do burn my letter, it seems so peevish & fretful. If I had time I'd write another.

I hear nothing from Miss Jannetta, & don't even know now where she is that I may write again. I do want so much a long talk with you. I can't write because I don't know how, what I want to say. I am glad to hear Maggie well. I was pained to show myself to you in the guise wh this letter wears, but John, it is well to see me as I am. My greatest fault I fear just now is that of loving you far too much. Do have a care for me & over me, for I feel Darling, as tho' I stood at the North Pole with the storms of the whole world howling about me in my isolation.

Yours,
S.C.P. McDowell.

[marginal note] Why not let me write you a letter at New York?

Princeton Aug: 8 1856.

My *dear Sally,*

Your letter reached me this forenoon. I expect another to-night. Edward must have been late at the Office, for it was not postmarked till the 5th (Tuesday).

Do you remember my telling you that we had burned years ago in a sort of foolish impulse a whole packet of letters. To my amazement, yesterday in going to a great chest of mine which I have never opened, but wh. had been packed by Louisa Benedict I found this very packet. I cant tell you how astonished I was. I seized them eagerly & with an avidity you can hardly understand ranged them in their dates (letter & answer) & began to read them as tho' they had been a book. My mind is still reeling with the excitements that the very backs & countenances of these old letters have produced. You will scarcely enter into such an idea & perhaps scarcely remember the statement about the burning, but I can hardly write this letter just in the midst of such sadly surprised & agitated feelings without speaking of it to you. Here is a whole world of agitation & feeling bound together in these leaves of paper & carrying me by a sort of spell over leagues & leagues of what it seems strange to think of as the actual journey of the past.

8 o'clock

Your letter is just here. Maggie fairly *rolled* in my arms with the delight of having your letter. The grand idea seemed to be—*a Poem on her*—it seemed too strange to be true. The fact is, it lies in the young Lady's vein. She likes to

40. McDowell's cousin John Randolph Benton (1829–1852).

advance very rapidly towards womanhood & all forms of womanly experience. I think if you would send her a bed quilt or arm chairs for housekeeping she would feel exceedingly gratified & would not perhaps be struck with its being so very premature if you were to send her her preserves or some perishable house-gear for use within a twelve-month. Mother often laughs at her. You know I told you I folded your letters lengthwise & make a pack of them of this shape[41] taking care that the dates should be up. Judge of my amazement to find that Maggie had noticed it & religiously imitated it & had all my letters & yours & little Sam Hagemans & the Potters' collected & made into such a pack & tied round with a string. Your poetry tho' strikes her in so new a way (& Darling it is very good) that I dont know how she'll dispose of it.

Your proposal about the morning I like, & it will make no change in my plans (if not my habits) except the hour. I am ashamed to say that I never rise before seven. I have long tried to do so & failed. I have a great mind to try again. From 8 to 9 would not suit you would it?

I feel your plan to be one by which I should gain so much if I could accomplish it that I mean to try. But, Sally, I fear it is hopeless. *Here* they would laugh at me if I said I would rise at 5. But *beauty* may accomplish what conscience cant. I mean to try.

As to preaching you need not be afraid that I shall be overslaughed. I am more in danger of being overslaughed by preaching. I have had three applications to preach on Sunday one at Burlington, one in Princeton at the 2d Ch. & one in N.Y. where I am going. I have one for next Sunday which I have declined for I shall be tired. I have *promised* to supply two pulpits the Sunday following. Of course one I shall have to be released from. Then I preach the Sunday after. Dont be anxious, Sally. If you love me you must love me for what I am & that is something that craves for its intellectual work something aside from the pulpit & in my own opinion more important.

A queer thing happened to me in New York. A man named McClelland had lived in Richmond 12 *years* ago. *I* was in Richmond four weeks. I went there just from the Seminary at Dr Plumer's request to assist him in editing the paper & preaching awhile.[42] I preached about five Sundays. Mr McC who knew nothing of all this as far as I was concerned began to tell me how a promising preacher of my name had been in Richmond in '43 (on his way to Florida or Texas he didnt remember which!) that he had often tho't of him since—"he was a promising young man". I asked him what sort of a looking man he was? He said he was a "little man—*good looking*." Now arent you ashamed, Sally, not observing that. I

41. Miller drew a picture here of a stack of papers.

42. Robert McClelland belonged to the First Presbyterian Church in Richmond in 1842, and in 1845 he was building contractor, trustee, and deacon for the Second Presbyterian until his return to New York City in 1854. While pastor of Richmond's First Presbyterian Church, William Swan Plumer also edited the *Watchman of the South*, a Presbyterian newspaper.

was perfectly silent & the conversation passed to something else.—Tell me when you write if the later hour will at all do if not I will make a desperate effort for five. Good night.

affly
JM

[marginal note] August: 9th. I rose at 5 1/2 this morning & fulfilled our engagement. Let us continue it. I will tell you if I fail.

Colalto,
Saturday, August 9. 1856.

My *dear John,*

Your change of days from Wednesday to Thursday works admirably. The letter that has, heretofore, come on Saturday night, and rested all day Sunday in the P.O. came this morning. It is a great relief to me; for waiting from Thursday till Monday was rather long for an impatient body like me. Besides, as my mail reaches me about 6 in the morning the waiting seems much longer than just the interval of two mail-days would warrant. Altogether the *regular* writing is a very great & very happy improvement. I am now *sure* of my letter three days in the week; and therefore the intervening times bring no disappointments to me.

I am sorry to hear that one of my letters should have failed to reach you in proper time. It may have been too late to be mailed the morning it was sent. I remember twice last week to have sent letters a little late; but as our Post Master is accommodating, expected he wd mail them notwithstanding. I shall guard against that cause of detention more carefully in future. But still, John, accidents will sometimes break upon our best & steadiest plans. You must then, when my letters fail just conclude that the *mail* is in fault. Which of my letters to Maggie laid so long on yr table undiscovered? And *how* did it happen? You had, two or three letters ago, laughingly commented upon my deceiving you by enclosing Maggie's letters to you, & I, of course, concluded my first letter to you had then been received: had it been?

No, John, certainly not: how could I disown our relations to each other, when fairly and properly questioned about them? Few people broach the subject to me, and I never thrust it upon any one. But Susan knows of the continuance of our engagement; Mary too, tho' to neither of them, did I, in speaking of you, announce the fact in distinct terms. I was so free in my manner of speaking that I don't recollect that the necessity of any such direct avowal occurred to me. Nib probably, knows it from Susan. I never speak to her at all about it. I understood from Cantey last Winter that she had said "Why, the marriage might as well (*or better,* I don't remember exactly which) take place, as the engagement continue". Miss Jannetta too knows of it. She told me Aunt Eliza had asked her about the posture of affairs, "hoping we were off". I told Miss Jannetta, not to tell her anything about it; for if she wanted to know unequivocally, & was interested in the matter, the honorable way was to come *to me*, & not go to a friend in my house. Nannie Carrington, however, as she was here so long & with me in Rich'd, must know enough to have no doubt of it. I told Dr Graham of it too, who never hesitates to ask whatever he wishes to know. He said Aunt Sally had inquired of him, hoping the thing was ended. Cousin John, almost from the day you left, has forborne to ask, evidently wishing not to be informed, as to my decision. I have thought it not altogether a friendly thing in him, especially as he had voluntarily lent himself to it, in its earlier stages.

Dr White & I talked about it one morning, a few days before I went to Halifax; and he repeated his opinion of it; which was, that there was no impropriety in it—& that I was, at liberty to continue it if I chose. Mr Blair also asked me something, I forget what, that led to my telling him. There is no secresy enjoined on any of these persons, except, as I mentioned, in Miss Jannetta's case, and they may have mentioned it to others; for aught I know, to dozens.

As to James, you mistake me. I have no great opinion of his judgment any way. I don't feel that he is to be considered, hereafter in my matters, and especially this one of ours, at all in the light of an Adviser or Counsellor. I wouldn't ask his opinion or counsel. Nothing but a strong sense of christian duty, which would not allow me to do any thing to *rupture* our natural tie, would reduce me to recieve any *offer* of advice from him: therefore as to *myself* individually I stand aloof from anything like an appeal to him; but it is as to his influence, or the tendency of it upon Lilly that I am anxious. He is *her brother;* and as such has the right, & ought, in all brotherly honor & fidelity to use it, to protect her against what *he* may deem an injury to her. He is terribly afraid of public opinion: I shrink from telling you how great & how controlling, I think this fear of his is;—it is enough for me to believe that it would lead him to exert all his power to tear that child from me, *if* he found the world adverse to me. This, however, is not unknown to you: You know how he acted last winter; and you will know still more when I tell you, that in the face of his declaration to you "that if Sally persists in this marriage, I will *go with her thro' thick and thin*" he said to Lilly, "if your Sister chooses to go on with this thing *I will have nothing more to do with her."* Now you see, in *his* case public opinion is to be tested, before we *know* how he will act, and this makes a difficulty. We have to decide as to our course & actually enter upon it before we know how he will think or act. In regard to him, therefore, it is more necessary that we endeavor to arrive at some true conclusion as to the feeling of the Community. To do that, I will, as soon as I can, ask Dr White what he thinks and Knows. Would it be wise to get him to *sound* some few others? But, John, I hate what seems to be this *asking permission* of society.

You so often speak of my being cut off from my friends by this thing. I consider that that has been pretty effectually done already. I have not had a line from Uncle Tom, even on business, when I wrote most urgently to him, since he knew of our engagement last Summer or Fall—indeed, altho' my brother Tom has been much with him *not even a message*. And, John, he knew to some extent, at least, how solitary I was all Winter & Spring; and knowing me must have known that I suffered greatly from these heavy outside pressures—and yet not one word of kindness! Well, Aunt Sally, has been as kind as she could be all things considered; but *can* I rely upon an affection which when the world presses against me with all its force, will allow her to add her own weight to it,—allow her to urge my brother, who could himself acknowledge almost at the very moment his obligations to me—saying "you know Sister, you have been a Mother to me"—urge *him* to desert me, & boldly say she thought my whole family ought to combine to put me down,—*and* then, when the world is appeased by my sacrifice of happiness come & make an offer to *help me*! *When* I want a friend—is when I am in difficulty—not when I am out of it. And the affection that ebbs & flows as fortune ebbs & flows can hardly be called steady. And yet I believe she loves me; and I love her a good deal in spite of my strong feeling at her conduct. But I can't go to her house; and that because I *wouldn't* be under *Uncle Floyd's* roof. And I imagine he hopes never to see me again, after his recantation of his *voluntary* letter, of last July, which letter has never been returned to me, in spite of Aunt Sally's promise to do it—no doubt, in consequence of "his having entirely changed his sentiments".

Uncle William, I understood from Aunt Eliza said substantially that he didn't approve the step; but if I chose to marry he didn't know what better was to be done than for my family to gather round me & support me. Aunt Eliza entertains the same sentiment, which by the by is the natural & true one; And the one which I agreed to, when *Aunt Sally* years ago urged it as directing her conduct to a near relation who had recently made a marriage alike shocking to decency and morality. No difference of manner ever appeared, so far as I ever heard of, to this kinsman in any of us. I know, for myself, I rec'd a visit from his Wife, who had been the abhorred Stepmother of his first wife, without being insulted my self or insulting her; and I remember assuring him warmly of my recognition of our relationship. And, since his death, I have whenever able been cousinly and kind to his children. But poor fellow! I always felt sorry for him any how.

Now, John, this makes the circle of my nearest relations outside of my own brothers & Sisters; and this, as far as I can gather from my own Knowledge & the report of others is their attitude to me. I consider their relation to my marriage project, & all its consequences, & the risks of a continued engagement as worthy of consideration only so far as it tells upon the world at large. It is painful to me [to] have old friendships ruptured it is true, but our feelings now to each other are just in that state, as to make it very easy and almost certain that a coolness will spring up, if not from this affair of ours, from some other sudden & less important difference. It is already evident, that old memories and a sort of religious principle are all that keep us together; but as these two influences exist in the parties but not together in *each person*, they may soon be over-stepped by passion or caprice.

It is very sad to me to feel that in my difficulties, the only persons who have exhibited to me in person any unkindness & insult have been my nearest of blood. No doubt, I am somewhat wrong, in not endeavoring to conciliate them. Everybody loves the delicate flattery of being deferred to—but, beyond the requirements of good manners, I wd feel a hypocrite to attempt it. But, in all solemnity, I try to *suppress* the uprisings of wrath & bitterness against them. (It is true I make a much stronger effort in some cases than in others)—and I do often feel towards them the working of the old & warm & grateful affection; but when it comes to a judgment upon their conduct, it is the same old thing. A man may defraud me, & I may forgive him heartily, & try to do him good; but according to my judgment he is a defrauder still, & I *must not trust* him again. Is there anything wrong in that? especially if I try to strip my cool judgment of everything like irritation and unkindness.

Do you know I feel ashamed to speak of my kinfolk in a tone that *seems* abusive. I do not deny to them many high & estimable traits of character. I do not deny them kind feelings & generous impulses in the general—I am only stating what I conceive to be facts in their conduct to me, and my feeling in consequence of it to them, & my anxiety about it as bearing upon Lilly's comfort in any further decisions of our own. And along with it all I have this thought. I *may* by a conciliatory course of conduct; and the sacrifice of my engagement to you; & the absolute abandonment of *my* views upon this marriage question, be able to win back and establish friendly relations with my near kindred; but, I have found them, even at the moment that they are professing the strongest affection for me, willing and ready to desert me upon a difference of opinion, and to join with the world in the opprobrium it would heap upon me; and I know too, that, if their affection was strong enough to outride any such opposition from the public, they are yet too distant from me, too much engrossed by their own families & their own pursuits, to render it possible for their attachment to be a thing of daily happiness & comfort to me:—Now, am I, for a precarious, and, at best, insufficient attachment like this, called upon to give up one which *is* a daily comfort, & as far as any earthly thing can be, a daily happiness: But, (& here comes the most painful of all this class of anxieties to me) may not this last attachment *fail*, in an exigent moment, from outside pressure, as the other has done? The ties of blood & early affection & family pride were not, all together, able to withstand these difficulties; how much reason have you to hope that a later affection without these ties, can surmount them? You are a human being, John, and I must admit the *possibility* of *danger* here. Believing that you love me passionately & returning that love with all my heart, and having the *thought* of that danger agony to me, I must yet admit there does exist a possibility of it. But, John, my faith in you triumphs over these terrors. I receive in the pleasure of your love a rich & full compensation for the sacrifice of these lesser affections. As long as you are warm & true, though I should sorrow over the loss of these old friendships, yet I would not have cause to repent of my decision.

So far then, all is said tha[t] can be, as to the effect of my friends opinions about us.

What they may think & feel, if it could just be confined to themselves, would not, by a great deal, be the thing that troubles me most. What they feel about us as affecting Lilly, if it cd be restricted in its effect to her and us alone, wd not be the greatest affliction to me. But I want, above all things, Darling, to *feel sure* that we are not doing wrong in the sight of God either by following wrong principles; or by doing a *lawful* thing which may yet be inconsistent with the highest standard of christian duty—of christian expediency. This idea of christian expediency is evolved by this public opinion & prejudice that we talk so much about. *How far* in a case like ours we are, upon this principle, bound to yield to public clamor which *may*, & *may not be* enlightened morality it is hard to decide—And on the other hand, how far it is proper for us, to attempt to make public opinion yield to us, it is also difficult to say. These were some of the difficulties that came up when the marriage was abandoned—and these same difficulties, tho' to a less extent, are opposed to a continued engagement. If there was nothing *morally* wrong in the marriage, there can scarcely be any thing morally wrong in an engagement. If the marriage was abandoned because of inexpediency, then I see nothing wrong in the waiting, under an engagement of marriage, for an expedient time to marry. Except perhaps this, that in our case it would seem that the death of another was the basis of our contract: & yet, I have often heard of marriages, which were delayed expressly upon such grounds; as, for instance, a child with the care of a Parent, refuses to marry until that Parent dies, and yet may properly remain engaged to be married during the many years that that parent continues to live.

My dear John, I think over this thing, until my mind seems to wind itself into a thousand knots. I pray over it—that I may be able to give it up under what may seem to be, higher claims upon me. My affection begs for its Gratification in a right to pour itself upon you, even when the question of marriage is kept in abeyance to this social prejudice.

And then I fear for you. I fear often, that I may, by an unreserved expression of affection impose new claims upon what you talk of us as *yr honor,* when perhaps some conscientious scruple is struggling for a fair hearing and a just control. O John! don't let me do you any wrong of this sort. If you love me, do do it in a way that God will bless. My affection craves that sort of love from you; & my reason teaches me, that it is the only sort that will out-ride our trials, that *can* secure our happiness.

I have written part of my letter this morning, Monday, having picked it from Saturday's writing. It seems a volume; but long as it is it may not give you any very clear idea of what I think:—writing is a poor exchange for talking.

It occurred to me, yesterday, that it might be well for me, in the way of deferring to them for counsel, to apprise the Reids of yr coming & thus forestall any expression of opposition to it, & perhaps secure their favor. I have no time to write all I think of it—for I am late now—but write what you think about it, for I wont say anything to them till I hear from you.

Correct the mis-spelled word in my last letter to Maggie. I declare I am getting nervous about this thing of spelling.

I was so shocked & pained to hear of the death of a niece of Mrs Mortons who all Winter & Spring used to come to my pew and seemed to have a sort of romantic interest in me. And I was greatly attracted to her, by her high character & unselfishness.

God bless you. Affec'ly
S.C.P. McDowell.

Princeton Aug: 11th 1856.

My dearest Sally,

I am just back from New York where I have had a very pleasant Sunday & where I have finished the series of Sundays that I was to preach in that particular church. The Pastor is on the Ocean & returns by Tuesday week. Dr McGill went with me & what do you think our talk was about?—Speculation in Copper Mining stock. The Doctor is going to show me how I can realize an income of $1000 a year out of $1500 & I am falling into the snare as softly as any mortal ever suffered himself to be entangled. Would not that be nice? $1000 a year. I could then extend a helping hand to you.

I bro't home the buttons & found them very neatly done, & can hardly restrain myself from sending them in this letter. Would you like to see them?

What *can* I do for you in your troubles. I feel more anxious about you than probably you are about yourself. *Darling, darling,* you will not be prospered if you talk so about your uncle. He is your *mother's brother* & both your Mother & Father loved him. You never wrote me such a naughty letter. Moreover, if he hears of your speeches you only can be the loser. Isolated as you are what is more natural than that you should circle yourself round by warm friendships in your own household & if men provoke you as all men sometimes will, *silence* I find is one of the highest priveleges of the injured especially where nothing can be done to redress either their rights or their honor.

What can I do for you, Darling? How can I enterfere so as to give you the least relief in all your pressing difficulties. Indeed, Sally, how do you live on from day to day? As *I* understand your affairs with *all* your means working badly I cant see how my poor daughter maintains herself, & I feel an anxiety I can hardly describe.

Let me *urge* you not to say one word against either uncles or brothers. Dont *lose* them as your friends. Let your position be more & more a pleasant one in your own home & if personal misfortune comes it will not then be mixed with other elements of weakness, which rest assured in this wicked world become greater instead of less when a person really falls into ruinous misfortune.

Dearest, do you really love me enough to hear me talk in a right earnest way. Then I would *implore* you not to alienate your brother James. I *personally* would feel a remorse about it. I would feel that I had divided your family & would have all the unhappiness of having been a disloger of your peace.

My engagements in N.Y. end so far as I have made any yet with the 5th Sunday in September. As soon after that as you think it wise for me to come, I want to see you. I have left it so long that the plan agitates me with painful impatience.

I want to talk over all these matters with you. Do you know my *bitterness* when I think how *much* could be avoided of embarrassment if I could marry you throws back upon me the whole question of our being married at once. I feel more pressed to do it both by love & sorrow than ever before & it is only because of old inveterate remstances[43] of judgment that I dont again sue to you for an immediate marriage. I have nursed myself so long in the gentle influence of your love that it has given me a sort of *household* feeling of right to regulate the day of our marriage like everything else, & that I have only to say, Sally wont you consent to marry me now to win your consent to confide all in my word. Is it so? Sally? Would you marry me at once if I solemnly assured you that I thot the time had come when we might do it wisely?

But, Dearest, you *must* cherish your relations. I would rather see you bankrupt than at variance with *all* your family & if you provoke them by severe speeches the public will turn against you & think the *many* more likely to be in the right than the one.

Do I ever wear anything you ever gave me? Why, bless you, Darling, I wear your spectacles every day. I try others & they dont seem so comfortable. I have written my whole book & all my letters with your pen & it is good yet. And presently I mean to fix my wrist-bands & wear the buttons. Do you wear anything I ever gave you? Kiss me for good-bye Dearest & dont quarrel with me.

Yours *affly*
Jno Miller.

Princeton, Aug: 11th 1856.

My dear Sally,

I have just received your naughty letter of the 7th. I'll tell you what I think of you, Sally. I think you ought to be somebody's darling pet wife, & as I cant conceive of the idea of your being any one's else tha[n] mine I feel so sadly the bitterness that keeps you from my arms. As I have often told you one of the forlornnesses of my present disappointment is that with an eager longing to shelter you in your interests & with a growing insight into the fact that nature has been true to her devices & has made you a *woman* & not a man, I am not able to take my own wife to my bosom & shelter in those ways in which every woman needs the protection of a husband. You were never meant to battle with the rough things of life. You have all a woman's leanings & now that I have waited

---

43. Miller possibly meant "remonstrances."

to see what you would do to extricate yourself from your different difficulties, I feel assured that tho they are manageable & a good male adviser might slowly wind you out of the coil you have suffered to encircle you, yet you will never do it & I am *so* anxious lest it gather & gather till it entirely encumber all your means of living.

I feel so worried in all this.

I have been repeatedly on the point of telling you some of my thoughts about you. *But*, Dearest, it is so needful that you should master & understand your position *yourself*, that I hate to say anything that would induce you to alter your plans or wait another period of weeks till I could talk with you on my visit.

Still my visit is so near now that I think I will tell you all that is in my heart.— You were within a few hours of being my wife. I feel toward you as tho' you were my wife now. I feel all that readiness & *desire* to serve you & manage if I could all your property as tho' I were your husband. And I have turned over that thought in all forms with the most anxious reflection. I would like to treat you *now* as tho' you were my wife & share my purse with you, &, indeed, if my purse were not so meager an affair & I were able to do all I want I would *insist* that you let your property lie quiet [and] gather up its resources under careful management.[44]

Colalto
Tuesday Aug: 12. 1856.

My dear John,

Such a surprise & disappointment as it was to me this morning to empty the mail bag & find no letter from you! I dont think such a failure has occurred before for weeks. I thought it over & over & at last was impressed by the idea of the letter having come & by some carelessness having been over looked at the Post Office. I didn't, however, send a second time to the Office. But being in town an hour after breakfast, what should happen but that the Post Master followed me into a store & gave me *your letter*! He has omitted to send it with the others, he said. I put it in my pocket walked down to the Hotel to see Mr Mann upon a little business, sat down with Lilly in his parlor, & read my delayed letter with no slight satisfaction, I assure you.

O, yes, John, I remember distinctly of yr telling me of yr having burnt a packet of letters, and of yr regret for it since. And my affection is greatly gratified at your telling me now of yr mistake & of their recovery. I am glad to know that you will let me share, as far as it is possible in all that interests or concerns you. It would be very painful to me to feel that you should think there was anything in my temper or feelings to forbid yr talking to me of the past with as much freedom as you please. I love to think that you will so rely upon my affection as to have nothing pent up & kept back from me, the speaking of which wd be either a relief or a

---

44. The letter ends here with space remaining on the sheet. It was probably mailed with the one written earlier that day.

pleasure to you. And, John, I am a little proud to think that with all a woman's jealousies upon such subjects, my attachment is able to bear such a trial. It could furnish no stronger proof of its strength; for you know, Darling, how covetous I am of your whole heart; & how sensitive lest I may not possess it all.

Like you I find half past *five* too early an hour at this season; but then 8 is too late for me. Indeed my early rising owes its origin in part to the desire to secure a quiet hour before breakfast, which, with us comes tolerably early. Suppose we try from 6 to 7, if you can manage, without great discomfort, to rise that early. I would like the hour to be a suitable & convenient one to both. My household arrangements—I mean particularly in regard to servants, restricts me, pretty much to the hour I have named. I thought of an evening hour; but it would not answer so well, even, if there could be entire freedom from interruption in it, wh: wd not be possible. So then we'll try the one named, allowing it to become later & later as the season advances.

I hope to obtain much good from this plan; and you cannot tell, John, what a strong load of affection & interest & union it is already becoming. To make the arrangement complete, if you are reading with any regularity or system, tell me when you are reading & how, & let me go along with you.

Do my letters show any improvement of spirits of late? I am *so* much better than I was. I have regained all my lost pounds, & my old energy & efficiency begins to return. A week or two after I came home I suffered dreadfully. I was a distress to Lilly at times, I was so wretched. I was painfully loaded with care & anxiety, with no one to counsel with, or aid me. But now, tho' my cares are not much lessened in number, I find I can bear them better. And my mind is quieter under our own special troubles; & has something nearer akin to repose in regard to them than ever before. How long it will last I cant predict. How it came about, I don't know either. I can have some conjecture it is true, but know nothing certainly. It is not the result of indifference or passiveness—for I love you with deeper & stronger emotion than ever I have done. And, John, I love you with a calmer confidence; which brings to me a fuller & more peaceful happiness.

Wednesday morning.

I forgot to say the other day that there might be some risk in directing my letters "to Mrs M D. Lexington:"—if you inserted "Colalto", then there cd be none provided they came to this Office at all. Sometimes my letters take a trip to Lex, Ky, before they reach me: & numbers of the Breckinridge's letters from Va, have never been sent out of the State, but have come to this place & been sent to me with my mail.

I am glad Maggie fancied her versified letter. I wrote Susie (James' little girl) such an one a year or more ago which was a great pleasure & prize to her. And if it pleases the little folk, it is certainly worth all the trouble it costs me, which when I am in the humor is not a great deal. But there are times when I can no more make two lines rhyme than I can build a house or cut a field of wheat.

We are luxuriating in a gentle rain this morning. You can't tell how much we have suffered for want of it this summer. Our Gardens are so late, that it is scarcely a week since the first tomatoes of mine were brought to table; & they were miserable things that looked as if they had escaped the drought by "the skin of their teeth"—or rather were in such case as to be all skin to our teeth.

I have not seen Dr White yet. As soon as I can I will do it. He has not been well of late & has had several deaths in his family, which while they could not cause any very heavy distress, have yet had their effect upon the old gentleman's feelings. I am afraid his Pastorate is drawing near its end here; but I am cautious about any such expression of opinion.

God bless you my dear John. With all my heart Yours,

S.C.P. McDowell.

Princeton, Aug: 12th 1856.

My sweetest Darling,

I think I must adopt the practise as I sit near my desk of seizing my pen & writing anything that strikes me. I am just reading from the April's Westminster an article on the "English Law of Divorce". You may not know that Palmerston, as one act of his administration has in view a total change of the Div: system.[45] Heretofore only about two cases of women being div: so as to be permitted to marry again have ever occurred in England & those cases not yours at all but I imagine cases of the *nullity* of the original marriage. It has been this practise in England that has reacted & produced the hardships in this country. The new law proposes a new & better system of process & at the same time to allow a *woman* to divorce her husband. The Tribune says that the husband is to be able to divorce the wife for infidelity; & the wife the husband for infidelity coupled with cruelty. Parliament rose, I fear, without passing this bill, tho' it will be bro't on again when Par: sits again & the Reviews are evidently smoothing the way for its passage. If it passes hundreds of women waiting for such relief will no doubt use it & the immediate number of divorces will be very great & the effect on public opinion on Epis.[46] & others, *here* & *there*, immense.

I seize however my pen to say how often my mind boils over with a feeling of impatience at our imprisonment & restraint. I reason in this way. Sally is as pure as an angel. She has been deeply oppressed. Nature has been true to her patterns in making her what she is, & she is most engagingly & *helplessly* a woman. She needs a husband more than any one I know & as a husband in the abstract torments me with the idea of imagining any husband but me, I am always thinking in an egotistical way, Darling, that you need me. That you would fare better in my arms

45. Henry John Temple, Viscount Palmerston (1784–1865), British prime minister (1855–1856; 1859–1865). The *Westminster Review*.

46. That is, Episcopalians.

& indeed, like a stone, my own beloved Treasure, you tend towards me with a sort of longing gravitation. Isnt it so, Dearest? There occurs to me my perfect willingness *as concerns me* to marry you, if it seemed right, if it drew upon me the world in arms. You are more than the world. And I would rather live in a cottage with you, than the idol of any city. These New Yorkers have been flattering me lately telling me of my interesting sermons & going over parts of them & asking Dr McGill to send me three times instead of once as he at first determined & so I am taking the places of others who had been going. And, Darling, this flattery comes to me just as it always has from the leading men of the church who discuss my sermons & talk them over & are set to thinking by them & so I get a fresh taste of the old excitements of Pastoral life. And yet I say truly I would rather farm on Rocky Hill & *right*[47] philosophy & have you my darling Wife & become wedded to you as I think husband & wife may till your very loveliness of person becomes a robe about me a sort of shadowy & more beautiful portion of myself, than live in all the acceptance of an orator & marry the most unchallenged woman that I can dream of or that the world can furnish. Still I am thrown back by difficulties more serious than just social dishonour & I have promised to talk over all this when I see you. And so I keep my day-dreams to myself—fearing this:—(& tell me if it is so, Sally) that if I talk to you of these flashings up of expectation I set your yearnings again in motion & destroy your repose of mind & keep you from that serious settlement of feeling which is requisite to steady you in the practical duties of life. I am constantly feeling—"Well, I *will* marry her, in spite of congregated opposition." But when judgment pulls me off of my horse again & writes <u>Veto</u> upon all my intensest dreaming then I keep it all to myself & dont tell you what I thought of lest I keep you in that frightful see-saw which you suffered from in a bitterer period of your life. But Sally, tell me—Did T ever *write* to you protesting your innocence. I know he did orally.[48] Have you *letters* in which he says he charged you falsely? Moreover, are you *sure* that you cannot find Dr Tyler's letter. If you cannot, had not I better write a confidential letter & draw from him a full statement in reply before the old man dies.

I sometimes have a fancy like this coming over me. "I am a public character. I *must* remain more or less under the eye of the public. I love Sally & would not resign her for my life. Is not a more public relation to her than I now hold better for me. Is the clandestine look of a reserved & uncertain engagement the wisest to be talked of & whispered about where I go. Is it not my policy to be more than commonly *declared* in my attachment to let people *know* that we are engaged & to let all our movements assume the aspect as time passes of a fixed & understood relation.["]

Then I think, when, Sally, asks me how she had better live & where she had better go if she breaks up her expensive establishment, had I not better advise

---

47. Miller meant "write."
48. "T" refers to Francis Thomas.

her to go where in her peculiar circumstances she could be sheltered & kept right before the public *in the house of some minister*. White now would be such a man, but he I see you do not like, nor would there be congeniality as to his family. Then there is "Brother" Ross. I know you do not like him. And his home would be very dull & you would not like to be under obligation; but Mary; may not that be the very place for some months or a year if you should break up your establishment *as I feel sure you should*. Does not Mary need you? Would not that reverse the obligation? Is there not some call in Providence for you to look after a poor sick sister? Might not I come to you there more freely—(the home of a minister & preaching for him &c) than any other place on earth & if it would be oppressively dull might not *reading* & writing to me & my occasional visits & a sense of service to your sister & a knowledge that being brought down to your own mere board you would be recovering from debt, would not all these keep you cheerful & happy. I must talk over all these things when I see you. If you have such an exculpatory letter from Thomas please send it to me. Pardon me for just one sentence of a little wanton violence to taste:—I would so like to see one of your *early* letters in which you were pouring out your heart in its longings—the ardour of a girl 19 years of age. I would so like to satisfy my jealousy that you did not love then more warmly than now. I *dare* you to be so entirely mine as to show me anything you have & to send me the warmest letter you ever wrote to any one but me. I can imagine the hot heart of a girl of twenty so much more fondly clinging to her lover than a staid matron of after years & I know I am just *surrendering* a delicate taste but Darling, are you not mine. And is not all of you mine. And is there anything you will not show me. At least will not a time come when you will have become so much a lover as to let me put my hand into the very bowels of your secretary. I know you will laugh & say that never lover was treated more confidentially & that I have somehow a strange way of ravishing your very bosom of all its secrets, but dare you trust me so far as to let me have just what I please. Were your letters ever returned to you or did you keep copies? & if so be naughty enough to give me torment in seeing you caressing with the fondest tenderness of speech tho' it be 15 years ago somebody else than me. It would strike me so strangely. Copy it over & obliterate all the names if you please—but (Sally, aint I wild?) prove to me that there is nothing in the wide creation if I ask for that I may not have. Goodbye for this morning.

Wednesday 9 1/2 P.M.

My noble Sally, that you should be willing to sacrifice all your worldly relationships to your affection for me draws me to you under an influence of which you have very little conception. I do not mean to answer your letter to night. I go to Phila early in the morning to see the Dentist & on other errands. And I will answer you carefully on Friday. I had no conception of such a state of things as you describe. By a natural reserve which I also have felt in any little unpleasant speech that I may have heard you have not told me. That your Uncle

Tom should refuse to answer your letter (unless perhaps embarrassed & kept from it by other causes) & that your Aunt Sally should talk of "putting you down" which means I suppose ruining you & casting you out of all society seems to me—well no matter! Not one brother or brother-in-law or sister or aunt or cousin that I have or know anything about would take any such ground.

The question narrows itself down to this:—not shall we continue engaged for we are now engaged & matters improve (do they not?) rather than grow worse i.e. your brothers &c return to you. Not, shall we write to each other? for that seems to be allowed us. But shall I go see you? for that seems the public & dangerous avowal & exposure.

Now, Darling, as a great proof of your passion for me & instinct of love & confidence, believe me when I tell you three things:—First, it is as impossible that I should cease loving you or that I should be forced from you by any such exigent necessity as that of which you speak as that the heavens should fall or that your own love should cease or grow indifferent to me. Sally, in the crowd of our *real* cares, do banish that one. To fail of all your earthly friendships & then at the last & most trying moment fail of his for whose sake you gave up all the rest would indeed be painting me as a fiend. I cant conceive of anything more happy than my friendship also failing if the time of your abandonment by others finds me such a miscreant as this. Dear Sally, banish all that from your mind. You have nothing earthly to fear in respect to my attachment so long as you care to value it. You are giving yourself "agony" for nothing. My visits even are not necessary to my steadiness. And my steadiness does not arise from a great romantic purpose to *sacrifice* myself to a principle of honour, but from a passion that has taken you far more into the chambers of my being & made you much more my *mistress* than you have ever known. You have more *power* over me *both* from honour & from *passion* & *now* from every generous impulse than to make it necessary for you to venture a tho't upon any question of *our lot being cast together*. So much for <u>me,</u> Darling. Now, Secondly, about myself I am perfectly independant about the visit. It cant hurt me let it turn out as badly as it may. I have not one instinct of self-protection that even so much as raises the question about it. As respects my ministry I dont feel my conscience awake to any difficulty. And as respects my standing I feel quite independant of any effect of the kind. My friends will treat me on my return from such a visit just as they have always done. But, Thirdly, I *do* feel strongly the effect upon you. Nay as to my self, I should have one sense of pain & that is at the shame of compromising you. If I thought I would do so I would quite refuse to go. I would do as the Major said take your cards in my hand & judge for you & not by the exquisite pleasure of seeing you once again wh. at best is a selfish pleasure (& wh. would not affect my loyalty to you) by stripping you of all the amenities of your usual society. I should dread the result to you. I should dread its effect on your health, nay on your very affection to me. Tell me, Darling, would you love me if I repelled all your friends. So then I *fear* about the visit, not from any judgment of mine but from what you now tell me. But my verdict is this:—you must decide. It cant hurt me. It can hurt you. Therefore, in all generosity you must decide. Go ask Dr White *confidentially* as your Pastor. Ask him also not to ask other people but what he knows of them already. Dont ask the Reids till you have determined whether I am to come for I would not appear to such people to yield & give up the point. If I thought your Aunt Sally's mode of talking was the prevalent one about you I would have every instinct of honour shrinking from subjecting a lady by my presence to such serious sacrifices & exposures. And, Dearest, I say clearly. If you cant tell me conscientiously that you think in these respects you will be safe *I cant come.*

And yet, my own Beloved, I dare hardly say so. I have been feasting upon the thot of what was before me & night after night as I lie awake thinking of you I walk up that road in front of your house & see your white dress round the bushes & presently fold you in my arms. But then I am used to sorrow. I gave up my marriage & surely I can give up seeing you. If I have to write for twenty years without once seeing your face I wont on my account sacrifice you for the pleasure of having you in my arms. So Darling think & pray & write.

Yours affly
JM.

[marginal notes] Honor bright! Sally. It was these rough assaults upon you of which you never told me that made you so thin & nervous in the Spring? Was it not?

By the way your Aunt Sally <u>couldnt</u> have put you down if we had married. She forgets that there are no holes to a married home. Virginia people cant put people down across 3 states & in the bosom of another family.

Thursday Morn.

Dear Girl,

I must write you a long letter further on this point. I wish I had known these *serious* speeches sooner. Why didnt you tell me. Our road forks here into two paths. One of wh. we must choose—either to let our love be the fond & persecuted thing of a reserved & private attachment or to come boldly out & avow a distinct engagement along with a purpose not immediately to marry. I feel much more resolute to press the last than I did to press our marriage—but I will not decide for you how far *I will shut you up* to no *love but mine*—how far I will force you to give up your friends for me.

I want also to speak of this thing in its *pecuniary* relations. You *must* extricate your property. It is now your great work. If your friends leave you & press you for your debts what could you do. Every sentiment of prudence & self respect finds you to give yourself with self denial & care to this one work of extricating your means of living. But, Darling, I weary you. I am yours, to use me as you please. I never felt so devoted to any mortal as I now do to you. Think over all I say

& remember the danger of my deserting you you may leave quite out of your account & dont fear to say as loving things as you feel.

Yours fondly
Jno.

Colalto,
Thursday, Aug: 14. 1856.

Oh John! I tell you the truth; *I do feel so bad.* I feel just like I had had a *real scolding,* (as, indeed I have had;) and that I partly deserved it, which makes it harder yet. Well, I mean to behave in future, since you are so displeased that I don't reverence "my Mother's brother" as I should do one, who standing in that relation, seems to me, some times to forget it himself. But I am wrong; and *indeed* I will try to do better hereafter. But, John, I am not the only one in the family who has trouble with Uncle Tom because of money.—Uncle William & Aunt Eliza have gone quite as far, if not a good deal farther than I in their words & deeds both. And there has been almost a rupture between Aunt Eliza & he growing out of money matters & other things; and a coolness between he & Uncle, which perhaps, the visit Uncle is now making him may serve to dispel. I feel sorry for all this; &, tho' I sympathize with Aunt Eliza in her grievances, yet I was candid enough to tell her, in a particular case that she mentioned last Fall, I think, that she behaved not well to her brother. And yet, every body likes Uncle Tom & thinks him mighty kind. And we all, have borne with him, & liked & liked untill—I don't know what. And we are sorry too, because of his money pressure, & would not complain or think hardly of him if he would only treat us a little more civilly when we approach him on business. Mr Carrington is the only one of us all who has been decided and uncompromising with him & I think he is more likely to retain his good will than any of the rest.[49] However, what I want is a real friendly spirit to a kinsman whom I used to love very warmly; and I mean to try to get it;—and I mean to quit laughing at his peculiarities, and quit saying sharp things, and quit talking depreciatingly of him—that is, quit expressing my opinion of him, if it is not so high as that I hear others express. But look here, John! what do you think of this? Nannie Carrington has a great reputation amongst us for amicability, and prudent speaking, and yet she told Aunt Sally last winter "She didn't like her Uncle Tom; & if he came to her Mother's house she would insult him!" *I* never came near making any such speech in all my worries.

I know if you were to see Uncle Tom you wd like him;—he is very thoroughly a gentleman in his bearing, with a style of conversation, that from its grace & ornament is, to many people, exceedingly attractive. There is nothing of the petit-maître about him with all his care of fashion in his dress & manner, but the contrary—he is manly, and rather dignified. And above all, John, in my heart I

---

49. McDowell's brother-in-law Charles Scott Carrington.

believe him to be a *true christian*, and a useful one. He has, with a strong hand torn away old usages at the Salt works, and established upon christian principles, a new system of operations there. And I honor him for it; for I know how strong the conviction of duty which enabled him to affect such a reform as he has done. When he was a little boy—not so little either 12 or 15 years old, he lived with my Parents, and went to college; and this gave them a half-parental fondness for him ever afterwards.

Did you mean to say that my letter was haughty or naughty? I would rather not take my choice of the two evils thus left to me by yr bad writing, so you will please tell me when you write again which you said. I am sorry you should think me either, especially the last; for that would bring me under the condemnation of *actual transgression;* whilst the other, I could easily slip from my shoulders to my old Father Adam's as original sin, and feel pretty well rid of the burden.

But indeed, John; in sober earnest; I do feel *bad* at your lecture. I feel sorry you shd think I need it & sorry that I did need it; and sorry you should find anything in me that didn't please you. But then, on the other hand, I am obliged to you for it. I thank you, for taking me in hand, and correcting, or endeavoring to correct me when I am wrong. I thank you for wisely and affectionately grasping your end of the check-string you have thrown round my neck, and drawing it hard enough for me to feel. I shant love you the less but only the more for all *such* checks.

As to James—he has nothing he can *reasonably* complain of, in me; Unless, he gets mad with a hurried note I wrote him a few days since about Tom. I was sorry afterwards I had written it in a hurry, for I might have been more cautious & choice in my language if I had had more time.

You don't know everything that has exasperated me in that quarter, or perhaps you would be more patient with me. However, I don't mean to justify *any* bitterness on my part as a *habit* of thought & feeling. I do try to root it out of my mind in this case; and I think, when I consider that it is *I,* I have been not unsuccessful. It distresses me that there should be any feud between us—that *we,* children of the same parents, should be at variance with each other;—that he, whom of all men God has made the nearest in blood to me, should yet be looked upon as an enemy. And I am struggling against all this feeling; but I don't *do* any thing to *conciliate* him: that is, I never write to him unless he write to me. I never, when I do write, ask with any special interest about himself or his wife, or his children: I never ask for counsel or say any thing that wd seem to be a call for sympathy, or make an exhibit of my affairs to any extent. I am never affectionate in my expressions or tone; but always *civilly kind*. Hearing the other day that Susie had been extremely ill, I wrote (the letter not specially for that purpose however) some such sentence as this—"I am sorry to hear of Susan's sickness; but hope now she will soon be well. Give my love to her & Sally; for I remember them both with great affection".[50] But in the summer earlier when

---

50. Susan and Sarah (Sally) Benton McDowell, daughters of James McDowell IV.

he wrote that he wished one of the little girls could be with me that she might have the benefit of this climate & cheer me in my solitude, I did not respond by asking for her. And yet, I love that little Sally, & wd have considered her a treasure in my loneliness.

But *what* can I do, John? *How* would you have me write? Sometimes I think I do myself injustice, by seeming both to you & him to have a harsher & unkinder feeling than I really do have. I can't bear James should think or Uncle Tom or any of them that I am putting away my anger and suing to them for peace because of any point I had to gain either in society or in pecuniary matters. I have no such ends. And if I ever have, as in truth, John, I think I have to some extent been, above this sort of evil feeling in my conduct to them, I have been so from the urging of mere principle more, a great deal more than from any other cause. Now write me a good long letter about all I have said to you; and scold me well where you think I need it, and love me, John, ever so much, even if I do have all these faults.

I don't know that you can help me in my property difficulties, and some other difficulties too. I am, all the time hoping that Providence will show me the way out of them. Lilly begs me to keep her at home this winter, & try a private teacher. Sometimes I incline to make the experiment till January. Then again, by way of curtailing, as in some aspects, it seems, all my expenses, I think I had better rent my house & hire my servants & live myself elsewhere. Then again I can't determine *where* I cd live less expensively than at home, *if* I had Lilly & her Teacher with me.

Lilly's expenses with her teacher, in my house wd be as well as I can make the calculation now, scarcely more than half that they have been this past year; and I have little doubt that the mental improvement would be more satisfactory. But, whether, hereafter she may not be dissatisfied with this plan, & question the integrity of my motives in it, if it should fail in advancing her education, is a question that weighs with me. I am extremely anxious, & have always been that she should have, what few girls *do* have a good English education. This wd be my great aim in getting a private teacher. However, I am just mentioning this a part of an arrangement for myself.—If it shd upon the trial not seem a proper plan for Lilly, then in January I am left in the same difficulty in which I find myself now; and looking to that possibility I doubt whether it be right for *me* even seriously to entertain the thought of such a purpose. And so I am wound up & up until I come back & stand still.

If your friend Dr McGill could only invest for me $10.000, so that it would bring me rateably the same amount of income that you say an investment of $1.500 wd bring you, why, I will forthwith sell off a part of my farm in town lots & send him the money. Let me see how it wd work. If you are to get 1.000 upon $1.500, why then upon $10.000 I should get $6.550! which wd help me amazingly. I could then have this house, *without* an Overseer. What a nice air-castle one can build upon this copper bottom!

I am anxious Lilly should go to Virginia Preston's wedding at Smithfield, the old family residence in a week or two, as there is to be a gathering of all the kin there.[51] If she does, I shall go with her as far as Aunt Eliza's and pay her a visit until Lilly returns. After that Uncle William may come down, to make his promised visit to me. Would you like to come when he is here? If so, then I will find out *certainly* when he will come. If not then after I get back from Fincastle I will write to you fixing your visit without any reference to any other persons. If Miss Jannetta only is here, I don't care whether Uncle comes or not. I mean, if your visit and his should both come together, then I should have no great anxiety about such things as household matters, for Miss Jannetta wd take them in hand and leave me free to meet Uncle's demands upon my thoughts and time and yours too. Only this I should feel bound to do—i.e. let Uncle know, of your proposed visit, so that he should not think *it* had been planned with any intention of having his presence here, at the time it was made as sort of a tacit approval of our relations, and a sanction of them by him.

As you say Maggie has such proclivities to womanhood, hand her the receipts enclosed & tell her to try her skill in the kitchen. No Preston table in Va at this season is ever without one of the two dishes—and they are both pretty good. I have been as careful, as old Mrs Glass of famous memory, to make the receipts plain. As the proverb has long settled the fact that "the proof of the pudding is in the eating", after Maggie has put hers to that test, tell her to write to me what she thinks of it.

I am glad you found the ring again. Do you know John, I fancied you had laid aside *my* spectacles? I am so glad you wear them; and I hope you will never have the chance of finding any other's comfortable.

I caught cold a night or two ago, and am made very uncomfortable by it. My eyes and throat and head & chest all suffer some from it—enough to remind me to bring my long letter to an end.

Your letter came straight this morning, and I hope your new plan will bring me another again on Saturday.

You say yr preaching engagements extend to the 5*th* Sunday in Sep'r; has September that many Sundays? Perhaps you meant to say "August"? Well, if you have engagements for Sepr, or if it is likely you will have any for that month, make them; and come after they are over. I want to see you very much, but not when you have work to do. Is the book finished? Oh, I have news for you! Mr Massie told me the other evening that he thought *I* had more turn for *Metaphysics* than any Preston, man or woman, he had ever seen! Now! Think what abstractionists the rest of the Prestons must be. It may be, you haven't thought as well of me,

51. Virginia Ann Emily Preston (1834–1898) married Robert Stark Means, M.D. (1833–1874), on Aug. 26, 1856.

as you should after all! But goodbye. Pray tell me how much you love me. I'm afraid you'll forget how.

Yours Affec'ly,
S.C.P. McDowell

Princeton, Aug: 15th 1856

My sweetest Sally,

I just have your nice warm letter. *Usually* you manage to cheat me out of the little endearments that a woman (I fancy, tho' I dont know much about it) usually lavishes upon her lover, and that by all kinds of excuses. Dearest, for you to tell me that you shrink from telling me how much you love me sometimes from the very dread of increasing my feeling on the score of honour &—is just about the coolest piece of effrontery I ever suffered from. When I come to think of it you do treat me scandalously—to tell me what a "volcano" your heart is—how as you once said to the Major it might come down "over leaping all barriers"—how pent up the warmth of your nature was and all that sort of rhetoric and then treat a poor youth who has been thrown into your power by a short romantic history and who cant get away from you—who like a poor sun-fish struck by a torpedo cant quit it or like a poor bird gazed at by a snake is so enchanted that it cant fly away & yet keep me on the poor crumbs of a few tender expressions, scattered up & down in a long correspondence, so that if like old M.S.S. they were written in red characters they would hardly alter the black letter look of the whole series of letters. Look here, Sally, some day I am going to do something right wicked. I'm going[52] to seal a letter with black wax or make you think I'm fearfully sick or drop the correspondence suddenly & let our sexton & undertaker write you word I'm dead & invite you to the funeral just to see whether all your high-flown stories about what you would say if you could & so on have the least bit of meaning in them except just to make me hold quiet & adore a divinity that dont care a wax candle about me. Sally dear, I think at this late day your talking about reserves in telling me you're half distracted in love with me, if you really are, is the greatest nonsense that one woman ever tried to perpetrate upon her victim & that to call your letters *love*-letters would be so funny particularly when naturally you're so volcanic. Fie, Sally, you haven't even said you passionately loved me & indeed you have denied it & said as to passion you dont know whether you have any of that or not. You think not. You're very volcanic but you don't think you have any passion. I've thought of advertising in the matrimonial column of the Ledger giving my age & weight &c & asking whether there isnt somebody who could treat me a little better. If there is you know it wouldnt interfere

---

52. Miller repeated "going."

with you for if you have no passion surely you couldnt be jealous of somebody who had.

Come here, Sally, think about that word again. Tell me now without any perverseness, *don't* you love me passionately?

I went to Phil. yesterday. I saw Leyburn. I quietly asked him what would be the effect of a visit &c. He said at once & truly, He could not conceive of its impropriety or its ill effect in your neighborhood. He said that he had thought *in your neighborhood* they seemed prepared for the marriage. He told me moreover he had met Mr. Kennedy, U.S. Sen, who had spoke to him of Thomas—told him he was living in a log cabin in Allegheny Co. very much renounced by everybody. Leyburn asked him whether *he* had a conviction that T. was libertine in character during his marriage. K. told him, unquestionably—that that was the cause of the sympathy with the op. party, & that he had heard that he had been seen at that time travelling to Balto in the company of disorderly characters.[53]

Dearest, in respect to my visit I have come to a complete conclusion. As respects *my self & family & ministry* I choose to come. You cant judge for me & I hold you not responsible & really will not allow you to prohibit me on these accounts. In respect to *your* friends how can I judge? Of course it would be folly. I therefore will assume no responsibility. Unless you can tell me you think it will not estrange them *I will not come*. The pain I should feel would not for one moment influence me. It would not be as painful as not marrying you last December & really when I came to weight your interests at that time my passionate longing after you *seemed to have no weight at all*. I hardly thought of it in settling the question. To cool your friends & desolate your home & give you the ceaseless feeling of a proud woman lifting up her head *with an effort of self-dependance* all the time would be in me not only wicked but puerile & base. The longing I have for you therefore; I dont think of. After the shock at our wedding it seems to me almost *natural* that I should be restrained & disappointed. & Therefore, Sally, I throw all responsibility on you. Report to me honestly & *soon* for I can bear disappointment better than suspense.

If you estrange your friends you make your pecuniary matters worse for you can ask from them fewer delays. And Darling, how can I with the least show of honour cut you off at a time of critical pecuniary distress by a step of mine & repel your natural guardians & helpers when I am so useless & can give you so little help myself. If you were independant & comfortable I would feel differently. Would it not be mean, a woman as you are, to cut you off from your male helpers & be so helpless myself. You *must* clear this up in yr mind, Dearest. The morning

---

53. Anthony Kennedy (1810–1892) was serving in the Maryland legislature when elected to the United States Senate. He took office on Mar. 4, 1857. "Op. party" means the "opposition party," that is, Whigs.

hour will suit best. If I can keep it, it will make me a better Christian. I will begin & read Matthew.[54] Indeed I did begin & found some things I will write to you of in the first chapters.

Affly
JM.

Colalto,
Thursday Aug: 16. 1856.

Dear John,

I saw a synopsis of the Matter to which you refer in Parlaiment; and as far as they were given read the points of the projected Divorce bill. I was struck with them; but chiefly I believe, with the fact that such wrongs as were inflicted by the old law of Divorce in England had remained thus long unredressed. I do not percieve that the *social* standing of a Divorcée will be, at all, improved under the new law, tho' pecuniarily she will be much benefitted. I think it well that the social feeling should be very stringent upon that whole subject of Divorce; but I complain that it is without *just* discrimination. It is a horrible necessity only which shd justify an appeal to a Civil Tribunal for relief and release, and that necessity ought to be acknowledged by a proper sympathy by the public—But I don't like to talk about it.

Dr White called just after I had written my last letter to you. I told him you were coming in a few weeks & asked what effect he thought yr visit wd have here. He thought the same people wd talk now who had done it before; but he was decidedly of opinion that we should not be influenced by that, but shd act resolutely upon our own conclusions. He said moreover I had well tested the feelings of the people here last Fall when the marriage was to have taken place & had found that the people I cared for had stuck to me. Among others he named the Reids. He thinks we should not defer so much to public opinion any how, in a case like ours; and does not believe that what we call *expediency* should be or can be for any length of time made to over-ride the simple Truth. He advises that nothing be said to anybody either by way of announcement of yr visit, or by way of conference in regard to it; but that when you are ready to come, why just come. As to Lilly, he does not think that she can be compromised by our relations. I told him the ground her Aunt Sally had taken. He seemed surprised—had not heard it—characterized it as "cruel", but did not speak as tho' he attached any special importance to it as affecting Lilly or I. After he thinks more of all I said to him he may come to different conclusions; in which case he will, I am sure, tho' there was no such arrangem't made, let me hear from him.

Why, John, what makes you think I don't like the Doctor? I was only miffed at some little thing he had said of you a year ago; but you mistake, I do like him.

54. A New Testament gospel.

I w'dn't like to board in his family however for reasons entirely aside from any personal feeling to him.

Uncle Tom didn't refuse to answer my letter by way of insult to me, but from carelessness & mortification to confess he cdn't pay me. I wrote to him in Jan'y telling him I had to take up a note in Bank for $500 which matured early the following month, & as other means to which I had looked had failed I must apply to him for the payment of a bond of his which he held for something above that amount. After some weeks I think—or perhaps it was only 10 or 12 days he sent me word thro' Mr Massie that he wd send me a check by mail. But no check & no further notice has ever since been taken[55] of me or my note—except a line in a letter to Aunt Eliza, who had written to him on business at the same time, which *we* thought referred to my letter, & which was this—"a *protest* by a county bank is nothing like one by a City bank"—nothing like so embarrassing & ruinous in its consequences I suppose he meant. I was *hard pressed* by his refusal, tho' I waited for the promised check as long as possible. My Kentucky rents proved, in fact, nothing. I *threatened* to sell my carriage & horses & wd have done, if I hadn't known I shd do it then at a terrible sacrifice; but, at last I renewed my note in Bank by a curtail of 30 pr ct & when it fell due again, paid it off, without ever applying to this Millionaire Uncle. I thought the worse of Uncle Tom about this affair, because of the circumstances under which he had borrowed the money from me two or three years before.

As to Aunt Sally's opinion, as I gave it to you, I have no idea that it is the common one among my kin. I think *she* feels *more called upon* to be very decided because of her Husband's unfortunate letter to me. *She must be strong enough to prove that he could not have ever favored the marriage*, if by any chance I should say that he had done it. I may do her injustice here; I hope I do. I have always thought Uncle Floyd at the bottom of that whole letter transaction. I have pretty well made up my mind that that letter has been withheld by him, &: that he means should it ever, in any conspicuous way, be brought before the public to make the statement of its existence, or at any rate, of its contents, a question of *veracity* between us, *he & I*. After this suspicion fastened upon me, I thought it well enough to speak to one or two friends about the letter & its fate. I therefore told Dr. Graham of it—giving its history without any comment upon it. I told him too that Uncle Floyd said "he had entirely changed his sentiments since that letter had been written"—at least his Wife had so reported. The Dr instantly said—"Yes! public opinion has changed his sentiments; and now he wishes to destroy the proof of his change". The Dr rather reproached me for giving up the original letter, & in reply to my emphatic disapproval of all fear of trusting such a thing as that in the hands of any such near relation, laughingly bade me be more wise in future. But, you know, John, we didn't value that letter for any aid in the ethical questions it gave us. I only began to esteem it, when I found, or

---

55. McDowell repeated "been taken."

suspected rather, that *he* was looking to a crisis in my affairs in which the with-holding of his letter might be of consequence to him, & when the exhibiting of it might be of importance to me. You will think this a terrible onslaught upon my Uncle—but, John, I am only speaking freely now, because these things run into our matters,—and I tell you the Virginia Press & the Virginia Public have gone as far as this; before me in its judgment of the Gentleman. For some years I have had my faith in him in a tottering state; but, of course, it has had no tendency to diminish, but on the contrary has rather increased my attachment to my Aunt; & nothing perhaps wd have shaken that, but her present unnatural position to me. As it is, you can't think how my heart is drawn to her, when I hear of her bad health & loneliness. She *is*, in spite of this affair of mine a fine woman. Nobody can be perfect—& if I were ever thrown with her again, I should find it easy in her good qualities to forget my grievances. She has been very affectionate and tender in her love to me up to this time; & after Aunt Mary died some years ago, she used to say she felt more like opening her heart to me than to anybody else.[56] And she often spoke freely of her innermost feelings; and since this coolness between us, it would often have been a pleasure to me to have been able to assure her that all such revealings were *safe* with me still. All these things are very sad—but, I am trying to feel to them as *sorrows* & to throw away the idea of their being injuries or insults to me, except when I have to form upon them a judgment to direct my course of action.

No; it was not these things that were such a burden to me in the spring.

How strange of you John! And yet I wish I could gratify you. I haven't a scrap of such a letter you ask for; if I had, you might have it. There were not many of them, & I took no copies of them; why should I? Those written before I was married, were all carefully kept—every scrap of every kind that had a line of mine upon it was put away. I remember even some cards of invitation to a May party at Miss English's. All that were written after that time were kept too. You know I left Annapolis intending to return in a few days? I never did go back; & after several years everything that I had left was packed up & sent back to me. I was obliged, to look into these boxes for papers etc, etc, and then found that *all* of my letters & *all of his*, had been retained. *Mine* of course he had, but his had been withdrawn from my writing desk & kept. Afterwards, in his quarrel with LeGrand, something was said about these letters, I don't know now what, but he thought it was a call upon him to restore them, which he instantly with much emphasis & emotion too I believe, refused to do, saying "they were his Treasures."[57] When my old friend Fendall told me of it—I said "Well, let him have them; & you, Mr. Fendall will prepare the deed of gift to him". "No" sd he,

---

56. Mary Thorton Carter Preston (1805–1842) married a cousin, John M. Preston (1788–1861) of Abingdon.

57. John Carroll Legrand (1814–1861), Maryland lawyer, served as secretary of state under Gov. Francis Thomas before his appointment by Thomas to be chief justice of the Maryland Supreme Court.

"I'll do no such thing; he shant have them". But, of course I have never asked for them, & where they are, or if they exist at all, I don't know.

But I have no idea that even "the warmest" of them could rouse your jealousy. I have no idea that any one of them or all of them together ever did speak half as much as any one of scores of yours. I have no thought now that the *feeling* that dictated them was as strong & deep, or any warmer than that that flows to you. It seem to me a dream that I ever even knew him. A horrible night-mare that catastrophe of my life seems to me now. And then I am so wholly given up to you in all my affection that it seems *impossible* I ever could, at any time have loved anybody but you. I cannot believe any girl could love with a fresher or even more romantic attachment than that I cherish for you, Darling. I have not *seen* any certainly; and I have seen four Sisters married in a fewer number of years. Cantey used to say last Summer, she has not the same degree of feeling; & quoted the same opinion of us from somebody else. And John I am loving you more & more. I find in you more to love; and I would like to have you throw your arms round me & let me bury in yr bosom all remembrance of the past. I would rejoice to have your love wipe away, as even now it is doing, all those wretched years from my heart's dial. O John! Nobody knows *how* sad all that period of life was to me. But I thank God, for much that was good in it, & all that was merciful. If I ever do get to Heaven I may look back upon it as the *brightest* spot in my life, "count it all joy" that its sufferings were decreed to me. And strange as it may look, sometimes when the mood is on me I would like to talk *to you* about these past sorrows, John. I feel so entirely secure in your sympathy. I know you would let me say all that my feelings wd prompt at the time, allowing me to without you could grow weary or worried by the recital of all these troubles—or that you cd do otherwise than *participate*, like an other self, in them. And then to lay my head in yr bosom, my own precious John and feel at rest there. But—I forget. Somehow, these old recollections so strangely merged into & mixed up with present feelings make me sad, & I am led under the pressure of them to speak, perhaps too freely even to you. So goodnight.

It just occurs to me after trying to impress it upon my memory, to suggest to you to look in Phil: for a kind of thin letter paper almost like tissue paper, but tough & capable of being written on on both sides without blotting. It is such as European travelers used when letter-postage was high. I have not seen any for a long time. It is very soft & light & compressible—2 or 3 sheets wd scarcely weigh as much as this one, on which I write.

My cold is better—tho' I cough and am hoarse yet—not much however.

Monday Morning

I have some doubt whether you can read my letter. If not a "scrappy" I think you may fairly call it a "scratchy" letter. However, make out of it what you can.

I am pretty sure I shall never be able to find that letter of Dr Tyler's that I once told you of. It was written about the time of *his* trouble with Mr Thomas in Frederick; and contained statements as to his professional connection with him which wd, no doubt, now be valuable. These statements were greatly obscured to me by the number of technical terms introduced; but they were plain enough to make a shocking history of the past. One sentence I distinctly remember as connected with an account of the transaction which ha[d] given ground to his adversary's charge of "maiming,"—it was this. "Thus, you see, Governor, that if my *professional skill* had been less successful, your family would have been saved these afflictions".

I have once or twice thought it wd be well if we could have old Dr Tyler's written statement; but wouldn't it be very unpleasant for you to seek for it. The old man is a garrulous old creature; rather meek at best.

I have often thought that Mr Fendall could probably supply or obtain more information upon this whole subject than any one else. He was more thorough and accurate in his investigation & knowledge of the case than all the rest of the Lawyers engaged in it, put together. He was fond of me; & I think took a deeper personal interest in the thing than any other person employed in it. Besides, he is prudent, & wonderfully gifted in silence. All my papers were in his keeping for some time, but they are now in the Bank of the Metropolis at Washington City, subject to my order. There may be among them letters from Dr Tyler bearing upon this same point as the one lost here; but I hardly believe there can be. By the bye Mr. Fendall, told me he thought of carefully writing out the whole case—perhaps he may have done it. If you think it advisable I cd without any difficulty, appeal to him on any point you may desire:—or you could do it yourself, if you preferred it. A note from me to the old Gentleman wd open the way to any conference you cd wish with him. I have great trust in him.

No. In all of Mr Thomas' letters since our separation he has never made a full & frank disavowal of all his *alleged* suspicions, or an unequivocal & distinct recantation of all his charges. He would near it, but never did it fully as I thought a man who wished me to return to him as his wife should have done.

I find among a few old letters, an original one from him, written a fortnight after my Father's death which I enclose.[58] I took no notice of it, and after some time (a month or so) it was followed by another, to which I replied in a brief note, a copy of which you already have—*Two* others, I think; *one* certainly followed, this after another interval of some months, & to those I replied in a long letter, of which also, you have a copy. Since then I have been entirely silent. These letters were returned to him; but I have copies of them.

You can keep the letter as, I don't like to trust it backwards & forwards by mail. I stop now to copy, before I send it to you. You can't think how I hate to talk of this matter.

---

58. James McDowell III died on Aug. 24, 1851. Thomas's letter is dated Sept. 3, 1851.

My cold increases, I am afraid. I cough a good deal & am rather too uncomfortable about my throat & chest to have my mind entirely without anxiety. Little Mac is sick, & I feel anxious about him. The music came this morning. I don't know that *I* am the person meant; if I am, I consider it a great impertinence. If I am the person meant, *Hewitt* never furnished those verses.[59] He is a composer of the *music* of ballads—not, that I recollect of, of the words. What do you think of all I say. I am hoping for a long letter tomorrow.

With all my heart Yours
S.C.P. McDowell

[Enclosure: Francis Thomas to Sally C. P. McDowell][60]

Alleghany County
Sept. 3–1851

I had long cherished the hope dearest Sally, that my repeated efforts at reconciliation & reunion wd have been crowned with success during the life of yr Father. Deeply sensible, long ago, how much I had to atone for in having disturbed that happy family circle now so cruelly broken for ever on earth, it was a warmly cherished wish of my heart to be permitted to share its sorrows, in the full belief that I cd assist to restore its peace & happiness. And this I was especially anxious to do while yr Father & mine yet lived. Circumstances that I did not know how to control frustrated all my attempts. And they have gone. Your noble Mother has gone beyond the reach of those consolations I longed to offer to their wounded spirits.

Sorrowing deeply over these melancholy events, sympathizing with my whole heart in your recent heavy calamity I will not resist the impulse that prompts me to appeal earnestly to you to grant me one interview that we may not too go hence without exchanging sincere assurances of a perfect forgiveness for acts in which we were both entirely free from malice. With affectionate respect I am Most sincerely

Your friend
Francis Thomas

59. John Hill Hewitt (1801–1890), author and composer of popular ballads.

60. After copying the letter, McDowell added, "Upon second thought, I send a copy instead of the *original* letter. If you want the original, I'll get somebody else to copy it, or certify to the correctness of *my* copy, then send it to you."

PART EIGHT

"I want to love you not only with my heart, but with my mind too."

August 1856–September 1856

Princeton, Aug: 18th 1856

Indeed I shant do any such thing. I have told you, "I love you" till I think you believe Jersey vegetation grows without either rain or sunshine that corn can be cut off of our Jersey cobs and kept "*on a boil*" without any care of replanting & I'll tell you what, Sally, I'm going to keep all about the state of my affections a great secret till I have given you an opportunity to overtake me. Indeed, I have been very uncivil all this time, for I remember when I was young an old cook book that I used to read told us always to let Ladies go first on all occasions. Sally, you've never yet told me once (we were married—I was going to say) once we were engaged that you loved me so much that you didn't care how soon or how thoroughly I knew it.

Oh! let me tell you some things before I forget it. I meant to say "the 5th Sunday of *August*.["] I shall not be engaged later than that. You must not write to N.Y. because I dont stay in the city long enough to get your letter. I would give more than I can tell if you *would* enter with warmth & intelligence into my metaphysical feelings. By the way before I close up this letter I hope to be able to tell you that I have bought a part of Allamby. I received last week $50 for preaching in New York & expect $30 more. Meanwhile a laboring man who owns part of the Allamby tract has come to me & asked me to buy it (5 acres for 90 dollars). I go with him this afternoon & if I find chestnut rails as he tells me enough to sell for 50 dollars when cut! & other wood beside! I mean to buy it & it will be mine before I sleep. He lives at a distance & cannot get as much in cash from any one else. (Oh! I said *naughty* not *haughty*—dont flatter yourself, Darling) so then I shall have made my first purchase on the tract &, mind you, it is *new* Allamby not the one 5 miles off, but the one overlooking

721

Princeton where the brightest summit & the place for building will be but two miles. O Sally, if you would love me & enter with all the cordiality of a refined & earnest lover into my schemes of *thinking* I should have hopes of a sort of Paradise, but if my wife is only a tender lover & a sweet & constant companion that will be very nice to be sure but nothing to compare with my own congenial fellow student. But Sally this you will never be. You love the warmth & fire of pulpit usefulness. I love the insinuating subtilty of those influences of thought which new mould opinions & which give *command* to the orator how & in what forms he shall minister the truth. You like Robert Breckinridge. I like Jonathan Edwards & would rather be a tenth part of Jonathan Edwards than fifty Robert Breckenridges or the best preacher that England ever reared. Still, Sally, we wont quarrel. Do you know what I have been thinking of lately. I have been watching you in all your difficulties & tho' you say I scold you, I think you the very loveliest of women. You behave like an angel—(I mean just with a little tinsy winsy bit of the fallen sort about you.) I want to send you a book. It is called the Flower of the Family.[1] I bought it for you this morning. Tell me whether you have it & if not I will send it on. When you have read it give it to Lilly. I think it will make you both better. Julie lent a copy to my Mag. It would have made you laugh to see me sitting reading here all alone in my room till I couldnt see the page & had to stop again & again to wipe my eyes. Either love has made me cry easily as you know brandy sometimes does or else that is a very good book.

Why, as to your uncle I would rather visit you alone for then I could have you all to myself. You know we meet seldom & I do so want quite to monopolize you. But if you can gain any point by it I acquiesce with all my heart. Do keep well with your friends. *All* men are partly devils, & therefore if gross faults would excuse family feuds no such things as families could exist. I would, however, have tho't better of you in your way of talking about your Uncle Tom, if you had told me at the beginning all the facts.

Maggie has made off with the receipts & from the schemy look her eyes had I take it my corn bed will have to pay for it & perhaps this very morning. She sends her thanks & has made me read that part of the letter to her & twice over.

I'll tell you how much I love you some other time. But, Sally, just tell me this. You have *long* said you loved me *as much* as you ever loved any mortal. You tell me now, "I love you with deeper & stronger emotion than ever I have done.["] Now tell me, Sally, then; dont you *now* love me *more* than you ever loved any other body. I rose this morning at 6. I mean to do still better. The book is almost finished. I think I will not finish the [r]est till after I see you.

Yours affly
Jno Miller.

1. *The Flower of the Family: A Book for Girls* by E[lizabeth] Prentiss (1818–1878) was published about 1853.

[marginal notes] Did you ever read any part of my letters to other people?

About the Copper McGill is going to tell me rumors when he comes home.

I am now in the whirl of impatience to press you again in my arms. Do arrange for it soon & so as to be *home* those weeks or about.

6 1/2 o'clock. I have been out & the lot is bought. This therefore is the date of the great Allamby tract being first occupied by the Millers.

Colalto,
Monday 6 P.M. Aug: 18. 1856.

My *dear John,*

It has been cloudy all day; but only within an hour or two have we had, what we need so much, a real rain. Now, it rains gently, but with a certain dismal & *resolved* look about the clouds, as tho' it meant to persevere for days to come. I sincerely hope it may; but it looks cheerless; and is so damp & cold that I am not only wearing a flannel wrapper but have, in addition, thrown a large, thick shawl round me, and find it very pleasant.

I wrote to you a part of a letter this morn'g in such a hurry that I had no time to glance over it, but I fancy it gave some intelligible answers to some of your questions. I ought not to write now; for tomorrow when I get another letter from you, I shall need *all my paper* for its reply;—(do you know I feel foolishly sensitive about letting our P.M., whom I never speak to except upon business, see so many letters to you bearing a double stamp?)—but, as I sat here by the window after I shut up my book, I feel so strongly drawn to a little talk with you, that I thought I might indulge the impulse for once.

It is an old story, this of our affection: One might think we had worn it thread bare in our very many discussions of it; but it comes day by day, very like the day itself a sort of new creation. It seems capable of much addition yet—and instead of wearing out from *use*, only seems to gain fresh vigor by it. I often love to tell you about it, and I delight above all things to have you tell me. I can't be as free in the use of terms and expressions as you can—I often reject those that come bubbling up warm & strong from my heart, & search out calmer ones. I don't know why, but I feel a sort of shame in *always* saying as hot things as I feel. No doubt you laugh to hear me say so, & wonder *how* I cd say any warmer things than I have said. But, John, I have told you a thousand times and surely you believe it by this time, that I love you with all the power of my nature. I love you with that sort of affection that exacts from itself the best that can be given; and longs for every good quality & every possible attraction, just that it may make the gift of them all to you. I love you too with a *submissive* sort of feeling as tho' it were a pleasure simply to yield to the requirements of your affection. But then, I *must* have an entire belief in your love to bring all this about in mine. This I Love. But the tea bell rings, & the night is almost here.

Tuesday afternoon

Dear John,

I have wasted two or three sheets in the attempt to write to you. Somehow none of them pleased me; & now in answer to all you say about the visit I say this—I'll take the responsibility of deciding, as you wish me to take it, for myself and my family upon all I know of them; and I say *whenever you can arrange for your visit, then make it*. Now, remember, this is *my* decision. I know more of my family than you do. I know better how I am cicumstanced in regard to them than you do. I do not believe that your visit would make the slightest change in the feelings or conduct of any of my Sisters to me, unless indeed Nib might be drawn off by her husband, who will be sure to shape his course to please James & the Prestons. Susan sd to me this summer, "There has been no change in the feelings of us, Sisters, to you Sister on account of this thing." Now beyond these nearest relations, *why* should I care? I have already showed you how little Uncle Tom has seemed to care for me in any way. And James has acted so little like a brother that he has lost all claim to be considered. I am not precuniarily involved with my brothers or Uncle. Uncle Tom [is] in my debt, & if Tom wd receive it a check upon him for a few hundred dollars wd free me from all money matters with him. If they were disposed to injure they cd only do it, *pecuniarily*, thro' Lilly; & not much then; for I cd not be forced to do more than I am already endeavoring to do to extricate myself from her.

My great fear has been for Lilly's comfort; but should all my Aunts and Uncles turn against me, I hardly think it cd hurt her seriously. As it is, & as I told her the other day, nothing would induce me to allow her to go to her Aunt Sally's house, if she lived in Washington as she may do, should Buchanan be elected. I gave her my reasons for this, telling her too they had been of quite long standing, & had been just such as had influenced others of the family in going to her house. Then Aunt Eliza, will probably go South—or at any rate leave Fincastle this Winter & there wd be another link cut. So upon looking narrowly into the whole difficulty I do not percieve that she could lose much, by their taking stand against me. I try to take care of her. God has mixed up her destiny with mine; & I hope he will over-rule for good to her any mistake I may make. And, as being responsible for her too, I have decided this thing. When you come on I can tell you more of all these family troubles.

I feel much inclined to believe that a calm, cool, determined carrying out of our own purpose will do more to defeat & disarm family opposition than any deference to it, will do toward conciliation. I think if we had carried out the marriage last Fall, we or at least *I* would have stood with them no worse, & probably better than I do now. If they wd take out their abuse upon me I could wear as quiet a countenance under it as old Dr Musgrave; but when they come down upon you, aspersing your honor, then I feel like I could, to use Willie Breckinridge's favorite phrase, "pitch right into them."

Now, Darling, when will you come?

Tom came today, having finally left his Uncle. I think he means to stay with me until he can make out his plans—probably till October. I should hardly need Miss Jannetta if he were here at the time of your visit.

My cough is better—but I am not well, & my head aches as I bend over my letter. Our Town, has had a good deal of sickness in it. Old Dr Junkin was alarmingly ill a few days since; & Dr Graham has a grown son still, or was late yesterday, dangerously sick. We have all been unusually well. Lilly much improved. She is a great comfort to me John, despite my anxiety about her. She is, of course, entirely familiar with yr writing, & if she happens to see me with yr letters, she laughs & asks me about "my Gospel". "Sister, you will be such a good woman; you read so much Gospel". She is very busy with a Nube which she says is for your Maggie. She complained to me the other day that she had to play *second* to you now in my affection—& thought it hard to step down from being no 1 there.

Pick up, without asking, except to know if it fits, a stocking or sock (whichever he wears), of Allie's & send it to me in a letter, pretty soon. When you come on can't you bring me a good daguerrotype of those little folk.

But good-bye. If I can I'll add a little tomorrow morning.

Wednesday morning

I have often heard statements similar to that made by Mr Kennedy to Dr Leyburn. I believe many of them. I once told you, I believe, of the German Gardener & his young wife at Frederick. I have long thought that poor man's sin was only that of imputation, tho' he bore trouble enough to have been the real transgressor. Other things rise up too that awaken strong suspicion—indeed I have the most entire belief in the existence of long standing vice of that kind.[2] I ought, perhaps, to be more sorry than I am to acknowledge it.

I am so uneasy about dear little Mac. He has suddenly become so thin and feeble & pale. Early this morn'g as Lilburn was riding him by the house he recognized it, & called for "Auntie"; but Lilburn rode on.[3] As they came back he called again, & would come in. I went down to see him, & he stretched his arms to me to take him, & asked for his breakfast. I took him & had a "batter-cake" which he begged for more. He eat, almost greedily, but seemed very feeble & had lost his spirits. He says he loves "Auntie a heart-full" & claims that she loves him as much. I do love him a great deal, and am hungry for him when he goes away.

Write me a good long letter when you write again. The Fall seems just upon us. It is cool & pleasant all the days.

What do you think of my renting every thing here except the farm to Tom? I couldn't rent him the farm now unless he would employ my new Overseer, which

2. Namely, that Thomas had committed adultery.
3. Lilburn was a trusted servant (slave) first of James McDowell III and then of the Massie family.

wd be a very useless expense for him. Indeed his renting my house wd be a bad scheme for him, tho' it might be a good one for me.

I am still undetermined about Lilly. She almost rebels against the Gills again. John, tell me; how are we to read the *ways* of Providence? I don't mean to read it like fulfilled Prophecy, that is easy enough—but to read it as a present lesson.

I am still battling with a sick head ache, tho' I think my cough is better this morning.

God help you—Do you know I can't bear to say "dearest", tho' you seem to fancy it. Cousin Virginia Breckinridge always says *"dearest"* to Uncle Robert, & I have taken up a sort of horror & disgust at the epithet from that.[4]

Affectionately Yours,
S.C.P. McDowell

Princeton, Aug: 19th 1856

I am tired, My Dear, of studying & sitting still all day & yet the hard cold rain which we have had since 10 o'clock & which has put an end to all appearance of drought keeps me from walking out & taking exercise. The thing most like recreation is writing to you; &, Dear, get near me. Here, let me draw this chair close by my table & fancy you in it, & now, Sweetest, let us have a good long talk.

I never dreamed of loving you before that morning in Lex: That I have often told you. But, Sally, I never thot you very interesting. I had heard you had behaved purely & nobly in all your troubles—at least that you had entirely escaped all challenge in your very trying circumstances & that struck me as very remarkable. But I never thot of you somehow as fine looking or attractive in any way & when I had seen you, you looked small & withered. When you broke in upon me that morning it was like making a new acquaintance with all the rapidity of old acquaintanceship. You looked lovely. You welcomed me kindly. You gave me so cordial & kind a welcome that it quite upset my poor hermit equilibrium. You looked so lovely that I could have *folded* you at once to my arms in that very mornings interview. How surprised you would have been if I had done it. And, Darling, you did not let me rest. You pursued me in my dreams. You came full armed out of other peoples mouths like Minerva out of the head of Jupiter & you looked so sweet and pretty & had such nice fat cheeks & I remember such a pretty white neck & such speaking eyes that I had no chance at all. A poor sallow student with nothing to claim for myself but a lot of black letter folios & a horrible old sad spirited character the idea of having much a magnificent creature as my own was perfectly intoxicating. Moreover castles began at once to go up & beautiful forests & this lovely apparition walked about in them all as if they were her own.

---

4. Robert Jefferson Breckinridge's second wife was Virginia Hart Shelby (1809–1859).

Honour bright Sally, didnt you see what an impression you were making on me before I told you. Tell me honestly—didnt you see you were making a conquest & is there no instinct in a woman that tells her when she is having a victory upon a poor *misèrable* like me. Sally, I dont think I ever asked you that question before. Did you positively not dream I loved you till I told you so that night in the straits. Sally, describe that scene to me in the Straits. Tell me all I said. My! how queenly you looked as you strode on before me. Your very feet as you drew off your dress from them as they stumbled thro' the dew seemed like Judas to "lift up the heel" against me".[5] The horrors of that night I shall never forget. And yet your very first utterance spoke volumes. You said, "I shall never waver". Now if you had hated me you wouldnt have said that. Or if you had not some little *care* for me, you would not have talked of "not wavering" for that implies temptation. I took fire from that very word. Tell me, my Love, did you care for me the least then?

Wednesday 9 P.M.

I have just read your letter. What do I think of what you say? Why, Darling, just *one thing*. That is all I can now think about in all that letter. How much Sally, *does love me*. And yet, poor Child, how you break off—"I forget." You must have old Puritan blood in you where love like flax or cotton is to be measured by the pound. Havnt you an old Bible somewhere in the house where in the list "A man shall not love his grandmother &c["] the printer has made a mistake & added "a woman shall not love her husband" or a lass shall not love her lover more than "juss a little". Here for the first time you get a little eloquent about your love & when your confessions are just freely on their way, you bring all up, with that exclamation Oh, but I forget, I'd like to know what you forget. Suppose I made you tell me what it is you forget.

If you can treat Mr Fendall so confidentially & can *depend* upon him to be silent I wish you would write to him asking 1. if proofs of Mr. T's irregular life came out in the trials. 2. if there were proofs of irregularity in his more recent history &c &, 3. if not, whether—however Darling, I so little know how well you are acquainted with Mr F. or how far such a letter will embarrass you that I will wait & talk with you about it in L. I dont want these parties however to die without leaving us all they have within their reach.

When am I to come to see you. My engagements are now so congenial that I think I would be half happy if it were not for one thing & that is a sad longing all the time to see you & a sense of *want* all the time if you know what that is, an incapacity to settle down & feel contented & *fixed* like other men. I had no conception that such a feeling could exist for whole years together.

I rose this morning a little after six. Our "Prayers" are at seven Winter & Summer; & Breakfast some ten minutes after. So that unless I rise at 5 1/2 wh. I mean to do I cant dress & secure the hour. Still, Dearest, I have done better than usual since we began & that early part of Matthew which I selected because I had

5. John 13:18.

been collecting some German Commentaries for it has already interested me a great deal. Dearest, listen to it. "Be thou there until I bring thee word."[6] So other people have had their troubles as well as me. Poor Mary was not even allowed to go home & bid her friends goodbye. And do you know I never noticed before how nicely the Providences fitted in together. The Magi who got them into this trouble *opened their treasures* & presented them gold & frankincense & myrrh; & no doubt this was what they travelled with on their trip to Egypt. Dont you wish that the wise man of the East who has got you into all this trouble had a little more of the gold & a little less of the disposition to get honest families into hot water. You never touched me more in a letter than by that word Jehovah Jireh. It was fulfilled to Mary & it will be fulfilled to us if we have the same submissive spirit. God bless you *dearest.*

JM

Thursday Mrn. 8 1/2 o clock

I forgot to tell you that I am wearing your buttons. I found a seamstress sewing in the entry the other day & learning that she belonged to the children I stopped their work & brot out a quantity of mine—among the rest the making of a quantity of button holes. They fit admirably. But just think, Dearest, what a lot of gold I carry about me—I that had such starched & *hard* notions. But alas! I've got my wrists in the hand cuffs & there's no telling where I wont go to.

What *was* the thing that "was such a burden to you in the Spring?"

I am growing so impatient about the visit. Next Sunday week is the last I shall be engaged in New York. I would like to start soon after that. Other things being equal I would like to find you alone—I mean not engrossed by your uncle or by any formal guests. Miss Gordon or Miss Polly could properly matronize you & Lilly would be there of course, but if you have any body else you know you will treat them shockingly. Moreover the time when we can deliberately walk into a separate room & turn away from all guests is passed. We no longer can take the liberties of young lovers & I would have to sit often with others or stay away when in my brief visit I would want to be *slowly* bringing up my wits in long trains of endless confabulations with you. Wont it be enlivening? Still Sally, do as is best. I would be glad to see you if all our meetings had to be on chairs & just opposite McDowell's tavern between that & John Lyle's Book Store. You wouldnt go to *sleep* there at any rate & that would be an immense gain over some of our interviews.

May I stay *three weeks?*

I have indeed bought the first slice of Allamby. I went to see it yesterday. It is quite well wooded. A farmer whom I met there told me half *the wood* was worth all I gave & as I cyphered out the acres the other day I found as near as I could calculate that there was 7 1/2 acres instead of 5. Indeed it is so much of a bargain

6. Matt. 2:13.

that as the check is not delivered yet I mean to put the owner on his guard & give him a chance to draw back. So I may not get it after all. He is a poor labourer, and the ghosts of his famished wife & orphans would haunt us if such a stretch of our fine park 10 years hence should be tho't of as bought under any kind of mistake for 90 dollars. I will set him on his guard & then if he chooses to sell (& I am not sure he can do better) we shall have the land with a safe conscience. I have gained one thing by not marrying you & that is that I have not to buy as this poor man has to ask his wife whether he may sell a few acres or not. I never could see why women grumble so about not having their rights.

We're going to have corn work to-day—so they tell me. Margaret sends her love. I was amused at Mary. She said she had *had* the recipe for pudding. And the objection to it was it took so much corn. I would like to know how you're sorry to have corn pudding without its being _all_ corn.

[marginal note] We have ship letter paper in the house I think. I will write on it for my next letter.

Colalto,
Thursday Aug: 21. 1856

My *dear John,*

I am afraid you are getting to be a "fast youth." Speculating in Stocks and buying lots all in a breath! What next? Will I give you joys of your "chestnut rails & wood beside", tho' I must say such an account of Allamby does not well accord with my notions & experience of farming. I have, I wouldn't like to say how many acres here that may be described somewhat after your own style—"cedar posts & rocks beside"; but the income they yield me wd scarcely suffice for the meagre living of a half crazed hermit-philosopher. However, John, I hope your new purchase will make us all rich some of these days;—in the mean time I'm quite sure it will furnish us any number of castles.

How odd those people should *pay* you for preaching! And yet it is very well, and no doubt it is a custom founded upon just and proper grounds, but I never heard of such a thing in Virginia. And I am curious to know how much those New Yorkers think your sermons worth, in gold and silver. How much "material aid" do they give you for the spiritual food with which you supply them? I never heard you preach but once: I didn't hear that sermon well for I was rather drowsy. I can't, therefore, say I thought it worth much to our people generally; but John, I can tell you it has *cost me* a great deal. I have "paid dear" for that Sunday I know. What do you think about it; has it been *worth* any thing to you?

Honor bright! You really do think that I behave pretty well? Well, John I thank you for saying so; but, in truth I can only claim a little commendation. But, tho' of course you mean me to cut off two thirds of what you say as mere exaggeration, yet I am heartily pleased & content with what remains. I am never offended at your scolding; for somehow, you manage to do it well, and seem not to love me the less when you try to make me correct my faults; but I enjoy a little praise *powerful much*. I feel so proud (!) now I can toss my head & tell you "I don't care if you did say my letter was '*naughty*' for now you don't mean any such thing."

It's very hard, in this world, Darling, even to try to "behave"—much harder, of course, to do it. And then I have been some wee bit spoiled & when people thwart me & contradict me I am terribly tempted to "come down upon 'em like a thousand of brick".

Ain't you a nice fellow! Who have you been "reading parts of *my* letters" to, that you come making such a charge against me. Did you want to shelter your misdemeanor's in that way, under similar offences in me if you could only be sure I had committed them? Come John, tell me the truth; how far have you transgressed? And *who* cd have the patience to listen to you? In good earnest, have you been so foolish?

And so you wont tell me how much you love me! Well John I am very sorry; particularly as you seem to think that your crop of affection has been short this year; & that if you use even a little of it this early in the season you will not, when planting-time comes have enough left to secure our living for another year. That's very sad—but you may keep your ears, grains & cob if you will only just throw the *husks* to me. I am too starved to be proud or particular; so I'll take the husks & and thank ye too.

I can't *always* tell with unequivocal distinctness whether "I love you more than I ever loved any other body" or not; but I love you far too much for you to have the faintest shadow of jealousy of anybody else. It[7] isn't possible I could have loved more than I do you & my affection for you is a far higher compliment (if there can be that) than an earlier one was.—Under its influence there is no impossibility of my becoming even a Metaphysician—a Jonathan Edwards—in petticoats! Imagine such a thing if you can.

I hope by this time Maggie has given you a specimen of corn soup that will do credit to my receipt.

I have read & so has Lilly "The Flower of the Family". I am sorry now that it happens so. Two years ago I read it with very great pleasure. Little Mary Leabrook had it here the first summer you came to Virginia.

I shall tell you something about yr visit when I write tomorrow morning; for now it depends a good deal upon Lilly's going on Saturday to Virginia Preston's wedding. She don't want to go, but I am anxious she should. All the Kin are to be represented there, & I choose she shall assert her claims & fill her place amongst them.

Friday morning 7 1/2

I can't yet decide about yr visit—that is, as to the time of it. My plan is to send Lilly to Smithfield either tomorrow or Monday if I can do it, let her stay till after the wedding, & then come back as far as Aunt Eliza's, where by next

---

7. McDowell added another "is" here.

Friday I will meet her. Uncle William will be there at that time, & while I am getting Lilly back, I can make him a visit. I intend if it be possible to pay him this piece of attention. I worried myself dreadfully last summer to do it; & after it was done thought he put little value upon it; but no matter, it is due to him from me & so if my conscience is clear in the matter, I care very little how he esteems it. Miss Jannetta is at Aunt Eliza's, & I will bring her down with me; then by the middle of Sep'r you can come on.

I think it is fair to tell Tom, as he is staying with me, of your visit when it is absolutely fixed as to the time &c. This I shall do easily enough for him to quit me, if he chooses to do it, so long before you come as that it shall not look to the public as if he had deserted on account of you com'g. I have no idea of seeming to his friends to inviegle him into anything like a favoring of me or my conduct; but shall leave him an open course.

I am kind to him because he is my brother. I have invited him to my house because I thought he was in a fair way to be unpleasantly treated & sneeringly thought of where he was; as things now stand between his Uncle & himself. I have had no thought as to any effect his being here wd have upon my plans either in private or to the public. It was clearly & wholly for his own sake, & not one particle for mine in any way, that I have asked him here. I am glad he is here I am sure. And I shan't quarrel with him if he chooses to leave me now, tho', of course, I shall not think well of him if he does it. I don't think however, that he will—tho' I don't know.—last Fall tells a sad tale as to the constancy of friends.

I was called to breakfast after writing the above, & before it was quite over Mac came in, & then Nib & Mr Massie—so I hurry off my letter.

Always Yours
S.C.P. McD.

Princeton, Aug: 23 1856

My *blessed Daughter*,

Did anybody ever call Dr Bob, *blessed* for if they did I'll never call you so again. How happy you made me with your good *warm* letter. It is like a royal robe & even when *sables* mix with the ermine it covers me all round with the most voluptuous embraces. Indeed, Darling, it isn't good for a cold student like me to fall into the possession of so beautiful a woman. And when you remember how much more happily[8] you write than most persons—indeed of either sex, you ought to pity a poor Tantalus like me who is brought, like the ghosts of Milton from the ribs of metaphysical ice back to that tortured glow that frozen people have when they are slowly & achingly carried back to life.[9] Dear Sally, I do *long*

---

8. An illegible word is interlined here.

9. In Greek mythology, King Tantalus, condemned to Hades for his crimes, suffered extreme thirst and hunger. He stood in water that receded whenever he tried to drink and the fruit dangling about his head withdrew whenever he reached for it.

so for your letter days to come. I do feast so upon those yellow envelopes. I do tremble so when I break the seal. My heart beats as tho' I were on the eve of our actual marriage. And when I find your white arms round me in the letter & your warm heart beating almost convulsively with mine it nearly crazes me. I live in the most extraordinary *vibrations*. Nothing can be more cold than the vault of a groping metaphysics & *nothing* can be more warm than that fold of generous devotion in which you wrap me when your heart speaks right out in your letters. And yet, Precious, you never did write me just in this way. I never got the ermine coat of your love fully round me in any of your letters. I always felt cold a little. There was always a big tatter somewhere or a snugness in the stuff so that I was always pulling at it to get it round me. I dont think you ever relaxed every muscle & let me hold you like a little child in my arms. And yet I dont know.—I was trying the other day to think how you could say you loved me more passionately. You have said "you longed to nestle at my side".—"You loved me with all the strength of your nature".—You thought of me almost without intermission.—You spoke my name sometimes for the mere pleasure of hearing the sound.—Being my wife was the most fervent desire of your nature.—When throwing your arms about me in an agony of pleasure you were just ready to claim me as your husband you sank back to the conviction that it could never be. *Did* you not say this, my Dearest? Was it a high *effort* to love me or do these things come welling up of their own accord? Can you honestly say you feel them when I utter them altogether? Well; tho they are so sweet & so tender & so full of *abandon* as tho' you could not more completely throw yourelf upon my confidence than in this tempest of your passion, yet do you know it all seems cold to me. I an ceaselessly looking for something else. I read such a thing & my first impulse is Oh! I wish it were the time for Sally's next letter. When *will* she tell me all her heart? Or when will she *have* all her heart in such a glow of attachment as to warm me so that I shall feel entirely relieved.

But, Sally, love or my love at least is a hungry passion & I am not sure it ever could be satisfied. I think I would be happy now if my heart would be content to go into the house that your love has built for it & enjoy *that* for it does, apart from my "own restlessness" (as Eddie calls it) make me very happy. But I no sooner get into this house than I treat it just as tho' it were a turnpike & push right thro' it to the furthest door & throw that wide open & reach out my arms & hungrily ask for something *more more* all the time. Instead of going into the rooms which are made luxurious by the softness of your affection & gazing on your picture & studying *near* it & throwing myself upon the bed which your own confidence has made for me & sleeping all night as tho' your sweet breathings were just by me on the pillow I am casting all away in moody impatience. This visit makes me positively unhappy. It *burns* me with the impatience of a throbbing fever to be with you. And when you are actually in my arms & all my ideals of your loveliness are realized & the warm palpitating reality is *mine* at least for the few moments that I fold you to my bosom, your body will absolutely *load* me with the most perverse & untimely recollections, for example, that I must have you, that my visit is just for a day, that I must be condemned to fold with the rapture of passion an image which is not mine, which returns my affection warmly & with an agony, that yet must make away from my arms again as tho' it were something forbid & that I must *someday* go thro' the torture of walking over that style again like a man going to the scaffold & of lumbering away in that old coach with the *last* image of affection that sad one of my poor passionate Sally, weeping or as I perversely think trying to weep on that old stone threshold & with one hand upon the door. But you'll get so tired of Me! Does all this strike you as nonsense? Sally.

Now about my visit I do thank you so much for letting me come. It is a poor love that gratifies itself at the expense of the lady & as you save me from doing that & prefer the visit, I can come in that most luxurious of all ways with my honour & my love both smiled upon & gratified. Now *when* shall I come. As soon after next Monday week as you will let me I would like to set out. Choose the best day. If your Uncle William is there while I am there you will *surely* offend him by neglecting him. So find distinctly when he'll come & let our time be some time else. Don't you think so?

Wont it be nice? Alas! tho', it will be so soon over. I cant get the *daguerres.* Our man here is miserable. I mean to try & send with this Allie's sock.

Tell me when you get this letter when you write.

How gravely you all talk about my book. I mean to take Sam's advice & be very careful.[10] I am *determined* to do what is right about it. Original thinking (or what thinks itself so) ought not to cease in the world. *No one* could advise me to be still & do nothing. All I ought to do is to be very cautious & *certain* & that God helping me I mean to be. Tell me if this letter seems to you utter nonsense. If it does you are not as much in love as I am. I will try to remember the ship paper. By the way you sometimes pay double when your letter is single. You did so last. I have a little scale on my desk. Do I ever do the reverse. You once told me I did. *Do take care of yourself.* Your own illnesses I always *brood over.* They seem like robberies of me. One thing strikes me about you. If you owe Tom money & cant pay him & he wants your house & thinks he can do well by it you are almost *bound* to consider the thing well. But dont get involved with your brothers in farming or the more perishable parts of your estate.

Yours fondly
Jno Miller.

[on scrap] I enclose Allie's sock. Put down your head here Sally, I want to whisper something. Closer!

No, No, now hold still.

---

10. Samuel Miller Jr. had offered to read his brother's manuscript and urged great caution lest a hasty publication destroy his reputation as a theologian and "close against you forever every door of Church preferment. . . ." He concluded with some Latin aphorisms (Samuel Miller Jr. to John Miller [Aug. ?, 1856]).

If you mean to knit A. some socks I advise you to make them "roomy" because you know his feet will grow considerably before you get them done. May I stay three weeks when I come. Dont forget to tell me. Poor Mac! I hope nothing will befall him. If I will go Europe & stay till T's death, will you come to Allamby & take charge of my children? So that they may learn thus early to call you, *Mother*.

Colalto,
Saturday Aug: 23. 1856.

My *dear John*,

What do think of this? Tom wants to rent from me for three years, taking my farm, farming implements, house & furniture and three negro men for $1.200 pr annum. This would leave me two or more servants, who could probably be hired for $200 more, and my Louisville lots at $200 to furnish an income. In addition to the $1.600 that derived the first year, I will sell him the wheat I am now sowing, or claim about 3/4 of the crop in July next, giving him 1/4 for the cutting and threshing, which even in such a poor crop as that of this year would give him something like $100—ample pay for keeping the fences up & cows out during the Spring & Summer.

At first view this looks wonderfully well; but then it leaves me without a home; & covering as it does *three years* makes a vagrant of Lilly too at a very important period of her life. I might it is true board with Tom; but somehow I am opposed to that. Sometimes I think it would be better for me to take them to board with me, & make Tom a sort of partner with me on the farm.

However, if I rented as I have stated I should have from rent, the sale of wheat & of my Carriage, & other things; & from my Louisville lots, the hire of serv'ts & rent of the Military about $2.500 the first year. This I think is a moderate calculation. If I could really obtain it, it would relieve all pressing difficulties. I would then, by the transfer of Washington lots, & the Military have pretty nearly squared with Lilly. Uncle Tom's debt would make my last payment upon this place & discharge a small debt to Nib. If need be my Saline land will nearly pay Mary what I owe her: And thus freed from debt, I shall have my farm here, with a house & stock & negroes to fall back upon at the end of three years, & my four Louisville lots beside! Meantime I must have a home for myself & Lilly. Boarding for a woman is an idle selfish way of living; but with, say, $1.300 a year for myself & $1000 for Lilly I might, if I thought proper take a house & live plainly in Rich'd. Yet there are strong social objections to my going to any city to live—not so much on my own account, as on hers, circumstanced as we are.

You speak of my living with Mary for a year or so. I couldn't do it. That miserable affair which those rich people in Charlotte have built & call "a nice little Parsonage" would not allow me. There is only one chamber in the house besides Mary's that has a fire-place in it, & that one is a passage-way to two other rooms about as large as this sheet of paper. Of course if Mary Ross comes from school this winter she will need this passage-chamber. I can't do without fire in the winter, & don't think I could have any comfort in those wee rooms in that enervating climate in the Summer. These inconveniences, I wd not regard when *visiting*, but they are formidable in a home. I hardly know what to think of doing.

I couldn't accomplish my wish about Lilly's visit. Her expenses have been so heavy this year that I was not willing she should go to the expense of $25 or 30 now, as when I came to examine more carefully it seemed likely she would do. I have not however, given up my thought of going up to see Uncle. It is probable I shall go on Saturday or Monday, & stay a few days. He may return here with me. If he does you must delay till he goes, of which I will write to you immediately.

I think Mr Fendall entirely to be trusted. I think him silent & prudent or prudently silent, if that is better, & if you will distinctly tell me you wish it I'll write to him immediately. But good night now. I am nodding at every word.

Monday morning

An offer, from the Proprietor of the Alum Spring, of $18 a month for Edward, made me send him right over on Saturday. This throws me into a feeling of constant scuffle, and draws heavily upon my time in the morning—consequently I was an hour later than our engagement Saturday morn. However, I was only a few minutes behind hand to-day; & will manage to be punctual hereafter.

I never knew until Friday from Tom that James had actually offered the Military for sale. Saturday morn'g I had a letter from him stating that he had offered; & this morning Mr Carrington writes me the same thing. I am worried;—for I wrote to James in March *distinctly* saying I could not have him, at his prices for my Agent & Lilly's in the sale of that land;—nor wd I have anybody who wdn't do the service for the pay fixed by the Law of Virginia, which never exceeded 5 pr ct. I have had no communication with him since on the subject. I am pretty sure Mary knew nothing of the sale, tho' she had consented to give him 6 pr ct in the Winter, which she now regrets. I know Venable too *forbid* Cantie to employ him as her agent.[11] I suppose he didn't want to have any money dealings with his new kin—and he was right. Now I am troubled. Mr. Carrington is annoyed too; & I mean to find Massie today & see what he says. However, independent of them all I mean to write to James that as he has undertaken this without my consent, I will not pay him any thing but such a sum as I think right. Indeed, I think I shall *forbid the* sale of my interest & Lilly's altogether. I can't imagine by what mistake he has considered himself employed by us. I can't think it right for me, crippled pecuniarily as I am to *give* James $4 or 500 to spend at the St. Lawrence next Winter, or to put into a moiré antique & point lace for a dinner dress for Lizzy.

Our friend, Dr White, has got into trouble with Col Smith of the Institute. The Dr with his straight-forward truthfulness is no match for such a wily, equivocating adversary, who has already, by his peculiar skill, obtained an advantage over him.

---

11. Charles Scott Venable had married Margaret Cantey McDowell the previous January.

The Dr seems much annoyed, & no doubt anxious as to the effect the matter is to have upon his own people. A very little now, will decide him to leave here.

I don't mean to tell you how much I love you any more. I think it makes you too presumptuous, &, as little Susan Taylor says "sufficious." I suppose I may say, however, I am every day filled with the thought of your coming.

Affectionately,
S.C.P. McDowell

Princeton, Sunday Aug 24th 1856.

My dear Wife,

Ever since I can remember I have turned to the 37 Ps 3,4,5, vs. "Trust in the Lord, & do good: so shalt thou dwell in the land and verily thou shalt be fed. Delight thyself also in the Lord & he shall give thee the desires of thy heart. Commit thy way unto the Lord, trust also in him & he shall bring it to pass. Rest in the Lord & wait patiently for him". With these I have joined Prov: 3:5,6. ["]Trust in the Lord with all thine heart; & lean not to thine own understanding. In all thy ways acknowledge him, & he shall direct thy paths." I have always singled out this:—"Delight thyself also in the Lord & he shall give thee the desires of thine heart." I have never fulfilled the duty, but yet poorly as I have lived I have wonderfully received the promise. If there is anything I ever did fervently desire it was leisure to press certain studies. I scarcely dreamed I ever should have it, but I suppose a *thousand* times I have quoted to myself this text & wondered if God ever would give me the great desire of my heart. It seemed Eutopian. The idea of profound leisure & particularly of a life *all* given to congenial pursuits seemed to me utterly out of my reach, pecuniarily, ministerially, & *morally*. I feared I never would have enough motive to sanction it, & I have often tho't & said that if I ever did reach it I would open my eyes the morning after it had been arranged with the most profound feeling of repose. Well, Sally, this very Eutopian thing I now possess; & my conscience which I have been consulting to-day seems to acquiesce in the idea that it may last forever. I cannot say that I have delighted in God, but in this great life concern he has certainly given me the desires of my heart. It is not the first time. When I was a student I meant to be a missionary. I was bent on going to China. I used to read all the works on that Empire I could lay my hands on. One of my plans was never to marry. I tho't it mean & therefore wrong to seduce a poor woman into an attachment which must in all probability end in ill health & death. I still believe missionaries should go single. And as women can do little more in these hot counties than rear their children I thot it a mere *indulgence* to carry a poor woman to die in those climates so fatal to *female* constitutions. And yet, Sally, (you will laugh but you must hear me thro' in all my garrulous experience) I had the most heaven like notions of the bliss of having a wife. I tho't those fellows who had no such vocation as I & could marry, were angels a sort of higher being in respect to pleasure & the idea of having some sweet creature as your own as much so as old Turretin that we used to learn Theology out of seemed to me a kind of higher state that only those could be promoted into who were the special favorites of heaven. Well, I got all ready, went to see old Walter Lowrie, was told by him to go see Dr Hodge (of Phila) & was told by him that I had a constitution safe for this country but that might not last six months under the tropics.[12] So, Sally, I lost my crown of martyrdom; & little Maggie & Allie & to be sure a great many sorrows & a great deal of happiness wasted upon a sad & melancholy temperament have all come into existence since that day of my release from missionary.

But you will be tired of me, my Blessed. The moral of all this is, Delight thyself also in the Lord & he shall give thee the desires of thy heart. I dont know why he has embittered this period so. But, Sally, I see *some* good in it. Were you not a little too worldly for a hermit's wife? Were you not a little too much accustomed to the waste & luxury of the South & its free living? And may not God be setting his finger upon me by not letting me have all I want just as once? & upon you by bringing you down to a little more of that exactness of thinking which will be necessary in weighing out the water-crepes at the prophet's table? May there not be things wanting to your character which these last troubles were wanted to supply & may we not rest on the Lord & wait patiently for him with some hope that we shall see one day a clear path thro' all these wanderings. Here ends the first great lesson I ever read to you.

I believe, Darling, your great policy is *silence* in all these home troubles. If you do not *recognise waverings* or remark upon them, they never become fixed & people forget that they had them & become your fast friends. I was on the eve of asking the other day, Who it was "aspersed my honour"? & what they said of me. But I will give you an example of what I think wise by mistrusting my own hot temper & asking no such question. I *know* so little of your friends & have been so reserved in any communication with them, that I would be sadly roused if I found any one of them had taken liberties with my acts especially as they have come before them in such simple & straightforward presentations. The worst thing I ever heard of your brother was that sentence in that private letter.

I am very impatient to see you & was half hoping you would send for me next week. I can *wait* a great deal better when I am *made* to, than when I am vexed & torn by immediate expectation. Good bye for now. I am just riding out with the children to the "New Purchase". Maggie inaugurated it by forgetting her bonnet there last Saturday & we were partly home before she found her mistake. We

---

12. Francis Turretin (1623–1687), theologian and author of *Theologia Elenchtica*, a staple text at Princeton Theological Seminary. Walter F. Lowrie (1784–1868), former U.S. senator from Pennsylvania and corresponding secretary of the Presbyterian Board of Foreign Missions from 1836 until his death. Archibald Alexander Hodge (1823–1886), Presbyterian minister who served as a missionary in India until health problems forced his return to the United States.

hope to find it to-day tho' if we cant we have one comfort all ready as in most such cases. It was nearly worn enough.

My darling, Daughter, any kind of love that *you* know any thing about you may safely ascribe to me for the style in which I love you is a thing you have no idea of. I could take your love into my heart & drive a coach & six all round it, so warmly am I yours.

Jno Miller.

Monday, Aug: 25

Oh, Sally, thats mean. So you refuse to tell me whether you read my letters. Well then I know you do. And tho' I have kept yours like the Black Art, & have never read any except some of the more serious parts of one or two of them to Mother for a certain purpose soon after our disappointment in the marriage yet now I'm going to give the whole pack to Godey[13] for immediate publication, begging him to be particular about the name, Sally Campbell Preston MacDowell & to publish it in large capitals with a portrait and autograph so[14]

yours till death   Her + Mark.
Sally Ross Campbell Preston Carrington Henry Floyd MacDowell.

I am going to write hereafter in strict metaphysical language ready for your next reading. Which ones did you read? O Sally to think that I should have been addressing those letters of mine some of them so badly written to a promiscuous Virginia audience. I am glad however that they are all so reserved & modest & that there is nothing that might not have been written by the most timid maiden or that might not serve as a model for the same class of general correspondence. O Sally, you are so expert in getting out of a difficulty.[15]

Pay, why certainly. Addison Alexander & Dr Hodge & all these Professors derive pocket money year by year for preaching. It is only in a certain case however—where a church is vacant or where an *arrangement* is made for the absence of a Pastor. If a Pastor asks me himself to preach I have always declined remuneration. So when a young licentiate Dr Boardman was to be absent a Sunday or two & asked me to preach & I did so & *their* usual fee $10 was offered me & I refused it I think I was probably eccentric in doing & that no other body would.[16] Where I have been preaching this Summer the Pastor was in Europe. The arrangement was to have two services up to a certain point in the Summer & then but one. I went one Sunday & preached twice & two Sundays & preached once. For *each* of three Sundays I have received $20 in a check for $60 making $15 a sermon. From my mountain den which I hope now to fill for life I hope

13. *Godey's Lady's Book*, the most popular women's magazine in nineteenth-century America.

14. Here Miller drew the picture of a face.

15. At this point Miller drew a picture of a large duck.

16. Samuel Ward Boardman (1830–1890) held a resident licentiate in 1856 at Andover Theological Seminary in Massachusetts.

often to do this & to make it help in the dates and water crepes which are all that a philosopher eats. In one of my *half*-Sundays Dr McGill (who was paid in the same way) asked me to preach the other part of the day for him. I did so: And the other day he was for offering me $10 as half of that days remuneration. I decline it. But he of course was paid for it, tho' not more than I for the days service in the other church. When I promised to preach in the Rutgers St Church on the 4th & 5th Sundays in Aug: it was for Dr. McGill who expected to be absent. He failed to get off by the 4th Sunday & therefore, filled the place himself. I go next Sunday. The corn soup was admirable only with my pestilent metaphysics I was wondering whether it wasnt the *corn* that made it so & therefore was troubled with painful doubts whether without the flour & water the great principle of the thing couldnt be met. I wish you'd send me a receipt for softening an ungrateful mistress.

Colalto,
Tuesday 10 P.M. Augt 26. '56

My *dear* John,

Were you ever struck by these verses of Longfellow's?—there is nothing new, of course in the sentiment but his well polished verse makes the old truth pleasantly emphatic.[17]

"Let us be patient! these severe afflictions
        Not from the ground arise,
"But often times celestial benedictions
        Assume this dark disguise.
"We see but dimly thro' the mists & vapors
        Amid these earthly damps
"What seem to us but sad, funereal tapers
        May be Heaven's distant lamps."
        * * * * * * * * * *
"And tho' at times impetuous with emotion
        And anguish long suppressed,
"The swelling heart is moaning like the ocean
        That cannot be at rest—
"We will be patient, & assuage the feeling
        We may not wholly stay
"By silence sanctifying, not concealing
        The grief that must have way."

Don't you like them? They fall very soothingly, upon me, & the two first verses are often in my mind. They often fall in with the current of my thoughts & feelings.

17. Henry Wadsworth Longfellow wrote *Resignation* in 1848, following the death of his young daughter.

At any rate, my mind is much quieter than it was. I am anxious and disturbed and often sad, miserably sad about our troubles, yet; but the anguish and tumult of feeling that seemed to wear out my very existence—or rather that seemed to leave me existence just that it might be ceaselessly quivering under torture, has calmed down. I am quiescent, if not acquiescent. I ought to be both. I don't want to be indifferent & passionless, but submissive to what seems a decree of Providence. Your love is a great gift to me; & I love all the pleasure that my warm return of it can give. This, of course, makes life less cheerless to me, tho' it adds much to its anxieties & cares.

Sure enough John, women are queer creatures. You know how often, & how strongly I tell you I love you. You know how pained I wd be to have this fact questioned by others, & how surprised I am to hear it doubted by you, & yet when you say to me "that I am half distracted in love with you," I feel for the moment really mad—I have a sort of notion of being treated with some indignity. I am ashamed that you should tell me such a thing. A curious specimen of contradictions I am! But no matter, I have never contradicted my affection for you, Darling. But, John, I'm so tired & sleepy I can't write another line—so good night.

Wednesday 7 1/2 A.M.

I write a *scrappy* this morning, following your example & being pressed for time.

Do buy Allamby if possible. Can't you pay the man say $30 more, which however would be something less than the rate of the 5 acres, which I believe were $18 pr acre, but which would satisfy him. Or cant you pay him the full $18 pr acre, if he will wait yr convenience, as I think he might do. I want you to have it.

Allie's sock gave me quite a sensation. Some how I hadn't exactly realized that he was a human being. I was surprised to see it so large; & yet it is precisely the size of one I had already commenced for him. How curious, John, that such an unsightly thing as a cotton sock can stir me so. I take it, & spread it out and wonder at the glow of feeling it has all the time the power to sustain. Is it strange that I should feel to yr children as I do to none others upon earth? I love little Mac astonishingly. I often put on my bonnet, & walk over to town for nothing in the world but to see that child; & yet I have a very different sort of emotion to Maggie & Allie. I suppose I shall love Susan's little boy—but never as much as if he had been named McDowell, as he ought to have been.

By the way, I had a letter from Mary yesterday giving more cheerful accounts of her health. She concluded by saying, "Thank Mr Miller for his kind remembrance of me (I had delivered yr message to her) & give my most affectionate regards or love to him". I would send you the letter but for a sentence or two in it, which she would not be willing for you to see, not that they relate in the most remote manner to us, but are of a private nature. It is the most affectionate letter I ever received from her. She was, as far as I can learn more disposed to uphold me & more indignant at James's conduct than any of them, except Susan. This, I think, is in part to be attributed to Mr Ross's opinion of the matter. Cantey was greatly provoked with her brother; but she is not steady or sure as Mary is in any thing.

No, indeed; I do not think yr letter all nonsense. On the contrary, I will thank you for as more of the same kind as you will be able to give me. And, pray, John, keep Metaphysics out of yr mind when you take my letters; and don't go groping among my sentences & phrases to see "if more or less is meant than meets the ear". Don't be suspicious of me Darling, & worry yourself & me by seeking after *mental reservations*, when you read my letters. I wouldn't tell you so often & so strongly of my affection if I didn't love you. I wouldn't know how to do it. I think, John, I *must* know by this time whether or not I love you. I must know enough to judge how much vitality this attachment has. I have tried it long enough, & under such variety of difficulties & such great ones too, as to have a pretty just idea of its capacity for endurance, & its steadiness; and I think—I *know* I never knew a stronger affection for any human being. And yet when you seem to want more warmth of emotion than you think I bestow, I wish I could meet all your wishes, tho' they are so unreasonable. I then almost wish I had a blind sort of devotion to you which could see no fault in you. And yet, I am sure, that could not please you. You would soon tire of a senseless kind of affection, which could not be at any time a thing to rest upon. I wouldn't care to love you in that way. I want to love you not only with my heart, but with my mind too. I want to have that sort of feeling which does for the wear & tear of life; & is not simply a beautiful garment for a holiday occasion. This sort of love, I think I give you, made glowing & bright & warm by all that is kindling and enthusiastic in my nature. You have no need to quarrel with me, Darling, on this score. If ever a woman opened her treasures of love & faith and poured them out lavishly, I think I have done it. I may not have the same amount of treasure it is true—I have, however, thought I had much more than most women,—but whatever I have, I have given you.

I am glad to find so strong an Ally in "Sam." All he says is sensible and true; (for by the Latin which however pure & wise was all *Greek* to me; but which I suppose, *done* into English wd have been some admonitory aphorism;) but I think he errs in making a secondary consideration, the principal one. I haven't time to write about it now. I have been so busy patching that tattered "ermine" of yours that the mail hour is just here.

Oh! What do you mean by this sentence: "Tell me when you get this letter when you write". Do you mean, at what time of the day I write to you? or, what? I write sometimes in the morning—then in the afternoon—then at night, without any regularity or system! I am well again. My cough hung about me till I grew uneasy; but I have escaped it this morning entirely. Lilly says "Sister you look so well." I am greatly grieved to lose my hair so rapidly.

Affectionately,
S.C.P. McD.

Princeton, Aug: 27th 1856

So, Sally, you are "every day filled with the tho't of my coming." Well, Sally, you are very easily filled. I wish *I* was filled with it. It makes me feel Oh, so empty.—And so hungry for the day to come. I quite quarreled with your long letter of figures tho' in some respects it is one of the most gratifying you ever wrote. It bears the marks of a strong *will* at least to make your way out of unpleasant unhealthy embarrassments & Darling, *when I think of it* I feel quite delighted, that my Wife, is an energetic as well as lovely woman. But the mischief is I *cant* think of it. The little sentence at the end of your letter I look at again & again while the rest deserves only a business reading & moreover, Lover, I so long to see you that I have no spirit for anything else.

As to Tom can he *pay* the $1200? Has he property to meet it? Will it be a good arrangement for him? I think it an *admirable* arrangement for you if it will be safe, or at least promising both for him & for you. Can his overseer guide him in the management? If you could reconcile yourself to living with him or to *returning* to live with him after rambling among your friends some months what a guide you might be to him both in the care of your own & of his estate. How would it do for you to take a cottage in Lexington itself such as Mr Morton or Mr Turveytop live in? Has it not struck you that if it is on Lilly's account that you cant lead a vagrant life as you call it that perhaps Lilly ought to be at least an equal partner in the expence of housekeeping. I wish Tom could learn farming as a business & by the help of a good overseer or *head-workman* which is better establish himself in a settled & self-sustaining life. But, dear Sally, I entreat you not to follow such counsels. Written at the distance of 100 leagues they are both "presumptuous" & "sufficous" especially as I see by your last letter that your own energy & executive gifts are higher than I had supposed. If you can extricate yourself with a clear safe property of $10.000 & an income of $600 a year, It will be doing better than I at one time supposed. And yet with proper management I think your property is all that you suppose.

But, Dearest, do have a stray sheet in all your letters in which to conjugate the verb "aimer" just a little for my common comfort.[18] If you would just write "I love you, John" round & round your letters just as five dollars—five dollars—five dollars—is written all round our Jersey notes I would like it so much better. I can read such things as a man said he could French the other day "just as well as English" whereas some of your cypherings about the Military & Saline works & especially about Mr Prestons debt are not much more intelligible than high Sanscrit.

Oh! the sleeve buttons. Sally, these are such jolly sleeve buttons. I wear 'em now & I think I like 'em better than anything else you ever gave me. I confess I do like gold sleeve-buttons. They feel now just as if I was born in em & indeed I cant realize now that I wasnt. Sally, if I die I mean to give mine to Allie & I

---

18. "Aimer" is the French verb for "love."

want you to leave yours to Maggie will you? marked just as they are. I shall come on now just as soon as you send for me so please send for me soon. I regret one thing & that is that that ugly equinoctial storm will be brewing up just as we are fairly at rest in each others arms. Wont that be incongruous? You dont tell me whether I may stay six weeks.

By the way let us put off about Fendall till I see you.

Maggie worries me a little by being pale & unwell this Summer. I love her more than I can explain & more—at least I feel it more when I fear about her health. I have never felt so much as lately what a snare *you* are to my piety. You do me good but you do me harm too by filling too many of my tho'ts. You seem to go *before me* in all these experiences. I am just beginning to feel how you absorb the feeling that might go to what is higher. Pray for me Sally. Indeed I need our prayers very much indeed. A good woman may do *every thing* almost for her lover even at the distance of many miles by praying for him as earnestly as some wives that I know do for their husbands.

By the way, it just occurs to me to say, what, however, will be almost unnecessary, that it would be highly imprudent & improper for *me* ever to be *mentioned* in connection with your business plans. I know Sally, it will have struck you & therefore I need hardly speak of it. But it would be *so* unfortunate if in a moment of forgetfulness you Should say, "that struck Mr M. too" or "Mr M. says just so". Excuse me for giving so common-place a caution. But in a fit of absence of mind there is no telling what a gay young woman like you might not say. I am as silent as death about your troubles *here*. No one hears of them. And I would so hate that any of your sisters should dream that I was standing among them an admitted counsellor in the private matters of your household. Here, Sally, let me kiss those pouting lips of yours. I dont think you are a fool. But I do think its good for all the children of Adam & (especially) all the daughters of Eve to be reminded just a tinsee winsie little of almost anything that could possibly be mad enough to happen. So goodbye & dont look cross at me.

Yours till marriage (I dont know how we'll get on afterward[)]

Jno Miller.

Colalto,
Thursday 6. P.M. Aug't: 28 '56

My *dear* John,

Don't be too distressed, I beg you, about yr "promiscuous Va audience". As Miss Dix once said to me about her letters, "I have too much care of your reputation to show them!" Are you satisfied now? But no, John, the truth is this. When Miss Jannetta was here, I used sometimes to read, here & there, in your letters to her. Since then, I keep them to myself. Once or twice at Susan's when I sat with her & read yr letters & others in her room I wd read a sentence or so upon some general topic as, for instance, the Brooks & Sumner affair. Cantey used to be very curious about them; & occasionally I would gratify her curiosity by a few sentences. I thought she enjoyed them not a little. But I tell you they are cautiously given. But you oughtn't to ask me so many questions; for you always bring me to confession; and then, I never know whether I am absolved or not. I aint, any such thing, at all like the duck in the picture (why didn't you write under it "this is a duck," that I might know certainly what you meant by your *line* engraving?) or like the duck in the story. As you are so fond of ducks pray answer me these conundrums—"Why do ducks go in & out of the water?" What is the difference between a duck with two wings & a duck with one?" See if yr metaphysics will help you in such *light literature* as this.

What I thought of objecting to in "Sam's" note about your book was this. He deprecates the publication of anything heteodox in its teachings *because* it will cut you off from all church preferment.—"it will ruin you as a theologian". Now it wd be absurd & false both, for me to say that *I* did not feel about it on this Ground too; but my greatest anxiety is on another account. I am fearful for the *Truth's* sake. I could bear to see you ruined as a Theologian, provided *you* did nothing towards ruining Theology. It is a fearful thing to tamper with truths which reach forward into eternity, & underlie all of ones immortal hopes. "Original thinking" may, before one is well aware of it, issue in presumptuous sinning. It may be that the seizing "of the timbers of our faith," may like Samson's act have only strength enough to make you a suicide & a murderer.[19] But this is the dark view of the thing. There is another & a better one; &, tho' I have no more metaphysics in me than if my brain had been made of lead, yet I kindle at the thought of new discoveries of such truths as will make God appear to man more glorious; & will tend to make man happier in the present service & anticipated enjoyment of his Maker. If you can be such a discoverer, you will be doing a great work for the world. But, John, success here, whilst it might be a great gain to others, may be ruin to you. I think it requires great humility & entire consecration to God, to enable any one to bear without injury to his own soul, successful efforts for the good of others, & even for God's glory. You should be very earnest to be yrself a *partaker* of the benefits that you hope may result from your studies. Do you know, I was surprised to find, in reading lately a short autobiography of Edwards, that he was a man of such genuine & humble piety. Somehow I had not thought of him as being so before—if indeed, I had thought much about him in any way.—It is most natural that a man of great mental power should possess strong religious sentiment. I have often observed that in spite of the depravity of our nature, the intellect is ever groping up towards the source whence it issued. And that Edwards should have great intellectual religion, & that the aspirations of his Genius should seek gratification in Theology as a science was all according to nature's law. But that he was an humble, heart-rending, self-denying earnest christian, was new to me. However this is all apart from my subject. Ain't I fond

19. See Judg. 14–16.

of wandering away into episodes. I think I must have caught the habit from old Dr Junkin, who has as many episodes in a single sermon, as the Mississippi has branches, or the Amazon mouths.

Friday morning

I thank you very much for your sermon-letter. I feel about it much as little Mac about his pictures, who no sooner sees one than he cries out, "More, Auntie, more". But, John, I was amused at you too. With the spirit of the old profession about you, you summed up all by a "practical application" of all your moralizing to *me & my defects*. You seemed to forget *you* could be united with me in these teachings. The fact is that you are so accustomed to hearing me " 'fess" when you charge any fault upon me, that you are beginning to think that nobody sins but me, especially in matters when you & I stand together. Now listen—Speaking of our disappointment &c "But I see *some* good in it. Were you (Oh Yes! *me*, of course) not a little too worldly for a hermit's wife? (Pray, was the hermit without worldliness himself when he chose such a wife?) Were you not a little too much accustomed to the waste & luxury of the South & its free living? (If so, I deserved the greater commendation for my willingness to forego these things.) May there not be things wanting to yr character which these last troubles were wanted to supply?" &c. &c. Yes—there may be. And as you look upon *my* heart as coming under your care in the department of "Domestic Missions", I thank you for your efforts. But, Darling, whilst I am greatly pleased to acknowledge mine as belonging to the Home, I hope you don't make a foreign field of yr own heart.

In good earnest; I agree to most that you say. I always feel that I *need* whatever trouble comes upon me; & I am anxious when it comes that it should be turned into a blessing. I long to sow such seed in this seed-time of tears, as that when the harvest comes, this in-gathering may be one of great joy. I have known already something of what it was to go forth weeping to sow & returning laden with sheaves. I have known what it was again & again to thank God with a full heart, for all his afflictions. They have been heavy enough & dark enough & many; yet, if they have been, as many have, overruled for good—then they were not too heavy or dark or numerous.

I go up to Fincastle on Monday. Don't write to me there.

I find our Circuit Court meets here about the 12th of Sep't; at which time the town is full of lawyers from other Counties. This wd make Mann's house disagreable to you, wouldn't it. But as they will be here 2 weeks, I hate to delay your visit till that is over.

Tell me, have you an engagement still in Phil: for the 3d of Oct.

I have written to James forbidding the sale of the Military in September. I find there is universal dissatisfaction about it; but everyone had consented to it but me; & as I had two shares, I thought it unpardonable in James to proceed in opposition to my wishes, as tho' he meant to force me into a concurrence. I talked to Massie about it telling him my intentions. He was glad, I think, to get rid of James' 6 pr ct agency; & said *he* would do whatever I did. I told him I wanted no support from him in my proceedings. Having two shares, I held the balance of power in my own hands any how; & if I had but one, I wd still feel, tho' in a less degree, of course, independent of his co-operation or that of any other of the family. I wrote James very civilly; but very decidedly. Mary writes to me, her dependance is upon *my* refusal to unite with the others. Susan consented to his terms as first proposed, saying to me "My hope was that you would object". Cantey had much the same feeling. I blamed them all, & told Massie so, the other day for their want of candor to James. It was wrong to allow him to think they were content when they gave their consent to him, when they were all very much the reverse.

I kept a copy of my letter to James. I felt anxious to do the thing kindly both on my own account and his; and think I succeeded. I know it will be a mortification to him to withdraw the advertisement of the land; & perhaps an inconvenience to lose the commission upon the sale, but I *couldn't* allow it. It will make him mad, I'm sure, especially as, in addition to this thwarting of his wishes, I have within a day or two refused to become an endorser for him in Bank. I feel sorry for him, & anxious about him too. But John, I am not able to give $300 to him for what I can have done for probably 1/3 of that sum. And I could not in justice to Lilly pay it either.

Tell me, honestly, am I too free in speaking to you of all these things. Often I fear I am. You are not my Husband; and yet you seem so like it, that *naturally* I talk to you of all my affairs. I hardly feel that my interests *can* be separate from yours—or that you can consider them so.

And so the corn soup was good! Well I told you that beforehand. I never heard of *Metaphysics* descending to corn soup before. It must be a sort of a clown that great philosophy of yours. But goodbye.

Affec'ly
S.C.P. McDowell.

Princeton, Aug: 30th 1856

Oh, Sally, you *are so* stupid. You are the stupidest Sally I ever—loved. What do I mean by:—"Tell me when you get this letter when you write?" Why, "Tell me (when you write) when you get this letter." Oh, Sally, you are so tumm. You will be asking next what I mean when I say, "Oh, Sally, when you read, you are such a sweet creature": & telling me you never read any such thing in all your life. Still, beggars musnt be choosers, & as I never remember begging for anything so hard as I did for you I suppose as you suggest I must take you as you are, & if you are not so very sensible, why, if youre good, & as you are somewhat good looking we'll try to get on the best we can. But, Sally, I'm in such a panic about that hair of yours. It was so handsome. And I was so ravished by the tho't of its having been so long & beautiful. Do keep it in. You must brush it a great deal & wash it in cold water, &, Sally, as I cant live where I can enjoy it now you must cut it all off & wear a beautiful cap & let it grow out again & then by the time I have gotten ready Allamby it will have grown out all new & beautiful.

Why do you want me to have Allamby. Oh, by the way, I have found that there are *not* 7 1/4 acres. The deed calls for it, but when with a little brass chain of Mother's I came to measure the tract it was but five. So I mean to say nothing to the man & when I go to New York to-night I mean to get from him the deed. But tell me why you wish me to have it. Have I ever [illegible] you with the least bit of interest to live there & call it your home.

Longfellow is really beautiful. I never observed it before. It is sweet, & I *know*, truthful. For if we are real Christians & I do *hope* we are, these dark passages must be bright avenues in the journey of life.

I am so glad you are more at rest. You seem to me my most dangerous treasure. And when I am struggling against the temptation of thinking & planning about you to the neglect of all that is religious, it seems so idle for you to waste my anxiety or fear that my heart at least *can* change in making you its permanent object. Dear, Sally, I am so <u>glad</u> you love me. I cant describe it by a better word. You know if you didnt love me I could release myself from you without a moments qualm. Then you know how much is contained in the feeling when I say that far off & dismal as my treasure in you is, yet I exult when I think of it. I have a sort of pride of your love. I clutch it as a man does his money. I love to think of it. And I have had forcibly to expel it & to resolve that all thro' Sunday & all thro' the mornings of every day I will not read your letters & I will not let you be sitting by my side playing with my fingers & beating your pretty little foot against the table where I read. The fact is, Sally, you have no modesty. You've come into my room without knocking & when I show manifest signs of wishing you away. And when I take you on my lap & smooth your hair & kiss you & begin to talk with you about some interesting plan, you see the start with which I wake up to your having come & the evident desire I have that you should be off any where else than where you are.

I am going soon to take a day & reflect over all my life & all my course as far as I can map it out for the future. Perhaps I will postpone it till after I have seen you. If I can make up my mind, as I nearly have, that this is my future home, & *determine* upon it as far as I consistently can, I will go on & buy other pieces of Allamby. I hope by selling the wood to some contractor after I buy the land to possess myself of much of that for nothing. And if by any management of a wise kind I could in time become possessed of a certain square (bounded by roads) of 800 acres I would not care if I absorbed in doing it all my patrimony as if I could have my hermitage upon it that 800 acres would fully & comfortably support us. But then I have no idea I could get it all. Its value as a whole is much more than my patrimony. And if by buying it in pieces & selling parts of the timber I could gradually take it up, I should meet *some* of the owners who would observe what I was after & refuse to sell inasmuch as the *number* of those who own the tract is very large & some of them seem settled upon it for life. But, Oh, Darling, it is so magnificent. Surrounded by a stone wall it would be one of the most beautiful seats in Am[erica].

And then there are two dangers, first to my piety. Could it flourish if worldly matters were so much to my mind? & second to my influence. I have already to be as quiet as these woods which I so much love & talk as little & act as little as I possibly can. For as my studies are private & only these land purchases in the light of day, people will think me secular & I shall do harm & injure the ministry by too much secularization. I am getting into the way of not thinking of these things in the morning & of not saying one unnecessary word about them when I am moving about in the afternoon. Sally, will you love Allamby? & will you be willing to live there? I wish when we were just in love & the eye of others was less upon us I had hurried you off by steamboat to Trenton & hired a Buggy & driven you to these summits. The farther one "Old Allamby" is 4 miles from P. & this where I have bought 1 1/4 at the nearest point. We could have stolen up to certain places of view & seen Princeton & the Valley North of the Hill stretched out in opposite directions under our feet. Goodbye till I get back fr. N.Y. I love you tenderly.

Jno Miller.

I have a package of this paper for you. But I send some now that you may never have any excuse.

Colalto
Saturday Aug 30. 1856

My Dear John,

This isn't the first time you furnished me with paper, but I believe it is the first time that you have made me feel that I *asked* for it. I don't know that I quite did that; but if I had, I don't imagine it wd have been a terrible crime. There is no knowing how far one may be reduced in this world! This is the identical paper I used to laugh at so.

I go up on Monday to Fincastle; and as I start early will not have time to add a line before I go. I therefore write this afternoon before I commence my packing &c. I shall probably stay a week, unless I find things at Aunt Eliza's in such condition as shall change my purpose. Your letters will come here; & the one only that comes on Tuesday will be sent up to me & will reach me Thursday morning. Just think, it will be nearly a week before I can hear from you again. Your usual amount of trash from me will go on from Fincastle; tho' I can't tell whether it will reach you on the same days as heretofore.

I think it likely, from what you told me this afternoon that Uncle William will not come down at all. He intends spending only a short time with his sister now, & then return to Carolina.

I have not thought Tom's idea of renting from me a good one for him; and have advised him again & again to buy a farm for himself, and have told him to expend upon it the money he must pay me for the use of mine. Only the other day my representations of the greater gain to him from such a plan were so strong that he has said nothing to me since about renting from me. I think it best for him to avoid all plans that are merely temporary; & wish him to buy a small tract of land and settle upon it immediately, with the purpose of making it a home for life. But he is hard to please, and the vision of the meadow at the Salt works stretching out 330 acres, & having 70 men at once, for days together cutting its long grass, always interferes with a practical view of his own finances, & what *they* can bring in meadow, & corn, & wood & all other kinds of lots. I don't know the lady he is to marry, but I hope she may be a prudent & energetic woman who will *manage* him well; for like all the other Preston men he will have to yield to that destiny.

I don't know a house that I could get in town if I wanted it. In fact, I am just at the end of all my planning. I don't know what to do. I wish I was a man that I might scuffle for myself. I think I'd go to Kansas, only I don't fancy fighting very much.[20]

I wish you were here now. The weather is beyond expression delightful, and I should enjoy your visit so much the more if we could be allowed by the weather to do as we please.

Cousin John, & probably Cousin Elizabeth Cocke will be here now in a few days. I mean to let the lady wait, a longer time than ever before, for my call. I think I'll make it in the afternoon before I expect you to come. She'll flare up as soon as she hears of your arrival; & I want to have her in my debt at the time. If she returns my visit *after* you come well; if not, then *she* has broken up our intercourse, & I am spared the risk of submitting to or repelling any indignity she might offer if I were, being in her debt a call, to return it. Don't you think that wise!

Why, certainly it would be improper for me to quote you in any of my business matters. I have no idea of doing such a thing. I verily believe, John, that if you were to examine my head phrenologically you would set out with the idea of measuring the depths of its hollows—the *most* of a good thing you wd never think of; but the *least* of it your mind would be for discovering. Especially *caution*, you wd expect to find, entirely below the soundings.

What is the matter with Maggie, John? Are you only anxious about her, or is she really not well? Is she never going to write to me any more? I said to Lilly this morn'g; "Lilly would you like to ask Maggie to come to see us?" "I couldn't ask her, Sister," she said; "but I'd be very glad if she would come". And afterwards, she asked me if I was going to get you to bring her on as if she still thought of the matter.

---

20. A reference to the conflict between free-soil and proslavery forces in Kansas.

Some weeks ago, I was surprised by a visit from a Seceder Preacher (you know about these old Scotch Seceders in yr part of the world don't you?) who lives a few miles from town.[21] I have known him by sight a number of years, & Father always liked him, but I knew nothing of him personally. He came to ask some help for his new church. There had been a long war between his sect & ours for the possession of the church in which they have both been preaching for a good many years, alternately. Finally a law suit was instituted, and in its progress I was appealed to for the old church papers which had been in my Grandfather's hands, & were then in mine. My conduct in the matter, which I don't now at all remember, pleased this Dr Thompson, as he told me, & gave him upon my own account a sort of regard for me, added to that he already felt on my Father's.[22] Well, we had a long talk upon church affairs, & my Parents & Grandparents until my heart warmed under it all, and when he apologized for coming to me for aid, I very promptly & heartily said—"Why, you should make no apology for yr application. I should have felt myself badly treated if you had passed me by. I can't give you much, to be sure, but the little I give, I give with a great deal of pleasure! It wd be great presumption in me [to] disown a church which accepts the same Confession of Faith that I do; And," I went on laughingly to say, "if you choose to sing psalms of bad metre, why that's your look out not mine. You must get that word con-so-la-ti-on fitted to yr music the best way you can. But I feel an interest in all these things in our Neighborhood; and like to be called on to help. These people have been friends of my family for generations; In an exigent hour they were friends of truest kind to me; & I am bound to them by very strong ties of gratitude". I suppose I spoke warmly, for he replied with great significance "Yes Madam, this County is your friend"; & repeated it very emphatically. I was much impressed by his manner, & thanked him most cordially for his offer to do anything for me when I thought he cd do it.

I was more struck by this, as only a day or two before I had a very warm assurance of sympathy given in the most delicate manner, from an old gentleman, who had stepped in one morning on business. I had never spoken to him up to this morning's interview; but my troubles have given to every body here the feeling of being acquainted with me, & when I meet them, they demean themselves to me as acquaintances. This old gentleman was so sudden & warm in his peculiar way, that I was moved to tears in an instant, & could for a moment scarcely control them. I have not seen him since, but he has sent me frequent messages by different

---

21. After the Marrow controversy in Scotland, some Presbyterians withdrew from the kirk in the name of liturgical and theological conservatism. In colonial America they formed their own presbytery and, in 1782, joined with descendants of the Convenanter tradition to form the Associate Reformed Synod.

22. Horatio Thompson (1799–1882), Presbyterian minister of the Associate Reformed Church, served at Timber Ridge Church in Rockbridge. The conflict in 1854 was over joint use of the stone church at Timber Ridge. Eventually Thompson provided the land for his congregation to build a brick church in 1857.

people. I was glad to have him talk to me of my Grandfather McDowell, who was a grand old gentleman, with his powerful mind & will. None of his Grandsons are like him—neither was my Father.

Now, John, take a long breath, here's something for you after all that egotism. I wonder if you ever heard it before! I wonder if you won't tire of hearing it so often! Does it never seem foolish in me to say how much I love you, and how much I think of you. I wish I had some new words to say it in, that it might have the look of freshness upon it. And yet it has a reality of freshness in it, tho' it does wear the same old word-garment. It is a fresh thing, Darling. It is no stagnant pool, this affection of mine: no artificial lake kept bound within certain limits; no Dead Sea sort of thing, which unlike all seas, has no outlet or inlet,—but it is a fresh, full flowing, stream. Sometimes it goes merrily rippling along, bubbling & sparkling & babbling in a kind of joyous song; and then again it swells out too broad & deep for any but a sighing happiness—a moaning joy, if you can at all comprehend these paradoxes. It is, at one time a plaything—at another a pleasure—still again a great wealth of happiness—& again often & often an inexplicable comfort. It draws into its great bosom all kinds of emotion & sensation—it is anxious, fearful, timid, sensitive, easily wounded: it is angry & joyous: it is hopeful & hopeless: it is trustful & suspicious too: it is energetic & yet faint-hearted: it is jealous, & yet generous too:—it is stormy & yet calm and O! *so* peaceful. I come, & lay my head like a child upon your knee, & am lost in the peaceful repose of a still happiness. It follows me all day long,—mixes itself up with all my thoughts—is my last consciousness at night, & first again when the day dawns. It mingles with my own being; &, as belonging to it almost, with my holiest aspirations; and often utters its prayer with a fervor which I would like to eject into others. It folds its arms about me, and is part of all my life both real & ideal. It is a dream, John, this love of mine—a vision—a passion—a hope—an every day reality, & necessity. Can I say any thing more? Can *you* say any thing more or as much? And now the night is here.

God bless you my own Love, and make us helps & not hindrances to each other in his service.

Aff.
S.C.P. McD.

Sunday night.

My own dear Love! Now my heart, in its fullness murmurs up to you. I have been sitting almost alone since dark; for Tom went to church, & Lilly read her Bible, & went to sleep. I have been reading most of the time, but my mind has been busy in its thoughts of you as my eye ran over the pages of my book— Not foolishly full of you have they been, but anxiously. I wonder, John, if I am "a snare to you" as you say. I wonder if I am indeed an injury to you. I may be; but I have always hoped & prayed to be far otherwise. Long ago, that is, when I first loved you, my *ambition* was to be a useful & helpful wife to you as a Minister. My own religious aspirations so far as this world was concerned, were all fully met in such a destiny;—& and my love for you prompted me to seek to be all to you that a good wife could be. My heart too was full of those little children. I loved them because they were yours—I had no other reason for loving them—and I was anxious to discharge *well* my duty to them in the most difficult of all relations. Thus for yrself, & yr church & yr children I was oh! so desirous to be a good & not an evil. But it may be, that the connections have done harm to all of you, & God has in Mercy to you interposed & broken up all our plans. And it may be that in mercy to me too He has seen fit to bring to nought all my ambitions. But, John, does it seem wrong to have been so anxious to be a good wife? And yet I might have failed to be that. I might not have suited any Minister. I was too proud perhaps—you all say I am—& yet I should have been *proud* to do all that was required of me; & do it well.

Anyhow, God has ordered differently. The great desire of my heart has not been granted. I know I too much coveted this, as it seemed to me unspeakable blessing. I more than half forgot that any other world was worth seeking for, in the happiness that this world seemed to be offering. I built upon it, too much of all my hope; & poured out to it treasures of affection. It was all disappointed. It was a far more terrible blow to me than you have ever imagined; but from the beginning I wanted to submit unquestioningly to it, & to have it become a means of spiritual good. I can't tell you, all the tossings & struggles, & battles I have had with it; (but latterly it has seemed to me, that God *was* making a blessing to me of this dreadful trial. It has *driven* me to Him until now my going to him is a pleasure. I am more peaceful, more obedient, more occupied with the great future, than for a long time before. I am more concerned with the heart-service in all my ways than heretofore. Yet, hand in hand with all this goes my affection for you. I am perfectly sure I love you far more than I ever did. And yet I am day by day praying to love you so subordinately as that at any given moment, should it appear the Will of God, I cd give you up without hesitation—without pain I could not do it. I am so earnest that God should sanctify our affection, & recognize with favor our relation. I don't want to do you any harm. My Darling, I love you too much for that. Neither do I want to jeopardize my own eternal safety by persisting in any course which He will not sanction. Therefore John, let us pray that in all our connection we may have the guidance & approval of God.

Once only before, I believe, I have written to you on Sunday. Somehow, I have scarcely the feeling it can be wrong to do it tonight.

How far apart we are! & yet, at this moment we may be very near to each other. You, away off in a crowded, noisy City, & I here, so quiet that I hear no sound but the ticking of my watch, & Lilly's regular breathing, seem hopelessly distant; & yet my thought brings you right to me. I half offer you this vacant chair beside me, and almost hear you speak to me. I am not sure I ever saw you more distinctly than I do now; and you look as solemn & grave as you pause to speak to me as tho' my own heart's earnest feeling had cast its shadow upon yr face. But it will, in reality be many days before I shall have yr answer. Who knows but that I may *hear* it when it is given. Good-night now—I hope you have done a good day's work to-day.

> *God bless you my dear John. Yr own*
> *S.C.P. McD.*

Fincastle
Wednesday Sep. 3. 1856

My Dear John,

I catch a moment to write you a note. I have nothing pleasant to say; but the contrary. I find Miss Jannetta partly engaged here for this month. I talked to her a little about it yesterday, but we were soon interrupted. She rebels against your visit, & thinks it would be an injury to me. She says, our ruptured marriage has already done me sufficient damage. My heart sank as she talked, but I have not yet abandoned my intention of having the visit. I will have a fuller talk with her today if possible, tho' she is busy getting little Mary ready to go off tomorrow with her Father. If I insist I believe she will go now with me, or come in October as her engagement here is by the month. I have been greatly grieved by this difficulty. It seems only the foreshadowing of an endifinite series of difficulties. I lay awake, I can't tell how long before daylight, thinking it all over, and trying to determine what course was best. I am sad about it and troubled. My heart struggles for the gratification of its affection; but, the day is past for me to allow it to triumph over every thing—and yet, I know, that it is strong enough to over-master almost every thing that religious principle would not forbid.

I am so sad, John. I hope God will direct us, & provide for us. The old watchword comes up again most comfortingly & cheeringly, & I lean upon it with all my strength. "Jehovah-jireh!" I thank God, that he has allowed his name to lighten a dark future, & cheer a cheerless present.

They are all in anxiety here. Aunt Eliza is about selling this place, which has been her patrimony, & their refuge in adversity. She is very sad about it. Uncle William has not yet returned from Va Preston's wedding; but will be here tonight probably.

I will write again tomorrow or next day, & tell you more of what she says of our matter. I go home on Saturday. Today I will, I hope, have yr letter that came to Lex: yesterday.

God bless you my dear John,

> *Affectionately*
> *S.C.P. McDowell*

Princeton Sep 4th 1856

My *Dear Sally,*

"I so sorry."

Well, Sally, *your* letter before the last wasn't put into the mail in time &
didn't reach me till Monday night. Then it told me not to write to Fincastle
& as I never fancied you would have the letter sent me I rested on my oars &
dropped one writing day. And now my poor dear Darling will expect a letter &
wonder about it & (I think) will be disappointed. I think so, Sally, from your
sweet letter that I have just received. Then you *do* love me, Sally? I never knew
you pour your love along in such a genial measure. I'll tell you what I think
about our love. I think it has passed into the condition which exists in husband
& wife when they are happily married. I think it has grown so far that it would
require almost a life time to wear it out again—that it would bear for example
a right hard quarrel in which we shouldn't speak to each other (or write) for
weeks & yet force us back to each other. What do you think—Sally? Suppose
I should treat you badly (not wanting—for by the way I think few husbands
treat their wives badly thro' mere malice) but suppose I should grossly offend
you & we should have a high quarrel; I think, we should "crawl" back to each
other after a few weeks. I do indeed. I think we have a sort of all life love.
What think *you?* So your love *is* a "passion". Well you never expressed it before.
Is it?

So you thought you recognized the paper. Look sharp at *this* & tell me what
you think.

O, Sally, I am abusing so your buttons. I looked a[t] them the other day &
find that in my hard wear they look quite worn. The face is quite visibly dulled
& they look quite [illegible] all round. I was quite shocked, & was going to take
them off & send them. But I thot perhaps, you would *like* them to look used, &
that if I wouldn't "rist" on 'em quite so hard or give them such heavy cuffs you
would like me to keep them warm on my arm till I can give them to you. I am
sorry they are dulled for they were right handsome, &, perhaps, are so still.

As to whether you talk too freely to me I answer nothing that it is right for
you to *think* is it wrong for you to tell me. Why, Darling, how do you & I differ?
Are we not all one creature. But you must take care of what you *think* of your
own blood. *I am glad you refused to endorse for James.* Father had a sort of horror
of being surety. And used to tell us, "My sons, never endorse for a man beyond a
sum which you are willing to *give* him". If I tho't I had the least rightful authority
over you I would "*forbid*" your endorsing, a là Venable, as one of the maddest
things you could do.

I have *bought* the lot & have the deed. I gave him but $93 or $94, the difference
(fr. $90) being some expences I have offered to pay. The lot is but 5 acres. I mean
to get more if I can. My plans of life are maturing very firmly. I will tell you them
when I see you.

And now, my Love, when is that to be? If those lawyers were all devils (& I fear some of them are) & all stopped at Mann's so that Man's soul was as blest with devils as John Bunyan speaks of in the Holy War it wouldnt influence me the slightest. So, Darling, I am now waiting for *you*. When you say the word (& if you think I had better not expose our affair to the notice of so many of these gentlemen I would wait) I shall start at once. Presbytery meets in Phila Oct 3d but if I were not happening to pass thro' Phila I would not go from *here* to it. Of course, therefore, I would not let it interfere with Va. I thought yesterday when [I] got your letter, of starting at any rate for Lexington *next* Monday Sept 8th. But when I thot that you might stay in Fin: or bring on some one or form some plan inconsistent with such a movement I determined to stay. But if your next letter should chance to tell of your return to Lex. & should announce that you are free from any inconsistent engagement I think I will start on Monday yet. Tho' you must not *expect* me. Indeed if *you* would *rather* I should wait till those lawyers go or till the first week of October I will delay till then. I am so *starving* to see you. Darling, if we were married we would have no such *high* feelings as these—would we? We would have *happier* feelings, but none so tempestuous.

Maggie is a great deal better—indeed, I think her sound again. She will write before long. Tho' it is a very solemn undertaking, these letters to her.

Dearest, how sweet that letter was to me! It was the only love-letter you ever wrote to me. Now that the ice is broken (& by the way there was a little broken ice about the edges yet) please go on & tell me *how* you love me & just how much.

As to my Sunday letters having all their lessons for *you* & none for poor me— why, Child, who ever heard of a man preaching to *himself* by way of Lexington P.O. You must be crazy. Suppose I were to write 300 hundred miles off such sentences as the old divines put in their diaries:—"*I* must be a much better child &c &c." how funny it would sound.

Now, I see, Sally, When you spoke of my philosophy, in many of your letters you meant *yourself*. Oh, I see. When you say, philosophy was a *great* evil, you meant my *little* friend at Lexington. O, yes! It was an allegory.—that philosophy would ruin me &c!

Goodbye, My own beloved Darling,

Yours fondly
Jno Miller

Fincastle
Friday Sep'r 5. 1856

My *Dear John*,

I lent my carriage to Virginia yesterday, & having stayed all night she did not return in time today for me to send a letter to the Post Office.[23] I felt troubled; for I know you will be anxious to hear from me.

23. McDowell's cousin Virginia Preston Carrington.

I am in a terrible whirl of people. Uncle William came two or three days since, & Va, & Campbell, & three others, filling this small house so full that I am turning round skimpily in a little chamber with 3 others to share it with me. I can only write in a snatchy style.

Miss Jannetta feels obliged to stay here for two months longer. This throws me out of your visit. I can't undertake to tell you, what amount of feeling this is to cost me. I don't feel it now, as I shall do, for there are so many to call upon my thoughts & attention, that I have not much left for myself. But tomorrow, & when I get home, & feel that this little taper that for weeks had been glimmering in the dark future, has like all the rest been extinguished—I shall sink back to the darkness & sorrow that has been decreed me. I don't mean to complain. My heart swells & my eyes fill as I write,—but I am used to sorrow. And when God sees fit, no doubt I shall be relieved. But when & how, I can't even dream.

Uncle met me most affectionately, expressing again & again his pleasure at seeing me. He is far more cordial & affectionate than when I last saw him—&, I believe, he & Aunt Eliza are my chief friends in the family, tho' I don't think his friendship very warm or very considerate.

I was sure I should have a letter from you today; but after waiting hours & hours, I have received none. I hardly felt as if I could summon strength to write to you under the disappointment, but have made out this far. Oh, John, my heart is so heavy & sad, and I am so grieved and perplexed. Do you think if our affection & relations were perfectly right, that God would thwart and trouble us so? I have thought a thousand times, under most anxious searchings it was not wrong; & yet often & often felt too—"well, it may be". I can't think about it with any reason now.

I go home tomorrow, & will write on Monday as usual.

God bless you. Do tell me—does yr love stand steady under all these discouragements, or is it getting a little weary.

Yr letter of last Saturday was sent to me here, & came Wednesday.

Affec'ly
S.C.P. McDowell

Princeton, Sept 6 56.
3 P.M.

My sweet Darling

I just have your note from Fincastle. I so mourn over the omission of a letter or anything that could sadden you & I so long to be with you that I may console you in our trouble.

Dearest, when I bore up under the postponement of our marriage I consoled myself by the thought of our frequent visits & I am not sure that this difficulty does not distress me more than the other. It was my favorite notion & then was & still is my settled opinion that we might meet often & that the oftener we met, that is, within certain limits, the better for keeping up the exact intelligence of our relations. I am perfectly sure that if we meet *ever* before our marriage it will be becoming more & more difficult to do so if it be postponed.

And, my own beloved I *dare* not injure you. If Miss J. says it will injure you, she has got it from your friends, & it is a proof that it *will* injure you beyond a cavil. The only question is, will it injure you so *seriously* as to forbid the sacrifice. Of course Miss J's testimony fills me with fear about this. If I become convinced that you will have to give up your whole circle of Va friends or any serious part of them for me I *will not see you*. And, Darling, what will be the consequence? *Why that, we will have to bear this suffering of not meeting in person—but only corresponding.* That is all—no more,—no less. Well, Sally, my own Sally, this is terrible, but then not distracting or agonizing at least it ought not to be so to you. It ought not to throw you back into your old sadnesses or make you sick or make you old as other things have done. For what is it? *A mere piece of self-denial.* The loss of you would overwhelm me but the patient waiting for you is a thing of a class which long sorrow has accustomed me to, tho' this is rather a painful case. And you even more than I ought to bear it for you are not so perversely impatient as I am.

I have one favour to ask of you. I have everything at stake in this matter—your health, your reputation, my own conscience & peace of mind. Sally Darling grant me one request, grant it solemnly before our common Father. Nay Dearest, do not look away, but think of it & make a solemn promise—*that all doubts of my constancy shall be thrown to the winds*, that you will not revive those old agonies which have worn your health & thinned your hair & while my treasure in your love & in your loveliness have increased, have lessened my wealth in your sweet person & made me tremble lest when I see you again the fair domain of your beauty will have been spoiled & wasted. Dont laugh at me, Sally but *promise*— that if your verdict is that I shant see you & the consequence that we do not meet till we are married & that not for ten years, that you will feel just as established in your right & just as *fixed* in your modes of feeling as tho I were actually at your feet or we had actually been married for a score of years. Promise me this, my Darling.

I dont doubt *your* love. Why should you be doubting mine. I dont say you will prove faithless. Why should you suppose I will. You say, "Human nature &c." Well have *wives* no human nature. Do not betrothed wives desert betrothed husbands nay *most generally* chafe at, & break the match. And if I have been at all deceived in too great caution about our marriage have I not special reasons for alarm at this last fear of my being entirely excluded from your person. And yet I scatter all such fears to the winds. I believe you love me passionately or *violently* dear Sally, if you dislike the other word. I believe these troubles only fold me more closely in your embrace. I believe if all obstacles were removed & you were free to-morrow to marry any one in the land you would impatiently fulfil your affection to me. So, Darling, promise! Remember, it must be a solemn promise—that you will never dream of it as a doubt, but that you & I are for each other as the only man & woman in the world.

Then, Sweetest, that anguish disposed of, what is all this other but *mere endurance*. It ought not to be a *morbid* sorrow. It ought not to make you either sick or old: But is a mere matter of Christian endurance.

Still, Sally, *I* with my bad organization & hungry restlessness ought to be excused for fretting a little under this new shape of a most unexpected & unreasonable vexation. I want you to do two things. I want you first to get from Miss J. definitely, what she means by "our ruptured marriage as having done you damage". Does she mean, it would have been better to go on? Tell me exactly all about these things. Throw off all reserve—& tell me what *you* have tho't or hinted of a difference of opinion on this subject. Then get from Miss J. her distinct reasons for thinking a visit hurtful. Ask if she realizes the fact that if not *now* then never can we meet without even more talk that if we meet at all it ought to be in publicly recognized relations. Ask her if we are never to meet. If she gives solid reasons for her judgment, I will not divorce you from your family & injure Lilly for the mere pleasure of a personal caress. I would write letters to you rather for twenty years. I had intended to tell you of a great day of *meditation* that I have been keeping. My plans of life are very steadily fixing themselves. I will write them in my next.

Your poor sad husband.
John

[Written across the next-to-last page] Jehovah Jireh!
[marginal note] Get the [illegible] & read Nos 72 & 73 Nouradain & Amana.

Lexington, Sept 8. 1856

My *dear* John,

It was too late after I got home & got my hunger appeased Saturday night to write to you. I found your letter, written Thursday morning waiting for me, and was glad to know from it that you *had* omitted our writing day. I was anxious lest the letter had been sent on from here to Fincastle, & had been delayed or lost there. It is safer to send letters from here to Liverpool, than to Fincastle.

I am grieved about your visit. I hardly know what to think of it. As I said to you before, so far as my own family is concerned I would let you make it, but I shrink from doing what might compromise me with every body. And yet I hardly know why I should, for troubled and suffering as I have been for months, the world's favor if I had possessed it most fully would have given little comfort. I had, insensibly, stored up a great deal of pleasure in the anticipation of yr visit, and I feel the disappointment very much.

I am worried about a great many things, I don't know what to do with Lilly. I don't know what to do with myself. I can fall upon no plan for either of us, which is without grave objections. Indeed Lilly has so cramped herself & me too by her expenditures that I have no means till January to send her from home. In fact it will take everything I can collect then, of my own to meet her bills & the most imperative of my own. Her Uncle Tom will not pay the interest upon the 2 or $3.000 he has of hers, tho' at this moment he has 300.000 bushels of salt ($100.000) ready for market, besides plaster, cattle &c &c. However as soon as he gets this to market, he may be willing to settle his business with us all. He is neither dishonest nor dishonorable, but culpably negligent & procrastinating, embarrassing all who have any business connection with him. Aunt Eliza is selling her home, when the $6.000 which she claims & I think he owes her, would relieve her from debt & all its disquietudes. He denies her claim, however, and does nothing to aid her! He is, it seems to us from recent accounts inexhaustibly rich, & we hope he will pay off his debts this year. His land alone about the Salt works, is worth $100.000; & the 3 acres containing the salt wells &c have been assessed at $300.000. Then there are Negroes in scores, & cattle & horses, & a great mansion in Abingdon finer than the finest in Western Va., with some 30 rooms all finished & furnished & unoccupied except occasionally during the year.

I am so much out of spirits, & really feeling so unwell to-day that my pen drags heavily. I have no energy for any thing that would rouse me to mental excitement.

Never mind about the buttons. I had rather they wd look worn. I shall like them all the better for your using them.

Have you any wish to try the effect of a "right high quarrel" between us? I believe we have never had one of any sort yet, which I must assure you is owing to my forbearance.

> *God bless You. Affec'ly*
> *S.C.P. McDowell*

(Sep'r)[24]
Princeton Nov: 8th 1856

My sweetest Darling,

I cannot deny that this last stroke is one of keen suffering to me. One of the first wild thoughts that it threw into my mind was that of a clandestine meeting. If you had a thick wood wrapping around your house as Allamby will have my temptation to it would be very great. If I could get (under any reasonable appearance) away from the public eye so long as the journey would take any mad project of seeing you would have wild charms to me. I *rebel* against this last verdict. And tho' I know I am a clergyman & you are a Christian lady & our steps must be led not merely by what we regard safe, but by what we regard right & proper yet I cant tell you how I feel already as a sort of outlaw on whom society has set one of her fingers of oppression.

But, Sally, I want you to find out distinctly what Miss J. has to stand upon in her very strong opinion. You must write to her & she must explain to you

---

24. McDowell corrected the month.

both her remarks—the damage done you by your ruptured marriage—& this that she regards as worse. I have had another impulse & that was to write a long full letter to your Aunt Carrington, the object of it being to set *you* right by a simple narrative—telling her, first, what is actually true that when I suffered myself to become interested in you I had not the most distant dream that our marriage would be either wrong or objected against—that from my Presbyterian training & knowledge of your previous history I supposed all the world admitted the propriety of marriage—that I addressed you therefore without a gleam of scruple & was surprised at the difficulties you threw in my way—that I resisted those reasons when presented as objections & considered them as only sensitive & over scrupulous objections of one naturally feeling strongly in such peculiar circumstances. However, Sally, I need not detail the letter. I would have written it & sent it for you to read if I had brought myself to conclude upon it. I would have let Mrs Carrington feel that the letter was written not for any purpose of asking her countenance, but simply as a respectful attention to the feelings of your family in respect to their natural & very obvious interest in you.

The fact is, your uncles & aunts & even James &—Mrs Cocke love you more probably than you have any idea & we are much too likely to do *last* & as a mere expression of impatience in respect to coolness that we have fancied existed, before the very mischief that leads to irreparable breaches in families.

But, dearest Sally, all this is aside from what I want chiefly to write to you about, & that is my strong & in these trials most yearning & solicitous affection I do feel so tenderly towards you, Darling, in these new instances of the pain you have from loving me. I so long to be with you. I so long to marry you that I may take you under my own care & a great consolation in all this business is first, that it cannot put farther off our *marriage* & that when our marriage occurs it will be divested of all that has been disagreeable throughout your history.

Did you talk with Mrs C.? What did she say about this visit?

I mean, when our minds are settled a little in respect to this distress to write you a long letter about my plans here. They are assuming a more *solid* appearance—less of the air castle. The rest of my life (in all *family* aspects) is devoted to you & to my children. I have no plans but those that connect themselves with you.

And if I must give up this visit (of wh. I am not yet convinced) I think I will love you more *tenderly* than ever before.

Yours devotedly
Jno.

Colalto,
Wednesday Sep: 10. 1856

My *dear* John,

I wanted to write you a real letter by this morning's mail, but yesterday afternoon I went out to attend to a piece of business for Miss Jannetta, & as it was our regular prayer-meeting night I did not get home till 9 o'clock. Now I am hurried; Tom is just starting to Fincastle to look after a farm I heard of there that is now for sale, and we are all in a fuss about his buggy &c. &c.

I shall take a quieter moment to write you fully about our immediate vexations & troubles. At present I am rather flurried, tho' having seen Tom off at least, I shall get quieter every word I write.

My anxiety, John, is not about my relations—"friends" as you call them;— they are not so deporting themselves to me, as to make me feel at all like relying upon them for anything but injury & abuse. That I do not of course, mean all of them—but I do mean that Abingdon junto of Floyd & Uncle Tom. I know more than I can tell you. But if I had no other proof, of *how far* they have gone, I had it in the excited & angry emotion with wh Miss Jannetta said to me the other day—"Oh! I think your friends have done you more harm than good". Heretofore she has been excusing & defending them. My suspicion, is not only mine but Aunt Eliza's, that Uncle Floyd means to make his letter to me last summer which you saw, & wh he had witheld from me, a matter of veracity between us. More than this—or in support of this, I suspect he is on another point endeavoring to weaken my assertions or statement. Aunt Eliza appeals to me to know if Dr White ever was consulted, or ever was in favor of my marriage, as it is understood he denies both. Now who understands this? Uncle William comes straight from Uncle Floyds town & Uncle Tom's house, & these inquiries are made of me. Why certainly these "friends" with whom he had been have been, I *suspect* saying something like this to him: "*Sally says,* she consulted Dr White about her marriage & that he favored it; but the Doctor *denies* that she ever did ask his advice; or that he ever did approve of her contemplated step." Fortunately I have *a letter* from Dr White, written last winter to Lilly principally upon this subject which contains these sentences—"Just recollect yr Sister's high character for intelligence & piety, & that many, very many of the wisest & best people in the land, & especially in her own State think that her course in this matter perfectly justifiable &c &c"—"I know perhaps as much as any one else what yr Sister's motives, principles & feelings in this subject are; & instead of censuring I admire & respect her more than I can express. I firmly believe that the law both of God & Man sustains her course".

Hence with *such* friends as these I can have no concern; but it is as to the opinions of others that I am concerned. However, we'll talk of this again.

Oh John! I am so sad & troubled. When these vexations & difficulties spring up, I always feel that they draw you away from me. And worse than that, when they come setting up the notion of their being something morally wrong in our relations, I shrink away from you. But John I have thought over this thing anxiously & carefully, am I deceived about it: Does God forbid it? Inexpedient our marriage might be, as Society is constituted;—but immoral—& disallowed by God I don't think it would be. If then the marriage be right, the engagement of marriage cannot be wrong.

And, John, after my spasms of fear on this point pass off, you can't tell how warmly I creep back to yr side, & how sweetly I luxuriate in the abundance & under the shelter of yr affection. It seems the only living thing on earth to me, & I draw upon it as tho' it must impart its own vitality to me. I long to see you often, but have always doubted that I ever should; & yet I have known no diminished attachment, but much the reverse, from yr absence. As you suffer from our disappointment as much as I do, I ought not to burden you with my sorrow about it—but ought, rather to endeavor to cheer you. I am interrupted again. God bless you my own dear John.

Yours,
S.C.P. McD.

Princeton, Sep 11th 1856.
Thursday Morn.

My *dear Sally*,

Your mournful little note has just been brought in by Allie who had been down town. I had not given up the hope that you wd still encourage me to come & I have that dreary feeling which a life always rather dismal, has, when a pleasant future is suddenly all taken away. I was out late last night at my sister Sarah's (Mrs Hageman) where the Henrys who are now here had been invited & were all at tea except the Prof himself who was not in town. One of the young daughters is a most fascinating woman. If it were not that I have no spirits for that sort of enterprise I would try to plague you a little with eloquence on her bright cheeks & handsome figure: but, Darling, I am the poorest person in the world to tease *you*, for I am so far gone in the beautiful passion, that I feel *for both sides*, that is, if I could *conceive* of you as the least jealous I would feel all the pang of it myself. Do you think if I were to go off on a rhapsody upon her beautiful face & eyes & to show by my enthusiasm how much I had been moved I could stir in you the least suspicion of me. Mrs Henry is really a very pleasant woman, much improved since her residence in W. & really possessing very simple and agreable manners.[25] They kept Mary & me out so late that for the first time I am writing all my letter after breakfast & of course hurrying to get it into the mail.

Enclosed is your postage. It is so long since I counted your letters that I fear it is not quite up to high water mark. The modern habit of prepaying makes the adjustment of postage so different from what it used to be that I was only waked up from my lethargy on the subject by a funny thing that happened in the country the other day. I went out to see the Janeways. One of the daughters a most bright little woman was receiving the visits of a country fellow who had got to college but whose father was a farmer of Dr J's parish. He was evidently a good deal scared & in high excitement. And the lady perfectly self-possessed was

---

25. Harriet L. Alexander Henry (1808–1882).

trying to reassure him & thereby embarrassing him more than ever. Presently I heard him stammer out a request that she would ride (on horseback) with him. (He had come on horseback) and to my no little amusement she replied *that she had no horse* in which he acquiesced as an all sufficient difficulty. Now as in Jersey sending a horse is part & parcel of a proper proposal to ride I began to laugh at our young friend in my own mind & quite flattered myself how much wiser I would have been, when on going home by a queer connection this postage came into my mind—how I had invited a lady to a long gallop over hill & dale of a diversified correspondence & how I had most complacently suffered her to furnish her own horse—how moreover I had been once laughed at for writing to a lady in old postage times several times & leaving a charge of 25 cts unpaid on each letter & then—*Moral*—how when we attempt to laugh at country lovers we must think carefully of what we are about ourselves. However, here is the postage, & now by all Jersey law, as well as by the rules of all Christendom I stand discharged & are at liberty to laugh at other people just as I please. 'Tho by the way, Darling, I do remember going two or three times to your house & falling into more dependant ways even than young *Vandyke*, for you managed it so that I should half invite myself to a ride with three or four young ladies in the ladies' carriage horses driver & all.[26]

Cheer up, dear Sally, there are good times in store for you yet. Preserve your health. Keep everything that is perishable of life or strength with great care thro' these dark days—that when the good time comes—you may not have lost anything of value in the time of darkness. Good-bye.

Yours affly,
Jno Miller.

Tell me what yr aunt & Miss J. *said.*

Colalto,
Thursday, Sept' 11. 1856

My *dear John,*

I can't tell you how much I wd prize a quiet hour with you "face to face". It would be an inexpressible enjoyment even tho' I were not allowed to speak a single word;—indeed, it wd be a great pleasure, even if words were prohibited to you too—tho' that wd be a very tantalizing pleasure I must admit. Yet just to know that we were once more together—just to look right straight up into yr very eyes—not into this shadowy face that by shutting my own eyes, I can often recall—but into the living & breathing face that I love:—just to feel that I am in some sort sheltered at yr side;—O John! What a *rest* it would be to me. But John, it wd be no pleasure to me if it were a stolen interview—"a clandestine meeting".

26. Anthony Van Dyke (1599–1641), Flemish artist, appointed court painter by Charles I of England.

I turn away, with instinctive horror from any such concealments. If I see you again we must strip our meetings of all look of being proscribed. I chafe madly against all secrecy. And you too John, would like it no better than I should. It would be entirely inconsistent with all my knowledge or notion of you to see you willing even for a clandestine meeting. It is only a wild fancy, Darling, born of that desperate sort of feeling that our troubles have occasioned. I know well the wildness & torture of such mad dreams. My whole soul often seems raving mad under the tumult & swell & conflict of its excited feelings. I can do nothing. I often lie down—And often when I am lying down this mental agony comes on, & I am prompted by mere restlessness to move about—But we are both wrong in this rebellious impatience. It is as sinful as it is distressing; and it takes away from us the little comfort we might claim.

I often think that our present circumstances are the very ones, for the exercise of the highest christian virtues & graces. It is easy enough to *trust* God, when we see things are going as we wish. Such a trust is not worthy the name. But now, when the future is all dark; when the present even is so dark that we are obliged to stand still, not having light enough to see where to put the foot next;—now when every thing seems against us;—when we are perplexed by these adverse notions & conduct of others,—now is the time for us to seek the support that God only can give—to cultivate, by constant exercise, the faith that he has already given—& be submissive & hopeful & patient. I was much struck with this exhortation in one of the Epistles—I think of Peter—"Commit thy way inunto the Lord, *in well doing*". This well-doing if it does not hasten the time for our "inheriting the promises,"[27] certainly does cheer us in the interval of waiting & anxiety. I take a great moral lesson from little Mac & his wants, which are something like this. He comes over here & spies on my table a peach. He seizes it & brings it eagerly to me—"Auntie, peel it, peel it". "No—Mac is sick; Auntie can't let him have it". The little fellow frets some but runs off. A little while after he comes back with an apple, his face as eager and expectant & joyous as possible. "No—Mac, I tell him again—You musn't have it". He swells up & his eyes are full of tears & his little mouth is all awry, & tho' he submits, he is nevertheless, sorely grieved & tempted to rebel. I take him in my arms, and smooth his curls gently, & *promise* him, he shall have a whole basket of apples if he will wait till the morning—or he shall have *one* if he will hold it in his hand & give it to his Mother, when he gets home, to peel for him. Very soon the hurried, burdened breathing, calms down; the little mouth gets straight again; & tho' the tears are on his cheeks, his eyes brighten. He takes his apple, *believes all my promises*, plays about in the yard awhile, & then goes home, where the first thing he does is to show his treasure & claim his reward—"Mama peel it, peel it". Now the *principle* of faith in that toddling little fellow, with his great red apple in his hand, in no wise differs from the principle of faith which we have if [we] be real christians; and our exercise

27. Heb. 6:12.

of it ought certainly to be as easy and as prompt as his. We know that if we do not get exactly what we ask for, we shall have what is better far, than that we ask or hope for even. And when our paroxysms of agony come on we ought to grasp the promises & soothe ourselves with them. I try to practice in this regard, what I am preaching to you and often succeed in quieting myself.

Much as I love you, my own dear John, and I love you with all my heart, yet I don't want that affection to absorb all affection of a higher kind; but, on the contrary, I would have it over-ruled & guided by this higher one. I would value my love to you, so much more than I do if I found it made me a more earnest, & faithful & sincere christian, both by its troubles & its pleasures. I don't see why it shouldn't do it, especially when its present difficulties call for the developement of every christian sentiment & emotion & act.

Friday 7 A.M.

It would be well-right useless for me to write to Miss Jannetta to explain her remarks to me. She said she did not hear our matter much spoken of in Aunt Eliza's family. She has been in Rich however since she left here, & it was there she heard the most about it, I gathered from her way of talking. Her opinion was, that I had lost standing, on account of my purpose to marry—but that the marriage concluded might make that loss more decided & apparent & greater. She thought also, under present circumstances, a visit from you, would not be proper—why, she did not explain.

I have always thought with her, that the public intention to marry placed me, upon that whole subject, just where in society the actual marriage wd have done. Mr Blair gave to me in Rich: the same opinion. I have heard it once again from another person. Few speak to me on the subject. But under this public committal, I have not been made to feel anything of public censure. I am, every where treated with the same attention as formerly. I doubt whether the marriage wd have changed things very materially. At any rate, I did not recede from the marriage on account of this supposed or exhibited state of public feeling. I had looked at that in the distance until I had overcome in great measure, my fear of it. I submitted to another motive and a more powerful feeling, which has been to me the saddest & most grievous & most torturing of all the feelings that the whole affair awakened. It is true, I often bring every thing I can seize upon to quiet it & am often entirely acquiescent, but I fight a hard battle for my peace.

If Miss Jannetta gives up her engagement in Fincastle, & I can get her a school here, I still hope *a little,* to be able to have a visit from you. It makes the present very cheerless, this disappointment, but the sources of pleasure are one after another fast drying up. I feel much as a man wounded in battle who has suffered the amputation of both legs & one arm—"well—it is a relief to know that I can repeat these sufferings only once more." I have only one tie, this letter-tie that is left in existence; when it is broken as, no doubt it will be like all the rest, I shall then suffer my last agony. But John, I know you suffer too. Of course it is a *pleasure* to me to know that you do, at that the same time that my heart loosens its hold upon my own sorrows that it may give all its sympathies to yours—if I can, at all feel, that yr sorrows & mine *have* a distinct & separate existence. After all is said as to our sorrows tho', I must always come back & tell you that there is a mingling with them of real pleasure. Your love to me, is an unfailing spring of comfort,—& my love to you is in itself an enjoyment. When things go smoothly with us, yr love brightens all to me; & when they go roughly, why, I have a certain sort of pleasure in sharing in yr troubles & distress. And we may one day have these crooked things made straight to us. Then let us be patient.

Please, John, *do me the favor* never again to write such a sentence as this to me. "The fact is yr Uncles & Aunts & James—& Mrs Cocke love you more probably than you have any idea of" &c &c. I know the *facts* better than you do, & such expressions from you always fret me. I should like to know what form *of affection* that can be which would seize me by the throat & thrust me, as a leper, out of the pale of society. I am trying & wishing to forgive these people, but it is not by calling evil, good; but by endeavoring to forgive the evil as evil, & excusing it as best I can.

No, don't write to Aunt Eliza. You owe no "deference" to my family; and ten to one, not she, but some of the others would either misapprehend or misconstrue any letter you would write. If you are ever to be my husband, that is not the attitude I wd like you to assume to them. You & yr motives are as much entitled to their respect & deference—& far more—than their notions & prejudices are entitled to yr notice or consideration. I never mentioned my affairs to Aunt Eliza when last there, as they, at present, stand. She was too much occupied & harassed by her own arrangements for me, even if I had wished to consult her about mine.

Whilst these near kin are standing against you to me, more distant relations are very gratifyingly kind & affectionate. When I meet them they are kinder than before—one of them at least—& I have met only a few—and others are prompt & full in all our indirect & direct communications. I have this hour the most overflowingly affectionate letter from Sally Breckinridge now in Balt.

If you think my letter fretful & peevish, pray scold me soundly for it. I am not perfect, my Darling—but very anxious that you should love me just as much as tho' I were. Won't you love me with all yr heart, in the very face of my faults. Oh John when you mourn over my getting old & ugly I long that you should be able to take up the words of that sweet little Scotch ballad, which no doubt you have heard a hundred times—Mary of Argyle.

"Tho' thy voice may lose its sweetness,
    And thine eye its brightness too;
"Tho' my step may lack its fleetness
    And thy hair its sunny hue;
"Still to me thou will be dearer

Than all the world shall own,—
"I have loved thee for thy beauty
 But not for that alone;
"I have watched thy heart, dear Mary,
 And its goodness was the will
"That has made thee mine forever
 Bonny Mary of Argyle."

How happy I should be to think I was good enough to be loved for that alone! But don't you love me anyhow?

       Yours
      S.C.P. McDowell

Princeton Sept. 13th 56.

My Darling,

I love you so much that when decisions pass out of my hands & are left with you I feel a dreary helplessness of spirit which I can hardly paint to you. I hover over you most anxious in my own account & yours in respect to what is to be your verdict. There is more in the attitude of your friends than "you can tell me", & therefore, of course I cannot judge. I only repeat, that if my visit is to strip you of your Preston society I will not pay it. Margaret B. is here, & tells me that you are *greatly* loved in all the West where you have been & I cant but believe that in Va they love you more than you imagine & therefore, respecting their relation to you, much more than you now do, I am resolved that I will not impair or disturb it.

But then, Sally, I am not sure that you are judging right. Recollect, first, that if we drop my visits to you we cannot take them up again. *That* after years of absence will seem like a new courtship & wear the aspect of new wavering. You must distinctly recognize then a *final arrest* of *visits* till we are married or till T's death. That *looks* terrible. Again as our engagement & correspondence will continue it is only *cloaking* & seeming afraid of a state of things which will always be *oozing* out (to use just the word for such a slow continued occasion of talk) in other ways—for instance thro' the P.O. & thro' our own occasional explanations of our position when either of us are questioned. Third, the disapprobation *visits* would excite would spend its force chiefly upon us—whereas marriage would implicate our children so that the former *cannot* be so serious as the latter. Still I stand by my old assertion. Much as it costs me if you are to part (not with *me*, but) with my visits or else with your whole or chief family connection *I refuse to see you.* I cant consent that my selfish gratification should be paid for by *one* of us, that one the lady & at so dear a price. I infer from several things that have been in your letters that ill things have been said of me. Life has worn so upon me by many distresses that insults like that of your Bro James do not sting so much as they *burn*, they fail to rouse me with a feeling of pain so much as they exasperate my pride & fill me with contempt & indignation.

Dear Sally, one truth I can give you means of enjoying (if it is an enjoyment to you) without any fear or wavering & that is that I love you beyond anything that your highest fancy enables you to conceive. God bless you & direct you.

JM.

Colalto, Sept: 13. 1856
Saturday afternoon.

My *dear John*,

Enclosed is *your* postage. If you esteem it most fair & *polite* to pay for *my* letters to you, you will hardly find fault with me for my accuracy & exactness in paying for yrs to me. And, lest we should quarrel as to the *number* of our letters, we will take it for granted that we hold an even balance in our correspondence; & therefore the monied value of your letters is no greater than mine, as their number is about the same. Now John, honestly—aint you ashamed to have been guilty of such an "eccentric" piece of folly. In these days, people who write upon business enclose stamps for the replies necessary; but I believe none others do. In the present case, I think you have stumbled upon a piece of very bad taste, wh wd offend me seriously, if ever repeated.

Don't you remember once asking me if I was at all jealous tempered, & of my answering that I was? I was in sober earnest in my reply: it was unfortunately too true. I am not sure that every one of strong feeling has not a little of this poison mingled with all the pleasure of their affections. *I have*, I know. I suppose nature gave me a good deal, & a peculiar history has only cultivated it. Now this is the truth, & if you are ambitious of testing it, you can do it very easily. If you are anxious or willing even, for mere sport, to rouse so painful a feeling, with one who has, as you know, sorrows enough & pain enough without any such addition, why you could succeed in an effort almost immediately.—But, John, whilst you would rouse my jealousy, you wd by the same effort destroy my affection. I couldn't love you or trust you, if I thought you capable of wantonly giving me pain, by awakening my anxiety as to the reality & loyalty of yr attachment to me. I couldn't bear either the frivolous vanity that wd be mixed up with such an effort. But dear me! How gravely I talk. And yet I can't help it; for I wouldn't for the world that *now*, you should yrself do any thing, from any motive of pure caprice or thoughtlessness or any thing else, that wd stir up one suspicion in my mind of your affection. If we were together you might *say* many a harmless thing, which, being absent from each other as we are, and troubled and thwarted, & anguished by our difficulties, you cannot *write* without causing some unpleasant feeling. I beg you will spare me, all playfulness, even upon so tender a subject. I tell you all this just that you *may* do it. You don't know what you do, when you venture even a little upon this dangerous topic. I think it wrong & foolish in me; but it would take a life of 8 centuries, & all the piety of all the old Testament worthies to wear out this temper with me. Don't you laugh at what I say: & don't get worried at it either: you can at least comfort yourself by knowing that if I loved you less, I should have less fear of the agony & the outbreak of this terrible feeling.

I wonder John, if you are *really* worthy of all the thought and all the love I pour out upon you. Someday, when you are in an honest mood tell me whether you are or not. I have nobody else to ask, & little chance to know you without an *envelope*, so I must trust to yr own truthfulness. I love you very much for some things that[28] I see & know—& a great deal for others that I take for granted belong to you, & then still more, for a number of qualities that rise up & stretch across my mind like a Milky Way—inspiring me by all that it offers to my imagination.

If I had anyone to stay with me, I would not, I think abandon all hope of seeing you yet—tho' I have given up all for the present.

John, tell me, do you think our present relations, if they are known, are doing you any injury as a Minister? Do you think they wd be likely to interfere in, if you wished it, yr obtaining a church anywhere? Do write me what yr future plans are. Our recent disappointment has so upset me, that I have forgotten every thing else. What have you determined about the book? Have you submitted it to Sam's examination? You have confidence in Prof: Henry's judgment & ability, why not ask *him* to give you a candid opinion about it? You need to be cautious, & you must forgive me, if I seem foolishly to admonish you to be so. I am anxious for the book & for you too as its Author.

Rev Mr Vaughen, from Lynchburg is preaching here just now. A very young man, & excellent preacher. He has improved too in many respects. He wrote an elaborate review of the University lectures, when the book came out, in which he touched *you* off; but I forgot entirely what he sd of you. He spent his strength in praising Uncle Robert, I remember. Dr Lewis Green has lately turned round, & came out fiercely *against* Uncle Robert. Something relating to Robinson's appointment to Danville, I believe turned him from a worshipper to an enemy of his.[29] I do mourn to see Preacher's showing passions like our own.

Tomorrow is our Communion. I am looking to it, with a degree of pleasure unfelt for a long time. How much we need now & then to be brought into the very presence of the King, with all our burdens & petitions in our hands. Often we are admitted to this presence-chamber; but the Master is absent—or, at any rate, we do not percieve him, & we seem to come back with our troubles fastened upon us. But then sometimes, we do meet the Master at his own banquet: he even goes up with us to the feast, and we return from his presence with joy & rejoicing, laden with precious gifts.

But good-bye now. I may add a note on Monday.

---

28. McDowell repeated "that."

29. Lewis Warner Green (1806–1863), Presbyterian minister and president of Hampden Sydney College in Virginia from 1848 to 1856. A Baltimore pastor and writer for the *Presbyterian Critic*, Stuart Robinson was appointed professor of church polity and pastoral theology at Danville Theological Seminary in Kentucky in 1856.

Monday Sep. 15. [1856]

Such delightful weather we have! Mere existence is a pleasure in it, & yet one can be sad under it too.

Miss Jannetta writes me, the letter receiv'd this morn'g, that she has concluded to remain where she is, five months longer.

Do write to me very freely & plainly as tho' you were talking to yourself, what you think of our whole affair, past, present, & future. I have hard work to bear up under its repeated & sudden shocks & disappointments. These, added to other difficulties have made sad inroads upon my strength. Every thing has come to a stand with me. I don't know what to turn to or where to look for aid of any kind. I am not willing to complain, for I know, or believe rather, that a higher power than any on earth *will* interpose to relieve me, but when & how I cannot imagine. I am pained to be so desponding and to have so little cheerful submission in these dark days. Yesterday morning I was chilly & cold & throwing myself on Lilly's couch, I covered up my head & shut my eyes & took David's method of comforting myself by *remembering* how God had dealt with me in the past. With a clearness never known before, I thought I could see, from one important event to another, the leadings of Providence. I could put my finger first on one thing, then another & another, all dark & trying at the moment, but all issuing in some thing *better* than I had or cd have expected; & all better than what had preceded them. A progress not from good to bad & from bad to worse; but on the contrary, even as regards this world, from bad to good, & from good to better. I found, I had every reason for trust & much for hope as to the future. My life has been a stormy one—but its storms have been over-ruled for good thus far. I cannot remember that I ever have passed any year of more unmitigated suffering than this last. It may seem strange to you, that I should say so. I have never before been entirely without human aid & sympathy. But for your affection, & I believe I have had more affection from you than sympathy John, haven't I? but for that, I shd have been without any strong earthly tie. Lilly is a strong bond, stronger perhaps than I am aware of, yet I have had all my power of emotion emptied upon you, & thus it seems as if yrs was the only tie on earth worth talking of. In this exigency, & feeling yr inability to aid me, I have been shut up to simple trust in God. I know this to be a sure refuge, & I feel myself *waiting,* to see what he will order me to do now. My heart rather springs up under its load as I thus take this attitude & wait; & welling out of its dark depths there is a little rippling brooklet of Hope yet.

John, don't my letters weary you? I am a poor *"help"* to you at present, but change places with me, Darling, & you be my help & comfort. You often have been. Sometimes when I read yr old letters I thank you anew for their encouraging & comforting spirit.

Your's affect'ly
S.C.P. McDowell.

Little Mac is entirely well & getting bad enough.

Princeton, Sep: 15th 1856.

My Darling,

Do you remember in Bleak House the phantom among the brick-kilns. I am often haunted by the recollection of it as I remember the story. There has been a phantom hovering about our correspondence. I never catch sight of it fully: at least I never did till this letter. Here at a time in the road it stands facing me, but then plunges into the woods. *Now, Darling, you must tell me what it is.* You say, "at any rate I did not recede from the marriage on account of the supposed or exhibited state of public feeling. I had looked at that in the distance until I had overcome in great measure my fear of it. I submitted to another motive and a more powerful feeling, which has been to me the saddest & most grievous & most torturing of all the feelings that the whole affair awakened. It is true I often bring everything I can seize upon to quiet it & am often entirely acquiescent, but I fight a hard battle for my peace."

Now, you must tell me what this is, Darling, I *beg* it. If it mortifies your pride or some feeling connected with your self respect is hiding something of this sort from me, still I *beg*. Sally, *in your next letter* tell me all this thing which once or twice you have indistinctly hinted at. If you think it too great a proof of your affection, recollect, Dearest, in *asking* it I give you a greater. I deliberately put myself in a position where my honour more than ever binds me permanently to your side. This is where I want to be. It does not need honour to keep me there. This letter-tie that you speak of *shall not* be broken. But then, Darling, I want this *last* proof of your devotion the surrender of what you evidently have long kept from me & which in this last letter starts out inadvertently into such sudden [premises?]. Dearest dont tell me *partly* what you dream or leave me half in doubt again by some indistinct expression but tell me all that you are thinking of & give me one of those thrilling pleasures with which you sometimes fill me when I feel that you are entirely my own.

My sweet dear Sally, I admire you so in this last most noble revelation of yourself—I mean in this last letter. You are so *like* me—I mean, Darling, what you once made me very proud by saying, you do express so beautifully in your actions what I admire & love. We do grow together so the more of your letters I break open & read that it is a perfect treat to me to see how you anticipate my haste & quiet it in every possible anxiety. I read lately all your letters to Maggie B. I had hardly imagined you would so agree with me in my love of reserve on all these matters. Then, Darling, your behaviour at Fincastle. My *passion* for you is beginning to settle into *all* the elements of esteem.

But Darling, answer this letter. I do *beg* you not to put me off. I am late this evening.

Yours very affly
JM

Colalto,
Tuesday Sep'r 16. 1856

My *dear John,*

I am tired to-night; & have a dull pain pressing upon my head that admonishes me to go to bed as quickly as possible. But I am generally so flurried & interrupted in the morning that I shall write part of my letter to-night in spite of such admonitions. We had old Dr Baker (of Texas) to make a rambling address at our prayer-meeting to-night; & then Cousin John & I took an old-fashioned talk in the porch after we came over, so that I am late with my writing.[30]

I want to find out, if I can in some quiet way, whether Miss Jannetta's idea about your visit is likely to be largely sympathized with by other friends, before I absolutely give it up. I wanted to ask Dr White again about it; but he has been busy lately & I forbore to trouble him with my concerns: tomorrow he goes away for some days. The thought of not seeing you at all for years, if ever again, when it stands out as a likely to be a naked reality, is dreadful to me. I am overcome by it. Then too, the appearance & reality of secrecy as to our engagement, as tho' we were concealing something wrong, is exceedingly dis-agreable. Sometimes I feel rebellious at it. As to yr 3d difficulty, under present circumstances, I look at it differently from you. If your visits were so disapproved by the public as to bring down its censure upon *us,* they would, in all practical results be, to my mind, as injurious as our marriage—&, in the same way & to the same extent:—indeed, John, I am not sure a public disapproval of yr visits would not go farther to do me serious injury, & would be more apt to thrust itself painfully upon me in my social relations, than the marriage. I would feel my position more shaken & less likely to be recovered than if we had proceeded last Fall as we had intended.

Now, in saying this, you must not think that I am urging the marriage *now.* However, full my right might be, yet you would not any more find me consenting to do such a thing now, than you wd have done in any of the earlier stages of our acquaintance. As things stand, in certain particulars, I *could not reasonably desire even, the consummation of our engagement;* therefore, you cannot misconstrue my difference of opinion with you on this point. And you must let me express it unreservedly without fearing that you can at all wound my pride, by mistaking me.

Wednesday 8 A.M.

I burnt last night, as you requested, the fly-leaf of your last letter. I am glad to know that Maggie Breckinridge is at home again. Somehow I didn't quite like her being at Niagara. By the way, don't you be so foolish as to ask her to show you my letters to her. I don't remember what they were about—nothing however I am sure that need be contraband to you; but I don't want you to do it just because it would look *rather foolish* in you. I don't know that I would have

---

30. Daniel Baker (1791–1857), an evangelist, founder, and agent for Austin College.

thought of yr having any such curiosity, if you had not told me that it had risen up, exactly in this spot.

I enclose you James' letter about the Ky land.[31] I heard thro' Willie Breckinridge the sale he made 3 years ago was considered a bad one. As to the Iron business—a foundry that he bought two years since, he was unfortunate & lost heavily. Col Brant, one of the keenest business men in the City of St Louis urged him to buy it.[32] He did so, & found he "had fallen among thieves." In his disaster, his father-in-law, this same Col Brant, turned aside & left him to struggle out as best he could. I have never had, any belief in his business capacity. He is energetic & industrious when he seizes hold of anything; but he loses all his labor, by letting go too quickly. He has no steady perseverance. Just now, I am troubled about him. He has written me (the letter before the enclosed) a sad account of his present difficulties & embarrassments. I cd but remark the strength of the old habit that turned him back to me when real *trouble* came. And, I felt gratified too, at the testimony he bore in thus returning, to my forbearance &c, &c, under our recent difficulty. I always wanted to bear myself to him, as that he shd feel he could rely upon my interest and support when it was needed. I have written a plain & full & encouraging letter,—such as perhaps, no other friend, wd feel at liberty to write to him. I told him I would not advise him for, "advice unasked was usually an offensive impertinence" but I would give my *opinion* about his affairs. My heart warmed to him in his troubles; and it scarcely occurred to me there had been a misunderstanding between us. I am always sorry for him and about him, tho' he does make me desperately mad too. I often wish I could tell him *all* that seems to me to be the Truth in his connections, of a business & social kind too; but, you know, tho' I speak freely yet there are important points I hardly can do more than allude to. I don't draw back from this entire honesty of expression from fear of his being offended with me,—I don't think that is to be considered when we can do a friend any real good,—but, because I hate to wound him.

As the days pass on I grow more & more anxious about my winter arrangements; & more & more in the dark about them; but I am hoping that something will "turn up" yet, to guide me.

What makes you write me such little bits of letters? O! let me beg that you will when you see fit to emphasize a word be careful to write it plainly. Sometimes, your important words, are utterly unreadable. Not that you don't write *well*—I think you write *beau-ti-ful-ly*; but this just happens now & then.

John, what makes you interject such expressions as this—"One truth I can give you the means of enjoying (*if it is an enjoyment to you*) &c." You know, that that "Truth" *is* my great happiness; and you know I like to have it repeated every day, & many times in the day; and you know that I am returning it to you very

31. This letter has not been located.
32. Joshua Bosworth Brant (1790–1861), retired military officer and businessman in St. Louis and father of Elizabeth Lovejoy Brant McDowell.

warmly and constantly. How much do you *really* think I love you. As Mac tells me—"a heartful"? Or just a little? Tell me, in good earnest.

Did you ever hear Dr Baker? A preacher sd to Mr Vaughen last night at Mr. Morton's tea table "Dr Baker says he can preach 4 times a day without fatigue!" "Indeed!," I put in, "did he say as much for his hearers"? I had no business, you know to say anything; but *one* service a day from the old gentleman is an abundance for me. Yet I respect his fervour & glowing piety & old age. I involuntarily bow, to a man who tells me such a fact as this—"For forty years I have preached the glorious Gospel of the Son of God!"

But goodbye. Yours
S.C.P. McDowell

Princeton Sept 17th 1856

My sweetest Sally,

I have no letter. I hope to get one to-morrow, but I shall not receive it before I must mail this. Tell me whether you get it on Saturday morning.

I asked Maggie the other day how the event of our marriage would have impressed your friends in Kentucky & the West. She said few had spoke to her of it. Dr. R. B. & the Porters & her brother Sam had alluded to it, & *that from all she could infer her uncle & others were pleased with the news.* She tho't your standing in the W. would not have been affected, that, possibly, Kentucky was more liberal in its judgments on such matters than other states but that the only reserve that she heard expressed was one of some little surprise that from a common impression of my mothers strict views about her family I should have ventured upon such a step. This was all she said. You see it was very favorable.

When you write again give me your opinion about *my visit itself* irrespective of your views about Miss J's presence. The main question is, Is the visit admissible itself. The question when Miss J. can join you or some one else is wholly secondary. I do so much want to go on. Your expression that "you have yet a little hope" that I may has excited me again & made me impatient.

I have just been drawing the deed to-night of another lot. This is the second. Perhaps I spoke to you of it before. I bôt the other of a labourer. I buy this of a millionaire & as very often happens I think my bargain with the laborer is rather the better of the two. Still I dont know. I pay my $100 & get only five acres, making ten in all. That is rather slow work, for a man who aspires to the whole hill, Isnt it? Still it gives me footing for a house for you, & that is a very sweet idea. If it be not a home to live in, perhaps it may be a home to die in & it gives me a mournfully sad pleasure to think even of our dying together, Darling.

You ask me, Will I love you with all your faults? Darling, I am in this condition[33] & if the bandage is ever removed from my eyes I fear I will make *so many*

---

33. A drawing appears in the center of the letter showing a figure with a blindfold.

discoveries. *Dearest* they say Virginia B was such a sweet lady before her marriage, the very idol of a warm circle of friends & tho' with your usual taste you have not told me the scandals of her now, yet from one of our Princeton rumourmongers, they heard the other day what a sad life they lead of it now. Then when Maggie told me how lovely she had been (tho' I believe Gov Shelby in *his* time tried to kill himself twice) I had a sort of shudder.[34] My very ears had a sort of pulled feeling & I thought how, suppose we were married of a Friday, & on Saturday you were to undertake to throw me out of the window or lead me such a life, there up among the rocks that after being worn to such a shadow that I could endure it no longer I were to try to open a vein in my arm & find myself so wasted that like Seneca my blood would not flow.[35] It has quite horrified me. Tell me, dear Sally, by all that was tender in Mrs Shelby's love are you just like her? Will you lead me a *storm*-life? What did you mean when you said you were not calculated to make me a merry comfortable home? Will you fly into furious passion when I am laboring & toiling to behave & to keep your heavy hands off of me? In a word, Loveliest of your sex, are you (like the Witch of Danville) beautiful indeed outwardly, but in your heart full of fierce tempests & all unreasonableness?[36] I so scared.

Sally, promise me one thing. You know I am a frail man not very fit to take my own part in any personal encounter. Promise me that you will never resort to personal violence at least in the first year of our married history. And Sally, above all dont go out & say that I beat you when no body is by because these Jersey neighbours who know my degree of physical strength will laugh at me so when they think how preposterous such an idea is.

Poor Sally! This may find you in the midst of distress & low spirits & may jar so unreasonably upon your feelings. Well, Dearest, come into my arms & like my own little Maggie when she is sick or unhappy nestle there as the only really warm shelter that you have. Poor little thing she comes to me at all hours & sometimes when I am most engaged & quite unceremoniously takes away my book or pulls me back from my writing & climbs into my lap & there caresses me & fondles me with all the ardour of the most forlorn dependance on me for affection. I love the little thing beyond expression. She sleeps in the room next to me & in the morning before I am up steals into my room & climbs up into my bed & tries to cherish her poor numb drooged Pop'pàa as she calls him into some thing like sense & recollection. There is but one other person that loves

34. Virginia Hart first married Alfred Shelby (1804–1832); she became the wife of McDowell's uncle Robert Jefferson Breckinridge in 1847. So troubled was this marriage that at one point in early 1856, the couple considered divorce (James C. Klotter, *The Breckinridges of Kentucky, 1760–1981* [Lexington: University Press of Kentucky, 1986], 58). Isaac Shelby (1750–1826), the father of Virginia Hart Shelby Breckinridge's first husband, was governor of Kentucky from 1792 to 1796 and again from 1812 to 1816.

35. Lucius Annaeus Seneca (4 B.C.?–65 A.D.), Roman statesman and philosopher, was ordered by Nero to kill himself.

36. The Witch of Danville is another reference to Virginia Hart Shelby Breckinridge. The Breckinridges lived in Danville, Ky.

me like her in the world & she I believe loves me more than anything human tho' my chief reason for thinking so is the blindness of my passion for her.

Affly
Jno Miller.

[marginal note] It is rather against my rule to repeat scandal even to you. Dont betray me.

Colalto,
Sep: 18. 1856

My *dear* John,

You never *ask* for anything that I am not immediately disposed to give it to you: of course, when you *"beg"*, I find it well-nigh impossible to resist. I am not reluctant to tell you everything in my mind from any motive that could give you a moment's uneasiness. I have not it is true, emptied my thoughts to you upon the *one* point of our postponed marriage, but my silence has been from no wrong feeling. I could not help the workings of my own mind, any more than you cd control the conclusions of yours; but I could be silent under them, especially when I felt that a candid avowal of them might expose me to such suspicions of my motive as my pride revolted at. And yet I would like to feel free to talk to you of all that is in my mind. I would do it, if you were here, but I don't like to attempt to write about this particular trouble, lest I should fail to do it properly. I am concealing nothing—keeping nothing back out of any unworthy feeling. I don't want to wound you, as I might do by my clumsy writing; neither am I willing to subject myself to any misconception.

But, John, if you will be cautious in yr judgment, & not attribute any want of affection or confidence to me, I will tell you what it is that has pained me so in all that matter. It costs my pride a good deal; but, I shall speak as plainly as I can. I can't bear anything that seems uncandid in a matter, where all our comfort depends upon our perfect confidence in each other.

The thing that has been such a trouble to me was the fact as Cousin John stated it—"Mr M is *not* willing to marry you", and that from, I often & often have feared other reasons than those given. As long, John, as you make me feel that this unwillingness arose entirely & absolutely from consideration for my reputation & happiness and that it was a strong sacrifice of yr own feelings & wishes for my welfare, I am content. But, I feel that nothing else could excuse it. And sometimes when a doubt crosses my mind that this *may not* have been the *controlling*, tho' as you have often & often avowed it, it must have been an existing motive, I am terribly wounded.

From the very first moment in all this affair, I had been perfectly honest & candid with you. I *pressed* upon you my fears for your children & your ministry. Nothing that has since been urged against the marriage by anybody was unthought of or unspoken of by me before there was any publicity given to the affair. My very affection suggested & painted to you—aye, & painted in strong colors too *all* the difficulties since raised. We talked over freely & fully & frequently all the points involving conscience & morals, and after months of this anxious combating of opinions I yielded. I foresaw better than you did the consequences of the step. I felt that the very first public avowal of a marriage engagement, was a surrendering in the eyes of the world, much of the dignity of my position; and it cost me not a little to go that far. But I loved you, & felt that yr affection & our own home would pay me for all I was giving up. It was a pain to me to lose the affection & respect of others if for nothing else for this reason, that in my peculiar circumstances, I would have been proud to have brought them as my marriage-portion to you. I thought it a large & rich possession, which would be a pleasure & comfort to us both. It may be I was mistaken as to the amount. However that might be, still if I couldn't bring that to you, I was ready to go without it, if you would not feel the loss affect your love to me. That was *the* great thing to me—that love was to recompense me for every loss—was to be to me home & friends & station—just everything. And after all our discussions of our difficulties were over, I gave myself up to it without any question of yr steadiness.

When our troubles came on in Nov: I yielded to a proper submission on yr part to yr Presbytery,—That being over, when you returned, with new views as to the marriage, can you wonder that I was deeply pained. I agreed then, I agree still, that it was a true & high sentiment wh wd protect me, from insult and injury in a connection which wd not injure you. I felt it was the truest honor that forbade you to carry out yr wishes for the marriage, when you supposed that marriage wd entail only disgrace & disquietude upon me. I could ask no stronger evidence of affection than such a sacrifice wd give. And even if yr sense of honor had not dictated this course, but some newly awakened conscientious scruple had arrested the matter, however disastrous & painful to me, still I should have supported you in a decision based on such grounds. I believe both these feelings actuated you at the time of our postponement. I believed it then, tho' my own mind took a different view of things. My feeling was that horrible fear that your affection if we were married, for which I was sacrificing everything would not stand the test of this public disapproval. I would not jeopard that. I was ready to brave the censure & neglect of the world; but I could not consent to run the risk of having *you* turn against me in our own home. My anxiety whispered to me you were not so strong as before, & my jealous affection has tortured into a thousand agonizing shapes, the *reasons* for your "unwillingness" to proceed. These are torment to me—tho' when I come to look at all I know of you & to believe that your assigned reasons, are your controlling reasons, I not only acquiesce, but love you the more for yr strong anxiety to protect me at such a cost of personal feeling. It does not lessen my affection, of course, that you should take a different view from mine, of *what* is the best protection of my character & the best guarantee of my happiness.

I do believe you love me. I do believe you are willing to give up a great deal to that affection. I *do* think sincerely that you ought not to be willing & ought not to give up everything to it. I think, moreover it is my business to keep you from yielding any important opinion or principle to it. Don't you know, John, how anxious I have been about that from the beginning? And yet, Darling, these racking fears & fancies—do tell me they are but fancies,—will get possession of me, & I have to fight hard before I can conquer or drive them away.

If I had ever felt at perfect liberty to speak my opinion of what seemed to me the true course in the matter, I might have escaped some of my suffering by having had my mind changed by the discussion; but in such a case, a woman's rights are always ignored by others & she fails to urge them herself out of the horror she feels at even seeming to assume the attitude of the wooer; and out of the shame she could not brook of appearing to thrust herself upon an unwilling lover. Besides, John, in my case, according to my perception & belief I did adopt, for myself & you too the true course. Our different reasonings issued in the same conclusion. Moreover, when I found that you were planning & feeling not for yourself alone, but anxiously for me too, I have been willing just to place what was my all of earthly sufferings in your hands. If you had been seeking under this storm of public censure, a discharge for any reason, I should never have hesitated:—but you were only seeking a *delay* which you urged for reasons based upon what you thought best for me, I have let go other advisers & have trusted to you.

No doubt much of this seems contradictory to you. It is so, because it attempts to tell you of a strong conflict of strong feelings. But the prevailing & powerful habit of my mind has always directed my course—this has been, I think if you will look back you will see, a straight one of steady affection. If, from other opinions than yours, my anxieties are excited—if from peculiar circumstances, I feel my pride wounded, still I never question your honor & your full title to my regard & confidence, and my affection has, under all this internal strife, kept on growing & growing. These things have been to my pride often what jealousy is to ones love—kindling the fire & supplying the fuel.

I wish I could talk over all this to you. After making the attempt to write, I feel how imperfect & futile even it has been. I have written too under many interruptions. But I send it as it is. Where I have been wrong you will forgive me. I never find I have been unjust to you in thought or word without suffering far more than you would possibly do from it; & my heart comes boiling & swelling back to you, as tho' in its increased warmth & fullness it would obliterate every wrong emotion. Whatever else you charge me with, you can not seriously feel that I do not love you with all the power of my nature. I have not loved you with any half-way affection; & tho' I may seem to you to have been unfair and unreasonable in my feeling often, yet I have never failed to bear full & fervent testimony to all that was honorable & generous in you. I had nothing but my love to give to you, for much that you have actually surrendered for me, tho', had the opportunity been fully granted, I should not have been behindhand, in sacrifice too.

But we oughtn't to talk of *sacrifice*—I am sure, I get very good pay in yr affection, which, I must weary you, by telling you so often, is almost my whole of happiness.

I had something else to say, but I can't, I am so late for the mail this morning—for part of my letter has been written to-day (Friday).

God bless you & direct us both.

Affec'ly
S.C.P. McDowell.

Princeton, Sept. 20th 1856.

My *dear Sally*,

Your *two* letters reached me together last night. One of them was post-marked two days earlier & must have gone wrong in some way.

One reason why letter writing is distasteful to me is that I would so like to have you in my arms when I talk to you about all these matters. For example I would like to take this miscarried letter & call you to me just like little Maggie & say—

Foolish Child, isnt it a Kind Providence that when those pretty fingers of yours go running wildly over the paper, that you are writing to an enamoured old gentleman who is too fond to be affronted. What do you think of such sentences as these. "If you esteem it *polite* (underscored) to pay for my letters" & "Aint you ashamed to have been guilty of such an "eccentric piece of folly?" "I think you have stumbled upon a piece of very bad taste, wh wd offend me seriously if ever repeated." Sally, what exactly were you thinking about when you wrote me such sentences. If *I* had had $10 sent me I would have thought, Well, certainly under the old regime it would have been right for a lover to prepay his letters to his betrothed wife; at any rate John says it was & that he was *actually laughed at* for not doing it which makes my laughing at him now the other way a little hard. Now a mere change of P.O. rule cant have made it so different as to have made it utterly preposterous in him to do the same thing in virtually the same way. I'll just take the $10 & laugh at him when I write again for his exactness, or I'll throw the note into some common charity or I'll send it back with a love of a little letter laughing at the good old soul in a loving quiet gentle way. I think he loves me. I think if I hadnt been in some money trouble he would have sent me on stamps, & envelopes long ago. I dare say he hesitated about sending *this*, but in carrying out his starched notions of etiquette, I should misconnect the act & make it a paltry one as in my original depravity I am in danger of doing. Therefore, I will treat my lover as they do the sun as a great luminous whole without looking at the spots on it, &—a great deal more of the same "old tiny" character.

Then I would kiss you & make you get off my knee as I do Maggie when she tires me & make you sit down on her little stool & say—

My Child

About this jealousy:—I dont think it right to take a body seriously when she herself tells me, "I know I am wrong & foolish", but then I have so good a chance of telling you how much I love you. Instead of being fascinated by any one else, I have been trying all day to recall who I was talking about. I cant possibly remember. I have always had a notion. (I am just writing to you now as I think—you tell me to do so) I have always had a notion I could marry anybody. It is one of my idiosyncrisies. In thinking of a wife I have always let my mind wander freely over the whole creation not doubting that the person I should select would be mine. And indeed, Darling, my experience has somewhat confirmed this cer[t]ainty for the moment I have chosen in each case I have with some discouragements won my way to the object. Now with this breadth of view I certainly have prepared the way for a high statement of my passion for you when I tell you, that with this boyish feeling of being able to win anybody I sought for (which I confess is very egotistical & foolish[)]: nevertheless *with this feeling,* there is no one in all my memory whom I would consent to marry & no one who can in the least impress me so absorbing is my passion & idolatry for you. Now, Darling, this may be very good to prove me very Quixotic & vain & all that. That I admit. That is one of the penalties of telling an idle fellow like me to tell you all he thinks. But it is also very good to show you my engrossing admiration & if *true* to show you how little anxiety you need have on the danger of an assault upon your jealousy.

"Am I worthy &c." Why, Sally, it is so flattering a connection that you ask this in, in connection with what seems to have been my teasing you a little & this poor shuttle cock of an enclosure that I can hardly recover sufficiently to say I am. If you mean, am I worthy of *you?* I say unequivocally I am not. If you mean, Am I worthy of all your tho't & care &c.? Well, I fear not. Darling, I wish you had a chance to know *how much I love you.* That I think is my great claim.

Dear me! I have been interrupted & my letter is late. I am sorry it is so foolish a one. I wanted to speak of things much more serious. I will write a day earlier, & a long letter for I have much to say.

Yours affly,
Jno Miller

Colalto, Saturday Sep'r 21. 1856.[37]

My *dear John,*

I have no good reason for it—& yet, perhaps, I have too,—but tonight, for the first time in several weeks I sit down to write without a weight upon my spirits. Usually I come to you *so* sad & troubled, but somehow this afternoon, I have had a little reprise, I am *light-hearted* once more. When I am dispirited, I come to you for rest; & now that I am cheerful, I come to you to share my pleasure with

---

37. Saturday was actually Sept. 20, 1856.

you. I have nothing to tell you that cd inspire you, but I am just disenthralled for a time, & use my liberty by coming, like Maggie, and claiming my place beside you. My only comfort when I am sorrowful is to sit by yr side, & fancy, at least, that I feel yr hand gently laid upon my head. And when a bright moment comes, I find myself more than ever drawn to you & enjoying yr sympathy. How closely we seem bound together. I hardly think a thought at *my end* of the line that it doesn't immediately tingle at yours.

Yes, yr letter of the 17th came by last nights mail. All yr letters, written on Thursday come to me Saturday morning. I don't know why mine don't go to you regularly. I may be too late sometimes; or our P.M. may be too early in doing up his mail. I *try* to send you a letter Monday, Wednesday & Friday mornings.

Now, John, don't be too much frightened when I tell you *I am* in real solemn earnest thought like Cousin Virginia Breckinridge! I am like, so like several of Aunt Harts daughters, Cousin Va amongst them, as to have it frequently remarked by others, & noticed even by myself. Dr Davidson of New Brunswick took a great fancy to me on account of my resemblance to "his old friend Mrs Shelby".[38] Stuart Robinson commented upon it also: Ain't you scared! I think, however I am more like the other sisters who are less handsome than Cousin Va. I never heard of her being "the idol" of her family & friends. She was thought a beauty; & was very pretty; but I never knew of her being particularly liked among her kin. My parents were exceptions, if she was. She has been kind enough to me when I have met her, which is more than many of the family can say, but I don't like her. I don't blame her alone for all their family discord, which is no secret anywhere—but I blame her for much that I have heard. An angel would be sorely tried in that household; & yet there is much that is really noble to be found in it. "Madam Shelby" as Cousin Nat Hart,[39] her brother, used to call her, is a miserably bad step mother; but then you cd expect nothing else from one who was a neglectful & careless mother to her own children—I imagine she makes no great difference in the matter of *care*, between Charlie & her own little John,[40] tho', of course, she loves Johnny and does not *throw away* any affection upon Charlie. Gov Shelby, between whom & my Grandfather Preston's family there was a feud for a time growing out of the fact of his claiming the honor of the King's Mountain engagement, which was really due to Grandmama's father, Col Campbell,—was not "madam's" husband. It was his son Alfred, (who was not esteemed a genius) that enjoyed that honor. It is very sad, the state of things there. No concealment is practiced in regard to their troubles, because no control is exercised upon their tempers. It must, necessarily, do an injury to Uncle Robert as a Minister, & as

38. McDowell's great-aunt Susannah Preston (1772–1833) married Nathaniel Hart (1770–1844). Robert Davidson (1808–1876), Presbyterian pastor in New Brunswick, N.J.

39. Her brother, Nathaniel Hart (1805–1854).

40. Charles Henry Breckinridge (1844–1867) was the last child of Robert Jefferson Breckinridge by his first wife, Ann Sophonisba Preston. After his marriage to Virginia Hart Shelby, he had three children, the youngest being John Robert Breckinridge (1850–?).

a christian, besides keeping him always boiling over & uncomfortable. For my own part I ought to love Uncle Robert very much—he has been very kind to me, always treating me respectfully & considerately. He never quarrelled or spoke sharply to me, & I have been a good deal with him, but was kind & affectionate & has had it in his power to be useful to me too. So, John, I ought not to speak ill of him, tho' of course, I can't justify a great deal that he does.

This paper isn't pleasant for me to write on—I am constantly jabbing my pen thro' it—does it serve you so too?

I think I have answered you in regard to yr visit—at least as to my opinion of it. I will write again of it, But good night now. I am so tired & sleepy. For two nights I have been up till past midnight, & I am suffering one of the consequences of such folly to-night.

Monday. Sep 22.

I can hardly make up an opinion about yr visit, as a thing by itself, because we are not to look at it in that way. If I can write to you & think of you & feel to you as the one whom I may, some day or other have for my husband, I can't see *why* I mightn't, properly, receive a visit from you. But it is as to the effect of such a thing upon others; It is this great knotty, hydra headed question of *expediency* that comes up constantly, in all my thinking of it. I can't form much of an opinion from what I know, at present, of public feeling; but judging from the past, I am not sure that I don't feel there is more danger to me, that is to my position, from a visit, than there wd have been in the marriage. However I will talk to Dr White about it again when he comes, & see if he can give me any more light upon the subject.

Sometimes, as I meet the warm hearted affectionate interest of some old lady-friends here, it pops into my head "Why not trust them & ask their counsel?" But, I draw back. I don't like to ask anybody. I feel not only reserved, but cautious about it.

Tom came back yesterday afternoon from an unsuccessful trip as far West as Montgomery. I am satisfied, however, at his having made the effort.

Do you know, John, how many fears I have about—*what* do you think? Now, pray don't you laugh, for I am "speaking the words of Truth & Soberness". Why, *about loving you too much.* I feel & fear intensely about that. I would certainly *desire* of all things that my love to you should be the strongest of all earthly affection. If you are ever to be my husband, if—but that I could not submit to—if, I was going to say, I didn't love you supremely, I wd earnestly endeavor to do it as a matter both of happiness & propriety; but I am so terribly controlled by my affection, that I want the high & steady & strong principle of love to God, to control *always* this master-passion of love to you. I want always to feel certain that *it* holds the reins, & that it guides and checks as secondary & subservient, all my attachment to you. You may think, that I love you *less* than you have seen others love. That may be; I don't know how much other people love. I don't know how much greater their capacity for loving may be than mine. I only know that I love you with all power of my heart, of my whole heart. And I fear that is too much. I am trying to bring it to its right position. I want to make it "know its place"; and, Darling, I want you to help me in the work. I shudder to think that yr love to me *cd* bring evil with it; & I pray that mine to you may not, in any way do you harm. Some day when you think of me & my anxieties & difficulties more than common, just throw your arm round me & draw me to you, & *pray* for me as tho' I were indeed your own self.

Dr Baker is here yet—preaching every day,—sometimes twice or three times a day. I like him much better than at first, as a mere preacher.

I met him for a moment somewhere the other evening, without his knowing who I was. However, yesterday, as he passed me in the aisle, I spoke, & he paused to tell me he wd like particularly to make my acquaintance. He had known Father—they were, he said, at College together, (I think he is mistaken) & he respected him much. I asked him to come to see me which he promised to do. I was not a little pleased at the old gentleman's manner to me. I never shall get entirely accustomed to the *deferential* look & manner of these *old* people to me. If I had been a thousand, the old Dr. couldn't have thrown more respect into his countenance. I observed it too, with Uncle William when in Fincastle. They may *talk* of me as they please, but when we meet face to face, I often observe this thing with them. But this all seems like mere vanity. It may be—but I think this demeanor from others to me, a cause for real gratitude.

Send me the buttons you are wearing. I send mine to you. Don't polish them at all, I want to get them from you a little dimmed.

God bless you—Affec'ly Yours
S.C.P. McDowell

Princeton, Sept 22nd [1856]

My dear Sally,

I love you the more for being a little proud but still it is mighty inconvenient. Don't you think your heart should have melted into a little more confidence all thro' these *winter* months in spite of this casing of pride. Don't you think these confessions ought to have stolen out to your lover at some sly time thro' some gap in the hedge. And Dearest, *now* you don't tell me everything. You say, "If I had ever felt at perfect liberty to speak my opinion of what seemed to me the true *course* in the matter &c" and yet even now you don't speak it. Indeed I am in some confusion as to what it really was. Putting some things together fr. other letters I would have inferred that you thought the safer & better course was to go on & marry. And yet in this very letter to-day you say, "Besides, John, in my case according to my perception & belief I did adopt for myself & you too the true course. Our different reasoning issued in the same conclusion". Now, my own Darling Sally, accepting the assurance I so often give you that you seem to me as my wife—that we seem like husband & bride kept separate from each other by some unholy spell—giving yourself up to my arms just as tho' you were my lawful wife & receiving in return the assurance that, *I am planning all my living for the next 40 years with the distinct* arrangement that there is to be a place for you,—banishing all the doubts which torment you & giving me that *last* proof of your affection that with some reason to doubt me (if you choose) you throw yourself entirely upon my truth, *do* tell me, I *"beg"* it, it seems you will do anything if I beg it: now Sally, with all the honour that it implies, I *beg* that you will treat me as your husband & regard yourself as already wooed & now treat the question of our marriage as happier families do the question of a new house or a return of the husband from sea as one altogether of expediency. My love would *riot* so upon that sort of nourishment, & it would tie me to you by bonds of passion the strength & temper of which I cannot even yet conceive.

Now as to myself, two unworthy courses might have been mine. One to have come back deceived as to my love & wavered as to the marriage from want of affection. I wont reply to such an idea. Your heart must be like poor "Legion"[41] in the gospel if you have any such conception.

Still I *will* say what I *know* you will believe me in, that one of the sadnesses I have lately felt (& pretty poignantly) is this, "Well, John, you have managed pretty successfully to make the very flower & centre of your age one of isolation & banishment, to give yourself a feeling of strained *expectation*—all thro' your better years, & to realize most bitterly some lady's remark when she heard of all our disappointment [']Well, poor things, *I pity them.*[']"

Now, as to the second unworthiness it might have been you seem to imply a preferring *on my own account* to delay. That you think would have been wrong. And yet, Sally, on my own account in a certain way I *did* prefer it. On account of my ministerial standing *I never yet have had a twinge.* I may be wrong but I never have. On myself as a citizen or on myself as a man or a Christian or even as *now* a father this thing has never for a moment weighed. But on myself as *reached thro' you,* on myself as mad for your affronts or shrinking with remorse for your social unhappiness I have thought a good deal—nay as your husband & the father of your children under the cloud of *your* injuries I have felt a good deal. Therefore, when Mrs H. said, "If you love that lady dont marry her" my heart instantly responded then if that be true, Dont marry her, for her own sake, & *if you love her,* dont marry her for *yours.* Is that unworthy, Sally? or a [wry] self-love? Perhaps it is a foolish truism for me to draw any such distinction. I think the whole truth lies somehow this way:—"The man does not suffer; it is the woman". "*No, no:*" must be the reply, "the man suffers *thro*" the woman, that is, in those relations of his life in wh. his happiness is wounded *in* hers & her offsprings. Now tell me what you think of all this; taking with you tho' the fact that I am never free from agitations as to the question, Whether it might not have been far happier for us

41. Mark 5:9, 15; Luke 8:30.

if we had married or if, Sally, had yielded to my first letter & given herself up so promptly that nothing could have interfered.

Now, as to the moral question, when I courted you that question was at rest. There *was* no such question in my mind. Now it is there of course with all its pros & cons. You know what reverses of information I have gone thro' in respect even to the facts in the case. My mind is always getting new light upon it; & lately I have thought more of the *desertion* matter & am disposed to make more of it than I formerly did. My opinion fortifies itself also in this way. In doubtful things, even if this were so, we are to hear the church, for Xt says, "Whatsoever ye shall bind on earth shall be bound in heaven."[42] I do not think this is a case even where he that doubteth is damned if he act, because this is an affair of duty. I have involved your affections & made an engagement & done that when no voice either within or without forbid me & therefore I am not at liberty to refrain from marrying just because there *is* a question & because in the very opinions of others there might be a margin of some doubt. That might forbid me to seek an engagement, but not forbid me to consummate it if you were involved.

Darling, my whole view of this matter is this. We love each other. We are engaged. We never mean to be otherwise. So long as the safety of your high taste & your social safety demand it let us forbear to marry. Let us be to each other all we can be without it. *Let us visit.* That is my opinion. Let us assert our engagement before all comers & have it understood. If any one says, It will hurt you more than the marriage, *deny it.* It is not so. Still, if *you* say it will hurt you very *near* as much or at all seriously then my course is taken. I will not visit you. Let us form all our plans for a happy future—if not in this world, why—Darling—in a better. I am prepared for this sort of life & have steeled myself to a long exile. If you fear bankruptcy & are brot to desire so extreme a measure I will be your trustee—that is I will be the same as a trustee using you for what is executive & taking regular steps thro' years to save all for you I can of your estate. Meanwhile I will study philosophy & try to get possession of Allamby. If we die, why, Darling, after seeing each other at intervals thro a term of years, that will be all of our pleasures. If we live why we will finish the troubled journey together. Kiss me Darling. All this in subordination to Providence who *has* helped us both & who will help us in time to come.

But one word more. I do not mean by all this to *exclude* the idea of marriage. My love, if you approve it & can out of your high region of prudish modesty get to me the idea that you approve it—it would fill me with a glow of the most fascinating interest & I should with a new element of hope & a strong glow of agitated affection enter with you on the test whether we may really do it.

God bless you my own beloved Sally. You are dearer to me than ever. That letter in which you rap me on the fingers for a little P.O. attention to you (& which is of course very agreeable to me to think of) charmed me with its piety.

42. Matt. 16:18, 18:18.

I have a treasure in you, my love. Only God, like my own poor Father, seems to have given you to me very much as he gave me a willow tree with liberty to think about it, but not to go much where it was & above all not to get up into its weeping & affectionate caresses. But what a long letter. Darling, thaw all the ice in your heart, & go on telling me a thousand things you have been keeping from me.

Yours Truly,
Jno Miller.

Colalto,
Tuesday, Sepr 23. 1856

Do you know, John, that one thing that makes me love you so much, is yr forbearance with me. If, when I worry you, you should get mad & speak sharply as *I* am apt to do, we should, long ago, have parted by mutual consent. But, when you quickly rebuke me without any passion even tho' I feel you may be hurt, you master me completely. No matter, how small the matter may be, I am ashamed of my conduct in it, and annoyed at myself. I would be sorry too—I am in a certain way, sorry to have worried you in the least—yet I am scarcely sorry to find out, even in such ways, new occasions & new reasons for loving you. I have often noticed this in you, & always with fresh admiration & love. I have never that I remember, been mean enough to take advantage of it & allow myself deliberately to say any thing that would wound you. Indeed I can't recollect ever, either in speaking or writing, having, but once, permitted myself to utter a word that I even suspected might pain you. You cannot think even in trifles that I am indifferent or careless as to yr feelings. I suffer more, perhaps, in being the offender than you do from the offense. But then, John, you always stand out from under the annoyances & unreasonableness of my temper so calmly & properly, that involuntarily I respect & love you. Indeed, I don't know but that you should vote me yr thanks for placing the picture in so becoming a light.

Your letter of the 20th owing to some carelessness at the Office here, was late getting to me this morning. I felt disappointed that it did not come earlier; but it was just as pleasant & then it did come. Do lecture me well, whenever you see I need it; which is often enough no doubt. There is nobody to do it but you; and if you want me to be as good as any poor sinner can be, pray use all the means in yr hand—they are neither few nor weak.

Tom has decided pretty much to go to Missouri. I am sorry he has; but am not inclined to interpose objections. He must *buy* his experience himself. Poor fellow! he seems so sad at the thoughts of going tomorrow. Lilly too is troubled by it; & my heart has another weight put upon it. I hope the Lord will take care of him. I am more and more confident of His faithfulness to his Covenant-engagements. I have a mournful sort of feeling creeping over me at Tom's going, that I have not had before. He seems thrown without shelter of any kind upon the world. It is true, he is old enough, and indeed ought, long ago, to have been pushing his way in the world, yet I can't get rid of these feelings.

I shant write tomorrow morning for I shall have some little things of Tom's to fix; and tonight I am hardly fit to write, being both tired & sick—my eyes & head can neither do much service now.

I do long, John, to talk to you often, about things I can't talk to others about. I want to tell you of mental disquietudes that agitate me very greatly. I have a natural turning to you as the depository of all my anxieties of every kind. But, you know, writing is a poor channel of communication for such things, and often as I purpose writing, almost as often I abandon the attempt. I am not alluding to any class of anxiety that need arouse any disquieting feeling with you. To be sure our relations are always a prolific cause of excitement to me. I fear, I am making an idol of you. I pray against it, but somehow as week after week passes, I find my affection not diminished, but augmented. When I think as I often do, that God as a mere test of faith, demands you at my hands—oh how I shrink from the full surrender. But good night. I cant write more. God bless you my precious John.

Affec'ly
S.C.P. McDowell

Wednesday 6 A.M.

As you percieve I am taking a minute or so from our morning hour, but it is just to give one more expression of affection before I send off my letter, which I do much earlier than usual. You cant tell how full my heart is of love to you. So far from wishing to conceal it from you as I often used to feel, I am pained that I cant tell you as I wd like how much I love you.

You laugh at my slow knitting. I have a pr of socks nearly finished for Allie wh I have half a notion to send that he may try them before I knit any more. I can knit him a pr in less than two days, but I only pick up that sort of work at odd times.

Affec'ly Yours,
S.C.P. McD.

Princeton Sept 25th 1856.

My *darling Sally*,

It is really becoming almost *comfortable* to write to you. The *act* makes me nervous & impatient, but the thing written is so exquisitely congenial to me. It is so *true* that I love you & just to repeat it over in ever varying forms & find my love having new hues just like these fruits at every season of the year is wondrously captivating. I predict that you & I will love each other with an uncommon *constancy*. Tho' our love is bred under hardships yet it is not a hardship bred by love. It is not the interruption of chafing & altercation such as so often comes when people are actually married. It is a love baptized by sorrow & I think we already love each other more than most married people. You ask me, "John, how much do you really think I love you". Sally, I have put away all doubt on that subject. I know you are much too proud for me to venture it. But still I will! I believe, my Dear, you love me with a passionate fondness. Come, Sally, if it isnt so, don't leave me under such an awkward mistake. Tell me in your next letter if it is not so. I believe our troubles have bound us together till we have passed the power to recall what we have given to each other. Indeed, Sally, I think a little with the Major that there is a wildness about our passion that makes us dependant now on each other almost for life itself. Now Dearest, write whether this is so.

You seem to me so congenial in your tastes & sense of honour. Have you observed no similarity between us in these respects? Your letters *lately* are *so* much after my mind—that at this late day & when tried all round your honour should seem never to sleep but to maintain itself under all possible experiences. And yet, Sally, you say you *ought* to love me. Tell me, Dearest, is your love at all cherished in this way or am I right in considering it a wild passion?

I send you the buttons. But I give them to you only on certain conditions. Recollect they are not yours & it is dishonest to appropriate them unless you comply. I conjure you to deal solemnly with me in these agreements. 1st That when you put them on it shall be the clasping of your chains *to me*. I send them as *fetters*. You are not to put them on unless you are to be considered my *bond* woman—sold over to another body & mind—<u>mine</u> in that most solemn & tender way in which the only owners of you are (not yourself, but) God & I. As entirely my property as a little fluttering heart & a lovely tasteful woman *can* be the property of another. Indeed, Sally, I have a most Oriental notion of the bliss just of *owning* you as tho' you were a part of this beautiful first house of ours & the great swarth [of] rocks that rise in the midst of it were not more helplessly my property than you are. Come Sally, have you passion enough to give up your own proper ownership. If not you musnt put on the buttons. You must send 'em back. If *so* then remember there are certain things my pretty liege which you must not do. You must not talk about your being an injury to me or my giving you up. You must not talk about whether it is right for you to continue our relations. You must not speak about your last tie being murdered, your last pretty limb being "cut off". You must quit talking on all those subjects. You must consider yourself if deceived or in any way mistaken in my love or in my faith as hopelessly lost & just give yourself up to all the hazards of a supreme faith in me whatever my faith to you. You must consider yourself like poor Hannibal with your ships burnt behind you & then if lost & deceived like him nevertheless as having ventured all in your passion for me.[43] If I am *true* then your instincts have served you & you are safe in my passionate affection, if your instincts have deceived you still it is too late to retract & after you put on these buttons you pass by the period

---

43. Hannibal (247?–183? B.C.), a Cathaginian general in the Second Punic War. After landing his army in Europe, he ordered his ships burned to prevent his soldiers from returning home.

of *thought* & give yourself up as having ventured all of your being. Come, Sally, do you agree—That is your first promise.

Then Secondly, you promise to *abandon* all those painful doubts which have been agitating you in respect to my affection—to take up the load of our separation as the only load of a serious kind wh. we bear to write me no more sad letters.—to feel: "John is not deceiving me but if he is, it is so hopelessly bad that no care or thought on my part can retrieve it & just to *trust* me as tho' we were indeed one flesh, & as tho' our counselings like the judgments of God *must* govern us & we can only submit.["] If there be any bliss I have on earth it is the thought of hopeful study & usefulness in companionship with you. No body can be more honoured than you are by a sense of emptiness & loneliness & absence *always* in the conditions I love the best. My life now is an *endurance* & it seems melancholy to me that the centre of my life should be one of expectancy & suspense. Now, Darling, will you not give up all anxieties & just fall into my arms & repose upon me as if I were fidelity itself. Tell me (when you write) whether you will.

Then, Thirdly, I exact this (and by the way, when you write you may of course make your exactions & make conditions for *your* buttons, but I thot of it first & so take mine separately) you will write at the transition but I exact *this:*—*that you go to bed at 9 1/2 o'clock.* Recollect, Sally, you shant have the buttons unless you comply. *As a habit* you are to go to bed at 9 1/2 o'clock. Your health is worn upon & this is my defence of my own claim to you in that direction. Nothing prostrates me so as late hours. Your low spirits each morn are partly that. This may make the whole difference between good & bad health, beauty & old age when I come to marry you. *Do you promise?* Here I break off. Moth[er] calls me for a drive.

Yours fondly,
JM.

Colalto
Thursday Sep. 25. 1856.

My *dear John,*

I am writing in the full glare of noonday; and feel as strangely about it as tho' a hot sun & a bright light had no business to be prying into my letters to you. It seems a down right impertinance, strongly akin to eaves-dropping.

I thank you so much for all you say and propose about my property matters. But why should you feel it necessary to speak *to me* with so much caution? Do you have the least fear I shall misconstrue your motives, or not understand them, or be offended at your offers? It is very late in the day for such fears to spring up, if they do exist. I am, perhaps, a little rampant under P.O. advancements, but then, you know that—wasn't so very wrong after all. No; I am greatly obliged to you, and much inclined to accept, tho' not willing to accede to *all* your requirements— as, for instance, I cannot agree that you shall, in cases of loss from yr advice, make up that loss from yr own funds. These pecuniary troubles are a great burden to me. I am so anxious to be freed from them. But then, John, they would be a great trouble to you, for you are so distant from all my scattered pieces of property.

You are worried that while I make so many plans, I am still sitting still. That is precisely the trouble with me. I am willing to sell distant lands to meet my liabilities. I am willing to practice any personal economy that will be necessary; but when I think of *where* I am to live then I am without ability to plan any longer. I want to get rid of the expense and annoyance of this great house with its infirmary of sick negroes. I can't live here by myself. I am not willing to ask any one to find a home with me, first because it might by & by prove a trouble & restraint to us both; & then, would increase my expenses. I want to rent my house, but where then am I to go? and for how long? I can't board in town—I fancy the scandal & tittle-tattle of a little village like this is too serious for *me* to be exposed to. Our family has always kept aloof from it, by living on this inaccessible hill. Even a small house, if it could be rented, wd still fix me in bonds to these invalid servants, & still entail more expense than is pleasant upon me. Then as to going to Susan's or Mary's to spend a year! I couldn't do it. I might divide the winter between them, but when the summer comes, & Lilly wants a home & I am sighing for one too, where are we to go? I, too am very averse to wasting my time as a visitor. However, in a matter of necessity likings & dislikings are not much considered.

When I give up my home here, I am depriving Lilly & myself too of a home just when it is most important.

I am hampered as no other woman is. I feel that constantly. It is not for *me* to go about where I please. I am subject to remark & scrutiny; and am in such circumstances, that I am too proud to accept any other than the mere courtesies of life from any body. If I send Lilly to Richd, I would like to go with her: But the city is full of acquaintances, who would be ready & pressing in their offers of hospitality &c, &c. These offers wd subject me to two very unpleasant difficulties. I must accept all & thereby be thrown too much & too frequently into society; or accept none & thereby be thrown out of all. And here again if I should be willing to receive them, I am, every woman is, dependent upon the attentions of gentlemen, in many ways that, of course, you at once perceive. I am exceedingly averse to placing myself in a position to make these necessary. There is no human being in Rich that I would consent should stand Sponsor for me in Society.—Nor is there, any where else.

John Atkinson, who was here yesterday, proposes to me to send Lilly to Mr Major[44] in Geo Town, & take rooms with her for myself. This wd have some, tho fewer, of the objections I have been talking of; and, in truth, as it presents the fairest front of any of my previous schemes I am rather seriously considering it. I wrote this morning to Mr Major for his Circular, & when it comes, shall have

---

44. A school in Georgetown.

some guide at least in the matter of expense. I feel hurried to a decision as the frost whitens the ground in the morning, & the wind moans thru' the house.

I think I need scarcely[45] yr exhortation to more entire confidence. If I were your wife I could hardly go buzzing into yr ears any more than I do now of all that concerns me. I wonder you don't sometimes express a wee bit of impatience. For an impatient man, bent upon his own way, you seem wonderfully patient under the trials I subject you to. John, you are an odd sort of man any how. You manage me as you please; & I never know until I have actually done what you wanted, that I never intended to do it; & never thought of such a thing as permitting you to order and control me in such a way. That first lesson in Washington, was the "conquering whipping", tho' it was about a little thing.

"You are going to walk this morning?" You asked with an impressive sort of quietness.

"Yes; after a little while". Some minutes passed & the walk seemed forgotten. I suppose I was not very anxious for it at any rate.

But again—"You will walk this morning?" with more emphasis.

"O Yes! presently". Again a long pause; then suddenly with very polite decision, "You will put on yr bonnet, & we will go now."

I never had another thought, & never knew one other earthly thing till I was out in the street, & it was too late then when my senses came back to even think of resistance. I am mad now—or wd be, if I wasnt amused at the recollection of how you just moved me about as you have seen toy geese in a bowl of water, made to bob about after the magnet in a child's hand. I never made you come round to my will,—because, some how I never had any will for you to come round to. But it's no hardship that to me. I am very happy often in having a Master to guide & direct;—so happy, that I think it selfish to keep all the pleasure to myself, & would generously offer you a chance now & then at such experience. Wont you "swop" places with me some of these days? Never mind I'll come down upon you like Cousin Virginia all of a sudden, & scatter you in a jiffy. And I'll do just like her. I'll sink my voice to its lowest & sweetest tone and look at you with the gentlest of smiles and say *Dearest*," & at the very same moment I'll be stirring up the whole house into a bedlam, and pouring fire upon yr brain.

I am going over to pay a visit or two to some strangers. I hate to visit, & get off from all regular visiting of the town people by attending to their guests. This summer I have not used the carriage at all, & when I see a stranger whom I must attend to, immediately I am weak in the knees. That tiresome walk breaks many a hospitable tie. Old Dr. Baker said when he came over the other evening, "Such a bad walk, madam; so many stiles!" (Observe *I* spell the word right; (for a wonder!) & remember *you* spelt it wrong.) But good bye till I get back.

45. The number "2" is superimposed over "need" and the number "1" over "scarcely," as if to reverse their order in the sentence.

9 P.M.

My ladies were not in when I called. I was rather sorry as I lost the effect of my "best bib & tucker" upon them. When I take the trouble to dress I like to be fully rewarded for it.

I was pleasantly surprised this morn'g by a visit from Cousin Ballard Preston, Sec'y of the Navy under Genl Taylor. I am not particularly fond of him, but have received most cordial attention from him for a number of years. His Father was Gov Preston, a younger brother of my Grandfather, a most amiable & excellent gentleman.[46] He served in the last War, & was severely wounded at Plattsburg & very lame, in consequence, all his life. It was not a great while after this exploit that he was made Gov, on which occasion John Randolph said of him:— "This is a case in wh an ounce of lead outweighs a pound of brains". As you may judge, he was not renowned for his cleverness. I have a notion that none of those old Prestons (the men, I mean, were remarkable for mind except the youngest who was Cousin John's father. But the women were all so with perhaps a single exception. Aunt Floyd, was a wonder. My Grandmother McDowell too was a woman of eminent good sense—Aunt Hart, likewise. Aunt Madison too, was greatly admired for very superior conversational ability: she was a beauty besides.[47] There were several others of inferior grade. The women were clever & the men handsome. I am not sure, that these peculiarities are not to be found even in the present generation. By the bye have you read that article in the last Westminster Review on "Inheritance"? I am quite anxious to get it from hearing Uncle William speak of it—so if you have a copy, or can lay yr hands upon one, send it to me. I hear the same article appears in the last Eclectic, but I rarely see that now.[48]

By an old Spanish grant, recently allowed by Congress, Uncle John, in right of his Wife, has come into possession of from 40 to 60.000 acres of Louisiana land valued at about $100 per acre! He is already a millionaire.[49] Such a stupendous fortune! But I dont think I wd have Old Hamptons blood in my children's veins for the whole of it. Aunt Caroline is a fine woman & so is her Mother; but that horrid old father wd taint ten generations at least. When I was at the Homas (Uncle John's sugar plantation above New Orleans) I used to shudder at the thought of being in the same house where Old Genl Hampton had lived. I found out, however, he never had been there, as Uncle John had built the house. He

46. President Zachary Taylor (1784–1850) had been a general in the Mexican War. Ballard Preston's father was Gov. James Patton Preston (1774–1843).

47. Francis Preston's sisters included Letitia Preston Floyd (1779–1852), Sarah Preston McDowell, Susannah Preston Hart, and Elizabeth Preston Madison (1762–1837).

48. The *Westminster Review* was published in both New York and London from 1824 to 1914. The *Eclectic Review* was published in London from 1805 to 1868.

49. John Smith Preston married Caroline Martha Hampton (1807–1883), daughter of Gen. Wade Hampton (1752–1835), a wealthy planter and congressman from South Carolina, and his third wife, Mary Cantey (1780–1863).

was a perfect monster of wickedness; & yet his children & grandchildren aspire to the first stand in America.

I have written you a gossipping sort of letter, not untainted by scandal.

With all my heart Yours
S.C.P. McDowell.

Friday Morning

I wrote a half a page or so last night about our postponed marriage; but concluded to let the whole subject alone for a day or two. I am so fearful of saying anything that might be wrong in its influence upon you or any one else. I am like my Father in such things. Aunt Benton used to say of him, "Oh James is so afraid of doing wrong that he lets the time for doing right pass from him".

Did you get a letter from me enclosing one from James? And now, I think of it, did I ever send you an engraving of my Father?

Thank Maggie for her letter, which I will answer, when I think she has a pretty sharp appetite, & can relish such plain fare as I must set before her. By the bye John, don't ask her ever again for my letters. You see there's nothing in them & it looks so absurd in you to be asking for such things.

Princeton Sept 27th 1856

My own dear Sally,

You cant tell what pleasure it gives me to hear you expressing your love so tenderly. It is a species of auricular confession that I think has no harm in it & of wh. I like to be made the priest. Indeed, Sally, we are coming to a time when we are falling into each other's possession without any of those reserves which pride or a kind of separate self-respect feels itself bound always to keep up. You seem to have come to a time when you love to tell me you love me & Sally if you knew how forlorn I am you would prepare for me this generous kind of pleasure in every letter that you hereafter write. If we are ever separated—if we are ever torn apart, or become driven from each others embrace or injured by either's unfaithfulness then of course you will revolt at all the tenderness you ever have shown me. Then, Dearest, the abandon with which you are blind to this & with which you genuinely give up all fear of me in every respect, in which you yield yourself to my possession without one fear that I will ever deceive you is a fine tribute of your love. Oh how I do revel in it. It is like the gifts of *kings*. It makes me love you so, to see you forgetting yourself in me. And, Darling, it is not a selfish love either. How *could* I be reconciled to any thing different. If I am worth loving, that is, if I have an unalterable *sealed* affection—a purpose wrought into it of the foremost temper to seek you as my wife & to follow that eager waiting if it leads me to the very limit of the grave how *could* I be satisfied that you should be different—that you should be building safeguards for yourself that I know are suited for some other being than I am & that you should lie in my arms with that constrained wakeful endlessly guarded disquiet which wears upon your strength & is so useless a loss of a higher & more generous happiness.

Sally, suppose *as a great gift to me* you allow your affection to ravish from you for me the last trace of your self-reserve & have no more cautions & no more concealed feelings & no more shielded pride but indulge a species of love in which giving up your pride to me is a pleasure—in which you *have* no pride & no distinctiveness of nature or character to keep up in the eye of your lover— in which we are moulded together & however we defend ourselves against the world cease to do so against ourselves; and if you think all this is unsafe & after having made you dependant upon me for your self-respect & received the very last expressions of your passion & having rifled your heart of everything that a proud woman might wish to retain even from a husband as a last admission of her dependance upon him for her happiness—I might after all be driven off or drawn off or be cherishing some lasting reserve—Sally, if you think anything like this, then make the throwing down of your defence against it & a generous taking of the risk or still better a passionate forgetting that there is any risk at all your *gift* to me, Sally, of spontaneous affection. I don't know whether you understand me, & yet you must for your letters are (or *have* been) full of what I want you to abandon & you have absolutely kept from me for a year an admission which a year ago would have helped me to make you so much happier.

Besides, Sally, it would clear your mind on other parts. It would reconcile you to the dismalnesses of yr position. It would make you less dependant on your friends. It would be giving you a path with *some* flowers upon it that would last you quite to the grave. And as I take it a passionate love such as mine, Darling, is at least to a woman more than half of life it would be repaying you more than all for everything of social friendship or kindred that you may happen to give up.

You may think, Darling, I am an exacting lover especially for one who feels himself denied the usual priveleges of one but would you have me less exacting, or would you be pleased if in all the points I have mentioned I were less easily satisfied.

Write in your next just all that you think of what I have written & tell me whether I may flatter myself of the Currency of such an all trusting & surrendering devotion.

Evening 6 3/4 o clock

I intended to read this when I came in, but the mail prevents me. I do hope Sally the lowest point of your spirits has been touched & that you will be more comforted hereafter. God bless you. Write me *long* letters & throw away all reserve & write your *tho'ts* for you know you & I are the same forever.

Yours affly
Jno Miller.

Colalto,
Saturday Sep: 27. 1856.

My dear John,

You must remember that when I am frankly telling you my opinion as to our marriage that I am only doing as you ask—"treating it, as happier families wd the building of a house, &c, &c, as a thing of expediency." I am looking at it thro' one pair of glasses; *you* are seeing it thro' another. I am using simply the right that belongs to me of standing on an *equal* footing with you in the matter—not usurping anything, nor abandoning anything;—not claiming, & yet not yielding anything because I am a woman, &, by courtesy, might ask some things, & by common usage, *must not* mention others. We stand, as you intimate, like *married people*, who are *alike* interested in what we are talking about.

First then, I did yield to the postponement of our marriage for the reason I have given: I thought you were not willing for it, & for the reason that you have only *repeated* in one of yr late letters. I did not think the reason, under the circumstances, such as *my* mind would have seized upon & held, but since it was a strong one with you & I feared wd sway yr feelings to me afterward, I retreated from the marriage. You observed it at the time that I did not accept it as controlling my mind & asked me if I were in your place if I wouldn't act differently. I replied evasively as to my own opinion, but, I believe, directly as to yours, something to this effect—that if I held yr opinions I would act upon them as you did—Now John, nearly a year has passed since then, and I have gone thro' every variety of feeling, and have seen the working of public opinion on this thing, and I say still, my opinion is stronger under the actual trial than then when we were theorizing about the future. That future is, to an extent, sufficient for a fair experiment, the past now, and I am only confirmed in the views then presented by my mind. *We committed a great mistake in consenting to any delay, if there was then no conscientious* interposition; if there was, then we should thank God for stopping things where they then were.

Since you were shaping your course with reference to my feelings & my happiness, & to yours as touched thru' mine, & not in answer to other influences wh, to tell you the truth, at that moment I could not have acknowledged honorable, I can speak more freely just here. Mrs Hunter's remark—"if you love that lady don't marry her"—was, to my mind entirely out of place. She is a looker on; I am the actor in the scene. *She supposes— I know.* It came too late. If she had said this to you when she first heard of our engagement it would have been well enough. "But," you say, "she had not then the least of idea of the strength of public opposition which she afterwards had." That is true. But, she knew there would [be] some opposition—she knew there would be *much* difficulty, and she did not weigh fairly both sides of the question before the exigence came. She thought, it may have been kindly for me, I don't know—but any how she thought, "that lady will lose her position, & destroy John's happiness & prospects if this marriage goes on: he ought to love her enough & regard himself enough not to be willing to allow that." She did not turn to think "What becomes of the lady if the marriage *is* stopped? Is her position not already affected by this public committal? Is she to be left to struggle alone against this strong tide of public disfavor? Is her happiness not *as* likely to suffer from the retreat as it wd do from the going on? Are her prospects battered or otherwise by this course of proceeding? In either event the man does not materially suffer from the world's censure, but *in both* the women does,—now, which of the two is the *least* likely to injure her?" She was wrong in her judgment as to the *best* for *me* certainly, all things considered *outside* of your feelings. I would, knowing now, as none can know perhaps but me, all the woman has to bear in such a case, have given far different advice. John, I pray you wont think me indelicate in speaking so plainly. You urge me to be perfectly candid & I am prompted by my own feelings to be so. I am not ashamed of having such feelings as I am telling you of; I only shrink from expressing them, because it looks as if I were pleading for the marriage. However if you *can* suspect me of such an unwomanly thing, why you will just have to do it; for *now* I am going to tell you my whole mind as to this matter—that is, as far as I can do it in writing. I think the truest *delicacy even,*—certainly the truest principle, is in perfect honesty.

I would have counselled you thus.—"If you love that lady marry her. This opposition only makes stronger all her claims upon you. You should, in this public exposure throw over her the mantle of yr protection. You should draw her to your side, and defend her under the title, the authority of which all must admit. You should, guard her, as none but her husband could do, against all assaults upon her feelings,—" &c. &c. If I had been *without* position, & looked to a marriage with you to give me one; if I had deceived you, in any particular in regard to my character & circumstances, and thus seduced you into an engagement; if I had been guilty of any of the evils laid to my charge; if I had from any unworthy motive lent myself to the marriage, why upon the discovery of any of these unworthinesses of course, you wd have been discharged. If, at a late moment, scruples as to yr ministerial duty, had arisen; then too, I should have counseled differently. If, even, under the representations of others, conscientious difficulties upon the morality of the marriage had been awakened at the last hour; then again, I should have urged you to stop short. But—

I had a position fully equal, in spite of all the past, to your own. I felt it was *abating* not *increasing* the dignity and safety of it to exchange it with all its isolation, for that of your wife: I had been honest, not only in speaking of all that concerned me, but, had frequently exhibited to you the difficulties suggested by my mind, that might follow upon your marriage with me under existing circumstances: I was innocent of all the charges hurled against me by the most devilish insanity: And I loved you:—You felt no anxiety as to yr Ministry: then, upon all these grounds you were safe in forming the marriage no matter how the world stormed. I am not so sure, as to the conscientious difficulty. I dont know how great it was, or with any definite information, what the nature of it is. However, if it was serious it *ought* to outweigh every other call upon you. The marriage cd neither be proper nor happy where it existed.

But you feared for me—feared your own happiness as assailed thro' mine. I dont wonder at it. I always thought, it was almost ungenerous in me to be willing to allow you to be thus assailed. But, John, I forewarned you; and yet I felt even in the face of all, that, if we loved one another & cd be certain that we were not acting against the law & will of God, we might still bear up against it, &, in time over-ride these storms.

In the same way I felt for our children. My children must always have a certain degree of pain in my history. This sort of sorrow will be their inheritance: it is entailed upon them, & I cant cut it off. But if *I* do what it right, I have no very great fear of any harm being done them. I would *not tempt* Providence, but I can trust God for myself & them, if I have his sanction for *my* acts. I would, of course, be most anxious to know what the right & true course for *me* is; having determined that I can safely & cheerfully leave all the consequences to God. If I can trust him for myself & you, I certainly can for such unreal and visionary beings as our children,—and, should they ever have an actual existence, for such real beings as they will then become. If nothing else is sure, the blessings of the Covenant are; & they are, to *christians and their children.* So we need, after all, to be specially earnest in settling this whole question rightly for our own selves. The interests of these hypothetic personages are all mingled with our own, that we could not if we would separate them, and they are so dear to us both that we are not likely to forget or disregard them.

Looking back, I think our decision a wrong judgment. My happiness has certainly not been promoted by it. My position certainly has not been strengthened [by] it. But it was not the less a decree of Providence, than if it had been the wisest course even according to Man's wisdom. As such I recognize it; and painful as all these months have been, I feel sure they have taught me some lessons that have benefited me, and that may benefit me more in time to come. I suffer much still, but I am acquiescent, and desire to commit this whole thing absolutely to God. I have been so terribly anxious to have my mind free from the faintest shadow upon the moral question involved in the whole affair, that I cant always decide whether I am not helped by the delay of our plans. I pray over it & think about it, but without very clear increase of wisdom. I therefore commit it to a Higher Power and am ready to wait till He shall bid us go forward.

I talk very little to any one about our plans—indeed have never disclosed them fully to any body. Cousin John never alludes even remotely to them to me nor I to him. Besides him I have no friend here to whom I wd speak. Dr White knows only what you choose to tell him.

I have written away, as thoughts came into my mind, & without any care or arrangement of them, & fear you will have some difficulty in getting at my meaning. I cant re-write my letter tho'. If you dont understand me tell me when you write again.

Your letter with the buttons came safely this morning. You're too late with yr conditions. The buttons have been mine a long time already. You're a polite fellow! I shant have the buttons unless I'll wear them as a badge of servitude! You must be my "bond-woman"! Not I, forsooth! A "bond-woman"! Why Man, *what are you talking about*. If to be your wife is to be a slave; and if to be yr betrothed wife is to be a bond-woman, I shall just scamper out of these fetters & chains of our engagement in a hurry.

John you do make such horrid bad puns. If I had the pure zeal of yr friend Dungan, I wd session you for it. John hold my paper up to the light & see if you can count the number of times I've jabbed my pen thro' it. Wont you send me a blunt pen to go along with this thin paper.

What do you call me when you speak of me? I dont know why, but I am curious to know.

Several times lately you refer to newly discovered traits of character, in my letters. I am puzzled to know what you allude to, & feel[50] disappointed at my inability to recall what I said, or remember what I did. But then I am so glad I cant; for, whenever you see these things peeping out again you will be sure to have them in their full, pure nature. Not knowing what they are, I shall never be tempted to affect them on any occasion; or thrust them upon you just to call forth yr admiration. So don't tell me, unless you shd sometimes think my *humble* opinion of myself needed encouragement.

Why, John, you are so absurd in yr requirements. You say I am not to write you any more *sad* letters. Suppose I cant write any other kind—am I not to write any? or am I to affect gayety when I dont feel it? And am I never to come to tell you my troubles? Why, if I am to be debarred all this, I might as well just let somebody else have my little man. And I am never to have any more *doubts* of *you* either! Dear me! if you were to take them all away of a sudden I should be so light Id soon mount away out of yr sight. Did you ever hear of that henpecked husband who became so thin under his grievances that he had to put 25 cents in his pocket to keep him from flying away? Well, I should be like him. Go to bed at half-past nine too! Did ever! My own precious darling, love of a turtle dove I am afraid you're losing yr senses.

But I'll tell you what I'll do. I'll do the best I can with these spirits of mine, & these doubts & my health and good looks. Cousin Va used to sleep day & night to keep herself young and handsome; & she succeeded; but I think we must do something else in this world beside look pretty.

I went out at 3 1/2 this afternoon to a meeting at the lecture-room, and am finishing my letter to-night. Such strange things do happen in this world. I am going to tell you one. I don't know that I ought exactly, yet I will. As I was coming

---

50. McDowell repeated "feel."

over home this afternoon, Cousin John joined me and we came on very pleasantly. Latterly his reserve has worn off a good deal and our old relations seemed almost wholly re-established. He comes oftener to see me & seems altogether himself; so that I rarely of late had any feeling of worry excited by his manner. You remember, I told you I had, some time ago. Well, we walked along very cosily until we got to that stile, where I ran off from you that famous Sunday night, when suddenly he put his hand on my shoulder, as I walked rather in advance of him, & said, "Sally, tell me what are your relations with Dr Miller now?" I was exceedingly startled & a little mystified by this "Doctor", but turned full upon him and said "Do you mean John Miller, Cousin John?" "Yes." "Why do you ask?" said I. "Because", he answered as nearly as I can recollect, "if they remain unchanged I can come to see you as often as I please". I told him, ["]they were unchanged but there need not be any difficulty in his coming to see me—why would there be?" He said—"Well, it is a shield to me to know that you belong to another. And you know you fascinate every body, etc, etc,." I was astonished—but I am so glad we are thus safely grounded in our old friendship. I dont think there was any great reason for this caution on his part, for there is no very emmenant danger of his ever being willing to enter the lists with you. Do you think, John, he could have imagined I should fall in love with him, & was protecting me against that mistake. How mad I wd be if I could think so. But I dont think any such thing, and I do love him, for he has always been so kind and affectionate, & I am glad in the future that things will go on straight with us. He will never have any more thought of me than if I were yr wife; & I shall not be discomforted by thinking that, perhaps he might. Is there any thing wrong in my telling you this?

I have written you a tremendous letter. Oh John! let me tell you one thing before I stop. You dont know what awful *readings* yr bad writing subjects you to. The other day there was this sentence in yr letter—"You dont know how my love wd *riot* on such nourishment". I read along "You dont know how my love wd"—Gracious! thought I, what an *uggy*[51] word!—& how odd;—"would"— yes—there it stands in black & white,—"would *rot* on such" &c. What do you think of that John?

If I can, on Monday when I send off my letter I want to put one of Ally's socks in it. Let him try it on, & see how it feels. I will keep the other for a measure & make in the others any alterations you suggest. They are not fine, but quite fine enough to wear well & keep him warm. I imagine it wd be a fantastic piece of folly in me to send the child, just for their looks, socks that wd be of no use to him. Anyhow if he was my child, he wouldn't get any better if as good; and that settles the matter.

When you read one of these long, "scrappy" letters (what elegant language you use!) of mine, do I ever seem to be talking to you? Do I ever seem near enough for you to look right into my face as I speak? You are a constant presence to me—an

51. McDowell meant "ugly."

invisible companion. I love you with all my heart. Pray for me, my own Darling, that I may not love you too much. Nine o'clock is coming, & you know I've got my orders, (wh I only mean to mind some times) so Goodnight.

God bless you. Yours
S.C.P. McDowell

Monday 8 1/2 A.M.

I add a line or two this morning. My opinion about our marriage difficulties is given simply as an opinion: it is not meant to control our plans. You are to feel yrself as free to follow yr own as you were before mine was given. I did not express my views at the formative period—indeed, I could not have done it any earlier than the present time, without subjecting myself to misconception. You needed to have all the knowledge of me that these last 10 months has given before you would have listened with any patience and without some disgust at such plain talk as mine has, of late, been. I feel quite sure you will not misunderstand me now. Indeed, John I think you will see from it all that I have loved you much more than you ever believed. If I didn't love you very sincerely & candidly now, you could not have extorted all this from me, even if I *could* have submitted my judgment to yours in the first instance. But I am glad to have told it all to you. I am keeping back nothing. I could *tell* you more, if you were at my side, but it wd all be of the same sort—nothing new. Hereafter, I shall feel free to express any difference of sentiment with you; and I shall be all the happier, in our forlorn sort of happiness from this entire unreserve and candour.

Now John, tell me all you think of my behavior in this thing: tell me honestly. I wont send Ally's sock. I'm in a hurry & cant fix it up!

Affec'ly,
S.C.P. McDowell.

PART NINE

"So, good bye My dear Mrs McDowell."

September 1856–October 1856

Princeton Sept 27th[1] 56
Sunday

My *dear Sally,*

I have a *rule*, not always well kept whenever I am to settle any important step to hold a day of special inquiry & prayerful meditation in respect to my duty. Such days I have kept repeatedly lately in respect to you & when a letter more than commonly sad has come to my hand I have given up the morning or the Sabbath as the case might be to such thots & then felt that *that* time ought very much to decide my opinion. When you say that my affection rather than "sympathy" has been given to you I am reminded that much of these meditations led in the same way & led to thoughts which so far I have kept *secret* & this has given a silence on these vexed subjects to my letters. I have been keeping such a season to day & my reason for it was the sadness that filled my mind after your letter. That sentence that these "difficulties are making sad inroads on your strength" just touched me on one point on which I am most sadly anxious; indeed your letter seems to me as almost the limit of despair & perhaps it is time that I should break a secret which heretofore I have not thought it wise to tell.

You remember weeks ago I spoke of wandering out in the woods on Sunday night. I wrote to you how I had resolved that as your life & mine was now united I must insist when your trouble became extreme on coming to your relief. I went much further at that time & have since & to day my thots fall in the same old channel. I have just destroyed a long closely written letter telling you what this channel is. The whole subject embarrasses me.

1. The date should be Sept. 28.

801

You must know I think your moneyed difficulties much more serious than you do yourself. I will not go over the painful strain for wh. I destroyed the other letter. But recollect. You have a ward. If you become a bankrupt, it may waste your health. That is the worst for *you*. But if you make her a bankrupt or touch a cent of her money it is in law *a crime.* Dearest you are not well enough for me to go into all lengths on this subject. Now your course bewilders me. You have told me of many plans, but you have pursued none. You are still in that great house & you say, No one tells you what else to do. *I* have told you, Darling, that boarding or visiting for a time or staying with a sister or keeping a smaller house is better than such an establishment that almost any other mode in wh: you could place yourself was better for one person & a sick servant than such a great wasteful establishment. But still I am "bewildered" because I dont know all your difficulties & think you *must* have some reason for doing as you do. Still lately Dearest, I have grown quite *benumbed* on the whole subject. I look on it with a sort of terror. And if I seem silent in my sympathy it is because, (for the cause that I burnt that letter & hate to send this one) I hate when you are pained already to pain you more & am stayed also by the hope that some last plan you have mentioned will be carried into execution.

So now, Dearest, I am going to tell you my secret & why it has been a secret, even tho' the time for divulging it has not at all come. It is this. The only hope I can at all see for my aiding you is by becoming your *counsellor*. In almost all my studies of the subject I have fallen upon that same plan. Its nature has been this:—First, not to forget that for every executive *step* necessary to extricate your property you are legally competent &, therefore, you need no help there. You can *take all the moves* upon the business chess board. You can write checks & sign notes & sell property & buy it. You do not need a trustee to so such things for you. Therefore, secondly, what you do need is to know what moves to take. Now, Darling, I dont meant to impeach your business skill. All I mean is that you are taking no moves. All my meditations have led me to but one plan in which I could aid you & that was to have the whole game put into my hands to find out what piece first to move & so on & try at least to save enough of the pieces to pay Lilly. Now this I have been willing to do, but I have not been willing [to] offer to do it because I thot you were not ready for that yet. Indeed, Sally, my objections have been three fold. first that I have been constantly hoping that you would begin & play the game skillfully yourself. Secondly, I tho't my distance & the delicacy of my position made the Major or some other friend better. Both *these* objections I have now given up.

The third was always the most serious one & exists yet. It is this. If I should begin & advise you how to move & conduct you step by step by letter as I would through the whole game your affairs would still turn out worse than your friends or even yourself would think they ought to. You would meet with losses. Property after you had sold it might appreciate. Your friends not knowing your embarrassments would think your property injured. And indeed it might prove too late by the best management to save it all. Why do I speak then of the plan as a secret? Why for this reason—I have always rejected it. I have never seen a time when I thought it wise to offer it. I have never seen a time when I tho't you would accept it. And yet I thought it of sense enough to *keep it* like a keg of wine unbroached that it *might* serve if possible at some very evil time. Well in this last letter you do seem to sigh over your difficulties as if you thought them very extreme & certainly in a way to fill me with the most painful sympathy. Darling, I can help you in no other way than in that I have mentioned & it is only when you have made your circumstances more desperate that you will allow me, I fear, to help you in so thorough a way.

Now of the detail. I have reflected a great deal over it. I have even gone so far as to settle the conditions. Let me first say however the plan rests upon the foundation that you are my betrothed wife—that that relation is fixed—that if we survive T. we are to end our lives together, & that this plan is one by which your husband who is helpless without it can preserve to you your health & fiduciary honour. The plan provides of course that you are to take every step & that I am to be unknown in the matter. You are to buy & sell just as the law empowers you. The whole thing is to be *done* by you. But Darling, off here or in my occasional visits for I mean to speak of that presently I would be the man in the automaton that directs the move. I would begin of course with a complete knowledge of your affairs. I would deliberate carefully about the first step to take. It might be the sale of a field hand or the sale of your Louisville lots or the cutting of a street out by the church. I dont know what. But I would give you a great deal to do in answering all sorts of questions & perhaps asking some of your neighbours. And I would hope slowly & somewhat perilously & through self-denials to get Lilly at least out without an impeachment of your honour.

Now as to the conditions. They would be, First, that I should not be known in the matter. Second, that I should never touch or see your money or ever borrow or vest it. Thirdly, that you should solemnly promise never while unmarried to *will* anything to me or above all to my children who as minors could not decline it & never during our unmarried life to make me any costly or remunerative present. Fourthly, that if I ever loaned you money as I should propose to do to save some property of yours or to bear expense while certain changes were going on I should never have anything but 6 per ct interest & not that unless the sum were large & the time unindurable. Fifthly, that I am in no wise to be benefitted by my management mediately or immediately & if I lead you into any heavy loss by mistake or maladministration I am to make it good.

This phantom of a plan is all that ever occurs to me as a means of helping you. I believe that I could sit down at your board & play out the game with my Northern skill quite successfully. And now as the main thing is, what skill have I in such matters, all I can say is that I have high reputation for executive ability. At Frederick Sam Tyler told me after I had touched some of the springs of their church machinery that he would recommend me to his namesake for Secretary of the Treasury. And at Phil. I was the head & front of that Ch. Ex. scheme &c &c. But Sally, you are not ripe for such a desperate remedy yet. You must come down nearer to my level of view in respect to your affairs. It is only when the sick man as poor Nicholas said of Turkey is pronounced desperate & when perhaps it will be too late even for my skilful hand that my offer will be brought to bear.[2]

Still tell me what you think of it.

I should want you to resign everything to me & with a power of veto to be sure if I was actually allowing you to burn down your house & yet with great caution even that I should want you to take your moves just as I should say.

Now as to my visit. Here also, Darling, I wanted you to speak first. I feel unwilling that *you* should be involved in order to give me a visit. Still now as the result of all my meditation I am in favor of the visit. That is *my* verdict. It will not hurt me. You ask me whether it would interfere with my settlement. I think not. But what difference does that make. I am *declining* settlements. I have declined one within a fortnight. *I* desire the visit as concerns *me*. On the other hand I will not pay it against your opinion. Your opinion must be that it will not cause the desertion of your relatives or *of course* I will not see you. Darling, make up your mind on this subject *soon*. I am tormented by the delay. To-day I am in wretched spirits. I have been driving my children away from me a thing I dont often do unless I am in the slough of Despond. Pray for me, Dearest. You have a very unhappy wretch for a lover.

All this letter I have written on Sunday. I thot it a holy duty to offer you what I could & to send you the sympathy that I seemed to lack. Moreover all that I have said here I hope is the direction of the Spirit for I have prayed for it sedulously.

One feature of your case that disturbs me is that Lilly should not have her money *now* when she wants it. From 15 to 17 is the important time with ladies, they need every facility. Her money might tempt some rogue hereafter. It would help her to see thro' him by being spent on her now.[3] One thing is certain, Darling, you shall not be a defaulter to her. That species of debt I would *force* you to receive from me if it took all our living. So Dearest, pray & think over it all & whenever you become perfectly desperate you may hand over the whole game to me. But remember I shall put you in short allowance at once.

Yours *affly*
JM.

Colalto
Tuesday, Sep: 30. 1856.

My *dear* John,

Do you know I had no letter today? It is the first failure in a long time. I was so sure I should have one; and some how I had a feeling it was to be one of more

2. Nicholas I (1796–1855), czar of Russia from 1825.
3. That is, by an education.

serious import than usual; and as I heard my little mail-carrier coming on thro' the passage my heart throbbed as tho' it were yourself not your letter that I was expecting. I was *so* disappointed; even the nerves of my body seemed fretted and sore. However, I hope for one tomorrow morning. You are so punctual and so careful to spare me all annoyance from this kind of disappointment that I never feel like grumbling at you or blaming you, when it does sometimes occur.

I was just thinking today, that I had almost ceased to talk to you about your visit. I have been full of other things of late when I have written to you; and have had no chance of seeing Dr White. Old Dr Baker & the equinoctial rains have rendered a visit to him impracticable. Besides I am so troubled about Lilly's arrangements that I have not thought of your visit as much as I did before. If I decide to go with Lilly, I shall want you to make your visit here before I go, if you are to make it at all.

Wednesday, 8 1/2 A.M.

I was so stupid last night that I put up my letter in despair. An accident happened to the Stage last night, & the mail only reached here an hour or two ago. I have not yet had mine, but hope still a little for a letter from you.

I have tried your prescription of 9 1/2 o'clock. Thus far, it has been very uncomfortable. I am awake with the first noises of the morning, and lie waiting for 5 to be struck by the town clock. At this season, you may know how dark every thing looks even when that hour comes. I am so restless too and cold, that I lose half of the good of my early napping.

I am going over to town. If I get yr letter then & have time, I will add a line to this; if not, won't this content you?

John, does it seem to you that I am more careless & unreserved in my writing to you than formerly? I feel the difference very decidedly myself. I am much happier in our letter-intercourse. I dont often feel the check-rein that used to draw me back from entire abandon with my pen. I am less harassed too with anxieties about your affection and yr concerns. In short, I have growing and deepening upon me the feeling of trust that belongs only to a wife. Now if you ever behave amiss, & betray this trust, what do you think would be bad enough for you?

What of the book?

Have you read a little volume by a Dr Young called "The Christ of History"? There is one of a title almost the same, "The Christ *in* History," yet widely different in its aim & far inferior every way to this.[4] I like this little book extremely:—apart from other merits its style of scholarly simplicity is very captivating, especially when you consider how perfectly suited it is to the subject discussed.

But Goodbye.

Affectionately Yours
S.C.P. McDowell

4. John Young (1805–1881), *The Christ of History: An Argument Grounded in the Facts of His Life on Earth*, was published in New York by R. Carter. *The Christ in History*, by Robert Turnbull (1809–1877), published in Boston, went through several editions.

Princeton, Sept 30th 56.
Tuesday, 8 1/2 o clock

Dear Sally,

I have delayed my writing to the last moment thinking of this trusteeship. I spent a long time yesterday in one of my "set studies" of the matter & still do not seem to have finished.

1. As to "trouble" (which you mention) that is *nothing.* It would be no trouble for me to look after you in any way.

2. As to skill, I am not modest enough to be much in doubt about that.

But then Dearest, I have just *one* objection & that is that such a relation could *hardly* be kept secret. My counsel would *leak* out somewhere & tho' you took all the steps yet you would be acting so differently that every one would suspect there was some one behind the throne. Then you know the busy tattle of people would say, "Oh, he is only looking after [']her property.[']" So much for the very work itself. Then Sally, in your proud reserve you have kept people from knowing how tried you are. Many think you rich I have no doubt. Then if in meddling with your estate I bring it down to its absolute value & make it wholly safe & serviceable it may be reduced so much from what people think it that I shall have the credit of ruining it. These results it seems to me can hardly be avoided.

The question, therefore, seems to be this:—How much do you *need* such an adviser. *You* have been proud even to me. You have not told me what your sufferings are. I have been alarmed by several things. First, the trial to your health that you have lately spoken of. It has alarmed me beyond measure. For tho' I know it has connection with *our* difficulties yet I have suspected more. Second, your economy in one or two directions. And, *third,* the current of poor Lilly just at this *flowering* season of her education when above all other times her money ought to be flowing to her aid. Sally, these things scare me. And I feel very much this way:—If you are at all safe in your moneyed position when you candidly & fairly judge I would rather not interfere. Do tell me, my Love, with perfect frankness. If you are sore pressed & in trouble beyond what I know then, Sally, I beg you to tell me. If you are reduced to straits & are in danger of violating Lilly's interests at an important time or else wrecking your whole estate, My own Darling, show me the regard of making me a confidant. You profess to tell me everything. It is almost a crime if in so important a matter you are "*proud*". If you are reduced to straits & without James or Tom or Uncle Tom or the Major (of whom moreover I am a little afraid) or Col Reid or anybody to help you, then I will *certainly* be your trustee. I have no doubt when I come to study it all out this will be my decision. Tell me therefore, are you at your last move? or have you a safe game that you can yet play for some time to come? I do not care for popular scandal on my own account. And, if I am doing right (& for that I pray) I will save you from violating your trusts & impoverishing Lilly's education & you & I must do the best we can to keep me out of view. I have 3 things at stake, your health, your self-respect, & the integrity of your trust, if you tell me that these are in danger (*I think*) I will offer to be trustee.

Write me therefore with great precision & decisiveness & if you love me be perfectly frank & communicative & keep your pride if you have it not for your alter ego but for the world without.

Recollect, tho: if you accept my offer & accede to conditions, you must go right to work not rashly but firmly with great regularity. I shall overwhelm you with questions & give you a great deal to do. You wanted work & I shall give it you. Everything must pass thro' your hands & be written & done by you. And I am only your soul inside of you doing some of your thinking & helping you to extricate yourself.

Write me at once & definitely.

Yours in haste
Jno Miller

Tell me when you write just how you are. Are you thin. Are you pale. Are you weak. Are[5] you handsome and & in good robust spirits!

Princeton, Oct. 2d 1856

Poor dear Sally,

Nothing could so entirely exonerate you from the charge of indelicacy about which you inquire my opinion as the whole tone & bearing of this letter. Here is information of feelings about which I have asked & entreated you to trust me & paved the way for a full revelation of all by every mode of speech that I could possibly use. I have told you we had passed the point of courtship & had reached tho' without marriage the point when we must jointly sit down & *contribute our ideas* & yet you write with a forced air as tho' you had quite unsexed yourself & your very witticisms on other pages wear the constrained look as tho' your mind had been bent to take a hard step which your reason approved but which your habits all shrunk from. Sally McDowell you're a lovely woman & tho' you have your faults like all your race yet your loveliness does not consist in mere fascination but in solid gifts of character which this letter in many ways which reveal themselves to your lover strongly yet almost *convulsively* displays.[6]

But, Darling, this letter has filled me with the most agitating feelings. I received it last night. I read it twice, the last time in bed & lay awake thinking of it. I must write this morning. And yet I am not at all ready to reduce to order the tumultuous & opposite feelings which views unexpectedly decided occasion.[7] I have a wild excitement of hope. I think I see that one *limb* in

---

5. Miller repeated "are."
6. Miller badly jumbled the conclusion of this paragraph.
7. Miller probably meant: "feelings which unexpectedly decided views occasion."

all my previous judgments has almost entirely dropped away. I feel as poor Gulliver would if *half* the cords that bound him to the ground were suddenly severed.[8] This excites me with an almost new expectation. But then on the other hand I fear that like Gulliver the liberty I have gained will only bring into pressure & force the other bonds on which then my whole confinement would depend.

Still even in so disturbed a moment I see *some* things. 1st As I have all along declared that *my* social preferences ought not to come into this question. In an ordinary courtship they ought not, but in one where I have really seduced you against your reasoning preeminently they ought not. I agree perfectly with you that save only the question of conscience it would not be "honorable" in me to make *my own* social fears a means of severing an arrangement which I had sued for against the very forewarnings that such fears would imply. Yet tho' it would be "honorable" to neglect such fears & insist upon the marriage if the other party consented yet it would be painful to win her consent in the midst of her *knowledge* that her husband had fear of the alliance and, therefore, it is with peculiar satisfaction that I am still able to say that as far as I know my own heart I would *prefer* the marriage as far as concerns my own social fears. If this were all I *would selfishly desire it.* Indeed I would eagerly embrace it. And, Darling, take all this strictly I beg you. As to all *my* social position (unexpected as was the opposition & altered the views in certain quarters) I *desire* the marriage. I have a contempt for men's treatment when my *taste* is at rest as well as my conscience & therefore with this distinct knowledge you might have written your letter more freely than you did.

2d. I gave you the choice as to our marriage & when the Major interfered I insisted that you should decide; (not that I did not influence you,) but you knew before the receipt of James letter I had assented to an arrangement for the following Wednesday. *Now so I feel still*—that barring the question of *conscience* the decision is with you. I have *said* the decision was yours. That I have felt in honour bound to say to all comers. But, Dearest, I say this with several convictions. 1st That you are *mistaken* in thinking your position would be unchanged by marriage. I have become *convinced* it would be. You have no idea of the storm under wh. Mrs H. made that speech[9] & under which Mr C[ornelius] came to retract his advice & Bp P[otter]. I grieve over any sense of less pleasant position *now* indeed I have *remorse* whenever I think of [it]. Your letter gives me the keenest anguish. But marriage would be worse & worse in a storm & tempest at least in my region of which Bp P. & Dr L[eyburn] & others had no idea. When those newspaper fragments came out Phil was in a perfect blaze. Now you rightly say *I* could stand this. But could you?

---

8. Lemuel Gulliver is the central figure in the satire *Gulliver's Travels* written by Jonathan Swift (1667–1745) and published in 1726.

9. Margaret Benedict Hunter's warning, "if you love that lady don't marry her."

Could I stand it, when it came in the *least* shape of scoff or negligence to you? I cannot tell how all this will settle down in my mind when I come to reflect as I shall before the next letter. But I imagine the decision will be this. Guard Sally as much as you can. Warn her as much as you are able. Hold her back till all her woman's sagacity which is not small has been used upon the question. Keep her fr. the marriage for *her* sake if you can, but then as you *prefer* it for yourself & are only secondarily influenced by *her* loss of position give *her* the decision & let the final verdict be hers, as respects all not involving conscience.

But then the moral question has been collecting facts & storing principles which so little did I come to that have not yet been canvassed & made out. So forbidden was I to marry you for *your* sake, that *for conscience sake* I have not lately settled the inquiry. Still I have thot a great deal of it. I would preferring *seeing* you to talk of this, but as I cant, now, I will write.

I conjure you now, Sally, that the ice is broken you will *keep* your whole mind before me on these subjects.

In great haste for the mail.

Yours
Jno Miller

I will send James letter.

Colalto
Friday Oct 3. 1856

My dear John,

No letter yesterday; none to-day. Tuesday's missing letter came Wednesday; it had been written in time to come on the regular day, but no doubt, there was some mail detention somewhere, that threw it a day later. But yesterday was a regular day too. The letter failed then & fails to-day also. And I am much more worried than you can imagine, or I choose to tell. The reason of its detention may be very good & satisfactory when I hear it, but the period of waiting between this & then is, to say the least, not comfortable. I am all the time half crazy with my accumulated troubles, & when these disappointments occur I am wonderfully fretted.

I wrote to Mr Major yesterday asking if he would receive me as a boarder, in case I sent Lilly to him. I am not pleased with the plan altogether—indeed shrink from it, but I know not what else to do. Indeed I dont care much what becomes of me. I may, after receiving his answer, make up my mind to go immediately,—that is, to break up my establishment here, for I may go to see Mary before settling down anywhere. In fact if it were not so expensive moving about in the interior of Va, I would not go to Geo. Town till January.

I saw Dr White—he says nothing new as to your visit. He says people will talk, but I have the right, he conceives to do as I please.[10] If you make it, I would rather it should be before I leave here. It is true, such a visit would be less noticed & commented upon in Geo. Town than here; but I have no intention or thought of any concealment about it.

Aunt Eliza comes to pay me a short visit next week. She has sold her home & is much inclined to settle in Charlottesville while her boys are at the University. If her girls remain any time with me you might come during their visit. Of that I will write to you more fully and certainly when I know more of their movements than I do at present. I *suppose* I want to see you just now; for I am so worried this morning I know nothing accurately of either past or present feelings. I fancy I am not well; my nerves all flutter & my head aches after a night of much disquiet.

Dont it seem strange?—I am not ["]terrified by dreams" as one of the old Testament worthies acknowledged himself to be, but I'm often excited by them.[11] For years I have never dreamt a single dream that I know of, but one, & that strange to say, was, this Summer of your little Maggie, in which my Mother is not the chief character. I have not that longing for her & thought of her when awake that wd warrant such nightly visitations, but such is the fact. She is always sick too in these dreams and an object of my care, stirring my feelings until I am excited by them when I am awake. O what a comfort it wd be if even once, and in a dream we cd change places, & she become the watcher & I the one watched once more! Last night I was roused from troubled attendance upon her, with such a sense of oppression that I called Lilly from her bed to throw up the window & open a shutter, cold & dark as it was. I longed for the day light; but after listening awhile for the clock, (my watch had run down) it rung out 4. I fell asleep after a long time & felt better when I waken again, but am still flurried, & discomposed. I see Miss Dix has returned; I'll write to her to take me in charge as a—something, I dont know what, that wd be glad to be thought not responsible nor fit to take of myself.

I ought to be more generous than to send you such a letter, but you had better know me in all of my moods. If you were sitting by me, perhaps I should quarrel with you, or speak so sharp you wouldn't know me. But in spite of all, I do believe I love you with all power of a strong passion; So goodbye.

Affectionately yours
S.C.P. McDowell

10. White had actually written much more than that. In a letter to her pastor McDowell had posed a series of questions about "the scriptural morality & expediency" of a marriage and the attitudes White had observed among the ministry and in the local community. In his reply the minister reassured her that she was free to marry and had the general approbation of churchmen and laity with whom he had consulted. White himself thought the marriage "desirable"; and the only disapproval he noted came "chiefly by ladies who had given little attention to the subject" (William L. White to Mrs. McDowell, Oct. 3, 1856).

11. Job 7:13–14.

Princeton Oct 4th 1856
8 1/2 A.M.
Mail closes at 9.

Dear Sally,

No man since Adam (who had at all the spirit of a man) could receive such a letter as you wrote me without having his heart all turned in one direction. The great obstructions to our marriage which six days ago I *knew* would hold their places till T's death crush & yield around me like drift. I am excited all day & sleepless much of the night. That such a lovely creature should bury her honour & all her treasured friendships & still triumph in her affection & cling so *madly* to *me* gives my wild passions hope that they havent enjoyed for many a long day.

I have a great deal to tell you. But to get it I have had as usual to come close up to the hour of the mail.

I cast aside all books & went straight into my study & began the study of our case in these new discoveries. I have completed a great deal of the reasoning.

I. I seduced you into the engagement.

II. I broke down your scruples & treated your fears even about yourself as wild dreams.

III. You had at the time a manifest shrinking from the *announcement* of an engagement; & said very emphatically that the consummation should very soon follow such a public committal.

IIII. Your forewarnings have been realized.

IV. For *me* after seducing you into a public committal & to the verge of marriage & after a solemn engagement to marry, to draw back on any ground short of conscience & *your good* would therefore as you say be cruel & dishonorable.

V. This sweeps out of the way all questions about my own social position at once & simplifies the question tho' that has been the condition the question with me as you know always.

VI. I have a right to make a stand for *your* good & have done so & up to your letter had given up the wedding till T's death. I still warn you. I still may ask you as I do whether even if your present position is not a pleasant one you are not attracted (as I am for you) *by the delight* there would be in having waited in the event of T's speedy death. (By the way, Sally, I hate such questions but do tell me for once what is the *chance* of that life. Is it an insecure & wasted one, or does [it][12] wear the promise of one of usual length. Wicked as it is I have been [trying?] to find this out! Do you know *anything?*)

VII. Viewing you as I would my children therefore, I have a right to warn you & to check you & to guard you & perhaps even to forbid you as the Major once suggested, inasmuch as the moment you are married you are under my care.

---

12. Miller wrote "the."

I feel inclined to do all these things but the last. Therefore VIII. The whole decision short of the moral question is after due deliberation *in your* hands. I have therefore yesterday to say it all in a few sentences determined after warning you of the storm you will suffer to throw away all possible questions for my self but the single one of conscience.

Therefore, Sally, I plunged at once into that. All else seems finished. I studied it carefully yesterday with an unfinished result. I went at night to Dr. McGill's, my fathers biographer & my personal friend & our best preacher confessedly in Princeton & *for the first time* I had ever said a word laid the whole matter before him. To my amazement he told me he had seen you & your fa[mily] & had been thinking over all our case. *He had not a doubt of the propriety of the marriage.* He would follow it if he were I to the bitter end. Still he would study it for me. We talked three hours. I hinted at wherein I had embarrassed your position. He had not tho't of it but now clearly recognized it. He had been in a company of the Alexanders before our intended wedding day. They had not hinted at any disapproval. Still I have learned to doubt these things.

Now, my own Beloved, quiet yourself. Dont let this excitement wear upon you more. Steady yourself by *this:*—We will both do what *God* seems to direct. I have now done but this aspect of the question.

Now, to treat this, I have determined to spend *a week of prayer.* This will reach you on Tuesday. I shall then have been three days in my room thro the forenoon hours. *Join* me *there. Let the week decide* with an earnest committing of all to God. If the moral question seems doubtful let us postpone the match: & also if *you* are afraid of the consequences. If not—not. Pray for *me* that my readings & studies may be final for I hope I shall settle my mind on this moral question which I have never vested all in before.

Still, Sally, think seriously of yourself & whether in poverty & with *some* seclusion to put the worst face upon it you can find your happiness in *me.* Can you my own Darling. *Tell me.* Can you. I love you with passionate fervor.

I write in extreme haste & have not reread my letter.

Knowing that you will be agitated I will write *every day* till this matter is decided. *Do you w[rite] too.* And, Dearest, as a *reasonable creature* dispel every prudery & separate feeling & urge every point with perfect *abandon.* Answer *all* my arguments.

Yours affectionately
JM

[marginal note] Write over a hard quire of white paper or even sheet of it & this paper will not catch the pen.

Saturday (Oct 4, 56)[13]
Evening Mail

6 1/2 clock.

My Sweetest Wife,

It seems we have been married 18 months. I told Dr McGill when he informed me that if that was so we had led a very uncomfortable married life & not a very *exemplary* one. It seems that Dr Pressly held that betrothal was marriage—that the wedding was a mere circumstance.[14] So, Duck, I have not been so wrong in making you behave & using a little authority.

I scribble a note to-night to say that I have been in the Sem. Library all day & tho' I dont want after all that has occurred to harrass you with another disappointment, & tho' this very suspense & excitement is wearing yet I must tell you that this day ends with the controversy in our favour. I have struck some very fruitful veins & have some new facts.

But, Sally, let us contemplate nothing else than a negative result & then we will not be disappointed. I have certainly now left all but the moral question to you.

But, Sally, think. Do you love me so passionately that you can find your happiness only in me & bear whatever storm this thing may stir up. Could you be happy with me alone? *Could* you Sally.

Yrs affly
Jno Miller.

I cant find an odd Eclectic or Westminster at our store. They wont sell it.

I will send ours. But you must send it back as soon as read. What on earth do you want such a paper for.

Colalto,
Saturday Oct 4. '56 3 p.m.

Dear John,

A new era in farm life has suddenly been ushered in. You Northern people can form only a faint idea of the panic created on one of our farms when a Negro is found bold enough to lift his hand against his Master, or his Master's white subordinate. I am in the midst of such a panic now. Late yesterday afternoon I was called to the door by the Overseer to hear that Alfred had actually resisted his authority, & having given him repeated blows, had, as in the scuffle he had slipped & fallen, jumped upon him & choked him severely. I was greatly startled, but entirely self-collected and capable of giving all safe and proper directions. It was nearly night, and I deferred any punishment till this morning, when all

---

13. McDowell supplied the date in parentheses.

14. John Taylor Pressly (1795–1870), Presbyterian minister and former professor of theology at Allegheny Seminary, Allegheny, Pa.

parties would be calmer, and I cd act most judiciously. I called up Alfred after I had sent away Moore (the Overseer) & heard his story. He wept profusely & seemed distressed at the occurrence, but evidently felt that he had done no wrong. This morn'g I sent for Mr Massie (I had sent last night for both him & the Town Constable, but it was too late for them to come). I determined when he came to carry out my first impulse, which was—to make Moore give the whipping, & the Constable be present to assist him in case of repeated resistance, as Moore was not so strong as Alfred—whilst Mr Massie was to stand by and see that the punishment was humanely given.

Since writing the above, I have had Alfred punished, and all things seem quiet. It has been a real trial to me. It is my first experience in such matters, and yet I felt it necessary to be both determined and composed. When the Officer & Mr Massie came, I sent a Messenger to the different fields & called all the hands (no great number!) with Moore to the house. They stood on the pavement by the back porch, whilst the white men, (Moore & the Constable) & Mr Massie stood on the steps. I took a stand apart from any of them, on the porch, and told Alfred of his fault & his punishment & Sam also, for he was incidentally engaged in the thing too. I never was called upon before to stand as Master stands here, as *Judge too* and was much agitated. I spoke, however, very emphatically, telling them that as my slaves they must submit to me in the person of my Overseer, but, at the same time they must look to me as their protector. I would protect them *against* an Overseer when necessary; & protect the Overseer against them &c &c. As I finished Alfred said, very respectfully, "Miss Sally, will you allow me to speak a few words for myself?" I consented.

"I am yr slave Madam. I am bound to submit to whatever you lay upon me; but am I to allow an Overseer to *impose* on me?" "Alfred," said I, "I am your protector. You are not to take the law in your own hands. If an Overseer threatens your life—or puts it in danger, you are to escape from him to me: you are not to undertake to defend yourself". He had set up the plea that he was acting in self-defence. My Overseer seems a kindhearted creature and certainly has evinced no unkindness to them. On the contrary every thing has gone on most satisfactorily and peacefully since he came.

These occurrences are dreadful. My whole household looks haggard. A tornado seems to have swept over us. But I feel relieved and thankful that it is all over with no damage to life or limb of any concerned. God have mercy on these poor creatures and their miserable Masters. My feelings have always been sadly wrought upon by their condition. In this case I had, several times, the inclination or threatened crumbling away of my resolution, but I was able, at last, to carry it out. I don't know what I shall be able to do next. The Providence of God has placed me again & again in, to me, terribly trying circumstances and—I have gone thro' them, whether with scars or not I dont know, but it seems to me I am a good deal unlike the Sally McDowell I knew years ago. However I must say, I am a much improved person in many respects tho' by no means perfect yet. When I look at Lilly and remember that my troubles commenced when I was just her age, I am astonished at the past. I wonder how she would have acted under similar difficulties. But do you know, that at Lilly's age (16) I was a much graver & more reserved person than you have ever known me to be. John, do you think I would have fancied you, if we had been thrown together then? I'm sure I shouldn't; for then I looked upon *boys* as the most despicable of wild animals.

Monday 8 A.M.

Dear John,

I had written quite a long letter on Saturday; but this morning I have determined not to send it. Your letter of Thursday receiv'd Saturday is not the one you intend me to accept as expressing fully or distinctly what you mean to say upon the matters it attends to, therefore it isn't worth while for me to attempt an answer to it. By the way John, did you intermit a letter last week? If you didn't it is lost, for one failed entirely—The one that should have come on Thursday.

I have shrunk greatly from the revelation of my opinions, recently made; but I am far happier in having no reserves with you. And all these late letters from you on our differences of opinion have not loosened but only tightened the bond between us. I love you, as I always hoped to do, & longed to be able to do, more and more the better I know you. I never could bear to think of your not being one who would grow upon my affection. You do not disappoint me; and my love for you increases in degree and in strength till it has all the *power* but none of the *blindness* of passion. I love you, as I am proud to do, & happy to do, which is far better, *intelligently*. I wouldn't care to have a fire in my heart, to which my mind didn't supply the fuel. I dont want to love you as my husband unless I can respect you—and I cant respect except upon the full use of my reason & judgment. And this is the love I do have for you. It never kindles into enthusiasm except it has been taught to do so by the workings of my mind. Is this something of a *philosophical* affection? Well, no matter; it is the sort I have, and you can judge for yourself whether it be not the most elevated, the most pure, the most steady. If you are not content with this type, why, according to my notions, you must *come down* to some other, which I wouldn't consent to feel, and which you must be very different from all my belief of you, if you would be satisfied to receive. As it is, believe me, I love you with all my heart & with all the confidence that the full approbation of my reason must inspire. Now, Darling, are you content? If you are not, what more do you want.

Our whole connection is different from any other engagement, and sanctions and requires more than any common one. We risk more than people commonly do, and we *ought* to be more unreserved & candid than wd be at all proper in ordinary cases. We should have an *inexorable habit of Trust* in each other, and at the same time the most careful watching against everything that would threaten even to invade this confidence. This care I think can be entirely consistent with perfect candor, and need impose no barrier-restraint upon either of us. What do you think?

As you may suppose this trouble on the plantation is likely to give a new cast to my plans for the future. It has been so sad a trouble to us all. I had a long talk with Alfred & his Wife yesterday, which I think, will be something like an amollient to their wounds. I told Alfred, that tho' I had ordered his punishment, yet it was my pleasure to tell him that he had so borne himself under it that my confidence in him & my respect for him had not, in the least, diminished. The thing has been a great distress to me, but he had behaved well, under his punishment, (which by the by, I have learned since was really exceedingly severe) and I felt it right to tell him so. In the future, I hope he wd, submit quietly to Mr Moore, & prove to us all the principles & determination he expressed. He has indeed behaved well; and he & Moore are here, at work this morn'g together, at the trees &c in the yard, both deporting themselves satisfactorily to me. But you cant tell how it has affected the whole concern. You ought to thank God every day that the responsibilities & distresses connected with slavery have not been imposed upon you. It is a heavy evil, which however we would have managed better, if there had been no Northern interference.

But I'm in a hurry. God bless you my own dear John.

Aff'ly
S.C.P. McDowell

Princeton Oct 6th 1856.
Monday 7. a.m.

"This is none other than the finger of God"!

You filled me with strange feelings some weeks ago when without a ray apparently of any light in respect to the future you spoke of lying on yr bed & *"comforting yourself in God"*. That was the *saucy* letter which nevertheless I admired so. When I heard you in those circumstances say that tho' you knew of nothing yet, you were *sure* the Almighty would interpose for your relief I felt quite *awed* & was half converted to the same conviction.

Now to *you* the interposition cannot appear so remarkable because it may seem to come from yourself. Indeed as a sensitive woman you shiver at the thought of having overstept your own delicate notions of propriety in that most important letter. But to me who am the *recipient* of the Providence, it seems almost like [a] miracle.

Last week I was as sure we would not be married till T. died as any man not the controller of Providence could possibly be. I was fixed in plans which were beginning actually to mature & of which I spoke as the burden of a long letter I was about to write. What is more startling I made repeated offers for part of that great square of mountain which I want ultimately to possess & urged one man to take $1000 & another annual instalments of $750 for four years ($3000) &

another $900 for a part where there was a house & barn, another $500 an offer wh he accepted & of which I was just treating. I dont mean that I made these offers all together, but one by one with the intention of buying any part of that square of the hill that was offered so low as that the *wood* would pay for it. Then I had actually bought two plots of 5 acres each & in my idle times was shaping our ultimate life & picturing you in your old age as the central figure in the picture.

Therefore, Sally, the Providence comes to me when I was exhibiting all that steadiness of patience & submission to what I thot right & wise that a Christian man ought to feel.

You may know then how much I was struck with a remark of Dr McGill's. I asked him "Doctor, has our position been damaged or not by stopping our marriage (instead of going right on) & then returning to it again?["] He replied with great earnestness, "I have repeatedly thought of that very thing. I think the arrest places you in a *better* position. It shows thinking people that you were not enraged by your passions—that tho' firm in your own convictions, yet when the church was disturbed you paused to review the whole matter & if now you go forward people will say, Well this was not an "enamoured & naive" who threw all away for the lady, here is a man who thinks & must know what he is about. Moreover it shows a moral courage which the church will admire (not to be betrayed by rashness) but to pause to reflect upon the altered circumstances & then face all results."

I do feel, therefore, that I have met with a very decided Providence in my favour; I had submitted entirely to God. I had given up the marriage thro' T's life as a thing too *costly* to you. I *had really submitted entirely to my duty.* And now comes this letter releasing me as far as you can from considerations of your position & really throwing me back upon the recollection that *I had given the decision to you.*

Now, Sally, love, yesterday wrought no change in my convictions indeed confirmed them. I find myself now that my mind is turned that way returning to my old belief, on which I wooed you, viz. that the marriage is right. My mind *cant* see otherwise. Indeed I have some new beliefs. I would not as I now think about the thing *consent* to an action of the church for that would seem to imply that the State act was defective. Turning all my strength upon that for several days *I am convinced it was not.* I am convinced you have been a free woman ever since that act. I would not have it touched. My mind is stronger the more I study. And I would be ready with the most searching argument to *prove* that legally & morally you have a right (especially as concerns *our church*) to marry whom you please.

Still, Sally, as my child I tremble for you. I hardly dare let you marry. Do you think your father would? As isolated I covet the marriage. As your husband & the mother of my children I tremble about it (*socially*). That alone could have sunk me in so profound a patience till T's death.

Then furthermore, I cant enrich you. I cant place you by money in an entrenched position. I cant give parties & entertain to win people to a true appreciation of you. I'm a poor student. Sally, how much do you love me? That's the great question after all. If you love me merely as a husband with enough of your heart disengaged to make social relations *necessary* for God's sake Sally, by all that is solemn in death & judgment I beg you Darling dont marry me. But if you love me, Sally, so that this picture satisfies you—a secluded home—a *cold* society—a revolt from the very attentions we receive from the suspicion that they have a patronizing air—insult from those that shun us & disgust at those who seem to smile at us just to spare our feelings—all these morbid things—then poverty & a good deal of self denial & a loss of your Virginia abundance—if all these things dont terrify you but you think you can find your happiness in *me* & absolutely in *my* society & that of your own children & mine you can find your main reliance for pleasure the remainder of your life—then Sally, after being thus thoroughly warned I discharge my own conscience & (if God gives me my decision on Friday night as he seems to be giving it to me now tho' you know I am not to believe anything as fixed till then) abide by the choice which I at the first promised to allow to you.

And, Dearest, your pride will not suffer in the least in having written me the letter when I tell you that since I received it I have neither eat (I mean like Bro. Ross) nor slept. It has filled me with impatience & excitement & revealed in another magnificent chamber worthy of a queen the breadth & luxuriance of my love.

Are you *sorry* you wrote me the letter. If you dont give up your prudery, Love, I'll tease you about it. I'll propose that those little "hypothetical" friends of ours keep the date of that letter as a great family festival as a thing to which they owe their own existence. I'll call it your famous coup d'etat that is if I can keep out of reach of some still more famous coup d'orielle & then I'll catch you in my arms as I mean to do any how & bless God for giving me such a wife & feel solemnly the pleasure of being brot with my family so near the blessings of Jehovah as your child-like faith in him has taught me to expect to be brought.

But Oh, Sally I have so much to say to you & here is the hateful mail coming in on us again.

Sally, in order to save two, or three letters tell me at once two or three things. I have my own thoughts about the 4th of them but with perfect abandon about all tell me yours.

1. If we marry, when?
2. Now? or
3. At the death of my mother.
4. If not to wait till this last event, how shall we be supported? You ask me often whether I do not fear for my ministry. I do not. For *my* ministry is the laborious completion of certain studies which are unless my conscience has decided wrong *my vocation*. My conscience *would be disturbed if I wilfully incapacitated myself for these studies*. Besides, if I *sought* a church either before or after marriage I expose myself & you to such scenes as in Phila. Then Sally, what can we do? If I wait

till my Mother's death I can arrange a support. I felt thankful that those bargains were declined on the hill for it leaves me with command of money. But I have only $4.500 & that vested so that if I sell the principal I can get but $3.000 or a little over. This would carry us along bravely for a time but how then? Dont let us act rashly in this new start that Providence has given me. Tell me your thoughts freely. I see how a marriage this Fall might passionately too, as I would like it, help matters in some directions but dont let us be visionaries or do anything foolish that we would censure in your brother Tom. I went down & sounded Mother last night. She seemed still to feel that there ought to be some way that such a thing could be properly done, but sounded off by saying that we had better let matters lie for the present & "let patience have her perfect work." This is a fav[orite] text of hers. I sounded her to see how a vigorous step on my part would affect her in her declining months.

In haste as usual & begging you to be as communicative as I am.

Yours sincerely and affly,
JM

Cant one find out about T's promise of life. It would be sad to marry if he was near his end.

Tuesday Oct: 7. 1856

My *dear John,*

I write you a hurried note this morning. I have only about 3/4 of an hour to write in. Lest you should have any anxiety about the letter I reported as missing yesterday, I will tell you first & foremost that it came to-day, with nothing upon its face to account for its lingering.

Of course, I did feel that the candid avowal of my different opinion would influence you in some way or other, I could not tell how. I was most anxious about it: if it were a wrong one, I shrunk from any wrong influence upon you:—if it were the true one it involved heavy responsibilities, so in this perplexity and disquietude I have earnestly prayed that, if I were wrong my views might fall to the ground & do no harm to any one. Since your letter came on Saturday I have thought more narrowly on the whole subject; and yesterday morning felt exceedingly anxious to look into the moral question again and settle it beyond a doubt. I gave up some hours of the morning to it. I besought most earnestly and sincerely to be taught *the Truth.* I prayed over it with my whole heart and thought it out with all the ability I had, and my mind goes back to its old conclusions with, perhaps, as solid conviction as I can expect to attain. I am too hurried to write, my thinkings now, but shall do it by tomorrow's mail. However, I may say, that by way of attaining entire accuracy and exactness of decision, in the afternoon I wrote a note to my old friend Fendall, which this days mail takes to him; and in three or four days I shall have his reply, which I will send to you.

My dear John, you cant feel more than I, the necessity of prayer in this matter. I feel there is much involved in it—our own happiness & usefulness—the honour & purity of our religious profession—the welfare of your children, & my own Lilly all of whom seem to occupy the same position in this thing,—and more remotely in time, but even more nearly in interest our own children. It is reasonable & proper that we should earnestly & specially ask for Guidance first, and help afterwards. And I join you, and feel the stronger, that I know we ask unitedly. Above all things, let us ask *submissively*.

O yes! I knew Dr. McGill when Moderator of the Assembly in Baltimore, & have met him since at our own house & else where I believe—but my acquaintance with him was slight. I remember to have heard that Addison Alexander professed great interest in our matter about the time of our failure last Fall.

God bless and direct us.

Aff.
S.C.P. McD.

[marginal note] James writes me this morning of the death of his little boy. It is a sad blow to him.

Princeton, Oct 9th 1856 (Oct 7)[15]

Look up at this date, Sally. So help me God you shall think of it in after life. If there can be any change from the agony of a suffering life to all that affection can do entirely to set you at your ease, that day shall inaugurate it.

I have read your last letter with but one feeling & that is that it is *unendurable* that one I passionately love should be reduced to such despair. Nobly as you have cast yourself upon God I cannot understand that you should be reduced to such extreme of entire surrender as to say you "dont care what becomes of you" unless it is the dark fact of the light which means to mark the coming of the morning. I feel therefore, that it is God that is leading me to you when I say, "*Sally I have scattered all doubts even on your account to the winds & come to beg that you will marry me at the very earliest possible day*". No matter for the questions I asked you. I will take your love as one that would go with me to prison or to judgment as a thing for granted. Maynt I, Sally? I will rely on your love as a "passion" & as of the warmest feeling. If it is not then you have frightfully deceived me. We have loved each other in wild & romantic histories & have had more reasons than others to have grown together into a perfect unity. I shall rely on this. And if we go live in the woods, in a sort of Coventry & in poverty too, I believe you will consent. As to the means of living I mean to let that matter drift. We have reached a point where for your very life & health & for my warm love of you

---

15. Miller missed the date. McDowell corrected it in parentheses.

marriage seems a first necessity. Dont it, Darling? Afterward if I break stone I must find some livelihood.

One thing only I reserve—*I will not live at Colalto on your money* even if it were possible. That I am resolved upon. If I must seek a charge—well, I *must;* & give up some of my higher vocation. At any rate I wont, if your property should all recover itself to-morrow.—*I wont live upon it.* I wont have the appearance of doing so. It is a humility that you cant ask of me. Still dont let this worry you. My Darling, dont let anything worry you. Your turn has come for some relief,— perhaps mine for some new embarrassments. Dont take rashly any steps. Only remember this:—I am determined to marry you *the very earliest day possible* for which I can win your assent. I mean Tuesday, Wednesday or Wednesday week &c. the very first day I can persuade you to select. So form the plan & announce the day to me.

I spoke of thinking on till Friday. But I find that is useless. I did not vow to do so & I cant bear to leave you in distress. I believe I have reached a prayerful decision, & if so then that is the voice of God.

I. As to the moral question I am *convinced,* with more intelligence & reason than when I first courted you.

II. As to public opinion it is false & *I wont submit to it.* It is an Episcopal (English Church) prejudice.[16] It will be changed in England before we are ten years older & then it will be too late for us & for our children.

III. As to the doctrine of expediency I am a metaphysician, not a Pastor; one who seeks to live alone, not who courts society; besides, there are expediencies on the other side. I am breaking the heart of a noble lady. *Aint I,* Sally? I am breaking solemn vows & protestations; & if I go much further I will carry the remorse of these things to my grave.

What do you think I did yesterday? I had ready the money ($100) for the second lot I bought & had expected the owner a rich New Orleans Merchant to come for it on Friday. He called later than the right hour & I was out. He had given me the deed, but had told Hageman before whom he acknowledged it that I had taken up his offer promptly or he would not let me have the lot for there was wood enough on it to pay for it.[17] (*This* by the way was not true.) Yesterday I rode out with the money. I laughingly told him what H. had said, & laughingly added Mr Tulane, if it is a matter of indifference to you it has ceased to be so with me. Within a week my plans have undergone an alternation which gives me a use for that money & makes me less able to use the lot. I am here with the money, but if you like I will give up the bargain & pay all expenses of the deed &c. He promptly agreed & so, Sally, my first management is already made for the wedding.

16. Miller interlined this sentence.

17. Paul Tulane (1801–1887), a New Orleans businessman and philanthropist, came from Princeton and later retired there. John F. Hageman, Miller's brother-in-law.

Does it not seem strange? Without the least variation of my principles, my mind has completely revolutionized itself in ten days & that all because a lovely woman who is bringing a blessing to me by her faith & prayers has been sensible & honest.

And now, Darling, after having told you the worst in previous letters I have a right now to turn & comfort you. You know you will be very much sheltered by me & will have a very different life even if the storm does blow from what you have before had. But as to the storm itself:—I feel a little like that poor antidiluvian who after being out in the weather all night & in terrible alarm trying to get into the Ark, when he found he could not succeed turned away with the remark (which tradition has faithfully handed down) that "Och & be jabers, he didn't think there was going to be such a tirrible fresh innyhow." I both from study & from temper have no use for the world any how & you (for whom I chiefly fear) if I am indeed that "unseen presence" that your love flatters me I am may be satisfied when that "little" star from being an occult planet begins actually to twinkle. But here settles down all my anxiety. Can a gruffy student, surly & not willing always to be bothered make a lovely woman accustomed to the world happy all day by the mere darkness of his frowns.

No, I have another anxiety. It is this. You know you are so thin. Is it so, Sally. I fancy you haggard & forlorn. Last year you know you were happy & you grew fat & handsome. Lilly tells me you played about like a kitten. This year all the springs of life have been exhausted. Now I have one anxiety. Put your ear down here & I will tell you. (I am glad I'm 400 miles off so you cant box my ears) I will tell you; put your ear lower. (Dr McGill tells me you are my wife & I have a right to say what I please) Now listen. I am afraid Preston will be such a care-worn hollow eyed feeble little fellow so "hypothetical" & "visionary" in his look & manner. This is my only anxiety. Now hadnt we better wait, till you have gambolled about the floor again & the springs of life have filled up. But good bye. The mail again.

Yours affly
Jno Miller.

Dont announce till after Friday's letter. I mean to go on shutting myself up till then. But ruminate over plans. Dont sell Colalto unless you get $15000 for it or make any other plan. Perhaps if mother will advance me to $5000 more than I have I will buy it *before* our marriage & give Lilly a mortgage on it. How would that do?

Princeton, Oct 7th 1856

My dear Sally,

As I hope your agitations will be over before this reaches you I am tempted to subside into my old times of writing but I will not yet a while. This morning you received my first response to your long letter. I can conceive the "*rest*", if you really love me & confide in me with which you sank down upon my shoulder & felt yourself at last not altogether given up to yourself.

Darling, my policy now is to ask no more questions & get no more various opinions, nor care for them. If you feel as I do about this whole matter & can enter into my tastes we are independant of the world.
I would,

First, offend no body by coldness or any peculiar manner.

Secondly, court no one by attention or any peculiar care.

Third, ask no one any opinion or appear to hesitate about any part of our movement as tho' we dreamed it was improper.

If we court people or are specially attentive to those who side with us we shall have a set of Mr Poindexters about us who will do us harm with those we would really value.

Let us live exactly like other people. And if you love me as I certainly love you I venture to predict *we* will hardly hear the storm however it may howl.

Hearing last Spring that Bill Alexander (our candidate for Governor) had talked about you in a gossiping way (not disrespectfully), to Hageman, my brother-in-law! & offered to lend him one of Thomas's pamphlets, I told H. to accept his offer & take it from him & lend it to me.[18] He did so. And I shall either destroy it or send it to you. The Gov. shall not have it to gossip with. I have been reading it, my Love, & it almost made me weep to think how you had been victimized & I felt thankful that by your honesty you & a kind Providence had kept me from victimizing you again.

I will tell you the interpretation of your dream. Your mother appearing to you as the object of your care means that our prayer is heard & that your Kindness & gentleness to her has found favour with God & is to give you a blessing in return. And whereas my poor darling Maggie appeared also once in your dream, that means that you are not to intermit altogether your attentions to others & that my poor motherless child is to be the next object of your care. Poor dear Maggie I hope she will not need it on a bed of death. She worries me now by a recurring unwellness which the cool weather does not seem to drive away.

I am glad your Aunt Eliza is near you. I hope you will win her without any undue effort to some sympathy with you in your wishes. By the way if Lilly should be kept with you it would be better. James may poison her so in Geo Town & moreover she would feel more & more alien to me. Still if *we* went to the North as I think we ought after we are married she would hardly go with us & unless you left her with Mrs Massie she would have no place to stay. Besides she ought to be at school & might not wish to be at the wedding. Still it is unfortunate

---

18. William Cowper Alexander (1806–1874), a Princeton lawyer and son of Archibald Alexander, was defeated in the election by William A. Newell. The pamphlet was *The Statement of Francis Thomas* that he published in 1845 attacking his estranged wife.

that she should be away fr. your influence just at this time. If she were with you for these first months of your marriage *she would never leave you till her own*. Cant Mrs. C. help you in this?

I am thinking seriously of buying Colalto at once. I would give (including some ground rents which I will explain another time) about $15000. If you could get more from someone else I am not sure but that you had better take it. I would pay in this way.—I would give Lilly a five years mortgage upon the place of $10000 which would have the treble advantage, first, of unburdening you; second, of *securing* her interests; & third of preventing any body if difficulty is made from wresting her means, (by appealing to your honour,) suddenly & ruinously out of your hands. Then I would give you some $3.200 in cash to pay your most pressing debts with & the rest in certain ground rents $1800 which tho' not convertible instantly into money, at par are nevertheless certain, like land—& pay an unfailing interest, so that you could hypothecate them also for the payment of your debts. This all depends on whether I can get the $3333 as an advance from Mother. (She gives us cash on the interest of that already.)[19] If I could; then I would have over and above, some $2000 of other funds which I would use of course to pay other debts & set things in motion or give you in place of the gr. rents if you like &c. How would you like such a plan? The advantage I should hope to reap from it would be a chance to sell Colalto slowly & have a house there till it was sold & till the rest of my patrimony is received without the pain which I would not submit to of living on your acres. Perhaps eventually we might buy this large house in which I was born & live in it. This house itself would be a social entree element in Princeton.

But I am getting quite garrulous. Good night.

> *Yours affly*
> JM.

Be on your guard. You know I'm a Northerner. I'll cheat you out of your barn if you don't care.

Colalto
Wednesday Oct: 8. 56.

Dear John,

I write a note this morning before breakfast, commencing as the clock strikes 8.

I am scarcely able to write intelligently as I am oppressed by a sort of sick headache, and can do nothing very comfortably.

I know nothing of the person you inquire about, more than you have yourself told me.[20] Dr Graham, I think, told me he had seen him either in the Winter, or Spring & that he looked dreadfully old, and rather rejected the idea of his acknowledged, being his real age. However, I have a very strong, almost defiant

---

19. The sentence in parentheses is interlined.
20. That is, Francis Thomas.

feeling about that. I always go back to the belief, "why, if it be *right* to marry, why make that man's living or dying a question with us?" It is true there is a wide difference between lawfulness & expediency, and we ought not to overlook it, or trample upon it; nevertheless, I have a strong sympathy with old Dr Baker, & my heart is stirred as I repeat his remark—"my friends, when I stand upon the Word of God I am as strong as an Archangel". I know, if I act according to the Word of God, I am strong. I *have* an indestructible foundation; but I don't always *feel* this in a way to be a comfort to me. However in our case, if we settle the great moral question in our favor, I think we may trust God for the rest. You dont know, John, how much occasion I have had for doing this in all the past. You don't know, how many and remarkable have been the special providences I have had to observe & be thankful for. Besides this, my reason teaches me the propriety and reasonableness of an implicit acceptance & confidence in all of the promises of the Bible.

You know, how wonderfully my social standing has been preserved. I suppose there has not been in America a case of such terrible assault upon a wife's character, which has been so signally defeated. Many an innocent wife, no doubt, has suffered & fallen nearly under her husband's attack—but, for me, God willed it otherwise. There was everything *against* me, but He ruled *for* me. And since then, I have led a vagrant life; living in different communities, among different kinds of people, in circumstances of much exposure. I was young and handsome and unusually attractive, (now I don't say this out of vanity, but as marking out the case truly and strongly), and yet, under all and thro all, no voice has been raised against me;—and more than that, I *myself* have stood firmly, not only receiving respect, but respecting myself. Now, why is this? & how is it? Truly very simply and naturally—it has been, out and out, God's work—not mine in any part.

Again, last Fall, in all the furor & fuss—no one assailed my character so far as I have heard;—and why not? God has restrained people, & not allowed me to suffer from "evil tongues."

Now, all these things lead me first to look to God for guidance, & then to *trust* him, avoiding carefully every thing that would seem like a tempting of providence. And I believe if it be, for solid reasons, proper for me to marry you, I can confide our social position & our children's interests very fully in His hands.—indeed, tho' I have a nervous agitation about it, I have scarcely a *real fear* that He will allow either to suffer. If we, ourselves, be christians, and endeavor to act as becomes our character as such, our children are safe. God is no more likely to forget *them* in his covenant engagement to us, than he has been to forget the Rechabites in His promise to old Jonadab, their worthy Ancestor.[21] This may all seem "*stuff*" to you; but the more of this same stuff I have, the happier I am; And I don't think it foolish either—but, on the contrary very good wisdom.

21. The Rechabites were an Israelite clan praised by the prophet Jeremiah for their fidelity to the traditions of their ancestor Jonadab (Jer. 35). Jonadab ben Rechab, chieftain of the Rechabites, accompanied Jehu in his chariot when he slaughtered the followers of Ahab in Samaria (2 Kings 10:15*ff*.).

I have written in a hurry. You needn't be afraid of any *prudery* in me. I shall talk—I do talk, very freely upon all subjects, both real & "*hypothetical*". Monday's letter came this morning. To all yr questions as to "time" &c, which by the way are rather premature, I will write in due season.

God bless you, my dear John.

Aff'y,
S.C.P. McDowell

Wednesday Oct. 8 [1856]

My dear Wife,

I may now soon expect your first "gun" in response & I trust you will have listened to my request that you will write every day. I am still searching into the moral question & my work yesterday still left me in advance of anything I would need to give me sufficient conviction to go forward in the matter. Indeed I am triumphantly entrenched in my old view of the question & again take a strong *interest* in it as one needing to be set straight in popular opinion.

I am beginning to worry over the fiscal part of the matter & fear some little embroglio there; but still as you have long since told me that you are "peculiarly fitted to be a poor man's wife" I am going to take you at your word. Harrassed as you have been I am not going to suffer you to be in suspense & unsheltered in your feelings on the ground of a difficulty in maintenance. I will abide by my offer of breaking stone & at any rate, Darling, with a professional education & good health we ought not absolutely to starve. What is the *whole amount* now of your indebtedness? Dont allow any future installment or liability to be lost sight of. Tell me a sum beyond which you are *sure* your liabilities present & prospective do not go even when all your store bills & minor accounts are called in. Don't hesitate to tell me even if it be two millions of dollars. You are *worth* four millions. And then tell me whom the main sums are owing to & which are most pressing to be paid off. Dont take any important steps now till I hear from you in respect to these things for I am ruminating over plans by which I *may* be able to give a happy turn to *all* such matters. Be *certain all* you communicate.

Yours affly
Jno Miller.

Princeton, Oct. 8th 1856

Dearest Wife,

I am a strange creature. The moment reason gives the rein to any passion I possess I am pitiably devoured with the most eager impatience. So long as judgment declares I *shant* do a thing I am wonderfully stoical, but the moment I have hope I am painfully dissatisfied. This is the preamble with which I come to my petition of this evening which is that in fixing your plans you will make our wedding day as soon as you are able.

I am quite sure that we are right. My old letters when I first became a writer may turn out even as to the social point to be the wisest I have yet written. At any rate I have no doubt that the love which you so generously express is one which if it *have* its basis in your intelligent taste & liking which mine for you certainly has will last long enough to make us satisfied *in ourselves* & independant in that way of the movements of society.

I am so sorry you have had that scene on your farm. I wish I could have been there to see the whole attitude and mien of my own lovely mistress when she orders the stripes which she has usually reserved for me to be laid on the back of another. I fear I am a little free of some of the less womanly graces in my wife for instance, *intellect & courage.* I dont care how blue my wife should be, nor would I love her any the less delicately but with the hotter passion if I saw the blood of all the Caesars tingling & mantling in her cheek.

I am going to write you on my next regular day a long letter describing my plan that I shall have tho't out. I have not completed it all yet. But it is becoming promisingly simple & I think will not *deflect* much the original intention. I suppose your "trousseau" of last year is still partly in existence. I shall trust to your girlish ingenuousness & womanly good sense if you are actually *in straits* for money at least to let me know. Nothing prevents my enclosing some but your disrespect to my age & fatherly feelings on that score some months back & my feeling that there would be a sort of meanness after you had struggled so heroically so far to impair your sense of independance at the last moment.

I am so jaded by impatient excitements & loss of sleep that I mean to intermit writing till my next regular time. But dont *you* do so. By the way, I *did* write the letter that failed. I forget what it had in it.

I want you to send me the long letter you wrote on Saturday & didnt send. If you burnt it write what was in it. Dont excuse yourself fr. this, Darling, I *"beg".*

I rode out on the Hill this afternoon to tell the people with whom I was negociating of my altered purpose. I will tell you when I write of my whole Rocky Hill plan & how far I am able to make this. I am now forming agree[ments] with it. God bless you. Hurry & get ready. I shall be ready next week!

> *Yours lovingly*
> *Jno Miller.*

[marginal notes] So you do use the word passion at last. Why did you hesitate so?

Just say, Dear Husband, in one of your letters. I want to see how it will look. Dont forget.

> *Thursday Morn.*

Blessings on you, my dear, Daughter. Hurry & give yourself into my arms. Now that I have thoroughly put you on your guard I feel much disposed to follow my own sweet will & despise what others told me & think light of our difficulties.

I doubt whether our troubles will have any other result than to chasten a little the flow of Va hospitality & bring it down to a better Jersey standard where people take the liberty between these two great cities to stay in their house for six months at a time without turning the key in one spare chamber. Cheer up Darling. It is an ill wind that blows no body any good. And if as I now firmly believe *I am called to this step* (aint that a nice call Sally?) by Jehovah Jireh the God who has listened to your prayers, then we shall have good *heavenly* company if we are saved the trouble of much that is earthly. By the way you will find me a good deal of a recluse anyhow. How will you like that, Sally. Your fathers picture you must keep for me at Colalto.

Colalto
Thursday Oct 9. 1856

My dear John,

I did not write this morning, tho' I wanted to do it, because I had only time for a mere note; and tho' I knew you would be disappointed, yet I thought, on the whole, it would be more satisfactory for me to delay till I had more time. This afternoon I have fixed myself, you perceive, with my stitched sheets for a whole volume.

Tuesday's letter came this morning. I don't, by any means, intend to hold you to its proposal. I don't want you to act prematurely under the emotion excited by a letter of mine written in unusually low spirits; but when you have entirely finished all your thinking and studying and reasoning, and are calmly able to come to a final decision, then will be the true time for you to form plans for the future. I dont want to hurry you to a rash, or what may afterwards, seem a rash step, by mere *compassion* for me. I am a reasonable woman, and therefore will allow others the use of such motives as I feel would *properly* influence me in their circumstances, and tho' my letter was written, as you must know, without any design of leading you to a decision, to which I did not, at that time know, your mind was tending, yet I am willing it should weigh with you, among the *lesser* reasons that are to help you in making up your conclusion.

You absolve me from answering *all* the questions of your other letters; but I wont be absolved. There are some I choose to answer—one, at least; as, at a critical moment like this it becomes of *vital* importance to us both; that is, as to whether, (I don't quote you verbatim) I *love* you enough to bear all the consequences of marrying you?—whether my love is strong enough to out-ride all the storms against us and make me happy under them. I answer you *honestly*, John. I say to you, what I *feel*, You must not feel *chilled* if I speak *cautiously*, this is neither a time nor a subject for flippant or inconsiderate speech. I have often said to you that I loved you as I ever loved any human being—sometimes I have thought I loved you *more* than I ever loved before. At any rate, my nature has never, (and this is the point I am often making with myself) shown itself *capable* of a higher or warmer or steadier affection than that I feel for you, and therefore I judge that all its *capacity* of loving is fully engaged in my attachment to you. But I dont love you blindly. I see faults in you (not a great many, however, I must in all candor say), and I percieve in you things that will be *annoyances* to me; but this is just what I have seen & felt to all whom I have loved, & they have not diminished the volume or the swell of my affection for them. And I think I do love you enough to be able to say that I *can* as you say, "find my happiness for the rest of my life in you & our children & yours." Yet, I will suffer I know under the social prejudice against us. Even now, the prospect of it, as it comes out in its darkest picturing makes me tremble, at times, and feel almost as if it were, or wd be, insupportable; but then, I turn to look at myself, as I know myself in all my moods and feelings, and I come back to the decision, that, in spite of all, I shall *gain* in the matter of happiness. *I* expect, and you must too, if I marry you, that I shall occasionally give way to spells of feeling that will make you suffer *for* me, as well as *with* me, on this very account; but we must not allow a *paroxysm* to determine the question of general health and comfort. I have suffered from some such cause for years: it is nothing new to me. I cant tell you the agony I undergo. I have, sometimes, gone off by myself, and wept as if my heart would break,—then again I am denied the relief of tears, and suffer in silence. But, John, if I am your wife, I wd have the inexpressible comfort of going to you for—not relief, for I have long known that *that* was beyond human power, but for a *companionship* in sorrow, wh, as you may suppose, I have never known. Others have felt for me; you, I shall look upon you as so much of myself as that you will feel *with* me. Therefore to me, even in this dark side of the picture, there is some light.

But, John, it is selfish in me—certainly scarcely less than ungenerous, to be willing to bring upon you any portion of my sorrows. It seems hard that I should allow my misfortunes to overshadow any household but, (I am speaking very plainly), I do consider, that with all these misfortunes, I am, apart from family connexsions, & in my own person, equal to any man in America. This is no boasting. I think of myself "*soberly* (?) as I ought to think" according to Paul's exhortation; nevertheless I take account of my peculiar circumstances, & feel that they may tinge with a want of generosity my willingness to marry anybody.

My anxiety principally has been as to *your* affection, whether it can keep warm and steady under the neglect and slight put upon me. What do you think, John?

It may seem strange to you that I shd express so little fear about your children. To tell you the Truth my fears about them have much subsided. Their friends will have, in their interest for them, every incentive to make the best of the marriage for their sake and will shelter them as much as possible from any damage on account of it. My Lilly is much worse off than they. She could not, perhaps, be worse off than with me, as matters now stand; will she be better off if I take her in my ricketty little life-boat? God only knows.

Now let me tell you something. I was trying to recollect to-day the *exact* time but could not; yet it was, I am sure *before* any of these last letters of yours were received, that praying more earnestly and specially than common about this particular matter of ours, I upon *two* occasions begged that an answer might be given in a way that I could understand, and proposed this form myself.— "If the Marriage be right—(I am not sure, I wish I could recollect with perfect distinctness the very words, that I did not say "according to the will of God" in the sense of its being *expedient* as well as *lawful*) then, that our *minds* shd be inclined (in the strong meaning which "bent" would have better expressed) to it; if wrong that our minds shd be disinclined (*bent against*) to it?" Do you think, from the workings of your own mind that this prayer has been answered or not. By the time this reaches you, you will have gone thro' all yr thinking upon the subject & will be able to tell me with some certainty. I could not tell *satisfactorily* whether it had been answered to me, as my feelings fluctuated a good deal under my thought about the thing; and as, without an expression of opinion from you a bending of *my* mind for or against the marriage could sound nothing. To-day however, I find it rather steadying itself in one way.

Now, John don't think me visionary. I *do* believe that God answers prayer; but when I am conscious of so much sin, it becomes me to speak with much diffidence, and circumspection, as to the belief that he will, in any remarkable specific way answer mine. And yet, it would be wrong in me to doubt that he could or would do it, inasmuch as the want of merit in the Suppliant is *not* the thing regarded, but it is the fullness of the merit of Christ that obtains the hearing and the answer. I would not presume; but certainly there can be no sin in taking God at his word. *And if it be true that He inclines us to this step, then we are perfectly safe in taking it.* We need not fear for ourselves or our children. All the needful strength would be given me in the assurance that we were doing right. If I am right, I can *perfectly* trust all the interests involved to God, & feel sure that He will take good care of them all even as concerns this life. "Hypothetic" as these beings are, I yet shrink from the thought of *my* bringing injury upon my children. All my pride of race augments this feeling: all my love for them makes me tremble at the idea of their being wounded in their feelings & injured in their prospects thro' me. But I have a sort of feeling that they *will not be*. A thousand times in my life, I have comforted myself by repeating Job's question,—"Remember, I pray thee, whoever perished, being innocent?"[22] God has wonderfully protected me heretofore; and if I am convinced that he approves the marriage, why John, I wouldn't have any thing to fear. I wd be scared no doubt at the noise & fuss people will make; but then I should have *no reason* to be so.

Tell me, do you think this sounds foolish and visionary? I may *talk* foolishly, but the *thing* I talk about is not folly, but sublime verity. It is a Truth, that God hears his people and guides them and protects, or as the Catechism says, "*defends* them". And in this matter of ours it is strange, how little I think of such a thing

22. Job 4:7.

as confiding in man. If we want any thing from man our best way is to ask God to dispose them to give it to us. I wish you were here, that I might talk to you, this thing of writing is so clumsy and slow and obscure.

In this stage of the matter it is idle for me to speak of plans. However, I may say this much. You need never fear my asking you to live at Colalto, or to do anything with *my* property that the most fastidious person wd object to. But if from the debris of my estate any thing worth talking about is secured, you must remember that I *could* not own it in any such *separate* way, as would deny to you the comfort of it. If you can manage it well, you are certainly *entitled* to its use; & you couldn't expect me, under any circumstances of enjoyment from it, to *enjoy* it in any other way than by sharing it with you. You mustn't conjure up a separate interest of this kind; nor worry at any *apparent* inequality, but look at things as they are, and no doubt, you will *detect* some good reason for making or wishing to make no change in them. I am not sure that it is not best, even to our views of things, that we are poor; and if we should marry, should be constrained to the "seclusion" you speak of. You talk of "Va abundance" as tho' I felt to it as the murmuring Jews did to the "flesh-pots of Egypt," as if it were a thing worth bartering a Canaan for.[23] I am amused at it. You exaggerate it very much. We often have as poor a table as any laborer in the Town; and for months together during the last 18 months I have been my own chamber-maid. We are often, as troubled by our servants, tho' they are slaves, as you can be. Cousin Elizabeth Cocke was telling me this evening that her maid, who was banished for a year from the house to "the quarters," told her not long ago—that "she was the devil and was going straight to hell, & she believed she too was going along with her!" A happy prospect to her no doubt! And a man-servant of hers came & stood in her presence with his hat on, until, at last she asked him if he hadn't been taught that it was proper to take his hat off. Whereupon he told her, "He did take his hat off *to his Master*!" It is true, I never had such impertinance to bear, but still negroes are as provoking often as white servants; & what is worse, cant be discharged at pleasure.

John, indeed you must behave better. I wont have you telling me *all* your "anxieties." Please pick up some of the "prudery" I have thrown off.

By the by, I had forgotten till this minute to tell you *how* I look. People tell me I never looked better. I have regained all the flesh I lost in the Spring; and when (indeed this paper is horrid—look how it takes)[24] this Fall weather flushes my face, you yrself wd declare you had never seen me look better. But I am rapidly losing my hair, wh is a distress to me. I wouldn't care so much, if you weren't so foolishly fond of beauty, but I am anxious to be as handsome as possible. Now, Good night. I am just as tired, as you will be when you have read this far.

23. Exod. 16:2–3.
24. Her ink bled through the thin stationary.

Friday 8 A.M.

I add a line only as it is time for breakfast now. Yr Wednesday's letter has just come. I'll write to you about my debts another time. I am hard pressed in money matters. But John dont you believe that these difficulties would drive me to your arms. They do not seem entirely unmanageable even by me, tho' they harass and cramp me greatly.

Dont tare up or destroy or put out of the way the pamphlet Alexander gave to Hageman, but have it ready to restore to him *whenever he asks for it*. I would not allow him to trace its destruction to you, as tho' you feared its effect. I cant imagine how any *gentleman* would care to preserve such a thing. However, I have always had my doubts about the genuine tone & feeling of that whole race:— there are cases of real & true sentiment amongst them,—but the *want* of that rather characterizes the whole family.

I agree in all you say as to our bearing to others. Cousin John used to say, I had a way of *looking* entirely composed, as if no thought of *my* being *wrong* entered my head. This, if true, will help the matter. And as a general thing people respect my motives, & will not rudely assail me.

I am so sorry to hear Maggie isn't well. I wish she had been with me this summer gaining strength upon the Alum water.

In a hurry Yours
S.C.P. McDowell

I did try the hard paper under this but it did precious little good. In future, I shant have to write such long letters, and will take paper of a firmer texture, so dont send me any more like this.

Princeton, Friday Evening
Oct 10th '56.

My Darling Sally,

Your letter of Wednesday has just come in & I am strangely *fascinated* with this account of T's apparent age. I never thought before of the possibility of this deception. I am so impatient now finally to possess you that I can scarcely think of anything else; but Oh, if that old wretch should die just after our wedding or in one year or even two years what force it would give to poor Mothers counsels. But still, My Love, I am more fascinated with the idea of our wedding & as the considerations of prudence are all on your account & are now all in your keeping I luxuriate in the idea of winning you if I can & of making myself happy in your affection.

I have spent the week in far more careful thought than I shall probably ever have again on this question & all with one result. I am stronger in my view. I think desertion a valid ground of divorce. I believe, therefore, there are four grounds with you either of which would justify your marriage, first, a State divorce along *with* the *fact* of unfaithfulness; second a divorce by a State very strict in[25] its practice, who has given the right reasons to its courts when *they* divorce, divorces, itself without giving any reasons at all, was possessed by common fame of the fact of unfaithfulness at the time, & called for such specifications as your father gave & as have been said to be insufficient by the force of a law just enacted & soon abrogated not now in force & not vital to the act of repudiation. Thirdly, those specifications which were tried & proved contained T's pamphlet & these proofs of "malitious desertion"; & fourthly, the Maryland legislature exhibits in its record in one view the fact of a divorce and a malitious desertion both at once. The result therefore of my week's thought could not have been more favorable.

I have gone farther & sketched a plan during my week's thinking.

The great object of my life is certain theological studies. I know you get tired of this thought, but it would be discouraging waywardness in me if *I* got tired of it or lingered away from the pulpit without an absorbing & in my view superior design. When I came to Princeton I had resigned the idea of marrying you before T's death & I began carefully to agitate some plan that would be an arrangement for life. I determined to stay in Princeton. I began to think whether I could connect with my favorite pursuit any official duty. I considered several. I thought over the idea of a charge. Well a city charge I knew would arrest all study & a country charge in the end would prove nearly as dissipating & less useful; so I rejected both. I thought of a professorship or a presidency in some college if I could get it. Well, Pres: Woolsey & Prof. Fowler I knew had left colleges or would like to for private study & I knew fr. all I had heard & seen that both engrossed your labour quite as much as the pastorate, indeed a country pastorate would do so less than either.[26] I saw nothing existent therefore but an entire cessation, & determined therefore to place myself in the path of an independent living. By acting carefully I knew I could maintain my children during Mother's life & at her death I meant to go on until you could join us with our residence in this village. So far my plan had worked well. I had had part of a year of leisurely study. I have lived under circumstances that confirm my conviction as to the best mode of prosecuting my duty. I have the approbation of my conscience in the matter & were it not for the *dismalness* of such a life impatient & hungry with an ungratified affection my year would have been a very congenial one. Lately I had begun to purchase that hill land. A thousand acres lying in a circle of roads I thought would be a beautiful home to be preparing for you during your uncertain banishment & I found that the wood part of it could be purchased in small tracts so as to be owned eventually for perhaps *less* than nothing. This then was my simple plan. 1st A devotion to philosophy. 2d a residence in Princeton. 3rd A preparation by afternoon superintendance of that beautiful home for us

25. Miller repeated "in."

26. Theodore Dwight Woolsey (1801–1889), Congregational minister and president of Yale College from 1846 to 1871. Samuel Fowler (1818–1865) of Sussex County, N.J.

on the skirts of the village. Three things helped me in this, first, an income of which I have talked to you of $270 a year; second, a distribution which mother has recently been making to each of us of $200 a year & thirdly, about a hundred dollars for preaching at different places. This so far has supported us boarding as we do with Mother & prevented my diminishing my means.

Now that I have hope of marrying you my aim has been to arrange some plan for us that will not interfere with my cherished vocation. To seek a charge would in other respects be evil, because till public opinion settles down it would be a much less safe position than one of independance. And even a professorship might expose us just at this stage to scenes I might be driven to resent.

I have thought, therefore, of this. If mother would give me the principal of $200 ($3333) instead of this interest, I could take from my own means enough to make it $5000 & give this to you for Colalto, making up $15000 by means of a mortgage for $10000 to Lilly. This I might do now, so that before our marriage the public might know that I had bought Colalto.—then be married—then come to the North on a long Winter visit—then return with the children to the farm & settle down to a regular application to my pursuits. My skill in farming you know nothing about. But I think I could guide an overseer so as to pay Lilly her interest, pay the overseer, give us all that support that comes off of such an establishment & enough more to give us a moderate sufficiency besides. The $5000 would pay your most pressing debts. I would have an income of some $160 more or might take more of my principal & pay off other liabilities; at any rate the essential feature would be my public purchase of Calalto which would relieve the difficulty I would feel of living there were it yours. Then if we survive Mother I might be a bidder for our own homestead here, (for by that time we might have reduced or partially sold Colalto,) the advantage in which would be that by settling first in the village & in so good a home we would avoid the appearance of stealing from public view & besides that whoever of us sons will own this property & run the necessary streets must greatly increase by the rate of them his own means of living as it consists of 17 acres of farm land in the midst of the town. That as our intermediate home might leave us at last as it became cluttered up with homes free to move to the Hill & thus rejoin the other arrangement. This is a rough sketch of my general outlook & plan of living having this advantage that it does nothing de novo[27] but would contemplate your house or this in circumstances in which *some* arrangement for them has actually to be made.

This plan, however, depends upon a certain advanced sum by Mother & I was in hopes that your letter to night might be more definite than it is that it might be sure to speak to her on the whole subject. I fear a little about Mother. She is feeble & burdened with age & if she were to assume an attitude of distress or

27. Latin, meaning brand new.

opposition I would be greatly perplexed. I wouldnt like to charge myself with hastening her descent down the declivity of life. If she from any cause, also, were to refuse what I speak of I should be somewhat at sea again.

Colalto were I to buy it would be about what I may expect from [my] own patrimonial estate. Mother is worth about $100.000. About $60.000 of that is willed already (by Father) & willed so that I would have but about $4000 of it. But Mother has had a plan to use the balance to make us all equal. Before she conceived this, however, she made a will which did not accomplish this fully, but arranged matters so that I would have about $12.000 of the estate which with what I now have of my own would be about $16.000 (that is, as I say, about equivalent to Colalto). She intends to equalize us further by destroying this will & making another. But the inroads of time may undermine that purpose & render her (unconsciously to herself) incapable of the required decision. I would dislike Mother to be so offended with me as to throw me back upon Father's old dotation of $4000;[28] but this I feel even in extreme old age she is too kind a Mother to do & I have strong hopes, as soon as I hear your decision that I may approach her on the whole subject & find what is dearer to me than her money her blessing & a sense that I have not wronged her in her old age. Let us, therefore, have the talk over with *her* before you *announce* anything publicly. But you can be taking your steps & whenever I hear from you with sufficient definiteness I will broach the subject to her & we will have that anxiety over. You will tell me too before long what you think of my plan for Colalto.

Meanwhile, I have taken a step which you will smile at & which I intended at first not to tell you. Williams is my bosom friend in Frederick. Under the seal of profound secrecy even from his wife I have ventured with all the taste with which I could manage it to ask him for a true account of T's health. I did this soon after my letter to you. I hope to hear to-morrow or Monday. If that catastrophe were unmistakeably approaching *I* for one would not be too "defiant" to prefer that it should pass first.

And now, Darling Sally, I have gone thro' a long *long* letter. I have told you all the work of the week. I wish you were nearer to me than 400 miles. And, Sally, why do you write me such short letters? & your head-ache makes you cold to me—almost *cool* to use a stronger word. Have I offended you? And why do you say that speculating upon when we may marry is "premature." Oh, Sally, youre a sad heart ache to me sometimes, not that you are not kind & that you are not loving nearly all the time, but that you are so *lovely* as to create a hunger that your words do not appease. Oh, if the Gods decree that any one should fall in love with you they ought to decree that the blind God should shoot very skillfully at you too, & make *your* wound as deep & rankling as the one that your loveliness makes *him* suffer. I feel right disposed to grumble. You were to write me a long

28. A "dotation" is an endowment.

letter &, Love, tho' your head-aches, yet even with a throbby head couldnt you say one kind thing when I have been waiting for it all day!

Yours very affectionately
Jno Miller.

I have now not one thing to interrupt my eager looking for our marriage except a wistful thought about T's life & a tinge of anxiety about mother. All else is disposed of. And these do not prevent my impatience to receive your answer. Write to me every day.

[marginal note] My book I hold in abeyance. *Now* I will not publish it at once, but guard against but wait till some mos. after our marriage. I am testing it in every way I can. I *cant* upset it.

Colalto,
Satur'y Oct 11, 1856

Dear John,

I shall write you a full business letter this afternoon; at present I scratch off a note, that the interval of waiting may not be so long. I have had no letter from you this morning, as I expected. Your letter yesterday spoke of a sort of weariness under the burden of a daily letter, but; as you are very steady to your promises I thought you would hold out till to-day. I should not be surprised if I find a letter from you lying in my box yet.

Remember when you use such expressions as these, "if you do not love me you have frightfully deceived me," that I sympathize in all the fears you can have on the subject. If I do not love you, I have frightfully deceived myself.

Set your mind at rest; "a surly gruff student, not always willing to be bothered" *can not* "make a woman happy under the darkness of his frowns!" Whoever dreamt of any body being made happy by such a dismal thing as "dark frowns." If yr philosophy teaches the possibility of happiness under such a condition of things it will be a God-send to all the bad tempered oppressors in the land, but of poor account to any forlorn sufferer; and as I am one of this last sort, it will not do Darling, for me. I shall want something brighter from you than frowns, especially if I am to have them from everybody else.

You talk of "my agitations being over"—why, John, they are yet to come, and will be in full force only when your letter written *yesterday* shall be received. Up to that, nothing you have said is of a binding nature to either of us. I wont accept any offer from you, or listen to any plan, made in the first excitement of the new turn given to our matters. You must be yourself, calm and resolved, having *finished* all yr deliberations. My own mind is steadier and quieter than formerly—so changed too, in many respects during the last year that it seems almost a new creation to me. This past has been a year of great suffering and sorrow to me, but, whatever the issue of our present deliberations, I shall never regret that it, with all its teachings has been added to my existence. I have not changed in my love to you, except that I love you more, but that very affection has different and worthier lights in it Now.

I shall be impatient to hear from you—I would say, *every day*, but you must regulate that by yr other occupations. I can't myself write every day. I am unusually occupied.

God bless you, my dear John.

Affection'y
S.C.P. McDowell

Colalto,
Monday Oct 13. 1856

Dear John,

I ought to have written Saturday evening as I intended, but I was tired & put it off till this morning. Now I am hurried, as I always am, in the morning. I find our present excitements wear upon me. Yesterday I was anxious & flurried, and getting to bed early to quiet myself, & get rested, I gave myself the chance to lie awake for an hour or so before a human being stirred on the premises. The result of all which is, that I am so nervous to-day, that every part of my body feels as if it had a terrible fight with which it yet quivers.

As to my debts about which you ask, I cannot be entirely certain, but I think the following schedule is nearly right.—

To Lilly	$12.000
Last payment on Colalto	4.000
To Mary	2.000
To Nib	500
Store bills etc. etc.	1.500
	$20.000

To meet these liabilities I have set apart certain pieces of property. But to give you some idea of my *ability* to meet them I give you a list of all *my possessions* as they at present stand.

Colalto recently assessed at about $19.000

1/8 of the Military	5.500
1/8 of Saline (rising in value)	1.500
1/8 of Uncle Tom's bond	1.300
My Grandmother's legacy about	3.500
Lot in Washington	6.000
4 small lots in Louisville	5.000
10 negroes	5.000
Household property, farming utensils, stock	2.000
	$49.300

If these different pieces of property were thrust into market just now, no doubt they would, in some cases, be cruelly sacrificed—but they are all safe investments at present except the Washington City lot. If Buchanan is elected I should like to hold on to it, giving Lilly a mortgage upon it for its present estimated value of $6.000. If Fremont is elected, which scarcely however seems possible, then it wont be worth a song to me. However, with all this array of thousands I *am pressed* for a few hundreds, which I am inclined to borrow from a neighboring Bank—or the Bank of Va at Richd. If my farming next year succeeds it will re-imburse me; & by renewing my note with a curtail of 20 pr cent every three months, or 2 months as the case may be, I fancy I could manage—*tolerably*. Still it may be difficult to do this, as money is so scarce in our State that even the Banks are slow to lend. My great anxiety is to get rid of Lilly's claim upon me; for as it stands now I am paying her 6 pr cent, when I can get only 3 or 4 or, at most, five upon my investments. If my Sisters wd take drafts upon our worshipful Uncle, I could have paid off my debt upon this place in June, but they want their money & dont want to wait for Uncle Tom, who has never yet felt the impulse of the 19th century in his business. I get mad at him—that is, I feel indignant, when I hear of his building, or projecting Hotels, I dont believe he is actually building them yet, and putting up ware-houses, on a large scale, and see him look, with *apparent* unconcern at Aunt Eliza selling off the home of her children when if he had met her claim upon him of $6.000 it wd have saved her: Or if he had loaned her the amount—or given it to her—or allowed her the use of his name in Bank, she might have kept her patrimony. But John, I do believe much money makes people mean. Uncle Tom with his Million is nothing like as honorable and generous as Aunt Eliza in her poverty. He promised to educate Campbell Carrington—advanced $50 (!) five years ago, and stopped. Now Campbell, who is a gallant fellow, goes this fall to the University upon his own means. He & Jimmy both worked last year like high spirited independent boys should work, & go this year to the University together, on their own means. I bid them God speed, with my whole heart.

It isn't worthwhile to send you the old letter you ask for: there is nothing of any interest in it now.

For my next letter I shall tell you more of my notions for the future. I am concerned about Lilly. I cant bear to think of her leaving me. She must go to school, but now she has her head full of my going with her. She has been wonderfully contented all summer here, and often says she is very happy with me alone. She deports herself to me like a child, hates to be away from me, and asks me till sometimes, I am a little impatient, "Sister do you love me"? Just the other day she laughingly said to me—"Truly, Sister, I am courting you every day". She is hot-tempered like the rest of her race, but more affectionate—yet I dont know.

James is in St Louis, with no intention that I have heard of leaving there. At a distance, he cant influence Lilly. I doubt whether any one else would attempt it, unless Massie & Nib would try their hand, neither of whom I think could effect much as Lilly is less fond of them than any other members of the family. She likes Mr Massie perhaps better than Bro Ross; but Nib less than any of her Sisters.

Dont trouble your money investments or arrangements with the purpose of aiding me; but take mine in hand, and disentangle and re-arrange them, so that they may avail us something hereafter.

Old Dr Ruffner is here, preaching well, but looking very tottering.[29]

God bless you. Aff'y
S.C.P. McDowell

Princeton, Oct 13th 1856.

Ha! Ha!

So you see some faults in me (not many tho') & *annoyances*! That's plain talk certainly! Well, Darling, I shant ask you what they are because after you have confided them to me you'll be going off looking for more. I mean to keep these in your [illegible] memories & then, Dearest, if I should be so happy as to show you that where I have annoyed you it has sprung from peculiarities of circumstance you will be all the happier for not having charged upon your husband peccadillos that he did not possess.

Sally, Dear, I now feel discharged from any further *honesties* of setting you upon your guard against any of the evils that could possibly follow our marriage. I have earned the right now if any poor suitor ever did of falling back upon my own individual hopes & pressing with all my power this marriage. You will see by what I enclose[30] that there is nothing that prudence could demand of us in one direction; & as to my Mother's peace I *could* not consult it any more than in some case of extreme necessity as for example if what I told her drove her to her room or to her bed, a thing that I regard *impossible*. You know I first spoke to her months ago in no other way in first announcing to her our engagement than one of entire deference to her claim. I told her I would not go on to an engagement (in her life time I meant) if it *seriously* disturbed her peace. Perhaps I was wrong in even saying as much. At any rate I said it & therein I felt free from all possible alarm on the part of conscience as to whether I honored my Mother. My mind therefore is all made up. You will write to me more definitely in your letter received tomorrow & then I shall speak to Mother & then—*Darling*, you cant tell how I wrestle with these few days of delay.

I must be strangely constituted. John Miller is a far greater annoyance to me than he can be to you. He is a perfect burden to me. I long to get rid of him. Wont you take him? And tho resting quiet all summer under a sense of a sort of philosophic necessity no sooner does he conjure up a little hope than he comes boisterously to me at all hours of the day, clamoring to know how the thing is coming on & perfectly impatient (a man that expected to wait for years) because now he must wait thro' these weeks of October.

29. Henry Ruffner, Presbyterian minister, former president of Washington College, and father of Miller's friend William Henry Ruffner.

30. The enclosure from John Williams has not been located.

The fact is, Sally, this same John Miller needs caring for a little. He cant work in such a frame as this. He is now held by no reserves. What friends laid upon him, in respect to you he has thoroughly discharged. The flood-gates of honour no longer hold for an instant his own personal desires, & your convenience & the possibilities of the case as to the time seem to him like worthless reeds that he chafes against in a most suffering impatience. Will it not be possible for us to marry early in November?

Ill tell you what I have been doing. If you will consent to accept invitations that are made to you at suitable points I want to distribute them on our journey so that they will prove certain actual facts in respect to the attitude of our friends. For example Prof. Henry since he came here has been teezing me again & again to pay him a visit. Then his wife took it up told me they had a room which they would keep ready for me at the Col. meeting. Then Prof. Henry told me of his wife's wish & spoke of it again on Friday when I called after a party at his brothers & finally he met me today & said, "You are not sure that you will be there in January will you not be there anytime this Winter?" Whereupon I took his arm & crossed over from the group where we were standing & said, "Prof. Henry it is a matter I speak of with reserve, but I may say to *you* thus only that the next time I am in Washington will probably be going on & returning from my marriage." He seemed evidently a good deal moved by the announcement & said with great feeling—"I'm glad of that. I'm glad of it for you both." ["]Well," said he, "Mr Miller, then is the time I claim a visit. I knew Gov. McDowell well & he was kind to me & Mrs Henry *shall* have a visit". I told him I had paused as perhaps a minister ought & had studied this whole subject calmly. I hadnt a doubt of our right. I told him, Public Opinion so far as it spoke different was false & I wouldnt submit to it & if I could win you to my view as I hoped I could we would be married this Winter. I was astonished to see how moved he was. The tears absolutely came into his eyes & he pressed my hand right warmly & applauded this particular opinion. He then made me *promise* that I would let Mrs Henry know in time to send you an invitation & promised that he would say nothing about the wedding till it was announced except to Mrs Henry. Now Dearest, we must accept that invitation. If they get us once into the Smithsonian building they will keep us there several days & if such men as Prof Henry come out warmly on our side I shall have small compunction on what some men call my *crime* in persuading you to marry me.

And now, Sweetest, I am going to take the luxury of following my own wish in all this matter of an immediate wedding if I never speak again of your hazards you must consider me as feeling that all those conversations are over. If you find me concealing from you sometimes the slightly speeches of others you must consider me as just treating them as I feel, that is, utterly despising them. And if you find me really talking inconsistently with all this anxiety for you & really saying things that seem to betoken a belief that there is no social danger you must only feel that I am settling upon my original belief & after giving due influence to our friends & due warning to you that I am getting back to my feeling that there is no really serious danger.

And now, Daughter, my heart warms tenderly to you in a *way* utterly impossible under its old anxieties. It feels healthily that you are my wife. It *claims* you with the most eager confidence & it exults that the time has come when it may put away all sage calculations for you that are a denial to itself & court & beg for you like any other suitor.

My happiness is in your hands far more than my own personal sacrifice of it has left you willing to imagine. And if you have injured me in anything it has been, Darling, that you not have acknowledged in some sort of confiding freedom at least from watchful anxieties that I was worthy of you in one respect, that I love *your* happiness more painstakingly than I do my own.

Yesterday I was in Brunswick. Dr Davidson was sick. After preaching I was invited to dinner at Col Neilson's.[31] While there I was wishing you could have been with me. A former wife was my sister-in-law, a lady of whose beauty there are wild traditions yet in this region. *He* is a Director of the "Monopoly" a friend of Com. Stocktons. He lives on an old ancestral farm of [800?] acres just out of Brunswick & his wife who was a Bleecker of one of the old families of Albany is a lovely woman whom you would very much like.[32] While there I thought of writing to you, but an extra meeting took me home sooner than I expected. I must tell you an old secret. You must not repeat it. The mother of my poor children who was Mrs Neilson's sister was often at her house & some years after her death was addressed by this brother-in-law. I could not help thinking yesterday as I saw his handsome hospitality & was sitting in his fine house & recollected his fortune of perhaps half a million how different in these respects at least was her actual fortune in a husband. Mrs Neilson is so nice. If *she* had heard from me the same news as Prof. H. I have no doubt she would have pressed on us the same invitation.

What can Williams mean by Thomas taking up those papers. Is it worth inquiring about? But, Sally, throwing away as I hope you will now do all thought about any of these matters; & giving yourself up as you naturally must to the care & protection of your husband I hope you will just turn all your thought to the matter of our marriage. I am now so entirely at sea in the dreamy reveries of my happiness in this respect that I really am not fit for a thing until this ceremony is safely over. Is the first part of Nov: too early for you to get ready?

I do think you are an incorrigible "boaster" almost as much so as I. And yet I do listen with a sort of exultant throb to the thought that one whom *I know* to be one of the loveliest of her Kind, or as Dr. Van R. expresses it *"that magnificent woman"* is to be within a few weeks my own possession.

31. Miller interlined here: "I went later." James Neilson (1784–1862), a businessman from New Brunswick, N.J. His third wife was Harriet Benedict (1811–1840), the older sister of Miller's first wife.

32. Neilson's wife was Catherine Bleecker Neilson (1809–1893).

Mrs Neilson wanted to know whether when our cards of invitation to the wedding of the Col's granddaughter who is to be married next week, came, I would write word that I would come.[33] I told her I would if I could. So I may see her soon again.

I do feel so *happy* this afternoon. Writing my own letter & taking my own part & as the boys used to express it, "not trying to shinny on both sides at once" gives such a feeling of lightness. Man is a selfish animal. And I find it "goes" much more naturally to let you look out for yourself & get you if I can.

Soliloquy. And yet I would like to know what *annoyance* I am to Sally. And yet perhaps it is better; because now she wont be disappointed with me when we are married. Indeed I *tell* her, she knew I had faults & she had no business to marry me. And yet I would like to know how I annoy her: because now in this blind period of my love I hate to have the gloss of a proud success worn off which I feel for winning so beautiful a creature. Perhaps it is because I talk slow & am small & ugly—or perhaps I lack the *physique*. James who understands these things tells us so.—or perhaps I am not well-behaved. Sally, ought to allow for the flutter & stir of her own presence in these things. Sally aint lenient to me in these matters. No matter if they *are* so, she knew them all before marriage & if they are not I'm a *martyr* & she shall give me three or four extra kisses for wronging me so before we were married.

Sally, Dear, I'm in earnest. I do beg you to bring this thing to an end. Im doing no good now as long as we are separated & I shall recover my good sense & usefulness only at yr side.

Yours affy,
Jno Miller

[marginal notes] [A]s to the "bending" of my mind of which I see a question in your letter—nothing could be more complete. I am settled in a way that seems final & complete.

Remember you need not wait for my interviw with Mother. Every thing waits now only for you.

Colalto
Oct: 14. '56 8 1/2 A.M.

Dear John,

I am late this morn'g. I didn't intend to write at all to-day, until yr letter came & determined me otherwise.

I said all planning for our marriage was "premature" in the letter you speak of, because, at that time, I did not consider your own mind fully made up about it, and I could not bear you should act upon any hasty or half-formed

33. Augusta Griffin (1835–?) married Ezekiel Chambers Wickes on Oct. 22, 1856. She was a granddaughter of Colonel Neilson by his first wife, Rivine Foreman (1791–1823).

judgment arising from a seeming or even real pressure of my opinion. Besides I wanted to be careful of my own feelings. I did not wish them to flow full & strong in a direction, from which, hereafter, they might be turned again most painfully.

I think I have refrained too, in all the letters of this past week, except one, in giving any strong expression of my own affection, or my own feelings in this new turn of affairs. I could have done both; I didn't choose to do either. I wrote you, I would not receive any proposed change from our present relations as, a sober & definite one, until all your deliberations were ended, and the whole allotted period for them entirely exhausted. Up to that, I was free to express my views, but I did not feel it to be entirely honorable or delicate to bias your judgment or hamper your final decision by frequent and strong iteration of my affection. Once, when it was a strong point for yr *judgment* to act upon, I spoke it out *honestly*—that was enough. If it has come in since, in any of my letters it has been incidentally.

Your letter makes me anxious. The old uneasinesses about yr profession come up. I cant *map* out the future, but I feel I ought not to disqualify you for your duty as a Minister. You speak of yr higher vocation. That has, always seemed, most uncertain to me. I have thought the test of two or three years would go against it. Then, that term of absence from the public eye, diminishes your chance of re-establishment as a Pastor, or of obtaining a Professorship, &c &c, even if you were unmarried & unassailable on that score. A Country charge I am convinced wouldn't suit you, even if it could be joined with yr favorite pursuit. But still these we can talk of again; what I want to say now is that I wont bind you to me as to any plan for an immediate marriage until you have *first* talked fully and candidly to your Mother. If she feels to it in such a way as to make you withdraw from it, why, it is far better you should be untrammelled by my consent to it: if she presents no obstacle then it is easy for us to come to an immediate determination.

I rather, at first glance, object to your plan about Colalto. It wont suit you, I think to live here. At any rate, it seems wisest for me to pay off Lilly as I have told you, than for you to embarrass your means to do it.

I have rather longed for your reasoning on the moral question. I have anxieties about it, which I have begun to think must grow out of my feelings, more than my reasonings. I want to come up to the law of God in matters; & not have that Law changed for any case. I believe in this thing of "desertion" as a ground of Divorce only so far as I find it bring about the criminality which according to the New Testament, annuls the marriage. Even then, the question comes up, how far the separation in the first instance was right. But I am hurried. I do love you John and am

wholly yours,
S.C.P. McDowell

Princeton, Oct 15th 1856
Morning

Darling,

It seems hard to be without a letter since Monday night & perhaps it ought to make *me* think how *you* feel as tho you were suddenly brought to a short allowance when in waiting till you make your reply I sink suddenly back to our old days. I hope tonight's letter will contain something definite for I want to go to Mother with the whole thing & be able to speak without the slightest uncertainty.

In this waiting mood I have been thinking of your Aunt Floyd's threat. Like most men, I suppose, I have a sort of exultant wish to see how the lady means to accomplish it. I suppose I may be sufficiently respectful & yet say that I have recurred to it with a sort of ineffable disdain. And besides an amused curiosity to see how your good Aunt means in this Motherly enterprise to proceed, I have the intention to *allow* you no communication with your family that is not attended on their part with the utmost respect. Still I have no intention to blow the trumpets of menace beforehand because I think that these various oppositions may be very likely to settle down when it is known that our own purpose is resolved & final.

Do you want to know what pleasure is my *highest* in this contemplated wedding? (Well I dont know that I can say the *highest* either for that would be saying that I am so good a man as to make such a pleasure exceed a more thrilling & immediate possession) but the strongest the most valued, when I come to reflect. What do you think it is, Sally? It is that I am bringing into my family a lady *of much trust in God*. It will be worth towers of strength to us, Sally. It will continue our family in being long after the best position & the most unchallenged & undoubted social steps might have proved incapable to uphold it. You have no idea how I prize these letters in which you ask me so strangely if I think you visionary. Darling, I am telling you the unvarnished truth when I tell you that your trust & faith appear to me so express & settled that I am expecting more good from them in our family destiny that I could wisely hope from the most delightful circumstances in all other respects that you could name. God *will* take care of those who trust him. And as I have brought my thinking to a point in which my mind is quite certain in respect to duty I am beginning to enjoy far more than I can describe the idea of our actual & speedy wedding.

I do hope, Sally, you will not embarrass it with unnecessary delays. And as I have gone thro all my part of the decision & have nothing to do but wait now till I am overtaken by you I hope Sally, that in acting for us both you will bring us into each others arms as soon as the circumstances of the case will possibly allow.

I dont feel willing to be away from you & now that it is determined we will marry I see no good for two persons like us to be long apart.

Thursday Oct 16
Morning

Poor John! No letter last night—an utter & blank disappointment! I am looking for one this morn. Yet I fear that Edward was late & that I shant hear till to-night.

I received last night in an enclosure that looked so much like yours that I was tantalized by it the enclosed invitation. I find I cant accept because Synod (which I ought to attend) assembles on Tuesday off at Norristown quite in the opposite direction.

I will write again to-morrow (that is, by the next mail) if I get a letter from you.

Affectionately
Your disappointed Husband
Jno Miller

Colalto
Wed'y Oct 15. 1856

Dear John

I have just received Mr Fendall's letter which I enclose.[34] You perceive it is entirely unsatisfactory and, upon the point of interest, worthless. I do not admit the correctness of his conclusion from the *omission* of a charge of libertinism in Uncle's speech. Uncle had material enough for all his purposes beside that; It is true a flagrant exhibition of such criminality such as Cost Johnson practised in Washington, might have been used by him with effect; yet even it wd have been, no more *convincing* to the multitude, than the universally received rumor of his misconduct in this particular was.[35] However, I am disappointed at Mr F's letter; but not discouraged.

It is very important, John, to me on many accounts that we should come to some *decision* on the matter. My comfort greatly needs it. The suspense & agitation I have been suffering with its attendent wakefulness and excitement & weariness is almost more than I can bear. I beg you will write me, conclusively, what your opinions and plans are. This writing work is slow and, at best, unsatisfactory. I have not wished to hurry you, but I do feel that the disquietude &c that I undergo, ought to be controlled by a final conclusion. So, I hope you have had yr talk with yr Mother before this reaches you. Indeed I am hoping for an *answer* to this letter before it can get to you. I hope you have anticipated it in one already written. My anxieties are great on the whole subject, and bear upon me so that I am losing my strength to control or support them. Yesterday I felt miserably. This morning I am troubled again.

34. This letter has not been located.

35. William Cost Johnson (1806–1860), a Washington, D.C., attorney. Previously he had served four terms as a Whig in the United States House of Representatives from Maryland. Francis Thomas defeated him in that state's gubernatorial election in 1841.

Write me Dr McGill's views of the moral question. Old Dr Ruffner dines with me to-day, and if I can summon the courage, I shall have a full talk with him on that point. I wd trust, his judgment before Dr White's a good deal; & besides I want a talk with somebody, and can rely upon him.

Would you believe it? We are in the midst of snow! Monday I was walking in a lace shawl & crepe bonnet; to day I am hovering over the fire in snow & clouds.

I am *so* troubled, Darling—say do you love me a very great deal.

In great haste. Aff'y
S.C.P. McDowell

Thursday 8. A.M.

Dear John,

It was so cold & snowy yesterday, I hated to send a servant with my letter at the mail hour, & consequently, it is here for me to add to this morning.

No letter from you *Yesterday*! None to-day! I think it hard under all the disquietude of the present, and am much dispirited about it. Do, I beg as a *mercy* to me, write me a letter that will show that you have reached a *conclusion*, on this matter. You deceive yourself, when you say you have left the decision with me. And, at any rate, the decision should not be *absolutely* with *either*, but with both. We must agree upon it together—not you take the whole out of my hands, & decide for me, & I submit to your decision;—nor I assume the responsibility alone, & you submit to my decree, but we must be united in it—and this way of doing it by letters is slow, unsatisfactory & subjects us beside to misapprehension & misconstruction one of another.

I think it proper that you defer to yr Mother—but not, after all that has passed, that you place the whole thing under her control. In the first instance, she waived any such responsibility; afterwards, when the marriage was determined upon, she wrote to me saying she did not wish us to recede from it; when it was disappointed last Winter, she was rather for yr asserting your right to go on; now, she still recognizes your right to proceed;—and thus under the whole aspect of this group of facts, a *respectful appeal* to her is all that seems to be required, under the circumstances. I would not have you omit any attention to her;—so far from it, you see I have already united with you in deferring to her feelings, *before* I would say aught to bind you so to me that you *could not* honorably yield to her judgment if it were *adverse* to my decision but, John, she ought not to forget or disregard the fact of my having some claim to consideration in the matter. I dont say a word in any unkind spirit to her. As your Mother, I couldnt do otherwise than feel very respectfully to her—but loving you as I do, I have a stronger & warmer sentiment than mere respect for her. Of all things, I would delight that she should love me; and sometimes as my heart bubbles up to yr Mother, I long that *she* should have wakened for me a little of the feeling of being mine too.

One thing, I observe in your sketch of yr opinions upon the moral question, which is, that you restrict the word "desertion" to its narrow & common acceptation. Old Dr McFarland & others, & Dr Ruffner yesterday gave it a wider scope—Dr McFarland you remember sd—"If a man treats his wife in such a way that it is impossible for her to live with him, *he deserts her.*" This comes with full force upon my case. Dr Ruffner offered & I gladly accepted his offer, to *write* out his opinion. He spoke cautiously as if he did not want to commit himself *unadvisedly.* His fear about our marrying was of personal violence from Thomas as he had heard of his saying, "he would kill any man whom I wd marry." He heard moreover that he had followed me like a shadow when I was last in Phil: wh, you know isn't true. I told him Thomas was a coward. For years I couldn't bear to admit that fact: but he is. He didn't behave, above suspicion of cowardice in his duel with Price and he acted like a craven, on the Bank Committee in Phil, in '35 or '36, I forget which.[36]

I write in terrible haste.

It is so cold. Snow & sleet night before last; & clouds & rain yesterday as tho' it were real winter.

My "head aches" dont make me "cool" to you Darling. I am hot enough. I even long to tell you so. And last night as I sat thinking of you, I wd have hailed it a privilege to be able to write you just how my love wrapped itself about you, and what a joy it wd be to let it flow out unfearingly to you. Do write to me my own little man—and dont be offended too quickly, or offended at all at any thing I may say.

God bless you my precious John.

Yours
S.C.P. McDowell.

Princeton, Oct 17th 1856
8 1/2 A.M.
Mail closes at 9.

My *Darling Sally,*

Here seems to be a point where I ought to say over again all I have ever said about "philosophy." I express that when I think of the socialities of a Pastor's life, his *immediate* usefulness & then of the $2000 or $3000 which (tho' with great deduction for expence) I might use for lifting off our heavy liabilities it requires steadiness to hold my own mind to the ideas I have cherished. And indeed, Darling, it does require the usual effort of perseverance to hold my mind upon its predestined track. But when you speak as tho you did not understand fully yet the tone of my feeling it seems honorable to go over again & say as I did so early in my courtship, that I have this *drawback* of a zeal for metaphysics; that I consider it *my highest duty* to keep my life as near as I can upon that track—that

---

36. William Price (?–1868), Maryland lawyer and politician. Thomas challenged him, but neither man was injured in the exchange in Aug. 1840.

it is my highest taste—that if I had wilfully trammel'd myself so as to forbid this pursuit I would count it a great sin (such a sin as you fear lest you & I commit in respect to my ministry) & that I think it most probable that (except under some pressure of a mere pecuniary kind) I shall never hold office again either in a College or in a Church. I cant *explain* this to you any more than the studies themselves, but you surely would not respect me if after all I have said I should deliberately yield & swerve from my purpose of life.

I talked with Dr Davidson the other day. He warned me about a country charge & told me I would be quite disappointed—that they would leave me as little time as a city & added that *his* town charge was so keeping him from certain works as that a year ago he listened to a proposal for change that he might have leisure for one or two efforts at authorship.

And then, Dearest, I think that this *sense of duty* (which I would give anything to make you feel is intense & final) agrees just in these present months with our circumstances. I could not settle *before* our marriage because that would destroy all our independance in meeting the shock of public opinion. I could not settle just after our marriage for that would be exposing us to the chaffering comments of every parish about you & our position in life. Therefore a residence *at first* unsettled seems wise in the very nature of the case. Then, Dearest, agreeing with that is the fact that your circumstances are such as to require immediate & considerable attention. *To me* at least who have never been in debt largely & to whom a large incumbrance would be a matter of anxiety it seems inconsistent with an immediate pastoral settlement. Then, lastly, it does *not* seem inconsistent as that sort of afternoon employment which might follow for some period of time intense morning study. Look at all these things, My Darling Sally, & as I am morbidly sensitive on some points *do* take them in & contemplate them broadly before you comment to give your final decision. Your mention of them at this late moment agitates me the fear that this hated philosophy has after all not shown her features yet in all their length and breadth.

As to the purchase of Colalto it recommends itself to me for these hastily stated reasons, First, it would give me room for employing my business time in a way to increase our support, as finally a like tract might do at Princeton. Second, Colalto cant safely be left, perhaps. It is a part of your property liable to abuse. Third, We could sell it as soon as possible—as soon as under any other arrangement & perhaps sooner & better. Fourth, my owning it & paying off $5000 of your debt in that way is the only way in which it seems to me now I could honorably occupy it. As to the price I ought, perhaps, to offer more but I *cant*. I havent got it. I havent got this. Besides I will give in all I have to pay off debts in the wisest and rapid way & that is all that in any case could be done. Besides I expect an agricultural depression after a year or two & if Colalto will produce at once $19000 in good available means or even $16000 it would be a serious question to me whether you had not better sell it.

Still, Darling, about these matters you are responsible for a wise judgment. Do give it beforehand.

I am sorry to write in such haste.

I will speak to Mother to-day. For, Darling, tho you dont say so (at which I complain a little) I think Mother in her feeble age, will not be disturbed about it prematurely.

I will look over yr letter & go on answering it in another letter for to-morrow. *Dearest* Sally. Do all *you* can to avoid unnecessary delays.

I will rule of the moral question. I am perfectly convinced.[37]*

> *Yrs affly,*
> JM

I hate to write a hasty letter because it lays a rough hand on the fact how tenderly I love you.

Colalto,
Friday Oct: 17. 1856.

My dear John I write you a rapid note. Your letter of the 13th came an hour ago. I cd not answer it immediately having a pressing note of another kind to write first.

I have always thought if we were to decide to be married, it ought to be at once—and looking at it the other day some day early in Nov: seemed the best time. We might slip in quietly in the general fuss of the election and its excitements. If we wait till the calm after that it gives the newspapers an opportunity to fill up their impoverished Columns with our business. I dont care particularly what day, between the last of Oct: which is Thursday & the 4th of Nov:—my idea is the sooner the better. We had better come a little in advance of the political excitement of that period, than behind it. As to business arrangements, they can be attended to afterwards.

I speak with a business air & in a very practical way of an event that involves everything to me, and often & often agitates me more than I can express.

I am troubled somewhat at Shriver's news. That man, John, has the sleepless malignity of a demon.[38] Nothing but the Grave will ever still his untiring, undecaying malice. What he means I cant conjecture, unless he is preparing another printed attack upon me, wh wd be more disagreable than hurtful.

I am ready for whatever plan you make as to accepting invitations &c. I shall make no communication of this thing till the last moment here, beyond one or two friends, and Lilly. I shall not I think, write to James or the others, until you actually come on. I will run no risk of another disappointment, or further trouble.

37. Here Miller placed a mark and then in the margin another mark and added: "except you are *not* convinced. Then of course it would be imprudent & wicked."

38. "That man" refers to Francis Thomas.

I wish I had time to say a little from my heart of hearts this morn'g.

You know, you are not as honest as I, or you could use the word "annoyance" to some of my ways too.

However, Goodbye. & God bless you. I shall write tomorrow.

Affe'y
S.C.P. McDowell

Princeton, Oct 17, 1856.

Dear Sally,

I come right home from the P.O. & go on writing. My walk in the cold has given me two ideas:—first, that I must not be hurried in writing as the Post Master had to make up a separate package to send my letter: & then, secondly, that I must not press you so hastily. I shall endanger your whole peace & tranquility in coming to a decision. I do not mean to let you see even the most distant selvage of your free papers under any morbid idea of honour; on the contrary I mean to win you now if I possibly can & as soon as I can. But I mean to do it honorably & I cant do that unless I leave you the freest opportunity of judgment & unless I save myself from the slightest possibility of appearing to sink down after our wedding or to fall off into any pursuits or eccentricities as they might possibly be thought of which you were not beforehand & *very early* beforehand entirely admonished.

Now, My Dearest, I do not mean that I am going to be a hard-hearted neglecter of all changes of circumstances that may occur; but I mean to say that my sense of duty is to use a taste which I find within me & such faculties as God may supply to do a work of attempted discovery & investigation & that continued, if successful, thro life, as a higher labor & grander vocation than any possible parish. This is my *conscience*. If you allow me to win you, you must recognize me as such a man. I would have preferred (on the one point of honor) to have let my first book come out & try my taste & my perseverance, but, Darling, I am absorbed in the other object now & want to win you at once. I have a love for the pulpit & should fall back to it with delight *sooner* than to a professorship if this purpose failed & unless it engrosses me as it does now & *grows* in me & widens & deepens its studies & pauses for one publication till it can assuage the whole ground of investigation, I shall soon tumble back to my profession exorcised of the devils that possessed me & with my mind[39] by dint of a good deal of profound & careful study enriched for the labours of the parish. This, of course, however, is *my* view of the matter. You must consider whether it is safe (other preachers with wh. I have conversed say, it is) & give me the advantage in our marriage of a quiet persuasion that I have not deceived you in my contemplated undertakings.

Now, therefore, I will speak to Mother this morning & yet to make such a step consistent with all I have said I will not consider that step as closing your

39. Interlined above this sentence, Miller added "(P.S. perhaps *empty* swept & garnished!!)."

deliberations, only mine; *I* am already determined the moment this is done, as indeed with a highly improbable exception (Her utter frustration & distress) I am already & then I will have nothing in my hand but the mere anxiety & suspense.

Here I will stop, Sally, & at suitable time this morning I will find Mother disengaged & speak all before her. God bless my dear Mother, & us both!

12 1/2 A.M.

Well! Mother & I have had a long talk. It has turned out better than I expected. She insisted first upon the opinion being given of some church body & when I showed her that that was impossible & if it were would imply a doubt of the legislative action she seemed to give that up but said I ought to consult again with the ministers; when I said that would appear like wavering but that I meant to *tell* the ministers in respect to my purpose, she seemed with much hesitation to give that up also. I wish I had finished the conversation there. But as I paused a moment she said I will tell you what I advise. I advise that Mrs. McDowell & you determine to wait two years. In that time things will clear & the public will respect you the more. I told her I could see no essential difference & that I could not feel that the advantage would equal the sacrifice. Still she insisted upon this & gave her counsel so strongly as to take off a little the pleasure of the interview.

You see, therefore, Sally, that *I* have finished all my decision & the verdict is left with you. I am your suitor now for an immediate marriage. I do not mean to destroy your tranquility of choice, but I do mean to say that every day I am now away from you is an agitating self-denial & every pause in your decision a painful suspense.

As to the moral question I would have sent you more, but my search has been so great. Calovius & Chemnitius & Bellarmine & Hartmann & a whole parcel of these fellows are rather hard to digest into a letter & I dont know that I can give you even the heads of my thought, but, for God's sake, be settled before we marry.[40]

I believe desertion *without* "unfaithfulness" is a perfect ground to act on. So our "book" says. I think so because 1 Cor 7:15 says so directly.[41] So even the Papists consider it tho they say it means the desertion of the "unbelieving" that is those not Papists because their marriage has not been a sacrament. But the whole tone of the chapter gives warrant to the inference of our confession: First it commands that married people shall not live apart & by the way *your* condition is sinful except in very peculiar cases (if any) *unless* you are divorced. The Bible contemplates no *separate* condition without effective divorce. Therefore it says v. 10 "Let not the wife depart from her husband. But & if she depart (a thing which

---

40. European theologians and scripture scholars. Abraham Calov (1612–1686), Martin Chemnitz (1522–1586), Robert Francis Bellarmine (1542–1621), and Friedrich Hartmann (sixteenth century) or Johann Hartmann (sixteenth century).

41. 1 Cor. 7:15 states: "If the unbeliever wishes to separate, however, let him do so. The believing husband or wife is not bound in such cases. God has called you to live in peace."

he dont sanction) let her remain unmarried, or be reconciled to her husband; & let not the husband put away his wife".[42] Leaving a command, therefore, so plain that no *believer* need be considered in any provision for desertion (just as no good Christian *could* be in the attitude toward his wife that Thomas is) he goes on next to speak of *unbelievers*. He says, "But if the unbelieving depart let him depart. A brother or a sister is not *under bondage* in such cases.["][43] Now nearly all commentators say that means are *free* (& may marry). If not what could it mean? The few who deny that it means that, say that it means are not under bondage of anxiety or bound to try to be reconciled or to follow up & thrust themselves upon the husband. This is absurd. So far as wise methods of reconciliation are concerned they *are* bound. All else would be a meaningless subject of counsel. It means are not bound in the sense in which the 11th verse says one *is* bound that is, as our book explains it. The one who departs[44] must remain unmarried, but the one departed from, not. This view is confirmed by the thirty ninth verse where the word *bound* is used plainly in this sense.[45]

Now if it be said why does Xt say in Matt: there is but *one* cause of separation that is unfaithfulness.[46] I say, so that there *is* but one ground & therefore Paul here *forbids* separation but is here treating of a further question that is, What is to be done when people *will* & *do* separate (For remember I say the Bible forbids *separation* just as it does remarriage.) Why, the *separator* is to remain unmarried the other is free. This for a multitude of reasons that cannot all be stated here is the only consistent theory of the passage & leaves only the question, Who deserted in your case? Plainly Thomas. He forced you to leave him. It was only by entreating to stay or at any rate *staying* that you held your place with him five or six times & finally at Annapolis your friends insisted that your removal should be his work & tho in the last extreme your father sent for you, yet to say after your letter that Thomas quotes (in which you say, "If you are determined to put me away &c") that you were not *constrained* to go home by him would be idle. The fact that his affections would revive & he would wish you back only shows that he added torture to desertion for that he would not finally have kept you is seen from his pamphlet where in the event of your refusing to return he turns again & wilfully & brutally maligns & then divorces you. Moreover these paroxysms were inveterate for as you know he has returned to them afterward. Now that this was not a brutal & horrid case of desertion no man in his *sane* senses could deny. That he tortured you as a cat does a mouse, fondling you between the acts of his ordering you out of the house (for I take it only mild villains desert in another way that is leave their houses to their wives) & turning upon you so soon after your reconciliations as to make your living with him impossible is in

42. 1 Cor. 7:10–11.
43. 1 Cor. 7:15.
44. Here Miller interlined "is Thomas."
45. "A wife is bound to her husband as long as he lives" (1 Cor. 15:39).
46. See Matt. 5:32, 19:9.

my view as much more thoroughly a case of desertion than the mere running off of a man from his wife as one dark act can be darker than another. Now the proofs of *this* desertion your father put into the courts before the Legislature. So that I will do nothing for one moment to throw into suspicion the divorce of the Va Legislature as one quite on Scriptural ground. Then there is the whole ground of unfaithfulness untouched & additional. The Va legislature too I believe in my heart acted upon them. They *never tell* their reasons in the enactment. The court finding was only a temporary expedient & *is* now dismised as supererogatory— & I believe that many a good man in the Legislature looked over the facts of the finding & added to them also his own private & the public's knowledge of Thomas's unfaithfulness. So that on any of four grounds I am satisfied on the moral question.

Write back when you receive this & if any doubts remain tell them & I will write much more fully. I can do it. By the way tell me if the above discussion of T's treatment of *you* does not answer to the facts.

Sat. 18th Morning

I am under a constant impulse to hasten you—& yet I wont. Your act shall be deliberate. But, Darling, dont hesitate for the object of avoiding the *appearance* of haste, *to me*. It would be w (wicked &) heartless.[47] You have been my wife in all feelings of *mine* for quite a year. And, Darling, havn't I been your husband. *I have now entirely established my own sense of duty*. I am waiting entirely for yours. If you in any future letter speak of yourself as leaving time for some imagined "last reasonings" of myself you will be unreasonable & wrong. I have a stormy intolerant impatience which the moment it gets any outlook storms at me & makes me quite sick & wretched. If you want any sane part left of your poor weary-spirited lover, you will listen to his suit or give him his quietus some way or other just as soon now as you consistently are able.

Oh, Sally, I go to Norristown on Tuesday (to Synod). Any letter that *leaves Lexington* on Tuesday Wednesday or Thursday morning (not later) had better be directed to "Norristown, Pennsylvania". I will have any *before* that sent after me from here.

I am still determined to buy Colalto if I can, if you will sell it, as the best plan (even if we sell it soon after) of starting honorably after our Northern visits in a life which may take that course afterwards wh Prov[idence] chooses to direct. To go to some other region & leave your debts & involved property there would seem to me almost impracticable, & to go there in a *languid* village where business is not done in a day would keep me longer a public pensioner upon you than I would altogether relish. Still, Darling, the decision to sell is yours. But be prompt.

Yrs fondly
JM.

---

47. Miller wrote "wicked &" in very tiny script.

Colalto,
Sat'y Oct: 18. 1856.

Dear John,

Write me in your next some thing of your winter plans. Some arrangements I must make here with reference to them, and had better do it before you come on. Lilly too must be at school. I had partly concluded to send her to Geo: Town, but if I am to be—look here John! Where am I to be? farther North, I shall want to have her nearer & will try to prevail upon her to go back to Miss Gill's or Mrs Carey's, I believe it is now.

You use the right word—my feelings too are more "healthy" under our changed prospects. And they have recognized the change so quickly. I have had no rush of boisterous emotion, no clamoring excitement, but a gentle waking up of my whole heart as if the day in its calm light had dawned upon it. The clouds that had gathered above it, and the shadows that laid upon it seem all breaking away, and, for a little while I have had granted me a certain "rapture of ripose"[48] that Byron, I believe, talked of, but I suppose, poor fellow, had little experience of.

And yet, John, I am fearful too. I shall never be anything else till I am actually your Wife. I thank God for what we already have, and hope to realize the full measure of our present prospects.

I can write a note only. I am always hurried, & you must not expect hereafter a letter every day.

With all my heart Yours
S.C.P. McDowell

Elizabethtown, N.J. Sunday
Oct 19th 1856

Sally,

I do so long to have a letter from you *all* about your love. I do so long to have the time come when I can just enjoy your love without all these doubts & questions about our affair. Indeed, Sally, when we are married there'll be that blessed advantage that our step will have been *taken* & we shall stand in quite a different position on all these questions.

My Love, suppose you give up all questions *now* & if your conscience only is at ease give yourself into my arms. I *must necessarily* take care of all these matters of your honor, &c. Why should we both be troubled about it. I am not *afraid* of anything that lies before us. I am very cool & collected in respected to the whole matter. I am corroded with impatience to have it consummated. I have always told you I had a contempt for the world. I dont consider it a high quality. Some rogues have it. But it is a very helpful one just now. And what sensitiveness I

---

48. From Byron's poem *The Giaour; A Fragment of a Turkis Tale*, published in 1813, line 75.

have chiefly lies in a hot-tempered dread of *your* not having respect. If I get into any trouble it will be that of angry resentment.

But stop! This is not very good for Sunday. I am here preaching. Dr Magie & Kirnan (Dr. Murray) are the neighboring Pastors.[49] I preach for Dr Magie. His church is large and crowded with hearers & I have had a very pleasant Sunday. I wish you were with me now that it is all over. God is very good to me in promising me the gift of you. For do you know, Dearest, God has made me a parent of you! I love to think of it just as a great generous gift like his own grace. O if you would turn out to be in any way badly mated with me either by my fault or yours, how it will contradict many pleasant dreams of you connected with the Providence of God. But, Sally, Child, we wont be badly mated, will we? You'll love me, & I'll love you and then if we quarrel & fight sometimes the storm'll blow over & you & I will be found among the wrecks of its fury daintily winning each other to peace. How sweet those reconciliations will be! Wont they, Sally?

I write now because I cant to-morrow. I shall be on the road at the time of the first mail. This place is near New York. I go back to Princeton to-morrow & to Synod on Tuesday. The Jersey Synod meets here.

Darling, there is a great secret I have been keeping from you. I feel so warm to you to-night that I cant keep it any longer. I have a remorse for keeping it so long. But as by this time you have probably written me your judgment & it will not influence your decision & that I might keep you believing the worst of me, as the most honorable course was the only reason of my keeping it *I will tell you*. I *am* aiming after a certain office. I told you I thought it quite probable I never might fill any. So I do. But a certain office like a European Professorship such as Brown had in Edinburgh or such as Reid had in Glasgow—calling for a lecture but once a week some 50 in all annually is my beau ideal of what would suit me. I fear it will never be had in this country but it may. I am *resolved* to push certain inquiries. Such a lecture wouldnt interrupt me & yet would be a strong & useful position.

How I do long to have you near me. I think you will be disappointed with me in some respects but find me much better in others. As to *you* I think I *must* be disappointed for now you seem to me like a great extraordinary mercy to a poor undeserving transgressor. Indeed you do, Sally. Do you think you *will* be so really.

But come I'm not writing as becomes the day & therefore I'll stop. I hope you are not going to say "again" & "again" & "again" in the torturing way you once said it.

Yours very affectionally
Jno Miller.

49. David Magie (1795–1865) and Nicholas Murray (1802–1861), both of Elizabethtown, N.J.

Colalto
Monday Oct: 20. 1856

My *dear* John,

I am sorry my letters have been delayed; but by this time you have received them all.

I am beginning to realize much that is to come upon me, and feel to a degree entirely unexpected by me the pain of giving up my own home, and the risk of finding new friends, and being able to make a new home happy. Lilly too, awakens so much anxiety. She behaved nobly when I told her of our change of plans; said much that was kind & thoughtful, & among other things assured me "you will never, Sister, hear me say one word to add to your troubles in this matter." She thinks she would rather not go to school until the "fuss" about the marriage is quiet; but I am unwilling for such delay, and unwilling too to leave her where she may be alienated from me. I object on that account to sending her to Geo: Town. If Buchanan is elected, of which since Penn'a has gone for him there seems little doubt, Uncle Floyd is one of his Cabinet—at least that is understood *privately*. I think it improbable, for his party is exceeding small in Va, whilst Hunter's and Wise's are both large, & so adverse to Floyd that this will coalesce at any moment to throw him over board.[50] However I know he never works for nothing & it is possible he & Buchanan have already agreed that a Cabinet appointment is to be his pay. In that case they will live in Wash: & Aunt Sally will try her best, kindly, she wd think to draw Lilly to her house, wh wd be against me. At any rate I have told Lilly she should never go to her Aunt's any where, if Uncle Floyd was at home. Aunt Sally is entirely wrapped up in him: she thinks he is just the Angel Gabriel himself whom it is no sin to fall down before & worship. We, on the contrary, believe his angelic tendencies are downward and upward. I cant make you understand how terribly my heart is wrung at the thought of that child being torn from me. But I hope things will turn out better than we now expect. Public opinion, that shifting thing, *may* re-act in our favor; yet we are not to hope for that.

I am very sorrowful under all the anxieties & fears, and hopes even of the present. I lie awake thinking over them all. I feel it to be a great venture; but then the prize is a great prize too. I am most anxious to be thoroughly right in the highest sense. I cant help hoping I am. If I am, I have no reason to fear. I have a great idea of the self-support of such a conviction; and more than this *self*-support, is the promised help of the Almighty. "There be many that ask, who will show us any good: Lord! lift *thou* up the light of the countenance upon us."[51]

---

50. John Buchanan Floyd served as secretary of war in President James Buchanan's cabinet from Mar. 6, 1857, until his resignation on Dec. 31, 1860. Robert Mercer Taliaferro Hunter (1809–1887) was a U.S. senator from Virginia from 1847 to 1861. He and Henry Wise, Virginia's governor from 1856 to 1859, were Democrats.

51. Ps. 4:6.

This is strength enough. Yet it is true as somebody says "that tho' God may show us that our way is right, he has not promised to make it right in the eyes of others".

I have said nothing of our matters to any one beyond my own home; but if I meet Cousin John to-day or tomorrow I shall tell him. I am not free from the idea of there being some uncertainty in the thing yet. I am very much concerned we should act properly to every body regardless of their offences to us; and that not from any mean pusilanimous spirit, but simply because it is right. It is very hard, I know, but we can, at least make the attempt. I take the safe side now, and rely upon nobody. I shant then be disappointed. Hence I look with great caution upon Mr Henry's offer. Mrs H. may have notions which will make her draw back from her husband's invitation; or else join in it with visible reluctance & constraint. If we want help from man as certainly we do, it is best we go to a higher source to obtain it. And do John; let us do our part well. "When a man's ways are right in the sight of the Lord, he maketh even his enemies to be at peace with him"![52]

We have delightful Indian Summer now, after the wintry weather of last week. Write as often as you can. God bless you.

Yours
S.C.P. McDowell

Princeton, Oct 20th 1856

Most joyfully, Darling Sally, do I accept the issue made in your mornings letter. *I decide that we be married immediately.* Now be a good girl & have no wavering about the matter. Moreover *I assume the whole responsibility.* I have never wanted you, to bear an accountability for listening to my earnest solicitations for your love, but only (on my old string) to be harping upon the point of *honor.* A lady did say, "If you love Mrs McD, dont marry her". I listened to the speech & showed an inclination to yield if your feelings were alarmed (as mine were about you). They were not, & so I went forward to marry you. In a few hours they *were* by your brother's letter & by further discoveries of my anxiety & the Major's & then you decided accordingly & we postponed the wedding. All I wish to secure is a feeling of not *seducing* you my own Beloved, of not alluring you selfishly to discredit. The fear that I shall do so is not an *internal* fear. It is not a fear bred of my own instincts. It is not a fear supported by my own thinkings. But then my thinking may be warped by passion & I have suffered to be printed on me the judgment of others. *It was honorable in me to have it so.* But now that you are all awake to your own position & have long considered &, Darling, *could live in a cottage with me* if all any friend says of us were realized, that is, Sally, you love me passionately & are ready for the wedding my honor is satisfied. I claim you as baptized into my love so that you could *live* for that if with no other (Is it so Sally?) & now that my *care for you* is satisfied the responsibility I entirely assume.

52. Prov. 16:7.

I have a firm conviction of the morality of our wedding.

Believing that your passions are involved & that we have grown to be incorporated together & are *dependant* upon each other for *health* & for the very *possibilities* of a tolerable existence—*I think it our duty to marry. Intolerable* as the rapture is, the idea of approaching you as your husband & folding you in my arms has (for once in a mans life) *the common blending of the keenest selfishness & the highest duty,* & I am willing to take the whole responsibility (before the world I mean, I cannot of course before God tho I *would*) of all that is moral & all that is wise & all that is expedient in this whole question.

Therefore, Darling, come into the confiding *restfulness* of a trusting & affectionate wife. *I* will take care of you & God will help me in it. I have not a wavering fear. That ought to be a comfort to you. I am free from all agitations or thought about this thing now except the sleeplessness of passion. So cheer up, Dearest. My task is *done* in snaring you. And now I can take you to my *care.*

As to "personal violence", what on earth has that to do with the question. How possibly could a *man* twist his mind so that that could become a point. It cannot touch conscience. And the only way I see that it can affect the question is favorably, for if anything of that sort were attempted it would make a favorable detour in public opinion. All I have to say is, that I wonder *men* in Va can mention those things to women & dont see what earthly good Ruffner gets by repeating it to *you* when all know that it has nothing to do with the legitimate question.

And now, Dearest, give yourself up entirely to my care. Dont let there be any more iterations of letters you say in your wearied utterance, John, you "*decide*" "conclude for me". Now, Sweetest I take you at your word. <u>I decide for an immediate marriage.</u> Dont worry one moment. You have in fact by force of this letter passed out from the stormy exposures of caring for yourself. I'll take care of you. Poor weary child, how I do feel for you in all you have endured. Be my own Daughter. Nestle in my bosom thro the rest of your saddened life. And tho I have no *joys* to bring you that can come from the depths of my poor desert bosom, yet Darling you can be a sun-beam to me. If you will only love me with an *unreasonable* passion (for you are wrong when you say that if you knew me I am "not one that would care that you should love me with a blind passion") if you will only love me so that you could live off in the forest & be happy *with me* (Will you, Darling?) I shall consider that a rich bestowment on me in my faithful & fervent suit to you.

Now Sweet One, dismiss all your troubles. "Gambol about the floor," for all our position is like (only a great deal firmer) our position last year. Get ready like a good girl. And all this Thomas business & public opinion business & social position business I'll look after without any care to you.

So far I had written when I got your next note. God bless you, my own Wife! By the way I had left my table & gone down stairs & when I came back Mag: B[reckinridge] met me at the door & told me of this letter & I found right among these open sheets. I wonder if honest good girls like M. are never tempted just to *read a line* of what is all underscored & laid out so plain before her. I hope not.

You women who have feeble shallow feelings cant judge of the *tumult* when a beautiful creature mentions her wedding day! When it is made so beautifully near & certain it is more than poor mortals like me can bear. Dear Sally, Thursday will suit me perfectly, either of the days. Only write & make all certain. But let me beg:—Dont conceal anything. Tell every body. Dont seem ashamed of it. Tell James. Let every one know it respectfully & at once. I would like to avoid the appearance of stealth. And moreover this rumour about Thomas leads me to wish to avoid the appearance of anything *unannounced* as tho' we were afraid of him.

So much to-night. I will still go to Synod. It will not interfere. As soon as you fix the *day* I will tell all right & left & many of my friends sooner.

I will write to-morrow & every day of the few till <u>*you are mine*</u>!

Yours half-happy for once,
Jno Miller

Fendalls letter dont influence me at all. I think I have said that before in this letter.

I could defend our course in any assembly; tho I feel confident no church body will oblige me to do it. I will not change my Presbytery, tho I should feel more entirely safe here than in Phil. Still it is skulking & I wont do it.

God bless you! My own Darling.

Now write me one or two good warm letters. You have no earthly excuse for not doing it. Go to bed early, & take care of your health. Suppose we stay in Lex: a day or two & dont "bother" ourselves to set out at once? Write every day of course. And fix everything soon & "nicely".

Princeton Oct 21st 56.

Darling Sally,

Just on way for Synod. Received your letter last night inquiring about Winter plans. My plans had connected themselves somewhat with the purchase of Colalto but as I *will* not torture you with even the misgiving of delay I assent to your wish that "business arrangements be postponed till after our wedding" & tho I am a little anxious, Darling, about these *crawlings* that I sometimes have of perhaps a morbid self-respect I will not assault either your pleasure or mine by the trouble of business delays.

My plan so far as I have formed it is simple. 1. *To be married.* 2. To stay or not at Colalto a day or half a day or not as you think best. 3d To go North & spend a couple of months or less or *more* as the aspect of the social sky (whether stormy or otherwise) leads us to choose in paying such visits as my friends invite us to pay. 4th *Then* to form a further plan & either go to Lexington if an honorable arrangement can be made & begin the disentangling of your difficulties or if the entangling is not such when we come to inspect it as make that necessary fix what other residence our light at that time will direct. Prof. Henrys invitation which (when it comes from Mrs H. you ought to accept) it might seem better to accept on some journey back to Va. Or should we pay that visit first of all? If so, Darling, say so at once & I will write word as I promised to Prof. Henry.

I am looking now on Thursday Nov 1st as our most probable wedding day.[53] If you fix another or *fix* that write me word at once.

I will be back from Sy. here on Sat or Mon. after announcing our marriage to Dick & Spence & the Bp &c in a day or two from this. Courage, Darling. I think all will go well. Judge Hepburn declares for you very strongly.[54]

Yours fondly
JM.

Colalto
Wed'y Oct 22. 1856.
8 A.M.

Dear John,

A man came on business before I was dressed yesterday morn'g and stayed an hour; and Cousin John & Phebe soon after breakfast so that I could not have written if I had intended to do it.[55]

I write now before breakfast, but at a late hour.

I believe I am as much settled upon the moral question of our Marriage, as my mind can be upon any point in ethics. I have anxieties about it; but not more than upon anything else in which my feelings are strongly engaged. I hope I have been entirely sincere and painstaking in the multitude of efforts I have made to come to a clear & full & fair conclusion on the whole subject. My mind is far more comfortable & "healthier" in its tone now in this regard than it was a year ago. And, John, I think, I am, perhaps, as assured as *I* could, with my mental organization ever reasonably expect to be.

No doubt I shall be happier when I am your wife, but, at present, I am much & painfully harassed by our peculiar difficulties, as well as those that always will flow in upon any woman who cares or thinks much, at such a time as this. The pleasure my affection for you furnishes, alternates with these distracting anxieties and makes them endurable. You mustn't doubt my love for you in the midst of these expressions of uneasiness & disquiet. It is no sign that it is lost or diminished that I feel thus strongly about things.

You are entirely right in your description of Thomas' conduct to me. My life was one of torture—all the more dreadful that it was mixed up with moods of tenderness. If you had been present you cd not have caught the look of things

---

53. Nov. 1, 1856, was actually a Saturday.
54. Samuel Hepburn (1782–1865) was a circuit judge in Pennsylvania.
55. Phebe Alexander Preston (1839–1873), a daughter of "Cousin John." Her husband was her first cousin, Edmund Randolph Cocke (1841–1922).

with more accuracy or described them more truly. I sat watching a cat, the other day, torturing a forlorn little mouse—I was just that poor suffering thing; without, however, the perfect certainty of death. I think I was in danger often of that fatal end, tho' I was unaware of it: and yet I dont know; he has all the cowardice of an opossin, & whilst he wd have killed me if he cd have concealed the deed, never wd, unless he had been in one of his storming passions, when there was a prospect of discovery.[56]

Lilly thinks she would like to go to Phil:, *if* I could get her boarding in a suitable private family. I like the notion of putting her at Dr Leyburn's very much, and think I shall write to him about it. He has a niece, from this town living with him, & might on that account be willing to take Lilly. What do you think of it? By the bye she says, "Ask Mr Miller if he doesn't think Sister might let her take a buggy ride with a young gentleman. Sister says she wont let her, because she dont think it right; but *she* says she *will* (!) *go*. She wants a ride, and Sister's horses are halt & blind, & her driver in the field, & so she cant have the carriage; mayn't she go in the buggy?"

I still think we had better be married early next month. If you leave home Friday the 1st you will get here Saturday night.[57] Monday we might be married & leave here the next day or in a day or two. There will be no reason for delay, but much for going off immediately. But John tell me, where are you going to stow me away after we leave here? I dont want you to *thrust* me upon your friends. I'd rather wait.

Such a long letter from Elizabethtown! Dr Murray is something of an acquaintance. I wish he wd renew to me his invitation to his house given some years ago, as I fancied the merry old gentleman with his white teeth. Lilly worries me *so* I cant write another word. She puts wax on my paper, & behaves like a baby.

Affe'y
S.C.P. McDowell

Norristown, Oct: 22d 56.
Wednesday noon.

My darling Sally,

I have been made nervous by the tho't that *possibly* I did not mail (before I left home) a note that I wrote yesterday. It answered your question about my Winter plans. They are to stay one or two days or not as you like in Lexington to come North, to go at once to Princeton (unless you prefer to stop a day or more with Mrs Henry) then to accept other invitations in Phil & elsewhere & to spend so much of the Winter as this consumes at the North *then* (if you think it best not to sell me Colalto or I cant get the advance fr. our estate to buy it) choose with our best lights where we will live.

56. An opossum, when threatened, pretends to be dead rather than fight back.
57. Friday was Oct. 31, 1856.

I spoke of *Thursday* Nov 1st as the day you mentioned for our wedding. I find Nov 1st is not Thursday. Still Nov 1st whatever day it is will be quite practicable for me or almost any other day that you choose to appoint of wh. I can hear definitely.

God bless you Dear Sally, I love you tumultously & can hardly *bear* the excitement of possessing you.

I have not talked to Spence &c yet, & of course to no one else first because mother came with me to town, goes back in a day or two & I dont want her to be excited with their sudden speeches.

I have no hesitations. That's enough for you to know. I owe you many thanks for your honesty & love.

God will take care of *you* & as to me I have no special anxieties unless I seduce you into some harm.

Yours affly
Jno Miller.

I may go home before Sunday.

Have no anxieties about *the day* when you have once settled it. I will be on hand.

Colalto Thursday Oct 23, 1856

Dear John,

I have had such a horror of another appointed and then disappointed marriage that I have forborne to say one word as to my plans to any of my friends. I wanted very much to speak to Cousin John; but tho' I have rather sought him yet I have not been able to catch him for a single minute's talk. Now, however, I shall speak to Nib & some few friends, & write to my brothers and Sisters who are absent.

If we are to make a visit to Prof: Henry, let it be as we go on after we are married, considering the 4th or 5th of Nov, as the time for the wedding.

I thank you for all you say that is comforting and re-assuring. I need both comfort and support. I cant throw away my anxious thoughts for the future, any more than I can throw away my heart itself; but I think they are assenting as the interval for your coming diminishes. I have the great solace of an abiding trust in God. I often question my *right* to this confidence, and wonder if it can be a strong self-delusion, but in almost all of my dark foreboding, it springs up to cheer me, and re-assure me. I have the strongest belief that God will fulfil his promises to his People. If I ever asked with earnest sincerity for anything in my life it has been for God's guidance in this matter. I can not think, therefore, that the "wisdom" he has promised can have been withheld. I cannot feel that He will allow me to ask wisdom, & yet give me only self-delusion, as an answer to my oft-repeated & most express petition. And yet if I should prove to be decei'd, why, I shall still have no doubt of God's Truth, but a deeper belief & stronger confirmation of the desperate deceitfulness of the human heart.

I dont know *how* to write to you now Darling. I have said so much of all my affection to you, that you must be quite sure of it by this time. Indeed I feel so much your wife that it wd be more natural in me to write to you about household matters & the common cares of a family. I might pick up most naturally your unfinished story of the empty "sugar barrel", and add to it certain troubles which my diminished storeroom, at present makes quite apparent.

I dont know where my brother Tom is now. He was visiting his lady-love when he wrote last, whose illness had detained him at her Father's. Wasn't that awkward?

God bless you, my dear John.

Affec'ly
S.C.P. McDowell.

When did you meet Judge Hepburn.

Norristown, Oct: 23d 56.

My *dear Sally,*

You do abuse me dreadfully. You tell me I musnt tell you "*all* my anxieties["] & therefore I have no confidante at all. I am vexed beyond measure. Here they have put me in the house of an old aristocratic family here thinking that I would live like a prince & company have come in from Europe & I am intruded upon by another clergyman as my fellow lodger. I have often said I would go to a tavern sooner than consent to this & yet here I am unable to move & no one to sympathize with me. Sally I do so wish you would hurry & take me under your care for I am of all men most miserable. If I were comfortably in your arms people would let me alone. And I shall be a martyr to these ancient barbarians till you appear for my relief.

I feel *firm* in all the path I am treading. I have told some of the ministers & am mighty satisfied with the result. No preacher has yet found fault with me.

I hope to have a letter here soon. I have none yet.

Yrs in haste
Jno Miller.

Colalto
Thursday Oct 23. 1856
10 1/2 P.M.

My *dear John,*

I shall be too busy to write even a note tomorrow morn'g, so I write to-night in a most uncomfortable way. I have been in bed half an hour, & find writing & lying down not very compatible comforts.

You would not think me cold to-night, as you something charge me with being, if you could just open my heart & take a peep into it. You would never quarrel again either about the wrapping that my little man wears—& say it is "thread-bare" & "patched" &c; but you wd grow warm & contented under an affection so full & glowing. I do love you, my own darling John, with all my heart; and, for the first time, I believe, since our decision, I am so relieved from my anxieties, & so given up to the pleasures of the future that I am really impatient for you, to come. O John, I do hope we may be a happiness to each other. I feel like throwing away every particle of reserve, and just coming and begging you like a "poor weary child" that you will fold me in your warm embrace and keep me sheltered & safe there for-ever. I have had such a storm-life, that I need a little rest, and you wont be ashamed of me, John, if I ask you to draw me to your bosom that I may find it there. You talk of the pleasure of "possession"—I can tell you the pleasure of being possessed is not less great. Such a sense of relief & content steals over me at the thought of belonging to you! But that mayn't last, Darling. I may grow rampant & fight for the "freedom of my own will" & way after the novelty of servitude wears off.

Monday, John, or Tuesday, the 4th or 5th of Nov, & not the 1st.[58] Somehow I'd rather be married in the morning. I hate to be married in a dark dress, & cannot go to the expense of getting a light one, both of wh difficulties wd be avoided by being married in the morn'g. You wdn't like me to wear a white dress, would you! But, goodnight.

Friday 8 A.M.

I had a talk with Cousin John yesterday even'g. He was very cheering in all he said; & our whole interview was most satisfactory & gratifying. I was extremely pleased at his cordial interest in all that concerned me even down to little things. I said, as I spoke of my sorrow at giving up my home, "And, Cousin John, I shall miss that little Mac dreadfully." "Well, *he* is a sweet fellow, but then you'll have your own two little children to take his place",—And he said it with such a heartsome recognition of my *proprietorship* (is it so John really?) in those little folk, and on that account, of his own interest for them, that I was, oh, so much pleased. He spoke of you too in a way to gratify; and altogether my heart was much lightened by our meeting.

And now, my own precious John, I am letting my affection have its own way, and it comes leaping over all barriers of all kinds, and offering itself for my constant & joyful companion. Cousin John said last even'g, "Why, Sally, already your eyes sparkle as if life was brightening to them." God grant it may be brighter to us both. Do you know you didn't send me any letter this morn'g? But I find the disappointment easier to bear now. And now throw your arms round me, Darling, and draw me close to you, and wipe away the light kiss that closed our first moonlight meeting so many weary months ago by the stronger and warmer one that claims me for your own Wife.

God bless us both. Your own
S.C.P. McDowell

58. Again, McDowell had not checked her calendar. Monday was Nov. 3, 1856.

Synod. Oct 24th 1856

Dear Sally,

I go I think tomorrow (Saturday) to Phil & Princeton. I have received no letter yet directed to Norristown. I received the one writ on Monday & sent fr. Princeton. It does not *appoint finally* our wedding day. My Darling if you dont take care I shant know when to go on & shall fail to be present at my own *marriage*.

I feel every disposition, Dearest, to take the office of sustaining your confidence in the step we are taking. I think it both *right* & *safe*, & tho you may be exposed to some reflections (to wh I have felt all along sad to expose you) yet as you love me I think we will get rid of all our troubles & ride out in time every difficulty.

I have mentioned our plan to members of this Synod (3 or 4) Dr Leyburn, Dr Boardman, Judge Sharswood and a Mr Belville & the result has by no means discouraged me.[59] Dr B. said he rather "rejoiced that some form of protest was to be made against what he regarded as an unchristian public sentiment". I would cheer you on in every possible way my Dear Sally in your kind compliance with my suit & hope Heaven will reward you for the steadiness of your love to one who perfectly adores you.

I will have other letters that come sent on from here to Princeton tho I hope for one here this afternoon or tomorrow morn.

The complaint I made in my last letter was singularly soon over. As I sealed my letter a young sister of my hostess stood at my elbow & said a guest had gone & asked whether I would not like another room. I hesitated so in replying that she saw what the answer ought to be & I am now installed in a fine square chamber looking out upon a fine landscape.

So good bye Sally. These last days are sad burdens to me. Dont delay unnecessarily, or out of any fears. Give yourself up to me Darling. I've proved my love for you by waiting so long.

> *Yours affectionately,*
> *Jno Miller*

Princeton, Oct. 25th 1856

My dearest Wife,

I can realize enough of the timorousness that must (as you say) assail *every* woman on the brink of her marriage to feel glad that so lovely a creature is to be entrusted to me & to feel tenderly the weight of the charge & the sacredness of the feelings that are to be exposed to my keeping. All men appear to be semi-barbarians, dear Sally, *except me:* And if you were my sister I would look with a sort of shudder at the thought of any one having you in such entire possession except one whom I could regard as myself or as like myself, so intolerant am I of any other of my sex & so amazed am I all the time at *any* woman for entrusting

---

59. George Sharswood (1810–1883), presiding judge of the district court in Philadelphia, 1848–1867. Jacob Belville (1820–1907), Presbyterian pastor in Hartsville, Pa.

themselves to their care. I wonder if women feel so. Do you wonder how I *could* love any one but you & feel a sort of shudder of disgust at the idea of any one else being endurable to me in my arms.

Well I have returned from Norristown. I received two letters there—one via Princeton & one direct to Norristown. That last announced Monday week as our wedding day. I hail it with a sort of rapture. If you dont change it (as I hope you will not) I shall leave home on next Friday (which however is not "Nov 1" but Oct 31st) & go right on & if I hear that there is a stage from Goshen (is there?) I shall see you at nine *next Saturday night*!! Why not keep that night as an anniversary rather than our wedding day? It is the night we meet *never-to-separate*.

As to "*thrusting* you upon my relatives" that is just the thing that I shant do. The very stand I take is of *seeking* no civility: But only doing two thin[g]s[60]—first, make people intelligent as to myself & then *accept* what civilities they chose to offer. It is natural in you to feel so Darling Sally. But believe me your dignity & self-respect is a thing of my constant care & I shall *permit* no attentions that are grudgingly & as tho per force bestowed. If you equal me in pride I shall be sorry for it will augur badly for the common sense of our house.

You're a petty woman—wouldnt let Lilly when a year younger go alone to my (preacher's) study & not wish me to say whether she may ride alone with a gay young student. Do you think I am going to give an opinion either on the one hand to annoy Lilly or on the other just to be contradicted by you?

As to the boarding question would Lilly consent to join our party & come North & visit with us?

I enclose a circular of wh. I heard wonderful things when in Elizabeth-Town. I will tell you what I heard when I see you.

I have told Mrs Potter & Dick of our speedy marriage. Mrs P. was very cordial & Dick enough so to make me very comfortable. I shall tell Mary to night & *write* to Spence who was too busy when I saw him for my purpose.

God bless you Dear Sally. Dont have a fear of *me* or of any one. God who *directs* our step will make *me* to you I trust all you have ever imagined & as to others He will take care that we have as much of the favour of the world as is consistent with our good.

Good night!

> Yours *affly*
> Jno Miller.

Princeton Oct 27th 56.

Dear Sally,

I hurry a letter to the P.O. I have told Mother the *day* & find her *more* satisfied than I had hoped yet still seeking to long after some church action or else some delay. I have also told Mary & the children. The children are in high feather.

---

60. Miller wrote "thinks."

And Maggie insists she is going with me tho of course she is not. By the way after this I do not mean to tell you who likes our match & who not. I have suffered so from being prejudiced ag. people beforehand that I mean to leave *you* to estimate people yourself.

I think our matters are going on very well.

My temperament thro some original mistake must be half that of a girl for with the passions of a most tempestuous affection I have such an organization as leaves me perfectly *tortured* with the rudeness of the impatience with which I long to meet you again. The fact is you are too lovely a creature to be the darling of any one & with all the passions of a man I have the yearning restlessness to see you of the most womanly sensibility. The fact is, Sally, I guess you will have comparatively with yourself a most stormy sort of lover.

Yours in haste.
Jno Miller

I will write daily.

Colalto
Oct 28 [27]. 1856
Monday 9. AM.[61]

My *dear John,*

If you could see the number of letters lying on my Table, written, this morning, you wdn't wonder that my note to you shd be short.

Monday the third of November I think will be our wedding-day. We have had strange confusion of ideas about the days of the month heretofore—but that is right now. If you leave home Friday you reach here at 12 or 1 o'clock Saturday night. Sunday intervenes, & Monday we can be married. I dont want you to come earlier than Saturday; you wd be so dreadfully in the way.

I have written to James today, & told our plans to our friends here. Cousin John says you're a lucky fellow.

I'm in such a hurry. Your wee notes came from Norristown, being the perfection of pink outside, but not quite the pink of perfection inside![62]

Dear John I love you. I cant tell you how very, very much.

God bless you. Affe'ly
S.C.P. McDowell

Princeton Oct 28th 56

Bless you Sally, you may get married in sky green if you will quit pushing the day along from one day to another. I wont be married on Tuesday. I have got my

---

61. Monday was Oct. 27, 1856.
62. Miller had written on pink stationary from Norristown.

868 "If You Love That Lady Don't Marry Her"

expectations raised for Monday & if you prefer the morning I do too. Monday morning will be just ten hours earlier than Monday evening. If that seems to hasten you too much in leaving Col-alto we will stay just as long as tho we were married on Tuesday, but, Darling, I suffer so from suspense & excitement that you must keep to that very nice sounding date, Nov 3d, as in all coming time our wedding day. Now remember Sally dont make it later. As to your wedding dress if we are married in the morning (which I altogether like) it will make no difference whatever.

But Alas! Alas! Dearest, there is no sky without a cloud. Mother (on reflection) takes a much more serious view of our step, & tho it dont influence me practically in the least, yet it does affect me painfully. She accused me of fickleness & vacillation, says she is sure I have *over persuaded you*, & moreover that it will appear sudden & wayward to the public, that I have been giving out an intention to spend some years in Princeton & that she predicts trouble. Well, it only has two effects on me, first, one of extreme pain that in Mother's feeble old age I should do anything to distress her (& moreover I had been counting much as I still do on a blessing from my respect to the fifth Commandment) & secondly, one of disappointment for after her predictions of trouble I feel less able to go to her for any more immediate use of my patrimony to avoid the very trouble that she so seriously predicts. Still I feel that I have done my duty & what need I have more. It is to me plain as day-light that I am not to leave you struggling under a thousand difficulties after the vows of affection I have made you & moreover that it would be foolish and of this Mother as she knows nothing could not judge after having betrothed you as a wife & made you therefore nearer to me than my children that I should leave you swimming in a stream where social embarrassments & business distress could possibly seem too great even for both of us together. So cheer up Sweetest. I have no doubt of my duty, & tho your loveliness might make me doubt of my unbiassed judgment yet fondly as I long for you I had given you up for a time, & that convinces me that I have judged coolly & conscientiously in the matter.

Mother is an old lady of near eighty. I love her with all my heart. I know you will never speak of her impatiently to me & that for my sake you will most respectfully seek her love. I know too, you will be pleased with her!

My plan is to come on from Lex. to Princeton—to pay our visit here & then go to Phil: to pay some visits there. People are so fickle however that we must hold our plans somewhat less firmly than in usual cases & mould them to circumstances. So in your outgivings dont *commit* yourself to others to any more explicit course for the Winter.

God bless you, My Dearest for your fond letter. I have lost all doubts that you love me. I feel *yours* so fully that you almost seem like myself. I no more doubt of your passion for me. Sally, we seem so alike in some things—Isnt it so? And *ought* not people who have become so absorbed in each other to go forward decisively to consummate a marriage.

"Dred" has one good sentence in it.[63] I will quote it: "For my part," said Nina, ["]I should go right on. I have noticed that people try all they can to stop a person who is taking an unusual course; & when they are perfectly certain that they cant stop them then they turn round & fall in with them; & I think that will be the case with you."

By the way I like this sentence:—"Nature only sends such men once in a century or two. They are road-makers for the rest of the world. They are quarry-masters, that quarry out marble enough for a generation to work up."

Sally, will you *help me* with your woman's-love to keep as far as I am able in the path that my conscience marks out for me?

Yours with sad impatience
Jno Miller

Dont fear the *embarrassments* of yr Northern journey. I am a favorite with many of my friends & tho you may miss your Va *heartiness* of manners yet in our Northern style (*believe me, Dearest*) you will be placed perfectly at your ease by more than usual kindness. Don't be afraid, Sally!

Tuesday Oct 29 [28]. 56[64]

My *dear John*,

This letter brings my part of our correspondence to a close. When I write to you again it will be under different relations and a new title. I cant say I have any great regret at the idea of giving up my pen; and yet it has been a source of great comfort and pleasure to me during the last two years. By the bye, John, it has just occurred to me. Look far back in your package of letters and you will find one dated *Nov. 2d.* It is *the* one that you always referred to as determining our fate. It is no unpleasant coin[ci]dence that our *wedding-day* falls almost upon that anniversary. I remember the date well, for the letter was written the night dear little Mac was born.

When you come on Saturday night, unless the roads are astonishingly good you will get to Town too late to come over. However I will wait for you till 12. But if you are later than that dont think of coming till morn'g.

I haven't the least fear that you will take every care of my feelings in all yr plans. You need hardly have assured me you wd; & yet I thank you for that piece of thoughtfulness.

My rampant Cousin, Mrs Cocke is here. I have done my part in the way of civility most heroically. She responded coolly, at first, and has since taken up the suspicion of my purpose & intermitted all attentions. I want you to see her: I used to love her & she has been very very kind to me, and so in all our present

---

63. *Dred: Tale of the Great Dismal Swamp*, by Harriet Beecher Stowe (1811–1896), was published in 1856.

64. Tuesday was Oct. 28, 1856.

attitude I allow her full play as the aggressor, hoping for her all the pleasure that such a course can yield.

Your affection gives me a great feeling of independence as to that of other people. I hope it may always be so. I have no Utopian views of married life; but I have all the hope of its comfort and pleasure that an earnest love to you and a reasonable notion of life can afford.

This will reach you the day you leave home. God bless us both my dear John in an existence wh is henceforth to be inseparable in this world.

With all my heart Yours
S.C.P. McDowell
for the last time.

Princeton Oct 29th 1856.

My *dear Sally*,

It ought to give you as much pleasure as pain to hear what I am going to say because it shows how firm I am against all the attitude that can be assumed even by those I love best. I would not tell you were it not that you *have* to know it in order not to commit yourself in a way that would expose it publicly.

Mother, whose health is feeble, came into my room & told me yesterday that after deliberation she was *opposed* to the suddenness of my movement & could not approve it: & then to my utter horror & surprise went on to make me understand that she could not repeat her invitation (Dont be pained by this, Darling; she is an *old* lady & you will see it turned out better) to us to pay her an immediate visit for the state of her health would make the uncertainties of her feeling & the over excitement of our presence & the calls of others a real danger to her life. Besides she felt unprepared to give her public testimony in favour of the marriage. I was perfectly thunderstruck. Every thing looked *black* about me. Apart from the pain of Mother's attitude itself I knew that such a stand from my own family would do us life long mischief & I at once determined that as *pride* could have no proper play toward my Mother that I would try to shape things so as to alter her purpose. I told her very respectfully that the marriage *would* take place—that I had formed a *full* judgment & she would not respect me if I changed it—that I would marry you now at all hazards let it cost what it might & as I had deferred to her most handsomely in the beginning saying I would not *form* the engage: if it seriously grieved her I considered myself as having gone on from there to a point when I could not expect the blessing of God if I had retracted—that as to her stand now I promptly acquiesced in it as I had determined to *solicit* no attentions but only to accept those that were offered; but that I begged she would consider that as the owner of my father's house & having power to decide against me in Princeton she would be inflicting upon her son a deliberate injury that would last as far as it had any power at all for life. I reminded her then of what had been said in Balt: (about "darkening her door &c" you know—a thing *quite* untrue) she said she could not help it. She did not feel prepared now to give her voice in *favor* of the match. Knowing Mother's firmness of purpose I began to consider the blow as one that must be submitted to, & had begun to shape a proposal to you that after our marriage on Monday we alter our course so as not to come near Princeton, to expose ourselves to the public bruiting of such a stand till it had been changed in some way. I went on however to tell Mother how the very *inexpediency* of the marriage that she feared was *created* by her step—if she thot the match not *morally* wrong but made so by public opposition she was *creating* that opposition & that at a time too late to go back for her opinion. She said I ought to have told her sooner & given her a longer time to become settled on the whole question. She said a great deal more of like character which I need not repeat but finally said that her *health* was the ground that she wished given to you for that she was not prepared to put it even so publicly as with you on the ground of a decided opposition.

I led the conversation in this connection in such a way as to lead her to the point that "a flying visit["] that would not give time for many calls from the town or the *continuance* in her feeble health of such an excitement could be made now & then a longer one if she lived could be arranged (when her judgment settled down) some weeks or months afterward. And when I told her that if we came at all she like the English must settle the length of our visit she mentioned "*two days.*" Now, Darling, this is very sad seeing that it is my own Mother whom I love very much. But one or two things as I reflect upon it quite take away its bitterness & make me feel that it makes little difference. 1st Mother is very old & is losing her memory & her hesitation & fright at the suddenness of this business does not prove anything of a serious kind. 2d Mother is very candid & very reserved. She is very candid & has therefore told me the worst & she is very reserved & will let nothing be seen by others. By the way *I* shall let her opposition drop into the most *silent* chamber of my memory. I shall not tell it even to my brothers & you must not lisp it to any one. We mustnt spread the fire ourselves: besides, *she will change.* 3d you must *accept* her invitation without a feeling. *Pride* has no place with a good old mother of eighty. Accept it in perfect silence & without lisping to any one any other connection of our haste than a temporary return to Phil. to pay some pressing visits there. Indeed as we go thro I think it probable[65] we may be importuned to stay & we can insist on pushing on to Princeton as a proper thing but promise to return soon. My word for it if you win upon Mother as you do on others she will insist before the Winter is over on a longer visit. Still I cant be *certain* of anything & in the rough jerking surprises to which we have been subject since our engagement I want to say *4th* that in my judgment we ought not to *commit ourselves* publicly to any length or route of journeying. We ought to have our plans quite in our grasp & be able to change them without exciting surprise at a moments warning. This is why I tell you all so frankly & in

---

65. Miller wrote "improbable" but meant the reverse.

a way so disagreeable to myself. Dont fear, Sally, *I* am looking forward without a *quiver* to our wedding. Inconveniences & pressures will come chiefly upon me. With God's help I will carry you though. I dont consider Mothers step at her age at all a serious one now that it can be concealed from the public. Mother will out grow it. And Mary is already sympathizing more with me for the very fact of Mother's opposition. Meet Mother with perfect unconstraint as tho you knew nothing but the feebleness of her health. I think the bustle of attentions & visits here *would* enfeeble her & tho that is rather an unmaternal reason & therefore not the whole of hers yet it can stand for it with *you* & we will make some other stand for it with the public.

Mother when she saw how promptly I acquiesced in her first decision acquiesced (tho with evident unwillingness) in my taking the children. She seemed to wish them at least to stay till we are settled more, & she renewed the offer that I should *give* Allie to her to adopt & bring up & *endow*. Of course I could not consent to that. Could I Sally?

I cant tell how they will behave in Phil. Indeed now when my own Mother has disappointed me I calculate upon nothing. I only know that my *conscience* is perfectly *unanimous* & that a woman ought to be content with a love that can burn as mine now does so warm & *defiant* in my bosom.

The day may grow quite dark about us Beloved One, but no matter. My tastes fit me for the *forest* even if men dont care for us & *your* tastes I will try to gratify by the warmth & character of my affection. How much difficulty of other sorts will that counterbalance.

Dont appear anxious to others & dont *be* anxious Jehovah Jireh. Many things you know have gone better than our hopes. And if nothing else occurs (tho we must be prepared to change our plans endlessly & without the *appearance* of changing them) that is we must make none fixedly) the opinion of my mother concealed as it is & with the turn it has now taken is chiefly serious in depressing & saddening herself, & me on her account.

In haste

Yours affly
Jno Miller.

Monday A.M. *Remember*

Princeton Oct 30th 1856.

So, Mrs McDowell,

My letters are not the pink of perfection. Well, Madam, remember, *I will never write to you again.* I have become interested in a Mrs Miller, a tall fine looking woman with bright eyes and very seductive in her manners, so much like you in many particulars that you deserve to be outwitted by her. She has no great opinion

(?) of you, moreover, & has made it a condition of our continued intimacy that I will never address a letter to you again. So, good bye My dear Mrs McDowell. We have had many a happy hour together, but I am tired of you & willing to get your very name out of my remembrance, & as soon as I can.

Mrs Miller's name (originally Millar) is a contraction in the course of ages for mi-laird i.e. My Lord, her husbands ancestors having risen to what they have since become from one of the petty "lairds" of the old country. She is a lady *every inch* & that is saying a good deal for her inches are pretty numerous & the family blood will not be much diluted by mingling with the warm rich current that flows in her pretty blue veins.

Mary expresses her great regret that Mother has taken the stand she has & insists that as she *has* a special nervous fear of the excitement of company & denies herself nearly always to her own visitors that this is the reason of her step. I did not tell Mary, however, all she said, nor will I tell any one but you. Mothers memory is failing & she will forget it herself; so it is not worth while to tell others & thus help to set fire to our own position. Still I have no doubt that Mary is more than half right. I heard in Norristown much *more to comfort* you, than the worried & affectionate anxieties of my poor infirm Mother could possibly overbalance. So, Darling, let us *thank* God & consider ourselves as in advance of our expectations so far.

I leave here to-morrow P.M. at 3 & will push right thro of course & reach you Sat. night. If I reach Lex. betw: 12 & 1 as you say I shall *not* come over. So go to bed at 7 or 8 like a good girl.

I received the enclosed note from Judge Carleton late of the Supreme Ct. of Louisiana.[66] I cant make out its meaning however. Suppose I write him word that I have broken with Mrs McDowell & never mean to write to her again. I think tho he does not intend to refer to my private matters at all.

I am feeling more & more assured that I am not doing you violence as Mrs H. would once have me fear. If you love me passionately as I *know* you do a husband returning your passion with one still more intense & devoted is certainly a large balance to throw into the scale against any prejudice of others. But good bye Mrs. McDowell, this is the last flourish JM of Oh so long a correspondence. I'm glad I'm done, aint you?

> *Your fond husband*
> *Jno Miller.*

P.S. I could not defend myself to Mother by stating the strong reasons for my "haste" in duty to *you* for Mothers-in-law do not appreciate such reasons &

---

66. Henry Carleton (1785–1863) wrote a short note to Miller from Philadelphia on Oct. 28, 1856, inviting him "to call at No. 371 Spruce Street, where you will find a friend who will be glad to take you by the right hand." He also invited Miller to bring his book so they could discuss it. On the back of this letter, Miller penciled his postscript to McDowell.

strong as I might have made the case in respect to one like you committed to me & in trouble & moreover in the hey-dey of life still Mother would have rebelled against it. It is, of course, evident that I shld keep all such reasonings to myself. Therefore I have left Mother accusing me that I have led you into this last haste & overpowered your better judgment.

JM.

"Those years of trial."

August 1871

Allamby Aug: 7th 1871

My dear Wife,

I find this thing of separation has grown to be quite *impossible*. You have now been gone just three weeks, and do you know I seriously feel as tho I could not endure it again. There was something in those long sad years, Sally, in which we were waiting to marry which has made us love each other more passionately than most people and tho I look with a sort of shudder on those years of trial and remember how Death might have carried one of us to the grave before we ever reached a quiet home in each others arms yet romance gilds over that time of my life with some pleasant feelings. And Dearest, how free we were. . . .

Do you remember the morning we lay awake talking about little Bess & about your fear that the nurse gave her some kind of drug to keep her quiet?[1] I laughed at you at the time & indeed was so bewitched with that pretty new night cap that I smothered up your face in the pillow to keep you quiet about such nonsense. But, Sally, you're just like Mary. You have a second sight. Yesterday as I came in suddenly upon her a little phial dropped out of her dress & "Godfrey's Cordial" in good plain characters was there on the label. If I didn't know you would be home on Friday I would send her off. As it is I watch her very closely. Bessy seems well & is as merry as a cricket.

The German edition of the "Ontology" has been sent me. The translation is very good. In the preface is a brief sketch of my life & among other things what do you think of their saying, "Herr Miller is married to a most lovely & beautiful ("herrliche") lady who makes the romantic & exquisite spot that he has chosen as his home a most hospitable one to the savans who come to visit him. Tho' evidently much younger than himself & we are told not at all inclined to the same studies yet she is a lady of eminent taste & remarkable conversational gifts".

1. "Little Bess" was Elizabeth Henry Miller (1860–1936).

875

Little do they know, Dearest, how long this same "herrliche" woman had to be waited for & how much of this great youth they give you is due to the good care I took of you all thro' our separation.

. . . . . .

And now, Sally, dont for the world put off your return. The carriage will go for you to the Barin on Friday & if my Lecture is over I shall be with it. Give my love to Lilly Brachford and tell Mr Brachford I heard he has the handsomest wife but one that Lexington ever produced. Do you remember that day you were left alone at the Hotel in Richmond waiting for her. I can hardly tell you how I felt. The fact is you were entirely too venturesome in those times. Dear, dear, Wife I always was anxious about you. I wouldnt undergo the troubles of that period for a great deal again. And yet as I told you there is a witchery about it that makes even that time seem bright with a sort of paler lustre. Dearest, we ought to be thankful that God has brought us together at all & often as I have knelt with you in our room & thanked God because he has relieved us from our sufferings, yet I never can feel duly grateful for all the fond blessings of a life which seems to have atoned already for all its miseries.

Preston wishes to add a postscript & I leave room.[2]

> *Your affectionate Husband*
> *Jno Miller*

By the way dont forget the sugar. The last of the barrel will be gone to day. Brown & Peters are the corner of Arch & 10th. You needn't be anxious about Bess.

---

2. Enclosed is a letter from "your affectionate son, Preston Miller."

Index

Legend:
JM = John Miller
McD = Sally McDowell
* = name or term is mentioned throughout the text and only the most significant page citations are given

877